W9-DFR-655

ALMANAC OF
BUSINESS
AND
INDUSTRIAL
FINANCIAL
RATIOS

2012 EDITION

LEO TROY, Ph.D.

CCH
a Wolters Kluwer business

Editorial Staff

Production...Christopher Zwirek
Design .... Craig Arritola

ISBN: 978-0-8080-2785-0

© 2011, CCH. All Rights Reserved.
4025 W. Peterson Avenue
Chicago, IL 60646-6085
1 800 248 3248
www.CCHGroup.com

Printed in the United States of America

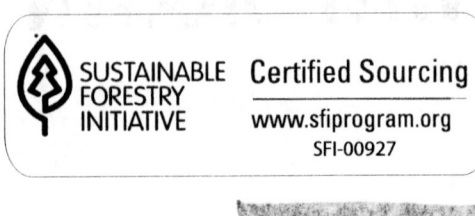

SUSTAINABLE FORESTRY INITIATIVE

Certified Sourcing

www.sfiprogram.org

SFI-00927

Dedicated

To Alexander, Suzannah, Dale, Ariel Sarah Troy, Abigayle Hannah Troy, and Rachel Ilana Troy

Preface

Now in its 43rd Edition, the *Almanac of Business and Industrial Financial Ratios* provides a precise benchmark for evaluating an individual company's financial performance. The performance data is derived from the latest available IRS figures on U.S. and international companies, and tracks 50 operating and financial factors in nearly 200 industries. The *Almanac* provides competitive norms in actual dollar amounts for revenue and capital factors, as well as important average operating costs in percent of net sales. It also provides other critical financial factors in percentage, including debt ratio, return on assets, return on equity, profit margin, and more. Beyond its reliable insights into corporate behavior, the *Almanac* can be used by other countries looking to model their economies on American performance.

Also included with the text, in a special pocket provided in the inside cover of the book, is a CD-ROM that contains all the materials found in the book including the explanatory discussion, the data tables, and the supporting index. Also included on the CD, but not in the book itself, is a special template that allows the reader to add individual company data of interest to compare and contrast with data from the book.

2012 Edition Highlights

The 2012 Edition of the *Almanac of Business and Industrial Financial Ratios* has been updated to include the following:

- **Broad scope:** *2012 Almanac* features the North American Industry Classification System (NAICS), so you can benchmark or analyze results consistently with corporations in the United States, Canada, and Mexico.

- **Most industry types:** *2012 Almanac* highlights most industry types, including industries with advanced technologies and newly emerging industries such as paging and wireless communications.

- **A truer picture** of corporate financial performance, since the data isn't based on a mixed bag of averages that might include partnerships or sole proprietors. *2012 Almanac* features a homogeneous universe of American corporate financial performance.

- **Many classifications:** *2012 Almanac* analyzes 195 industries with 50 financial performance items.

- **Benchmarks:** *2012 Almanac* provides 13 benchmarks, including such critical measures as Receipts to Cash Flow, Debt to Total Assets, and Return on Equity both before and after taxes.

- **Analytical tables:** *Table I, Corporations with and without Net Income (All Corporations), and Table II, Corporations with Net Income.*

- **Easier apples-to-apples comparisons:** Each table is divided into 13 asset sizes.

- **More comprehensive:** Total receipts of all corporations covered by *2012 Almanac* is $28.6 trillion, making the *Almanac* the Anatomy of American Corporate Capitalism.

Leo Troy, Ph. D.

October 2011

About the Author

Dr. Leo Troy is Professor of Economics at Rutgers University. He has been a faculty member of Rutgers for 50 years. In addition to authoring the widely praised *Almanac*, he has written many other books and articles published in leading journals. Professor Troy has been the recipient of numerous awards including two from the National Science Foundation, and two Fulbright grants. In addition, he has received numerous awards from private foundations. Dr. Troy received his Ph.D. from Columbia University and is a member of Phi Beta Kappa. He is a veteran of World War II with three battle stars and the combat infantry badge. He is the father of two children and is also a grandfather of three girls, including twins.

Acknowledgments

I wish to acknowledge the contributions of five people in particular for the development of the 43rd Edition of the *Almanac:* Phil Wilson, Alan Kovar of Brighton Best, Lawrence R. Chodor, CPA, CVA, Wiss & Company, Marvin Sunshine, and Karen Kane.

Philip is responsible for the programming, which dealt with a very large amount of data, covering both the current and trend information. Alan, drawing upon his knowledge and experience as a CPA and Partner of Wiss and Company of Livingston, N.J., contributed significantly to the new content of the book. To Marvin Sunshine, Esq, my appreciation for actions and support that helped make the *Almanac* a continuing publication. Karen Kane is acknowledged for her contributions to the graphics of this issue.

Special acknowledgement is due my late friends and colleagues, Stan Katz, CPA, and Professor Emeritus of Accounting, Rutgers University, John Gilmour. I thank, too, Professor of Accounting, Rutgers University, David Zaumeyer, Ph.D., CPA, for recommending several ratios that continue to be included in the *Almanac*. I thank Mr. Ka-Neng Au, Business Librarian, Rutgers University, for significant contributions to the *Almanac*.

I wish to recognize, too, the cooperation of members of the Statistics of Income Division of the Internal Revenue Service—in particular, Ken Szeflinksi, Martha A. Harris, and Phyllis J. Whiles of the Corporation Returns Analysis Section. Without their data and its reliability, the Almanac would not be possible. Responsibility for the use of their facts and figures is, of course, solely my own. In this regard, I recall the valuable assistance I received from Barry Rosenstein, MBA, CPA, in checking procedures, in earlier editions, and which have continued into the current one. Finally, I wish to recognize the help of Suzannah B. Troy in bringing about the 43rd annual edition of the *Almanac*. I anticipate continuation of her valuable assistance in subsequent editions.

INTRODUCTION

QUESTIONS, ANSWERS AND COMMENTS ON THE *ALMANAC*
Some users have requested further information on the use of the *Almanac's* ratios and statistics. This Q & A addition to the *Almanac* is in response to that demand.

1. What are the general purposes of the Almanac?

The goal of the *Almanac* is to provide users with a reliable and comprehensive source of standard financial ratios and financial statistics on all corporations, public and private, including those filing 1120S returns in the United States. Excluded are all individual proprietorships and partnerships. The *Almanac* makes available key business and financial statistics, which are consistent and neutral (unbiased by any commercial publisher or trade association).

2. What is the source and reliability of the Almanac's results?

The *Almanac's* results are computed from the Department of the Treasury, Internal Revenue Service's statistical sampling of the tax returns of all corporations. Dividends received from foreign corporations are included in total receipts of those corporations affected. The statistics apply to the company rather than the establishment.

3. Are international comparisons available?

Yes. Because of the adoption of a common system of industrial classification by the U.S., Canada and Mexico, known as the North American Industrial Classification System of industries (NAICS), under the North American Free Trade Agreement, users in Canada and Mexico can compare and contrast their results with those corporations in the United States.

4. What about comparisons within the U.S?

These are the most important applications of the *Almanac*. Results are available for each and every corporation within the U.S., whether public or private, and include small business corporations, those which file the 1120S tax return. Therefore, users can compare their corporate performance with that of their industry and asset size group of corporate enterprise in the United States.

5. How many corporations are covered in the Almanac?

The *Almanac's* results are derived from more than 5.8 million corporation tax returns. Furthermore, the user can easily determine the number of enterprises for the total of each industry and by each of the 12 asset size groups. This makes for a total of 13 asset size comparisons.

6. What about differences in the size of corporations?

In addition to the results for each industry, the *Almanac* displays 12 columns of performance by the size of assets. Again, this makes for a total of 13 asset size comparisons.

7. Does the Almanac distinguish between the profitability of corporations?

In a word, yes. Each industry is divided between two tables: Table I reports the results of all corporations in an industry, that is, those with and without net income. It is followed by a second table for the same industry, Table II, which reports only those corporations with net income.

8. How many items of information are there for each industry?

There are 50 indicators of corporate performance in each table and each industry and for all asset size groups, except where the IRS' data sample is too small, or it does not supply the necessary information.

9. Who are the users of the Almanac?

Accountants, corporate managers, business consultants, investors evaluating a corporate takeover, entrepreneurs considering new businesses, lawyers, and students of accounting, business, and management.

10. What accounting time period is covered?

The Internal Revenue Service provides the most recent statistics publicly available for the *Almanac*. For the 2012 *Almanac*, these statistics apply to the accounting period from July 2008 through June 2009.

WHAT'S NEW IN THIS EDITION

Beginning with the year 2002, the *Almanac of Business and Industrial Financial Ratios* began using the North American Industry Classification System (NAICS). NAICS replaces the Internal Revenue Service's own system, which it had used for many years, an adaptation of Standard Industrial Classification (SIC); all previous *Almanacs* had used that adaptation.

The new industrial classification system is the product of the North American Free Trade Agreement (NAFTA), and it replaces the existing classification systems not only of the United States but also of Canada and Mexico. Hence, the new system applies uniformly to the three countries, and users of the *Almanac 2012*, utilizing the new international industrial classification system, can now compare their results with corporations in all three nations.

In the United States, the new manual was created by the Office of Management and Budget (OMB). The NAICS system gives special attention to industries producing and furnishing advanced technologies, new and emerging industries, as well as service industries in general. NAICS divides the economy into 21 sectors, five in the predominantly goods-producing area, and 16 in the service producing area.

INDUSTRY SECTORS

In 2007, NAICS was revised and reorganized; several of those changes apply to the *Almanac 2012*. The Real Estate Investment Trust category (525930) was deleted. In its place, Mortgage REIT's were reclassified to Other Financial Vehicles (525995) while Equity REIT's were reclassified either to Lessors of Buildings (531115) or Lessors of Miniwarehouses, Self-Storage Units and other Real Estate (531135), depending on the content of the REIT portfolio.

The other major changes were in the information sector. The Internet Publishing and Broadcasting category (516100) was deleted and reclassified with Other Information Services (519100). Internet Service Providers (518115) were reclassified to Telecommunications (517000). Web Search Portals (also part of 518115) were reclassified to the expanded category, Other Information Services (519100). The remainder of the 518115 category was reorganized as Data processing, Hosting and Related Services (518210).

The source of the IRS's data are the tax returns of all *active* public and private corporations. Because the *Almanac's* data are derived only from corporate tax returns, there is a mixture of corporate with the financial performance of partnerships and individual proprietorships; the *Almanac's* information constitutes a **homogeneous universe**. The tax returns are classified by the IRS on the basis of the business activity which accounts for a corporation's largest percentage of total receipts. Large corporations with dissimilar business activities are included in only one industry, despite operations that are unrelated to the industry in which they are grouped.

The data developed by the IRS are derived from a stratified probability sample of corporation income tax returns. Where the sample data from the sample are small and should those numbers be used in a denominator, the result is reported as a dot (·) in the *Almanac*. Returns of the largest corporations are generally in the sample from year to year, but comparability can be affected by consolidations and mergers, changes in the law and the tax forms, and changes in the industrial classification system used over the years.

REPRESENTATIVE INDUSTRIES

The *Almanac* reports on nearly 200 industries. Minor industries are denoted by a six-digit code; major industries are designated by a three-digit industry code; industrial sectors by a two-digit code; and industrial divisions by a two-digit code. When the data are the same for minor, major, sector, and industrial division, the IRS reports only the industrial division, and similarly for other identities applicable to the major and sectoral industries; the *Almanac* follows this procedure.

Almanac 2012 continues the previous coverage of reporting information: for all industries, **Table I, Corporations with and without Net Income** (that is, the entire universe of active reporting corporations), and **Table II, Corporations with Net Income**, a subset of the universe. In the *Almanac 2012*, Table I covers over 5.8 million enterprises (corporations), and Table II covers 3.2 million corporations with net income. This implies that 2.6 million corporations reported deficits. The IRS defines net income (or deficit) as the companies' net profit or loss from taxable sources of income reduced by allowable deductions. Total receipts of the 5.8 million corporations reported in *Almanac 2012* was $28.6 trillion, down by $0.2 trillion.

The *Almanac* continues to report performance results not only by the total for each industry, but by 12 other asset size groups (a total of 13 asset size groups), providing 50 items of data and/or ratios on corporate performance:

Total

Zero
$1 to $500,000
$500,001 to $1,000,000
$1,000,001 to $5,000,000
$5,000,001 to $10,000,000
$10,000,001 to $25,000,000
$25,000,001 to $50,000,000
$50,000,001 to $100,000,000
$100,000,001 to $250,000,000
$250,000,001 to $500,000,000
$500,000,001 to $2,500,000,000
$2,500,000,001 or more

All data in Tables I and II cover an accounting period identified on all tables and are the most recent information available from the IRS. For the *Almanac 2012*, the accounting period is July 2008 through June 2009. The dating of the data is counterbalanced by the most extensive industrial coverage available in any report on financial performance, the number of items of corporate performance, and their availability in thirteen asset size groups. Moreover, the timing of the data are also counterbalanced by the stability of the *Almanac's* values as past trends have indicated. Therefore, the *Almanac's* financial results are reliable in assessing current corporate performance.

Beyond its reliable insights into corporate behavior on a micro basis, its comprehensive and detailed coverage make the *Almanac* the **Anatomy of American Corporate Capitalism**. In this macro sense, it constitutes **the** example to those countries desirous of modeling their economies on the American performance.

How to Use the Almanac

On the micro level, the *Almanac* multiplies manyfold the power of financial analysis to evaluate an individual company's financial performance: In contrast to many standard reports, the *Almanac* gives management, and analysts independent of any company, more of the fundamental analytical tools needed to compare their company with companies in the same industry and of the same asset size. The *Almanac* can enhance the value of any company's annual report because it affords the analyst and the stockholder detailed background of financial information for comparison.

All items and ratios are listed in Both Table I and Table II. No figures are reported in the *Almanac* when the IRS has either suppressed the underlying data, or the sample size, or other reasons affecting a calculated result, and where the ratio/item was not applicable to an industry. The 50 tax-based items that provide that financial analysis are as follows:

1. Number of Enterprises

These are the count of corporate tax returns filed by active corporations on one of the Form 1120-series returns.

SPECIAL NOTE: Net Sales is used to compute the percentage of items 3 to 7 to Net Sales for all industries, except Finance, Insurance, and Real Estate (FIRE). For the FIRE industries, Total Receipts are used to compute the percentage of items 3 to 7.

Revenues ($ in thousands), Items 2 to 9

2. Operating Income (Net Sales)

This is the IRS item Business Receipts, the gross operating receipts reduced by the cost of returned goods and allowances.

3. Interest

Taxable interest includes interest on U.S. Government obligations, loans, notes, mortgages, arbitrage bonds, nonexempt private activity bonds, corporate bonds, bank deposits, and tax refunds; interest received from tax-exempt state or local municipal bonds and ESOP loans are not included in this item.

4. Rents

These are the gross amounts received from the use or occupancy of property by corporations whose principal activities did not involve operating rental properties.

5. Royalties

These are gross payments received for the use of property rights before taking deductions.

6. Other Portfolio Income

These consist of cash, notes, and accounts receivable, less allowance for bad debts and inventories.

7. Other Receipts

These receipts include such items as income from minor operations, cash discounts, claims, license rights, judgments, and joint ventures.

8. Total Receipts

Total receipts are the sum of ten items: 1. Business receipts; 2. Interest; 3. Interest on government obligations: state and local; 4. Rents; 5. Royalties; 6. Net capital gains (excluding long-term gains from regulated investment companies); 7. Net gain, noncapital assets; 8. Dividends received from domestic corporations; 9. Dividends received from foreign corporations; 10. Other receipts.

9. Average Total Receipts

Total receipts divided by the number of enterprises.

OPERATING COSTS/OPERATING INCOME, ITEMS 10 TO 22

10. Cost of Operations

This is the IRS's Costs of Goods Sold; it consists of the costs incurred in producing the goods or furnishing the services that generated the corporations' business receipts.

11. Salaries and Wages

These include the amount of salaries and wages paid as well as bonuses and director's fees, but no contributions to pension plans (see item 16) nor compensation of officers (see item 20).

12. Taxes Paid

Excludes Federal Income Taxes; they are the amounts paid for ordinary state and local taxes, social security, payroll taxes, unemployment insurance taxes, excise taxes, import and tariff duties, and business license and privilege taxes.

13. Interest Paid

These amounts consist of interest paid on all business indebtedness.

14. Depreciation

The charges allowed are governed principally by the IRS rules in effect in 1997, basically enacted in 1986, but also include other modifications. Hence, depreciation could represent amounts computed by different sets of rules.

15. Amortization and Depletion

Most amortization is calculated on a straight-line basis. Depletion is allowed for the exhaustion of natural deposits and timber.

16. Pensions, Profit-Sharing, Stock Bonus, and Annuity Plans

These are amounts deducted during the current year for qualified pension, profit-sharing, or other funded deferred compensation plans.

17. Employee Benefits

These are employer contributions to death benefit, insurance, health, accident, and sickness, and other welfare plans.

18. Advertising

Amounts include promotion and publicity expenses.

19. Other Expenses

These include expenses for repairs, bad debts, rent paid on business property, domestic production activities, contributions and gifts, and expenses not allocable to specific deductible items.

20. Officers' Compensation

Salaries, wages, stock bonuses, bonds, and other forms of compensation are included in this item.

21. Operating Margin

This is the net income after all operating costs have been deducted.

22. Operating Margin Before Officers' Compensation

This measure takes into account the effect of Officers' Compensation on the operating margin.

SELECTED AVERAGE BALANCE SHEET ITEMS ($ IN THOUSANDS) ITEMS 23 TO 29

23. *Average Net Receivables*

The total of Notes and Accounts Receivable, less Allowance for Bad Debts, divided by the number of enterprises. Notes and Accounts Receivable are the gross amounts arising from business sales or services to customers on credit in the course of ordinary trade or business. This includes commercial paper, charge accounts, current intercompany receivables, property investment loans, and trade acceptances.

24. *Average Inventories*

Total inventories are divided by the number of enterprises. Inventories include finished goods, partially finished goods, new materials and supplies acquired for sale, merchandise on hand or in transit, and growing crops reported as assets by agricultural enterprises.

25. *Average Net Property, Plant and Equipment*

This includes depreciable assets less accumulated depreciation, depletable assets less accumulated depletion, and land; the sum is divided by the number of enterprises. Depreciable assets consist of end-of-year balance sheet tangible property, such as buildings and equipment used in trade or business, or held for the production of income, and that has a useful life of one year or more. The amount of accumulated depreciation represents the portion written off in the current year, as well as in prior years. Depletable assets represent the end-of-year value of mineral property, oil and gas wells, and other natural resources; standing timber; intangible development and drilling costs capitalized; and leases and leaseholds, subject to depletion. Accumulated depletion represents the cumulative adjustment of these assets.

26. *Average Total Assets*

Total Assets (and Total Liabilities) are amounts reported in the end-of-year balance sheet. Total Assets are net amounts after reduction from accumulated depreciation, accumulated amortization, accumulated depletion, and the reserve for bad debts. Total Liabilities include the claims of creditors and stockholders' equity, and were net after reduction by the cost of treasury stock. The average of total assets was obtained by dividing it by the number of enterprises.

27. *Average of Notes and Loans Payable, and Mortgages*

These liabilities were separated on the balance sheet according to the time to maturity of the obligations. Time to maturity was based on the date of the balance sheet, rather than the date of issue of the obligations. The total was divided by the number of enterprises.

28. *Average of All Other Liabilities*

These included accounts payable, and other liabilities including other current liabilities. The total was divided by the number of enterprises.

29. *Average Net Worth*

Net Worth represents the stockholders' equity in the corporation (total assets minus the claims of creditors). It consists of Capital Stock, Paid-In Capital Surplus, Retained Earnings Appropriated, Retained Earnings Unappropriated, less cost of treasury stock.

SELECTED FINANCIAL RATIOS, NUMBER OF TIMES TO ONE, RATIOS 30 TO 44

30. Current Ratio

The items that used Current Assets for this ratio are Cash; Notes and Accounts Receivable, Less: Allowance for Bad Debts; Inventories; Government Obligations; Tax-Exempt Securities; and Other Current Assets. For Current Liabilities, the following items were included: Accounts Payable; Mortgages and Notes Maturing in Less than 1 Year; and Other Current Liabilities.

This ratio, rated highest by CPAs as a measure of liquidity, gauges the ability of a company to meet its short-term financial obligations should it be compelled to liquidate its assets. However, it is not an absolute measure of the company's ability to meet its obligations. It is obtained by dividing current assets by current liabilities. The standard guideline has been a ratio of 2 to 1; however, some companies have found that in their experience, a ratio less than 2 to 1 is adequate, while others consider a larger one to be necessary. The ratio is affected by the method of valuation of inventory (LIFO or FIFO) and by inflation. The *Almanac* provides measures that can be treated as standards by size of asset.

31. Quick Ratio

This ratio is also known as the "Acid Test Ratio" because it is often used to estimate a company's general liquidity. There is some disagreement about the inclusion of inventory in the numerator because it may be slow moving, obsolete, or pledged to specific creditors, and, therefore, not be readily convertible into cash. The *Almanac* adopts a conservative approach and does not include the item in calculating the ratio. Excluding inventories and other current assets, the numerator is the same as that used in determining current assets. The denominator, current liabilities, is unchanged. The ratio of 1 to 1 has been considered a reasonable standard, but it is jeopardized because accounts and notes receivable may not be convertible into cash at face value and at short notice. The *Almanac* provides measures that can be treated as standards by size of asset.

32. Net Sales to Working Capital

This is an efficiency, or turnover, ratio that measures the rate at which current assets less current liabilities (Working Capital) is used in making sales. (In industries in Finance, Insurance, and Real Estate, total receipts rather than net sales is used.) A low ratio indicates a less efficient (profitable) use of working capital in making sales. The *Almanac* provides measures that can be treated as standards by size of asset. Working Capital is the difference between current assets and current liabilities.

33. Coverage Ratio

This ratio measures the number of times all interest paid by the company is covered by earnings before interest charges and taxes (EBIT). For that reason, the ratio is also known as the "times interest earned ratio." The ratio indicates the company's ability to service its debt based on its income.

34. Total Asset Turnover

The ratio is an efficiency ratio because it indicates the effectiveness of the company's use of its total assets in generating sales. It is measured by dividing net sales by total assets.

35. *Inventory Turnover*

Inventory turnover measures the liquidity of the inventory. It is computed by dividing the cost of goods sold by the average inventory. The result shows the number of times that the average inventory can be converted into receivables or cash. The ratio reflects both on the quality of the inventory and the efficiency of management. Typically, the higher the turnover rate, the more likely profits will be higher.

SPECIAL NOTE: Inventory turnover is not computed for industries in Finance, Insurance, and Real Estate.

36. *Receivables Turnover*

This ratio measures the liquidity of accounts receivable. It indicates the average collection period throughout the year. It is obtained by dividing sales average by net receivables. It is not computed in the Finance, Insurance, and Real Estate industries (although it is calculated for all other industries even though conventional analysis typically omits it) for many of the industries in the *Almanac*.

37. *Total Liabilities to Net Worth*

This ratio indicates the extent to which the company's funds are supplied by short- and long-term creditors compared to its owners. It is an indicator of the company's long-term debt paying ability. The ratio is one of the most important bearing on the company's capital structure. Net worth is defined in ratio 29.

38. *Current Assets to Working Capital*

The dependence of Working Capital in part on current assets is important to understanding this part of the source of Working Capital. Current Assets are defined in ratio 30 and Working Capital is defined in ratio 32.

39. *Current Liabilities to Working Capital*

The dependence of Working Capital in part on current liabilities is important to understanding this part of the source of Working Capital. Current Liabilities are defined in ratio 30 and Working Capital is defined in ratio 32.

40. *Working Capital to Net Sales or Total Receipts*

The purpose of this ratio is to determine the working capital needed in relation to projected sales or receipts. Working Capital is defined in ratio 32.

41. *Inventory to Working Capital*

This ratio, by showing the proportion of Working Capital invested in Inventory, indicates the part of Current Assets that are least liquid. Inventories which exceed working capital indicate that current liabilities exceed liquid current assets. Working Capital is defined in ratio 32.

42. *Total Receipts to Cash Flow*

Cash Flow is the difference between cash receipts and cash disbursements. The ratio of total receipts to cash flow could suggest steps which management might take to improve the company's cash position.

43. *Cost of Goods to Cash Flow*

This ratio can be the basis for projections of cash requirements needed to fund projected costs of production. Cash flow is defined in ratio 42.

44. *Cash Flow to Total Debt*

This ratio indicates the extent to which a company could service its total debt from cash flow. It is analogous to the coverage ratio; refer to ratio 33. Cash flow is defined in ratio 42.

SELECTED FINANCIAL FACTORS (IN PERCENTAGES), ITEMS 45 TO 50

45. *Debt Ratio (Total Liabilities to Total Assets)*

This ratio indicates the company's ability to pay all its debts. It measures the creditors' and owners' of the company's ability to withstand losses. It is an indicator of the long-run solvency of the firm.

46. *Return on Total Assets*

The ratio combines the turnover and profit ratios (Sales/Total Assets x [times] Profit/Sales) and yields the return on investment (Total Assets). The result is the end product of the DuPont System of financial analysis. The system takes into account both operating income and operating assets. In Table I of each industry, the Return on Investment (ROI) is net income less deficit before income taxes divided by total assets. In Table II of each industry, the ROI is net income before income taxes divided by Total Assets. Total Assets are used because management has discretion in the investment of the resources provided by both the creditors and owners.

47. *Return on Equity Before Income Taxes*

This ratio measures the profitability of the company's operations to owners, before income taxes. For Table I this is net income, less deficit before income taxes and before credits. For Table II this is net income minus income tax before credits.

48. *Return on Equity After Income Taxes*

This ratio measures the profitability of the company's operations to owners, after income taxes. For Table I this is net income, less deficit and minus income tax before credits. For Table II this is net income minus income tax and before credits.

49. *Profit Margin (Before Income Tax)*

This is net income before income tax divided by net sales (or total receipts) and indicates the contribution of sales to the profitability of the company. Competition, capital structure, and operating characteristics cause the margin to vary within and among industries. For Table I, net income less deficit and before income taxes is the numerator; for Table II it is net income before tax.

50. *Profit Margin (After Income Tax)*

This ratio is the same as ratio 49 except that income taxes are taken into account.

Table of Contents

Page references to tables for industries with net income are in italic

PRINCIPAL BUSINESS ACTIVITY (BASED ON NAICS)

ALMANAC
of Business and Industrial
FINANCIAL RATIOS

43rd ANNUAL EDITION
2012

Table I

Corporations with and without Net Income

AGRICULTURAL PRODUCTION

MONEY AMOUNTS AND SIZE OF ASSETS IN THOUSANDS OF DOLLARS

Item Description for Accounting Period 7/08 Through 6/09		Total	Zero Assets	Under 500	500 to 1,000	1,000 to 5,000	5,000 to 10,000	10,000 to 25,000	25,000 to 50,000	50,000 to 100,000	100,000 to 250,000	250,000 to 500,000	500,000 to 2,500,000	2,500,000 and over
Number of Enterprises	1	99073	10476	55029	16410	15172	1045	588	165	93	66	17	12	0
Revenues ($ in Thousands)														
Net Sales	2	108809500	1083467	12997189	12355259	21297545	7746668	8331876	4141793	7539086	9640162	6897577	16778877	0
Interest	3	312827	9461	30740	43883	87341	27866	15374	12137	10609	15894	17623	41899	0
Rents	4	941914	23382	181865	181366	327781	41197	21118	18484	19538	60753	13389	53040	0
Royalties	5	152260	1309	35633	12551	20791	6361	4830	9960	8105	31036	2682	19003	0
Other Portfolio Income	6	1334617	81664	256990	140527	350717	94263	89730	96055	33647	78980	21968	90077	0
Other Receipts	7	12613485	318411	3294794	2875063	4267967	918348	383450	256714	286267	140745	109131	-237403	0
Total Receipts	8	124164603	1517694	16797211	15608649	26352142	8834703	8846378	4535143	7897252	9967570	7062370	16745493	0
Average Total Receipts	9	1253	145	305	951	1737	8454	15045	27486	84917	151024	415434	1395458	•
Operating Costs/Operating Income (%)														
Cost of Operations	10	53.6	8.9	21.6	38.6	34.0	52.9	63.7	64.7	64.9	75.7	79.3	81.5	•
Salaries and Wages	11	7.0	8.9	9.8	7.7	10.3	6.8	7.0	6.4	5.4	4.7	3.3	3.9	•
Taxes Paid	12	1.8	3.6	2.6	2.5	2.8	2.0	1.4	1.3	1.0	1.2	1.0	0.6	•
Interest Paid	13	2.5	3.8	2.8	2.6	3.5	3.1	1.9	3.1	1.6	1.8	1.2	1.9	•
Depreciation	14	6.3	7.9	9.7	8.7	9.7	6.3	4.5	5.7	3.7	4.0	3.2	2.5	•
Amortization and Depletion	15	0.3	0.0	0.1	0.1	0.2	0.3	0.1	0.4	0.4	0.4	0.7	0.5	•
Pensions and Other Deferred Comp.	16	0.2	0.1	0.1	0.3	0.1	0.1	0.1	0.3	0.2	0.2	0.3	0.2	•
Employee Benefits	17	1.0	1.0	1.3	1.0	1.0	0.8	0.8	0.6	1.0	0.7	0.6	1.6	•
Advertising	18	0.3	0.5	0.3	0.3	0.3	0.3	0.5	0.2	0.2	0.3	0.2	0.5	•
Other Expenses	19	39.2	86.0	74.2	58.9	59.9	44.0	24.5	27.1	24.2	12.2	11.4	10.1	•
Officers' Compensation	20	1.8	1.3	4.1	3.3	2.3	1.8	1.5	1.0	1.0	0.7	0.5	0.4	•
Operating Margin	21	•	•	•	•	•	•	•	•	•	•	•	•	•
Operating Margin Before Officers' Comp.	22	•	•	•	•	•	•	•	•	•	•	•	•	•

Selected Average Balance Sheet ($ in Thousands)

Net Receivables 23	90	0	2	36	61	323	1713	2830	9037	19403	50819	205813	•
Inventories 24	116	0	12	43	138	854	2537	3783	11199	18708	54526	94370	•
Net Property, Plant and Equipment 25	503	0	91	404	1072	3849	6167	14052	27495	53858	126497	306429	•
Total Assets 26	1097	0	191	699	1941	6829	14853	34266	68067	142787	326934	1204894	•
Notes and Loans Payable 27	614	0	178	470	1134	4409	7213	17798	27333	55093	125985	501754	•
All Other Liabilities 28	170	0	13	50	216	850	2369	3958	12673	27449	51531	430086	•
Net Worth 29	313	0	-1	178	592	1569	5271	12510	28061	60244	149417	273054	•

Selected Financial Ratios (Times to 1)

Current Ratio 30	1.4	•	1.4	1.5	1.3	1.2	1.5	1.3	1.5	2.3	1.2
Quick Ratio 31	0.7	•	0.9	1.0	0.7	0.5	0.7	0.5	0.7	1.0	0.6
Net Sales to Working Capital 32	11.5	•	15.2	14.2	14.4	25.3	7.4	10.7	9.1	5.0	19.6
Coverage Ratio 33	1.0	5.7	1.9	1.9	0.9	•	1.0	0.6	1.8	1.5	•
Total Asset Turnover 34	1.0	•	1.2	1.1	0.7	1.1	1.0	0.7	1.2	1.2	1.2
Inventory Turnover 35	5.1	•	4.3	6.7	3.5	4.6	3.6	4.3	4.7	5.9	12.1
Receivables Turnover 36	13.0	•	86.3	23.9	23.5	21.4	8.1	9.3	7.7	8.2	11.0
Total Liabilities to Net Worth 37	2.5	•	•	2.9	2.3	3.4	1.8	1.7	1.4	1.2	3.4
Current Assets to Working Capital 38	3.7	•	3.4	3.0	4.6	7.1	3.0	4.7	3.0	1.8	6.8
Current Liabilities to Working Capital 39	2.7	•	2.4	2.0	3.6	6.1	2.0	3.7	2.0	0.8	5.8
Working Capital to Net Sales 40	0.1	•	0.1	0.1	0.1	0.0	0.1	0.1	0.1	0.2	0.1
Inventory to Working Capital 41	1.3	•	0.8	0.6	1.5	3.1	1.3	1.6	1.2	0.8	2.2
Total Receipts to Cash Flow 42	3.4	1.2	1.9	2.1	2.2	3.2	4.9	5.4	4.4	10.2	25.8
Cost of Goods to Cash Flow 43	1.8	0.1	0.4	0.8	0.8	1.7	3.1	3.5	2.9	6.7	21.0
Cash Flow to Total Debt 44	0.4	•	0.7	0.7	0.5	0.4	0.3	0.2	0.5	0.2	0.1

Selected Financial Factors (in Percentages)

Debt Ratio 45	71.4	•	100.5	74.5	69.5	77.0	64.5	63.5	58.8	57.8	54.3	77.3
Return on Total Assets 46	2.5	•	6.7	5.4	2.2	•	1.8	1.3	3.3	3.3	2.3	•
Return on Equity Before Income Taxes 47	•	•	•	9.9	•	•	•	•	3.5	3.5	1.7	•
Return on Equity After Income Taxes 48	•	•	•	8.1	•	•	•	•	2.9	2.1	•	•
Profit Margin (Before Income Tax) 49	•	18.1	2.6	2.3	•	•	•	•	1.2	1.5	0.6	•
Profit Margin (After Income Tax) 50	•	16.8	2.2	1.9	•	•	•	•	1.0	0.9	•	•

1

Table II

Corporations with Net Income

AGRICULTURAL PRODUCTION

MONEY AMOUNTS AND SIZE OF ASSETS IN THOUSANDS OF DOLLARS

Item Description for Accounting Period 7/08 Through 6/09		Total	Zero Assets	Under 500	500 to 1000	1,000 to 5,000	5,000 to 10,000	10,000 to 25,000	25,000 to 50,000	50,000 to 100,000	100,000 to 250,000	250,000 to 500,000	500,000 to 2,500,000	2,500,000 and over
Number of Enterprises	1	52313	4465	28877	9616	8505	402	276	71	•	•	8	7	0
Revenues ($ in Thousands)														
Net Sales	2	54833880	666967	8378967	8900621	9975170	3244060	4941946	1829019	•	•	3474736	3782062	0
Interest	3	221746	7967	26268	39456	65868	21781	10625	7257	•	•	9587	15448	0
Rents	4	593340	3909	81353	117986	245706	30474	15928	5760	•	•	4130	11314	0
Royalties	5	116479	1309	8577	12551	15746	5631	4574	9799	•	•	2682	17431	0
Other Portfolio Income	6	879437	76566	192487	111291	210681	70229	63235	81096	•	•	12997	6105	0
Other Receipts	7	10256738	301078	2483834	2531684	3309437	550659	459377	200026	•	•	72824	100973	0
Total Receipts	8	66901620	1057796	11171486	11713589	13822608	3922834	5495685	2132957	•	•	3576956	3933333	0
Average Total Receipts	9	1279	237	387	1218	1625	9758	19912	30042	•	•	447120	561905	•
Operating Costs/Operating Income (%)														
Cost of Operations	10	44.3	4.5	15.2	39.0	19.7	35.3	65.8	62.9	•	•	74.9	67.7	•
Salaries and Wages	11	7.6	11.5	8.4	6.8	12.7	6.7	5.0	6.6	•	•	4.2	8.3	•
Taxes Paid	12	2.0	4.6	2.1	2.3	3.1	2.2	1.2	1.5	•	•	1.3	0.6	•
Interest Paid	13	2.0	2.8	2.2	2.0	3.5	2.0	1.4	1.8	•	•	1.0	1.1	•
Depreciation	14	7.1	7.2	9.4	7.5	12.9	5.4	3.4	6.9	•	•	4.0	4.7	•
Amortization and Depletion	15	0.3	0.0	0.0	0.1	0.0	0.1	0.1	0.5	•	•	1.3	1.6	•
Pensions and Other Deferred Comp.	16	0.2	0.1	0.1	0.3	0.2	0.1	0.2	0.2	•	•	0.3	0.2	•
Employee Benefits	17	1.1	1.1	1.3	0.9	0.9	1.0	0.7	0.5	•	•	0.6	3.3	•
Advertising	18	0.3	0.3	0.3	0.2	0.3	0.2	0.2	0.1	•	•	0.1	0.9	•
Other Expenses	19	43.2	62.7	73.1	58.7	67.7	54.2	23.4	22.7	•	•	8.5	10.0	•
Officers' Compensation	20	2.3	1.9	3.8	3.5	3.0	2.7	1.5	1.4	•	•	0.5	0.6	•
Operating Margin	21	•	3.4	•	•	•	•	•	•	•	•	3.4	0.9	•
Operating Margin Before Officers' Comp.	22	•	5.3	•	•	•	•	•	•	•	•	3.9	1.6	•

Selected Average Balance Sheet ($ in Thousands)

	•	•	•	•	•	•	•	•	•	•
Net Receivables 23	79	0	3	41	37	356	2116	3247	•	41800	88771
Inventories 24	107	0	8	36	160	1109	2657	3166	•	51797	69797
Net Property, Plant and Equipment 25	457	0	84	366	1026	2955	5673	14006	•	114580	228078
Total Assets 26	1032	0	210	713	1860	7021	15491	34365	•	302366	714142
Notes and Loans Payable 27	426	0	107	438	834	3345	5603	11938	•	95504	118586
All Other Liabilities 28	116	0	10	46	137	1005	2009	5000	•	50618	139636
Net Worth 29	490	0	93	229	889	2671	7879	17426	•	156244	455921

Selected Financial Ratios (Times to 1)

	•	•	•	•	•	•	•	•	•	•
Current Ratio 30	1.8	•	2.2	2.1	1.5	1.4	2.0	1.6	•	2.2	1.8
Quick Ratio 31	1.1	•	1.6	1.6	0.8	0.7	1.1	1.0	•	1.0	1.1
Net Sales to Working Capital 32	7.0	•	8.6	9.9	7.5	11.2	4.9	6.6	•	6.0	5.0
Coverage Ratio 33	6.8	23.1	8.7	6.1	5.1	6.3	7.0	7.2	•	7.1	5.5
Total Asset Turnover 34	1.0	•	1.4	1.3	0.6	1.1	1.2	0.7	•	1.4	0.8
Inventory Turnover 35	4.3	•	5.5	9.9	1.4	2.6	4.4	5.1	•	6.3	5.2
Receivables Turnover 36	12.4	•	71.2	26.7	24.5	17.8	7.8	7.1	•	•	•
Total Liabilities to Net Worth 37	1.1	•	1.3	2.1	1.1	1.6	1.0	1.0	•	0.9	0.6
Current Assets to Working Capital 38	2.2	•	1.8	1.9	2.8	3.6	2.0	2.6	•	1.8	2.2
Current Liabilities to Working Capital 39	1.2	•	0.8	0.9	1.8	2.6	1.0	1.6	•	0.8	1.2
Working Capital to Net Sales 40	0.1	•	0.1	0.1	0.1	0.1	0.2	0.2	•	0.2	0.2
Inventory to Working Capital 41	0.7	•	0.3	0.3	1.0	1.6	0.7	0.7	•	0.7	0.6
Total Receipts to Cash Flow 42	2.3	1.0	1.6	1.8	1.6	2.0	3.6	4.2	•	8.2	8.3
Cost of Goods to Cash Flow 43	1.0	0.0	0.2	0.7	0.3	0.7	2.4	2.7	•	6.1	5.6
Cash Flow to Total Debt 44	0.8	•	1.6	1.1	0.8	1.0	0.7	0.4	•	0.4	0.3

Selected Financial Factors (in Percentages)

	•	•	•	•	•	•	•	•	•	•
Debt Ratio 45	52.5	•	55.6	67.9	52.2	62.0	49.1	49.3	•	48.3	36.2
Return on Total Assets 46	13.9	•	26.9	15.9	11.4	14.8	11.1	10.0	•	10.4	4.5
Return on Equity Before Income Taxes 47	24.9	•	53.6	41.3	19.1	32.8	18.7	16.9	•	17.3	5.8
Return on Equity After Income Taxes 48	23.1	•	51.8	39.2	17.9	29.3	17.7	15.0	•	13.0	3.9
Profit Margin (Before Income Tax) 49	11.7	61.9	17.2	10.2	14.5	10.9	8.2	11.5	•	6.2	4.9
Profit Margin (After Income Tax) 50	10.8	59.8	16.6	9.7	13.6	9.7	7.8	10.2	•	4.7	3.3

2

Table I

Corporations with and without Net Income

FORESTRY AND LOGGING

MONEY AMOUNTS AND SIZE OF ASSETS IN THOUSANDS OF DOLLARS

Item Description for Accounting Period 7/08 Through 6/09	Total	Zero Assets	Under 500	500 to 1,000	1,000 to 5,000	5,000 to 10,000	10,000 to 25,000	25,000 to 50,000	50,000 to 100,000	100,000 to 250,000	250,000 to 500,000	500,000 to 2,500,000	2,500,000 and over
Number of Enterprises **1**	9942	1603	5564	1401	1235	13	82	25	9	0	4	5	0

Revenues ($ in Thousands)

Net Sales **2**	13125485	966002	1547548	3776555	3452020	191229	1170584	739452	419928	0	936783	325384	0
Interest **3**	228209	8409	2797	646	3388	62	3107	825	379	0	18003	190592	0
Rents **4**	52695	18877	8122	521	12371	72	3371	2174	111	0	2542	4535	0
Royalties **5**	21126	5	0	3094	13754	0	2707	0	0	0	0	1566	0
Other Portfolio Income **6**	299835	181098	1484	2744	43066	4361	32979	4481	4373	0	2303	22949	0
Other Receipts **7**	172834	5202	38045	20319	38001	-5419	11256	-7099	-8246	0	59764	21009	0
Total Receipts **8**	13900184	1179593	1597996	3403879	3562600	190305	1224004	739833	416545	0	1019395	566035	0
Average Total Receipts **9**	1398	736	287	2430	2885	14639	14927	29593	46283	•	254849	113207	•

Operating Costs/Operating Income (%)

Cost of Operations **10**	58.8	19.5	62.5	46.5	51.6	85.6	83.4	92.3	85.8	•	82.6	77.9	•
Salaries and Wages **11**	8.2	9.9	5.7	10.6	11.7	3.6	5.8	1.1	3.8	•	4.1	0.0	•
Taxes Paid **12**	2.1	0.6	1.9	2.4	2.8	0.6	1.6	1.9	1.0	•	0.9	4.1	•
Interest Paid **13**	4.4	7.0	2.1	1.8	2.4	0.8	2.4	1.1	3.0	•	2.2	81.2	•
Depreciation **14**	6.4	3.0	6.0	8.1	9.8	3.9	3.5	1.1	6.3	•	1.1	3.9	•
Amortization and Depletion **15**	0.5	0.5	0.5	•	0.1	•	0.2	0.8	0.2	•	3.3	3.3	•
Pensions and Other Deferred Comp. **16**	0.4	0.4	•	0.0	1.2	0.0	0.2	0.1	0.2	•	0.5	•	•
Employee Benefits **17**	1.2	0.2	2.7	1.0	1.7	0.1	0.3	0.2	1.1	•	1.3	•	•
Advertising **18**	0.1	0.1	0.0	0.1	0.2	0.0	0.1	0.0	0.1	•	0.1	•	•
Other Expenses **19**	21.5	76.2	12.8	23.2	21.1	11.7	6.6	4.6	8.5	•	8.1	39.8	•
Officers' Compensation **20**	2.6	0.8	5.2	3.1	3.0	1.0	2.4	0.4	1.4	•	0.7	•	•
Operating Margin **21**	•	•	0.7	3.1	•	•	•	•	•	•	•	•	•
Operating Margin Before Officers' Comp. **22**	•	•	6.0	6.2	•	•	•	•	•	•	•	•	•

Selected Average Balance Sheet ($ in Thousands)

Item												
Net Receivables 23	53	0	2	18	90	338	604	1102	1929	•	38743	25133
Inventories 24	72	0	7	22	122	3271	3811	3160	2338	•	3679	4328
Net Property, Plant and Equipment 25	868	0	53	475	1287	2653	6353	20413	27258	•	133864	846194
Total Assets 26	1801	0	83	710	1950	8463	15201	36315	72167	•	326687	1964360
Notes and Loans Payable 27	1028	0	79	623	1428	1165	4871	6424	19050	•	55017	1235510
All Other Liabilities 28	92	0	5	49	147	2810	721	1830	13014	•	51368	34258
Net Worth 29	681	0	-1	37	375	4488	9608	28061	40103	•	220302	694592

Selected Financial Ratios (Times to 1)

Item												
Current Ratio 30	3.6	•	3.7	1.1	1.2	0.6	2.7	4.8	1.3	•	1.4	21.3
Quick Ratio 31	2.9	•	3.2	0.4	0.8	0.2	0.9	2.0	0.3	•	0.9	21.1
Net Sales to Working Capital 32	3.3	•	18.3	143.4	37.1	•	4.1	4.9	8.6	•	12.5	0.1
Coverage Ratio 33	0.9	1.6	2.9	3.2	0.1	•	•	•	•	•	2.7	0.6
Total Asset Turnover 34	0.7	•	3.4	3.4	1.4	1.7	0.9	0.8	0.6	•	0.7	0.0
Inventory Turnover 35	10.8	•	25.0	51.5	11.8	3.8	3.1	8.6	17.1	•	52.6	11.7
Receivables Turnover 36	22.3	•	142.7	131.8	24.7	14.5	18.4	27.0	16.3	•	5.3	3.0
Total Liabilities to Net Worth 37	1.6	•	•	18.3	4.2	0.9	0.6	0.3	0.8	•	0.5	1.8
Current Assets to Working Capital 38	1.4	•	1.4	12.5	6.3	•	1.6	1.3	4.1	•	3.4	1.0
Current Liabilities to Working Capital 39	0.4	•	0.4	11.5	5.3	•	0.6	0.3	3.1	•	2.4	0.0
Working Capital to Net Sales 40	0.3	•	0.1	0.0	0.0	•	0.2	0.2	0.1	•	0.1	10.1
Inventory to Working Capital 41	0.2	•	0.1	2.6	1.4	•	0.9	0.6	0.5	•	0.2	0.0
Total Receipts to Cash Flow 42	5.9	1.3	7.1	4.4	7.6	47.0	2813.9	694.3	•	•	9.9	•
Cost of Goods to Cash Flow 43	3.5	0.2	4.5	2.1	3.9	40.2	2347.5	640.6	•	•	8.2	•
Cash Flow to Total Debt 44	0.2	•	0.5	0.8	0.2	0.1	0.0	0.0	•	•	0.2	•

Selected Financial Factors (in Percentages)

Item												
Debt Ratio 45	62.2	•	100.9	94.8	80.8	47.0	36.8	22.7	44.4	•	32.6	64.6
Return on Total Assets 46	2.9	•	20.3	19.2	0.2	•	•	•	•	•	4.3	1.5
Return on Equity Before Income Taxes 47	•	•	•	252.0	•	•	•	•	•	•	4.1	•
Return on Equity After Income Taxes 48	•	•	•	251.7	•	•	•	•	•	•	2.9	•
Profit Margin (Before Income Tax) 49	•	3.9	4.0	3.9	•	•	•	•	•	•	3.8	•
Profit Margin (After Income Tax) 50	•	3.9	3.6	3.8	•	•	•	•	•	•	2.7	•

Table II

Corporations with Net Income

FORESTRY AND LOGGING

MONEY AMOUNTS AND SIZE OF ASSETS IN THOUSANDS OF DOLLARS

Item Description for Accounting Period 7/08 Through 6/09	Total	Zero Assets	Under 500	500 to 1,000	1,000 to 5,000	5,000 to 10,000	10,000 to 25,000	25,000 to 50,000	50,000 to 100,000	100,000 to 250,000	250,000 to 500,000	500,000 to 2,500,000	2,500,000 and over
Number of Enterprises **1**	4053	520	2053	968	471	5	24	8	0	0	4	0	0
Revenues ($ in Thousands)													
Net Sales **2**	7618277	705659	1015797	2356976	1471473	62421	494741	672716	0	0	838494	0	0
Interest **3**	110564	0	2523	634	1742	9	2966	775	0	0	101915	0	0
Rents **4**	24481	0	8122	521	9075	72	3371	1755	0	0	1565	0	0
Royalties **5**	19555	0	0	3094	13754	0	2707	0	0	0	0	0	0
Other Portfolio Income **6**	118463	39178	662	2678	33642	4361	31033	4878	0	0	2033	0	0
Other Receipts **7**	132742	17	37510	20287	25850	163	5531	6232	0	0	37151	0	0
Total Receipts **8**	8024082	744854	1064614	2384190	1555536	67026	540349	686356	0	0	981158	0	0
Average Total Receipts **9**	1980	1432	519	2463	3303	13405	22515	85794	•	•	245290	•	•
Operating Costs/Operating Income (%)													
Cost of Operations **10**	55.6	1.4	60.5	44.8	56.8	52.9	77.7	89.5	•	•	83.1	•	•
Salaries and Wages **11**	6.9	10.3	2.2	11.6	5.7	11.0	7.0	1.0	•	•	3.2	•	•
Taxes Paid **12**	1.5	0.5	1.4	1.6	2.2	1.7	2.0	1.4	•	•	1.2	•	•
Interest Paid **13**	2.1	0.9	2.1	1.3	2.0	2.4	0.5	0.4	•	•	7.6	•	•
Depreciation **14**	5.6	1.8	5.2	8.1	9.4	11.8	2.1	1.6	•	•	0.9	•	•
Amortization and Depletion **15**	0.4	•	0.7	•	0.2	•	0.4	0.5	•	•	1.5	•	•
Pensions and Other Deferred Comp. **16**	0.6	•	•	0.0	2.5	0.0	0.3	0.0	•	•	0.5	•	•
Employee Benefits **17**	1.5	0.0	3.4	1.0	2.4	0.3	1.4	0.2	•	•	1.2	•	•
Advertising **18**	0.0	0.0	0.0	0.0	0.1	0.0	0.1	0.0	•	•	0.1	•	•
Other Expenses **19**	20.4	82.6	9.6	23.0	14.3	22.9	8.2	3.5	•	•	5.4	•	•
Officers' Compensation **20**	2.8	0.3	6.2	2.5	4.5	3.2	3.2	0.2	•	•	0.4	•	•
Operating Margin **21**	2.6	2.1	8.6	6.2	0.0	•	•	1.5	•	•	•	•	•
Operating Margin Before Officers' Comp. **22**	5.4	2.5	14.9	8.7	4.6	•	0.4	1.8	•	•	•	•	•

Selected Average Balance Sheet ($ in Thousands)

Net Receivables 23	58	0	0	25	51	460	567	3060	36160	•
Inventories 24	60	0	3	1	44	3244	4024	13162	1918	•
Net Property, Plant and Equipment 25	402	0	59	378	899	2987	6054	9004	121830	•
Total Assets 26	1175	0	126	672	1722	7707	14445	33547	596690	•
Notes and Loans Payable 27	650	0	126	532	951	3029	2134	6163	324787	•
All Other Liabilities 28	91	0	13	20	232	535	613	4452	40284	•
Net Worth 29	433	0	-13	120	540	4143	11698	22932	231619	•

Selected Financial Ratios (Times to 1)

Current Ratio 30	1.8	•	3.1	1.0	1.6	5.3	5.2	4.9	1.6	•
Quick Ratio 31	1.1	•	2.6	0.5	1.3	1.5	2.8	1.7	1.2	•
Net Sales to Working Capital 32	15.7	•	17.5	265.7	13.7	4.1	7.1	4.5	11.0	•
Coverage Ratio 33	4.8	9.4	7.3	6.7	3.9	1.5	13.1	9.1	2.5	•
Total Asset Turnover 34	1.6	•	3.9	3.6	1.8	1.6	1.4	2.5	0.4	•
Inventory Turnover 35	17.5	•	87.3	1519.4	40.6	2.0	4.0	5.7	90.9	•
Receivables Turnover 36	23.2	•	2138.5	113.3	18.9	6.8	14.7	•	1.6	•
Total Liabilities to Net Worth 37	1.7	•	•	4.6	2.2	0.9	0.2	0.5	1.6	•
Current Assets to Working Capital 38	2.3	•	1.5	26.1	2.7	1.2	1.2	1.3	2.7	•
Current Liabilities to Working Capital 39	1.3	•	0.5	25.1	1.7	0.2	0.2	0.3	1.7	•
Working Capital to Net Sales 40	0.1	•	0.0	0.0	0.1	0.2	0.1	0.2	0.1	•
Inventory to Working Capital 41	0.4	•	0.1	0.1	0.1	0.0	0.5	0.7	0.1	•
Total Receipts to Cash Flow 42	4.1	1.1	4.9	4.0	7.2	5.5	13.6	19.4	6.4	•
Cost of Goods to Cash Flow 43	2.3	0.0	3.0	1.8	4.1	2.9	10.6	17.4	5.4	•
Cash Flow to Total Debt 44	0.6	•	0.7	1.1	0.4	0.6	0.6	0.4	0.1	•

Selected Financial Factors (in Percentages)

Debt Ratio 45	63.2	•	110.5	82.2	68.7	46.2	19.0	31.6	61.2	•
Return on Total Assets 46	16.0	•	61.2	31.3	14.1	5.9	9.9	10.1	6.8	•
Return on Equity Before Income Taxes 47	34.4	•	•	149.8	33.3	3.8	11.3	13.1	10.7	•
Return on Equity After Income Taxes 48	31.3	•	•	149.7	31.8	2.7	8.5	9.9	7.3	•
Profit Margin (Before Income Tax) 49	7.9	7.7	13.5	7.4	5.8	1.3	6.4	3.6	11.8	•
Profit Margin (After Income Tax) 50	7.2	7.7	12.8	7.3	5.5	0.9	4.8	2.7	8.1	•

Table I

Corporations with and without Net Income

SUPPORT ACTIVITIES AND FISHING, HUNTING AND TRAPPING

MONEY AMOUNTS AND SIZE OF ASSETS IN THOUSANDS OF DOLLARS

Item Description for Accounting Period 7/08 Through 6/09	Total	Zero Assets	Under 500	500 to 1,000	1,000 to 5,000	5,000 to 10,000	10,000 to 25,000	25,000 to 50,000	50,000 to 100,000	100,000 to 250,000	250,000 to 500,000	500,000 to 2,500,000	2,500,000 and over
Number of Enterprises **1**	28278	6909	16072	3077	1713	281	167	44	10	5	0	0	0
Revenues ($ in Thousands)													
Net Sales **2**	28338219	363661	4888410	3556348	7701126	2750367	4836412	1377642	918311	1945943	0	0	0
Interest **3**	30760	0	3236	1080	12662	6567	3732	1801	916	768	0	0	0
Rents **4**	34713	101	101	1136	25125	5943	1574	646	64	24	0	0	0
Royalties **5**	25161	0	0	0	5006	870	0	18045	0	1241	0	0	0
Other Portfolio Income **6**	274194	81823	24814	37385	56709	60331	7879	1167	1085	3000	0	0	0
Other Receipts **7**	773622	-16974	129683	157570	162540	60825	103845	114495	21630	40005	0	0	0
Total Receipts **8**	29476669	428611	5046244	3753519	7963168	2884903	4953442	1513796	942006	1990981	0	0	0
Average Total Receipts **9**	1042	62	314	1220	4649	10267	29661	34404	94201	398196	•	•	•
Operating Costs/Operating Income (%)													
Cost of Operations **10**	61.9	24.3	41.8	24.8	73.0	75.8	74.8	81.0	65.1	75.9	•	•	•
Salaries and Wages **11**	8.3	5.9	10.1	9.1	7.2	6.0	9.6	4.8	9.8	9.5	•	•	•
Taxes Paid **12**	1.6	5.4	2.2	1.7	1.4	1.4	1.6	1.4	1.3	0.8	•	•	•
Interest Paid **13**	1.2	1.1	1.2	1.1	0.8	1.7	1.1	2.5	1.3	1.3	•	•	•
Depreciation **14**	4.0	7.5	3.3	7.6	3.7	5.1	2.4	3.0	2.9	3.0	•	•	•
Amortization and Depletion **15**	0.1	•	0.1	0.1	0.2	0.2	0.1	0.0	0.2	0.2	•	•	•
Pensions and Other Deferred Comp. **16**	0.1	•	0.0	0.1	0.1	0.1	0.2	0.3	0.2	0.1	•	•	•
Employee Benefits **17**	0.6	2.1	0.6	0.5	0.4	0.7	0.6	0.6	1.3	0.5	•	•	•
Advertising **18**	0.2	0.2	0.5	0.1	0.1	0.2	0.2	0.1	0.7	0.2	•	•	•
Other Expenses **19**	20.4	45.3	32.9	53.4	13.6	11.1	8.0	10.8	10.7	6.0	•	•	•
Officers' Compensation **20**	2.5	14.6	6.9	2.1	1.8	1.5	0.8	1.0	0.8	0.3	•	•	•
Operating Margin **21**	•	•	0.5	•	•	•	0.6	•	5.6	2.2	•	•	•
Operating Margin Before Officers' Comp. **22**	1.6	8.2	7.3	1.5	•	•	1.4	•	6.4	2.5	•	•	•

Selected Average Balance Sheet ($ in Thousands)

Net Receivables 23	71	0	4	27	241	1231	3091	5728	12746	43423
Inventories 24	67	0	5	20	173	934	2758	3940	15627	81889
Net Property, Plant and Equipment 25	187	0	29	288	852	3323	3837	8693	14433	76236
Total Assets 26	540	0	85	693	1977	7338	15162	33993	71590	316221
Notes and Loans Payable 27	242	0	67	345	977	2568	5710	15286	24028	87080
All Other Liabilities 28	117	0	25	79	360	1456	4452	6555	22254	74229
Net Worth 29	181	0	-8	269	641	3314	5000	12152	25308	154912

Selected Financial Ratios (Times to 1)

Current Ratio 30	1.7	•	2.3	1.6	2.0	1.7	1.5	1.3	1.4	2.3
Quick Ratio 31	1.0	•	1.7	1.0	1.4	1.2	0.7	0.8	0.8	1.1
Net Sales to Working Capital 32	9.7	•	17.1	11.4	11.1	7.6	9.8	9.0	8.2	3.7
Coverage Ratio 33	3.6	11.3	4.0	5.4	2.3	1.7	3.7	2.7	7.5	4.3
Total Asset Turnover 34	1.9	•	3.6	1.7	2.3	1.3	1.9	0.9	1.3	1.2
Inventory Turnover 35	9.2	•	23.2	14.5	19.0	7.9	7.9	6.4	3.8	3.6
Receivables Turnover 36	14.3	•	53.4	27.4	18.5	8.3	10.2	5.6	8.1	11.1
Total Liabilities to Net Worth 37	2.0	•	•	1.6	2.1	1.2	2.0	1.8	1.8	1.0
Current Assets to Working Capital 38	2.4	•	1.8	2.7	2.0	2.4	3.2	3.9	3.5	1.8
Current Liabilities to Working Capital 39	1.4	•	0.8	1.7	1.0	1.4	2.2	2.9	2.5	0.8
Working Capital to Net Sales 40	0.1	•	0.1	0.1	0.1	0.1	0.1	0.1	0.1	0.3
Inventory to Working Capital 41	0.7	•	0.3	0.2	0.4	0.6	1.1	1.1	1.1	0.8
Total Receipts to Cash Flow 42	5.2	2.1	3.5	2.0	8.3	13.5	11.0	7.9	6.0	11.2
Cost of Goods to Cash Flow 43	3.2	0.5	1.5	0.5	6.1	10.3	8.2	6.4	3.9	8.5
Cash Flow to Total Debt 44	0.5	•	0.9	1.4	0.4	0.2	0.3	0.2	0.3	0.2

Selected Financial Factors (in Percentages)

Debt Ratio 45	66.4	•	108.9	61.3	67.6	54.8	67.0	64.3	64.6	51.0
Return on Total Assets 46	7.9	•	17.7	10.1	4.0	3.9	7.9	6.2	12.1	7.0
Return on Equity Before Income Taxes 47	17.0	•	•	21.2	7.1	3.5	17.5	10.8	29.7	11.0
Return on Equity After Income Taxes 48	15.4	•	•	20.6	5.4	1.5	15.7	9.2	26.5	11.0
Profit Margin (Before Income Tax) 49	3.1	11.4	3.7	4.9	1.0	1.2	3.0	4.2	8.2	4.4
Profit Margin (After Income Tax) 50	2.8	11.4	3.6	4.8	0.8	0.5	2.7	3.6	7.3	4.4

Table II

Corporations with Net Income

SUPPORT ACTIVITIES AND FISHING, HUNTING AND TRAPPING

MONEY AMOUNTS AND SIZE OF ASSETS IN THOUSANDS OF DOLLARS

Item Description for Accounting Period 7/08 Through 6/09		Total	Zero Assets	Under 500	500 to 1,000	1,000 to 5,000	5,000 to 10,000	10,000 to 25,000	25,000 to 50,000	50,000 to 100,000	100,000 to 250,000	250,000 to 500,000	500,000 to 2,500,000	2,500,000 and over
Number of Enterprises	1	12483	2704	6735	1812	893	181	120	24	•	•	0	0	0
Revenues ($ in Thousands)														
Net Sales	2	22282133	172074	3399791	2749754	5700913	1921476	4286388	1249353	•	•	0	0	0
Interest	3	23874	0	810	896	9440	5900	3480	1769	•	•	0	0	0
Rents	4	20492	101	59	28	16117	2060	1574	466	•	•	0	0	0
Royalties	5	24292	0	0	0	5006	0	0	18045	•	•	0	0	0
Other Portfolio Income	6	197541	81823	21059	2361	20118	60258	6901	942	•	•	0	0	0
Other Receipts	7	676334	22684	66233	153387	148241	57685	52499	113997	•	•	0	0	0
Total Receipts	8	23224666	276682	3487952	2906426	5899835	2047379	4350842	1384572	•	•	0	0	0
Average Total Receipts	9	1861	102	518	1604	6607	11311	36257	57690	•	•	•	•	•
Operating Costs/Operating Income (%)														
Cost of Operations	10	63.8	8.3	43.2	26.6	77.4	71.2	73.8	82.6	•	•	•	•	•
Salaries and Wages	11	8.2	•	7.3	9.7	8.0	6.0	10.1	3.9	•	•	•	•	•
Taxes Paid	12	1.4	2.0	1.5	1.6	1.4	1.6	1.7	1.0	•	•	•	•	•
Interest Paid	13	0.9	•	0.8	0.7	0.5	1.6	1.0	1.0	•	•	•	•	•
Depreciation	14	2.9	5.9	2.2	4.5	2.1	5.7	2.1	2.1	•	•	•	•	•
Amortization and Depletion	15	0.1	•	0.0	0.2	0.0	0.1	0.1	0.0	•	•	•	•	•
Pensions and Other Deferred Comp.	16	0.1	•	0.0	0.2	0.1	0.2	0.2	0.3	•	•	•	•	•
Employee Benefits	17	0.5	4.3	0.3	0.4	0.3	0.8	0.6	0.5	•	•	•	•	•
Advertising	18	0.2	0.0	0.4	0.0	0.1	0.1	0.2	0.0	•	•	•	•	•
Other Expenses	19	16.0	43.6	26.8	48.0	7.7	10.8	6.9	9.0	•	•	•	•	•
Officers' Compensation	20	2.2	16.5	5.8	2.3	1.9	1.8	0.7	0.9	•	•	•	•	•
Operating Margin	21	3.7	19.4	11.7	5.8	0.6	0.3	2.7	•	•	•	•	•	•
Operating Margin Before Officers' Comp.	22	5.9	35.9	17.5	8.2	2.5	2.1	3.4	•	•	•	•	•	•

Selected Average Balance Sheet ($ in Thousands)

Net Receivables 23	128	0	3	34	227	1766	3864	8668
Inventories 24	127	0	6	16	295	1117	3160	5980
Net Property, Plant and Equipment 25	227	0	25	266	591	3009	3762	6870
Total Assets 26	793	0	110	686	1947	7577	15292	32788
Notes and Loans Payable 27	247	0	46	223	495	2328	5537	8309
All Other Liabilities 28	177	0	18	73	357	1536	5195	8304
Net Worth 29	370	0	46	390	1095	3713	4561	16175

Selected Financial Ratios (Times to 1)

Current Ratio 30	2.0	•	4.7	2.2	2.7	2.1	1.4	1.7
Quick Ratio 31	1.2	•	4.1	1.4	1.6	1.6	0.7	1.0
Net Sales to Working Capital 32	8.5	•	13.4	9.6	9.6	5.7	13.4	6.4
Coverage Ratio 33	10.1	•	20.0	18.2	9.3	5.1	5.3	10.9
Total Asset Turnover 34	2.3	•	4.6	2.2	3.3	1.4	2.3	1.6
Inventory Turnover 35	8.9	•	35.4	24.6	16.8	6.8	8.3	7.2
Receivables Turnover 36	14.0	•	58.5	23.5	23.4	6.3	10.9	•
Total Liabilities to Net Worth 37	1.1	•	1.4	0.8	0.8	1.0	2.4	1.0
Current Assets to Working Capital 38	2.0	•	1.3	1.8	1.6	1.9	3.7	2.4
Current Liabilities to Working Capital 39	1.0	•	0.3	0.8	0.6	0.9	2.7	1.4
Working Capital to Net Sales 40	0.1	•	0.1	0.1	0.1	0.2	0.1	0.2
Inventory to Working Capital 41	0.6	•	0.1	0.2	0.4	0.3	1.4	0.7
Total Receipts to Cash Flow 42	5.0	0.8	3.0	1.9	10.8	8.0	10.6	6.0
Cost of Goods to Cash Flow 43	3.2	0.1	1.3	0.5	8.4	5.7	7.8	5.0
Cash Flow to Total Debt 44	0.9	•	2.6	2.7	0.7	0.3	0.3	0.5

Selected Financial Factors (in Percentages)

Debt Ratio 45	53.4	•	58.2	43.2	43.7	51.0	70.2	50.7
Return on Total Assets 46	19.8	•	69.1	26.9	14.9	11.9	12.1	16.6
Return on Equity Before Income Taxes 47	38.2	•	156.9	44.8	23.6	19.5	32.8	30.6
Return on Equity After Income Taxes 48	36.5	•	155.7	44.1	21.7	16.7	30.1	28.4
Profit Margin (Before Income Tax) 49	7.9	80.2	14.3	11.5	4.1	6.8	4.2	9.5
Profit Margin (After Income Tax) 50	7.6	80.2	14.2	11.3	3.7	5.9	3.8	8.8

Table I

Corporations with and without Net Income

OIL AND GAS EXTRACTION

MONEY AMOUNTS AND SIZE OF ASSETS IN THOUSANDS OF DOLLARS

Item Description for Accounting Period 7/08 Through 6/09	Total	Zero Assets	Under 500	500 to 1,000	1,000 to 5,000	5,000 to 10,000	10,000 to 25,000	25,000 to 50,000	50,000 to 100,000	100,000 to 250,000	250,000 to 500,000	500,000 to 2,500,000	2,500,000 and over
Number of Enterprises **1**	20953	3121	12688	1544	2049	524	455	202	126	101	55	52	34
Revenues ($ in Thousands)													
Net Sales **2**	223177375	2495043	6372673	1297267	5059247	3130873	3308407	3374658	3120798	7104510	8691606	20416838	158805455
Interest **3**	2469555	11996	4649	1976	23470	9305	24920	24266	39594	48877	234946	130877	1914679
Rents **4**	226225	2559	0	12165	12923	313	57133	9794	17889	10256	518	1882	100793
Royalties **5**	906694	57002	29185	13097	124134	56087	152677	26755	34200	45076	14661	77022	276797
Other Portfolio Income **6**	16644214	123674	71241	32956	216049	110318	286007	197171	120882	414355	289270	1686974	13095318
Other Receipts **7**	10325139	145962	143570	12243	297010	343983	328371	278528	584752	271129	319321	1182291	6417978
Total Receipts **8**	253749202	2836236	6621318	1369704	5732833	3650879	4157515	3911172	3918115	7894203	9550322	23495884	180611020
Average Total Receipts **9**	12110	909	522	887	2798	6967	9137	19362	31096	78160	173642	451844	5312089
Operating Costs/Operating Income (%)													
Cost of Operations **10**	50.6	4.5	58.1	23.8	23.4	40.3	27.8	27.2	19.1	41.7	43.0	25.8	57.8
Salaries and Wages **11**	3.9	10.4	3.2	5.7	11.4	7.9	10.6	5.8	12.2	5.2	4.2	3.9	3.0
Taxes Paid **12**	2.7	1.5	2.2	4.2	4.4	2.8	4.2	4.0	5.2	3.3	2.4	3.9	2.4
Interest Paid **13**	4.0	4.5	0.2	2.7	1.3	0.5	2.0	3.6	2.7	3.6	4.7	6.3	4.1
Depreciation **14**	7.0	8.5	2.3	2.7	6.0	5.6	9.8	11.2	14.4	10.0	6.4	10.1	6.5
Amortization and Depletion **15**	5.6	9.4	1.2	1.2	3.2	2.2	6.2	10.2	11.2	7.7	9.8	13.9	4.3
Pensions and Other Deferred Comp. **16**	0.4	1.1	0.5	0.0	0.2	0.4	0.6	0.4	1.3	0.1	0.7	0.3	0.4
Employee Benefits **17**	0.4	0.9	0.2	0.1	2.0	0.4	0.9	0.5	1.0	0.6	0.4	0.3	0.3
Advertising **18**	0.1	0.0	0.1	0.3	0.1	0.1	0.2	0.1	0.1	0.0	0.0	0.0	0.0
Other Expenses **19**	27.3	43.3	15.9	25.6	30.6	24.8	36.5	36.2	36.8	33.6	24.4	38.8	25.3
Officers' Compensation **20**	1.5	8.5	5.2	2.5	6.4	3.2	3.3	2.5	2.5	2.0	0.8	1.3	1.0
Operating Margin **21**	•	7.4	10.9	31.1	11.1	11.7	•	•	•	•	3.3	•	•
Operating Margin Before Officers' Comp. **22**	•	15.9	16.1	33.7	17.4	14.9	1.3	0.9	•	4.1	•	•	•

Selected Average Balance Sheet ($ in Thousands)

Net Receivables 23	1723	0	8	138	212	966	1858	2793	7360	12898	31649	61800	772061
Inventories 24	225	0	3	48	19	57	155	375	775	2096	3199	7294	104363
Net Property, Plant and Equipment 25	12773	0	43	73	721	1243	4493	14854	27668	82031	199087	712033	5884097
Total Assets 26	24500	0	140	701	2471	7350	15824	34598	70348	157347	340024	1123596	11338515
Notes and Loans Payable 27	6797	0	48	190	797	1087	2996	10082	16168	49997	87444	377986	3069182
All Other Liabilities 28	7024	0	11	216	767	1950	3517	7166	14395	32069	48081	263380	3519544
Net Worth 29	10679	0	80	295	908	4314	9310	17350	39785	75282	204499	482230	4749789

Selected Financial Ratios (Times to 1)

Current Ratio 30	0.9	•	4.9	2.0	1.3	1.7	1.9	1.2	1.8	1.5	1.2	1.0	0.8
Quick Ratio 31	0.6	•	3.5	1.6	1.0	1.2	1.5	0.9	1.4	1.1	0.9	0.7	0.5
Net Sales to Working Capital 32	•	•	7.9	3.9	9.5	3.6	2.1	9.9	2.5	5.5	14.6	67.8	•
Coverage Ratio 33	3.9	5.7	76.9	14.6	19.1	53.5	12.8	5.0	7.9	1.9	3.8	2.7	3.6
Total Asset Turnover 34	0.4	•	3.6	1.2	1.0	0.8	0.5	0.5	0.4	0.4	0.5	0.3	0.4
Inventory Turnover 35	24.0	•	83.6	4.1	30.3	42.1	13.1	12.1	6.1	14.0	21.2	13.9	25.9
Receivables Turnover 36	5.4	•	45.1	7.9	11.6	4.7	4.1	4.8	3.2	4.2	5.6	4.5	5.4
Total Liabilities to Net Worth 37	1.3	•	0.7	1.4	1.7	0.7	0.7	1.0	0.8	1.1	0.7	1.3	1.4
Current Assets to Working Capital 38	•	•	1.3	2.1	4.5	2.4	2.1	6.0	2.3	3.1	6.8	31.4	•
Current Liabilities to Working Capital 39	•	•	0.3	1.1	3.5	1.4	1.1	5.0	1.3	2.1	5.8	30.4	•
Working Capital to Net Sales 40	•	•	0.1	0.3	0.1	0.3	0.5	0.1	0.4	0.2	0.1	0.0	•
Inventory to Working Capital 41	•	•	0.0	0.2	0.0	0.0	0.1	0.3	0.1	0.1	0.3	1.5	•
Total Receipts to Cash Flow 42	3.1	1.7	3.6	1.7	2.0	2.0	2.0	2.3	2.0	3.2	3.1	2.3	3.4
Cost of Goods to Cash Flow 43	1.6	0.1	2.1	0.4	0.5	0.8	0.6	0.6	0.4	1.4	1.3	0.6	2.0
Cash Flow to Total Debt 44	0.3	•	2.4	1.2	0.8	1.0	0.5	0.4	0.4	0.3	0.4	0.3	0.2

Selected Financial Factors (in Percentages)

Debt Ratio 45	56.4	•	42.7	57.9	63.3	41.3	41.2	49.9	43.4	52.2	39.9	57.1	58.1
Return on Total Assets 46	6.9	•	53.8	47.2	25.6	23.4	11.6	8.6	7.6	3.1	8.3	5.9	6.0
Return on Equity Before Income Taxes 47	11.7	•	92.6	104.6	66.1	39.2	18.2	13.6	11.8	3.2	10.2	8.5	10.4
Return on Equity After Income Taxes 48	7.7	•	90.6	102.1	61.8	37.4	16.0	11.6	9.9	0.6	5.9	6.1	6.0
Profit Margin (Before Income Tax) 49	11.7	21.1	14.8	36.7	24.3	28.3	23.3	14.1	18.9	3.4	13.2	10.5	10.5
Profit Margin (After Income Tax) 50	7.7	10.8	14.5	35.8	22.7	27.0	20.5	12.1	16.0	0.6	7.7	7.5	6.1

Table II

Corporations with Net Income

OIL AND GAS EXTRACTION

MONEY AMOUNTS AND SIZE OF ASSETS IN THOUSANDS OF DOLLARS

Item Description for Accounting Period 7/08 Through 6/09	Total	Zero Assets	Under 500	500 to 1,000	1,000 to 5,000	5,000 to 10,000	10,000 to 25,000	25,000 to 50,000	50,000 to 100,000	100,000 to 250,000	250,000 to 500,000	500,000 to 2,500,000	2,500,000 and over
Number of Enterprises 1	15237	2082	9133	1299	1713	391	307	114	79	52	25	26	16
Revenues ($ in Thousands)													
Net Sales 2	163341950	1539020	3040679	1186465	4544356	2962506	2621874	2749790	2554856	5571258	5574244	9369888	121627012
Interest 3	1794265	616	4174	1781	20231	5783	15016	13327	19425	29543	78192	69748	1536428
Rents 4	200372	0	0	12165	12923	277	56474	3608	9527	8586	22	1835	94955
Royalties 5	820330	30711	27333	13097	115805	56087	145145	25376	33535	44388	11970	45211	271671
Other Portfolio Income 6	15432291	38735	71206	31572	214291	107223	266330	180190	106355	355414	235691	1530515	12294766
Other Receipts 7	9989257	61316	139109	8901	271835	289193	279297	239520	602750	231488	288320	1221427	6356109
Total Receipts 8	191578465	1670398	3282501	1253981	5179441	3421069	3384136	3211811	3326448	6240677	6188439	12238624	142180941
Average Total Receipts 9	12573	802	359	965	3024	8750	11023	28174	42107	120013	247538	470716	8886309
Operating Costs/Operating Income (%)													
Cost of Operations 10	52.2	1.7	29.8	21.0	23.6	41.7	25.6	28.5	17.9	42.8	42.5	26.8	59.6
Salaries and Wages 11	3.3	4.1	2.4	4.6	10.2	6.0	8.9	5.4	11.6	3.8	2.0	3.4	2.7
Taxes Paid 12	2.6	1.1	3.4	4.3	4.1	2.5	4.2	4.0	5.4	3.2	2.1	3.2	2.3
Interest Paid 13	3.4	3.5	0.2	0.3	1.0	0.3	1.3	2.0	1.7	1.9	2.5	5.4	3.8
Depreciation 14	6.2	9.3	3.7	1.5	5.4	5.1	8.0	7.3	10.9	7.0	4.0	9.8	5.9
Amortization and Depletion 15	4.3	2.3	1.7	1.2	2.8	2.1	5.7	6.0	5.7	4.5	4.3	13.1	3.7
Pensions and Other Deferred Comp. 16	0.5	0.0	1.0	0.0	0.1	0.3	0.6	0.4	1.6	0.1	0.1	0.4	0.5
Employee Benefits 17	0.3	0.9	0.5	0.1	2.0	0.3	0.8	0.4	0.9	0.4	0.3	0.2	0.2
Advertising 18	0.1	0.0	0.1	0.2	0.1	0.0	0.1	0.1	0.1	0.0	0.0	0.0	0.1
Other Expenses 19	23.0	23.0	21.3	21.3	27.3	21.7	25.7	25.8	31.7	23.8	14.8	32.3	22.3
Officers' Compensation 20	1.4	2.7	9.9	2.7	5.9	2.3	2.8	2.3	2.0	1.7	0.5	1.6	0.9
Operating Margin 21	2.8	51.4	26.0	43.0	17.5	17.6	16.2	17.8	10.5	10.8	26.8	•	•
Operating Margin Before Officers' Comp. 22	4.1	54.1	35.9	45.7	23.4	19.9	19.1	20.1	12.5	12.5	27.3	3.7	5.3

Selected Average Balance Sheet ($ in Thousands)

Net Receivables 23	1863	0	10	157	190	751	1755	3143	7824	13252	42080	72459	1395887
Inventories 24	222	0	2	55	17	45	168	439	628	3292	5414	8644	162131
Net Property, Plant and Equipment 25	11653	0	46	60	657	1461	3753	13065	26486	69031	163032	549628	9291539
Total Assets 26	23495	0	158	674	2408	7275	16173	35626	70658	159066	328831	1102797	18058550
Notes and Loans Payable 27	5631	0	51	25	509	630	1483	7286	11212	34640	76176	305440	4398021
All Other Liabilities 28	7082	0	8	178	490	1606	2711	6868	13860	31230	91385	208143	5882363
Net Worth 29	10781	0	99	472	1410	5039	11979	21472	45586	93196	161270	589214	7778166

Selected Financial Ratios (Times to 1)

Current Ratio 30	1.0	•	5.9	2.7	1.7	2.2	2.9	1.4	2.2	2.2	1.6	1.6	0.8
Quick Ratio 31	0.7	•	4.2	2.3	1.3	1.6	2.4	1.2	1.7	1.6	1.2	1.1	0.5
Net Sales to Working Capital 32	•	•	4.2	2.9	5.2	3.8	1.6	6.6	2.3	3.9	6.1	4.5	•
Coverage Ratio 33	7.4	17.9	158.0	186.3	33.8	114.8	35.2	18.5	25.0	13.1	16.3	7.4	5.6
Total Asset Turnover 34	0.5	•	2.1	1.4	1.1	1.0	0.5	0.7	0.5	0.7	0.7	0.3	0.4
Inventory Turnover 35	25.2	•	42.7	3.5	37.8	70.0	13.0	15.7	9.2	13.9	17.5	11.2	28.0
Receivables Turnover 36	5.0	•	29.6	7.4	13.5	5.8	4.6	6.8	3.9	5.2	5.4	2.9	4.9
Total Liabilities to Net Worth 37	1.2	•	0.6	0.4	0.7	0.4	0.4	0.7	0.5	0.7	1.0	0.9	1.3
Current Assets to Working Capital 38	•	•	1.2	1.6	2.4	1.9	1.5	3.2	1.8	1.9	2.6	2.7	•
Current Liabilities to Working Capital 39	•	•	0.2	0.6	1.4	0.9	0.5	2.2	0.8	0.9	1.6	1.7	•
Working Capital to Net Sales 40	•	•	0.2	0.3	0.2	0.3	0.6	0.2	0.4	0.3	0.2	0.2	•
Inventory to Working Capital 41	•	•	0.0	0.2	0.0	0.0	0.0	0.2	0.1	0.1	0.2	0.1	•
Total Receipts to Cash Flow 42	2.7	1.2	1.9	1.5	1.8	1.9	1.7	1.9	1.5	2.4	2.2	1.8	3.1
Cost of Goods to Cash Flow 43	1.4	0.0	0.6	0.3	0.4	0.8	0.4	0.5	0.3	1.0	0.9	0.5	1.9
Cash Flow to Total Debt 44	0.3	•	3.0	2.9	1.4	1.8	1.2	0.9	0.9	0.7	0.6	0.4	0.2

Selected Financial Factors (in Percentages)

Debt Ratio 45	54.1	•	37.2	30.1	41.5	30.7	25.9	39.7	35.5	41.4	51.0	46.6	56.9
Return on Total Assets 46	11.6	•	72.1	66.2	35.6	34.7	24.4	24.6	19.4	16.8	27.4	13.0	9.0
Return on Equity Before Income Taxes 47	21.9	•	114.1	94.2	59.1	49.7	32.0	38.6	28.8	26.4	52.4	21.0	17.1
Return on Equity After Income Taxes 48	16.5	•	112.0	92.3	55.8	47.7	29.5	35.8	26.3	22.3	40.5	17.0	11.5
Profit Margin (Before Income Tax) 49	22.1	59.9	33.9	48.6	31.4	33.1	44.9	34.4	40.6	23.0	37.9	34.3	17.5
Profit Margin (After Income Tax) 50	16.6	43.2	33.3	47.7	29.6	31.7	41.4	31.9	37.1	19.4	29.3	27.8	11.8

Table I

Corporations with and without Net Income

COAL MINING

MONEY AMOUNTS AND SIZE OF ASSETS IN THOUSANDS OF DOLLARS

Item Description for Accounting Period 7/08 Through 6/09	Total	Zero Assets	Under 500	500 to 1,000	1,000 to 5,000	5,000 to 10,000	10,000 to 25,000	25,000 to 50,000	50,000 to 100,000	100,000 to 250,000	250,000 to 500,000	500,000 to 2,500,000	2,500,000 and over
Number of Enterprises **1**	1240	•	538	•	181	•	47	20	15	16	0	8	6
Revenues ($ in Thousands)													
Net Sales **2**	33158083	•	254265	•	984404	•	867124	1633151	1343412	2281927	0	7706100	15145725
Interest **3**	473802	•	392	•	828	•	1616	35	919	4612	0	32604	431726
Rents **4**	25369	•	234	•	2916	•	24	0	0	485	0	3666	18044
Royalties **5**	288572	•	21733	•	3768	•	26	0	344	19347	0	43555	199777
Other Portfolio Income **6**	315152	•	0	•	1043	•	29631	339	19250	4346	0	46069	163212
Other Receipts **7**	1253582	•	-1	•	5872	•	10017	15442	18420	33739	0	369427	775606
Total Receipts **8**	35514560	•	276623	•	998831	•	908438	1648967	1382345	2344456	0	8201421	16734090
Average Total Receipts **9**	28641	•	514	•	5518	•	19328	82448	92156	146528	•	1025178	2789015
Operating Costs/Operating Income (%)													
Cost of Operations **10**	66.2	•	59.2	•	38.1	•	70.9	48.4	68.1	67.7	•	74.8	65.1
Salaries and Wages **11**	2.1	•	0.4	•	6.3	•	3.5	6.4	2.5	3.7	•	1.3	1.9
Taxes Paid **12**	5.7	•	10.3	•	3.9	•	3.1	3.9	4.7	3.2	•	4.7	7.0
Interest Paid **13**	3.8	•	•	•	0.1	•	1.7	0.6	2.9	3.0	•	4.2	5.0
Depreciation **14**	5.5	•	0.4	•	2.6	•	7.3	3.2	6.9	9.5	•	5.4	5.5
Amortization and Depletion **15**	5.2	•	1.2	•	1.2	•	2.8	1.6	3.6	3.4	•	4.6	7.5
Pensions and Other Deferred Comp. **16**	0.8	•	•	•	•	•	0.1	0.2	0.2	0.3	•	0.8	1.0
Employee Benefits **17**	3.1	•	•	•	1.3	•	2.3	2.2	2.0	3.2	•	3.1	3.9
Advertising **18**	0.1	•	•	•	•	•	0.0	0.0	0.0	0.0	•	0.1	0.1
Other Expenses **19**	15.4	•	23.5	•	36.9	•	15.6	33.8	11.5	17.1	•	5.6	16.8
Officers' Compensation **20**	0.8	•	•	•	1.1	•	0.9	0.9	0.4	0.9	•	0.3	0.5
Operating Margin **21**	•	•	5.0	•	8.6	•	0.9	•	•	•	•	•	•
Operating Margin Before Officers' Comp. **22**	•	•	5.0	•	9.7	•	•	•	•	•	•	•	•

Selected Average Balance Sheet ($ in Thousands)

Net Receivables 23	13926	1	646	1596	9724	8668	20710	106776	2577465
Inventories 24	1063	0	25	1106	1591	2680	4342	37008	129483
Net Property, Plant and Equipment 25	17511	9	573	5626	10398	30445	86695	464015	2555807
Total Assets 26	47504	113	2356	13746	35121	67315	182649	1159994	7125602
Notes and Loans Payable 27	12512	0	1431	5070	10483	27796	62615	504682	1526386
All Other Liabilities 28	25070	45	851	3750	8622	26908	55624	520241	4166287
Net Worth 29	9922	68	74	4926	16015	12611	64410	135071	1432929

Selected Financial Ratios (Times to 1)

Current Ratio 30	1.1	2.3	1.3	1.0	1.7	0.9	0.9	1.7	1.1
Quick Ratio 31	1.0	1.0	1.3	0.9	1.4	0.6	0.7	1.4	0.9
Net Sales to Working Capital 32	12.6	8.2	16.5	106.6	11.7	•	•	7.2	14.2
Coverage Ratio 33	0.6	136.1	•	•	0.8	1.0	0.8	1.4	0.2
Total Asset Turnover 34	0.6	4.2	2.3	1.3	2.3	1.3	0.8	0.8	0.4
Inventory Turnover 35	16.7	•	83.8	11.8	24.8	22.7	22.2	19.5	12.7
Receivables Turnover 36	2.3	1142.8	10.5	9.5	•	9.9	7.9	7.2	1.2
Total Liabilities to Net Worth 37	3.8	0.7	30.9	1.8	1.2	4.3	1.8	7.6	4.0
Current Assets to Working Capital 38	9.0	1.8	4.0	23.4	2.4	2.4	•	2.4	17.4
Current Liabilities to Working Capital 39	8.0	0.8	3.0	22.4	1.4	•	•	1.4	16.4
Working Capital to Net Sales 40	0.1	0.1	0.0	0.0	0.1	0.1	•	0.1	0.1
Inventory to Working Capital 41	0.6	•	0.1	3.7	0.2	•	•	0.3	0.9
Total Receipts to Cash Flow 42	11.6	4.8	2.2	11.1	4.3	15.9	22.4	18.6	15.7
Cost of Goods to Cash Flow 43	7.7	2.9	0.8	7.8	2.1	10.8	15.2	13.9	10.2
Cash Flow to Total Debt 44	0.1	2.2	1.1	0.2	1.0	0.1	0.1	0.1	0.0

Selected Financial Factors (in Percentages)

Debt Ratio 45	79.1	40.0	96.9	64.2	54.4	81.3	64.7	88.4	79.9
Return on Total Assets 46	1.2	57.6	23.4	•	1.1	4.0	•	4.9	0.4
Return on Equity Before Income Taxes 47	•	96.1	740.6	•	•	0.7	•	11.6	•
Return on Equity After Income Taxes 48	•	74.2	731.9	•	•	0.1	•	5.9	•
Profit Margin (Before Income Tax) 49	•	13.8	10.0	•	•	0.1	•	1.6	•
Profit Margin (After Income Tax) 50	•	10.6	9.9	•	•	0.0	•	0.8	•

Table II

Corporations with Net Income

COAL MINING

MONEY AMOUNTS AND SIZE OF ASSETS IN THOUSANDS OF DOLLARS

Item Description for Accounting Period 7/08 Through 6/09	Total	Zero Assets	Under 500	500 to 1,000	1,000 to 5,000	5,000 to 10,000	10,000 to 25,000	25,000 to 50,000	50,000 to 100,000	100,000 to 250,000	250,000 to 500,000	500,000 to 2,500,000	2,500,000 and over
Number of Enterprises **1**	487	7	115	•	103	21	15	6	7	4	0	•	0
Revenues ($ in Thousands)													
Net Sales **2**	14418794	226234	254265	•	628224	559458	258868	366112	806043	664612	•	•	0
Interest **3**	161347	32	392	•	751	744	637	35	147	520	•	•	0
Rents **4**	10308	0	234	•	0	0	24	0	0	0	•	•	0
Royalties **5**	100204	0	21733	•	3768	0	0	0	0	64	•	•	0
Other Portfolio Income **6**	135684	15382	0	•	0	13436	683	50	2274	3223	•	•	0
Other Receipts **7**	581739	7574	-1	•	5373	1828	671	8258	5973	23899	•	•	0
Total Receipts **8**	15408076	249222	276623	•	638116	575466	260883	374455	814437	692318	•	•	0
Average Total Receipts **9**	31639	35603	2405	•	6195	27403	17392	62409	116348	173080	•	•	•
Operating Costs/Operating Income (%)													
Cost of Operations **10**	58.8	78.0	59.2	•	15.0	60.5	69.6	74.7	62.9	46.9	•	•	•
Salaries and Wages **11**	1.5	0.3	0.4	•	9.3	0.2	1.6	2.3	3.5	7.5	•	•	•
Taxes Paid **12**	4.3	5.2	10.1	•	2.2	9.0	1.4	1.9	4.6	1.6	•	•	•
Interest Paid **13**	3.3	0.8	•	•	0.1	1.4	2.7	1.2	1.1	0.3	•	•	•
Depreciation **14**	4.7	4.2	0.4	•	1.4	3.0	3.5	3.4	7.1	9.4	•	•	•
Amortization and Depletion **15**	6.5	3.9	1.2	•	1.8	1.5	3.8	2.4	5.3	4.5	•	•	•
Pensions and Other Deferred Comp. **16**	0.9	0.2	•	•	•	0.0	0.1	0.2	0.3	0.2	•	•	•
Employee Benefits **17**	3.9	3.6	•	•	1.9	1.1	0.9	0.8	1.6	2.2	•	•	•
Advertising **18**	0.1	0.0	•	•	•	0.0	0.0	0.0	0.0	0.0	•	•	•
Other Expenses **19**	12.7	12.5	22.4	•	46.6	19.3	12.0	6.0	7.9	22.3	•	•	•
Officers' Compensation **20**	1.2	0.2	•	•	1.6	0.2	0.7	2.6	0.5	0.7	•	•	•
Operating Margin **21**	2.1	•	6.4	•	20.0	3.7	3.7	4.4	5.2	4.3	•	•	•
Operating Margin Before Officers' Comp. **22**	3.3	•	6.4	•	21.6	3.9	4.4	7.1	5.7	5.0	•	•	•

Selected Average Balance Sheet ($ in Thousands)

Net Receivables 23	3302	0	4	•	466	292	730	16176	13609	33661
Inventories 24	1308	0	0	•	43	215	3177	1205	959	6729
Net Property, Plant and Equipment 25	16562	0	41	•	533	3157	1453	4917	34777	70792
Total Assets 26	38079	0	223	•	2146	5816	14089	32439	73699	191168
Notes and Loans Payable 27	12114	0	0	•	735	4211	4287	20768	16961	35944
All Other Liabilities 28	16771	0	211	•	468	1155	2982	6526	18852	45334
Net Worth 29	9195	0	11	•	943	451	6819	5146	37886	109890

Selected Financial Ratios (Times to 1)

Current Ratio 30	1.3	•	0.8	•	3.2	0.8	1.3	3.9	1.8	1.3
Quick Ratio 31	0.9	•	0.5	•	3.0	0.4	0.8	3.4	1.6	1.1
Net Sales to Working Capital 32	15.6	•	•	•	6.2	•	14.1	3.9	10.7	12.5
Coverage Ratio 33	3.7	2.6	•	•	213.7	5.6	2.6	6.4	6.4	27.9
Total Asset Turnover 34	0.8	•	9.9	•	2.8	4.6	1.2	1.9	1.6	0.9
Inventory Turnover 35	13.3	•	•	•	21.1	75.1	3.8	37.8	75.6	11.6
Receivables Turnover 36	2.3	•	1142.8	•	12.0	19.7	6.1	4.6	10.0	7.1
Total Liabilities to Net Worth 37	3.1	•	18.5	•	1.3	11.9	1.1	5.3	0.9	0.7
Current Assets to Working Capital 38	4.9	•	•	•	1.5	•	4.9	1.3	2.3	4.5
Current Liabilities to Working Capital 39	3.9	•	•	•	0.5	•	3.9	0.3	1.3	3.5
Working Capital to Net Sales 40	0.1	•	•	•	0.2	•	0.1	0.3	0.1	0.1
Inventory to Working Capital 41	0.6	•	•	•	0.0	•	1.4	0.1	0.1	0.5
Total Receipts to Cash Flow 42	5.6	24.2	4.8	•	1.5	5.8	7.4	8.9	10.1	3.8
Cost of Goods to Cash Flow 43	3.3	18.9	2.8	•	0.2	3.5	5.2	6.6	6.4	1.8
Cash Flow to Total Debt 44	0.2	•	2.2	•	3.4	0.9	0.3	0.3	0.3	0.5

Selected Financial Factors (in Percentages)

Debt Ratio 45	75.9	•	94.9	•	56.0	92.3	51.6	84.1	48.6	42.5
Return on Total Assets 46	9.5	•	•	•	61.6	36.4	8.8	15.0	11.5	7.6
Return on Equity Before Income Taxes 47	28.9	•	2927.0	•	139.5	385.2	11.3	79.8	18.9	12.8
Return on Equity After Income Taxes 48	24.4	•	2320.4	•	138.3	384.9	9.2	71.9	18.4	12.7
Profit Margin (Before Income Tax) 49	9.0	1.2	15.2	•	21.6	6.5	4.5	6.7	6.2	8.4
Profit Margin (After Income Tax) 50	7.6	1.1	12.0	•	21.4	6.5	3.6	6.1	6.1	8.4

10

Table I

Corporations with and without Net Income

METAL ORE MINING

MONEY AMOUNTS AND SIZE OF ASSETS IN THOUSANDS OF DOLLARS

Item Description for Accounting Period 7/08 Through 6/09	Total	Zero Assets	Under 500	500 to 1,000	1,000 to 5,000	5,000 to 10,000	10,000 to 25,000	25,000 to 50,000	50,000 to 100,000	100,000 to 250,000	250,000 to 500,000	500,000 to 2,500,000	2,500,000 and over
Number of Enterprises 1	2031	•	1692	•	127	•	29	27	12	16	5	12	9
Revenues ($ in Thousands)													
Net Sales 2	42929999	•	38487	•	50773	•	150873	46602	450079	363208	678467	5753209	35188086
Interest 3	894107	•	379	•	1984	•	1190	1262	5438	9877	2556	61557	808843
Rents 4	36509	•	6434	•	180	•	1593	219	0	1876	101	89	26017
Royalties 5	474025	•	26841	•	0	•	0	0	98	74	0	162571	284411
Other Portfolio Income 6	4417750	•	564	•	16028	•	3	239	2248	17210	294510	145168	3932388
Other Receipts 7	1346821	•	35195	•	21719	•	141342	1869	43100	6753	153828	54947	870103
Total Receipts 8	50099211	•	107900	•	90684	•	295001	50191	500963	398998	1129462	6177541	41109848
Average Total Receipts 9	24667	•	64	•	714	•	10172	1859	41747	24937	225892	514795	4567761
Operating Costs/Operating Income (%)													
Cost of Operations 10	56.8	•	0.3	•	116.6	•	84.1	98.7	46.3	58.9	65.7	64.5	55.0
Salaries and Wages 11	2.2	•	15.8	•	58.3	•	13.9	34.4	9.7	10.1	0.0	0.5	2.2
Taxes Paid 12	2.1	•	12.4	•	6.4	•	1.5	2.5	2.3	1.4	0.8	2.5	2.1
Interest Paid 13	3.2	•	4.3	•	24.7	•	2.6	6.8	0.5	4.2	2.2	1.3	3.6
Depreciation 14	5.5	•	2.7	•	34.0	•	3.1	14.2	4.5	22.7	5.7	4.3	5.5
Amortization and Depletion 15	11.3	•	13.5	•	26.6	•	2.4	31.8	5.9	13.3	11.8	10.2	11.6
Pensions and Other Deferred Comp. 16	0.3	•	11.0	•	•	•	•	•	0.2	0.4	•	0.2	0.3
Employee Benefits 17	0.8	•	2.7	•	8.8	•	1.1	1.7	1.5	2.1	5.5	0.1	0.8
Advertising 18	0.0	•	•	•	0.6	•	0.4	6.2	0.2	0.1	•	0.0	0.0
Other Expenses 19	11.6	•	108.3	•	238.7	•	64.1	126.2	39.1	44.3	12.6	8.4	10.6
Officers' Compensation 20	0.7	•	60.7	•	2.6	•	3.3	1.4	0.3	3.1	0.1	0.4	0.7
Operating Margin 21	5.3	•	•	•	•	•	•	•	•	•	•	7.5	7.7
Operating Margin Before Officers' Comp. 22	6.1	•	•	•	•	•	•	•	•	•	•	7.9	8.4

Selected Average Balance Sheet ($ in Thousands)

Net Receivables 23	15862	0	24	958	80	4365	4515	7808	48944	3491419
Inventories 24	3231	0	10	115	172	4142	12875	11594	63149	608474
Net Property, Plant and Equipment 25	15965	8	724	8011	10695	19071	50263	221835	504483	2605901
Total Assets 26	67886	102	2058	16642	30897	68125	150471	350805	1085942	13094848
Notes and Loans Payable 27	9410	36	1255	6401	11483	40141	56213	64091	163274	1633122
All Other Liabilities 28	25616	37	3615	3590	3958	12325	27484	105689	183701	5307542
Net Worth 29	32861	28	-2812	6650	15456	15660	66774	181025	738967	6154184

Selected Financial Ratios (Times to 1)

Current Ratio 30	1.6	17.0	0.7	1.8	0.7	2.6	2.8	0.6	1.7	1.6
Quick Ratio 31	1.3	17.0	0.4	0.6	0.5	1.7	1.2	0.3	1.1	1.4
Net Sales to Working Capital 32	2.5	0.3	•	2.2	•	3.0	0.8	•	4.4	2.2
Coverage Ratio 33	8.4	12.0	•	8.4	•	2.4	•	29.5	12.4	8.4
Total Asset Turnover 34	0.3	0.2	0.2	0.3	0.1	0.6	0.2	0.4	0.4	0.3
Inventory Turnover 35	3.7	•	44.4	37.9	9.9	4.2	1.0	7.7	4.9	3.5
Receivables Turnover 36	1.5	542.1	27.4	2.9	•	6.6	6.1	8.0	13.5	1.2
Total Liabilities to Net Worth 37	1.1	2.6	•	1.5	1.0	3.4	1.3	0.9	0.5	1.1
Current Assets to Working Capital 38	2.6	1.1	•	2.3	•	1.6	1.6	•	2.4	2.6
Current Liabilities to Working Capital 39	1.6	0.1	•	1.3	•	0.6	0.6	•	1.4	1.6
Working Capital to Net Sales 40	0.4	3.2	•	0.5	•	0.3	1.3	•	0.2	0.5
Inventory to Working Capital 41	0.4	•	•	0.1	•	0.4	0.7	•	0.6	0.4
Total Receipts to Cash Flow 42	3.4	0.7	•	1.2	1.2	3.0	•	3.1	5.0	3.2
Cost of Goods to Cash Flow 43	1.9	0.0	•	1.0	•	1.4	•	2.0	3.2	1.7
Cash Flow to Total Debt 44	0.2	0.5	•	0.4	•	0.2	•	0.3	0.3	0.2

Selected Financial Factors (in Percentages)

Debt Ratio 45	51.6	72.0	236.6	60.0	50.0	77.0	55.6	48.4	32.0	53.0
Return on Total Assets 46	8.4	11.5	•	6.8	0.7	0.7	•	24.8	7.4	9.0
Return on Equity Before Income Taxes 47	15.2	37.7	48.1	14.9	•	1.7	•	46.5	10.0	16.8
Return on Equity After Income Taxes 48	9.9	31.9	48.1	9.9	•	•	•	32.3	5.9	11.3
Profit Margin (Before Income Tax) 49	23.7	47.1	•	19.0	•	•	•	62.0	15.4	26.5
Profit Margin (After Income Tax) 50	15.4	39.8	•	12.7	•	0.7	•	43.1	9.1	17.8

Table II

Corporations with Net Income

METAL ORE MINING

MONEY AMOUNTS AND SIZE OF ASSETS IN THOUSANDS OF DOLLARS

Item Description for Accounting Period 7/08 Through 6/09		Total	Zero Assets	Under 500	500 to 1,000	1,000 to 5,000	5,000 to 10,000	10,000 to 25,000	25,000 to 50,000	50,000 to 100,000	100,000 to 250,000	250,000 to 500,000	500,000 to 2,500,000	2,500,000 and over
Number of Enterprises	1	792	0	691	59	0	16	4	0	5	0	•	•	6
Revenues ($ in Thousands)														
Net Sales	2	39558074	0	38007	2469	0	207746	149154	0	447837	0	•	•	3410306
Interest	3	830045	0	0	39	0	946	326	0	3215	0	•	•	26583
Rents	4	27738	0	0	0	0	0	1593	0	0	0	•	•	64
Royalties	5	471308	0	26841	0	0	0	0	0	0	0	•	•	162571
Other Portfolio Income	6	4405134	0	0	15966	0	9148	0	0	15738	0	•	•	137383
Other Receipts	7	1390083	0	35054	1456	0	24008	140544	0	43199	0	•	•	121916
Total Receipts	8	46682382	0	99902	19930	0	241848	291617	0	509989	0	•	•	3858823
Average Total Receipts	9	58942	•	145	338	•	15116	72904	•	101998	•	•	•	643137
Operating Costs/Operating Income (%)														
Cost of Operations	10	54.9	•	•	•	•	98.1	85.0	•	53.8	•	•	•	47.9
Salaries and Wages	11	2.1	•	•	36.4	•	0.2	4.2	•	7.9	•	•	•	0.2
Taxes Paid	12	2.2	•	5.2	2.4	•	0.1	0.5	•	1.6	•	•	•	4.1
Interest Paid	13	3.1	•	4.3	16.2	•	0.3	0.3	•	1.3	•	•	•	1.0
Depreciation	14	5.3	•	2.2	8.3	•	0.1	0.4	•	5.1	•	•	•	5.0
Amortization and Depletion	15	11.5	•	10.6	•	•	1.4	0.0	•	5.5	•	•	•	14.7
Pensions and Other Deferred Comp.	16	0.3	•	11.1	•	•	•	•	•	0.4	•	•	•	0.4
Employee Benefits	17	0.8	•	•	10.7	•	•	•	•	1.4	•	•	•	0.0
Advertising	18	0.0	•	•	•	•	•	0.0	•	0.0	•	•	•	0.0
Other Expenses	19	10.4	•	48.8	326.5	•	4.6	5.0	•	13.9	•	•	•	9.3
Officers' Compensation	20	0.7	•	44.5	•	•	0.8	0.3	•	0.3	•	•	•	0.2
Operating Margin	21	8.6	•	•	•	•	•	4.1	•	8.7	•	•	•	17.0
Operating Margin Before Officers' Comp.	22	9.3	•	17.7	•	•	4.4	4.4	•	9.0	•	•	•	17.2

Selected Average Balance Sheet ($ in Thousands)

Net Receivables 23	39987	13141	553	6919	0	11	38688
Inventories 24	7556	8963	0	0	0	0	60536
Net Property, Plant and Equipment 25	33736	35123	3091	9826	13	529	504408
Total Assets 26	155046	87367	6624	19404	113	753	1027576
Notes and Loans Payable 27	19024	11339	503	0	28	1339	141787
All Other Liabilities 28	61153	52421	10100	3243	0	322	182436
Net Worth 29	74870	23606	-3978	16161	85	-907	703352

Selected Financial Ratios (Times to 1)

Current Ratio 30	1.7	2.4	0.2	4.6	363.9	0.3	1.8
Quick Ratio 31	1.4	1.4	0.2	3.1	363.9	0.3	1.2
Net Sales to Working Capital 32	2.3	3.6	•	3.2	0.6	•	5.0
Coverage Ratio 33	10.0	18.3	38.7	292.9	32.3	26.2	31.6
Total Asset Turnover 34	0.3	0.6	2.0	1.9	0.5	0.1	0.6
Inventory Turnover 35	3.6	5.4	•	•	•	•	4.5
Receivables Turnover 36	1.4	7.3	46.9	6.6	•	7.3	7.3
Total Liabilities to Net Worth 37	1.1	2.7	•	0.2	0.3	•	0.5
Current Assets to Working Capital 38	2.5	1.7	•	1.3	1.0	•	2.2
Current Liabilities to Working Capital 39	1.5	0.7	•	0.3	0.0	•	1.2
Working Capital to Net Sales 40	0.4	0.3	•	0.3	1.8	•	0.2
Inventory to Working Capital 41	0.4	0.6	•	•	•	•	0.5
Total Receipts to Cash Flow 42	3.1	3.2	9.1	1.0	0.6	1.2	2.9
Cost of Goods to Cash Flow 43	1.7	1.7	9.0	0.8	•	•	1.4
Cash Flow to Total Debt 44	0.2	0.4	0.1	12.0	3.4	0.0	0.6

Selected Financial Factors (in Percentages)

Debt Ratio 45	51.7	73.0	160.1	16.7	24.7	220.4	31.6
Return on Total Assets 46	10.2	24.5	21.8	192.1	68.5	23.5	17.7
Return on Equity Before Income Taxes 47	19.0	85.8	•	229.8	88.1	•	25.1
Return on Equity After Income Taxes 48	12.9	63.2	•	215.0	83.4	•	16.5
Profit Margin (Before Income Tax) 49	28.4	22.6	10.8	99.6	136.1	406.7	31.0
Profit Margin (After Income Tax) 50	19.4	16.7	9.7	93.2	128.7	405.3	20.4

Table I

Corporations with and without Net Income

NONMETALLIC MINERAL MINING AND QUARRYING

MONEY AMOUNTS AND SIZE OF ASSETS IN THOUSANDS OF DOLLARS

Item Description for Accounting Period 7/08 Through 6/09		Total	Zero Assets	Under 500	500 to 1,000	1,000 to 5,000	5,000 to 10,000	10,000 to 25,000	25,000 to 50,000	50,000 to 100,000	100,000 to 250,000	250,000 to 500,000	500,000 to 2,500,000	2,500,000 and over
Number of Enterprises	1	5243	1522	2008	187	963	269	171	54	31	24	6	7	3
Revenues ($ in Thousands)														
Net Sales	2	28763498	792033	411409	85792	3836466	2308272	2320593	1709843	1497329	2908596	1992401	4343733	6557031
Interest	3	66336	3119	98	580	3022	4400	2957	3185	5353	15630	699	15199	12093
Rents	4	37288	141	0	0	384	5	1440	3389	458	3365	186	3306	24615
Royalties	5	32527	464	359	0	222	1522	155	1109	0	657	6	11286	16746
Other Portfolio Income	6	409204	848	4540	25457	27711	21454	52236	21747	20003	13420	10940	7399	203451
Other Receipts	7	497388	62295	14466	798	37002	27787	48081	10339	19676	39882	22886	155001	59174
Total Receipts	8	29806241	858900	430872	112627	3904807	2363440	2425462	1749612	1542819	2981550	2027718	4535924	6873110
Average Total Receipts	9	5685	564	215	602	4055	8786	14184	32400	49768	124231	337853	647989	2291037
Operating Costs/Operating Income (%)														
Cost of Operations	10	65.2	65.8	69.5	74.7	66.9	61.0	65.8	68.9	69.8	69.3	69.0	65.7	59.6
Salaries and Wages	11	4.4	3.4	1.4	3.2	3.3	3.5	4.9	4.2	5.4	3.8	5.6	4.0	5.3
Taxes Paid	12	1.9	1.8	5.5	3.3	2.1	2.0	1.8	1.2	1.4	1.1	1.5	1.7	2.6
Interest Paid	13	2.8	2.5	2.0	1.9	1.2	2.0	2.1	1.8	2.3	1.7	1.9	3.8	4.7
Depreciation	14	7.2	2.5	4.1	8.6	4.6	7.1	9.4	7.9	7.7	8.5	5.4	5.4	9.7
Amortization and Depletion	15	2.6	4.5	0.0	0.6	0.3	0.7	2.1	2.3	1.6	2.8	2.7	4.6	3.5
Pensions and Other Deferred Comp.	16	0.9	1.0	•	0.2	0.4	0.4	0.5	0.6	0.6	1.1	0.8	0.8	1.7
Employee Benefits	17	2.2	4.2	•	1.8	1.5	2.0	1.8	1.0	2.6	2.1	0.6	3.2	2.6
Advertising	18	0.2	0.4	0.7	0.0	0.2	0.6	0.2	0.4	0.2	0.1	0.2	0.3	0.1
Other Expenses	19	10.9	18.8	16.0	37.7	10.5	12.8	11.0	8.8	13.6	8.9	8.3	7.6	12.5
Officers' Compensation	20	1.4	3.1	0.0	7.0	2.2	2.4	2.6	1.8	1.6	1.6	0.8	0.7	0.3
Operating Margin	21	0.4	•	0.9	•	6.8	5.4	•	1.1	•	•	3.2	2.2	•
Operating Margin Before Officers' Comp.	22	1.8	•	0.9	•	9.1	7.8	0.4	2.9	0.6	0.6	4.0	2.9	•

Selected Average Balance Sheet ($ in Thousands)

Net Receivables 23	598	0	0	79	348	884	2106	3124	6427	17320	39665	74938	214387
Inventories 24	526	0	4	68	156	457	1730	4383	6530	15260	35499	56407	255550
Net Property, Plant and Equipment 25	3011	0	30	215	998	2756	7844	13500	30043	62845	188016	317199	2045257
Total Assets 26	7388	0	78	552	2175	6200	16648	34863	67227	157979	345551	970040	5081461
Notes and Loans Payable 27	2491	0	63	382	708	2992	4253	10104	17262	41751	130878	232698	2051515
All Other Liabilities 28	1800	0	17	180	236	677	2058	3861	15297	31218	100206	347728	1380029
Net Worth 29	3097	0	-1	-10	1232	2531	10337	20898	34668	85009	114466	389614	1649917

Selected Financial Ratios (Times to 1)

Current Ratio 30	1.5	•	2.2	1.7	3.3	2.1	2.8	2.3	2.4	2.0	1.8	1.7	0.7
Quick Ratio 31	0.9	•	1.5	1.4	2.8	1.6	1.7	1.2	1.6	1.0	1.2	1.0	0.2
Net Sales to Working Capital 32	8.7	•	29.7	3.4	5.4	6.6	3.4	4.5	3.4	4.4	7.3	6.3	•
Coverage Ratio 33	2.5	1.1	3.8	•	8.4	4.9	2.1	2.9	•	1.8	3.6	2.8	1.5
Total Asset Turnover 34	0.7	•	2.6	0.8	1.8	1.4	0.8	0.9	0.7	0.8	1.0	0.6	0.4
Inventory Turnover 35	6.8	•	36.6	5.0	17.0	11.5	5.2	5.0	5.2	5.5	6.5	7.2	5.1
Receivables Turnover 36	8.8	•	929.7	•	11.5	8.5	6.6	•	6.8	6.8	7.2	9.1	9.6
Total Liabilities to Net Worth 37	1.4	•	•	•	0.8	1.4	0.6	0.7	0.9	0.9	2.0	1.5	2.1
Current Assets to Working Capital 38	2.9	•	1.9	2.3	1.4	1.9	1.5	1.7	1.7	2.0	2.2	2.4	•
Current Liabilities to Working Capital 39	1.9	•	0.9	1.3	0.4	0.9	0.5	0.7	0.7	1.0	1.2	1.4	•
Working Capital to Net Sales 40	0.1	•	0.0	0.3	0.2	0.2	0.3	0.2	0.3	0.2	0.1	0.2	•
Inventory to Working Capital 41	0.9	•	•	0.5	0.2	0.3	0.4	0.6	0.4	0.5	0.7	0.8	•
Total Receipts to Cash Flow 42	10.0	6.5	8.0	12.2	6.5	6.1	11.1	10.4	29.9	13.5	10.0	9.6	15.0
Cost of Goods to Cash Flow 43	6.5	4.3	5.6	9.1	4.4	3.7	7.3	7.2	20.8	9.3	6.9	6.3	8.9
Cash Flow to Total Debt 44	0.1	•	0.3	0.1	0.6	0.4	0.2	0.2	0.0	0.1	0.1	0.1	0.0

Selected Financial Factors (in Percentages)

Debt Ratio 45	58.1	•	101.7	101.9	43.4	59.2	37.9	40.1	48.4	46.2	66.9	59.8	67.5
Return on Total Assets 46	5.0	•	19.9	•	17.9	13.6	3.6	4.8	•	2.4	6.6	6.7	2.9
Return on Equity Before Income Taxes 47	7.1	•	•	340.8	27.8	26.4	3.0	5.2	•	2.0	14.4	10.7	2.8
Return on Equity After Income Taxes 48	5.4	•	•	355.9	27.1	25.7	2.8	4.0	•	0.5	10.5	6.9	1.4
Profit Margin (Before Income Tax) 49	4.0	0.4	5.6	•	8.6	7.8	2.3	3.4	•	1.4	5.0	6.7	2.1
Profit Margin (After Income Tax) 50	3.1	•	5.5	•	8.4	7.6	2.1	2.7	•	0.3	3.6	4.3	1.0

Table II

Corporations with Net Income

NONMETALLIC MINERAL MINING AND QUARRYING

MONEY AMOUNTS AND SIZE OF ASSETS IN THOUSANDS OF DOLLARS

Item Description for Accounting Period 7/08 Through 6/09	Total	Zero Assets	Under 500	500 to 1,000	1,000 to 5,000	5,000 to 10,000	10,000 to 25,000	25,000 to 50,000	50,000 to 100,000	100,000 to 250,000	250,000 to 500,000	500,000 to 2,500,000	2,500,000 and over
Number of Enterprises **1**	2110	3	890	•	771	174	88	33	14	13	•	7	0
Revenues ($ in Thousands)													
Net Sales **2**	21619041	485873	224050	•	3608246	1590214	1398699	1256649	904171	1743837	•	8596398	0
Interest **3**	29307	455	0	•	1309	3354	1388	934	2557	3623	•	14575	0
Rents **4**	32027	141	0	•	167	5	644	2204	275	2749	•	25684	0
Royalties **5**	23764	464	359	•	0	1	155	481	0	342	•	21962	0
Other Portfolio Income **6**	277608	606	0	•	27700	21408	47403	17626	12987	5190	•	112582	0
Other Receipts **7**	235725	8388	14457	•	34640	23905	38962	13675	547	31108	•	46775	0
Total Receipts **8**	22217472	495927	238866	•	3672062	1638887	1487251	1291569	920537	1786849	•	8817976	0
Average Total Receipts **9**	10530	165309	268	•	4763	9419	16901	39138	65753	137450	•	1259711	•
Operating Costs/Operating Income (%)													
Cost of Operations **10**	62.7	70.6	59.1	•	68.9	55.0	58.3	67.2	69.1	65.4	•	58.3	•
Salaries and Wages **11**	4.0	0.7	0.0	•	3.2	3.2	5.6	4.4	4.5	4.1	•	4.2	•
Taxes Paid **12**	1.9	0.6	2.4	•	1.9	2.0	2.0	1.2	1.3	1.2	•	2.3	•
Interest Paid **13**	2.6	0.2	1.2	•	1.1	1.8	1.6	1.1	1.7	1.2	•	4.5	•
Depreciation **14**	6.7	1.7	4.3	•	3.8	7.9	8.1	7.5	7.8	7.5	•	7.9	•
Amortization and Depletion **15**	2.7	3.1	0.0	•	0.2	0.5	2.7	1.5	1.8	3.2	•	4.3	•
Pensions and Other Deferred Comp. **16**	0.9	0.7	•	•	0.4	0.4	0.6	0.6	0.4	0.9	•	1.4	•
Employee Benefits **17**	2.0	2.4	•	•	1.3	1.8	2.1	1.0	1.5	2.7	•	2.7	•
Advertising **18**	0.2	0.3	1.2	•	0.2	0.6	0.2	0.4	0.1	0.2	•	0.2	•
Other Expenses **19**	10.2	15.7	23.5	•	8.9	13.6	11.3	8.6	6.9	9.6	•	10.2	•
Officers' Compensation **20**	1.1	1.0	0.0	•	1.7	2.7	2.6	1.8	0.9	1.0	•	0.4	•
Operating Margin **21**	5.0	3.1	8.1	•	8.3	10.4	5.0	4.7	4.1	3.0	•	3.4	•
Operating Margin Before Officers' Comp. **22**	6.1	4.1	8.2	•	10.0	13.2	7.6	6.5	5.0	4.1	•	3.8	•

Selected Average Balance Sheet ($ in Thousands)

Net Receivables 23	1117	0	0	•	419	1074	2249	3644	8756	21177	•	134636
Inventories 24	915	0	9	•	171	439	1803	5937	8622	15876	•	142240
Net Property, Plant and Equipment 25	5236	0	20	•	1024	2008	7361	13424	30522	65834	•	988091
Total Assets 26	12475	0	52	•	2122	6101	17137	33618	71374	155300	•	2373204
Notes and Loans Payable 27	4211	0	36	•	725	2396	3335	8790	17814	29089	•	876143
All Other Liabilities 28	2908	0	1	•	292	375	1700	3569	14666	30118	•	659372
Net Worth 29	5355	0	15	•	1105	3330	12101	21258	38894	96093	•	837690

Selected Financial Ratios (Times to 1)

Current Ratio 30	1.7	•	0.6	•	2.5	3.4	3.3	2.4	3.5	2.3	•	1.0
Quick Ratio 31	1.0	•	0.6	•	2.0	2.9	2.4	1.3	2.4	1.4	•	0.5
Net Sales to Working Capital 32	8.4	•	•	•	8.2	4.4	3.4	4.5	3.5	3.9	•	85.4
Coverage Ratio 33	4.0	30.4	12.9	•	10.5	8.3	8.2	7.8	4.5	5.4	•	2.3
Total Asset Turnover 34	0.8	•	4.9	•	2.2	1.5	0.9	1.1	0.9	0.9	•	0.5
Inventory Turnover 35	7.0	•	16.9	•	18.9	11.5	5.1	4.3	5.2	5.5	•	5.0
Receivables Turnover 36	8.5	•	506.3	•	12.9	7.1	5.6	8.4	5.8	5.4	•	•
Total Liabilities to Net Worth 37	1.3	•	2.4	•	0.9	0.8	0.4	0.6	0.8	0.6	•	1.8
Current Assets to Working Capital 38	2.5	•	•	•	1.7	1.4	1.4	1.7	1.4	1.7	•	25.4
Current Liabilities to Working Capital 39	1.5	•	•	•	0.7	0.4	0.4	0.7	0.4	0.7	•	24.4
Working Capital to Net Sales 40	0.1	•	•	•	0.1	0.2	0.3	0.2	0.3	0.3	•	0.0
Inventory to Working Capital 41	0.7	•	•	•	0.3	0.2	0.3	0.7	0.3	0.3	•	9.9
Total Receipts to Cash Flow 42	7.5	5.1	4.4	•	6.4	4.4	5.6	7.3	9.2	8.6	•	10.0
Cost of Goods to Cash Flow 43	4.7	3.6	2.6	•	4.4	2.4	3.3	4.9	6.3	5.6	•	5.8
Cash Flow to Total Debt 44	0.2	•	1.6	•	0.7	0.7	0.6	0.4	0.2	0.3	•	0.1

Selected Financial Factors (in Percentages)

Debt Ratio 45	57.1	•	70.7	•	47.9	45.4	29.4	36.8	45.5	38.1	•	64.7
Return on Total Assets 46	8.5	•	78.1	•	24.6	23.0	11.9	9.7	6.9	5.8	•	5.5
Return on Equity Before Income Taxes 47	14.8	•	245.9	•	42.7	37.0	14.8	13.4	9.8	7.7	•	8.8
Return on Equity After Income Taxes 48	12.3	•	241.5	•	41.7	36.2	14.4	11.6	8.4	5.1	•	5.8
Profit Margin (Before Income Tax) 49	7.7	5.1	14.8	•	10.1	13.5	11.2	7.5	5.9	5.5	•	6.0
Profit Margin (After Income Tax) 50	6.5	4.0	14.5	•	9.8	13.2	11.0	6.5	5.0	3.7	•	4.0

Table I

Corporations with and without Net Income

SUPPORT ACTIVITIES FOR MINING

MONEY AMOUNTS AND SIZE OF ASSETS IN THOUSANDS OF DOLLARS

Item Description for Accounting Period 7/08 Through 6/09	Total	Zero Assets	Under 500	500 to 1,000	1,000 to 5,000	5,000 to 10,000	10,000 to 25,000	25,000 to 50,000	50,000 to 100,000	100,000 to 250,000	250,000 to 500,000	500,000 to 2,500,000	2,500,000 and over
Number of Enterprises **1**	9040	1084	5655	1010	851	133	122	69	33	23	18	24	18
Revenues ($ in Thousands)													
Net Sales **2**	93260051	2000982	3634788	2249100	3577655	1259986	2412487	3321418	1925872	2809377	2600023	16255005	51213358
Interest **3**	987302	10368	1288	2094	4845	6456	2276	4945	5965	4923	25281	84544	834316
Rents **4**	1004430	11794	1066	0	3320	4702	22188	50	435	3463	81528	219728	656156
Royalties **5**	469965	26	10	652	0	40795	21265	6859	755	513	726	11158	387206
Other Portfolio Income **6**	1653750	121869	944	38611	8626	7695	86449	35188	10867	7173	28593	280438	1027299
Other Receipts **7**	2366713	184196	2669	1479	25825	222582	-20168	71461	89065	27625	27571	263897	1470511
Total Receipts **8**	99742211	2329235	3640765	2291936	3620271	1542216	2524497	3439921	2032959	2853074	2763722	17714770	55588846
Average Total Receipts **9**	11033	2149	644	2269	4254	11596	20693	49854	61605	124047	153540	713115	3088269
Operating Costs/Operating Income (%)													
Cost of Operations **10**	42.8	37.0	22.9	20.9	33.0	38.1	40.8	54.0	36.9	49.9	51.3	47.3	43.6
Salaries and Wages **11**	10.3	13.9	21.8	20.3	10.1	21.6	14.8	10.1	18.0	11.8	10.9	9.8	8.2
Taxes Paid **12**	1.8	1.7	3.6	3.8	2.2	2.9	2.6	2.4	2.1	1.9	2.5	1.9	1.4
Interest Paid **13**	3.3	1.5	1.3	0.9	0.7	1.0	0.6	2.0	3.5	3.4	3.2	3.3	4.0
Depreciation **14**	11.8	19.3	3.1	6.7	5.9	10.5	10.2	6.8	14.3	14.3	16.5	17.1	11.1
Amortization and Depletion **15**	0.6	0.3	0.1	0.0	0.1	0.1	0.5	0.3	0.6	1.0	1.4	1.2	0.6
Pensions and Other Deferred Comp. **16**	0.9	0.9	0.8	0.6	0.2	0.2	0.5	0.3	0.5	0.2	0.7	0.3	1.3
Employee Benefits **17**	1.8	2.6	0.3	0.5	1.4	1.8	0.7	1.2	1.6	0.9	2.5	1.4	2.3
Advertising **18**	0.1	0.1	0.4	0.3	0.3	0.4	0.2	0.2	0.1	0.2	0.1	0.1	0.1
Other Expenses **19**	18.8	22.4	24.1	19.9	31.6	37.1	22.8	17.1	25.8	14.9	10.7	15.6	18.2
Officers' Compensation **20**	1.6	6.0	8.3	5.9	5.9	3.9	3.0	1.2	0.9	0.7	0.9	1.0	0.6
Operating Margin **21**	6.0	•	13.3	20.2	8.6	•	3.2	4.5	•	0.9	•	0.9	8.6
Operating Margin Before Officers' Comp. **22**	7.6	0.3	21.6	26.0	14.6	•	6.2	5.8	•	1.6	0.2	1.9	9.3

Selected Average Balance Sheet ($ in Thousands)

Net Receivables 23	2498	0	13	80	567	1145	3755	7730	9671	33092	79758	147834	818517
Inventories 24	560	0	1	20	17	299	581	585	2442	3417	6576	30923	214246
Net Property, Plant and Equipment 25	6361	0	51	225	528	2265	4582	10075	28580	71202	89619	587170	2038739
Total Assets 26	15672	0	152	646	2050	6750	15030	36007	70565	158734	363610	1259037	5025776
Notes and Loans Payable 27	4616	0	86	209	355	2240	2646	10644	34387	58855	87617	394696	1435244
All Other Liabilities 28	3756	0	30	73	420	1430	5413	12137	17174	37078	88019	257713	1248676
Net Worth 29	7301	0	36	365	1276	3079	6971	13225	19004	62801	187974	606628	2341856

Selected Financial Ratios (Times to 1)

Current Ratio 30	1.9	•	2.6	1.8	2.9	2.5	2.0	1.6	1.4	1.7	1.4	2.3	1.8
Quick Ratio 31	1.4	•	2.5	1.6	2.5	2.1	1.6	1.1	1.1	1.4	1.2	1.6	1.3
Net Sales to Working Capital 32	4.6	•	11.9	20.0	4.5	5.3	4.4	9.0	8.7	5.9	5.0	4.0	4.0
Coverage Ratio 33	5.2	8.1	11.4	24.9	15.9	5.5	13.6	5.1	1.3	1.8	3.1	2.9	5.6
Total Asset Turnover 34	0.7	•	4.2	3.4	2.1	1.4	1.3	1.3	0.8	0.8	0.4	0.5	0.6
Inventory Turnover 35	7.9	•	149.7	23.6	81.8	12.1	13.9	44.5	8.8	17.8	11.3	10.4	5.8
Receivables Turnover 36	4.7	•	70.3	18.1	7.8	6.9	6.1	8.2	6.0	4.3	1.9	4.3	4.3
Total Liabilities to Net Worth 37	1.1	•	3.2	0.8	0.6	1.2	1.7	1.7	2.7	1.5	0.9	1.1	1.1
Current Assets to Working Capital 38	2.1	•	1.6	2.3	1.5	1.7	2.0	2.8	3.6	2.4	3.7	1.7	2.2
Current Liabilities to Working Capital 39	1.1	•	0.6	1.3	0.5	0.7	1.0	1.8	2.6	1.4	2.7	0.7	1.2
Working Capital to Net Sales 40	0.2	•	0.1	0.0	0.2	0.2	0.2	0.1	0.1	0.2	0.2	0.2	0.2
Inventory to Working Capital 41	0.3	•	0.0	0.2	0.0	0.1	0.2	0.2	0.4	0.2	0.2	0.2	0.3
Total Receipts to Cash Flow 42	4.2	4.2	3.0	2.6	3.6	2.8	4.1	5.0	4.6	9.7	9.1	6.1	3.8
Cost of Goods to Cash Flow 43	1.8	1.6	0.7	0.5	1.2	1.1	1.7	2.7	1.7	4.8	4.7	2.9	1.7
Cash Flow to Total Debt 44	0.3	•	1.8	3.0	1.5	0.9	0.6	0.4	0.2	0.1	0.1	0.2	0.3

Selected Financial Factors (in Percentages)

Debt Ratio 45	53.4	•	76.2	43.6	37.8	54.4	53.6	63.3	73.1	60.4	48.3	51.8	53.4
Return on Total Assets 46	11.1	•	62.4	79.2	21.5	8.0	11.2	13.5	3.8	4.5	4.0	5.2	12.5
Return on Equity Before Income Taxes 47	19.2	•	238.9	134.8	32.3	14.4	22.3	29.5	3.4	4.9	5.3	7.1	22.1
Return on Equity After Income Taxes 48	13.4	•	237.6	131.4	28.8	8.8	18.6	24.1	0.4	0.9	3.6	4.9	14.5
Profit Margin (Before Income Tax) 49	13.6	10.6	13.5	22.1	9.8	4.7	7.9	8.1	1.1	2.5	6.8	6.3	18.2
Profit Margin (After Income Tax) 50	9.5	8.4	13.4	21.5	8.7	2.9	6.6	6.6	0.1	0.5	4.7	4.4	12.0

Table II

Corporations with Net Income

SUPPORT ACTIVITIES FOR MINING

MONEY AMOUNTS AND SIZE OF ASSETS IN THOUSANDS OF DOLLARS

Item Description for Accounting Period 7/08 Through 6/09	Total	Zero Assets	Under 500	500 to 1,000	1,000 to 5,000	5,000 to 10,000	10,000 to 25,000	25,000 to 50,000	50,000 to 100,000	100,000 to 250,000	250,000 to 500,000	500,000 to 2,500,000	2,500,000 and over
Number of Enterprises 1	6060	1061	3334	736	649	59	95	46	20	14	9	•	•
Revenues ($ in Thousands)													
Net Sales 2	82626019	1136767	3018696	1990568	2764295	808245	2275341	2686917	1406809	1955550	1283730	•	•
Interest 3	842866	7369	693	1942	3790	3368	2055	3759	1825	3765	16768	•	•
Rents 4	923297	5253	23	0	9	86	22188	0	435	2599	16990	•	•
Royalties 5	467768	0	0	652	0	40795	20301	6827	517	0	312	•	•
Other Portfolio Income 6	1611585	121869	0	38359	8250	6668	86449	33447	5673	6781	27818	•	•
Other Receipts 7	2253715	164554	2477	671	23093	219809	-24421	69357	83390	21718	37029	•	•
Total Receipts 8	88725250	1435812	3021889	2032192	2799437	1078971	2381913	2800307	1498649	1990413	1382647	•	•
Average Total Receipts 9	14641	1353	906	2761	4313	18288	25073	60876	74932	142172	153627	•	•
Operating Costs/Operating Income (%)													
Cost of Operations 10	42.3	38.1	23.6	17.6	22.2	30.3	41.8	53.3	36.0	52.3	62.2	•	•
Salaries and Wages 11	9.9	6.8	16.2	21.4	10.8	26.6	14.0	9.3	18.6	7.4	8.5	•	•
Taxes Paid 12	1.8	0.7	3.5	3.9	2.1	3.1	2.6	2.5	2.0	2.0	2.3	•	•
Interest Paid 13	2.7	1.7	1.2	0.5	0.4	0.6	0.5	1.6	2.1	2.3	2.1	•	•
Depreciation 14	10.6	20.2	2.6	6.7	4.8	8.2	7.7	4.4	10.4	7.6	8.5	•	•
Amortization and Depletion 15	0.6	0.0	0.1	0.0	0.0	0.1	0.3	0.3	0.4	0.7	0.2	•	•
Pensions and Other Deferred Comp. 16	1.0	1.5	0.9	0.7	0.2	0.1	0.5	0.3	0.6	0.3	0.9	•	•
Employee Benefits 17	1.8	1.4	0.2	0.3	0.7	2.4	0.6	1.2	1.3	0.7	1.4	•	•
Advertising 18	0.1	0.0	0.4	0.4	0.2	0.4	0.2	0.2	0.1	0.2	0.1	•	•
Other Expenses 19	19.0	24.8	24.0	19.6	38.6	41.9	20.6	15.9	25.7	15.8	0.2	•	•
Officers' Compensation 20	1.4	3.4	9.2	5.4	5.5	3.8	2.9	1.3	1.1	0.8	1.2	•	•
Operating Margin 21	8.7	1.4	18.0	23.4	14.4	•	8.4	9.7	1.8	10.0	12.4	•	•
Operating Margin Before Officers' Comp. 22	10.1	4.9	27.2	28.8	19.9	•	11.3	11.0	2.8	10.8	13.6	•	•

Selected Average Balance Sheet ($ in Thousands)

Net Receivables 23	3368	0	8	59	629	1962	3850	9275	12875	38936	114222
Inventories 24	786	0	2	10	21	244	711	604	2757	4931	9814
Net Property, Plant and Equipment 25	7817	0	66	226	440	2043	4547	7895	22473	45792	55094
Total Assets 26	19814	0	197	654	2074	7040	15470	38694	70952	147167	362687
Notes and Loans Payable 27	4929	0	78	139	196	1322	2143	9336	29224	56185	57765
All Other Liabilities 28	5045	0	20	49	415	1260	5354	15219	16391	31126	101040
Net Worth 29	9840	0	99	466	1463	4458	7973	14139	25337	59856	203881

Selected Financial Ratios (Times to 1)

Current Ratio 30	2.0	•	4.6	2.3	3.8	3.1	2.5	1.7	1.8	2.2	1.9
Quick Ratio 31	1.4	•	4.4	2.2	3.2	2.8	1.9	1.2	1.4	1.8	1.7
Net Sales to Working Capital 32	4.3	•	9.4	19.8	3.7	4.9	4.1	7.9	5.6	4.3	2.1
Coverage Ratio 33	7.1	17.5	16.0	53.4	39.0	27.1	28.8	9.5	5.0	6.2	11.7
Total Asset Turnover 34	0.7	•	4.6	4.1	2.1	1.9	1.5	1.5	1.0	0.9	0.4
Inventory Turnover 35	7.3	•	128.0	49.0	44.8	17.0	14.1	51.5	9.2	14.8	9.0
Receivables Turnover 36	4.6	•	135.6	26.8	6.6	4.9	7.5	8.5	5.9	4.0	•
Total Liabilities to Net Worth 37	1.0	•	1.0	0.4	0.4	0.6	0.9	1.7	1.8	1.5	0.8
Current Assets to Working Capital 38	2.0	•	1.3	1.8	1.4	1.5	1.7	2.5	2.2	1.8	2.2
Current Liabilities to Working Capital 39	1.0	•	0.3	0.8	0.4	0.5	0.7	1.5	1.2	0.8	1.2
Working Capital to Net Sales 40	0.2	•	0.1	0.1	0.3	0.2	0.2	0.1	0.2	0.2	0.5
Inventory to Working Capital 41	0.3	•	0.0	0.1	0.0	0.0	0.2	0.1	0.4	0.2	0.1
Total Receipts to Cash Flow 42	3.7	2.5	2.6	2.4	2.6	1.9	3.7	3.9	3.5	5.2	6.0
Cost of Goods to Cash Flow 43	1.6	1.0	0.6	0.4	0.6	0.6	1.5	2.1	1.3	2.7	3.7
Cash Flow to Total Debt 44	0.4	•	3.5	6.0	2.7	2.8	0.9	0.6	0.4	0.3	0.1

Selected Financial Factors (in Percentages)

Debt Ratio 45	50.3	•	49.7	28.8	29.5	36.7	48.5	63.5	64.3	59.3	43.8
Return on Total Assets 46	13.4	•	88.9	107.4	33.1	32.3	20.9	23.5	10.2	13.4	9.6
Return on Equity Before Income Taxes 47	23.2	•	165.8	148.1	45.7	49.2	39.2	57.6	23.0	27.7	15.7
Return on Equity After Income Taxes 48	16.8	•	165.0	144.4	41.6	40.5	35.0	50.0	19.2	20.9	12.7
Profit Margin (Before Income Tax) 49	16.8	27.7	18.2	25.5	15.7	16.0	13.0	14.0	8.3	11.9	22.4
Profit Margin (After Income Tax) 50	12.1	23.9	18.1	24.9	14.3	13.2	11.7	12.1	6.9	8.9	18.2

Table I

Corporations with and without Net Income

ELECTRIC POWER GENERATION, TRANSMISSION AND DISTRIBUTION

MONEY AMOUNTS AND SIZE OF ASSETS IN THOUSANDS OF DOLLARS

Item Description for Accounting Period 7/08 Through 6/09	Total	Zero Assets	Under 500	500 to 1,000	1,000 to 5,000	5,000 to 10,000	10,000 to 25,000	25,000 to 50,000	50,000 to 100,000	100,000 to 250,000	250,000 to 500,000	500,000 to 2,500,000	2,500,000 and over
Number of Enterprises **1**	1337	74	629	195	148	52	60	24	25	33	16	34	47
Revenues ($ in Thousands)													
Net Sales **2**	359185861	497289	168479	99104	150320	129587	1265988	588718	3080576	3815740	1793238	17307801	330289022
Interest **3**	4917596	264339	117	229	4731	2869	1496	30113	16103	44864	70529	409572	4072634
Rents **4**	1370725	2647	0	0	0	1422	0	0	1584	179	18571	16841	1329481
Royalties **5**	391321	0	0	0	0	0	0	0	200	0	0	23268	367853
Other Portfolio Income **6**	6176564	17202	0	941	180011	946	13770	6262	960	3691	3030	839350	5110397
Other Receipts **7**	9401363	56158	299	22622	1039	2942	8313	24192	45941	178688	383250	546725	8131198
Total Receipts **8**	381443430	837635	168895	122896	336101	137766	1289567	649285	3145364	4043162	2268618	19143557	349300585
Average Total Receipts **9**	285298	11319	269	630	2271	2649	21493	27054	125815	122520	141789	563046	7431927
Operating Costs/Operating Income (%)													
Cost of Operations **10**	60.7	29.5	90.5	•	66.6	50.7	85.9	76.8	78.7	75.4	65.0	63.2	60.2
Salaries and Wages **11**	3.4	2.8	6.3	5.4	4.3	12.3	4.1	3.0	2.9	2.3	3.0	4.1	3.3
Taxes Paid **12**	3.4	3.8	0.9	8.2	3.4	5.1	0.5	0.9	0.7	0.9	1.9	2.0	3.6
Interest Paid **13**	5.3	78.5	0.9	0.8	4.1	4.6	2.2	2.1	1.6	3.4	9.5	5.3	5.3
Depreciation **14**	7.9	23.2	0.8	1.5	9.5	10.6	2.3	2.4	0.9	3.2	8.0	8.4	8.0
Amortization and Depletion **15**	0.7	1.2	•	•	0.3	0.2	0.2	0.2	0.4	0.3	0.2	1.0	0.7
Pensions and Other Deferred Comp. **16**	1.0	0.1	•	•	•	1.2	0.6	0.0	0.1	0.2	0.1	0.8	1.1
Employee Benefits **17**	1.0	0.3	•	0.6	2.0	2.2	0.2	0.4	1.1	0.4	0.6	0.7	1.1
Advertising **18**	0.1	0.0	0.1	0.1	0.1	1.0	0.1	0.6	0.1	0.4	0.1	0.1	0.1
Other Expenses **19**	21.7	47.4	19.8	48.9	113.8	28.5	8.4	35.9	14.6	18.1	55.9	24.0	21.5
Officers' Compensation **20**	0.4	•	•	22.3	2.1	3.6	0.6	0.9	0.5	0.9	0.4	0.4	0.3
Operating Margin **21**	•	•	•	12.1	•	•	•	•	•	•	•	•	•
Operating Margin Before Officers' Comp. **22**	•	•	•	34.4	•	•	•	•	•	•	•	•	•

Selected Average Balance Sheet ($ in Thousands)

Net Receivables 23	45964	0	29	0	86	1106	1897	15582	13041	13799	21129	92998	1204166
Inventories 24	10562	0	72	12	0	112	517	240	1610	2910	4400	43148	263413
Net Property, Plant and Equipment 25	338551	0	3	152	178	1908	5632	9252	19602	58190	179452	696607	8999149
Total Assets 26	651358	0	128	763	2154	6620	15938	41189	68209	162359	376147	1263463	17276364
Notes and Loans Payable 27	256556	0	63	0	799	1929	5736	18980	28230	61527	205130	584388	6724899
All Other Liabilities 28	223265	0	43	166	549	995	5285	29886	21394	43553	141144	338136	5990464
Net Worth 29	171537	0	23	597	805	3696	4917	-7677	18584	57279	29874	340938	4561001

Selected Financial Ratios (Times to 1)

Current Ratio 30	1.0	•	2.4	3.7	7.0	3.3	1.1	1.0	1.2	1.9	0.9	1.0	1.0
Quick Ratio 31	0.6	•	1.0	3.7	2.2	3.1	0.9	0.8	0.9	1.4	0.5	0.8	0.5
Net Sales to Working Capital 32	•	•	3.6	1.1	1.0	1.6	44.6	24.3	28.7	6.1	•	43.4	•
Coverage Ratio 33	1.1	0.8	1.1	46.8	5.2	•	•	•	1.3	1.2	•	1.1	1.1
Total Asset Turnover 34	0.4	•	2.1	0.7	0.5	0.4	1.3	0.6	1.8	0.7	0.3	0.4	0.4
Inventory Turnover 35	15.4	•	3.4	•	•	11.3	35.1	78.3	60.3	30.0	16.5	7.5	16.0
Receivables Turnover 36	6.6	•	18.2	4.8	12.7	2.6	13.1	1.6	11.0	8.4	7.1	5.6	6.6
Total Liabilities to Net Worth 37	2.8	•	4.7	0.3	1.7	0.8	2.2	•	2.7	1.8	11.6	2.7	2.8
Current Assets to Working Capital 38	•	•	1.7	1.4	1.2	1.4	9.6	28.6	5.5	2.1	•	22.9	•
Current Liabilities to Working Capital 39	•	•	0.7	0.4	0.2	0.4	8.6	27.6	4.5	1.1	•	21.9	•
Working Capital to Net Sales 40	•	•	0.3	0.9	1.0	0.6	0.0	0.0	0.0	0.2	•	0.0	•
Inventory to Working Capital 41	•	•	1.0	•	•	0.1	1.0	0.1	0.5	0.2	•	3.5	•
Total Receipts to Cash Flow 42	6.0	3.6	•	1.4	5.7	15.7	32.2	5.5	7.7	6.7	2.9	6.5	6.0
Cost of Goods to Cash Flow 43	3.6	1.1	•	•	3.8	7.9	27.7	4.2	6.0	5.1	1.9	4.1	3.6
Cash Flow to Total Debt 44	0.1	•	2.2	0.1	0.1	0.1	0.1	0.1	0.3	0.2	0.1	0.1	0.1

Selected Financial Factors (in Percentages)

Debt Ratio 45	73.7	•	82.5	21.7	62.6	44.2	69.1	118.6	72.8	64.7	92.1	73.0	73.6
Return on Total Assets 46	2.4	•	•	24.6	10.2	•	•	•	3.7	2.8	•	2.3	2.5
Return on Equity Before Income Taxes 47	0.9	•	•	30.8	22.0	•	•	41.1	3.3	1.1	•	0.7	1.1
Return on Equity After Income Taxes 48	•	•	•	30.8	5.7	•	•	45.4	1.2	0.1	•	•	0.0
Profit Margin (Before Income Tax) 49	0.6	•	•	36.2	17.4	•	•	•	0.5	0.6	•	0.5	0.7
Profit Margin (After Income Tax) 50	•	•	•	36.2	4.5	•	•	•	0.2	0.0	•	•	0.0

Table II

Corporations with Net Income

ELECTRIC POWER GENERATION, TRANSMISSION AND DISTRIBUTION

MONEY AMOUNTS AND SIZE OF ASSETS IN THOUSANDS OF DOLLARS

Item Description for Accounting Period 7/08 Through 6/09	Total	Zero Assets	Under 500	500 to 1,000	1,000 to 5,000	5,000 to 10,000	10,000 to 25,000	25,000 to 50,000	50,000 to 100,000	100,000 to 250,000	250,000 to 500,000	500,000 to 2,500,000	2,500,000 and over
Number of Enterprises **1**	807	•	•	177	19	25	8	•	11	12	10	16	28
Revenues ($ in Thousands)													
Net Sales **2**	218244566	•	•	99104	146007	49103	83673	•	1212012	2441986	1535203	9859035	20310984
Interest **3**	2914951	•	•	149	2487	2533	295	•	1253	17828	36550	197215	2395194
Rents **4**	846939	•	•	0	0	0	0	•	263	135	18571	10175	817795
Royalties **5**	384550	•	•	0	0	0	0	•	193	0	0	23268	361089
Other Portfolio Income **6**	3803884	•	•	941	180011	946	13289	•	24	1126	2162	771150	2814879
Other Receipts **7**	4494736	•	•	22564	740	428	550	•	28830	152001	43293	341694	3888187
Total Receipts **8**	230689626	•	•	122758	329245	53010	97807	•	1242575	2583076	1635779	11202537	212588128
Average Total Receipts **9**	285861	•	•	694	17329	2120	12226	•	112961	215256	163578	700159	7592433
Operating Costs/Operating Income (%)													
Cost of Operations **10**	59.7	•	•	•	68.5	3.8	66.8	•	77.4	87.4	69.0	63.5	59.0
Salaries and Wages **11**	3.3	•	•	2.1	0.0	6.2	7.2	•	5.3	1.5	3.4	3.7	3.3
Taxes Paid **12**	3.2	•	•	7.8	2.4	6.2	1.4	•	1.1	0.6	1.7	2.6	3.2
Interest Paid **13**	5.2	•	•	0.8	3.7	7.1	0.1	•	1.5	1.2	8.2	4.8	5.1
Depreciation **14**	7.7	•	•	0.0	7.2	13.3	3.2	•	1.0	1.2	6.2	7.9	7.8
Amortization and Depletion **15**	0.7	•	•	•	•	•	0.1	•	0.5	0.2	0.1	0.8	0.7
Pensions and Other Deferred Comp. **16**	0.6	•	•	•	•	1.8	1.2	•	0.3	0.2	0.1	1.1	0.6
Employee Benefits **17**	1.0	•	•	0.1	1.4	•	1.2	•	2.2	0.3	0.7	0.8	1.0
Advertising **18**	0.1	•	•	0.0	•	0.0	•	•	0.1	0.2	0.1	0.1	0.1
Other Expenses **19**	19.4	•	•	38.5	103.1	16.0	9.2	•	4.8	7.2	11.3	18.2	19.7
Officers' Compensation **20**	0.4	•	•	19.7	•	3.0	0.7	•	0.8	0.2	0.5	0.3	0.4
Operating Margin **21**	•	•	•	31.0	•	42.7	9.0	•	5.1	•	•	•	•
Operating Margin Before Officers' Comp. **22**	•	•	•	50.7	•	45.7	9.6	•	5.9	0.1	•	•	•

Selected Average Balance Sheet ($ in Thousands)

Net Receivables 23	41379	•	0	591	2046	1282	•	7570	13227	17557	129837	1097647
Inventories 24	13402	•	8	0	116	480	•	1167	6072	4807	30598	363748
Net Property, Plant and Equipment 25	322293	•	160	0	2241	2905	•	24601	52336	195495	770662	8737364
Total Assets 26	633042	•	780	3428	5914	15664	•	64067	166092	369601	1390576	17187644
Notes and Loans Payable 27	249869	•	0	5	2350	972	•	19149	71646	207479	646718	6703793
All Other Liabilities 28	224110	•	183	661	1286	7083	•	25493	41013	105192	342145	6173995
Net Worth 29	159064	•	597	2762	2278	7610	•	19424	53432	56929	401713	4309856

Selected Financial Ratios (Times to 1)

Current Ratio 30	1.1	•	3.4	5.0	5.9	1.9	•	1.0	1.9	1.5	1.4	1.1
Quick Ratio 31	0.6	•	3.4	1.2	5.7	1.7	•	0.6	1.2	1.0	1.1	0.6
Net Sales to Working Capital 32	23.3	•	1.3	2.9	0.7	5.1	•	125.1	7.8	8.7	7.9	26.4
Coverage Ratio 33	1.9	•	70.4	11.7	8.0	305.6	•	6.0	6.9	1.6	3.0	1.8
Total Asset Turnover 34	0.4	•	0.7	2.2	0.3	0.7	•	1.7	1.2	0.4	0.4	0.4
Inventory Turnover 35	12.0	•	•	•	0.6	14.5	•	73.1	28.9	22.0	12.8	11.7
Receivables Turnover 36	5.9	•	4.8	14.1	1.9	2.2	•	12.4	9.3	12.0	4.5	5.9
Total Liabilities to Net Worth 37	3.0	•	0.3	0.2	1.6	1.1	•	2.3	2.1	5.5	2.5	3.0
Current Assets to Working Capital 38	9.9	•	1.4	1.3	1.2	2.1	•	22.5	2.1	2.9	3.8	11.2
Current Liabilities to Working Capital 39	8.9	•	0.4	0.3	0.2	1.1	•	21.5	1.1	1.9	2.8	10.2
Working Capital to Net Sales 40	0.0	•	0.8	0.3	1.4	0.2	•	0.0	0.1	0.1	0.1	0.0
Inventory to Working Capital 41	1.0	•	•	•	0.0	•	•	1.8	0.3	0.4	0.3	1.2
Total Receipts to Cash Flow 42	5.0	•	1.2	3.7	1.6	5.4	•	8.5	8.1	7.7	5.6	5.0
Cost of Goods to Cash Flow 43	3.0	•	•	2.5	0.1	3.6	•	6.6	7.1	5.3	3.5	2.9
Cash Flow to Total Debt 44	0.1	•	2.5	3.1	0.3	0.2	•	0.3	0.2	0.1	0.1	0.1

Selected Financial Factors (in Percentages)

Debt Ratio 45	74.9	•	23.4	19.4	61.5	51.4	•	69.7	67.8	84.6	71.1	74.9
Return on Total Assets 46	4.2	•	39.9	96.0	19.0	17.3	•	15.8	9.9	5.6	6.5	4.0
Return on Equity Before Income Taxes 47	7.9	•	51.4	109.0	43.2	35.5	•	43.5	26.3	13.8	15.0	7.2
Return on Equity After Income Taxes 48	5.9	•	51.4	72.1	41.4	24.4	•	38.9	23.2	10.2	12.8	5.2
Profit Margin (Before Income Tax) 49	4.7	•	54.8	39.2	50.1	25.8	•	7.7	7.0	5.1	9.8	4.3
Profit Margin (After Income Tax) 50	3.5	•	54.8	25.9	48.0	17.8	•	6.9	6.2	3.8	8.3	3.1

Table I

Corporations with and without Net Income

NATURAL GAS DISTRIBUTION

MONEY AMOUNTS AND SIZE OF ASSETS IN THOUSANDS OF DOLLARS

Item Description for Accounting Period 7/08 Through 6/09	Total	Zero Assets	Under 500	500 to 1,000	1,000 to 5,000	5,000 to 10,000	10,000 to 25,000	25,000 to 50,000	50,000 to 100,000	100,000 to 250,000	250,000 to 500,000	500,000 to 2,500,000	2,500,000 and over
Number of Enterprises **1**	556	10	248	116	78	4	34	11	12	7	7	11	18
Revenues ($ in Thousands)													
Net Sales **2**	122947127	8278	6864	69350	392666	111452	1197422	1964727	492739	4641262	6309643	14728596	93024127
Interest **3**	1760399	600	0	0	1824	7	9711	375	53171	813	4474	111620	1577803
Rents **4**	121351	0	0	2809	0	37	0	0	2137	0	1067	5435	109866
Royalties **5**	41029	0	0	0	0	0	0	0	28	0	4105	1936	34958
Other Portfolio Income **6**	2240311	0	0	0	1950	14	914	2674	29244	8652	54	57015	2139793
Other Receipts **7**	6519716	5718	0	3328	1243	457	4198	80172	2196863	3477	91090	175940	3957235
Total Receipts **8**	133629933	14596	6864	75487	397683	111967	1212245	2047948	2774182	4654204	6410433	15080542	100843782
Average Total Receipts **9**	240342	1460	28	651	5098	27992	35654	186177	231182	664886	915776	1370958	5602432
Operating Costs/Operating Income (%)													
Cost of Operations **10**	73.8	6.0	67.3	73.4	75.7	81.8	90.4	96.2	73.8	95.4	96.2	86.8	68.5
Salaries and Wages **11**	3.7	5.4	•	•	4.5	0.5	1.1	2.3	12.5	0.7	0.6	2.0	4.4
Taxes Paid **12**	2.4	4.7	3.0	0.8	0.8	0.7	0.6	0.4	3.8	0.1	0.6	1.8	2.8
Interest Paid **13**	3.9	5.0	•	•	0.9	0.3	0.7	0.2	4.3	0.3	1.1	2.1	4.6
Depreciation **14**	5.7	5.7	•	•	10.4	4.5	1.2	0.2	5.9	0.5	1.0	3.0	6.8
Amortization and Depletion **15**	0.6	0.1	•	•	0.0	0.3	0.0	0.0	0.7	0.1	0.4	0.4	0.7
Pensions and Other Deferred Comp. **16**	0.4	0.3	•	•	1.0	•	0.1	0.0	0.7	0.1	0.1	0.3	0.4
Employee Benefits **17**	0.9	114.5	•	0.1	0.4	1.0	0.2	0.1	1.5	0.1	0.3	0.5	1.1
Advertising **18**	0.0	0.0	•	•	0.0	0.0	0.0	0.0	0.1	0.1	0.0	0.0	0.0
Other Expenses **19**	14.2	223.0	200.3	27.6	6.4	3.5	3.6	2.1	532.0	2.4	2.3	6.1	14.5
Officers' Compensation **20**	0.3	0.0	•	3.3	1.4	0.7	0.6	0.5	1.4	0.2	0.2	0.3	0.3
Operating Margin **21**	•	•	•	•	•	6.7	1.7	•	•	•	•	•	•
Operating Margin Before Officers' Comp. **22**	•	•	•	•	0.1	7.4	2.2	•	•	0.2	•	•	•

Selected Average Balance Sheet ($ in Thousands)

Net Receivables 23	35606	0	0	204	444	633	4154	31056	5707	42691	42291	121714	958397
Inventories 24	11754	0	0	121	218	735	3506	3509	21741	38955		110226	261966
Net Property, Plant and Equipment 25	193105	0	0	28	943	4218	5904	4900	29356	30357	90457	480667	5585155
Total Assets 26	463348	14	571	2336	8230	14312	42904	73703	149745	308109		1290927	13227150
Notes and Loans Payable 27	125750	0	1	339	1418	797	4817	12604	22103	37791	111648	447635	3512544
All Other Liabilities 28	232470	0	4	166	622	2148	3022	24519	1254018	110923	90153	510751	5929429
Net Worth 29	105128	0	8	66	295	5285	6473	5781	-1202417	1031	106308	332540	3785178

Selected Financial Ratios (Times to 1)

Current Ratio 30	1.1	•	2.6	3.3	1.7	1.5	1.3	2.5	0.8	1.3	1.2	1.1	
Quick Ratio 31	0.5	•	2.6	3.3	1.6	1.2	1.2	1.8	0.5	0.6	0.5	0.4	
Net Sales to Working Capital 32	28.6	•	3.3	1.6	10.1	13.6	19.6	1.7	•	28.8	15.1	34.5	
Coverage Ratio 33	1.7	•	•	1.0	27.7	5.3	10.7	•	1.8	•	0.5	1.9	
Total Asset Turnover 34	0.5	•	2.0	1.0	2.2	3.4	2.5	4.2	0.6	4.4	2.9	1.0	0.4
Inventory Turnover 35	13.9	•	•	31.4	104.6	43.3	49.0	8.6	29.1	22.3	10.5	13.5	
Receivables Turnover 36	3.8	•	•	2.8	15.9	12.0	7.0	6.5	•	14.6	3.1		
Total Liabilities to Net Worth 37	3.4	•	0.6	7.6	6.9	1.2	6.4	•	144.2	1.9	2.9	2.5	
Current Assets to Working Capital 38	13.1	•	1.6	1.4	2.4	4.0	1.6	•	4.6	5.1	17.9		
Current Liabilities to Working Capital 39	12.1	•	0.6	0.4	1.4	0.4	3.0	0.6	•	3.6	4.1	16.9	
Working Capital to Net Sales 40	0.0	•	0.3	0.6	0.1	0.1	0.1	0.6	•	0.0	0.1	0.0	
Inventory to Working Capital 41	1.6	•	•	•	0.1	0.3	0.5	0.2	•	1.2	1.5	1.8	
Total Receipts to Cash Flow 42	7.3	•	3.4	4.7	21.4	10.0	15.9	26.3	0.2	43.3	115.1	27.5	6.8
Cost of Goods to Cash Flow 43	5.4	•	2.3	3.4	16.2	8.1	14.4	25.3	0.2	41.3	110.8	23.8	4.6
Cash Flow to Total Debt 44	0.1	•	1.5	0.3	0.1	0.9	0.3	0.1	0.1	0.1	0.0	0.1	

Selected Financial Factors (in Percentages)

Debt Ratio 45	77.3	•	39.1	88.4	87.4	35.8	54.8	86.5	1731.4	99.3	65.5	74.2	71.4
Return on Total Assets 46	3.2	•	•	3.7	1.8	25.3	8.6	9.6	•	•	2.7	1.2	3.5
Return on Equity Before Income Taxes 47	6.0	•	32.1	•	38.0	15.5	64.3	166.0	•	2.5	•	•	5.9
Return on Equity After Income Taxes 48	2.9	•	27.3	•	25.1	63.0	109.4	•	2.6	•	•	•	3.5
Profit Margin (Before Income Tax) 49	2.9	•	3.5	•	7.2	2.1	0.3	•	•	•	0.3	•	4.3
Profit Margin (After Income Tax) 50	1.4	•	3.0	•	4.8	2.0	0.2	•	•	•	0.2	•	2.5

Table II

Corporations with Net Income

NATURAL GAS DISTRIBUTION

MONEY AMOUNTS AND SIZE OF ASSETS IN THOUSANDS OF DOLLARS

Item Description for Accounting Period 7/08 Through 6/09	Total	Zero Assets	Under 500	500 to 1,000	1,000 to 5,000	5,000 to 10,000	10,000 to 25,000	25,000 to 50,000	50,000 to 100,000	100,000 to 250,000	250,000 to 500,000	500,000 to 2,500,000	2,500,000 and over
Number of Enterprises **1**	449	•	•	116	13	4	17	•	7	•	0	8	•
Revenues ($ in Thousands)													
Net Sales **2**	85978600	•	•	69350	204025	111452	1107564	•	429324	•	0	12887070	•
Interest **3**	1282729	•	•	0	942	7	811	•	2191	•	0	24284	•
Rents **4**	69840	•	•	2809	0	37	0	•	2133	•	0	2660	•
Royalties **5**	39072	•	•	0	0	0	0	•	26	•	0	0	•
Other Portfolio Income **6**	2087152	•	•	0	1950	14	853	•	918	•	0	50348	•
Other Receipts **7**	3872805	•	•	3328	901	457	173	•	6645	•	0	186696	•
Total Receipts **8**	93330198	•	•	75487	207818	111967	1109401	•	441237	•	0	13151058	•
Average Total Receipts **9**	207862	•	•	651	15986	27992	65259	•	63034	•	•	1643882	•
Operating Costs/Operating Income (%)													
Cost of Operations **10**	75.6	•	•	73.4	83.6	81.8	92.2	•	76.7	•	•	88.3	•
Salaries and Wages **11**	3.5	•	•	•	0.5	0.5	0.8	•	3.0	•	•	1.1	•
Taxes Paid **12**	2.1	•	•	0.8	0.1	0.7	0.4	•	2.4	•	•	1.6	•
Interest Paid **13**	3.5	•	•	•	0.4	0.3	0.1	•	1.6	•	•	1.0	•
Depreciation **14**	4.9	•	•	•	0.3	4.5	0.3	•	5.1	•	•	2.3	•
Amortization and Depletion **15**	0.5	•	•	•	•	0.3	0.0	•	0.3	•	•	0.1	•
Pensions and Other Deferred Comp. **16**	0.4	•	•	•	0.1	•	0.1	•	0.7	•	•	0.2	•
Employee Benefits **17**	1.0	•	•	0.1	0.3	1.0	0.1	•	1.5	•	•	0.5	•
Advertising **18**	0.0	•	•	•	0.0	0.0	0.0	•	0.0	•	•	0.0	•
Other Expenses **19**	10.6	•	•	27.6	2.4	3.5	1.7	•	4.6	•	•	3.7	•
Officers' Compensation **20**	0.2	•	•	3.3	0.7	0.7	0.5	•	1.2	•	•	0.3	•
Operating Margin **21**	•	•	•	•	11.5	6.7	3.9	•	3.0	•	•	0.9	•
Operating Margin Before Officers' Comp. **22**	•	•	•	•	12.2	7.4	4.4	•	4.2	•	•	1.2	•

Selected Average Balance Sheet ($ in Thousands)

Net Receivables 23	38106	204	668	633	4159	8453	156963
Inventories 24	10575	0	609	218	1366	5108	168091
Net Property, Plant and Equipment 25	163186	28	0	4218	1495	32027	471092
Total Assets 26	437192	571	2255	8230	13142	75518	1225181
Notes and Loans Payable 27	93418	339	632	797	3111	13697	374981
All Other Liabilities 28	211284	166	1337	2148	3467	23729	456678
Net Worth 29	132491	66	286	5285	6564	38092	393521

Selected Financial Ratios (Times to 1)

Current Ratio 30	1.2	3.3	1.4	3.5	2.4	1.7	1.3
Quick Ratio 31	0.5	3.3	1.3	2.7	1.8	0.8	0.5
Net Sales to Working Capital 32	12.1	1.6	41.3	12.8	11.0	5.4	15.7
Coverage Ratio 33	2.8	•	30.8	27.7	34.9	4.6	3.9
Total Asset Turnover 34	0.4	1.0	7.0	3.4	5.0	0.8	1.3
Inventory Turnover 35	13.7	•	21.6	104.6	44.0	9.2	8.5
Receivables Turnover 36	•	2.8	17.7	8.6	19.3	9.0	•
Total Liabilities to Net Worth 37	2.3	7.6	6.9	0.6	1.0	1.0	2.1
Current Assets to Working Capital 38	6.5	1.4	3.3	1.4	1.7	2.5	4.9
Current Liabilities to Working Capital 39	5.5	0.4	2.3	0.4	0.7	1.5	3.9
Working Capital to Net Sales 40	0.1	0.6	0.0	0.1	0.1	0.2	0.1
Inventory to Working Capital 41	0.7	•	•	•	0.2	0.5	1.6
Total Receipts to Cash Flow 42	7.7	4.7	6.4	10.0	17.9	10.8	19.0
Cost of Goods to Cash Flow 43	5.8	3.4	5.3	8.1	16.5	8.3	16.8
Cash Flow to Total Debt 44	0.1	0.3	1.2	0.9	0.6	0.2	0.1

Selected Financial Factors (in Percentages)

Debt Ratio 45	69.7	88.4	87.3	35.8	50.1	49.6	67.9
Return on Total Assets 46	4.3	3.7	95.9	25.3	20.3	5.9	5.2
Return on Equity Before Income Taxes 47	9.2	32.1	731.7	38.0	39.5	9.2	12.1
Return on Equity After Income Taxes 48	6.1	27.3	636.2	25.1	36.7	6.4	8.6
Profit Margin (Before Income Tax) 49	6.4	3.5	13.3	7.2	4.0	5.7	3.0
Profit Margin (After Income Tax) 50	4.3	3.0	11.6	4.8	3.7	4.0	2.1

20

Table I

Corporations with and without Net Income

WATER, SEWAGE AND OTHER SYSTEMS

MONEY AMOUNTS AND SIZE OF ASSETS IN THOUSANDS OF DOLLARS

Item Description for Accounting Period 7/08 Through 6/09	Total	Zero Assets	Under 500	500 to 1,000	1,000 to 5,000	5,000 to 10,000	10,000 to 25,000	25,000 to 50,000	50,000 to 100,000	100,000 to 250,000	250,000 to 500,000	500,000 to 2,500,000	2,500,000 and over
Number of Enterprises **1**	5314	671	3465	462	475	118	56	33	•	•	4	•	3
Revenues ($ in Thousands)													
Net Sales **2**	8216562	38782	724297	449372	442184	368028	247388	263200	•	•	234118	•	3486509
Interest **3**	44928	26	1541	1307	1771	726	2711	9137	•	•	2709	•	14401
Rents **4**	30484	0	891	0	1924	0	404	2324	•	•	447	•	4151
Royalties **5**	84	0	0	0	0	0	0	84	•	•	0	•	0
Other Portfolio Income **6**	69532	0	731	18562	3591	0	28682	2989	•	•	89	•	8914
Other Receipts **7**	196230	1	5794	1292	21780	5220	12346	1656	•	•	2356	•	120527
Total Receipts **8**	8557820	38809	733254	470533	471250	373974	291531	279390	•	•	239719	•	3634502
Average Total Receipts **9**	1610	58	212	1018	992	3169	5206	8466	•	•	59930	•	1211501
Operating Costs/Operating Income (%)													
Cost of Operations **10**	32.0	•	4.6	27.0	32.9	41.2	57.0	22.3	•	•	23.6	•	30.7
Salaries and Wages **11**	9.0	•	8.4	19.4	11.7	6.9	7.5	13.2	•	•	6.2	•	8.8
Taxes Paid **12**	7.3	0.1	3.3	3.2	4.0	6.7	5.4	10.1	•	•	9.0	•	9.7
Interest Paid **13**	8.7	•	3.8	0.9	7.4	3.2	4.2	6.7	•	•	11.8	•	11.1
Depreciation **14**	15.9	1.4	4.5	3.9	11.4	13.4	10.3	11.2	•	•	26.9	•	20.1
Amortization and Depletion **15**	0.7	•	0.0	0.0	0.1	0.0	0.3	0.2	•	•	0.3	•	1.3
Pensions and Other Deferred Comp. **16**	1.8	•	1.3	0.2	0.4	0.3	0.6	0.8	•	•	4.1	•	2.3
Employee Benefits **17**	2.7	•	3.5	1.9	1.3	1.7	3.6	2.8	•	•	3.0	•	3.2
Advertising **18**	0.2	•	0.3	0.2	0.3	0.1	0.4	0.0	•	•	0.1	•	0.2
Other Expenses **19**	30.1	118.5	52.5	26.6	33.9	23.7	15.1	32.3	•	•	16.1	•	35.8
Officers' Compensation **20**	2.7	76.5	9.9	6.0	4.9	3.5	3.4	3.8	•	•	2.5	•	0.2
Operating Margin **21**	•	•	7.9	10.5	•	•	•	•	•	•	•	•	•
Operating Margin Before Officers' Comp. **22**	•	•	17.8	16.5	•	2.7	•	0.5	•	•	•	•	•

Selected Average Balance Sheet ($ in Thousands)

Net Receivables 23	217	0	8	175	55	338	1395	1095	•	•	•	•	6897	•	202423
Inventories 24	50	0	2	32	31	4	43	149	•	•	•	•	1238	•	11837
Net Property, Plant and Equipment 25	4822	0	109	294	1705	5197	9352	19327	•	•	•	•	301914	•	4982669
Total Assets 26	6880	0	166	694	2492	6373	15372	32596	•	•	•	•	373836	•	6831802
Notes and Loans Payable 27	2576	0	54	155	1543	3113	3226	6831	•	•	•	•	146751	•	2544636
All Other Liabilities 28	2193	0	24	137	688	1720	6019	11090	•	•	•	•	143966	•	2145541
Net Worth 29	2111	0	88	401	261	1540	6127	14675	•	•	•	•	83120	•	2141625

Selected Financial Ratios (Times to 1)

Current Ratio 30	0.7	•	2.2	2.1	2.8	1.0	1.5	1.5	•	•	•	•	0.5	•	0.5
Quick Ratio 31	0.5	•	2.0	2.0	2.4	0.6	1.2	1.1	•	•	•	•	0.4	•	0.3
Net Sales to Working Capital 32	•	•	7.0	4.9	2.8	118.2	4.0	5.6	•	•	•	•	•	•	•
Coverage Ratio 33	0.2	•	3.4	18.1	0.7	1.2	3.4	1.4	•	•	•	•	0.9	•	•
Total Asset Turnover 34	0.2	•	1.3	1.4	0.4	0.5	0.3	0.2	•	•	•	•	0.2	•	0.2
Inventory Turnover 35	9.9	•	5.1	8.2	9.7	350.6	57.9	11.9	•	•	•	•	11.1	•	30.1
Receivables Turnover 36	6.7	•	20.0	8.7	14.4	8.2	3.0	6.7	•	•	•	•	3.5	•	6.3
Total Liabilities to Net Worth 37	2.3	•	0.9	0.7	8.5	3.1	1.5	1.2	•	•	•	•	3.5	•	2.2
Current Assets to Working Capital 38	•	•	1.8	1.9	1.6	36.0	3.1	2.9	•	•	•	•	•	•	•
Current Liabilities to Working Capital 39	•	•	0.8	0.9	0.6	35.0	2.1	1.9	•	•	•	•	•	•	•
Working Capital to Net Sales 40	•	•	0.1	0.2	0.4	0.0	0.2	0.2	•	•	•	•	0.2	•	0.2
Inventory to Working Capital 41	•	•	0.1	0.0	0.1	0.1	0.0	0.2	•	•	•	•	0.2	•	0.2
Total Receipts to Cash Flow 42	10.7	5.2	1.8	2.7	3.6	6.9	7.7	3.5	•	•	•	•	8.8	•	3.5
Cost of Goods to Cash Flow 43	3.4	•	0.1	0.7	1.2	2.8	4.4	0.8	•	•	•	•	2.1	•	•
Cash Flow to Total Debt 44	0.0	•	1.5	1.2	0.1	0.1	0.1	0.1	•	•	•	•	0.0	•	0.1

Selected Financial Factors (in Percentages)

Debt Ratio 45	69.3	•	47.0	42.2	89.5	75.8	60.1	55.0	•	•	•	•	77.8	•	68.7
Return on Total Assets 46	0.4	•	16.2	22.6	1.9	2.0	4.1	2.3	•	•	•	•	1.7	•	•
Return on Equity Before Income Taxes 47	•	•	21.6	36.9	•	1.6	7.3	1.5	•	•	•	•	•	•	•
Return on Equity After Income Taxes 48	•	•	21.2	35.6	•	0.9	4.3	0.7	•	•	•	•	•	•	•
Profit Margin (Before Income Tax) 49	•	•	9.1	15.2	•	0.8	10.2	2.7	•	•	•	•	•	•	•
Profit Margin (After Income Tax) 50	•	•	8.9	14.7	•	0.4	5.9	1.2	•	•	•	•	•	•	•

Table II

Corporations with Net Income

WATER, SEWAGE AND OTHER SYSTEMS

MONEY AMOUNTS AND SIZE OF ASSETS IN THOUSANDS OF DOLLARS

Item Description for Accounting Period 7/08 Through 6/09	Total	Zero Assets	Under 500	500 to 1,000	1,000 to 5,000	5,000 to 10,000	10,000 to 25,000	25,000 to 50,000	50,000 to 100,000	100,000 to 250,000	250,000 to 500,000	500,000 to 2,500,000	2,500,000 and over
Number of Enterprises **1**	2773	267	1894	284	181	82	29	21	•	•	0	•	0
Revenues ($ in Thousands)													
Net Sales **2**	4485249	38782	522934	210851	290689	330584	133557	221625	•	•	0	•	0
Interest **3**	22518	26	913	1000	1503	535	1014	1670	•	•	0	•	0
Rents **4**	18794	0	0	0	0	0	385	1772	•	•	0	•	0
Royalties **5**	0	0	0	0	0	0	0	0	•	•	0	•	0
Other Portfolio Income **6**	61532	0	731	18562	1914	0	27964	661	•	•	0	•	0
Other Receipts **7**	104571	0	5454	1084	107	4136	7642	1265	•	•	0	•	0
Total Receipts **8**	4692664	38808	530032	231497	294213	335255	170562	226993	•	•	•	•	•
Average Total Receipts **9**	1692	145	280	815	1625	4088	5881	10809	•	•	•	•	•
Operating Costs/Operating Income (%)													
Cost of Operations **10**	33.8	•	5.2	9.7	33.9	41.7	55.5	20.0	•	•	•	•	•
Salaries and Wages **11**	7.7	•	7.6	28.0	10.4	5.6	9.4	13.3	•	•	•	•	•
Taxes Paid **12**	6.7	0.1	2.3	3.0	2.8	7.0	4.2	11.0	•	•	•	•	•
Interest Paid **13**	5.7	•	1.4	0.4	5.0	3.1	3.4	3.9	•	•	•	•	•
Depreciation **14**	14.0	1.4	4.6	2.9	6.3	12.3	7.5	10.3	•	•	•	•	•
Amortization and Depletion **15**	0.5	•	0.0	0.1	0.1	0.0	0.2	0.1	•	•	•	•	•
Pensions and Other Deferred Comp. **16**	1.6	•	1.1	•	0.4	0.3	0.9	0.7	•	•	•	•	•
Employee Benefits **17**	2.0	•	2.6	2.5	0.8	1.7	3.1	2.3	•	•	•	•	•
Advertising **18**	0.1	•	0.2	0.1	0.2	0.1	0.0	0.0	•	•	•	•	•
Other Expenses **19**	20.7	97.4	53.7	15.5	29.3	19.8	10.6	30.9	•	•	•	•	•
Officers' Compensation **20**	1.8	•	2.5	3.7	3.6	3.5	5.8	2.7	•	•	•	•	•
Operating Margin **21**	5.4	1.0	18.8	34.4	7.2	4.8	•	4.7	•	•	•	•	•
Operating Margin Before Officers' Comp. **22**	7.2	1.0	21.3	38.1	10.8	8.4	5.1	7.5	•	•	•	•	•

Selected Average Balance Sheet ($ in Thousands)

Net Receivables 23	226	0	10	102	71	417	1996	1207
Inventories 24	25	0	3	1	36	3	71	99
Net Property, Plant and Equipment 25	4087	0	143	317	1055	5011	7693	23251
Total Assets 26	5619	0	223	698	2506	6344	16016	32663
Notes and Loans Payable 27	1785	0	71	18	1820	2032	3053	7051
All Other Liabilities 28	1903	0	17	18	352	1652	6191	12579
Net Worth 29	1930	0	135	661	334	2659	6772	13033

Selected Financial Ratios (Times to 1)

Current Ratio 30	1.0	•	6.0	18.3	4.4	0.9	1.9	2.6
Quick Ratio 31	0.8	•	5.3	18.1	3.9	0.6	1.4	2.0
Net Sales to Working Capital 32	89.3	•	4.4	2.1	2.0	•	2.2	4.5
Coverage Ratio 33	2.7	•	15.0	103.6	2.6	3.0	8.9	2.8
Total Asset Turnover 34	0.3	•	1.2	1.1	0.6	0.6	0.3	0.3
Inventory Turnover 35	21.9	•	5.2	82.6	15.1	659.0	35.9	21.3
Receivables Turnover 36	5.8	•	17.3	14.6	16.4	8.0	2.0	•
Total Liabilities to Net Worth 37	1.9	•	0.6	0.1	6.5	1.4	1.4	1.5
Current Assets to Working Capital 38	31.2	•	1.2	1.1	1.3	•	2.1	1.6
Current Liabilities to Working Capital 39	30.2	•	0.2	0.1	0.3	•	1.1	0.6
Working Capital to Net Sales 40	0.0	•	0.2	0.5	0.5	•	0.4	0.2
Inventory to Working Capital 41	2.0	•	0.1	0.0	0.1	•	0.0	0.0
Total Receipts to Cash Flow 42	3.8	1.0	1.4	1.8	2.9	6.4	5.4	3.1
Cost of Goods to Cash Flow 43	1.3	•	0.1	0.2	1.0	2.7	3.0	0.6
Cash Flow to Total Debt 44	0.1	•	2.2	11.3	0.3	0.2	0.1	0.2

Selected Financial Factors (in Percentages)

Debt Ratio 45	65.7	•	39.4	5.2	86.7	58.1	57.7	60.1
Return on Total Assets 46	4.5	•	26.7	47.5	8.2	5.9	8.7	3.5
Return on Equity Before Income Taxes 47	8.4	•	41.1	49.6	37.2	9.4	18.4	5.7
Return on Equity After Income Taxes 48	7.1	•	40.7	48.4	35.4	8.8	13.0	4.4
Profit Margin (Before Income Tax) 49	10.0	1.1	20.1	44.2	7.7	6.2	27.0	7.0
Profit Margin (After Income Tax) 50	8.5	1.1	19.9	43.1	7.4	5.8	19.1	5.4

Table I

Corporations with and without Net Income

COMBINATION GAS AND ELECTRIC

MONEY AMOUNTS AND SIZE OF ASSETS IN THOUSANDS OF DOLLARS

Item Description for Accounting Period 7/08 Through 6/09	Total	Zero Assets	Under 500	500 to 1,000	1,000 to 5,000	5,000 to 10,000	10,000 to 25,000	25,000 to 50,000	50,000 to 100,000	100,000 to 250,000	250,000 to 500,000	500,000 to 2,500,000	2,500,000 and over
Number of Enterprises **1**	31	0	0	0	0	0	0	0	•	•	0	•	26
Revenues ($ in Thousands)													
Net Sales **2**	247399781	0	0	0	0	0	0	0	•	•	0	•	245803199
Interest **3**	970286	0	0	0	0	0	0	0	•	•	0	•	961140
Rents **4**	851331	0	0	0	0	0	0	0	•	•	0	•	845087
Royalties **5**	30322	0	0	0	0	0	0	0	•	•	0	•	30322
Other Portfolio Income **6**	2051120	0	0	0	0	0	0	0	•	•	0	•	2046484
Other Receipts **7**	3701186	0	0	0	0	0	0	0	•	•	0	•	3683740
Total Receipts **8**	255004026	0	0	0	0	0	0	0	•	•	0	•	253369972
Average Total Receipts **9**	8225936	•	•	•	•	•	•	•	•	•	•	•	9744999
Operating Costs/Operating Income (%)													
Cost of Operations **10**	67.0	•	•	•	•	•	•	•	•	•	•	•	67.0
Salaries and Wages **11**	3.5	•	•	•	•	•	•	•	•	•	•	•	3.5
Taxes Paid **12**	2.9	•	•	•	•	•	•	•	•	•	•	•	2.9
Interest Paid **13**	4.2	•	•	•	•	•	•	•	•	•	•	•	4.2
Depreciation **14**	6.7	•	•	•	•	•	•	•	•	•	•	•	6.7
Amortization and Depletion **15**	2.2	•	•	•	•	•	•	•	•	•	•	•	2.2
Pensions and Other Deferred Comp. **16**	1.0	•	•	•	•	•	•	•	•	•	•	•	1.0
Employee Benefits **17**	1.0	•	•	•	•	•	•	•	•	•	•	•	1.0
Advertising **18**	0.1	•	•	•	•	•	•	•	•	•	•	•	0.1
Other Expenses **19**	13.7	•	•	•	•	•	•	•	•	•	•	•	13.7
Officers' Compensation **20**	0.2	•	•	•	•	•	•	•	•	•	•	•	0.2
Operating Margin **21**	•	•	•	•	•	•	•	•	•	•	•	•	•
Operating Margin Before Officers' Comp. **22**	•	•	•	•	•	•	•	•	•	•	•	•	•

Selected Average Balance Sheet ($ in Thousands)

Net Receivables 23	660822	780685
Inventories 24	364792	432850
Net Property, Plant and Equipment 25	7390661	8742336
Total Assets 26	13298289	15733362
Notes and Loans Payable 27	5206015	6161331
All Other Liabilities 28	5200652	6154989
Net Worth 29	2891621	3417042

Selected Financial Ratios (Times to 1)

Current Ratio 30	1.1	1.1
Quick Ratio 31	0.5	0.5
Net Sales to Working Capital 32	31.0	30.4
Coverage Ratio 33	1.1	1.1
Total Asset Turnover 34	0.6	0.6
Inventory Turnover 35	14.7	14.6
Receivables Turnover 36	11.4	11.4
Total Liabilities to Net Worth 37	3.6	3.6
Current Assets to Working Capital 38	8.6	8.4
Current Liabilities to Working Capital 39	7.6	7.4
Working Capital to Net Sales 40	0.0	0.0
Inventory to Working Capital 41	1.4	1.4
Total Receipts to Cash Flow 42	8.7	8.7
Cost of Goods to Cash Flow 43	5.8	5.8
Cash Flow to Total Debt 44	0.1	0.1

Selected Financial Factors (in Percentages)

Debt Ratio 45	78.3	78.3
Return on Total Assets 46	2.9	2.9
Return on Equity Before Income Taxes 47	1.7	1.7
Return on Equity After Income Taxes 48	•	•
Profit Margin (Before Income Tax) 49	0.6	0.6
Profit Margin (After Income Tax) 50	•	•

23

Table II

Corporations with Net Income

COMBINATION GAS AND ELECTRIC

MONEY AMOUNTS AND SIZE OF ASSETS IN THOUSANDS OF DOLLARS

Item Description for Accounting Period 7/08 Through 6/09	Total	Zero Assets	Under 500	500 to 1,000	1,000 to 5,000	5,000 to 10,000	10,000 to 25,000	25,000 to 50,000	50,000 to 100,000	100,000 to 250,000	250,000 to 500,000	500,000 to 2,500,000	2,500,000 and over
Number of Enterprises **1**	15	0	0	0	0	0	0	0	•	0	0	•	•

Revenues ($ in Thousands)

Item Description for Accounting Period 7/08 Through 6/09	Total	Zero Assets	Under 500	500 to 1,000	1,000 to 5,000	5,000 to 10,000	10,000 to 25,000	25,000 to 50,000	50,000 to 100,000	100,000 to 250,000	250,000 to 500,000	500,000 to 2,500,000	2,500,000 and over
Net Sales **2**	115094578	0	0	0	0	0	0	0	•	0	0	•	•
Interest **3**	554094	0	0	0	0	0	0	0	•	0	0	•	•
Rents **4**	742700	0	0	0	0	0	0	0	•	0	0	•	•
Royalties **5**	5	0	0	0	0	0	0	0	•	0	0	•	•
Other Portfolio Income **6**	1816337	0	0	0	0	0	0	0	•	0	0	•	•
Other Receipts **7**	2560573	0	0	0	0	0	0	0	•	0	0	•	•
Total Receipts **8**	120768287	0	0	0	0	0	0	0	•	0	0	•	•
Average Total Receipts **9**	8051219	•	•	•	•	•	•	•	•	•	•	•	•

Operating Costs/Operating Income (%)

Item Description for Accounting Period 7/08 Through 6/09	Total	Zero Assets	Under 500	500 to 1,000	1,000 to 5,000	5,000 to 10,000	10,000 to 25,000	25,000 to 50,000	50,000 to 100,000	100,000 to 250,000	250,000 to 500,000	500,000 to 2,500,000	2,500,000 and over
Cost of Operations **10**	56.9	•	•	•	•	•	•	•	•	•	•	•	•
Salaries and Wages **11**	4.8	•	•	•	•	•	•	•	•	•	•	•	•
Taxes Paid **12**	3.9	•	•	•	•	•	•	•	•	•	•	•	•
Interest Paid **13**	4.0	•	•	•	•	•	•	•	•	•	•	•	•
Depreciation **14**	8.8	•	•	•	•	•	•	•	•	•	•	•	•
Amortization and Depletion **15**	4.4	•	•	•	•	•	•	•	•	•	•	•	•
Pensions and Other Deferred Comp. **16**	1.3	•	•	•	•	•	•	•	•	•	•	•	•
Employee Benefits **17**	1.3	•	•	•	•	•	•	•	•	•	•	•	•
Advertising **18**	0.1	•	•	•	•	•	•	•	•	•	•	•	•
Other Expenses **19**	14.1	•	•	•	•	•	•	•	•	•	•	•	•
Officers' Compensation **20**	0.2	•	•	•	•	•	•	•	•	•	•	•	•
Operating Margin **21**	0.1	•	•	•	•	•	•	•	•	•	•	•	•
Operating Margin Before Officers' Comp. **22**	0.4	•	•	•	•	•	•	•	•	•	•	•	•

Selected Average Balance Sheet ($ in Thousands)

Net Receivables **23**	836137
Inventories **24**	417373
Net Property, Plant and Equipment **25**	8709518
Total Assets **26**	15469386
Notes and Loans Payable **27**	4931682
All Other Liabilities **28**	6430493
Net Worth **29**	4107211

Selected Financial Ratios (Times to 1)

Current Ratio **30**	1.2
Quick Ratio **31**	0.6
Net Sales to Working Capital **32**	17.7
Coverage Ratio **33**	2.4
Total Asset Turnover **34**	0.5
Inventory Turnover **35**	10.5
Receivables Turnover **36**	•
Total Liabilities to Net Worth **37**	2.8
Current Assets to Working Capital **38**	5.9
Current Liabilities to Working Capital **39**	4.9
Working Capital to Net Sales **40**	0.1
Inventory to Working Capital **41**	1.0
Total Receipts to Cash Flow **42**	6.5
Cost of Goods to Cash Flow **43**	3.7
Cash Flow to Total Debt **44**	0.1

Selected Financial Factors (in Percentages)

Debt Ratio **45**	73.4
Return on Total Assets **46**	4.7
Return on Equity Before Income Taxes **47**	10.2
Return on Equity After Income Taxes **48**	6.8
Profit Margin (Before Income Tax) **49**	5.5
Profit Margin (After Income Tax) **50**	3.7

24

Table I

Corporations with and without Net Income

CONSTRUCTION OF BUILDINGS

MONEY AMOUNTS AND SIZE OF ASSETS IN THOUSANDS OF DOLLARS

Item Description for Accounting Period 7/08 Through 6/09	Total	Zero Assets	Under 500	500 to 1,000	1,000 to 5,000	5,000 to 10,000	10,000 to 25,000	25,000 to 50,000	50,000 to 100,000	100,000 to 250,000	250,000 to 500,000	500,000 to 2,500,000	2,500,000 and over
Number of Enterprises **1**	231765	41947	139701	17684	24633	4067	2564	648	278	142	42	•	•
Revenues ($ in Thousands)													
Net Sales **2**	578631972	9971556	68844961	25986338	109406682	43380680	75640738	38035235	36827035	39417150	21681619	•	•
Interest **3**	1321616	11677	27357	21362	76218	34533	41037	27245	22829	38036	52760	•	•
Rents **4**	529034	199	33769	29680	66541	24240	60149	24035	18872	51313	75348	•	•
Royalties **5**	34442	0	0	0	7	1	0	0	12	11296	109	•	•
Other Portfolio Income **6**	1166524	23729	132170	19704	111685	44219	64933	40838	25641	44707	337799	•	•
Other Receipts **7**	4227919	191492	473901	275294	514219	220886	101992	233491	189849	163030	451420	•	•
Total Receipts **8**	585911507	10198653	69512158	26332378	110175352	43704559	75908849	38360844	37084238	39725532	22599055	•	•
Average Total Receipts **9**	2528	243	498	1489	4473	10746	29606	59199	133397	279757	538073	•	•
Operating Costs/Operating Income (%)													
Cost of Operations **10**	86.2	84.0	68.8	80.1	85.4	86.7	89.1	89.6	91.1	91.7	91.0	•	•
Salaries and Wages **11**	3.4	3.9	5.3	3.9	3.2	2.6	2.5	2.7	2.1	2.1	3.4	•	•
Taxes Paid **12**	0.9	0.8	1.7	1.2	1.0	0.9	0.6	0.5	0.5	0.5	0.7	•	•
Interest Paid **13**	0.9	1.3	0.7	1.0	0.7	0.7	0.5	0.6	0.5	0.6	0.8	•	•
Depreciation **14**	0.7	0.8	1.2	0.9	0.7	0.7	0.5	0.5	0.4	0.5	0.6	•	•
Amortization and Depletion **15**	0.1	0.0	0.0	0.0	0.0	0.0	0.0	0.0	0.0	0.0	0.1	•	•
Pensions and Other Deferred Comp. **16**	0.2	0.0	0.3	0.2	0.2	0.2	0.2	0.1	0.2	0.2	0.2	•	•
Employee Benefits **17**	0.6	0.9	0.8	0.6	0.5	0.8	0.7	0.4	0.7	0.4	0.4	•	•
Advertising **18**	0.3	0.4	0.6	0.3	0.2	0.2	0.2	0.2	0.2	0.2	0.2	•	•
Other Expenses **19**	6.9	19.7	14.2	7.3	5.3	4.7	3.0	3.7	2.7	3.1	3.4	•	•
Officers' Compensation **20**	1.9	2.5	5.2	3.3	2.4	1.9	1.6	1.4	0.9	0.7	0.7	•	•
Operating Margin **21**	•	•	1.2	1.4	0.5	0.7	1.1	0.2	0.6	•	0.7	•	•
Operating Margin Before Officers' Comp. **22**	•	•	6.4	4.6	2.8	2.6	2.7	1.5	1.5	0.7	1.5	•	•

Selected Average Balance Sheet ($ in Thousands)

Net Receivables 23	337	0	13	78	394	1415	4617	8985	22174	48162	91717
Inventories 24	371	0	14	197	519	1979	3695	8211	15627	36091	67352
Net Property, Plant and Equipment 25	164	0	24	145	304	722	1766	3963	6600	14919	31643
Total Assets 26	1449	0	100	729	2184	6942	15234	33794	69670	145043	341273
Notes and Loans Payable 27	558	0	66	425	975	2832	5230	12625	20394	40829	108767
All Other Liabilities 28	565	0	31	178	778	2779	6823	14343	34257	70335	132331
Net Worth 29	326	0	3	126	431	1330	3180	6826	15018	33879	100175

Selected Financial Ratios (Times to 1)

Current Ratio 30	1.5	•	1.5	1.6	1.5	1.5	1.4	1.4	1.4	1.4	1.7
Quick Ratio 31	0.8	•	0.9	0.7	0.6	0.6	0.8	0.8	0.8	0.8	1.0
Net Sales to Working Capital 32	6.6	•	24.1	7.6	8.7	5.9	8.1	8.1	8.9	8.9	5.4
Coverage Ratio 33	0.1	•	3.8	3.8	2.6	3.2	3.9	2.6	3.3	2.3	4.2
Total Asset Turnover 34	1.7	•	5.0	2.0	2.0	1.5	1.9	1.7	1.9	1.9	1.5
Inventory Turnover 35	5.8	•	24.6	6.0	7.3	4.7	7.1	6.4	7.7	7.0	7.0
Receivables Turnover 36	7.6	•	40.3	16.4	11.5	6.2	6.3	5.9	5.9	5.5	5.9
Total Liabilities to Net Worth 37	3.4	•	32.0	4.8	4.1	4.2	3.8	4.0	3.6	3.3	2.4
Current Assets to Working Capital 38	2.8	•	3.0	2.7	3.1	3.0	3.3	3.5	3.8	3.7	2.5
Current Liabilities to Working Capital 39	1.8	•	2.0	1.7	2.1	2.0	2.3	2.5	2.8	2.7	1.5
Working Capital to Net Sales 40	0.2	•	0.0	0.1	0.1	0.2	0.1	0.1	0.1	0.1	0.2
Inventory to Working Capital 41	0.8	•	0.7	0.9	1.0	1.0	0.8	1.1	0.9	1.0	0.6
Total Receipts to Cash Flow 42	20.5	20.5	7.0	11.8	18.4	19.6	28.2	25.5	31.6	33.0	23.5
Cost of Goods to Cash Flow 43	17.7	17.2	4.8	9.4	15.7	17.0	25.1	22.8	28.8	30.2	21.4
Cash Flow to Total Debt 44	0.1	•	0.7	0.2	0.1	0.1	0.1	0.1	0.1	0.1	0.1

Selected Financial Factors (in Percentages)

Debt Ratio 45	77.5	•	97.0	82.7	80.3	80.8	79.1	79.8	78.4	76.6	70.6
Return on Total Assets 46	0.1	•	14.2	7.4	3.9	3.2	3.8	2.9	3.4	2.4	5.1
Return on Equity Before Income Taxes 47	•	•	347.1	31.3	12.0	11.5	13.5	8.8	10.9	5.8	13.3
Return on Equity After Income Taxes 48	•	•	338.9	29.6	10.9	10.1	12.6	7.6	10.0	4.4	9.4
Profit Margin (Before Income Tax) 49	•	•	2.1	2.7	1.2	1.4	1.5	1.0	1.2	0.7	2.6
Profit Margin (After Income Tax) 50	•	•	2.1	2.5	1.1	1.3	1.4	0.9	1.1	0.5	1.8

Table II
Corporations with Net Income

CONSTRUCTION OF BUILDINGS

MONEY AMOUNTS AND SIZE OF ASSETS IN THOUSANDS OF DOLLARS

Item Description for Accounting Period 7/08 Through 6/09	Total	Zero Assets	Under 500	500 to 1,000	1,000 to 5,000	5,000 to 10,000	10,000 to 25,000	25,000 to 50,000	50,000 to 100,000	100,000 to 250,000	250,000 to 500,000	500,000 to 2,500,000	2,500,000 and over
Number of Enterprises 1	122593	16465	78170	9750	13668	2279	1580	368	170	•	29	•	•
Revenues ($ in Thousands)													
Net Sales 2	436881081	4191055	50551696	19341725	81417876	32848102	64549781	32817236	31183063	•	19880627	•	•
Interest 3	426671	685	12268	13106	48739	24324	33274	19918	13126	•	39605	•	•
Rents 4	278189	172	7493	20769	26013	12351	31755	6668	17758	•	60183	•	•
Royalties 5	33039	0	0	0	7	1	0	0	12	•	0	•	•
Other Portfolio Income 6	788269	21976	85950	8423	92707	25969	53419	33675	19298	•	290665	•	•
Other Receipts 7	2648268	77416	156694	262910	376600	200506	3604	160475	197763	•	348582	•	•
Total Receipts 8	441055517	4291304	50814101	19646933	81961942	33111253	64671833	33037972	31431020	•	20619662	•	•
Average Total Receipts 9	3598	261	650	2015	5997	14529	40932	89777	184888	•	711023	•	•
Operating Costs/Operating Income (%)													
Cost of Operations 10	85.0	59.3	66.4	78.0	84.1	84.9	88.2	88.8	90.5	•	91.6	•	•
Salaries and Wages 11	2.6	4.2	4.5	3.0	2.8	2.3	2.2	2.2	1.8	•	2.6	•	•
Taxes Paid 12	0.7	0.8	1.5	1.1	0.9	0.9	0.5	0.4	0.4	•	0.6	•	•
Interest Paid 13	0.3	0.9	0.5	0.7	0.4	0.3	0.2	0.2	0.1	•	0.4	•	•
Depreciation 14	0.5	1.0	1.0	0.6	0.6	0.7	0.5	0.4	0.4	•	0.6	•	•
Amortization and Depletion 15	0.0	0.1	0.0	0.0	0.0	0.0	0.0	0.0	0.0	•	0.1	•	•
Pensions and Other Deferred Comp. 16	0.2	0.0	0.3	0.2	0.2	0.2	0.2	0.1	0.2	•	0.1	•	•
Employee Benefits 17	0.5	0.1	0.8	0.5	0.5	0.8	0.6	0.4	0.7	•	0.3	•	•
Advertising 18	0.2	0.3	0.5	0.3	0.2	0.2	0.1	0.1	0.1	•	0.1	•	•
Other Expenses 19	4.6	23.6	13.3	7.0	4.6	4.0	2.4	2.9	2.0	•	1.9	•	•
Officers' Compensation 20	1.9	3.8	5.0	3.1	2.3	1.8	1.6	1.4	0.9	•	0.6	•	•
Operating Margin 21	3.3	5.9	6.2	5.5	3.4	3.9	3.4	3.2	2.9	•	1.1	•	•
Operating Margin Before Officers' Comp. 22	5.2	9.7	11.2	8.6	5.7	5.7	5.1	4.6	3.8	•	1.7	•	•

Selected Average Balance Sheet ($ in Thousands)

	•	•	•	•	•	•	•	•	•	•
Net Receivables 23	468	0	13	101	545	2050	6485	14199	32553	114707
Inventories 24	254	0	14	163	420	1609	2565	5301	8317	41096
Net Property, Plant and Equipment 25	130	0	20	112	252	752	1237	2703	4360	30068
Total Assets 26	1341	0	97	707	2196	6989	15176	34145	69189	339096
Notes and Loans Payable 27	262	0	43	275	667	1811	2544	4808	6139	58847
All Other Liabilities 28	689	0	25	215	890	3107	8437	19557	45268	169732
Net Worth 29	391	0	29	217	639	2072	4195	9780	17782	110518

Selected Financial Ratios (Times to 1)

	•	•	•	•	•	•	•	•	•	•
Current Ratio 30	1.4	•	1.7	2.0	1.6	1.7	1.4	1.4	1.3	1.4
Quick Ratio 31	1.0	•	1.1	1.0	0.9	1.0	1.0	1.1	1.1	1.0
Net Sales to Working Capital 32	11.5	•	23.4	7.1	8.7	6.5	11.2	11.1	14.3	9.6
Coverage Ratio 33	14.7	9.9	14.0	11.2	10.9	18.3	20.0	24.2	38.9	14.1
Total Asset Turnover 34	2.7	•	6.6	2.8	2.7	2.1	2.7	2.6	2.7	2.0
Inventory Turnover 35	12.0	•	31.1	9.5	11.9	7.6	14.1	14.9	20.0	15.3
Receivables Turnover 36	7.4	•	46.0	18.5	11.2	5.4	6.2	5.9	5.6	6.5
Total Liabilities to Net Worth 37	2.4	•	2.4	2.3	2.4	2.4	2.6	2.5	2.9	2.1
Current Assets to Working Capital 38	3.4	•	2.4	2.0	2.5	2.5	3.5	3.6	4.5	3.4
Current Liabilities to Working Capital 39	2.4	•	1.4	1.0	1.5	1.5	2.5	2.6	3.5	2.4
Working Capital to Net Sales 40	0.1	•	0.0	0.1	0.1	0.2	0.1	0.1	0.1	0.1
Inventory to Working Capital 41	0.4	•	0.5	0.5	0.5	0.4	0.4	0.4	0.2	0.4
Total Receipts to Cash Flow 42	12.8	3.3	5.6	8.0	12.9	13.1	19.3	16.6	20.0	20.0
Cost of Goods to Cash Flow 43	10.9	2.0	3.7	6.2	10.9	11.1	17.0	14.8	18.1	18.3
Cash Flow to Total Debt 44	0.3	•	1.7	0.5	0.3	0.2	0.2	0.2	0.2	0.2

Selected Financial Factors (in Percentages)

	•	•	•	•	•	•	•	•	•	•
Debt Ratio 45	70.9	•	70.2	69.3	70.9	70.4	72.4	71.4	74.3	67.4
Return on Total Assets 46	12.1	•	48.0	21.7	12.2	10.2	10.2	10.5	10.0	10.3
Return on Equity Before Income Taxes 47	38.8	•	149.5	64.4	38.1	32.6	35.1	35.2	37.8	29.3
Return on Equity After Income Taxes 48	36.7	•	148.0	62.6	36.7	31.0	33.9	33.9	36.5	24.1
Profit Margin (Before Income Tax) 49	4.3	8.2	6.7	7.0	4.1	4.7	3.6	3.9	3.7	4.7
Profit Margin (After Income Tax) 50	4.0	7.9	6.6	6.8	3.9	4.5	3.5	3.7	3.5	3.9

Table I

Corporations with and without Net Income

HEAVY AND CIVIL ENGINEERING CONSTRUCTION

MONEY AMOUNTS AND SIZE OF ASSETS IN THOUSANDS OF DOLLARS

Item Description for Accounting Period 7/08 Through 6/09		Total	Zero Assets	Under 500	500 to 1,000	1,000 to 5,000	5,000 to 10,000	10,000 to 25,000	25,000 to 50,000	50,000 to 100,000	100,000 to 250,000	250,000 to 500,000	500,000 to 2,500,000	2,500,000 and over
Number of Enterprises	1	23150	1619	10037	3419	5089	1547	875	305	144	76	16	17	5
Revenues ($ in Thousands)														
Net Sales	2	224030658	738462	9371053	5883279	26122912	25834343	29488685	22530961	18639024	17702194	10042974	23251222	34425549
Interest	3	351931	135	5861	7901	37620	18274	23138	15352	20619	26062	11425	72026	113519
Rents	4	114519	0	3729	10617	24022	1058	23642	16794	11817	5234	1232	10141	6233
Royalties	5	81217	0	0	0	0	0	2433	188	23498	15	26552	7470	21061
Other Portfolio Income	6	1219927	51461	54083	56507	188782	126291	117001	187588	85501	124455	27308	69754	131195
Other Receipts	7	3257288	8679	-48436	6000	161226	93530	105244	221450	203984	381522	84091	485751	1554247
Total Receipts	8	229055540	798737	9386290	5964304	26534562	26073496	29760143	22972333	18984443	18239482	10193582	23896364	36251804
Average Total Receipts	9	9894	493	935	1744	5214	16854	34012	75319	131836	239993	637099	1405668	7250361
Operating Costs/Operating Income (%)														
Cost of Operations	10	77.6	47.2	58.9	62.6	67.3	77.5	80.1	79.9	80.0	79.1	84.0	77.9	86.2
Salaries and Wages	11	3.6	2.6	9.2	6.8	5.6	2.8	2.6	3.0	2.7	3.0	1.7	4.0	3.0
Taxes Paid	12	1.3	1.6	2.7	2.2	1.7	1.2	1.0	0.8	0.7	0.7	0.6	2.6	0.8
Interest Paid	13	0.6	1.4	0.6	0.9	0.7	0.6	0.5	0.4	0.5	0.6	0.5	0.9	0.4
Depreciation	14	3.4	4.4	3.4	4.3	4.8	3.6	3.6	3.5	3.7	3.5	3.6	3.3	1.6
Amortization and Depletion	15	0.2	0.1	0.1	0.0	0.0	0.0	0.0	0.1	0.1	0.2	0.3	0.6	0.5
Pensions and Other Deferred Comp.	16	0.4	0.0	0.4	0.4	0.4	0.6	0.3	0.3	0.7	0.4	0.3	0.3	0.1
Employee Benefits	17	0.9	1.0	0.6	1.0	1.1	1.0	1.0	1.1	1.0	1.4	0.5	1.0	0.4
Advertising	18	0.1	0.4	0.5	0.2	0.1	0.1	0.1	0.1	0.1	0.1	0.0	0.2	0.0
Other Expenses	19	7.8	46.7	17.7	13.8	13.0	6.8	5.8	5.6	5.6	6.9	3.4	7.0	6.9
Officers' Compensation	20	2.1	1.1	6.3	5.8	4.2	2.8	1.9	1.6	1.3	1.3	0.9	0.6	0.7
Operating Margin	21	2.1	•	•	2.0	1.0	3.2	3.1	3.6	3.5	2.9	4.2	1.7	•
Operating Margin Before Officers' Comp.	22	4.1	•	6.1	7.8	5.2	5.9	4.9	5.2	4.9	4.2	5.1	2.3	0.1

Selected Average Balance Sheet ($ in Thousands)

Net Receivables 23	1386	0	41	115	520	2159	5452	10943	20270	39163	85561	184831	1356111
Inventories 24	122	0	3	21	47	205	431	854	2048	5060	13747	21979	51898
Net Property, Plant and Equipment 25	1313	0	85	283	761	1849	4050	8678	17618	36116	103604	205186	1045450
Total Assets 26	5298	0	211	686	2181	6996	15649	33752	69744	150934	348816	858462	6120813
Notes and Loans Payable 27	1008	0	113	233	649	1700	3169	6258	14590	28299	61596	156436	575941
All Other Liabilities 28	2063	0	44	139	554	2307	5339	11912	24514	50504	110400	386417	3289932
Net Worth 29	2227	0	54	313	977	2989	7141	15581	30640	72131	176119	315609	2254940

Selected Financial Ratios (Times to 1)

Current Ratio 30	1.5	•	1.5	1.9	1.8	1.7	1.8	1.7	1.6	1.6	1.9	1.3	1.1
Quick Ratio 31	1.2	•	1.2	1.5	1.5	1.4	1.4	1.4	1.3	1.3	1.4	0.9	0.9
Net Sales to Working Capital 32	10.2	•	26.3	10.6	10.0	8.8	7.4	8.1	8.2	7.0	6.9	15.5	35.2
Coverage Ratio 33	8.5	2.1	1.0	4.9	4.5	7.8	8.5	14.2	10.9	11.6	13.2	6.0	13.2
Total Asset Turnover 34	1.8	•	4.4	2.5	2.4	2.4	2.2	2.2	1.9	1.5	1.8	1.6	1.1
Inventory Turnover 35	61.5	•	205.6	51.2	73.4	63.1	62.6	69.1	50.6	36.4	38.4	48.5	114.4
Receivables Turnover 36	7.0	•	30.5	11.8	8.7	6.9	5.8	6.9	6.1	6.0	6.7	6.9	6.6
Total Liabilities to Net Worth 37	1.4	•	2.9	1.2	1.2	1.3	1.2	1.2	1.3	1.1	1.0	1.7	1.7
Current Assets to Working Capital 38	3.2	•	2.9	2.1	2.3	2.4	2.3	2.4	2.7	2.6	2.1	4.8	16.4
Current Liabilities to Working Capital 39	2.2	•	1.9	1.1	1.3	1.4	1.3	1.4	1.7	1.6	1.1	3.8	15.4
Working Capital to Net Sales 40	0.1	•	0.0	0.1	0.1	0.1	0.1	0.1	0.1	0.1	0.1	0.1	0.0
Inventory to Working Capital 41	0.1	•	0.1	0.2	0.1	0.1	0.1	0.1	0.1	0.2	0.1	0.3	0.3
Total Receipts to Cash Flow 42	11.0	2.7	8.3	8.3	9.0	12.8	14.0	12.4	12.5	11.3	13.3	10.9	9.9
Cost of Goods to Cash Flow 43	8.5	1.3	4.9	5.2	6.1	9.9	11.2	9.9	10.0	8.9	11.2	8.5	8.5
Cash Flow to Total Debt 44	0.3	•	0.7	0.6	0.5	0.3	0.3	0.3	0.3	0.3	0.3	0.2	0.2

Selected Financial Factors (in Percentages)

Debt Ratio 45	58.0	•	74.3	54.3	55.2	57.3	54.4	53.8	56.1	52.2	49.4	63.2	63.2
Return on Total Assets 46	9.0	•	2.3	10.8	7.6	11.1	9.7	13.1	10.9	9.9	11.1	8.6	6.3
Return on Equity Before Income Taxes 47	18.9	•	18.8	18.8	13.2	22.7	18.7	26.3	22.5	18.9	20.3	19.4	15.7
Return on Equity After Income Taxes 48	16.4	•	17.8	17.8	11.4	20.8	17.2	23.6	20.8	17.2	19.0	13.7	12.5
Profit Margin (Before Income Tax) 49	4.4	1.6	3.4	3.4	2.5	4.1	4.0	5.6	5.3	5.9	5.7	4.5	5.1
Profit Margin (After Income Tax) 50	3.8	0.1	3.2	3.2	2.2	3.7	3.6	5.0	4.9	5.3	5.3	3.2	4.1

Table II

Corporations with Net Income

HEAVY AND CIVIL ENGINEERING CONSTRUCTION

MONEY AMOUNTS AND SIZE OF ASSETS IN THOUSANDS OF DOLLARS

Item Description for Accounting Period 7/08 Through 6/09	Total	Zero Assets	Under 500	500 to 1,000	1,000 to 5,000	5,000 to 10,000	10,000 to 25,000	25,000 to 50,000	50,000 to 100,000	100,000 to 250,000	250,000 to 500,000	500,000 to 2,500,000	2,500,000 and over
Number of Enterprises 1	13135	954	4798	1853	3140	1267	657	243	123	62	16	17	5
Revenues ($ in Thousands)													
Net Sales 2	192386712	362864	5780622	4125767	18821978	22601265	23303256	18209754	16345476	15115985	10042974	23251222	34425549
Interest 3	318031	134	2928	4738	25433	14485	17968	13203	19429	22742	11425	72026	113519
Rents 4	80395	0	4	124	13675	652	16332	15958	10872	5171	1232	10141	6233
Royalties 5	80132	0	0	0	0	0	1388	188	23458	15	26552	7470	21061
Other Portfolio Income 6	1018937	51461	21930	51475	144136	87333	87480	163642	66447	116777	27308	69754	131195
Other Receipts 7	3192927	8680	7336	5029	148969	70463	83569	213044	173525	358224	84091	485751	1554247
Total Receipts 8	197077134	423139	5812820	4187133	19154191	22774198	23509993	18615789	16639207	15618914	10193582	23896364	36251804
Average Total Receipts 9	15004	444	1212	2260	6100	17975	35784	76608	135278	251918	637099	1405668	7250361
Operating Costs/Operating Income (%)													
Cost of Operations 10	77.5	47.0	57.9	57.1	65.8	76.5	78.2	78.2	79.4	78.2	84.0	77.9	86.2
Salaries and Wages 11	3.3	4.5	6.7	8.1	5.3	2.6	2.4	2.9	2.6	2.8	1.7	4.0	3.0
Taxes Paid 12	1.2	2.4	2.6	2.1	1.7	1.1	1.0	0.9	0.7	0.7	0.6	2.6	0.8
Interest Paid 13	0.5	0.7	0.3	0.6	0.5	0.5	0.5	0.4	0.4	0.5	0.5	0.9	0.4
Depreciation 14	3.1	4.1	1.9	3.3	4.4	3.3	3.2	3.1	3.4	3.2	3.6	3.3	1.6
Amortization and Depletion 15	0.2	0.2	0.0	0.0	0.0	0.0	0.0	0.0	0.1	0.2	0.3	0.6	0.5
Pensions and Other Deferred Comp. 16	0.4	0.0	0.2	0.5	0.5	0.6	0.4	0.3	0.7	0.4	0.3	0.3	0.1
Employee Benefits 17	0.9	1.8	0.3	1.1	0.9	1.0	1.1	1.2	1.0	1.4	0.5	1.0	0.4
Advertising 18	0.1	0.1	0.5	0.2	0.1	0.1	0.1	0.1	0.1	0.1	0.0	0.2	0.0
Other Expenses 19	7.3	32.6	16.0	14.1	12.1	6.7	5.9	5.7	5.4	6.3	3.4	7.0	6.9
Officers' Compensation 20	1.9	1.0	6.1	5.4	4.3	2.8	2.1	1.6	1.3	1.3	0.9	0.6	0.7
Operating Margin 21	3.7	5.5	7.4	7.4	4.5	4.9	5.2	5.5	5.0	5.0	4.2	1.7	*
Operating Margin Before Officers' Comp. 22	5.6	6.4	13.5	12.7	8.8	7.6	7.2	7.1	6.4	6.2	5.1	2.3	0.1

Selected Average Balance Sheet ($ in Thousands)

Net Receivables 23	2088	0	23	117	549	2155	5595	10858	20405	40793	85561	184831	1356111
Inventories 24	185	0	4	16	55	216	464	785	2062	5734	12599	24828	51898
Net Property, Plant and Equipment 25	1840	0	66	240	770	1773	3841	7491	16506	32170	103604	205186	1045450
Total Assets 26	8050	0	196	675	2313	7075	15989	33050	69893	152012	348116	858462	6120813
Notes and Loans Payable 27	1272	0	66	234	527	1481	2692	5311	11854	22355	61596	156436	575941
All Other Liabilities 28	3259	0	39	105	613	2299	5557	12050	25356	50024	110400	386417	3289932
Net Worth 29	3519	0	90	336	1172	3295	7740	15689	32683	79633	176119	315609	2254940

Selected Financial Ratios (Times to 1)

Current Ratio 30	1.5	•	2.4	2.5	1.8	1.8	1.9	1.8	1.7	1.8	1.9	1.3	1.1
Quick Ratio 31	1.2	•	1.8	2.1	1.6	1.5	1.5	1.5	1.4	1.4	1.4	0.9	0.9
Net Sales to Working Capital 32	9.9	•	18.5	10.2	10.2	8.5	7.0	7.8	7.5	6.3	6.9	15.5	35.2
Coverage Ratio 33	13.3	31.8	28.4	15.0	13.7	11.8	14.3	22.1	18.5	18.1	13.2	6.0	13.2
Total Asset Turnover 34	1.8	•	6.2	3.3	2.6	2.5	2.2	2.3	1.9	1.6	1.8	1.6	1.1
Inventory Turnover 35	61.5	•	190.1	79.7	71.3	63.1	59.7	74.7	51.1	33.2	41.9	42.9	114.4
Receivables Turnover 36	6.8	•	46.2	13.1	8.4	7.0	5.4	6.5	6.0	6.0	•	•	6.6
Total Liabilities to Net Worth 37	1.3	•	1.2	1.0	1.0	1.1	1.1	1.1	1.1	0.9	1.0	1.7	1.7
Current Assets to Working Capital 38	3.1	•	1.7	1.7	2.2	2.2	2.2	2.3	2.5	2.3	2.1	4.8	16.4
Current Liabilities to Working Capital 39	2.1	•	0.7	0.7	1.2	1.2	1.2	1.3	1.5	1.3	1.1	3.8	15.4
Working Capital to Net Sales 40	0.1	•	0.1	0.1	0.1	0.1	0.1	0.1	0.1	0.2	0.1	0.1	0.0
Inventory to Working Capital 41	0.1	•	0.1	0.1	0.1	0.1	0.1	0.1	0.1	0.2	0.1	0.3	0.3
Total Receipts to Cash Flow 42	9.6	2.8	5.3	5.7	7.1	10.9	10.8	9.9	10.8	9.6	13.3	10.9	9.9
Cost of Goods to Cash Flow 43	7.4	1.3	3.1	3.2	4.7	8.3	8.5	7.8	8.6	7.5	11.2	8.5	8.5
Cash Flow to Total Debt 44	0.3	•	2.1	1.2	0.7	0.4	0.4	0.4	0.3	0.4	0.3	0.2	0.2

Selected Financial Factors (in Percentages)

Debt Ratio 45	56.3	•	54.0	50.3	49.3	53.4	51.6	52.5	53.2	47.6	49.4	63.2	63.2
Return on Total Assets 46	12.2	•	51.1	31.3	17.6	15.5	14.4	18.4	13.6	13.9	11.1	8.6	6.3
Return on Equity Before Income Taxes 47	25.8	•	107.2	58.8	32.2	30.5	27.6	36.9	27.6	25.1	20.3	19.4	15.7
Return on Equity After Income Taxes 48	23.0	•	106.3	57.0	29.7	28.4	25.7	33.6	25.7	23.2	19.0	13.7	12.5
Profit Margin (Before Income Tax) 49	6.2	22.1	8.0	8.9	6.3	5.6	6.0	7.7	6.8	8.2	5.7	4.5	5.1
Profit Margin (After Income Tax) 50	5.5	19.0	7.9	8.6	5.8	5.3	5.6	7.0	6.3	7.6	5.3	3.2	4.1

28

Table I

Corporations with and without Net Income

LAND SUBDIVISION

MONEY AMOUNTS AND SIZE OF ASSETS IN THOUSANDS OF DOLLARS

Item Description for Accounting Period 7/08 Through 6/09	Total	Zero Assets	Under 500	500 to 1,000	1,000 to 5,000	5,000 to 10,000	10,000 to 25,000	25,000 to 50,000	50,000 to 100,000	100,000 to 250,000	250,000 to 500,000	500,000 to 2,500,000	2,500,000 and over
Number of Enterprises **1**	40204	5940	17881	4277	9307	1551	768	264	123	57	21	15	0
Revenues ($ in Thousands)													
Net Sales **2**	27709149	1999974	2918543	896515	8305415	1646801	3277590	1731687	1350417	2320834	1531655	1729718	0
Interest **3**	218540	745	4242	2956	32010	5491	8422	14450	21219	23607	41733	63663	0
Rents **4**	434346	24052	7732	2193	25116	32352	42618	9281	26847	145735	30450	87970	0
Royalties **5**	28149	0	0	0	7385	5966	13521	149	0	1083	0	45	0
Other Portfolio Income **6**	372715	44740	2590	17292	56434	16437	27575	16819	51324	65232	3472	70801	0
Other Receipts **7**	1000524	-8562	22441	128066	677930	927	23002	115552	6874	-37936	116322	-44091	0
Total Receipts **8**	29763423	2060949	2955548	1047022	9104290	1707974	3392728	1887938	1456681	2518555	1723632	1908106	0
Average Total Receipts **9**	740	347	165	245	978	1101	4418	7151	11843	44185	82078	127207	•
Operating Costs/Operating Income (%)													
Cost of Operations **10**	81.5	104.1	65.7	66.9	81.1	89.8	87.9	77.4	88.2	80.2	48.6	102.2	•
Salaries and Wages **11**	8.0	2.4	8.6	3.8	8.2	5.6	5.0	10.4	9.5	6.6	19.3	11.5	•
Taxes Paid **12**	2.6	0.7	2.5	3.2	1.7	2.8	1.5	3.4	3.0	2.4	9.0	4.0	•
Interest Paid **13**	6.3	3.6	1.8	9.6	3.9	7.4	5.3	8.5	9.3	7.0	11.4	17.6	•
Depreciation **14**	2.7	2.9	0.8	1.2	2.6	2.0	2.1	3.7	4.8	3.2	6.3	3.0	•
Amortization and Depletion **15**	0.3	0.1	0.2	0.0	0.0	0.1	0.2	0.2	0.4	0.2	1.0	1.4	•
Pensions and Other Deferred Comp. **16**	0.5	0.0	•	0.1	0.9	0.4	0.1	0.3	0.3	0.4	0.6	0.4	•
Employee Benefits **17**	0.6	0.0	0.5	0.3	0.3	0.4	0.3	0.8	0.9	0.9	2.2	1.9	•
Advertising **18**	0.7	0.1	0.3	0.2	0.4	1.4	0.6	1.8	1.3	0.8	2.0	0.9	•
Other Expenses **19**	18.6	30.8	13.8	30.0	12.7	16.3	10.2	21.3	25.8	22.7	29.1	30.0	•
Officers' Compensation **20**	2.8	1.7	6.7	5.6	2.6	1.4	1.4	2.3	3.5	2.8	0.8	2.8	•
Operating Margin **21**	•	•	•	•	•	•	•	•	•	•	•	•	•
Operating Margin Before Officers' Comp. **22**	•	5.7	•	•	•	•	•	•	•	•	•	•	•

Selected Average Balance Sheet ($ in Thousands)

Line Item													
Net Receivables 23	150	0	5	15	161	149	679	2797	4369	12690	57863	28394	•
Inventories 24	676	0	27	303	489	2703	5355	8808	19818	32066	92093	267497	•
Net Property, Plant and Equipment 25	643	0	49	126	587	1914	4027	10114	16167	40621	93558	265965	•
Total Assets 26	2346	0	132	694	2138	6995	15511	34493	67693	145993	356584	872860	•
Notes and Loans Payable 27	1479	0	93	571	1227	5073	10829	22101	46299	80588	204296	489655	•
All Other Liabilities 28	365	0	8	87	306	762	2194	5533	10007	26219	84232	164664	•
Net Worth 29	502	0	30	36	605	1160	2487	6859	11386	39186	68055	218541	•

Selected Financial Ratios (Times to 1)

Line Item													
Current Ratio 30	•	2.1	3.1	3.5	2.3	3.2	2.1	2.1	2.5	1.6	1.9	1.3	•
Quick Ratio 31	•	0.5	1.0	0.4	0.6	0.2	0.3	0.5	0.5	0.5	0.8	0.3	•
Net Sales to Working Capital 32	•	1.1	3.8	0.7	1.4	0.4	0.9	0.7	0.5	1.6	0.9	1.2	•
Coverage Ratio 33	•	•	1.2	0.6	•	•	•	0.7	0.9	•	•	•	•
Total Asset Turnover 34	•	0.3	1.2	0.3	0.4	0.2	0.3	0.2	0.2	0.3	0.2	0.1	•
Inventory Turnover 35	•	0.8	4.0	0.5	1.5	0.4	0.7	0.6	0.5	1.0	0.4	0.4	•
Receivables Turnover 36	•	4.3	27.3	8.2	4.7	5.8	5.7	2.2	2.6	3.2	1.5	3.0	•
Total Liabilities to Net Worth 37	•	3.7	18.5	2.5	5.0	5.2	4.0	4.9	2.7	4.2	3.0		•
Current Assets to Working Capital 38	•	1.9	1.4	1.8	1.4	1.9	1.9	1.7	2.6	2.1	4.0		•
Current Liabilities to Working Capital 39	•	0.9	0.4	0.8	0.4	0.9	0.9	0.7	1.6	1.1	3.0		•
Working Capital to Net Sales 40	•	0.9	1.4	0.7	2.6	1.1	1.5	2.0	0.6	1.2	0.8		•
Inventory to Working Capital 41	•	1.0	1.0	0.8	1.0	1.1	0.9	0.9	1.2	1.0	2.2		•
Total Receipts to Cash Flow 42	•	8.7	4.3	19.5	•	•	•	•	2.7	1.6	14.0		•
Cost of Goods to Cash Flow 43	•	5.7	2.9	15.8	•	•	•	•	5.7	6.8			•
Cash Flow to Total Debt 44	•	0.2	0.1	0.0	•	•	•	•	0.2	0.0			•

Selected Financial Factors (in Percentages)

Line Item											
Debt Ratio 45	78.6	•	77.2	94.9	71.7	83.4	84.0	80.1	83.2	73.2	80.9	75.0
Return on Total Assets 46	•	•	2.6	1.6	•	•	•	•	•	•	•	•
Return on Equity Before Income Taxes 47	•	•	1.6	•	•	•	•	•	•	•	•	•
Return on Equity After Income Taxes 48	•	•	1.5	•	•	•	•	•	•	•	•	•
Profit Margin (Before Income Tax) 49	•	•	0.3	•	•	•	•	•	•	•	•	•
Profit Margin (After Income Tax) 50	•	•	0.3	•	•	•	•	•	•	•	•	•

Table II

Corporations with Net Income

LAND SUBDIVISION

MONEY AMOUNTS AND SIZE OF ASSETS IN THOUSANDS OF DOLLARS

Item Description for Accounting Period 7/08 Through 6/09	Total	Zero Assets	Under 500	500 to 1,000	1,000 to 5,000	5,000 to 10,000	10,000 to 25,000	25,000 to 50,000	50,000 to 100,000	100,000 to 250,000	250,000 to 500,000	500,000 to 2,500,000	2,500,000 and over
Number of Enterprises **1**	12887	2117	4928	1748	3294	515	191	54	21	10	5	4	0
Revenues ($ in Thousands)													
Net Sales **2**	13981253	1103625	2054953	642615	4761726	878944	1459630	722201	383509	1309370	591460	73220	0
Interest **3**	94273	667	4010	1748	11544	3930	4270	2688	3885	4308	31164	26058	0
Rents **4**	154118	16795	0	662	17290	24958	21587	3095	5744	15749	1438	46800	0
Royalties **5**	27157	0	0	0	7368	5966	13521	0	0	257	0	45	0
Other Portfolio Income **6**	200717	17834	2579	17262	39443	13899	11759	5670	3038	32976	2540	53717	0
Other Receipts **7**	705511	27646	14229	61897	248790	26930	35405	7465	23977	31531	50791	176851	0
Total Receipts **8**	15163029	1166567	2075771	724184	5086161	954627	1546172	741119	420153	1394191	677393	376691	0
Average Total Receipts **9**	1177	551	421	414	1544	1854	8095	13724	20007	139419	135479	94173	•
Operating Costs/Operating Income (%)													
Cost of Operations **10**	74.2	72.8	70.7	60.1	78.6	71.7	75.9	77.3	65.7	77.8	62.4	73.0	•
Salaries and Wages **11**	3.5	2.5	2.1	2.0	1.6	2.7	4.4	4.6	6.7	4.3	13.6	64.4	•
Taxes Paid **12**	1.4	0.7	1.1	1.5	0.8	2.6	1.4	1.7	2.5	1.7	2.0	25.0	•
Interest Paid **13**	2.2	1.5	0.7	3.5	1.3	3.9	1.8	2.0	3.3	2.0	4.7	66.3	•
Depreciation **14**	1.1	0.3	0.2	0.9	1.1	1.9	1.2	0.7	1.0	1.4	2.9	5.7	•
Amortization and Depletion **15**	0.1	0.0	0.0	0.0	0.0	0.0	0.2	0.1	0.1	0.0	0.0	1.5	•
Pensions and Other Deferred Comp. **16**	0.3	•	•	0.1	0.3	0.0	0.1	0.1	0.1	0.7	1.2	8.2	•
Employee Benefits **17**	0.4	•	0.6	0.1	0.2	0.0	0.4	0.4	0.4	0.9	0.5	4.8	•
Advertising **18**	0.3	0.1	0.0	0.3	0.2	0.7	0.2	0.7	0.6	0.6	1.7	2.2	•
Other Expenses **19**	8.6	8.8	7.1	7.0	7.3	8.5	5.7	5.5	7.1	10.1	21.4	106.6	•
Officers' Compensation **20**	2.5	2.6	6.4	2.9	1.5	1.4	1.7	1.1	3.2	2.4	0.3	19.7	•
Operating Margin **21**	5.6	10.7	11.0	21.5	7.3	6.7	7.0	6.0	9.4	•	•	•	•
Operating Margin Before Officers' Comp. **22**	8.1	13.3	17.4	24.4	8.7	8.0	8.7	7.1	12.6	0.4	•	•	•

Selected Average Balance Sheet ($ in Thousands)

	(1)	(2)	(3)	(4)	(5)	(6)	(7)	(8)	(9)	(10)	(11)	(12)	(13)
Net Receivables 23	147	0	8	4	183	83	905	5254	4365	27216	65606	14088	•
Inventories 24	724	0	44	313	481	3278	6623	13433	38641	70624	99047	92358	•
Net Property, Plant and Equipment 25	568	0	52	110	541	2144	3565	8809	9014	53307	121988	373738	•
Total Assets 26	2001	0	157	720	2202	7036	15571	33027	68653	146788	381167	825083	•
Notes and Loans Payable 27	997	0	37	329	942	4415	10157	19758	42460	63086	199364	296858	•
All Other Liabilities 28	273	0	-0	91	220	1074	2100	5236	8524	45876	46643	130890	•
Net Worth 29	731	0	120	300	1039	1546	3315	8033	17669	37826	135160	397334	•

Selected Financial Ratios (Times to 1)

	(1)	(2)	(3)	(4)	(5)	(6)	(7)	(8)	(9)	(10)	(11)	(12)
Current Ratio 30	2.7	3.5	3.4	3.1	5.7	2.3	1.5	2.8	1.1	3.9	2.5	•
Quick Ratio 31	0.7	1.4	0.4	0.9	0.3	0.4	0.5	0.6	0.6	1.7	1.1	•
Net Sales to Working Capital 32	1.7	7.7	1.2	1.9	0.5	1.6	2.2	0.7	26.2	0.8	0.2	•
Coverage Ratio 33	7.6	17.2	10.8	12.2	4.9	8.3	5.3	6.8	3.1	1.8	4.3	11.7
Total Asset Turnover 34	0.5	2.7	0.5	0.7	0.2	0.5	0.4	0.3	0.9	0.3	0.0	•
Inventory Turnover 35	1.1	6.7	0.7	2.4	0.4	0.9	0.8	0.3	1.4	0.7	0.1	•
Receivables Turnover 36	5.1	36.3	12.1	6.3	6.2	5.4	2.2	2.6	4.0	•	•	•
Total Liabilities to Net Worth 37	1.7	0.3	1.4	1.1	3.5	3.7	3.1	2.9	2.9	1.8	1.1	•
Current Assets to Working Capital 38	1.6	1.4	1.4	1.5	1.2	1.8	3.1	1.6	13.7	1.3	1.7	•
Current Liabilities to Working Capital 39	0.6	0.4	0.4	0.5	0.2	0.8	2.1	0.6	12.7	0.3	0.7	•
Working Capital to Net Sales 40	0.6	0.1	0.8	0.5	2.0	0.6	0.5	1.5	0.0	1.2	5.7	•
Inventory to Working Capital 41	0.9	0.4	1.2	0.6	1.0	1.1	1.2	0.9	3.9	0.7	0.9	•
Total Receipts to Cash Flow 42	4.9	5.5	2.6	5.2	4.5	5.9	8.0	4.2	8.0	4.7	0.6	4.4
Cost of Goods to Cash Flow 43	3.7	3.9	1.6	4.1	3.2	4.4	6.2	2.8	6.2	2.9	0.4	3.2
Cash Flow to Total Debt 44	0.2	2.0	0.3	0.2	0.1	0.1	0.1	0.1	0.2	0.1	0.1	•

Selected Financial Factors (in Percentages)

	(1)	(2)	(3)	(4)	(5)	(6)	(7)	(8)	(9)	(10)	(11)	(12)
Debt Ratio 45	63.5	23.6	58.4	52.8	78.0	78.7	75.7	74.3	74.2	64.5	51.8	•
Return on Total Assets 46	9.0	34.0	19.3	10.0	4.6	7.2	4.3	5.9	5.7	2.6	6.4	•
Return on Equity Before Income Taxes 47	21.4	41.9	42.0	19.5	16.8	29.8	14.3	19.6	15.0	3.2	10.1	•
Return on Equity After Income Taxes 48	20.5	41.8	41.7	19.0	16.1	27.6	13.9	18.9	13.1	2.8	8.3	•
Profit Margin (Before Income Tax) 49	14.4	12.0	34.2	14.1	15.2	12.9	8.6	18.9	4.3	3.7	220.1	16.5
Profit Margin (After Income Tax) 50	13.8	12.0	34.0	13.7	14.6	12.0	8.4	18.3	3.8	3.2	180.5	16.1

Table I
Corporations with and without Net Income

ELECTRICAL CONTRACTORS

MONEY AMOUNTS AND SIZE OF ASSETS IN THOUSANDS OF DOLLARS

Item Description for Accounting Period 7/08 Through 6/09	Total	Zero Assets	Under 500	500 to 1,000	1,000 to 5,000	5,000 to 10,000	10,000 to 25,000	25,000 to 50,000	50,000 to 100,000	100,000 to 250,000	250,000 to 500,000	500,000 to 2,500,000	2,500,000 and over
Number of Enterprises **1**	58613	5927	44328	3063	3949	883	•	69	40	9	•	•	•
Revenues ($ in Thousands)													
Net Sales **2**	101449361	1043348	23573820	6739331	20779359	15440643	•	5894817	7373712	3262699	•	•	•
Interest **3**	64163	111	7150	2679	17455	10670	•	4286	1477	1579	•	•	•
Rents **4**	11109	0	4484	8	2464	1606	•	1671	582	48	•	•	•
Royalties **5**	6	0	0	0	0	6		0	0	0			
Other Portfolio Income **6**	91768	2061	12616	2497	18571	8629	•	3096	3091	2835	•	•	•
Other Receipts **7**	1163724	598	137925	9120	102121	31705	•	32768	39400	28649	•	•	•
Total Receipts **8**	102780131	1046118	23735995	6753635	20919970	15493259	•	5936638	7418262	3295810	•	•	•
Average Total Receipts **9**	1754	177	535	2205	5298	17546	•	86038	185457	366201	•	•	•
Operating Costs/Operating Income (%)													
Cost of Operations **10**	67.7	54.1	50.8	64.1	71.5	74.7	•	78.3	77.7	77.4	•	•	•
Salaries and Wages **11**	6.9	12.7	9.7	7.1	6.2	5.3	•	4.1	5.6	7.8	•	•	•
Taxes Paid **12**	1.9	2.3	2.9	2.1	2.1	1.3	•	0.9	1.1	1.1	•	•	•
Interest Paid **13**	0.5	0.9	0.6	0.4	0.5	0.3	•	0.2	0.2	0.8	•	•	•
Depreciation **14**	1.3	2.1	1.9	1.1	1.1	0.9	•	1.3	0.7	1.5	•	•	•
Amortization and Depletion **15**	0.1	•	0.0	0.0	0.1	0.0	•	0.0	0.1	0.3	•	•	•
Pensions and Other Deferred Comp. **16**	0.7	•	0.7	0.5	0.5	1.0	•	0.4	0.4	0.6	•	•	•
Employee Benefits **17**	2.3	0.1	1.3	3.1	2.5	2.2	•	1.6	1.7	0.8	•	•	•
Advertising **18**	0.3	0.3	0.5	0.4	0.4	0.1	•	0.1	0.1	0.1	•	•	•
Other Expenses **19**	9.5	24.6	16.9	12.6	8.0	5.7	•	4.7	3.9	4.8	•	•	•
Officers' Compensation **20**	4.8	5.3	9.2	5.9	4.0	3.6	•	2.3	2.1	1.7	•	•	•
Operating Margin **21**	4.0	•	5.6	2.7	3.2	4.8	•	6.1	6.4	3.2	•	•	•
Operating Margin Before Officers' Comp. **22**	8.8	3.0	14.8	8.6	7.2	8.3	•	8.4	8.5	4.9	•	•	•

Selected Average Balance Sheet ($ in Thousands)

Net Receivables 23	259	0	15	255	794	3112	18511	36828	83936
Inventories 24	25	0	9	62	92	238	631	1251	3360
Net Property, Plant and Equipment 25	76	0	21	91	261	496	3576	4876	15627
Total Assets 26	638	0	93	687	1858	6769	36102	69970	173442
Notes and Loans Payable 27	108	0	45	130	354	805	2999	5926	39046
All Other Liabilities 28	261	0	30	217	768	2720	17744	33943	87565
Net Worth 29	270	0	18	340	736	3245	15359	30101	46830

Selected Financial Ratios (Times to 1)

Current Ratio 30	1.8	•	1.7	2.2	1.7	1.8	1.8	1.6	1.4
Quick Ratio 31	1.4	•	1.2	1.7	1.4	1.5	1.6	1.4	1.2
Net Sales to Working Capital 32	8.4	•	21.9	7.3	9.2	6.9	6.7	8.4	9.7
Coverage Ratio 33	12.5	•	11.9	8.0	9.6	15.6	28.9	32.3	6.4
Total Asset Turnover 34	2.7	•	5.7	3.2	2.8	2.6	2.4	2.6	2.1
Inventory Turnover 35	47.0	•	30.6	22.7	41.0	54.8	106.0	114.4	83.5
Receivables Turnover 36	6.9	•	35.0	7.3	7.1	5.9	4.4	5.1	3.7
Total Liabilities to Net Worth 37	1.4	•	4.1	1.0	1.5	1.1	1.4	1.3	2.7
Current Assets to Working Capital 38	2.3	•	2.5	1.8	2.5	2.2	2.3	2.5	3.5
Current Liabilities to Working Capital 39	1.3	•	1.5	0.8	1.5	1.2	1.3	1.5	2.5
Working Capital to Net Sales 40	0.1	•	0.0	0.1	0.1	0.1	0.2	0.1	0.1
Inventory to Working Capital 41	0.1	•	0.4	0.3	0.2	0.1	0.0	0.0	0.1
Total Receipts to Cash Flow 42	7.8	4.9	4.9	7.6	10.3	10.8	11.1	10.7	15.3
Cost of Goods to Cash Flow 43	5.3	2.6	2.5	4.8	7.3	8.0	8.7	8.3	11.9
Cash Flow to Total Debt 44	0.6	•	1.5	0.8	0.5	0.5	0.4	0.4	0.2

Selected Financial Factors (in Percentages)

Debt Ratio 45	57.8	•	80.2	50.5	60.4	52.1	57.5	57.0	73.0
Return on Total Assets 46	15.7	•	39.2	10.7	12.4	14.1	16.6	18.9	10.3
Return on Equity Before Income Taxes 47	34.2	•	181.8	18.9	28.0	27.4	37.7	42.6	32.2
Return on Equity After Income Taxes 48	32.0	•	179.9	18.2	25.8	25.5	35.2	39.6	27.1
Profit Margin (Before Income Tax) 49	5.3	•	6.3	2.9	3.9	5.1	6.8	7.0	4.2
Profit Margin (After Income Tax) 50	5.0	•	6.2	2.8	3.6	4.7	6.3	6.5	3.5

Table II
Corporations with Net Income

ELECTRICAL CONTRACTORS

Money Amounts and Size of Assets in Thousands of Dollars

Item Description for Accounting Period 7/08 Through 6/09	Total	Zero Assets	Under 500	500 to 1,000	1,000 to 5,000	5,000 to 10,000	10,000 to 25,000	25,000 to 50,000	50,000 to 100,000	100,000 to 250,000	250,000 to 500,000	500,000 to 2,500,000	2,500,000 and over
1 Number of Enterprises	36672	3532	27468	1701	2804	733	320	63	•	•	•	0	0
Revenues ($ in Thousands)													
2 Net Sales	83656715	790437	16892418	3900430	16401994	14236100	13089219	5702447	•	•	•	0	0
3 Interest	51859	111	4445	2012	12992	9197	4716	3864	•	•	•	0	0
4 Rents	4991	0	0	8	2464	1429	248	212	•	•	•	0	0
5 Royalties	6	0	0	0	0	6	0	0	•	•	•	0	0
6 Other Portfolio Income	57483	92	10697	1837	11034	6952	5248	2321	•	•	•	0	0
7 Other Receipts	1134021	1	124261	4689	99741	29837	44513	32094	•	•	•	0	0
8 Total Receipts	84905075	790641	17031821	3908976	16528225	14283521	13143944	5740938	•	•	•	0	0
9 Average Total Receipts	2315	224	620	2298	5895	19486	41075	91126	•	•	•	0	0
Operating Costs/Operating Income (%)													
10 Cost of Operations	68.7	48.6	50.4	63.7	69.3	74.8	74.3	78.9	•	•	•	•	•
11 Salaries and Wages	6.4	10.2	8.9	7.8	6.4	5.4	4.4	4.1	•	•	•	•	•
12 Taxes Paid	1.7	1.5	2.7	2.1	2.2	1.3	1.0	0.8	•	•	•	•	•
13 Interest Paid	0.4	0.6	0.4	0.2	0.4	0.3	0.3	0.2	•	•	•	•	•
14 Depreciation	1.1	0.9	1.1	1.2	1.2	0.8	0.8	0.9	•	•	•	•	•
15 Amortization and Depletion	0.1	•	0.0	0.0	0.1	0.0	0.0	0.0	•	•	•	•	•
16 Pensions and Other Deferred Comp.	0.7	•	0.4	0.7	0.6	0.7	1.2	0.4	•	•	•	•	•
17 Employee Benefits	2.4	0.0	1.1	3.2	2.7	2.2	3.9	1.7	•	•	•	•	•
18 Advertising	0.3	0.3	0.5	0.6	0.3	0.1	0.2	0.1	•	•	•	•	•
19 Other Expenses	7.9	20.4	15.6	7.8	7.2	5.5	4.4	4.2	•	•	•	•	•
20 Officers' Compensation	4.4	5.5	8.4	5.3	4.2	3.4	3.0	2.3	•	•	•	•	•
21 Operating Margin	6.1	11.9	10.6	7.3	5.4	5.5	6.5	6.5	•	•	•	•	•
22 Operating Margin Before Officers' Comp.	10.5	17.4	18.9	12.6	9.6	8.9	9.5	8.8	•	•	•	•	•

Selected Average Balance Sheet ($ in Thousands)

Net Receivables 23	348	0	18	219	837	3345	8545	19086
Inventories 24	30	0	9	73	105	263	386	498
Net Property, Plant and Equipment 25	98	0	22	92	300	507	1208	2642
Total Assets 26	845	0	109	700	2022	6601	15945	36475
Notes and Loans Payable 27	116	0	37	78	349	748	1978	1677
All Other Liabilities 28	343	0	29	211	822	2754	7975	18907
Net Worth 29	386	0	43	411	851	3098	5993	15892

Selected Financial Ratios (Times to 1)

Current Ratio 30	1.8	•	2.1	2.4	1.8	1.9	1.7	1.7
Quick Ratio 31	1.5	•	1.6	1.8	1.5	1.7	1.4	1.5
Net Sales to Working Capital 32	7.9	•	15.4	7.0	8.7	7.0	7.3	7.0
Coverage Ratio 33	22.1	20.5	30.3	35.8	17.1	18.9	23.4	45.5
Total Asset Turnover 34	2.7	•	5.6	3.3	2.9	2.9	2.6	2.5
Inventory Turnover 35	51.4	•	33.0	19.9	38.5	55.3	78.7	143.2
Receivables Turnover 36	6.7	•	33.3	7.3	7.2	6.0	4.9	4.7
Total Liabilities to Net Worth 37	1.2	•	1.5	0.7	1.4	1.1	1.7	1.3
Current Assets to Working Capital 38	2.2	•	1.9	1.7	2.3	2.1	2.5	2.4
Current Liabilities to Working Capital 39	1.2	•	0.9	0.7	1.3	1.1	1.5	1.4
Working Capital to Net Sales 40	0.1	•	0.1	0.1	0.1	0.1	0.1	0.1
Inventory to Working Capital 41	0.1	•	0.3	0.2	0.1	0.1	0.1	0.0
Total Receipts to Cash Flow 42	7.4	3.3	4.1	7.3	8.8	10.2	10.2	11.3
Cost of Goods to Cash Flow 43	5.1	1.6	2.0	4.7	6.1	7.6	7.6	8.9
Cash Flow to Total Debt 44	0.7	•	2.3	1.1	0.6	0.5	0.4	0.4

Selected Financial Factors (in Percentages)

Debt Ratio 45	54.2	•	60.3	41.2	57.9	53.1	62.4	56.4
Return on Total Assets 46	21.6	•	66.4	25.5	19.1	18.0	18.4	18.1
Return on Equity Before Income Taxes 47	45.1	•	161.7	42.1	42.7	36.3	46.9	40.7
Return on Equity After Income Taxes 48	42.6	•	160.4	41.1	40.1	33.8	44.8	38.0
Profit Margin (Before Income Tax) 49	7.6	11.9	11.4	7.6	6.2	5.8	6.9	7.1
Profit Margin (After Income Tax) 50	7.2	11.5	11.3	7.4	5.8	5.4	6.6	6.7

Table I

Corporations with and without Net Income

PLUMBING, HEATING, AND AIR-CONDITIONING CONTRACTORS

MONEY AMOUNTS AND SIZE OF ASSETS IN THOUSANDS OF DOLLARS

Item Description for Accounting Period 7/08 Through 6/09	Total	Zero Assets	Under 500	500 to 1,000	1,000 to 5,000	5,000 to 10,000	10,000 to 25,000	25,000 to 50,000	50,000 to 100,000	100,000 to 250,000	250,000 to 500,000	500,000 to 2,500,000	2,500,000 and over
Number of Enterprises **1**	77945	7798	60677	3925	4300	710	•	96	29	5	•	•	•
Revenues ($ in Thousands)													
Net Sales **2**	129206344	842472	38400355	9219201	29479593	13985927	•	8001914	4903752	1597716	•	•	•
Interest **3**	65331	482	7527	6825	21091	8813	•	1444	2149	1001	•	•	•
Rents **4**	6970	0	1399	253	2520	781	•	0	546	0	•	•	•
Royalties **5**	1917	0	1917	0	0	0	•	0	0	0	•	•	•
Other Portfolio Income **6**	181048	12	12773	72948	52240	21452	•	692	1562	159	•	•	•
Other Receipts **7**	458923	18707	95519	7844	87256	37265	•	14182	14419	3620	•	•	•
Total Receipts **8**	129920533	861673	38519490	9307071	29642700	14054238	•	8018232	4922428	1602496	•	•	•
Average Total Receipts **9**	1667	110	635	2371	6894	19795	•	83523	169739	320499	•	•	•
Operating Costs/Operating Income (%)													
Cost of Operations **10**	66.8	37.2	51.6	57.8	70.6	74.2	•	78.9	75.9	81.4	•	•	•
Salaries and Wages **11**	7.9	9.1	12.7	9.5	6.5	6.3	•	4.5	5.7	4.1	•	•	•
Taxes Paid **12**	1.9	3.0	2.8	2.8	1.8	1.3	•	0.9	1.6	3.3	•	•	•
Interest Paid **13**	0.5	1.4	0.7	0.5	0.4	0.3	•	0.2	0.1	0.7	•	•	•
Depreciation **14**	1.2	3.2	1.7	2.0	0.9	1.1	•	0.7	0.8	0.4	•	•	•
Amortization and Depletion **15**	0.1	0.2	0.0	0.0	0.0	0.1	•	0.0	0.1	0.6	•	•	•
Pensions and Other Deferred Comp. **16**	0.5	0.6	0.3	0.6	0.6	0.4	•	0.9	0.4	0.2	•	•	•
Employee Benefits **17**	2.0	0.5	1.5	2.6	2.4	2.9	•	2.6	3.3	0.4	•	•	•
Advertising **18**	0.7	1.8	1.2	1.7	0.7	0.3	•	0.1	0.1	0.1	•	•	•
Other Expenses **19**	9.7	40.8	15.4	15.0	8.7	5.6	•	3.7	4.8	3.0	•	•	•
Officers' Compensation **20**	4.9	1.7	8.3	6.0	4.5	3.2	•	2.4	1.6	1.8	•	•	•
Operating Margin **21**	3.7	0.6	3.7	1.3	2.9	4.3	•	5.2	5.6	4.1	•	•	•
Operating Margin Before Officers' Comp. **22**	8.6	2.2	12.0	7.4	7.5	7.6	•	7.5	7.2	5.8	•	•	•

Selected Average Balance Sheet ($ in Thousands)

Net Receivables	23	224	0	26	246	998	3099	•	17754	38683	74910
Inventories	24	25	0	7	54	146	387	•	1639	942	788
Net Property, Plant and Equipment	25	64	0	28	159	253	691	•	2222	6460	4742
Total Assets	26	506	0	104	704	2154	6935	•	33163	69281	151366
Notes and Loans Payable	27	104	0	57	162	430	818	•	1966	4580	15419
All Other Liabilities	28	235	0	31	254	968	3520	•	19367	40049	111638
Net Worth	29	167	0	17	288	756	2597	•	11831	24651	24308

Selected Financial Ratios (Times to 1)

Current Ratio	30	1.6	•	1.6	1.6	1.7	1.6	•	1.4	1.4	1.0
Quick Ratio	31	1.3	•	1.4	1.3	1.4	1.3	•	1.2	1.2	0.9
Net Sales to Working Capital	32	11.9	•	25.9	12.4	9.7	9.1	•	9.6	9.8	85.3
Coverage Ratio	33	10.3	3.1	6.8	5.5	9.5	19.2	•	36.2	41.6	7.7
Total Asset Turnover	34	3.3	•	6.1	3.3	3.2	2.8	•	2.5	2.4	2.1
Inventory Turnover	35	44.2	•	45.9	25.0	33.2	37.7	•	40.2	136.3	330.3
Receivables Turnover	36	7.4	•	25.1	9.3	7.0	5.5	•	4.5	5.3	4.0
Total Liabilities to Net Worth	37	2.0	•	5.2	1.4	1.8	1.7	•	1.8	1.8	5.2
Current Assets to Working Capital	38	2.8	•	2.7	2.7	2.5	2.6	•	3.3	3.4	32.3
Current Liabilities to Working Capital	39	1.8	•	1.7	1.7	1.5	1.6	•	2.3	2.4	31.3
Working Capital to Net Sales	40	0.1	•	0.0	0.1	0.1	0.1	•	0.1	0.1	0.0
Inventory to Working Capital	41	0.2	•	0.3	0.3	0.2	0.2	•	0.2	0.1	0.2
Total Receipts to Cash Flow	42	8.5	2.7	5.9	7.3	10.2	12.2	•	12.4	10.2	18.5
Cost of Goods to Cash Flow	43	5.7	1.0	3.1	4.2	7.2	9.1	•	9.8	7.7	15.1
Cash Flow to Total Debt	44	0.6	•	1.2	0.8	0.5	0.4	•	0.3	0.4	0.1

Selected Financial Factors (in Percentages)

Debt Ratio	45	67.0	•	83.8	59.1	64.9	62.6	•	64.3	64.4	83.9
Return on Total Assets	46	15.5	•	28.4	9.2	12.4	14.4	•	13.9	14.9	10.6
Return on Equity Before Income Taxes	47	42.4	•	149.7	18.3	31.6	36.4	•	37.8	40.9	57.5
Return on Equity After Income Taxes	48	39.8	•	147.5	17.2	29.7	34.6	•	36.7	39.4	57.5
Profit Margin (Before Income Tax)	49	4.3	2.8	4.0	2.2	3.5	4.8	•	5.4	6.0	4.4
Profit Margin (After Income Tax)	50	4.0	2.7	3.9	2.1	3.3	4.6	•	5.2	5.7	4.4

Table II

Corporations with Net Income

PLUMBING, HEATING, AND AIR-CONDITIONING CONTRACTORS

MONEY AMOUNTS AND SIZE OF ASSETS IN THOUSANDS OF DOLLARS

Item Description for Accounting Period 7/08 Through 6/09	Total	Zero Assets	Under 500	500 to 1,000	1,000 to 5,000	5,000 to 10,000	10,000 to 25,000	25,000 to 50,000	50,000 to 100,000	100,000 to 250,000	250,000 to 500,000	500,000 to 2,500,000	2,500,000 and over
Number of Enterprises 1	52063	3899	41194	2525	3346	599	377	87	•	•	•	•	•
Revenues ($ in Thousands)													
Net Sales 2	107833851	392815	27514885	6395283	24993731	12876307	14306019	7690201	•	•	•	•	•
Interest 3	51920	482	3927	4692	17787	6227	7744	1234	•	•	•	•	•
Rents 4	6412	0	1277	253	2214	651	1095	0	•	•	•	•	•
Royalties 5	0	0	0	0	0	0	0	0					
Other Portfolio Income 6	164001	0	4908	71948	45353	21280	12392	542	•	•	•	•	•
Other Receipts 7	408855	623	79907	5544	82320	32630	86411	13154	•	•	•	•	•
Total Receipts 8	108465039	393920	27604904	6477720	25141405	12937095	14413661	7705131	•	•	•	•	•
Average Total Receipts 9	2083	101	670	2565	7514	21598	38233	88565	•	•	•	•	•
Operating Costs/Operating Income (%)													
Cost of Operations 10	67.5	29.1	49.3	58.3	69.9	73.9	79.4	78.7	•	•	•	•	•
Salaries and Wages 11	7.4	10.8	12.8	8.7	6.1	6.2	3.9	4.4	•	•	•	•	•
Taxes Paid 12	1.8	3.0	2.8	2.3	1.8	1.3	0.9	0.9	•	•	•	•	•
Interest Paid 13	0.3	1.2	0.5	0.4	0.3	0.2	0.3	0.1	•	•	•	•	•
Depreciation 14	1.1	3.7	1.5	1.4	0.9	1.2	0.8	0.6	•	•	•	•	•
Amortization and Depletion 15	0.1	•	0.0	0.0	0.0	0.1	0.0	0.0	•	•	•	•	•
Pensions and Other Deferred Comp. 16	0.5	1.3	0.3	0.7	0.6	0.4	0.5	1.0	•	•	•	•	•
Employee Benefits 17	2.1	•	1.6	2.4	2.4	3.1	1.9	2.7	•	•	•	•	•
Advertising 18	0.6	1.4	1.0	1.6	0.8	0.3	0.1	0.1	•	•	•	•	•
Other Expenses 19	8.6	27.8	14.5	13.3	8.4	5.3	4.0	3.5	•	•	•	•	•
Officers' Compensation 20	4.5	1.6	8.1	6.0	4.4	3.0	2.5	2.4	•	•	•	•	•
Operating Margin 21	5.6	20.0	7.7	4.9	4.4	4.9	5.6	5.7	•	•	•	•	•
Operating Margin Before Officers' Comp. 22	10.2	21.6	15.8	10.9	8.8	7.9	8.1	8.1	•	•	•	•	•

Selected Average Balance Sheet ($ in Thousands)

Net Receivables 23	294	0	26	262	1038	3379	8477	19102	•
Inventories 24	31	0	7	58	163	422	332	1744	•
Net Property, Plant and Equipment 25	69	0	26	122	247	715	1080	2260	•
Total Assets 26	637	0	106	700	2261	7076	15187	33314	•
Notes and Loans Payable 27	96	0	39	137	383	726	1697	1815	•
All Other Liabilities 28	295	0	26	231	980	3564	7562	19591	•
Net Worth 29	246	0	40	332	898	2786	5928	11908	•

Selected Financial Ratios (Times to 1)

Current Ratio 30	1.6	•	1.9	2.0	1.8	1.6	1.6	1.5
Quick Ratio 31	1.4	•	1.7	1.7	1.4	1.3	1.4	1.3
Net Sales to Working Capital 32	10.7	•	21.0	9.7	9.3	10.4	7.5	9.4
Coverage Ratio 33	19.2	18.3	17.4	15.2	16.9	25.6	19.7	41.1
Total Asset Turnover 34	3.3	•	6.3	3.6	3.3	3.0	2.5	2.7
Inventory Turnover 35	45.8	•	50.0	25.4	32.0	37.7	90.8	39.9
Receivables Turnover 36	7.1	•	27.9	8.5	7.4	5.5	4.8	4.4
Total Liabilities to Net Worth 37	1.6	•	1.6	1.1	1.5	1.5	1.6	1.8
Current Assets to Working Capital 38	2.6	•	2.1	2.0	2.3	2.8	2.6	3.1
Current Liabilities to Working Capital 39	1.6	•	1.1	1.0	1.3	1.8	1.6	2.1
Working Capital to Net Sales 40	0.1	•	0.0	0.1	0.1	0.1	0.1	0.1
Inventory to Working Capital 41	0.2	•	0.2	0.2	0.2	0.2	0.1	0.2
Total Receipts to Cash Flow 42	7.9	2.4	5.0	6.2	9.0	11.7	11.1	11.8
Cost of Goods to Cash Flow 43	5.3	0.7	2.5	3.6	6.3	8.7	8.8	9.3
Cash Flow to Total Debt 44	0.7	•	2.0	1.1	0.6	0.4	0.4	0.3

Selected Financial Factors (in Percentages)

Debt Ratio 45	61.4	•	61.9	52.6	60.3	60.6	61.0	64.3
Return on Total Assets 46	21.4	•	53.6	23.7	17.4	17.1	16.7	16.0
Return on Equity Before Income Taxes 47	52.5	•	132.6	46.8	41.2	41.6	40.6	43.7
Return on Equity After Income Taxes 48	49.9	•	131.3	45.3	39.2	39.6	38.8	42.5
Profit Margin (Before Income Tax) 49	6.2	20.3	8.0	6.1	5.0	5.4	6.3	5.9
Profit Margin (After Income Tax) 50	5.9	20.1	7.9	5.9	4.7	5.1	6.1	5.7

Table I

Corporations with and without Net Income

OTHER SPECIALTY TRADE CONTRACTORS

MONEY AMOUNTS AND SIZE OF ASSETS IN THOUSANDS OF DOLLARS

Item Description for Accounting Period 7/08 Through 6/09		Total	Zero Assets	Under 500	500 to 1,000	1,000 to 5,000	5,000 to 10,000	10,000 to 25,000	25,000 to 50,000	50,000 to 100,000	100,000 to 250,000	250,000 to 500,000	500,000 to 2,500,000	2,500,000 and over
Number of Enterprises	1	335013	65387	233684	15382	16928	2001	1223	248	90	44	17	•	•
Revenues ($ in Thousands)														
Net Sales	2	397850758	7693415	124839731	36812283	94712764	32604779	41719510	18906012	12701998	11373200	9178248	•	•
Interest	3	232440	2633	25393	17076	59169	23988	26519	10158	14295	14682	7751	•	•
Rents	4	152049	128	22904	7740	28327	6293	9598	10431	2583	695	26	•	•
Royalties	5	47779	0	242	3348	0	0	135	3993	16	7	30266	•	•
Other Portfolio Income	6	1158219	235775	334859	77752	180762	48202	76578	63922	40764	61712	11330	•	•
Other Receipts	7	2166961	199990	540647	73284	566151	168991	221959	135114	118477	24430	94270	•	•
Total Receipts	8	40608206	8131941	125763776	36991483	95547173	32852253	42054299	19129630	12878133	11474726	9321891	•	•
Average Total Receipts	9	1199	124	538	2405	5644	16418	34386	77136	143090	260789	548347	•	•
Operating Costs/Operating Income (%)														
Cost of Operations	10	64.7	43.4	52.1	58.7	68.7	75.3	76.9	78.5	76.4	77.7	73.8	•	•
Salaries and Wages	11	7.8	7.5	11.4	9.7	7.0	5.0	4.2	3.9	5.1	4.6	4.5	•	•
Taxes Paid	12	1.9	1.9	2.6	2.2	1.8	1.4	1.1	0.9	1.0	0.9	0.9	•	•
Interest Paid	13	0.7	1.2	0.7	0.7	0.6	0.5	0.5	0.5	0.6	0.8	2.0	•	•
Depreciation	14	2.3	2.5	2.0	2.6	2.4	1.9	2.3	2.4	1.9	3.0	2.0	•	•
Amortization and Depletion	15	0.1	0.3	0.0	0.0	0.0	0.0	0.1	0.0	0.3	0.3	0.9	•	•
Pensions and Other Deferred Comp.	16	0.4	0.0	0.3	0.4	0.4	0.7	0.5	0.7	0.3	0.6	0.3	•	•
Employee Benefits	17	1.4	0.4	1.5	1.3	1.3	1.6	2.0	1.4	1.3	0.9	0.5	•	•
Advertising	18	0.4	1.3	0.7	0.5	0.2	0.3	0.2	0.1	0.1	0.1	0.2	•	•
Other Expenses	19	13.0	31.9	18.6	16.8	11.5	7.1	6.1	6.4	8.4	5.7	7.3	•	•
Officers' Compensation	20	4.4	8.1	7.0	5.5	3.7	2.9	2.4	1.4	1.7	1.5	1.0	•	•
Operating Margin	21	2.9	1.6	3.1	1.7	2.3	3.3	3.9	3.9	3.0	3.9	6.7	•	•
Operating Margin Before Officers' Comp.	22	7.3	9.6	10.1	7.2	5.9	6.2	6.3	5.2	4.7	5.4	7.7	•	•

Selected Average Balance Sheet ($ in Thousands)

Net Receivables 23	132	0	12	174	733	3092	6712	15235	29784	49243	100823
Inventories 24	19	0	5	37	111	369	615	1258	1897	4320	4206
Net Property, Plant and Equipment 25	91	0	30	209	494	1161	2639	6556	9808	28378	42095
Total Assets 26	397	0	88	721	2022	6808	15176	34220	72564	146230	318122
Notes and Loans Payable 27	129	0	55	254	576	1559	3087	6451	14195	27185	113260
All Other Liabilities 28	131	0	21	182	633	2656	6113	14457	32109	61623	104586
Net Worth 29	137	0	12	286	813	2593	5976	13312	26260	57421	100276

Selected Financial Ratios (Times to 1)

Current Ratio 30	1.6	•	1.3	2.0	1.7	1.7	1.6	1.6	1.5	1.6	1.4
Quick Ratio 31	1.3	•	1.1	1.6	1.4	1.3	1.3	1.3	1.3	1.3	1.1
Net Sales to Working Capital 32	12.4	•	49.3	10.9	9.6	8.0	7.9	8.4	8.1	7.2	11.7
Coverage Ratio 33	6.4	7.2	6.5	4.3	6.2	9.0	10.1	11.9	8.6	6.6	5.2
Total Asset Turnover 34	3.0	•	6.1	3.3	2.8	2.4	2.2	2.2	1.9	1.8	1.7
Inventory Turnover 35	39.5	•	55.7	37.7	34.5	33.3	42.6	47.5	56.8	46.5	94.7
Receivables Turnover 36	8.5	•	43.1	13.6	7.2	4.7	5.1	4.8	4.7	4.8	6.2
Total Liabilities to Net Worth 37	1.9	•	6.2	1.5	1.5	1.6	1.5	1.6	1.8	1.5	2.2
Current Assets to Working Capital 38	2.6	•	3.9	2.0	2.3	2.5	2.6	2.7	2.9	2.7	3.4
Current Liabilities to Working Capital 39	1.6	•	2.9	1.0	1.3	1.5	1.6	1.7	1.9	1.7	2.4
Working Capital to Net Sales 40	0.1	•	0.0	0.1	0.1	0.1	0.1	0.1	0.1	0.1	0.1
Inventory to Working Capital 41	0.2	•	0.5	0.2	0.2	0.2	0.1	0.1	0.1	0.1	0.1
Total Receipts to Cash Flow 42	7.5	2.9	5.4	6.5	9.0	12.4	12.5	11.5	9.6	12.3	7.9
Cost of Goods to Cash Flow 43	4.8	1.3	2.8	3.8	6.2	9.4	9.6	9.0	7.3	9.6	5.8
Cash Flow to Total Debt 44	0.6	•	1.3	0.8	0.5	0.3	0.3	0.3	0.3	0.2	0.3

Selected Financial Factors (in Percentages)

Debt Ratio 45	65.4	•	86.1	60.4	59.8	61.9	60.6	61.1	63.8	60.7	68.5
Return on Total Assets 46	13.7	•	27.6	9.5	10.4	10.8	11.8	12.3	9.6	10.0	17.4
Return on Equity Before Income Taxes 47	33.3	•	167.8	18.4	21.6	25.3	26.9	28.9	23.4	21.5	44.4
Return on Equity After Income Taxes 48	31.4	•	165.5	17.4	20.0	22.7	25.0	27.3	20.5	19.1	42.1
Profit Margin (Before Income Tax) 49	3.9	7.3	3.8	2.2	3.1	4.0	4.7	5.1	4.3	4.8	8.3
Profit Margin (After Income Tax) 50	3.6	7.2	3.8	2.1	2.9	3.6	4.4	4.8	3.8	4.2	7.8

35

Table II

Corporations with Net Income

OTHER SPECIALTY TRADE CONTRACTORS

MONEY AMOUNTS AND SIZE OF ASSETS IN THOUSANDS OF DOLLARS

Item Description for Accounting Period 7/08 Through 6/09		Total	Zero Assets	Under 500	500 to 1,000	1,000 to 5,000	5,000 to 10,000	10,000 to 25,000	25,000 to 50,000	50,000 to 100,000	100,000 to 250,000	250,000 to 500,000	500,000 to 2,500,000	2,500,000 and over
Number of Enterprises	1	204569	35726	145661	9279	11078	1493	990	217	74	•	12	•	•
Revenues ($ in Thousands)														
Net Sales	2	294506917	5178943	85728768	24897927	65976046	26667122	35490710	16645537	10973550	•	7870258	•	•
Interest	3	173102	932	13815	10146	42599	18228	22730	8532	12664	•	3827	•	•
Rents	4	49493	53	9594	397	15400	5090	5302	10414	2583	•	26	•	•
Royalties	5	44431	0	242	0	0	0	135	3993	16	•	30266	•	•
Other Portfolio Income	6	773047	213339	191611	66131	100086	20731	46048	53579	34112	•	2322	•	•
Other Receipts	7	1370456	62082	94696	36674	541556	116851	156017	141094	102968	•	88985	•	•
Total Receipts	8	296917446	5455349	86038726	25011275	66675687	26828022	35720942	16863149	11125893	•	7995684	•	•
Average Total Receipts	9	1451	153	591	2695	6019	17969	36082	77710	150350	•	666307	•	•
Operating Costs/Operating Income (%)														
Cost of Operations	10	63.8	38.2	50.1	55.5	66.0	73.5	76.4	78.4	75.4	•	74.4	•	•
Salaries and Wages	11	7.2	5.8	10.1	10.3	7.5	5.0	4.0	3.5	4.9	•	4.1	•	•
Taxes Paid	12	1.7	1.5	2.5	2.0	1.8	1.4	1.0	0.9	1.0	•	0.9	•	•
Interest Paid	13	0.5	1.0	0.5	0.5	0.4	0.3	0.4	0.5	0.4	•	0.9	•	•
Depreciation	14	1.8	2.1	1.5	2.4	1.9	1.5	1.8	2.2	1.6	•	1.4	•	•
Amortization and Depletion	15	0.1	0.0	0.0	0.0	0.0	0.0	0.0	0.0	0.1	•	0.3	•	•
Pensions and Other Deferred Comp.	16	0.5	0.1	0.3	0.3	0.5	0.8	0.5	0.7	0.3	•	0.4	•	•
Employee Benefits	17	1.4	0.5	1.5	1.4	1.3	1.8	2.0	1.4	1.3	•	0.4	•	•
Advertising	18	0.4	1.2	0.7	0.4	0.2	0.3	0.1	0.1	0.1	•	0.2	•	•
Other Expenses	19	11.7	27.4	17.6	15.9	10.4	6.7	5.6	5.7	8.1	•	7.0	•	•
Officers' Compensation	20	4.2	8.1	6.6	5.2	4.0	3.0	2.4	1.4	1.8	•	1.0	•	•
Operating Margin	21	6.8	14.0	8.5	6.2	5.9	5.7	5.7	5.1	5.0	•	9.2	•	•
Operating Margin Before Officers' Comp.	22	11.0	22.2	15.1	11.4	9.8	8.8	8.1	6.5	6.9	•	10.1	•	•

Selected Average Balance Sheet ($ in Thousands)

Net Receivables 23	167	0	11	182	767	3361	7177	15609	32245	124484
Inventories 24	23	0	6	29	116	440	527	1182	1748	4206
Net Property, Plant and Equipment 25	88	0	27	216	427	932	2199	6087	9198	29602
Total Assets 26	459	0	89	728	2036	6759	15279	34422	72600	326833
Notes and Loans Payable 27	106	0	39	195	392	1044	2485	6192	10761	67914
All Other Liabilities 28	157	0	19	127	615	2841	6276	14536	34022	123499
Net Worth 29	197	0	32	405	1028	2874	6518	13694	27817	135420

Selected Financial Ratios (Times to 1)

Current Ratio 30	1.8	•	1.8	2.8	2.2	1.8	1.7	1.6	1.6	1.6
Quick Ratio 31	1.5	•	1.4	2.3	1.8	1.4	1.4	1.4	1.4	1.2
Net Sales to Working Capital 32	10.2	•	29.7	9.3	7.3	7.4	7.4	8.0	7.3	9.1
Coverage Ratio 33	15.8	21.4	18.2	14.5	18.5	21.9	17.1	15.1	17.7	13.4
Total Asset Turnover 34	3.1	•	6.6	3.7	2.9	2.6	2.3	2.2	2.0	2.0
Inventory Turnover 35	40.0	•	52.2	50.7	34.0	29.9	52.0	50.9	64.0	116.0
Receivables Turnover 36	7.8	•	49.3	13.2	6.8	4.5	4.9	4.7	4.4	•
Total Liabilities to Net Worth 37	1.3	•	1.8	0.8	1.0	1.4	1.3	1.5	1.6	1.4
Current Assets to Working Capital 38	2.2	•	2.3	1.6	1.8	2.3	2.4	2.7	2.7	2.7
Current Liabilities to Working Capital 39	1.2	•	1.3	0.6	0.8	1.3	1.4	1.7	1.7	1.7
Working Capital to Net Sales 40	0.1	•	0.0	0.1	0.1	0.1	0.1	0.1	0.1	0.1
Inventory to Working Capital 41	0.1	•	0.3	0.1	0.1	0.2	0.1	0.1	0.1	0.1
Total Receipts to Cash Flow 42	6.3	2.4	4.4	5.1	7.2	10.1	10.7	10.7	8.0	6.7
Cost of Goods to Cash Flow 43	4.0	0.9	2.2	2.9	4.7	7.4	8.2	8.4	6.1	5.0
Cash Flow to Total Debt 44	0.9	•	2.3	1.6	0.8	0.5	0.4	0.3	0.4	0.5

Selected Financial Factors (in Percentages)

Debt Ratio 45	57.1	•	64.6	44.4	49.5	57.5	57.3	60.2	61.7	58.6
Return on Total Assets 46	25.5	•	62.0	26.5	21.4	17.5	15.8	15.2	13.8	23.3
Return on Equity Before Income Taxes 47	55.6	•	165.9	44.4	40.1	39.3	35.0	35.7	34.1	52.1
Return on Equity After Income Taxes 48	53.5	•	164.4	43.3	38.2	36.6	32.8	33.9	30.8	49.6
Profit Margin (Before Income Tax) 49	7.6	19.4	8.9	6.7	6.9	6.3	6.4	6.4	6.4	10.8
Profit Margin (After Income Tax) 50	7.3	19.2	8.8	6.5	6.6	5.9	6.0	6.0	5.8	10.2

36

Table I

Corporations with and without Net Income

ANIMAL FOOD AND GRAIN AND OILSEED MILLING

MONEY AMOUNTS AND SIZE OF ASSETS IN THOUSANDS OF DOLLARS

Item Description for Accounting Period 7/08 Through 6/09		Total	Zero Assets	Under 500	500 to 1,000	1,000 to 5,000	5,000 to 10,000	10,000 to 25,000	25,000 to 50,000	50,000 to 100,000	100,000 to 250,000	250,000 to 500,000	500,000 to 2,500,000	2,500,000 and over
Number of Enterprises	1	1528	423	387	0	415	98	94	45	25	27	5	4	5
Revenues ($ in Thousands)														
Net Sales	2	133366788	317242	146106	0	2693553	3630076	4363884	5576787	4878440	8634915	1852129	3797225	97976432
Interest	3	403500	2	241	0	774	306	2078	1673	3302	12618	4248	10898	367360
Rents	4	207166	0	0	0	20	0	90	849	263	345	1775	944	202880
Royalties	5	405594	0	0	0	0	0	0	0	14	1257	825	60665	342834
Other Portfolio Income	6	643213	0	0	0	697	810	1254	5309	4762	26594	24889	79489	499411
Other Receipts	7	3251340	4399	0	0	80572	-5079	2580	61014	30852	62632	1251	91309	2921806
Total Receipts	8	138777601	321643	146347	0	2775616	3626113	4369886	5645632	4917633	8738361	1885117	4040530	102310723
Average Total Receipts	9	90823	760	378	•	6688	37001	46488	125458	196705	323643	377023	1010132	20462145
Operating Costs/Operating Income (%)														
Cost of Operations	10	83.9	88.1	69.8	•	87.3	84.8	84.5	85.6	84.6	84.4	68.8	84.2	83.9
Salaries and Wages	11	2.5	4.5	5.1	•	3.8	4.1	3.0	3.0	2.7	3.1	6.8	2.0	2.2
Taxes Paid	12	0.5	0.5	8.0	•	0.5	0.5	0.6	0.5	0.8	0.5	1.3	0.3	0.5
Interest Paid	13	1.5	0.2	0.4	•	0.6	0.3	0.4	0.7	0.8	1.2	2.6	1.7	1.7
Depreciation	14	1.6	1.5	1.0	•	1.4	2.1	2.5	1.8	1.8	2.3	3.6	4.2	1.4
Amortization and Depletion	15	0.2	0.0	0.1	•	0.0	0.0	0.0	0.1	0.1	0.3	0.9	0.7	0.2
Pensions and Other Deferred Comp.	16	0.6	•	•	•	0.0	0.0	0.1	0.2	0.2	0.3	1.1	0.7	0.8
Employee Benefits	17	0.6	0.6	3.6	•	0.3	0.6	0.4	0.6	0.5	0.8	0.8	0.9	0.6
Advertising	18	4.0	0.1	0.1	•	0.4	0.1	0.5	0.4	0.3	0.3	0.9	0.7	5.3
Other Expenses	19	4.4	4.9	20.0	•	4.4	6.9	4.8	5.8	5.0	5.9	9.7	5.0	4.0
Officers' Compensation	20	0.4	•	8.3	•	1.3	0.3	1.1	0.6	0.6	1.0	1.1	1.3	0.2
Operating Margin	21	•	•	•	•	•	0.3	2.0	0.6	2.7	•	2.3	•	•
Operating Margin Before Officers' Comp.	22	0.1	•	•	•	1.2	0.7	3.1	1.2	3.2	0.8	3.4	•	•

Selected Average Balance Sheet ($ in Thousands)

Net Receivables 23	4112	0	10	•	435	1703	4396	8015	17191	29769	45443	105096	655402
Inventories 24	6462	0	21	•	751	1010	2476	10371	16174	30507	55755	85481	1381590
Net Property, Plant and Equipment 25	10895	0	50	•	833	2949	5452	13029	21171	54844	134675	334056	2175207
Total Assets 26	51198	0	109	•	2390	6565	15357	37499	76144	162234	379598	1027298	12226349
Notes and Loans Payable 27	21412	0	71	•	1555	1115	4449	11357	22956	48953	140307	332626	5415788
All Other Liabilities 28	15392	0	278	•	707	3115	3874	11995	17665	44641	81394	238690	3779878
Net Worth 29	14394	0	-241	•	128	2335	7034	14147	35523	68640	157897	455982	3030683

Selected Financial Ratios (Times to 1)

Current Ratio 30	1.3	•	0.7	•	1.1	1.1	1.6	1.4	1.8	1.8	2.3	1.6	1.2
Quick Ratio 31	0.5	•	0.3	•	0.4	0.8	1.0	0.7	0.9	0.9	1.3	0.7	0.4
Net Sales to Working Capital 32	23.4	•	•	•	80.1	159.8	13.9	22.9	9.8	10.2	4.9	8.5	33.2
Coverage Ratio 33	3.5	7.3	•	•	6.0	1.9	6.0	3.7	5.3	1.8	2.5	4.3	3.6
Total Asset Turnover 34	1.7	•	3.5	•	2.7	5.6	3.0	3.3	2.6	2.0	1.0	0.9	1.6
Inventory Turnover 35	11.4	•	12.7	•	7.5	31.1	15.8	10.2	10.2	8.9	4.6	9.3	11.9
Receivables Turnover 36	19.1	•	44.5	•	14.9	18.9	12.2	13.4	13.0	11.4	7.3	9.9	24.1
Total Liabilities to Net Worth 37	2.6	•	•	•	17.7	1.8	1.2	1.7	1.1	1.4	1.4	1.3	3.0
Current Assets to Working Capital 38	4.5	•	•	•	17.6	15.4	2.7	3.8	2.3	2.3	1.8	2.7	6.1
Current Liabilities to Working Capital 39	3.5	•	•	•	16.6	14.4	1.7	2.8	1.3	1.3	0.8	1.7	5.1
Working Capital to Net Sales 40	0.0	•	•	•	0.0	0.0	0.1	0.0	0.1	0.1	0.2	0.1	0.0
Inventory to Working Capital 41	1.6	•	•	•	10.1	3.2	1.0	1.6	1.0	1.0	0.6	0.8	2.1
Total Receipts to Cash Flow 42	15.7	24.0	40.9	•	16.5	23.8	17.0	15.0	14.2	17.6	8.6	12.3	15.8
Cost of Goods to Cash Flow 43	13.2	21.1	28.6	•	14.4	20.2	14.4	12.8	12.0	14.9	5.9	10.4	13.2
Cash Flow to Total Debt 44	0.2	•	0.0	•	0.2	0.4	0.3	0.4	0.3	0.2	0.2	0.1	0.1

Selected Financial Factors (in Percentages)

Debt Ratio 45	71.9	•	321.1	•	94.7	64.4	54.2	62.3	53.3	57.7	58.4	55.6	75.2
Return on Total Assets 46	9.1	•	•	•	9.8	2.7	7.8	8.1	10.9	4.5	6.5	6.8	9.8
Return on Equity Before Income Taxes 47	23.2	•	25.7	•	153.1	3.6	14.2	15.7	19.0	4.9	9.4	11.7	28.3
Return on Equity After Income Taxes 48	15.5	•	25.7	•	149.3	2.1	13.3	14.5	15.3	2.0	8.1	7.7	18.4
Profit Margin (Before Income Tax) 49	3.8	1.0	•	•	3.0	0.2	2.2	1.8	3.5	1.1	4.0	5.6	4.4
Profit Margin (After Income Tax) 50	2.5	0.6	•	•	2.9	0.1	2.0	1.7	2.8	0.4	3.5	3.7	2.8

Table II

Corporations with Net Income

ANIMAL FOOD AND GRAIN AND OILSEED MILLING

MONEY AMOUNTS AND SIZE OF ASSETS IN THOUSANDS OF DOLLARS

Item Description for Accounting Period 7/08 Through 6/09	Total	Zero Assets	Under 500	500 to 1,000	1,000 to 5,000	5,000 to 10,000	10,000 to 25,000	25,000 to 50,000	50,000 to 100,000	100,000 to 250,000	250,000 to 500,000	500,000 to 2,500,000	2,500,000 and over
Number of Enterprises **1**	1340	413	346	0	383	54	64	29	22	18	•	•	4
Revenues ($ in Thousands)													
Net Sales **2**	123179377	317242	143940	0	2570256	1486724	3262424	3449933	4745459	6110632	•	•	3797225
Interest **3**	392369	0	241	0	774	306	1789	942	3037	7437	•	•	10898
Rents **4**	206867	0	0	0	20	0	90	849	263	46	•	•	944
Royalties **5**	405160	0	0	0	0	0	0	0	14	1257	•	•	60665
Other Portfolio Income **6**	608221	0	0	0	697	319	784	5306	4755	16682	•	•	79489
Other Receipts **7**	3259984	4399	1	0	80572	68	22290	53612	30006	55537	•	•	91309
Total Receipts **8**	128051978	321641	144182	0	2652319	1487417	3287377	3510642	4783534	6191591	•	•	4040530
Average Total Receipts **9**	95561	779	417	•	6925	27545	51365	121057	217433	343977	•	•	1010132
Operating Costs/Operating Income (%)													
Cost of Operations **10**	83.9	88.1	70.1	•	87.2	90.1	83.2	82.4	84.5	82.2	•	•	84.2
Salaries and Wages **11**	2.3	4.5	4.2	•	4.0	2.7	3.1	3.4	2.7	3.0	•	•	2.0
Taxes Paid **12**	0.5	0.5	7.8	•	0.5	0.4	0.6	0.8	0.8	0.5	•	•	0.3
Interest Paid **13**	1.5	0.2	0.4	•	0.5	0.1	0.4	0.6	0.7	0.9	•	•	1.7
Depreciation **14**	1.5	1.5	0.5	•	1.4	0.4	2.3	1.9	1.6	2.0	•	•	4.2
Amortization and Depletion **15**	0.1	•	0.0	•	0.0	0.0	0.0	0.1	0.1	0.2	•	•	0.7
Pensions and Other Deferred Comp. **16**	0.7	•	•	•	0.0	0.0	0.2	0.4	0.2	0.3	•	•	0.7
Employee Benefits **17**	0.6	0.6	3.7	•	0.2	0.3	0.4	0.8	0.5	1.0	•	•	0.9
Advertising **18**	4.3	0.1	0.1	•	0.4	0.1	0.4	0.3	0.2	0.4	•	•	0.7
Other Expenses **19**	4.1	4.7	3.7	•	3.4	3.5	3.8	5.9	4.8	5.6	•	•	5.0
Officers' Compensation **20**	0.3	•	8.4	•	1.2	0.8	1.3	0.8	0.6	0.8	•	•	1.3
Operating Margin **21**	0.1	•	1.1	•	1.3	1.6	4.3	2.7	3.2	3.1	•	•	•
Operating Margin Before Officers' Comp. **22**	0.4	•	9.5	•	2.4	2.4	5.7	3.5	3.8	3.9	•	•	•

Selected Average Balance Sheet ($ in Thousands)

	•	•	•	•	•	•	•	•	•	•	•
Net Receivables 23	4234	0	11	•	420	2555	4711	8665	19030	34020	105096
Inventories 24	6797	0	12	•	676	1518	2827	11204	16465	34764	86542
Net Property, Plant and Equipment 25	11133	0	18	•	891	731	5823	12812	21295	49633	334056
Total Assets 26	52600	0	81	•	2410	6390	16435	39766	77173	169292	1027298
Notes and Loans Payable 27	23022	0	18	•	1064	314	3610	10906	22959	53646	332626
All Other Liabilities 28	16357	0	69	•	527	2730	3523	13412	19383	38840	238690
Net Worth 29	13221	0	-6	•	819	3346	9301	15447	34830	76806	455982

Selected Financial Ratios (Times to 1)

	•	•	•	•	•	•	•	•	•	•	•
Current Ratio 30	1.3	•	0.7	•	1.9	2.0	2.0	1.5	1.8	1.8	1.6
Quick Ratio 31	0.5	•	0.3	•	0.7	1.6	1.3	0.8	0.9	0.9	0.7
Net Sales to Working Capital 32	21.5	•	•	•	9.7	9.8	10.1	17.0	9.7	9.9	8.5
Coverage Ratio 33	4.0	8.7	4.0	•	9.9	21.8	15.2	8.7	6.6	5.7	4.3
Total Asset Turnover 34	1.7	•	5.2	•	2.8	4.3	3.1	3.0	2.8	2.0	0.9
Inventory Turnover 35	11.3	•	25.0	•	8.7	16.3	15.0	8.7	11.1	8.0	9.2
Receivables Turnover 36	19.2	•	74.3	•	19.9	8.6	11.1	10.6	14.3	10.0	•
Total Liabilities to Net Worth 37	3.0	•	•	•	1.9	0.9	0.8	1.6	1.2	1.2	1.3
Current Assets to Working Capital 38	4.2	•	•	•	2.1	2.0	2.0	3.2	2.2	2.3	2.7
Current Liabilities to Working Capital 39	3.2	•	•	•	1.1	1.0	1.0	2.2	1.2	1.3	1.7
Working Capital to Net Sales 40	0.0	•	•	•	0.1	0.1	0.1	0.1	0.1	0.1	0.1
Inventory to Working Capital 41	1.5	•	•	•	1.2	0.4	0.7	1.2	1.0	1.0	0.8
Total Receipts to Cash Flow 42	14.9	23.7	24.2	•	14.9	22.5	12.6	10.7	13.3	11.3	12.3
Cost of Goods to Cash Flow 43	12.5	20.9	17.0	•	13.0	20.3	10.5	8.8	11.2	9.3	10.4
Cash Flow to Total Debt 44	0.2	•	0.2	•	0.3	0.4	0.6	0.5	0.4	0.3	0.1

Selected Financial Factors (in Percentages)

	•	•	•	•	•	•	•	•	•	•	•
Debt Ratio 45	74.9	•	107.7	•	66.0	47.6	43.4	61.2	54.9	54.6	55.6
Return on Total Assets 46	10.5	•	8.7	•	13.8	7.6	16.8	15.0	13.3	10.7	6.8
Return on Equity Before Income Taxes 47	31.2	•	•	•	36.5	13.9	27.8	34.1	25.0	19.5	11.7
Return on Equity After Income Taxes 48	21.6	•	•	•	35.8	12.1	26.8	32.5	20.6	15.6	7.7
Profit Margin (Before Income Tax) 49	4.5	1.3	1.3	•	4.5	1.7	5.1	4.4	4.0	4.4	5.6
Profit Margin (After Income Tax) 50	3.1	0.8	1.2	•	4.4	1.5	4.9	4.2	3.3	3.5	3.7

Table I

Corporations with and without Net Income

SUGAR AND CONFECTIONERY PRODUCT

MONEY AMOUNTS AND SIZE OF ASSETS IN THOUSANDS OF DOLLARS

Item Description for Accounting Period 7/08 Through 6/09	Total	Zero Assets	Under 500	500 to 1,000	1,000 to 5,000	5,000 to 10,000	10,000 to 25,000	25,000 to 50,000	50,000 to 100,000	100,000 to 250,000	250,000 to 500,000	500,000 to 2,500,000	2,500,000 and over
Number of Enterprises **1**	1288	9	90	•	•	•	38	15	18	0	5	7	3
Revenues ($ in Thousands)													
Net Sales **2**	52003129	1506439	289381	•	•	•	1659156	930525	2336125	0	2581332	3084660	38138605
Interest **3**	244395	6972	61	•	•	•	781	597	1174	0	1084	103679	129462
Rents **4**	53732	16233	0	•	•	•	1	3977	0	0	5	25355	7974
Royalties **5**	376098	168232	0	•	•	•	11507	1267	0	0	2439	80250	112403
Other Portfolio Income **6**	2401835	264686	0	•	•	•	1507	57	1246	0	695	80513	2052391
Other Receipts **7**	571486	95268	2647	•	•	•	9054	6204	12533	0	6858	76892	360389
Total Receipts **8**	55650675	2057830	292089	•	•	•	1682006	942627	2351078	0	2592413	3451349	40801224
Average Total Receipts **9**	43207	228648	3245	•	•	•	44263	62842	130615	•	518483	493050	13600408
Operating Costs/Operating Income (%)													
Cost of Operations **10**	56.2	46.4	63.1	•	•	•	81.7	78.3	69.7	•	78.4	62.7	51.6
Salaries and Wages **11**	6.6	28.6	7.4	•	•	•	3.0	2.1	6.4	•	5.2	5.6	6.1
Taxes Paid **12**	1.0	1.8	1.6	•	•	•	0.7	0.7	0.9	•	0.6	1.0	0.9
Interest Paid **13**	3.8	2.7	0.8	•	•	•	0.7	1.0	1.2	•	2.8	8.3	4.1
Depreciation **14**	2.8	5.4	3.0	•	•	•	1.6	3.4	2.8	•	2.5	6.1	2.5
Amortization and Depletion **15**	1.4	5.5	0.6	•	•	•	0.0	0.1	0.4	•	0.8	5.6	1.2
Pensions and Other Deferred Comp. **16**	0.8	0.3	0.1	•	•	•	0.2	0.2	0.5	•	0.4	0.6	1.0
Employee Benefits **17**	1.3	2.7	1.3	•	•	•	0.4	0.3	1.9	•	0.7	2.1	1.3
Advertising **18**	5.2	10.4	0.1	•	•	•	0.4	0.6	2.1	•	2.5	0.6	6.3
Other Expenses **19**	20.0	28.6	14.0	•	•	•	10.3	10.7	12.1	•	9.7	20.6	21.6
Officers' Compensation **20**	1.2	13.4	9.4	•	•	•	1.5	1.8	1.1	•	0.9	1.0	0.6
Operating Margin **21**	•	•	•	•	•	•	•	0.8	1.0	•	•	•	2.8
Operating Margin Before Officers' Comp. **22**	0.8	•	8.0	•	•	•	0.9	2.6	2.1	•	•	•	3.4

Selected Average Balance Sheet ($ in Thousands)

Net Receivables 23	4567	0	•	•	430	•	•	2731	6641	13162	•	63520	40788	1566500
Inventories 24	3684	0	•	•	339	•	•	5452	10255	20660	•	89382	66269	987393
Net Property, Plant and Equipment 25	8463	0	•	•	325	•	•	5366	13745	22895	•	100019	267146	2505933
Total Assets 26	67815	0	•	•	1258	•	•	17007	33253	78642	•	378128	1225347	24550294
Notes and Loans Payable 27	33196	0	•	•	278	•	•	4436	7532	24667	•	241319	420788	12508597
All Other Liabilities 28	21474	0	•	•	224	•	•	5648	8078	20000	•	152602	322726	7935446
Net Worth 29	13145	0	•	•	756	•	•	6922	17642	33974	•	-15792	481833	4106252

Selected Financial Ratios (Times to 1)

Current Ratio 30	0.7	•	•	2.3	•	1.4	1.6	1.7	•	0.8	•	1.4	0.5
Quick Ratio 31	0.3	•	•	1.5	•	0.5	0.7	0.7	•	0.4	•	0.3	0.3
Net Sales to Working Capital 32	•	•	•	6.3	•	14.9	9.1	7.5	•	•	•	7.0	•
Coverage Ratio 33	3.5	•	•	0.5	•	2.1	3.0	2.3	•	0.1	•	0.7	4.3
Total Asset Turnover 34	0.6	•	•	2.6	•	2.6	1.9	1.7	•	1.4	•	0.4	0.5
Inventory Turnover 35	6.2	•	•	6.0	•	6.5	4.7	4.4	•	4.5	•	4.2	6.6
Receivables Turnover 36	8.6	•	•	4.9	•	16.3	8.1	11.0	•	8.1	•	5.3	8.3
Total Liabilities to Net Worth 37	4.2	•	•	0.7	•	1.5	0.9	1.3	•	•	•	1.5	5.0
Current Assets to Working Capital 38	•	•	•	1.8	•	3.2	2.7	2.4	•	•	•	3.7	•
Current Liabilities to Working Capital 39	•	•	•	0.8	•	2.2	1.7	1.4	•	•	•	2.7	•
Working Capital to Net Sales 40	0.2	•	•	0.2	•	0.1	0.1	0.1	•	•	•	0.1	•
Inventory to Working Capital 41	•	•	•	0.6	•	1.9	1.3	1.3	•	•	•	1.3	•
Total Receipts to Cash Flow 42	4.3	5.6	•	10.1	•	10.7	8.9	8.4	•	25.0	•	7.8	3.6
Cost of Goods to Cash Flow 43	2.4	2.6	•	6.4	•	8.8	7.0	5.8	•	19.6	•	4.9	1.9
Cash Flow to Total Debt 44	0.2	•	•	0.6	•	0.4	0.4	0.3	•	0.1	•	0.1	0.2

Selected Financial Factors (in Percentages)

Debt Ratio 45	80.6	•	•	39.9	•	59.3	46.9	56.8	•	104.2	•	60.7	83.3
Return on Total Assets 46	8.0	•	•	1.1	•	3.7	5.9	4.7	•	0.2	•	2.2	9.2
Return on Equity Before Income Taxes 47	29.6	•	•	•	•	4.9	7.4	6.1	•	86.7	•	•	42.2
Return on Equity After Income Taxes 48	19.2	•	•	•	•	3.1	6.7	5.6	•	86.7	•	•	28.0
Profit Margin (Before Income Tax) 49	9.6	•	•	•	•	0.8	2.1	1.6	•	•	•	•	13.6
Profit Margin (After Income Tax) 50	6.2	•	•	•	•	0.5	1.9	1.5	•	•	•	•	9.0

Table II

Corporations with Net Income

SUGAR AND CONFECTIONERY PRODUCT

MONEY AMOUNTS AND SIZE OF ASSETS IN THOUSANDS OF DOLLARS

Item Description for Accounting Period 7/08 Through 6/09	Total	Zero Assets	Under 500	500 to 1,000	1,000 to 5,000	5,000 to 10,000	10,000 to 25,000	25,000 to 50,000	50,000 to 100,000	100,000 to 250,000	250,000 to 500,000	500,000 to 2,500,000	2,500,000 and over
Number of Enterprises **1**	573	0	413	30	58	•	16	11	11	0	•	•	3
Revenues ($ in Thousands)													
Net Sales **2**	42637027	0	15269	54727	210574	•	520275	690586	1673411	0	•	•	38138605
Interest **3**	233234	0	0	0	39	•	103	568	1012	0	•	•	129462
Rents **4**	33399	0	0	0	0	•	0	3625	0	0	•	•	7974
Royalties **5**	150463	0	0	0	0	•	11443	1215	0	0	•	•	112403
Other Portfolio Income **6**	2126325	0	0	728	0	•	1232	57	1241	0	•	•	2105391
Other Receipts **7**	406932	0	4	497	1106	•	1913	5577	10411	0	•	•	360389
Total Receipts **8**	45587380	0	15273	55952	211719	•	534966	701628	1686075	0	•	•	40801224
Average Total Receipts **9**	79559	•	37	1865	3650	•	33435	63784	153280	•	•	•	13600408
Operating Costs/Operating Income (%)													
Cost of Operations **10**	53.5	•	37.3	63.4	55.4	•	74.3	78.7	70.6	•	•	•	51.6
Salaries and Wages **11**	6.1	•	0.5	14.0	9.7	•	4.5	1.4	6.4	•	•	•	6.1
Taxes Paid **12**	0.9	•	0.6	0.4	1.7	•	1.0	0.5	1.1	•	•	•	0.9
Interest Paid **13**	4.1	•	0.1	1.2	0.1	•	1.1	1.0	1.0	•	•	•	4.1
Depreciation **14**	2.6	•	0.0	2.4	2.0	•	1.6	3.6	2.6	•	•	•	2.5
Amortization and Depletion **15**	1.1	•	0.1	•	•	•	0.1	0.1	0.1	•	•	•	1.2
Pensions and Other Deferred Comp. **16**	0.9	•	•	•	0.2	•	0.2	0.1	0.5	•	•	•	1.0
Employee Benefits **17**	1.3	•	•	•	1.2	•	0.3	0.2	1.4	•	•	•	1.3
Advertising **18**	5.8	•	4.5	0.1	0.1	•	0.5	0.5	2.3	•	•	•	6.3
Other Expenses **19**	20.6	•	20.4	12.4	13.9	•	11.0	8.4	11.0	•	•	•	21.6
Officers' Compensation **20**	0.8	•	5.3	4.2	11.7	•	1.9	1.9	1.0	•	•	•	0.6
Operating Margin **21**	2.3	•	31.1	1.8	4.0	•	3.6	3.7	2.1	•	•	•	2.8
Operating Margin Before Officers' Comp. **22**	3.1	•	36.4	6.0	15.7	•	5.5	5.6	3.1	•	•	•	3.4

Selected Average Balance Sheet ($ in Thousands)

Net Receivables 23	9041	•	1	150	331	•	2145	7922	16192	•	1566500
Inventories 24	6567	•	22	252	352	•	8897	8603	21373	•	987393
Net Property, Plant and Equipment 25	14661	•	0	432	242	•	6309	14550	22733	•	2505933
Total Assets 26	137012	•	10	968	1141	•	16575	34497	82664	•	24550294
Notes and Loans Payable 27	68424	•	0	243	61	•	4730	7716	22485	•	12508597
All Other Liabilities 28	44407	•	1	365	139	•	4710	8548	25674	•	7935446
Net Worth 29	24181	•	8	360	941	•	7135	18233	34506	•	4106252

Selected Financial Ratios (Times to 1)

Current Ratio 30	0.6	•	6.8	0.8	4.4	•	1.4	1.6	1.7	•	0.5
Quick Ratio 31	0.3	•	6.7	0.2	2.8	•	0.3	0.8	0.6	•	0.3
Net Sales to Working Capital 32	•	•	4.3	•	5.3	•	12.7	8.7	7.4	•	•
Coverage Ratio 33	4.1	•	265.2	4.3	63.6	•	6.8	6.5	3.8	•	4.3
Total Asset Turnover 34	0.5	•	3.7	1.9	3.2	•	2.0	1.8	1.8	•	0.5
Inventory Turnover 35	6.1	•	0.6	4.6	5.7	•	2.7	5.7	5.0	•	6.6
Receivables Turnover 36	8.1	•	1.0	24.4	5.1	•	8.5	7.2	10.8	•	8.3
Total Liabilities to Net Worth 37	4.7	•	0.2	1.7	0.2	•	1.3	0.9	1.4	•	5.0
Current Assets to Working Capital 38	•	•	1.2	•	1.3	•	3.6	2.6	2.5	•	•
Current Liabilities to Working Capital 39	•	•	0.2	•	0.3	•	2.6	1.6	1.5	•	•
Working Capital to Net Sales 40	•	•	0.2	•	0.2	•	0.1	0.1	0.1	•	•
Inventory to Working Capital 41	•	•	0.0	•	0.4	•	2.5	1.1	1.4	•	•
Total Receipts to Cash Flow 42	3.8	•	2.1	6.3	6.2	•	6.3	7.9	8.2	•	3.6
Cost of Goods to Cash Flow 43	2.0	•	0.8	4.0	3.5	•	4.7	6.2	5.8	•	1.9
Cash Flow to Total Debt 44	0.2	•	10.0	0.5	2.9	•	0.5	0.5	0.4	•	0.2

Selected Financial Factors (in Percentages)

Debt Ratio 45	82.4	•	17.2	62.8	17.5	•	57.0	47.1	58.3	•	83.3
Return on Total Assets 46	9.1	•	115.1	9.9	14.6	•	14.7	11.5	7.1	•	9.2
Return on Equity Before Income Taxes 47	38.9	•	138.5	20.5	17.4	•	29.1	18.4	12.4	•	42.2
Return on Equity After Income Taxes 48	26.2	•	138.5	20.5	13.4	•	24.9	17.5	11.7	•	28.0
Profit Margin (Before Income Tax) 49	12.6	•	31.1	4.1	4.5	•	6.4	5.3	2.8	•	13.6
Profit Margin (After Income Tax) 50	8.5	•	31.1	4.1	3.5	•	5.5	5.1	2.6	•	9.0

40

Table I

Corporations with and without Net Income

FRUIT AND VEGETABLE PRESERVING AND SPECIALTY FOOD

MONEY AMOUNTS AND SIZE OF ASSETS IN THOUSANDS OF DOLLARS

Item Description for Accounting Period 7/08 Through 6/09		Total	Zero Assets	Under 500	500 to 1,000	1,000 to 5,000	5,000 to 10,000	10,000 to 25,000	25,000 to 50,000	50,000 to 100,000	100,000 to 250,000	250,000 to 500,000	500,000 to 2,500,000	2,500,000 and over
Number of Enterprises	1	925	392	•	•	245	•	78	38	33	15	5	7	5
Revenues ($ in Thousands)														
Net Sales	2	50060268	3327607	•	•	1826916	•	2166862	1953626	4354571	4533593	2981763	9748517	16195657
Interest	3	72368	4214	•	•	269	•	982	1993	1931	1259	2301	16369	42612
Rents	4	16785	0	•	•	1207	•	14	513	2119	1242	733	5704	5252
Royalties	5	269651	481	•	•	12	•	0	0	0	0	0	9936	256949
Other Portfolio Income	6	862289	1378	•	•	1188	•	417	5892	1637	1899	623	5855	843281
Other Receipts	7	960432	168275	•	•	1761	•	5073	52572	22696	14994	24009	45210	618591
Total Receipts	8	52241793	3501955	•	•	1831353	•	2173348	2014596	4382954	4552987	3009429	9831591	17962342
Average Total Receipts	9	56478	8934	•	•	7475	•	27863	53016	132817	303532	601886	1404513	3592468
Operating Costs/Operating Income (%)														
Cost of Operations	10	67.5	50.0	•	•	82.0	•	74.7	77.3	78.8	78.6	73.5	64.0	61.9
Salaries and Wages	11	4.7	5.4	•	•	2.0	•	6.5	4.4	3.1	3.2	4.2	7.1	4.2
Taxes Paid	12	0.8	0.9	•	•	1.7	•	1.0	0.9	0.5	0.8	0.9	0.8	0.7
Interest Paid	13	1.8	1.7	•	•	1.1	•	1.3	1.5	1.2	1.0	1.0	2.1	2.5
Depreciation	14	2.5	1.8	•	•	1.9	•	2.6	3.3	2.5	2.3	3.3	2.8	2.5
Amortization and Depletion	15	0.9	0.6	•	•	0.4	•	0.3	0.3	0.2	0.1	0.3	1.0	1.6
Pensions and Other Deferred Comp.	16	0.5	1.1	•	•	0.2	•	0.1	0.3	0.3	0.2	0.1	0.5	0.8
Employee Benefits	17	1.1	1.0	•	•	0.6	•	0.8	0.6	1.1	0.6	1.2	2.2	0.6
Advertising	18	2.6	0.0	•	•	0.2	•	1.3	0.4	0.7	0.3	2.7	6.3	3.0
Other Expenses	19	15.4	35.6	•	•	3.8	•	10.7	8.5	7.8	8.5	10.0	12.5	20.2
Officers' Compensation	20	0.7	0.6	•	•	3.4	•	1.3	1.4	0.6	0.6	0.4	0.4	0.4
Operating Margin	21	1.6	1.4	•	•	2.7	•	•	1.1	3.1	3.7	2.6	0.3	1.5
Operating Margin Before Officers' Comp.	22	2.3	2.0	•	•	6.2	•	0.8	2.5	3.7	4.4	2.9	0.7	2.0

Selected Average Balance Sheet ($ in Thousands)

Net Receivables 23	4766	0	•	•	•	418	•	•	3049	6128	12076	26212	47746	98755	381813
Inventories 24	7439	0	•	•	•	425	•	•	5922	9362	23056	78983	98918	202288	395119
Net Property, Plant and Equipment 25	8519	0	•	•	•	1020	•	•	4072	9436	19916	45689	121803	245144	629306
Total Assets 26	51785	0	•	•	•	2656	•	•	14216	34438	72086	165524	343624	995449	6091335
Notes and Loans Payable 27	13994	0	•	•	•	1151	•	•	5441	12599	25148	53804	107463	365122	1349923
All Other Liabilities 28	12436	0	•	•	•	411	•	•	5064	8317	17647	43530	91489	282687	1244039
Net Worth 29	25355	0	•	•	•	1093	•	•	3712	13522	29291	68189	144671	347641	3497373

Selected Financial Ratios (Times to 1)

Current Ratio 30	1.4	•	•	•	•	2.0	•	•	1.4	1.6	1.6	1.9	1.6	1.8	1.2
Quick Ratio 31	0.6	•	•	•	•	1.1	•	•	0.6	0.7	0.5	0.5	0.5	0.7	0.6
Net Sales to Working Capital 32	13.9	•	•	•	•	13.5	•	•	11.3	6.5	8.8	5.8	9.3	8.8	22.2
Coverage Ratio 33	4.5	5.0	•	•	•	3.8	•	•	0.9	3.7	4.0	5.1	4.6	1.6	6.4
Total Asset Turnover 34	1.0	•	•	•	•	2.8	•	•	2.0	1.5	1.8	1.8	1.7	1.4	0.5
Inventory Turnover 35	4.9	•	•	•	•	14.4	•	•	3.5	4.2	4.5	3.0	4.4	4.4	5.1
Receivables Turnover 36	12.3	•	•	•	•	17.2	•	•	9.0	9.5	12.8	10.9	12.5	12.1	10.4
Total Liabilities to Net Worth 37	1.0	•	•	•	•	1.4	•	•	2.8	1.5	1.5	1.4	1.4	1.9	0.7
Current Assets to Working Capital 38	3.8	•	•	•	•	2.0	•	•	3.8	2.6	2.7	2.2	2.6	2.3	7.1
Current Liabilities to Working Capital 39	2.8	•	•	•	•	1.0	•	•	2.8	1.6	1.7	1.2	1.6	1.3	6.1
Working Capital to Net Sales 40	0.1	•	•	•	•	0.1	•	•	0.1	0.2	0.1	0.2	0.1	0.1	0.0
Inventory to Working Capital 41	1.9	•	•	•	•	0.9	•	•	2.1	1.4	1.7	1.4	1.7	1.1	3.0
Total Receipts to Cash Flow 42	5.6	2.5	•	•	•	18.4	•	•	13.3	9.6	10.4	9.8	7.9	8.7	3.8
Cost of Goods to Cash Flow 43	3.8	1.2	•	•	•	15.1	•	•	9.9	7.4	8.2	7.7	5.8	5.6	2.4
Cash Flow to Total Debt 44	0.4	•	•	•	•	0.3	•	•	0.2	0.3	0.3	0.3	0.4	0.2	0.3

Selected Financial Factors (in Percentages)

Debt Ratio 45	51.0	•	•	•	•	58.8	•	•	73.9	60.7	59.4	58.8	57.9	65.1	42.6
Return on Total Assets 46	8.4	•	•	•	•	11.4	•	•	2.2	8.6	9.1	9.4	7.8	4.6	8.4
Return on Equity Before Income Taxes 47	13.4	•	•	•	•	20.4	•	•	•	16.1	16.8	18.4	14.4	4.7	12.4
Return on Equity After Income Taxes 48	9.3	•	•	•	•	20.3	•	•	•	13.4	14.5	16.1	10.0	3.1	8.1
Profit Margin (Before Income Tax) 49	6.3	6.6	•	•	•	3.0	•	•	•	4.2	3.7	4.2	3.5	1.2	13.3
Profit Margin (After Income Tax) 50	4.4	4.0	•	•	•	3.0	•	•	•	3.5	3.2	3.6	2.4	0.8	8.8

Table II

Corporations with Net Income

FRUIT AND VEGETABLE PRESERVING AND SPECIALTY FOOD

MONEY AMOUNTS AND SIZE OF ASSETS IN THOUSANDS OF DOLLARS

Item Description for Accounting Period 7/08 Through 6/09		Total	Zero Assets	Under 500	500 to 1,000	1,000 to 5,000	5,000 to 10,000	10,000 to 25,000	25,000 to 50,000	50,000 to 100,000	100,000 to 250,000	250,000 to 500,000	500,000 to 2,500,000	2,500,000 and over
Number of Enterprises	1	393	•	0	0	209	54	44	27	27	•	5	•	5
Revenues ($ in Thousands)														
Net Sales	2	43463240	•	0	0	1716998	1614315	1106106	1559362	3872856	•	2981763	•	16195657
Interest	3	71048	•	0	0	0	17	974	1751	1871	•	2301	•	42612
Rents	4	15384	•	0	0	0	0	14	375	2063	•	733	•	5252
Royalties	5	269639	•	0	0	0	2274	0	0	0	•	0	•	256949
Other Portfolio Income	6	859662	•	0	0	0	117	97	5826	1631	•	623	•	843281
Other Receipts	7	898416	•	0	0	178	6599	2463	14039	21749	•	24009	•	618591
Total Receipts	8	45577389	•	0	0	1717176	1623322	1109654	1581353	3900170	•	3009429	•	17962342
Average Total Receipts	9	115973	•	•	•	8216	30062	25219	58569	144451	•	601886	•	3592468
Operating Costs/Operating Income (%)														
Cost of Operations	10	67.0	•	•	•	82.7	74.0	73.0	75.5	78.9	•	73.5	•	61.9
Salaries and Wages	11	4.7	•	•	•	1.9	4.1	5.2	4.1	3.0	•	4.2	•	4.2
Taxes Paid	12	0.8	•	•	•	1.6	1.4	0.8	0.9	0.5	•	0.9	•	0.7
Interest Paid	13	1.7	•	•	•	1.1	0.4	0.9	1.2	1.0	•	1.0	•	2.5
Depreciation	14	2.5	•	•	•	1.9	2.7	2.4	2.7	2.3	•	3.3	•	2.5
Amortization and Depletion	15	0.8	•	•	•	0.4	0.3	0.1	0.4	0.1	•	0.3	•	1.6
Pensions and Other Deferred Comp.	16	0.6	•	•	•	0.2	0.0	0.1	0.2	0.3	•	0.1	•	0.8
Employee Benefits	17	1.1	•	•	•	0.5	2.1	0.9	0.5	1.1	•	1.2	•	0.6
Advertising	18	2.1	•	•	•	0.2	•	0.4	0.4	0.6	•	2.7	•	3.0
Other Expenses	19	15.4	•	•	•	2.9	8.2	8.1	6.8	7.7	•	10.0	•	20.2
Officers' Compensation	20	0.6	•	•	•	2.4	0.2	1.4	1.6	0.6	•	0.4	•	0.4
Operating Margin	21	2.6	•	•	•	4.2	6.4	6.6	5.8	3.8	•	2.6	•	1.5
Operating Margin Before Officers' Comp.	22	3.2	•	•	•	6.6	6.7	8.0	7.4	4.4	•	2.9	•	2.0

Selected Average Balance Sheet ($ in Thousands)

Net Receivables 23	9920	453	2207	2375	6983	12661	47746	381813
Inventories 24	15421	424	1659	7194	10111	22961	98918	437597
Net Property, Plant and Equipment 25	17666	1120	1905	4283	7668	19472	121803	629306
Total Assets 26	112213	2839	6939	14052	32897	71848	343624	6091335
Notes and Loans Payable 27	28380	1243	1756	3696	11189	23699	107463	1349923
All Other Liabilities 28	25209	422	2437	3926	6921	17613	91489	1244039
Net Worth 29	58623	1174	2746	6429	14787	30536	144671	3497373

Selected Financial Ratios (Times to 1)

Current Ratio 30	1.5	1.9	1.3	2.0	2.3	1.6	1.6	1.2
Quick Ratio 31	0.6	0.9	0.7	0.7	1.0	0.6	0.5	0.6
Net Sales to Working Capital 32	11.2	15.4	29.4	5.4	4.4	8.6	9.3	22.2
Coverage Ratio 33	5.5	4.8	17.5	8.4	6.9	5.5	4.6	6.4
Total Asset Turnover 34	1.0	2.9	4.3	1.8	1.8	2.0	1.7	0.5
Inventory Turnover 35	4.8	16.0	13.3	2.6	4.3	4.9	4.4	4.6
Receivables Turnover 36	12.2	17.4	15.2	8.7	9.6	14.1	12.5	•
Total Liabilities to Net Worth 37	0.9	1.4	1.5	1.2	1.2	1.4	1.4	0.7
Current Assets to Working Capital 38	3.2	2.1	4.4	2.0	1.8	2.6	2.6	7.1
Current Liabilities to Working Capital 39	2.2	1.1	3.4	1.0	0.8	1.6	1.6	6.1
Working Capital to Net Sales 40	0.1	0.1	0.0	0.2	0.2	0.1	0.1	0.0
Inventory to Working Capital 41	1.6	1.0	1.8	1.2	1.0	1.6	1.7	3.0
Total Receipts to Cash Flow 42	5.2	16.5	7.7	7.7	8.4	9.7	7.9	3.8
Cost of Goods to Cash Flow 43	3.5	13.7	5.7	5.6	6.3	7.7	5.8	2.4
Cash Flow to Total Debt 44	0.4	0.3	0.9	0.4	0.4	0.4	0.4	0.3

Selected Financial Factors (in Percentages)

Debt Ratio 45	47.8	58.7	60.4	54.2	55.1	57.5	57.9	42.6
Return on Total Assets 46	9.4	15.5	31.8	14.0	14.8	10.9	7.8	8.4
Return on Equity Before Income Taxes 47	14.7	29.7	75.9	26.9	28.2	21.1	14.4	12.4
Return on Equity After Income Taxes 48	10.5	29.6	75.2	26.0	24.8	18.3	10.0	8.1
Profit Margin (Before Income Tax) 49	7.8	4.2	7.0	6.9	7.2	4.5	3.5	13.3
Profit Margin (After Income Tax) 50	5.6	4.2	6.9	6.6	6.3	3.9	2.4	8.8

Table I

Corporations with and without Net Income

DAIRY PRODUCT

MONEY AMOUNTS AND SIZE OF ASSETS IN THOUSANDS OF DOLLARS

Item Description for Accounting Period 7/08 Through 6/09	Total	Zero Assets	Under 500	500 to 1,000	1,000 to 5,000	5,000 to 10,000	10,000 to 25,000	25,000 to 50,000	50,000 to 100,000	100,000 to 250,000	250,000 to 500,000	500,000 to 2,500,000	2,500,000 and over
Number of Enterprises **1**	855	0	602	0	102	37	37	31	20	13	5	8	0
Revenues ($ in Thousands)													
Net Sales **2**	43905936	0	113358	0	1296315	1137405	2010476	3073309	3034843	4088351	3670822	25481058	0
Interest **3**	35487	0	551	0	837	1110	648	1161	4668	6025	157	20331	0
Rents **4**	5951	0	0	0	0	521	1701	36	659	1080	123	1831	0
Royalties **5**	60943	0	0	0	0	0	0	0	3724	10	47884	9325	0
Other Portfolio Income **6**	81612	0	34	0	170	347	1281	2402	2890	493	16824	57172	0
Other Receipts **7**	133217	0	-1	0	2099	469	7190	4344	23227	14477	14418	66990	0
Total Receipts **8**	44223146	0	113942	0	1299421	1139852	2021296	3081252	3070011	4410436	3750228	25636707	0
Average Total Receipts **9**	51723	•	189	•	12739	30807	54630	99395	153501	316187	750046	3204588	•
Operating Costs/Operating Income (%)													
Cost of Operations **10**	79.3	•	57.1	•	84.6	88.8	79.6	78.8	80.1	81.6	76.6	78.6	•
Salaries and Wages **11**	4.0	•	15.0	•	3.6	1.2	4.9	4.8	4.6	2.8	4.8	4.0	•
Taxes Paid **12**	0.8	•	6.7	•	0.8	0.3	0.9	0.7	0.8	0.6	0.7	0.9	•
Interest Paid **13**	1.4	•	2.3	•	0.8	0.1	1.0	0.5	0.8	0.7	1.5	1.8	•
Depreciation **14**	2.4	•	7.3	•	1.7	0.8	2.6	1.8	3.3	3.6	2.4	2.3	•
Amortization and Depletion **15**	0.4	•	0.3	•	•	0.0	0.0	0.1	0.2	0.1	0.4	0.6	•
Pensions and Other Deferred Comp. **16**	0.6	•	1.2	•	0.2	0.1	0.4	0.5	0.3	0.3	0.7	0.7	•
Employee Benefits **17**	0.7	•	1.7	•	0.7	0.6	0.6	0.7	0.9	1.0	1.4	0.5	•
Advertising **18**	1.2	•	1.8	•	0.1	0.7	0.5	0.3	0.6	1.5	1.9	1.4	•
Other Expenses **19**	6.7	•	32.3	•	5.8	3.4	6.0	8.2	7.0	5.4	8.4	6.7	•
Officers' Compensation **20**	0.6	•	4.1	•	1.6	1.6	2.1	1.0	0.7	0.3	0.6	0.3	•
Operating Margin **21**	1.9	•	•	•	•	2.3	1.4	2.6	0.7	2.3	0.6	2.3	•
Operating Margin Before Officers' Comp. **22**	2.4	•	•	•	1.6	3.9	3.5	3.6	1.4	2.5	1.2	2.6	•

Selected Average Balance Sheet ($ in Thousands)

Net Receivables 23	3699	21	765	1728	4086	7162	13271	21713	47111	231448
Inventories 24	2967	11	1021	1636	4771	4354	11971	26033	61365	146111
Net Property, Plant and Equipment 25	8432	132	1272	2130	7045	12434	25140	56657	121068	553851
Total Assets 26	25023	292	3477	6450	16975	33297	70640	140752	313840	1769165
Notes and Loans Payable 27	10425	329	1206	824	7324	7454	18949	38162	118669	823976
All Other Liabilities 28	7861	16	857	1916	3909	9440	16295	31842	84286	619327
Net Worth 29	6736	-53	1414	3710	5743	16404	35395	70748	110885	325862

Selected Financial Ratios (Times to 1)

Current Ratio 30	1.5	1.0	1.5	2.2	1.9	1.7	1.9	2.0	1.5	1.4
Quick Ratio 31	0.8	0.6	0.8	1.2	0.9	0.9	1.0	1.1	0.7	0.7
Net Sales to Working Capital 32	15.8	•	18.2	13.1	12.7	14.1	9.4	10.5	18.8	19.1
Coverage Ratio 33	2.8	•	1.3	21.9	3.0	6.9	3.2	4.9	2.9	2.6
Total Asset Turnover 34	2.1	0.6	3.7	4.8	3.2	3.0	2.1	2.2	2.3	1.8
Inventory Turnover 35	13.7	9.5	10.5	16.7	9.1	17.9	10.2	9.9	9.2	17.1
Receivables Turnover 36	14.1	17.3	11.2	19.6	12.0	15.6	12.2	14.8	11.4	14.7
Total Liabilities to Net Worth 37	2.7	•	1.5	0.7	2.0	1.0	1.0	1.0	1.8	4.4
Current Assets to Working Capital 38	2.8	•	2.9	1.8	2.1	2.5	2.1	2.0	3.1	3.3
Current Liabilities to Working Capital 39	1.8	•	1.9	0.8	1.1	1.5	1.1	1.0	2.1	2.3
Working Capital to Net Sales 40	0.1	•	0.1	0.1	0.1	0.1	0.1	0.1	0.1	0.1
Inventory to Working Capital 41	0.9	•	1.3	0.8	1.1	0.7	0.8	0.8	1.4	0.9
Total Receipts to Cash Flow 42	12.8	•	24.5	19.1	15.0	10.5	13.3	13.5	10.4	12.6
Cost of Goods to Cash Flow 43	10.1	•	20.7	16.9	11.9	8.3	10.7	11.0	8.0	9.9
Cash Flow to Total Debt 44	0.2	•	0.3	0.6	0.3	0.6	0.3	0.3	0.3	0.2

Selected Financial Factors (in Percentages)

Debt Ratio 45	73.1	118.1	59.3	42.5	66.2	50.7	49.9	49.7	64.7	81.6
Return on Total Assets 46	8.0	•	3.7	12.3	9.5	9.6	5.6	7.8	9.9	8.3
Return on Equity Before Income Taxes 47	19.4	104.2	2.0	20.4	18.5	16.7	7.6	12.4	18.3	27.7
Return on Equity After Income Taxes 48	16.1	104.2	1.5	20.0	15.6	14.4	5.8	11.1	18.3	22.2
Profit Margin (Before Income Tax) 49	2.5	•	0.2	2.5	2.0	2.8	1.8	2.8	2.8	2.8
Profit Margin (After Income Tax) 50	2.1	•	0.2	2.4	1.6	2.4	1.4	2.5	2.8	2.3

Table II

Corporations with Net Income

DAIRY PRODUCT

MONEY AMOUNTS AND SIZE OF ASSETS IN THOUSANDS OF DOLLARS

Item Description for Accounting Period 7/08 Through 6/09	Total	Zero Assets	Under 500	500 to 1,000	1,000 to 5,000	5,000 to 10,000	10,000 to 25,000	25,000 to 50,000	50,000 to 100,000	100,000 to 250,000	250,000 to 500,000	500,000 to 2,500,000	2,500,000 and over
Number of Enterprises 1	180	0	0	0	68	24	33	23	11	•	•	•	0
Revenues ($ in Thousands)													
Net Sales 2	39959745	0	0	0	961710	679649	1760074	2176233	1870276	•	•	•	0
Interest 3	24576	0	0	0	301	175	406	481	4269	•	•	•	0
Rents 4	4512	0	0	0	0	0	1492	4	105	•	•	•	0
Royalties 5	13059	0	0	0	0	0	0	0	3724	•	•	•	0
Other Portfolio Income 6	79474	0	0	0	170	190	1279	2078	1566	•	•	•	0
Other Receipts 7	104876	0	0	0	2099	406	6603	4168	20102	•	•	•	0
Total Receipts 8	40186242	0	0	0	964280	680420	1769854	2182964	1900042	•	•	•	0
Average Total Receipts 9	223257	•	•	•	14181	28351	53632	94911	172731	•	•	•	•
Operating Costs/Operating Income (%)													
Cost of Operations 10	79.6	•	•	•	85.2	83.8	81.7	80.2	79.8	•	•	•	•
Salaries and Wages 11	3.8	•	•	•	3.4	0.9	3.8	3.7	4.0	•	•	•	•
Taxes Paid 12	0.8	•	•	•	0.8	0.4	0.7	0.6	0.6	•	•	•	•
Interest Paid 13	1.4	•	•	•	0.5	0.2	1.1	0.3	0.7	•	•	•	•
Depreciation 14	2.3	•	•	•	1.5	1.0	2.5	1.6	2.6	•	•	•	•
Amortization and Depletion 15	0.4	•	•	•	•	•	0.0	0.1	0.0	•	•	•	•
Pensions and Other Deferred Comp. 16	0.6	•	•	•	0.3	0.1	0.2	0.4	0.2	•	•	•	•
Employee Benefits 17	0.6	•	•	•	0.6	0.9	0.4	0.6	0.7	•	•	•	•
Advertising 18	1.2	•	•	•	0.0	1.1	0.4	0.3	0.3	•	•	•	•
Other Expenses 19	6.3	•	•	•	4.5	4.2	4.9	6.6	7.8	•	•	•	•
Officers' Compensation 20	0.6	•	•	•	1.9	2.6	2.2	1.2	0.9	•	•	•	•
Operating Margin 21	2.6	•	•	•	1.2	4.9	2.2	4.4	2.3	•	•	•	•
Operating Margin Before Officers' Comp. 22	3.1	•	•	•	3.1	7.5	4.5	5.6	3.2	•	•	•	•

Selected Average Balance Sheet ($ in Thousands)

Net Receivables 23	15115	•	803	1222	4042	6264	15545
Inventories 24	12368	•	1026	1749	4962	4642	16042
Net Property, Plant and Equipment 25	34807	•	808	1819	6267	11370	22669
Total Assets 26	104541	•	3110	5834	16176	32853	69261
Notes and Loans Payable 27	42824	•	928	1116	7765	7168	18642
All Other Liabilities 28	34522	•	675	1914	3813	7423	16270
Net Worth 29	27196	•	1507	2804	4599	18262	34349

Selected Financial Ratios (Times to 1)

Current Ratio 30	1.5	•	2.2	1.9	1.9	1.8	2.1
Quick Ratio 31	0.7	•	1.2	1.0	0.9	1.0	1.1
Net Sales to Working Capital 32	16.4	•	12.4	15.2	11.7	11.5	8.3
Coverage Ratio 33	3.2	•	3.8	29.4	3.6	14.3	6.3
Total Asset Turnover 34	2.1	•	4.5	4.9	3.3	2.9	2.5
Inventory Turnover 35	14.3	•	11.7	13.6	8.8	16.3	8.5
Receivables Turnover 36	14.8	•	12.4	•	12.1	16.6	10.5
Total Liabilities to Net Worth 37	2.8	•	1.1	1.1	2.5	0.8	1.0
Current Assets to Working Capital 38	2.8	•	1.8	2.1	2.1	2.2	1.9
Current Liabilities to Working Capital 39	1.8	•	0.8	1.1	1.1	1.2	0.9
Working Capital to Net Sales 40	0.1	•	0.1	0.1	0.1	0.1	0.1
Inventory to Working Capital 41	0.9	•	0.8	0.9	1.1	0.6	0.6
Total Receipts to Cash Flow 42	12.6	•	23.0	12.2	15.3	10.1	9.5
Cost of Goods to Cash Flow 43	10.0	•	19.6	10.2	12.5	8.1	7.5
Cash Flow to Total Debt 44	0.2	•	0.4	0.8	0.3	0.6	0.5

Selected Financial Factors (in Percentages)

Debt Ratio 45	74.0	•	51.6	51.9	71.6	44.4	50.4
Return on Total Assets 46	9.5	•	9.0	24.9	12.7	14.3	11.4
Return on Equity Before Income Taxes 47	25.1	•	13.7	50.1	32.2	23.9	19.4
Return on Equity After Income Taxes 48	21.3	•	13.0	49.3	28.1	21.1	16.1
Profit Margin (Before Income Tax) 49	3.1	•	1.5	5.0	2.8	4.6	3.9
Profit Margin (After Income Tax) 50	2.6	•	1.4	4.9	2.4	4.1	3.2

Table I

Corporations with and without Net Income

MEAT AND SEAFOOD PROCESSING

MONEY AMOUNTS AND SIZE OF ASSETS IN THOUSANDS OF DOLLARS

Item Description for Accounting Period 7/08 Through 6/09	Total	Zero Assets	Under 500	500 to 1,000	1,000 to 5,000	5,000 to 10,000	10,000 to 25,000	25,000 to 50,000	50,000 to 100,000	100,000 to 250,000	250,000 to 500,000	500,000 to 2,500,000	2,500,000 and over
Number of Enterprises **1**	3257	8	2409	116	366	92	116	62	37	31	11	6	4
Revenues ($ in Thousands)													
Net Sales **2**	114656621	349921	2253641	190171	2629437	1517324	6875222	6508616	7025472	12155083	7402668	11539661	56209406
Interest **3**	126098	35	65	467	3852	213	3236	3052	517	6330	9806	22483	76041
Rents **4**	21865	0	0	172	856	1603	1009	954	81	189	2885	534	13583
Royalties **5**	34164	0	0	0	0	0	0	0	0	0	234	27364	6566
Other Portfolio Income **6**	430361	23817	0	1750	16907	254	3911	13366	2453	25957	5180	16394	320371
Other Receipts **7**	597938	664	31	77	6493	43290	6337	18386	17086	84546	40802	60869	319356
Total Receipts **8**	115867047	374437	2253737	192637	2657545	1562684	6889715	6544374	7045609	12272105	7461575	11667305	56945323
Average Total Receipts **9**	35575	46805	936	1661	7261	16986	59394	105554	190422	395874	678325	1944551	14236331
Operating Costs/Operating Income (%)													
Cost of Operations **10**	86.8	88.3	76.1	67.8	72.7	83.6	83.0	83.7	85.2	85.6	84.7	80.6	90.8
Salaries and Wages **11**	2.8	3.2	4.0	5.8	5.2	2.9	3.5	4.3	2.9	2.5	3.2	6.4	1.7
Taxes Paid **12**	0.5	0.3	1.4	3.0	1.3	1.3	0.6	0.6	0.4	0.5	0.6	0.4	0.3
Interest Paid **13**	0.9	0.0	0.5	0.0	1.0	1.3	0.5	0.7	0.9	0.7	1.5	0.8	0.9
Depreciation **14**	1.8	1.1	1.1	1.7	2.5	2.2	1.4	1.9	2.2	2.3	2.1	2.4	1.6
Amortization and Depletion **15**	0.1	•	0.4	•	0.0	0.3	0.1	0.1	0.1	0.2	0.3	0.3	•
Pensions and Other Deferred Comp. **16**	0.4	0.1	•	0.1	0.5	0.3	0.2	0.2	0.1	0.1	0.2	0.3	0.6
Employee Benefits **17**	0.7	0.5	0.3	0.7	1.6	0.9	1.1	0.5	1.0	0.8	1.2	2.1	0.3
Advertising **18**	0.6	0.0	1.3	4.0	0.5	0.1	0.6	0.6	1.7	0.7	0.5	0.6	0.4
Other Expenses **19**	5.2	3.5	13.1	13.0	9.5	10.0	5.7	5.5	4.7	5.5	4.8	9.2	3.7
Officers' Compensation **20**	0.5	0.0	1.6	4.6	2.2	1.6	1.7	0.5	0.5	0.6	0.5	0.4	0.2
Operating Margin **21**	•	3.0	0.2	•	3.1	•	1.6	1.4	0.2	0.6	0.3	•	•
Operating Margin Before Officers' Comp. **22**	0.3	3.0	1.8	4.0	5.3	•	3.3	1.9	0.7	1.1	0.8	•	•

Selected Average Balance Sheet ($ in Thousands)

Net Receivables 23	1957	0	12	114	406	1570	3508	6648	13279	22794	60142	64070	743818
Inventories 24	3107	0	1	66	222	582	2700	7472	16744	37557	77320	245280	1273199
Net Property, Plant and Equipment 25	4568	0	33	100	1520	1608	5146	11522	27841	59305	97416	274206	1796700
Total Assets 26	14624	0	108	794	3161	6261	15043	33487	68906	158575	360883	1006411	6062552
Notes and Loans Payable 27	4886	0	65	5	2276	3853	5401	13862	23892	51489	177386	318603	1684844
All Other Liabilities 28	3938	0	25	46	580	1816	3262	6794	15845	44494	95797	174983	1877972
Net Worth 29	5800	0	17	743	305	592	6380	12830	29170	62593	87700	512824	2499735

Selected Financial Ratios (Times to 1)

Current Ratio 30	1.7	•	0.8	5.7	1.7	1.1	2.3	1.5	1.4	1.5	1.4	1.8	1.9
Quick Ratio 31	0.7	•	0.5	4.2	1.2	0.7	1.3	0.7	0.6	0.7	0.6	0.4	0.7
Net Sales to Working Capital 32	13.4	•	•	7.6	15.8	55.1	13.0	18.1	17.7	14.9	14.1	10.6	12.1
Coverage Ratio 33	2.0	438.2	1.4	33.1	5.4	•	4.6	3.7	1.6	3.1	1.8	•	2.1
Total Asset Turnover 34	2.4	•	8.7	2.1	2.3	2.6	3.9	3.1	2.8	2.5	1.9	1.9	2.3
Inventory Turnover 35	9.8	•	580.8	16.7	23.5	23.7	18.2	11.8	9.7	8.9	7.4	6.3	10.0
Receivables Turnover 36	17.7	•	76.0	15.9	14.6	12.8	16.6	16.7	14.7	15.4	13.9	15.1	20.4
Total Liabilities to Net Worth 37	1.5	•	5.2	0.1	9.4	9.6	1.4	1.6	1.4	1.5	3.1	1.0	1.4
Current Assets to Working Capital 38	2.4	•	•	1.2	2.4	10.4	1.8	3.0	3.4	2.8	3.8	2.3	2.1
Current Liabilities to Working Capital 39	1.4	•	•	0.2	1.4	9.4	0.8	2.0	2.4	1.8	2.8	1.3	1.1
Working Capital to Net Sales 40	0.1	•	•	0.1	0.1	0.0	0.1	0.1	0.1	0.1	0.1	0.1	0.1
Inventory to Working Capital 41	1.2	•	•	0.3	0.5	1.6	0.6	1.4	1.6	1.3	2.0	1.1	1.2
Total Receipts to Cash Flow 42	20.8	13.6	10.1	11.6	9.3	18.8	15.9	15.7	22.5	17.7	20.1	20.4	26.8
Cost of Goods to Cash Flow 43	18.1	12.0	7.9	7.7	6.8	15.7	13.2	13.2	15.1	17.0	16.5		24.3
Cash Flow to Total Debt 44	0.2	•	1.0	2.7	0.3	0.2	0.4	0.3	0.2	0.1	0.2	0.2	0.1

Selected Financial Factors (in Percentages)

Debt Ratio 45	60.3	•	83.8	6.5	90.3	90.5	57.6	61.7	57.7	60.5	75.7	49.0	58.8
Return on Total Assets 46	4.2	•	5.8	1.0	11.7	•	9.1	8.4	3.7	5.5	4.9	•	4.4
Return on Equity Before Income Taxes 47	5.2	•	10.7	1.1	98.5	•	16.8	16.0	3.2	9.4	9.0	•	5.6
Return on Equity After Income Taxes 48	3.5	•	9.8	0.9	94.7	•	14.0	14.6	2.2	8.1	4.9	•	3.7
Profit Margin (Before Income Tax) 49	0.9	10.0	0.2	0.5	4.2	•	1.8	2.0	0.5	1.5	1.2	•	1.0
Profit Margin (After Income Tax) 50	0.6	6.6	0.2	0.4	4.0	•	1.5	1.8	0.3	1.3	0.6	•	0.7

45

Table II

Corporations with Net Income

MEAT AND SEAFOOD PROCESSING

MONEY AMOUNTS AND SIZE OF ASSETS IN THOUSANDS OF DOLLARS

Item Description for Accounting Period 7/08 Through 6/09	Total	Zero Assets	Under 500	500 to 1,000	1,000 to 5,000	5,000 to 10,000	10,000 to 25,000	25,000 to 50,000	50,000 to 100,000	100,000 to 250,000	250,000 to 500,000	500,000 to 2,500,000	2,500,000 and over
Number of Enterprises **1**	1821	8	1273	59	271	•	89	42	22	18	8	0	•
Revenues ($ in Thousands)													
Net Sales **2**	75206438	349921	1684141	148188	1880717	•	5259535	4936550	4612457	7352538	5262338	0	•
Interest **3**	63355	35	0	19	3833	•	3103	2863	396	5854	4750	0	•
Rents **4**	13993	0	0	0	856	•	753	954	69	185	2885	0	•
Royalties **5**	1407	0	0	0	0	•	0	0	0	0	234	0	•
Other Portfolio Income **6**	196953	23817	0	281	8134	•	330	12961	2238	25444	4808	0	•
Other Receipts **7**	373219	664	0	79	5263	•	4001	12829	9156	34453	54414	0	•
Total Receipts **8**	75855365	374437	1684141	148567	1898803	•	5267722	4966157	4624316	7418474	5329429	0	•
Average Total Receipts **9**	41656	46805	1323	2518	7007	•	59188	118242	210196	412137	666179	•	•
Operating Costs/Operating Income (%)													
Cost of Operations **10**	87.0	88.3	79.8	73.2	71.7	•	81.6	84.4	82.7	82.7	78.5	•	•
Salaries and Wages **11**	2.4	3.2	2.4	1.9	4.4	•	3.6	3.1	3.4	2.6	3.6	•	•
Taxes Paid **12**	0.4	0.3	0.5	1.7	1.2	•	0.6	0.5	0.4	0.5	0.7	•	•
Interest Paid **13**	0.7	0.0	0.4	0.0	1.0	•	0.4	0.5	0.6	0.6	1.3	•	•
Depreciation **14**	1.7	1.1	1.2	1.7	2.5	•	1.5	1.6	1.9	2.6	3.3	•	•
Amortization and Depletion **15**	•	•	0.5	•	0.0	•	0.1	0.1	0.0	0.1	0.3	•	•
Pensions and Other Deferred Comp. **16**	0.3	0.1	•	0.1	0.6	•	0.2	0.1	0.1	0.1	0.3	•	•
Employee Benefits **17**	0.4	0.5	•	0.9	1.8	•	1.1	0.6	1.1	0.7	1.2	•	•
Advertising **18**	0.5	0.0	1.6	5.1	0.4	•	0.7	0.5	1.9	0.8	0.3	•	•
Other Expenses **19**	4.5	3.5	11.5	12.0	7.8	•	6.5	5.5	4.6	4.9	7.4	•	•
Officers' Compensation **20**	0.4	0.0	0.6	2.9	3.0	•	0.8	0.5	0.5	0.8	0.5	•	•
Operating Margin **21**	1.7	3.0	1.4	0.5	5.6	•	3.1	2.6	2.7	3.6	2.7	•	•
Operating Margin Before Officers' Comp. **22**	2.1	3.0	2.0	3.4	8.6	•	3.8	3.2	3.2	4.4	3.2	•	•

Selected Average Balance Sheet ($ in Thousands)

Net Receivables 23	2338	0	0	224	409	•	3164	7512	15485	21601	43192
Inventories 24	3760	0	0	93	204	•	3029	8489	20004	42451	63672
Net Property, Plant and Equipment 25	5327	0	38	150	1427	•	5261	10271	24093	70145	148346
Total Assets 26	15886	0	148	688	3256	•	15219	35349	70829	161825	375583
Notes and Loans Payable 27	4443	0	73	10	1177	•	4258	12942	21673	42167	165470
All Other Liabilities 28	4652	0	36	61	360	•	2656	6130	17109	44562	85149
Net Worth 29	6791	0	40	617	1719	•	8305	16278	32048	75096	124964

Selected Financial Ratios (Times to 1)

Current Ratio 30	1.8	•	0.6	6.6	1.9	•	2.9	1.7	1.5	1.7	1.3
Quick Ratio 31	0.8	•	0.1	4.8	1.4	•	1.6	0.8	0.7	0.8	0.6
Net Sales to Working Capital 32	14.1	•	•	7.3	12.0	•	11.4	13.7	15.3	13.0	19.6
Coverage Ratio 33	4.7	438.2	4.2	39.5	7.9	•	8.4	7.5	5.6	8.7	4.1
Total Asset Turnover 34	2.6	•	8.9	3.6	2.1	•	3.9	3.3	3.0	2.5	1.8
Inventory Turnover 35	9.6	•	3390.9	19.7	24.4	•	15.9	11.7	8.7	8.0	8.1
Receivables Turnover 36	16.4	•	1424.8	•	15.2	•	17.0	16.0	13.7	13.6	•
Total Liabilities to Net Worth 37	1.3	•	2.7	0.1	0.9	•	0.8	1.2	1.2	1.2	2.0
Current Assets to Working Capital 38	2.3	•	•	1.2	2.1	•	1.5	2.3	3.0	2.4	4.2
Current Liabilities to Working Capital 39	1.3	•	•	0.2	1.1	•	0.5	1.3	2.0	1.4	3.2
Working Capital to Net Sales 40	0.1	•	•	0.1	0.1	•	0.1	0.1	0.1	0.1	0.1
Inventory to Working Capital 41	1.1	•	•	0.3	0.5	•	0.5	1.1	1.4	1.1	1.9
Total Receipts to Cash Flow 42	16.4	13.6	10.5	13.1	8.3	•	11.8	12.7	14.9	12.8	9.9
Cost of Goods to Cash Flow 43	14.2	12.0	8.4	9.6	5.9	•	9.6	10.7	12.3	10.6	7.7
Cash Flow to Total Debt 44	0.3	•	1.2	2.7	0.5	•	0.7	0.5	0.4	0.4	0.3

Selected Financial Factors (in Percentages)

Debt Ratio 45	57.3	•	73.2	10.3	47.2	•	45.4	54.0	54.8	53.6	66.7
Return on Total Assets 46	8.6	•	16.2	2.8	16.1	•	14.3	12.7	10.7	12.8	9.1
Return on Equity Before Income Taxes 47	15.8	•	46.2	3.1	26.6	•	23.1	23.8	19.4	24.5	20.6
Return on Equity After Income Taxes 48	13.3	•	45.5	2.5	25.7	•	20.2	22.2	17.9	22.7	16.7
Profit Margin (Before Income Tax) 49	2.6	10.0	1.4	0.8	6.6	•	3.2	3.3	3.0	4.5	3.9
Profit Margin (After Income Tax) 50	2.2	6.6	1.4	0.6	6.4	•	2.8	3.1	2.7	4.2	3.2

Table I

Corporations with and without Net Income

BAKERIES AND TORTILLA

MONEY AMOUNTS AND SIZE OF ASSETS IN THOUSANDS OF DOLLARS

Item Description for Accounting Period 7/08 Through 6/09	Total	Zero Assets	Under 500	500 to 1,000	1,000 to 5,000	5,000 to 10,000	10,000 to 25,000	25,000 to 50,000	50,000 to 100,000	100,000 to 250,000	250,000 to 500,000	500,000 to 2,500,000	2,500,000 and over
Number of Enterprises **1**	3895	475	2782	0	317	115	119	34	22	11	8	12	0
Revenues ($ in Thousands)													
Net Sales **2**	45261656	1132181	1011231	0	1186861	1886940	3885392	2152575	2942352	2384981	5313086	23366057	0
Interest **3**	61674	108	44	0	251	321	2134	494	810	1878	6819	48817	0
Rents **4**	12178	47	3179	0	67	769	0	250	85	231	32	7517	0
Royalties **5**	91882	0	0	0	0	0	146	0	1	32820	6038	52878	0
Other Portfolio Income **6**	831664	47643	6482	0	326	9455	3328	1815	4433	402	37251	720528	0
Other Receipts **7**	1957196	8860	1147	0	13957	4404	13254	3155	14607	48628	21896	1827287	0
Total Receipts **8**	48216250	1188839	1022083	0	1201462	1901889	3904254	2158289	2962288	2468940	5385122	26023084	0
Average Total Receipts **9**	12379	2503	367	•	3790	16538	32809	63479	134649	224449	673140	2168590	•
Operating Costs/Operating Income (%)													
Cost of Operations **10**	65.7	72.4	42.7	•	57.2	77.5	73.5	68.6	66.9	65.8	72.9	62.5	•
Salaries and Wages **11**	7.8	7.9	18.1	•	8.8	2.3	5.1	8.3	10.1	9.4	6.9	8.0	•
Taxes Paid **12**	1.7	1.3	3.9	•	2.1	0.5	1.3	1.1	1.6	1.5	1.0	1.9	•
Interest Paid **13**	1.8	1.8	1.9	•	0.5	0.9	0.6	1.3	0.9	1.6	1.2	2.4	•
Depreciation **14**	3.1	2.8	2.9	•	3.5	3.8	2.8	4.6	3.7	4.4	2.5	2.8	•
Amortization and Depletion **15**	0.6	1.0	0.4	•	0.4	0.1	0.1	0.3	0.4	0.6	1.1	0.8	•
Pensions and Other Deferred Comp. **16**	1.0	0.4	0.0	•	0.3	0.1	0.5	0.5	1.3	1.8	0.2	1.3	•
Employee Benefits **17**	3.1	2.1	0.5	•	0.8	0.8	1.1	1.3	3.3	3.3	1.4	4.4	•
Advertising **18**	1.6	1.8	1.1	•	1.0	0.1	0.5	0.7	0.9	1.0	1.5	2.3	•
Other Expenses **19**	16.4	13.0	22.1	•	16.8	11.9	7.9	12.1	9.1	14.0	9.7	21.2	•
Officers' Compensation **20**	1.0	0.4	14.9	•	5.0	1.0	1.8	1.5	1.2	0.9	0.4	0.2	•
Operating Margin **21**	•	•	•	•	3.6	0.9	4.9	•	0.8	•	1.1	•	•
Operating Margin Before Officers' Comp. **22**	•	•	6.5	•	8.6	1.9	6.6	1.2	2.0	1.6	•	•	•

Selected Average Balance Sheet ($ in Thousands)

Net Receivables 23	907	0	4	•	233	1075	2540	4041	10846	21515	101133	133385	•
Inventories 24	534	0	9	•	121	564	1574	3178	5987	12383	41860	87791	•
Net Property, Plant and Equipment 25	2418	0	51	•	771	2723	6461	17640	30250	63594	93242	436696	•
Total Assets 26	7598	0	104	•	1897	6069	14663	35339	67789	135544	393014	1577641	•
Notes and Loans Payable 27	2576	0	129	•	544	3027	4966	17887	22135	48260	73528	528923	•
All Other Liabilities 28	2355	0	41	•	306	3175	3138	10557	17312	47601	129362	493805	•
Net Worth 29	2667	0	-66	•	1047	-133	6560	6895	28342	39682	190124	554914	•

Selected Financial Ratios (Times to 1)

Current Ratio 30	1.0	•	0.6	•	2.4	0.7	1.6	1.0	1.2	1.0	1.5	0.8	•
Quick Ratio 31	0.6	•	0.4	•	1.2	0.5	1.0	0.6	0.8	0.7	1.0	0.5	•
Net Sales to Working Capital 32	•	1.0	•	•	7.7	•	13.4	288.3	30.3	139.4	9.7	•	•
Coverage Ratio 33	3.3	•	•	•	10.4	2.9	10.1	0.9	2.6	0.5	3.0	3.6	•
Total Asset Turnover 34	1.5	•	3.5	•	2.0	2.7	2.2	1.8	2.0	1.6	1.7	1.2	•
Inventory Turnover 35	14.3	•	16.7	•	17.7	22.6	15.3	13.7	14.9	11.5	11.6	13.9	•
Receivables Turnover 36	13.4	•	29.5	•	21.8	18.3	12.9	15.1	12.0	11.0	7.3	15.0	•
Total Liabilities to Net Worth 37	1.8	•	•	•	0.8	1.2	1.2	4.1	1.4	2.4	1.1	1.8	•
Current Assets to Working Capital 38	•	•	•	•	1.7	•	2.6	45.1	5.2	29.8	2.9	•	•
Current Liabilities to Working Capital 39	•	•	•	•	0.7	•	1.6	44.1	4.2	28.8	1.9	•	•
Working Capital to Net Sales 40	•	•	•	•	0.1	•	0.1	0.0	0.0	0.0	0.1	•	•
Inventory to Working Capital 41	•	•	•	•	0.3	•	0.7	15.8	1.2	7.6	0.7	•	•
Total Receipts to Cash Flow 42	6.2	21.8	15.4	•	6.1	9.9	8.6	10.4	12.9	9.9	9.6	4.6	•
Cost of Goods to Cash Flow 43	4.1	15.8	6.6	•	3.5	7.7	6.3	7.1	8.6	6.5	7.0	2.9	•
Cash Flow to Total Debt 44	0.4	•	0.1	•	0.7	0.3	0.5	0.2	0.3	0.2	0.3	0.4	•

Selected Financial Factors (in Percentages)

Debt Ratio 45	64.9	•	162.9	•	44.8	102.2	55.3	80.5	58.2	70.7	51.6	64.8	•
Return on Total Assets 46	8.9	•	•	•	10.6	6.9	13.2	2.2	4.7	1.4	6.3	10.6	•
Return on Equity Before Income Taxes 47	17.6	•	40.4	•	17.4	•	26.6	•	6.8	•	8.7	21.8	•
Return on Equity After Income Taxes 48	11.9	•	40.4	•	17.1	•	24.7	•	5.5	•	7.5	13.7	•
Profit Margin (Before Income Tax) 49	4.0	0.0	•	•	4.9	1.7	5.3	•	1.4	•	2.5	6.2	•
Profit Margin (After Income Tax) 50	2.7	•	•	•	4.8	1.6	5.0	•	1.2	•	2.1	3.9	•

Table II

Corporations with Net Income

BAKERIES AND TORTILLA

MONEY AMOUNTS AND SIZE OF ASSETS IN THOUSANDS OF DOLLARS

Item Description for Accounting Period 7/08 Through 6/09	Total	Zero Assets	Under 500	500 to 1,000	1,000 to 5,000	5,000 to 10,000	10,000 to 25,000	25,000 to 50,000	50,000 to 100,000	100,000 to 250,000	250,000 to 500,000	500,000 to 2,500,000	2,500,000 and over
Number of Enterprises **1**	1025	•	687	0	133	•	87	16	15	•	8	7	0
Revenues ($ in Thousands)													
Net Sales **2**	33801079	•	383948	0	739744	•	2890874	904977	2332795	•	5313086	17778291	0
Interest **3**	48355	•	0	0	102	•	1809	13	610	•	6819	38092	0
Rents **4**	11617	•	3179	0	67	•	0	0	52	•	32	7517	0
Royalties **5**	55529	•	0	0	0	•	146	0	1	•	6038	49344	0
Other Portfolio Income **6**	783450	•	0	0	50	•	3328	1577	4178	•	37251	715694	0
Other Receipts **7**	242024	•	833	0	1598	•	10082	1682	11073	•	21896	179481	0
Total Receipts **8**	34942054	•	387960	0	741561	•	2906239	908249	2348709	•	5385122	18768419	0
Average Total Receipts **9**	34090	•	565	•	5576	•	33405	56766	156581	•	673140	2681203	•
Operating Costs/Operating Income (%)													
Cost of Operations **10**	65.9	•	39.6	•	53.1	•	69.4	67.9	64.8	•	72.9	64.0	•
Salaries and Wages **11**	6.8	•	17.6	•	7.9	•	5.5	6.1	10.5	•	6.9	6.3	•
Taxes Paid **12**	1.5	•	4.6	•	1.6	•	1.3	0.6	1.6	•	1.0	1.8	•
Interest Paid **13**	1.8	•	2.5	•	0.7	•	0.5	1.5	0.8	•	1.2	2.4	•
Depreciation **14**	2.9	•	0.8	•	2.7	•	2.8	4.3	3.1	•	2.5	3.0	•
Amortization and Depletion **15**	0.6	•	0.7	•	0.1	•	0.1	0.1	0.2	•	1.1	0.6	•
Pensions and Other Deferred Comp. **16**	0.8	•	0.0	•	0.3	•	0.7	0.3	1.4	•	0.2	1.0	•
Employee Benefits **17**	2.7	•	1.1	•	0.6	•	1.3	1.6	3.5	•	1.4	3.4	•
Advertising **18**	1.7	•	0.7	•	0.9	•	0.5	0.5	0.9	•	1.5	2.3	•
Other Expenses **19**	13.0	•	21.7	•	13.2	•	8.7	10.8	9.2	•	9.7	15.1	•
Officers' Compensation **20**	0.7	•	8.9	•	2.8	•	1.7	2.4	1.4	•	0.4	0.2	•
Operating Margin **21**	1.7	•	1.8	•	16.3	•	7.5	4.0	2.7	•	1.1	•	•
Operating Margin Before Officers' Comp. **22**	2.5	•	10.8	•	19.1	•	9.2	6.4	4.1	•	1.6	0.1	•

Selected Average Balance Sheet ($ in Thousands)

Net Receivables 23	2713	0	336	2482	3121	13053	101133	181029
Inventories 24	1591	16	179	1364	2958	6055	35914	132423
Net Property, Plant and Equipment 25	6716	56	1009	5774	18018	28079	93242	599390
Total Assets 26	21548	100	1985	14271	30509	69663	393014	2092845
Notes and Loans Payable 27	6590	209	634	3654	18500	20017	73528	671479
All Other Liabilities 28	6603	106	333	2781	7016	19461	129362	663321
Net Worth 29	8355	-215	1018	7836	4994	30186	190124	758045

Selected Financial Ratios (Times to 1)

Current Ratio 30	1.0	0.3	1.9	1.9	1.1	1.3	1.5	0.7
Quick Ratio 31	0.6	0.2	1.4	1.2	0.6	0.9	1.0	0.4
Net Sales to Working Capital 32	•	•	15.0	11.0	54.1	25.7	9.7	•
Coverage Ratio 33	5.0	2.2	25.9	16.2	3.9	5.4	3.0	4.7
Total Asset Turnover 34	1.5	5.6	2.8	2.3	1.9	2.2	1.7	1.2
Inventory Turnover 35	13.6	14.1	16.4	16.9	13.0	16.6	13.5	12.3
Receivables Turnover 36	12.9	60.1	21.0	13.8	13.1	•	8.1	14.2
Total Liabilities to Net Worth 37	1.6	•	0.9	0.8	5.1	1.3	1.1	1.8
Current Assets to Working Capital 38	•	•	2.1	2.1	8.0	4.5	2.9	•
Current Liabilities to Working Capital 39	•	•	1.1	1.1	7.0	3.5	1.9	•
Working Capital to Net Sales 40	•	•	0.1	0.1	0.0	0.0	0.1	•
Inventory to Working Capital 41	•	•	0.5	0.5	2.6	1.0	0.7	•
Total Receipts to Cash Flow 42	6.6	6.8	3.9	6.7	7.7	10.3	9.6	5.7
Cost of Goods to Cash Flow 43	4.3	2.7	2.1	4.6	5.2	6.6	7.0	3.7
Cash Flow to Total Debt 44	0.4	0.3	1.5	0.8	0.3	0.4	0.3	0.3

Selected Financial Factors (in Percentages)

Debt Ratio 45	61.2	314.8	48.7	45.1	83.6	56.7	51.6	63.8
Return on Total Assets 46	13.3	30.1	48.2	19.8	10.8	9.2	6.3	13.8
Return on Equity Before Income Taxes 47	27.5	•	90.3	33.9	49.0	17.2	8.7	29.9
Return on Equity After Income Taxes 48	20.5	•	89.5	31.8	48.9	15.5	7.5	19.7
Profit Margin (Before Income Tax) 49	7.0	2.9	16.5	8.0	4.3	3.3	2.5	8.9
Profit Margin (After Income Tax) 50	5.2	2.9	16.4	7.5	4.3	3.0	2.1	5.9

Table I

Corporations with and without Net Income

OTHER FOOD

MONEY AMOUNTS AND SIZE OF ASSETS IN THOUSANDS OF DOLLARS

Item Description for Accounting Period 7/08 Through 6/09	Total	Zero Assets	Under 500	500 to 1,000	1,000 to 5,000	5,000 to 10,000	10,000 to 25,000	25,000 to 50,000	50,000 to 100,000	100,000 to 250,000	250,000 to 500,000	500,000 to 2,500,000	2,500,000 and over
Number of Enterprises 1	4228	959	1853	313	609	144	180	73	38	32	17	7	4
Revenues ($ in Thousands)													
Net Sales 2	119027056	338896	192866	661361	3934329	2539700	5837409	5477136	5171750	8221332	8303433	8763034	69585811
Interest 3	2533491	245	9	187	575	1174	2827	13821	5962	8924	36952	21488	2441327
Rents 4	97720	0	0	0	263	0	950	258	3603	805	16584	2127	73129
Royalties 5	913759	0	0	0	0	1215	0	484	31140	15206	8056	676	856982
Other Portfolio Income 6	398082	204	0	0	27143	6561	1027	874	25479	17347	31139	70144	218166
Other Receipts 7	434101	3004	0	390	25596	6740	47643	37811	28626	21198	100142	153569	9381
Total Receipts 8	123404209	342349	192875	661938	3987906	2555390	5889856	5530384	5266560	8284812	8496306	9011038	73184796
Average Total Receipts 9	29187	357	104	2115	6548	17746	32721	75759	138594	258900	499783	1287291	18296199
Operating Costs/Operating Income (%)													
Cost of Operations 10	71.2	76.1	23.2	75.7	73.8	69.7	73.9	77.5	70.7	71.0	71.9	75.0	70.0
Salaries and Wages 11	5.5	3.3	12.7	3.2	7.5	8.4	6.4	4.8	5.8	5.8	6.8	4.6	5.1
Taxes Paid 12	1.1	1.4	3.7	3.7	1.3	1.4	1.0	0.7	1.0	1.0	0.9	0.8	1.2
Interest Paid 13	4.2	1.8	19.7	0.7	0.9	0.9	0.9	1.2	1.5	2.0	1.5	2.9	6.0
Depreciation 14	2.3	1.0	7.2	0.8	1.6	2.6	3.3	2.0	2.4	2.6	3.3	2.9	2.0
Amortization and Depletion 15	0.4	0.3	0.6	0.0	0.1	0.0	0.0	0.2	0.7	0.6	0.5	1.3	0.4
Pensions and Other Deferred Comp. 16	1.1	0.0	0.8	•	0.3	0.4	0.2	0.3	0.3	0.3	0.4	0.7	1.6
Employee Benefits 17	1.2	0.2	•	0.4	1.0	0.8	1.1	1.2	1.3	1.2	1.0	1.8	1.2
Advertising 18	3.3	4.9	5.8	0.3	0.5	0.6	1.1	0.9	2.2	3.3	2.6	0.5	4.4
Other Expenses 19	9.7	11.4	39.5	8.6	9.0	9.5	8.5	7.8	9.9	10.9	9.6	9.8	9.7
Officers' Compensation 20	0.5	1.4	2.4	3.3	2.7	3.6	1.3	1.0	1.0	1.0	0.8	0.4	0.1
Operating Margin 21	•	•	•	3.2	1.3	2.1	2.4	2.5	3.2	0.2	0.8	•	•
Operating Margin Before Officers' Comp. 22	•	•	•	6.6	4.1	5.6	3.7	3.4	4.1	1.3	1.6	•	•

Selected Average Balance Sheet ($ in Thousands)

Net Receivables 23	71292	0	4	42	531	1614	3345	6931	11230	21243	42764	155524	74203951
Inventories 24	2150	0	4	71	490	1669	3441	8547	14937	27537	49297	163906	961142
Net Property, Plant and Equipment 25	4617	0	49	227	710	2457	5576	8202	21999	38979	101421	291809	2780436
Total Assets 26	116512	0	78	807	2360	7105	16041	33919	73868	159437	346458	1230838	115494740
Notes and Loans Payable 27	11524	0	78	154	875	3758	5780	11028	26233	63459	98797	550347	9262571
All Other Liabilities 28	78887	0	16	185	732	2150	3313	10768	18545	42891	94766	385699	81230378
Net Worth 29	26101	0	-17	468	754	1196	6948	12123	29090	53087	152894	294793	25001791

Selected Financial Ratios (Times to 1)

Current Ratio 30	1.0	•	0.9	1.0	1.7	1.5	2.0	1.5	1.8	1.5	1.9	1.7	1.0
Quick Ratio 31	0.9	•	0.7	1.0	0.9	0.7	1.0	0.6	0.9	0.6	0.8	0.8	0.9
Net Sales to Working Capital 32	•	•	•	292.1	10.1	13.1	7.1	12.4	9.1	11.3	7.1	8.1	•
Coverage Ratio 33	1.8	0.6	0.2	5.5	3.9	4.1	4.8	3.9	4.3	1.5	3.0	1.8	1.6
Total Asset Turnover 34	0.2	•	1.3	2.6	2.7	2.5	2.0	2.2	1.8	1.6	1.4	1.0	0.2
Inventory Turnover 35	9.3	•	5.9	22.5	9.7	7.4	7.0	6.8	6.4	6.6	7.1	5.7	12.7
Receivables Turnover 36	0.4	•	•	32.2	15.1	9.9	10.5	12.9	12.0	12.1	12.2	8.9	0.3
Total Liabilities to Net Worth 37	3.5	•	•	0.7	2.1	4.9	1.3	1.8	1.5	2.0	1.3	3.2	3.6
Current Assets to Working Capital 38	•	•	•	26.6	2.4	3.0	2.0	3.2	2.3	3.2	2.2	2.5	•
Current Liabilities to Working Capital 39	•	•	•	25.6	1.4	2.0	1.0	2.2	1.3	2.2	1.2	1.5	•
Working Capital to Net Sales 40	•	•	•	0.0	0.1	0.1	0.1	0.1	0.1	0.1	0.1	0.1	•
Inventory to Working Capital 41	•	•	•	2.1	1.0	1.2	0.9	1.6	1.0	1.3	0.8	1.0	•
Total Receipts to Cash Flow 42	9.3	11.7	10.0	12.5	10.5	9.6	10.0	10.7	7.7	11.4	10.1	9.6	8.8
Cost of Goods to Cash Flow 43	6.6	8.9	2.3	9.4	7.7	6.7	7.4	8.3	5.4	8.1	7.3	7.2	6.2
Cash Flow to Total Debt 44	0.0	•	0.1	0.5	0.4	0.3	0.4	0.3	0.4	0.2	0.2	0.1	0.0

Selected Financial Factors (in Percentages)

Debt Ratio 45	77.6	•	121.5	42.0	68.1	83.2	56.7	64.3	60.6	66.7	55.9	76.0	78.4
Return on Total Assets 46	1.8	•	5.6	10.6	10.0	8.9	8.4	10.2	12.0	4.8	6.6	5.3	1.5
Return on Equity Before Income Taxes 47	3.6	•	96.8	14.9	23.2	39.9	15.3	21.2	23.5	4.8	10.0	10.0	2.7
Return on Equity After Income Taxes 48	2.5	•	110.9	14.9	21.2	33.9	14.2	19.8	18.8	2.5	5.3	5.6	1.7
Profit Margin (Before Income Tax) 49	3.4	•	•	3.3	2.7	2.7	3.3	3.4	5.0	1.0	3.1	2.4	3.8
Profit Margin (After Income Tax) 50	2.3	•	•	3.3	2.5	2.3	3.0	3.2	4.0	0.5	1.7	1.3	2.5

Table II

Corporations with Net Income

OTHER FOOD

MONEY AMOUNTS AND SIZE OF ASSETS IN THOUSANDS OF DOLLARS

Item Description for Accounting Period 7/08 Through 6/09		Total	Zero Assets	Under 500	500 to 1,000	1,000 to 5,000	5,000 to 10,000	10,000 to 25,000	25,000 to 50,000	50,000 to 100,000	100,000 to 250,000	250,000 to 500,000	500,000 to 2,500,000	2,500,000 and over
Number of Enterprises	1	1247	15	57	296	505	101	152	54	29	19	10	•	•
Revenues ($ in Thousands)														
Net Sales	2	106997353	308250	63585	658598	3322762	2300329	5109069	4563588	4259680	5145897	6042834	•	•
Interest	3	2525647	0	8	0	425	1103	2281	13683	5246	6764	34222	•	•
Rents	4	81420	0	0	0	263	0	931	199	2078	266	2426	•	•
Royalties	5	893634	0	0	0	0	1215	0	0	31095	3654	49	•	•
Other Portfolio Income	6	363305	0	0	0	27076	266	796	870	25428	11059	18660	•	•
Other Receipts	7	295498	-1444	0	377	24765	1828	36289	38515	26254	6815	76638	•	•
Total Receipts	8	111156857	306806	63593	658975	3375291	2304741	5149366	4616855	4349781	5174455	6174829	•	•
Average Total Receipts	9	89139	20454	1116	2226	6684	22819	33877	85497	149992	272340	617483	•	•
Operating Costs/Operating Income (%)														
Cost of Operations	10	70.6	76.0	29.4	75.9	75.2	69.4	72.4	76.9	69.9	66.9	72.0	•	•
Salaries and Wages	11	5.3	2.4	0.8	3.1	6.7	7.7	5.9	5.0	5.5	6.1	5.5	•	•
Taxes Paid	12	1.1	1.4	3.5	3.6	1.2	1.3	0.9	0.7	1.0	1.0	0.9	•	•
Interest Paid	13	4.3	0.6	0.0	0.7	0.9	0.8	0.8	1.1	1.3	1.5	1.4	•	•
Depreciation	14	2.2	0.7	3.0	0.8	1.4	1.9	3.0	1.6	2.3	3.0	3.1	•	•
Amortization and Depletion	15	0.3	0.0	•	0.0	0.0	0.0	0.0	0.1	0.5	0.3	0.5	•	•
Pensions and Other Deferred Comp.	16	1.2	0.0	2.3	•	0.3	0.4	0.2	0.4	0.4	0.4	0.3	•	•
Employee Benefits	17	1.2	0.2	•	0.4	0.9	0.7	1.1	1.4	1.2	1.0	1.1	•	•
Advertising	18	3.4	0.6	1.0	0.3	0.5	0.6	1.0	0.7	2.4	4.5	2.2	•	•
Other Expenses	19	9.5	5.1	36.0	8.5	7.5	8.9	8.8	7.5	9.8	8.1	8.5	•	•
Officers' Compensation	20	0.5	0.5	2.5	2.9	2.7	3.5	1.3	1.1	1.1	0.9	0.7	•	•
Operating Margin	21	0.2	12.3	21.4	3.6	2.7	4.6	4.5	3.5	4.9	6.3	3.9	•	•
Operating Margin Before Officers' Comp.	22	0.7	12.8	24.0	6.5	5.4	8.1	5.8	4.6	5.9	7.2	4.6	•	•

Selected Average Balance Sheet ($ in Thousands)

Net Receivables 23	240932	0	120	44	546	1923	3496	7477	12200	23948	53668
Inventories 24	6048	0	46	56	491	1918	3111	8352	16397	31357	49646
Net Property, Plant and Equipment 25	13707	0	53	240	687	2661	5394	8136	23049	44803	113896
Total Assets 26	386232	0	416	802	2351	7382	16006	34151	74900	153891	373146
Notes and Loans Payable 27	34598	0	1	163	742	2947	5029	10202	23020	61869	88466
All Other Liabilities 28	265017	0	99	196	766	2603	2957	9437	19946	43134	85756
Net Worth 29	86618	0	316	443	843	1833	8020	14512	31934	48888	198924

Selected Financial Ratios (Times to 1)

Current Ratio 30	1.0	•	3.9	1.0	1.7	1.3	2.2	1.6	2.0	1.7	2.2
Quick Ratio 31	0.9	•	3.6	0.9	0.9	0.7	1.2	0.7	1.1	0.8	1.1
Net Sales to Working Capital 32	•	•	4.6	•	10.4	20.8	6.5	10.8	7.7	8.2	6.4
Coverage Ratio 33	2.0	19.5	2273.8	5.9	5.8	7.0	7.9	5.4	6.6	5.5	5.5
Total Asset Turnover 34	0.2	•	2.7	2.8	2.8	3.1	2.1	2.5	2.0	1.8	1.6
Inventory Turnover 35	10.0	•	7.1	30.3	10.1	8.2	7.8	7.8	6.3	5.8	8.8
Receivables Turnover 36	0.4	•	6.4	39.8	14.6	10.3	10.9	13.5	12.4	10.2	12.2
Total Liabilities to Net Worth 37	3.5	•	0.3	0.8	1.8	3.0	1.0	1.4	1.3	2.1	0.9
Current Assets to Working Capital 38	•	•	1.4	•	2.5	3.9	1.8	2.6	2.0	2.3	1.8
Current Liabilities to Working Capital 39	•	•	0.4	•	1.5	2.9	0.8	1.6	1.0	1.3	0.8
Working Capital to Net Sales 40	•	•	0.2	•	0.1	0.0	0.2	0.1	0.1	0.1	0.2
Inventory to Working Capital 41	•	•	0.1	•	1.0	1.6	0.8	1.2	0.8	1.0	0.6
Total Receipts to Cash Flow 42	8.4	6.3	1.9	12.2	10.3	8.2	8.0	9.7	6.7	7.5	8.2
Cost of Goods to Cash Flow 43	6.0	4.8	0.6	9.2	7.8	5.7	5.8	7.4	4.7	5.0	5.9
Cash Flow to Total Debt 44	0.0	•	5.9	0.5	0.4	0.5	0.5	0.4	0.5	0.3	0.4

Selected Financial Factors (in Percentages)

Debt Ratio 45	77.6	•	24.0	44.7	64.1	75.2	49.9	57.5	57.4	68.2	46.7
Return on Total Assets 46	2.0	•	57.5	12.1	14.5	17.3	12.7	14.3	16.2	14.6	12.2
Return on Equity Before Income Taxes 47	4.5	•	75.6	18.2	33.5	59.9	22.2	27.4	32.3	37.7	18.7
Return on Equity After Income Taxes 48	3.3	•	51.4	18.2	31.4	54.3	21.1	25.8	26.7	33.5	12.5
Profit Margin (Before Income Tax) 49	4.5	11.8	21.4	3.6	4.3	4.8	5.3	4.7	7.0	6.8	6.1
Profit Margin (After Income Tax) 50	3.3	11.8	14.6	3.6	4.0	4.4	5.0	4.4	5.8	6.0	4.1

Table I

Corporations with and without Net Income

SOFT DRINK AND ICE

MONEY AMOUNTS AND SIZE OF ASSETS IN THOUSANDS OF DOLLARS

Item Description for Accounting Period 7/08 Through 6/09	Total	Zero Assets	Under 500	500 to 1,000	1,000 to 5,000	5,000 to 10,000	10,000 to 25,000	25,000 to 50,000	50,000 to 100,000	100,000 to 250,000	250,000 to 500,000	500,000 to 2,500,000	2,500,000 and over
Number of Enterprises **1**	225	•	0	•	46	•	29	22	16	12	9	4	6
Revenues ($ in Thousands)													
Net Sales **2**	56660912	•	0	•	265421	•	1256505	1703872	1954684	2928696	3856594	3343293	40346263
Interest **3**	643717	•	0	•	245	•	469	857	1692	9790	10185	2329	617897
Rents **4**	46477	•	0	•	0	•	238	0	137	1247	4736	230	39881
Royalties **5**	1504844	•	0	•	0	•	0	0	0	0	11056	10	1493777
Other Portfolio Income **6**	1361361	•	0	•	5823	•	4299	520	514	10804	2894	1285	1315490
Other Receipts **7**	1876159	•	0	•	436	•	23617	4633	9606	51832	67052	75065	1607049
Total Receipts **8**	62093470	•	0	•	271925	•	1285128	1709882	1966633	3002369	3952517	3422212	45420357
Average Total Receipts **9**	275971	•	•	•	5911	•	44315	77722	122915	250197	439169	855553	7570060
Operating Costs/Operating Income (%)													
Cost of Operations **10**	52.3	•	•	•	60.3	•	76.0	70.7	63.8	72.7	57.2	57.8	47.3
Salaries and Wages **11**	12.1	•	•	•	13.1	•	8.4	6.5	9.2	8.1	13.8	14.8	12.5
Taxes Paid **12**	1.6	•	•	•	2.4	•	1.1	1.4	1.2	1.3	2.3	1.6	1.6
Interest Paid **13**	3.6	•	•	•	0.4	•	0.4	1.0	1.2	1.1	3.3	2.9	4.2
Depreciation **14**	4.7	•	•	•	8.1	•	2.4	2.8	3.1	3.8	5.6	4.6	4.9
Amortization and Depletion **15**	1.0	•	•	•	0.3	•	0.1	0.0	0.4	0.9	0.6	1.5	1.2
Pensions and Other Deferred Comp. **16**	1.0	•	•	•	0.8	•	0.1	0.5	0.2	0.3	0.5	0.3	1.2
Employee Benefits **17**	2.2	•	•	•	1.7	•	0.9	2.0	1.9	1.7	2.2	3.0	2.3
Advertising **18**	7.7	•	•	•	1.8	•	1.5	7.4	2.5	0.9	2.7	0.4	9.8
Other Expenses **19**	15.7	•	•	•	16.0	•	9.4	4.5	8.2	8.1	13.1	16.9	17.4
Officers' Compensation **20**	0.4	•	•	•	9.5	•	1.2	1.5	0.8	0.5	0.6	0.6	0.2
Operating Margin **21**	•	•	•	•	•	•	•	1.6	7.4	0.5	0.6	•	•
Operating Margin Before Officers' Comp. **22**	•	•	•	•	•	•	•	3.1	8.3	1.0	•	•	•

Selected Average Balance Sheet ($ in Thousands)

Item									
Net Receivables 23	38355	418	3381	7826	12779	22172	40410	114410	1169759
Inventories 24	12496	396	2335	5501	13653	29271	36998	•	318336
Net Property, Plant and Equipment 25	62189	868	4112	8094	23194	50989	108350	241872	1781207
Total Assets 26	324391	2780	16294	38150	64405	148137	342280	776628	10392231
Notes and Loans Payable 27	157616	590	3534	18002	21753	36022	166835	470565	5120846
All Other Liabilities 28	88493	331	2911	13387	13868	31706	115027	272456	2789902
Net Worth 29	78282	1859	9848	6760	28784	80409	60417	33607	2481483

Selected Financial Ratios (Times to 1)

Item									
Current Ratio 30	0.9	•	2.3	1.4	2.6	2.2	1.6	1.8	0.8
Quick Ratio 31	0.6	•	1.4	0.9	1.7	1.5	1.1	1.2	0.6
Net Sales to Working Capital 32	•	•	10.5	18.4	8.6	9.1	13.7	8.5	•
Coverage Ratio 33	3.6	•	2.9	2.6	7.8	3.6	1.1	0.3	3.9
Total Asset Turnover 34	0.8	•	2.1	2.7	1.9	1.6	1.3	1.1	0.6
Inventory Turnover 35	10.5	•	8.8	14.1	13.8	13.0	8.4	13.1	10.0
Receivables Turnover 36	5.7	•	3.9	10.6	9.5	10.2	11.1	5.9	5.0
Total Liabilities to Net Worth 37	3.1	•	0.5	0.7	1.2	0.8	4.7	22.1	3.2
Current Assets to Working Capital 38	•	•	1.8	1.6	1.8	2.6	2.3	3.7	•
Current Liabilities to Working Capital 39	•	•	0.8	0.6	0.8	1.6	1.3	2.7	•
Working Capital to Net Sales 40	•	•	0.1	0.1	0.1	0.1	0.1	0.1	•
Inventory to Working Capital 41	•	•	0.6	0.5	1.1	0.4	0.6	•	•
Total Receipts to Cash Flow 42	4.8	121.4	12.7	20.5	6.9	10.6	9.5	8.7	3.9
Cost of Goods to Cash Flow 43	2.5	73.2	9.6	14.5	4.4	7.7	5.4	5.0	1.9
Cash Flow to Total Debt 44	0.2	•	0.1	0.5	0.3	0.2	0.1	0.5	0.2

Selected Financial Factors (in Percentages)

Item									
Debt Ratio 45	75.9	33.1	39.6	82.3	55.3	45.7	82.3	95.7	76.1
Return on Total Assets 46	9.9	•	2.8	6.0	17.4	6.7	4.7	0.9	10.8
Return on Equity Before Income Taxes 47	29.5	•	2.9	22.2	34.0	8.9	2.8	•	33.6
Return on Equity After Income Taxes 48	19.1	•	1.2	20.1	32.8	7.6	•	•	21.8
Profit Margin (Before Income Tax) 49	9.2	•	0.6	1.9	8.0	2.9	0.4	•	12.4
Profit Margin (After Income Tax) 50	5.9	•	0.3	1.8	7.7	2.5	•	•	8.1

Table II

Corporations with Net Income

SOFT DRINK AND ICE

MONEY AMOUNTS AND SIZE OF ASSETS IN THOUSANDS OF DOLLARS

Item Description for Accounting Period 7/08 Through 6/09	Total	Zero Assets	Under 500	500 to 1000	1,000 to 5,000	5,000 to 10,000	10,000 to 25,000	25,000 to 50,000	50,000 to 100,000	100,000 to 250,000	250,000 to 500,000	500,000 to 2,500,000	2,500,000 and over
Number of Enterprises 1	109	0	0	•	29	15	16	15	13	8	•	•	•
Revenues ($ in Thousands)													
Net Sales 2	36071837	0	0	•	241509	240576	836183	1072832	1705442	2127200	0	0	•
Interest 3	624697	0	0	•	71	160	56	856	1546	5126	0	0	•
Rents 4	41403	0	0	•	0	9	0	0	137	1247	0	0	•
Royalties 5	1493788	0	0	•	0	0	0	0	0	0	0	0	•
Other Portfolio Income 6	1346430	0	0	•	5796	19072	348	457	514	10146	0	0	•
Other Receipts 7	1779490	0	0	•	284	35834	16991	4268	9557	38839	0	0	•
Total Receipts 8	41357645	0	0	•	247660	295651	853578	1078413	1711196	2182558	0	0	•
Average Total Receipts 9	379428	•	•	•	8540	19710	53349	71894	132092	272820	•	•	•
Operating Costs/Operating Income (%)													
Cost of Operations 10	46.2	•	•	•	57.9	59.7	78.2	58.0	62.0	70.9	•	•	•
Salaries and Wages 11	10.7	•	•	•	10.4	14.5	5.5	8.8	9.4	8.2	•	•	•
Taxes Paid 12	1.4	•	•	•	2.1	2.4	0.9	1.6	1.2	1.4	•	•	•
Interest Paid 13	3.8	•	•	•	0.2	0.0	0.3	1.0	1.0	0.6	•	•	•
Depreciation 14	4.2	•	•	•	1.9	2.6	2.5	3.0	2.7	3.5	•	•	•
Amortization and Depletion 15	0.9	•	•	•	•	0.1	0.1	0.0	0.4	0.7	•	•	•
Pensions and Other Deferred Comp. 16	1.1	•	•	•	0.9	0.7	0.1	0.7	0.2	0.4	•	•	•
Employee Benefits 17	2.1	•	•	•	1.8	1.8	0.5	2.6	1.8	2.0	•	•	•
Advertising 18	11.5	•	•	•	1.4	6.3	1.8	11.1	2.6	0.8	•	•	•
Other Expenses 19	19.6	•	•	•	8.7	17.9	6.1	5.5	9.0	8.2	•	•	•
Officers' Compensation 20	0.4	•	•	•	9.1	0.7	0.9	2.4	0.8	0.6	•	•	•
Operating Margin 21	•	•	•	•	5.5	•	3.2	5.3	8.7	2.8	•	•	•
Operating Margin Before Officers' Comp. 22	•	•	•	•	14.6	•	4.1	7.7	9.5	3.4	•	•	•

Selected Average Balance Sheet ($ in Thousands)

Net Receivables 23	62657	595	1307	3767	7201	13534	25582
Inventories 24	20658	443	567	2536	5872	4992	11652
Net Property, Plant and Equipment 25	76729	344	2027	5104	6449	18691	45357
Total Assets 26	454499	2445	8100	16808	35701	64740	150808
Notes and Loans Payable 27	222732	102	0	1518	12772	17857	28954
All Other Liabilities 28	137577	253	931	2812	9423	13009	32032
Net Worth 29	94190	2090	7168	12478	13506	33874	89822

Selected Financial Ratios (Times to 1)

Current Ratio 30	0.9	4.2	4.0	2.5	3.1	2.5	1.8
Quick Ratio 31	0.6	2.9	3.1	1.5	2.0	1.8	1.3
Net Sales to Working Capital 32	•	10.0	5.7	12.3	6.9	8.6	11.7
Coverage Ratio 33	5.1	54.5	493.5	18.0	7.0	10.3	9.9
Total Asset Turnover 34	0.7	3.4	2.0	3.1	2.0	2.0	1.8
Inventory Turnover 35	7.4	10.9	16.9	16.1	7.1	16.3	16.2
Receivables Turnover 36	4.1	3.8	15.7	•	8.7	10.6	•
Total Liabilities to Net Worth 37	3.8	0.2	0.1	0.3	1.6	0.9	0.7
Current Assets to Working Capital 38	•	1.3	1.3	1.7	1.5	1.7	2.3
Current Liabilities to Working Capital 39	•	0.3	0.3	0.7	0.5	0.7	1.3
Working Capital to Net Sales 40	0.1	0.1	0.2	0.1	0.1	0.1	0.1
Inventory to Working Capital 41	•	0.3	0.3	0.6	0.5	0.4	0.5
Total Receipts to Cash Flow 42	3.3	7.3	5.1	9.3	10.5	6.0	8.3
Cost of Goods to Cash Flow 43	1.5	4.2	3.1	7.3	6.1	3.7	5.9
Cash Flow to Total Debt 44	0.3	3.2	3.4	1.3	0.3	0.7	0.5

Selected Financial Factors (in Percentages)

Debt Ratio 45	79.3	14.5	11.5	25.8	62.2	47.7	40.4
Return on Total Assets 46	14.0	28.0	32.1	17.3	13.5	21.1	10.5
Return on Equity Before Income Taxes 47	54.5	32.2	36.2	22.0	30.6	36.4	15.9
Return on Equity After Income Taxes 48	36.7	28.7	29.6	19.7	29.1	35.1	14.1
Profit Margin (Before Income Tax) 49	15.5	8.1	16.2	5.2	5.8	9.4	5.4
Profit Margin (After Income Tax) 50	10.5	7.2	13.2	4.7	5.5	9.1	4.8

Table I

Corporations with and without Net Income

BREWERIES

MONEY AMOUNTS AND SIZE OF ASSETS IN THOUSANDS OF DOLLARS

Item Description for Accounting Period 7/08 Through 6/09	Total	Zero Assets	Under 500	500 to 1,000	1,000 to 5,000	5,000 to 10,000	10,000 to 25,000	25,000 to 50,000	50,000 to 100,000	100,000 to 250,000	250,000 to 500,000	500,000 to 2,500,000	2,500,000 and over
Number of Enterprises **1**	257	0	93	0	135	0	15	8	0	4	0	0	3
Revenues ($ in Thousands)													
Net Sales **2**	23435472	0	63542	0	342808	0	273785	408635	0	810183	0	0	21536518
Interest **3**	113105	0	60	0	0	0	147	91	0	1419	0	0	111387
Rents **4**	25054	0	0	0	0	0	344	0	0	515	0	0	24195
Royalties **5**	382668	0	0	0	0	0	0	0	0	0	0	0	382668
Other Portfolio Income **6**	485171	0	659	0	0	0	0	2	0	1631	0	0	482878
Other Receipts **7**	219938	0	0	0	0	0	823	4524	0	6337	0	0	208257
Total Receipts **8**	24661408	0	64261	0	342808	0	275099	413252	0	820085	0	0	22745903
Average Total Receipts **9**	95959	•	691	•	2539	•	18340	51656	•	205021	•	•	7581968
Operating Costs/Operating Income (%)													
Cost of Operations **10**	42.9	•	81.5	•	76.1	•	58.6	62.7	•	56.0	•	•	41.2
Salaries and Wages **11**	16.7	•	•	•	0.6	•	6.9	7.2	•	8.4	•	•	17.7
Taxes Paid **12**	12.0	•	2.8	•	2.4	•	5.2	3.8	•	2.8	•	•	12.8
Interest Paid **13**	4.4	•	•	•	1.6	•	1.8	2.1	•	0.2	•	•	4.7
Depreciation **14**	4.6	•	1.8	•	3.2	•	8.6	6.7	•	7.7	•	•	4.4
Amortization and Depletion **15**	0.6	•	•	•	•	•	0.1	0.2	•	0.3	•	•	0.6
Pensions and Other Deferred Comp. **16**	1.9	•	•	•	•	•	0.2	0.3	•	0.5	•	•	2.1
Employee Benefits **17**	1.6	•	•	•	•	•	1.5	1.5	•	1.2	•	•	1.6
Advertising **18**	5.7	•	•	•	0.1	•	2.4	2.5	•	4.3	•	•	5.9
Other Expenses **19**	11.3	•	1.4	•	9.2	•	8.2	8.4	•	16.5	•	•	11.3
Officers' Compensation **20**	3.5	•	•	•	•	•	3.4	1.0	•	0.9	•	•	3.7
Operating Margin **21**	•	•	12.6	•	6.8	•	3.1	3.6	•	1.3	•	•	•
Operating Margin Before Officers' Comp. **22**	•	•	12.6	•	6.8	•	6.5	4.5	•	2.2	•	•	•

Selected Average Balance Sheet ($ in Thousands)

Net Receivables **23**	5200	68	43	1448	9407	14586	389639
Inventories **24**	3664	65	198	1496	2508	9417	274111
Net Property, Plant and Equipment **25**	34342	0	876	10128	27976	82954	266743
Total Assets **26**	308074	323	1790	15124	47065	185482	25852712
Notes and Loans Payable **27**	138908	4	1419	6968	16138	10647	11743716
All Other Liabilities **28**	54689	165	219	2632	11572	34718	4579681
Net Worth **29**	114478	154	151	5524	19355	140116	9529315

Selected Financial Ratios (Times to 1)

Current Ratio **30**	0.3	0.9	3.5	1.3	2.7	2.7	0.2
Quick Ratio **31**	0.2	0.5	2.0	0.7	1.9	2.1	0.1
Net Sales to Working Capital **32**	•	•	4.7	20.4	5.9	4.2	•
Coverage Ratio **33**	1.2	•	5.2	2.9	3.2	13.4	1.1
Total Asset Turnover **34**	0.3	2.1	1.4	1.2	1.1	1.1	0.3
Inventory Turnover **35**	10.7	8.6	9.8	7.1	12.8	12.0	10.8
Receivables Turnover **36**	15.6	9.6	82.1	13.9	9.8	16.0	15.9
Total Liabilities to Net Worth **37**	1.7	1.1	10.8	1.7	1.4	0.3	1.7
Current Assets to Working Capital **38**	•	•	1.4	4.8	1.6	1.6	•
Current Liabilities to Working Capital **39**	•	•	0.4	3.8	0.6	0.6	•
Working Capital to Net Sales **40**	•	•	0.2	0.0	0.2	0.2	•
Inventory to Working Capital **41**	•	•	0.5	1.9	0.5	0.2	•
Total Receipts to Cash Flow **42**	11.9	6.6	8.5	10.4	8.3	5.5	12.7
Cost of Goods to Cash Flow **43**	5.1	5.4	6.5	6.1	5.2	3.1	5.2
Cash Flow to Total Debt **44**	0.0	0.6	0.2	0.2	0.2	0.8	0.0

Selected Financial Factors (in Percentages)

Debt Ratio **45**	62.8	52.5	91.5	63.5	58.9	24.5	63.1
Return on Total Assets **46**	1.5	29.0	11.8	6.5	7.4	2.8	1.4
Return on Equity Before Income Taxes **47**	0.6	61.0	113.3	11.8	12.4	3.4	0.3
Return on Equity After Income Taxes **48**	0.3	49.4	113.3	5.8	11.9	3.4	0.0
Profit Margin (Before Income Tax) **49**	0.7	13.7	6.8	3.6	4.7	2.3	0.4
Profit Margin (After Income Tax) **50**	0.3	11.1	6.8	1.8	4.5	2.3	0.0

Table II

Corporations with Net Income

BREWERIES

MONEY AMOUNTS AND SIZE OF ASSETS IN THOUSANDS OF DOLLARS

Item Description for Accounting Period 7/08 Through 6/09	Total	Zero Assets	Under 500	500 to 1,000	1,000 to 5,000	5,000 to 10,000	10,000 to 25,000	25,000 to 50,000	50,000 to 100,000	100,000 to 250,000	250,000 to 500,000	500,000 to 2,500,000	2,500,000 and over
Number of Enterprises **1**	246	0	•	0	135	0	•	•	0	•	0	0	0

Revenues ($ in Thousands)

Item	Total	Zero Assets	Under 500	500 to 1,000	1,000 to 5,000	5,000 to 10,000	10,000 to 25,000	25,000 to 50,000	50,000 to 100,000	100,000 to 250,000	250,000 to 500,000	500,000 to 2,500,000	2,500,000 and over
Net Sales **2**	19762425	0	•	0	342808	0	•	•	0	•	0	0	0
Interest **3**	19677	0	•	0	0	0	•	•	0	•	0	0	0
Rents **4**	24259	0	•	0	0	0	•	•	0	•	0	0	0
Royalties **5**	166194	0	•	0	0	0	•	•	0	•	0	0	0
Other Portfolio Income **6**	432129	0	•	0	0	0	•	•	0	•	0	0	0
Other Receipts **7**	89420	0	•	0	0	0	•	•	0	•	0	0	0
Total Receipts **8**	20494104	0	•	0	342808	0	•	•	0	•	0	0	0
Average Total Receipts **9**	83309	•	•	•	2539	•	•	•	•	•	•	•	•

Operating Costs/Operating Income (%)

Item	Total	Zero Assets	Under 500	500 to 1,000	1,000 to 5,000	5,000 to 10,000	10,000 to 25,000	25,000 to 50,000	50,000 to 100,000	100,000 to 250,000	250,000 to 500,000	500,000 to 2,500,000	2,500,000 and over
Cost of Operations **10**	40.2	•	•	•	76.1	•	•	•	•	•	•	•	•
Salaries and Wages **11**	17.5	•	•	•	0.6	•	•	•	•	•	•	•	•
Taxes Paid **12**	13.0	•	•	•	2.4	•	•	•	•	•	•	•	•
Interest Paid **13**	3.0	•	•	•	1.6	•	•	•	•	•	•	•	•
Depreciation **14**	4.6	•	•	•	3.2	•	•	•	•	•	•	•	•
Amortization and Depletion **15**	0.6	•	•	•	•	•	•	•	•	•	•	•	•
Pensions and Other Deferred Comp. **16**	2.2	•	•	•	•	•	•	•	•	•	•	•	•
Employee Benefits **17**	1.8	•	•	•	•	•	•	•	•	•	•	•	•
Advertising **18**	4.4	•	•	•	0.1	•	•	•	•	•	•	•	•
Other Expenses **19**	11.2	•	•	•	9.2	•	•	•	•	•	•	•	•
Officers' Compensation **20**	4.0	•	•	•	•	•	•	•	•	•	•	•	•
Operating Margin **21**	•	•	•	•	6.8	•	•	•	•	•	•	•	•
Operating Margin Before Officers' Comp. **22**	1.3	•	•	•	6.8	•	•	•	•	•	•	•	•

Selected Average Balance Sheet ($ in Thousands)

Net Receivables 23	3762	43
Inventories 24	3729	198
Net Property, Plant and Equipment 25	34512	876
Total Assets 26	269861	1790
Notes and Loans Payable 27	116591	1419
All Other Liabilities 28	49675	219
Net Worth 29	103595	151

Selected Financial Ratios (Times to 1)

Current Ratio 30	0.3	3.5
Quick Ratio 31	0.1	2.0
Net Sales to Working Capital 32		4.7
Coverage Ratio 33	1.6	5.2
Total Asset Turnover 34	0.3	1.4
Inventory Turnover 35	8.7	9.8
Receivables Turnover 36	15.2	82.1
Total Liabilities to Net Worth 37	1.6	10.8
Current Assets to Working Capital 38		1.4
Current Liabilities to Working Capital 39		0.4
Working Capital to Net Sales 40		0.2
Inventory to Working Capital 41		0.5
Total Receipts to Cash Flow 42	10.9	8.5
Cost of Goods to Cash Flow 43	4.4	6.5
Cash Flow to Total Debt 44	0.0	0.2

Selected Financial Factors (in Percentages)

Debt Ratio 45	61.6	91.5
Return on Total Assets 46	1.5	11.8
Return on Equity Before Income Taxes 47	1.4	113.3
Return on Equity After Income Taxes 48	1.1	113.3
Profit Margin (Before Income Tax) 49	1.8	6.8
Profit Margin (After Income Tax) 50	1.4	6.8

Table I

Corporations with and without Net Income

WINERIES AND DISTILLERIES

MONEY AMOUNTS AND SIZE OF ASSETS IN THOUSANDS OF DOLLARS

Item Description for Accounting Period 7/08 Through 6/09	Total	Zero Assets	Under 500	500 to 1,000	1,000 to 5,000	5,000 to 10,000	10,000 to 25,000	25,000 to 50,000	50,000 to 100,000	100,000 to 250,000	250,000 to 500,000	500,000 to 2,500,000	2,500,000 and over
Number of Enterprises 1	2045	•	619	•	436	•	49	40	22	9	5	0	5
Revenues ($ in Thousands)													
Net Sales 2	23398884	•	76731	•	831025	•	406931	953588	1051106	791524	2050353	0	16656130
Interest 3	75893	•	0	•	1614	•	720	533	3508	1217	11657	0	56362
Rents 4	11546	•	0	•	336	•	0	172	2027	796	67	0	8147
Royalties 5	471421	•	0	•	0	•	0	2485	0	0	198	0	468738
Other Portfolio Income 6	98856	•	11590	•	1017	•	5466	6542	4820	261	113	0	67178
Other Receipts 7	596131	•	11096	•	13583	•	8840	6072	14247	18946	36397	0	481601
Total Receipts 8	24652731	•	99417	•	847575	•	421957	969392	1075708	812744	2098785	0	17738156
Average Total Receipts 9	12055	•	161	•	1944	•	8611	24235	48896	90305	419757	•	3547631
Operating Costs/Operating Income (%)													
Cost of Operations 10	54.4	•	90.0	•	37.7	•	44.9	51.8	61.3	61.3	47.1	•	56.1
Salaries and Wages 11	6.7	∘	3.1	•	16.5	•	14.4	9.8	8.6	7.5	6.2	•	5.6
Taxes Paid 12	10.8	•	3.3	•	6.8	•	3.5	3.9	7.2	6.6	16.3	•	11.5
Interest Paid 13	5.1	•	2.9	•	1.6	•	5.1	1.7	2.4	2.8	2.5	•	6.0
Depreciation 14	3.5	•	10.7	•	5.1	•	7.7	6.9	5.5	6.7	6.1	•	2.3
Amortization and Depletion 15	1.8	•	0.0	•	0.1	•	0.1	0.2	0.9	1.9	0.9	•	2.3
Pensions and Other Deferred Comp. 16	1.0	•	•	•	0.5	•	0.3	0.4	0.4	0.3	0.6	•	1.2
Employee Benefits 17	1.4	•	0.2	•	3.7	•	0.8	1.3	0.7	1.2	0.9	•	1.4
Advertising 18	5.1	•	1.4	•	1.6	•	1.0	1.6	1.5	3.9	2.0	•	6.4
Other Expenses 19	8.6	•	60.6	•	24.3	•	17.4	12.7	10.3	6.2	13.8	•	6.3
Officers' Compensation 20	1.2	•	39.0	•	7.4	•	1.8	2.8	1.4	1.0	0.4	•	0.5
Operating Margin 21	0.4	•	•	•	•	•	3.1	6.8	•	0.4	3.0	•	0.4
Operating Margin Before Officers' Comp. 22	1.7	•	•	•	2.1	•	4.9	9.6	1.3	1.4	3.5	•	0.9

Selected Average Balance Sheet ($ in Thousands)

Net Receivables 23	1592	5	72	932	3189	5248	11574	31423	528119
Inventories 24	3998	0	1001	4720	8850	22390	44904	178488	844993
Net Property, Plant and Equipment 25	3171	93	353	3760	15324	25227	42618	140994	639392
Total Assets 26	17272	124	1683	14254	35551	69011	130731	597813	5095506
Notes and Loans Payable 27	8879	222	414	7888	9064	21096	45024	197986	2891092
All Other Liabilities 28	3273	5	144	3596	6385	9265	27812	107514	1024623
Net Worth 29	5120	-103	1126	2771	20102	38650	57896	292313	1179791

Selected Financial Ratios (Times to 1)

Current Ratio 30	2.4	0.2	6.7	2.1	2.0	2.1	1.9	2.3	2.4
Quick Ratio 31	0.7	0.1	1.6	0.3	0.7	0.6	0.4	0.2	0.9
Net Sales to Working Capital 32	3.1		1.7	1.9	3.0	3.0	2.5	2.2	3.6
Coverage Ratio 33	2.2			2.3	6.1	1.9	2.1	3.2	2.3
Total Asset Turnover 34	0.7	1.0	1.1	0.6	0.7	0.7	0.7	0.7	0.7
Inventory Turnover 35	1.6		0.7	0.8	1.4	1.3	1.2	1.1	2.2
Receivables Turnover 36	6.8	49.0	27.9	11.6	8.9	7.2	8.8	16.8	6.2
Total Liabilities to Net Worth 37	2.4		0.5	4.1	0.8	0.8	1.3	1.0	3.3
Current Assets to Working Capital 38	1.7		1.2	1.9	2.0	1.9	2.1	1.7	1.7
Current Liabilities to Working Capital 39	0.7		0.2	0.9	1.0	0.9	1.1	0.7	0.7
Working Capital to Net Sales 40	0.3		0.6	0.5	0.3	0.3	0.4	0.5	0.3
Inventory to Working Capital 41	1.1		0.8	1.5	1.1	1.3	1.5	1.3	1.0
Total Receipts to Cash Flow 42	8.2		6.5	5.3	5.5	10.2	12.8	7.2	8.6
Cost of Goods to Cash Flow 43	4.5		2.5	2.4	2.8	6.2	7.9	3.4	4.8
Cash Flow to Total Debt 44	0.1		0.5	0.1	0.3	0.2	0.1	0.2	0.1

Selected Financial Factors (in Percentages)

Debt Ratio 45	70.4	183.6	33.1	80.6	43.5	44.0	55.7	51.1	76.8
Return on Total Assets 46	7.5			6.9	6.8	3.2	4.0	5.4	8.9
Return on Equity Before Income Taxes 47	14.0	97.8		20.4	10.0	2.8	4.7	7.6	21.3
Return on Equity After Income Taxes 48	9.2	97.8		17.5	9.1	1.5	4.1	5.7	13.7
Profit Margin (Before Income Tax) 49	6.3			6.8	8.4	2.2	3.1	5.4	7.6
Profit Margin (After Income Tax) 50	4.1			5.8	7.7	1.3	2.7	4.0	4.9

Table II

Corporations with Net Income

WINERIES AND DISTILLERIES

MONEY AMOUNTS AND SIZE OF ASSETS IN THOUSANDS OF DOLLARS

Item Description for Accounting Period 7/08 Through 6/09		Total	Zero Assets	Under 500	500 to 1,000	1,000 to 5,000	5,000 to 10,000	10,000 to 25,000	25,000 to 50,000	50,000 to 100,000	100,000 to 250,000	250,000 to 500,000	500,000 to 2,500,000	2,500,000 and over
Number of Enterprises	1	431	0	•	•	47	106	33	32	9	•	•	0	•
Revenues ($ in Thousands)														
Net Sales	2	20100833	0	•	•	135619	384392	336896	798729	518838	•	•	0	•
Interest	3	60899	0	•	•	479	191	102	516	1227	•	•	0	•
Rents	4	9178	0	•	•	0	0	0	172	57	•	•	0	•
Royalties	5	471421	0	•	•	0	0	0	2485	0	•	•	0	•
Other Portfolio Income	6	85271	0	•	•	986	1448	116	3235	1521	•	•	0	•
Other Receipts	7	486204	0	•	•	3572	15549	5124	6969	1482	•	•	0	•
Total Receipts	8	21213806	0	•	•	140656	401580	342238	812106	523125	•	•	0	•
Average Total Receipts	9	49220	•	•	•	2993	3788	10371	25378	58125	•	•	•	•
Operating Costs/Operating Income (%)														
Cost of Operations	10	54.4	•	•	•	17.6	37.0	47.2	51.1	56.1	•	•	•	•
Salaries and Wages	11	6.1	•	•	•	11.6	15.0	12.8	9.2	9.4	•	•	•	•
Taxes Paid	12	11.4	•	•	•	3.2	4.9	3.0	2.2	2.5	•	•	•	•
Interest Paid	13	5.1	•	•	•	0.5	5.0	3.0	0.8	1.5	•	•	•	•
Depreciation	14	2.7	•	•	•	7.3	8.1	5.1	6.4	4.6	•	•	•	•
Amortization and Depletion	15	2.0	•	•	•	0.2	0.1	0.0	0.1	0.8	•	•	•	•
Pensions and Other Deferred Comp.	16	1.1	•	•	•	3.0	0.4	0.3	0.4	0.1	•	•	•	•
Employee Benefits	17	1.3	•	•	•	3.0	1.2	0.5	1.1	0.4	•	•	•	•
Advertising	18	5.3	•	•	•	1.4	0.7	1.1	1.4	2.0	•	•	•	•
Other Expenses	19	6.9	•	•	•	39.2	13.8	15.6	14.6	8.0	•	•	•	•
Officers' Compensation	20	0.9	•	•	•	8.3	1.0	1.8	2.5	1.4	•	•	•	•
Operating Margin	21	2.7	•	•	•	4.7	12.9	9.5	10.3	13.1	•	•	•	•
Operating Margin Before Officers' Comp.	22	3.6	•	•	•	13.1	13.9	11.3	12.8	14.6	•	•	•	•

Selected Average Balance Sheet ($ in Thousands)

Net Receivables 23	6656	•	91	221	1176	3201	7172
Inventories 24	14409	•	1571	2448	6054	8644	27502
Net Property, Plant and Equipment 25	10137	•	432	3917	3562	14116	18569
Total Assets 26	65066	•	2550	7893	14496	35790	75706
Notes and Loans Payable 27	35447	•	561	4995	6538	6734	15978
All Other Liabilities 28	12913	•	294	689	4579	6719	7203
Net Worth 29	16705	•	1695	2208	3380	22336	52525

Selected Financial Ratios (Times to 1)

Current Ratio 30	2.4	•	7.2	4.5	1.9	2.2	2.6
Quick Ratio 31	0.8	•	3.0	0.8	0.3	0.8	1.0
Net Sales to Working Capital 32	3.3	•	1.6	1.2	2.2	2.8	2.7
Coverage Ratio 33	2.7	•	19.7	4.5	4.7	16.2	10.3
Total Asset Turnover 34	0.7	•	1.1	0.5	0.7	0.7	0.8
Inventory Turnover 35	1.8	•	0.3	0.5	0.8	1.5	1.2
Receivables Turnover 36	6.6	•	11.5	14.0	10.8	10.1	5.9
Total Liabilities to Net Worth 37	2.9	•	0.5	2.6	3.3	0.6	0.4
Current Assets to Working Capital 38	1.7	•	1.2	1.3	2.1	1.8	1.6
Current Liabilities to Working Capital 39	0.7	•	0.2	0.3	1.1	0.8	0.6
Working Capital to Net Sales 40	0.3	•	0.6	0.8	0.5	0.4	0.4
Inventory to Working Capital 41	1.0	•	0.7	1.0	1.7	1.0	0.9
Total Receipts to Cash Flow 42	7.5	•	2.9	3.6	4.3	4.3	5.4
Cost of Goods to Cash Flow 43	4.1	•	0.5	1.3	2.0	2.2	3.0
Cash Flow to Total Debt 44	0.1	•	1.1	0.2	0.2	0.4	0.5

Selected Financial Factors (in Percentages)

Debt Ratio 45	74.3	•	33.5	72.0	76.7	37.6	30.6
Return on Total Assets 46	10.0	•	10.1	10.2	9.9	8.9	11.7
Return on Equity Before Income Taxes 47	24.6	•	14.4	28.5	33.4	13.3	15.2
Return on Equity After Income Taxes 48	17.6	•	9.8	27.3	29.9	12.4	13.0
Profit Margin (Before Income Tax) 49	8.8	•	8.5	17.3	11.1	11.9	13.9
Profit Margin (After Income Tax) 50	6.3	•	5.8	16.6	9.9	11.1	11.9

Table I

Corporations with and without Net Income

TOBACCO MANUFACTURING

MONEY AMOUNTS AND SIZE OF ASSETS IN THOUSANDS OF DOLLARS

Item Description for Accounting Period 7/08 Through 6/09	Total	Zero Assets	Under 500	500 to 1,000	1,000 to 5,000	5,000 to 10,000	10,000 to 25,000	25,000 to 50,000	50,000 to 100,000	100,000 to 250,000	250,000 to 500,000	500,000 to 2,500,000	2,500,000 and over
Number of Enterprises 1	37	0	0	0	0	10	9	9	0	0	0	6	3
Revenues ($ in Thousands)													
Net Sales 2	42352436	0	0	0	0	353926	470602	822189	0	0	0	7880600	32825119
Interest 3	224923	0	0	0	0	816	279	3957	0	0	0	32255	187616
Rents 4	1491201	0	0	0	0	0	0	72	0	0	0	0	1491129
Royalties 5	518199	0	0	0	0	0	0	3374	0	0	0	325596	189229
Other Portfolio Income 6	4926991	0	0	0	0	0	1271	5332	0	0	0	9308	4911081
Other Receipts 7	530133	0	0	0	0	4975	1040	17771	0	0	0	15614	490731
Total Receipts 8	50043883	0	0	0	0	359717	473192	852695	0	0	0	8263373	40094905
Average Total Receipts 9	1352537	•	•	•	•	35972	52577	94744	•	•	•	1377229	13364968
Operating Costs/Operating Income (%)													
Cost of Operations 10	44.0	•	•	•	•	48.1	78.7	60.6	•	•	•	30.4	46.2
Salaries and Wages 11	4.3	•	•	•	•	0.4	8.2	1.9	•	•	•	4.5	4.3
Taxes Paid 12	15.7	•	•	•	•	37.0	1.1	20.1	•	•	•	6.9	17.7
Interest Paid 13	4.1	•	•	•	•	0.3	0.2	2.6	•	•	•	2.5	4.5
Depreciation 14	2.0	•	•	•	•	2.4	0.8	0.2	•	•	•	1.8	2.1
Amortization and Depletion 15	1.1	•	•	•	•	0.0	0.0	0.4	•	•	•	1.9	0.9
Pensions and Other Deferred Comp. 16	1.3	•	•	•	•	•	0.5	0.1	•	•	•	0.8	1.5
Employee Benefits 17	1.3	•	•	•	•	0.6	0.7	0.6	•	•	•	0.3	1.6
Advertising 18	1.7	•	•	•	•	0.1	2.2	0.6	•	•	•	0.5	2.0
Other Expenses 19	12.6	•	•	•	•	2.3	11.9	9.2	•	•	•	26.5	9.5
Officers' Compensation 20	0.9	•	•	•	•	9.4	2.7	1.1	•	•	•	1.7	0.6
Operating Margin 21	11.2	•	•	•	•	•	•	2.6	•	•	•	22.3	9.2
Operating Margin Before Officers' Comp. 22	12.1	•	•	•	•	8.7	•	3.7	•	•	•	24.0	9.8

Selected Average Balance Sheet ($ in Thousands)

Net Receivables 23	29147	733	1867	4105	50073	238974
Inventories 24	104989	2566	4879	11911	210128	815692
Net Property, Plant and Equipment 25	117362	2026	1347	1350	164725	1103167
Total Assets 26	1575404	6354	18256	49526	1502457	16200538
Notes and Loans Payable 27	459300	83	1885	38203	441957	460247
All Other Liabilities 28	783962	3478	4476	19621	662428	8260129
Net Worth 29	332141	2793	11895	-8298	398072	3280162

Selected Financial Ratios (Times to 1)

Current Ratio 30	1.4	2.1	3.4	1.2	1.3	1.4
Quick Ratio 31	0.9	0.6	0.9	0.7	0.6	1.0
Net Sales to Working Capital 32	8.0	15.9	5.4	14.7	8.5	7.8
Coverage Ratio 33	9.1	4.4	•	3.5	11.7	8.8
Total Asset Turnover 34	0.7	5.6	2.9	1.8	0.9	0.7
Inventory Turnover 35	4.8	6.6	8.4	4.7	1.9	6.2
Receivables Turnover 36	32.7	68.5	28.9	20.7	34.6	32.6
Total Liabilities to Net Worth 37	3.7	1.3	0.5	•	2.8	3.9
Current Assets to Working Capital 38	3.7	1.9	1.4	5.1	4.1	3.7
Current Liabilities to Working Capital 39	2.7	0.9	0.4	4.1	3.1	2.7
Working Capital to Net Sales 40	0.1	0.1	0.2	0.1	0.1	0.1
Inventory to Working Capital 41	0.8	1.3	0.7	2.1	1.6	0.6
Total Receipts to Cash Flow 42	2.6	31.6	25.5	8.0	1.9	2.7
Cost of Goods to Cash Flow 43	1.2	15.2	20.0	4.9	0.6	1.3
Cash Flow to Total Debt 44	0.4	0.3	0.3	0.2	0.6	0.3

Selected Financial Factors (in Percentages)

Debt Ratio 45	78.9	56.0	34.8	116.8	73.5	79.8
Return on Total Assets 46	26.7	6.8	16.3	•	26.1	27.1
Return on Equity Before Income Taxes 47	112.7	11.9	•	•	90.1	118.6
Return on Equity After Income Taxes 48	74.9	7.9	•	•	60.9	78.5
Profit Margin (Before Income Tax) 49	32.7	0.9	•	6.3	27.3	35.5
Profit Margin (After Income Tax) 50	21.7	0.6	•	6.3	18.5	23.5

Table II

Corporations with Net Income

TOBACCO MANUFACTURING

MONEY AMOUNTS AND SIZE OF ASSETS IN THOUSANDS OF DOLLARS

Item Description for Accounting Period 7/08 Through 6/09	Total	Zero Assets	Under 500	500 to 1,000	1,000 to 5,000	5,000 to 10,000	10,000 to 25,000	25,000 to 50,000	50,000 to 100,000	100,000 to 250,000	250,000 to 500,000	500,000 to 2,500,000	2,500,000 and over
Number of Enterprises **1**	31	0	0	0	0	10	•	•	0	0	0	6	3
Revenues ($ in Thousands)													
Net Sales **2**	41825402	0	0	0	0	353926	•	•	0	0	0	7880600	32825119
Interest **3**	220687	0	0	0	0	816	•	•	0	0	0	32255	187616
Rents **4**	1491129	0	0	0	0	0	•	•	0	0	0	0	1491129
Royalties **5**	514826	0	0	0	0	0	•	•	0	0	0	325596	189229
Other Portfolio Income **6**	4920395	0	0	0	0	0	•	•	0	0	0	9308	4911081
Other Receipts **7**	519618	0	0	0	0	4975	•	•	0	0	0	15614	490731
Total Receipts **8**	49492057	0	0	0	0	359717	•	•	0	0	0	8263373	40094905
Average Total Receipts **9**	1596518	•	•	•	•	35972	•	•	•	•	•	1377229	13364968
Operating Costs/Operating Income (%)													
Cost of Operations **10**	43.5	•	•	•	•	48.1	•	•	•	•	•	30.4	46.2
Salaries and Wages **11**	4.2	•	•	•	•	0.4	•	•	•	•	•	4.5	4.3
Taxes Paid **12**	15.9	•	•	•	•	37.0	•	•	•	•	•	6.9	17.7
Interest Paid **13**	4.1	•	•	•	•	0.3	•	•	•	•	•	2.5	4.5
Depreciation **14**	2.0	•	•	•	•	2.4	•	•	•	•	•	1.8	2.1
Amortization and Depletion **15**	1.1	•	•	•	•	0.0	•	•	•	•	•	1.9	0.9
Pensions and Other Deferred Comp. **16**	1.3	•	•	•	•	•	•	•	•	•	•	0.8	1.5
Employee Benefits **17**	1.3	•	•	•	•	0.6	•	•	•	•	•	0.3	1.6
Advertising **18**	1.6	•	•	•	•	0.1	•	•	•	•	•	0.5	2.0
Other Expenses **19**	12.6	•	•	•	•	2.3	•	•	•	•	•	26.5	9.5
Officers' Compensation **20**	0.9	•	•	•	•	9.4	•	•	•	•	•	1.7	0.6
Operating Margin **21**	11.5	•	•	•	•	•	•	•	•	•	•	22.3	9.2
Operating Margin Before Officers' Comp. **22**	12.4	•	•	•	•	8.7	•	•	•	•	•	24.0	9.8

Selected Average Balance Sheet ($ in Thousands)

Net Receivables **23**	34139	733	50073	238974
Inventories **24**	123541	2566	210128	771226
Net Property, Plant and Equipment **25**	139695	2026	164725	1103167
Total Assets **26**	1873498	6354	1502457	16200538
Notes and Loans Payable **27**	542824	83	441957	4460247
All Other Liabilities **28**	933452	3478	662428	8260129
Net Worth **29**	397222	2793	398072	3280162

Selected Financial Ratios (Times to 1)

Current Ratio **30**	1.4	2.1	1.3	1.4
Quick Ratio **31**	0.9	0.6	0.6	1.0
Net Sales to Working Capital **32**	8.1	15.9	8.5	7.8
Coverage Ratio **33**	9.1	4.4	11.7	8.8
Total Asset Turnover **34**	0.7	5.6	0.9	0.7
Inventory Turnover **35**	4.7	6.6	1.9	6.6
Receivables Turnover **36**	32.6	68.5	34.6	3.9
Total Liabilities to Net Worth **37**	3.7	1.3	2.8	3.9
Current Assets to Working Capital **38**	3.8	1.9	4.1	3.7
Current Liabilities to Working Capital **39**	2.8	0.9	3.1	2.7
Working Capital to Net Sales **40**	0.1	0.1	0.1	0.1
Inventory to Working Capital **41**	0.8	1.3	1.6	0.6
Total Receipts to Cash Flow **42**	2.6	31.6	1.9	2.7
Cost of Goods to Cash Flow **43**	1.1	15.2	0.6	1.3
Cash Flow to Total Debt **44**	0.4	0.3	0.6	0.3

Selected Financial Factors (in Percentages)

Debt Ratio **45**	78.8	56.0	73.5	79.8
Return on Total Assets **46**	26.8	6.8	26.1	27.1
Return on Equity Before Income Taxes **47**	112.7	11.9	90.1	118.6
Return on Equity After Income Taxes **48**	75.0	7.9	60.9	78.5
Profit Margin (Before Income Tax) **49**	33.2	0.9	27.3	35.5
Profit Margin (After Income Tax) **50**	22.1	0.6	18.5	23.5

Table I

Corporations with and without Net Income

TEXTILE MILLS

MONEY AMOUNTS AND SIZE OF ASSETS IN THOUSANDS OF DOLLARS

Item Description for Accounting Period 7/08 Through 6/09	Total	Zero Assets	Under 500	500 to 1,000	1,000 to 5,000	5,000 to 10,000	10,000 to 25,000	25,000 to 50,000	50,000 to 100,000	100,000 to 250,000	250,000 to 500,000	500,000 to 2,500,000	2,500,000 and over
Number of Enterprises **1**	1828	423	906	136	176	71	62	21	17	8	5	4	0
Revenues ($ in Thousands)													
Net Sales **2**	11387635	100746	457780	207804	519644	1124051	1408197	676543	1794829	1425637	1730524	1941881	0
Interest **3**	47165	1313	0	826	3020	2832	2327	1651	2358	2325	1446	29066	0
Rents **4**	10879	0	0	0	453	1241	5085	44	1508	0	980	1567	0
Royalties **5**	37300	0	0	0	0	0	0	0	6	7501	0	29793	0
Other Portfolio Income **6**	78676	24596	0	0	7375	758	1031	11761	4904	14503	11093	2654	0
Other Receipts **7**	118774	4018	0	93	4834	3194	20045	1779	22704	14564	15087	32459	0
Total Receipts **8**	11680429	130673	457780	208723	535326	1132076	1436685	691778	1826309	1464530	1759130	2037420	0
Average Total Receipts **9**	6390	309	505	1535	3042	15945	23172	32942	107430	183066	351826	509355	•
Operating Costs/Operating Income (%)													
Cost of Operations **10**	76.3	94.8	51.6	75.4	69.3	88.6	79.7	61.3	78.1	80.3	81.2	69.6	•
Salaries and Wages **11**	5.7	11.6	4.6	2.5	5.1	4.7	5.6	3.5	6.0	4.7	5.0	8.5	•
Taxes Paid **12**	1.3	2.3	3.0	1.2	1.8	1.7	0.8	1.4	1.1	0.5	1.3	1.6	•
Interest Paid **13**	2.2	2.2	2.7	0.1	0.4	1.1	1.4	4.4	0.8	2.2	2.2	4.4	•
Depreciation **14**	2.9	8.5	0.3	0.8	1.8	1.1	3.7	3.5	2.9	4.0	3.8	2.0	•
Amortization and Depletion **15**	0.4	0.0	0.0	•	•	0.2	0.1	0.6	0.0	0.1	0.7	1.0	•
Pensions and Other Deferred Comp. **16**	0.5	0.1	0.1	•	0.1	0.1	0.2	0.1	0.6	0.5	0.7	1.1	•
Employee Benefits **17**	1.4	3.7	0.0	0.7	2.3	0.2	1.3	0.3	1.2	1.3	1.8	2.5	•
Advertising **18**	0.3	0.4	0.1	0.0	0.3	0.0	0.3	0.1	0.7	0.1	0.2	0.2	•
Other Expenses **19**	9.9	33.7	24.4	25.4	14.3	5.8	7.1	7.1	8.9	5.6	7.5	13.9	•
Officers' Compensation **20**	1.9	0.8	12.7	5.0	3.2	1.3	1.5	1.8	1.3	0.7	1.3	1.1	•
Operating Margin **21**	•	•	0.5	•	1.4	•	•	15.9	•	0.0	•	•	•
Operating Margin Before Officers' Comp. **22**	•	•	13.2	4.5	4.5	•	•	17.7	0.7	0.7	•	•	•

Selected Average Balance Sheet ($ in Thousands)

Item												
Net Receivables 23	102068	62450	25962	9339	3125	3930	1318	301	94	91	0	896
Inventories 24	78403	80594	33471	16559	4152	4470	2003	510	95	18	0	1035
Net Property, Plant and Equipment 25	89739	114319	49720	19351	7990	4261	962	369	43	12	0	1225
Total Assets 26	713570	393866	141137	67174	29765	16240	6899	2120	582	155	0	5366
Notes and Loans Payable 27	273477	114491	55939	12088	16976	6568	3397	797	113	83	0	1945
All Other Liabilities 28	198261	55803	32923	18701	4727	1979	2060	601	271	65	0	1216
Net Worth 29	241832	223571	52275	36385	8062	7693	1443	723	197	8	0	2206

Selected Financial Ratios (Times to 1)

Item											
Current Ratio 30	1.3	3.3	1.9	1.9	3.2	1.3	3.4	3.5	1.4	•	2.0
Quick Ratio 31	0.8	1.5	1.0	0.7	1.8	0.9	2.0	1.1	1.3	•	1.0
Net Sales to Working Capital 32	10.4	3.2	6.1	6.7	3.2	3.9	2.7	5.0	13.3	•	5.2
Coverage Ratio 33	0.8	•	2.3	1.1	1.2	5.2	11.6	•	1.2	•	1.1
Total Asset Turnover 34	0.7	0.9	1.3	1.6	1.4	1.1	1.4	2.6	3.3	•	1.2
Inventory Turnover 35	4.3	3.5	4.3	5.0	4.0	4.8	7.0	12.1	14.4	•	4.6
Receivables Turnover 36	3.5	5.2	5.5	11.3	5.5	11.7	12.0	7.4	4.7	•	5.9
Total Liabilities to Net Worth 37	2.0	0.8	1.7	0.8	1.1	2.7	3.8	1.9	18.1	•	1.4
Current Assets to Working Capital 38	4.6	1.4	2.2	2.1	1.5	2.1	4.1	1.4	3.2	•	2.0
Current Liabilities to Working Capital 39	3.6	0.4	1.2	1.1	0.5	1.1	3.1	0.4	2.2	•	1.0
Working Capital to Net Sales 40	0.1	0.3	0.2	0.1	0.3	0.3	0.1	0.2	0.1	•	0.2
Inventory to Working Capital 41	1.4	0.7	0.7	1.1	0.5	0.7	1.9	0.2	0.3	•	0.8
Total Receipts to Cash Flow 42	10.7	47.1	16.0	14.9	19.0	4.7	6.6	10.1	6.4	•	14.5
Cost of Goods to Cash Flow 43	7.4	38.2	12.8	11.6	15.2	2.9	4.6	7.6	3.3	•	11.0
Cash Flow to Total Debt 44	0.1	0.0	0.1	0.2	0.1	0.3	0.3	0.4	0.5	•	0.1

Selected Financial Factors (in Percentages)

Item											
Debt Ratio 45	66.1	43.2	63.0	45.8	52.6	72.9	79.1	65.9	66.1	94.8	58.9
Return on Total Assets 46	2.5	•	6.2	1.4	2.5	24.7	•	6.7	•	10.3	2.7
Return on Equity Before Income Taxes 47	•	•	9.3	0.3	1.0	73.7	•	17.8	•	30.7	0.4
Return on Equity After Income Taxes 48	•	•	8.3	•	1.0	49.8	•	17.3	•	30.7	•
Profit Margin (Before Income Tax) 49	•	•	2.7	0.1	0.3	18.4	•	4.4	•	0.5	0.1
Profit Margin (After Income Tax) 50	•	•	2.4	•	0.3	12.5	•	4.2	•	0.5	•

Table II

Corporations with Net Income

TEXTILE MILLS

MONEY AMOUNTS AND SIZE OF ASSETS IN THOUSANDS OF DOLLARS

Item Description for Accounting Period 7/08 Through 6/09	Total	Zero Assets	Under 500	500 to 1,000	1,000 to 5,000	5,000 to 10,000	10,000 to 25,000	25,000 to 50,000	50,000 to 100,000	100,000 to 250,000	250,000 to 500,000	500,000 to 2,500,000	2,500,000 and over
Number of Enterprises **1**	847	0	651	53	75	•	27	8	9	4	•	0	0
Revenues ($ in Thousands)													
Net Sales **2**	5173204	0	256764	205051	280664	•	753792	373361	1168840	829229	•	0	0
Interest **3**	9956	0	0	1	587	•	6	101	189	139	•	0	0
Rents **4**	5917	0	0	0	0	•	2837	0	730	0	•	0	0
Royalties **5**	6	0	0	0	0	•	0	0	0	0	•	0	0
Other Portfolio Income **6**	43282	0	0	0	7073	•	1026	10903	4825	13726	•	0	0
Other Receipts **7**	48461	0	0	56	4223	•	13578	1150	10557	3013	•	0	0
Total Receipts **8**	5280826	0	256764	205108	292547	•	771239	385515	1185141	846107	•	0	0
Average Total Receipts **9**	6235	•	394	3870	3901	•	28564	48189	131682	211527	•	•	•
Operating Costs/Operating Income (%)													
Cost of Operations **10**	67.3	•	32.5	76.2	70.7	•	76.6	40.2	78.3	76.6	•	•	•
Salaries and Wages **11**	6.4	•	8.2	2.1	3.8	•	5.6	3.1	6.1	2.9	•	•	•
Taxes Paid **12**	1.2	•	2.1	1.1	1.1	•	0.4	1.6	0.8	0.4	•	•	•
Interest Paid **13**	1.5	•	4.1	0.1	0.4	•	1.5	3.8	0.6	1.4	•	•	•
Depreciation **14**	2.6	•	0.6	0.7	1.7	•	3.1	2.1	2.4	4.8	•	•	•
Amortization and Depletion **15**	0.2	•	0.0	•	•	•	0.0	0.0	0.0	0.1	•	•	•
Pensions and Other Deferred Comp. **16**	0.5	•	0.1	•	0.1	•	0.0	0.0	0.4	0.1	•	•	•
Employee Benefits **17**	1.3	•	•	0.0	3.3	•	0.6	0.4	1.3	1.2	•	•	•
Advertising **18**	0.3	•	•	0.0	0.0	•	0.5	0.1	0.7	0.0	•	•	•
Other Expenses **19**	10.4	•	31.0	14.5	11.4	•	5.9	9.7	6.5	5.9	•	•	•
Officers' Compensation **20**	2.3	•	18.7	4.9	1.0	•	2.0	2.5	0.9	0.5	•	•	•
Operating Margin **21**	5.8	•	2.5	0.3	6.4	•	3.7	36.6	1.9	6.0	•	•	•
Operating Margin Before Officers' Comp. **22**	8.2	•	21.3	5.2	7.4	•	5.7	39.1	2.9	6.5	•	•	•

Selected Average Balance Sheet ($ in Thousands)

Net Receivables 23	837	82	237	405	2973	3969	11921	25256
Inventories 24	1238	17	239	745	6013	4717	20300	20052
Net Property, Plant and Equipment 25	1094	15	108	246	4135	9630	18008	73921
Total Assets 26	4817	132	548	1967	16642	27482	67824	154011
Notes and Loans Payable 27	1306	83	108	563	4399	8431	10238	61990
All Other Liabilities 28	1121	81	212	261	2527	7320	18127	27859
Net Worth 29	2391	-33	228	1143	9716	11732	39459	64162

Selected Financial Ratios (Times to 1)

Current Ratio 30	2.1	1.0	1.4	4.6	3.3	1.3	1.9	2.2
Quick Ratio 31	1.1	0.9	0.9	2.3	1.6	0.6	0.8	1.3
Net Sales to Working Capital 32	5.1	87.0	36.6	3.3	3.6	13.9	7.0	7.0
Coverage Ratio 33	6.2	1.6	3.6	28.5	4.9	11.5	6.7	6.7
Total Asset Turnover 34	1.3	3.0	7.1	1.9	1.7	1.7	1.9	1.3
Inventory Turnover 35	3.3	7.6	12.3	3.6	3.6	4.0	5.0	7.9
Receivables Turnover 36	5.7	3.6	13.1	6.1	9.3	15.4	11.1	•
Total Liabilities to Net Worth 37	1.0	•	1.4	0.7	0.7	1.3	0.7	1.4
Current Assets to Working Capital 38	1.9	25.2	3.8	1.3	1.4	4.5	2.1	1.8
Current Liabilities to Working Capital 39	0.9	24.2	2.8	0.3	0.4	3.5	1.1	0.8
Working Capital to Net Sales 40	0.2	0.0	0.0	0.3	0.3	0.1	0.1	0.1
Inventory to Working Capital 41	0.8	3.7	1.3	0.6	0.5	2.2	1.0	0.7
Total Receipts to Cash Flow 42	6.8	5.2	9.8	5.3	10.3	2.3	13.2	8.3
Cost of Goods to Cash Flow 43	4.6	1.7	7.5	3.8	7.9	0.9	10.4	6.4
Cash Flow to Total Debt 44	0.4	0.5	1.2	0.9	0.4	1.3	0.3	0.3

Selected Financial Factors (in Percentages)

Debt Ratio 45	50.4	124.9	58.4	41.9	41.6	57.3	41.8	58.3
Return on Total Assets 46	12.1	19.9	3.5	21.0	12.5	74.1	7.4	12.7
Return on Equity Before Income Taxes 47	20.4	•	6.1	34.8	17.1	158.4	10.8	25.9
Return on Equity After Income Taxes 48	16.7	•	5.2	34.1	17.1	115.3	9.4	24.4
Profit Margin (Before Income Tax) 49	8.0	2.5	0.4	10.6	6.0	39.8	3.3	8.0
Profit Margin (After Income Tax) 50	6.5	2.5	0.3	10.4	5.9	29.0	2.9	7.5

Table I

Corporations with and without Net Income

TEXTILE PRODUCT MILLS

MONEY AMOUNTS AND SIZE OF ASSETS IN THOUSANDS OF DOLLARS

Item Description for Accounting Period 7/08 Through 6/09		Total	Zero Assets	Under 500	500 to 1,000	1,000 to 5,000	5,000 to 10,000	10,000 to 25,000	25,000 to 50,000	50,000 to 100,000	100,000 to 250,000	250,000 to 500,000	500,000 to 2,500,000	2,500,000 and over
Number of Enterprises	1	1767	397	441	120	575	69	89	46	10	6	9	5	0
Revenues ($ in Thousands)														
Net Sales	2	24970957	369638	367775	231487	2380558	622320	3177992	2862462	1390058	1241626	4456300	7870743	0
Interest	3	61087	0	1219	482	337	113	1733	644	573	1112	11631	43243	0
Rents	4	3142	0	0	0	0	0	0	777	0	2142	0	222	0
Royalties	5	48810	0	0	0	0	0	0	0	0	231	10783	37796	0
Other Portfolio Income	6	98303	0	0	24256	0	1492	6306	3127	1277	3595	8202	50049	0
Other Receipts	7	734087	2	60	4834	14146	82404	5881	11434	11050	11385	44896	547993	0
Total Receipts	8	25916386	369640	369054	261059	2395041	706329	3191912	2878444	1402958	1260091	4531812	8550046	0
Average Total Receipts	9	14667	931	837	2175	4165	10237	35864	62575	140296	210015	503535	1710009	•
Operating Costs/Operating Income (%)														
Cost of Operations	10	71.4	51.5	79.6	60.6	59.7	65.8	84.4	78.5	82.2	82.3	74.4	62.9	•
Salaries and Wages	11	9.7	13.1	4.4	6.7	10.5	6.3	3.5	6.7	6.0	4.2	6.4	16.8	•
Taxes Paid	12	1.3	1.0	1.3	2.5	2.2	1.6	0.4	0.7	0.9	0.7	1.2	1.7	•
Interest Paid	13	2.0	1.0	1.0	0.7	1.2	3.2	0.8	1.4	1.1	2.4	3.0	2.6	•
Depreciation	14	2.8	•	0.9	0.2	4.1	5.9	1.4	1.6	1.9	3.0	2.2	4.0	•
Amortization and Depletion	15	0.5	•	•	0.0	0.1	0.0	1.2	0.3	0.4	0.4	0.6	0.6	•
Pensions and Other Deferred Comp.	16	0.5	•	•	0.7	0.3	0.3	0.1	0.4	0.3	0.5	0.5	1.0	•
Employee Benefits	17	1.9	•	0.3	4.9	0.9	2.3	1.3	1.0	1.1	2.1	1.6	3.1	•
Advertising	18	0.7	0.3	0.0	1.2	0.8	0.1	0.4	0.5	0.8	0.3	0.9	1.0	•
Other Expenses	19	11.5	11.4	13.2	15.0	19.3	10.9	6.0	7.2	7.2	7.7	8.2	16.2	•
Officers' Compensation	20	1.7	19.6	4.5	11.3	2.9	7.5	1.1	1.3	0.5	1.1	1.2	0.6	•
Operating Margin	21	•	2.1	•	•	•	•	•	0.4	•	•	•	•	•
Operating Margin Before Officers' Comp.	22	•	21.7	•	7.5	0.9	3.5	0.5	1.7	•	•	1.0	•	•

Selected Average Balance Sheet ($ in Thousands)

Net Receivables 23	1298	0	71	50	466	782	3019	6844	16282	24180	49604	119263	•
Inventories 24	2215	0	26	374	512	1764	5940	10592	14707	55219	52071	295516	•
Net Property, Plant and Equipment 25	2052	0	18	172	570	2874	3267	7026	16887	33588	59996	309500	•
Total Assets 26	10924	0	152	627	2125	5831	15369	35253	76869	136616	360790	1942290	•
Notes and Loans Payable 27	3993	0	325	270	1010	5848	3815	8776	21440	58592	194139	567947	•
All Other Liabilities 28	2566	0	82	377	443	944	4183	10090	16722	35278	90071	421397	•
Net Worth 29	4365	0	-255	-20	672	-961	7371	16386	38706	42746	76580	952946	•

Selected Financial Ratios (Times to 1)

Current Ratio 30	1.6	•	1.2	0.8	1.5	2.0	2.3	1.6	2.1	1.4	1.3	1.6	•
Quick Ratio 31	0.7	•	0.8	0.3	0.7	1.0	0.8	0.7	1.2	0.6	0.6	0.7	•
Net Sales to Working Capital 32	8.0	•	43.3	•	9.8	6.2	5.6	7.4	6.1	10.4	14.8	6.7	•
Coverage Ratio 33	0.8	3.2	•	13.0	•	3.9	1.0	1.7	•	•	1.5	0.3	•
Total Asset Turnover 34	1.3	•	5.5	3.1	1.9	1.5	2.3	1.8	1.8	1.5	1.4	0.8	•
Inventory Turnover 35	4.6	•	25.7	3.1	4.8	3.4	5.1	4.6	7.8	3.1	7.1	3.4	•
Receivables Turnover 36	10.8	•	17.7	6.8	10.3	6.7	11.0	8.3	9.4	5.5	13.2	13.5	•
Total Liabilities to Net Worth 37	1.5	•	•	•	2.2	•	1.1	1.2	1.0	2.2	3.7	1.0	•
Current Assets to Working Capital 38	2.7	•	7.0	2.9	2.9	2.0	2.6	1.9	1.9	3.4	4.3	2.6	•
Current Liabilities to Working Capital 39	1.7	•	6.0	1.9	1.9	1.0	1.7	0.9	0.9	2.4	3.3	1.6	•
Working Capital to Net Sales 40	0.1	•	0.0	0.1	0.1	0.2	0.2	0.1	0.2	0.1	0.1	0.1	•
Inventory to Working Capital 41	1.2	•	2.3	1.4	1.0	1.0	1.0	1.2	0.7	1.7	2.1	1.1	•
Total Receipts to Cash Flow 42	11.1	7.4	21.5	4.7	6.8	5.2	22.5	15.3	26.2	44.7	13.1	8.7	•
Cost of Goods to Cash Flow 43	7.9	3.8	17.1	2.9	4.1	3.4	18.9	12.0	21.5	36.8	9.7	5.4	•
Cash Flow to Total Debt 44	0.2	•	0.1	0.6	0.4	0.3	0.2	0.2	0.1	0.0	0.1	0.2	•

Selected Financial Factors (in Percentages)

Debt Ratio 45	60.0	•	267.1	103.2	68.4	116.5	52.0	53.5	49.6	68.7	78.8	50.9	•
Return on Total Assets 46	2.2	•	•	29.8	•	19.6	1.9	4.1	•	6.3	•	0.5	•
Return on Equity Before Income Taxes 47	•	•	15.9	•	•	•	0.0	3.5	•	•	10.4	•	•
Return on Equity After Income Taxes 48	•	•	16.6	•	•	•	•	3.1	•	•	5.7	•	•
Profit Margin (Before Income Tax) 49	•	2.1	8.9	•	9.5	•	0.9	•	•	•	1.6	•	•
Profit Margin (After Income Tax) 50	2.1	•	8.5	•	9.2	•	0.8	•	•	•	0.9	•	•

61

Table II

Corporations with Net Income

TEXTILE PRODUCT MILLS

MONEY AMOUNTS AND SIZE OF ASSETS IN THOUSANDS OF DOLLARS

Item Description for Accounting Period 7/08 Through 6/09	Total	Zero Assets	Under 500	500 to 1,000	1,000 to 5,000	5,000 to 10,000	10,000 to 25,000	25,000 to 50,000	50,000 to 100,000	100,000 to 250,000	250,000 to 500,000	500,000 to 2,500,000	2,500,000 and over
Number of Enterprises **1**	1215	•	167	•	443	63	49	29	7	0	0	0	0

Revenues ($ in Thousands)

	Total	Zero Assets	Under 500	500 to 1,000	1,000 to 5,000	5,000 to 10,000	10,000 to 25,000	25,000 to 50,000	50,000 to 100,000	100,000 to 250,000	250,000 to 500,000	500,000 to 2,500,000	2,500,000 and over
Net Sales **2**	12391575	•	301407	•	1768294	444260	1898016	2018930	1057100	0	0	0	0
Interest **3**	47333	•	1146	•	319	113	1397	510	293	0	0	0	0
Rents **4**	476	•	0	•	0	0	0	311	0	0	0	0	0
Royalties **5**	25694	•	0	•	0	0	0	0	0	0	0	0	0
Other Portfolio Income **6**	77050	•	0	•	0	0	5546	2933	696	0	0	0	0
Other Receipts **7**	222141	•	60	•	12690	77264	2364	6337	8117	0	0	0	0
Total Receipts **8**	12764269	•	302613	•	1781303	521637	1907323	2029021	1066206	0	0	0	0
Average Total Receipts **9**	10506	•	1812	•	4021	8280	38925	69966	152315	•	•	•	•

Operating Costs/Operating Income (%)

	Total	Zero Assets	Under 500	500 to 1,000	1,000 to 5,000	5,000 to 10,000	10,000 to 25,000	25,000 to 50,000	50,000 to 100,000	100,000 to 250,000	250,000 to 500,000	500,000 to 2,500,000	2,500,000 and over
Cost of Operations **10**	70.5	•	76.4	•	58.2	60.1	83.2	76.1	78.2	•	•	•	•
Salaries and Wages **11**	7.9	•	5.3	•	11.9	6.2	2.8	7.6	5.1	•	•	•	•
Taxes Paid **12**	1.1	•	1.2	•	2.2	1.3	0.4	0.6	0.8	•	•	•	•
Interest Paid **13**	1.9	•	0.2	•	0.9	3.0	0.7	1.3	0.5	•	•	•	•
Depreciation **14**	2.3	•	0.3	•	2.2	7.6	1.3	1.4	2.7	•	•	•	•
Amortization and Depletion **15**	0.3	•	•	•	0.1	0.1	0.2	0.3	0.3	•	•	•	•
Pensions and Other Deferred Comp. **16**	0.6	•	•	•	0.2	0.5	0.1	0.3	0.2	•	•	•	•
Employee Benefits **17**	1.3	•	0.3	•	1.2	0.1	1.2	0.7	1.3	•	•	•	•
Advertising **18**	0.7	•	0.0	•	1.1	0.2	0.2	0.5	0.5	•	•	•	•
Other Expenses **19**	9.5	•	11.1	•	18.5	11.7	5.5	7.3	6.0	•	•	•	•
Officers' Compensation **20**	2.5	•	3.9	•	2.9	9.4	1.4	1.2	0.8	•	•	•	•
Operating Margin **21**	1.4	•	1.2	•	0.6	•	3.2	2.7	3.5	•	•	•	•
Operating Margin Before Officers' Comp. **22**	3.9	•	5.1	•	3.5	9.3	4.5	3.9	4.3	•	•	•	•

Selected Average Balance Sheet ($ in Thousands)

Net Receivables 23	1299	143	526	847	3849	7646	15148
Inventories 24	1889	59	584	1521	6187	11409	20418
Net Property, Plant and Equipment 25	1216	17	342	2706	3439	4702	27430
Total Assets 26	7070	303	1906	5529	15722	34132	84614
Notes and Loans Payable 27	2139	116	723	3760	4004	8874	15036
All Other Liabilities 28	1669	152	467	394	3810	12184	17365
Net Worth 29	3263	35	716	1375	7909	13073	52213

Selected Financial Ratios (Times to 1)

Current Ratio 30	2.0	1.2	1.5	2.3	2.6	1.4	2.2
Quick Ratio 31	1.1	0.8	0.7	1.3	1.1	0.6	1.1
Net Sales to Working Capital 32	5.4	38.6	10.0	4.4	5.4	9.8	6.2
Coverage Ratio 33	3.3	7.4	2.5	6.7	7.0	3.5	9.1
Total Asset Turnover 34	1.4	6.0	2.1	1.3	2.5	2.0	1.8
Inventory Turnover 35	3.8	23.3	4.0	2.8	5.2	4.6	5.8
Receivables Turnover 36	8.3	17.7	8.3	6.0	10.0	8.6	•
Total Liabilities to Net Worth 37	1.2	7.7	1.7	3.0	1.0	1.6	0.6
Current Assets to Working Capital 38	2.0	6.1	3.2	1.7	1.6	3.4	1.9
Current Liabilities to Working Capital 39	1.0	5.1	2.2	0.7	0.6	2.4	0.9
Working Capital to Net Sales 40	0.2	0.0	0.1	0.2	0.2	0.1	0.2
Inventory to Working Capital 41	0.7	2.2	1.5	0.8	0.9	1.4	0.8
Total Receipts to Cash Flow 42	8.4	10.9	6.0	3.6	12.8	11.3	12.2
Cost of Goods to Cash Flow 43	6.0	8.3	3.5	2.2	10.7	8.6	9.6
Cash Flow to Total Debt 44	0.3	0.6	0.6	0.5	0.4	0.3	0.4

Selected Financial Factors (in Percentages)

Debt Ratio 45	53.9	88.5	62.5	75.1	49.7	61.7	38.3
Return on Total Assets 46	9.0	10.8	4.7	25.9	11.3	9.1	8.8
Return on Equity Before Income Taxes 47	13.7	81.3	7.5	88.8	19.2	17.1	12.7
Return on Equity After Income Taxes 48	11.7	68.2	6.1	87.3	16.7	16.4	12.5
Profit Margin (Before Income Tax) 49	4.4	1.6	1.3	17.3	3.9	3.2	4.4
Profit Margin (After Income Tax) 50	3.7	1.3	1.1	17.0	3.4	3.1	4.3

Table I

Corporations with and without Net Income

APPAREL KNITTING MILLS

MONEY AMOUNTS AND SIZE OF ASSETS IN THOUSANDS OF DOLLARS

Item Description for Accounting Period 7/08 Through 6/09		Total	Zero Assets	Under 500	500 to 1,000	1,000 to 5,000	5,000 to 10,000	10,000 to 25,000	25,000 to 50,000	50,000 to 100,000	100,000 to 250,000	250,000 to 500,000	500,000 to 2,500,000	2,500,000 and over
Number of Enterprises	1	190	0	86	34	21	10	24	5	3	4	3	0	0
Revenues ($ in Thousands)														
Net Sales	2	6666713	0	78131	51663	37336	172372	680525	258985	211050	738573	4438078	0	0
Interest	3	6035	0	0	0	2318	8	1699	158	25	1298	530	0	0
Rents	4	40	0	0	0	0	0	13	0	16	12	0	0	0
Royalties	5	45299	0	0	0	0	0	0	104	0	10193	35002	0	0
Other Portfolio Income	6	41975	0	0	8782	2321	33	823	150	0	3841	26026	0	0
Other Receipts	7	-3648	0	0	139	-1	0	-9040	70	1214	-2099	6067	0	0
Total Receipts	8	6756414	0	78131	60584	41974	172413	674020	259467	212305	751818	4505703	0	0
Average Total Receipts	9	35560	•	908	1782	1999	17241	28084	51893	70768	187954	1501901	•	•
Operating Costs/Operating Income (%)														
Cost of Operations	10	72.3	•	53.5	78.8	74.1	63.5	79.7	80.5	67.0	73.9	71.3	•	•
Salaries and Wages	11	7.9	•	22.4	7.0	2.2	5.3	6.0	3.7	5.0	5.4	8.8	•	•
Taxes Paid	12	1.2	•	0.1	1.6	3.8	0.7	1.3	0.5	0.7	1.1	1.2	•	•
Interest Paid	13	2.9	•	1.3	0.5	0.5	1.4	0.6	1.3	1.1	1.9	3.7	•	•
Depreciation	14	1.5	•	6.5	0.5	0.8	5.1	1.1	2.5	1.2	3.0	1.0	•	•
Amortization and Depletion	15	0.3	•	•	•	•	0.0	0.0	0.7	0.3	0.8	0.3	•	•
Pensions and Other Deferred Comp.	16	0.3	•	•	•	0.1	0.2	0.0	0.2	0.9	0.3	0.3	•	•
Employee Benefits	17	1.4	•	•	0.2	0.6	1.1	0.6	0.3	0.3	1.9	1.6	•	•
Advertising	18	3.9	•	0.2	1.4	7.7	0.2	0.1	1.6	9.9	4.5	4.5	•	•
Other Expenses	19	7.7	•	12.7	10.8	12.1	7.9	6.1	10.2	7.6	8.5	7.4	•	•
Officers' Compensation	20	0.8	•	•	13.3	5.0	2.0	1.6	1.2	1.7	0.8	0.4	•	•
Operating Margin	21	•	•	3.4	•	•	12.5	2.8	•	4.3	•	•	•	•
Operating Margin Before Officers' Comp.	22	0.7	•	3.4	•	•	14.5	4.4	•	6.1	•	•	•	•

Selected Average Balance Sheet ($ in Thousands)

Net Receivables 23	4106	224	162	124	1035	3054	6658	10005	29826	162158
Inventories 24	8284	8	531	1353	702	2088	17578	15144	47939	392218
Net Property, Plant and Equipment 25	3083	5	11	64	4275	1820	4179	11819	38233	95998
Total Assets 26	26001	286	938	2755	7954	15328	28884	60845	162591	1134038
Notes and Loans Payable 27	14597	74	25	13	1983	2155	15443	22224	53650	778626
All Other Liabilities 28	7963	183	51	470	2315	1700	4781	15261	33462	406015
Net Worth 29	3442	29	862	2272	3656	11473	8460	23360	75479	-50602

Selected Financial Ratios (Times to 1)

Current Ratio 30	2.9	1.5	18.1	1.4	1.6	3.5	5.0	2.5	3.2	2.8
Quick Ratio 31	1.0	1.5	7.6	1.2	1.0	2.6	2.1	1.2	1.1	0.7
Net Sales to Working Capital 32	3.5	9.3	1.7	9.1	13.0	4.3	3.1	3.6	3.0	3.4
Coverage Ratio 33	1.5	3.5	•	11.4	9.8	4.2	•	5.6	1.2	1.4
Total Asset Turnover 34	1.3	3.2	1.6	0.6	2.2	1.8	1.8	1.2	1.1	1.3
Inventory Turnover 35	3.1	57.7	2.3	1.0	15.6	10.8	2.4	3.1	2.8	2.7
Receivables Turnover 36	7.7	8.1	18.8	4.5	26.1	8.6	5.1	14.1	6.5	7.6
Total Liabilities to Net Worth 37	6.6	8.7	0.1	0.2	1.2	0.3	2.4	1.6	1.2	•
Current Assets to Working Capital 38	1.5	2.9	1.1	3.4	2.7	1.4	1.3	1.7	1.5	1.5
Current Liabilities to Working Capital 39	0.5	1.9	0.1	2.4	1.7	0.4	0.3	0.7	0.5	0.5
Working Capital to Net Sales 40	0.3	0.1	0.6	0.1	0.1	0.2	0.3	0.3	0.3	0.3
Inventory to Working Capital 41	0.8	0.1	0.6	0.6	0.8	0.2	0.7	0.8	0.9	0.9
Total Receipts to Cash Flow 42	14.3	7.8	•	21.9	5.5	16.6	16.1	9.2	15.1	14.9
Cost of Goods to Cash Flow 43	10.3	4.2	16.2	16.2	3.5	13.2	13.0	6.2	11.2	10.6
Cash Flow to Total Debt 44	0.1	0.5	•	0.2	0.7	0.4	0.2	0.2	0.1	0.1

Selected Financial Factors (in Percentages)

Debt Ratio 45	86.8	89.7	8.0	17.5	54.0	25.2	70.5	61.6	53.6	104.5
Return on Total Assets 46	6.0	15.0	5.8	3.9	30.2	4.3	•	7.0	2.5	6.6
Return on Equity Before Income Taxes 47	16.1	104.5	6.4	4.3	59.1	4.4	•	14.9	0.7	•
Return on Equity After Income Taxes 48	12.2	88.8	6.4	3.5	59.1	3.6	•	10.0	0.3	•
Profit Margin (Before Income Tax) 49	1.6	3.4	3.6	5.5	12.5	1.8	•	4.9	0.3	1.3
Profit Margin (After Income Tax) 50	1.2	2.9	3.6	4.5	12.5	1.5	•	3.3	0.1	0.9

Table II

Corporations with Net Income

APPAREL KNITTING MILLS

Money Amounts and Size of Assets in Thousands of Dollars

Item Description for Accounting Period 7/08 Through 6/09	Total	Zero Assets	Under 500	500 to 1,000	1,000 to 5,000	5,000 to 10,000	10,000 to 25,000	25,000 to 50,000	50,000 to 100,000	100,000 to 250,000	250,000 to 500,000	500,000 to 2,500,000	2,500,000 and over
Number of Enterprises **1**	169	0	86	34	•	4	11	•	•	0	•	0	0
Revenues ($ in Thousands)													
Net Sales **2**	6264025	0	78131	51663	•	56593	580531	•	•	0	•	0	0
Interest **3**	4270	0	0	0	•	0	223	•	•	0	•	0	0
Rents **4**	16	0	0	0	•	0	0	•	•	0	•	0	0
Royalties **5**	36581	0	0	0	•	0	0	•	•	0	•	0	0
Other Portfolio Income **6**	37842	0	0	8782	•	0	712	•	•	0	•	0	0
Other Receipts **7**	5311	0	0	139	•	0	0	•	•	0	•	0	0
Total Receipts **8**	6348045	0	78131	60584	•	56593	581466	•	•	•	•	•	•
Average Total Receipts **9**	37562	•	908	1782	•	14148	52861	•	•	•	•	•	•
Operating Costs/Operating Income (%)													
Cost of Operations **10**	72.0	•	53.5	78.8	•	20.6	80.6	•	•	•	•	•	•
Salaries and Wages **11**	7.9	•	22.4	7.0	•	11.9	5.3	•	•	•	•	•	•
Taxes Paid **12**	1.2	•	0.1	1.6	•	2.1	1.4	•	•	•	•	•	•
Interest Paid **13**	2.9	•	1.3	•	•	0.0	0.3	•	•	•	•	•	•
Depreciation **14**	1.4	•	6.5	0.5	•	4.1	1.2	•	•	•	•	•	•
Amortization and Depletion **15**	0.3	•	•	•	•	0.0	0.0	•	•	•	•	•	•
Pensions and Other Deferred Comp. **16**	0.3	•	•	•	•	0.2	0.0	•	•	•	•	•	•
Employee Benefits **17**	1.4	•	•	•	•	•	0.7	•	•	•	•	•	•
Advertising **18**	4.1	•	0.2	0.2	•	0.7	0.0	•	•	•	•	•	•
Other Expenses **19**	7.3	•	12.7	10.8	•	15.8	4.7	•	•	•	•	•	•
Officers' Compensation **20**	0.7	•	•	13.3	•	2.1	1.1	•	•	•	•	•	•
Operating Margin **21**	0.5	•	3.4	•	•	42.5	4.6	•	•	•	•	•	•
Operating Margin Before Officers' Comp. **22**	1.2	•	3.4	•	•	44.6	5.7	•	•	•	•	•	•

Selected Average Balance Sheet ($ in Thousands)

Net Receivables 23	4217	224	162	1510	5901
Inventories 24	8061	8	531	864	1446
Net Property, Plant and Equipment 25	2892	5	11	1664	3211
Total Assets 26	26357	286	938	7041	17048
Notes and Loans Payable 27	15285	74	25	52	1874
All Other Liabilities 28	8547	183	51	417	2666
Net Worth 29	2525	29	862	6572	12508

Selected Financial Ratios (Times to 1)

Current Ratio 30	2.9	1.5	18.1	11.7	3.0
Quick Ratio 31	0.9	1.5	7.6	9.5	2.6
Net Sales to Working Capital 32	3.6	9.3	1.7	3.0	5.8
Coverage Ratio 33	1.7	3.5		1093.0	16.7
Total Asset Turnover 34	1.4	3.2	1.6	2.0	3.1
Inventory Turnover 35	3.3	57.7	2.3	3.4	29.4
Receivables Turnover 36	8.3	8.1	18.8	18.7	8.6
Total Liabilities to Net Worth 37	9.4	8.7	0.1	0.1	0.4
Current Assets to Working Capital 38	1.5	2.9	1.1	1.1	1.5
Current Liabilities to Working Capital 39	0.5	1.9	0.1	0.1	0.5
Working Capital to Net Sales 40	0.3	0.1	0.6	0.3	0.2
Inventory to Working Capital 41	0.8	0.1	0.6	0.2	0.2
Total Receipts to Cash Flow 42	13.7	7.8		1.8	13.1
Cost of Goods to Cash Flow 43	9.9	4.2		0.4	10.6
Cash Flow to Total Debt 44	0.1	0.5		16.6	0.9

Selected Financial Factors (in Percentages)

Debt Ratio 45	90.4	89.7	8.0	6.7	26.6
Return on Total Assets 46	7.2	15.0	5.8	85.4	15.2
Return on Equity Before Income Taxes 47	31.8	104.5	6.4	91.4	19.5
Return on Equity After Income Taxes 48	25.8	88.8	6.4	91.4	17.9
Profit Margin (Before Income Tax) 49	2.2	3.4	3.6	42.4	4.6
Profit Margin (After Income Tax) 50	1.8	2.9	3.6	42.4	4.2

Table I

Corporations with and without Net Income

CUT AND SEW APPAREL CONTRACTORS AND MFRS.

MONEY AMOUNTS AND SIZE OF ASSETS IN THOUSANDS OF DOLLARS

Item Description for Accounting Period 7/08 Through 6/09	Total	Zero Assets	Under 500	500 to 1,000	1,000 to 5,000	5,000 to 10,000	10,000 to 25,000	25,000 to 50,000	50,000 to 100,000	100,000 to 250,000	250,000 to 500,000	500,000 to 2,500,000	2,500,000 and over
Number of Enterprises 1	6095	1587	3251	339	571	117	142	41	21	14	7	7	0
Revenues ($ in Thousands)													
Net Sales 2	39898245	202094	1075756	539798	3229584	2661263	4997769	2501284	2389689	3133386	3223095	15944528	0
Interest 3	147504	0	186	698	2869	262	1731	351	1101	7580	90	132636	0
Rents 4	26073	0	0	0	328	0	0	797	2133	965	0	21849	0
Royalties 5	816587	0	0	0	470	0	91	8755	403	373	8440	798055	0
Other Portfolio Income 6	128973	3334	0	0	1533	10	14100	601	7120	149	799	101325	0
Other Receipts 7	1040164	0	11937	358	20784	60154	70751	16188	31794	16167	39249	772784	0
Total Receipts 8	42057546	205428	1087879	540854	3255568	2721689	5084442	2527976	2432240	3158620	3271673	17771177	0
Average Total Receipts 9	6900	129	335	1595	5702	23262	35806	61658	115821	225616	467382	2538740	•
Operating Costs/Operating Income (%)													
Cost of Operations 10	65.2	41.5	61.4	55.1	68.3	72.2	76.4	70.1	69.3	65.4	58.0	60.7	•
Salaries and Wages 11	10.5	35.5	3.8	15.4	10.2	8.6	6.2	8.8	10.9	10.3	10.9	12.3	•
Taxes Paid 12	2.0	4.7	3.1	1.5	1.8	2.7	2.1	2.7	1.7	1.8	1.8	1.7	•
Interest Paid 13	2.0	0.9	0.6	1.1	1.3	1.0	1.1	1.8	1.0	1.5	2.1	3.1	•
Depreciation 14	1.7	0.2	1.3	2.9	0.6	0.3	0.8	1.2	1.6	1.7	2.7	2.3	•
Amortization and Depletion 15	0.7	•	0.0	0.0	0.1	0.0	0.2	0.3	0.2	0.3	0.7	1.3	•
Pensions and Other Deferred Comp. 16	0.4	•	•	0.2	0.2	0.1	0.1	0.1	0.5	0.4	0.3	0.7	•
Employee Benefits 17	1.4	0.0	1.9	0.6	0.9	0.3	0.4	0.7	1.2	1.4	1.9	1.9	•
Advertising 18	2.6	•	0.3	0.7	1.2	2.2	0.7	1.9	1.8	2.5	4.7	3.5	•
Other Expenses 19	15.6	23.2	26.7	23.3	13.4	11.4	9.2	11.3	9.1	10.2	14.2	20.7	•
Officers' Compensation 20	2.2	5.9	7.6	3.1	4.5	2.1	3.0	1.8	1.5	1.6	1.5	1.6	•
Operating Margin 21	•	•	•	•	•	•	•	•	1.2	3.0	1.3	•	•
Operating Margin Before Officers' Comp. 22	•	•	0.7	•	2.1	1.2	2.8	1.1	2.7	4.6	2.8	•	•

Selected Average Balance Sheet ($ in Thousands)

Item												
Net Receivables 23	918	0	17	106	297	2519	3303	4386	12919	29201	54361	475116
Inventories 24	1036	0	22	186	1030	3598	5438	14143	22567	36831	116608	296708
Net Property, Plant and Equipment 25	529	0	11	206	195	484	1529	3319	8224	22284	57946	244156
Total Assets 26	4444	0	98	698	2335	7593	15581	32307	67884	149094	376438	2089176
Notes and Loans Payable 27	1352	0	91	350	938	2842	4576	6637	17529	45246	99803	619060
All Other Liabilities 28	1468	0	30	127	667	1454	4393	11471	17753	43231	107215	776101
Net Worth 29	1624	0	-23	221	730	3298	6612	14199	32602	60617	169420	694015

Selected Financial Ratios (Times to 1)

Item												
Current Ratio 30	2.0	1.9	1.5	2.1	2.1	1.6	1.8	2.2	2.1	2.3	2.1	
Quick Ratio 31	1.0	1.2	0.7	0.8	1.0	0.6	0.4	0.9	0.8	0.9	1.3	
Net Sales to Working Capital 32	5.0	10.4	15.0	5.5	6.7	8.5	5.6	4.6	4.2	3.8	4.4	
Coverage Ratio 33	1.7	•	•	•	2.3	2.4	1.2	4.1	3.5	2.4	1.7	
Total Asset Turnover 34	1.5	3.4	2.3	2.4	3.0	2.3	1.9	1.7	1.5	1.2	1.1	
Inventory Turnover 35	4.1	9.4	4.7	3.7	4.6	4.9	3.0	3.5	4.0	2.3	4.7	
Receivables Turnover 36	6.9	21.6	12.4	16.8	9.6	10.8	8.6	8.5	8.8	4.3	•	
Total Liabilities to Net Worth 37	1.7	•	2.2	2.2	1.3	1.4	1.3	1.1	1.5	1.2	2.0	
Current Assets to Working Capital 38	2.0	2.1	2.9	1.9	1.9	2.8	2.3	1.8	1.9	1.7	1.9	
Current Liabilities to Working Capital 39	1.0	1.1	1.9	0.9	0.9	1.8	1.3	0.8	0.9	0.7	0.9	
Working Capital to Net Sales 40	0.2	0.1	0.1	0.2	0.1	0.1	0.2	0.2	0.2	0.3	0.2	
Inventory to Working Capital 41	0.8	0.7	1.6	1.1	0.9	1.3	1.2	0.9	0.7	0.9	0.6	
Total Receipts to Cash Flow 42	7.8	14.3	8.7	7.0	11.6	9.0	11.4	10.7	10.7	9.9	7.3	6.0
Cost of Goods to Cash Flow 43	5.1	5.9	5.3	3.9	7.9	6.5	8.7	7.5	7.4	6.5	4.2	3.7
Cash Flow to Total Debt 44	0.3	0.3	0.5	0.3	0.6	0.3	0.3	0.2	0.3	0.3	0.3	0.3

Selected Financial Factors (in Percentages)

Item												
Debt Ratio 45	63.4	123.8	68.4	68.7	56.6	57.6	56.1	52.0	59.3	55.0	66.8	
Return on Total Assets 46	5.2	•	•	•	7.2	6.0	4.0	6.7	8.1	6.1	5.7	
Return on Equity Before Income Taxes 47	6.0	82.2	•	•	9.5	8.3	1.6	10.6	14.2	7.9	7.1	
Return on Equity After Income Taxes 48	2.8	82.8	•	•	8.3	7.9	1.5	9.0	13.1	6.8	1.4	
Profit Margin (Before Income Tax) 49	1.5	•	•	•	1.4	1.6	0.4	3.0	3.8	2.9	2.2	
Profit Margin (After Income Tax) 50	0.7	•	•	•	1.2	1.5	0.4	2.6	3.5	2.5	0.4	

65

Table II

Corporations with Net Income

CUT AND SEW APPAREL CONTRACTORS AND MFRS.

MONEY AMOUNTS AND SIZE OF ASSETS IN THOUSANDS OF DOLLARS

Item Description for Accounting Period 7/08 Through 6/09		Total	Zero Assets	Under 500	500 to 1,000	1,000 to 5,000	5,000 to 10,000	10,000 to 25,000	25,000 to 50,000	50,000 to 100,000	100,000 to 250,000	250,000 to 500,000	500,000 to 2,500,000	2,500,000 and over
Number of Enterprises	1	2051	298	1067	66	386	101	89	12	13	•	•	•	0
Revenues ($ in Thousands)														
Net Sales	2	25867437	1569	523557	168711	2016133	2258078	3336482	1054841	1549739	•	•	•	0
Interest	3	91321	0	186	1	1452	253	155	0	929	•	•	•	0
Rents	4	15410	0	0	0	19	0	0	0	2133	•	•	•	0
Royalties	5	620619	0	0	0	281	0	0	0	403	•	•	•	0
Other Portfolio Income	6	81507	0	0	0	1506	10	710	10	7040	•	•	•	0
Other Receipts	7	820045	0	1	359	20293	59753	30968	8114	22249	•	•	•	0
Total Receipts	8	27496339	1569	523744	169071	2039684	2318094	3368315	1062965	1582493	•	•	•	•
Average Total Receipts	9	13406	5	491	2562	5284	22951	37846	88580	121730	•	•	•	•
Operating Costs/Operating Income (%)														
Cost of Operations	10	63.2	1.5	44.4	37.0	65.5	71.2	74.3	75.5	71.9	•	•	•	•
Salaries and Wages	11	9.9	2.4	5.8	23.3	7.8	8.6	5.6	6.1	8.7	•	•	•	•
Taxes Paid	12	1.6	0.3	2.2	2.5	1.6	2.3	1.7	1.4	0.9	•	•	•	•
Interest Paid	13	2.2	0.1	0.7	0.2	1.1	1.1	0.8	0.5	0.8	•	•	•	•
Depreciation	14	1.5	0.1	1.1	0.3	0.8	0.4	0.6	1.2	1.0	•	•	•	•
Amortization and Depletion	15	0.4	•	0.1	0.0	0.0	0.0	0.1	0.0	0.2	•	•	•	•
Pensions and Other Deferred Comp.	16	0.4	•	•	•	0.2	0.1	0.1	0.2	0.3	•	•	•	•
Employee Benefits	17	1.4	•	0.8	0.4	0.6	0.3	0.4	0.6	0.6	•	•	•	•
Advertising	18	2.8	•	0.3	1.3	1.9	2.6	0.6	0.4	0.6	•	•	•	•
Other Expenses	19	14.9	1.8	33.4	30.3	10.7	12.2	8.1	5.3	8.0	•	•	•	•
Officers' Compensation	20	2.0	•	5.4	3.4	4.9	1.4	3.3	1.5	1.9	•	•	•	•
Operating Margin	21	•	93.8	5.8	1.3	5.0	•	4.4	7.2	5.1	•	•	•	•
Operating Margin Before Officers' Comp.	22	1.7	93.8	11.2	4.7	9.9	1.3	7.7	8.7	7.0	•	•	•	•

Selected Average Balance Sheet ($ in Thousands)

Net Receivables 23	1689	0	32	8	286	2479	2991	6056	15133
Inventories 24	2233	0	50	351	1206	3183	5233	21513	26344
Net Property, Plant and Equipment 25	960	0	17	81	264	422	1071	4049	6141
Total Assets 26	8947	0	158	562	2519	7876	15001	32111	67853
Notes and Loans Payable 27	2651	0	82	174	825	2907	2467	6236	11465
All Other Liabilities 28	2935	0	34	220	661	1440	5341	5792	17888
Net Worth 29	3361	0	43	168	1033	3529	7193	20083	38501

Selected Financial Ratios (Times to 1)

Current Ratio 30	2.3	•	3.2	1.5	2.5	2.2	1.7	2.3	2.4
Quick Ratio 31	1.1	•	1.8	0.2	1.1	1.0	0.6	0.7	1.1
Net Sales to Working Capital 32	4.6	•	6.6	15.4	4.1	6.0	8.4	5.6	4.4
Coverage Ratio 33	3.9	1473.0	8.9	10.0	6.7	3.3	7.8	16.6	9.8
Total Asset Turnover 34	1.4	•	3.1	4.5	2.1	2.8	2.5	2.7	1.8
Inventory Turnover 35	3.6	•	4.4	2.7	2.8	5.0	5.3	3.1	3.3
Receivables Turnover 36	6.8	•	18.7	15.3	15.9	•	10.7	5.8	7.5
Total Liabilities to Net Worth 37	1.7	•	2.7	2.4	1.4	1.2	1.1	0.6	0.8
Current Assets to Working Capital 38	1.8	•	1.4	2.9	1.7	1.8	2.5	1.7	1.7
Current Liabilities to Working Capital 39	0.8	•	0.4	1.9	0.7	0.8	1.5	0.7	0.7
Working Capital to Net Sales 40	0.2	•	0.2	0.1	0.2	0.2	0.1	0.2	0.2
Inventory to Working Capital 41	0.7	•	0.6	2.5	0.9	0.9	1.0	0.7	0.8
Total Receipts to Cash Flow 42	5.7	1.1	3.3	3.7	7.1	7.8	8.4	8.6	7.5
Cost of Goods to Cash Flow 43	3.6	0.0	1.5	1.4	4.6	5.5	6.3	6.5	5.4
Cash Flow to Total Debt 44	0.4	•	1.3	1.7	0.5	0.7	0.6	0.8	0.5

Selected Financial Factors (in Percentages)

Debt Ratio 45	62.4	•	73.1	70.2	59.0	55.2	52.0	37.5	43.3
Return on Total Assets 46	12.2	•	20.3	7.7	15.0	10.1	15.3	23.2	14.2
Return on Equity Before Income Taxes 47	24.2	•	66.8	23.1	31.0	15.7	27.8	34.9	22.5
Return on Equity After Income Taxes 48	19.6	•	65.8	22.9	30.2	14.4	27.3	34.8	20.3
Profit Margin (Before Income Tax) 49	6.4	93.8	5.8	1.5	6.1	2.5	5.3	8.0	7.3
Profit Margin (After Income Tax) 50	5.2	93.8	5.7	1.5	6.0	2.3	5.2	8.0	6.6

Table I

Corporations with and without Net Income

APPAREL ACCESSORIES AND OTHER APPAREL

MONEY AMOUNTS AND SIZE OF ASSETS IN THOUSANDS OF DOLLARS

Item Description for Accounting Period 7/08 Through 6/09	Total	Zero Assets	Under 500	500 to 1,000	1,000 to 5,000	5,000 to 10,000	10,000 to 25,000	25,000 to 50,000	50,000 to 100,000	100,000 to 250,000	250,000 to 500,000	500,000 to 2,500,000	2,500,000 and over
Number of Enterprises 1	4212	1529	1880	205	484	11	66	25	7	5	0	0	0
Revenues ($ in Thousands)													
Net Sales 2	10315577	181436	990679	918733	2258147	205232	1591707	1386121	716207	2067317	0	0	0
Interest 3	19237	9	127	0	2683	361	816	2281	416	12545	0	0	0
Rents 4	604	0	0	0	0	102	2	79	420	0	0	0	0
Royalties 5	2725	0	0	0	0	0	1107	30	110	1479	0	0	0
Other Portfolio Income 6	8977	0	0	0	7899	53	141	61	158	664	0	0	0
Other Receipts 7	90269	-1	7044	306	12883	841	13754	6362	1987	47090	0	0	0
Total Receipts 8	10437389	181444	997850	919039	2281612	206589	1607527	1394934	719298	2129095	0	0	•
Average Total Receipts 9	2478	119	531	4483	4714	18781	24356	55797	102757	425819	•	•	•
Operating Costs/Operating Income (%)													
Cost of Operations 10	63.4	58.3	52.7	84.6	64.5	81.9	62.7	71.1	70.6	49.2	•	•	•
Salaries and Wages 11	10.6	23.7	8.8	7.2	10.6	12.0	12.7	7.0	8.1	13.4	•	•	•
Taxes Paid 12	2.2	0.9	1.8	0.8	2.1	1.6	1.8	1.8	1.1	4.5	•	•	•
Interest Paid 13	1.9	2.5	0.3	1.2	1.1	1.4	1.7	2.4	1.3	4.1	•	•	•
Depreciation 14	1.2	0.4	0.2	0.4	0.8	0.4	1.7	1.8	1.0	1.9	•	•	•
Amortization and Depletion 15	0.3	0.0	0.1	0.0	0.1	0.0	0.3	0.2	0.2	0.8	•	•	•
Pensions and Other Deferred Comp. 16	0.2	0.0	0.2	•	0.6	0.0	0.3	0.2	0.0	0.0	•	•	•
Employee Benefits 17	1.0	0.0	0.3	0.4	1.0	1.3	1.6	1.0	0.5	1.3	•	•	•
Advertising 18	1.5	0.4	1.2	0.3	0.8	2.7	1.4	3.0	0.8	2.5	•	•	•
Other Expenses 19	13.9	13.4	21.7	10.2	10.0	15.7	10.4	12.2	12.0	20.7	•	•	•
Officers' Compensation 20	3.5	•	9.7	3.1	6.2	3.5	2.0	1.4	2.6	0.9	•	•	•
Operating Margin 21	0.2	0.3	3.0	•	2.3	•	3.4	•	1.9	0.7	•	•	•
Operating Margin Before Officers' Comp. 22	3.6	0.3	12.7	•	8.5	•	5.4	•	4.5	1.5	•	•	•

Selected Average Balance Sheet ($ in Thousands)

Net Receivables 23	278	0	25	61	476	1597	3023	8257	18245	66242
Inventories 24	457	0	58	533	720	2779	6412	11961	24419	86972
Net Property, Plant and Equipment 25	149	0	3	48	276	678	1745	4417	5664	40944
Total Assets 26	1365	0	170	734	2094	6284	16247	36698	73560	338297
Notes and Loans Payable 27	569	0	86	466	554	958	6372	17240	41449	144032
All Other Liabilities 28	462	0	51	413	653	2431	3108	8234	20303	174135
Net Worth 29	333	0	33	-145	887	2894	6767	11224	11808	20130

Selected Financial Ratios (Times to 1)

Current Ratio 30	1.6	•	2.9	1.4	1.9	1.9	1.8	1.8	1.8	1.1
Quick Ratio 31	0.7	•	1.5	0.4	0.9	1.5	0.6	0.6	0.8	0.5
Net Sales to Working Capital 32	6.9	•	5.0	24.7	7.1	7.5	4.7	4.4	4.1	24.0
Coverage Ratio 33	1.7	1.1	11.6	•	4.0	•	3.7	0.4	2.9	1.9
Total Asset Turnover 34	1.8	•	3.1	6.1	2.2	3.0	1.5	1.5	1.4	1.2
Inventory Turnover 35	3.4	•	4.8	7.1	4.2	5.5	2.4	3.3	3.0	2.3
Receivables Turnover 36	8.8	•	15.3	42.2	9.0	8.9	6.9	6.8	5.5	8.2
Total Liabilities to Net Worth 37	3.1	•	4.2	•	1.4	1.2	1.4	2.3	5.2	15.8
Current Assets to Working Capital 38	2.6	•	1.5	3.3	2.1	2.1	2.2	2.3	2.2	11.0
Current Liabilities to Working Capital 39	1.6	•	0.5	2.3	1.1	1.1	1.2	1.3	1.2	10.0
Working Capital to Net Sales 40	0.1	•	0.2	0.0	0.1	0.1	0.2	0.2	0.2	0.0
Inventory to Working Capital 41	1.3	•	0.7	2.2	1.1	0.4	1.2	1.0	0.9	5.3
Total Receipts to Cash Flow 42	8.5	12.7	4.9	•	8.8	•	8.1	13.3	7.6	5.5
Cost of Goods to Cash Flow 43	5.4	7.4	2.6	•	5.7	•	5.1	9.5	5.4	2.7
Cash Flow to Total Debt 44	0.3	•	0.8	•	0.4	•	0.3	0.2	0.2	0.2

Selected Financial Factors (in Percentages)

Debt Ratio 45	75.6	•	80.7	119.7	57.6	53.9	58.3	69.4	83.9	94.0
Return on Total Assets 46	5.9	•	12.6	•	9.9	•	9.4	1.3	5.0	9.5
Return on Equity Before Income Taxes 47	10.1	•	59.6	252.7	17.6	•	16.5	•	20.4	74.5
Return on Equity After Income Taxes 48	5.3	•	59.6	254.5	16.6	•	13.8	•	12.6	41.4
Profit Margin (Before Income Tax) 49	1.4	0.3	3.7	•	3.3	•	4.6	•	2.4	3.6
Profit Margin (After Income Tax) 50	0.7	•	3.7	•	3.1	•	3.9	•	1.5	2.0

Table II

Corporations with Net Income

APPAREL ACCESSORIES AND OTHER APPAREL

MONEY AMOUNTS AND SIZE OF ASSETS IN THOUSANDS OF DOLLARS

Item Description for Accounting Period 7/08 Through 6/09	Total	Zero Assets	Under 500	500 to 1,000	1,000 to 5,000	5,000 to 10,000	10,000 to 25,000	25,000 to 50,000	50,000 to 100,000	100,000 to 250,000	250,000 to 500,000	500,000 to 2,500,000	2,500,000 and over
Number of Enterprises 1	2156	469	973	160	•	0	48	•	•	•	0	0	0
Revenues ($ in Thousands)													
Net Sales 2	7269594	114137	666400	630407	•	0	1455111	•	•	•	•	•	•
Interest 3	16557	9	0	0	•	0	141	•	•	•	•	•	•
Rents 4	420	0	0	0	•	0	0	•	•	•	•	•	•
Royalties 5	2695	0	0	0	•	0	1107	•	•	•	•	•	•
Other Portfolio Income 6	8770	0	0	0	•	0	83	•	•	•	•	•	•
Other Receipts 7	43985	0	4202	0	•	0	10338	•	•	•	•	•	•
Total Receipts 8	7342021	114146	670602	630407	•	0	1466780	•	•	•	•	•	•
Average Total Receipts 9	3405	243	689	3940	•	•	30558	•	•	•	•	•	•
Operating Costs/Operating Income (%)													
Cost of Operations 10	63.1	86.1	52.1	80.8	•	•	61.2	•	•	•	•	•	•
Salaries and Wages 11	9.3	7.1	9.8	2.0	•	•	12.7	•	•	•	•	•	•
Taxes Paid 12	2.3	0.2	1.2	0.8	•	•	1.8	•	•	•	•	•	•
Interest Paid 13	1.5	0.4	0.1	1.3	•	•	1.8	•	•	•	•	•	•
Depreciation 14	1.1	0.0	0.0	0.5	•	•	1.7	•	•	•	•	•	•
Amortization and Depletion 15	0.1	0.1	0.0	0.0	•	•	0.3	•	•	•	•	•	•
Pensions and Other Deferred Comp. 16	0.3	0.1	0.2	•	•	•	0.3	•	•	•	•	•	•
Employee Benefits 17	1.1	0.0	0.4	0.6	•	•	1.5	•	•	•	•	•	•
Advertising 18	1.6	0.3	1.6	0.3	•	•	1.4	•	•	•	•	•	•
Other Expenses 19	10.3	3.2	11.4	10.0	•	•	10.3	•	•	•	•	•	•
Officers' Compensation 20	4.3	•	11.9	2.3	•	•	1.9	•	•	•	•	•	•
Operating Margin 21	5.2	2.6	11.2	1.4	•	•	5.1	•	•	•	•	•	•
Operating Margin Before Officers' Comp. 22	9.5	2.6	23.1	3.8	•	•	7.0	•	•	•	•	•	•

Selected Average Balance Sheet ($ in Thousands)

Net Receivables 23	367	0	43	78	3753
Inventories 24	591	0	42	323	7115
Net Property, Plant and Equipment 25	171	0	1	53	2080
Total Assets 26	1652	0	186	697	16817
Notes and Loans Payable 27	592	0	13	457	8272
All Other Liabilities 28	382	0	64	301	3606
Net Worth 29	678	0	109	-61	4940

Selected Financial Ratios (Times to 1)

Current Ratio 30	2.1	•	2.9	1.8	1.7
Quick Ratio 31	0.8	•	1.6	0.6	0.6
Net Sales to Working Capital 32	5.2	•	5.7	16.4	5.5
Coverage Ratio 33	5.3	8.1	126.6	2.1	4.3
Total Asset Turnover 34	2.0	•	3.7	5.7	1.8
Inventory Turnover 35	3.6	•	8.4	9.9	2.6
Receivables Turnover 36	8.9	•	10.7	56.1	9.0
Total Liabilities to Net Worth 37	1.4	•	0.7	•	2.4
Current Assets to Working Capital 38	1.9	•	1.5	2.3	2.4
Current Liabilities to Working Capital 39	0.9	•	0.5	1.3	1.4
Working Capital to Net Sales 40	0.2	•	0.2	0.1	0.2
Inventory to Working Capital 41	0.9	•	0.7	1.5	1.3
Total Receipts to Cash Flow 42	7.1	23.4	5.3	11.3	7.3
Cost of Goods to Cash Flow 43	4.5	20.2	2.8	9.1	4.5
Cash Flow to Total Debt 44	0.5	•	1.7	0.5	0.4

Selected Financial Factors (in Percentages)

Debt Ratio 45	58.9	•	41.3	108.8	70.6
Return on Total Assets 46	15.6	•	43.9	15.2	13.8
Return on Equity Before Income Taxes 47	30.9	•	74.2	•	36.2
Return on Equity After Income Taxes 48	26.5	•	74.2	•	31.1
Profit Margin (Before Income Tax) 49	6.2	2.6	11.8	1.4	5.9
Profit Margin (After Income Tax) 50	5.3	1.8	11.8	1.3	5.1

Table I

Corporations with and without Net Income

LEATHER AND ALLIED PRODUCT MANUFACTURING

MONEY AMOUNTS AND SIZE OF ASSETS IN THOUSANDS OF DOLLARS

Item Description for Accounting Period 7/08 Through 6/09	Total	Zero Assets	Under 500	500 to 1,000	1,000 to 5,000	5,000 to 10,000	10,000 to 25,000	25,000 to 50,000	50,000 to 100,000	100,000 to 250,000	250,000 to 500,000	500,000 to 2,500,000	2,500,000 and over
Number of Enterprises **1**	2035	293	1529	0	153	0	30	13	9	4	0	5	0
Revenues ($ in Thousands)													
Net Sales **2**	8311846	249553	308599	0	504371	0	774177	909284	940281	1683140	0	2942440	0
Interest **3**	32072	9628	3	0	580	0	615	678	4156	3966	0	12446	0
Rents **4**	513	8	0	0	6	0	15	0	124	347	0	13	0
Royalties **5**	168539	973	0	0	0	0	0	0	3938	1742	0	161886	0
Other Portfolio Income **6**	44137	0	0	0	1722	0	19223	0	60	1851	0	21283	0
Other Receipts **7**	51910	21	802	0	516	0	2891	4688	4984	2050	0	35957	0
Total Receipts **8**	8609017	260183	309404	0	507195	0	796921	914650	953543	1693096	0	3174025	0
Average Total Receipts **9**	4230	888	202	•	3315	•	26564	70358	105949	423274	•	634805	•
Operating Costs/Operating Income (%)													
Cost of Operations **10**	65.8	62.4	29.9	•	64.6	•	71.3	77.6	66.8	69.8	•	62.4	•
Salaries and Wages **11**	11.1	36.7	29.6	•	9.8	•	10.7	5.9	9.9	6.9	•	11.8	•
Taxes Paid **12**	1.7	1.4	3.4	•	3.2	•	0.8	1.9	1.7	1.0	•	2.0	•
Interest Paid **13**	2.6	18.8	0.6	•	0.1	•	0.8	0.4	2.0	0.4	•	4.4	•
Depreciation **14**	1.7	1.0	2.2	•	0.4	•	2.0	1.4	1.4	1.5	•	2.2	•
Amortization and Depletion **15**	0.5	•	0.2	•	0.0	•	0.3	0.0	1.0	0.1	•	0.9	•
Pensions and Other Deferred Comp. **16**	0.6	0.0	0.2	•	0.3	•	0.4	0.3	0.3	0.7	•	1.0	•
Employee Benefits **17**	0.9	1.6	1.4	•	0.3	•	1.8	1.0	1.0	0.5	•	0.8	•
Advertising **18**	3.2	0.6	2.8	•	1.1	•	3.4	0.5	2.4	2.1	•	5.6	•
Other Expenses **19**	13.4	13.4	30.2	•	16.3	•	11.1	6.9	14.3	9.0	•	15.9	•
Officers' Compensation **20**	1.9	1.5	5.2	•	3.7	•	1.2	1.5	1.2	3.5	•	1.0	•
Operating Margin **21**	•	•	•	•	0.2	•	•	•	•	4.6	•	•	•
Operating Margin Before Officers' Comp. **22**	•	•	•	•	3.9	•	•	•	•	8.0	•	•	•

Selected Average Balance Sheet ($ in Thousands)

Net Receivables 23	782	0	25	44	2821	9703	13891	54948	198065
Inventories 24	747	0	31	501	5180	8704	21325	70061	111411
Net Property, Plant and Equipment 25	310	0	8	178	1506	4058	8277	31468	58545
Total Assets 26	3733	0	133	1616	17003	30155	73227	232660	930882
Notes and Loans Payable 27	1042	0	145	50	3544	6485	20048	31814	278503
All Other Liabilities 28	1734	0	5	851	2242	6524	13965	74030	563270
Net Worth 29	957	0	-17	714	11217	17146	39213	126816	89110

Selected Financial Ratios (Times to 1)

Current Ratio 30	1.3	7.2	1.5	3.3	2.7	3.9	1.7	0.9
Quick Ratio 31	0.7	4.1	0.4	1.6	1.4	2.0	0.8	0.5
Net Sales to Working Capital 32	9.1	2.9	8.2	2.8	5.0	2.7	6.8	•
Coverage Ratio 33	1.2	•	8.0	•	9.1	0.8	14.8	1.2
Total Asset Turnover 34	1.1	1.5	2.0	1.5	2.3	1.4	1.8	0.6
Inventory Turnover 35	3.6	2.0	4.2	3.6	6.2	3.3	4.2	3.3
Receivables Turnover 36	4.8	10.2	81.9	8.3	7.9	7.3	8.5	2.9
Total Liabilities to Net Worth 37	2.9	•	1.3	0.5	0.8	0.9	0.8	9.4
Current Assets to Working Capital 38	4.8	1.2	3.2	1.4	1.6	1.3	2.5	•
Current Liabilities to Working Capital 39	3.8	0.2	2.2	0.4	0.6	0.3	1.5	•
Working Capital to Net Sales 40	0.1	0.3	0.1	0.4	0.2	0.4	0.1	•
Inventory to Working Capital 41	1.6	0.5	1.2	0.6	0.7	0.6	1.1	•
Total Receipts to Cash Flow 42	9.2	5.0	8.4	10.8	10.6	8.8	8.6	7.9
Cost of Goods to Cash Flow 43	6.1	1.5	5.4	7.7	8.2	5.9	6.0	5.0
Cash Flow to Total Debt 44	0.2	0.3	0.4	0.4	0.5	0.3	0.5	0.1

Selected Financial Factors (in Percentages)

Debt Ratio 45	74.4	112.9	55.8	34.0	43.1	46.4	45.5	90.4
Return on Total Assets 46	3.4	•	1.2	•	8.5	2.3	10.7	3.4
Return on Equity Before Income Taxes 47	2.2	63.3	2.4	•	13.3	•	18.3	6.4
Return on Equity After Income Taxes 48	•	63.3	2.1	•	13.3	•	15.2	•
Profit Margin (Before Income Tax) 49	0.5	•	0.5	•	3.3	•	5.5	1.0
Profit Margin (After Income Tax) 50	•	•	0.5	•	3.3	•	4.6	•

Table II

Corporations with Net Income

LEATHER AND ALLIED PRODUCT MANUFACTURING

MONEY AMOUNTS AND SIZE OF ASSETS IN THOUSANDS OF DOLLARS

Item Description for Accounting Period 7/08 Through 6/09	Total	Zero Assets	Under 500	500 to 1,000	1,000 to 5,000	5,000 to 10,000	10,000 to 25,000	25,000 to 50,000	50,000 to 100,000	100,000 to 250,000	250,000 to 500,000	500,000 to 2,500,000	2,500,000 and over
Number of Enterprises **1**	1095	4	935	0	116	0	17	•	5	4	0	•	0
Revenues ($ in Thousands)													
Net Sales **2**	6902091	45292	264144	0	242873	0	616696	•	545294	1683140	0	•	0
Interest **3**	13736	0	0	0	88	0	608	•	1916	3966	0	•	0
Rents **4**	505	0	0	0	6	0	15	•	124	347	0	•	0
Royalties **5**	120783	0	0	0	0	0	0	•	911	1742	0	•	0
Other Portfolio Income **6**	18755	0	0	0	1349	0	11430	•	23	1851	0	•	0
Other Receipts **7**	14846	0	0	0	196	0	1612	•	3365	2050	0	•	0
Total Receipts **8**	7070716	45292	264144	0	244512	0	630361	•	551633	1693096	0	•	0
Average Total Receipts **9**	6457	11323	283	•	2108	•	37080	•	110327	423274	•	•	•
Operating Costs/Operating Income (%)													
Cost of Operations **10**	65.1	27.1	31.1	•	48.7	•	65.6	•	64.5	69.8	•	•	•
Salaries and Wages **11**	9.7	•	17.1	•	11.3	•	11.9	•	10.2	6.9	•	•	•
Taxes Paid **12**	1.7	•	2.4	•	5.0	•	0.8	•	1.5	1.0	•	•	•
Interest Paid **13**	0.5	•	0.7	•	•	•	0.7	•	1.5	0.4	•	•	•
Depreciation **14**	1.8	0.4	2.6	•	0.3	•	2.3	•	1.6	1.5	•	•	•
Amortization and Depletion **15**	0.4	•	0.2	•	0.0	•	0.2	•	0.4	0.1	•	•	•
Pensions and Other Deferred Comp. **16**	0.4	•	0.2	•	0.1	•	0.5	•	0.2	0.7	•	•	•
Employee Benefits **17**	0.9	•	1.6	•	0.3	•	1.8	•	1.1	0.5	•	•	•
Advertising **18**	3.4	•	3.0	•	1.6	•	4.2	•	1.8	2.1	•	•	•
Other Expenses **19**	10.8	•	26.4	•	25.4	•	10.8	•	8.8	9.0	•	•	•
Officers' Compensation **20**	2.1	•	6.1	•	4.8	•	1.2	•	1.1	3.5	•	•	•
Operating Margin **21**	3.3	72.5	8.6	•	2.5	•	0.0	•	7.4	4.6	•	•	•
Operating Margin Before Officers' Comp. **22**	5.4	72.5	14.6	•	7.3	•	1.2	•	8.5	8.0	•	•	•

Selected Average Balance Sheet ($ in Thousands)

Net Receivables 23	1305	0	0	35	3666	11824	54948
Inventories 24	1088	0	17	296	8492	20574	74431
Net Property, Plant and Equipment 25	502	0	13	141	2542	8836	31468
Total Assets 26	4220	0	122	1336	19378	67686	232660
Notes and Loans Payable 27	562	0	102	2	4189	16812	31814
All Other Liabilities 28	1379	0	1	838	3289	15418	74030
Net Worth 29	2280	0	18	496	11899	35456	126816

Selected Financial Ratios (Times to 1)

Current Ratio 30	2.0		3.1	1.3	2.7	3.2	1.7
Quick Ratio 31	1.2		1.1	0.3	1.1	1.5	0.8
Net Sales to Working Capital 32	4.3		11.9	9.1	4.0	3.8	6.8
Coverage Ratio 33	12.9		13.5		4.0	6.7	14.8
Total Asset Turnover 34	1.5		2.3	1.6	1.9	1.6	1.8
Inventory Turnover 35	3.8		5.2	3.4	2.8	3.4	3.9
Receivables Turnover 36	4.7		24.2	57.8	7.6		6.5
Total Liabilities to Net Worth 37	0.9		5.6	1.7	0.6	0.9	0.8
Current Assets to Working Capital 38	2.0		1.5	4.6	1.6	1.5	2.5
Current Liabilities to Working Capital 39	1.0		0.5	3.6	0.6	0.5	1.5
Working Capital to Net Sales 40	0.2		0.1	0.1	0.3	0.3	0.1
Inventory to Working Capital 41	0.7		1.0	1.2	0.9	0.7	1.1
Total Receipts to Cash Flow 42	6.9		3.0	4.7	8.3	6.6	8.6
Cost of Goods to Cash Flow 43	4.5		0.9	2.3	5.4	4.2	6.0
Cash Flow to Total Debt 44	0.5		0.9	0.5	0.6	0.5	0.5

Selected Financial Factors (in Percentages)

Debt Ratio 45	46.0		84.9	62.9	38.6	47.6	45.5
Return on Total Assets 46	9.8		21.4	4.2	5.6	16.3	10.7
Return on Equity Before Income Taxes 47	16.7		131.0	11.3	6.8	26.5	18.3
Return on Equity After Income Taxes 48	13.9		131.0	10.8	5.9	22.9	15.2
Profit Margin (Before Income Tax) 49	6.0	72.5	8.6	2.7	2.2	8.6	5.5
Profit Margin (After Income Tax) 50	5.0	72.5	8.6	2.6	1.9	8.6	4.6

70

Table I
Corporations with and without Net Income

WOOD PRODUCT MANUFACTURING

MONEY AMOUNTS AND SIZE OF ASSETS IN THOUSANDS OF DOLLARS

Item Description for Accounting Period 7/08 Through 6/09		Total	Zero Assets	Under 500	500 to 1,000	1,000 to 5,000	5,000 to 10,000	10,000 to 25,000	25,000 to 50,000	50,000 to 100,000	100,000 to 250,000	250,000 to 500,000	500,000 to 2,500,000	2,500,000 and over
Number of Enterprises	1	11223	512	6143	1611	2087	426	256	76	49	37	12	13	0
Revenues ($ in Thousands)														
Net Sales	2	66253147	249694	4044299	3008704	9509281	6879912	6776143	4646914	4223644	6988855	5389187	14536516	0
Interest	3	160554	4	649	476	5775	4409	3734	4058	5351	22547	46251	67299	0
Rents	4	26185	0	1617	17	3415	555	3199	1676	4620	2314	4230	4543	0
Royalties	5	22480	0	0	0	0	0	167	1219	92	8002	0	13001	0
Other Portfolio Income	6	317071	3463	15806	1797	14479	24872	10552	17237	17653	21751	89205	100259	0
Other Receipts	7	545057	1807	20810	14455	33688	25052	35217	32577	39336	122651	25908	193551	0
Total Receipts	8	67324494	254968	4083181	3025449	9566638	6934800	6829012	4703681	4290696	7166120	5554781	14915169	0
Average Total Receipts	9	5999	498	665	1878	4584	16279	26676	61891	87565	193679	462898	1147321	•
Operating Costs/Operating Income (%)														
Cost of Operations	10	76.9	98.3	52.8	62.6	72.4	81.9	77.2	85.2	84.1	83.2	84.2	76.0	•
Salaries and Wages	11	6.5	1.9	12.4	11.6	7.2	3.9	5.7	4.2	4.3	5.7	4.8	7.3	•
Taxes Paid	12	1.3	0.3	2.8	2.5	1.5	1.0	1.4	0.9	0.8	1.0	1.0	1.4	•
Interest Paid	13	1.7	1.0	1.1	1.7	0.9	0.8	1.3	1.2	2.1	2.5	1.9	2.7	•
Depreciation	14	3.8	0.6	2.7	3.0	2.4	2.5	4.5	2.6	4.0	4.4	4.8	4.9	•
Amortization and Depletion	15	0.5	•	0.1	0.1	0.1	0.0	0.1	0.3	0.3	0.8	0.4	1.3	•
Pensions and Other Deferred Comp.	16	0.4	•	0.1	0.0	0.2	0.2	0.3	0.2	0.2	0.2	0.3	1.0	•
Employee Benefits	17	1.4	4.3	1.6	0.9	0.9	1.0	1.3	1.2	1.2	1.2	0.9	2.5	•
Advertising	18	0.6	0.1	0.4	0.2	0.2	0.5	0.3	0.4	0.5	0.5	1.3	1.2	•
Other Expenses	19	9.2	8.8	18.6	14.6	10.8	5.9	8.4	6.1	6.5	9.4	7.8	8.7	•
Officers' Compensation	20	1.7	0.4	6.1	3.7	3.4	1.5	1.5	0.8	0.8	0.9	0.3	0.5	•
Operating Margin	21	•	•	1.2	•	0.0	0.7	•	•	•	•	•	•	•
Operating Margin Before Officers' Comp.	22	•	•	7.3	2.7	3.4	2.2	•	•	•	•	•	•	•

Selected Average Balance Sheet ($ in Thousands)

Net Receivables 23	504	0	18	129	491	1128	2430	6094	8089	13054	53686	94274	•
Inventories 24	723	0	13	162	539	2175	4303	8912	16295	23578	54119	125151	•
Net Property, Plant and Equipment 25	1596	0	64	189	542	2664	6273	10958	26019	70451	159659	516539	•
Total Assets 26	4072	0	144	659	2074	6971	15369	36169	71321	151127	394120	1227888	•
Notes and Loans Payable 27	1641	0	87	617	906	2577	5914	11468	26581	59236	159556	469758	•
All Other Liabilities 28	827	0	22	158	350	999	2180	5862	11888	38290	83894	286563	•
Net Worth 29	1604	0	35	-116	817	3395	7275	18840	32852	53601	150669	471567	•

Selected Financial Ratios (Times to 1)

Current Ratio 30	1.7	•	1.7	1.4	2.2	2.4	1.9	2.1	1.8	1.8	1.3	1.2	•
Quick Ratio 31	0.8	•	1.1	0.6	1.3	1.0	0.8	1.0	0.8	0.8	0.5	0.5	•
Net Sales to Working Capital 32	9.2	•	24.1	16.7	6.6	7.0	7.2	5.4	6.5	7.7	11.9	22.9	•
Coverage Ratio 33	•	•	3.0	0.8	1.7	3.0	0.0	•	•	•	•	•	•
Total Asset Turnover 34	1.4	•	4.6	2.8	2.2	2.3	1.7	1.7	1.2	1.2	1.1	0.9	•
Inventory Turnover 35	6.3	•	26.8	7.2	6.1	6.1	4.8	5.8	4.5	6.7	7.0	6.8	•
Receivables Turnover 36	11.6	•	30.6	15.4	9.4	13.7	10.3	9.1	9.9	12.0	9.9	12.6	•
Total Liabilities to Net Worth 37	1.5	•	3.1	•	1.5	1.1	1.1	0.9	1.2	1.8	1.6	1.6	•
Current Assets to Working Capital 38	2.5	•	2.3	3.8	1.9	1.7	2.1	1.9	2.3	2.3	4.3	5.6	•
Current Liabilities to Working Capital 39	1.5	•	1.3	2.8	0.9	0.7	1.1	0.9	1.3	1.3	3.3	4.6	•
Working Capital to Net Sales 40	0.1	•	0.0	0.1	0.2	0.1	0.1	0.2	0.2	0.1	0.1	0.0	•
Inventory to Working Capital 41	1.1	•	0.5	1.8	0.7	0.9	1.1	0.7	1.1	0.8	1.6	2.4	•
Total Receipts to Cash Flow 42	23.1	•	7.0	11.4	12.1	18.1	18.7	40.0	51.0	255.9	350.5	54.0	•
Cost of Goods to Cash Flow 43	17.8	•	3.7	7.1	8.8	14.8	14.5	34.1	42.9	212.9	295.2	41.0	•
Cash Flow to Total Debt 44	0.1	•	0.9	0.2	0.3	0.3	0.2	0.1	0.0	0.0	0.0	0.0	•

Selected Financial Factors (in Percentages)

Debt Ratio 45	60.6	•	75.7	117.6	60.6	51.3	52.7	47.9	53.9	64.5	61.8	61.6	•
Return on Total Assets 46	•	•	15.0	3.6	3.5	5.3	0.0	•	•	•	•	•	•
Return on Equity Before Income Taxes 47	•	•	41.3	6.7	3.5	7.1	•	•	•	•	•	•	•
Return on Equity After Income Taxes 48	•	•	39.1	7.3	2.7	6.8	•	•	•	•	•	•	•
Profit Margin (Before Income Tax) 49	•	•	2.2	•	0.6	1.5	•	•	•	•	•	•	•
Profit Margin (After Income Tax) 50	•	•	2.1	•	0.5	1.4	•	•	•	•	•	•	•

Table II

Corporations with Net Income

WOOD PRODUCT MANUFACTURING

MONEY AMOUNTS AND SIZE OF ASSETS IN THOUSANDS OF DOLLARS

Item Description for Accounting Period 7/08 Through 6/09	Total	Zero Assets	Under 500	500 to 1,000	1,000 to 5,000	5,000 to 10,000	10,000 to 25,000	25,000 to 50,000	50,000 to 100,000	100,000 to 250,000	250,000 to 500,000	500,000 to 2,500,000	2,500,000 and over
Number of Enterprises **1**	5408	261	2591	732	1262	379	118	34	14	11	0	5	0
Revenues ($ in Thousands)													
Net Sales **2**	36691483	0	2809397	2085078	6616357	6147087	3754013	1933282	1475911	2089917	0	9780440	0
Interest **3**	25981	4	499	62	4483	2169	2247	2567	1398	4167	0	8384	0
Rents **4**	9737	0	1617	0	2976	504	1315	1197	1224	0	0	905	0
Royalties **5**	18918	0	0	0	0	0	101	0	0	8002	0	10815	0
Other Portfolio Income **6**	101766	3463	14551	1600	12018	24303	4474	6991	81	7493	0	26793	0
Other Receipts **7**	266294	841	9365	11103	21855	22766	11071	7694	14723	35843	0	131035	0
Total Receipts **8**	37114179	4308	2835429	2097843	6657689	6196829	3773221	1951731	1493337	2145422	0	9955372	0
Average Total Receipts **9**	6863	17	1094	2866	5276	16350	31976	57404	106667	195038	•	1991674	•
Operating Costs/Operating Income (%)													
Cost of Operations **10**	70.9	•	53.6	56.2	70.0	82.5	75.1	78.7	79.1	65.9	•	69.2	•
Salaries and Wages **11**	7.2	•	11.9	13.5	6.9	3.4	5.0	4.1	4.6	6.5	•	9.0	•
Taxes Paid **12**	1.4	•	2.4	2.7	1.3	1.0	1.2	1.0	0.6	1.8	•	1.2	•
Interest Paid **13**	0.9	•	0.5	1.3	0.5	0.7	0.9	1.0	1.2	1.3	•	1.3	•
Depreciation **14**	2.7	•	2.5	3.0	1.8	2.4	3.2	3.0	3.2	3.9	•	3.0	•
Amortization and Depletion **15**	0.3	•	0.0	0.0	0.0	0.0	0.0	0.2	0.2	0.1	•	0.9	•
Pensions and Other Deferred Comp. **16**	0.4	•	0.1	0.0	0.2	0.2	0.2	0.3	0.3	0.3	•	1.1	•
Employee Benefits **17**	1.5	•	0.6	1.2	1.0	0.9	1.2	1.2	1.4	0.5	•	3.0	•
Advertising **18**	0.7	•	0.4	0.1	0.2	0.5	0.2	0.5	0.4	1.6	•	1.4	•
Other Expenses **19**	8.8	•	16.8	14.4	9.3	5.2	7.1	6.7	6.3	12.0	•	8.2	•
Officers' Compensation **20**	1.6	•	3.3	2.9	3.0	1.2	1.4	0.7	1.0	1.4	•	0.6	•
Operating Margin **21**	3.5	•	7.9	4.5	5.9	2.1	4.6	2.7	1.7	4.6	•	1.2	•
Operating Margin Before Officers' Comp. **22**	5.2	•	11.2	7.5	8.9	3.3	6.0	3.4	2.7	6.1	•	1.8	•

Selected Average Balance Sheet ($ in Thousands)

Net Receivables 23	518	0	26	156	482	1132	3236	7761	8894	16911	125707
Inventories 24	769	0	10	132	590	2122	4346	12316	24646	20277	179614
Net Property, Plant and Equipment 25	1071	0	71	222	521	2584	5527	10223	19858	67111	358813
Total Assets 26	3658	0	176	666	2087	6916	15235	35762	72423	182256	1510402
Notes and Loans Payable 27	1079	0	99	547	568	2281	4956	11182	16575	45126	381031
All Other Liabilities 28	872	0	29	194	292	954	2278	4798	11805	41117	543228
Net Worth 29	1707	0	48	-75	1226	3681	8000	19782	44043	96013	586143

Selected Financial Ratios (Times to 1)

Current Ratio 30	1.7	•	2.0	1.4	2.5	2.7	2.2	2.1	2.9	1.4	1.0
Quick Ratio 31	0.8	•	1.3	0.8	1.6	1.1	1.2	1.0	1.3	0.6	0.3
Net Sales to Working Capital 32	9.8	•	21.2	24.5	6.5	6.4	6.7	4.8	4.6	8.2	283.7
Coverage Ratio 33	6.1	•	18.8	5.1	13.1	5.4	6.9	4.6	3.5	6.6	3.3
Total Asset Turnover 34	1.9	•	6.1	4.3	2.5	2.3	2.1	1.6	1.5	1.0	1.3
Inventory Turnover 35	6.3	•	57.5	12.1	6.2	6.3	5.5	3.6	3.4	6.2	7.5
Receivables Turnover 36	11.7	•	30.7	16.7	10.3	14.7	9.5	5.7	7.8	10.1	15.0
Total Liabilities to Net Worth 37	1.1	•	2.7	•	0.7	0.9	0.9	0.8	0.6	0.9	1.6
Current Assets to Working Capital 38	2.4	•	2.0	3.5	1.7	1.6	1.8	1.9	1.5	3.2	59.1
Current Liabilities to Working Capital 39	1.4	•	1.0	2.5	0.7	0.6	0.8	0.9	0.5	2.2	58.1
Working Capital to Net Sales 40	0.1	•	0.0	0.0	0.2	0.2	0.1	0.2	0.2	0.1	0.0
Inventory to Working Capital 41	1.0	•	0.2	1.3	0.5	0.9	0.8	0.7	0.7	1.0	25.7
Total Receipts to Cash Flow 42	8.9	•	4.9	7.2	7.6	15.0	9.6	11.9	12.5	5.9	10.3
Cost of Goods to Cash Flow 43	6.3	•	2.6	4.0	5.3	12.4	7.2	9.4	9.9	3.9	7.1
Cash Flow to Total Debt 44	0.4	•	1.7	0.5	0.8	0.3	0.5	0.3	0.6	0.4	0.2

Selected Financial Factors (in Percentages)

Debt Ratio 45	53.3	•	72.9	111.3	41.2	46.8	47.5	44.7	39.2	47.3	61.2
Return on Total Assets 46	10.4	•	57.0	27.4	17.7	8.3	12.5	7.4	5.9	8.8	5.6
Return on Equity Before Income Taxes 47	18.6	•	199.0	•	27.8	12.8	20.4	10.5	7.0	14.2	10.0
Return on Equity After Income Taxes 48	17.5	•	195.1	•	26.9	12.5	18.6	10.0	5.9	12.1	9.0
Profit Margin (Before Income Tax) 49	4.7	•	8.8	5.2	6.5	2.9	5.1	3.7	2.9	7.2	3.0
Profit Margin (After Income Tax) 50	4.4	•	8.6	5.1	6.3	2.8	4.7	3.5	2.5	6.1	2.7

72

Table I

Corporations with and without Net Income

PULP, PAPER, AND PAPERBOARD MILLS

MONEY AMOUNTS AND SIZE OF ASSETS IN THOUSANDS OF DOLLARS

Item Description for Accounting Period 7/08 Through 6/09	Total	Zero Assets	Under 500	500 to 1,000	1,000 to 5,000	5,000 to 10,000	10,000 to 25,000	25,000 to 50,000	50,000 to 100,000	100,000 to 250,000	250,000 to 500,000	500,000 to 2,500,000	2,500,000 and over
Number of Enterprises **1**	385	•	0	•	217	•	29	20	11	10	10	18	10
Revenues ($ in Thousands)													
Net Sales **2**	98758295	•	0	•	992522	•	1114337	1202581	1280087	2214864	4417060	20544693	66554196
Interest **3**	1320756	•	0	•	850	•	1280	3676	1131	12412	8095	122152	1168825
Rents **4**	21206	•	0	•	25	•	75	75	126	2	3588	3298	14017
Royalties **5**	93715	•	0	•	0	•	0	0	0	0	0	6121	87595
Other Portfolio Income **6**	8549736	•	0	•	0	•	310	442	2	21445	18700	74744	8433715
Other Receipts **7**	1908043	•	0	•	44276	•	9564	2590	6934	14689	16729	162277	1648199
Total Receipts **8**	110651751	•	0	•	1037673	•	1125566	1209364	1288280	2263412	4464172	20913285	77906547
Average Total Receipts **9**	287407	•	•	•	4782	•	38813	60468	117116	226341	446417	1161849	7790655
Operating Costs/Operating Income (%)													
Cost of Operations **10**	80.5	•	•	•	80.2	•	84.6	84.5	85.3	92.1	78.9	79.6	80.3
Salaries and Wages **11**	4.4	•	•	•	1.4	•	5.2	4.8	2.8	2.1	6.7	3.1	4.7
Taxes Paid **12**	0.9	•	•	•	0.4	•	0.8	0.8	0.5	0.4	0.9	0.6	0.9
Interest Paid **13**	4.2	•	•	•	0.9	•	1.0	1.2	2.1	1.6	2.5	2.7	5.0
Depreciation **14**	4.4	•	•	•	0.8	•	2.9	1.5	5.1	3.6	3.8	5.7	4.3
Amortization and Depletion **15**	0.5	•	•	•	0.6	•	0.1	0.0	0.3	0.2	0.6	0.4	0.5
Pensions and Other Deferred Comp. **16**	0.6	•	•	•	•	•	0.1	1.0	0.2	0.3	1.1	0.8	0.5
Employee Benefits **17**	1.7	•	•	•	0.3	•	1.1	2.0	1.2	1.2	2.4	1.8	1.7
Advertising **18**	0.2	•	•	•	0.2	•	0.1	0.1	0.5	0.3	0.3	0.3	0.2
Other Expenses **19**	9.2	•	•	•	17.4	•	5.0	5.8	6.5	3.6	5.7	6.4	10.5
Officers' Compensation **20**	0.3	•	•	•	0.9	•	0.8	1.2	0.3	0.7	0.4	0.5	0.2
Operating Margin **21**	•	•	•	•	•	•	•	•	•	•	•	•	•
Operating Margin Before Officers' Comp. **22**	•	•	•	•	•	•	•	•	•	•	•	•	•

Selected Average Balance Sheet ($ in Thousands)

Net Receivables 23	49259	•	265	•	4153	7058	14037	12322	53204	139942	1528873
Inventories 24	23860	•	198	•	3381	3870	16324	23478	36289	142724	559304
Net Property, Plant and Equipment 25	123438	•	114	•	6354	7308	30697	55609	137980	581643	3439412
Total Assets 26	391882	•	1274	•	18221	33165	70170	144289	372816	1111372	12334257
Notes and Loans Payable 27	161900	•	701	•	10546	8813	34824	41491	165400	421883	5162672
All Other Liabilities 28	117401	•	80	•	6105	20393	19680	39008	89598	331526	3709133
Net Worth 29	112582	•	493	•	1570	3960	15666	63790	117817	357964	3462452

Selected Financial Ratios (Times to 1)

Current Ratio 30	1.0	•	11.7	•	1.4	1.2	1.5	1.8	2.2	1.7	0.9
Quick Ratio 31	0.6	•	9.1	•	0.9	0.6	0.7	0.8	0.9	0.9	0.6
Net Sales to Working Capital 32	289.9	•	7.1	•	14.5	20.6	10.0	9.4	5.1	8.2	•
Coverage Ratio 33	2.3	•	2.7	•	0.4	•	•	0.1	1.2	1.0	2.7
Total Asset Turnover 34	0.7	•	3.6	•	2.1	1.8	1.7	1.5	1.2	1.0	0.5
Inventory Turnover 35	8.7	•	18.5	•	9.6	13.1	6.1	8.7	9.6	6.4	9.6
Receivables Turnover 36	6.0	•	16.0	•	•	7.3	7.4	12.6	10.9	5.6	5.6
Total Liabilities to Net Worth 37	2.5	•	1.6	•	10.6	7.4	3.5	1.3	2.2	2.1	2.6
Current Assets to Working Capital 38	103.3	•	1.1	•	3.7	6.4	2.9	2.2	1.8	2.5	•
Current Liabilities to Working Capital 39	102.3	•	0.1	•	2.7	5.4	1.9	1.2	0.8	1.5	•
Working Capital to Net Sales 40	0.0	•	0.1	•	0.1	0.0	0.1	0.1	0.2	0.1	•
Inventory to Working Capital 41	27.4	•	0.2	•	1.3	1.2	1.4	1.1	0.5	1.0	•
Total Receipts to Cash Flow 42	9.2	•	10.6	•	40.0	38.6	99.2	•	•	24.8	6.8
Cost of Goods to Cash Flow 43	7.4	•	8.5	•	33.9	32.6	84.5	•	•	19.7	5.5
Cash Flow to Total Debt 44	0.1	•	0.6	•	0.1	0.1	0.0	•	•	0.1	0.1

Selected Financial Factors (in Percentages)

Debt Ratio 45	71.3	•	61.3	•	91.4	88.1	77.7	55.8	68.4	67.8	71.9
Return on Total Assets 46	6.3	•	8.6	•	0.9	•	•	•	0.4	2.7	7.3
Return on Equity Before Income Taxes 47	12.4	•	13.9	•	•	•	•	•	•	•	16.3
Return on Equity After Income Taxes 48	9.3	•	13.8	•	•	•	•	•	•	•	13.0
Profit Margin (Before Income Tax) 49	5.4	•	1.5	•	•	•	•	•	•	•	8.5
Profit Margin (After Income Tax) 50	4.1	•	1.5	•	•	•	•	•	•	•	6.8

73

Table II
Corporations with Net Income

PULP, PAPER, AND PAPERBOARD MILLS

MONEY AMOUNTS AND SIZE OF ASSETS IN THOUSANDS OF DOLLARS

Item Description for Accounting Period 7/08 Through 6/09	Total	Zero Assets	Under 500	500 to 1,000	1,000 to 5,000	5,000 to 10,000	10,000 to 25,000	25,000 to 50,000	50,000 to 100,000	100,000 to 250,000	250,000 to 500,000	500,000 to 2,500,000	2,500,000 and over
Number of Enterprises 1	226	0	0	•	117	9	12	9	6	5	5	8	•
Revenues ($ in Thousands)													
Net Sales 2	64474844	0	0	•	776214	235704	571723	458435	763170	1017117	1841710	7227548	•
Interest 3	1220958	0	0	•	850	0	0	211	857	11580	2081	102112	•
Rents 4	18638	0	0	•	25	0	0	55	126	0	3010	2526	•
Royalties 5	84092	0	0	•	0	0	0	0	0	0	0	3824	•
Other Portfolio Income 6	8515985	0	0	•	0	378	238	100	0	9657	17518	65716	•
Other Receipts 7	1666284	0	0	•	44277	2609	9553	557	5729	3178	7627	33004	•
Total Receipts 8	75980801	0	0	•	821366	238691	581514	459358	769882	1041532	1871946	7434730	•
Average Total Receipts 9	336198	•	•	•	7020	26521	48460	51040	128314	208306	374389	929341	•
Operating Costs/Operating Income (%)													
Cost of Operations 10	79.2	•	•	•	81.9	79.5	75.7	80.3	85.4	85.5	72.9	76.0	•
Salaries and Wages 11	4.7	•	•	•	0.3	4.3	8.2	4.0	1.8	0.8	6.9	3.7	•
Taxes Paid 12	1.0	•	•	•	0.1	1.2	1.0	0.6	0.3	0.3	1.2	0.8	•
Interest Paid 13	4.2	•	•	•	1.2	0.9	0.8	0.5	0.9	2.0	2.6	1.6	•
Depreciation 14	4.1	•	•	•	0.9	1.1	3.7	1.5	3.0	3.0	5.0	4.1	•
Amortization and Depletion 15	0.4	•	•	•	0.8	0.0	0.2	0.0	0.1	0.2	0.5	0.2	•
Pensions and Other Deferred Comp. 16	0.6	•	•	•	•	0.1	0.1	1.0	0.2	0.3	0.6	0.6	•
Employee Benefits 17	1.7	•	•	•	0.1	0.2	1.4	2.5	1.4	1.4	2.2	1.0	•
Advertising 18	0.2	•	•	•	0.1	0.0	0.1	0.0	0.2	0.5	0.3	0.1	•
Other Expenses 19	10.0	•	•	•	17.6	9.5	6.0	6.4	4.3	4.4	6.3	7.6	•
Officers' Compensation 20	0.3	•	•	•	0.5	0.9	0.9	0.4	0.4	1.2	0.6	0.6	•
Operating Margin 21	•	•	•	•	•	2.3	2.0	2.9	2.0	0.6	0.9	3.8	•
Operating Margin Before Officers' Comp. 22	•	•	•	•	•	3.2	2.8	3.2	2.4	1.8	1.5	4.4	•

Selected Average Balance Sheet ($ in Thousands)

Net Receivables 23	50682	372	2222	4830	5379	16281	16923	36578	114701
Inventories 24	27093	219	2802	4308	5526	18321	27618	32220	154920
Net Property, Plant and Equipment 25	138012	102	3445	8667	4850	27751	42797	193834	420848
Total Assets 26	495734	1468	9340	22026	29564	67371	132851	380838	907374
Notes and Loans Payable 27	195053	1301	2752	7143	3611	20632	55989	152066	205857
All Other Liabilities 28	138040	144	492	3989	31779	18951	31905	103057	271281
Net Worth 29	162641	24	6096	10893	-5827	27789	44956	125715	430236

Selected Financial Ratios (Times to 1)

Current Ratio 30	1.0	4.9	8.8	1.9	0.8	1.8	1.9	1.8	1.8
Quick Ratio 31	0.6	4.8	4.5	1.1	0.3	0.9	1.1	0.7	1.1
Net Sales to Working Capital 32	•	16.0	4.8	9.3	•	7.8	7.9	6.4	8.2
Coverage Ratio 33	3.7	3.1	4.7	5.5	7.8	4.3	2.5	2.0	5.3
Total Asset Turnover 34	0.6	4.5	2.8	2.2	1.7	1.9	1.5	1.0	1.0
Inventory Turnover 35	8.3	24.8	7.4	8.4	7.4	5.9	6.3	8.3	4.4
Receivables Turnover 36	5.9	15.3	•	•	5.6	9.1	7.7	10.3	4.1
Total Liabilities to Net Worth 37	2.0	60.6	0.5	1.0	•	1.4	2.0	2.0	1.1
Current Assets to Working Capital 38	•	1.3	1.1	2.1	•	2.3	2.1	2.2	2.3
Current Liabilities to Working Capital 39	•	0.3	0.1	1.1	•	1.3	1.1	1.2	1.3
Working Capital to Net Sales 40	•	0.1	0.2	0.1	•	0.1	0.1	0.2	0.1
Inventory to Working Capital 41	•	0.0	0.5	0.8	•	1.1	0.8	0.6	0.7
Total Receipts to Cash Flow 42	5.9	8.2	9.0	13.7	12.8	16.3	16.2	14.7	8.5
Cost of Goods to Cash Flow 43	4.6	6.7	7.2	10.3	10.3	13.9	13.9	10.7	6.4
Cash Flow to Total Debt 44	0.1	0.6	0.9	0.3	0.1	0.2	0.1	0.1	0.2

Selected Financial Factors (in Percentages)

Debt Ratio 45	67.2	98.4	34.7	50.5	119.7	58.8	66.2	67.0	52.6
Return on Total Assets 46	9.1	16.4	12.2	9.7	6.1	7.1	7.6	5.0	8.6
Return on Equity Before Income Taxes 47	20.3	688.4	14.7	16.0	•	13.2	13.5	7.5	14.6
Return on Equity After Income Taxes 48	16.7	685.7	13.6	15.9	•	10.5	9.4	5.5	10.3
Profit Margin (Before Income Tax) 49	11.6	2.5	3.4	3.7	3.1	2.9	3.0	2.6	7.0
Profit Margin (After Income Tax) 50	9.5	2.5	3.2	3.6	3.1	2.3	2.1	1.9	4.9

Table I

Corporations with and without Net Income

CONVERTED PAPER PRODUCT

MONEY AMOUNTS AND SIZE OF ASSETS IN THOUSANDS OF DOLLARS

Item Description for Accounting Period 7/08 Through 6/09	Total	Zero Assets	Under 500	500 to 1,000	1,000 to 5,000	5,000 to 10,000	10,000 to 25,000	25,000 to 50,000	50,000 to 100,000	100,000 to 250,000	250,000 to 500,000	500,000 to 2,500,000	2,500,000 and over
Number of Enterprises **1**	2843	•	988	995	•	•	164	81	36	21	9	12	7
Revenues ($ in Thousands)													
Net Sales **2**	90776221	•	1267987	7602518	•	•	6304787	5357081	3776383	5176556	3755925	10706020	42757313
Interest **3**	1096418	•	20	35	•	•	3629	2868	5274	1409	12027	22340	1045056
Rents **4**	30431	•	0	0	•	•	2495	1021	1586	268	2236	12885	7642
Royalties **5**	1701484	•	0	0	•	•	0	2073	55	1315	3839	10555	1683054
Other Portfolio Income **6**	1017947	•	496	4780	•	•	3440	6867	11556	23022	58488	73964	779889
Other Receipts **7**	894176	•	959	34702	•	•	24713	21418	21111	9382	9997	66869	672126
Total Receipts **8**	95516677	•	1269462	7642035	•	•	6339064	5391328	3815965	5521952	3842512	10892633	46945080
Average Total Receipts **9**	33597	•	1285	7680	•	•	38653	66560	105999	248188	426946	907719	6706440
Operating Costs/Operating Income (%)													
Cost of Operations **10**	71.9	•	79.2	68.8	•	•	77.3	77.8	80.6	77.3	73.9	76.8	67.5
Salaries and Wages **11**	8.6	•	4.2	10.1	•	•	5.5	6.3	5.1	5.6	7.5	5.4	11.0
Taxes Paid **12**	0.9	•	1.5	1.7	•	•	0.9	1.2	0.8	0.8	1.1	0.8	0.8
Interest Paid **13**	3.2	•	1.8	1.1	•	•	1.2	1.2	1.7	1.2	1.8	4.0	4.6
Depreciation **14**	3.5	•	0.8	2.2	•	•	2.9	3.4	4.0	2.5	2.6	4.1	4.1
Amortization and Depletion **15**	0.6	•	0.0	0.1	•	•	0.2	0.1	0.3	0.2	1.0	0.7	0.8
Pensions and Other Deferred Comp. **16**	1.8	•	0.0	0.3	•	•	0.2	0.6	0.4	0.5	0.5	0.6	3.4
Employee Benefits **17**	1.8	•	1.1	2.2	•	•	1.1	1.7	1.4	1.3	2.6	2.1	1.9
Advertising **18**	0.6	•	0.1	0.2	•	•	0.1	0.2	0.2	0.4	0.8	0.2	0.9
Other Expenses **19**	8.5	•	11.4	8.6	•	•	7.6	5.5	5.7	7.3	9.0	6.9	9.3
Officers' Compensation **20**	0.9	•	6.6	2.4	•	•	1.6	1.3	0.9	0.8	0.5	0.4	0.4
Operating Margin **21**	•	•	•	2.2	•	•	1.4	0.8	•	1.9	•	0.6	•
Operating Margin Before Officers' Comp. **22**	•	•	•	4.7	•	•	3.0	2.1	•	2.8	•	•	•

Selected Average Balance Sheet ($ in Thousands)

Net Receivables 23	4203	61	829	3750	7864	12192	30198	40844	129414	925400
Inventories 24	2944	27	521	3485	7509	15439	26231	54081	93746	522032
Net Property, Plant and Equipment 25	7659	30	797	5747	12638	23780	38029	110248	292059	1783546
Total Assets 26	43766	173	2449	15743	34679	68895	133749	323252	894845	13740447
Notes and Loans Payable 27	16955	752	1083	6806	12164	24199	48784	93591	499744	5023189
All Other Liabilities 28	9202	57	678	4643	8197	17186	33198	93229	221601	2690093
Net Worth 29	17609	-636	688	4294	14318	27510	51767	136432	173500	6027165

Selected Financial Ratios (Times to 1)

Current Ratio 30	1.1	1.7	1.3	1.4	1.5	1.4	1.6	1.3	1.2	1.0
Quick Ratio 31	0.5	1.3	0.8	0.7	0.9	0.7	0.9	0.6	0.7	0.4
Net Sales to Working Capital 32	24.9	22.9	23.1	17.4	10.3	10.6	10.5	13.6	26.2	88.1
Coverage Ratio 33	2.6	•	3.5	2.7	2.1	1.0	3.3	1.6	1.0	3.1
Total Asset Turnover 34	0.7	7.4	3.1	2.4	1.9	1.5	1.8	1.3	1.0	0.4
Inventory Turnover 35	7.8	38.0	10.1	8.5	6.9	5.5	7.3	5.7	7.3	7.9
Receivables Turnover 36	7.1	17.0	8.9	•	7.8	7.9	8.0	8.0	6.4	6.4
Total Liabilities to Net Worth 37	1.5	•	2.6	2.7	1.4	1.5	1.6	1.4	4.2	1.3
Current Assets to Working Capital 38	8.5	2.5	4.7	3.8	2.8	3.3	2.5	4.1	7.2	39.5
Current Liabilities to Working Capital 39	7.5	1.5	3.7	2.8	1.8	2.3	1.5	3.1	6.2	38.5
Working Capital to Net Sales 40	0.0	0.0	0.0	0.1	0.1	0.1	0.1	0.1	0.0	0.0
Inventory to Working Capital 41	2.2	0.6	1.4	1.6	1.1	1.6	1.1	1.7	2.5	7.7
Total Receipts to Cash Flow 42	11.4	•	12.8	14.1	20.4	23.4	12.4	14.5	20.9	8.5
Cost of Goods to Cash Flow 43	8.2	•	8.8	10.9	15.8	18.8	9.6	10.7	16.0	5.7
Cash Flow to Total Debt 44	0.1	•	0.3	0.2	0.2	0.1	0.2	0.2	0.1	0.1

Selected Financial Factors (in Percentages)

Debt Ratio 45	59.8	467.4	71.9	72.7	58.7	60.1	61.3	57.8	80.6	56.1
Return on Total Assets 46	6.0	•	12.0	7.8	5.0	2.6	7.3	3.9	3.9	6.2
Return on Equity Before Income Taxes 47	9.1	13.2	30.6	17.9	6.4	0.1	13.1	3.5	•	9.5
Return on Equity After Income Taxes 48	6.0	13.2	30.6	15.9	4.8	•	10.8	2.2	•	6.1
Profit Margin (Before Income Tax) 49	5.0	•	2.8	2.0	1.4	0.0	2.7	1.1	•	9.4
Profit Margin (After Income Tax) 50	3.3	•	2.8	1.8	1.0	•	2.3	0.7	•	6.0

Table II

Corporations with Net Income

CONVERTED PAPER PRODUCT

MONEY AMOUNTS AND SIZE OF ASSETS IN THOUSANDS OF DOLLARS

Item Description for Accounting Period 7/08 Through 6/09		Total	Zero Assets	Under 500	500 to 1,000	1,000 to 5,000	5,000 to 10,000	10,000 to 25,000	25,000 to 50,000	50,000 to 100,000	100,000 to 250,000	250,000 to 500,000	500,000 to 2,500,000	2,500,000 and over
Number of Enterprises	1	1907	•	441	•	763	118	128	56	21	16	6	•	•
Revenues ($ in Thousands)														
Net Sales	2	70509891	•	810592	•	6041282	2325935	4851167	3995176	2466357	4073707	2624749	•	•
Interest	3	989002	•	20	•	29	1874	3248	1941	2918	1197	10511	•	•
Rents	4	17769	•	0	•	0	1745	2092	906	1567	261	2155	•	•
Royalties	5	1693010	•	0	•	0	0	0	0	55	852	2949	•	•
Other Portfolio Income	6	942857	•	0	•	4780	2002	2382	6232	3944	22568	58457	•	•
Other Receipts	7	794132	•	63	•	33488	24569	23463	20460	6102	3399	8991	•	•
Total Receipts	8	74946661	•	810675	•	6079579	2356125	4882352	4024715	2480943	4101984	2707812	•	•
Average Total Receipts	9	39301	•	1838	•	7968	19967	38143	71870	118140	256374	451302	•	•
Operating Costs/Operating Income (%)														
Cost of Operations	10	69.3	•	79.4	•	65.9	80.4	75.3	75.1	79.6	76.3	71.2	•	•
Salaries and Wages	11	9.7	•	1.7	•	11.1	3.6	6.1	6.3	4.9	5.7	8.7	•	•
Taxes Paid	12	1.0	•	1.3	•	1.8	1.0	0.9	1.2	1.0	0.8	1.4	•	•
Interest Paid	13	3.2	•	0.1	•	1.0	0.8	1.2	0.9	1.2	1.1	1.1	•	•
Depreciation	14	3.3	•	0.4	•	1.9	2.1	2.8	3.3	3.0	2.7	2.5	•	•
Amortization and Depletion	15	0.6	•	•	•	0.0	0.0	0.2	0.1	0.3	0.2	0.8	•	•
Pensions and Other Deferred Comp.	16	2.1	•	0.0	•	0.4	0.2	0.2	0.6	0.4	0.4	0.7	•	•
Employee Benefits	17	1.9	•	1.6	•	2.3	0.8	1.2	1.7	1.5	1.2	3.4	•	•
Advertising	18	0.7	•	0.0	•	0.1	0.1	0.1	0.1	0.1	0.3	0.9	•	•
Other Expenses	19	8.6	•	7.5	•	8.8	6.2	7.1	5.9	4.7	7.5	9.1	•	•
Officers' Compensation	20	0.9	•	6.0	•	2.6	1.9	1.7	1.4	0.9	0.9	0.5	•	•
Operating Margin	21	•	•	2.0	•	4.0	2.9	3.3	3.3	2.5	2.8	•	•	•
Operating Margin Before Officers' Comp.	22	•	•	8.0	•	6.6	4.8	5.0	4.7	3.4	3.8	0.2	•	•

Selected Average Balance Sheet ($ in Thousands)

Item										
Net Receivables 23	4921	•	25	864	1737	3612	7294	13693	32949	39649
Inventories 24	3520	•	32	541	1488	3224	8016	17690	26097	56742
Net Property, Plant and Equipment 25	8443	•	24	797	2045	5759	13667	20748	37680	111958
Total Assets 26	56064	•	73	2503	7165	15199	34799	70027	138967	306856
Notes and Loans Payable 27	20062	•	28	957	2262	6207	11324	21143	49827	66607
All Other Liabilities 28	11233	•	46	555	1672	4619	7471	15923	28474	86917
Net Worth 29	24770	•	-1	991	3232	4373	16003	32961	60667	153332

Selected Financial Ratios (Times to 1)

Item										
Current Ratio 30	1.1	•	0.9	1.6	2.2	1.3	1.6	1.6	1.7	1.4
Quick Ratio 31	0.5	•	0.5	1.1	1.4	0.7	0.9	0.8	1.0	0.7
Net Sales to Working Capital 32	27.5	•	•	13.4	8.1	19.4	10.9	7.8	9.6	12.2
Coverage Ratio 33	3.4	•	25.7	5.7	6.1	4.4	5.2	3.4	4.3	3.9
Total Asset Turnover 34	0.7	•	25.1	3.2	2.8	2.5	2.1	1.7	1.8	1.4
Inventory Turnover 35	7.3	•	45.5	9.7	10.6	8.9	6.7	5.3	7.4	5.5
Receivables Turnover 36	6.7	•	18.4	9.7	•	7.9	7.9	7.4	7.9	8.3
Total Liabilities to Net Worth 37	1.3	•	•	1.5	1.2	2.5	1.2	1.1	1.3	1.0
Current Assets to Working Capital 38	10.0	•	•	2.8	1.8	4.1	2.7	2.6	2.4	3.6
Current Liabilities to Working Capital 39	9.0	•	•	1.8	0.8	3.1	1.7	1.6	1.4	2.6
Working Capital to Net Sales 40	0.0	•	•	0.1	0.1	0.1	0.1	0.1	0.1	0.1
Inventory to Working Capital 41	2.3	•	•	0.8	0.6	1.6	1.0	1.2	0.9	1.5
Total Receipts to Cash Flow 42	9.2	•	19.6	10.0	12.4	11.8	12.6	16.0	11.0	11.7
Cost of Goods to Cash Flow 43	6.4	•	15.6	6.6	9.9	8.9	9.5	12.8	8.4	8.3
Cash Flow to Total Debt 44	0.1	•	1.3	0.5	0.4	0.3	0.3	0.2	0.3	0.2

Selected Financial Factors (in Percentages)

Item										
Debt Ratio 45	55.8	•	100.9	60.4	54.9	71.2	54.0	52.9	56.3	50.0
Return on Total Assets 46	7.2	•	52.3	17.7	13.8	12.8	10.2	7.0	8.8	6.1
Return on Equity Before Income Taxes 47	11.5	•	•	36.8	25.7	34.2	17.9	10.5	15.5	9.1
Return on Equity After Income Taxes 48	8.2	•	•	36.8	23.2	32.4	15.9	8.4	12.9	7.3
Profit Margin (Before Income Tax) 49	7.7	•	2.0	4.6	4.2	4.0	4.0	2.9	3.7	3.2
Profit Margin (After Income Tax) 50	5.5	•	2.0	4.6	3.8	3.6	3.6	2.4	3.1	2.6

Table I

Corporations with and without Net Income

PRINTING AND RELATED SUPPORT ACTIVITIES

MONEY AMOUNTS AND SIZE OF ASSETS IN THOUSANDS OF DOLLARS

Item Description for Accounting Period 7/08 Through 6/09		Total	Zero Assets	Under 500	500 to 1,000	1,000 to 5,000	5,000 to 10,000	10,000 to 25,000	25,000 to 50,000	50,000 to 100,000	100,000 to 250,000	250,000 to 500,000	500,000 to 2,500,000	2,500,000 and over
Number of Enterprises	1	32728	3987	22628	2621	2613	404	282	111	33	16	18	12	3
Revenues ($ in Thousands)														
Net Sales	2	87977121	617048	10593400	5802396	14463222	6222728	7483656	6137775	2657131	2559666	6447346	12837866	12154888
Interest	3	251180	5	2397	309	14100	1395	5202	4344	4003	2870	27415	112837	76303
Rents	4	31385	0	315	5303	5008	663	5553	802	108	5058	1904	3557	3115
Royalties	5	94672	0	1490	0	336	1147	8988	130	0	21331	29299	6832	25120
Other Portfolio Income	6	409181	99473	31147	121809	39630	24497	9458	5406	12476	3230	26531	35522	1
Other Receipts	7	840552	9527	-6553	96937	117490	53939	77061	136474	37023	29342	28999	206466	53845
Total Receipts	8	89604091	726053	10622196	6026754	14639786	6304369	7589918	6284931	2710741	2621497	6561494	13203080	12313272
Average Total Receipts	9	2738	182	469	2299	5603	15605	26915	56621	82144	163844	364527	1100257	4104424
Operating Costs/Operating Income (%)														
Cost of Operations	10	61.2	54.2	46.3	51.0	64.7	62.7	66.6	72.9	62.7	65.2	64.3	61.4	62.6
Salaries and Wages	11	10.8	7.1	12.0	16.5	9.7	14.3	9.7	8.8	9.8	8.4	11.3	10.3	9.3
Taxes Paid	12	2.0	3.1	2.7	3.1	2.0	1.6	1.5	1.0	1.5	1.6	1.7	1.3	2.6
Interest Paid	13	2.4	1.3	0.8	1.1	1.3	0.8	1.8	1.6	2.3	3.2	3.4	4.4	4.3
Depreciation	14	4.1	8.0	2.1	2.9	4.3	3.3	5.2	4.5	5.5	4.7	4.1	5.5	4.0
Amortization and Depletion	15	0.7	0.8	0.1	0.1	0.2	0.1	0.2	0.4	0.5	2.3	1.3	1.9	0.9
Pensions and Other Deferred Comp.	16	0.4	3.7	0.2	0.6	0.3	0.1	0.3	0.3	0.3	0.4	1.2	0.6	0.2
Employee Benefits	17	1.7	1.6	1.0	1.0	1.5	1.5	1.6	2.0	2.3	1.5	2.9	2.3	1.6
Advertising	18	0.9	0.3	0.6	0.7	0.5	0.4	0.4	0.4	2.4	2.6	0.3	2.7	0.3
Other Expenses	19	13.0	29.7	24.1	16.7	10.9	10.7	9.9	7.9	11.7	9.8	13.3	10.6	12.2
Officers' Compensation	20	3.2	8.1	8.9	4.8	5.2	2.8	2.6	2.0	2.7	1.5	0.7	0.5	0.4
Operating Margin	21	•	•	1.2	1.7	•	1.5	0.3	•	•	•	•	•	1.6
Operating Margin Before Officers' Comp.	22	2.8	•	10.1	6.4	4.7	4.3	2.9	0.2	1.0	0.2	•	•	2.0

Selected Average Balance Sheet ($ in Thousands)

Net Receivables **23**	410	0	25	196	522	1933	3939	8950	11720	21858	54922	188757	1370831
Inventories **24**	135	0	6	47	216	995	1909	3790	8606	11488	24056	54522	228923
Net Property, Plant and Equipment **25**	504	0	35	247	863	2094	6010	9812	22367	38828	75456	345200	771030
Total Assets **26**	2086	0	102	717	2258	6934	15865	34893	66385	151232	381836	1236580	6906431
Notes and Loans Payable **27**	993	0	86	486	1225	1687	6300	11497	26459	82469	140481	517365	3803542
All Other Liabilities **28**	644	0	38	212	517	1388	3928	7616	19195	29357	118130	565526	1923764
Net Worth **29**	449	0	-23	19	516	3859	5636	15779	20732	39406	123225	153689	1179125

Selected Financial Ratios (Times to 1)

Current Ratio **30**	1.3	•	1.3	1.6	1.5	2.3	1.6	2.0	1.3	1.5	1.6	0.8	1.2
Quick Ratio **31**	0.9	•	1.1	1.3	1.1	1.5	1.1	1.4	0.8	0.9	1.1	0.5	0.8
Net Sales to Working Capital **32**	15.2	•	35.9	15.6	15.0	6.5	9.1	6.3	12.1	11.0	7.3	•	12.2
Coverage Ratio **33**	1.7	0.6	2.8	6.1	1.5	4.3	2.0	1.4	1.1	1.3	0.4	1.3	1.7
Total Asset Turnover **34**	1.3	•	4.6	3.1	2.5	2.2	1.7	1.6	1.2	1.1	0.9	0.9	0.6
Inventory Turnover **35**	12.2	•	35.6	24.0	16.6	9.7	9.3	10.6	5.9	9.1	9.6	12.0	11.1
Receivables Turnover **36**	7.0	•	18.8	11.5	8.7	7.9	6.5	6.3	6.2	7.7	6.8	6.2	3.9
Total Liabilities to Net Worth **37**	3.6	•	•	37.4	3.4	0.8	1.8	1.2	2.2	2.8	2.1	7.0	4.9
Current Assets to Working Capital **38**	4.5	•	4.2	2.7	3.1	1.8	2.7	2.0	4.3	3.2	2.6	•	6.7
Current Liabilities to Working Capital **39**	3.5	•	3.2	1.7	2.1	0.8	1.7	1.0	3.3	2.2	1.6	•	5.7
Working Capital to Net Sales **40**	0.1	•	0.0	0.1	0.1	0.2	0.1	0.2	0.1	0.1	0.1	•	0.1
Inventory to Working Capital **41**	0.7	•	0.5	0.3	0.5	0.5	0.6	0.4	1.1	0.9	0.5	•	0.7
Total Receipts to Cash Flow **42**	9.4	5.2	5.6	6.4	13.9	10.0	11.4	16.9	10.3	12.3	12.7	10.9	7.5
Cost of Goods to Cash Flow **43**	5.8	2.8	2.6	3.3	9.0	6.3	7.6	12.3	6.5	8.1	8.1	6.7	4.7
Cash Flow to Total Debt **44**	0.2	•	0.7	0.5	0.2	0.5	0.2	0.2	0.2	0.1	0.1	0.1	0.1

Selected Financial Factors (in Percentages)

Debt Ratio **45**	78.5	•	122.3	97.4	77.1	44.3	64.5	54.8	68.8	73.9	67.7	87.6	82.9
Return on Total Assets **46**	5.0	•	10.4	20.5	4.9	8.1	5.8	3.5	3.1	4.5	1.4	5.1	4.2
Return on Equity Before Income Taxes **47**	9.3	•	•	656.7	7.1	11.2	8.1	2.2	1.1	4.2	•	10.6	9.9
Return on Equity After Income Taxes **48**	6.9	•	•	654.9	6.3	11.0	6.6	1.4	•	2.3	•	4.6	5.9
Profit Margin (Before Income Tax) **49**	1.5	•	1.5	5.5	0.7	2.8	1.7	0.6	0.3	1.0	•	1.5	2.9
Profit Margin (After Income Tax) **50**	1.1	•	1.4	5.5	0.6	2.8	1.4	0.4	•	0.6	•	0.7	1.7

Table II

Corporations with Net Income

PRINTING AND RELATED SUPPORT ACTIVITIES

MONEY AMOUNTS AND SIZE OF ASSETS IN THOUSANDS OF DOLLARS

Item Description for Accounting Period 7/08 Through 6/09		Total	Zero Assets	Under 500	500 to 1,000	1,000 to 5,000	5,000 to 10,000	10,000 to 25,000	25,000 to 50,000	50,000 to 100,000	100,000 to 250,000	250,000 to 500,000	500,000 to 2,500,000	2,500,000 and over
Number of Enterprises	1	17089	2296	10746	1886	1568	305	169	75	16	13	6	8	0
Revenues ($ in Thousands)														
Net Sales	2	49332288	265158	5456465	4310384	9472949	5024002	4705611	4622381	1424020	2117625	2519153	9414540	0
Interest	3	123353	5	1994	69	8520	329	3329	2367	2416	2829	1106	100389	0
Rents	4	21500	0	79	5241	1947	301	1332	729	60	5058	156	6598	0
Royalties	5	59642	0	0	0	0	0	8983	130	0	21331	264	28934	0
Other Portfolio Income	6	323858	93645	24675	111871	28441	23054	7066	4927	11596	3144	9287	6151	0
Other Receipts	7	550927	6586	5811	60492	43968	33423	54811	125705	10023	22650	5727	181730	0
Total Receipts	8	50411568	365394	5489024	4488057	9555825	5081109	4781132	4756239	1448115	2172637	2535693	9738342	0
Average Total Receipts	9	2950	159	511	2380	6094	16659	28291	63417	90507	167126	422616	1217293	•
Operating Costs/Operating Income (%)														
Cost of Operations	10	57.3	27.1	42.3	47.1	65.5	61.2	66.0	73.8	54.1	61.6	67.6	45.5	•
Salaries and Wages	11	11.1	3.2	9.8	18.0	9.2	14.7	8.6	7.7	10.8	9.6	9.5	12.9	•
Taxes Paid	12	1.9	3.9	3.0	3.3	1.6	1.7	1.3	0.8	1.6	1.6	1.5	1.8	•
Interest Paid	13	1.9	2.4	0.4	0.9	0.9	0.6	1.2	1.3	2.0	2.5	1.2	5.4	•
Depreciation	14	3.5	5.5	1.5	2.3	2.9	2.6	3.8	3.8	5.5	4.8	4.3	5.1	•
Amortization and Depletion	15	0.7	1.2	0.1	0.1	0.2	0.1	0.2	0.2	0.4	1.9	0.9	2.3	•
Pensions and Other Deferred Comp.	16	0.5	0.7	0.2	0.8	0.3	0.1	0.3	0.3	0.3	0.5	1.6	0.7	•
Employee Benefits	17	1.7	0.7	1.1	0.9	1.4	1.4	1.4	1.6	2.2	1.4	2.7	2.7	•
Advertising	18	1.0	0.6	0.5	0.7	0.7	0.4	0.5	0.4	4.3	3.1	0.2	2.0	•
Other Expenses	19	12.3	37.4	21.6	14.7	8.8	10.2	9.6	7.2	14.7	10.7	7.2	14.7	•
Officers' Compensation	20	3.7	17.5	10.6	4.8	4.9	2.8	2.7	2.1	2.0	1.4	0.7	0.8	•
Operating Margin	21	4.6	•	9.0	6.7	3.7	4.2	4.3	1.0	2.1	1.1	2.7	6.0	•
Operating Margin Before Officers' Comp.	22	8.3	17.5	19.6	11.4	8.6	7.0	7.0	3.0	4.1	2.5	3.4	6.8	•

Selected Average Balance Sheet ($ in Thousands)

Net Receivables 23	359	0	25	208	561	2099	4340	9502	11228	21040	51526	219304
Inventories 24	169	0	7	36	219	941	1872	4031	11372	11512	46994	61613
Net Property, Plant and Equipment 25	476	0	30	191	680	1720	5391	10012	20138	33195	98985	355626
Total Assets 26	1982	0	106	724	2224	6841	16238	35916	67559	154161	356626	1891609
Notes and Loans Payable 27	748	0	54	246	842	1241	4599	10342	25121	59482	73673	858918
All Other Liabilities 28	496	0	21	172	509	1315	4021	7749	20092	24323	105306	523165
Net Worth 29	739	0	31	306	874	4286	7617	17825	22346	70357	177647	509525

Selected Financial Ratios (Times to 1)

Current Ratio 30	1.8	•	2.6	2.2	1.7	2.9	1.8	1.9	1.3	1.6	1.4	1.6
Quick Ratio 31	1.2	•	2.2	1.9	1.3	1.8	1.3	1.4	0.9	1.0	0.8	0.9
Net Sales to Working Capital 32	8.2	•	12.6	9.8	12.0	5.4	7.2	7.2	12.9	9.0	13.5	6.1
Coverage Ratio 33	4.6	17.0	26.4	13.2	6.2	9.4	6.1	4.0	2.9	2.4	3.9	2.7
Total Asset Turnover 34	1.5	•	4.8	3.2	2.7	2.4	1.7	1.7	1.3	1.1	1.2	0.6
Inventory Turnover 35	9.8	•	30.0	30.1	18.1	10.7	9.8	11.3	4.2	8.7	6.0	8.7
Receivables Turnover 36	6.4	•	15.9	8.4	8.4	8.4	•	6.6	5.4	8.6	4.8	5.5
Total Liabilities to Net Worth 37	1.7	•	2.4	1.4	1.5	0.6	1.1	1.0	2.0	1.2	1.0	2.7
Current Assets to Working Capital 38	2.3	•	1.6	1.8	2.5	1.5	2.3	2.1	4.6	2.7	3.3	2.8
Current Liabilities to Working Capital 39	1.3	•	0.6	0.8	1.5	0.5	1.3	1.1	3.6	1.7	2.3	1.8
Working Capital to Net Sales 40	0.1	•	0.1	0.1	0.1	0.2	0.1	0.1	0.1	0.1	0.1	0.2
Inventory to Working Capital 41	0.4	•	0.1	0.2	0.4	0.4	0.5	0.4	1.2	0.7	1.1	0.2
Total Receipts to Cash Flow 42	6.6	1.6	4.3	5.3	10.4	8.4	7.7	11.7	6.2	8.8	11.7	4.8
Cost of Goods to Cash Flow 43	3.8	0.4	1.8	2.5	6.8	5.1	5.1	8.6	3.3	5.4	7.9	2.2
Cash Flow to Total Debt 44	0.3	•	1.6	1.0	0.4	0.8	0.4	0.3	0.3	0.2	0.2	0.2

Selected Financial Factors (in Percentages)

Debt Ratio 45	62.7	•	70.6	57.8	60.7	37.4	53.1	50.4	66.9	54.4	50.2	73.1
Return on Total Assets 46	12.6	•	48.0	36.8	14.7	14.3	12.1	8.9	7.7	6.5	5.4	9.3
Return on Equity Before Income Taxes 47	26.6	•	156.7	80.6	31.5	20.5	21.6	13.3	15.0	8.4	8.0	21.9
Return on Equity After Income Taxes 48	23.8	•	156.0	80.5	30.7	20.2	19.8	12.3	12.2	7.1	6.0	15.7
Profit Margin (Before Income Tax) 49	6.8	37.8	9.6	10.8	4.6	5.3	5.9	3.9	3.8	3.6	3.4	9.5
Profit Margin (After Income Tax) 50	6.1	37.4	9.6	10.8	4.4	5.2	5.4	3.5	3.1	3.1	2.6	6.8

Table I

Corporations with and without Net Income

PETROLEUM REFINERIES (INCLUDING INTEGRATED)

MONEY AMOUNTS AND SIZE OF ASSETS IN THOUSANDS OF DOLLARS

Item Description for Accounting Period 7/08 Through 6/09	Total	Zero Assets	Under 500	500 to 1,000	1,000 to 5,000	5,000 to 10,000	10,000 to 25,000	25,000 to 50,000	50,000 to 100,000	100,000 to 250,000	250,000 to 500,000	500,000 to 2,500,000	2,500,000 and over
Number of Enterprises **1**	569	379	0	0	107	9	26	0	8	9	0	12	19

Revenues ($ in Thousands)

	Total	Zero Assets	Under 500	500 to 1,000	1,000 to 5,000	5,000 to 10,000	10,000 to 25,000	25,000 to 50,000	50,000 to 100,000	100,000 to 250,000	250,000 to 500,000	500,000 to 2,500,000	2,500,000 and over
Net Sales **2**	2223596695	6814653	0	0	7190	22726	632521	0	2085820	4186873	0	456895162	164157395
Interest **3**	16755071	0	0	0	27	298	1814	0	5104	7014	0	75042	16665772
Rents **4**	1406005	0	0	0	0	0	283	0	0	814	0	17696	1387212
Royalties **5**	1247198	0	0	0	0	0	0	0	0	3	0	159	1247036
Other Portfolio Income **6**	29431239	0	0	0	0	0	5047	0	544	11954	0	54275	29359418
Other Receipts **7**	44931384	162581	0	0	89948	20384	176	0	36274	12126	0	325012	44284886
Total Receipts **8**	2317367592	6977234	0	0	97165	43408	639841	0	2127742	4218784	0	461617000	2257101719
Average Total Receipts **9**	4072702	18410	•	•	908	4823	24609	•	265968	468754	•	3846808	118794827

Operating Costs/Operating Income (%)

	Total	Zero Assets	Under 500	500 to 1,000	1,000 to 5,000	5,000 to 10,000	10,000 to 25,000	25,000 to 50,000	50,000 to 100,000	100,000 to 250,000	250,000 to 500,000	500,000 to 2,500,000	2,500,000 and over
Cost of Operations **10**	90.6	101.6	•	•	1.7	142.6	75.2	•	93.5	94.7	•	92.8	90.5
Salaries and Wages **11**	1.1	•	•	•	18.4	•	4.5	•	0.8	0.9	•	1.7	1.1
Taxes Paid **12**	1.4	0.0	•	•	2.4	4.2	1.5	•	0.2	0.2	•	1.5	1.4
Interest Paid **13**	1.0	•	•	•	29.1	10.8	0.5	•	0.8	1.0	•	0.7	1.0
Depreciation **14**	0.8	•	•	•	0.6	26.3	1.7	•	1.6	0.9	•	1.8	0.8
Amortization and Depletion **15**	0.3	•	•	•	•	•	0.0	•	0.1	0.1	•	0.4	0.3
Pensions and Other Deferred Comp. **16**	0.3	•	•	•	•	•	0.2	•	0.0	0.0	•	0.1	0.4
Employee Benefits **17**	0.2	•	•	•	•	•	0.4	•	0.2	0.1	•	0.2	0.2
Advertising **18**	0.0	•	•	•	0.8	0.1	0.0	•	0.0	0.1	•	0.0	0.0
Other Expenses **19**	3.2	0.1	•	•	282.6	7.6	14.8	•	1.8	4.1	•	3.2	3.2
Officers' Compensation **20**	0.1	•	•	•	•	•	2.9	•	0.1	0.1	•	0.2	0.1
Operating Margin **21**	1.0	•	•	•	•	•	•	•	0.6	•	•	•	1.0
Operating Margin Before Officers' Comp. **22**	1.0	•	•	•	•	•	1.2	•	0.8	•	•	1.1	1.1

Selected Average Balance Sheet ($ in Thousands)

	C1	C2	C3	C4	C5	C6	C7	C8	C9	C10
Net Receivables 23	1133301	0	74	49	2135	•	9915	19728	127379	33842059
Inventories 24	60466	0	1	178	1163	•	2612	28648	199121	1668680
Net Property, Plant and Equipment 25	422000	0	11	5058	2631	•	31304	62713	640057	12184587
Total Assets 26	3344493	0	2250	7794	14523	•	81781	156622	1292211	99197777
Notes and Loans Payable 27	411431	0	213	7455	3782	•	16968	50073	406309	12023889
All Other Liabilities 28	1543777	0	130	25	2311	•	27974	53140	343155	45974478
Net Worth 29	1389285	0	1907	314	8430	•	36838	53408	542747	41199411

Selected Financial Ratios (Times to 1)

	C1	C2	C3	C4	C5	C6	C7	C8	C9	C10
Current Ratio 30	1.0	•	0.2	•	1.7	•	1.2	1.3	1.7	1.0
Quick Ratio 31	0.9	•	0.2	•	1.3	•	0.9	0.7	0.8	0.9
Net Sales to Working Capital 32	919.0	•	•	1.0	8.1	•	55.6	26.9	20.0	•
Coverage Ratio 33	7.3	•	35.9	0.9	•	•	4.4	•	•	7.5
Total Asset Turnover 34	1.2	•	0.0	0.3	1.7	•	3.2	3.0	2.9	1.1
Inventory Turnover 35	58.5	•	1.7	20.2	15.7	•	93.3	15.4	17.7	61.8
Receivables Turnover 36	3.3	•	1.7	2.3	14.0	•	36.5	10.8	24.6	3.2
Total Liabilities to Net Worth 37	1.4	•	0.2	23.8	0.7	•	1.2	1.9	1.4	1.4
Current Assets to Working Capital 38	308.7	•	•	1.0	2.5	•	6.7	4.0	2.5	•
Current Liabilities to Working Capital 39	307.7	•	•	•	1.5	•	5.7	3.0	1.5	•
Working Capital to Net Sales 40	0.0	•	•	1.0	0.1	•	0.0	0.0	0.0	•
Inventory to Working Capital 41	14.0	•	•	0.1	0.5	•	1.0	1.5	0.8	•
Total Receipts to Cash Flow 42	12.8	130.8	0.1	20.6	8.9	•	26.0	46.6	109.3	12.5
Cost of Goods to Cash Flow 43	11.6	132.9	0.0	29.4	6.7	•	24.3	44.1	101.4	11.3
Cash Flow to Total Debt 44	0.2	•	2.5	0.0	0.4	•	0.2	0.1	0.0	0.2

Selected Financial Factors (in Percentages)

	C1	C2	C3	C4	C5	C6	C7	C8	C9	C10
Debt Ratio 45	58.5	•	15.2	96.0	42.0	•	55.0	65.9	58.0	58.5
Return on Total Assets 46	8.8	•	31.2	3.3	•	•	10.9	•	•	8.9
Return on Equity Before Income Taxes 47	18.2	•	35.8	•	•	•	18.6	•	•	18.5
Return on Equity After Income Taxes 48	11.8	•	35.8	•	•	•	15.7	•	•	12.0
Profit Margin (Before Income Tax) 49	6.5	0.7	1015.8	•	•	•	2.6	•	•	6.7
Profit Margin (After Income Tax) 50	4.2	0.4	1015.8	•	•	•	2.2	•	•	4.3

79

Table II

Corporations with Net Income

PETROLEUM REFINERIES (INCLUDING INTEGRATED)

MONEY AMOUNTS AND SIZE OF ASSETS IN THOUSANDS OF DOLLARS

Item Description for Accounting Period 7/08 Through 6/09		Total	Zero Assets	Under 500	500 to 1,000	1,000 to 5,000	5,000 to 10,000	10,000 to 25,000	25,000 to 50,000	50,000 to 100,000	100,000 to 250,000	250,000 to 500,000	500,000 to 2,500,000	2,500,000 and over
Number of Enterprises	1	150	•	0	0	•	4	12	0	4	•	0	•	16
Revenues ($ in Thousands)														
Net Sales	2	2180592236	•	0	0	•	0	557033	0	1931600	•	0	•	•2150710220
Interest	3	16439387	•	0	0	•	298	930	0	1028	•	0	•	•1639276
Rents	4	1371547	•	0	0	•	0	283	0	0	•	0	•	•1368387
Royalties	5	1247055	•	0	0	•	0	0	0	0	•	0	•	•1247036
Other Portfolio Income	6	29222048	•	0	0	•	0	1066	0	18	•	0	•	•29182192
Other Receipts	7	43236083	•	0	0	•	17788	195	0	20261	•	0	•	•42729428
Total Receipts	8	2272108356	•	0	0	•	18086	559507	0	1952907	•	0	•	•2241636539
Average Total Receipts	9	15147389	•	•	•	•	4522	46626	•	488227	•	•	•	•140102284
Operating Costs/Operating Income (%)														
Cost of Operations	10	90.5	•	•	•	•	•	72.1	•	93.3	•	•	•	90.5
Salaries and Wages	11	1.1	•	•	•	•	•	3.4	•	0.5	•	•	•	1.1
Taxes Paid	12	1.4	•	•	•	•	•	1.1	•	0.2	•	•	•	1.4
Interest Paid	13	1.0	•	•	•	•	•	0.3	•	0.2	•	•	•	1.0
Depreciation	14	0.8	•	•	•	•	•	1.4	•	0.8	•	•	•	0.8
Amortization and Depletion	15	0.3	•	•	•	•	•	•	•	0.0	•	•	•	0.3
Pensions and Other Deferred Comp.	16	0.3	•	•	•	•	•	0.2	•	0.0	•	•	•	0.4
Employee Benefits	17	0.2	•	•	•	•	•	0.2	•	0.2	•	•	•	0.2
Advertising	18	0.0	•	•	•	•	•	0.0	•	0.0	•	•	•	0.1
Other Expenses	19	3.1	•	•	•	•	•	12.5	•	0.2	•	•	•	3.1
Officers' Compensation	20	0.1	•	•	•	•	•	3.0	•	0.1	•	•	•	0.1
Operating Margin	21	1.2	•	•	•	•	•	5.6	•	4.6	•	•	•	1.2
Operating Margin Before Officers' Comp.	22	1.2	•	•	•	•	•	8.6	•	4.7	•	•	•	1.2

Selected Average Balance Sheet ($ in Thousands)

Net Receivables 23	4275179	•	•	111	3393	16658	•	40032313
Inventories 24	219733	•	•	88	2370	7780	•	1948495
Net Property, Plant and Equipment 25	1506482	•	•	534	2519	25415	•	13958505
Total Assets 26	12429271	•	•	5276	18464	86734	•	116071836
Notes and Loans Payable 27	1426718	•	•	1523	1690	13691	•	13336581
All Other Liabilities 28	5785620	•	•	57	2469	21449	•	54116518
Net Worth 29	5216933	•	•	3696	14305	51594	•	48618736

Selected Financial Ratios (Times to 1)

Current Ratio 30	1.0	•	•	•	4.7	2.4	•	1.0
Quick Ratio 31	0.9	•	•	•	3.5	1.8	•	0.9
Net Sales to Working Capital 32	•	•	•	•	5.2	16.5	•	•
Coverage Ratio 33	7.8	•	•	•	19.0	38.5	•	7.8
Total Asset Turnover 34	1.2	•	•	•	2.5	5.6	•	1.2
Inventory Turnover 35	59.9	•	•	•	14.1	62.4	•	57.9
Receivables Turnover 36	3.3	•	•	•	15.3	•	•	•
Total Liabilities to Net Worth 37	1.4	•	•	0.4	0.3	0.7	•	1.4
Current Assets to Working Capital 38	•	•	•	1.0	1.3	1.7	•	•
Current Liabilities to Working Capital 39	•	•	•	•	0.3	0.7	•	•
Working Capital to Net Sales 40	•	•	•	•	0.2	0.1	•	•
Inventory to Working Capital 41	•	•	•	•	0.3	0.3	•	•
Total Receipts to Cash Flow 42	12.6	•	•	•	6.2	17.7	•	12.5
Cost of Goods to Cash Flow 43	11.4	•	•	•	4.5	16.5	•	11.3
Cash Flow to Total Debt 44	0.2	•	•	2.7	1.8	0.8	•	0.2

Selected Financial Factors (in Percentages)

Debt Ratio 45	58.0	•	•	29.9	22.5	40.5	•	58.1
Return on Total Assets 46	9.0	•	•	80.0	16.1	32.3	•	9.0
Return on Equity Before Income Taxes 47	18.7	•	•	114.2	19.6	52.9	•	18.7
Return on Equity After Income Taxes 48	12.2	•	•	75.4	17.3	48.7	•	12.2
Profit Margin (Before Income Tax) 49	6.7	•	•	•	6.1	5.7	•	•
Profit Margin (After Income Tax) 50	4.4	•	•	•	5.3	5.2	•	•

Table I

Corporations with and without Net Income

ASPHALT PAVING, ROOFING, OTHER PETROLEUM AND COAL PRODUCTS

MONEY AMOUNTS AND SIZE OF ASSETS IN THOUSANDS OF DOLLARS

Item Description for Accounting Period 7/08 Through 6/09	Total	Zero Assets	Under 500	500 to 1,000	1,000 to 5,000	5,000 to 10,000	10,000 to 25,000	25,000 to 50,000	50,000 to 100,000	100,000 to 250,000	250,000 to 500,000	500,000 to 2,500,000	2,500,000 and over
Number of Enterprises **1**	712	11	255	66	177	96	65	12	13	13	0	4	0
Revenues ($ in Thousands)													
Net Sales **2**	16253230	30317	134301	189986	826735	1803665	2292447	732918	1942049	4155677	0	4145134	0
Interest **3**	21881	0	0	80	43	1071	711	1035	1375	12283	0	5283	0
Rents **4**	5427	0	0	0	2	1688	3398	7	8	322	0	3	0
Royalties **5**	2237	0	0	0	0	0	0	828	1405	4	0	0	0
Other Portfolio Income **6**	213920	21302	0	21849	9060	888	827	1331	1829	8214	0	148622	0
Other Receipts **7**	180819	2099	0	127	118424	2597	9762	2657	12409	35661	0	-2918	0
Total Receipts **8**	16677514	53718	134301	212042	954264	1809909	2307145	738776	1959075	4212161	0	4296124	0
Average Total Receipts **9**	23423	4883	527	3213	5391	18853	35495	61565	150698	324012	•	1074031	•
Operating Costs/Operating Income (%)													
Cost of Operations **10**	73.8	67.4	60.1	70.8	69.1	68.6	80.6	72.7	82.1	78.0	•	65.9	•
Salaries and Wages **11**	4.9	32.2	8.2	5.4	1.1	10.7	4.6	2.9	2.5	4.9	•	4.3	•
Taxes Paid **12**	1.1	2.3	2.7	2.1	2.5	0.8	0.9	1.4	0.6	0.7	•	1.6	•
Interest Paid **13**	2.2	1.5	1.0	0.1	0.0	0.6	1.0	0.9	0.9	1.5	•	5.9	•
Depreciation **14**	2.6	12.0	7.5	3.8	0.6	1.9	3.2	1.5	2.2	2.7	•	3.1	•
Amortization and Depletion **15**	0.2	•	•	•	0.0	0.0	0.2	0.1	0.4	0.2	•	0.2	•
Pensions and Other Deferred Comp. **16**	0.2	•	•	0.0	0.0	0.6	0.1	0.1	0.2	0.3	•	0.1	•
Employee Benefits **17**	1.0	1.3	•	0.0	2.4	0.4	0.9	0.7	0.8	0.7	•	1.6	•
Advertising **18**	0.8	1.1	0.5	0.1	0.3	2.3	0.9	0.5	1.6	0.3	•	0.6	•
Other Expenses **19**	9.6	37.6	20.4	11.0	22.4	9.3	6.4	8.4	3.7	5.8	•	15.1	•
Officers' Compensation **20**	1.3	•	•	8.1	5.5	2.8	1.0	2.2	1.5	0.6	•	0.3	•
Operating Margin **21**	2.1	•	•	•	•	1.9	0.1	8.5	3.5	4.3	•	1.4	•
Operating Margin Before Officers' Comp. **22**	3.5	•	•	6.7	1.5	4.7	1.2	10.8	5.0	4.8	•	1.7	•

Selected Average Balance Sheet ($ in Thousands)

	1	2	3	4	5	6	7	8	9	10	11	
Net Receivables 23	2165	0	0	370	908	1168	4214	5574	16392	26070	87781	•
Inventories 24	2213	0	0	0	550	834	2544	8135	15447	26142	148708	•
Net Property, Plant and Equipment 25	3840	0	51	312	497	1756	6032	7438	15316	47568	286259	•
Total Assets 26	16016	0	53	845	2140	6414	16226	38333	67145	204218	1324194	•
Notes and Loans Payable 27	5045	0	229	128	3408	1713	5754	8206	16105	59407	325868	•
All Other Liabilities 28	7407	0	0	446	2750	1184	4452	9707	16973	42869	865005	•
Net Worth 29	3563	0	-176	271	-4018	3517	6020	20420	34068	101942	133321	•

Selected Financial Ratios (Times to 1)

	1	2	3	4	5	6	7	8	9	10	11	
Current Ratio 30	1.5	•	0.9	0.6	2.2	1.2	2.2	2.6	2.2	1.2		•
Quick Ratio 31	0.7	•	0.9	0.4	1.7	0.8	1.1	1.5	0.7	0.5		•
Net Sales to Working Capital 32	11.0	387.0	•	7.4	21.2	5.9	5.5	6.0	25.8			•
Coverage Ratio 33	3.1	15.3	0.5	95.4	258.0	4.6	1.8	11.0	5.6	4.9	1.9	•
Total Asset Turnover 34	1.4	•	10.0	3.4	2.2	2.9	2.2	1.6	2.2	1.6	0.8	•
Inventory Turnover 35	7.6	•	•	5.9	15.5	11.2	5.5	7.9	9.5	4.6		•
Receivables Turnover 36	9.6	17.6	7.9	4.9	11.9	9.6	8.1	8.5	11.0	10.3		•
Total Liabilities to Net Worth 37	3.5	•	2.1	0.8	1.7	0.9	1.0	1.0	8.9			•
Current Assets to Working Capital 38	3.1	1.0	•	1.8	5.1	1.9	1.6	1.8	7.6			•
Current Liabilities to Working Capital 39	2.1	•	•	0.8	4.1	0.9	0.6	0.8	6.6			•
Working Capital to Net Sales 40	0.1	0.0	•	0.1	0.0	0.2	0.2	0.2	0.0			•
Inventory to Working Capital 41	1.0	•	•	0.3	1.7	0.7	0.6	0.6	3.2			•
Total Receipts to Cash Flow 42	9.3	7.6	6.6	10.0	17.8	6.1	14.0	9.5	9.3			•
Cost of Goods to Cash Flow 43	6.9	4.6	4.7	6.8	14.4	4.5	11.5	7.4	6.2			•
Cash Flow to Total Debt 44	0.2	0.3	0.8	0.7	0.2	0.6	0.3	0.3	0.1			•

Selected Financial Factors (in Percentages)

	1	2	3	4	5	6	7	8	9	10	11	
Debt Ratio 45	77.8	•	434.1	67.9	287.7	45.2	62.9	46.7	49.3	50.1	89.9	•
Return on Total Assets 46	10.0	•	5.1	35.2	25.1	8.4	3.8	16.2	11.7	11.2	8.5	•
Return on Equity Before Income Taxes 47	30.5	•	1.3	108.8	•	11.9	4.4	27.6	18.9	17.8	39.1	•
Return on Equity After Income Taxes 48	24.0	•	1.3	74.0	•	9.9	2.6	21.2	16.4	14.3	26.1	•
Profit Margin (Before Income Tax) 49	4.8	21.6	•	10.2	11.4	2.2	0.7	9.2	4.3	5.7	5.0	•
Profit Margin (After Income Tax) 50	3.7	20.3	•	7.0	11.2	1.9	0.4	7.1	3.7	4.6	3.4	•

81

Table II

Corporations with Net Income

ASPHALT PAVING, ROOFING, OTHER PETROLEUM AND COAL PRODUCTS

MONEY AMOUNTS AND SIZE OF ASSETS IN THOUSANDS OF DOLLARS

Item Description for Accounting Period 7/08 Through 6/09		Total	Zero Assets	Under 500	500 to 1,000	1,000 to 5,000	5,000 to 10,000	10,000 to 25,000	25,000 to 50,000	50,000 to 100,000	100,000 to 250,000	250,000 to 500,000	500,000 to 2,500,000	2,500,000 and over
Number of Enterprises	1	401	•	0	66	•	78	35	12	10	•	0	•	0
Revenues ($ in Thousands)														
Net Sales	2	11658642	•	0	189986	•	1635468	1430652	732918	1637467	•	0	•	0
Interest	3	16302	•	0	80	•	105	709	1035	909	•	0	•	0
Rents	4	5422	•	0	0	•	1688	3393	7	8	•	0	•	0
Royalties	5	832	•	0	0	•	0	0	828	0	•	0	•	0
Other Portfolio Income	6	203525	•	0	21849	•	888	454	1331	1824	•	0	•	0
Other Receipts	7	170289	•	0	127	•	1417	6907	2657	11346	•	0	•	0
Total Receipts	8	12055012	•	0	212042	•	1639566	1442115	738776	1651554	•	0	•	0
Average Total Receipts	9	30062	•	•	3213	•	21020	41203	61565	165155	•	•	•	•
Operating Costs/Operating Income (%)														
Cost of Operations	10	75.1	•	•	70.8	•	67.0	79.1	72.7	82.6	•	•	•	•
Salaries and Wages	11	4.7	•	•	5.4	•	11.6	4.1	2.9	2.2	•	•	•	•
Taxes Paid	12	1.3	•	•	2.1	•	0.8	0.9	1.4	0.7	•	•	•	•
Interest Paid	13	1.5	•	•	0.1	•	0.4	0.6	0.9	0.5	•	•	•	•
Depreciation	14	2.2	•	•	3.8	•	1.1	3.0	1.5	2.2	•	•	•	•
Amortization and Depletion	15	0.1	•	•	•	•	0.0	0.1	0.1	0.0	•	•	•	•
Pensions and Other Deferred Comp.	16	0.3	•	•	0.0	•	0.7	0.1	0.1	0.2	•	•	•	•
Employee Benefits	17	0.9	•	•	0.0	•	0.4	0.9	0.7	0.6	•	•	•	•
Advertising	18	0.9	•	•	0.1	•	2.5	1.4	0.5	1.8	•	•	•	•
Other Expenses	19	7.1	•	•	11.0	•	8.7	6.3	8.4	3.2	•	•	•	•
Officers' Compensation	20	1.7	•	•	8.1	•	2.9	1.1	2.2	1.6	•	•	•	•
Operating Margin	21	4.2	•	•	•	•	3.9	2.4	8.5	4.4	•	•	•	•
Operating Margin Before Officers' Comp.	22	5.9	•	•	6.7	•	6.8	3.5	10.8	6.0	•	•	•	•

Selected Average Balance Sheet ($ in Thousands)

Net Receivables 23	2769	370	1131	4908	5574	15154
Inventories 24	2584	0	932	3925	6832	16684
Net Property, Plant and Equipment 25	4151	312	1444	5546	7438	14834
Total Assets 26	19941	845	6318	18500	38333	66664
Notes and Loans Payable 27	6795	128	1185	4293	8206	12068
All Other Liabilities 28	6682	446	1323	5277	9707	15938
Net Worth 29	6463	271	3810	8929	20420	38659

Selected Financial Ratios (Times to 1)

Current Ratio 30	1.7	0.9	2.8	1.7	2.2	2.9
Quick Ratio 31	0.9	0.9	2.2	1.0	1.1	1.6
Net Sales to Working Capital 32	8.0	•	6.8	9.2	5.9	5.5
Coverage Ratio 33	6.1	95.4	10.9	6.7	11.0	11.9
Total Asset Turnover 34	1.5	3.4	3.3	2.2	1.6	2.5
Inventory Turnover 35	8.5	•	15.1	8.2	6.5	8.1
Receivables Turnover 36	9.7	7.9	15.5	7.9	•	
Total Liabilities to Net Worth 37	2.1	2.1	0.7	1.1	0.9	0.7
Current Assets to Working Capital 38	2.4	•	1.5	2.4	1.9	1.5
Current Liabilities to Working Capital 39	1.4	•	0.5	1.4	0.9	0.5
Working Capital to Net Sales 40	0.1	•	0.1	0.1	0.2	0.2
Inventory to Working Capital 41	0.7	•	0.3	0.9	0.7	0.6
Total Receipts to Cash Flow 42	8.3	6.6	8.4	11.5	6.1	13.0
Cost of Goods to Cash Flow 43	6.2	4.7	5.6	9.1	4.5	10.7
Cash Flow to Total Debt 44	0.3	0.8	1.0	0.4	0.6	0.5

Selected Financial Factors (in Percentages)

Debt Ratio 45	67.6	67.9	39.7	51.7	46.7	42.0
Return on Total Assets 46	13.3	35.2	15.0	8.4	16.2	14.0
Return on Equity Before Income Taxes 47	34.3	108.8	22.6	14.8	27.6	22.0
Return on Equity After Income Taxes 48	28.0	74.0	20.2	12.6	21.2	19.2
Profit Margin (Before Income Tax) 49	7.6	10.2	4.1	3.2	9.2	5.2
Profit Margin (After Income Tax) 50	6.2	7.0	3.7	2.7	7.1	4.5

Table I

Corporations with and without Net Income

BASIC CHEMICAL

MONEY AMOUNTS AND SIZE OF ASSETS IN THOUSANDS OF DOLLARS

Item Description for Accounting Period 7/08 Through 6/09		Total	Zero Assets	Under 500	500 to 1,000	1,000 to 5,000	5,000 to 10,000	10,000 to 25,000	25,000 to 50,000	50,000 to 100,000	100,000 to 250,000	250,000 to 500,000	500,000 to 2,500,000	2,500,000 and over
Number of Enterprises	1	1313	468	91	244	150	59	105	63	31	21	20	35	25
Revenues ($ in Thousands)														
Net Sales	2	196240868	4867474	90680	582726	811798	863962	3236994	3531445	4396284	4830705	6976518	34366898	131685383
Interest	3	3125206	8191	0	0	3582	590	3790	1941	3405	15377	26168	191660	2870504
Rents	4	431523	118	0	0	0	0	1262	4324	386	18973	3242	10000	393217
Royalties	5	3519535	18153	0	0	1118	0	26	0	1410	25135	31353	188478	3253863
Other Portfolio Income	6	4415687	81550	0	0	5666	5763	3009	6868	5190	7146	39537	670733	3590221
Other Receipts	7	4678904	61848	0	11488	3551	5041	15506	20916	46916	148185	101503	452219	3811732
Total Receipts	8	212411723	5037334	90680	594214	825715	875356	3260587	3565494	4445591	5045521	7178321	35879988	145604920
Average Total Receipts	9	161776	10764	996	2435	5505	14837	31053	56595	143664	240263	358916	1025143	5824197
Operating Costs/Operating Income (%)														
Cost of Operations	10	80.4	85.6	73.8	65.2	75.5	70.5	74.1	72.1	85.3	81.9	76.4	80.3	80.8
Salaries and Wages	11	5.8	7.3	3.7	6.0	6.2	4.1	6.1	5.8	3.1	5.9	5.0	4.4	6.2
Taxes Paid	12	0.8	0.7	1.0	0.6	1.4	2.0	1.1	1.0	0.6	0.8	0.4	0.7	0.8
Interest Paid	13	4.5	2.0	0.0	0.2	0.5	0.2	0.6	1.0	0.9	1.4	2.2	3.1	5.5
Depreciation	14	3.5	2.1	0.1	0.7	2.9	7.8	2.7	3.1	2.4	3.8	4.5	4.2	3.4
Amortization and Depletion	15	0.8	0.6	•	•	0.0	•	0.3	0.3	0.3	0.5	0.7	1.0	0.8
Pensions and Other Deferred Comp.	16	1.0	0.3	0.0	•	0.4	0.3	0.3	0.6	0.4	0.5	0.7	0.8	1.1
Employee Benefits	17	1.3	0.6	2.9	0.8	1.0	0.3	1.2	1.2	0.5	0.7	1.1	1.6	1.4
Advertising	18	0.5	0.1	0.0	0.1	0.1	0.1	0.4	0.2	0.1	0.1	0.2	0.2	0.7
Other Expenses	19	8.1	5.0	7.4	11.8	9.1	7.3	8.3	7.9	7.2	8.1	12.6	7.5	8.2
Officers' Compensation	20	0.5	0.9	6.1	4.3	4.4	0.9	2.3	1.8	1.1	0.8	0.7	0.6	0.3
Operating Margin	21	•	•	4.9	10.3	•	6.3	2.6	5.0	•	•	•	•	•
Operating Margin Before Officers' Comp.	22	•	•	11.0	14.6	2.8	7.3	4.9	6.8	•	•	•	•	•

Selected Average Balance Sheet ($ in Thousands)

Net Receivables **23**	49216	0	90	222	739	3129	3451	7960	12942	25345	77472	146787	2231168
Inventories **24**	13767	0	152	106	475	437	3628	6732	11263	25289	37026	105813	472416
Net Property, Plant and Equipment **25**	39955	0	7	134	283	3733	4973	9522	21446	46116	112466	293807	1475098
Total Assets **26**	250818	0	348	770	2339	8325	15098	34447	71670	166717	371091	1190810	10787335
Notes and Loans Payable **27**	113705	0	2	116	310	9674	4500	9210	25525	51655	142078	484702	5036579
All Other Liabilities **28**	72340	0	45	111	519	1676	2976	8156	17453	49020	96776	332512	3152174
Net Worth **29**	64772	0	301	543	1510	-3025	7622	17082	28691	66042	132237	373596	2598581

Selected Financial Ratios (Times to 1)

Current Ratio **30**	1.0	•	7.1	3.3	3.0	1.3	2.5	1.8	1.8	1.2	1.9	1.3	0.9
Quick Ratio **31**	0.7	•	3.8	2.1	2.0	1.0	1.3	1.0	1.2	0.6	1.2	0.7	0.7
Net Sales to Working Capital **32**	94.1	•	3.6	5.4	4.9	14.4	5.8	6.2	8.5	22.1	4.8	11.4	•
Coverage Ratio **33**	1.5	0.2	2241.0	51.0	1.2	35.7	6.4	6.8	0.3	0.9	0.3	1.2	1.6
Total Asset Turnover **34**	0.6	•	2.9	3.1	2.3	1.8	2.0	1.6	2.0	1.4	0.9	0.8	0.5
Inventory Turnover **35**	8.7	•	4.8	14.7	8.6	23.6	6.3	6.0	10.7	7.5	7.2	7.5	9.0
Receivables Turnover **36**	3.0	•	3.8	16.6	5.7	5.2	8.1	7.8	10.8	6.9	5.1	6.7	2.3
Total Liabilities to Net Worth **37**	2.9	•	0.2	0.2	0.4	0.5	•	1.0	1.0	1.5	1.8	2.2	3.2
Current Assets to Working Capital **38**	49.0	•	1.2	1.4	1.5	4.4	1.7	2.2	2.2	6.8	2.1	4.0	•
Current Liabilities to Working Capital **39**	48.0	•	0.2	0.4	0.5	3.4	0.7	1.2	1.2	5.8	1.1	3.0	•
Working Capital to Net Sales **40**	0.0	•	0.3	0.2	0.2	0.1	0.2	0.2	0.1	0.0	0.2	0.1	•
Inventory to Working Capital **41**	9.0	•	0.5	0.2	0.3	0.5	0.7	0.9	0.7	2.2	0.6	1.2	•
Total Receipts to Cash Flow **42**	14.3	46.4	10.6	4.3	14.4	7.6	10.3	8.4	19.1	15.1	11.8	20.4	13.5
Cost of Goods to Cash Flow **43**	11.5	39.7	7.8	2.8	10.9	5.3	7.6	6.1	16.3	12.4	9.0	16.4	10.9
Cash Flow to Total Debt **44**	0.1	•	2.0	2.4	0.5	0.2	0.4	0.4	0.2	0.2	0.1	0.1	0.0

Selected Financial Factors (in Percentages)

Debt Ratio **45**	74.2	•	13.5	29.5	35.4	136.3	49.5	50.4	60.0	60.4	64.4	68.6	75.9
Return on Total Assets **46**	4.1	•	14.2	38.8	1.4	13.8	8.1	11.4	0.5	1.8	0.6	3.0	4.3
Return on Equity Before Income Taxes **47**	5.4	•	16.3	54.0	0.4	•	13.5	19.6	•	•	•	1.3	6.5
Return on Equity After Income Taxes **48**	2.5	•	16.3	54.0	•	•	10.7	16.9	•	•	•	•	3.4
Profit Margin (Before Income Tax) **49**	2.4	•	4.9	12.3	0.1	7.6	3.3	6.0	•	•	0.5	•	3.2
Profit Margin (After Income Tax) **50**	1.1	•	4.9	12.3	7.5	2.6	5.2	•	0.1	•	0.5	•	1.7

Table II

Corporations with Net Income

BASIC CHEMICAL

MONEY AMOUNTS AND SIZE OF ASSETS IN THOUSANDS OF DOLLARS

Item Description for Accounting Period 7/08 Through 6/09	Total	Zero Assets	Under 500	500 to 1,000	1,000 to 5,000	5,000 to 10,000	10,000 to 25,000	25,000 to 50,000	50,000 to 100,000	100,000 to 250,000	250,000 to 500,000	500,000 to 2,500,000	2,500,000 and over
Number of Enterprises 1	677	5	91	189	113	59	88	48	17	14	11	23	18
Revenues ($ in Thousands)													
Net Sales 2	123799032	3154836	90680	438339	637559	863962	2906936	2726876	3187551	3111603	4645261	18537441	83497986
Interest 3	2277608	5325	0	0	3244	590	3341	1510	1376	12141	13804	136541	2099736
Rents 4	416155	0	0	0	0	0	1262	2162	386	18341	1758	6684	385561
Royalties 5	2805130	593	0	0	1118	0	26	0	0	19200	30877	174238	2579078
Other Portfolio Income 6	3897839	44197	0	0	1615	5763	3008	4670	5018	6915	39049	586328	3201275
Other Receipts 7	3163733	20546	0	0	998	5041	11188	14428	22458	132860	96025	293241	2566952
Total Receipts 8	136359497	3225497	90680	438339	644534	875356	2925761	2749646	3216789	3301060	4826774	19734473	94430588
Average Total Receipts 9	201417	645099	996	2319	5704	14837	33247	57284	189223	235790	438798	858021	5240588
Operating Costs/Operating Income (%)													
Cost of Operations 10	76.7	89.2	73.8	66.2	80.6	70.5	73.4	69.9	85.3	76.4	71.3	72.3	77.7
Salaries and Wages 11	6.4	1.2	3.7	3.7	3.8	4.1	5.9	5.1	2.3	8.0	6.4	6.1	6.8
Taxes Paid 12	0.8	0.5	1.0	0.1	1.0	2.0	1.0	1.1	0.5	0.9	0.5	0.9	0.9
Interest Paid 13	4.1	1.5	0.0	•	0.3	0.2	0.5	0.8	0.7	0.9	2.0	3.5	5.0
Depreciation 14	3.8	0.8	0.1	0.5	1.3	7.8	2.4	3.0	2.2	2.8	3.5	3.5	4.1
Amortization and Depletion 15	0.7	0.5	•	•	0.0	•	0.2	0.2	0.4	0.2	0.5	1.2	0.6
Pensions and Other Deferred Comp. 16	1.0	0.1	0.0	•	0.2	0.3	0.2	0.7	0.4	0.4	1.0	1.1	1.1
Employee Benefits 17	1.6	0.2	2.9	0.0	0.4	0.3	1.1	1.1	0.4	0.7	1.1	2.2	1.7
Advertising 18	0.7	0.1	0.0	0.1	0.1	0.1	0.4	0.2	0.1	0.2	0.2	0.3	0.9
Other Expenses 19	8.1	2.2	7.4	11.2	4.7	7.3	7.7	7.8	4.2	7.8	11.2	8.7	8.3
Officers' Compensation 20	0.5	0.3	6.1	1.3	3.6	0.9	2.4	1.8	1.3	1.0	0.8	0.8	0.3
Operating Margin 21	•	3.5	4.9	16.9	4.1	6.3	4.7	8.5	2.2	0.7	1.6	•	•
Operating Margin Before Officers' Comp. 22	•	3.8	11.0	18.2	7.7	7.3	7.1	10.3	3.5	1.7	2.4	0.2	•

Selected Average Balance Sheet ($ in Thousands)

Net Receivables 23	85237	0	225	90	786	3129	3632	7492	15470	26331	93858	165127	2846654
Inventories 24	18442	0	78	152	486	347	3791	6207	13302	23593	35746	86744	489174
Net Property, Plant and Equipment 25	52121	0	151	7	217	3733	4067	8879	20670	37354	102527	224120	1503956
Total Assets 26	348475	0	784	348	2346	8325	14699	33911	67143	165976	390242	1199857	10928107
Notes and Loans Payable 27	148102	0	0	2	181	9674	3137	7748	16490	31920	106199	417541	4862615
All Other Liabilities 28	81845	0	137	45	457	1676	2772	7124	16480	52034	117793	371611	2432838
Net Worth 29	118528	0	646	301	1708	-3025	8790	19040	34173	82023	166251	410706	3632654

Selected Financial Ratios (Times to 1)

Current Ratio 30	1.0	•	4.6	7.1	3.3	1.3	2.9	2.0	2.0	1.8	2.0	1.3	0.9
Quick Ratio 31	0.8	•	3.2	3.8	2.3	1.0	1.6	1.2	1.2	1.0	1.3	0.8	0.8
Net Sales to Working Capital 32	•	•	4.7	3.6	4.9	14.4	5.3	5.5	9.6	6.4	4.7	9.5	•
Coverage Ratio 33	2.9	4.9	•	2241.0	19.9	35.7	11.4	12.9	5.6	8.6	3.9	2.9	2.6
Total Asset Turnover 34	0.5	•	3.0	2.9	2.4	1.8	2.2	1.7	2.8	1.3	1.1	0.7	0.4
Inventory Turnover 35	7.6	•	19.6	4.8	9.4	29.8	6.4	6.4	12.0	7.2	8.4	6.7	7.4
Receivables Turnover 36	2.1	•	15.0	3.8	5.4	5.2	8.2	9.0	11.2	6.4	5.4	5.4	1.5
Total Liabilities to Net Worth 37	1.9	•	0.2	0.2	0.4	0.7	0.7	0.8	1.0	1.0	1.3	1.9	2.0
Current Assets to Working Capital 38	•	•	1.3	1.2	1.4	4.4	1.5	2.0	2.0	2.2	2.0	3.9	•
Current Liabilities to Working Capital 39	•	•	0.3	0.2	0.4	3.4	0.5	1.0	1.0	1.2	1.0	2.9	•
Working Capital to Net Sales 40	•	•	0.2	0.3	0.2	0.1	0.2	0.2	0.1	0.2	0.2	0.1	•
Inventory to Working Capital 41	•	•	0.0	0.5	0.3	0.5	0.6	0.8	0.7	0.7	0.5	1.1	•
Total Receipts to Cash Flow 42	8.7	14.7	3.6	10.6	11.8	7.6	8.9	6.6	16.1	7.8	6.5	8.9	8.7
Cost of Goods to Cash Flow 43	6.7	13.1	2.4	7.8	9.5	5.3	6.6	4.6	13.7	5.9	4.6	6.5	6.8
Cash Flow to Total Debt 44	0.1	•	4.7	2.0	0.7	0.2	0.6	0.6	0.4	0.3	0.3	0.1	0.1

Selected Financial Factors (in Percentages)

Debt Ratio 45	66.0	•	17.5	13.5	27.2	136.3	40.2	43.9	49.1	50.6	57.4	65.8	66.8
Return on Total Assets 46	6.1	•	50.0	14.2	13.2	13.8	13.2	17.0	10.7	10.2	8.2	6.9	5.6
Return on Equity Before Income Taxes 47	11.6	•	60.7	16.3	17.2	•	20.1	27.9	17.3	18.2	14.2	13.2	10.3
Return on Equity After Income Taxes 48	8.5	•	60.7	16.3	14.7	•	17.3	24.8	14.9	14.3	9.8	10.4	7.2
Profit Margin (Before Income Tax) 49	7.5	5.7	16.9	4.9	5.2	7.6	5.4	9.4	3.2	6.7	5.6	6.7	8.1
Profit Margin (After Income Tax) 50	5.5	3.9	16.9	4.9	4.4	7.5	4.6	8.3	2.7	5.3	3.9	5.6	5.7

Table I

Corporations with and without Net Income

RESIN, SYNTHETIC RUBBER AND FIBERS AND FILAMENTS

MONEY AMOUNTS AND SIZE OF ASSETS IN THOUSANDS OF DOLLARS

Item Description for Accounting Period 7/08 Through 6/09	Total	Zero Assets	Under 500	500 to 1,000	1,000 to 5,000	5,000 to 10,000	10,000 to 25,000	25,000 to 50,000	50,000 to 100,000	100,000 to 250,000	250,000 to 500,000	500,000 to 2,500,000	2,500,000 and over
Number of Enterprises 1	1166	31	652	177	199	9	34	15	18	12	9	6	3
Revenues ($ in Thousands)													
Net Sales 2	44657263	187838	137684	631370	1199930	61035	939654	775797	1610960	2927171	4251992	8689826	23244008
Interest 3	1297666	76	0	0	116	38	1022	1342	2550	2361	8556	37003	1244602
Rents 4	63729	16	0	0	0	0	0	0	0	190	561	1724	61237
Royalties 5	770518	6	0	0	0	0	0	456	44	179	9576	6032	754225
Other Portfolio Income 6	238305	0	0	13952	464	1226	293	10605	1742	23583	58899	9033	118508
Other Receipts 7	1705701	434	12	0	2082	7	4583	3075	6604	14733	-3216	62157	1615230
Total Receipts 8	48733182	188370	137696	645322	1202592	62306	945552	791275	1621900	2968217	4326368	8805775	27037810
Average Total Receipts 9	41795	6076	211	3646	6043	6923	27810	52752	90106	247351	480708	1467629	9012603
Operating Costs/Operating Income (%)													
Cost of Operations 10	77.1	85.2	37.7	70.4	67.0	72.7	76.5	78.5	73.2	84.6	88.5	86.4	71.7
Salaries and Wages 11	2.3	8.4	•	8.8	5.0	7.5	3.9	4.4	4.7	3.9	3.4	2.9	0.9
Taxes Paid 12	0.5	0.7	1.2	2.1	1.5	1.2	0.9	0.8	1.0	0.5	0.8	0.5	0.3
Interest Paid 13	4.3	5.9	0.0	0.4	2.4	2.5	1.5	4.1	1.2	2.1	1.8	1.4	6.6
Depreciation 14	4.8	3.2	3.5	0.1	2.2	5.4	4.1	2.5	3.7	3.2	2.3	3.1	6.5
Amortization and Depletion 15	0.3	0.6	0.1	•	0.1	•	0.4	0.7	0.4	0.6	0.3	0.0	0.3
Pensions and Other Deferred Comp. 16	0.8	8.3	•	•	1.6	0.1	0.2	0.2	0.6	0.3	0.3	0.6	0.9
Employee Benefits 17	1.9	0.7	1.5	1.9	3.5	0.3	1.3	1.5	0.8	0.6	1.3	0.4	2.9
Advertising 18	0.3	0.1	0.9	0.3	0.2	0.1	0.6	0.4	0.2	0.2	0.1	0.1	0.3
Other Expenses 19	15.5	123.2	91.7	14.4	15.1	12.9	8.9	7.4	6.2	5.8	5.7	3.7	22.9
Officers' Compensation 20	0.4	0.2	3.9	4.0	4.0	2.3	1.6	0.7	0.8	0.8	0.4	0.3	0.1
Operating Margin 21	•	•	•	•	•	•	0.1	•	7.1	•	•	0.5	•
Operating Margin Before Officers' Comp. 22	•	•	•	1.5	1.4	•	1.7	•	8.0	•	•	0.8	•

Selected Average Balance Sheet ($ in Thousands)

Item													
Net Receivables 23	5574	0	21	220	550	1637	3898	7170	13044	27436	74318	81665	1453105
Inventories 24	4621	0	2	150	649	6464	3170	6311	10205	25317	44598	134897	1090818
Net Property, Plant and Equipment 25	14720	0	37	37	684	2419	6235	11211	21979	50956	96913	512656	3879949
Total Assets 26	94723	0	177	815	2895	7541	16864	35192	71132	158556	320166	1098191	31929320
Notes and Loans Payable 27	15641	0	414	267	556	3090	5465	18140	16609	82351	119509	449915	4087001
All Other Liabilities 28	35852	0	37	167	180	3797	5344	15238	16918	45881	137898	339473	12378852
Net Worth 29	43230	0	-274	380	2159	654	6055	1813	37606	30325	62759	308803	15463467

Selected Financial Ratios (Times to 1)

Item													
Current Ratio 30	1.5	•	3.7	3.5	3.4	5.8	1.5	1.2	2.7	1.1	1.0	2.0	1.5
Quick Ratio 31	0.8	•	1.9	2.3	1.8	3.5	0.9	0.5	1.5	0.6	0.6	0.8	0.9
Net Sales to Working Capital 32	8.1	•	2.1	8.6	5.6	1.6	10.4	17.8	4.0	35.4	•	8.4	6.7
Coverage Ratio 33	1.5	•	•	0.3	•	1.3	1.5	1.3	7.7	0.5	•	2.3	1.8
Total Asset Turnover 34	0.4	•	1.2	4.4	2.1	0.9	1.6	1.5	1.3	1.5	1.5	1.3	0.2
Inventory Turnover 35	6.4	•	32.0	16.8	6.2	0.8	6.7	6.4	6.4	8.2	9.4	9.3	5.1
Receivables Turnover 36	5.5	•	15.7	14.6	10.4	1.7	7.1	6.6	7.0	8.6	7.4	16.1	3.9
Total Liabilities to Net Worth 37	1.2	•	•	1.1	0.3	10.5	1.8	18.4	0.9	4.2	4.1	2.6	1.1
Current Assets to Working Capital 38	3.1	•	1.4	1.4	1.4	1.2	3.2	6.0	1.6	11.6	•	2.0	3.1
Current Liabilities to Working Capital 39	2.1	•	0.4	0.4	0.4	0.2	2.2	5.0	0.6	10.6	•	1.0	2.1
Working Capital to Net Sales 40	0.1	•	0.5	0.1	0.2	0.6	0.1	0.1	0.3	0.0	•	0.1	0.1
Inventory to Working Capital 41	1.0	•	0.0	0.5	0.7	0.5	1.0	2.7	0.5	3.6	•	0.9	0.9
Total Receipts to Cash Flow 42	7.5	•	2.1	8.1	25.2	11.8	14.4	13.0	7.7	28.6	70.0	22.4	4.6
Cost of Goods to Cash Flow 43	5.8	•	0.8	5.7	16.9	8.6	11.0	10.2	5.7	24.2	62.0	19.3	3.3
Cash Flow to Total Debt 44	0.1	•	0.2	1.0	0.3	0.1	0.2	0.1	0.3	0.1	0.0	0.1	0.1

Selected Financial Factors (in Percentages)

Item													
Debt Ratio 45	54.4	•	255.0	53.3	25.4	91.3	64.1	94.8	47.1	80.9	80.4	71.9	51.6
Return on Total Assets 46	2.6	•	•	0.7	•	•	3.6	7.8	11.3	1.5	•	4.3	2.9
Return on Equity Before Income Taxes 47	2.0	31.3	31.3	•	•	•	3.3	33.2	18.5	•	•	8.5	2.6
Return on Equity After Income Taxes 48	0.8	31.3	31.3	•	•	•	1.4	14.0	16.2	•	•	3.7	1.6
Profit Margin (Before Income Tax) 49	2.3	•	•	•	•	•	0.7	1.2	7.8	•	•	1.8	5.2
Profit Margin (After Income Tax) 50	0.9	•	•	•	•	•	0.3	0.5	6.8	•	•	0.8	3.3

85

Table II

Corporations with Net Income

RESIN, SYNTHETIC RUBBER AND FIBERS AND FILAMENTS

MONEY AMOUNTS AND SIZE OF ASSETS IN THOUSANDS OF DOLLARS

Item Description for Accounting Period 7/08 Through 6/09	Total	Zero Assets	Under 500	500 to 1,000	1,000 to 5,000	5,000 to 10,000	10,000 to 25,000	25,000 to 50,000	50,000 to 100,000	100,000 to 250,000	250,000 to 500,000	500,000 to 2,500,000	2,500,000 and over
Number of Enterprises **1**	522	•	259	103	•	5	18	10	14	7	5	•	0
Revenues ($ in Thousands)													
Net Sales **2**	31859562	•	36529	284185	•	41170	590340	481792	1472568	1829012	2077901	•	0
Interest **3**	1261014	•	0	0	•	29	351	1095	2067	1587	3767	•	0
Rents **4**	63729	•	0	0	•	0	0	0	0	190	561	•	0
Royalties **5**	759615	•	0	0	•	0	0	456	0	10	4917	•	0
Other Portfolio Income **6**	182897	•	0	0	•	1226	24	4	1742	1760	57127	•	0
Other Receipts **7**	1639742	•	0	0	•	6	2195	1635	4916	9892	9065	•	0
Total Receipts **8**	35766559	•	36529	284185	•	42431	592910	484982	1481293	1842451	2153338	•	0
Average Total Receipts **9**	68518	•	141	2759	•	8486	32939	48498	105807	263207	430668	•	•
Operating Costs/Operating Income (%)													
Cost of Operations **10**	73.1	•	12.6	39.1	•	57.9	77.5	77.0	74.0	80.4	85.6	•	•
Salaries and Wages **11**	1.8	•	•	10.3	•	8.7	3.3	3.7	4.0	4.8	3.4	•	•
Taxes Paid **12**	0.5	•	0.3	2.0	•	0.7	0.9	0.7	0.9	0.7	0.8	•	•
Interest Paid **13**	5.3	•	•	•	•	0.1	1.1	1.5	0.9	0.8	0.9	•	•
Depreciation **14**	4.9	•	2.0	0.0	•	2.7	3.7	2.8	3.4	2.0	2.3	•	•
Amortization and Depletion **15**	0.3	•	•	•	•	•	0.0	0.6	0.4	0.3	0.5	•	•
Pensions and Other Deferred Comp. **16**	0.9	•	•	•	•	0.2	0.3	0.3	0.6	0.3	0.4	•	•
Employee Benefits **17**	2.3	•	•	•	•	0.4	1.5	1.5	0.9	0.9	1.0	•	•
Advertising **18**	0.3	•	•	0.1	•	0.1	0.8	0.6	0.3	0.2	0.1	•	•
Other Expenses **19**	17.9	•	76.3	17.5	•	2.4	6.2	7.0	4.4	5.7	5.0	•	•
Officers' Compensation **20**	0.3	•	•	3.9	•	3.5	1.4	1.0	0.8	1.1	0.7	•	•
Operating Margin **21**	•	•	8.8	27.1	•	23.2	3.3	3.3	9.5	2.8	•	•	•
Operating Margin Before Officers' Comp. **22**	•	•	8.8	31.1	•	26.7	4.8	4.3	10.3	3.9	•	•	•

Selected Average Balance Sheet ($ in Thousands)

	1	2	3	4	5	6	7	8	9
Net Receivables 23	9784	0	371	1371	6041	7079	13811	27534	50174
Inventories 24	8808	0	122	10805	4376	5953	12064	27619	37023
Net Property, Plant and Equipment 25	25697	5	1	498	5379	13431	21787	31945	94982
Total Assets 26	193807	59	741	7161	16376	36261	72284	149449	299077
Notes and Loans Payable 27	28665	8	4	147	4614	6001	13505	32841	13914
All Other Liabilities 28	74139	48	125	6221	6001	17093	17127	38391	113502
Net Worth 29	91004	3	613	794	5761	13167	41652	78218	171661

Selected Financial Ratios (Times to 1)

	1	2	3	4	5	6	7	8	9
Current Ratio 30	1.6	1.1	5.8	6.9	2.1	1.3	2.9	2.5	1.4
Quick Ratio 31	0.9	1.1	4.9	4.0	1.3	0.6	1.6	1.1	0.9
Net Sales to Working Capital 32	6.1	22.1	4.5	1.5	5.8	12.8	4.0	4.9	12.3
Coverage Ratio 33	2.2	•	•	250.1	4.4	3.7	12.5	5.4	5.4
Total Asset Turnover 34	0.3	2.4	3.7	1.1	2.0	1.3	1.5	1.7	1.4
Inventory Turnover 35	5.1	•	8.8	0.4	5.8	6.2	6.5	7.6	9.6
Receivables Turnover 36	4.4	•	7.7	1.4	5.2	5.4	•	8.5	•
Total Liabilities to Net Worth 37	1.1	21.6	0.2	8.0	1.8	1.8	0.7	0.9	0.7
Current Assets to Working Capital 38	2.7	8.5	1.2	1.2	1.9	4.6	1.5	1.7	3.6
Current Liabilities to Working Capital 39	1.7	7.5	0.2	0.2	0.9	3.6	0.5	0.7	2.6
Working Capital to Net Sales 40	0.2	0.0	0.2	0.7	0.2	0.1	0.3	0.2	0.1
Inventory to Working Capital 41	0.9	•	0.2	0.5	0.6	1.9	0.5	0.5	1.1
Total Receipts to Cash Flow 42	5.2	1.2	2.4	3.5	12.7	9.6	7.4	11.7	13.7
Cost of Goods to Cash Flow 43	3.8	0.1	0.9	2.0	9.9	7.4	5.5	9.4	11.8
Cash Flow to Total Debt 44	0.1	2.1	9.1	0.4	0.2	0.2	0.5	0.3	0.2

Selected Financial Factors (in Percentages)

	1	2	3	4	5	6	7	8	9
Debt Ratio 45	53.0	95.6	17.3	88.9	64.8	63.7	42.4	47.7	42.6
Return on Total Assets 46	3.7	21.1	101.0	27.2	9.7	7.3	16.0	7.5	6.6
Return on Equity Before Income Taxes 47	4.2	476.4	122.2	244.8	21.4	14.7	25.5	11.7	9.3
Return on Equity After Income Taxes 48	3.0	476.4	122.2	162.4	17.5	10.7	22.8	9.7	7.0
Profit Margin (Before Income Tax) 49	6.3	8.8	27.1	23.6	3.8	4.0	10.1	3.5	3.8
Profit Margin (After Income Tax) 50	4.5	8.8	27.1	15.7	3.1	2.9	9.0	2.9	2.9

Table I

Corporations with and without Net Income

PHARMACEUTICAL AND MEDICINE

MONEY AMOUNTS AND SIZE OF ASSETS IN THOUSANDS OF DOLLARS

Item Description for Accounting Period 7/08 Through 6/09		Total	Zero Assets	Under 500	500 to 1,000	1,000 to 5,000	5,000 to 10,000	10,000 to 25,000	25,000 to 50,000	50,000 to 100,000	100,000 to 250,000	250,000 to 500,000	500,000 to 2,500,000	2,500,000 and over
Number of Enterprises	1	1240	24	490	4	186	175	120	74	46	47	12	28	33
Revenues ($ in Thousands)														
Net Sales	2	324628654	3340310	122944	0	580534	1959099	1981698	2378712	2450421	5069883	3031865	21097413	282615774
Interest	3	6718829	93822	172	28	2713	7161	20290	26854	29987	64960	58295	447715	5966832
Rents	4	159414	350	814	0	182	0	457	378	139	1714	0	11243	144138
Royalties	5	25948549	394000	0	0	1925	634	1555	43534	28574	144162	123463	372222	24838479
Other Portfolio Income	6	15167302	450585	1408	0	527	3175	414	25748	1578	41944	13867	472280	14155777
Other Receipts	7	25221456	1175431	39308	0	2854	62319	35299	100933	157468	82075	433288	1433806	21698674
Total Receipts	8	397844204	5454498	164646	28	588735	2032388	2039713	2576159	2668167	5404738	3660778	23834679	349419674
Average Total Receipts	9	320842	227271	336	7	3165	11614	16998	34813	58004	114994	305065	851239	10588475
Operating Costs/Operating Income (%)														
Cost of Operations	10	51.2	10.0	32.4	•	53.8	68.4	66.5	59.4	50.5	47.2	25.5	50.5	51.8
Salaries and Wages	11	14.5	63.1	24.2	•	15.6	6.8	11.8	12.6	17.9	13.7	14.1	12.6	14.2
Taxes Paid	12	1.5	5.8	2.9	•	2.6	2.2	1.6	2.2	3.3	1.9	1.5	1.7	1.5
Interest Paid	13	4.1	1.4	5.5	•	4.2	2.5	2.2	3.1	1.7	2.6	2.5	4.1	4.2
Depreciation	14	3.2	2.7	5.4	•	3.9	3.1	4.0	4.8	4.6	4.2	2.2	2.8	3.2
Amortization and Depletion	15	1.7	1.4	1.0	•	1.2	1.0	2.0	3.3	1.5	2.9	3.0	2.1	1.6
Pensions and Other Deferred Comp.	16	2.0	0.0	•	•	0.2	0.5	0.3	0.6	0.7	0.4	0.4	0.5	2.2
Employee Benefits	17	3.5	2.6	0.8	•	1.7	2.5	1.6	2.6	1.9	2.6	3.3	1.9	3.7
Advertising	18	4.5	2.6	0.0	•	1.0	0.3	1.4	1.4	1.3	2.9	1.9	2.8	4.8
Other Expenses	19	24.5	82.6	85.5	•	44.6	15.2	18.3	26.4	33.0	27.2	38.5	23.8	23.6
Officers' Compensation	20	0.7	22.7	14.2	•	8.3	4.4	3.8	3.8	3.1	2.6	1.3	1.0	0.3
Operating Margin	21	•	•	•	•	•	•	•	•	•	•	5.9	•	•
Operating Margin Before Officers' Comp.	22	•	•	•	•	•	•	•	•	•	•	7.2	•	•

Selected Average Balance Sheet ($ in Thousands)

Net Receivables 23	83133	0	12	0	234	1119	2956	5299	8993	16345	47480	123718	2935674
Inventories 24	33691	0	9	1705	294	1760	2671	4251	8171	16100	38801	131429	1075459
Net Property, Plant and Equipment 25	60916	0	40	0	715	2932	3843	8461	13978	31577	42635	119004	2054885
Total Assets 26	691553	0	110	622	2488	8278	15616	35452	75582	159561	327567	1095110	24408786
Notes and Loans Payable 27	213087	0	270	2270	1179	1620	5284	12081	15996	39727	53750	269333	7614140
All Other Liabilities 28	211770	0	105	262	1097	1039	4502	13454	26245	39957	85352	316526	7504488
Net Worth 29	266696	0	-265	-1909	212	5620	5830	9916	33341	79876	188466	509251	9290159

Selected Financial Ratios (Times to 1)

Current Ratio 30	1.1	•	0.3	1.0	1.1	3.7	1.5	1.6	2.1	2.4	3.2	1.9	1.1
Quick Ratio 31	0.6	•	0.2	1.0	0.8	2.1	1.0	1.1	1.2	1.4	1.9	1.0	0.5
Net Sales to Working Capital 32	10.5	•	•	•	30.3	3.3	5.2	3.8	2.4	2.6	1.9	3.2	15.5
Coverage Ratio 33	4.7	•	•	•	•	•	•	•	•	0.5	11.6	3.6	5.1
Total Asset Turnover 34	0.4	•	2.3	•	1.3	1.4	1.1	0.9	0.7	0.7	0.8	0.7	0.4
Inventory Turnover 35	4.0	•	9.0	•	5.7	4.3	4.1	4.5	3.3	3.2	1.7	2.9	4.1
Receivables Turnover 36	2.7	•	19.5	•	11.8	8.9	5.8	6.6	6.6	7.1	5.1	7.1	2.4
Total Liabilities to Net Worth 37	1.6	•	•	•	10.7	0.5	1.7	2.6	1.3	1.0	0.7	1.2	1.6
Current Assets to Working Capital 38	8.2	•	26.8	•	11.5	1.4	2.9	2.6	1.9	1.7	1.5	2.1	12.5
Current Liabilities to Working Capital 39	7.2	•	25.8	•	10.5	0.4	1.9	1.6	0.9	0.7	0.5	1.1	11.5
Working Capital to Net Sales 40	0.1	•	•	•	0.0	0.3	0.2	0.3	0.4	0.4	0.5	0.3	0.1
Inventory to Working Capital 41	1.4	•	•	•	2.9	0.5	0.8	0.5	0.4	0.4	0.2	0.6	2.0
Total Receipts to Cash Flow 42	3.3	•	3.1	3.0	32.2	10.7	20.6	9.8	5.4	4.5	1.6	3.4	3.3
Cost of Goods to Cash Flow 43	1.7	•	0.3	1.0	17.3	7.3	13.7	5.8	2.7	2.1	0.4	1.7	1.7
Cash Flow to Total Debt 44	0.2	•	0.2	•	0.0	0.4	0.1	0.1	0.2	0.3	1.1	0.4	0.2

Selected Financial Factors (in Percentages)

Debt Ratio 45	61.4	•	340.6	407.1	91.5	32.1	62.7	72.0	55.9	49.9	42.5	53.5	61.9
Return on Total Assets 46	7.3	•	•	•	•	•	•	•	•	0.9	22.5	10.0	7.5
Return on Equity Before Income Taxes 47	14.9	•	36.0	223.2	•	•	•	•	•	•	35.8	15.5	15.9
Return on Equity After Income Taxes 48	9.6	•	38.1	223.2	•	•	•	•	•	•	26.4	10.5	10.5
Profit Margin (Before Income Tax) 49	15.2	•	•	•	•	•	•	•	•	•	26.7	10.5	17.2
Profit Margin (After Income Tax) 50	9.8	•	•	•	•	•	•	•	•	•	19.7	7.1	11.4

Table II

Corporations with Net Income

PHARMACEUTICAL AND MEDICINE

MONEY AMOUNTS AND SIZE OF ASSETS IN THOUSANDS OF DOLLARS

Item Description for Accounting Period 7/08 Through 6/09		Total	Zero Assets	Under 500	500 to 1,000	1,000 to 5,000	5,000 to 10,000	10,000 to 25,000	25,000 to 50,000	50,000 to 100,000	100,000 to 250,000	250,000 to 500,000	500,000 to 2,500,000	2,500,000 and over
Number of Enterprises	1	458	•	48	0	•	131	62	32	24	24	•	22	29
Revenues ($ in Thousands)														
Net Sales	2	298430888	•	57834	0	•	1816001	1081025	1533069	1802124	3506809	•	17334521	267968259
Interest	3	6388180	•	103	0	•	1618	7783	8232	6529	13968	•	374707	5860246
Rents	4	154400	•	0	0	•	0	328	0	51	1583	•	10249	141841
Royalties	5	25047233	•	0	0	•	0	1555	16159	28300	97129	•	337972	24317810
Other Portfolio Income	6	14814174	•	1408	0	•	3167	268	2	1571	28815	•	461856	14127555
Other Receipts	7	23309339	•	20600	0	•	2105	27426	62161	19531	47883	•	1142665	20719439
Total Receipts	8	368144214	•	79945	0	•	1822891	1118385	1619623	1858106	3696187	•	19661970	333135150
Average Total Receipts	9	803808	•	1666	•	•	13915	18038	50613	77421	154008	•	893726	11487419
Operating Costs/Operating Income (%)														
Cost of Operations	10	51.3	•	19.4	•	•	67.6	56.0	57.8	49.6	46.9	•	48.0	51.7
Salaries and Wages	11	13.9	•	6.2	•	•	5.0	9.2	7.8	12.9	11.0	•	12.9	14.2
Taxes Paid	12	1.5	•	2.3	•	•	1.9	1.3	1.6	1.8	1.6	•	1.9	1.5
Interest Paid	13	4.0	•	2.5	•	•	0.9	1.2	0.7	0.8	1.6	•	4.4	4.0
Depreciation	14	3.2	•	1.5	•	•	2.8	3.2	4.5	3.8	3.1	•	2.8	3.2
Amortization and Depletion	15	1.6	•	•	•	•	0.3	0.2	1.1	0.6	2.0	•	1.9	1.6
Pensions and Other Deferred Comp.	16	1.9	•	•	•	•	0.4	0.3	0.2	0.8	0.4	•	0.5	2.0
Employee Benefits	17	3.5	•	0.0	•	•	2.5	1.2	1.7	1.2	1.9	•	1.7	3.7
Advertising	18	4.6	•	0.0	•	•	0.3	1.3	0.8	1.4	2.5	•	3.2	4.9
Other Expenses	19	23.8	•	42.1	•	•	6.8	14.0	15.9	13.1	19.8	•	22.6	23.8
Officers' Compensation	20	0.4	•	•	•	•	3.8	3.7	1.7	1.9	1.8	•	1.0	0.2
Operating Margin	21	•	•	26.0	•	•	7.6	8.4	6.3	12.0	7.4	•	•	•
Operating Margin Before Officers' Comp.	22	•	•	26.0	•	•	11.5	12.1	8.0	13.9	9.2	•	•	0.2

Selected Average Balance Sheet ($ in Thousands)

Net Receivables 23	213693	0	•	1374	2987	7574	13885	22159	132920	3208325
Inventories 24	83807	14	•	1861	2928	4905	11801	23836	146783	1150383
Net Property, Plant and Equipment 25	151872	0	•	3364	3701	9479	14928	32367	117096	2221096
Total Assets 26	1742404	242	•	8521	15247	32776	72631	151573	1079388	26285630
Notes and Loans Payable 27	524826	1	•	1713	2693	9039	14454	35432	260190	8014671
All Other Liabilities 28	533331	125	•	883	4303	9653	19333	28014	313909	8092152
Net Worth 29	684247	116	•	5925	8252	14084	38843	88127	505289	10178807

Selected Financial Ratios (Times to 1)

Current Ratio 30	1.1	1.9	•	4.8	2.3	1.8	2.6	2.3	1.9	1.1
Quick Ratio 31	0.6	1.4	•	2.6	1.6	1.1	1.4	1.3	1.0	0.5
Net Sales to Working Capital 32	11.0	10.8	•	4.0	3.3	5.0	2.9	3.7	3.4	15.0
Coverage Ratio 33	5.6	27.2	•	10.3	11.0	17.8	19.1	9.3	4.3	5.5
Total Asset Turnover 34	0.4	5.0	•	1.6	1.1	1.5	1.0	1.0	0.7	0.4
Inventory Turnover 35	4.0	17.2	•	5.0	3.3	5.6	3.2	2.9	2.6	4.2
Receivables Turnover 36	2.6	17.3	•	10.1	5.2	6.9	•	6.5	6.8	2.5
Total Liabilities to Net Worth 37	1.5	1.1	•	0.4	0.8	1.3	0.9	0.7	1.1	1.6
Current Assets to Working Capital 38	8.7	2.1	•	1.3	1.8	2.3	1.6	1.8	2.1	12.2
Current Liabilities to Working Capital 39	7.7	1.1	•	0.3	0.8	1.3	0.6	0.8	1.1	11.2
Working Capital to Net Sales 40	0.1	0.1	•	0.3	0.3	0.2	0.3	0.3	0.3	0.1
Inventory to Working Capital 41	1.4	0.0	•	0.5	0.5	0.5	0.5	0.6	0.6	1.9
Total Receipts to Cash Flow 42	3.1	1.0	•	8.2	4.2	4.0	3.8	3.3	3.1	3.2
Cost of Goods to Cash Flow 43	1.6	0.2	•	5.5	2.4	2.3	1.9	1.6	1.5	1.6
Cash Flow to Total Debt 44	0.2	10.0	•	0.7	0.6	0.6	0.6	0.7	0.4	0.2

Selected Financial Factors (in Percentages)

Debt Ratio 45	60.7	52.1	•	30.5	45.9	57.0	46.5	41.9	53.2	61.3
Return on Total Assets 46	8.3	332.5	•	14.4	14.9	18.6	16.4	14.4	13.7	7.9
Return on Equity Before Income Taxes 47	17.3	669.1	•	18.7	25.1	40.8	29.0	22.0	22.5	16.6
Return on Equity After Income Taxes 48	11.6	619.0	•	16.3	23.2	33.6	24.5	15.4	16.1	11.1
Profit Margin (Before Income Tax) 49	18.1	64.2	•	8.0	11.9	12.0	15.0	13.3	14.4	18.3
Profit Margin (After Income Tax) 50	12.2	59.4	•	7.0	11.0	9.9	12.7	9.3	10.3	12.2

Table I

Corporations with and without Net Income

PAINT, COATING, AND ADHESIVE

MONEY AMOUNTS AND SIZE OF ASSETS IN THOUSANDS OF DOLLARS

Item Description for Accounting Period 7/08 Through 6/09	Total	Zero Assets	Under 500	500 to 1,000	1,000 to 5,000	5,000 to 10,000	10,000 to 25,000	25,000 to 50,000	50,000 to 100,000	100,000 to 250,000	250,000 to 500,000	500,000 to 2,500,000	2,500,000 and over
Number of Enterprises **1**	1328	50	80	349	647	77	54	30	15	12	0	9	5
Revenues ($ in Thousands)													
Net Sales **2**	43269924	14779	81145	1050649	3551131	971070	1496420	1395014	1407680	2270683	0	7320949	23710405
Interest **3**	508710	0	0	58	993	716	858	592	1335	12451	0	63017	428690
Rents **4**	13109	0	0	0	403	0	691	1143	57	1417	0	6258	3140
Royalties **5**	443893	0	0	0	0	0	0	251	1858	2085	0	49415	390284
Other Portfolio Income **6**	771300	25278	0	0	5157	1274	13311	8801	2024	2717	0	112515	600224
Other Receipts **7**	570608	0	0	1703	12303	35072	-24516	5341	7607	31491	0	205298	296307
Total Receipts **8**	45577544	40057	81145	1052410	3569987	1008132	1486764	1411142	1420561	2320844	0	7755452	25429050
Average Total Receipts **9**	34320	801	1014	3016	5518	13093	27533	47038	94704	193404	•	861939	5085810
Operating Costs/Operating Income (%)													
Cost of Operations **10**	66.4	78.2	43.0	63.6	64.4	67.0	70.4	69.4	68.2	69.3	•	68.1	65.6
Salaries and Wages **11**	9.3	22.2	31.6	5.8	7.1	9.8	9.4	9.5	9.3	8.9	•	9.2	9.8
Taxes Paid **12**	1.4	7.4	1.2	2.9	1.5	4.0	0.9	1.3	1.3	1.8	•	1.5	1.3
Interest Paid **13**	2.7	•	•	1.2	0.6	1.0	1.1	0.4	1.4	2.0	•	3.3	3.4
Depreciation **14**	2.3	0.6	1.6	1.4	0.5	3.2	1.9	2.1	2.7	3.3	•	2.7	2.3
Amortization and Depletion **15**	0.9	13.7	•	0.0	0.2	0.1	0.2	0.2	1.2	1.0	•	1.5	0.9
Pensions and Other Deferred Comp. **16**	1.8	0.2	•	0.6	0.4	0.1	0.5	0.6	1.7	1.4	•	1.2	2.6
Employee Benefits **17**	1.8	2.1	•	1.1	0.7	2.1	1.1	1.2	1.7	1.5	•	2.1	2.0
Advertising **18**	1.0	4.0	4.6	0.1	1.6	0.3	0.7	0.4	1.3	0.3	•	0.6	1.3
Other Expenses **19**	13.8	25.8	38.4	10.4	14.4	15.2	12.1	10.7	10.3	10.1	•	12.6	15.0
Officers' Compensation **20**	1.3	•	•	5.6	5.6	4.4	2.6	2.4	1.4	1.4	•	0.7	0.4
Operating Margin **21**	•	•	•	7.4	2.9	•	•	1.7	•	•	•	•	•
Operating Margin Before Officers' Comp. **22**	•	•	•	13.0	8.5	•	1.6	4.1	0.8	0.3	•	•	•

Selected Average Balance Sheet ($ in Thousands)

Net Receivables 23	3686	0	75	372	359	1348	3290	5699	14366	26831	•	83323	557342
Inventories 24	3503	0	0	210	444	1709	3777	7407	13684	18561	•	118300	436294
Net Property, Plant and Equipment 25	5181	0	22	131	229	1108	2644	4919	18235	40554	•	167185	808821
Total Assets 26	31038	0	156	752	2031	6066	14798	31340	75213	174976	•	1009205	5022435
Notes and Loans Payable 27	10428	0	553	373	385	2847	5951	5141	14576	64280	•	281668	1840990
All Other Liabilities 28	12439	0	16	225	360	1358	6336	5811	22872	34841	•	249434	2515662
Net Worth 29	8172	0	-413	155	1285	1861	2511	20388	37766	75855	•	478102	665784

Selected Financial Ratios (Times to 1)

Current Ratio 30	1.1	•	0.7	1.5	2.9	1.4	1.2	4.0	1.2	2.3	•	1.4	0.9
Quick Ratio 31	0.5	•	0.4	0.9	1.8	0.7	0.6	2.4	0.7	1.2	•	0.7	0.4
Net Sales to Working Capital 32	25.5	•	•	15.0	6.6	14.6	21.0	3.4	14.3	5.0	•	9.7	•
Coverage Ratio 33	2.0	•	•	7.4	6.5	•	•	8.5	1.4	1.7	•	1.9	1.9
Total Asset Turnover 34	1.0	•	6.5	4.0	2.7	2.1	1.9	1.5	1.2	1.1	•	0.8	0.9
Inventory Turnover 35	6.2	•	•	9.1	8.0	4.9	5.2	4.4	4.7	7.1	•	4.7	7.1
Receivables Turnover 36	7.4	•	•	•	12.4	6.1	7.3	6.2	5.9	8.9	•	6.1	7.8
Total Liabilities to Net Worth 37	2.8	•	•	3.9	0.6	2.3	4.9	0.5	1.0	1.3	•	1.1	6.5
Current Assets to Working Capital 38	9.0	•	•	3.1	1.5	3.8	6.5	1.3	5.2	1.8	•	3.8	•
Current Liabilities to Working Capital 39	8.0	•	•	2.1	0.5	2.8	5.5	0.3	4.2	0.8	•	2.8	•
Working Capital to Net Sales 40	0.0	•	•	0.1	0.2	0.1	0.0	0.3	0.1	0.2	•	0.1	•
Inventory to Working Capital 41	2.6	•	•	1.0	0.5	1.6	3.0	0.5	1.9	0.6	•	1.0	•
Total Receipts to Cash Flow 42	7.4	•	9.4	6.7	6.4	26.9	11.8	8.4	10.8	11.3	•	7.8	6.7
Cost of Goods to Cash Flow 43	4.9	•	4.0	4.2	4.1	18.0	8.3	5.8	7.4	7.8	•	5.3	4.4
Cash Flow to Total Debt 44	0.2	•	0.2	0.8	1.1	0.1	0.2	0.5	0.2	0.2	•	0.2	0.2

Selected Financial Factors (in Percentages)

Debt Ratio 45	73.7	•	364.3	79.4	36.7	69.3	83.0	34.9	49.8	56.6	•	52.6	86.7
Return on Total Assets 46	5.8	•	•	35.0	10.7	•	•	5.2	2.3	3.7	•	5.1	6.3
Return on Equity Before Income Taxes 47	11.2	•	49.8	146.7	14.3	•	•	7.0	1.3	3.5	•	5.2	23.0
Return on Equity After Income Taxes 48	6.7	•	49.8	146.7	13.9	•	•	5.9	•	2.1	•	3.3	11.9
Profit Margin (Before Income Tax) 49	2.8	116.7	•	7.6	3.3	•	•	3.1	0.5	1.4	•	3.1	3.2
Profit Margin (After Income Tax) 50	1.7	98.5	•	7.6	3.2	•	•	2.6	•	0.8	•	1.9	1.7

Table II

Corporations with Net Income

PAINT, COATING, AND ADHESIVE

MONEY AMOUNTS AND SIZE OF ASSETS IN THOUSANDS OF DOLLARS

Item Description for Accounting Period 7/08 Through 6/09		Total	Zero Assets	Under 500	500 to 1,000	1,000 to 5,000	5,000 to 10,000	10,000 to 25,000	25,000 to 50,000	50,000 to 100,000	100,000 to 250,000	250,000 to 500,000	500,000 to 2,500,000	2,500,000 and over
Number of Enterprises	1	886	50	0	349	400	5	32	21	9	8	0	•	•
Revenues ($ in Thousands)														
Net Sales	2	35656304	14779	0	1050649	2707058		755016	1019339	758765	1677038	0	•	•
Interest	3	494412	0	0	58	829		71	381	694	11158	0	•	•
Rents	4	12343	0	0	0	0		653	826	49	1417	0	•	•
Royalties	5	401810	0	0	0	0		0	238	279	0	0	•	•
Other Portfolio Income	6	709933	25278	0	0	3095		12583	8734	1677	2075	0	•	•
Other Receipts	7	538665	0	0	1703	5781	29681	385	4206	2472	29678	0	•	•
Total Receipts	8	37813467	40057	0	1052410	2716763	29681	768708	1033724	763936	1721366	0	•	•
Average Total Receipts	9	42679	801	•	3016	6792	5936	24022	49225	84882	215171	•	•	•
Operating Costs/Operating Income (%)														
Cost of Operations	10	65.3	78.2	•	63.6	65.2	•	67.0	66.7	64.8	68.2	•	•	•
Salaries and Wages	11	9.5	22.2	•	5.8	5.6	•	9.3	9.8	7.5	8.5	•	•	•
Taxes Paid	12	1.5	7.4	•	2.9	1.5	•	0.7	1.4	1.1	2.1	•	•	•
Interest Paid	13	2.4	*	•	1.2	0.4	•	0.9	0.3	2.0	2.1	•	•	•
Depreciation	14	2.2	0.6	•	1.4	0.4	•	1.5	1.9	2.9	2.6	•	•	•
Amortization and Depletion	15	1.0	13.7	•	0.0	0.3	•	0.2	0.2	1.5	0.7	•	•	•
Pensions and Other Deferred Comp.	16	2.1	0.2	•	0.6	0.5	•	0.6	0.6	0.2	1.9	•	•	•
Employee Benefits	17	1.8	2.1	•	1.1	0.8	•	1.8	0.8	1.2	1.5	•	•	•
Advertising	18	1.1	4.0	•	0.1	1.8	•	0.8	0.2	0.8	0.4	•	•	•
Other Expenses	19	12.0	25.8	•	10.4	10.4	•	11.0	9.7	12.5	9.5	•	•	•
Officers' Compensation	20	1.3	•	•	5.6	6.7	•	3.0	2.7	1.4	1.6	•	•	•
Operating Margin	21	•	•	•	7.4	6.3	•	3.3	5.6	3.9	0.9	•	•	•
Operating Margin Before Officers' Comp.	22	1.2	•	•	13.0	13.0	•	6.3	8.3	5.3	2.5	•	•	•

Selected Average Balance Sheet ($ in Thousands)

Net Receivables 23	4417	0		372	494	0	2965	5749	10166	29703
Inventories 24	4285	0		164	626	13504	4085	8357	14917	22468
Net Property, Plant and Equipment 25	6216	0		131	117	0	2297	4995	16865	32580
Total Assets 26	38175	0		752	2142	6418	14111	32353	71852	189505
Notes and Loans Payable 27	9653	0		373	479	0	4968	3353	19136	69076
All Other Liabilities 28	15633	0		225	478	0	2167	4440	13189	43538
Net Worth 29	12889	0		155	1186	6418	6975	24560	39527	76891

Selected Financial Ratios (Times to 1)

Current Ratio 30	1.1			1.5	2.8		2.1	5.4	1.3	2.5
Quick Ratio 31	0.5			0.9	1.8		1.1	3.3	0.7	1.4
Net Sales to Working Capital 32	26.2			15.0	6.5		5.8	2.8	14.3	4.4
Coverage Ratio 33	3.6			7.4	17.6		6.6	22.3	3.4	2.7
Total Asset Turnover 34	1.1			4.0	3.2		1.7	1.5	1.2	1.1
Inventory Turnover 35	6.1			11.6	7.0		3.9	3.9	3.7	6.4
Receivables Turnover 36	7.5			9.3	10.3		5.3	5.6	5.3	7.9
Total Liabilities to Net Worth 37	2.0			3.9	0.8		1.0	0.3	0.8	1.5
Current Assets to Working Capital 38	9.6			3.1	1.6		1.9	1.2	4.4	1.7
Current Liabilities to Working Capital 39	8.6			2.1	0.6		0.9	0.2	3.4	0.7
Working Capital to Net Sales 40	0.0			0.1	0.2		0.2	0.4	0.1	0.2
Inventory to Working Capital 41	2.6			1.0	0.5		0.8	0.4	1.9	0.5
Total Receipts to Cash Flow 42	6.5			6.7	6.7		6.8	6.6	6.4	9.8
Cost of Goods to Cash Flow 43	4.3			4.2	4.4		4.6	4.4	4.1	6.7
Cash Flow to Total Debt 44	0.2			0.8	1.1		0.5	0.9	0.4	0.2

Selected Financial Factors (in Percentages)

Debt Ratio 45	66.2			79.4	44.6		50.6	24.1	45.0	59.4
Return on Total Assets 46	9.2			35.0	22.2	27.8	9.8	11.5	8.2	6.2
Return on Equity Before Income Taxes 47	19.8			146.7	37.9	27.8	16.9	14.5	10.5	9.6
Return on Equity After Income Taxes 48	15.5			146.7	37.2	27.8	14.7	13.3	7.7	7.4
Profit Margin (Before Income Tax) 49	6.4	116.7		7.6	6.6		5.0	7.3	4.9	3.5
Profit Margin (After Income Tax) 50	5.0	98.5		7.6	6.5		4.3	6.7	3.6	2.7

Table I

Corporations with and without Net Income

SOAP, CLEANING COMPOUND, AND TOILET PREPARATION

MONEY AMOUNTS AND SIZE OF ASSETS IN THOUSANDS OF DOLLARS

Item Description for Accounting Period 7/08 Through 6/09	Total	Zero Assets	Under 500	500 to 1,000	1,000 to 5,000	5,000 to 10,000	10,000 to 25,000	25,000 to 50,000	50,000 to 100,000	100,000 to 250,000	250,000 to 500,000	500,000 to 2,500,000	2,500,000 and over
Number of Enterprises 1	2195	1040	402	186	301	134	58	19	19	12	5	8	11
Revenues ($ in Thousands)													
Net Sales 2	96314912	168827	436719	252621	2433162	1751553	1960155	955388	1926382	2455103	2966965	9008620	71999418
Interest 3	773419	0	52	125	891	822	1189	3863	1103	12571	6516	24870	721416
Rents 4	74024	0	0	0	1965	829	1292	474	167	3803	234	7523	57737
Royalties 5	3266647	0	0	0	7436	0	792	1256	382	1589	3237	170515	3081441
Other Portfolio Income 6	5729078	1149	0	36284	2337	1803	481	3195	9	20466	50463	460111	5152781
Other Receipts 7	3810738	3538	4	1198	6394	46136	10475	7746	36390	46373	19967	182899	3449615
Total Receipts 8	109968818	173514	436775	290228	2452185	1801143	1974384	971922	1964433	2539905	3047382	9854538	84462408
Average Total Receipts 9	50100	167	1087	1560	8147	13441	34041	51154	103391	211659	609476	1231817	7678401
Operating Costs/Operating Income (%)													
Cost of Operations 10	43.9	34.4	74.6	64.0	58.8	54.0	67.3	63.1	66.4	57.2	64.8	50.7	39.3
Salaries and Wages 11	9.9	18.3	3.6	10.3	11.8	22.0	10.0	12.3	8.3	9.9	8.9	10.4	9.5
Taxes Paid 12	1.8	9.2	2.6	3.0	1.9	0.9	1.3	1.7	1.4	1.4	1.4	3.4	1.7
Interest Paid 13	4.2	0.3	0.0	1.1	0.4	0.3	0.7	0.9	2.7	3.4	1.3	4.3	4.7
Depreciation 14	2.6	1.4	0.4	1.2	0.9	4.8	2.3	1.6	2.2	1.7	2.4	2.2	2.8
Amortization and Depletion 15	1.6	0.0	0.0	0.0	0.0	0.2	0.1	1.0	1.6	1.5	0.5	0.8	1.9
Pensions and Other Deferred Comp. 16	1.9	0.1	•	0.3	1.0	0.6	0.4	0.5	0.1	0.4	0.8	0.7	2.3
Employee Benefits 17	1.8	0.7	0.1	3.6	0.9	0.5	1.8	1.2	1.3	0.6	0.8	2.0	1.9
Advertising 18	7.1	5.6	0.1	1.2	1.5	0.5	2.0	2.1	1.7	8.6	5.1	8.2	7.8
Other Expenses 19	24.1	38.1	11.8	24.6	13.7	16.4	10.3	14.4	18.4	15.0	12.1	19.9	26.7
Officers' Compensation 20	1.1	1.3	10.7	6.8	5.4	3.7	2.1	2.2	3.3	1.0	1.1	1.6	0.7
Operating Margin 21	•	•	•	•	3.7	•	1.7	•	•	•	0.9	•	0.7
Operating Margin Before Officers' Comp. 22	1.1	•	6.8	•	9.1	•	3.8	1.1	•	0.2	2.0	•	1.4

Selected Average Balance Sheet ($ in Thousands)

Net Receivables 23	14573	0	85	581	91	1316	3985	7287	20926	33644	69602	82336	2673361
Inventories 24	4176	0	62	454	95	1046	4151	6701	11844	25674	56946	174786	567565
Net Property, Plant and Equipment 25	7814	0	30	291	52	2112	4086	5861	10304	27786	85759	133876	1307576
Total Assets 26	113924		349	755	2442	6567	14687	33262	66260	169027	399265	1300478	20999727
Notes and Loans Payable 27	31307	0	0	410	789	564	4070	11096	37545	81378	147067	648274	5483097
All Other Liabilities 28	28580	0	15	496	43	2161	4348	8846	21139	41186	125942	358393	5224205
Net Worth 29	54038	334	-77	1535	496	3843	6268	13320	7576	46462	126256	293811	10292425

Selected Financial Ratios (Times to 1)

Current Ratio 30	0.9	•	•	2.7	4.8	1.8	1.5	1.8	1.6	1.6	1.0	1.6	0.8
Quick Ratio 31	0.6	•	•	1.3	3.5	1.1	0.8	1.0	0.9	0.9	0.5	0.6	0.6
Net Sales to Working Capital 32	•	•	3.6	6.6	2.6	8.4	11.0	6.8	6.9	7.3	•	7.8	•
Coverage Ratio 33	5.0	•	•	12.7	•	•	4.6	1.7	•	1.8	3.7	2.5	5.5
Total Asset Turnover 34	0.4	•	3.1	3.3	1.8	2.0	2.3	1.5	1.5	1.2	1.5	0.9	0.3
Inventory Turnover 35	4.6	•	13.0	10.5	9.2	6.8	5.5	4.7	5.7	4.6	6.7	3.3	4.5
Receivables Turnover 36	3.0	•	•	15.4	•	11.0	7.8	5.9	6.1	7.2	7.7	7.2	2.5
Total Liabilities to Net Worth 37	1.1	•	0.0	0.6	•	0.7	1.3	1.5	7.7	2.6	2.2	3.4	1.0
Current Assets to Working Capital 38	•	•	1.1	1.6	1.3	2.3	3.1	2.2	2.6	2.7	•	2.6	•
Current Liabilities to Working Capital 39	•	•	0.1	0.6	0.3	1.3	2.1	1.2	1.6	1.7	•	1.6	•
Working Capital to Net Sales 40	•	•	0.3	0.2	0.4	0.1	0.1	0.1	0.1	0.1	•	0.1	•
Inventory to Working Capital 41	•	•	0.2	0.5	0.2	0.8	1.2	0.9	0.9	1.0	•	1.1	•
Total Receipts to Cash Flow 42	3.2	3.4	13.8	6.5	10.4	7.8	8.7	7.7	20.4	6.4	7.4	5.9	2.7
Cost of Goods to Cash Flow 43	1.4	1.2	10.3	3.8	6.6	4.2	5.9	4.8	13.5	3.6	4.8	3.0	1.0
Cash Flow to Total Debt 44	0.2	•	5.1	1.4	0.2	0.6	0.5	0.3	0.1	0.3	0.3	0.2	0.2

Selected Financial Factors (in Percentages)

Debt Ratio 45	52.6	•	4.4	37.1	110.1	41.5	57.3	60.0	88.6	72.5	68.4	77.4	51.0
Return on Total Assets 46	8.0	•	•	15.9	•	•	7.1	2.5	•	7.4	7.3	9.2	8.1
Return on Equity Before Income Taxes 47	13.5	•	•	23.3	20.1	•	13.0	2.7	•	12.0	16.9	24.1	13.5
Return on Equity After Income Taxes 48	8.9	•	•	21.9	70.6	•	10.5	1.8	•	8.4	12.2	16.8	8.9
Profit Margin (Before Income Tax) 49	16.7	•	•	4.4	•	•	2.4	0.7	•	2.7	3.6	6.3	21.3
Profit Margin (After Income Tax) 50	10.9	•	•	4.2	•	•	1.9	0.5	•	1.9	2.6	4.4	14.0

Table II

Corporations with Net Income

SOAP, CLEANING COMPOUND, AND TOILET PREPARATION

MONEY AMOUNTS AND SIZE OF ASSETS IN THOUSANDS OF DOLLARS

Item Description for Accounting Period 7/08 Through 6/09		Total	Zero Assets	Under 500	500 to 1,000	1,000 to 5,000	5,000 to 10,000	10,000 to 25,000	25,000 to 50,000	50,000 to 100,000	100,000 to 250,000	250,000 to 500,000	500,000 to 2,500,000	2,500,000 and over
Number of Enterprises	1	1089	413	90	111	269	107	53	7	10	8	•	•	•
Revenues ($ in Thousands)														
Net Sales	2	90329991	168827	124133	184576	2336231	1690452	1734368	534059	1069380	1839815	•	•	•
Interest	3	667934	0	46	0	885	95	1189	1955	327	3179	•	•	•
Rents	4	70317	0	0	0	1965	766	1292	437	19	626	•	•	•
Royalties	5	3160178	0	0	0	7436	0	792	115	170	1589	•	•	•
Other Portfolio Income	6	5601186	1149	0	36284	2335	1802	481	42	7	20466	•	•	•
Other Receipts	7	3708514	1104	0	1177	6355	11504	10251	4956	6744	43087	•	•	•
Total Receipts	8	103538120	171080	124179	222037	2355207	1704619	1748373	541564	1076647	1908762	•	•	•
Average Total Receipts	9	95076	414	1380	2000	8755	15931	32988	77366	107665	238595	•	•	•
Operating Costs/Operating Income (%)														
Cost of Operations	10	42.3	34.4	81.3	65.5	59.1	53.7	64.9	60.2	58.2	53.7	•	•	•
Salaries and Wages	11	9.9	18.3	2.2	7.2	11.6	21.9	10.5	11.8	8.9	9.8	•	•	•
Taxes Paid	12	1.9	4.9	0.7	2.7	1.9	0.8	1.2	1.4	1.7	1.3	•	•	•
Interest Paid	13	4.0	0.3	•	1.0	0.2	0.1	0.7	0.5	1.3	2.0	•	•	•
Depreciation	14	2.7	1.4	0.8	1.1	0.9	4.8	2.4	1.5	2.3	1.5	•	•	•
Amortization and Depletion	15	1.6	0.0	0.1	0.0	0.0	0.0	0.1	0.2	0.5	0.9	•	•	•
Pensions and Other Deferred Comp.	16	2.0	0.1	•	0.5	1.1	0.6	0.4	0.4	0.2	0.4	•	•	•
Employee Benefits	17	1.7	0.7	0.4	4.7	0.8	0.5	1.5	1.2	1.2	0.8	•	•	•
Advertising	18	7.5	2.8	0.0	0.2	1.5	0.3	2.2	2.7	1.7	10.9	•	•	•
Other Expenses	19	24.4	25.0	10.2	18.7	13.3	12.6	11.1	15.5	10.1	15.0	•	•	•
Officers' Compensation	20	1.0	1.3	3.5	4.4	5.3	3.5	2.4	2.3	5.2	1.0	•	•	•
Operating Margin	21	1.1	10.9	0.7	•	4.2	1.1	2.6	2.3	8.7	2.9	•	•	•
Operating Margin Before Officers' Comp.	22	2.1	12.2	4.2	•	9.6	4.6	5.0	4.7	13.9	3.9	•	•	•

Selected Average Balance Sheet ($ in Thousands)

	1	2	3	4	5	6	7	8	9	10
Net Receivables 23	28000	0	100	75	618	1515	3903	12585	21317	38040
Inventories 24	7619	0	59	102	433	946	3805	14307	16440	27102
Net Property, Plant and Equipment 25	14970	0	12	7	294	2484	4048	5973	9306	24487
Total Assets 26	221905	0	448	765	2585	6786	14616	39552	64784	164921
Notes and Loans Payable 27	59034	0	0	1047	294	254	4130	3327	18470	56379
All Other Liabilities 28	55898	0	20	55	531	2310	3883	14008	21374	38160
Net Worth 29	106973	0	428	-338	1761	4222	6604	22198	24940	70382

Selected Financial Ratios (Times to 1)

	1	2	3	4	5	6	7	8	9	10
Current Ratio 30	0.9	•	22.1	10.8	3.3	1.8	1.6	2.2	1.8	2.1
Quick Ratio 31	0.6	•	19.0	7.7	1.6	1.1	0.9	1.1	0.9	1.1
Net Sales to Working Capital 32	•	•	3.3	2.5	6.1	9.4	9.3	5.1	5.6	5.3
Coverage Ratio 33	5.6	45.0	•	16.0	21.8	19.7	6.2	9.0	8.4	4.4
Total Asset Turnover 34	0.4	•	3.1	2.2	3.4	2.3	2.2	1.9	1.7	1.4
Inventory Turnover 35	4.6	•	19.0	10.7	11.9	9.0	5.6	3.2	3.8	4.6
Receivables Turnover 36	3.0	•	27.6	14.7	16.1	12.3	7.8	4.2	•	7.1
Total Liabilities to Net Worth 37	1.1	•	0.0	•	0.5	0.6	1.2	0.8	1.6	1.3
Current Assets to Working Capital 38	•	•	1.0	1.1	1.4	2.3	2.7	1.8	2.3	1.9
Current Liabilities to Working Capital 39	•	•	0.0	0.1	0.4	1.3	1.7	0.8	1.3	0.9
Working Capital to Net Sales 40	•	•	0.3	0.4	0.2	0.1	0.1	0.2	0.2	0.2
Inventory to Working Capital 41	•	•	0.1	0.1	0.4	0.7	1.0	0.7	0.9	0.7
Total Receipts to Cash Flow 42	3.0	2.8	11.5	6.1	6.4	8.3	7.6	5.6	5.6	5.0
Cost of Goods to Cash Flow 43	1.3	1.0	9.4	4.0	3.8	4.4	4.9	3.4	3.2	2.7
Cash Flow to Total Debt 44	0.2	•	6.1	0.2	1.6	0.7	0.5	0.8	0.5	0.5

Selected Financial Factors (in Percentages)

	1	2	3	4	5	6	7	8	9	10
Debt Ratio 45	51.8	•	4.4	144.2	31.9	37.8	54.8	43.8	61.5	57.3
Return on Total Assets 46	8.4	•	2.3	33.2	17.5	4.8	9.1	8.2	17.7	12.1
Return on Equity Before Income Taxes 47	14.2	•	2.4	•	24.5	7.3	16.9	13.0	40.5	21.8
Return on Equity After Income Taxes 48	9.5	•	2.4	•	23.2	7.0	14.3	11.6	34.5	18.3
Profit Margin (Before Income Tax) 49	18.4	12.2	•	14.3	5.0	2.0	3.4	3.8	9.4	6.7
Profit Margin (After Income Tax) 50	12.2	12.2	10.4	4.7	1.9	2.9	3.4	3.8	8.0	5.6

Table I

Corporations with and without Net Income

CHEMICAL PRODUCT AND PREPARATION

MONEY AMOUNTS AND SIZE OF ASSETS IN THOUSANDS OF DOLLARS

Item Description for Accounting Period 7/08 Through 6/09	Total	Zero Assets	Under 500	500 to 1,000	1,000 to 5,000	5,000 to 10,000	10,000 to 25,000	25,000 to 50,000	50,000 to 100,000	100,000 to 250,000	250,000 to 500,000	500,000 to 2,500,000	2,500,000 and over
Number of Enterprises **1**	2780	356	1495	294	271	81	109	62	42	26	18	16	10
Revenues ($ in Thousands)													
Net Sales **2**	90797716	1167538	980679	426038	2106942	951824	3236406	2953531	3984815	5512959	6437940	17716662	45322381
Interest **3**	731313	1967	21	546	951	1998	6249	5428	14484	13780	28942	82385	574564
Rents **4**	27445	417	0	1911	0	2931	5945	444	181	235	773	2064	12544
Royalties **5**	541988	0	0	0	0	0	0	887	4166	27846	18082	37587	453420
Other Portfolio Income **6**	973820	26472	1	1017	1717	577	22388	1052	11079	10982	47164	255119	596252
Other Receipts **7**	1730218	33463	18962	1544	-25203	13225	33860	17479	20578	135512	86504	220285	1174009
Total Receipts **8**	94802500	1229857	999663	431056	2084407	970555	3304848	2978821	4035303	5701314	6619405	18314102	48133170
Average Total Receipts **9**	34102	3455	669	1466	7692	11982	30320	48046	96079	219281	367745	1144631	4813317
Operating Costs/Operating Income (%)													
Cost of Operations **10**	72.7	81.4	54.7	72.7	56.6	57.5	72.1	63.5	76.3	73.1	70.5	71.7	75.0
Salaries and Wages **11**	6.4	5.6	5.3	3.4	9.1	12.4	7.9	9.1	6.1	6.9	7.5	5.1	6.3
Taxes Paid **12**	1.1	0.9	3.0	2.2	1.7	2.1	1.2	1.5	1.1	1.0	1.1	1.3	0.9
Interest Paid **13**	2.6	1.5	0.5	0.8	0.3	1.7	0.7	1.1	1.9	2.0	2.9	1.7	3.4
Depreciation **14**	2.9	0.7	0.2	0.7	0.8	3.1	1.8	3.4	2.6	2.7	4.0	3.2	3.0
Amortization and Depletion **15**	1.1	0.0	0.3	•	0.0	0.2	0.2	0.4	0.5	0.8	1.8	0.9	1.4
Pensions and Other Deferred Comp. **16**	0.6	0.5	0.9	0.9	1.7	0.6	0.4	0.3	0.4	0.7	0.4	0.7	0.5
Employee Benefits **17**	0.9	0.6	1.5	•	1.3	2.0	0.8	0.5	1.0	1.1	1.4	1.3	0.7
Advertising **18**	0.5	0.1	0.3	0.3	0.5	0.5	0.8	0.7	0.5	0.4	0.4	1.1	0.2
Other Expenses **19**	9.7	7.8	18.1	13.8	16.5	17.8	11.1	17.8	8.7	9.7	10.5	8.5	8.9
Officers' Compensation **20**	0.9	0.4	12.1	6.3	6.1	4.2	2.2	2.4	1.5	0.6	0.9	1.0	0.1
Operating Margin **21**	0.5	0.4	3.1	•	5.4	•	0.8	•	•	1.0	•	3.5	•
Operating Margin Before Officers' Comp. **22**	1.5	0.9	15.2	5.2	11.6	2.2	3.0	1.8	0.9	1.6	4.5	4.5	•

Selected Average Balance Sheet ($ in Thousands)

Net Receivables 23	5212	0	60	138	961	1495	4306	6187	11999	24389	76846	133044	847500
Inventories 24	3807	0	30	217	556	1566	3768	6311	13981	30342	46843	165472	455509
Net Property, Plant and Equipment 25	6667	0	43	143	388	2281	3101	8770	17124	35075	82890	228836	1047031
Total Assets 26	40846	0	177	785	2305	7044	15558	34170	72750	159669	346192	1163399	7599311
Notes and Loans Payable 27	11362	0	58	185	352	2471	4788	8567	19896	52906	171143	349934	1920427
All Other Liabilities 28	14862	0	22	125	679	1413	4277	8678	20054	51912	99551	370064	3004040
Net Worth 29	14622	0	97	474	1274	3161	6492	16925	32801	54851	75498	443402	2674844

Selected Financial Ratios (Times to 1)

Current Ratio 30	1.4	•	2.0	2.2	2.1	1.9	2.1	1.9	1.9	1.5	1.3	1.4	1.3
Quick Ratio 31	0.7	•	1.4	1.0	1.4	1.0	1.2	1.0	1.0	0.6	0.8	0.7	0.6
Net Sales to Working Capital 32	7.3	•	13.0	6.2	8.0	5.8	5.2	5.3	4.9	8.4	9.1	9.0	6.9
Coverage Ratio 33	3.5	4.8	10.3	1.1	16.1	1.0	4.9	1.2	1.4	3.3	1.5	5.1	3.4
Total Asset Turnover 34	0.8	•	3.7	1.8	3.4	1.7	1.9	1.4	1.3	1.3	1.0	1.0	0.6
Inventory Turnover 35	6.2	•	12.1	4.9	7.9	4.3	5.7	4.8	5.2	5.1	5.4	4.8	7.5
Receivables Turnover 36	6.2	•	•	9.3	6.9	6.5	6.6	7.7	7.7	4.6	6.7	5.7	
Total Liabilities to Net Worth 37	1.8	•	0.8	0.7	0.8	1.2	1.4	1.0	1.2	1.9	3.6	1.6	1.8
Current Assets to Working Capital 38	3.5	•	2.0	1.9	1.9	2.1	1.9	2.1	2.1	3.0	4.2	3.5	4.0
Current Liabilities to Working Capital 39	2.5	•	1.0	0.9	0.9	1.1	0.9	1.1	1.1	2.0	3.2	2.5	3.0
Working Capital to Net Sales 40	0.1	•	0.1	0.2	0.1	0.2	0.2	0.2	0.2	0.1	0.1	0.1	0.1
Inventory to Working Capital 41	0.9	•	0.6	0.9	0.6	0.7	0.6	0.7	0.8	1.3	1.3	1.3	0.9
Total Receipts to Cash Flow 42	8.0	10.9	5.2	8.4	5.5	6.4	8.6	6.2	13.1	8.1	10.7	7.7	7.9
Cost of Goods to Cash Flow 43	5.8	8.8	2.8	6.1	3.1	3.7	6.2	4.0	10.0	5.9	7.6	5.5	5.9
Cash Flow to Total Debt 44	0.2	•	1.6	0.6	1.4	0.5	0.4	0.4	0.2	0.3	0.1	0.2	0.1

Selected Financial Factors (in Percentages)

Debt Ratio 45	64.2	•	45.3	39.6	44.7	55.1	58.3	50.5	54.9	65.6	78.2	61.9	64.8
Return on Total Assets 46	7.1	•	20.6	1.6	15.7	2.9	7.0	1.9	3.6	8.9	4.5	8.4	7.0
Return on Equity Before Income Taxes 47	14.1	•	34.1	0.2	26.6	0.0	13.4	0.5	2.5	18.1	7.2	17.8	14.2
Return on Equity After Income Taxes 48	8.7	•	34.1	•	24.4	•	11.5	•	•	13.6	2.2	12.2	8.4
Profit Margin (Before Income Tax) 49	6.3	5.8	5.0	0.1	4.4	0.0	2.9	0.2	0.9	4.7	1.5	7.1	8.4
Profit Margin (After Income Tax) 50	3.9	3.4	5.0	•	4.0	•	2.5	•	•	3.5	0.5	4.9	4.9

Table II

Corporations with Net Income

CHEMICAL PRODUCT AND PREPARATION

MONEY AMOUNTS AND SIZE OF ASSETS IN THOUSANDS OF DOLLARS

Item Description for Accounting Period 7/08 Through 6/09	Total	Zero Assets	Under 500	500 to 1,000	1,000 to 5,000	5,000 to 10,000	10,000 to 25,000	25,000 to 50,000	50,000 to 100,000	100,000 to 250,000	250,000 to 500,000	500,000 to 2,500,000	2,500,000 and over
1 Number of Enterprises	2091	11	1437	163	249	49	78	29	29	15	10	13	7
Revenues ($ in Thousands)													
2 Net Sales	67043239	1146375	952062	194821	2021302	694373	2567147	1939779	3236947	3720755	3405522	16686267	30477887
3 Interest	562227	1967	0	43	651	1222	1130	1316	10979	8819	16332	48864	470903
4 Rents	22608	417	0	1316	0	0	5945	327	169	235	642	1024	12532
5 Royalties	477499	0	0	0	0	0	0	0	4082	22022	1307	31321	418767
6 Other Portfolio Income	894734	26471	1	1017	1717	577	22279	983	10387	10847	30983	226964	562509
7 Other Receipts	1295239	33345	18847	887	364	446	18037	9407	18613	64690	50959	187202	892446
8 Total Receipts	70295546	1208575	970910	198084	2024034	696618	2614538	1951812	3281177	3827368	3505745	17181642	32835044
9 Average Total Receipts	33618	109870	676	1215	8129	14217	33520	67304	113144	255158	350574	1321665	4690721
Operating Costs/Operating Income (%)													
10 Cost of Operations	69.3	81.5	55.0	67.5	55.8	58.0	71.5	57.2	74.9	70.2	67.1	71.8	69.2
11 Salaries and Wages	6.7	5.5	4.2	6.5	8.9	10.0	7.2	9.0	6.1	5.6	8.0	5.0	7.5
12 Taxes Paid	1.2	0.8	2.9	2.4	1.7	1.9	1.3	1.4	1.1	0.9	1.1	1.3	1.1
13 Interest Paid	2.0	1.3	0.4	0.6	0.3	1.3	0.5	0.6	1.0	0.9	2.5	1.4	2.8
14 Depreciation	2.4	0.7	0.2	0.7	0.7	3.1	1.5	3.3	1.8	2.3	2.6	2.8	2.6
15 Amortization and Depletion	1.1	0.0	0.3	•	0.0	0.1	0.1	0.1	0.5	0.4	1.4	1.0	1.5
16 Pensions and Other Deferred Comp.	0.7	0.5	0.9	2.0	1.7	0.7	0.4	0.3	0.5	0.8	0.3	0.6	0.7
17 Employee Benefits	0.9	0.5	1.4	•	1.2	2.7	0.6	0.3	1.0	1.0	1.3	1.2	0.6
18 Advertising	0.5	0.0	0.3	0.2	0.2	0.2	0.8	0.6	0.5	0.4	0.7	1.2	0.2
19 Other Expenses	10.1	7.1	17.6	7.7	16.8	12.5	9.0	18.4	7.7	8.4	11.4	8.2	10.4
20 Officers' Compensation	1.0	0.4	12.1	10.6	6.2	4.1	2.0	2.3	1.4	0.6	0.9	0.8	0.1
21 Operating Margin	4.2	1.5	4.7	1.8	6.5	5.5	5.1	6.6	3.5	8.5	2.6	4.8	3.3
22 Operating Margin Before Officers' Comp.	5.2	1.9	16.8	12.3	12.7	9.6	7.0	8.9	4.9	9.1	3.5	5.6	3.4

Selected Average Balance Sheet ($ in Thousands)

Net Receivables 23	5417	0	60	45	994	1728	4399	7540	11768	25888	83996	149601	975074
Inventories 24	4081	0	19	196	483	2020	4227	9331	17619	34512	58776	182010	650342
Net Property, Plant and Equipment 25	5991	0	45	66	347	2095	3021	10234	12027	31607	42366	246605	1039648
Total Assets 26	42701	0	174	725	2226	6786	15108	33303	72942	158840	354974	1252166	8794732
Notes and Loans Payable 27	9467	0	45	88	306	2852	3969	7070	13696	36235	150079	336696	1738156
All Other Liabilities 28	15545	0	22	93	620	1540	3774	8114	18855	48907	94199	409277	3450644
Net Worth 29	17690	0	107	544	1300	2394	7366	18119	40391	73697	110696	506193	3605933

Selected Financial Ratios (Times to 1)

Current Ratio 30	1.4	•	1.9	2.5	2.4	1.6	2.1	1.9	2.4	1.8	1.3	1.3	1.3
Quick Ratio 31	0.6	•	1.3	0.8	1.6	0.8	1.2	1.1	1.2	0.8	0.7	0.7	0.5
Net Sales to Working Capital 32	7.0	•	14.4	7.0	7.7	9.4	5.7	7.0	4.3	6.7	8.5	10.3	5.9
Coverage Ratio 33	6.6	6.2	17.6	6.9	25.0	5.6	13.6	13.2	6.0	13.5	3.3	6.8	6.2
Total Asset Turnover 34	0.8	•	3.8	1.6	3.6	2.1	2.2	2.0	1.5	1.6	1.0	1.0	0.5
Inventory Turnover 35	5.4	•	19.2	4.1	9.4	4.1	5.6	4.1	4.7	5.0	3.9	5.1	4.6
Receivables Turnover 36	5.5	•	11.4	11.6	9.6	6.3	6.7	6.1	•	7.8	3.3	7.1	•
Total Liabilities to Net Worth 37	1.4	•	0.6	0.3	0.7	1.8	1.1	0.8	0.8	1.2	2.2	1.5	1.4
Current Assets to Working Capital 38	3.7	•	2.2	1.7	1.7	2.8	1.9	2.1	1.7	2.3	4.3	3.9	4.5
Current Liabilities to Working Capital 39	2.7	•	1.2	0.7	0.7	1.8	0.9	1.1	0.7	1.3	3.3	2.9	3.5
Working Capital to Net Sales 40	0.1	•	0.1	0.1	0.1	0.1	0.2	0.1	0.2	0.1	0.1	0.1	0.2
Inventory to Working Capital 41	1.0	•	0.6	1.1	0.5	1.1	0.7	0.8	0.7	0.9	1.4	1.4	0.9
Total Receipts to Cash Flow 42	5.9	9.9	4.8	10.1	4.8	6.1	7.5	4.3	9.0	5.5	7.1	7.3	5.2
Cost of Goods to Cash Flow 43	4.1	8.1	2.7	6.8	2.7	3.5	5.4	2.4	6.8	3.9	4.8	5.3	3.6
Cash Flow to Total Debt 44	0.2	•	2.0	0.7	1.8	0.5	0.6	1.0	0.4	0.5	0.2	0.2	0.2

Selected Financial Factors (in Percentages)

Debt Ratio 45	58.6	•	38.5	24.9	41.6	64.7	51.2	45.6	44.6	53.6	68.8	59.6	59.0
Return on Total Assets 46	9.6	•	26.9	6.6	25.1	14.9	16.2	15.8	9.5	19.6	7.9	9.6	8.7
Return on Equity Before Income Taxes 47	19.7	•	41.3	7.5	41.2	34.7	30.8	26.8	14.2	39.2	17.7	20.3	17.9
Return on Equity After Income Taxes 48	13.7	•	41.3	6.8	38.8	30.6	28.4	20.8	10.3	33.4	11.6	14.4	11.7
Profit Margin (Before Income Tax) 49	10.9	6.9	6.7	3.4	6.6	5.9	6.9	7.3	5.1	11.6	5.7	8.0	14.8
Profit Margin (After Income Tax) 50	7.6	4.5	6.7	3.1	6.2	5.2	6.4	5.6	3.7	9.9	3.8	5.7	9.7

Table I

Corporations with and without Net Income

PLASTICS PRODUCT

MONEY AMOUNTS AND SIZE OF ASSETS IN THOUSANDS OF DOLLARS

Item Description for Accounting Period 7/08 Through 6/09	Total	Zero Assets	Under 500	500 to 1,000	1,000 to 5,000	5,000 to 10,000	10,000 to 25,000	25,000 to 50,000	50,000 to 100,000	100,000 to 250,000	250,000 to 500,000	500,000 to 2,500,000	2,500,000 and over
Number of Enterprises **1**	9731	1761	2809	1288	2426	625	390	169	111	99	22	28	3
Revenues ($ in Thousands)													
Net Sales **2**	115107828	943814	1333680	2224040	12613538	8942959	11903348	9613008	11805944	19107141	8679717	21904276	6036363
Interest **3**	337771	900	388	2718	5589	4148	10891	9088	19688	80313	14283	161016	28750
Rents **4**	36588	0	0	227	1196	2957	1015	4026	3775	5436	5890	12067	0
Royalties **5**	150309	0	0	0	0	103	572	2669	8769	13160	39673	39388	45974
Other Portfolio Income **6**	548083	91	20848	1356	41832	3026	6592	25084	84845	115033	30301	182689	36391
Other Receipts **7**	733236	1096	7220	4206	33562	55034	88219	44131	57036	226824	49333	152487	14084
Total Receipts **8**	116913815	945901	1362136	2232547	12695717	9008227	12010637	9698006	11980057	19547907	8819197	22451923	6161562
Average Total Receipts **9**	12015	537	485	1733	5233	14413	30797	57385	107928	197454	400873	801854	2053854
Operating Costs/Operating Income (%)													
Cost of Operations **10**	74.7	68.5	50.4	57.5	69.1	72.0	74.8	75.8	72.6	79.8	77.0	78.2	73.0
Salaries and Wages **11**	5.3	7.3	15.5	9.0	5.2	6.8	6.2	5.7	7.1	4.2	5.1	3.8	3.6
Taxes Paid **12**	1.1	1.8	2.7	2.8	1.9	1.2	1.0	1.0	1.0	0.9	0.9	0.8	0.2
Interest Paid **13**	2.5	4.9	1.2	0.6	1.2	1.0	1.3	1.4	1.5	2.6	3.9	3.8	7.2
Depreciation **14**	3.7	2.8	1.0	4.0	2.8	3.1	3.2	4.3	3.7	4.0	3.6	4.4	4.3
Amortization and Depletion **15**	0.5	0.4	•	0.1	0.2	0.1	0.2	0.4	0.6	0.7	0.9	0.7	0.3
Pensions and Other Deferred Comp. **16**	0.4	0.4	0.0	0.1	0.2	0.4	0.3	0.4	0.5	0.4	0.5	0.3	0.5
Employee Benefits **17**	1.6	2.7	1.5	1.3	1.5	1.1	1.6	1.6	1.8	1.5	1.5	1.2	4.2
Advertising **18**	0.4	0.6	1.7	0.5	0.2	0.7	0.3	0.4	0.5	0.4	0.2	0.3	0.2
Other Expenses **19**	8.7	14.2	17.5	17.0	9.8	9.3	8.2	7.5	9.6	8.0	8.5	7.3	7.5
Officers' Compensation **20**	1.6	5.5	4.4	7.9	5.2	2.4	1.8	1.2	0.9	0.7	0.7	0.3	0.3
Operating Margin **21**	•	•	4.2	•	2.7	1.8	1.1	0.4	0.3	•	•	•	•
Operating Margin Before Officers' Comp. **22**	1.2	•	8.6	7.1	7.9	4.2	2.9	1.6	1.2	•	•	•	•

Selected Average Balance Sheet ($ in Thousands)

Net Receivables **23**	1479	0	31	197	573	1925	3572	6929	13821	23642	39880	125169	211531
Inventories **24**	1268	0	24	116	491	1247	3327	7289	13189	22580	50230	75200	238426
Net Property, Plant and Equipment **25**	2346	0	13	164	540	2400	4931	13110	19753	45305	91931	200356	441818
Total Assets **26**	9606	0	182	716	2072	7067	15599	36329	70641	154746	345559	889910	4900504
Notes and Loans Payable **27**	4118	0	87	435	942	2484	5130	12814	22670	59502	169859	476767	1923137
All Other Liabilities **28**	2345	0	38	171	581	1708	5123	8511	16924	44094	126944	214178	516148
Net Worth **29**	3143	0	56	110	549	2875	5345	15005	31047	51150	48755	198965	2461219

Selected Financial Ratios (Times to 1)

Current Ratio **30**	1.4	•	2.3	1.8	1.6	1.9	1.5	1.6	1.9	1.4	1.7	1.2	1.1
Quick Ratio **31**	0.8	•	1.3	1.4	1.0	1.2	0.8	0.9	1.0	0.7	0.8	0.7	0.5
Net Sales to Working Capital **32**	10.7	•	6.3	8.1	10.5	7.6	10.5	8.5	6.7	11.1	8.7	20.7	57.5
Coverage Ratio **33**	1.5	•	6.5	0.3	3.9	3.6	2.6	1.9	2.3	0.6	0.9	1.4	1.2
Total Asset Turnover **34**	1.2	•	2.6	2.4	2.5	2.0	2.0	1.6	1.5	1.2	1.1	0.9	0.4
Inventory Turnover **35**	7.0	•	9.8	8.6	7.3	8.3	6.9	5.9	5.9	6.8	6.1	8.1	6.2
Receivables Turnover **36**	7.9	•	13.3	8.3	8.8	8.1	8.4	7.7	7.8	8.3	6.4	7.0	8.2
Total Liabilities to Net Worth **37**	2.1	•	2.2	5.5	2.8	1.5	1.9	1.4	1.3	2.0	6.1	3.5	1.0
Current Assets to Working Capital **38**	3.3	•	1.8	2.3	2.7	2.2	3.0	2.6	2.2	3.6	2.5	7.2	16.8
Current Liabilities to Working Capital **39**	2.3	•	0.8	1.3	1.7	1.2	2.0	1.6	1.2	2.6	1.5	6.2	15.8
Working Capital to Net Sales **40**	0.1	•	0.2	0.1	0.1	0.1	0.1	0.1	0.2	0.1	0.1	0.0	0.0
Inventory to Working Capital **41**	1.1	•	0.3	0.4	1.0	0.7	1.2	1.0	0.8	1.3	1.0	2.1	5.7
Total Receipts to Cash Flow **42**	13.4	140.6	5.2	11.5	10.2	10.5	12.6	14.8	11.4	18.6	18.6	14.2	15.2
Cost of Goods to Cash Flow **43**	10.0	96.3	2.6	6.6	7.0	7.6	9.4	11.2	8.3	14.8	14.3	11.1	11.1
Cash Flow to Total Debt **44**	0.1	•	0.7	0.2	0.3	0.3	0.2	0.2	0.2	0.1	0.1	0.1	0.1

Selected Financial Factors (in Percentages)

Debt Ratio **45**	67.3	•	69.0	84.7	73.5	59.3	65.7	58.7	56.0	66.9	85.9	77.6	49.8
Return on Total Assets **46**	4.6	•	19.6	0.4	11.4	7.1	6.4	4.1	5.2	2.1	4.0	4.8	3.4
Return on Equity Before Income Taxes **47**	4.7	•	53.6	•	32.1	12.5	11.3	4.8	6.6	•	•	6.4	0.9
Return on Equity After Income Taxes **48**	3.2	•	53.6	•	29.8	12.1	9.5	3.5	4.7	•	•	4.7	0.1
Profit Margin (Before Income Tax) **49**	1.3	•	6.4	•	3.4	2.5	2.0	1.3	1.9	•	•	1.6	1.1
Profit Margin (After Income Tax) **50**	0.9	•	6.4	•	3.1	2.4	1.7	0.9	1.4	•	•	1.2	0.1

Table II

Corporations with Net Income

PLASTICS PRODUCT

MONEY AMOUNTS AND SIZE OF ASSETS IN THOUSANDS OF DOLLARS

Item Description for Accounting Period 7/08 Through 6/09		Total	Zero Assets	Under 500	500 to 1,000	1,000 to 5,000	5,000 to 10,000	10,000 to 25,000	25,000 to 50,000	50,000 to 100,000	100,000 to 250,000	250,000 to 500,000	500,000 to 2,500,000	2,500,000 and over
Number of Enterprises	1	6842	1479	•	881	1704	413	234	117	72	•	8	17	0
Revenues ($ in Thousands)														
Net Sales	2	69268556	585138	•	1465643	10310881	6143588	7288338	6564895	7823323	•	2872248	16792828	0
Interest	3	193519	537	•	2030	4116	2331	4253	4222	14246	•	5848	127487	0
Rents	4	18044	0	•	227	1192	2366	406	1463	1339	•	4536	4409	0
Royalties	5	104572	0	•	0	0	6	0	2669	8088	•	25658	64522	0
Other Portfolio Income	6	433311	91	•	894	35832	485	4942	20864	74908	•	22252	216671	0
Other Receipts	7	489401	4169	•	2949	21928	49503	72625	22202	46505	•	17564	102600	0
Total Receipts	8	70507403	589935	•	1471743	10373949	6198279	7370564	6616315	7968409	•	2948106	17308517	0
Average Total Receipts	9	10305	399	•	1671	6088	15008	31498	56550	110672	•	368513	1018148	•
Operating Costs/Operating Income (%)														
Cost of Operations	10	71.4	68.7	•	59.8	68.2	67.0	73.5	71.0	70.2	•	71.5	75.1	•
Salaries and Wages	11	5.6	4.4	•	5.1	5.3	7.9	5.3	6.2	6.9	•	6.1	4.4	•
Taxes Paid	12	1.2	1.4	•	2.6	1.7	1.3	1.0	1.2	1.1	•	1.0	0.8	•
Interest Paid	13	1.7	0.9	•	0.5	0.5	0.6	0.9	1.2	1.2	•	2.5	3.2	•
Depreciation	14	3.5	3.1	•	3.1	2.5	2.9	2.8	3.8	3.4	•	3.6	4.7	•
Amortization and Depletion	15	0.3	0.2	•	0.1	0.0	0.0	0.1	0.2	0.4	•	0.7	0.6	•
Pensions and Other Deferred Comp.	16	0.4	0.6	•	0.1	0.3	0.5	0.4	0.4	0.5	•	0.7	0.5	•
Employee Benefits	17	1.6	2.6	•	1.0	1.4	1.3	1.5	1.7	1.8	•	2.0	1.9	•
Advertising	18	0.4	0.8	•	0.6	0.2	0.9	0.2	0.5	0.5	•	0.2	0.2	•
Other Expenses	19	8.2	8.2	•	15.5	8.5	10.0	7.0	7.5	9.1	•	7.6	6.9	•
Officers' Compensation	20	2.0	2.6	•	7.4	5.6	2.7	1.7	1.4	1.0	•	0.7	0.4	•
Operating Margin	21	3.8	6.5	•	4.2	5.7	4.9	5.5	4.8	4.0	•	3.4	1.3	•
Operating Margin Before Officers' Comp.	22	5.8	9.1	•	11.6	11.3	7.6	7.3	6.2	4.9	•	4.1	1.7	•

Selected Average Balance Sheet ($ in Thousands)

Net Receivables 23	1236	0	•	214	676	1663	3822	7367	12993	•	48359	140175
Inventories 24	1154	0	•	112	545	1399	3964	7640	14789	•	42113	92764
Net Property, Plant and Equipment 25	1817	0	•	100	554	2362	4436	12424	19135	•	65371	253161
Total Assets 26	8140	0	•	636	2269	7059	15456	36052	71596	•	342752	1510256
Notes and Loans Payable 27	2780	0	•	83	692	1544	4390	11217	19462	•	157495	585235
All Other Liabilities 28	1562	0	•	152	545	1242	3599	7490	14849	•	97555	235599
Net Worth 29	3797	0	•	401	1032	4273	7468	17345	37286	•	87702	689422

Selected Financial Ratios (Times to 1)

Current Ratio 30	1.8	•	•	2.7	2.4	2.2	2.2	2.0	2.0	•	1.5	1.3
Quick Ratio 31	1.0	•	•	2.3	1.5	1.4	1.3	1.1	1.0	•	0.9	0.7
Net Sales to Working Capital 32	7.4	•	•	5.6	6.9	7.0	6.1	6.0	6.3	•	8.8	14.4
Coverage Ratio 33	4.5	8.8	•	9.6	13.4	11.3	8.0	5.6	6.2	•	4.4	2.4
Total Asset Turnover 34	1.2	•	•	2.6	2.7	2.1	2.0	1.6	1.5	•	1.0	0.7
Inventory Turnover 35	6.3	•	•	8.9	7.6	7.1	5.8	5.2	5.2	•	6.1	8.0
Receivables Turnover 36	7.5	•	•	7.5	9.1	7.9	6.9	6.9	7.6	•	•	•
Total Liabilities to Net Worth 37	1.1	•	•	0.6	1.2	0.7	1.1	1.1	0.9	•	2.9	1.2
Current Assets to Working Capital 38	2.2	•	•	1.6	1.7	1.9	1.8	2.0	2.0	•	3.0	4.7
Current Liabilities to Working Capital 39	1.2	•	•	0.6	0.7	0.9	0.8	1.0	1.0	•	2.0	3.7
Working Capital to Net Sales 40	0.1	•	•	0.2	0.1	0.1	0.2	0.2	0.2	•	0.1	0.1
Inventory to Working Capital 41	0.7	•	•	0.2	0.6	0.6	0.7	0.8	0.8	•	1.0	1.4
Total Receipts to Cash Flow 42	8.7	7.8	•	8.6	8.2	7.5	8.6	9.1	7.9	•	8.7	10.7
Cost of Goods to Cash Flow 43	6.2	5.4	•	5.1	5.6	5.0	6.3	6.5	5.6	•	6.2	8.1
Cash Flow to Total Debt 44	0.3	•	•	0.8	0.6	0.7	0.5	0.3	0.4	•	0.2	0.1

Selected Financial Factors (in Percentages)

Debt Ratio 45	53.4	•	•	36.9	54.5	39.5	51.7	51.9	47.9	•	74.4	54.4
Return on Total Assets 46	9.3	•	•	13.6	18.2	13.4	15.2	10.5	10.9	•	11.8	5.1
Return on Equity Before Income Taxes 47	15.5	•	•	19.3	37.1	20.1	27.5	17.9	17.6	•	35.6	6.6
Return on Equity After Income Taxes 48	13.7	•	•	18.0	35.4	19.7	25.3	16.3	15.1	•	27.9	5.3
Profit Margin (Before Income Tax) 49	5.8	7.3	•	4.7	6.3	5.8	6.6	5.5	6.0	•	8.7	4.6
Profit Margin (After Income Tax) 50	5.1	7.3	•	4.3	6.0	5.6	6.1	5.0	5.2	•	6.8	3.7

Table I

Corporations with and without Net Income

RUBBER PRODUCT

MONEY AMOUNTS AND SIZE OF ASSETS IN THOUSANDS OF DOLLARS

Item Description for Accounting Period 7/08 Through 6/09		Total	Zero Assets	Under 500	500 to 1,000	1,000 to 5,000	5,000 to 10,000	10,000 to 25,000	25,000 to 50,000	50,000 to 100,000	100,000 to 250,000	250,000 to 500,000	500,000 to 2,500,000	2,500,000 and over
Number of Enterprises	1	770	15	195	128	253	40	65	21	25	11	3	10	4
Revenues ($ in Thousands)														
Net Sales	2	56302233	386138	146749	350731	2222547	702953	2286943	977017	2144907	1962530	1308694	11638286	32174740
Interest	3	395024	63	5	37	4202	1414	955	3384	3831	4956	3849	85879	286448
Rents	4	15448	0	0	0	0	0	0	0	4207	355	645	1767	8474
Royalties	5	541889	0	508	0	0	0	92	104	3	1976	685	52742	485777
Other Portfolio Income	6	565769	0	12561	150	572	17797	1896	518	8919	4833	1554	75796	441171
Other Receipts	7	438963	1033	1462	373	5771	18478	10349	3923	10912	7114	7922	51741	319889
Total Receipts	8	58259326	387234	161285	351291	2233092	740642	2300235	984946	2172779	1981764	1323349	11906211	33716499
Average Total Receipts	9	75661	25816	827	2744	8826	18516	35388	46902	86911	180160	441116	1190621	8429125
Operating Costs/Operating Income (%)														
Cost of Operations	10	73.8	71.9	42.9	71.7	68.1	65.8	70.3	81.2	74.3	78.6	68.8	79.5	72.3
Salaries and Wages	11	5.9	5.2	12.2	5.8	9.7	5.1	6.8	6.0	6.1	5.2	4.1	4.0	6.4
Taxes Paid	12	1.2	1.1	3.9	1.1	1.9	1.0	1.2	1.0	1.8	0.7	0.8	0.4	1.5
Interest Paid	13	1.9	1.3	4.2	0.9	1.0	0.6	0.6	0.9	2.6	2.0	1.3	2.8	1.7
Depreciation	14	2.9	3.8	4.2	1.0	1.5	1.2	3.1	2.7	4.1	2.5	1.2	3.4	2.8
Amortization and Depletion	15	1.0	0.9	0.1	0.0	0.0	0.9	0.1	0.2	1.0	1.2	1.3	0.8	1.2
Pensions and Other Deferred Comp.	16	1.6	0.4	0.1	0.1	0.5	0.7	0.4	0.4	0.2	1.0	0.3	1.2	2.2
Employee Benefits	17	4.7	2.0	0.9	2.6	1.9	1.6	1.8	1.9	2.3	2.1	1.9	3.3	6.2
Advertising	18	1.2	0.9	1.0	0.1	0.2	0.2	2.3	0.6	0.5	0.1	1.6	0.6	1.6
Other Expenses	19	11.3	13.0	19.6	10.9	9.5	7.5	7.5	6.0	8.1	4.8	14.1	6.3	14.1
Officers' Compensation	20	0.7	0.0	2.9	6.8	3.8	12.8	1.2	1.7	1.2	0.6	0.9	0.5	0.1
Operating Margin	21	•	•	8.0	•	2.0	2.6	4.6	•	•	1.1	3.7	•	•
Operating Margin Before Officers' Comp.	22	•	•	10.9	5.7	5.8	15.3	5.8	•	•	1.8	4.6	•	•

Selected Average Balance Sheet ($ in Thousands)

Net Receivables 23	9769	0	23	177	1035	1658	3669	7033	11788	27182	53747	124954	1194064
Inventories 24	10074	0	25	485	818	2038	2953	9332	9700	22918	63792	137275	1246372
Net Property, Plant and Equipment 25	13612	0	41	90	778	1064	4824	12290	18691	33718	40717	226510	1606366
Total Assets 26	61314	0	440	808	3236	7060	14875	38292	67317	153984	313227	1147162	7090533
Notes and Loans Payable 27	19428	0	64	160	1089	1427	3290	13230	29828	54527	95507	384800	2155529
All Other Liabilities 28	28220	0	414	405	1159	1685	3613	16834	20370	46008	119961	430690	3741458
Net Worth 29	13666	0	-38	243	988	3948	7972	8228	17118	53448	97759	331671	1193547

Selected Financial Ratios (Times to 1)

Current Ratio 30	1.5	•	1.4	1.5	1.7	2.5	2.4	1.7	1.6	1.8	1.5	1.2	1.6
Quick Ratio 31	0.7	•	1.0	0.4	0.9	1.4	1.4	0.8	0.8	0.8	0.7	0.6	0.8
Net Sales to Working Capital 32	8.5	•	20.2	12.0	9.7	6.2	6.4	5.7	8.0	5.8	8.1	16.7	7.6
Coverage Ratio 33	•	0.9	5.2	•	3.5	14.4	9.9	•	0.6	2.1	4.7	1.0	•
Total Asset Turnover 34	1.2	•	1.7	3.4	2.7	2.5	2.4	1.2	1.3	1.2	1.4	1.0	1.1
Inventory Turnover 35	5.4	•	12.9	4.1	7.3	5.7	8.4	4.0	6.6	6.1	4.7	6.7	4.7
Receivables Turnover 36	6.9	•	26.1	30.9	8.0	8.7	9.9	5.6	8.0	6.6	5.1	9.3	6.1
Total Liabilities to Net Worth 37	3.5	•	•	2.3	2.3	0.8	0.9	3.7	2.9	1.9	2.2	2.5	4.9
Current Assets to Working Capital 38	2.9	•	3.3	3.1	2.4	1.7	1.7	2.5	2.8	2.3	2.9	5.4	2.8
Current Liabilities to Working Capital 39	1.9	•	2.3	2.1	1.4	0.7	0.7	1.5	1.8	1.3	1.9	4.4	1.8
Working Capital to Net Sales 40	0.1	•	0.0	0.1	0.1	0.2	0.2	0.2	0.1	0.2	0.1	0.1	0.1
Inventory to Working Capital 41	1.2	•	1.0	2.1	0.9	0.7	0.6	1.0	1.1	0.8	1.4	2.1	1.2
Total Receipts to Cash Flow 42	16.5	10.6	3.6	16.9	9.9	8.4	9.2	33.9	19.8	18.3	5.6	22.5	18.2
Cost of Goods to Cash Flow 43	12.2	7.6	1.6	12.1	6.7	5.5	6.5	27.5	14.7	14.4	3.8	17.9	13.2
Cash Flow to Total Debt 44	0.1	•	0.4	0.3	0.4	0.7	0.6	0.0	0.1	0.1	0.4	0.1	0.1

Selected Financial Factors (in Percentages)

Debt Ratio 45	77.7	•	108.5	70.0	69.5	44.1	46.4	78.5	74.6	65.3	68.8	71.1	83.2
Return on Total Assets 46	•	•	37.9	•	9.3	21.2	13.7	•	2.1	4.9	8.6	2.9	•
Return on Equity Before Income Taxes 47	•	•	•	•	21.7	35.3	23.0	•	7.6	•	21.6	0.4	•
Return on Equity After Income Taxes 48	•	•	•	•	21.5	27.1	21.8	•	•	5.6	20.0	•	•
Profit Margin (Before Income Tax) 49	•	•	17.9	•	2.4	7.9	5.2	•	•	5.6	2.3	4.8	0.1
Profit Margin (After Income Tax) 50	•	•	15.7	•	2.4	6.1	4.9	•	1.7	2.3	4.8	4.5	•

Table II

Corporations with Net Income

RUBBER PRODUCT

MONEY AMOUNTS AND SIZE OF ASSETS IN THOUSANDS OF DOLLARS

Item Description for Accounting Period 7/08 Through 6/09	Total	Zero Assets	Under 500	500 to 1,000	1,000 to 5,000	5,000 to 10,000	10,000 to 25,000	25,000 to 50,000	50,000 to 100,000	100,000 to 250,000	250,000 to 500,000	500,000 to 2,500,000	2,500,000 and over
Number of Enterprises **1**	400	4	•	46	135	37	52	7	11	•	0	6	0
Revenues ($ in Thousands)													
Net Sales **2**	15035915	94442	•	248909	1751947	611099	1543918	489996	814508	•	0	7112878	0
Interest **3**	28347	39	•	37	10	1399	690	3	1096	•	0	18141	0
Rents **4**	2544	0	•	0	0	0	0	0	655	•	0	1667	0
Royalties **5**	27931	0	•	0	0	0	0	0	0	•	0	25701	0
Other Portfolio Income **6**	102766	0	•	0	0	17797	1773	456	4941	•	0	60657	0
Other Receipts **7**	90282	209	•	248	1659	18293	8455	10423	1534	•	0	34917	0
Total Receipts **8**	15287785	94690	•	249194	1753616	648588	1554836	500878	822734	•	0	7253961	0
Average Total Receipts **9**	38219	23672	•	5417	12990	17529	29901	71554	74794	•	•	1208994	•
Operating Costs/Operating Income (%)													
Cost of Operations **10**	73.5	71.0	•	77.7	67.4	64.8	66.7	77.7	69.3	•	•	78.3	•
Salaries and Wages **11**	5.7	2.2	•	3.4	9.4	4.6	7.4	6.7	8.0	•	•	4.4	•
Taxes Paid **12**	0.9	2.5	•	1.2	2.0	1.1	1.2	0.9	1.8	•	•	0.4	•
Interest Paid **13**	1.2	0.3	•	0.3	0.6	0.5	0.5	0.5	1.3	•	•	1.3	•
Depreciation **14**	2.7	2.4	•	0.6	0.8	1.1	3.5	1.7	3.4	•	•	3.3	•
Amortization and Depletion **15**	0.4	0.0	•	0.0	0.0	1.0	0.0	0.2	0.5	•	•	0.5	•
Pensions and Other Deferred Comp. **16**	0.7	0.5	•	0.1	0.4	0.7	0.2	0.2	0.1	•	•	1.0	•
Employee Benefits **17**	2.5	2.9	•	0.9	2.2	1.0	1.5	1.9	1.7	•	•	3.3	•
Advertising **18**	0.4	•	•	0.2	0.1	0.0	0.7	0.2	0.4	•	•	0.4	•
Other Expenses **19**	6.5	16.4	•	6.0	7.5	7.7	8.0	3.2	7.7	•	•	5.0	•
Officers' Compensation **20**	1.8	•	•	8.3	4.2	14.4	1.3	1.7	1.4	•	•	0.5	•
Operating Margin **21**	3.6	1.7	•	1.2	5.4	3.0	8.9	5.2	4.3	•	•	1.4	•
Operating Margin Before Officers' Comp. **22**	5.4	1.7	•	9.5	9.5	17.4	10.2	6.9	5.7	•	•	2.0	•

Selected Average Balance Sheet ($ in Thousands)

Net Receivables 23	4375	0	•	259	1378	1526	3650	7922	10448	•	130436
Inventories 24	10216	0	•	458	1182	1780	3058	9865	11272	•	157843
Net Property, Plant and Equipment 25	5887	0	•	88	829	850	4511	6826	15952	•	226342
Total Assets 26	26325	0	•	918	3813	6720	14768	33666	62357	•	1022344
Notes and Loans Payable 27	6165	0	•	89	1177	951	2940	6386	20603	•	205252
All Other Liabilities 28	7750	0	•	206	1267	1599	2163	5982	11250	•	306994
Net Worth 29	12409	0	•	623	1369	4170	9666	21297	30503	•	510098

Selected Financial Ratios (Times to 1)

Current Ratio 30	1.8	•	•	3.3	2.0	3.1	3.9	2.9	2.0	•	1.6
Quick Ratio 31	0.8	•	•	1.3	1.1	1.7	2.3	1.5	1.0	•	0.6
Net Sales to Working Capital 32	7.0	•	•	9.5	8.9	5.4	4.0	4.6	5.6	•	8.6
Coverage Ratio 33	5.7	7.9	•	5.0	9.5	21.0	21.1	17.0	5.0	•	4.1
Total Asset Turnover 34	1.4	•	•	5.9	3.4	2.5	2.0	2.1	1.2	•	1.2
Inventory Turnover 35	2.7	•	•	9.2	7.4	6.0	6.5	5.5	4.6	•	5.9
Receivables Turnover 36	3.4	•	•	41.7	8.3	9.4	8.0	7.7	6.2	•	•
Total Liabilities to Net Worth 37	1.1	•	•	0.5	1.8	0.6	0.5	0.6	1.0	•	1.0
Current Assets to Working Capital 38	2.2	•	•	1.4	2.0	1.5	1.3	1.5	2.0	•	2.8
Current Liabilities to Working Capital 39	1.2	•	•	0.4	1.0	0.5	0.3	0.5	1.0	•	1.8
Working Capital to Net Sales 40	0.1	•	•	0.1	0.1	0.2	0.2	0.2	0.2	•	0.1
Inventory to Working Capital 41	0.9	•	•	0.8	0.7	0.6	0.4	0.7	0.8	•	1.1
Total Receipts to Cash Flow 42	10.0	6.2	•	21.3	8.8	7.7	6.5	9.7	9.5	•	14.3
Cost of Goods to Cash Flow 43	7.3	4.4	•	16.6	5.9	5.0	4.3	7.5	6.6	•	11.2
Cash Flow to Total Debt 44	0.3	•	•	0.9	0.6	0.8	0.9	0.6	0.2	•	0.2

Selected Financial Factors (in Percentages)

Debt Ratio 45	52.9	•	•	32.1	64.1	37.9	34.6	36.7	51.1	•	50.1
Return on Total Assets 46	9.7	•	•	9.8	20.7	23.6	20.3	16.3	7.9	•	6.4
Return on Equity Before Income Taxes 47	17.0	•	•	11.6	51.7	36.2	29.5	24.2	13.0	•	9.6
Return on Equity After Income Taxes 48	14.2	•	•	9.2	51.5	27.9	28.3	22.8	9.2	•	6.9
Profit Margin (Before Income Tax) 49	5.6	2.0	•	1.3	5.5	9.1	9.6	7.4	5.4	•	4.1
Profit Margin (After Income Tax) 50	4.7	1.4	•	1.1	5.4	7.0	9.2	6.9	3.8	•	3.0

Table I

Corporations with and without Net Income

CLAY, REFRACTORY AND OTHER NONMETALLIC MINERAL PRODUCT

MONEY AMOUNTS AND SIZE OF ASSETS IN THOUSANDS OF DOLLARS

Item Description for Accounting Period 7/08 Through 6/09	Total	Zero Assets	Under 500	500 to 1,000	1,000 to 5,000	5,000 to 10,000	10,000 to 25,000	25,000 to 50,000	50,000 to 100,000	100,000 to 250,000	250,000 to 500,000	500,000 to 2,500,000	2,500,000 and over
1 Number of Enterprises	2042	14	1147	501	222	5	62	40	21	17	5	9	0
Revenues ($ in Thousands)													
2 Net Sales	20005449	354826	1052719	1217245	1313420	74515	1576478	1768845	1382791	2498320	1259947	7506342	0
3 Interest	141905	5812	351	1473	174	0	594	2319	2293	5920	4148	118821	0
4 Rents	112802	0	0	0	0	0	399	0	66	1625	96	110616	0
5 Royalties	76893	0	0	0	0	0	2598	149	163	2047	464	71471	0
6 Other Portfolio Income	291001	1334	0	2086	348	0	1326	1283	905	1047	10015	272655	0
7 Other Receipts	330984	725	-13	5232	141	-975	11816	11519	22320	106022	15623	158579	0
8 Total Receipts	20959034	362697	1053057	1226036	1314083	73540	1593211	1784115	1408538	2614981	1290293	8238484	0
9 Average Total Receipts	10264	25907	918	2447	5919	14708	25697	44603	67073	153822	258059	915387	•
Operating Costs/Operating Income (%)													
10 Cost of Operations	67.4	81.2	49.4	48.2	72.3	59.8	73.1	71.4	69.1	70.3	65.7	68.4	•
11 Salaries and Wages	7.6	3.9	11.5	6.4	6.9	6.8	4.5	6.5	8.1	10.4	7.2	7.5	•
12 Taxes Paid	1.5	0.0	2.9	2.4	2.0	0.9	1.6	1.5	1.2	1.2	1.3	1.3	•
13 Interest Paid	2.4	2.4	0.6	0.3	0.8	•	1.0	0.9	2.9	2.3	1.4	4.1	•
14 Depreciation	4.3	16.0	3.2	1.8	2.1	0.3	2.2	3.9	5.5	4.7	4.8	4.9	•
15 Amortization and Depletion	0.1	0.0	•	0.1	0.2	•	0.8	0.2	0.9	•	0.7	0.8	•
16 Pensions and Other Deferred Comp.	1.1	0.7	4.1	1.0	0.1	0.3	0.3	0.3	0.4	1.6	1.0	1.1	•
17 Employee Benefits	2.4	1.3	0.3	12.8	0.5	•	1.0	2.3	0.9	2.2	2.3	2.1	•
18 Advertising	0.9	0.6	0.5	0.5	1.1	0.5	0.8	0.2	0.4	2.4	0.2	0.9	•
19 Other Expenses	12.3	5.9	20.4	12.1	13.8	6.4	8.3	7.4	9.4	14.8	10.9	13.4	•
20 Officers' Compensation	2.1	0.9	6.6	9.4	1.7	19.5	2.8	1.2	2.1	1.2	0.5	0.9	•
21 Operating Margin	•	•	0.5	5.0	•	5.5	3.7	4.2	•	•	4.0	•	•
22 Operating Margin Before Officers' Comp.	0.1	•	7.1	14.5	0.1	25.0	6.5	5.3	1.4	•	4.5	•	•

Selected Average Balance Sheet ($ in Thousands)

Net Receivables 23	1271	0	5	160	534	1172	2961	5409	9283	18040	46308	139142	•
Inventories 24	1524	0	53	138	729	3386	3642	7223	12594	34496	65086	123511	•
Net Property, Plant and Equipment 25	3191	0	70	229	795	616	5139	11610	28810	51508	100937	374695	•
Total Assets 26	11117	0	237	751	2263	7778	14282	33113	72691	146137	301745	1531509	•
Notes and Loans Payable 27	3802	0	110	171	1070	0	5367	9064	25756	46673	59309	554249	•
All Other Liabilities 28	3625	0	67	149	895	632	3970	7116	15811	44990	63884	566817	•
Net Worth 29	3691	0	60	430	298	7146	4945	16933	31124	54474	178552	410442	•

Selected Financial Ratios (Times to 1)

Current Ratio 30	1.8	•	2.3	2.8	1.2	11.1	1.7	2.5	2.4	1.7	3.6	1.5	•
Quick Ratio 31	0.9	•	1.4	1.6	0.7	4.2	0.8	1.1	1.1	0.6	2.1	0.8	•
Net Sales to Working Capital 32	5.4	•	10.3	7.4	22.7	2.3	8.2	4.4	3.4	4.8	2.3	5.9	•
Coverage Ratio 33	2.2	•	1.9	19.8	•	•	5.8	6.5	1.4	•	5.7	2.2	•
Total Asset Turnover 34	0.9	•	3.9	3.2	2.6	1.9	1.8	1.3	0.9	1.0	0.8	0.5	•
Inventory Turnover 35	4.3	•	8.5	8.5	5.9	2.6	5.1	4.4	3.6	3.0	2.5	4.6	•
Receivables Turnover 36	3.2	•	58.7	20.0	9.5	8.3	9.1	8.9	6.6	9.0	3.3	1.6	•
Total Liabilities to Net Worth 37	2.0	•	2.9	0.7	6.6	0.1	1.9	1.0	1.3	1.7	0.7	2.7	•
Current Assets to Working Capital 38	2.2	•	1.8	1.5	5.2	1.1	2.5	1.7	1.7	2.4	1.4	2.9	•
Current Liabilities to Working Capital 39	1.2	•	0.8	0.5	4.2	0.1	1.5	0.7	0.7	1.4	0.4	1.9	•
Working Capital to Net Sales 40	0.2	•	0.1	0.1	0.0	0.4	0.1	0.2	0.3	0.2	0.4	0.2	•
Inventory to Working Capital 41	0.9	•	0.7	0.6	2.2	0.6	1.2	0.8	0.7	1.2	0.5	0.9	•
Total Receipts to Cash Flow 42	9.1	•	7.7	11.6	9.1	11.3	9.8	9.3	11.8	11.0	6.5	8.0	•
Cost of Goods to Cash Flow 43	6.2	•	3.8	5.6	6.6	6.8	7.2	6.6	8.2	7.7	4.3	5.5	•
Cash Flow to Total Debt 44	0.1	•	0.7	0.7	0.3	2.1	0.3	0.3	0.1	0.1	0.3	0.1	•

Selected Financial Factors (in Percentages)

Debt Ratio 45	66.8	•	74.5	42.7	86.8	8.1	65.4	48.9	57.2	62.7	40.8	73.2	•
Return on Total Assets 46	4.7	•	4.3	19.6	•	8.0	10.2	7.9	3.7	•	6.8	4.9	•
Return on Equity Before Income Taxes 47	7.8	•	8.0	32.5	•	8.7	24.3	13.1	2.4	•	9.5	10.1	•
Return on Equity After Income Taxes 48	4.4	•	8.0	32.4	•	8.7	21.4	10.6	•	•	6.8	5.3	•
Profit Margin (Before Income Tax) 49	2.9	•	0.5	5.8	•	4.2	4.7	5.0	1.1	•	6.7	5.0	•
Profit Margin (After Income Tax) 50	1.7	•	0.5	5.7	4.2	4.2	4.2	4.1		•	4.8	2.6	•

Table II

Corporations with Net Income

CLAY, REFRACTORY AND OTHER NONMETALLIC MINERAL PRODUCT

MONEY AMOUNTS AND SIZE OF ASSETS IN THOUSANDS OF DOLLARS

Item Description for Accounting Period 7/08 Through 6/09		Total	Zero Assets	Under 500	500 to 1,000	1,000 to 5,000	5,000 to 10,000	10,000 to 25,000	25,000 to 50,000	50,000 to 100,000	100,000 to 250,000	250,000 to 500,000	500,000 to 2,500,000	2,500,000 and over
Number of Enterprises	1	995	8	311	450	122	5	41	29	•	7	•	6	0
Revenues ($ in Thousands)														
Net Sales	2	11675119	0	623058	1151174	809768	74515	1310670	1277959	•	1254621	•	3041252	0
Interest	3	84828	19	0	1473	0	0	567	2319	•	2570	•	73370	0
Rents	4	3770	0	0	0	0	0	399	0	•	1625	•	1584	0
Royalties	5	55550	0	0	0	0	0	550	149	•	702	•	53522	0
Other Portfolio Income	6	275420	0	0	2086	0	0	519	1249	•	943	•	259797	0
Other Receipts	7	144087	1218	0	4810	0	-975	13984	11511	•	87262	•	18082	0
Total Receipts	8	12238774	1237	623058	1159543	809768	73540	1326689	1293187	•	1347723	•	3447607	0
Average Total Receipts	9	12300	155	2003	2577	6637	14708	32358	44593	•	192532	•	574601	•
Operating Costs/Operating Income (%)														
Cost of Operations	10	63.0	•	41.0	47.4	72.8	59.8	72.2	66.9	•	79.0	•	56.8	•
Salaries and Wages	11	6.8	•	13.4	6.0	6.0	6.8	4.0	6.9	•	5.1	•	8.7	•
Taxes Paid	12	1.6	•	3.4	2.3	2.0	0.9	1.4	1.7	•	1.2	•	1.3	•
Interest Paid	13	1.9	•	0.8	0.2	0.3	•	0.7	1.0	•	1.7	•	4.0	•
Depreciation	14	3.4	•	4.6	1.9	0.5	0.3	2.0	3.9	•	2.4	•	4.8	•
Amortization and Depletion	15	0.6	•	•	0.1	0.2	•	0.8	0.3	•	0.3	•	0.8	•
Pensions and Other Deferred Comp.	16	0.7	•	0.0	1.1	0.0	0.3	0.3	0.4	•	0.4	•	1.1	•
Employee Benefits	17	2.9	•	0.0	13.4	0.0	•	1.1	1.8	•	2.3	•	2.7	•
Advertising	18	0.4	•	0.7	0.5	0.0	0.5	0.9	0.3	•	0.8	•	0.2	•
Other Expenses	19	10.8	•	24.3	11.6	15.9	6.4	7.3	8.7	•	7.0	•	12.1	•
Officers' Compensation	20	2.5	•	2.9	9.6	0.7	19.5	3.0	1.5	•	1.0	•	1.5	•
Operating Margin	21	5.6	•	8.9	5.9	1.5	5.5	6.4	6.5	•	•	•	5.9	•
Operating Margin Before Officers' Comp.	22	8.1	•	11.8	15.6	2.3	25.0	9.5	8.1	•	•	•	7.4	•

Selected Average Balance Sheet ($ in Thousands)

Net Receivables 23	•	1702	0	169	675	1172	3514	6297	• 16003	•	136140
Inventories 24	•	1647	81	149	852	3683	3700	8108	• 36631	•	64341
Net Property, Plant and Equipment 25	•	2653	223	165	87	616	4613	11179	• 45572	•	150483
Total Assets 26	•	10753	274	732	1507	7778	13813	34020	• 157006	•	895309
Notes and Loans Payable 27	•	2717	196	74	108	0	3039	6419	• 47409	•	266292
All Other Liabilities 28	•	3945	19	157	1343	632	3603	8510	• 36946	•	428684
Net Worth 29	•	4091	59	500	57	7146	7171	19091	• 72650	•	200333

Selected Financial Ratios (Times to 1)

Current Ratio 30	•	1.9	3.1	3.2	1.0	1.1	1.9	2.6	• 2.2	•	1.5
Quick Ratio 31	•	1.1	0.0	1.8	0.7	4.2	1.0	1.3	• 0.7	•	0.9
Net Sales to Working Capital 32	•	4.6	49.1	6.8	•	2.3	8.2	4.0	• 4.2	•	3.8
Coverage Ratio 33	•	6.8	12.4	36.4	6.2	•	12.6	8.8	• 4.8	•	6.1
Total Asset Turnover 34	•	1.1	7.3	3.5	4.4	1.9	2.3	1.3	• 1.1	•	0.6
Inventory Turnover 35	•	4.5	10.2	8.1	5.7	2.4	6.2	3.6	• 3.9	•	4.5
Receivables Turnover 36	•	6.2	112.1	21.4	7.5	25.4	9.8	•	• 9.7	•	3.8
Total Liabilities to Net Worth 37	•	1.6	3.6	0.5	25.6	0.1	0.9	0.8	• 1.2	•	3.5
Current Assets to Working Capital 38	•	2.1	1.5	1.5	•	1.1	2.1	1.6	• 1.8	•	2.9
Current Liabilities to Working Capital 39	•	1.1	0.5	0.5	•	0.1	1.1	0.6	• 0.8	•	1.9
Working Capital to Net Sales 40	•	0.2	0.0	0.1	•	0.4	0.1	0.3	• 0.2	•	0.3
Inventory to Working Capital 41	•	0.7	1.5	0.6	•	0.6	1.0	0.7	• 0.9	•	0.6
Total Receipts to Cash Flow 42	•	5.7	4.3	11.5	6.3	11.3	8.4	6.9	• 8.3	•	3.7
Cost of Goods to Cash Flow 43	•	3.6	1.8	5.4	4.6	6.8	6.1	4.6	• 6.6	•	2.1
Cash Flow to Total Debt 44	•	0.3	2.2	1.0	0.7	2.1	0.6	0.4	• 0.3	•	0.2

Selected Financial Factors (in Percentages)

Debt Ratio 45	•	62.0	78.4	31.6	96.2	8.1	48.1	43.9	• 53.7	•	77.6
Return on Total Assets 46	•	13.9	70.8	23.9	8.1	8.0	19.2	11.3	• 9.3	•	14.0
Return on Equity Before Income Taxes 47	•	31.1	301.8	34.0	181.7	8.7	34.0	17.9	• 15.9	•	52.2
Return on Equity After Income Taxes 48	•	24.8	301.8	33.8	179.6	8.7	30.9	14.8	• 14.3	•	37.2
Profit Margin (Before Income Tax) 49	•	10.8	8.9	6.6	1.5	4.2	7.6	7.7	• 6.4	•	20.6
Profit Margin (After Income Tax) 50	•	8.6	8.9	6.6	1.5	4.2	6.9	6.4	• 5.8	•	14.7

Table I

Corporations with and without Net Income

GLASS AND GLASS PRODUCT

MONEY AMOUNTS AND SIZE OF ASSETS IN THOUSANDS OF DOLLARS

Item Description for Accounting Period 7/08 Through 6/09		Total	Zero Assets	Under 500	500 to 1,000	1,000 to 5,000	5,000 to 10,000	10,000 to 25,000	25,000 to 50,000	50,000 to 100,000	100,000 to 250,000	250,000 to 500,000	500,000 to 2,500,000	2,500,000 and over
Number of Enterprises	1	2245	0	1389	344	394	52	29	14	6	6	4	7	0
Revenues ($ in Thousands)														
Net Sales	2	22537346	0	610520	707283	1552644	769461	1386653	498209	546064	1362149	1623210	13481155	0
Interest	3	102941	0	0	611	1250	135	1020	701	1404	3044	8350	86425	0
Rents	4	6683	0	0	0	145	149	858	571	468	10	0	4483	0
Royalties	5	101204	0	0	0	0	19	0	0	0	14279	36	86870	0
Other Portfolio Income	6	179280	0	0	52	190	260	236	1744	199	585	8494	167518	0
Other Receipts	7	143705	0	404	19	1905	289	2597	1624	4183	4886	18217	109581	0
Total Receipts	8	23071159	0	610924	707965	1556134	770313	1391364	502849	552318	1384953	1658307	13936032	0
Average Total Receipts	9	10277	•	440	2058	3950	14814	47978	35918	92053	230826	414577	1990862	•
Operating Costs/Operating Income (%)														
Cost of Operations	10	69.3	•	32.0	44.8	63.2	76.1	77.7	71.5	67.1	67.7	73.2	71.4	•
Salaries and Wages	11	6.8	•	19.1	11.9	8.8	9.1	4.8	4.1	5.1	9.0	2.8	6.2	•
Taxes Paid	12	1.6	•	3.0	2.6	1.8	0.8	1.2	1.8	1.6	1.6	1.7	1.6	•
Interest Paid	13	2.2	•	0.4	1.3	1.7	1.8	1.0	1.7	3.3	2.6	4.4	2.1	•
Depreciation	14	4.6	•	0.4	3.6	2.8	2.3	2.5	3.8	3.3	3.6	9.1	5.0	•
Amortization and Depletion	15	0.5	•	•	0.0	0.0	0.4	0.1	1.5	0.4	0.8	0.7	0.6	•
Pensions and Other Deferred Comp.	16	0.6	•	•	0.0	0.1	0.0	0.2	0.2	0.3	0.3	1.4	0.7	•
Employee Benefits	17	2.9	•	0.2	0.5	1.1	1.2	2.1	1.0	3.0	1.8	2.5	3.7	•
Advertising	18	0.4	•	3.0	1.1	0.5	0.2	0.2	0.2	0.2	0.5	0.1	0.3	•
Other Expenses	19	11.9	•	24.1	25.1	13.4	6.8	9.2	8.4	8.0	14.5	4.7	11.9	•
Officers' Compensation	20	1.6	•	8.0	9.6	8.4	1.6	1.2	1.0	1.3	0.8	0.5	0.3	•
Operating Margin	21	•	•	9.7	•	•	•	•	4.7	6.4	•	•	•	•
Operating Margin Before Officers' Comp.	22	•	•	17.6	9.1	6.6	1.3	0.9	5.7	7.7	•	•	•	•

Selected Average Balance Sheet ($ in Thousands)

	•	•	•	•	•	•	•	•	•	•	•
Net Receivables **23**	889	•	19	104	491	2123	3967	4329	11465	34381	47598	141341
Inventories **24**	1325	•	87	258	389	1458	3463	6406	14257	25920	54881	269375
Net Property, Plant and Equipment **25**	2702	•	10	189	834	2144	5452	11776	15211	43455	168721	599679
Total Assets **26**	10953	•	126	681	2203	7316	16294	40310	78221	166869	407832	2684579
Notes and Loans Payable **27**	3643	•	300	268	1407	2995	5566	13871	33654	72601	209925	732431
All Other Liabilities **28**	3785	•	8	188	299	2402	5282	5045	13358	51123	130645	1006739
Net Worth **29**	3524	•	-181	225	496	1919	5446	21393	31209	43145	67262	945409

Selected Financial Ratios (Times to 1)

	•	•	•	•	•	•	•	•	•	•	•
Current Ratio **30**	1.0	•	15.1	1.8	3.2	1.5	1.4	2.2	1.9	1.7	1.1	0.7
Quick Ratio **31**	0.4	•	3.8	0.8	2.0	0.8	0.8	1.2	1.0	1.2	0.5	0.2
Net Sales to Working Capital **32**	•	•	4.1	12.2	4.4	9.7	17.7	4.0	5.4	6.6	34.0	•
Coverage Ratio **33**	1.1	•	22.9	0.7	0.0	0.9	1.1	4.2	3.3	0.3	1.2	0.9
Total Asset Turnover **34**	0.9	•	3.5	3.0	1.8	2.0	2.9	0.9	1.2	1.4	1.0	0.7
Inventory Turnover **35**	5.2	•	1.6	3.6	6.4	7.7	10.7	4.0	4.3	5.9	5.4	5.1
Receivables Turnover **36**	9.2	•	17.5	11.0	8.5	7.9	13.7	7.6	6.3	7.9	6.8	9.7
Total Liabilities to Net Worth **37**	2.1	•	•	2.0	3.4	2.8	2.0	0.9	1.5	2.9	5.1	1.8
Current Assets to Working Capital **38**	•	•	1.1	2.2	1.4	3.2	3.7	1.8	2.1	2.4	11.4	•
Current Liabilities to Working Capital **39**	•	•	0.1	1.2	0.4	2.2	2.7	0.8	1.1	1.4	10.4	•
Working Capital to Net Sales **40**	•	•	0.2	0.1	0.2	0.1	0.1	0.2	0.2	0.2	0.0	•
Inventory to Working Capital **41**	•	•	0.8	1.0	0.5	1.3	1.3	0.7	0.8	0.7	5.1	•
Total Receipts to Cash Flow **42**	12.4	•	3.8	6.6	10.8	21.8	13.9	7.9	7.4	10.8	22.2	14.4
Cost of Goods to Cash Flow **43**	8.6	•	1.2	3.0	6.8	16.6	10.8	5.7	4.9	7.3	16.3	10.3
Cash Flow to Total Debt **44**	0.1	•	0.4	0.7	0.2	0.1	0.3	0.2	0.3	0.2	0.1	0.1

Selected Financial Factors (in Percentages)

	•	•	•	•	•	•	•	•	•	•	•
Debt Ratio **45**	67.8	•	243.5	67.0	77.5	73.8	66.6	46.9	60.1	74.1	83.5	64.8
Return on Total Assets **46**	2.2	•	35.4	2.6	0.1	3.3	6.2	6.2	12.6	1.2	5.4	1.3
Return on Equity Before Income Taxes **47**	0.6	•	•	•	•	0.7	9.0	22.1	6.2	•	6.2	•
Return on Equity After Income Taxes **48**	•	•	•	•	•	•	7.0	19.1	5.9	•	•	•
Profit Margin (Before Income Tax) **49**	0.2	•	9.7	•	•	0.1	5.4	7.6	•	•	1.0	1.0
Profit Margin (After Income Tax) **50**	•	•	9.7	•	•	0.1	4.2	6.6	•	•	•	1.0

Table II
Corporations with Net Income

GLASS AND GLASS PRODUCT

MONEY AMOUNTS AND SIZE OF ASSETS IN THOUSANDS OF DOLLARS

Item Description for Accounting Period 7/08 Through 6/09		Total	Zero Assets	Under 500	500 to 1000	1,000 to 5,000	5,000 to 10,000	10,000 to 25,000	25,000 to 50,000	50,000 to 100,000	100,000 to 250,000	250,000 to 500,000	500,000 to 2,500,000	2,500,000 and over
Number of Enterprises	1	1228	0	684	328	148	35	17	5	•	•	0	0	3
Revenues ($ in Thousands)														
Net Sales	2	14461680	0	461474	660099	943182	498512	943652	271011	•	•	0	0	8834115
Interest	3	55370	0	0	611	1176	85	193	196	•	•	0	0	44108
Rents	4	3195	0	0	0	145	149	858	301	•	•	0	0	1274
Royalties	5	6812	0	0	0	0	0	0	0	•	•	0	0	6812
Other Portfolio Income	6	165748	0	0	52	190	240	232	524	•	•	0	0	159737
Other Receipts	7	55834	0	404	19	447	1355	941	1	•	•	0	0	39686
Total Receipts	8	14748639	0	461878	660781	945140	500341	945876	272033	•	•	0	0	9085732
Average Total Receipts	9	12010	•	675	2015	6386	14295	55640	54407	•	•	•	•	3028577
Operating Costs/Operating Income (%)														
Cost of Operations	10	67.1	•	27.5	41.3	64.5	72.8	81.5	72.3	•	•	•	•	68.5
Salaries and Wages	11	7.2	•	22.2	12.2	9.5	8.4	3.0	2.9	•	•	•	•	6.8
Taxes Paid	12	1.6	•	3.2	2.6	1.6	0.9	0.9	0.6	•	•	•	•	1.6
Interest Paid	13	1.1	•	0.2	1.3	0.5	1.6	0.7	0.3	•	•	•	•	1.0
Depreciation	14	4.9	•	0.4	3.7	3.0	1.7	2.2	3.2	•	•	•	•	5.7
Amortization and Depletion	15	0.5	•	•	0.0	0.0	0.1	0.0	0.0	•	•	•	•	0.7
Pensions and Other Deferred Comp.	16	0.6	•	•	0.0	0.1	0.0	0.2	0.2	•	•	•	•	0.6
Employee Benefits	17	2.4	•	0.0	0.5	1.2	1.4	1.9	0.7	•	•	•	•	2.8
Advertising	18	0.5	•	2.0	1.1	0.2	0.2	0.0	0.1	•	•	•	•	0.5
Other Expenses	19	9.7	•	26.5	25.3	6.0	4.6	3.8	3.9	•	•	•	•	10.1
Officers' Compensation	20	1.7	•	3.6	9.9	12.0	2.0	1.1	0.8	•	•	•	•	0.2
Operating Margin	21	2.8	•	14.4	1.9	1.4	6.3	4.5	15.0	•	•	•	•	1.7
Operating Margin Before Officers' Comp.	22	4.5	•	18.0	11.7	13.4	8.4	5.6	15.7	•	•	•	•	1.9

Selected Average Balance Sheet ($ in Thousands)

		•							•	
Net Receivables 23	903	•	31	102	844	2088	5104	5904	•	166254
Inventories 24	1516	•	24	214	614	1137	2574	9504	•	424330
Net Property, Plant and Equipment 25	2840	•	8	193	585	1811	5287	8547	•	877391
Total Assets 26	9607	•	75	677	2658	6783	15973	36953	•	3007744
Notes and Loans Payable 27	2410	•	38	267	1258	2501	5398	3579	•	625001
All Other Liabilities 28	3349	•	10	188	314	1095	6778	10126	•	1159819
Net Worth 29	3849	•	26	222	1085	3187	3796	23248	•	1222924

Selected Financial Ratios (Times to 1)

		•							•	
Current Ratio 30	1.0	•	6.5	1.7	5.0	2.0	1.0	1.9	•	0.7
Quick Ratio 31	0.4	•	4.7	0.7	3.6	1.1	0.7	1.0	•	0.2
Net Sales to Working Capital 32	95.4	•	12.0	13.1	4.1	6.0	121.8	4.9	•	•
Coverage Ratio 33	5.6	•	62.4	2.5	3.9	5.3	7.3	59.1	•	5.8
Total Asset Turnover 34	1.2	•	9.0	3.0	2.4	2.1	3.5	1.5	•	1.0
Inventory Turnover 35	5.2	•	7.8	3.9	6.7	9.1	17.6	4.1	•	4.8
Receivables Turnover 36	8.9	•	14.1	15.1	7.1	8.7	13.5	•	•	9.5
Total Liabilities to Net Worth 37	1.5	•	1.8	2.1	1.4	1.1	3.2	0.6	•	1.5
Current Assets to Working Capital 38	24.0	•	1.2	2.3	1.2	2.0	21.2	2.1	•	•
Current Liabilities to Working Capital 39	23.0	•	0.2	1.3	0.2	1.0	20.2	1.1	•	•
Working Capital to Net Sales 40	0.0	•	0.1	0.1	0.2	0.2	0.0	0.2	•	•
Inventory to Working Capital 41	11.2	•	0.3	1.1	0.3	0.7	6.3	0.9	•	•
Total Receipts to Cash Flow 42	9.2	•	3.0	5.8	18.6	9.9	13.7	5.6	•	9.4
Cost of Goods to Cash Flow 43	6.2	•	0.8	2.4	12.0	7.2	11.2	4.0	•	6.5
Cash Flow to Total Debt 44	0.2	•	4.6	0.8	0.2	0.4	0.3	0.7	•	0.2

Selected Financial Factors (in Percentages)

		•							•	
Debt Ratio 45	59.9	•	64.9	67.2	59.2	53.0	76.2	37.1	•	59.3
Return on Total Assets 46	7.3	•	132.7	9.9	5.2	17.4	19.0	22.8	•	5.5
Return on Equity Before Income Taxes 47	15.0	•	371.7	18.0	9.5	30.0	69.1	35.7	•	11.3
Return on Equity After Income Taxes 48	11.4	•	371.7	14.1	7.2	28.4	57.8	30.5	•	7.4
Profit Margin (Before Income Tax) 49	4.9	•	14.5	2.0	1.6	6.7	4.7	15.3	•	4.7
Profit Margin (After Income Tax) 50	3.7	•	14.5	1.6	1.2	6.3	4.0	13.1	•	3.1

102

Table I

Corporations with and without Net Income

CEMENT, CONCRETE, LIME AND GYPSUM PRODUCT

MONEY AMOUNTS AND SIZE OF ASSETS IN THOUSANDS OF DOLLARS

Item Description for Accounting Period 7/08 Through 6/09	Total	Zero Assets	Under 500	500 to 1,000	1,000 to 5,000	5,000 to 10,000	10,000 to 25,000	25,000 to 50,000	50,000 to 100,000	100,000 to 250,000	250,000 to 500,000	500,000 to 2,500,000	2,500,000 and over
Number of Enterprises 1	4742	408	1837	709	1249	262	134	55	31	19	10	18	9
Revenues ($ in Thousands)													
Net Sales 2	72546289	746898	1039034	1243987	5191041	3750309	3272510	2290402	2711362	3473411	3795097	10767134	34265103
Interest 3	684436	732	474	1430	6987	6670	5871	1608	3967	5845	9620	167092	474140
Rents 4	102898	259	0	62	2403	1101	3457	405	1617	408	8055	62502	22629
Royalties 5	67563	310	0	0	0	0	5	116	1540	928	4385	28819	31459
Other Portfolio Income 6	474112	0	475	5215	33578	36504	19432	9821	13437	11029	17706	53056	273861
Other Receipts 7	750587	8653	3685	4515	57731	45177	27646	23869	28262	10117	-23330	267088	297173
Total Receipts 8	74625885	756852	1043668	1255209	5291740	3839761	3328921	2326221	2760185	3501738	3811533	11345691	35364365
Average Total Receipts 9	15737	1855	568	1770	4237	14656	24843	42295	89038	184302	381153	630316	3929374
Operating Costs/Operating Income (%)													
Cost of Operations 10	71.6	77.5	41.0	60.0	69.5	69.1	69.4	73.4	75.2	73.0	72.7	70.9	73.3
Salaries and Wages 11	5.8	1.1	18.6	8.1	6.2	5.6	7.6	5.5	4.6	5.3	4.1	4.2	6.1
Taxes Paid 12	1.5	1.5	6.2	2.0	2.0	2.0	2.2	1.4	1.3	1.5	1.2	1.2	1.3
Interest Paid 13	4.5	6.3	1.2	1.3	1.6	1.4	1.0	1.3	1.4	1.6	1.6	4.8	6.7
Depreciation 14	6.3	13.1	4.8	4.2	3.3	6.1	5.3	7.5	5.6	5.9	5.9	8.8	6.2
Amortization and Depletion 15	1.3	2.6	0.1	0.0	0.1	0.0	0.2	0.3	0.5	0.5	1.4	2.6	1.5
Pensions and Other Deferred Comp. 16	0.7	•	0.0	0.6	0.3	0.4	0.6	0.4	0.6	0.5	0.7	0.6	0.9
Employee Benefits 17	1.9	3.9	2.2	1.6	1.4	1.6	1.6	1.7	1.6	2.2	1.7	2.3	2.0
Advertising 18	0.4	0.2	0.2	0.9	1.0	0.2	0.6	0.5	0.5	0.4	0.3	0.2	0.3
Other Expenses 19	10.6	8.0	27.2	13.8	12.2	12.8	11.1	9.4	9.0	5.8	6.7	9.7	10.9
Officers' Compensation 20	1.0	0.2	4.8	4.8	3.4	3.6	1.6	2.1	0.9	0.9	0.8	0.6	0.2
Operating Margin 21	•	•	•	2.6	•	•	•	•	•	2.5	2.9	•	•
Operating Margin Before Officers' Comp. 22	•	•	•	7.4	2.5	0.6	0.5	•	•	3.4	3.7	•	•

Selected Average Balance Sheet ($ in Thousands)

Net Receivables **23**	2616	0	40	152	425	2156	3294	6376	14168	25853	52194	92147	802886
Inventories **24**	1630	0	16	70	288	1175	2095	4682	8482	14758	27702	71774	481465
Net Property, Plant and Equipment **25**	10082	0	74	296	795	3301	6417	16724	31881	60348	144967	577633	3315819
Total Assets **26**	24869	0	192	687	2285	7537	16107	34501	68031	147190	346571	1210646	8671092
Notes and Loans Payable **27**	8995	0	115	265	1199	3590	4484	12454	24235	45521	95242	397860	3199839
All Other Liabilities **28**	9134	0	44	116	449	1520	2753	3044	12379	29588	63573	293791	3865162
Net Worth **29**	6740	0	33	307	637	2427	8869	19003	31417	72082	187756	518994	1606091

Selected Financial Ratios (Times to 1)

Current Ratio **30**	1.3	•	1.3	2.9	1.8	1.4	2.2	2.4	1.9	2.0	2.4	1.1	1.1
Quick Ratio **31**	0.8	•	1.0	2.0	1.2	1.0	1.5	1.5	1.2	1.3	1.7	0.5	0.7
Net Sales to Working Capital **32**	13.2	•	29.0	7.7	8.0	11.9	5.5	4.8	6.3	6.4	4.8	24.1	32.6
Coverage Ratio **33**	0.4	•	•	3.6	1.6	0.6	1.6	•	1.3	3.1	3.0	0.9	0.1
Total Asset Turnover **34**	0.6	•	2.9	2.6	1.8	1.9	1.5	1.2	1.3	1.2	1.1	0.5	0.4
Inventory Turnover **35**	6.7	•	14.3	15.0	10.0	8.4	8.1	6.5	7.8	9.0	10.0	5.9	5.8
Receivables Turnover **36**	4.6	•	13.2	9.6	8.1	6.7	6.7	5.2	6.0	5.9	7.3	7.5	3.3
Total Liabilities to Net Worth **37**	2.7	•	4.8	1.2	2.6	2.1	0.8	0.8	1.2	1.0	0.8	1.3	4.4
Current Assets to Working Capital **38**	4.7	•	4.9	1.5	2.2	3.5	1.8	1.7	2.1	2.0	1.7	9.4	12.9
Current Liabilities to Working Capital **39**	3.7	•	3.9	0.5	1.2	2.5	0.8	0.7	1.1	1.0	0.7	8.4	11.9
Working Capital to Net Sales **40**	0.1	•	0.0	0.1	0.1	0.1	0.2	0.2	0.2	0.2	0.2	0.0	0.0
Inventory to Working Capital **41**	1.4	•	0.8	0.3	0.6	0.9	0.5	0.5	0.6	0.5	0.4	3.0	3.8
Total Receipts to Cash Flow **42**	21.3	•	7.3	8.0	11.2	13.5	11.2	22.0	14.2	14.7	12.6	15.0	60.1
Cost of Goods to Cash Flow **43**	15.3	•	3.0	4.8	7.8	9.3	7.8	16.2	10.7	10.7	9.2	10.6	44.0
Cash Flow to Total Debt **44**	0.0	•	0.5	0.6	0.2	0.2	0.3	0.1	0.2	0.2	0.2	0.1	0.0

Selected Financial Factors (in Percentages)

Debt Ratio **45**	72.9	•	82.8	55.4	72.1	67.8	44.9	44.9	53.8	51.0	45.8	57.1	81.5
Return on Total Assets **46**	1.1	•	•	12.2	4.8	1.5	2.4	•	2.4	6.1	5.4	2.2	0.2
Return on Equity Before Income Taxes **47**	•	•	•	19.8	6.4	•	1.7	•	1.3	8.5	6.6	•	•
Return on Equity After Income Taxes **48**	•	•	•	19.6	5.0	•	1.0	•	0.5	5.7	4.2	•	•
Profit Margin (Before Income Tax) **49**	•	•	•	3.5	1.0	•	0.6	•	0.5	3.3	3.3	•	•
Profit Margin (After Income Tax) **50**	•	•	•	3.4	0.8	•	0.4	•	0.2	2.2	2.1	•	•

Table II

Corporations with Net Income

CEMENT, CONCRETE, LIME AND GYPSUM PRODUCT

MONEY AMOUNTS AND SIZE OF ASSETS IN THOUSANDS OF DOLLARS

Item Description for Accounting Period 7/08 Through 6/09		Total	Zero Assets	Under 500	500 to 1,000	1,000 to 5,000	5,000 to 10,000	10,000 to 25,000	25,000 to 50,000	50,000 to 100,000	100,000 to 250,000	250,000 to 500,000	500,000 to 2,500,000	2,500,000 and over
Number of Enterprises	1	1987	0	832	375	502	127	73	30	19	•	•	12	0
Revenues ($ in Thousands)														
Net Sales	2	36544085	0	718460	713283	2605155	2506810	1878767	1331847	1880090	•	•	20561969	0
Interest	3	250792	0	260	208	3786	5185	2800	1251	3157	•	•	220687	0
Rents	4	23123	0	0	0	417	1027	1425	291	498	•	•	11502	0
Royalties	5	32471	0	0	0	0	0	5	0	52	•	•	28020	0
Other Portfolio Income	6	161698	0	475	5142	9425	30213	2558	2701	5665	•	•	89902	0
Other Receipts	7	390457	0	2619	2053	15202	7741	28452	22114	22331	•	•	273266	0
Total Receipts	8	37402626	0	721814	720686	2633985	2550976	1914007	1358204	1911793	•	•	21185346	0
Average Total Receipts	9	18824	•	868	1922	5247	20086	26219	45273	100621	•	•	1765446	•
Operating Costs/Operating Income (%)														
Cost of Operations	10	70.3	•	37.9	50.1	65.9	70.2	69.9	70.9	74.7	•	•	72.2	•
Salaries and Wages	11	5.0	•	17.5	10.0	5.3	4.8	6.2	5.7	4.7	•	•	4.3	•
Taxes Paid	12	1.3	•	5.1	2.8	1.5	1.9	1.8	1.3	1.4	•	•	1.0	•
Interest Paid	13	3.1	•	1.3	0.8	0.9	0.9	0.8	0.6	1.2	•	•	4.7	•
Depreciation	14	5.2	•	4.5	3.2	2.3	2.3	4.4	5.8	4.5	•	•	6.1	•
Amortization and Depletion	15	1.2	•	0.0	•	0.1	0.0	0.2	0.3	0.4	•	•	1.9	•
Pensions and Other Deferred Comp.	16	0.7	•	•	0.5	0.2	0.3	0.6	0.5	0.8	•	•	0.9	•
Employee Benefits	17	1.5	•	0.9	2.8	1.6	1.0	1.2	0.8	1.6	•	•	1.6	•
Advertising	18	0.4	•	0.1	1.4	1.7	0.2	0.6	0.7	0.6	•	•	0.2	•
Other Expenses	19	8.2	•	25.8	14.2	10.0	13.3	8.9	7.9	7.8	•	•	7.2	•
Officers' Compensation	20	1.1	•	5.0	4.7	3.3	3.7	1.4	2.7	1.1	•	•	0.2	•
Operating Margin	21	1.9	•	1.9	9.6	7.1	1.5	4.0	2.9	1.4	•	•	•	•
Operating Margin Before Officers' Comp.	22	3.0	•	6.9	14.3	10.4	5.3	5.4	5.6	2.4	•	•	0.0	•

Selected Average Balance Sheet ($ in Thousands)

Net Receivables 23	2219	4	171	428	2402	3837	5434	15833	202608
Inventories 24	2467	13	103	341	1567	2248	5172	9457	151163
Net Property, Plant and Equipment 25	8629	130	232	671	2450	5488	12644	30389	1121312
Total Assets 26	18848	214	718	2008	7913	14835	33386	67703	2312088
Notes and Loans Payable 27	6834	147	237	647	3173	4331	7678	22565	898163
All Other Liabilities 28	4523	16	72	310	1244	3256	2056	12402	619195
Net Worth 29	7491	51	410	1051	3497	7248	23653	32737	794730

Selected Financial Ratios (Times to 1)

Current Ratio 30	1.8	1.0	6.1	2.6	1.4	2.1	3.3	2.3	1.6
Quick Ratio 31	1.1	0.6	3.9	1.9	1.0	1.6	2.1	1.5	0.8
Net Sales to Working Capital 32	7.3	•	5.4	7.3	14.1	5.9	3.8	5.4	8.8
Coverage Ratio 33	2.4	2.8	14.3	10.0	4.6	8.2	9.3	3.6	1.6
Total Asset Turnover 34	1.0	4.0	2.6	2.6	2.5	1.7	1.3	1.5	0.7
Inventory Turnover 35	5.2	24.5	9.3	10.0	8.8	8.0	6.1	7.8	8.2
Receivables Turnover 36	3.5	145.5	8.1	7.2	6.6	5.9	•	5.4	11.2
Total Liabilities to Net Worth 37	1.5	3.2	0.8	0.9	1.3	1.0	0.4	1.1	1.9
Current Assets to Working Capital 38	2.2	•	1.2	1.6	3.4	1.9	1.4	1.8	2.7
Current Liabilities to Working Capital 39	1.2	•	0.2	0.6	2.4	0.9	0.4	0.8	1.7
Working Capital to Net Sales 40	0.1	•	0.2	0.1	0.1	0.2	0.3	0.2	0.1
Inventory to Working Capital 41	0.7	•	0.3	0.4	0.8	0.4	0.4	0.4	1.0
Total Receipts to Cash Flow 42	10.0	4.6	5.0	7.0	8.1	8.2	9.5	11.1	12.4
Cost of Goods to Cash Flow 43	7.0	1.8	2.5	4.6	5.7	5.7	6.7	8.3	9.0
Cash Flow to Total Debt 44	0.2	1.1	1.2	0.8	0.6	0.4	0.5	0.3	0.1

Selected Financial Factors (in Percentages)

Debt Ratio 45	60.3	76.1	42.9	47.7	55.8	51.1	29.2	51.6	65.6
Return on Total Assets 46	7.2	14.6	30.3	23.6	10.4	11.5	7.3	6.2	5.6
Return on Equity Before Income Taxes 47	10.6	39.2	49.3	40.5	18.4	20.7	9.1	9.2	6.3
Return on Equity After Income Taxes 48	8.4	37.8	49.0	38.4	13.8	19.1	8.6	7.9	4.3
Profit Margin (Before Income Tax) 49	4.3	2.3	10.6	8.2	3.3	5.8	4.9	3.0	2.9
Profit Margin (After Income Tax) 50	3.4	2.2	10.6	7.8	2.4	5.4	4.6	2.6	2.0

Table I

Corporations with and without Net Income

IRON, STEEL MILLS AND STEEL PRODUCT

MONEY AMOUNTS AND SIZE OF ASSETS IN THOUSANDS OF DOLLARS

Item Description for Accounting Period 7/08 Through 6/09		Total	Zero Assets	Under 500	500 to 1,000	1,000 to 5,000	5,000 to 10,000	10,000 to 25,000	25,000 to 50,000	50,000 to 100,000	100,000 to 250,000	250,000 to 500,000	500,000 to 2,500,000	2,500,000 and over
Number of Enterprises	1	4199	938	1668	315	763	170	159	63	44	32	18	17	12
Revenues ($ in Thousands)														
Net Sales	2	16729018	527264	1879938	1119481	4651191	3151087	5431188	4700652	5587276	9015827	7822591	23309565	99532959
Interest	3	595793	143	55	257	4471	8438	3635	1387	6686	7628	86123	67846	409123
Rents	4	71087	0	0	0	0	2	1871	1047	252	1437	15225	10134	41119
Royalties	5	447111	0	0	0	0	0	2381	68	139	21295	2147	7829	413249
Other Portfolio Income	6	361756	65477	29	29	467	8964	4983	3905	1854	8532	19274	29025	219214
Other Receipts	7	2579032	30175	5	10828	35193	24334	37064	30678	24572	77334	38444	458378	1812034
Total Receipts	8	170783797	623059	1880027	1130595	4691322	3192825	5481122	4737737	5620779	9132053	7983804	23882777	102427698
Average Total Receipts	9	40672	664	1127	3589	6149	18781	34472	75202	127745	285377	443545	1404869	8535642
Operating Costs/Operating Income (%)														
Cost of Operations	10	79.3	82.5	43.1	71.9	74.5	83.7	75.8	78.2	83.7	81.5	81.4	85.1	78.4
Salaries and Wages	11	2.5	4.7	22.6	6.3	4.8	4.6	4.3	3.7	3.3	3.1	2.5	1.6	1.8
Taxes Paid	12	0.9	1.6	2.7	2.3	1.2	0.7	1.0	0.8	0.7	1.0	0.7	0.5	1.0
Interest Paid	13	1.5	2.7	0.4	0.1	0.8	0.5	0.6	1.1	1.0	0.8	2.5	1.1	1.8
Depreciation	14	2.5	3.1	2.0	0.9	1.7	1.7	2.6	3.0	2.2	2.2	2.5	2.2	2.7
Amortization and Depletion	15	0.5	0.7	0.1	0.0	0.0	0.0	0.2	0.2	0.2	0.1	0.3	1.3	0.5
Pensions and Other Deferred Comp.	16	1.3	0.1	•	0.0	0.0	0.2	0.7	0.4	0.5	0.5	0.3	0.2	2.0
Employee Benefits	17	1.4	0.8	3.0	2.1	0.6	0.7	1.8	1.2	1.0	1.1	1.2	1.0	1.5
Advertising	18	0.1	0.5	0.0	0.2	0.1	0.1	0.1	0.3	0.1	0.3	0.1	0.1	0.0
Other Expenses	19	5.8	13.6	20.1	12.5	5.6	4.2	6.0	5.4	3.4	4.2	4.3	4.8	6.2
Officers' Compensation	20	0.7	2.8	4.3	3.2	6.0	2.1	1.9	1.6	1.3	0.5	0.6	0.2	0.3
Operating Margin	21	3.5	•	1.6	0.5	4.4	1.5	5.0	4.1	2.6	4.6	3.6	1.9	3.9
Operating Margin Before Officers' Comp.	22	4.2	•	6.0	3.7	10.4	3.6	6.9	5.6	4.0	5.1	4.2	2.1	4.1

Selected Average Balance Sheet ($ in Thousands)

Line Item													
Net Receivables 23	1020318	137367	46516	29103	13275	7619	4254	2031	436	314	38	0	4508
Inventories 24	920773	209628	83010	50049	19282	11001	3987	2433	544	81	25	0	4949
Net Property, Plant and Equipment 25	2083638	258075	83926	41580	14517	10070	4044	2196	479	96	92	0	8352
Total Assets 26	7233477	1091587	326113	157662	67263	35737	16224	7631	2324	692	197		30408
Notes and Loans Payable 27	2444657	184822	119262	31982	17305	13839	3661	1551	909	43	131	0	9301
All Other Liabilities 28	2455883	371625	105604	45690	27333	12084	4880	2379	559	379	71	0	10231
Net Worth 29	2332937	535139	101247	79991	22624	9814	7684	3700	855	269	-6	0	10876

Selected Financial Ratios (Times to 1)

Line Item													
Current Ratio 30	2.1	1.7	1.8	2.2	1.4	1.6	1.9	2.0	3.1	1.5	1.0	•	2.0
Quick Ratio 31	1.2	0.8	0.7	1.0	0.6	0.7	1.0	1.1	1.6	1.2	0.7	•	1.0
Net Sales to Working Capital 32	6.0	7.4	6.1	5.4	11.4	9.0	7.0	7.3	4.5	18.7	397.2	•	6.4
Coverage Ratio 33	4.8	5.0	3.2	8.6	4.2	5.3	10.5	7.0	7.4	11.7	5.4	2.9	5.0
Total Asset Turnover 34	1.1	1.3	1.3	1.8	1.9	2.1	2.1	2.4	2.6	5.1	5.7	•	1.3
Inventory Turnover 35	7.1	5.6	4.3	4.6	5.5	5.3	6.5	6.4	8.3	31.4	19.5	•	6.4
Receivables Turnover 36	8.0	8.8	8.9	8.3	9.8	7.1	8.0	8.6	13.0	12.5	32.0	•	8.4
Total Liabilities to Net Worth 37	2.1	1.0	2.2	1.0	2.0	2.6	1.1	1.1	1.7	1.6	•	•	1.8
Current Assets to Working Capital 38	1.9	2.4	2.3	1.8	3.8	2.6	2.1	2.0	1.5	3.0	35.8	•	2.1
Current Liabilities to Working Capital 39	0.9	1.4	1.3	0.8	2.8	1.6	1.1	1.0	0.5	2.0	34.8	•	1.1
Working Capital to Net Sales 40	0.2	0.1	0.2	0.2	0.1	0.1	0.1	0.1	0.2	0.1	0.0	•	0.2
Inventory to Working Capital 41	0.7	1.0	1.2	0.9	1.7	1.3	0.8	0.8	0.4	0.5	9.3	•	0.8
Total Receipts to Cash Flow 42	9.9	11.8	11.2	11.3	17.6	11.6	10.4	18.1	11.0	7.9	6.1	5.9	10.5
Cost of Goods to Cash Flow 43	7.8	10.1	9.1	9.2	14.7	9.1	7.9	15.1	8.2	5.7	2.6	4.9	8.3
Cash Flow to Total Debt 44	0.2	0.2	0.2	0.3	0.2	0.2	0.4	0.3	0.4	1.1	0.9	•	0.2

Selected Financial Factors (in Percentages)

Line Item													
Debt Ratio 45	67.7	51.0	69.0	49.3	66.4	72.5	52.6	51.5	63.2	61.1	102.8	•	64.2
Return on Total Assets 46	9.8	7.1	10.8	12.0	8.0	12.6	13.7	8.1	15.8	8.6	11.6	•	9.7
Return on Equity Before Income Taxes 47	24.1	11.5	24.0	20.8	18.1	37.1	26.2	14.4	37.2	20.3	•	•	21.7
Return on Equity After Income Taxes 48	15.6	7.0	17.5	15.8	14.5	32.1	24.1	11.7	35.7	19.9	•	•	14.8
Profit Margin (Before Income Tax) 49	6.8	4.5	5.6	5.9	3.2	4.9	5.9	2.9	5.2	1.5	1.7	5.1	5.9
Profit Margin (After Income Tax) 50	4.4	2.8	4.1	4.5	2.6	4.2	5.4	2.3	5.0	1.5	1.7	4.6	4.0

Table II
Corporations with Net Income

IRON, STEEL MILLS AND STEEL PRODUCT

MONEY AMOUNTS AND SIZE OF ASSETS IN THOUSANDS OF DOLLARS

Item Description for Accounting Period 7/08 Through 6/09	Total	Zero Assets	Under 500	500 to 1,000	1,000 to 5,000	5,000 to 10,000	10,000 to 25,000	25,000 to 50,000	50,000 to 100,000	100,000 to 250,000	250,000 to 500,000	500,000 to 2,500,000	2,500,000 and over
Number of Enterprises **1**	2903	714	1086	233	466	123	134	47	33	29	15	•	•
Revenues ($ in Thousands)													
Net Sales **2**	140448469	340224	1205553	975573	3293103	2040499	4725169	3752033	4317217	7796227	7315585	•	•
Interest **3**	449978	57	0	251	4311	8402	3609	951	4417	7241	77470	•	•
Rents **4**	69417	0	0	0	0	2	1871	1047	252	1437	15222	•	•
Royalties **5**	440188	0	0	0	0	0	2381	0	65	21295	2147	•	•
Other Portfolio Income **6**	265646	65477	0	29	176	8964	4708	3778	1479	7603	19272	•	•
Other Receipts **7**	2144831	29457	2	7523	14353	24116	36402	31782	30043	80623	35527	•	•
Total Receipts **8**	143818529	435215	1205555	983376	3311943	2081983	4774140	3789591	4353473	7914426	7465223	•	•
Average Total Receipts **9**	49541	610	1110	4220	7107	16927	35628	80630	131923	272911	497682	•	•
Operating Costs/Operating Income (%)													
Cost of Operations **10**	77.7	70.4	37.7	73.2	68.9	77.8	74.4	76.5	83.4	79.7	80.9	•	•
Salaries and Wages **11**	2.5	5.2	25.5	7.0	5.0	4.7	4.4	3.5	3.2	3.4	2.4	•	•
Taxes Paid **12**	1.0	1.5	3.1	2.1	1.4	0.8	1.1	0.8	0.7	1.1	0.7	•	•
Interest Paid **13**	1.5	3.4	0.3	0.2	0.8	0.6	0.5	0.9	1.0	0.7	2.2	•	•
Depreciation **14**	2.4	2.7	2.2	1.0	1.0	2.2	2.3	2.7	1.7	2.2	2.3	•	•
Amortization and Depletion **15**	0.6	0.5	0.2	0.0	0.0	•	0.1	0.1	0.2	0.1	0.3	•	•
Pensions and Other Deferred Comp. **16**	1.2	0.1	•	0.4	0.4	0.3	0.8	0.2	0.4	0.5	0.3	•	•
Employee Benefits **17**	1.3	0.8	2.9	1.8	0.4	1.0	1.9	1.1	0.8	1.2	1.2	•	•
Advertising **18**	0.1	0.7	0.0	0.1	0.2	0.1	0.1	0.3	0.1	0.3	0.1	•	•
Other Expenses **19**	5.8	5.2	20.5	10.7	5.7	5.3	5.5	5.6	3.1	4.2	4.2	•	•
Officers' Compensation **20**	0.7	2.7	3.3	2.8	7.7	2.7	2.1	1.6	1.2	0.5	0.6	•	•
Operating Margin **21**	5.2	6.8	4.2	1.3	8.5	4.5	6.8	6.7	4.1	6.1	4.7	•	•
Operating Margin Before Officers' Comp. **22**	5.9	9.4	7.5	4.1	16.3	7.2	8.9	8.4	5.3	6.6	5.3	•	•

Selected Average Balance Sheet ($ in Thousands)

Net Receivables 23	•	52581	28805	14419	8637	4361	1667	486	381	45	0	5785
Inventories 24	•	90770	49650	19801	11876	4167	2685	624	14	23	0	5962
Net Property, Plant and Equipment 25	•	68250	37174	11399	9400	3606	2605	357	107	122	0	9727
Total Assets 26	•	323859	154347	67440	35080	16246	7459	2339	729	261	0	36800
Notes and Loans Payable 27	•	109260	27444	15878	9885	3507	1676	1004	42	137	0	11910
All Other Liabilities 28	•	118178	43454	22367	11413	4345	1634	528	447	33	0	11980
Net Worth 29	•	96421	83448	29195	13782	8394	4150	806	240	91	0	12910

Selected Financial Ratios (Times to 1)

Current Ratio 30	•	1.7	2.2	1.8	1.7	2.0	2.2	3.5	1.3	3.5	•	2.0
Quick Ratio 31	•	0.7	1.0	0.8	0.8	1.1	1.4	1.7	1.3	2.3	•	1.1
Net Sales to Working Capital 32	•	6.1	5.1	6.8	8.9	6.6	6.6	4.5	27.7	11.7	•	6.1
Coverage Ratio 33	•	4.0	11.2	6.1	9.6	15.4	12.4	12.6	13.8	13.0	11.1	6.0
Total Asset Turnover 34	•	1.5	1.7	1.9	2.3	2.2	2.2	3.0	5.7	4.3	•	1.3
Inventory Turnover 35	•	4.3	4.3	5.5	5.1	6.3	4.8	7.8	214.5	17.9	•	6.3
Receivables Turnover 36	•	10.0	7.9	9.5	6.4	7.6	6.9	12.0	•	26.6	•	8.2
Total Liabilities to Net Worth 37	•	2.4	0.8	1.3	1.5	0.9	0.8	1.9	2.0	1.9	•	1.9
Current Assets to Working Capital 38	•	2.3	1.8	2.3	2.5	2.0	1.8	1.4	4.0	1.4	•	2.0
Current Liabilities to Working Capital 39	•	1.3	0.8	1.3	1.5	1.0	0.8	0.4	3.0	0.4	•	1.0
Working Capital to Net Sales 40	•	0.2	0.2	0.1	0.1	0.2	0.2	0.2	0.0	0.1	•	0.2
Inventory to Working Capital 41	•	1.2	0.9	1.0	1.2	0.7	0.6	0.3	0.1	0.4	•	0.7
Total Receipts to Cash Flow 42	•	10.1	9.6	13.8	8.8	8.8	9.9	7.7	8.3	5.0	2.6	9.1
Cost of Goods to Cash Flow 43	•	8.2	7.7	11.5	6.7	6.6	7.7	5.3	6.1	1.9	1.8	7.1
Cash Flow to Total Debt 44	•	0.2	0.4	0.2	0.4	0.5	0.5	0.6	1.0	1.3	•	0.2

Selected Financial Factors (in Percentages)

Debt Ratio 45	•	70.2	45.9	56.7	60.7	48.3	44.4	65.5	67.0	65.2	•	64.9
Return on Total Assets 46	•	13.5	14.5	11.5	19.7	18.1	15.9	29.9	13.1	19.4	•	12.0
Return on Equity Before Income Taxes 47	•	34.0	24.4	22.2	44.9	32.8	26.3	80.0	36.8	51.5	•	28.6
Return on Equity After Income Taxes 48	•	25.8	19.1	18.5	40.4	30.6	23.0	77.4	36.2	51.5	•	20.2
Profit Margin (Before Income Tax) 49	•	6.7	7.6	4.9	7.8	7.8	6.6	9.1	2.1	4.2	34.7	7.6
Profit Margin (After Income Tax) 50	•	5.1	5.9	4.1	7.0	7.3	5.8	8.8	2.1	4.2	33.9	5.4

Table I

Corporations with and without Net Income

NONFERROUS METAL PRODUCTION AND PROCESSING

MONEY AMOUNTS AND SIZE OF ASSETS IN THOUSANDS OF DOLLARS

Item Description for Accounting Period 7/08 Through 6/09		Total	Zero Assets	Under 500	500 to 1,000	1,000 to 5,000	5,000 to 10,000	10,000 to 25,000	25,000 to 50,000	50,000 to 100,000	100,000 to 250,000	250,000 to 500,000	500,000 to 2,500,000	2,500,000 and over
Number of Enterprises	1	773	4	84	0	391	54	99	55	22	18	17	23	6
Revenues ($ in Thousands)														
Net Sales	2	109911477	1274311	72698	0	2711728	3672147	4645744	5638334	3555465	6821108	10955977	34203452	36356512
Interest	3	1819452	5388	1	0	132	96	1387	4433	5921	14535	31272	155610	1600678
Rents	4	33299	25	0	0	3988	0	1632	139	57	196	2940	15172	9151
Royalties	5	116207	111	0	0	0	0	594	4363	37244	622	37	73236	
Other Portfolio Income	6	1675594	1798	1	0	1479	3606	7884	1584	11699	16995	12564	43585	1574399
Other Receipts	7	1473930	3205	4	0	25019	-1234	22273	19453	12980	60989	104921	264299	962020
Total Receipts	8	115029959	1284838	72704	0	2742346	3674615	4679514	5663943	3590485	6914445	11123943	34707130	40575996
Average Total Receipts	9	148810	321210	866	•	7014	68048	47268	102981	163204	384136	654350	1509006	6762666
Operating Costs/Operating Income (%)														
Cost of Operations	10	85.5	81.9	76.6	•	84.9	93.3	87.5	87.7	85.7	89.2	91.2	84.5	82.9
Salaries and Wages	11	2.5	3.7	4.2	•	0.8	1.8	2.1	2.3	2.9	1.8	1.8	2.7	2.9
Taxes Paid	12	0.5	0.4	1.0	•	0.5	0.2	0.6	0.5	0.7	0.4	0.3	0.6	0.5
Interest Paid	13	3.0	1.2	0.1	•	0.6	0.5	0.6	1.0	0.7	1.5	1.3	1.6	6.6
Depreciation	14	2.4	1.3	1.1	•	1.0	0.7	1.6	1.6	1.6	1.3	1.4	1.7	4.2
Amortization and Depletion	15	0.8	0.1	0.0	•	0.0	0.1	0.1	0.1	0.2	0.4	0.3	0.6	1.7
Pensions and Other Deferred Comp.	16	0.3	0.3	•	•	0.2	0.1	0.2	0.3	0.2	0.9	0.4	0.3	0.3
Employee Benefits	17	1.0	1.5	4.1	•	0.3	0.7	0.7	1.0	0.4	1.2	0.9	0.9	1.1
Advertising	18	0.1	0.1	0.0	•	0.1	0.0	0.0	0.1	0.0	0.0	0.0	0.1	0.1
Other Expenses	19	7.2	15.5	9.2	•	5.9	2.2	2.6	3.6	5.1	4.2	4.3	10.7	6.8
Officers' Compensation	20	0.4	0.4	6.1	•	0.9	0.6	1.6	1.1	0.6	0.5	0.2	0.5	0.0
Operating Margin	21	•	•	•	•	4.7	•	2.3	0.7	1.8	•	•	•	•
Operating Margin Before Officers' Comp.	22	•	•	3.6	•	5.6	0.3	3.9	1.8	2.3	•	•	•	•

Selected Average Balance Sheet ($ in Thousands)

Net Receivables 23	66186	0	106	323	1527	3557	7417	16916	24730	64174	148444	7476944
Inventories 24	12337	0	12	252	2491	3413	11505	18185	28987	76251	157687	414534
Net Property, Plant and Equipment 25	28464	0	47	346	2763	5164	8909	15827	33175	94177	246989	2081047
Total Assets 26	208439	0	243	1581	8143	16080	35968	70731	158718	358458	1069883	20226855
Notes and Loans Payable 27	76919	0	29	1011	3751	4611	15117	18565	54539	139429	408914	7400746
All Other Liabilities 28	60896	0	72	317	3602	4682	9918	17124	62317	117466	355612	5677457
Net Worth 29	70624	0	142	253	791	6787	10933	35042	41863	101564	305357	7148653

Selected Financial Ratios (Times to 1)

Current Ratio 30	1.1	•	2.2	3.7	1.1	2.0	1.5	2.0	1.7	1.5	1.6	1.0
Quick Ratio 31	0.9	•	2.1	2.5	0.5	1.2	0.6	1.2	0.8	0.7	0.8	0.9
Net Sales to Working Capital 32	12.3	•	8.1	8.0	141.0	9.7	12.8	7.6	11.8	11.8	8.6	22.0
Coverage Ratio 33	1.6	•	•	10.5	0.7	6.0	2.2	4.8	1.1	0.5	•	2.1
Total Asset Turnover 34	0.7	•	3.6	4.4	8.4	2.9	2.9	2.3	2.4	1.8	1.4	0.3
Inventory Turnover 35	9.9	•	56.6	23.4	25.5	12.0	7.8	7.6	11.7	7.7	8.0	12.1
Receivables Turnover 36	2.2	•	5.8	20.1	36.5	11.6	12.1	7.8	11.4	8.8	9.6	0.8
Total Liabilities to Net Worth 37	2.0	•	0.7	5.3	9.3	1.4	2.3	1.0	2.8	2.5	2.5	1.8
Current Assets to Working Capital 38	7.8	•	1.8	1.4	10.4	2.0	2.9	2.0	2.4	3.2	2.6	30.6
Current Liabilities to Working Capital 39	6.8	•	0.8	0.4	9.4	1.0	1.9	1.0	1.4	2.2	1.6	29.6
Working Capital to Net Sales 40	0.1	•	0.1	0.1	0.0	0.1	0.1	0.1	0.1	0.1	0.1	0.0
Inventory to Working Capital 41	1.0	•	0.1	0.4	4.7	0.7	1.4	0.6	1.0	1.3	0.9	1.4
Total Receipts to Cash Flow 42	21.9	10.5	43.2	9.8	71.1	19.8	26.1	14.7	29.6	33.3	93.4	12.4
Cost of Goods to Cash Flow 43	18.8	8.6	33.1	8.4	66.3	17.3	22.9	12.6	26.4	30.4	78.9	10.2
Cash Flow to Total Debt 44	0.0	•	0.2	0.5	0.1	0.3	0.2	0.3	0.1	0.1	0.0	0.0

Selected Financial Factors (in Percentages)

Debt Ratio 45	66.1	•	41.6	84.0	90.3	57.8	69.6	50.5	73.6	71.7	71.5	64.7
Return on Total Assets 46	3.4	•	28.1	2.6	10.6	6.2	7.8	3.9	1.2	•	•	4.2
Return on Equity Before Income Taxes 47	3.8	•	159.0	•	20.9	11.0	12.5	1.7	•	•	•	6.2
Return on Equity After Income Taxes 48	1.3	•	158.9	•	18.6	9.9	8.6	•	•	•	•	4.0
Profit Margin (Before Income Tax) 49	1.9	•	5.8	•	3.0	1.2	2.7	0.2	•	•	•	7.3
Profit Margin (After Income Tax) 50	0.7	•	5.8	•	2.7	1.1	1.9	•	•	•	•	4.7

Table II
Corporations with Net Income

NONFERROUS METAL PRODUCTION AND PROCESSING

MONEY AMOUNTS AND SIZE OF ASSETS IN THOUSANDS OF DOLLARS

Item Description for Accounting Period 7/08 Through 6/09	Total	Zero Assets	Under 500	500 to 1,000	1,000 to 5,000	5,000 to 10,000	10,000 to 25,000	25,000 to 50,000	50,000 to 100,000	100,000 to 250,000	250,000 to 500,000	500,000 to 2,500,000	2,500,000 and over
Number of Enterprises **1**	516	•	0	0	337	23	74	32	12	11	•	15	•
Revenues ($ in Thousands)													
Net Sales **2**	75266451	•	0	0	2654731	2351789	3697129	3353481	2387519	5056172	•	22753435	•
Interest **3**	1558206	•	0	0	48	17	994	552	2048	13139	•	67752	•
Rents **4**	14914	•	0	0	2505	0	1123	79	11	196	•	2762	•
Royalties **5**	83129	•	0	0	0	0	594	0	4363	622	•	4962	•
Other Portfolio Income **6**	1428542	•	0	0	1479	21	7420	1198	10655	1143	•	26844	•
Other Receipts **7**	1336367	•	0	0	24942	1793	17110	14975	2667	22055	•	270151	•
Total Receipts **8**	79687609	•	0	0	2683705	2353620	3724370	3370285	2407263	5093327	•	23125906	•
Average Total Receipts **9**	154433	•	•	•	7964	102331	50329	105321	200605	463030	•	1541727	•
Operating Costs/Operating Income (%)													
Cost of Operations **10**	84.0	•	•	•	85.7	93.4	86.7	86.3	83.0	89.0	•	82.1	•
Salaries and Wages **11**	2.4	•	•	•	0.8	1.4	1.9	2.1	2.9	2.0	•	2.8	•
Taxes Paid **12**	0.5	•	•	•	0.4	0.2	0.7	0.5	0.7	0.3	•	0.7	•
Interest Paid **13**	3.3	•	•	•	0.6	0.1	0.4	0.8	0.7	1.0	•	1.4	•
Depreciation **14**	2.6	•	•	•	1.0	0.4	1.0	1.2	1.2	0.9	•	1.7	•
Amortization and Depletion **15**	0.8	•	•	•	0.0	0.0	0.0	0.1	0.2	0.1	•	0.2	•
Pensions and Other Deferred Comp. **16**	0.2	•	•	•	0.2	0.0	0.2	0.2	0.2	0.2	•	0.4	•
Employee Benefits **17**	0.9	•	•	•	0.3	0.2	0.7	0.6	0.5	0.5	•	1.0	•
Advertising **18**	0.1	•	•	•	0.1	0.0	0.1	0.1	0.0	0.0	•	0.1	•
Other Expenses **19**	5.4	•	•	•	5.0	1.6	2.3	3.3	5.3	4.1	•	5.4	•
Officers' Compensation **20**	0.4	•	•	•	0.9	0.6	1.6	1.3	0.6	0.5	•	0.3	•
Operating Margin **21**	•	•	•	•	4.9	2.1	4.3	3.4	4.7	1.5	•	3.8	•
Operating Margin Before Officers' Comp. **22**	•	•	•	•	5.8	2.7	6.0	4.7	5.3	2.0	•	4.1	•

Selected Average Balance Sheet ($ in Thousands)

Net Receivables 23	85548	•	•	•	371	1703	3822	7616	19990	30855	•	146530
Inventories 24	14055	•	•	•	259	4145	3615	12777	21838	32926	•	194945
Net Property, Plant and Equipment 25	31206	•	•	•	246	1856	4107	6892	14962	22970	•	221437
Total Assets 26	259556	•	•	•	1644	8214	15689	37262	72894	149422	•	1040209
Notes and Loans Payable 27	87655	•	•	•	1010	1370	3248	12994	20113	51091	•	391138
All Other Liabilities 28	73817	•	•	•	360	3172	4238	9720	22474	52592	•	279867
Net Worth 29	98084	•	•	•	275	3672	8203	14549	30307	45739	•	369204

Selected Financial Ratios (Times to 1)

Current Ratio 30	1.2	•	•	3.8	1.7	2.6	1.8	2.1	2.0	•	2.9
Quick Ratio 31	1.0	•	•	2.6	1.1	1.6	0.8	1.4	1.0	•	1.5
Net Sales to Working Capital 32	9.5	•	•	7.9	41.3	8.0	9.4	7.7	10.0	•	4.7
Coverage Ratio 33	3.0	•	•	11.4	22.7	14.0	5.6	8.9	3.2	•	4.8
Total Asset Turnover 34	0.6	•	•	4.8	12.4	3.2	2.8	2.7	3.1	•	1.5
Inventory Turnover 35	8.7	•	•	26.1	23.0	12.0	7.1	7.6	12.4	•	6.4
Receivables Turnover 36	1.6	•	•	20.3	31.3	10.4	•	7.8	11.7	•	8.8
Total Liabilities to Net Worth 37	1.6	•	•	5.0	1.2	0.9	1.6	1.4	2.3	•	1.8
Current Assets to Working Capital 38	7.2	•	•	1.4	2.4	1.6	2.3	1.9	2.0	•	1.5
Current Liabilities to Working Capital 39	6.2	•	•	0.4	1.4	0.6	1.3	0.9	1.0	•	0.5
Working Capital to Net Sales 40	0.1	•	•	0.1	0.0	0.1	0.1	0.1	0.1	•	0.2
Inventory to Working Capital 41	0.8	•	•	0.4	0.8	0.5	1.1	0.6	0.8	•	0.6
Total Receipts to Cash Flow 42	11.2	•	•	10.6	29.9	14.8	15.6	10.5	18.4	•	10.3
Cost of Goods to Cash Flow 43	9.4	•	•	9.1	27.9	12.8	13.5	8.7	16.4	•	8.5
Cash Flow to Total Debt 44	0.1	•	•	0.5	0.8	0.5	0.3	0.4	0.2	•	0.2

Selected Financial Factors (in Percentages)

Debt Ratio 45	62.2	•	•	83.3	55.3	47.7	61.0	58.4	69.4	•	64.5
Return on Total Assets 46	5.6	•	•	31.4	28.4	17.3	13.4	16.9	10.0	•	10.1
Return on Equity Before Income Taxes 47	9.8	•	•	171.2	60.8	30.7	28.3	36.1	22.4	•	22.6
Return on Equity After Income Taxes 48	7.1	•	•	171.1	60.2	28.2	26.8	27.7	17.3	•	17.9
Profit Margin (Before Income Tax) 49	6.6	•	•	6.0	2.2	5.0	3.9	5.5	2.2	•	5.5
Profit Margin (After Income Tax) 50	4.8	•	•	6.0	2.2	4.6	3.7	4.2	1.7	•	4.4

Table I

Corporations with and without Net Income

FOUNDRIES

MONEY AMOUNTS AND SIZE OF ASSETS IN THOUSANDS OF DOLLARS

Item Description for Accounting Period 7/08 Through 6/09	Total	Zero Assets	Under 500	500 to 1,000	1,000 to 5,000	5,000 to 10,000	10,000 to 25,000	25,000 to 50,000	50,000 to 100,000	100,000 to 250,000	250,000 to 500,000	500,000 to 2,500,000	2,500,000 and over
Number of Enterprises 1	1515	94	929	26	264	97	49	24	12	7	6	6	0
Revenues ($ in Thousands)													
Net Sales 2	26236708	10549	1011823	96795	2343636	1189340	1434809	1757990	1324127	1828181	2662953	12576505	0
Interest 3	26382	251	0	0	1943	439	757	855	1789	1544	3193	15612	0
Rents 4	4675	0	0	0	575	77	1303	108	122	0	1437	1052	0
Royalties 5	35972	0	0	0	0	10661	0	2	296	3554	0	21459	0
Other Portfolio Income 6	98181	538	0	0	1798	889	527	28840	12425	5030	5825	42309	0
Other Receipts 7	251662	9008	0	0	61811	7687	5241	9811	9069	6685	32274	110076	0
Total Receipts 8	26653580	20346	1011823	96795	2409763	1209093	1442637	1797606	1347828	1844994	2705682	12767013	0
Average Total Receipts 9	17593	216	1089	3723	9128	12465	29442	74900	112319	263571	450947	2127836	•
Operating Costs/Operating Income (%)													
Cost of Operations 10	75.2	145.9	64.4	79.5	71.7	80.4	75.9	77.3	74.4	69.6	81.9	75.2	•
Salaries and Wages 11	4.6	8.2	6.8	11.9	5.0	4.2	3.9	4.7	5.9	9.5	3.1	3.9	•
Taxes Paid 12	1.0	1.3	2.3	0.1	1.0	1.0	0.9	1.3	1.0	0.8	0.6	1.0	•
Interest Paid 13	1.2	0.3	0.1	0.2	0.3	1.6	0.9	1.4	2.6	2.2	2.4	0.9	•
Depreciation 14	3.1	5.0	1.4	0.3	1.5	3.8	3.5	3.0	5.0	5.5	3.8	2.8	•
Amortization and Depletion 15	0.4	1.4	0.2	•	0.0	0.1	0.1	0.1	0.5	0.6	0.2	0.6	•
Pensions and Other Deferred Comp. 16	1.2	•	0.0	•	0.3	0.5	0.4	0.9	1.2	0.4	0.7	1.8	•
Employee Benefits 17	1.4	5.9	0.6	0.0	2.3	2.4	2.6	1.2	0.9	1.5	1.8	1.1	•
Advertising 18	0.1	•	0.1	0.0	0.1	0.2	0.1	0.2	0.3	0.0	0.2	0.1	•
Other Expenses 19	5.6	303.7	8.3	10.8	12.1	5.5	4.7	5.0	6.9	12.9	4.8	3.1	•
Officers' Compensation 20	1.5	•	3.9	13.2	5.9	2.0	2.3	1.2	0.8	0.3	0.7	0.7	•
Operating Margin 21	4.7	•	11.8	•	•	•	4.8	3.9	0.5	•	•	8.9	•
Operating Margin Before Officers' Comp. 22	6.2	•	15.7	•	5.7	0.4	7.1	5.1	1.4	•	0.5	9.6	•

Selected Average Balance Sheet ($ in Thousands)

	•	•	•	•	•	•	•	•	•	•	•	•
Net Receivables 23	2054	0	107	105	1084	1914	3822	7378	11848	40463	54703	236548
Inventories 24	2046	0	32	403	776	1541	2862	6734	11281	28213	49953	296009
Net Property, Plant and Equipment 25	3122	0	15	82	708	2363	5327	12929	24241	63591	132684	365652
Total Assets 26	13067	0	231	618	3296	6709	15506	35947	73568	205644	405718	1944301
Notes and Loans Payable 27	2846	0	138	0	496	3301	4200	15866	25041	83482	124440	252446
All Other Liabilities 28	3778	0	48	279	1342	1944	3086	10760	22965	79064	130352	518078
Net Worth 29	6443	0	45	340	1458	1464	8220	9321	25561	43098	150927	1173778

Selected Financial Ratios (Times to 1)

		•										
Current Ratio 30	2.0	•	4.1	1.9	1.7	1.8	2.1	1.4	2.4	1.5	1.9	2.3
Quick Ratio 31	1.1	•	3.5	0.5	1.1	1.1	1.2	0.7	1.6	0.8	1.0	1.2
Net Sales to Working Capital 32	6.0	•	7.4	14.6	9.8	6.9	6.4	13.0	4.5	9.1	6.4	4.9
Coverage Ratio 33	6.5	•	111.7	•	8.5	1.0	7.2	5.9	1.8	•	1.6	13.6
Total Asset Turnover 34	1.3	•	4.7	6.0	2.7	1.8	1.9	2.0	1.5	1.3	1.1	1.1
Inventory Turnover 35	6.4	•	21.9	7.4	8.2	6.4	7.8	8.4	7.3	6.4	7.3	5.3
Receivables Turnover 36	8.2	•	8.5	70.9	8.1	5.7	7.3	10.8	8.7	7.5	7.4	8.5
Total Liabilities to Net Worth 37	1.0	•	4.1	0.8	1.3	3.6	0.9	2.9	1.9	3.8	1.7	0.7
Current Assets to Working Capital 38	2.0	•	1.3	2.1	2.5	2.2	1.9	3.7	1.7	3.0	2.1	1.8
Current Liabilities to Working Capital 39	1.0	•	0.3	1.1	1.5	1.2	0.9	2.7	0.7	2.0	1.1	0.8
Working Capital to Net Sales 40	0.2	•	0.1	0.1	0.1	0.1	0.2	0.1	0.2	0.1	0.2	0.2
Inventory to Working Capital 41	0.8	•	0.2	1.6	0.8	0.8	0.7	1.5	0.4	1.2	0.8	0.7
Total Receipts to Cash Flow 42	9.8	•	5.8	•	9.2	21.6	11.7	10.5	13.9	12.6	21.0	8.1
Cost of Goods to Cash Flow 43	7.4	•	3.8	•	6.6	17.3	8.9	8.1	10.3	8.8	17.2	6.1
Cash Flow to Total Debt 44	0.3	•	1.0	•	0.5	0.1	0.3	0.3	0.2	0.1	0.1	0.3

Selected Financial Factors (in Percentages)

		•										
Debt Ratio 45	50.7	•	80.6	45.1	55.8	78.2	47.0	74.1	65.3	79.0	62.8	39.6
Return on Total Assets 46	10.2	•	56.3	•	7.9	3.0	11.7	16.6	7.0	•	4.2	12.5
Return on Equity Before Income Taxes 47	17.4	•	286.7	•	15.8	0.4	18.9	53.2	9.1	•	4.1	19.2
Return on Equity After Income Taxes 48	12.7	•	286.7	•	14.6	•	16.1	40.9	7.2	•	2.2	13.7
Profit Margin (Before Income Tax) 49	6.5	•	11.8	2.6	0.0	5.3	6.8	2.1	•		1.4	10.7
Profit Margin (After Income Tax) 50	4.7	•	11.8	2.4	•	4.5	5.2	1.7	•		0.8	7.7

Table II

Corporations with Net Income

FOUNDRIES

MONEY AMOUNTS AND SIZE OF ASSETS IN THOUSANDS OF DOLLARS

Item Description for Accounting Period 7/08 Through 6/09	Total	Zero Assets	Under 500	500 to 1,000	1,000 to 5,000	5,000 to 10,000	10,000 to 25,000	25,000 to 50,000	50,000 to 100,000	100,000 to 250,000	250,000 to 500,000	500,000 to 2,500,000	2,500,000 and over
Number of Enterprises 1	1014	•	572	0	223	49	42	20	7	4	•	•	0
Revenues ($ in Thousands)													
Net Sales 2	20822343	•	933473	0	2026944	631530	1263436	1438850	633119	836559	•	•	0
Interest 3	23135	•	0	0	1880	157	689	833	1321	634	•	•	0
Rents 4	4237	•	0	0	575	0	1303	108	0	0	•	•	0
Royalties 5	25312	•	0	0	0	0	0	2	296	3554	•	•	0
Other Portfolio Income 6	85380	•	0	0	1753	261	235	28811	2275	5030	•	•	0
Other Receipts 7	193878	•	0	0	59683	2708	4726	7870	-427	3500	•	•	0
Total Receipts 8	21154285	•	933473	0	2090835	634656	1270389	1476474	636584	849277	•	•	0
Average Total Receipts 9	20862	•	1632	•	9376	12952	30247	73824	90941	212319	•	•	•
Operating Costs/Operating Income (%)													
Cost of Operations 10	74.6	•	68.9	•	69.8	77.7	74.8	73.7	74.7	76.1	•	•	•
Salaries and Wages 11	4.2	•	4.5	•	5.6	2.9	3.9	5.4	4.8	4.4	•	•	•
Taxes Paid 12	1.0	•	2.1	•	1.1	0.9	0.8	1.4	0.9	0.5	•	•	•
Interest Paid 13	1.0	•	0.1	•	0.4	1.9	0.9	1.3	1.0	2.6	•	•	•
Depreciation 14	2.7	•	0.9	•	1.4	3.3	3.7	3.0	3.7	2.5	•	•	•
Amortization and Depletion 15	0.4	•	•	•	•	•	0.1	0.1	0.1	0.4	•	•	•
Pensions and Other Deferred Comp. 16	1.2	•	0.0	•	0.4	0.6	0.5	1.0	0.9	0.4	•	•	•
Employee Benefits 17	1.2	•	0.0	•	2.0	2.7	2.6	1.3	1.4	2.6	•	•	•
Advertising 18	0.1	•	0.1	•	0.1	0.2	0.1	0.2	0.6	0.0	•	•	•
Other Expenses 19	4.4	•	6.2	•	12.3	4.0	4.3	5.0	3.9	3.9	•	•	•
Officers' Compensation 20	1.5	•	4.2	•	5.9	2.1	2.4	1.4	1.2	0.7	•	•	•
Operating Margin 21	7.8	•	13.0	•	1.2	3.7	5.8	6.3	6.8	5.8	•	•	•
Operating Margin Before Officers' Comp. 22	9.3	•	17.2	•	7.1	5.9	8.3	7.6	8.0	6.5	•	•	•

Selected Average Balance Sheet ($ in Thousands)

	•	•	•	•	•	•	•	•
Net Receivables 23	2449	155	•	1198	2379	4177	6733	11884	29526
Inventories 24	2577	40	•	857	2284	2968	8588	13300	27578
Net Property, Plant and Equipment 25	3298	17	•	691	1963	5107	11707	17828	42206
Total Assets 26	15996	295	•	3484	6567	15930	34172	71414	188122
Notes and Loans Payable 27	2760	19	•	560	4077	4121	14687	10251	81077
All Other Liabilities 28	4270	63	•	1139	1665	3262	8360	10451	63913
Net Worth 29	8967	213	•	1785	825	8547	11125	50712	43132

Selected Financial Ratios (Times to 1)

	•	•	•	•	•	•	•	•
Current Ratio 30	2.2	4.4	•	1.7	2.5	2.1	1.7	4.6	1.7
Quick Ratio 31	1.3	4.0	•	1.2	1.4	1.3	0.9	3.3	0.9
Net Sales to Working Capital 32	5.4	7.6	•	8.6	4.7	6.2	8.8	2.6	7.7
Coverage Ratio 33	11.1	112.8	•	12.6	3.2	8.5	8.5	7.8	3.9
Total Asset Turnover 34	1.3	5.5	•	2.6	2.0	1.9	2.1	1.3	1.1
Inventory Turnover 35	5.9	27.8	•	7.4	4.4	7.6	6.2	5.1	5.8
Receivables Turnover 36	7.8	8.5	•	7.7	4.2	6.9	•	6.1	9.3
Total Liabilities to Net Worth 37	0.8	0.4	•	1.0	7.0	0.9	2.1	0.4	3.4
Current Assets to Working Capital 38	1.8	1.3	•	2.3	1.7	1.9	2.5	1.3	2.5
Current Liabilities to Working Capital 39	0.8	0.3	•	1.3	0.7	0.9	1.5	0.3	1.5
Working Capital to Net Sales 40	0.2	0.1	•	0.1	0.2	0.2	0.1	0.4	0.1
Inventory to Working Capital 41	0.7	0.1	•	0.7	0.7	0.7	1.0	0.3	1.1
Total Receipts to Cash Flow 42	8.2	6.0	•	8.1	13.2	10.9	8.1	9.4	9.6
Cost of Goods to Cash Flow 43	6.1	4.1	•	5.7	10.3	8.2	6.0	7.0	7.3
Cash Flow to Total Debt 44	0.4	3.3	•	0.7	0.2	0.4	0.4	0.5	0.1

Selected Financial Factors (in Percentages)

	•	•	•	•	•	•	•	•
Debt Ratio 45	43.9	27.8	•	48.7	87.4	46.3	67.4	29.0	77.1
Return on Total Assets 46	13.5	72.4	•	12.3	12.1	13.7	23.0	10.2	11.5
Return on Equity Before Income Taxes 47	22.0	99.4	•	22.2	66.2	22.5	62.3	12.5	37.3
Return on Equity After Income Taxes 48	17.0	99.4	•	21.0	62.1	19.4	49.9	10.9	31.4
Profit Margin (Before Income Tax) 49	9.6	13.0	•	4.4	4.2	6.4	9.6	7.0	7.7
Profit Margin (After Income Tax) 50	7.4	13.0	•	4.1	4.0	5.5	7.7	6.1	6.5

Table I

Corporations with and without Net Income

FORGING AND STAMPING

MONEY AMOUNTS AND SIZE OF ASSETS IN THOUSANDS OF DOLLARS

Item Description for Accounting Period 7/08 Through 6/09		Total	Zero Assets	Under 500	500 to 1,000	1,000 to 5,000	5,000 to 10,000	10,000 to 25,000	25,000 to 50,000	50,000 to 100,000	100,000 to 250,000	250,000 to 500,000	500,000 to 2,500,000	2,500,000 and over
Number of Enterprises	1	2538	94	1059	436	606	122	129	42	23	21	5	0	0
Revenues ($ in Thousands)														
Net Sales	2	21576574	1769743	229275	519134	3027273	1617332	3668573	2292243	2185173	3983872	2283955	0	0
Interest	3	39641	3127	176	216	1308	881	1780	137	1574	1383	29060	0	0
Rents	4	2631	110	0	253	119	55	43	12	347	1052	641	0	0
Royalties	5	9	0	0	0	7	0	0	2	0	0	0	0	0
Other Portfolio Income	6	121498	53272	17991	403	2208	1134	1656	892	1815	41841	288	0	0
Other Receipts	7	163068	11283	234	1993	6712	17212	22222	9055	24718	32191	37445	0	0
Total Receipts	8	21903421	1837535	247676	521999	3037627	1636614	3694274	2302341	2213627	4060339	2351389	0	0
Average Total Receipts	9	8630	19548	234	1197	5013	13415	28638	54818	96245	193349	470278	•	•
Operating Costs/Operating Income (%)														
Cost of Operations	10	75.4	83.8	47.0	65.4	72.8	73.5	75.7	74.6	79.3	77.1	72.8	•	•
Salaries and Wages	11	4.4	4.9	1.8	2.3	4.8	4.6	5.3	4.4	4.8	4.1	2.6	•	•
Taxes Paid	12	1.1	0.7	3.0	2.1	1.9	0.8	1.1	1.1	1.0	1.0	0.8	•	•
Interest Paid	13	1.7	2.0	0.4	1.0	1.2	0.5	0.8	0.9	1.4	2.4	4.9	•	•
Depreciation	14	3.0	1.2	3.6	0.8	2.7	2.2	3.0	3.6	3.6	4.7	2.0	•	•
Amortization and Depletion	15	0.2	0.5	•	0.1	0.0	0.2	0.2	0.4	0.4	0.3	0.2	•	•
Pensions and Other Deferred Comp.	16	0.6	0.9	0.4	0.4	0.9	0.2	0.6	0.4	0.4	0.3	1.5	•	•
Employee Benefits	17	2.2	3.3	3.0	1.5	2.1	2.2	2.1	2.0	2.4	2.7	0.5	•	•
Advertising	18	0.1	0.0	1.8	0.3	0.2	0.2	0.3	0.1	0.0	0.1	0.0	•	•
Other Expenses	19	6.6	6.1	36.0	18.5	7.3	7.6	5.6	5.5	4.4	7.0	3.5	•	•
Officers' Compensation	20	2.3	0.4	11.9	12.6	4.3	2.5	2.4	1.0	1.5	1.4	1.3	•	•
Operating Margin	21	2.2	•	•	•	1.8	5.6	3.0	6.1	0.7	•	9.9	•	•
Operating Margin Before Officers' Comp.	22	4.5	•	2.9	7.6	6.1	8.1	5.3	7.1	2.1	0.3	11.2	•	•

Selected Average Balance Sheet ($ in Thousands)

Net Receivables 23	1002	0	38	116	553	1575	3325	6838	12676	25195	77821	•
Inventories 24	1098	0	17	201	434	1624	3580	6221	8822	24090	100991	•
Net Property, Plant and Equipment 25	1400	0	13	95	691	1623	3834	10527	21699	46550	93750	•
Total Assets 26	5642	0	93	704	2407	7619	13919	31861	66277	153243	729974	•
Notes and Loans Payable 27	1641	0	6	142	833	1191	3851	9474	20174	45287	227384	•
All Other Liabilities 28	1655	0	6	126	1529	1193	3145	6626	15836	48280	201074	•
Net Worth 29	2346	0	81	436	45	5236	6923	15760	30268	59676	301516	•

Selected Financial Ratios (Times to 1)

Current Ratio 30	2.0	•	13.7	3.3	1.6	2.4	2.3	1.9	1.6	1.9	2.5	•
Quick Ratio 31	1.1	•	10.7	2.0	1.0	1.4	1.4	1.1	1.0	1.0	1.1	•
Net Sales to Working Capital 32	6.0	•	3.0	3.0	8.6	5.7	6.0	6.5	7.7	6.0	3.0	•
Coverage Ratio 33	3.1	1.0	•	•	2.7	14.5	5.4	8.1	2.4	1.3	3.6	•
Total Asset Turnover 34	1.5	•	2.3	1.7	2.1	1.7	2.0	1.7	1.4	1.2	0.6	•
Inventory Turnover 35	5.8	•	6.1	3.9	8.4	6.0	6.0	6.5	8.5	6.1	3.3	•
Receivables Turnover 36	7.7	•	•	•	8.7	7.8	6.9	7.9	8.1	8.0	5.8	•
Total Liabilities to Net Worth 37	1.4	•	0.2	0.6	53.0	0.5	1.0	1.0	1.2	1.6	1.4	•
Current Assets to Working Capital 38	2.0	•	1.1	1.4	2.7	1.7	1.8	2.1	2.6	2.2	1.7	•
Current Liabilities to Working Capital 39	1.0	•	0.1	0.4	1.7	0.7	0.8	1.1	1.6	1.2	0.7	•
Working Capital to Net Sales 40	0.2	•	0.3	0.3	0.1	0.2	0.2	0.2	0.1	0.2	0.3	•
Inventory to Working Capital 41	0.7	•	0.2	0.5	0.9	0.6	0.6	0.8	0.8	0.8	0.7	•
Total Receipts to Cash Flow 42	13.2	36.7	4.9	11.6	20.0	8.4	15.0	9.9	19.2	20.4	6.3	•
Cost of Goods to Cash Flow 43	10.0	30.7	2.3	7.6	14.6	6.2	11.4	7.4	15.2	15.7	4.6	•
Cash Flow to Total Debt 44	0.2	•	3.6	0.4	0.1	0.7	0.3	0.3	0.1	0.1	0.2	•

Selected Financial Factors (in Percentages)

Debt Ratio 45	58.4	•	13.2	38.1	98.1	31.3	50.3	50.5	54.3	61.1	58.7	•
Return on Total Assets 46	8.2	•	•	•	7.0	12.7	9.1	12.8	4.7	3.9	11.1	•
Return on Equity Before Income Taxes 47	13.4	•	•	•	239.1	17.2	14.9	22.7	5.9	2.4	19.5	•
Return on Equity After Income Taxes 48	11.7	•	•	•	218.8	15.3	13.7	20.9	4.6	•	18.4	•
Profit Margin (Before Income Tax) 49	3.7	•	•	•	2.1	6.8	3.6	6.6	1.9	0.7	12.9	•
Profit Margin (After Income Tax) 50	3.2	•	•	•	2.0	6.0	3.3	6.0	1.5	•	12.1	•

Table II

Corporations with Net Income

FORGING AND STAMPING

MONEY AMOUNTS AND SIZE OF ASSETS IN THOUSANDS OF DOLLARS

Item Description for Accounting Period 7/08 Through 6/09	Total	Zero Assets	Under 500	500 to 1,000	1,000 to 5,000	5,000 to 10,000	10,000 to 25,000	25,000 to 50,000	50,000 to 100,000	100,000 to 250,000	250,000 to 500,000	500,000 to 2,500,000	2,500,000 and over
Number of Enterprises **1**	1567	•	885	83	366	•	95	38	•	12	5	0	0
Revenues ($ in Thousands)													
Net Sales **2**	16325014	•	153243	150361	2298208	•	2610541	2144851	•	2253186	2283955	0	0
Interest **3**	36914	•	108	41	706	•	980	120	•	416	29060	0	0
Rents **4**	915	•	0	35	0	•	0	0	•	7	641	0	0
Royalties **5**	9	•	0	0	7	•	0	2	•	0	0	0	0
Other Portfolio Income **6**	69363	•	15050	403	1351	•	1132	718	•	2104	288	0	0
Other Receipts **7**	92512	•	236	298	455	•	17054	8731	•	6631	37445	0	0
Total Receipts **8**	16524727	•	168637	151138	2300727	•	2629707	2154422	•	2262344	2351389	0	0
Average Total Receipts **9**	10545	•	191	1821	6286	•	27681	56695	•	188529	470278	•	•
Operating Costs/Operating Income (%)													
Cost of Operations **10**	74.4	•	35.7	68.1	72.1	•	73.7	74.1	•	73.6	72.8	•	•
Salaries and Wages **11**	3.8	•	1.6	0.0	4.1	•	4.8	4.5	•	3.8	2.6	•	•
Taxes Paid **12**	1.1	•	3.9	2.6	1.6	•	1.1	1.0	•	1.1	0.8	•	•
Interest Paid **13**	1.5	•	0.6	0.2	0.7	•	0.6	0.8	•	1.4	4.9	•	•
Depreciation **14**	2.8	•	5.0	0.0	2.5	•	2.8	3.5	•	3.9	2.0	•	•
Amortization and Depletion **15**	0.2	•	•	•	0.0	•	0.1	0.4	•	0.2	0.2	•	•
Pensions and Other Deferred Comp. **16**	0.7	•	•	1.1	1.2	•	0.7	0.4	•	0.4	1.5	•	•
Employee Benefits **17**	2.0	•	3.6	2.1	2.0	•	2.3	1.8	•	2.0	0.5	•	•
Advertising **18**	0.1	•	2.7	0.7	0.1	•	0.4	0.1	•	0.0	0.0	•	•
Other Expenses **19**	4.8	•	29.5	15.3	5.6	•	4.2	5.6	•	3.4	3.5	•	•
Officers' Compensation **20**	2.1	•	12.1	9.6	4.2	•	3.0	0.9	•	1.8	1.3	•	•
Operating Margin **21**	6.3	•	5.1	0.3	5.9	•	6.3	6.7	•	8.6	9.9	•	•
Operating Margin Before Officers' Comp. **22**	8.4	•	17.2	9.9	10.1	•	9.3	7.7	•	10.4	11.2	•	•

Selected Average Balance Sheet ($ in Thousands)

Net Receivables 23	1194	35	216	672	3184	7040	23085	77821
Inventories 24	1315	4	486	485	3852	5739	33429	106809
Net Property, Plant and Equipment 25	1555	14	2	646	3560	9703	42208	93750
Total Assets 26	6669	80	620	2218	13712	31933	144672	729974
Notes and Loans Payable 27	1847	8	56	666	3277	8614	43091	227384
All Other Liabilities 28	1601	4	154	637	3063	6987	29236	201074
Net Worth 29	3221	69	410	914	7372	16331	72345	301516

Selected Financial Ratios (Times to 1)

Current Ratio 30	2.2	17.5	2.9	1.5	2.4	2.0	2.6	2.5
Quick Ratio 31	1.2	15.1	2.0	0.9	1.5	1.2	1.3	1.1
Net Sales to Working Capital 32	5.6	2.8	4.4	12.5	5.4	6.1	4.2	3.0
Coverage Ratio 33	5.9	25.1	5.3	9.7	11.9	9.7	7.5	3.6
Total Asset Turnover 34	1.6	2.2	2.9	2.8	2.0	1.8	1.3	0.6
Inventory Turnover 35	5.9	14.1	2.5	9.3	5.3	7.3	4.1	3.1
Receivables Turnover 36	7.9	6.5	4.2	8.8	6.6	9.1	6.6	
Total Liabilities to Net Worth 37	1.1	0.2	0.5	1.4	0.9	1.0	1.0	1.4
Current Assets to Working Capital 38	1.8	1.1	1.5	2.9	1.7	2.0	1.6	1.7
Current Liabilities to Working Capital 39	0.8	0.1	0.5	1.9	0.7	1.0	0.6	0.7
Working Capital to Net Sales 40	0.2	0.4	0.2	0.1	0.2	0.2	0.2	0.3
Inventory to Working Capital 41	0.7	0.1	0.5	1.0	0.6	0.7	0.7	0.7
Total Receipts to Cash Flow 42	9.8	3.6	10.7	13.8	10.6	9.3	8.9	6.3
Cost of Goods to Cash Flow 43	7.3	1.3	7.3	10.0	7.8	6.9	6.5	4.6
Cash Flow to Total Debt 44	0.3	4.2	0.8	0.3	0.4	0.4	0.3	0.2

Selected Financial Factors (in Percentages)

Debt Ratio 45	51.7	14.4	33.9	58.8	46.2	48.9	50.0	58.7
Return on Total Assets 46	14.2	34.0	3.0	19.0	15.3	14.2	13.4	11.1
Return on Equity Before Income Taxes 47	24.3	38.2	3.7	41.3	26.1	24.9	23.2	19.5
Return on Equity After Income Taxes 48	22.3	38.2	3.3	39.6	24.6	23.0	19.6	18.4
Profit Margin (Before Income Tax) 49	7.5	15.2	0.8	6.0	7.0	7.2	8.9	12.9
Profit Margin (After Income Tax) 50	6.9	15.2	0.7	5.8	6.6	6.6	7.6	12.1

Table I

Corporations with and without Net Income

CUTLERY, HARDWARE, SPRING AND WIRE MACHINE SHOPS, NUT, BOLT

MONEY AMOUNTS AND SIZE OF ASSETS IN THOUSANDS OF DOLLARS

Item Description for Accounting Period 7/08 Through 6/09	Total	Zero Assets	Under 500	500 to 1,000	1,000 to 5,000	5,000 to 10,000	10,000 to 25,000	25,000 to 50,000	50,000 to 100,000	100,000 to 250,000	250,000 to 500,000	500,000 to 2,500,000	2,500,000 and over
Number of Enterprises 1	20654	3647	11517	1665	2836	488	350	72	34	21	12	12	0
Revenues ($ in Thousands)													
Net Sales 2	70380749	395676	4970971	3594201	11636390	6325001	9159827	4043905	3392667	3923890	5245952	17692270	0
Interest 3	347061	845	3100	2248	10188	9203	5341	13671	3802	7940	12517	278206	0
Rents 4	33855	173	0	5212	7744	1014	4094	1287	942	6470	558	6361	0
Royalties 5	124861	22	0	0	44	0	77	125	1640	2849	3535	116569	0
Other Portfolio Income 6	436955	4941	13462	25712	34556	37680	18524	13838	14648	42732	57849	173011	0
Other Receipts 7	855735	4266	79981	4805	62866	22382	52586	34739	17434	195358	26520	354799	0
Total Receipts 8	72179216	405923	5067514	3632178	11751788	6395280	9240449	4107565	3431133	4179239	5346931	18621216	0
Average Total Receipts 9	3495	111	440	2181	4144	13105	26401	57050	100916	199011	445578	1551768	•
Operating Costs/Operating Income (%)													
Cost of Operations 10	64.8	36.0	50.2	56.4	64.4	67.8	70.1	70.4	76.1	74.7	69.1	60.7	•
Salaries and Wages 11	7.7	10.3	11.4	6.6	6.8	5.6	6.5	5.5	5.3	8.1	9.0	9.4	•
Taxes Paid 12	1.5	2.9	2.9	2.2	2.3	1.7	1.2	1.0	0.9	1.2	1.3	1.1	•
Interest Paid 13	2.8	1.2	1.3	1.4	1.5	0.6	1.2	1.1	1.4	1.4	3.1	6.8	•
Depreciation 14	3.3	9.0	2.9	5.5	4.1	3.7	4.4	3.9	2.6	3.4	2.1	1.9	•
Amortization and Depletion 15	0.8	0.4	0.0	0.0	0.1	0.1	0.2	0.2	0.5	0.4	0.8	2.4	•
Pensions and Other Deferred Comp. 16	0.6	0.4	0.6	0.5	0.4	0.5	0.5	0.5	0.6	0.5	1.0	0.8	•
Employee Benefits 17	2.0	0.2	1.4	2.5	2.1	1.7	2.1	1.5	1.5	1.8	2.6	2.1	•
Advertising 18	0.7	0.2	0.3	0.2	0.3	0.5	0.8	0.5	0.8	0.6	1.2	1.1	•
Other Expenses 19	10.9	26.6	19.0	11.0	8.8	9.5	8.3	7.2	7.2	7.8	9.9	14.2	•
Officers' Compensation 20	3.1	12.0	9.0	6.0	6.0	4.3	2.6	1.5	1.4	0.8	0.6	0.7	•
Operating Margin 21	1.7	0.9	1.1	7.7	3.1	4.1	2.3	6.6	1.5	0.8	•	•	•
Operating Margin Before Officers' Comp. 22	4.8	12.9	10.1	13.7	9.1	8.4	4.9	8.2	2.9	0.1	0.7	•	•

Selected Average Balance Sheet ($ in Thousands)

Net Receivables 23	508	0	31	176	436	1386	3116	6879	12774	30344	73429	365738
Inventories 24	403	0	20	84	341	1851	4105	9241	15460	29850	67732	168673
Net Property, Plant and Equipment 25	470	0	36	231	702	1678	4478	8620	17445	35625	52264	162368
Total Assets 26	3633	0	165	698	2224	6863	15627	33682	68560	167904	385840	3661031
Notes and Loans Payable 27	1458	0	86	397	1067	1265	5282	8632	22338	48591	212149	1502179
All Other Liabilities 28	839	0	24	198	479	1410	2959	7084	21219	41614	115856	845403
Net Worth 29	1336	0	56	103	678	4188	7386	17966	25003	77699	57836	1313449

Selected Financial Ratios (Times to 1)

Current Ratio 30	1.9	•	2.9	1.3	1.6	2.5	2.1	2.7	1.7	1.8	1.3	2.0
Quick Ratio 31	1.0	•	2.1	0.9	1.0	1.3	1.0	1.3	0.7	0.9	0.7	1.0
Net Sales to Working Capital 32	5.1	•	6.1	20.9	9.1	4.9	5.4	4.4	6.3	5.3	10.9	3.1
Coverage Ratio 33	2.7	3.9	3.4	7.2	3.7	9.4	3.6	8.1	2.9	5.3	1.4	1.9
Total Asset Turnover 34	0.9	•	2.6	3.1	1.8	1.9	1.7	1.7	1.5	1.1	1.1	0.4
Inventory Turnover 35	5.5	•	11.1	14.6	7.8	4.8	4.5	4.3	4.9	4.7	4.5	5.3
Receivables Turnover 36	6.3	•	12.4	12.6	9.9	9.8	8.2	7.7	8.1	6.0	6.6	3.4
Total Liabilities to Net Worth 37	1.7	•	2.0	5.8	2.3	0.6	1.1	0.9	1.7	1.2	5.7	1.8
Current Assets to Working Capital 38	2.1	•	1.5	4.1	2.6	1.7	1.9	1.6	2.4	2.2	4.2	2.0
Current Liabilities to Working Capital 39	1.1	•	0.5	3.1	1.6	0.7	0.9	0.6	1.4	1.2	3.2	1.0
Working Capital to Net Sales 40	0.2	•	0.2	0.0	0.1	0.2	0.2	0.2	0.2	0.2	0.1	0.3
Inventory to Working Capital 41	0.6	•	0.3	0.8	0.8	0.7	0.9	0.7	1.2	0.9	1.7	0.4
Total Receipts to Cash Flow 42	8.2	4.6	6.5	6.7	10.2	10.7	10.7	7.2	11.8	8.5	12.0	6.2
Cost of Goods to Cash Flow 43	5.3	1.7	3.3	3.8	6.6	7.3	7.5	5.1	9.0	6.4	8.3	3.7
Cash Flow to Total Debt 44	0.2	•	0.6	0.5	0.3	0.5	0.3	0.5	0.2	0.2	0.1	0.1

Selected Financial Factors (in Percentages)

Debt Ratio 45	63.2	•	66.1	85.3	69.5	39.0	52.7	46.7	63.5	53.7	85.0	64.1
Return on Total Assets 46	7.2	•	11.2	31.4	10.4	11.1	7.3	15.5	6.0	8.2	5.0	5.3
Return on Equity Before Income Taxes 47	12.4	•	23.4	183.6	24.9	16.2	11.3	25.5	10.8	14.3	10.0	7.1
Return on Equity After Income Taxes 48	9.7	•	22.5	174.8	21.5	12.9	9.1	23.7	8.2	10.6	5.3	4.5
Profit Margin (Before Income Tax) 49	4.9	3.5	3.0	8.7	4.1	5.2	3.2	8.2	2.7	6.0	1.3	6.3
Profit Margin (After Income Tax) 50	3.8	3.0	2.9	8.3	3.6	4.2	2.6	7.6	2.1	4.4	0.7	4.0

Table II

Corporations with Net Income

CUTLERY, HARDWARE, SPRING AND WIRE MACHINE SHOPS, NUT, BOLT

MONEY AMOUNTS AND SIZE OF ASSETS IN THOUSANDS OF DOLLARS

Item Description for Accounting Period 7/08 Through 6/09	Total	Zero Assets	Under 500	500 to 1,000	1,000 to 5,000	5,000 to 10,000	10,000 to 25,000	25,000 to 50,000	50,000 to 100,000	100,000 to 250,000	250,000 to 500,000	500,000 to 2,500,000	2,500,000 and over
Number of Enterprises 1	13457	1923	7655	1368	1793	378	225	57	25	16	7	9	0
Revenues ($ in Thousands)													
Net Sales 2	55248017	229881	3761650	3160859	8427116	4834476	6084994	3478501	2505118	3527246	3194679	16043497	0
Interest 3	325271	589	1642	1828	7764	8933	3959	12352	2592	5682	11015	268915	0
Rents 4	27719	173	0	5212	7579	759	1567	106	880	6469	558	4415	0
Royalties 5	120922	22	0	0	44	0	43	125	1640	1617	2154	115277	0
Other Portfolio Income 6	400918	4936	13457	25597	23922	36972	9330	11747	13912	42603	51460	166980	0
Other Receipts 7	593438	75	64323	1353	35229	13179	36891	34024	15952	20029	22326	350061	0
Total Receipts 8	56716285	235676	3841072	3194849	8501654	4894319	6136784	3536855	2540094	3603646	3282192	16949145	0
Average Total Receipts 9	4215	123	502	2335	4742	12948	27275	62050	101604	225228	468885	1883238	•
Operating Costs/Operating Income (%)													
Cost of Operations 10	62.6	24.4	48.3	55.2	62.0	62.9	67.8	69.5	73.9	73.9	68.8	59.1	•
Salaries and Wages 11	7.9	16.9	11.6	6.9	7.1	6.1	6.5	5.5	5.9	5.0	9.8	9.7	•
Taxes Paid 12	1.6	2.5	3.0	2.1	2.4	1.8	1.2	1.0	0.9	1.3	1.4	1.1	•
Interest Paid 13	2.9	1.6	0.8	1.3	1.2	0.6	0.9	1.1	0.9	1.0	2.1	7.3	•
Depreciation 14	2.9	4.7	2.5	5.4	3.3	3.5	3.4	3.1	2.7	3.3	2.0	1.9	•
Amortization and Depletion 15	0.8	•	0.0	0.0	0.0	0.1	0.1	0.1	0.2	0.3	0.5	2.3	•
Pensions and Other Deferred Comp. 16	0.6	0.6	0.4	0.6	0.4	0.5	0.6	0.4	0.5	0.4	1.5	0.5	•
Employee Benefits 17	1.9	0.2	1.4	2.4	1.7	1.7	1.9	1.4	1.2	1.2	2.9	2.3	•
Advertising 18	0.6	0.1	0.4	0.2	0.2	0.5	0.6	0.5	0.9	0.6	0.7	0.8	•
Other Expenses 19	10.8	28.1	15.8	10.7	8.3	9.8	8.0	6.8	7.2	7.2	9.0	14.6	•
Officers' Compensation 20	3.1	6.0	8.8	5.5	6.7	4.6	2.6	1.5	1.5	0.7	0.5	0.7	•
Operating Margin 21	4.5	14.8	6.9	9.7	6.8	7.9	6.3	9.1	4.1	5.2	1.0	•	•
Operating Margin Before Officers' Comp. 22	7.6	20.8	15.7	15.2	13.4	12.5	8.9	10.6	5.6	5.9	1.5	0.2	•

Selected Average Balance Sheet ($ in Thousands)

Item	•	•	•	•	•	•	•	•	•	•	•	•
Net Receivables 23	646	0	29	183	536	1485	3251	7337	13118	32434	88827	454018
Inventories 24	471	0	21	69	392	2023	4502	10168	17114	33397	63041	179311
Net Property, Plant and Equipment 25	509	0	38	238	601	1492	3944	7629	18076	38426	61236	196158
Total Assets 26	4659	0	154	685	2105	6987	15488	33525	68582	168757	399341	4617026
Notes and Loans Payable 27	1802	0	72	386	903	1146	4101	8352	17230	34327	204205	1923924
All Other Liabilities 28	1052	0	17	219	420	1387	2853	6858	20333	40871	121897	1044338
Net Worth 29	1804	0	65	81	782	4454	8534	18314	31019	93559	73239	1648764

Selected Financial Ratios (Times to 1)

Item	•	•	•	•	•	•	•	•	•	•	•	•
Current Ratio 30	2.1	•	4.0	1.3	2.2	2.8	2.5	2.7	2.0	2.2	1.3	2.0
Quick Ratio 31	1.1	•	3.0	0.9	1.5	1.5	1.4	1.2	0.9	1.1	0.7	1.0
Net Sales to Working Capital 32	4.5	•	6.0	26.1	6.5	4.2	4.6	4.5	5.1	4.6	12.8	2.9
Coverage Ratio 33	3.7	11.8	11.7	9.3	7.5	16.6	8.6	10.4	7.2	8.4	2.8	2.0
Total Asset Turnover 34	0.9	•	3.2	3.4	2.2	1.8	1.7	1.8	1.5	1.3	1.1	0.4
Inventory Turnover 35	5.5	•	11.1	18.4	7.4	4.0	4.1	4.2	4.3	4.9	5.0	5.9
Receivables Turnover 36	5.8	•	14.8	13.5	9.0	8.9	7.3	7.8	7.3	6.5	5.5	3.3
Total Liabilities to Net Worth 37	1.6	•	1.4	7.5	1.7	0.6	0.8	0.8	1.2	0.8	4.5	1.8
Current Assets to Working Capital 38	1.9	•	1.3	4.7	1.8	1.5	1.6	1.6	2.0	1.9	5.0	2.0
Current Liabilities to Working Capital 39	0.9	•	0.3	3.7	0.8	0.5	0.6	0.6	1.0	0.9	4.0	1.0
Working Capital to Net Sales 40	0.2	•	0.2	0.0	0.2	0.2	0.2	0.2	0.2	0.2	0.1	0.3
Inventory to Working Capital 41	0.5	•	0.3	0.6	0.5	0.6	0.7	0.8	1.0	0.8	1.7	0.3
Total Receipts to Cash Flow 42	6.6	2.7	5.2	5.9	7.8	7.3	7.6	6.3	8.9	7.8	9.6	5.6
Cost of Goods to Cash Flow 43	4.1	0.6	2.5	3.2	4.8	4.6	5.2	4.3	6.5	5.8	6.6	3.3
Cash Flow to Total Debt 44	0.2	•	1.1	0.7	0.5	0.7	0.5	0.6	0.3	0.4	0.1	0.1

Selected Financial Factors (in Percentages)

Item	•	•	•	•	•	•	•	•	•	•	•	•
Debt Ratio 45	61.3	•	57.8	88.2	62.8	36.3	44.9	45.4	54.8	44.6	81.7	64.3
Return on Total Assets 46	9.5	•	31.5	40.6	19.7	17.8	14.1	21.6	9.6	11.1	6.7	5.8
Return on Equity Before Income Taxes 47	18.0	•	68.3	308.0	46.0	26.3	22.6	35.7	18.3	17.7	23.7	8.3
Return on Equity After Income Taxes 48	14.9	•	67.1	294.4	41.3	22.3	19.7	33.5	15.4	13.6	17.4	5.6
Profit Margin (Before Income Tax) 49	7.9	17.4	9.0	10.8	7.6	9.1	7.1	10.7	5.7	7.5	3.8	7.7
Profit Margin (After Income Tax) 50	6.6	16.7	8.9	10.3	6.9	7.8	6.2	10.0	4.8	5.8	2.8	5.2

Table I
Corporations with and without Net Income

ARCHITECTURAL AND STRUCTURAL METALS

MONEY AMOUNTS AND SIZE OF ASSETS IN THOUSANDS OF DOLLARS

Item Description for Accounting Period 7/08 Through 6/09		Total	Zero Assets	Under 500	500 to 1,000	1,000 to 5,000	5,000 to 10,000	10,000 to 25,000	25,000 to 50,000	50,000 to 100,000	100,000 to 250,000	250,000 to 500,000	500,000 to 2,500,000	2,500,000 and over
Number of Enterprises	1	6631	123	3237	807	1714	322	274	90	32	13	9	10	0
Revenues ($ in Thousands)														
Net Sales	2	54076133	288066	2292860	1995065	9229576	4527541	8751806	5626411	3675661	3377513	4096576	10215061	0
Interest	3	113560	0	619	1987	4176	1722	6488	3297	3307	6143	10378	75443	0
Rents	4	10804	0	0	0	379	929	1276	185	220	632	0	7184	0
Royalties	5	34299	0	0	0	51	0	307	204	0	443	3	33291	0
Other Portfolio Income	6	183519	53378	761	7	3100	2531	3074	12579	5570	1477	11312	89728	0
Other Receipts	7	428876	10142	11823	10313	56986	38495	33606	21838	43852	13637	40873	147310	0
Total Receipts	8	54847191	351586	2306063	2007372	9294268	4571218	8796557	5664514	3728610	3399845	4159142	10568017	0
Average Total Receipts	9	8271	2858	712	2487	5423	14196	32104	62939	116519	261527	462127	1056802	•
Operating Costs/Operating Income (%)														
Cost of Operations	10	72.5	87.3	65.4	67.3	70.7	72.8	73.6	76.5	75.7	72.4	75.3	70.9	•
Salaries and Wages	11	6.2	14.7	5.4	9.1	5.7	4.8	6.1	5.7	5.1	6.7	5.0	7.8	•
Taxes Paid	12	1.3	1.7	1.7	2.7	1.4	1.7	1.0	1.2	1.0	1.2	1.0	1.3	•
Interest Paid	13	1.6	7.2	0.4	0.6	0.6	0.7	0.7	0.9	1.1	1.3	3.6	3.7	•
Depreciation	14	2.6	1.5	1.5	1.6	1.6	2.9	1.9	2.5	1.9	2.6	3.9	4.3	•
Amortization and Depletion	15	0.2	0.2	0.0	0.1	0.0	0.0	0.2	0.1	0.3	0.4	0.8	0.4	•
Pensions and Other Deferred Comp.	16	0.5	0.2	0.8	0.3	0.4	0.6	0.4	0.3	0.3	0.5	0.1	1.1	•
Employee Benefits	17	1.9	1.9	0.8	2.6	2.8	1.3	1.7	1.3	1.5	1.6	1.4	2.6	•
Advertising	18	0.5	0.3	0.4	0.6	0.2	0.3	0.3	0.3	0.6	0.8	0.2	1.1	•
Other Expenses	19	8.7	18.1	15.2	14.1	10.0	6.8	8.0	5.5	6.7	8.5	7.2	9.3	•
Officers' Compensation	20	2.2	2.2	7.6	4.6	3.7	3.2	2.3	1.4	1.0	0.5	1.3	0.4	•
Operating Margin	21	1.7	•	0.7	•	2.9	4.9	3.9	4.4	4.8	3.4	0.1	•	•
Operating Margin Before Officers' Comp.	22	3.9	•	8.4	1.2	6.6	8.1	6.2	5.8	5.8	3.8	1.5	•	•

Selected Average Balance Sheet ($ in Thousands)

	•	•	•	•	•	•	•	•	•	•	•	•
Net Receivables **23**	1217	0	67	161	889	2388	5960	9366	17016	27034	91493	123426
Inventories **24**	728	0	21	118	378	1422	2967	6491	11644	27619	26599	118712
Net Property, Plant and Equipment **25**	1220	0	39	200	430	1870	2847	7274	12444	37752	105739	319014
Total Assets **26**	5293	0	189	740	2349	6966	14948	34617	67990	154916	317259	1336020
Notes and Loans Payable **27**	1853	0	86	296	721	1723	3649	9351	20406	41700	187242	525652
All Other Liabilities **28**	1427	0	54	224	628	1776	4790	9019	21032	40646	97032	326126
Net Worth **29**	2012	0	49	220	1000	3467	6509	16247	26553	72571	32984	484242

Selected Financial Ratios (Times to 1)

	•	•	•	•	•	•	•	•	•	•	•	•
Current Ratio **30**	1.7	•	1.5	1.8	2.3	1.9	2.1	1.7	1.8	2.4	1.5	1.2
Quick Ratio **31**	1.1	•	1.1	1.2	1.7	1.4	1.4	1.0	1.1	1.3	1.1	0.6
Net Sales to Working Capital **32**	7.3	•	16.8	10.7	5.5	6.5	5.4	6.7	6.3	6.0	8.0	19.3
Coverage Ratio **33**	3.2	•	4.3	•	7.4	9.3	7.4	6.9	6.6	4.0	1.5	1.5
Total Asset Turnover **34**	1.5	•	3.7	3.3	2.3	2.0	2.1	1.8	1.7	1.7	1.4	0.8
Inventory Turnover **35**	8.1	•	21.7	14.1	10.1	7.2	7.9	7.4	7.5	6.8	12.9	6.1
Receivables Turnover **36**	6.2	•	10.3	15.2	6.5	4.6	6.0	7.0	7.1	8.3	5.9	5.1
Total Liabilities to Net Worth **37**	1.6	•	2.9	2.4	1.3	1.0	1.3	1.1	1.6	1.1	8.6	1.8
Current Assets to Working Capital **38**	2.4	•	3.2	2.2	1.8	2.1	1.9	2.5	2.2	1.7	3.2	6.4
Current Liabilities to Working Capital **39**	1.4	•	2.2	1.2	0.8	1.1	0.9	1.5	1.2	0.7	2.2	5.4
Working Capital to Net Sales **40**	0.1	•	0.1	0.1	0.2	0.2	0.2	0.1	0.2	0.2	0.1	0.1
Inventory to Working Capital **41**	0.7	•	0.5	0.7	0.4	0.4	0.5	0.7	0.7	0.6	0.6	2.2
Total Receipts to Cash Flow **42**	11.0	24.7	11.1	15.8	9.7	9.2	10.0	11.3	8.8	9.5	15.6	14.6
Cost of Goods to Cash Flow **43**	8.0	21.5	7.3	10.6	6.8	6.7	7.4	8.6	6.7	6.9	11.8	10.4
Cash Flow to Total Debt **44**	0.2	•	0.5	0.3	0.4	0.4	0.4	0.3	0.3	0.3	0.1	0.1

Selected Financial Factors (in Percentages)

	•	•	•	•	•	•	•	•	•	•	•	•
Debt Ratio **45**	62.0	•	74.1	70.3	57.4	50.2	56.5	53.1	60.9	53.2	89.6	63.8
Return on Total Assets **46**	7.6	•	6.4	•	9.5	13.2	10.9	10.8	12.5	9.0	7.6	4.3
Return on Equity Before Income Taxes **47**	13.7	•	18.9	19.3	19.3	23.6	21.6	19.6	27.1	14.4	22.9	4.1
Return on Equity After Income Taxes **48**	11.2	•	18.3	17.6	17.6	21.8	19.3	17.9	24.8	12.0	3.9	1.7
Profit Margin (Before Income Tax) **49**	3.4	•	1.3	•	3.6	5.8	4.4	5.1	6.3	4.0	1.7	1.9
Profit Margin (After Income Tax) **50**	2.8	•	1.3	•	3.3	5.4	3.9	4.6	5.7	3.3	0.3	0.8

Table II

Corporations with Net Income

ARCHITECTURAL AND STRUCTURAL METALS

MONEY AMOUNTS AND SIZE OF ASSETS IN THOUSANDS OF DOLLARS

Item Description for Accounting Period 7/08 Through 6/09		Total	Zero Assets	Under 500	500 to 1,000	1,000 to 5,000	5,000 to 10,000	10,000 to 25,000	25,000 to 50,000	50,000 to 100,000	100,000 to 250,000	250,000 to 500,000	500,000 to 2,500,000	2,500,000 and over
Number of Enterprises	1	4433	38	2257	190	1321	283	224	70	•	•	6	•	0
Revenues ($ in Thousands)														
Net Sales	2	38866673	73112	1184674	603558	7213564	4145704	6987325	5039304	•	•	2672531	•	0
Interest	3	48924	0	167	465	3735	1053	6001	2739	•	•	3067	•	0
Rents	4	5092	0	0	0	379	917	727	185	•	•	0	•	0
Royalties	5	18778	0	0	0	51	0	307	0	•	•	0	•	0
Other Portfolio Income	6	64292	29415	294	0	2605	1536	3001	11197	•	•	10779	•	0
Other Receipts	7	226760	1	11590	504	54199	32422	28533	15168	•	•	34489	•	0
Total Receipts	8	39232519	102528	1196725	604527	7274533	4181632	7025894	5068593	•	•	2720866	•	0
Average Total Receipts	9	8850	2698	530	3182	5507	14776	31366	72408	•	•	453478	•	•
Operating Costs/Operating Income (%)														
Cost of Operations	10	72.7	95.0	60.9	69.4	69.0	72.8	73.8	78.2	•	•	75.5	•	•
Salaries and Wages	11	5.4	12.1	5.5	3.5	5.9	4.5	5.3	4.6	•	•	3.8	•	•
Taxes Paid	12	1.2	0.5	1.9	2.5	1.5	1.7	1.0	1.0	•	•	0.9	•	•
Interest Paid	13	1.0	5.1	0.5	1.1	0.5	0.4	0.5	0.7	•	•	1.0	•	•
Depreciation	14	2.2	3.2	0.9	1.0	1.6	2.8	1.7	1.8	•	•	3.5	•	•
Amortization and Depletion	15	0.2	0.7	•	0.2	0.0	0.0	0.1	0.1	•	•	0.6	•	•
Pensions and Other Deferred Comp.	16	0.5	0.2	•	0.3	0.6	0.6	0.4	0.3	•	•	0.1	•	•
Employee Benefits	17	1.7	2.0	1.4	1.2	1.8	0.9	1.7	1.2	•	•	1.9	•	•
Advertising	18	0.3	0.2	0.3	0.8	0.3	0.3	0.3	0.3	•	•	0.1	•	•
Other Expenses	19	7.2	11.5	17.1	10.8	9.6	6.4	6.8	4.2	•	•	5.6	•	•
Officers' Compensation	20	2.3	3.4	8.0	7.5	3.8	3.2	2.5	1.4	•	•	1.4	•	•
Operating Margin	21	5.4	•	3.6	1.8	5.7	6.5	5.8	6.2	•	•	5.6	•	•
Operating Margin Before Officers' Comp.	22	7.7	•	11.6	9.3	9.5	9.7	8.4	7.6	•	•	7.1	•	•

Selected Average Balance Sheet ($ in Thousands)

Net Receivables 23	1373	0	58	179	873	2511	5841	10133	•	107306
Inventories 24	802	0	19	154	290	1318	3015	6660	•	25469
Net Property, Plant and Equipment 25	966	0	14	133	406	1867	2467	5803	•	112254
Total Assets 26	5163	0	141	646	2173	6917	15124	35130	•	313379
Notes and Loans Payable 27	1518	0	57	538	569	1162	2814	8517	•	102634
All Other Liabilities 28	1415	0	43	109	566	1481	5100	8960	•	115672
Net Worth 29	2231	0	40	-0	1038	4274	7211	17653	•	95072

Selected Financial Ratios (Times to 1)

Current Ratio 30	2.0	•	2.5	4.5	2.5	2.9	2.1	2.0	•	1.7
Quick Ratio 31	1.4	•	1.9	3.2	2.0	2.2	1.5	1.2	•	1.3
Net Sales to Working Capital 32	6.0	•	7.0	8.0	5.3	4.8	5.1	5.9	•	6.0
Coverage Ratio 33	7.6	2.3	10.2	2.8	15.5	21.1	13.5	10.8	•	8.4
Total Asset Turnover 34	1.7	•	3.7	4.9	2.5	2.1	2.1	2.0	•	1.4
Inventory Turnover 35	7.9	•	17.1	14.3	13.0	8.1	7.6	8.4	•	13.2
Receivables Turnover 36	5.6	•	6.9	10.1	6.5	4.7	5.7	7.8	•	•
Total Liabilities to Net Worth 37	1.3	•	2.5	•	1.1	0.6	1.1	1.0	•	2.3
Current Assets to Working Capital 38	2.0	•	1.7	1.3	1.7	1.5	1.9	2.0	•	2.5
Current Liabilities to Working Capital 39	1.0	•	0.7	0.3	0.7	0.5	0.9	1.0	•	1.5
Working Capital to Net Sales 40	0.2	•	0.1	0.1	0.2	0.2	0.2	0.2	•	0.2
Inventory to Working Capital 41	0.5	•	0.2	0.4	0.3	0.3	0.5	0.6	•	0.3
Total Receipts to Cash Flow 42	9.0	5.9	7.0	12.3	8.0	8.2	9.4	10.4	•	9.3
Cost of Goods to Cash Flow 43	6.5	5.6	4.2	8.6	5.5	6.0	6.9	8.2	•	7.0
Cash Flow to Total Debt 44	0.3	•	0.8	0.4	0.6	0.7	0.4	0.4	•	0.2

Selected Financial Factors (in Percentages)

Debt Ratio 45	56.8	•	71.3	100.1	52.2	38.2	52.3	49.7	•	69.7
Return on Total Assets 46	12.9	•	19.0	14.9	17.5	16.3	14.2	15.2	•	11.9
Return on Equity Before Income Taxes 47	25.8	•	59.7	•	34.3	25.1	27.6	27.4	•	34.7
Return on Equity After Income Taxes 48	22.4	•	58.7	•	32.1	23.4	25.1	25.4	•	24.8
Profit Margin (Before Income Tax) 49	6.6	6.4	4.6	2.0	6.5	7.3	6.4	6.7	•	7.4
Profit Margin (After Income Tax) 50	5.7	6.4	4.5	1.9	6.1	6.8	5.8	6.2	•	5.3

Table I

Corporations with and without Net Income

BOILER, TANK, AND SHIPPING CONTAINER

MONEY AMOUNTS AND SIZE OF ASSETS IN THOUSANDS OF DOLLARS

Item Description for Accounting Period 7/08 Through 6/09		Total	Zero Assets	Under 500	500 to 1,000	1,000 to 5,000	5,000 to 10,000	10,000 to 25,000	25,000 to 50,000	50,000 to 100,000	100,000 to 250,000	250,000 to 500,000	500,000 to 2,500,000	2,500,000 and over
Number of Enterprises	1	884	3	378	183	197	15	52	23	13	8	5	6	0
Revenues ($ in Thousands)														
Net Sales	2	22668565	114364	168506	241209	969969	218922	1622169	1215543	1228130	1247541	2457225	13184988	0
Interest	3	36555	0	0	0	1066	207	1695	440	1037	3431	13514	15165	0
Rents	4	11243	0	0	0	2260	0	260	0	114	1666	485	6458	0
Royalties	5	37356	0	0	0	0	0	0	0	0	657	187	36513	0
Other Portfolio Income	6	71537	15812	0	137	132	14	45882	1872	1753	134	6	5795	0
Other Receipts	7	228575	0	-8953	1127	270	0	12907	4014	7860	12009	21527	177812	0
Total Receipts	8	23053831	130176	159553	242473	973697	219143	1682913	1221869	1238894	1265438	2492944	13426731	0
Average Total Receipts	9	26079	43392	422	1325	4943	14610	32364	53125	95300	158180	498589	2237788	•
Operating Costs/Operating Income (%)														
Cost of Operations	10	78.6	67.2	70.4	56.8	72.7	67.1	78.0	72.3	75.2	68.1	78.8	81.7	•
Salaries and Wages	11	4.0	0.9	6.0	9.5	6.8	7.9	5.3	5.0	4.7	5.0	5.9	2.9	•
Taxes Paid	12	0.8	0.8	0.8	2.7	1.6	1.3	1.2	1.7	0.9	1.2	1.2	0.4	•
Interest Paid	13	2.3	1.1	2.7	0.2	0.2	0.3	1.1	1.0	1.1	4.4	2.4	2.6	•
Depreciation	14	3.7	2.5	2.0	0.5	1.3	2.5	1.9	2.2	3.0	3.5	0.8	5.0	•
Amortization and Depletion	15	0.7	•	•	•	•	0.0	0.2	0.2	0.9	0.8	0.5	0.9	•
Pensions and Other Deferred Comp.	16	0.6	•	0.8	0.7	0.7	0.2	0.8	0.4	0.9	0.7	0.2	0.6	•
Employee Benefits	17	1.9	•	•	0.2	2.8	1.8	1.5	2.7	2.2	1.1	1.0	2.1	•
Advertising	18	0.2	0.0	0.2	0.5	0.4	0.1	1.2	0.3	0.3	0.2	0.2	0.0	•
Other Expenses	19	4.2	19.4	31.5	7.6	6.4	8.4	6.3	6.0	7.9	8.7	3.5	2.4	•
Officers' Compensation	20	1.1	•	•	5.6	5.6	1.4	2.4	2.0	1.3	0.7	1.7	0.3	•
Operating Margin	21	2.0	8.0	•	15.7	1.6	9.0	0.2	6.1	1.7	5.5	3.8	1.0	•
Operating Margin Before Officers' Comp.	22	3.1	8.0	•	21.2	7.1	10.4	2.5	8.0	2.9	6.2	5.5	1.4	•

Selected Average Balance Sheet ($ in Thousands)

Net Receivables 23	2857	0	0	190	425	1489	4130	7731	12274	24815	55223	226295
Inventories 24	3017	0	0	130	595	1791	4220	5758	9996	23263	44783	162787
Net Property, Plant and Equipment 25	4445	0	71	370	277	1307	2614	6238	15204	37668	21320	479346
Total Assets 26	23274	0	71	835	1599	6618	17518	32088	66633	163343	381213	2375354
Notes and Loans Payable 27	8452	0	512	166	394	429	2569	9271	25433	75764	88623	906206
All Other Liabilities 28	7291	0	61	66	347	1285	5573	9702	15696	32310	224643	704006
Net Worth 29	7530	0	-502	603	859	4905	9376	13116	25504	55268	67947	765142

Selected Financial Ratios (Times to 1)

Current Ratio 30	1.5	•	5.1	2.2	4.0	2.3	2.1	1.5	1.3	1.3	1.4
Quick Ratio 31	0.7	•	3.6	0.9	3.2	1.3	1.3	0.7	0.8	0.6	0.6
Net Sales to Working Capital 32	9.7	•	3.5	7.0	4.2	4.9	4.6	8.7	9.5	13.2	12.6
Coverage Ratio 33	2.7	20.2	68.0	13.8	34.1	4.7	7.3	3.2	2.6	3.2	2.1
Total Asset Turnover 34	1.1	6.3	1.6	3.1	2.2	1.8	1.6	1.4	1.0	1.3	0.9
Inventory Turnover 35	6.7	•	5.7	6.0	5.5	5.8	6.6	7.1	4.6	8.7	11.0
Receivables Turnover 36	8.8	•	•	10.9	3.7	6.9	6.9	8.0	6.3	9.4	15.6
Total Liabilities to Net Worth 37	2.1	•	0.4	0.9	0.3	0.9	1.4	1.6	2.0	4.6	2.1
Current Assets to Working Capital 38	3.1	•	1.2	1.8	1.3	1.8	1.9	3.2	4.0	5.0	3.7
Current Liabilities to Working Capital 39	2.1	•	0.2	0.8	0.3	0.8	0.9	2.2	3.0	4.0	2.7
Working Capital to Net Sales 40	0.1	•	0.3	0.1	0.2	0.2	0.2	0.1	0.1	0.1	0.1
Inventory to Working Capital 41	1.1	•	0.3	1.0	0.1	0.6	0.5	1.1	1.1	1.6	1.5
Total Receipts to Cash Flow 42	16.2	2.6	6.0	19.9	6.6	13.7	9.3	11.9	7.0	13.6	25.5
Cost of Goods to Cash Flow 43	12.7	1.8	3.4	14.5	4.4	10.7	6.7	9.0	4.8	10.7	20.8
Cash Flow to Total Debt 44	0.1	•	0.9	0.3	1.3	0.3	0.3	0.2	0.2	0.1	0.1

Selected Financial Factors (in Percentages)

Debt Ratio 45	67.6	809.6	27.8	46.3	25.9	46.5	59.1	61.7	66.2	82.2	67.8
Return on Total Assets 46	6.6	•	25.9	6.4	20.6	8.9	12.5	5.1	10.9	10.1	5.1
Return on Equity Before Income Taxes 47	12.7	•	35.4	11.1	27.0	13.1	26.5	9.2	19.6	39.2	8.4
Return on Equity After Income Taxes 48	9.4	•	35.4	11.0	21.7	11.1	25.7	5.9	17.8	26.4	5.2
Profit Margin (Before Income Tax) 49	3.7	21.9	16.2	1.9	9.1	3.9	6.6	2.5	6.9	5.4	2.9
Profit Margin (After Income Tax) 50	2.8	21.9	16.2	1.9	7.3	3.3	6.4	1.6	6.3	3.7	1.8

Table II
Corporations with Net Income

BOILER, TANK, AND SHIPPING CONTAINER

Money Amounts and Size of Assets in Thousands of Dollars

Item Description for Accounting Period 7/08 Through 6/09		Total	Zero Assets	Under 500	500 to 1,000	1,000 to 5,000	5,000 to 10,000	10,000 to 25,000	25,000 to 50,000	50,000 to 100,000	100,000 to 250,000	250,000 to 500,000	500,000 to 2,500,000	2,500,000 and over
Number of Enterprises	1	416	•	0	183	137	•	36	17	10	•	5	•	0
Revenues ($ in Thousands)														
Net Sales	2	17309285	•	0	241209	673365	•	1181671	938401	948097	•	2457225	•	0
Interest	3	28757	•	0	0	919	•	1399	243	972	•	13514	•	0
Rents	4	6403	•	0	0	0	•	260	0	114	•	485	•	0
Royalties	5	35611	•	0	0	0	•	0	0	0	•	187	•	0
Other Portfolio Income	6	70506	•	0	137	131	•	45882	1656	1036	•	6	•	0
Other Receipts	7	190984	•	0	1127	200	•	6245	1054	3977	•	21527	•	0
Total Receipts	8	17641546	•	0	242473	674615	•	1235457	941354	954196	•	2492944	•	0
Average Total Receipts	9	42408	•	•	1325	4924	•	34318	55374	95420	•	498589	•	•
Operating Costs/Operating Income (%)														
Cost of Operations	10	78.6	•	•	56.8	69.3	•	73.8	72.1	74.5	•	78.8	•	•
Salaries and Wages	11	4.2	•	•	9.5	5.8	•	6.0	4.6	4.4	•	5.9	•	•
Taxes Paid	12	0.8	•	•	2.7	1.3	•	1.1	1.6	0.8	•	1.2	•	•
Interest Paid	13	2.1	•	•	0.2	0.2	•	1.0	0.9	1.0	•	2.4	•	•
Depreciation	14	3.4	•	•	0.5	1.6	•	1.7	2.2	3.0	•	0.8	•	•
Amortization and Depletion	15	0.2	•	•	•	•	•	0.1	0.1	0.3	•	0.5	•	•
Pensions and Other Deferred Comp.	16	0.4	•	•	0.8	0.6	•	1.0	0.4	1.0	•	0.2	•	•
Employee Benefits	17	1.7	•	•	0.2	2.1	•	2.0	1.9	1.5	•	1.0	•	•
Advertising	18	0.2	•	•	0.5	0.6	•	1.7	0.3	0.3	•	0.2	•	•
Other Expenses	19	3.2	•	•	7.6	7.8	•	7.0	4.5	5.9	•	3.5	•	•
Officers' Compensation	20	1.1	•	•	5.6	5.9	•	2.7	2.0	1.4	•	1.7	•	•
Operating Margin	21	3.9	•	•	15.7	4.9	•	1.9	9.4	5.9	•	3.8	•	•
Operating Margin Before Officers' Comp.	22	5.1	•	•	21.2	10.8	•	4.6	11.3	7.3	•	5.5	•	•

Net Receivables 23	4025	190	299	4066	7117	12086	55223
Inventories 24	5806	116	760	5601	7495	9680	44783
Net Property, Plant and Equipment 25	6735	370	310	2690	6991	15392	21320
Total Assets 26	31819	835	1597	18035	31611	66383	381213
Notes and Loans Payable 27	10921	166	462	2101	10408	17081	88623
All Other Liabilities 28	11641	66	357	6500	9459	14426	224643
Net Worth 29	9257	603	778	9434	11745	34876	67947

Current Ratio 30	1.5	5.1	1.9	2.4	2.2	2.1	1.3
Quick Ratio 31	0.7	3.6	0.6	1.2	1.3	1.0	0.6
Net Sales to Working Capital 32	9.2	3.5	8.5	4.6	4.4	5.5	13.2
Coverage Ratio 33	3.8	68.0	25.1	7.5	11.3	7.4	3.2
Total Asset Turnover 34	1.3	1.6	3.1	1.8	1.7	1.4	1.3
Inventory Turnover 35	5.6	6.5	4.5	4.3	5.3	7.3	8.7
Receivables Turnover 36	8.2	7.6	10.0	6.1	•	8.0	9.4
Total Liabilities to Net Worth 37	2.4	0.4	1.1	0.9	1.7	0.9	4.6
Current Assets to Working Capital 38	3.0	1.2	2.1	1.7	1.8	1.9	5.0
Current Liabilities to Working Capital 39	2.0	0.2	1.1	0.7	0.8	0.9	4.0
Working Capital to Net Sales 40	0.1	0.3	0.1	0.2	0.2	0.2	0.1
Inventory to Working Capital 41	1.2	0.3	1.4	0.7	0.6	0.8	1.6
Total Receipts to Cash Flow 42	13.8	6.0	11.0	10.5	7.7	9.0	13.6
Cost of Goods to Cash Flow 43	10.9	3.4	7.6	7.8	5.5	6.7	10.7
Cash Flow to Total Debt 44	0.1	0.9	0.5	0.4	0.4	0.3	0.1

Debt Ratio 45	70.9	27.8	51.3	47.7	62.8	47.5	82.2
Return on Total Assets 46	10.4	25.9	16.3	13.6	18.6	10.6	10.1
Return on Equity Before Income Taxes 47	26.5	35.4	32.0	22.5	45.5	17.5	39.2
Return on Equity After Income Taxes 48	20.7	35.4	31.9	19.7	44.9	14.5	26.4
Profit Margin (Before Income Tax) 49	5.9	16.2	5.1	6.5	9.7	6.4	5.4
Profit Margin (After Income Tax) 50	4.6	16.2	5.1	5.7	9.5	5.3	3.7

Table I

Corporations with and without Net Income

COATING, ENGRAVING, HEAT TREATING, AND ALLIED ACTIVITIES

MONEY AMOUNTS AND SIZE OF ASSETS IN THOUSANDS OF DOLLARS

Item Description for Accounting Period 7/08 Through 6/09	Total	Zero Assets	Under 500	500 to 1,000	1,000 to 5,000	5,000 to 10,000	10,000 to 25,000	25,000 to 50,000	50,000 to 100,000	100,000 to 250,000	250,000 to 500,000	500,000 to 2,500,000	2,500,000 and over
Number of Enterprises **1**	4253	257	2545	493	754	103	60	17	9	9	0	5	0
Revenues ($ in Thousands)													
Net Sales **2**	19510588	9085	1884065	720135	3772509	1355532	1386982	847425	835457	1515455	0	7183943	0
Interest **3**	109922	0	1651	318	813	3796	1611	949	2023	8339	0	90422	0
Rents **4**	18866	0	6957	935	2415	837	0	673	0	3635	0	3414	0
Royalties **5**	72601	0	0	0	0	0	0	0	61	15873	0	56666	0
Other Portfolio Income **6**	422472	0	82203	62	875	8831	154	849	915	12624	0	315958	0
Other Receipts **7**	151522	0	9213	25	9333	15759	12855	2392	14103	13671	0	74172	0
Total Receipts **8**	20285971	9085	1984089	721475	3785945	1384755	1401602	852288	852559	1569597	0	7724575	0
Average Total Receipts **9**	4770	35	780	1463	5021	13444	23360	50135	94729	174400	•	1544915	•
Operating Costs/Operating Income (%)													
Cost of Operations **10**	65.1	•	39.2	41.6	57.3	69.6	67.0	76.0	67.6	72.9	•	73.9	•
Salaries and Wages **11**	6.9	•	15.1	6.3	6.4	6.4	7.0	6.5	5.9	6.3	•	5.6	•
Taxes Paid **12**	1.6	1.0	3.8	1.9	2.2	0.9	1.4	1.0	1.6	1.4	•	1.1	•
Interest Paid **13**	3.6	•	1.5	0.5	1.1	2.0	1.3	1.4	1.6	3.9	•	7.0	•
Depreciation **14**	3.1	6.5	2.3	2.0	2.9	3.4	3.9	4.1	4.0	6.1	•	2.4	•
Amortization and Depletion **15**	0.7	•	0.0	•	0.0	0.0	0.1	0.2	0.4	1.8	•	1.4	•
Pensions and Other Deferred Comp. **16**	0.6	•	0.1	1.3	0.7	0.7	0.9	0.3	0.8	0.5	•	0.4	•
Employee Benefits **17**	2.0	•	2.7	1.2	2.6	0.6	2.3	2.6	1.0	1.4	•	1.9	•
Advertising **18**	0.6	•	0.3	0.4	0.2	0.0	0.2	0.1	0.3	0.1	•	1.2	•
Other Expenses **19**	11.8	81.0	26.1	28.1	12.6	7.2	7.4	4.8	7.5	5.9	•	10.3	•
Officers' Compensation **20**	3.8	•	14.4	4.3	6.7	3.9	4.5	1.3	1.7	2.2	•	0.3	•
Operating Margin **21**	0.2	17.5	•	12.5	7.5	5.4	4.0	1.7	7.7	•	•	•	•
Operating Margin Before Officers' Comp. **22**	4.1	17.5	8.8	16.8	14.1	9.3	8.5	3.0	9.3	•	•	•	•

Selected Average Balance Sheet ($ in Thousands)

Net Receivables 23	•	220239	24851	14328	5307	3074	2071	542	149	44	596	0
Inventories 24	•	265930	24942	8165	4693	1177	434	134	57	5	463	0
Net Property, Plant and Equipment 25	•	199297	51749	26960	14235	5218	2365	677	144	64	764	0
Total Assets 26	•	2041796	163641	70440	33984	14264	7611	2032	589	171	3948	0
Notes and Loans Payable 27	•	1082255	62685	12739	9980	4662	4350	700	141	172	1886	0
All Other Liabilities 28	•	328423	42855	21045	6109	2474	1022	309	101	76	717	0
Net Worth 29	•	63118	58102	36657	17895	7128	2239	1023	348	-77	1344	0

Selected Financial Ratios (Times to 1)

Current Ratio 30	•	1.7	1.6	2.2	1.8	2.1	2.8	2.1	3.3	1.1	1.8	•
Quick Ratio 31	•	0.8	0.9	1.7	1.1	1.6	2.3	1.7	2.5	1.1	1.1	•
Net Sales to Working Capital 32	•	5.8	8.4	5.7	8.1	5.7	5.4	10.1	5.2	67.1	7.2	•
Coverage Ratio 33	•	1.3	1.3	6.9	2.7	4.9	4.8	8.3	27.0	0.8	2.2	•
Total Asset Turnover 34	•	0.7	1.0	1.3	1.5	1.6	1.7	2.5	2.5	4.3	1.2	•
Inventory Turnover 35	•	4.0	4.9	7.7	8.1	13.2	21.1	21.4	10.6	52.8	6.5	•
Receivables Turnover 36	•	5.6	6.6	6.1	7.8	7.7	6.9	9.9	•	•	7.2	•
Total Liabilities to Net Worth 37	•	2.2	1.8	0.9	0.9	1.0	2.4	1.0	0.7	•	1.9	•
Current Assets to Working Capital 38	•	2.4	2.7	1.8	2.3	1.9	1.5	1.9	1.4	8.0	2.2	•
Current Liabilities to Working Capital 39	•	1.4	1.7	0.8	1.3	0.9	0.5	0.9	0.4	7.0	1.2	•
Working Capital to Net Sales 40	•	0.2	0.1	0.2	0.1	0.2	0.2	0.1	0.2	0.0	0.1	•
Inventory to Working Capital 41	•	1.0	1.1	0.3	0.7	0.4	0.2	0.3	0.2	0.5	0.7	•
Total Receipts to Cash Flow 42	•	10.8	27.2	6.4	18.9	9.5	7.8	6.1	2.8	5.9	8.1	1.6
Cost of Goods to Cash Flow 43	•	8.0	19.8	4.3	14.4	6.4	5.4	3.5	1.1	2.3	5.3	•
Cash Flow to Total Debt 44	•	0.1	0.1	0.4	0.2	0.3	0.3	0.8	2.2	0.5	0.2	•

Selected Financial Factors (in Percentages)

Debt Ratio 45	•	69.1	64.5	48.0	47.3	50.0	70.6	49.6	41.0	145.0	65.9	•
Return on Total Assets 46	•	6.5	5.3	15.0	5.5	10.3	16.5	22.0	32.6	5.3	9.2	•
Return on Equity Before Income Taxes 47	•	5.1	3.6	24.6	6.6	16.3	44.3	38.3	53.2	2.3	14.7	•
Return on Equity After Income Taxes 48	•	3.9	•	21.6	5.2	15.8	41.6	38.2	47.4	3.6	12.8	•
Profit Margin (Before Income Tax) 49	•	2.3	1.2	9.7	2.4	5.0	7.5	7.8	12.7	•	4.3	17.5
Profit Margin (After Income Tax) 50	•	1.7	•	8.5	1.9	4.9	7.1	7.8	11.3	•	3.8	17.5

119

Table II

Corporations with Net Income

COATING, ENGRAVING, HEAT TREATING, AND ALLIED ACTIVITIES

MONEY AMOUNTS AND SIZE OF ASSETS IN THOUSANDS OF DOLLARS

Item Description for Accounting Period 7/08 Through 6/09	Total	Zero Assets	Under 500	500 to 1,000	1,000 to 5,000	5,000 to 10,000	10,000 to 25,000	25,000 to 50,000	50,000 to 100,000	100,000 to 250,000	250,000 to 500,000	500,000 to 2,500,000	2,500,000 and over
Number of Enterprises 1	2828	257	1417	465	539	83	41	9	•	4	0	•	0
Revenues ($ in Thousands)													
Net Sales 2	16223869	9085	1080023	699333	2892395	1219476	1189027	408965	•	787385	0	•	0
Interest 3	98553	0	235	318	218	3481	66	693	•	2653	0	•	0
Rents 4	15699	0	6957	935	1254	66	0	0	•	3072	0	•	0
Royalties 5	71849	0	0	0	0	0	0	0	•	15183	0	•	0
Other Portfolio Income 6	348909	0	19824	62	39	8803	154	657	•	2965	0	•	0
Other Receipts 7	130297	0	1217	24	8596	12493	10380	1384	•	7943	0	•	0
Total Receipts 8	16899176	9085	1108256	700672	2902502	1244319	1199627	411699	•	819201	0	•	0
Average Total Receipts 9	5976	35	782	1507	5385	14992	29259	45744	•	204800	•	•	•
Operating Costs/Operating Income (%)													
Cost of Operations 10	64.7	•	30.0	40.9	58.0	70.2	64.9	67.8	•	59.0	•	•	•
Salaries and Wages 11	6.3	•	15.2	6.2	4.7	6.4	7.1	5.9	•	7.0	•	•	•
Taxes Paid 12	1.4	1.0	2.1	1.8	1.9	0.8	1.4	1.4	•	1.8	•	•	•
Interest Paid 13	3.6	•	0.6	0.3	0.7	2.0	1.0	1.2	•	1.7	•	•	•
Depreciation 14	2.7	0.5	3.1	2.0	2.3	3.0	3.5	4.6	•	3.3	•	•	•
Amortization and Depletion 15	0.7	•	•	•	0.0	0.0	0.0	0.4	•	1.7	•	•	•
Pensions and Other Deferred Comp. 16	0.6	•	0.1	1.3	0.7	0.8	1.0	0.6	•	0.3	•	•	•
Employee Benefits 17	1.8	•	1.3	1.3	2.1	0.6	2.1	3.3	•	1.9	•	•	•
Advertising 18	0.7	•	0.4	0.4	0.2	0.0	0.2	0.1	•	0.1	•	•	•
Other Expenses 19	11.2	81.0	19.9	27.8	12.2	6.0	6.5	4.2	•	11.0	•	•	•
Officers' Compensation 20	3.7	•	19.8	4.2	6.2	3.6	4.7	1.4	•	4.1	•	•	•
Operating Margin 21	2.7	17.5	7.5	13.8	11.1	6.6	7.3	9.2	•	8.2	•	•	•
Operating Margin Before Officers' Comp. 22	6.4	17.5	27.3	18.0	17.3	10.2	12.1	10.6	•	12.3	•	•	•

Selected Average Balance Sheet ($ in Thousands)

Net Receivables 23	765	0	33	150	571	2459	3707	5025	•	•	•	29069
Inventories 24	381	0	9	41	145	288	1352	1984	•	•	•	43081
Net Property, Plant and Equipment 25	867	0	79	141	696	2165	5771	15277	•	•	•	33972
Total Assets 26	5178	0	205	582	2257	7806	14185	35060	•	•	•	143840
Notes and Loans Payable 27	2385	0	64	88	478	4786	4231	7675	•	•	•	49702
All Other Liabilities 28	846	0	28	105	296	1051	2939	5261	•	•	•	37146
Net Worth 29	1947	0	113	389	1484	1969	7015	22124	•	•	•	56993

Selected Financial Ratios (Times to 1)

Current Ratio 30	1.9	•	3.3	3.3	2.4	2.9	2.0	2.4	•	•	•	2.1
Quick Ratio 31	1.2	•	3.3	2.7	2.0	2.4	1.5	1.9	•	•	•	1.2
Net Sales to Working Capital 32	6.5	•	11.7	5.3	9.0	5.5	7.6	5.4	•	•	•	5.9
Coverage Ratio 33	2.9	•	19.0	41.6	17.6	5.3	8.9	9.4	•	•	•	8.2
Total Asset Turnover 34	1.1	•	3.7	2.6	2.4	1.9	2.0	1.3	•	•	•	1.4
Inventory Turnover 35	9.7	•	25.1	15.0	21.4	35.8	13.9	15.5	•	•	•	2.7
Receivables Turnover 36	9.4	•	18.7	13.7	9.8	6.7	7.7	•	•	•	•	3.4
Total Liabilities to Net Worth 37	1.7	•	0.8	0.5	0.5	3.0	1.0	0.6	•	•	•	1.5
Current Assets to Working Capital 38	2.1	•	1.4	1.4	1.7	1.5	2.0	1.7	•	•	•	1.9
Current Liabilities to Working Capital 39	1.1	•	0.4	0.4	0.7	0.5	1.0	0.7	•	•	•	0.9
Working Capital to Net Sales 40	0.2	•	0.1	0.2	0.1	0.2	0.1	0.2	•	•	•	0.2
Inventory to Working Capital 41	0.6	•	0.0	0.2	0.2	0.1	0.4	0.2	•	•	•	0.7
Total Receipts to Cash Flow 42	6.9	1.6	4.9	2.7	5.1	7.6	7.6	8.4	•	•	•	5.3
Cost of Goods to Cash Flow 43	4.5	•	1.5	1.1	3.0	5.3	5.0	5.7	•	•	•	3.1
Cash Flow to Total Debt 44	0.3	•	1.7	2.9	1.4	0.3	0.5	0.4	•	•	•	0.4

Selected Financial Factors (in Percentages)

Debt Ratio 45	62.4	•	44.9	33.2	34.3	74.8	50.5	36.9	•	•	•	60.4
Return on Total Assets 46	11.8	•	39.8	37.1	28.9	20.1	18.9	14.1	•	•	•	19.1
Return on Equity Before Income Taxes 47	20.5	•	68.5	54.3	41.5	64.6	34.0	20.0	•	•	•	42.3
Return on Equity After Income Taxes 48	18.6	•	66.9	48.8	41.3	60.7	33.2	17.8	•	•	•	29.2
Profit Margin (Before Income Tax) 49	7.0	17.5	10.1	14.0	11.5	8.7	8.2	9.7	•	•	•	12.2
Profit Margin (After Income Tax) 50	6.3	17.5	9.9	12.6	11.4	8.1	8.0	8.7	•	•	•	8.5

Table I

Corporations with and without Net Income

OTHER FABRICATED METAL PRODUCT

MONEY AMOUNTS AND SIZE OF ASSETS IN THOUSANDS OF DOLLARS

Item Description for Accounting Period 7/08 Through 6/09	Total	Zero Assets	Under 500	500 to 1,000	1,000 to 5,000	5,000 to 10,000	10,000 to 25,000	25,000 to 50,000	50,000 to 100,000	100,000 to 250,000	250,000 to 500,000	500,000 to 2,500,000	2,500,000 and over
Number of Enterprises **1**	17228	1367	9988	1487	3076	635	349	152	75	49	19	20	9
Revenues ($ in Thousands)													
Net Sales **2**	140508059	1182569	5427086	3173938	18307262	8282071	10631929	9039748	8433092	8313734	7217133	18420723	42078772
Interest **3**	1326645	11549	3561	1730	8339	4252	6099	4402	7476	20730	16829	110148	1131529
Rents **4**	46356	11	14	1416	1152	150	2567	1348	3925	800	254	6363	28357
Royalties **5**	603286	3642	11634	0	0	441	1189	789	8734	14018	12836	39266	510737
Other Portfolio Income **6**	1305986	82040	12391	7328	33168	3842	20216	25582	19598	13907	66846	18673	1002394
Other Receipts **7**	1561316	102635	85549	17698	113094	52022	81202	39676	66706	94431	73040	179137	656129
Total Receipts **8**	145351648	1382446	5540235	3202110	18463015	8342778	10743202	9111545	8539531	8457620	7386938	18774310	45407918
Average Total Receipts **9**	8437	1011	555	2153	6002	13138	30783	59944	113860	172604	388786	938716	5045324
Operating Costs/Operating Income (%)													
Cost of Operations **10**	69.7	70.9	58.9	67.5	71.4	68.2	71.7	69.4	73.5	68.3	71.6	71.9	68.5
Salaries and Wages **11**	6.5	8.9	8.5	5.7	5.4	7.1	6.2	6.7	6.7	7.4	7.5	5.5	6.6
Taxes Paid **12**	1.3	0.9	2.7	1.3	1.8	1.2	1.0	1.1	0.9	1.2	1.2	1.3	1.3
Interest Paid **13**	2.5	1.4	0.9	1.2	0.8	0.8	0.8	1.2	1.0	2.1	1.5	3.0	5.0
Depreciation **14**	2.4	2.1	1.6	2.2	2.1	2.7	2.9	2.8	2.7	2.9	2.4	2.4	2.2
Amortization and Depletion **15**	1.0	0.3	0.1	0.2	0.0	0.0	0.2	0.3	0.3	0.6	0.4	0.9	2.7
Pensions and Other Deferred Comp. **16**	0.9	0.1	0.2	0.5	0.4	0.3	0.6	0.4	0.6	0.8	1.3	1.4	1.2
Employee Benefits **17**	1.9	1.1	1.4	1.0	1.6	1.5	1.3	1.5	1.9	1.5	2.1	1.6	2.6
Advertising **18**	0.9	0.1	0.3	0.3	0.5	0.4	0.3	0.7	0.5	0.8	1.2	0.3	1.9
Other Expenses **19**	8.8	9.8	15.3	12.3	9.3	7.4	6.6	8.1	7.1	6.8	8.1	7.2	9.9
Officers' Compensation **20**	2.0	3.7	8.1	5.2	4.7	4.0	2.2	2.1	1.5	1.3	1.2	0.6	0.2
Operating Margin **21**	2.2	0.7	2.0	2.5	2.1	6.4	6.1	5.8	3.3	6.0	1.7	3.9	•
Operating Margin Before Officers' Comp. **22**	4.1	4.4	10.1	7.8	6.7	10.3	8.4	8.0	4.8	7.4	2.9	4.5	•

Selected Average Balance Sheet ($ in Thousands)

Net Receivables 23	1114	0	39	207	682	1743	3922	7326	14837	22001	54391	117269	804920
Inventories 24	1091	0	23	194	582	2293	4616	9637	16602	28659	65673	166742	524230
Net Property, Plant and Equipment 25	1157	0	36	169	526	1656	4037	8546	17553	28589	69532	137051	796899
Total Assets 26	15110	0	159	722	2376	7020	16678	34322	69933	144312	320531	1027469	21767247
Notes and Loans Payable 27	6366	0	113	491	725	1660	4113	9752	16232	43151	80692	430482	9793630
All Other Liabilities 28	2261	0	42	178	656	1508	3944	10680	17340	44612	87985	288102	2374502
Net Worth 29	6484	0	4	53	995	3852	8621	13889	36360	56550	151854	308884	9559115

Selected Financial Ratios (Times to 1)

Current Ratio 30	1.7	•	1.7	1.8	2.1	2.6	2.4	1.9	2.0	1.8	2.6	1.8	1.3
Quick Ratio 31	0.9	•	1.1	1.2	1.3	1.4	1.2	1.0	1.0	0.9	1.2	0.8	0.6
Net Sales to Working Capital 32	6.2	•	13.8	11.0	6.7	4.4	4.7	5.8	5.4	5.3	3.9	5.2	8.6
Coverage Ratio 33	3.4	14.6	5.3	3.9	4.5	10.3	10.2	6.7	5.7	4.8	3.9	2.9	2.5
Total Asset Turnover 34	0.5	•	3.4	3.0	2.5	1.9	1.8	1.7	1.6	1.2	1.2	0.9	0.2
Inventory Turnover 35	5.2	•	13.9	7.4	7.3	3.9	4.7	4.3	5.0	4.0	4.1	4.0	6.1
Receivables Turnover 36	6.5	•	16.1	9.4	8.4	7.3	7.7	7.2	7.8	7.5	6.2	6.7	4.7
Total Liabilities to Net Worth 37	1.3	•	38.9	12.7	1.4	0.8	0.9	1.5	0.9	1.6	1.1	2.3	1.3
Current Assets to Working Capital 38	2.4	•	2.4	2.3	1.9	1.6	1.7	2.1	2.0	2.2	1.6	2.2	3.9
Current Liabilities to Working Capital 39	1.4	•	1.4	1.3	0.9	0.6	0.7	1.1	1.0	1.2	0.6	1.2	2.9
Working Capital to Net Sales 40	0.2	•	0.1	0.1	0.1	0.2	0.2	0.2	0.2	0.2	0.3	0.2	0.1
Inventory to Working Capital 41	0.8	•	0.6	0.7	0.7	0.7	0.8	0.9	0.8	0.9	0.6	1.0	1.0
Total Receipts to Cash Flow 42	8.1	4.0	7.2	8.2	10.9	7.8	8.4	7.8	10.1	7.8	10.4	8.6	7.1
Cost of Goods to Cash Flow 43	5.7	2.8	4.2	5.5	7.8	5.3	6.0	5.4	7.4	5.3	7.4	6.2	4.8
Cash Flow to Total Debt 44	0.1	•	0.5	0.4	0.4	0.5	0.5	0.4	0.3	0.2	0.2	0.1	0.1

Selected Financial Factors (in Percentages)

Debt Ratio 45	57.1	•	97.5	92.7	58.1	45.1	48.3	59.5	48.0	60.8	52.6	69.9	55.9
Return on Total Assets 46	4.6	•	17.3	13.7	9.2	14.6	14.5	13.5	8.9	11.8	6.7	8.0	2.6
Return on Equity Before Income Taxes 47	7.6	•	562.3	139.0	17.2	24.1	25.3	28.3	14.1	23.8	10.4	17.5	3.5
Return on Equity After Income Taxes 48	5.8	•	548.9	137.0	15.6	22.2	23.5	25.8	11.6	19.5	6.4	12.0	2.3
Profit Margin (Before Income Tax) 49	6.1	18.5	4.1	3.4	2.9	7.1	7.2	6.6	4.6	7.9	4.2	5.9	7.3
Profit Margin (After Income Tax) 50	4.6	13.1	4.0	3.4	2.6	6.6	6.7	6.0	3.7	6.5	2.6	4.0	4.7

Table II

Corporations with Net Income

OTHER FABRICATED METAL PRODUCT

MONEY AMOUNTS AND SIZE OF ASSETS IN THOUSANDS OF DOLLARS

Item Description for Accounting Period 7/08 Through 6/09	Total	Zero Assets	Under 500	500 to 1,000	1,000 to 5,000	5,000 to 10,000	10,000 to 25,000	25,000 to 50,000	50,000 to 100,000	100,000 to 250,000	250,000 to 500,000	500,000 to 2,500,000	2,500,000 and over
Number of Enterprises 1	10853	404	6294	1047	2007	561	284	120	58	38	13	16	9
Revenues ($ in Thousands)													
Net Sales 2	121621868	999100	3972314	2383278	13583730	7336855	9202489	7536036	6739397	7297318	4426006	16066573	42078772
Interest 3	1289289	11506	990	1573	5929	3597	3224	1956	6040	14914	15953	92079	1131529
Rents 4	39729	11	4	1376	25	150	2567	1348	3802	369	234	1487	28357
Royalties 5	582499	3642	0	0	0	441	789	195	8055	6818	12555	39266	510737
Other Portfolio Income 6	1230787	82040	75	1466	16169	2068	12740	21491	15754	6425	51689	18475	1002394
Other Receipts 7	1465374	108618	69163	16528	90984	39565	68307	35682	60282	89463	66384	164269	656129
Total Receipts 8	126229546	1204917	4042546	2404221	13696837	7382676	9290116	7596708	6833330	7415307	4572821	16382149	45407918
Average Total Receipts 9	11631	2982	642	2296	6825	13160	32712	63306	117816	195140	351755	1023884	5045324
Operating Costs/Operating Income (%)													
Cost of Operations 10	68.9	68.3	60.2	64.4	71.3	67.7	70.8	67.8	72.3	67.1	66.5	70.5	68.5
Salaries and Wages 11	6.3	9.5	6.0	5.6	5.1	6.6	5.9	6.8	6.6	7.1	8.0	5.8	6.6
Taxes Paid 12	1.3	0.9	2.0	1.3	1.5	1.1	1.0	1.1	0.9	1.3	1.4	1.4	1.3
Interest Paid 13	2.6	1.3	0.6	0.9	0.6	0.7	0.7	1.0	0.7	1.7	0.6	3.2	5.0
Depreciation 14	2.2	1.7	1.6	2.4	1.8	2.3	2.6	2.6	2.6	2.9	2.6	1.9	2.2
Amortization and Depletion 15	1.1	0.4	0.0	0.0	0.1	0.0	0.1	0.2	0.2	0.5	0.4	0.9	2.7
Pensions and Other Deferred Comp. 16	0.9	0.2	0.2	0.6	0.4	0.3	0.5	0.4	0.6	0.7	1.7	1.3	1.2
Employee Benefits 17	1.9	1.1	1.3	0.9	1.3	1.3	1.2	1.5	1.8	1.3	2.3	1.7	2.6
Advertising 18	0.9	0.1	0.3	0.2	0.5	0.3	0.3	0.7	0.5	0.8	0.5	0.3	1.9
Other Expenses 19	8.4	9.9	12.1	13.4	7.6	7.1	6.1	7.3	6.6	6.9	8.8	7.3	9.9
Officers' Compensation 20	1.8	3.8	8.3	5.3	4.4	4.0	2.3	2.4	1.5	1.4	1.8	0.6	0.2
Operating Margin 21	3.6	2.8	7.4	5.0	5.5	8.4	8.5	8.2	5.8	8.3	5.5	5.1	•
Operating Margin Before Officers' Comp. 22	5.5	6.6	15.7	10.3	9.9	12.4	10.7	10.6	7.3	9.7	7.3	5.7	•

Selected Average Balance Sheet ($ in Thousands)

Net Receivables 23	1549	33	230	781	1768	4103	7441	15336	24664	53483	123305	804920
Inventories 24	1512	21	167	649	2346	4808	10255	18155	33461	69460	183966	524230
Net Property, Plant and Equipment 25	1551	45	173	484	1494	3739	8165	16470	31602	78726	135108	796899
Total Assets 26	22721	140	712	2570	6951	16545	34101	70442	146676	318367	1088203	21767247
Notes and Loans Payable 27	9566	77	339	545	1354	3997	8976	12314	38392	46741	499211	9793630
All Other Liabilities 28	3186	34	165	649	1498	3710	7601	17809	43761	84168	307285	2374502
Net Worth 29	9970	29	208	1376	4099	8838	17525	40318	64524	187458	281708	9559115

Selected Financial Ratios (Times to 1)

Current Ratio 30	1.8	•	1.5	1.9	2.5	2.8	2.6	2.4	2.3	2.0	2.9	1.8	1.3
Quick Ratio 31	0.9	•	1.0	1.3	1.6	1.5	1.3	1.2	1.2	1.0	1.4	0.8	0.6
Net Sales to Working Capital 32	5.9	•	23.3	9.8	5.8	4.2	4.6	4.8	4.7	4.8	3.0	5.2	8.6
Coverage Ratio 33	4.1	19.6	15.8	7.6	12.1	13.5	14.3	10.1	11.3	6.7	17.0	3.2	2.5
Total Asset Turnover 34	0.5	•	4.5	3.2	2.6	1.9	2.0	1.8	1.6	1.3	1.1	0.9	0.2
Inventory Turnover 35	5.1	•	18.4	8.8	7.4	3.8	4.8	4.2	4.6	3.8	3.3	3.8	6.1
Receivables Turnover 36	6.3	•	19.3	11.7	8.5	7.2	7.8	7.3	7.4	7.5	5.3	6.8	4.7
Total Liabilities to Net Worth 37	1.3	•	3.8	2.4	0.9	0.7	0.9	0.9	0.7	1.3	0.7	2.9	1.3
Current Assets to Working Capital 38	2.3	•	3.0	2.1	1.7	1.6	1.6	1.7	1.8	2.0	1.5	2.2	3.9
Current Liabilities to Working Capital 39	1.3	•	2.0	1.1	0.7	0.6	0.6	0.7	0.8	1.0	0.5	1.2	2.9
Working Capital to Net Sales 40	0.2	•	0.0	0.1	0.2	0.2	0.2	0.2	0.2	0.2	0.3	0.2	0.1
Inventory to Working Capital 41	0.8	•	0.8	0.6	0.6	0.6	0.7	0.8	0.7	0.8	0.5	1.0	1.0
Total Receipts to Cash Flow 42	7.2	3.2	6.1	6.4	8.9	6.9	7.2	6.9	8.1	6.7	6.7	7.7	7.1
Cost of Goods to Cash Flow 43	5.0	2.2	3.7	4.1	6.4	4.7	5.1	4.7	5.8	4.5	4.4	5.5	4.8
Cash Flow to Total Debt 44	0.1	•	0.9	0.7	0.6	0.7	0.6	0.6	0.5	0.3	0.4	0.2	0.1

Selected Financial Factors (in Percentages)

Debt Ratio 45	56.1	•	79.3	70.8	46.5	41.0	46.6	48.6	42.8	56.0	41.1	74.1	55.9
Return on Total Assets 46	5.2	•	43.9	21.7	18.2	18.3	19.8	18.4	12.9	15.4	10.3	9.4	2.6
Return on Equity Before Income Taxes 47	8.9	•	198.4	64.6	31.2	28.7	34.4	32.3	20.6	29.7	16.4	25.2	3.5
Return on Equity After Income Taxes 48	7.1	•	195.5	63.8	29.4	26.7	32.3	29.8	17.7	24.9	11.7	17.6	2.3
Profit Margin (Before Income Tax) 49	7.9	24.5	9.1	5.9	6.3	9.0	9.4	9.0	7.2	10.0	9.1	7.1	7.3
Profit Margin (After Income Tax) 50	6.3	18.1	9.0	5.8	6.0	8.4	8.8	8.3	6.1	8.4	6.5	4.9	4.7

Table I

Corporations with and without Net Income

AGRICULTURE, CONSTRUCTION, AND MINING MACHINERY

MONEY AMOUNTS AND SIZE OF ASSETS IN THOUSANDS OF DOLLARS

Item Description for Accounting Period 7/08 Through 6/09		Total	Zero Assets	Under 500	500 to 1,000	1,000 to 5,000	5,000 to 10,000	10,000 to 25,000	25,000 to 50,000	50,000 to 100,000	100,000 to 250,000	250,000 to 500,000	500,000 to 2,500,000	2,500,000 and over
Number of Enterprises	1	3950	50	2219	341	950	148	102	42	39	23	13	12	11
Revenues ($ in Thousands)														
Net Sales	2	144198653	2236839	946032	887052	4240370	1703356	2870617	2617264	3745519	4905759	5128052	14126523	100791270
Interest	3	4044867	5012	86	539	1857	1280	6557	2166	5384	7104	24536	91051	3899296
Rents	4	1143744	0	0	529	7	3	2143	546	770	646	1281	75283	1362535
Royalties	5	1356962	0	0	0	0	0	541	0	230	1144	5238	85942	1263868
Other Portfolio Income	6	2167647	5758	674	25175	18898	5548	17316	766	12704	11660	2718	117070	1949362
Other Receipts	7	4092899	134830	1172	58732	15735	63685	22653	6167	28888	45699	15670	956912	2742753
Total Receipts	8	157304772	2382439	947964	972027	4276867	1773872	2919827	2626909	3793495	4972012	5177495	15452781	112009084
Average Total Receipts	9	39824	47649	427	2851	4502	11986	28626	62545	97269	216174	398269	1287732	10182644
Operating Costs/Operating Income (%)														
Cost of Operations	10	71.8	91.1	56.5	68.5	73.0	67.0	72.7	70.5	71.1	72.7	68.3	73.0	71.5
Salaries and Wages	11	6.1	1.5	8.0	11.1	6.8	8.7	7.6	7.1	6.4	6.8	7.8	6.6	5.9
Taxes Paid	12	0.8	0.4	2.0	0.6	1.2	1.2	1.3	1.0	1.2	0.9	1.0	0.9	0.7
Interest Paid	13	3.1	1.1	0.9	1.5	1.2	1.0	1.7	0.8	1.3	1.4	1.8	2.8	3.7
Depreciation	14	3.2	2.4	0.2	1.0	2.3	2.8	2.2	1.5	2.3	2.4	2.5	2.8	3.6
Amortization and Depletion	15	0.4	0.2	0.0	0.0	0.0	0.1	0.2	0.2	0.4	0.3	0.8	0.3	0.4
Pensions and Other Deferred Comp.	16	1.1	0.1	0.4	0.2	0.3	0.2	0.5	0.5	1.0	0.6	0.5	1.4	1.3
Employee Benefits	17	1.8	0.3	0.8	0.8	1.1	1.7	2.1	1.9	1.7	0.9	1.0	0.9	2.2
Advertising	18	0.4	1.4	0.3	0.7	0.6	2.0	1.1	0.6	0.7	0.6	0.6	0.7	0.2
Other Expenses	19	11.6	10.2	12.5	12.6	7.2	10.8	7.1	7.8	7.6	8.2	10.5	7.4	13.0
Officers' Compensation	20	0.6	0.1	7.8	1.7	2.8	3.8	2.2	1.8	1.2	0.8	0.6	0.4	0.3
Operating Margin	21	•	•	10.6	3.6	3.6	0.6	1.3	6.2	5.0	4.4	4.6	2.8	•
Operating Margin Before Officers' Comp.	22	•	•	18.4	2.9	6.4	4.5	3.5	8.0	6.3	5.2	5.2	3.3	•

Selected Average Balance Sheet ($ in Thousands)

Net Receivables 23	13324	0	20	99	353	1123	3997	8450	14871	27746	82553	191092	4245911
Inventories 24	5086	0	31	111	626	2748	5410	13177	17249	44205	81990	220000	1134714
Net Property, Plant and Equipment 25	5331	0	8	78	478	1319	2927	4947	11123	24267	57364	191628	1438201
Total Assets 26	48691	0	104	659	2156	6488	15805	35148	67362	155950	378195	1360251	14392927
Notes and Loans Payable 27	21511	0	67	119	729	1354	5573	8462	15629	31475	89166	393288	6886298
All Other Liabilities 28	14122	0	48	131	533	1498	4639	11944	21125	48878	125816	424530	4113500
Net Worth 29	13058	0	-11	408	894	3636	5594	14743	30607	75597	163212	542433	3393128

Selected Financial Ratios (Times to 1)

Current Ratio 30	1.5	•	1.6	2.7	2.1	1.8	1.9	2.0	2.0	1.9	2.2	1.6	1.4
Quick Ratio 31	1.0	•	0.5	1.6	1.1	0.6	0.9	0.8	1.0	0.7	1.2	0.7	1.0
Net Sales to Working Capital 32	5.0	•	14.0	10.7	7.0	6.2	5.2	4.7	4.3	4.5	3.4	6.5	4.8
Coverage Ratio 33	4.4	•	12.6	8.0	4.7	5.6	2.8	8.9	5.9	4.9	4.3	5.6	4.3
Total Asset Turnover 34	0.7	•	4.1	4.0	2.1	1.8	1.8	1.8	1.4	1.4	1.0	0.9	0.6
Inventory Turnover 35	5.2	•	7.9	16.0	5.2	2.8	3.8	3.3	4.0	3.5	3.3	3.9	5.8
Receivables Turnover 36	2.8	•	22.3	45.0	10.4	10.5	7.4	7.3	7.2	8.1	4.6	5.5	2.2
Total Liabilities to Net Worth 37	2.7	•	•	0.6	1.4	0.8	1.8	1.4	1.2	1.1	1.3	1.5	3.2
Current Assets to Working Capital 38	3.1	•	2.7	1.6	1.9	2.2	2.1	2.0	2.0	2.1	1.8	2.6	3.4
Current Liabilities to Working Capital 39	2.1	•	1.7	0.6	0.9	1.2	1.1	1.0	1.0	1.1	0.8	1.6	2.4
Working Capital to Net Sales 40	0.2	•	0.1	0.1	0.1	0.2	0.2	0.2	0.2	0.2	0.3	0.2	0.2
Inventory to Working Capital 41	0.7	•	1.4	0.6	0.8	1.3	1.0	1.0	0.9	1.1	0.6	1.1	0.7
Total Receipts to Cash Flow 42	5.7	16.1	5.4	5.6	10.2	7.5	12.4	7.7	8.0	8.3	7.4	5.5	5.2
Cost of Goods to Cash Flow 43	4.1	14.6	3.1	3.8	7.4	5.0	9.0	5.4	5.7	6.0	5.1	4.0	3.7
Cash Flow to Total Debt 44	0.2	•	0.7	1.9	0.3	0.5	0.2	0.4	0.3	0.3	0.2	0.3	0.2

Selected Financial Factors (in Percentages)

Debt Ratio 45	73.2	•	110.5	38.0	58.5	43.9	64.6	58.1	54.6	51.5	56.8	60.1	76.4
Return on Total Assets 46	10.4	•	47.8	48.5	11.6	10.3	8.2	13.1	10.8	9.7	7.9	13.6	10.0
Return on Equity Before Income Taxes 47	29.9	•	•	68.4	22.1	15.1	14.9	27.7	19.7	16.0	14.1	27.9	32.5
Return on Equity After Income Taxes 48	19.9	•	•	68.0	20.6	13.1	9.5	22.9	15.7	12.0	9.1	18.1	21.2
Profit Margin (Before Income Tax) 49	10.7	•	10.7	10.7	4.4	4.8	3.0	6.6	6.3	5.7	5.8	12.9	12.0
Profit Margin (After Income Tax) 50	7.1	•	10.7	10.7	4.1	4.1	1.9	5.4	5.0	4.3	3.8	8.3	7.9

Table II

Corporations with Net Income

AGRICULTURE, CONSTRUCTION, AND MINING MACHINERY

MONEY AMOUNTS AND SIZE OF ASSETS IN THOUSANDS OF DOLLARS

Item Description for Accounting Period 7/08 Through 6/09	Total	Zero Assets	Under 500	500 to 1,000	1,000 to 5,000	5,000 to 10,000	10,000 to 25,000	25,000 to 50,000	50,000 to 100,000	100,000 to 250,000	250,000 to 500,000	500,000 to 2,500,000	2,500,000 and over
Number of Enterprises **1**	3283	0	2132	226	690	56	65	•	29	16	9	•	11
Revenues ($ in Thousands)													
Net Sales **2**	134285592	0	884899	547175	3418517	696203	1821959	•	2962420	3756429	3330489	•	100791270
Interest **3**	4019088	0	80	345	1640	1258	5823	•	5269	4104	21003	•	3899296
Rents **4**	1442753	0	0	0	0	3	2082	•	754	269	1281	•	1362535
Royalties **5**	1356928	0	0	0	0	0	541	•	230	1109	5238	•	1263868
Other Portfolio Income **6**	2150171	0	0	23567	18507	2667	16221	•	9919	9879	2718	•	1949362
Other Receipts **7**	3898745	0	0	50302	8640	56268	18632	•	17367	28622	14518	•	2742753
Total Receipts **8**	147153277	0	884979	621389	3447304	756399	1865258	•	2995959	3800412	3375247	•	112009084
Average Total Receipts **9**	44823	•	415	2750	4996	13507	28696	•	103309	237526	375027	•	10182644
Operating Costs/Operating Income (%)													
Cost of Operations **10**	71.4	•	54.9	68.8	74.9	68.6	70.1	•	70.3	71.9	64.2	•	71.5
Salaries and Wages **11**	6.0	•	8.5	11.8	5.1	5.7	6.5	•	5.6	5.9	8.1	•	5.9
Taxes Paid **12**	0.7	•	2.1	0.3	1.0	1.2	1.3	•	1.2	0.9	1.0	•	0.7
Interest Paid **13**	3.2	•	0.6	2.0	0.8	0.8	1.1	•	0.8	1.1	2.1	•	3.7
Depreciation **14**	3.2	•	0.1	1.1	1.4	3.8	1.9	•	2.2	2.2	3.1	•	3.6
Amortization and Depletion **15**	0.4	•	0.0	0.0	0.1	0.2	0.0	•	0.1	0.3	1.1	•	0.4
Pensions and Other Deferred Comp. **16**	1.2	•	0.5	0.1	0.2	0.4	0.6	•	0.9	0.4	0.4	•	1.3
Employee Benefits **17**	1.9	•	0.8	1.0	0.5	1.0	2.3	•	1.4	0.8	1.4	•	2.2
Advertising **18**	0.3	•	0.1	0.5	0.6	0.2	0.8	•	0.6	0.6	0.6	•	0.2
Other Expenses **19**	11.6	•	12.5	7.9	5.7	8.5	7.6	•	7.3	7.9	9.4	•	13.0
Officers' Compensation **20**	0.5	•	8.3	1.5	2.8	3.1	1.8	•	1.4	0.8	0.8	•	0.3
Operating Margin **21**	•	•	11.6	5.2	6.9	6.5	6.1	•	8.2	7.3	7.9	•	•
Operating Margin Before Officers' Comp. **22**	0.1	•	19.9	6.6	9.7	9.6	7.9	•	9.6	8.1	8.7	•	•

Selected Average Balance Sheet ($ in Thousands)

Net Receivables **23**	15639	20	66	405	1236	4454	14690	29269	68950	4245911
Inventories **24**	5631	28	66	611	3281	5841	17169	43514	65125	1299684
Net Property, Plant and Equipment **25**	5921	4	49	374	1485	2660	10894	25122	67076	1438201
Total Assets **26**	56526	97	654	2066	6697	15457	66298	154164	372506	14392927
Notes and Loans Payable **27**	25194	54	86	412	1880	4456	11101	24972	101316	6886298
All Other Liabilities **28**	16250	49	84	510	945	3982	19435	49617	81000	4113500
Net Worth **29**	15082	-6	485	1144	3871	7019	35762	79575	190190	3393128

Selected Financial Ratios (Times to 1)

Current Ratio **30**	1.5	1.5	4.1	2.2	1.9	2.0	2.1	1.8	2.6	1.4
Quick Ratio **31**	1.0	0.5	2.9	1.5	0.8	1.1	1.1	0.8	1.4	1.0
Net Sales to Working Capital **32**	5.0	15.8	9.4	8.0	6.7	4.8	4.3	5.4	3.3	4.8
Coverage Ratio **33**	4.7	19.5	10.3	10.4	20.6	8.5	12.4	8.7	5.6	4.3
Total Asset Turnover **34**	0.7	4.3	3.7	2.4	1.9	1.8	1.5	1.5	1.0	0.6
Inventory Turnover **35**	5.2	8.0	25.4	6.1	2.6	3.4	4.2	3.9	3.6	5.0
Receivables Turnover **36**	2.7	23.4	60.0	9.3	8.6	5.9	7.3	8.5		3.2
Total Liabilities to Net Worth **37**	2.7		0.3	0.8	0.7	1.2	0.9	0.9	1.0	3.2
Current Assets to Working Capital **38**	3.2	3.0	1.3	1.8	2.1	2.0	1.9	2.2	1.6	3.4
Current Liabilities to Working Capital **39**	2.2	2.0	0.3	0.8	1.1	1.0	0.9	1.2	0.6	2.4
Working Capital to Net Sales **40**	0.2	0.1	0.1	0.1	0.1	0.2	0.2	0.2	0.3	0.2
Inventory to Working Capital **41**	0.7	1.5	0.3	0.6	1.1	0.8	0.8	1.1	0.6	0.7
Total Receipts to Cash Flow **42**	5.4	5.3	3.9	8.3	4.7	7.0	6.5	6.9	6.2	5.2
Cost of Goods to Cash Flow **43**	3.8	2.9	2.7	6.2	3.2	4.9	4.6	5.0	4.0	3.7
Cash Flow to Total Debt **44**	0.2	0.8	3.7	0.7	0.9	0.5	0.5	0.5	0.3	0.2

Selected Financial Factors (in Percentages)

Debt Ratio **45**	73.3	106.6	25.9	44.6	42.2	54.6	46.1	48.4	48.9	76.4
Return on Total Assets **46**	10.8	51.9	76.9	20.5	29.4	17.5	15.5	14.5	11.6	10.0
Return on Equity Before Income Taxes **47**	32.0		93.6	33.5	48.5	33.9	26.3	24.9	18.7	32.5
Return on Equity After Income Taxes **48**	21.6		93.1	31.9	43.6	27.1	21.8	19.4	12.6	21.2
Profit Margin (Before Income Tax) **49**	11.8	11.6	18.7	7.7	15.1	8.5	9.2	8.5	9.6	12.0
Profit Margin (After Income Tax) **50**	8.0	11.5	18.6	7.4	13.6	6.8	7.6	6.6	6.5	7.9

Table I

Corporations with and without Net Income

INDUSTRIAL MACHINERY

MONEY AMOUNTS AND SIZE OF ASSETS IN THOUSANDS OF DOLLARS

Item Description for Accounting Period 7/08 Through 6/09		Total	Zero Assets	Under 500	500 to 1,000	1,000 to 5,000	5,000 to 10,000	10,000 to 25,000	25,000 to 50,000	50,000 to 100,000	100,000 to 250,000	250,000 to 500,000	500,000 to 2,500,000	2,500,000 and over
Number of Enterprises	1	3013	486	780	372	544	489	155	74	46	37	14	11	5
Revenues ($ in Thousands)														
Net Sales	2	55346297	156051	347836	788712	3160380	5211191	3508729	3490732	3687337	5306258	5546307	8617872	15524894
Interest	3	330081	427	0	240	3035	2810	5988	10415	14495	42019	23334	53008	174311
Rents	4	63097	0	1694	0	522	138	2933	6090	2087	16511	21603	3953	7567
Royalties	5	189762	10	0	0	23	307	6258	583	7741	5122	12633	60454	96631
Other Portfolio Income	6	668198	456	0	0	4018	16186	6626	14551	8340	171939	39627	108545	297911
Other Receipts	7	529475	25199	1205	2869	78807	24823	9143	18804	64856	48410	41549	114068	99738
Total Receipts	8	57126910	182143	350735	791821	3246785	5255455	3539677	3541175	3784856	5590259	5685053	8957900	16201052
Average Total Receipts	9	18960	375	450	2129	5968	10747	22837	47854	82279	151088	406075	814355	3240210
Operating Costs/Operating Income (%)														
Cost of Operations	10	67.5	73.1	70.0	65.6	70.3	67.9	73.2	71.2	70.0	68.0	73.6	64.6	63.4
Salaries and Wages	11	9.7	6.5	5.1	5.2	6.2	9.6	8.6	8.2	9.1	10.2	6.3	9.9	12.3
Taxes Paid	12	1.1	1.2	1.0	3.5	1.0	1.3	1.2	1.3	1.4	1.2	0.9	1.3	0.8
Interest Paid	13	2.0	1.2	0.4	0.8	1.1	1.1	1.0	0.9	1.2	2.1	3.2	2.9	2.3
Depreciation	14	2.4	2.9	1.7	2.7	2.3	1.9	1.3	3.2	2.1	2.7	2.1	2.8	2.4
Amortization and Depletion	15	0.8	0.6	•	0.0	0.3	0.1	0.6	0.2	1.0	1.1	1.1	0.9	1.0
Pensions and Other Deferred Comp.	16	0.8	0.5	•	0.1	0.4	0.7	0.5	0.5	0.9	0.5	2.2	0.9	0.6
Employee Benefits	17	2.0	2.4	5.5	2.0	2.5	2.6	2.0	1.7	2.0	2.0	2.1	1.6	2.0
Advertising	18	0.5	0.3	0.7	1.2	0.4	0.4	0.7	0.5	0.5	0.4	0.4	0.4	0.5
Other Expenses	19	8.6	21.5	16.5	9.6	8.4	7.6	7.7	8.8	9.7	10.0	6.4	9.5	8.3
Officers' Compensation	20	1.8	9.2	6.0	6.0	5.1	3.4	3.1	3.5	1.4	1.3	0.8	1.0	0.7
Operating Margin	21	2.8	•	•	3.3	1.9	3.4	0.2	•	0.8	0.4	0.9	4.2	5.8
Operating Margin Before Officers' Comp.	22	4.6	•	•	9.3	6.9	6.7	3.3	3.4	2.2	1.7	1.7	5.2	6.4

Selected Average Balance Sheet ($ in Thousands)

Net Receivables 23	4678	0	42	281	878	1364	3536	7171	14504	26610	86887	210024	1311182
Inventories 24	2659	0	58	147	758	1683	3901	9166	11432	20339	68737	103012	403681
Net Property, Plant and Equipment 25	2286	0	37	64	520	1388	1620	7719	11623	19625	42118	70170	485519
Total Assets 26	21385	0	133	708	2610	6938	15359	34842	70752	142491	363741	1033304	5861584
Notes and Loans Payable 27	5150	0	8	358	989	2587	3241	9106	15340	35952	148117	314795	965480
All Other Liabilities 28	6515	0	58	205	729	1860	6797	9846	22501	36024	170944	343030	1576918
Net Worth 29	9719	0	66	145	892	2491	5322	15891	32911	70515	44681	375479	3319187

Selected Financial Ratios (Times to 1)

Current Ratio 30	1.6	•	2.1	3.2	2.1	1.5	1.9	1.8	2.2	1.4	1.2		1.7
Quick Ratio 31	1.0	•	1.0	2.0	1.0	0.8	1.0	1.1	1.3	0.8	0.7		1.2
Net Sales to Working Capital 32	4.6	•	9.6	4.6	6.0	4.6	5.5	4.3	4.2	3.6	6.5	13.3	3.1
Coverage Ratio 33	4.4	•	•	5.3	5.1	4.8	2.1	2.5	3.8	3.6	2.4	4.3	6.2
Total Asset Turnover 34	0.9	•	3.4	3.0	2.2	1.5	1.4	1.1	1.0	1.1	0.8		0.5
Inventory Turnover 35	4.7	•	5.4	9.4	5.4	4.3	4.2	3.7	4.9	4.8	4.2	4.9	4.9
Receivables Turnover 36	4.3	•	7.4	10.9	6.0	8.6	6.7	6.0	5.1	4.9	5.3	3.3	3.0
Total Liabilities to Net Worth 37	1.2	•	1.0	3.9	1.9	1.8	1.2	1.1	1.1	1.0	7.1	1.8	0.8
Current Assets to Working Capital 38	2.6	•	1.9	1.5	2.0	1.9	2.9	2.1	2.3	1.9	3.2	6.8	2.4
Current Liabilities to Working Capital 39	1.6	•	0.9	0.5	1.0	0.9	1.9	1.1	1.3	0.9	2.2	5.8	1.4
Working Capital to Net Sales 40	0.2	•	0.1	0.2	0.2	0.2	0.2	0.2	0.2	0.3	0.2	0.1	0.3
Inventory to Working Capital 41	0.7	•	0.9	0.5	0.8	0.7	1.1	0.8	0.6	0.5	1.3	1.7	0.5
Total Receipts to Cash Flow 42	8.1	7.8	22.5	9.3	9.8	10.4	13.9	11.9	8.7	9.3	11.6	6.2	6.3
Cost of Goods to Cash Flow 43	5.5	5.7	15.8	6.1	6.9	7.1	10.2	8.5	6.1	6.3	8.5	4.0	4.0
Cash Flow to Total Debt 44	0.2	•	0.3	0.4	0.3	0.2	0.2	0.2	0.2	0.2	0.1	0.2	0.2

Selected Financial Factors (in Percentages)

Debt Ratio 45	54.5	•	50.0	79.6	65.8	64.1	65.4	54.4	53.5	50.5	87.7	63.7	43.4
Return on Total Assets 46	7.6	•	•	13.5	12.7	8.2	3.1	3.1	7.9	5.3	8.5	9.6	7.5
Return on Equity Before Income Taxes 47	13.0	•	•	53.7	29.9	18.0	4.7	4.1	8.4	11.6	40.7	20.2	11.1
Return on Equity After Income Taxes 48	9.0	•	•	46.1	28.1	16.6	2.7	2.2	4.8	7.8	27.5	14.6	7.2
Profit Margin (Before Income Tax) 49	6.9	•	•	3.7	4.6	4.2	1.1	1.4	3.4	5.7	4.6	9.7	11.9
Profit Margin (After Income Tax) 50	4.7	•	•	3.1	4.3	3.9	0.6	0.7	2.0	3.8	3.1	7.0	7.7

Table II
Corporations with Net Income

INDUSTRIAL MACHINERY

MONEY AMOUNTS AND SIZE OF ASSETS IN THOUSANDS OF DOLLARS

Item Description for Accounting Period 7/08 Through 6/09	Total	Zero Assets	Under 500	500 to 1,000	1,000 to 5,000	5,000 to 10,000	10,000 to 25,000	25,000 to 50,000	50,000 to 100,000	100,000 to 250,000	250,000 to 500,000	500,000 to 2,500,000	2,500,000 and over
Number of Enterprises **1**	1195	•	0	295	354	305	102	36	34	27	•	•	•
Revenues ($ in Thousands)													
Net Sales **2**	43364852	•	0	590131	2493466	3912103	2366415	1914801	2754980	4090102	•	•	•
Interest **3**	286486	•	0	205	1852	2461	4060	7810	9779	28402	•	•	•
Rents **4**	49123	•	0	0	0	94	2933	4221	183	16085	•	•	•
Royalties **5**	145361	•	0	0	0	307	4676	583	314	4878	•	•	•
Other Portfolio Income **6**	628152	•	0	0	3326	15119	5214	3320	7456	167763	•	•	•
Other Receipts **7**	243150	•	0	2830	25566	22423	3268	15143	34650	44539	•	•	•
Total Receipts **8**	44717124	•	0	593166	2524210	3952507	2386566	1945878	2807362	4351769	•	•	•
Average Total Receipts **9**	37420	•	•	2011	7131	12959	23398	54052	82569	161177	•	•	•
Operating Costs/Operating Income (%):													
Cost of Operations **10**	65.3	•	•	60.9	69.5	65.1	72.0	66.9	70.4	67.7	•	•	•
Salaries and Wages **11**	9.8	•	•	3.9	5.6	10.2	7.0	7.8	7.9	10.2	•	•	•
Taxes Paid **12**	1.0	•	•	1.6	0.8	1.3	1.0	1.2	1.2	1.0	•	•	•
Interest Paid **13**	1.9	•	•	1.1	0.4	0.7	0.5	0.7	1.1	1.7	•	•	•
Depreciation **14**	1.9	•	•	3.5	1.9	1.4	1.2	1.8	1.8	2.4	•	•	•
Amortization and Depletion **15**	0.7	•	•	•	0.3	0.1	0.2	0.2	0.8	0.8	•	•	•
Pensions and Other Deferred Comp. **16**	0.8	•	•	0.2	0.3	0.9	0.5	0.7	0.9	0.6	•	•	•
Employee Benefits **17**	1.9	•	•	2.7	1.6	2.2	1.8	1.7	1.7	1.9	•	•	•
Advertising **18**	0.4	•	•	1.5	0.1	0.5	0.7	0.7	0.4	0.4	•	•	•
Other Expenses **19**	8.0	•	•	10.7	6.7	7.2	6.3	7.6	6.2	8.7	•	•	•
Officers' Compensation **20**	1.7	•	•	7.1	4.4	3.3	3.2	5.2	1.4	1.4	•	•	•
Operating Margin **21**	6.4	•	•	6.8	8.3	7.1	5.5	5.6	6.2	3.2	•	•	•
Operating Margin Before Officers' Comp. **22**	8.2	•	•	13.9	12.6	10.4	8.8	10.8	7.6	4.6	•	•	•

Selected Average Balance Sheet ($ in Thousands)

Net Receivables 23	8525	267	1090	1079	3659	7358	15070	27363
Inventories 24	5298	138	681	1888	3498	10795	12080	20634
Net Property, Plant and Equipment 25	3878	50	488	1422	1569	6560	11068	19649
Total Assets 26	41656	708	2732	7259	15241	34222	71156	142031
Notes and Loans Payable 27	9297	404	485	1572	1937	6800	11930	29688
All Other Liabilities 28	11611	5	843	1890	6717	11035	22142	41175
Net Worth 29	20747	299	1404	3797	6587	16387	37084	71168

Selected Financial Ratios (Times to 1)

Current Ratio 30	1.7	13.0	3.2	2.1	1.7	1.9	1.8	2.0
Quick Ratio 31	1.1	8.3	2.1	1.1	1.0	1.2	1.1	1.2
Net Sales to Working Capital 32	4.6	3.3	5.0	5.6	5.1	4.8	4.5	4.2
Coverage Ratio 33	6.5	7.5	23.0	12.2	14.2	10.8	8.5	6.7
Total Asset Turnover 34	0.9	2.8	2.6	1.8	1.5	1.6	1.1	1.1
Inventory Turnover 35	4.5	8.8	7.2	4.4	4.8	3.3	4.7	5.0
Receivables Turnover 36	4.2	12.6	6.4	9.6	6.7	5.3	4.8	5.3
Total Liabilities to Net Worth 37	1.0	1.4	0.9	0.9	1.3	1.1	0.9	1.0
Current Assets to Working Capital 38	2.4	1.1	1.5	1.9	2.5	2.1	2.3	2.0
Current Liabilities to Working Capital 39	1.4	0.1	0.5	0.9	1.5	1.1	1.3	1.0
Working Capital to Net Sales 40	0.2	0.3	0.2	0.2	0.2	0.2	0.2	0.2
Inventory to Working Capital 41	0.7	0.3	0.4	0.9	0.7	0.7	0.7	0.5
Total Receipts to Cash Flow 42	6.5	6.6	7.4	7.7	9.0	7.4	7.8	7.8
Cost of Goods to Cash Flow 43	4.3	4.0	5.1	5.0	6.5	4.9	5.5	5.3
Cash Flow to Total Debt 44	0.3	0.7	0.7	0.5	0.3	0.4	0.3	0.3

Selected Financial Factors (in Percentages)

Debt Ratio 45	50.2	57.7	48.6	47.7	56.8	52.1	47.9	49.9
Return on Total Assets 46	10.9	23.8	25.6	15.6	10.4	12.3	10.5	12.0
Return on Equity Before Income Taxes 47	18.5	48.8	47.6	27.4	22.5	23.4	17.7	20.3
Return on Equity After Income Taxes 48	13.7	44.1	45.8	25.9	20.0	19.6	13.5	15.2
Profit Margin (Before Income Tax) 49	10.6	7.3	9.5	8.1	6.4	7.2	8.1	9.6
Profit Margin (After Income Tax) 50	7.8	6.6	9.1	7.7	5.7	6.0	6.2	7.1

Table I
Corporations with and without Net Income

COMMERCIAL AND SERVICE INDUSTRY MACHINERY

MONEY AMOUNTS AND SIZE OF ASSETS IN THOUSANDS OF DOLLARS

Item Description for Accounting Period 7/08 Through 6/09		Total	Zero Assets	Under 500	500 to 1,000	1,000 to 5,000	5,000 to 10,000	10,000 to 25,000	25,000 to 50,000	50,000 to 100,000	100,000 to 250,000	250,000 to 500,000	500,000 to 2,500,000	2,500,000 and over
Number of Enterprises	1	1715	44	849	236	320	121	71	31	12	10	8	9	3
Revenues ($ in Thousands)														
Net Sales	2	38891072	538268	465229	491334	1756469	1225578	1656519	1272571	1152536	2067337	2320994	7225022	18719216
Interest	3	955249	21876	202	140	631	1884	1694	4170	1802	6490	9190	59085	848084
Rents	4	194960	15	1260	0	503	12	179	1026	1533	3488	347	133440	53158
Royalties	5	899051	1	0	0	0	0	18	0	776	83	10290	37310	850574
Other Portfolio Income	6	248859	0	712	0	1049	1942	18353	2260	1562	14881	11461	19645	176995
Other Receipts	7	1596851	12624	2237	63	14704	12293	5200	5641	10702	27577	5920	57638	1442248
Total Receipts	8	42786042	572784	469640	491537	1773356	1241709	1681963	1285668	1168911	2119856	2358202	7532140	22090275
Average Total Receipts	9	24948	13018	553	2083	5542	10262	23690	41473	97409	211986	294775	836904	7363425
Operating Costs/Operating Income (%)														
Cost of Operations	10	60.7	64.8	56.8	62.1	69.7	60.2	69.4	68.9	62.6	68.3	60.9	59.0	58.1
Salaries and Wages	11	13.8	14.6	11.1	2.6	10.8	14.4	9.6	10.2	11.8	12.2	12.3	13.4	15.7
Taxes Paid	12	1.9	4.2	1.7	1.8	1.5	1.5	1.5	1.4	1.3	1.7	1.5	1.6	2.3
Interest Paid	13	3.9	5.4	0.4	3.1	1.4	1.2	1.9	1.1	0.7	1.3	2.0	4.1	5.4
Depreciation	14	5.9	1.9	0.4	0.2	0.7	2.4	2.5	2.3	2.2	3.5	2.8	5.2	8.8
Amortization and Depletion	15	0.9	0.1	•	0.2	0.0	0.2	1.0	0.4	0.4	0.3	2.1	0.8	1.0
Pensions and Other Deferred Comp.	16	1.8	0.6	1.0	0.0	0.9	0.5	0.3	0.6	1.2	0.5	0.9	0.6	3.0
Employee Benefits	17	2.5	4.0	4.2	2.1	2.7	3.8	1.3	2.2	3.1	2.0	1.8	2.7	2.4
Advertising	18	1.6	0.9	0.3	0.6	0.6	2.4	0.9	0.6	2.2	0.9	0.7	0.7	2.3
Other Expenses	19	16.1	14.2	8.4	20.5	12.1	12.5	11.7	10.2	12.3	11.6	12.9	14.9	19.2
Officers' Compensation	20	1.1	0.5	4.2	5.8	3.6	2.7	1.5	2.3	1.6	1.2	1.0	0.8	0.6
Operating Margin	21	•	•	11.5	1.0	•	•	•	•	0.7	•	1.0	•	•
Operating Margin Before Officers' Comp.	22	•	•	15.7	6.8	0.9	•	•	2.1	2.3	•	1.9	•	•

Selected Average Balance Sheet ($ in Thousands)

Net Receivables 23	6428	0	28	171	499	1455	2604	6561	10627	45565	69489	104129	2720084
Inventories 24	2494	0	66	309	750	1523	4430	10094	16770	38800	42316	93507	442130
Net Property, Plant and Equipment 25	3368	0	21	50	188	1312	2589	5004	1115	29850	40344	119820	1118901
Total Assets 26	32932	0	159	889	2432	5993	14497	35722	70347	150219	347010	903320	13080352
Notes and Loans Payable 27	15143	0	34	997	803	1501	4605	7629	9423	34479	101461	367903	6707826
All Other Liabilities 28	10588	0	8	82	508	2440	4490	15270	24663	50824	129603	312779	4075614
Net Worth 29	7200	0	117	-191	1122	2053	5402	12823	36260	64917	115946	222638	2296912

Selected Financial Ratios (Times to 1)

Current Ratio 30	1.0	•	3.6	4.4	2.2	1.5	1.7	1.4	1.9	1.5	1.3	1.4	0.9
Quick Ratio 31	0.6	•	2.6	1.9	1.1	0.7	0.7	0.6	0.9	0.9	0.8	0.7	0.6
Net Sales to Working Capital 32	77.6	•	6.2	3.9	5.4	7.6	6.2	6.0	4.4	6.1	8.7	9.8	•
Coverage Ratio 33	1.4	0.1	32.2	1.3	•	0.5	1.0	2.1	4.2	0.1	2.3	1.2	1.5
Total Asset Turnover 34	0.7	•	3.4	2.3	2.3	1.7	1.6	1.1	1.4	1.4	0.8	0.9	0.5
Inventory Turnover 35	5.5	•	4.7	4.2	5.1	4.0	3.7	2.8	3.6	3.6	4.2	5.1	8.2
Receivables Turnover 36	3.4	•	7.6	14.8	12.5	8.0	9.0	6.6	6.7	4.4	5.4	5.9	2.2
Total Liabilities to Net Worth 37	3.6	•	0.4	•	1.2	1.9	1.7	1.8	0.9	1.3	2.0	3.1	4.7
Current Assets to Working Capital 38	44.6	•	1.4	1.3	1.9	2.8	2.5	3.8	2.1	2.8	4.1	3.6	•
Current Liabilities to Working Capital 39	43.6	•	0.4	0.3	0.9	1.8	1.5	2.8	1.1	1.8	3.1	2.6	•
Working Capital to Net Sales 40	0.0	•	0.2	0.3	0.2	0.1	0.2	0.2	0.2	0.2	0.1	0.1	•
Inventory to Working Capital 41	8.8	•	0.3	0.6	0.9	1.3	1.2	1.6	1.0	1.0	1.4	1.3	•
Total Receipts to Cash Flow 42	7.8	12.9	4.9	8.0	16.5	10.2	9.8	11.8	8.3	11.6	7.3	8.4	6.7
Cost of Goods to Cash Flow 43	4.7	8.4	2.8	5.0	11.5	6.1	6.8	8.1	5.2	7.9	4.4	5.0	3.9
Cash Flow to Total Debt 44	0.1	•	2.6	0.2	0.3	0.3	0.3	0.2	0.3	0.2	0.2	0.1	0.1

Selected Financial Factors (in Percentages)

Debt Ratio 45	78.1	•	26.6	121.5	53.9	65.8	62.7	64.1	48.5	56.8	66.6	75.4	82.4
Return on Total Assets 46	3.7	•	44.1	9.7	•	1.0	3.0	2.6	3.9	0.3	4.0	4.2	3.8
Return on Equity Before Income Taxes 47	4.7	•	58.3	•	•	•	0.1	3.8	5.8	•	6.9	2.3	6.9
Return on Equity After Income Taxes 48	1.4	•	56.3	•	•	•	•	1.5	4.5	•	4.1	•	3.1
Profit Margin (Before Income Tax) 49	1.5	•	12.4	1.0	•	•	0.0	1.2	2.2	•	2.7	0.6	2.5
Profit Margin (After Income Tax) 50	0.4	•	12.0	1.0	•	•	•	0.5	1.7	•	1.6	•	1.1

Table II

Corporations with Net Income

COMMERCIAL AND SERVICE INDUSTRY MACHINERY

MONEY AMOUNTS AND SIZE OF ASSETS IN THOUSANDS OF DOLLARS

Item Description for Accounting Period 7/08 Through 6/09	Total	Zero Assets	Under 500	500 to 1,000	1,000 to 5,000	5,000 to 10,000	10,000 to 25,000	25,000 to 50,000	50,000 to 100,000	100,000 to 250,000	250,000 to 500,000	500,000 to 2,500,000	2,500,000 and over
Number of Enterprises 1	1360	19	708	236	214	87	50	19	8	5	•	•	0
Revenues ($ in Thousands)													
Net Sales 2	26349309	154743	398467	491334	1594151	1023641	1204353	750674	929340	1225213	•	•	0
Interest 3	606112	147	0	140	171	1209	471	2076	1400	2832	•	•	0
Rents 4	12605	15	0	0	503	12	179	831	1511	3488	•	•	0
Royalties 5	482218	0	0	0	0	0	0	0	475	0	•	•	0
Other Portfolio Income 6	89873	0	2	0	695	1674	255	1861	989	786	•	•	0
Other Receipts 7	1315137	116	20	63	14061	5152	4165	4615	5238	23040	•	•	0
Total Receipts 8	28855254	155021	398489	491537	1609581	1031688	1209423	760057	938953	1255359	•	•	0
Average Total Receipts 9	21217	8159	563	2083	7521	11858	24188	40003	117369	251072	•	•	•
Operating Costs/Operating Income (%)													
Cost of Operations 10	55.4	54.5	54.2	62.1	69.2	61.4	68.3	67.3	60.2	66.5	•	•	•
Salaries and Wages 11	14.9	6.4	12.3	2.6	10.7	13.0	8.1	9.2	11.6	12.7	•	•	•
Taxes Paid 12	2.1	12.3	1.6	1.8	1.3	1.3	1.6	1.3	1.3	2.1	•	•	•
Interest Paid 13	4.3	0.7	0.0	3.1	0.5	1.0	0.9	0.6	0.3	0.3	•	•	•
Depreciation 14	6.3	1.4	0.2	0.2	0.4	1.1	1.3	2.3	2.1	1.9	•	•	•
Amortization and Depletion 15	1.0	•	•	0.2	0.0	0.1	0.3	0.2	0.3	0.4	•	•	•
Pensions and Other Deferred Comp. 16	1.3	0.3	1.1	0.0	1.0	0.5	0.3	0.6	1.4	0.8	•	•	•
Employee Benefits 17	2.7	1.0	4.7	2.1	2.7	3.6	1.4	1.5	3.4	2.3	•	•	•
Advertising 18	1.0	0.7	0.2	0.6	0.5	2.7	0.7	0.4	1.8	1.1	•	•	•
Other Expenses 19	15.6	10.1	6.8	20.5	8.2	10.8	9.0	6.6	10.9	11.4	•	•	•
Officers' Compensation 20	1.2	1.1	3.3	5.8	3.5	2.4	1.1	2.3	1.6	1.3	•	•	•
Operating Margin 21	•	11.5	15.4	1.0	2.1	2.1	7.1	7.7	5.0	•	•	•	•
Operating Margin Before Officers' Comp. 22	•	12.7	18.7	6.8	5.6	4.6	8.2	10.0	6.6	0.4	•	•	•

Selected Average Balance Sheet ($ in Thousands)

Net Receivables 23	6896	0	20	171	633	1526	2839	7120	11918	57753
Inventories 24	2329	0	58	190	922	1727	4972	11625	18415	35338
Net Property, Plant and Equipment 25	2650	0	5	50	181	949	2023	3716	12602	29093
Total Assets 26	30043	0	105	889	2859	5784	13671	33680	78374	153404
Notes and Loans Payable 27	14579	0	4	997	479	892	3506	4518	9546	23768
All Other Liabilities 28	8643	0	4	82	541	2864	3967	16645	24879	49737
Net Worth 29	6822	0	96	-191	1839	2029	6198	12516	43949	79899

Selected Financial Ratios (Times to 1)

Current Ratio 30	1.0	•	12.1	4.4	2.8	1.5	1.7	1.6	2.4	1.8
Quick Ratio 31	0.7	•	8.4	1.9	1.5	0.7	0.7	0.7	1.1	1.1
Net Sales to Working Capital 32	•	•	6.2	3.9	5.0	8.4	5.9	4.0	3.6	5.3
Coverage Ratio 33	2.3	18.7	2799.3	1.3	7.5	4.0	9.0	17.1	18.1	5.9
Total Asset Turnover 34	0.6	•	5.4	2.3	2.6	2.0	1.8	1.2	1.5	1.6
Inventory Turnover 35	4.6	•	5.2	6.8	5.6	4.2	3.3	2.3	3.8	4.6
Receivables Turnover 36	2.5	•	10.3	21.3	12.9	8.1	8.1	•	7.7	•
Total Liabilities to Net Worth 37	3.4	•	0.1	•	0.6	1.9	1.2	1.7	0.8	0.9
Current Assets to Working Capital 38	•	•	1.1	1.3	1.6	2.9	2.4	2.7	1.7	2.3
Current Liabilities to Working Capital 39	•	•	0.1	0.3	0.6	1.9	1.4	1.7	0.7	1.3
Working Capital to Net Sales 40	•	•	0.2	0.3	0.2	0.1	0.2	0.3	0.3	0.2
Inventory to Working Capital 41	•	•	0.3	0.6	0.7	1.3	1.3	1.2	0.8	0.8
Total Receipts to Cash Flow 42	6.2	5.3	4.6	8.0	11.6	8.4	6.5	7.7	6.6	8.6
Cost of Goods to Cash Flow 43	3.4	2.9	2.5	5.0	8.0	5.1	4.4	5.2	4.0	5.7
Cash Flow to Total Debt 44	0.1	•	14.4	0.2	0.6	0.4	0.5	0.2	0.5	0.4

Selected Financial Factors (in Percentages)

Debt Ratio 45	77.3	•	8.1	121.5	35.7	64.9	54.7	62.8	43.9	47.9
Return on Total Assets 46	6.4	•	82.9	9.7	9.1	7.9	14.9	11.1	9.4	2.9
Return on Equity Before Income Taxes 47	15.7	•	90.2	•	12.3	16.9	29.2	28.1	15.8	4.7
Return on Equity After Income Taxes 48	11.3	•	87.3	•	11.7	12.3	27.0	24.3	14.3	3.4
Profit Margin (Before Income Tax) 49	5.5	11.7	15.4	1.0	3.0	2.9	7.5	8.9	6.0	1.5
Profit Margin (After Income Tax) 50	4.0	7.8	14.9	1.0	2.9	2.1	6.9	7.7	5.4	1.1

Table I

Corporations with and without Net Income

VENTILATION, HEATING, A.C. & COMMERCIAL REFRIGERATION EQUIP.

MONEY AMOUNTS AND SIZE OF ASSETS IN THOUSANDS OF DOLLARS

Item Description for Accounting Period 7/08 Through 6/09	Total	Zero Assets	Under 500	500 to 1,000	1,000 to 5,000	5,000 to 10,000	10,000 to 25,000	25,000 to 50,000	50,000 to 100,000	100,000 to 250,000	250,000 to 500,000	500,000 to 2,500,000	2,500,000 and over
Number of Enterprises **1**	871	7	99	314	150	135	65	44	24	19	3	8	3
Revenues ($ in Thousands)													
Net Sales **2**	36288402	2964449	11823	673061	611824	1808177	1865140	2791861	2429232	3748135	1135498	9474639	8774562
Interest **3**	100320	9269	335	542	1656	1504	3422	3125	2608	9966	2528	46008	19357
Rents **4**	14536	0	0	0	52	392	465	283	2	2429	56	10858	0
Royalties **5**	120291	4166	0	108	0	0	1946	4234	3754	3379	297	94383	8025
Other Portfolio Income **6**	230408	2369	0	0	58665	295	3345	12124	3814	23393	255	122300	3847
Other Receipts **7**	405285	24356	932	332	1824	6108	8202	10203	11423	27729	20970	276421	16786
Total Receipts **8**	37159242	3004609	13090	674043	674021	1816476	1882520	2821830	2450833	3815031	1159604	10024609	8822577
Average Total Receipts **9**	42663	429230	132	2147	4493	13455	28962	64132	102118	200791	386535	1253076	2940859
Operating Costs/Operating Income (%)													
Cost of Operations **10**	72.6	75.3	83.8	52.7	64.9	75.6	74.7	65.3	75.5	71.0	73.7	71.8	75.6
Salaries and Wages **11**	7.1	8.4	54.9	8.5	11.3	5.8	8.1	8.7	6.7	7.7	8.2	8.0	4.6
Taxes Paid **12**	0.8	0.2	9.5	1.2	2.1	0.9	1.1	1.1	1.2	0.9	1.3	0.8	0.4
Interest Paid **13**	3.1	1.2	33.5	0.0	0.7	0.7	0.6	0.8	1.3	1.7	1.7	3.6	6.7
Depreciation **14**	1.7	1.9	2.3	0.9	1.8	1.5	1.6	1.5	2.6	2.3	1.9	1.8	1.4
Amortization and Depletion **15**	0.9	0.4	0.8	•	0.2	0.0	0.4	0.2	0.3	0.8	1.5	0.6	2.4
Pensions and Other Deferred Comp. **16**	0.8	0.0	•	1.8	2.9	0.6	0.5	0.6	0.5	1.1	0.1	1.2	0.8
Employee Benefits **17**	1.8	2.2	2.7	0.9	1.8	0.6	1.1	2.1	2.3	1.9	1.1	1.5	2.2
Advertising **18**	0.8	1.2	1.2	0.2	1.3	0.3	0.7	0.6	0.5	0.8	0.7	1.2	0.7
Other Expenses **19**	9.4	8.3	61.0	19.4	15.7	9.9	7.4	9.6	6.8	8.4	9.7	11.5	7.7
Officers' Compensation **20**	1.3	0.4	27.2	6.3	11.2	2.8	2.0	1.2	2.1	0.9	0.3	1.1	0.4
Operating Margin **21**	•	0.4	•	8.1	•	1.2	1.8	8.3	0.2	2.5	•	•	•
Operating Margin Before Officers' Comp. **22**	0.8	0.8	•	14.4	•	4.1	3.8	9.5	2.3	3.4	0.3	•	•

Selected Average Balance Sheet ($ in Thousands)

Item													
Net Receivables 23	6437	0	46	209	564	1967	4578	10421	13925	30912	142145	137742	659955
Inventories 24	4207	0	10	66	630	1506	3752	5231	14714	25365	53436	98032	363606
Net Property, Plant and Equipment 25	4360	0	54	119	250	1403	2837	7373	14001	25443	48976	122875	356502
Total Assets 26	47576	0	363	613	2599	7080	15186	35418	64112	158238	393656	1253993	7186958
Notes and Loans Payable 27	11397	0	310	4	959	1769	3716	7833	22648	46497	134417	481309	1081655
All Other Liabilities 28	24317	0	148	239	1078	1737	4052	13114	15860	59595	165511	491356	4644441
Net Worth 29	11862	0	239	-185	562	3573	7418	14471	25603	52145	93728	281328	1460862

Selected Financial Ratios (Times to 1)

Item													
Current Ratio 30	1.2	•	0.2	3.2	2.1	2.7	1.8	1.8	1.7	1.5	1.4	1.6	0.7
Quick Ratio 31	0.7	•	0.1	2.7	1.3	1.5	1.1	1.2	0.9	0.8	1.1	0.9	0.4
Net Sales to Working Capital 32	16.8	•	•	6.3	3.9	4.7	6.1	5.9	7.2	8.2	5.3	6.7	•
Coverage Ratio 33	1.7	2.5	•	392.3	•	3.6	5.7	12.7	1.8	3.6	2.2	2.0	0.7
Total Asset Turnover 34	0.9	•	0.3	3.5	1.6	1.9	1.9	1.8	1.6	1.2	1.0	0.9	0.4
Inventory Turnover 35	7.2	•	9.7	17.1	4.2	6.7	5.7	7.9	5.2	5.5	5.2	8.7	6.1
Receivables Turnover 36	6.7	•	1.5	12.9	6.4	7.4	6.7	7.1	5.3	7.5	2.8	11.0	4.2
Total Liabilities to Net Worth 37	3.0	•	•	0.3	3.6	1.0	1.0	1.4	1.5	2.0	3.2	3.5	3.9
Current Assets to Working Capital 38	6.0	•	•	1.4	1.9	1.6	2.2	2.2	2.5	3.1	3.3	2.6	•
Current Liabilities to Working Capital 39	5.0	•	•	0.4	0.9	0.6	1.2	1.2	1.5	2.1	2.3	1.6	•
Working Capital to Net Sales 40	0.1	•	0.2	0.2	0.3	0.2	0.2	0.2	0.1	0.1	0.2	0.1	•
Inventory to Working Capital 41	1.8	•	•	0.2	0.5	0.6	0.8	0.5	0.9	1.2	0.7	0.8	•
Total Receipts to Cash Flow 42	10.2	11.1	•	3.9	236.7	9.7	11.5	5.6	15.4	9.0	10.2	7.8	22.2
Cost of Goods to Cash Flow 43	7.4	8.3	•	2.1	153.6	7.3	8.6	3.7	11.6	6.4	7.5	5.6	16.8
Cash Flow to Total Debt 44	0.1	•	3.6	3.6	0.0	0.4	0.3	0.5	0.2	0.2	0.1	0.2	0.0

Selected Financial Factors (in Percentages)

Item													
Debt Ratio 45	75.1	•	150.9	24.9	78.4	49.5	51.2	59.1	60.1	67.0	76.2	77.6	79.7
Return on Total Assets 46	4.6	•	•	28.7	•	4.5	6.1	18.2	3.6	7.9	3.6	6.9	1.9
Return on Equity Before Income Taxes 47	7.6	•	107.2	38.2	•	6.4	10.3	41.0	4.0	17.3	8.2	15.5	•
Return on Equity After Income Taxes 48	4.3	•	107.3	37.5	•	5.1	6.7	32.3	2.9	11.1	1.8	9.8	•
Profit Margin (Before Income Tax) 49	2.2	1.8	•	8.2	•	1.7	2.7	9.3	1.0	4.6	2.0	3.7	•
Profit Margin (After Income Tax) 50	1.2	0.9	•	8.1	•	1.4	1.7	7.4	0.7	2.9	0.5	2.3	•

Table II
Corporations with Net Income

VENTILATION, HEATING, A.C. & COMMERCIAL REFRIGERATION EQUIP.

MONEY AMOUNTS AND SIZE OF ASSETS IN THOUSANDS OF DOLLARS

Item Description for Accounting Period 7/08 Through 6/09	Total	Zero Assets	Under 500	500 to 1,000	1,000 to 5,000	5,000 to 10,000	10,000 to 25,000	25,000 to 50,000	50,000 to 100,000	100,000 to 250,000	250,000 to 500,000	500,000 to 2,500,000	2,500,000 and over
Number of Enterprises **1**	595	•	•	314	49	106	45	41	12	•	0	•	0
Revenues ($ in Thousands)													
Net Sales **2**	24616488	•	•	673061	317229	1657657	1345612	2731522	1401909	•	•	•	•
Interest **3**	58126	•	•	542	684	728	998	2581	1200	•	•	•	•
Rents **4**	14483	•	•	0	0	392	465	283	2	•	•	•	•
Royalties **5**	108126	•	•	108	0	0	1946	4234	0	•	•	•	•
Other Portfolio Income **6**	161266	•	•	0	73	295	2355	11931	862	•	•	•	•
Other Receipts **7**	282664	•	•	332	3	2155	3335	9501	3929	•	•	•	•
Total Receipts **8**	25241153	•	•	674043	317989	1661227	1354711	2760052	1407902	•	•	•	•
Average Total Receipts **9**	42422	•	•	2147	6490	15672	30105	67318	117325	•	•	•	•
Operating Costs/Operating Income (%)													
Cost of Operations **10**	71.0	•	•	52.7	58.1	76.2	70.2	65.3	69.2	•	•	•	•
Salaries and Wages **11**	7.2	•	•	8.5	9.0	5.0	7.2	8.7	7.1	•	•	•	•
Taxes Paid **12**	0.9	•	•	1.2	1.9	0.8	1.0	1.1	1.2	•	•	•	•
Interest Paid **13**	1.5	•	•	0.0	0.2	0.6	0.4	0.7	1.3	•	•	•	•
Depreciation **14**	1.8	•	•	0.9	2.0	1.2	1.4	1.4	2.1	•	•	•	•
Amortization and Depletion **15**	0.5	•	•	•	0.4	0.0	0.5	0.1	0.3	•	•	•	•
Pensions and Other Deferred Comp. **16**	0.9	•	•	1.8	4.8	0.7	0.5	0.6	0.3	•	•	•	•
Employee Benefits **17**	1.5	•	•	0.9	0.2	0.6	1.0	2.1	2.1	•	•	•	•
Advertising **18**	0.8	•	•	0.2	0.2	0.2	0.4	0.5	0.7	•	•	•	•
Other Expenses **19**	9.2	•	•	19.4	13.6	7.2	5.3	9.0	6.5	•	•	•	•
Officers' Compensation **20**	1.5	•	•	6.3	6.8	2.7	2.3	1.1	3.2	•	•	•	•
Operating Margin **21**	3.1	•	•	8.1	2.7	4.9	9.6	9.2	5.8	•	•	•	•
Operating Margin Before Officers' Comp. **22**	4.6	•	•	14.4	9.6	7.6	12.0	10.3	8.9	•	•	•	•

Selected Average Balance Sheet ($ in Thousands)

Net Receivables 23	4741	•	•	209	364	2380	3787	11011	15922
Inventories 24	4416	•	•	79	1131	1484	3855	4652	20004
Net Property, Plant and Equipment 25	3984	•	•	119	426	1378	2991	6862	14478
Total Assets 26	28261	•	•	613	2874	6618	15338	34299	67065
Notes and Loans Payable 27	7624	•	•	4	758	1661	2934	7592	21458
All Other Liabilities 28	9576	•	•	148	1354	1851	3257	13799	14880
Net Worth 29	11061	•	•	461	762	3106	9148	12907	30727

Selected Financial Ratios (Times to 1)

Current Ratio 30	1.8	•	•	3.2	1.5	3.1	2.0	1.8	2.0
Quick Ratio 31	1.1	•	•	2.7	1.2	1.9	1.2	1.2	1.1
Net Sales to Working Capital 32	7.3	•	•	6.3	9.1	4.6	6.4	6.7	5.6
Coverage Ratio 33	5.1	•	•	392.3	14.2	9.8	23.7	15.0	5.6
Total Asset Turnover 34	1.5	•	•	3.5	2.3	2.4	1.9	1.9	1.7
Inventory Turnover 35	6.7	•	•	14.3	3.3	8.0	5.4	9.4	4.0
Receivables Turnover 36	6.6	•	•	•	5.3	7.7	7.0	7.5	4.1
Total Liabilities to Net Worth 37	1.6	•	•	0.3	2.8	1.1	0.7	1.7	1.2
Current Assets to Working Capital 38	2.2	•	•	1.4	3.0	1.5	2.0	2.3	2.0
Current Liabilities to Working Capital 39	1.2	•	•	0.4	2.0	0.5	1.0	1.3	1.0
Working Capital to Net Sales 40	0.1	•	•	0.2	0.1	0.2	0.2	0.2	0.2
Inventory to Working Capital 41	0.7	•	•	0.2	0.5	0.5	0.8	0.6	0.7
Total Receipts to Cash Flow 42	7.5	•	•	3.9	7.9	8.9	7.0	5.5	9.1
Cost of Goods to Cash Flow 43	5.3	•	•	2.1	4.6	6.7	4.9	3.6	6.3
Cash Flow to Total Debt 44	0.3	•	•	3.6	0.4	0.5	0.7	0.6	0.4

Selected Financial Factors (in Percentages)

Debt Ratio 45	60.9	•	•	24.9	73.5	53.1	40.4	62.4	54.2
Return on Total Assets 46	11.0	•	•	28.7	7.2	13.5	20.7	21.3	13.0
Return on Equity Before Income Taxes 47	22.6	•	•	38.2	25.2	25.8	33.3	52.9	23.4
Return on Equity After Income Taxes 48	17.4	•	•	37.5	17.4	23.9	29.1	42.5	21.6
Profit Margin (Before Income Tax) 49	6.0	•	•	8.2	3.0	5.1	10.2	10.2	6.1
Profit Margin (After Income Tax) 50	4.7	•	•	8.1	2.1	4.8	8.9	8.2	5.7

Table I

Corporations with and without Net Income

METALWORKING MACHINERY

MONEY AMOUNTS AND SIZE OF ASSETS IN THOUSANDS OF DOLLARS

Item Description for Accounting Period 7/08 Through 6/09	Total	Zero Assets	Under 500	500 to 1,000	1,000 to 5,000	5,000 to 10,000	10,000 to 25,000	25,000 to 50,000	50,000 to 100,000	100,000 to 250,000	250,000 to 500,000	500,000 to 2,500,000	2,500,000 and over
Number of Enterprises **1**	6782	758	3827	604	1211	173	128	39	21	12	4	5	0
Revenues ($ in Thousands)													
Net Sales **2**	26246888	196823	2083297	723932	5179496	1994826	2649587	1635795	1470646	2731399	1055806	6525281	0
Interest **3**	73163	0	1164	778	8969	1090	1459	2105	4587	11684	3018	38309	0
Rents **4**	14628	0	1185	4116	1168	2723	473	592	155	2605	1056	554	0
Royalties **5**	5587	0	0	0	0	0	259	0	55	3956	0	1317	0
Other Portfolio Income **6**	99406	25257	23289	170	7447	276	14070	3369	3083	11230	1825	9390	0
Other Receipts **7**	261376	-151	11838	12012	50197	10728	38816	17824	14216	32962	381	72554	0
Total Receipts **8**	26701048	221929	2120773	741008	5247277	2009643	2704664	1659685	1492742	2793836	1062086	6647405	0
Average Total Receipts **9**	3937	293	554	1227	4333	11616	21130	42556	71083	232820	265522	1329481	•
Operating Costs/Operating Income (%)													
Cost of Operations **10**	65.2	46.8	33.9	54.9	68.9	69.1	69.4	68.6	69.9	64.4	77.1	67.7	•
Salaries and Wages **11**	7.9	11.6	12.4	13.4	5.7	4.5	6.9	8.2	5.3	7.8	6.5	9.7	•
Taxes Paid **12**	1.6	3.2	4.5	2.9	1.8	1.4	1.4	1.2	1.2	1.3	1.2	0.8	•
Interest Paid **13**	2.1	0.4	2.0	2.3	0.9	1.1	1.1	1.5	1.4	2.1	2.7	4.1	•
Depreciation **14**	3.4	0.5	3.8	3.8	4.1	3.8	4.4	4.0	5.4	2.4	1.2	2.6	•
Amortization and Depletion **15**	0.4	•	0.0	0.1	0.0	0.2	0.2	0.3	0.3	0.4	0.3	1.2	•
Pensions and Other Deferred Comp. **16**	0.6	0.6	0.1	0.3	0.6	0.6	0.5	0.9	1.1	0.9	0.7	0.5	•
Employee Benefits **17**	2.6	2.5	2.1	6.0	1.5	0.5	3.0	2.3	2.2	2.3	1.6	4.4	•
Advertising **18**	0.4	0.2	0.1	0.3	0.2	0.2	0.5	0.7	0.5	0.5	0.3	0.7	•
Other Expenses **19**	11.3	13.1	31.8	13.3	9.7	9.1	8.1	10.7	7.7	10.6	4.5	10.3	•
Officers' Compensation **20**	2.9	17.2	10.0	7.7	4.1	4.3	2.4	1.8	1.3	0.8	0.5	0.3	•
Operating Margin **21**	1.4	4.0	•	•	2.6	5.2	2.1	•	3.7	6.4	3.3	•	•
Operating Margin Before Officers' Comp. **22**	4.3	21.2	9.4	2.8	6.7	9.5	4.5	1.7	5.0	7.3	3.8	•	•

Selected Average Balance Sheet ($ in Thousands)

Net Receivables 23	531	0	36	172	545	1670	3631	6003	11240	37632	42289	171633
Inventories 24	538	0	9	107	550	1186	3020	9936	13419	30006	88819	181653
Net Property, Plant and Equipment 25	636	0	48	249	683	1752	4265	9550	15525	35418	27297	214629
Total Assets 26	3607	0	142	743	2481	6564	15589	36352	67648	175809	363740	2185883
Notes and Loans Payable 27	1240	0	174	418	780	1425	4811	9525	15431	61798	96494	772861
All Other Liabilities 28	906	0	42	160	423	2128	4169	9888	14988	36472	101012	585918
Net Worth 29	1461	0	-73	165	1278	3011	6608	16939	37229	77538	166234	827104

Selected Financial Ratios (Times to 1)

Current Ratio 30	1.4	•	1.2	1.2	2.3	1.6	1.6	1.7	2.3	2.1	2.0	0.8
Quick Ratio 31	0.7	•	1.0	0.8	1.4	1.0	0.8	0.7	1.1	1.1	0.8	0.3
Net Sales to Working Capital 32	9.1	•	44.6	18.2	5.1	7.8	6.0	5.1	3.3	4.6	3.8	•
Coverage Ratio 33	2.8	44.5	1.6	•	5.5	6.5	4.6	1.9	4.7	6.9	2.9	1.1
Total Asset Turnover 34	1.1	•	3.8	1.6	1.7	1.8	1.3	1.2	1.0	1.3	0.7	0.6
Inventory Turnover 35	4.7	•	20.3	6.1	5.4	6.7	4.8	2.9	3.6	4.9	2.3	4.9
Receivables Turnover 36	7.4	•	16.6	6.8	7.1	7.1	6.6	5.2	6.4	6.1	5.1	9.0
Total Liabilities to Net Worth 37	1.5	•	•	3.5	0.9	1.2	1.4	1.1	0.8	1.3	1.2	1.6
Current Assets to Working Capital 38	3.5	•	6.5	6.2	1.8	2.7	2.7	2.4	1.8	1.9	2.0	•
Current Liabilities to Working Capital 39	2.5	•	5.5	5.2	0.8	1.7	1.7	1.4	0.8	0.9	1.0	•
Working Capital to Net Sales 40	0.1	•	0.0	0.1	0.2	0.1	0.2	0.2	0.3	0.2	0.3	•
Inventory to Working Capital 41	1.3	•	0.6	1.4	0.6	0.9	1.0	1.2	0.7	0.8	1.1	•
Total Receipts to Cash Flow 42	8.3	6.7	3.8	18.9	9.7	7.9	10.5	9.9	8.8	5.5	12.9	11.2
Cost of Goods to Cash Flow 43	5.4	3.1	1.3	10.4	6.7	5.5	7.3	6.8	6.2	3.6	9.9	7.6
Cash Flow to Total Debt 44	0.2	•	0.7	0.1	0.4	0.4	0.2	0.2	0.3	0.4	0.1	0.1

Selected Financial Factors (in Percentages)

Debt Ratio 45	59.5	•	151.3	77.8	48.5	54.1	57.6	53.4	45.0	55.9	54.3	62.2
Return on Total Assets 46	6.2	•	12.3	•	8.1	12.2	6.9	3.3	6.8	18.3	5.6	2.7
Return on Equity Before Income Taxes 47	9.9	•	•	•	12.9	22.5	12.8	3.4	9.8	35.4	8.0	0.8
Return on Equity After Income Taxes 48	8.2	•	•	•	12.4	21.5	12.1	2.2	8.0	28.3	4.5	0.2
Profit Margin (Before Income Tax) 49	3.7	16.7	1.3	•	3.8	5.9	4.1	1.4	5.2	12.0	5.0	0.5
Profit Margin (After Income Tax) 50	3.1	12.4	1.2	•	3.7	5.6	3.9	0.9	4.3	9.7	2.8	0.1

Table II

Corporations with Net Income

METALWORKING MACHINERY

MONEY AMOUNTS AND SIZE OF ASSETS IN THOUSANDS OF DOLLARS

Item Description for Accounting Period 7/08 Through 6/09		Total	Zero Assets	Under 500	500 to 1,000	1,000 to 5,000	5,000 to 10,000	10,000 to 25,000	25,000 to 50,000	50,000 to 100,000	100,000 to 250,000	250,000 to 500,000	500,000 to 2,500,000	2,500,000 and over
Number of Enterprises	1	3801	748	1602	351	830	125	88	26	16	•	•	•	0
Revenues ($ in Thousands)														
Net Sales	2	19808845	196319	1037712	487228	4229536	1514550	1843726	1059990	1192734	•	•	•	0
Interest	3	44448	0	481	743	4877	616	1133	1479	3604	•	•	•	0
Rents	4	13029	0	1185	4116	1168	2215	439	592	155	•	•	•	0
Royalties	5	4344	0	0	0	0	0	259	0	53	•	•	•	0
Other Portfolio Income	6	70010	25257	20154	155	4428	190	1489	3046	1283	•	•	•	0
Other Receipts	7	212844	20	9356	3412	47940	7277	18761	10880	9385	•	•	•	0
Total Receipts	8	20153520	221596	1068888	495654	4287949	1524848	1865807	1075987	1207214	•	•	•	0
Average Total Receipts	9	5302	296	667	1412	5166	12199	21202	41384	75451	•	•	•	•
Operating Costs/Operating Income (%)														
Cost of Operations	10	65.1	46.6	36.6	49.8	67.1	67.0	67.1	66.5	66.4	•	•	•	•
Salaries and Wages	11	6.7	11.7	0.5	15.0	5.8	3.6	5.0	7.8	6.2	•	•	•	•
Taxes Paid	12	1.4	3.2	4.6	2.9	1.8	1.4	1.2	1.0	1.2	•	•	•	•
Interest Paid	13	2.1	0.4	2.2	1.1	0.7	0.9	1.0	1.7	1.6	•	•	•	•
Depreciation	14	3.3	0.5	3.9	3.6	3.8	4.2	4.9	4.3	5.5	•	•	•	•
Amortization and Depletion	15	0.4	•	0.0	•	0.0	0.3	0.1	0.2	0.4	•	•	•	•
Pensions and Other Deferred Comp.	16	0.6	0.6	•	0.4	0.7	0.8	0.5	0.7	0.8	•	•	•	•
Employee Benefits	17	2.3	2.5	1.6	5.3	1.1	0.5	3.0	1.9	2.1	•	•	•	•
Advertising	18	0.4	0.2	0.0	0.2	0.2	0.2	0.3	0.8	0.6	•	•	•	•
Other Expenses	19	10.4	13.1	36.5	11.2	9.1	6.8	7.4	10.8	8.1	•	•	•	•
Officers' Compensation	20	2.6	17.2	9.4	7.8	4.0	4.3	2.3	1.9	1.5	•	•	•	•
Operating Margin	21	4.6	4.1	4.7	2.7	5.8	10.0	7.2	2.4	5.6	•	•	•	•
Operating Margin Before Officers' Comp.	22	7.2	21.3	14.1	10.5	9.8	14.3	9.5	4.4	7.0	•	•	•	•

Selected Average Balance Sheet ($ in Thousands)

	•	•	•	•	•	•	•	•	•
Net Receivables 23	701	0	47	179	590	1352	4045	5113	12451
Inventories 24	747	0	14	92	633	1060	3229	10170	14876
Net Property, Plant and Equipment 25	804	0	73	243	755	1916	4706	10030	15492
Total Assets 26	4631	0	211	746	2863	6221	16002	35847	68629
Notes and Loans Payable 27	1545	0	239	285	753	1217	4738	10240	18938
All Other Liabilities 28	1240	0	66	178	481	1420	4270	7385	14717
Net Worth 29	1846	0	-94	284	1629	3583	6995	18221	34974

Selected Financial Ratios (Times to 1)

	•	•	•	•	•	•	•	•	•
Current Ratio 30	1.5	•	1.3	1.6	2.5	2.2	1.5	1.6	2.1
Quick Ratio 31	0.8	•	0.9	1.2	1.5	1.5	0.8	0.6	1.0
Net Sales to Working Capital 32	8.0	45.3	27.4	9.3	4.8	6.1	6.0	6.4	3.7
Coverage Ratio 33	4.4	•	4.5	4.9	11.5	12.6	9.7	3.3	5.2
Total Asset Turnover 34	1.1	•	3.1	1.9	1.8	1.9	1.3	1.1	1.1
Inventory Turnover 35	4.5	•	16.8	7.5	5.4	7.7	4.4	2.7	3.3
Receivables Turnover 36	7.1	•	13.9	7.4	7.7	7.6	5.7	5.2	•
Total Liabilities to Net Worth 37	1.5	•	•	1.6	0.8	0.7	1.3	1.0	1.0
Current Assets to Working Capital 38	3.1	•	4.9	2.6	1.7	1.8	2.9	2.7	1.9
Current Liabilities to Working Capital 39	2.1	•	3.9	1.6	0.7	0.8	1.9	1.7	0.9
Working Capital to Net Sales 40	0.1	•	0.0	0.1	0.2	0.2	0.2	0.2	0.3
Inventory to Working Capital 41	1.1	0.7	0.7	0.5	0.6	0.5	0.9	1.4	0.7
Total Receipts to Cash Flow 42	6.9	6.6	2.8	9.6	7.4	6.7	7.9	8.0	7.6
Cost of Goods to Cash Flow 43	4.5	3.1	1.0	4.8	5.0	4.5	5.3	5.3	5.1
Cash Flow to Total Debt 44	0.3	•	0.8	0.3	0.6	0.7	0.3	0.3	0.3

Selected Financial Factors (in Percentages)

	•	•	•	•	•	•	•	•	•
Debt Ratio 45	60.1	•	144.4	62.0	43.1	42.4	56.3	49.2	49.0
Return on Total Assets 46	10.3	•	30.2	10.4	13.8	22.5	12.2	6.4	9.1
Return on Equity Before Income Taxes 47	20.1	•	•	21.7	22.2	36.0	25.0	8.8	14.4
Return on Equity After Income Taxes 48	17.7	•	•	20.6	21.6	34.7	24.0	7.1	11.9
Profit Margin (Before Income Tax) 49	7.1	16.9	7.7	4.4	7.1	10.6	8.4	3.9	6.7
Profit Margin (After Income Tax) 50	6.3	12.6	7.5	4.2	6.9	10.3	8.0	3.2	5.6

Table I

Corporations with and without Net Income

ENGINE, TURBINE AND POWER TRANSMISSION EQUIPMENT

MONEY AMOUNTS AND SIZE OF ASSETS IN THOUSANDS OF DOLLARS

Item Description for Accounting Period 7/08 Through 6/09	Total	Zero Assets	Under 500	500 to 1,000	1,000 to 5,000	5,000 to 10,000	10,000 to 25,000	25,000 to 50,000	50,000 to 100,000	100,000 to 250,000	250,000 to 500,000	500,000 to 2,500,000	2,500,000 and over
Number of Enterprises **1**	475	0	289	0	60	41	38	12	7	11	7	7	4
Revenues ($ in Thousands)													
Net Sales **2**	32245488	0	4940	0	366056	280698	875589	314961	378327	1872547	2593737	8212800	17345833
Interest **3**	216241	0	1	0	592	1273	1924	928	1648	18046	7585	18350	165895
Rents **4**	9847	0	0	0	0	0	0	0	0	2197	169	1825	5656
Royalties **5**	344188	0	0	0	0	0	0	0	0	463	12792	39252	291680
Other Portfolio Income **6**	320524	0	0	0	0	47	187	9222	281	9215	31303	30377	239892
Other Receipts **7**	445927	0	1	0	12	130	6584	2780	8862	16484	10349	37084	363642
Total Receipts **8**	33582215	0	4942	0	366660	282148	884284	327891	389118	1918952	2655935	8339688	18412598
Average Total Receipts **9**	70699	•	17	•	6111	6882	23271	27324	55588	174450	379419	1191384	4603150
Operating Costs/Operating Income (%)													
Cost of Operations **10**	72.0	•	43.8	•	62.7	66.4	66.1	75.7	70.0	73.2	71.9	78.8	69.1
Salaries and Wages **11**	7.5	•	0.8	•	12.6	3.5	5.9	11.7	11.1	8.0	6.3	5.9	8.2
Taxes Paid **12**	1.2	•	7.3	•	1.9	4.5	1.5	1.6	1.2	1.3	1.2	0.8	1.3
Interest Paid **13**	2.1	•	•	•	0.6	1.0	2.1	2.0	2.8	1.6	1.3	1.2	2.7
Depreciation **14**	2.7	•	0.2	•	0.5	2.3	4.2	7.1	2.7	3.4	2.4	2.2	2.9
Amortization and Depletion **15**	0.7	•	•	•	0.0	0.0	0.4	0.2	1.0	0.3	1.4	0.9	0.6
Pensions and Other Deferred Comp. **16**	1.4	•	•	•	0.1	0.2	0.4	0.3	0.2	0.4	0.5	1.6	1.6
Employee Benefits **17**	2.9	•	1.0	•	0.7	0.7	2.7	3.4	1.4	2.4	1.4	1.6	4.3
Advertising **18**	0.6	•	0.4	•	0.8	0.3	0.3	0.5	0.3	0.4	0.2	0.3	0.8
Other Expenses **19**	11.2	•	42.7	•	12.4	5.8	10.8	11.2	18.1	7.9	9.0	5.4	14.6
Officers' Compensation **20**	0.8	•	1.8	•	3.1	2.7	1.8	1.4	2.2	1.0	1.4	0.4	0.7
Operating Margin **21**	•	•	2.0	•	4.5	12.7	3.8	•	•	0.2	3.1	1.6	•
Operating Margin Before Officers' Comp. **22**	•	•	3.8	•	7.6	15.4	5.6	•	•	1.2	4.5	2.0	•

Selected Average Balance Sheet ($ in Thousands)

Item	1	2	3	4	5	6	7	8	9	10	11	12	13
Net Receivables 23	9765	•	0	•	294	980	2824	3471	10921	31337	91971	194525	501249
Inventories 24	9022	•	2	•	1496	949	3657	9034	17040	29547	29936	170195	515898
Net Property, Plant and Equipment 25	9712	•	0	•	422	3128	4523	8235	7871	34060	45549	135210	623469
Total Assets 26	60132	•	4	•	1993	6015	16212	30121	63652	172712	370821	959326	3890268
Notes and Loans Payable 27	14541	•	6	•	814	1761	5184	6552	17221	42374	101107	200972	951920
All Other Liabilities 28	25670	•	21	•	295	926	5015	8583	12745	58132	216239	385104	1724952
Net Worth 29	19921	•	-22	•	885	3328	6014	14985	33687	72206	53475	373251	1213396

Selected Financial Ratios (Times to 1)

Item	1	2	3	4	5	6	7	8	9	10	11	12	13
Current Ratio 30	1.4	•	0.2	•	2.4	3.0	1.4	1.6	2.5	1.8	1.1	1.5	1.3
Quick Ratio 31	0.7	•	0.2	•	1.5	1.7	0.5	0.7	1.4	1.0	0.7	0.7	0.6
Net Sales to Working Capital 32	10.0	•	•	•	7.5	3.8	7.8	4.0	2.4	4.1	24.2	7.9	14.9
Coverage Ratio 33	1.9	•	•	•	8.8	13.9	3.4	•	2.8	2.8	5.5	3.9	1.1
Total Asset Turnover 34	1.1	•	3.9	•	3.1	1.1	1.4	0.9	0.8	1.0	1.0	1.2	1.1
Inventory Turnover 35	5.4	•	4.8	•	2.6	4.8	4.2	2.2	2.2	4.2	8.9	5.4	5.8
Receivables Turnover 36	6.7	•	38.0	•	5.7	7.9	10.6	6.0	2.8	7.1	4.7	5.8	7.9
Total Liabilities to Net Worth 37	2.0	•	•	•	1.3	0.8	1.7	1.0	0.9	1.4	5.9	1.6	2.2
Current Assets to Working Capital 38	3.8	•	•	•	1.7	1.5	3.3	2.7	1.7	2.2	13.8	3.2	4.6
Current Liabilities to Working Capital 39	2.8	•	•	•	0.7	0.5	2.3	1.7	0.7	1.2	12.8	2.2	3.6
Working Capital to Net Sales 40	0.1	•	•	•	0.1	0.3	0.1	0.3	0.4	0.2	0.0	0.1	0.1
Inventory to Working Capital 41	1.3	•	•	•	0.6	0.6	1.5	1.3	0.6	0.9	1.8	1.2	1.6
Total Receipts to Cash Flow 42	9.5	•	2.3	•	7.3	5.5	9.4	•	13.0	10.8	8.4	13.2	8.4
Cost of Goods to Cash Flow 43	6.8	•	1.0	•	4.6	3.7	6.2	•	9.1	7.9	6.0	10.4	5.8
Cash Flow to Total Debt 44	0.2	•	0.3	•	0.8	0.5	0.2	•	0.1	0.2	0.1	0.2	0.2

Selected Financial Factors (in Percentages)

Item	1	2	3	4	5	6	7	8	9	10	11	12	13
Debt Ratio 45	66.9	•	592.4	•	55.6	44.7	62.9	50.2	47.1	58.2	85.6	61.1	68.8
Return on Total Assets 46	4.4	•	7.9	•	16.2	16.2	10.0	•	•	4.3	6.9	5.9	3.4
Return on Equity Before Income Taxes 47	6.2	•	•	•	32.3	27.2	19.1	•	•	6.7	39.4	11.2	1.3
Return on Equity After Income Taxes 48	3.1	•	•	•	28.2	17.7	17.2	•	•	4.3	25.2	7.4	•
Profit Margin (Before Income Tax) 49	1.8	•	2.0	•	4.7	13.2	5.0	•	2.8	5.4	5.7	3.6	0.4
Profit Margin (After Income Tax) 50	0.9	•	2.0	•	4.1	8.6	4.5	•	1.8	4.5	3.6	2.3	•

Table II

Corporations with Net Income

ENGINE, TURBINE AND POWER TRANSMISSION EQUIPMENT

MONEY AMOUNTS AND SIZE OF ASSETS IN THOUSANDS OF DOLLARS

Item Description for Accounting Period 7/08 Through 6/09		Total	Zero Assets	Under 500	500 to 1,000	1,000 to 5,000	5,000 to 10,000	10,000 to 25,000	25,000 to 50,000	50,000 to 100,000	100,000 to 250,000	250,000 to 500,000	500,000 to 2,500,000	2,500,000 and over
Number of Enterprises	1	416	0	•	0	39	30	30	•	4	8	•	•	0
Revenues ($ in Thousands)														
Net Sales	2	23322629	0	•	0	134020	280698	702693	•	269954	1541409	•	•	0
Interest	3	151847	0	•	0	497	1273	418	•	973	5147	•	•	0
Rents	4	7120	0	•	0	0	0	0	•	0	1932	•	•	0
Royalties	5	299940	0	•	0	0	0	0	•	0	463	•	•	0
Other Portfolio Income	6	288891	0	•	0	0	47	56	•	96	7743	•	•	0
Other Receipts	7	293268	0	•	0	0	130	6289	•	0	6158	•	•	0
Total Receipts	8	24363695	0	•	0	134517	282148	709456	•	271023	1562852	•	•	0
Average Total Receipts	9	58567	•	•	•	3449	9405	23649	•	67756	195356	•	•	•
Operating Costs/Operating Income (%)														
Cost of Operations	10	73.7	•	•	•	42.5	66.4	61.0	•	70.6	73.9	•	•	•
Salaries and Wages	11	5.2	•	•	•	15.5	3.4	6.2	•	4.1	7.8	•	•	•
Taxes Paid	12	1.1	•	•	•	2.0	4.5	1.7	•	0.7	1.1	•	•	•
Interest Paid	13	2.2	•	•	•	0.1	1.0	1.7	•	3.1	0.6	•	•	•
Depreciation	14	2.5	•	•	•	0.3	2.3	5.0	•	1.5	3.2	•	•	•
Amortization and Depletion	15	0.6	•	•	•	0.0	0.0	0.0	•	0.2	0.1	•	•	•
Pensions and Other Deferred Comp.	16	1.5	•	•	•	0.2	0.2	0.5	•	0.2	0.4	•	•	•
Employee Benefits	17	2.0	•	•	•	1.6	0.7	3.1	•	1.0	1.9	•	•	•
Advertising	18	0.2	•	•	•	1.3	0.3	0.4	•	0.1	0.5	•	•	•
Other Expenses	19	10.9	•	•	•	11.0	5.5	10.8	•	9.1	6.3	•	•	•
Officers' Compensation	20	0.8	•	•	•	8.1	2.7	2.1	•	1.9	1.0	•	•	•
Operating Margin	21	•	•	•	•	17.6	13.0	7.6	•	7.6	3.1	•	•	•
Operating Margin Before Officers' Comp.	22	•	•	•	•	25.7	15.7	9.7	•	9.5	4.1	•	•	•

Selected Average Balance Sheet ($ in Thousands)

Net Receivables 23	6690	47	1339	2768	12246	34689
Inventories 24	7636	1768	1116	3610	15408	34019
Net Property, Plant and Equipment 25	7262	73	2372	5526	4414	33961
Total Assets 26	44878	1520	6291	16294	60756	172812
Notes and Loans Payable 27	13030	18	1496	5777	22088	36782
All Other Liabilities 28	16526	101	1265	3672	10682	62932
Net Worth 29	15323	1402	3529	6845	27988	73098

Selected Financial Ratios (Times to 1)

Current Ratio 30	1.6	10.7	3.0	1.6	2.2	1.9
Quick Ratio 31	0.8	6.6	1.7	0.7	1.2	1.0
Net Sales to Working Capital 32	8.1	3.3	3.8	6.3	3.6	4.1
Coverage Ratio 33	3.0	262.4	14.3	6.0	3.6	8.7
Total Asset Turnover 34	1.2	2.3	1.5	1.4	1.1	1.1
Inventory Turnover 35	5.4	0.8	5.6	4.0	3.1	4.2
Receivables Turnover 36	6.9	2.6	8.6	10.4	•	7.2
Total Liabilities to Net Worth 37	1.9	0.1	0.8	1.4	1.2	1.4
Current Assets to Working Capital 38	2.6	1.1	1.5	2.6	1.8	2.1
Current Liabilities to Working Capital 39	1.6	0.1	0.5	1.6	0.8	1.1
Working Capital to Net Sales 40	0.1	0.3	0.3	0.2	0.3	0.2
Inventory to Working Capital 41	1.0	0.4	0.6	1.2	0.8	0.9
Total Receipts to Cash Flow 42	7.8	3.9	5.5	7.4	6.5	10.4
Cost of Goods to Cash Flow 43	5.8	1.7	3.7	4.5	4.6	7.7
Cash Flow to Total Debt 44	0.2	7.5	0.6	0.3	0.3	0.2

Selected Financial Factors (in Percentages)

Debt Ratio 45	65.9	7.8	43.9	58.0	53.9	57.7
Return on Total Assets 46	8.3	40.7	21.6	14.7	12.3	5.9
Return on Equity Before Income Taxes 47	16.3	44.0	35.9	29.3	19.2	12.3
Return on Equity After Income Taxes 48	11.7	40.0	23.7	27.2	12.7	9.1
Profit Margin (Before Income Tax) 49	4.4	17.9	13.5	8.5	8.0	4.7
Profit Margin (After Income Tax) 50	3.2	16.3	8.9	7.9	5.3	3.4

Table I

Corporations with and without Net Income

OTHER GENERAL PURPOSE MACHINERY

MONEY AMOUNTS AND SIZE OF ASSETS IN THOUSANDS OF DOLLARS

Item Description for Accounting Period 7/08 Through 6/09		Total	Zero Assets	Under 500	500 to 1,000	1,000 to 5,000	5,000 to 10,000	10,000 to 25,000	25,000 to 50,000	50,000 to 100,000	100,000 to 250,000	250,000 to 500,000	500,000 to 2,500,000	2,500,000 and over
Number of Enterprises	1	6203	725	3704	216	912	292	209	55	30	31	7	17	6
Revenues ($ in Thousands)														
Net Sales	2	67100635	249462	1808232	333155	3565271	3529288	5646358	2472190	2856516	5600267	3323412	15810561	21905922
Interest	3	553296	1237	453	81	1714	2442	3426	3898	3001	16310	10716	219825	290193
Rents	4	17472	0	241	451	193	2302	4426	3177	5	1953	1235	1977	1512
Royalties	5	665774	0	0	0	0	0	0	1885	1574	11724	1493	162247	486851
Other Portfolio Income	6	423072	0	7108	319	484	959	14086	3127	25626	50110	4314	199473	117470
Other Receipts	7	832734	2568	2018	408	14101	13021	50459	13829	5778	57370	3885	102638	566657
Total Receipts	8	69592983	253267	1818052	334414	3581763	3548012	5718755	2498106	2892500	5737734	3345055	16496721	23368605
Average Total Receipts	9	11219	349	491	1548	3927	12151	27362	45420	96417	185088	477865	970395	3894768
Operating Costs/Operating Income (%)														
Cost of Operations	10	69.3	89.1	46.1	68.3	59.4	68.1	71.2	73.2	72.2	69.3	66.8	66.8	73.7
Salaries and Wages	11	8.6	4.9	14.3	9.5	10.0	9.3	7.9	8.6	8.3	8.8	6.3	8.7	8.3
Taxes Paid	12	1.5	1.2	2.6	2.3	2.2	1.7	1.3	1.5	1.2	1.4	1.2	1.3	1.4
Interest Paid	13	2.8	4.0	1.4	1.6	0.6	1.0	1.0	1.1	1.5	1.5	1.2	3.2	4.6
Depreciation	14	2.1	4.3	2.3	2.2	2.1	2.0	2.1	1.9	2.4	2.0	2.8	2.2	1.9
Amortization and Depletion	15	0.8	0.6	0.1	0.0	0.1	0.2	0.2	0.3	0.5	0.6	0.7	0.8	1.2
Pensions and Other Deferred Comp.	16	0.9	0.2	0.1	0.3	0.4	0.2	0.5	0.2	0.5	1.1	0.7	1.2	1.2
Employee Benefits	17	2.4	1.7	1.2	3.5	1.9	2.1	2.1	1.7	2.0	1.7	1.9	3.2	2.5
Advertising	18	0.5	0.3	0.5	1.4	0.7	0.6	0.4	0.3	0.4	0.5	0.7	0.5	0.5
Other Expenses	19	9.6	12.2	19.0	14.5	11.4	9.7	8.2	9.1	6.4	9.0	10.1	9.4	9.4
Officers' Compensation	20	1.4	0.7	5.7	6.7	5.2	2.5	2.3	1.1	1.2	0.9	1.2	0.9	0.4
Operating Margin	21	0.2	•	6.7	•	6.0	2.4	2.8	1.0	3.4	3.2	6.3	1.7	•
Operating Margin Before Officers' Comp.	22	1.6	•	12.5	•	11.3	4.9	5.0	2.1	4.6	4.1	7.4	2.6	•

Selected Average Balance Sheet ($ in Thousands)

Net Receivables 23	1910	0	19	135	447	1398	4075	7476	14935	28700	46559	145540	922000
Inventories 24	1473	0	24	212	528	2200	4031	7865	15104	24407	58918	113516	508756
Net Property, Plant and Equipment 25	1227	0	56	210	401	1177	2626	4864	11216	18493	59606	103923	456254
Total Assets 26	12555	0	125	734	2029	7287	15915	32793	65671	156993	351931	863600	7361261
Notes and Loans Payable 27	4110	0	109	371	665	1639	6188	7005	22830	41243	67087	266853	2546736
All Other Liabilities 28	3581	0	22	226	473	2876	4482	9048	21698	47007	118052	276935	1955463
Net Worth 29	4864	0	-5	137	891	2773	5245	16740	21144	68743	166792	319812	2859063

Selected Financial Ratios (Times to 1)

Current Ratio 30	1.4	•	1.8	1.4	2.6	1.5	1.9	2.1	1.4	1.7	1.6	1.5	1.1
Quick Ratio 31	0.7	•	1.0	0.5	1.6	0.7	1.0	1.0	0.6	0.9	0.7	0.8	0.6
Net Sales to Working Capital 32	8.2	•	20.3	10.6	4.2	6.7	5.4	3.7	8.0	5.2	7.7	7.3	23.4
Coverage Ratio 33	2.6	•	6.3	•	12.5	4.0	5.0	2.8	4.2	4.8	6.8	3.2	1.6
Total Asset Turnover 34	0.9	•	3.9	2.1	1.9	1.7	1.7	1.4	1.4	1.2	1.3	1.1	0.5
Inventory Turnover 35	5.1	•	9.2	5.0	4.4	3.7	4.8	4.2	4.6	5.1	5.4	5.5	5.3
Receivables Turnover 36	5.8	•	21.6	12.9	7.7	8.3	6.0	5.7	6.7	6.1	7.3	7.3	4.2
Total Liabilities to Net Worth 37	1.6	•	•	4.3	1.3	1.6	2.0	1.0	2.1	1.3	1.1	1.7	1.6
Current Assets to Working Capital 38	3.7	•	2.2	3.4	1.6	2.9	2.2	1.9	3.5	2.4	2.6	3.0	12.6
Current Liabilities to Working Capital 39	2.7	•	1.2	2.4	0.6	1.9	1.2	0.9	2.5	1.4	1.6	2.0	11.6
Working Capital to Net Sales 40	0.1	•	0.0	0.1	0.2	0.1	0.2	0.3	0.1	0.2	0.1	0.1	0.0
Inventory to Working Capital 41	1.2	•	1.0	2.0	0.6	1.5	0.8	0.7	1.3	0.8	1.0	1.0	3.0
Total Receipts to Cash Flow 42	8.7	•	4.8	•	6.3	10.6	9.5	10.5	11.1	8.3	6.6	7.3	10.7
Cost of Goods to Cash Flow 43	6.0	•	2.2	•	3.8	7.3	6.8	7.7	8.0	5.8	4.4	4.8	7.9
Cash Flow to Total Debt 44	0.2	•	0.8	•	0.5	0.3	0.3	0.3	0.2	0.2	0.4	0.2	0.1

Selected Financial Factors (in Percentages)

Debt Ratio 45	61.3	•	104.4	81.3	56.1	62.0	67.0	49.0	67.8	56.2	52.6	63.0	61.2
Return on Total Assets 46	6.3	•	33.8	•	13.6	6.4	8.6	4.2	9.3	8.3	10.9	11.1	3.6
Return on Equity Before Income Taxes 47	10.2	•	•	•	28.6	12.7	20.8	5.3	22.1	15.0	19.7	20.7	3.4
Return on Equity After Income Taxes 48	6.7	•	•	•	27.1	9.6	18.1	3.1	16.4	9.8	11.2	14.3	1.3
Profit Margin (Before Income Tax) 49	4.6	•	7.3	•	6.5	2.9	4.0	2.0	4.9	5.7	6.9	7.1	2.7
Profit Margin (After Income Tax) 50	3.0	•	7.2	•	6.2	2.2	3.5	1.2	3.6	3.7	3.9	4.9	1.0

Table II

Corporations with Net Income

OTHER GENERAL PURPOSE MACHINERY

MONEY AMOUNTS AND SIZE OF ASSETS IN THOUSANDS OF DOLLARS

Item Description for Accounting Period 7/08 Through 6/09	Total	Zero Assets	Under 500	500 to 1,000	1,000 to 5,000	5,000 to 10,000	10,000 to 25,000	25,000 to 50,000	50,000 to 100,000	100,000 to 250,000	250,000 to 500,000	500,000 to 2,500,000	2,500,000 and over
Number of Enterprises 1	3247	•	2005	136	650	205	136	42	26	25	•	13	•
Revenues ($ in Thousands)													
Net Sales 2	54195567	•	1381857	198429	3136700	2610890	3915615	1799768	2415300	4250270	•	12817194	•
Interest 3	171417	•	453	81	1325	1661	1836	3427	2656	9991	•	47047	•
Rents 4	12438	•	0	451	193	430	2407	2814	5	1858	•	1532	•
Royalties 5	614754	•	0	0	0	0	0	1065	1574	763	•	160305	•
Other Portfolio Income 6	376403	•	7101	319	484	888	3613	2678	25297	47302	•	196254	•
Other Receipts 7	580426	•	1822	186	13581	5195	37149	9726	4899	42349	•	63882	•
Total Receipts 8	55951005	•	1391233	199466	3152283	2619064	3960620	1819478	2449731	4352533	•	13286214	•
Average Total Receipts 9	17232	•	694	1467	4850	12776	29122	43321	94220	174101	•	1022016	•
Operating Costs/Operating Income (%)													
Cost of Operations 10	67.6	•	38.8	61.3	58.3	62.9	69.6	72.4	68.8	66.1	•	64.8	•
Salaries and Wages 11	8.6	•	16.4	8.5	10.4	10.8	6.9	8.5	8.5	9.3	•	9.3	•
Taxes Paid 12	1.4	•	2.6	2.6	2.2	2.0	1.4	1.4	1.2	1.4	•	1.5	•
Interest Paid 13	1.6	•	1.3	0.4	0.5	0.7	0.8	0.9	1.6	1.3	•	1.7	•
Depreciation 14	2.0	•	1.1	0.8	1.9	2.1	1.7	2.1	2.4	2.3	•	2.1	•
Amortization and Depletion 15	0.7	•	0.0	•	0.1	0.0	0.2	0.2	0.6	0.5	•	0.7	•
Pensions and Other Deferred Comp. 16	1.0	•	0.1	0.2	0.5	0.5	0.5	0.3	0.6	0.8	•	1.3	•
Employee Benefits 17	2.1	•	1.3	2.5	1.6	1.6	1.8	1.2	2.0	1.4	•	3.4	•
Advertising 18	0.5	•	0.4	1.2	0.6	0.7	0.3	0.3	0.4	0.5	•	0.5	•
Other Expenses 19	9.2	•	17.8	10.6	9.8	10.1	6.7	7.1	7.0	8.8	•	8.9	•
Officers' Compensation 20	1.3	•	6.5	8.1	4.8	2.7	2.2	1.2	1.3	1.0	•	0.9	•
Operating Margin 21	4.0	•	13.6	3.7	9.4	5.8	7.9	4.5	5.5	6.5	•	4.9	•
Operating Margin Before Officers' Comp. 22	5.3	•	20.1	11.8	14.2	8.6	10.1	5.6	6.8	7.5	•	5.8	•

Selected Average Balance Sheet ($ in Thousands)

Net Receivables 23	3176	32	123	538	1517	4715	6683	14526	30518	153588
Inventories 24	2249	38	282	575	2602	4185	7313	13262	26205	147137
Net Property, Plant and Equipment 25	1851	56	129	339	1151	2367	5494	11393	20393	105995
Total Assets 26	16837	165	685	2150	7398	15386	32420	65264	153179	879844
Notes and Loans Payable 27	5009	54	79	336	1323	5224	5553	21621	36366	240110
All Other Liabilities 28	5374	27	107	579	2410	4440	7378	19912	37770	276982
Net Worth 29	6453	84	500	1236	3665	5722	19490	23732	79043	362751

Selected Financial Ratios (Times to 1)

Current Ratio 30	1.4	2.7	5.1	3.0	2.0	1.8	2.8	1.4	2.1	1.4
Quick Ratio 31	0.8	1.5	1.6	2.0	0.9	1.1	1.3	0.7	1.1	0.7
Net Sales to Working Capital 32	7.6	12.4	3.3	4.2	4.5	5.8	3.0	8.4	3.9	8.1
Coverage Ratio 33	6.0	11.8	10.6	22.8	10.1	12.5	7.4	5.4	7.8	7.0
Total Asset Turnover 34	1.0	4.2	2.1	2.2	1.7	1.9	1.3	1.4	1.1	1.1
Inventory Turnover 35	5.0	7.1	3.2	4.9	3.1	4.8	4.2	4.8	4.3	4.3
Receivables Turnover 36	6.1	18.3	10.3	8.0	7.9	5.1	5.7	7.4	5.4	•
Total Liabilities to Net Worth 37	1.6	1.0	0.4	0.7	1.0	1.7	0.7	1.8	0.9	1.4
Current Assets to Working Capital 38	3.4	1.6	1.2	1.5	2.0	2.2	1.6	3.6	1.9	3.4
Current Liabilities to Working Capital 39	2.4	0.6	0.2	0.5	1.0	1.2	0.6	2.6	0.9	2.4
Working Capital to Net Sales 40	0.1	0.1	0.3	0.2	0.2	0.2	0.3	0.1	0.3	0.1
Inventory to Working Capital 41	1.1	0.7	0.9	0.5	1.0	0.8	0.6	1.4	0.7	1.2
Total Receipts to Cash Flow 42	6.9	3.7	8.3	5.6	7.8	7.0	8.9	8.6	6.6	6.2
Cost of Goods to Cash Flow 43	4.6	1.4	5.1	3.3	4.9	4.9	6.4	5.9	4.4	4.0
Cash Flow to Total Debt 44	0.2	2.3	1.0	0.9	0.4	0.4	0.4	0.3	0.3	0.3

Selected Financial Factors (in Percentages)

Debt Ratio 45	61.7	49.1	27.1	42.5	50.5	62.8	39.9	63.6	48.4	58.8
Return on Total Assets 46	9.4	65.6	9.9	23.3	11.7	18.3	8.4	12.5	11.5	13.0
Return on Equity Before Income Taxes 47	20.5	117.8	12.3	38.8	21.3	45.4	12.1	28.0	19.5	26.9
Return on Equity After Income Taxes 48	15.5	117.4	9.1	37.3	17.9	41.7	9.7	22.2	13.9	19.6
Profit Margin (Before Income Tax) 49	7.9	14.3	4.2	9.9	6.1	9.0	5.5	7.1	9.1	9.9
Profit Margin (After Income Tax) 50	6.0	14.3	3.1	9.5	5.2	8.3	4.4	5.7	6.4	7.2

Table I

Corporations with and without Net Income

COMPUTER AND PERIPHERAL EQUIPMENT

MONEY AMOUNTS AND SIZE OF ASSETS IN THOUSANDS OF DOLLARS

Item Description for Accounting Period 7/08 Through 6/09	Total	Zero Assets	Under 500	500 to 1,000	1,000 to 5,000	5,000 to 10,000	10,000 to 25,000	25,000 to 50,000	50,000 to 100,000	100,000 to 250,000	250,000 to 500,000	500,000 to 2,500,000	2,500,000 and over
Number of Enterprises **1**	2611	840	865	174	380	122	104	42	23	20	12	17	12
Revenues ($ in Thousands)													
Net Sales **2**	194850172	202348	257857	360465	2070924	957626	2271415	2184768	2567919	3664414	3302762	13508133	163501542
Interest **3**	2726964	3958	103	227	5271	6503	5954	14011	10645	40388	63588	91406	2488911
Rents **4**	1163829	0	0	0	0	0	550	9	167	696	16	20099	1142292
Royalties **5**	25916916	0	0	0	0	0	0	5334	5080	24197	32761	242705	25606839
Other Portfolio Income **6**	3190023	17968	4105	0	103	1301	53648	1608	1282	51241	28376	273704	2756689
Other Receipts **7**	2388070	34231	308	1319	12384	7445	26547	-52422	26142	17405	63404	402992	1848311
Total Receipts **8**	230235974	258505	262373	362011	2088682	972875	2358114	2153308	2611235	3798341	3490907	14539039	197340584
Average Total Receipts **9**	88179	308	303	2081	5497	7974	22674	51269	113532	189917	290909	855238	16445049
Operating Costs/Operating Income (%)													
Cost of Operations **10**	63.4	52.2	60.0	47.0	54.3	60.2	62.5	52.8	71.5	67.2	56.4	66.7	63.3
Salaries and Wages **11**	16.1	36.5	15.5	32.6	16.6	25.7	17.3	21.4	13.3	14.8	16.1	15.1	16.0
Taxes Paid **12**	1.8	3.0	6.9	3.7	2.6	2.9	1.9	1.9	1.9	1.4	1.8	1.7	1.7
Interest Paid **13**	1.6	0.1	6.2	0.7	0.6	1.4	1.1	2.1	0.9	1.2	1.1	1.3	1.7
Depreciation **14**	3.5	3.3	1.3	0.5	1.7	2.3	2.8	2.2	1.4	2.2	2.5	2.6	3.7
Amortization and Depletion **15**	0.9	0.9	0.0	0.0	0.7	1.0	1.1	3.5	0.8	1.5	1.6	1.6	0.8
Pensions and Other Deferred Comp. **16**	0.5	0.0	0.5	0.6	1.4	0.3	0.2	0.1	0.3	0.2	0.4	0.8	0.5
Employee Benefits **17**	1.8	2.7	4.7	2.8	2.3	2.4	1.3	2.0	1.6	2.0	1.6	2.4	1.7
Advertising **18**	1.6	0.2	0.2	0.2	0.4	1.0	1.3	1.4	0.9	1.8	1.5	4.2	1.4
Other Expenses **19**	22.6	41.0	13.6	16.0	15.1	20.4	13.9	23.6	12.8	14.5	15.9	26.5	23.0
Officers' Compensation **20**	0.8	3.8	9.2	5.5	6.6	4.3	3.6	1.8	1.1	1.6	1.5	0.7	0.7
Operating Margin **21**	•	•	•	•	•	•	•	•	•	•	•	•	•
Operating Margin Before Officers' Comp. **22**	•	•	•	•	4.3	•	•	•	•	1.2	•	•	•

Selected Average Balance Sheet ($ in Thousands)

Net Receivables 23	19713	0	33	140	765	1435	3638	7340	16824	31642	37989	169058	3826298
Inventories 24	3819	0	17	314	436	1540	2459	5890	12636	18436	28381	72316	568523
Net Property, Plant and Equipment 25	8987	0	9	121	293	881	2044	2580	4730	14290	18088	72411	1754470
Total Assets 26	133182	0	99	895	2417	6888	15523	35534	70938	159002	337459	991198	26409879
Notes and Loans Payable 27	32562	0	171	423	675	1436	2774	9966	27434	29650	39697	181675	6572584
All Other Liabilities 28	48133	0	75	135	687	1783	4370	11436	26914	62409	89788	331476	9632918
Net Worth 29	52486	0	-146	338	1054	3669	8378	14132	16589	66943	207975	478047	10204376

Selected Financial Ratios (Times to 1)

Current Ratio 30	1.0	•	0.6	2.0	2.5	2.5	2.4	1.7	1.5	1.6	2.4	1.7	1.0
Quick Ratio 31	0.6	•	0.4	1.4	1.8	1.7	1.6	1.1	0.9	1.0	1.5	1.1	0.5
Net Sales to Working Capital 32	39.1	•	•	9.9	4.8	2.7	3.4	5.3	8.3	6.0	2.6	4.8	•
Coverage Ratio 33	6.8	•	•	•	•	•	•	•	•	•	5.7	•	8.7
Total Asset Turnover 34	0.6	•	3.0	2.3	2.3	1.1	1.4	1.5	1.6	1.2	0.8	0.8	0.5
Inventory Turnover 35	12.4	•	10.4	3.1	6.8	3.1	5.5	4.7	6.3	6.7	5.5	7.3	15.2
Receivables Turnover 36	3.4	•	16.2	6.6	7.7	4.6	5.6	5.2	5.9	5.8	4.8	4.2	3.2
Total Liabilities to Net Worth 37	1.5	•	•	1.7	1.3	0.9	0.9	1.5	3.3	1.4	0.6	1.1	1.6
Current Assets to Working Capital 38	24.9	•	•	2.0	1.7	1.7	1.7	2.5	3.0	2.7	1.7	2.5	•
Current Liabilities to Working Capital 39	23.9	•	•	1.0	0.7	0.7	0.7	1.5	2.0	1.7	0.7	1.5	•
Working Capital to Net Sales 40	0.0	•	•	0.1	0.2	0.4	0.3	0.2	0.1	0.2	0.4	0.2	•
Inventory to Working Capital 41	1.8	•	•	0.5	0.4	0.5	0.4	0.5	0.8	0.6	0.2	0.4	•
Total Receipts to Cash Flow 42	4.3	9.1	92.2	9.8	•	15.0	47.6	15.4	14.7	5.1	•	•	3.7
Cost of Goods to Cash Flow 43	2.7	4.8	43.3	5.3	•	9.4	25.1	11.0	9.9	2.9	•	•	2.3
Cash Flow to Total Debt 44	0.2	•	0.0	0.0	0.4	0.2	0.1	0.1	0.1	0.4	0.2	•	0.2

Selected Financial Factors (in Percentages)

Debt Ratio 45	60.6	•	247.4	62.3	56.4	46.7	46.0	60.2	76.6	57.9	38.4	51.8	61.4
Return on Total Assets 46	6.1	•	•	•	•	•	•	•	•	•	5.4	•	7.5
Return on Equity Before Income Taxes 47	13.2	33.4	•	•	•	•	•	•	•	•	7.2	•	17.2
Return on Equity After Income Taxes 48	7.5	33.4	•	•	•	•	•	•	•	•	6.2	•	11.0
Profit Margin (Before Income Tax) 49	9.3	•	•	•	•	•	•	•	•	•	5.4	•	12.9
Profit Margin (After Income Tax) 50	5.3	•	•	•	•	•	•	•	•	•	4.7	•	8.2

Table II

Corporations with Net Income

COMPUTER AND PERIPHERAL EQUIPMENT

MONEY AMOUNTS AND SIZE OF ASSETS IN THOUSANDS OF DOLLARS

Item Description for Accounting Period 7/08 Through 6/09	Total	Zero Assets	Under 500	500 to 1,000	1,000 to 5,000	5,000 to 10,000	10,000 to 25,000	25,000 to 50,000	50,000 to 100,000	100,000 to 250,000	250,000 to 500,000	500,000 to 2,500,000	2,500,000 and over
Number of Enterprises 1	826	310	63	28	249	62	48	16	12	10	8	11	9
Revenues ($ in Thousands)													
Net Sales 2	167142980	128641	153665	26917	1477724	743754	1397905	750275	1926803	1533959	2743472	7462112	148797752
Interest 3	2537363	3800	0	39	3132	1836	1825	543	2648	30583	35636	50391	2406930
Rents 4	1156921	0	0	0	0	0	0	9	167	420	0	14033	1142292
Royalties 5	25047472	0	0	0	0	0	0	199	4559	1642	27345	146200	24867528
Other Portfolio Income 6	2824790	17968	0	0	0	1301	53029	743	443	48675	647	26457	2675525
Other Receipts 7	1820534	14978	46	1320	236	6534	1700	681	22066	14497	62203	398384	1297891
Total Receipts 8	200530060	165387	153711	28276	1481092	753425	1454459	752450	1956686	1629776	2869303	8097577	181187918
Average Total Receipts 9	242772	534	2440	1010	5948	12152	30301	47028	163057	162978	358663	736143	20131991
Operating Costs/Operating Income (%)													
Cost of Operations 10	60.4	24.9	68.9	10.6	53.1	60.9	61.0	52.2	72.2	52.7	54.4	53.0	61.0
Salaries and Wages 11	16.0	41.7	2.1	32.9	11.0	13.0	12.6	18.1	9.7	21.2	16.2	21.2	15.8
Taxes Paid 12	1.8	2.5	3.6	6.1	2.3	2.3	1.1	1.7	1.9	1.7	1.7	2.6	1.8
Interest Paid 13	1.6	0.2	1.1	•	0.5	1.0	0.3	1.2	0.3	1.5	0.2	0.8	1.7
Depreciation 14	3.6	3.1	2.0	1.4	0.8	1.4	1.4	1.9	1.2	2.3	2.5	3.3	3.7
Amortization and Depletion 15	0.9	0.3	•	0.0	•	0.0	0.3	0.7	0.6	0.5	0.8	1.7	0.8
Pensions and Other Deferred Comp. 16	0.5	0.0	•	0.3	1.7	0.3	0.2	0.1	0.1	0.2	0.2	1.2	0.5
Employee Benefits 17	1.8	3.3	0.0	5.5	2.4	1.2	0.9	1.8	1.4	2.0	1.5	3.4	1.7
Advertising 18	1.7	0.3	0.1	2.7	0.3	0.3	0.9	1.1	0.5	2.4	1.7	6.2	1.5
Other Expenses 19	23.1	30.7	10.6	10.4	9.2	10.6	8.7	12.6	10.2	12.9	16.1	7.7	24.7
Officers' Compensation 20	0.8	3.7	11.5	28.8	6.5	2.2	2.1	2.4	0.7	1.6	1.4	0.7	0.7
Operating Margin 21	•	•	•	1.3	12.3	6.7	10.5	6.3	1.3	1.0	3.2	•	•
Operating Margin Before Officers' Comp. 22	•	•	11.4	30.1	18.8	8.9	12.6	8.8	2.0	2.6	4.6	•	•

Selected Average Balance Sheet ($ in Thousands)

Net Receivables 23	55625	0	181	69	870	1995	4369	8682	22045	29870	43084	172389	4715498
Inventories 24	10339	0	204	1519	570	2419	3194	7739	18562	16155	26923	66093	732830
Net Property, Plant and Equipment 25	24757	0	90	350	126	840	1852	3475	5895	13362	22720	85687	2097507
Total Assets 26	387199	0	483	886	2261	6920	14043	34908	72795	166063	353445	958099	33516206
Notes and Loans Payable 27	95304	0	217	0	525	1479	1471	2286	13076	34114	34938	96027	8504939
All Other Liabilities 28	136778	0	141	2	642	1891	3000	14296	31705	53394	98940	331707	11885018
Net Worth 29	155117	0	126	884	1094	3549	9572	18327	28015	78554	219567	530365	13126249

Selected Financial Ratios (Times to 1)

Current Ratio 30	1.0	•	1.2	203.7	2.8	3.4	2.5	1.5	2.1	2.9	1.7	1.0
Quick Ratio 31	0.6	•	0.5	203.2	1.7	2.3	1.6	0.8	1.3	1.9	1.2	0.5
Net Sales to Working Capital 32	59.0	•	40.0	2.1	3.3	3.8	3.3	9.2	3.4	2.6	4.1	•
Coverage Ratio 33	9.8	95.7	•	26.0	9.4	47.5	7.0	10.6	5.8	42.0	10.2	9.7
Total Asset Turnover 34	0.5	•	5.0	1.1	2.6	1.7	2.1	1.3	2.2	0.9	1.0	0.7
Inventory Turnover 35	11.8	•	8.2	0.1	5.5	5.6	3.0	3.2	6.2	5.0	6.9	5.4	13.8
Receivables Turnover 36	3.2	•	20.7	0.6	7.2	4.8	6.7	3.5	6.7	5.6	5.6	3.5	3.1
Total Liabilities to Net Worth 37	1.5	•	2.8	0.0	1.1	0.9	0.5	0.9	1.6	1.1	0.6	0.8	1.6
Current Assets to Working Capital 38	39.1	•	6.5	1.0	1.5	1.4	1.6	1.6	2.9	1.9	1.5	2.4	•
Current Liabilities to Working Capital 39	38.1	•	5.5	0.0	0.5	0.4	0.6	0.6	1.9	0.9	0.5	1.4	•
Working Capital to Net Sales 40	0.0	•	0.0	0.5	0.2	0.3	0.3	0.3	0.1	0.3	0.4	0.2	•
Inventory to Working Capital 41	2.6	•	3.3	0.0	0.4	0.4	0.3	0.3	0.9	0.3	0.2	0.3	•
Total Receipts to Cash Flow 42	3.5	3.2	20.5	6.3	5.2	5.5	5.6	5.6	8.5	6.5	4.5	8.4	3.3
Cost of Goods to Cash Flow 43	2.1	0.8	14.2	0.7	2.8	3.7	3.3	2.9	6.1	3.4	2.4	4.4	2.0
Cash Flow to Total Debt 44	0.3	•	0.3	66.5	1.0	0.6	1.2	0.5	0.4	0.3	0.6	0.2	0.2

Selected Financial Factors (in Percentages)

Debt Ratio 45	59.9	•	74.0	0.3	51.6	48.7	31.8	47.5	61.5	52.7	37.9	44.6	60.8
Return on Total Assets 46	8.4	•	5.7	6.8	34.1	15.5	30.7	11.1	6.9	8.1	7.9	5.9	8.3
Return on Equity Before Income Taxes 47	18.8	•	0.0	6.9	67.7	27.1	44.1	18.0	16.3	14.2	12.3	9.7	19.1
Return on Equity After Income Taxes 48	12.6	•	0.0	6.9	61.5	24.0	40.1	15.9	12.4	12.8	10.9	6.9	12.7
Profit Margin (Before Income Tax) 49	14.4	17.9	0.0	6.3	12.5	8.0	14.5	7.1	2.8	7.3	7.9	7.6	15.2
Profit Margin (After Income Tax) 50	9.7	17.9	0.0	6.3	11.3	7.1	13.2	6.2	2.2	6.6	7.0	5.4	10.1

Table I

Corporations with and without Net Income

COMMUNICATIONS EQUIPMENT

MONEY AMOUNTS AND SIZE OF ASSETS IN THOUSANDS OF DOLLARS

Item Description for Accounting Period 7/08 Through 6/09	Total	Zero Assets	Under 500	500 to 1,000	1,000 to 5,000	5,000 to 10,000	10,000 to 25,000	25,000 to 50,000	50,000 to 100,000	100,000 to 250,000	250,000 to 500,000	500,000 to 2,500,000	2,500,000 and over
Number of Enterprises **1**	1718	33	1001	162	203	107	70	61	22	20	8	17	13
Revenues ($ in Thousands)													
Net Sales **2**	136009890	2481831	235420	117236	979105	873008	1616046	2844601	1861277	2737139	3532720	19544672	99186836
Interest **3**	1185913	6071	181	253	1975	1290	3562	12446	4737	33069	16526	202975	902829
Rents **4**	333502	2297	0	15	0	2579	0	245	141	0	0	146743	181483
Royalties **5**	1969594	1324	0	0	0	0	526	359	3026	10649	816	57393	1895500
Other Portfolio Income **6**	1983754	19083	686	13783	118	103	4206	54577	407	32091	9192	87032	1762475
Other Receipts **7**	1062973	-3986	-1	87	-12346	17495	17687	24521	37746	17444	11463	172923	779939
Total Receipts **8**	142545626	2506620	236286	131374	968852	894475	1642027	2936749	1907334	2830392	3570717	20211738	104709062
Average Total Receipts **9**	82972	75958	236	811	4773	8360	23458	48143	86697	141520	446340	1188926	8054543
Operating Costs/Operating Income (%)													
Cost of Operations **10**	66.2	75.6	38.6	33.8	53.3	73.7	65.0	65.6	63.0	55.2	73.6	80.3	63.6
Salaries and Wages **11**	14.9	19.7	7.2	22.8	23.2	13.0	11.6	13.1	14.6	16.9	9.2	6.0	16.7
Taxes Paid **12**	1.1	1.8	3.0	5.6	3.3	2.0	1.4	1.6	1.7	1.5	0.7	0.5	1.1
Interest Paid **13**	1.9	3.6	1.2	1.6	2.1	1.3	5.2	1.1	1.1	1.9	0.8	1.3	2.1
Depreciation **14**	2.4	2.2	0.9	2.0	0.8	1.9	1.9	2.1	1.8	2.2	2.1	1.3	2.7
Amortization and Depletion **15**	1.5	1.4	•	0.8	2.9	1.1	0.9	1.9	1.1	1.4	0.6	0.9	1.7
Pensions and Other Deferred Comp. **16**	0.9	2.1	•	0.2	0.4	0.1	0.5	0.2	0.3	0.4	0.1	0.2	1.1
Employee Benefits **17**	1.8	3.7	0.1	3.1	1.1	2.7	1.5	1.6	1.8	2.3	1.3	1.1	1.9
Advertising **18**	1.0	0.2	0.4	1.5	1.3	0.5	0.6	0.5	0.5	0.7	0.3	0.4	1.3
Other Expenses **19**	8.6	2.4	44.1	22.5	20.5	10.6	12.9	16.2	11.8	16.5	8.8	8.0	8.1
Officers' Compensation **20**	0.7	2.4	16.1	11.3	7.2	4.1	2.8	1.8	1.2	1.3	0.6	0.4	0.4
Operating Margin **21**	•	•	•	•	•	•	•	•	1.2	•	1.8	•	•
Operating Margin Before Officers' Comp. **22**	•	•	4.5	6.0	•	•	•	•	2.4	1.1	2.4	•	•

Selected Average Balance Sheet ($ in Thousands)

Item													
Net Receivables **23**	17138	0	7	387	1047	5105	8522	16623	25473	74171	133632		1894338
Inventories **24**	5790	0	26	766	1000	3649	6256	10869	16002	51395	89356		499782
Net Property, Plant and Equipment **25**	8560	0	5	99	1031	1511	3158	4707	8864	33678	48991		991067
Total Assets **26**	107909	0	107	590	2350	6417	16643	35770	71091	148267	361516	1062888	11937194
Notes and Loans Payable **27**	22975	0	71	188	1128	1681	14073	8720	9411	31867	82659	175137	2535478
All Other Liabilities **28**	41367	0	30	42	1515	6498	14996	26265	27872	104192	343814		4720785
Net Worth **29**	43566	0	6	360	-338	-3928	12053	35415	88528	174665	543938		4680931

Selected Financial Ratios (Times to 1)

Item													
Current Ratio **30**	1.3	•	1.4	0.9	2.2	1.7	1.2	2.1	2.6	2.0	1.9		1.2
Quick Ratio **31**	0.8	•	1.0	0.5	1.2	1.0	0.8	1.4	1.6	1.4	1.0		0.8
Net Sales to Working Capital **32**	8.2	8.9	1.4	•	3.4	4.5	11.4	3.6	2.5	4.6	4.4		11.2
Coverage Ratio **33**	3.6	5.2	•	•	0.5	0.1	4.5	2.8	4.3	3.2			4.3
Total Asset Turnover **34**	0.7	•	2.2	2.1	1.3	1.4	1.3	0.9	1.2	1.1			0.6
Inventory Turnover **35**	9.1	•	3.5	3.4	6.0	4.1	4.9	4.9	4.7	6.3	10.3		9.7
Receivables Turnover **36**	4.9	•	30.3	10.4	9.6	5.2	6.0	4.6	4.7	5.6	8.1		4.3
Total Liabilities to Net Worth **37**	1.5	•	16.6	0.6	•	2.0	1.0	0.7	1.1	1.0			1.6
Current Assets to Working Capital **38**	3.9	•	3.4	1.1	1.8	2.4	5.4	1.9	1.6	2.0	2.1		5.5
Current Liabilities to Working Capital **39**	2.9	•	2.4	0.1	0.8	1.4	4.4	0.9	0.6	1.0	1.1		4.5
Working Capital to Net Sales **40**	0.1	•	0.1	0.7	0.3	0.2	0.1	0.3	0.4	0.2	0.2		0.1
Inventory to Working Capital **41**	0.6	•	1.1	0.4	0.5	0.7	1.5	0.4	0.3	0.5	0.3		0.7
Total Receipts to Cash Flow **42**	9.5	•	3.7	8.5	•	12.4	10.0	7.3	5.9	9.7	10.5		8.9
Cost of Goods to Cash Flow **43**	6.3	•	1.4	2.9	•	8.1	6.5	4.6	3.2	7.2	8.5		5.6
Cash Flow to Total Debt **44**	0.1	•	0.6	0.4	0.1	0.2	0.3	0.2	0.4	0.2	0.2		0.1

Selected Financial Factors (in Percentages)

Item													
Debt Ratio **45**	59.6	•	94.3	38.9	114.4	49.8	123.6	66.3	50.2	40.3	51.7	48.8	60.8
Return on Total Assets **46**	5.2	•	•	10.4	•	3.5	0.2	•	5.7	4.9	4.4	4.7	5.7
Return on Equity Before Income Taxes **47**	9.3	•	•	13.7	245.2	16.0	8.9	•	5.3	7.0	6.3		11.2
Return on Equity After Income Taxes **48**	5.6	•	•	•	246.3	17.1	5.7	•	2.9	3.4	5.3		7.1
Profit Margin (Before Income Tax) **49**	5.1	•	6.8	•	•	•	•	3.7	3.4	2.8	3.0		6.9
Profit Margin (After Income Tax) **50**	3.1	•	•	•	•	•	2.4	•	1.9	3.4	1.4	2.5	4.4

Table II

Corporations with Net Income

COMMUNICATIONS EQUIPMENT

MONEY AMOUNTS AND SIZE OF ASSETS IN THOUSANDS OF DOLLARS

Item Description for Accounting Period 7/08 Through 6/09		Total	Zero Assets	Under 500	500 to 1,000	1,000 to 5,000	5,000 to 10,000	10,000 to 25,000	25,000 to 50,000	50,000 to 100,000	100,000 to 250,000	250,000 to 500,000	500,000 to 2,500,000	2,500,000 and over
Number of Enterprises	1	974	9	686	34	54	82	31	33	11	11	•	•	7
Revenues ($ in Thousands)														
Net Sales	2	79739682	135589	101168	60428	495800	552922	990318	1934459	1097301	1805350	•	•	54506822
Interest	3	692952	202	0	241	94	166	731	6399	2338	17257	•	•	549831
Rents	4	301408	0	0	15	0	305	0	132	140	0	•	•	156423
Royalties	5	987872	0	0	0	0	0	526	0	3024	10338	•	•	938075
Other Portfolio Income	6	697208	72	0	13783	118	103	22	47771	38	32091	•	•	510784
Other Receipts	7	772023	215	0	12	54	23116	6861	10050	2420	12898	•	•	581518
Total Receipts	8	83191145	136078	101168	74479	496066	576612	998458	1998811	1105261	1877934	•	•	57243453
Average Total Receipts	9	85412	15120	147	2191	9186	7032	32208	60570	100478	170721	•	•	8177636
Operating Costs/Operating Income (%)														
Cost of Operations	10	63.3	31.5	32.6	12.2	57.2	67.2	61.2	66.0	56.0	60.3	•	•	58.3
Salaries and Wages	11	16.2	28.5	•	16.1	10.1	9.6	6.5	9.3	12.8	12.3	•	•	20.3
Taxes Paid	12	1.0	2.5	2.0	5.9	1.4	2.1	1.1	1.5	1.4	1.1	•	•	1.1
Interest Paid	13	1.6	12.7	0.5	0.5	0.3	0.9	4.3	0.9	0.7	2.0	•	•	1.9
Depreciation	14	2.7	6.3	•	1.3	0.3	1.6	1.3	1.8	2.0	2.3	•	•	3.3
Amortization and Depletion	15	0.8	0.2	•	1.6	•	0.1	0.3	0.3	0.9	0.2	•	•	0.9
Pensions and Other Deferred Comp.	16	0.9	•	•	0.3	0.3	0.1	0.9	0.3	0.4	0.5	•	•	1.2
Employee Benefits	17	0.8	2.0	•	1.8	0.8	1.7	0.9	1.0	1.9	2.4	•	•	0.6
Advertising	18	1.0	0.4	•	0.6	1.1	0.5	0.5	0.3	0.6	0.8	•	•	1.3
Other Expenses	19	5.6	12.3	13.6	17.9	9.3	8.1	6.6	13.9	13.0	10.9	•	•	4.3
Officers' Compensation	20	0.6	1.4	14.2	11.0	5.4	4.8	2.6	1.8	0.9	1.1	•	•	0.5
Operating Margin	21	5.6	2.2	37.2	30.9	13.9	3.3	13.8	2.9	9.4	6.1	•	•	6.5
Operating Margin Before Officers' Comp.	22	6.2	3.6	51.4	42.0	19.3	8.2	16.4	4.7	10.3	7.2	•	•	7.0

Selected Average Balance Sheet ($ in Thousands)

	1	2	3	4	5	6	7	8	9	10	11	12
Net Receivables 23	15399	0	5	11	544	1020	5323	10795	14900	27494	•	1729426
Inventories 24	5779	0	2	510	1843	736	3441	5433	11723	15746	•	509490
Net Property, Plant and Equipment 25	11437	0	0	77	194	955	1969	4658	5663	10649	•	1403500
Total Assets 26	116189	0	74	830	3736	6040	17126	36176	73330	147936	•	13625146
Notes and Loans Payable 27	20646	0	47	0	162	1692	20416	7465	8315	41211	•	2348721
All Other Liabilities 28	32824	0	1	29	1785	1068	7122	15226	27398	33074	•	3660257
Net Worth 29	62720	0	26	801	1789	3281	-10413	13485	37616	73651	•	7616168

Selected Financial Ratios (Times to 1)

	1	2	3	4	5	6	7	8	9	10	11	12
Current Ratio 30	1.3	•	1.5	25.7	1.6	2.1	2.5	1.2	2.1	3.0	•	1.1
Quick Ratio 31	0.8	•	1.5	11.6	0.8	1.2	1.6	0.8	1.4	1.8	•	0.8
Net Sales to Working Capital 32	11.6	•	5.7	2.5	8.6	3.3	3.8	14.0	4.0	2.7	•	35.7
Coverage Ratio 33	8.4	1.2	81.7	121.4	48.4	9.3	4.4	10.2	15.2	6.2	•	8.6
Total Asset Turnover 34	0.7	•	2.0	2.1	2.5	1.1	1.9	1.6	1.4	1.1	•	0.6
Inventory Turnover 35	9.0	•	21.4	0.4	2.8	6.2	5.7	7.1	4.8	6.3	•	8.9
Receivables Turnover 36	5.4	•	55.8	52.4	12.6	8.9	6.3	6.6	5.4	4.6	•	4.7
Total Liabilities to Net Worth 37	0.9	•	1.9	0.0	1.1	0.8	•	1.7	0.9	1.0	•	0.8
Current Assets to Working Capital 38	4.8	•	2.9	1.0	2.7	1.9	1.7	5.5	1.9	1.5	•	14.3
Current Liabilities to Working Capital 39	3.8	•	1.9	0.0	1.7	0.9	0.7	4.5	0.9	0.5	•	13.3
Working Capital to Net Sales 40	0.1	•	0.2	0.4	0.1	0.3	0.3	0.1	0.3	0.4	•	0.0
Inventory to Working Capital 41	0.8	•	0.1	0.3	1.0	0.4	0.4	1.5	0.4	0.3	•	2.2
Total Receipts to Cash Flow 42	7.5	12.9	2.1	2.1	4.7	7.1	5.0	6.1	4.7	5.4	•	7.4
Cost of Goods to Cash Flow 43	4.8	4.0	0.7	0.3	2.7	4.8	3.1	4.0	2.6	3.3	•	4.3
Cash Flow to Total Debt 44	0.2	•	1.5	29.7	1.0	0.3	0.2	0.4	0.6	0.4	•	0.2

Selected Financial Factors (in Percentages)

	1	2	3	4	5	6	7	8	9	10	11	12
Debt Ratio 45	46.0	•	65.1	3.5	52.1	45.7	160.8	62.7	48.7	50.2	•	44.1
Return on Total Assets 46	9.5	•	75.1	117.1	34.9	9.5	35.3	15.1	14.9	13.8	•	9.2
Return on Equity Before Income Taxes 47	15.5	•	212.4	120.3	71.4	15.7	•	36.6	27.1	23.3	•	14.6
Return on Equity After Income Taxes 48	10.9	•	209.9	79.4	70.6	12.8	•	31.3	20.9	18.0	•	9.9
Profit Margin (Before Income Tax) 49	11.9	2.5	37.2	54.2	13.9	7.6	14.6	8.4	10.2	10.5	•	14.3
Profit Margin (After Income Tax) 50	8.4	2.5	36.7	35.8	13.8	6.2	14.3	7.2	7.9	8.1	•	9.7

Table I

Corporations with and without Net Income

AUDIO AND VIDEO EQUIP., REPRODUCING MAGNETIC & OPTICAL MEDIA

MONEY AMOUNTS AND SIZE OF ASSETS IN THOUSANDS OF DOLLARS

Item Description for Accounting Period 7/08 Through 6/09		Total	Zero Assets	Under 500	500 to 1,000	1,000 to 5,000	5,000 to 10,000	10,000 to 25,000	25,000 to 50,000	50,000 to 100,000	100,000 to 250,000	250,000 to 500,000	500,000 to 2,500,000	2,500,000 and over
Number of Enterprises	1	1370	25	776	63	378	18	48	21	18	8	6	6	3
Revenues ($ in Thousands)														
Net Sales	2	32615450	0	149205	0	1154840	222547	825750	1138949	1729159	1627574	2703271	6775773	16288383
Interest	3	71320	347	0	301	3106	1344	2588	954	2705	8340	6210	26743	18681
Rents	4	10738	0	0	0	521	0	452	0	1058	0	3545	199	4963
Royalties	5	652281	0	0	0	0	0	0	0	0	0	45	432864	219372
Other Portfolio Income	6	541810	0	0	0	466	5	100	866	10361	18880	9182	362339	139611
Other Receipts	7	587602	0	0	0	1871	2417	16684	14327	3419	28893	27579	24105	468307
Total Receipts	8	34479201	347	149205	301	1160804	226313	845574	1155096	1746702	1683687	2749832	7622023	17139317
Average Total Receipts	9	25167	14	192	5	3071	12573	17616	55005	97039	210461	458305	1270337	5713106
Operating Costs/Operating Income (%)														
Cost of Operations	10	67.6	•	63.2	•	56.0	73.2	57.3	66.5	53.2	78.0	73.3	57.2	72.8
Salaries and Wages	11	11.8	•	•	•	15.8	10.5	18.8	7.7	15.5	9.9	11.3	17.8	9.0
Taxes Paid	12	1.1	•	1.7	•	1.7	1.1	1.6	1.3	2.1	1.0	1.1	1.6	0.8
Interest Paid	13	2.6	•	2.9	•	1.7	0.9	1.0	3.1	2.2	0.3	0.8	2.1	3.5
Depreciation	14	2.6	•	6.1	•	1.1	2.7	3.7	1.8	2.8	2.3	2.8	4.1	2.1
Amortization and Depletion	15	1.2	•	•	•	1.4	0.3	0.9	1.2	1.1	0.2	0.6	1.7	1.2
Pensions and Other Deferred Comp.	16	0.4	•	•	•	0.5	0.2	0.4	0.2	0.2	0.4	0.8	0.1	0.5
Employee Benefits	17	2.0	•	0.2	•	1.4	1.4	2.6	1.2	2.7	1.8	1.3	2.5	1.9
Advertising	18	1.8	•	0.0	•	2.3	0.2	1.2	1.2	2.0	0.5	1.1	2.6	1.8
Other Expenses	19	13.4	•	38.7	•	23.2	23.2	16.5	15.4	14.7	8.1	7.7	17.7	11.4
Officers' Compensation	20	0.7	•	0.1	•	3.2	3.9	3.9	1.7	1.4	1.1	0.7	0.5	0.2
Operating Margin	21	•	•	•	•	•	•	•	•	2.1	•	•	•	•
Operating Margin Before Officers' Comp.	22	•	•	•	•	•	•	•	0.5	3.5	•	•	•	•

Selected Average Balance Sheet ($ in Thousands)

Net Receivables **23**	3520	0	13	0	297	2279	2442	6987	14541	28764	50446	217648	764801
Inventories **24**	2917	0	21	14	467	1854	2431	8185	10841	29821	88604	259049	640551
Net Property, Plant and Equipment **25**	2266	0	9	26	164	740	1381	2735	11380	15960	52198	117052	516359
Total Assets **26**	37350	0	34	931	2050	7510	13556	34866	71395	158367	362707	1260916	12165819
Notes and Loans Payable **27**	11366	0	157	48	919	1750	3270	26869	25200	22336	63295	111298	4222079
All Other Liabilities **28**	8941	0	19	21	436	3487	3391	18181	22617	37428	129724	542532	2240228
Net Worth **29**	17043	0	-141	863	694	2274	6895	-10185	23578	98603	169688	607084	5703511

Selected Financial Ratios (Times to 1)

Current Ratio **30**	1.4	•	0.8	43.6	2.4	1.6	1.5	1.9	2.3	2.5	2.1	1.1	1.2
Quick Ratio **31**	0.7	•	0.6	43.0	1.5	0.9	1.1	0.8	1.2	1.5	0.9	0.7	0.6
Net Sales to Working Capital **32**	8.6	•	•	•	3.3	5.2	7.7	5.1	3.7	3.7	4.7	19.7	13.4
Coverage Ratio **33**	1.3	•	•	•	•	•	1.2	1.2	2.4	1.8	1.8	3.6	1.1
Total Asset Turnover **34**	0.6	•	5.6	•	1.5	1.6	1.3	1.6	1.3	1.3	1.2	0.9	0.4
Inventory Turnover **35**	5.5	•	5.8	3.4	3.7	4.9	4.1	4.4	4.7	5.3	3.7	2.5	6.2
Receivables Turnover **36**	6.2	•	4.6	•	9.2	3.3	5.0	9.2	8.4	5.1	7.8	2.5	14.2
Total Liabilities to Net Worth **37**	1.2	•	•	0.1	2.0	2.3	1.0	•	2.0	0.6	1.1	1.1	1.1
Current Assets to Working Capital **38**	3.6	•	•	1.0	1.7	2.6	3.0	2.1	1.8	1.7	1.9	9.8	5.1
Current Liabilities to Working Capital **39**	2.6	•	•	0.0	0.7	1.6	2.0	1.1	0.8	0.7	0.9	8.8	4.1
Working Capital to Net Sales **40**	0.1	•	•	•	0.3	0.2	0.1	0.2	0.3	0.3	0.2	0.1	0.1
Inventory to Working Capital **41**	1.0	•	•	•	0.5	0.8	0.5	1.0	0.6	0.4	0.7	2.0	1.6
Total Receipts to Cash Flow **42**	8.8	•	8.4	•	9.2	23.3	11.5	7.5	6.7	15.4	16.0	5.2	10.6
Cost of Goods to Cash Flow **43**	5.9	•	5.3	•	5.2	17.1	6.6	5.0	3.5	12.0	11.7	3.0	7.7
Cash Flow to Total Debt **44**	0.1	•	0.1	•	0.2	0.1	0.2	0.2	0.3	0.2	0.1	0.3	0.1

Selected Financial Factors (in Percentages)

Debt Ratio **45**	54.4	•	513.8	7.3	66.1	69.7	49.1	129.2	67.0	37.7	53.2	51.9	53.1
Return on Total Assets **46**	2.2	•	•	•	•	•	•	5.8	7.3	0.8	1.8	6.7	1.6
Return on Equity Before Income Taxes **47**	1.1	•	17.4	•	•	•	•	•	13.0	0.6	1.7	10.1	0.2
Return on Equity After Income Taxes **48**	0.6	•	17.4	•	•	•	•	•	9.6	•	0.9	8.5	0.1
Profit Margin (Before Income Tax) **49**	0.8	•	•	•	•	•	•	0.7	3.2	0.3	0.6	5.4	0.2
Profit Margin (After Income Tax) **50**	0.4	•	•	•	•	•	•	0.1	2.4	•	0.4	4.5	0.2

Table II

Corporations with Net Income

AUDIO AND VIDEO EQUIP., REPRODUCING MAGNETIC & OPTICAL MEDIA

MONEY AMOUNTS AND SIZE OF ASSETS IN THOUSANDS OF DOLLARS

Item Description for Accounting Period 7/08 Through 6/09	Total	Zero Assets	Under 500	500 to 1,000	1,000 to 5,000	5,000 to 10,000	10,000 to 25,000	25,000 to 50,000	50,000 to 100,000	100,000 to 250,000	250,000 to 500,000	500,000 to 2,500,000	2,500,000 and over
Number of Enterprises 1	656	0	288	0	290	10	32	15	10	3	•	•	0
Revenues ($ in Thousands)													
Net Sales 2	22059655	0	7490	0	928316	165516	727703	855038	1039264	629170	•	•	0
Interest 3	31962	0	0	0	1657	0	1882	382	612	5516	•	•	0
Rents 4	6797	0	0	0	491	0	443	0	180	0	•	•	0
Royalties 5	570448	0	0	0	0	0	0	0	0	0	•	•	0
Other Portfolio Income 6	406621	0	0	0	466	0	100	561	9795	16047	•	•	0
Other Receipts 7	353337	0	0	0	155	189	15641	8616	5138	315	•	•	0
Total Receipts 8	23428820	0	7490	0	931085	165705	745769	864597	1054989	651048	•	•	0
Average Total Receipts 9	35715	•	26	•	3211	16570	23305	57640	105499	217016	•	•	•
Operating Costs/Operating Income (%)													
Cost of Operations 10	65.6	•	53.2	•	49.0	77.0	59.0	68.2	51.1	63.2	•	•	•
Salaries and Wages 11	11.6	•	•	•	13.8	0.7	12.9	6.2	13.4	14.6	•	•	•
Taxes Paid 12	0.8	•	0.9	•	1.5	1.0	1.2	1.1	1.6	1.4	•	•	•
Interest Paid 13	2.6	•	0.1	•	0.2	0.8	0.5	3.1	2.1	0.6	•	•	•
Depreciation 14	2.1	•	•	•	0.9	0.6	2.5	1.2	2.3	1.9	•	•	•
Amortization and Depletion 15	1.0	•	•	•	0.1	•	1.0	0.5	0.6	0.2	•	•	•
Pensions and Other Deferred Comp. 16	0.3	•	•	•	0.6	0.3	0.5	0.1	0.3	0.9	•	•	•
Employee Benefits 17	1.9	•	•	•	1.1	1.3	2.1	1.2	3.4	2.7	•	•	•
Advertising 18	1.7	•	•	•	2.8	0.1	1.0	0.7	1.9	0.7	•	•	•
Other Expenses 19	12.8	•	33.1	•	19.7	12.5	12.0	11.9	13.3	8.0	•	•	•
Officers' Compensation 20	0.7	•	•	•	3.0	2.4	3.8	1.5	1.2	0.5	•	•	•
Operating Margin 21	•	•	12.7	•	7.3	3.3	3.6	4.2	8.7	5.2	•	•	•
Operating Margin Before Officers' Comp. 22	•	•	12.7	•	10.3	5.8	7.4	5.7	9.9	5.7	•	•	•

Selected Average Balance Sheet ($ in Thousands)

Net Receivables **23**	4600	0	241	2779	3114	7205	16039	17986
Inventories **24**	4643	9	564	1966	2900	7866	10487	46611
Net Property, Plant and Equipment **25**	2861	0	102	468	1376	1858	11192	10312
Total Assets **26**	59189	11	1863	6600	14322	32268	66033	171064
Notes and Loans Payable **27**	16216	5	320	2504	1073	24427	29636	41455
All Other Liabilities **28**	11400	1	276	3309	3267	18800	15062	59518
Net Worth **29**	31574	5	1267	787	9982	-10959	21335	70091

Selected Financial Ratios (Times to 1)

Current Ratio **30**	1.2	8.9	3.8	1.2	2.2	2.3	2.2	1.8
Quick Ratio **31**	0.6	1.7	2.5	0.6	1.7	1.0	1.4	1.2
Net Sales to Working Capital **32**	16.2	2.8	2.6	16.2	5.7	4.4	4.7	4.9
Coverage Ratio **33**	3.2	159.8	32.3	5.4	12.9	3.0	6.0	18.6
Total Asset Turnover **34**	0.6	2.5	1.7	2.5	1.6	1.8	1.6	1.2
Inventory Turnover **35**	4.8	1.6	2.8	6.5	4.6	4.9	5.1	2.8
Receivables Turnover **36**	6.5	•	9.4	3.6	5.2	10.0	8.5	4.5
Total Liabilities to Net Worth **37**	0.9	1.3	0.5	7.4	0.4	•	2.1	1.4
Current Assets to Working Capital **38**	5.6	1.1	1.4	5.8	1.8	1.7	1.8	2.2
Current Liabilities to Working Capital **39**	4.6	0.1	0.4	4.8	0.8	0.7	0.8	1.2
Working Capital to Net Sales **40**	0.1	0.4	0.4	0.1	0.2	0.2	0.2	0.2
Inventory to Working Capital **41**	2.2	0.9	0.4	1.5	0.3	0.8	0.6	0.5
Total Receipts to Cash Flow **42**	6.2	2.2	4.1	7.2	6.1	6.7	4.7	6.5
Cost of Goods to Cash Flow **43**	4.1	1.2	2.0	5.6	3.6	4.6	2.4	4.1
Cash Flow to Total Debt **44**	0.2	2.0	1.3	0.4	0.9	0.2	0.5	0.3

Selected Financial Factors (in Percentages)

Debt Ratio **45**	46.7	56.0	32.0	88.1	30.3	134.0	67.7	59.0
Return on Total Assets **46**	4.6	31.4	13.4	10.6	10.4	16.1	19.6	13.2
Return on Equity Before Income Taxes **47**	5.9	70.9	19.1	72.6	13.8	•	50.5	30.4
Return on Equity After Income Taxes **48**	5.2	70.9	16.4	60.0	12.3	•	43.8	20.2
Profit Margin (Before Income Tax) **49**	5.5	12.7	7.5	3.5	6.1	6.0	10.4	10.2
Profit Margin (After Income Tax) **50**	4.9	12.7	6.5	2.9	5.4	5.2	9.0	6.7

Table I

Corporations with and without Net Income

SEMICONDUCTOR AND OTHER ELECTRONIC COMPONENT

MONEY AMOUNTS AND SIZE OF ASSETS IN THOUSANDS OF DOLLARS

Item Description for Accounting Period 7/08 Through 6/09	Total	Zero Assets	Under 500	500 to 1,000	1,000 to 5,000	5,000 to 10,000	10,000 to 25,000	25,000 to 50,000	50,000 to 100,000	100,000 to 250,000	250,000 to 500,000	500,000 to 2,500,000	2,500,000 and over
Number of Enterprises **1**	5726	573	2482	487	1324	307	224	81	72	54	44	59	19
Revenues ($ in Thousands)													
Net Sales **2**	190901934	497183	762300	919012	6502799	3155738	5275426	2868504	5176771	8406240	12779112	39679496	104879353
Interest **3**	2289782	6231	1904	821	7475	10053	17584	17092	34485	64551	108907	474333	1546346
Rents **4**	49115	106	0	0	0	0	3186	32	5437	6366	11933	4873	17182
Royalties **5**	6454206	857	0	0	0	0	2837	19664	59119	7947	291074	908621	5164089
Other Portfolio Income **6**	5148749	837206	0	4563	24511	20783	16989	22806	38362	43768	120305	1086378	2933079
Other Receipts **7**	5788838	180	13346	1688	12957	17851	55020	68965	127637	567430	132942	1156426	3634394
Total Receipts **8**	210632624	1341763	777550	926084	6547742	3204425	5371042	2997063	5441811	9096302	13444273	43310127	118174443
Average Total Receipts **9**	36785	2342	313	1902	4945	10438	23978	37001	75581	168450	305552	734070	6219708
Operating Costs/Operating Income (%)													
Cost of Operations **10**	66.1	77.4	70.4	52.2	61.4	59.9	70.5	65.9	66.2	70.1	68.4	68.5	64.9
Salaries and Wages **11**	12.2	11.7	2.0	12.4	14.0	12.2	11.3	10.9	14.5	13.8	15.8	14.5	10.7
Taxes Paid **12**	1.2	1.4	1.4	2.4	2.4	1.7	1.7	2.0	1.4	1.6	1.5	1.2	0.9
Interest Paid **13**	1.8	0.5	0.2	0.6	1.4	0.9	1.3	1.1	1.7	1.9	1.2	2.6	1.7
Depreciation **14**	5.5	2.4	1.1	2.4	2.7	3.2	2.7	2.7	3.6	3.8	3.4	6.4	6.2
Amortization and Depletion **15**	1.4	2.1	0.0	0.5	0.3	0.6	0.5	0.5	1.4	1.1	2.8	1.1	1.6
Pensions and Other Deferred Comp. **16**	0.6	0.0	•	0.1	0.9	0.4	0.5	0.8	0.4	0.6	0.4	0.5	0.7
Employee Benefits **17**	2.0	3.4	0.3	2.8	1.6	2.1	1.6	2.1	1.7	1.6	2.3	2.2	2.0
Advertising **18**	1.4	0.1	0.4	0.2	0.4	1.1	0.4	0.5	0.5	0.8	0.4	0.4	2.2
Other Expenses **19**	11.8	23.5	36.9	21.5	11.8	12.9	10.4	12.6	15.2	13.8	9.2	10.7	11.9
Officers' Compensation **20**	1.1	5.6	3.4	8.0	5.6	3.6	3.1	2.8	2.1	1.2	0.9	0.9	0.5
Operating Margin **21**	•	•	•	•	•	1.5	•	•	•	•	•	•	•
Operating Margin Before Officers' Comp. **22**	•	•	•	5.1	3.1	5.1	1.0	•	•	•	•	•	•

Selected Average Balance Sheet ($ in Thousands)

Net Receivables **23**	8896	0	26	194	639	1446	3048	6191	10348	32570	49412	164438	1785567
Inventories **24**	3299	0	12	209	549	1903	3328	5631	8082	21207	34525	62455	490129
Net Property, Plant and Equipment **25**	7253	0	13	94	660	1458	2290	5137	11257	25137	47235	158709	1346856
Total Assets **26**	52264	0	161	762	2595	6797	15442	34666	72388	169496	334817	1077670	10211856
Notes and Loans Payable **27**	10930	0	96	399	914	1894	4388	9191	14717	31046	63560	299116	1866078
All Other Liabilities **28**	14990	0	54	140	754	1107	4428	5966	19641	50987	73358	287255	3077680
Net Worth **29**	26344	0	11	223	927	3796	6626	19508	38030	87463	197898	491299	5268098

Selected Financial Ratios (Times to 1)

Current Ratio **30**	1.8	•	1.6	3.7	1.7	3.0	2.2	2.0	2.2	2.3	2.4	1.8	1.7
Quick Ratio **31**	1.2	•	1.5	2.1	1.0	1.7	1.3	1.2	1.4	1.5	1.6	1.2	1.2
Net Sales to Working Capital **32**	3.6	•	6.6	4.7	7.4	3.5	4.2	3.7	3.2	2.7	3.0	3.4	3.8
Coverage Ratio **33**	4.6	268.6	•	•	4.3	•	•	3.3	•	0.0	0.1	2.1	7.2
Total Asset Turnover **34**	0.6	•	1.9	2.5	1.9	1.5	1.5	1.0	1.0	0.9	0.9	0.6	0.5
Inventory Turnover **35**	6.7	•	18.1	4.7	5.5	3.2	5.0	4.1	5.9	5.1	5.8	7.4	7.3
Receivables Turnover **36**	3.6	•	17.2	8.1	8.5	5.5	7.3	5.4	7.1	4.9	4.8	4.5	2.8
Total Liabilities to Net Worth **37**	1.0	•	13.2	2.4	1.8	0.8	1.3	0.8	0.9	0.9	0.7	1.2	0.9
Current Assets to Working Capital **38**	2.3	•	2.6	1.4	2.5	1.5	1.9	2.0	1.8	1.7	1.7	2.3	2.5
Current Liabilities to Working Capital **39**	1.3	•	1.6	0.4	1.5	0.5	0.9	1.0	0.8	0.7	0.7	1.3	1.5
Working Capital to Net Sales **40**	0.3	•	0.2	0.2	0.1	0.3	0.2	0.3	0.3	0.4	0.3	0.3	0.3
Inventory to Working Capital **41**	0.3	•	0.2	0.5	0.9	0.5	0.6	0.6	0.4	0.4	0.3	0.3	0.3
Total Receipts to Cash Flow **42**	7.4	0.6	6.3	9.3	16.6	8.0	19.2	8.1	12.1	10.6	18.4	12.9	5.7
Cost of Goods to Cash Flow **43**	4.9	0.5	4.4	4.8	10.2	4.8	13.6	5.4	8.0	7.4	12.6	8.8	3.7
Cash Flow to Total Debt **44**	0.2	•	0.3	0.4	0.2	0.4	0.1	0.3	0.2	0.2	0.1	0.1	0.2

Selected Financial Factors (in Percentages)

Debt Ratio **45**	49.6	•	93.0	70.7	64.3	44.1	57.1	43.7	47.5	48.4	40.9	54.4	48.4
Return on Total Assets **46**	5.3	•	•	•	•	6.0	•	3.8	•	0.1	0.2	3.5	6.7
Return on Equity Before Income Taxes **47**	8.3	•	•	•	•	8.3	•	4.7	•	•	•	4.0	11.3
Return on Equity After Income Taxes **48**	4.7	•	•	•	•	7.2	•	2.3	•	•	•	1.3	7.0
Profit Margin (Before Income Tax) **49**	6.5	144.3	•	•	•	3.1	•	2.6	•	•	•	2.9	10.7
Profit Margin (After Income Tax) **50**	3.7	142.9	•	•	•	2.7	•	1.3	•	•	•	0.9	6.7

Table II
Corporations with Net Income

SEMICONDUCTOR AND OTHER ELECTRONIC COMPONENT

MONEY AMOUNTS AND SIZE OF ASSETS IN THOUSANDS OF DOLLARS

Item Description for Accounting Period 7/08 Through 6/09	Total	Zero Assets	Under 500	500 to 1,000	1,000 to 5,000	5,000 to 10,000	10,000 to 25,000	25,000 to 50,000	50,000 to 100,000	100,000 to 250,000	250,000 to 500,000	500,000 to 2,500,000	2,500,000 and over
Number of Enterprises 1	3372	304	1281	365	872	233	137	44	37	26	24	36	13
Revenues ($ in Thousands)													
Net Sales 2	129638818	380301	276300	729305	5249990	2618570	3711080	1939757	3228461	4621078	7413981	23630206	75839789
Interest 3	1309575	5143	1901	634	883	3770	7228	7121	14894	24971	48091	294123	900817
Rents 4	34258	0	0	0	0	0	2713	32	204	1023	9952	3818	16516
Royalties 5	5810184	0	0	0	0	0	3	17803	7400	5703	128887	588398	5061991
Other Portfolio Income 6	3919596	837202	0	0	2714	18729	2718	2380	35228	9052	65071	813964	2132540
Other Receipts 7	2676221	-63	8882	276	6421	12426	43666	56046	67640	92943	75885	994998	1317096
Total Receipts 8	143338652	1222583	287083	730215	5260008	2653495	3767408	2023139	3353827	4754770	7741867	26325507	85268749
Average Total Receipts 9	42523	4022	224	2001	6032	11388	27499	45980	90644	182876	322578	731264	6559135
Operating Costs/Operating Income (%)													
Cost of Operations 10	60.3	80.1	54.4	50.3	58.3	57.6	68.7	61.2	66.5	66.1	63.3	63.4	58.2
Salaries and Wages 11	12.0	8.9	2.1	11.3	12.7	9.9	7.6	7.4	9.8	10.5	16.4	15.4	11.1
Taxes Paid 12	1.2	0.9	3.4	2.3	2.3	1.3	1.5	1.9	1.2	1.4	1.4	1.3	1.1
Interest Paid 13	1.1	0.5	0.4	0.3	1.1	0.6	0.6	0.7	1.4	1.1	0.6	2.2	0.8
Depreciation 14	5.6	0.7	1.2	0.7	2.5	2.1	2.0	2.1	2.5	3.1	3.4	5.1	6.9
Amortization and Depletion 15	0.9	2.7	•	0.2	0.2	0.6	0.2	0.3	0.9	0.4	0.4	1.4	1.0
Pensions and Other Deferred Comp. 16	0.7	•	•	0.0	0.9	0.4	0.7	1.1	0.3	0.4	0.4	0.5	0.9
Employee Benefits 17	2.2	3.7	0.3	2.0	1.5	2.0	1.4	1.6	1.4	1.5	2.4	2.4	2.3
Advertising 18	1.6	0.0	0.0	0.1	0.3	1.2	0.4	0.6	0.5	1.0	0.5	0.4	2.4
Other Expenses 19	9.2	15.1	21.4	16.9	9.7	10.0	6.5	10.9	9.5	10.6	7.4	8.3	9.4
Officers' Compensation 20	1.2	5.0	9.0	8.0	5.6	3.1	3.0	2.4	1.9	1.1	0.9	1.0	0.7
Operating Margin 21	3.9	•	7.8	8.0	5.0	11.2	7.3	9.9	4.2	2.8	3.0	•	5.1
Operating Margin Before Officers' Comp. 22	5.1	•	16.9	16.0	10.6	14.4	10.4	12.3	6.1	3.9	3.9	•	5.7

Selected Average Balance Sheet ($ in Thousands)

Net Receivables 23	10731	0	27	201	806	1643	3242	6972	10956	35543	48873	136712	2062745
Inventories 24	3319	0	12	187	582	1783	3804	6050	8731	24443	39462	61913	398894
Net Property, Plant and Equipment 25	8422	0	6	59	684	1039	2319	4378	8736	24112	44395	140712	1533744
Total Assets 26	56263	0	124	736	2587	6479	14846	33831	72739	170912	318934	981841	10143559
Notes and Loans Payable 27	8281	0	12	60	889	1497	2710	7497	15883	28701	37541	233190	1187086
All Other Liabilities 28	17774	0	19	151	559	991	4358	6870	17012	35603	69712	283431	3446556
Net Worth 29	30208	0	93	525	1140	3991	7779	19463	39844	106608	211681	465220	5509917

Selected Financial Ratios (Times to 1)

Current Ratio 30	1.8	•	3.9	4.0	2.0	3.5	2.3	2.7	2.4	2.6	2.1	1.8	1.7
Quick Ratio 31	1.3	•	3.2	2.1	1.2	2.0	1.2	1.6	1.6	1.7	1.4	1.1	1.3
Net Sales to Working Capital 32	3.4	•	4.0	4.5	7.0	3.6	4.5	3.6	3.7	2.8	3.9	3.4	3.2
Coverage Ratio 33	15.5	386.3	27.7	31.0	5.9	20.9	15.0	21.0	6.6	6.3	14.7	7.2	23.1
Total Asset Turnover 34	0.7	•	1.7	2.7	2.3	1.7	1.8	1.3	1.2	1.0	1.0	0.7	0.6
Inventory Turnover 35	7.0	•	9.7	5.4	6.0	3.6	4.9	4.5	6.6	4.8	5.0	6.7	8.5
Receivables Turnover 36	4.4	•	•	8.8	9.3	5.9	8.1	5.6	8.0	5.1	5.1	4.2	•
Total Liabilities to Net Worth 37	0.9	•	0.3	0.4	1.3	0.6	0.9	0.7	0.8	0.6	0.5	1.1	0.8
Current Assets to Working Capital 38	2.2	•	1.3	1.3	2.0	1.4	1.8	1.6	1.7	1.6	1.9	2.2	2.4
Current Liabilities to Working Capital 39	1.2	•	0.3	0.3	1.0	0.4	0.8	0.6	0.7	0.6	0.9	1.2	1.4
Working Capital to Net Sales 40	0.3	•	0.3	0.2	0.1	0.3	0.2	0.3	0.3	0.4	0.3	0.3	0.3
Inventory to Working Capital 41	0.3	•	0.2	0.6	0.8	0.4	0.7	0.5	0.4	0.4	0.4	0.3	0.2
Total Receipts to Cash Flow 42	4.7	0.5	3.8	5.2	9.1	5.1	7.7	4.3	6.8	6.7	7.9	6.6	4.0
Cost of Goods to Cash Flow 43	2.8	0.4	2.1	2.6	5.3	2.9	5.3	2.6	4.5	4.4	5.0	4.2	2.3
Cash Flow to Total Debt 44	0.3	•	1.9	1.8	0.5	0.9	0.5	0.7	0.4	0.4	0.4	0.2	0.3

Selected Financial Factors (in Percentages)

Debt Ratio 45	46.3	•	24.8	28.6	56.0	38.4	47.6	42.5	45.2	37.6	33.6	52.6	45.7
Return on Total Assets 46	11.7	•	21.2	22.8	14.5	22.9	17.3	19.3	11.4	7.2	7.9	10.8	11.3
Return on Equity Before Income Taxes 47	20.3	•	27.1	30.9	27.4	35.4	30.8	31.9	17.7	9.7	11.1	19.5	19.9
Return on Equity After Income Taxes 48	15.0	•	25.4	30.7	25.7	34.1	25.9	27.6	16.0	8.3	8.9	14.8	13.9
Profit Margin (Before Income Tax) 49	16.0	207.1	11.7	8.1	5.2	12.6	8.8	14.1	8.1	5.8	7.6	13.8	18.8
Profit Margin (After Income Tax) 50	11.8	205.2	11.0	8.1	4.9	12.1	7.4	12.2	7.3	5.0	6.1	10.5	13.2

Table I

Corporations with and without Net Income

NAVIGATIONAL, MEASURING, ELECTROMEDICAL, AND CONTROL

MONEY AMOUNTS AND SIZE OF ASSETS IN THOUSANDS OF DOLLARS

Item Description for Accounting Period 7/08 Through 6/09	Total	Zero Assets	Under 500	500 to 1,000	1,000 to 5,000	5,000 to 10,000	10,000 to 25,000	25,000 to 50,000	50,000 to 100,000	100,000 to 250,000	250,000 to 500,000	500,000 to 2,500,000	2,500,000 and over
Number of Enterprises **1**	3028	43	1625	159	642	171	179	68	40	41	14	26	19
Revenues ($ in Thousands)													
Net Sales **2**	99460512	548075	573083	156710	3968245	1730412	4222522	3298719	3640636	5805148	3295769	13582962	58638232
Interest **3**	1970108	989	127	872	4297	3219	11743	5554	7935	58075	58096	118192	1701010
Rents **4**	80378	165	0	792	687	3737	254	1844	7624	1953	1572	26625	35127
Royalties **5**	810364	0	0	0	0	0	70	20	9460	10091	2096	205899	582728
Other Portfolio Income **6**	1036705	17008	93	146	213	7772	5471	8164	30945	149527	5924	231344	580098
Other Receipts **7**	1532814	37324	112	2749	42336	17072	12791	41285	38005	87608	6361	358601	888565
Total Receipts **8**	104890881	603561	573415	161269	4015778	1762212	4252851	3355586	3734605	6112402	3369818	14523623	62425760
Average Total Receipts **9**	34640	14036	353	1014	6255	10305	23759	49347	93365	149083	240701	558601	3285566
Operating Costs/Operating Income (%)													
Cost of Operations **10**	60.4	38.0	36.3	56.7	59.5	59.0	62.1	54.7	65.1	57.3	53.3	58.2	62.1
Salaries and Wages **11**	13.7	19.8	10.4	11.9	14.3	15.7	12.7	16.1	11.5	14.9	15.7	15.4	12.9
Taxes Paid **12**	1.7	3.1	3.3	2.4	2.2	2.0	1.5	1.6	1.3	1.6	2.4	1.4	1.7
Interest Paid **13**	4.1	2.3	0.9	2.7	0.9	0.4	1.1	1.1	0.9	2.2	3.1	3.0	5.5
Depreciation **14**	2.0	3.1	1.3	1.3	1.3	1.7	2.0	2.1	2.2	2.6	2.4	2.6	1.9
Amortization and Depletion **15**	1.4	15.1	0.1	0.0	0.1	0.4	0.3	0.6	0.9	1.2	1.5	2.8	1.3
Pensions and Other Deferred Comp. **16**	1.2	0.4	0.0	•	0.4	0.4	0.7	0.5	0.5	0.5	1.1	0.7	1.7
Employee Benefits **17**	2.0	0.7	3.3	1.6	2.0	2.8	2.0	2.3	2.2	2.6	2.4	2.1	1.8
Advertising **18**	0.7	0.8	1.6	0.6	1.0	1.1	0.8	1.1	1.0	1.3	1.8	0.8	0.4
Other Expenses **19**	12.0	30.1	38.7	35.8	13.2	15.7	9.0	14.1	11.5	15.3	13.3	14.4	10.5
Officers' Compensation **20**	1.4	1.3	16.9	9.7	5.8	3.0	4.0	2.8	1.6	1.7	1.0	1.1	0.6
Operating Margin **21**	•	•		•	•	•	3.9	3.1	1.3	•	2.1	•	•
Operating Margin Before Officers' Comp. **22**	0.8	•	4.0	•	5.0	0.8	7.9	5.9	2.9	0.5	3.2	•	0.1

Selected Average Balance Sheet ($ in Thousands)

Net Receivables 23	6820	0	27	119	926	1490	3675	7577	15883	28249	56951	128846	664423
Inventories 24	3506	0	28	440	651	1407	3501	5884	10765	24157	25974	81317	258789
Net Property, Plant and Equipment 25	3594	0	10	113	238	1132	2096	5909	8115	17715	21278	82472	327883
Total Assets 26	63127	0	202	670	2809	6447	14760	33801	72060	163973	344610	1035504	7448130
Notes and Loans Payable 27	14156	0	197	523	894	964	3549	10402	14588	40755	74770	246920	1613703
All Other Liabilities 28	17874	0	25	146	1258	1585	3737	11047	18250	41871	76192	313160	2100272
Net Worth 29	31097	0	-20	1	658	3899	7474	12352	39221	81346	193648	475424	3734155

Selected Financial Ratios (Times to 1)

Current Ratio 30	1.0	•	1.4	2.8	1.3	2.7	2.3	1.6	2.3	2.1	2.2	1.1	0.8
Quick Ratio 31	0.6	•	0.9	1.8	0.8	1.5	1.4	0.8	1.4	1.2	1.4	0.7	0.5
Net Sales to Working Capital 32	54.4	•	8.0	2.8	14.3	3.6	4.0	6.3	3.6	3.7	2.8	13.6	•
Coverage Ratio 33	2.5	•	•	•	1.5	0.2	5.3	5.7	5.3	3.3	2.5	3.1	2.3
Total Asset Turnover 34	0.5	•	1.7	1.5	2.2	1.6	1.6	1.4	1.3	0.9	0.7	0.5	0.4
Inventory Turnover 35	5.7	•	4.6	1.3	5.6	4.2	4.2	4.5	5.5	3.4	4.8	3.7	7.4
Receivables Turnover 36	4.9	•	14.1	2.6	6.1	5.6	6.5	6.6	6.5	4.5	3.3	3.5	5.2
Total Liabilities to Net Worth 37	1.0	•	•	506.6	3.3	0.7	1.0	1.7	0.8	1.0	0.8	1.2	1.0
Current Assets to Working Capital 38	23.5	•	3.3	1.6	4.9	1.6	1.8	2.8	1.7	1.9	1.8	8.2	•
Current Liabilities to Working Capital 39	22.5	•	2.3	0.6	3.9	0.6	0.8	1.8	0.7	0.9	0.8	7.2	•
Working Capital to Net Sales 40	0.0	•	0.1	0.4	0.1	0.3	0.3	0.2	0.3	0.3	0.4	0.1	•
Inventory to Working Capital 41	6.1	•	1.2	0.5	1.0	0.6	0.6	0.9	0.5	0.6	0.3	1.9	•
Total Receipts to Cash Flow 42	6.8	4.4	5.5	8.4	10.3	7.8	8.4	5.8	7.7	6.0	6.4	6.0	7.0
Cost of Goods to Cash Flow 43	4.1	1.7	2.0	4.8	6.1	4.6	5.2	3.2	5.0	3.5	3.4	3.5	4.3
Cash Flow to Total Debt 44	0.1	•	0.3	0.2	0.3	0.5	0.4	0.4	0.4	0.3	0.2	0.2	0.1

Selected Financial Factors (in Percentages)

Debt Ratio 45	50.7	•	109.7	99.8	76.6	39.5	49.4	63.5	45.6	50.4	43.8	54.1	49.9
Return on Total Assets 46	5.2	•	•	•	2.9	0.1	9.1	8.8	6.3	6.3	5.2	4.7	5.3
Return on Equity Before Income Taxes 47	6.3	•	231.2	•	3.8	•	14.5	19.7	9.4	8.9	5.4	6.9	6.0
Return on Equity After Income Taxes 48	4.3	•	232.6	•	0.2	•	12.5	16.6	6.3	4.7	3.7	4.3	4.2
Profit Margin (Before Income Tax) 49	6.0	•	•	•	0.4	•	4.6	5.0	4.0	5.1	4.5	6.2	7.3
Profit Margin (After Income Tax) 50	4.0	•	•	•	0.0	•	4.0	4.2	2.7	2.7	3.0	3.9	5.0

Table II
Corporations with Net Income

NAVIGATIONAL, MEASURING, ELECTROMEDICAL, AND CONTROL

MONEY AMOUNTS AND SIZE OF ASSETS IN THOUSANDS OF DOLLARS

Item Description for Accounting Period 7/08 Through 6/09		Total	Zero Assets	Under 500	500 to 1,000	1,000 to 5,000	5,000 to 10,000	10,000 to 25,000	25,000 to 50,000	50,000 to 100,000	100,000 to 250,000	250,000 to 500,000	500,000 to 2,500,000	2,500,000 and over
Number of Enterprises	1	1329	5	576	0	375	117	105	47	27	28	10	21	16
Revenues ($ in Thousands)														
Net Sales	2	85634663	469643	148630	0	2663837	1351484	2882315	2499397	2711911	4563193	2613149	11781862	53944241
Interest	3	1415414	588	46	0	1900	937	3810	2919	5335	38544	49176	97024	1215134
Rents	4	72007	165	0	0	610	3737	141	1454	7624	1596	1129	26625	28926
Royalties	5	618671	0	0	0	0	0	0	20	6942	2035	1676	93848	514150
Other Portfolio Income	6	903595	16009	93	0	147	3198	2855	5411	26385	133274	5797	181003	529422
Other Receipts	7	1351398	36510	1	0	34915	15686	5441	34558	25379	75941	6804	234307	881859
Total Receipts	8	89995748	522915	148770	0	2701409	1375042	2894562	2543759	2783576	4814583	2677731	12414669	57118732
Average Total Receipts	9	67717	104583	258	•	7204	11752	27567	54123	103095	171949	267773	591175	3569921
Operating Costs/Operating Income (%)														
Cost of Operations	10	60.6	36.0	23.2	•	54.0	58.3	59.3	51.1	67.1	56.2	50.7	60.1	62.4
Salaries and Wages	11	12.9	15.7	•	•	14.7	11.9	10.5	16.9	9.5	14.0	15.8	13.6	12.5
Taxes Paid	12	1.6	3.5	1.9	•	2.4	1.6	1.4	1.6	1.2	1.4	2.5	1.5	1.5
Interest Paid	13	3.6	1.8	0.8	•	0.6	0.3	0.6	0.6	0.8	2.3	3.5	2.4	4.7
Depreciation	14	1.9	2.7	1.4	•	1.1	1.6	1.7	1.8	1.8	2.4	2.4	2.4	1.8
Amortization and Depletion	15	1.3	16.7	•	•	0.0	0.1	0.1	0.4	0.6	0.8	1.6	1.8	1.3
Pensions and Other Deferred Comp.	16	1.3	0.4	•	•	0.3	0.5	0.8	0.6	0.6	0.4	1.3	0.7	1.7
Employee Benefits	17	2.0	0.1	2.5	•	1.8	2.7	1.8	2.6	2.0	2.6	2.4	1.9	1.9
Advertising	18	0.6	0.9	•	•	0.9	0.8	0.4	0.9	0.8	1.4	2.2	0.8	0.4
Other Expenses	19	10.9	28.5	47.1	•	11.6	11.0	6.8	11.4	8.7	13.3	11.8	12.1	10.4
Officers' Compensation	20	1.2	1.2	20.4	•	5.1	2.5	4.1	3.1	1.4	1.7	1.1	1.2	0.6
Operating Margin	21	2.3	•	2.9	•	7.3	8.7	12.6	8.8	5.6	3.5	4.8	1.5	0.9
Operating Margin Before Officers' Comp.	22	3.4	•	23.2	•	12.5	11.2	16.6	11.9	7.0	5.2	6.0	2.6	1.4

Selected Average Balance Sheet ($ in Thousands)

Net Receivables **23**	13127	14	0	•	701	1789	4488	7788	16282	32567	62790	134612	707624
Inventories **24**	6732	12	0	•	601	1673	4621	6552	11510	25620	28868	73002	314434
Net Property, Plant and Equipment **25**	6567	9	0	•	277	1293	2210	5677	8142	19295	21142	70073	345334
Total Assets **26**	119897	161	0	•	2773	6364	15634	33711	73198	169722	362756	978656	7708291
Notes and Loans Payable **27**	24681	58	0	•	543	937	2297	9340	12599	43323	80070	217159	1553764
All Other Liabilities **28**	34454	1	0	•	880	1531	3008	10580	18630	46056	82306	298184	2224281
Net Worth **29**	60762	101	0	•	1350	3896	10330	13792	41970	80343	200380	463313	3930246

Selected Financial Ratios (Times to 1)

Current Ratio **30**	1.0	•	5.0	•	1.8	3.0	3.3	2.0	2.6	2.2	2.1	1.1	0.8
Quick Ratio **31**	0.6	•	3.9	•	1.2	1.7	2.1	1.1	1.5	1.3	1.3	0.7	0.5
Net Sales to Working Capital **32**	•	•	5.1	•	8.6	3.7	3.2	4.6	3.4	3.7	3.1	38.2	•
Coverage Ratio **33**	3.4	3.5	4.9	•	15.0	36.2	22.5	17.4	11.9	5.5	3.1	4.6	2.7
Total Asset Turnover **34**	0.5	•	1.6	•	2.6	1.8	1.8	1.6	1.4	1.0	0.7	0.6	0.4
Inventory Turnover **35**	5.8	•	5.0	•	6.4	4.0	3.5	4.2	5.9	3.6	4.6	4.6	6.7
Receivables Turnover **36**	4.9	•	•	•	8.2	5.0	5.6	6.8	7.1	4.4	3.7	•	•
Total Liabilities to Net Worth **37**	1.0	•	0.6	•	1.1	0.6	0.5	1.4	0.7	1.1	0.8	1.1	1.0
Current Assets to Working Capital **38**	•	•	1.3	•	2.2	1.5	1.4	2.0	1.6	1.8	1.9	20.0	•
Current Liabilities to Working Capital **39**	•	•	0.3	•	1.2	0.5	0.4	1.0	0.6	0.8	0.9	19.0	•
Working Capital to Net Sales **40**	•	•	0.2	•	0.1	0.3	0.3	0.2	0.3	0.3	0.3	0.0	•
Inventory to Working Capital **41**	•	•	0.2	•	0.4	0.6	0.5	0.7	0.5	0.5	0.3	5.0	•
Total Receipts to Cash Flow **42**	6.2	3.4	2.2	•	6.0	5.2	5.4	4.9	6.7	5.0	5.9	5.8	6.7
Cost of Goods to Cash Flow **43**	3.8	1.2	0.5	•	3.2	3.0	3.2	2.5	4.5	2.8	3.0	3.5	4.2
Cash Flow to Total Debt **44**	0.2	•	1.9	•	0.8	0.9	1.0	0.5	0.5	0.4	0.3	0.2	0.1

Selected Financial Factors (in Percentages)

Debt Ratio **45**	49.3	•	37.0	•	51.3	38.8	33.9	59.1	42.7	52.7	44.8	52.7	49.0
Return on Total Assets **46**	6.5	•	6.0	•	24.0	19.5	23.8	17.7	12.6	11.9	7.8	6.4	5.6
Return on Equity Before Income Taxes **47**	9.1	•	7.5	•	46.0	31.0	34.4	40.8	20.2	20.6	9.6	10.6	7.0
Return on Equity After Income Taxes **48**	6.7	•	6.8	•	43.0	28.1	31.9	36.7	15.9	14.5	7.2	7.4	4.9
Profit Margin (Before Income Tax) **49**	8.6	4.5	3.0	•	8.7	10.4	12.9	10.6	8.4	10.2	7.4	8.7	8.1
Profit Margin (After Income Tax) **50**	6.3	3.8	2.7	•	8.2	9.5	12.0	9.5	6.6	7.1	5.5	6.1	5.7

Table I

Corporations with and without Net Income

ELECTRICAL LIGHTING EQUIPMENT AND HOUSEHOLD APPLIANCE

MONEY AMOUNTS AND SIZE OF ASSETS IN THOUSANDS OF DOLLARS

Item Description for Accounting Period 7/08 Through 6/09		Total	Zero Assets	Under 500	500 to 1,000	1,000 to 5,000	5,000 to 10,000	10,000 to 25,000	25,000 to 50,000	50,000 to 100,000	100,000 to 250,000	250,000 to 500,000	500,000 to 2,500,000	2,500,000 and over
Number of Enterprises	1	1547	651	389	64	204	51	123	14	14	21	7	5	4
Revenues ($ in Thousands)														
Net Sales	2	148134316	579106	8591	2785	1075127	615162	4045001	911639	1104088	4164190	3899115	9990418	121739095
Interest	3	81921511	914	0	3	0	777	1439	306	17612	10419	511	37182	81852349
Rents	4	12640912	0	0	0	0	0	1071	0	0	591	54	16458	12622739
Royalties	5	1945439	241	0	0	0	0	213	0	10	2429	407	26586	1915553
Other Portfolio Income	6	431817	8	0	0	82	773	720	499	6046	5982	18589	35393	4250125
Other Receipts	7	33195657	1698	1	0	7635	28091	22294	2435	7256	32548	22537	77351	32993807
Total Receipts	8	282156052	581967	8592	2788	1082844	644803	4070738	914879	1135012	4216159	3941213	10183388	255373668
Average Total Receipts	9	182389	894	22	44	5308	12643	33095	65348	81072	200769	563030	2036678	63843417
Operating Costs/Operating Income (%)														
Cost of Operations	10	68.8	92.4	25.5	72.3	56.6	62.4	68.9	73.8	70.4	66.6	72.0	71.0	68.6
Salaries and Wages	11	11.1	17.0	0.8	6.6	17.7	11.6	10.8	5.7	6.1	9.0	4.7	6.5	11.7
Taxes Paid	12	0.4	0.4	0.9	1.3	3.7	1.6	1.1	1.1	1.3	1.2	1.0	1.3	0.2
Interest Paid	13	61.2	0.4	1.8	0.1	1.0	0.5	0.8	0.8	4.4	2.5	1.2	2.0	74.1
Depreciation	14	8.1	3.0	0.3	•	0.6	1.2	1.4	1.9	1.7	2.5	3.6	2.0	9.3
Amortization and Depletion	15	3.2	4.1	0.3	•	0.1	0.0	0.1	0.2	1.2	0.6	0.4	0.4	3.7
Pensions and Other Deferred Comp.	16	0.6	0.0	•	0.5	0.0	0.1	0.2	0.4	0.5	0.6	0.3	0.3	0.7
Employee Benefits	17	2.1	0.0	0.0	•	0.4	1.5	1.8	1.4	1.2	1.9	0.9	1.9	2.2
Advertising	18	1.8	0.3	3.9	5.1	0.8	1.0	0.6	2.7	1.0	2.4	4.0	2.8	1.6
Other Expenses	19	35.4	4.3	241.4	41.3	12.3	14.4	10.3	10.9	13.1	10.1	10.7	11.1	40.7
Officers' Compensation	20	0.4	0.3	2.0	6.7	1.3	3.5	1.5	1.5	1.6	1.3	0.6	0.1	0.3
Operating Margin	21	•	•	•	•	5.4	2.2	2.4	•	•	1.2	0.7	0.5	•
Operating Margin Before Officers' Comp.	22	•	•	•	•	6.7	5.7	3.9	1.2	2.5	2.5	1.3	0.6	•

Selected Average Balance Sheet ($ in Thousands)

	1	2	3	4	5	6	7	8	9	10	11	12	13
Net Receivables 23	123454	0	1	5	499	1129	4113	7262	9089	32137	54489	220570	46982214
Inventories 24	8008	0	9	79	655	4542	5213	15714	9670	32131	97468	198927	2167208
Net Property, Plant and Equipment 25	32730	0	0	0	276	909	2694	5030	9904	25946	92842	195323	11954794
Total Assets 26	518064	0	5	600	2122	7200	15564	34297	69230	165688	345879	1349027	196148627
Notes and Loans Payable 27	372207	0	24	6	784	1472	4073	6299	30940	50837	96327	279342	142849857
All Other Liabilities 28	100413	0	-20	4	794	2091	4662	14303	23171	50677	106529	471670	37452872
Net Worth 29	45443	0	2	591	543	3637	6829	13695	15119	64174	143022	598015	15845898

Selected Financial Ratios (Times to 1)

	1	2	3	4	5	6	7	8	9	10	11	12	13
Current Ratio 30	0.8	•	0.2	62.1	1.6	2.4	1.8	1.5	1.1	1.8	1.8	1.3	0.7
Quick Ratio 31	0.6	•	0.1	53.8	0.7	0.8	0.9	0.6	0.5	0.9	0.6	0.8	0.6
Net Sales to Working Capital 32	•	•	•	0.1	9.7	3.4	6.6	7.6	23.9	5.2	6.2	19.5	•
Coverage Ratio 33	1.1	•	•	•	7.2	14.3	4.8	1.1	1.1	2.1	2.3	2.4	1.1
Total Asset Turnover 34	0.2	•	4.3	0.1	2.5	1.7	2.1	1.9	1.1	1.2	1.6	1.5	0.2
Inventory Turnover 35	8.2	•	0.6	0.4	4.6	1.7	4.3	3.1	5.7	4.1	4.1	7.1	9.6
Receivables Turnover 36	0.8	•	8.5	16.3	9.8	4.8	8.0	6.3	8.9	6.4	7.7	6.6	0.7
Total Liabilities to Net Worth 37	10.4	•	2.2	0.0	2.9	1.0	1.3	1.5	3.6	1.6	1.4	1.3	11.4
Current Assets to Working Capital 38	•	•	•	1.0	2.7	1.7	2.2	2.9	9.6	2.2	2.2	4.8	•
Current Liabilities to Working Capital 39	•	•	•	0.0	1.7	0.7	1.2	1.9	8.6	1.2	1.2	3.8	•
Working Capital to Net Sales 40	•	•	•	13.6	0.1	0.3	0.2	0.1	0.0	0.2	0.2	0.1	•
Inventory to Working Capital 41	•	•	•	0.1	1.5	1.0	1.0	1.7	3.7	0.9	0.9	1.5	•
Total Receipts to Cash Flow 42	3.4	•	3.4	17.4	6.1	5.2	9.3	11.1	8.6	9.5	9.0	8.1	3.0
Cost of Goods to Cash Flow 43	2.3	•	0.9	12.6	3.5	3.2	6.4	8.2	6.1	6.3	6.5	5.7	2.1
Cash Flow to Total Debt 44	0.1	•	1.9	0.3	0.5	0.7	0.4	0.3	0.2	0.2	0.3	0.3	0.1

Selected Financial Factors (in Percentages)

	1	2	3	4	5	6	7	8	9	10	11	12	13
Debt Ratio 45	91.2	•	68.6	1.6	74.4	49.5	56.1	60.1	78.2	61.3	58.6	55.7	91.9
Return on Total Assets 46	12.9	•	•	•	17.7	12.4	8.1	1.7	5.5	6.1	4.6	7.1	13.0
Return on Equity Before Income Taxes 47	17.7	•	•	•	59.6	22.9	14.6	0.3	2.0	8.2	6.3	9.5	18.7
Return on Equity After Income Taxes 48	11.5	•	•	•	59.5	20.3	13.5	•	5.7	5.7	4.3	4.3	12.3
Profit Margin (Before Income Tax) 49	8.4	•	•	•	6.1	6.9	3.0	0.1	0.4	2.6	1.6	2.8	9.7
Profit Margin (After Income Tax) 50	5.5	•	•	•	6.1	6.1	2.8	•	1.9	1.9	1.1	1.3	6.4

147

Table II

Corporations with Net Income

ELECTRICAL LIGHTING EQUIPMENT AND HOUSEHOLD APPLIANCE

MONEY AMOUNTS AND SIZE OF ASSETS IN THOUSANDS OF DOLLARS

Item Description for Accounting Period 7/08 Through 6/09	Total	Zero Assets	Under 500	500 to 1,000	1,000 to 5,000	5,000 to 10,000	10,000 to 25,000	25,000 to 50,000	50,000 to 100,000	100,000 to 250,000	250,000 to 500,000	500,000 to 2,500,000	2,500,000 and over
Number of Enterprises 1	698	•	•	0	132	46	99	6	7	11	•	0	•
Revenues ($ in Thousands)													
Net Sales 2	135978261	•	•	0	854901	557904	3469749	466174	771993	2590537	•	0	•
Interest 3	81870019	•	•	0	0	212	499	63	283	6600	•	0	•
Rents 4	12640700	•	•	0	0	0	1071	0	0	387	•	0	•
Royalties 5	1920123	•	•	0	0	0	0	0	10	355	•	0	•
Other Portfolio Income 6	4294594	•	•	0	0	745	720	424	1990	5275	•	0	•
Other Receipts 7	33080515	•	•	0	0	27831	18145	961	4432	5672	•	0	•
Total Receipts 8	269784212	•	•	0	854901	586692	3490184	467622	778708	2608826	•	0	•
Average Total Receipts 9	386510	•	•	•	6477	12754	35254	77937	111244	237166	•	•	•
Operating Costs/Operating Income (%)													
Cost of Operations 10	68.2	•	•	•	52.3	63.8	66.9	76.6	67.8	63.0	•	•	•
Salaries and Wages 11	11.5	•	•	•	19.2	9.5	10.8	4.6	6.0	8.3	•	•	•
Taxes Paid 12	0.4	•	•	•	4.2	1.5	1.1	0.5	1.3	1.0	•	•	•
Interest Paid 13	66.5	•	•	•	0.2	0.6	0.6	0.4	1.6	1.0	•	•	•
Depreciation 14	8.5	•	•	•	0.2	1.1	1.4	1.5	1.2	2.5	•	•	•
Amortization and Depletion 15	3.4	•	•	•	0.1	•	0.1	0.0	0.8	0.3	•	•	•
Pensions and Other Deferred Comp. 16	0.6	•	•	•	•	0.1	0.3	0.4	0.5	0.8	•	•	•
Employee Benefits 17	2.1	•	•	•	0.1	1.3	1.9	1.0	1.0	2.3	•	•	•
Advertising 18	1.6	•	•	•	1.0	0.8	0.7	1.1	0.9	1.2	•	•	•
Other Expenses 19	37.4	•	•	•	11.7	11.8	9.6	5.4	10.8	10.7	•	•	•
Officers' Compensation 20	0.4	•	•	•	1.6	3.3	1.5	1.7	1.6	1.5	•	•	•
Operating Margin 21	•	•	•	•	9.2	6.3	5.1	6.8	6.5	7.5	•	•	•
Operating Margin Before Officers' Comp. 22	•	•	•	•	10.8	9.6	6.5	8.4	8.1	9.0	•	•	•

Selected Average Balance Sheet ($ in Thousands)

Net Receivables 23	268636	630	1107	4197	8413	14232	41806
Inventories 24	15186	605	2669	5567	21668	16926	43697
Net Property, Plant and Equipment 25	70334	51	871	2952	2777	6495	28326
Total Assets 26	1133111	1500	7317	15456	37512	70066	172386
Notes and Loans Payable 27	821564	109	1625	3334	4531	21058	32668
All Other Liabilities 28	214496	531	2000	4406	11655	16895	49332
Net Worth 29	97051	860	3692	7715	21326	32112	90386

Selected Financial Ratios (Times to 1)

Current Ratio 30	0.7	2.6	2.4	2.0	2.3	2.6	2.5
Quick Ratio 31	0.6	1.5	0.8	0.9	0.8	1.3	1.3
Net Sales to Working Capital 32		7.3	3.4	6.2	4.0	4.2	3.9
Coverage Ratio 33	1.1	38.9	21.2	10.0	16.8	5.5	9.6
Total Asset Turnover 34	0.2	4.3	1.7	2.3	2.1	1.6	1.4
Inventory Turnover 35	8.7	5.6	2.9	4.2	2.7	4.4	3.4
Receivables Turnover 36	0.8	8.9	13.9	8.0	5.4		5.3
Total Liabilities to Net Worth 37	10.7	0.7	1.0	1.0	0.8	1.2	0.9
Current Assets to Working Capital 38		1.6	1.7	2.0	1.8	1.6	1.7
Current Liabilities to Working Capital 39		0.6	0.7	1.0	0.8	0.6	0.7
Working Capital to Net Sales 40		0.1	0.3	0.2	0.3	0.2	0.3
Inventory to Working Capital 41		0.7	1.0	1.0	1.1	0.6	0.7
Total Receipts to Cash Flow 42	3.2	5.2	4.7	7.7	8.9	6.1	5.8
Cost of Goods to Cash Flow 43	2.2	2.7	3.0	5.1	6.8	4.1	3.7
Cash Flow to Total Debt 44	0.1	1.9	0.7	0.6	0.5	0.5	0.5

Selected Financial Factors (in Percentages)

Debt Ratio 45	91.4	42.7	49.5	50.1	43.1	54.2	47.6
Return on Total Assets 46	13.1	40.9	19.6	14.3	15.6	14.3	12.9
Return on Equity Before Income Taxes 47	19.4	69.4	37.1	25.7	25.8	25.5	22.0
Return on Equity After Income Taxes 48	13.0	69.3	34.3	24.5	23.9	19.9	18.8
Profit Margin (Before Income Tax) 49	9.7	9.2	11.3	5.7	7.1	7.4	8.5
Profit Margin (After Income Tax) 50	6.5	9.2	10.4	5.4	6.6	5.8	7.2

Table I

Corporations with and without Net Income

ELECTRICAL EQUIPMENT

MONEY AMOUNTS AND SIZE OF ASSETS IN THOUSANDS OF DOLLARS

Item Description for Accounting Period 7/08 Through 6/09	Total	Zero Assets	Under 500	500 to 1,000	1,000 to 5,000	5,000 to 10,000	10,000 to 25,000	25,000 to 50,000	50,000 to 100,000	100,000 to 250,000	250,000 to 500,000	500,000 to 2,500,000	2,500,000 and over
Number of Enterprises 1	1056	42	363	179	282	64	57	24	11	15	9	5	5
Revenues ($ in Thousands)													
Net Sales 2	47859655	21270	4038	378045	1316905	697286	1665457	1113182	1185731	2488931	3412955	5163938	30441916
Interest 3	718214	49	0	0	633	818	1305	1209	4621	12250	22245	7645	667439
Rents 4	93759	0	0	0	765	991	0	5	334	118	0	208	91338
Royalties 5	437457	6	0	0	0	0	55	348	2901	1632	15021	9798	407696
Other Portfolio Income 6	715806	595	0	0	13642	109	12000	2962	17196	11463	2474	12472	642890
Other Receipts 7	521928	401	0	0	3553	1247	3217	6715	4425	26625	5197	114112	356440
Total Receipts 8	50346819	22321	4038	378045	1335498	700451	1682034	1124421	1215208	2541019	3457892	5308173	32577719
Average Total Receipts 9	47677	531	11	2112	4736	10945	29509	46851	110473	169401	384210	1061635	6515544
Operating Costs/Operating Income (%)													
Cost of Operations 10	69.3	109.8	73.5	56.9	67.9	47.3	66.7	70.0	65.7	61.2	68.5	68.2	71.2
Salaries and Wages 11	7.7	21.0	0.1	6.0	11.6	6.7	8.7	6.9	7.8	12.4	7.6	7.0	7.2
Taxes Paid 12	1.1	4.8	9.4	2.1	1.8	2.2	1.2	0.9	1.1	1.4	2.0	0.7	1.0
Interest Paid 13	3.2	0.6	1.4	0.1	1.8	0.7	1.1	1.5	0.4	2.0	2.5	3.8	3.7
Depreciation 14	1.8	2.9	0.2	1.7	1.5	1.1	1.4	2.2	2.0	2.3	2.5	2.7	1.6
Amortization and Depletion 15	1.2	7.9	•	•	0.1	0.0	0.3	0.9	0.2	1.1	1.4	4.5	0.8
Pensions and Other Deferred Comp. 16	1.7	•	•	•	0.3	0.5	0.9	0.4	0.8	1.2	2.3	1.3	2.0
Employee Benefits 17	1.8	2.1	•	1.4	1.7	1.8	2.0	2.8	1.2	1.9	1.3	2.1	1.8
Advertising 18	0.5	1.2	0.2	0.5	0.3	0.5	0.3	0.3	0.6	0.9	0.3	0.8	0.4
Other Expenses 19	9.6	46.0	44.5	14.1	12.6	17.3	10.6	6.6	8.7	13.3	10.2	9.5	9.0
Officers' Compensation 20	1.4	20.0	29.9	15.4	4.9	9.3	2.2	1.7	1.4	1.3	1.1	0.6	0.9
Operating Margin 21	0.7	•	•	1.7	•	12.6	4.6	5.8	10.0	1.0	0.3	•	0.3
Operating Margin Before Officers' Comp. 22	2.0	•	•	17.1	0.4	21.9	6.8	7.5	11.4	2.3	1.4	•	1.2

Selected Average Balance Sheet ($ in Thousands)

Net Receivables 23	1737845	156148	98058	29348	17190	8041	3967	1111	592	172	0	11051
Inventories 24	459011	165466	41194	22139	16545	7667	3445	3193	1175	223	54	4718
Net Property, Plant and Equipment 25	677145	143277	67674	27875	9444	4856	2690	304	394	75	0	5347
Total Assets 26	11695628	1267426	361728	170680	71050	35585	13912	6858	2369	722	1	70356
Notes and Loans Payable 27	1842941	557456	138196	31111	8045	8352	3750	1053	1215	100	0	13867
All Other Liabilities 28	1825476	386972	112031	60586	24959	11597	3916	1729	878	181	0	13396
Net Worth 29	8027212	322998	111500	78983	38046	15637	6247	4076	276	442	0	43094

Selected Financial Ratios (Times to 1)

Current Ratio 30	1.0	1.5	2.0	1.5	2.2	1.7	2.1	2.4	2.0	2.9	2.6	1.2
Quick Ratio 31	0.7	0.7	1.2	0.9	1.1	0.9	1.2	1.4	0.8	1.7	0.9	0.8
Net Sales to Working Capital 32	•	8.9	3.6	7.7	4.6	5.7	5.9	3.5	4.7	5.2	21.8	16.3
Coverage Ratio 33	3.4	1.5	1.9	2.5	35.1	5.7	6.1	19.0	•	13.5	•	3.2
Total Asset Turnover 34	0.5	0.8	1.0	1.0	1.5	1.3	2.1	1.6	2.0	2.9	12.6	0.6
Inventory Turnover 35	9.4	4.3	6.3	4.6	4.3	4.2	5.7	1.6	2.7	5.4	0.2	6.7
Receivables Turnover 36	3.5	4.8	5.2	5.4	6.5	6.0	8.3	3.8	7.6	9.7	0.3	4.0
Total Liabilities to Net Worth 37	0.5	2.9	2.2	1.2	0.9	1.3	1.2	0.7	7.6	0.6	2.9	0.6
Current Assets to Working Capital 38	•	3.2	2.0	3.1	1.8	2.5	1.9	1.7	2.0	1.5	1.6	6.8
Current Liabilities to Working Capital 39	•	2.2	1.0	2.1	0.8	1.5	0.9	0.7	1.0	0.5	0.6	5.8
Working Capital to Net Sales 40	•	0.1	0.3	0.1	0.2	0.2	0.2	0.3	0.2	0.2	0.0	0.1
Inventory to Working Capital 41	•	1.2	0.5	1.0	0.7	1.0	0.7	0.6	1.1	0.6	0.8	1.7
Total Receipts to Cash Flow 42	6.8	10.5	10.4	7.0	5.0	8.3	7.6	3.6	13.5	8.0	•	7.3
Cost of Goods to Cash Flow 43	4.9	7.1	7.1	4.3	3.3	5.8	5.0	1.7	9.1	4.6	•	5.1
Cash Flow to Total Debt 44	0.2	0.1	0.1	0.3	0.7	0.3	0.5	1.1	0.2	0.9	•	0.2

Selected Financial Factors (in Percentages)

Debt Ratio 45	31.4	74.5	69.2	53.7	46.5	56.1	55.1	40.6	88.3	38.8	74.5	38.7
Return on Total Assets 46	6.6	4.6	4.9	4.9	20.6	10.9	13.9	21.8	•	5.4	•	6.6
Return on Equity Before Income Taxes 47	6.8	6.1	7.4	6.4	37.3	20.5	25.9	34.8	•	8.2	•	7.3
Return on Equity After Income Taxes 48	4.6	2.5	2.6	3.3	32.5	16.2	21.9	34.8	•	6.9	•	5.0
Profit Margin (Before Income Tax) 49	9.0	1.9	2.2	3.0	13.2	6.9	5.5	13.0	•	1.7	•	7.0
Profit Margin (After Income Tax) 50	6.1	0.8	0.8	1.6	11.5	5.5	4.7	13.0	•	1.4	•	4.7

Table II
Corporations with Net Income

ELECTRICAL EQUIPMENT

MONEY AMOUNTS AND SIZE OF ASSETS IN THOUSANDS OF DOLLARS

Item Description for Accounting Period 7/08 Through 6/09	Total	Zero Assets	Under 500	500 to 1,000	1,000 to 5,000	5,000 to 10,000	10,000 to 25,000	25,000 to 50,000	50,000 to 100,000	100,000 to 250,000	250,000 to 500,000	500,000 to 2,500,000	2,500,000 and over
Number of Enterprises **1**	490	•	•	126	212	•	46	21	11	9	•	0	5
Revenues ($ in Thousands)													
Net Sales **2**	42114870	•	•	306539	958631	•	1375947	972404	1185731	1702778	•	0	30411916
Interest **3**	687233	•	•	0	130	•	667	978	4621	8409	•	0	667439
Rents **4**	92100	•	•	0	394	•	0	5	334	29	•	0	91338
Royalties **5**	417147	•	•	0	0	•	0	348	2901	0	•	0	407696
Other Portfolio Income **6**	678966	•	•	0	213	•	545	2962	17196	2837	•	0	642890
Other Receipts **7**	397386	•	•	0	2114	•	2901	5254	4425	11539	•	0	356440
Total Receipts **8**	44387702	•	•	306539	961482	•	1380060	981951	1215208	1725592	•	0	32577719
Average Total Receipts **9**	90587	•	•	2433	4535	•	30001	46760	110473	191732	•	•	6515544
Operating Costs/Operating Income (%)													
Cost of Operations **10**	69.2	•	•	56.6	63.6	•	63.3	69.2	65.7	58.2	•	•	71.2
Salaries and Wages **11**	7.4	•	•	5.1	12.0	•	8.1	6.4	7.8	12.1	•	•	7.2
Taxes Paid **12**	1.1	•	•	1.8	1.7	•	1.2	0.8	1.1	1.8	•	•	1.0
Interest Paid **13**	3.0	•	•	0.2	1.6	•	0.8	0.8	0.4	1.5	•	•	3.7
Depreciation **14**	1.7	•	•	1.9	1.3	•	1.3	1.9	2.0	2.4	•	•	1.6
Amortization and Depletion **15**	0.8	•	•	•	0.0	•	0.1	0.6	0.2	1.1	•	•	0.8
Pensions and Other Deferred Comp. **16**	1.7	•	•	•	0.4	•	1.0	0.4	0.8	1.7	•	•	2.0
Employee Benefits **17**	1.7	•	•	1.8	0.9	•	1.7	3.1	1.2	1.8	•	•	1.8
Advertising **18**	0.4	•	•	0.6	0.2	•	0.3	0.3	0.6	1.1	•	•	0.4
Other Expenses **19**	9.2	•	•	14.0	10.8	•	9.3	7.0	8.7	10.4	•	•	9.0
Officers' Compensation **20**	1.3	•	•	15.8	4.8	•	2.3	1.7	1.4	1.5	•	•	0.9
Operating Margin **21**	2.3	•	•	2.1	2.7	•	10.6	7.7	10.0	6.5	•	•	0.3
Operating Margin Before Officers' Comp. **22**	3.6	•	•	18.0	7.5	•	13.0	9.3	11.4	8.0	•	•	1.2

Selected Average Balance Sheet ($ in Thousands)

Net Receivables 23	21060	222	562	3977	8539	17190	34057	1737845
Inventories 24	8097	302	1306	3249	6384	17173	23733	475093
Net Property, Plant and Equipment 25	9951	13	431	2434	4519	9444	29554	677145
Total Assets 26	136200	722	2306	13890	35039	71050	159500	11695628
Notes and Loans Payable 27	22743	141	1342	3260	5964	8045	25740	1842941
All Other Liabilities 28	23283	204	736	3443	12433	24959	47048	1825476
Net Worth 29	90174	377	228	7187	16642	38046	86713	8027212

Selected Financial Ratios (Times to 1)

Current Ratio 30	1.1	2.8	2.2	2.3	1.8	2.2	2.2	1.0
Quick Ratio 31	0.8	1.5	0.8	1.3	1.0	1.1	1.3	0.7
Net Sales to Working Capital 32	19.5	5.3	4.4	5.6	4.9	4.6	4.7	•
Coverage Ratio 33	4.0	13.7	2.9	14.9	12.6	35.1	6.2	3.4
Total Asset Turnover 34	0.6	3.4	2.0	2.2	1.3	1.5	1.2	0.5
Inventory Turnover 35	7.3	4.6	2.2	5.8	5.0	4.1	4.6	9.1
Receivables Turnover 36	4.2	8.1	7.4	8.7	7.1	•	5.6	•
Total Liabilities to Net Worth 37	0.5	0.9	9.1	0.9	1.1	0.9	0.8	0.5
Current Assets to Working Capital 38	7.9	1.5	1.8	1.8	2.3	1.8	1.8	•
Current Liabilities to Working Capital 39	6.9	0.5	0.8	0.8	1.3	0.8	0.8	•
Working Capital to Net Sales 40	0.1	0.2	0.2	0.2	0.2	0.2	0.2	•
Inventory to Working Capital 41	1.9	0.7	1.1	0.7	0.9	0.7	0.6	•
Total Receipts to Cash Flow 42	6.7	8.2	8.2	5.4	6.9	5.0	6.1	6.8
Cost of Goods to Cash Flow 43	4.6	4.6	5.2	3.4	4.8	3.3	3.5	4.9
Cash Flow to Total Debt 44	0.3	0.9	0.3	0.8	0.4	0.7	0.4	0.2

Selected Financial Factors (in Percentages)

Debt Ratio 45	33.8	47.8	90.1	48.3	52.5	46.5	45.6	31.4
Return on Total Assets 46	7.5	7.8	9.0	25.2	12.6	20.6	11.1	6.6
Return on Equity Before Income Taxes 47	8.4	13.8	59.7	45.4	24.4	37.3	17.1	6.8
Return on Equity After Income Taxes 48	6.0	11.7	56.5	41.1	19.8	32.5	12.4	4.6
Profit Margin (Before Income Tax) 49	8.8	2.1	3.0	10.9	8.8	13.2	7.8	9.0
Profit Margin (After Income Tax) 50	6.3	1.8	2.8	9.9	7.1	11.5	5.7	6.1

Table I
Corporations with and without Net Income

OTHER ELECTRICAL EQUIPMENT AND COMPONENT

MONEY AMOUNTS AND SIZE OF ASSETS IN THOUSANDS OF DOLLARS

Item Description for Accounting Period 7/08 Through 6/09	Total	Zero Assets	Under 500	500 to 1,000	1,000 to 5,000	5,000 to 10,000	10,000 to 25,000	25,000 to 50,000	50,000 to 100,000	100,000 to 250,000	250,000 to 500,000	500,000 to 2,500,000	2,500,000 and over
Number of Enterprises 1	3795	539	801	1083	631	330	192	88	57	36	20	14	3
Revenues ($ in Thousands)													
Net Sales 2	67510228	271282	646695	2321394	2975242	4023769	5322255	4506119	4616141	6691960	6191783	11674454	18269133
Interest 3	521313	814	752	13	2139	4155	6604	8177	19121	23842	46278	160592	248825
Rents 4	36146	0	0	138	50	1301	2248	0	1402	338	1822	4	28844
Royalties 5	250023	0	7073	0	0	0	1074	9992	2447	36050	27252	29933	136202
Other Portfolio Income 6	828689	59199	0	653	155	3371	3664	11097	6224	20686	17820	250868	454951
Other Receipts 7	782843	156686	27722	295292	14284	17137	18837	13748	79524	40643	-108992	52269	175693
Total Receipts 8	69929242	487981	682242	2617490	2991870	4049733	5354682	4549133	4724859	6813519	6175963	12168120	19313648
Average Total Receipts 9	18427	905	852	2417	4741	12272	27889	51695	82892	189264	308798	869151	6437883
Operating Costs/Operating Income (%)													
Cost of Operations 10	69.3	70.6	59.8	54.7	56.5	64.9	72.8	69.5	70.3	72.9	65.7	68.1	73.7
Salaries and Wages 11	8.9	19.6	24.8	13.4	9.4	9.0	7.0	10.1	8.9	8.8	8.7	9.0	7.9
Taxes Paid 12	1.3	3.7	2.5	2.5	1.8	1.7	1.5	1.2	1.4	1.2	1.1	1.2	1.0
Interest Paid 13	2.9	1.4	3.4	2.4	0.5	1.3	0.8	1.1	1.6	1.8	2.6	4.7	4.6
Depreciation 14	2.2	2.8	0.8	1.3	1.8	1.4	1.8	2.8	2.6	2.7	2.6	2.9	1.5
Amortization and Depletion 15	1.1	1.6	0.1	0.0	0.5	0.7	0.2	0.3	1.0	0.9	2.4	1.6	1.1
Pensions and Other Deferred Comp. 16	0.5	0.2	0.2	0.2	0.3	0.2	0.4	0.6	0.5	0.3	0.5	1.0	0.4
Employee Benefits 17	1.5	2.3	0.0	1.2	1.6	1.2	1.4	1.8	1.6	1.7	1.8	2.2	1.1
Advertising 18	1.2	0.4	0.3	0.2	0.7	0.7	0.4	0.4	0.7	0.6	0.9	1.5	2.2
Other Expenses 19	10.0	30.5	26.5	28.5	16.4	13.2	7.5	9.3	9.9	7.4	11.4	10.4	6.2
Officers' Compensation 20	1.6	6.4	3.7	5.3	5.9	3.7	2.4	1.8	1.7	1.8	0.6	0.9	0.3
Operating Margin 21	•	•	•	•	4.4	2.0	3.8	1.1	•	•	1.7	•	0.1
Operating Margin Before Officers' Comp. 22	1.1	•	•	•	10.3	5.8	6.2	2.9	1.5	1.7	2.3	•	0.4

Selected Average Balance Sheet ($ in Thousands)

Net Receivables 23	2467	0	61	232	397	1412	3721	8705	13670	30193	52360	158323	578616
Inventories 24	2307	0	103	126	510	2410	4716	9277	14606	26822	40264	107532	529236
Net Property, Plant and Equipment 25	1982	0	6	74	494	1120	2613	6345	11751	28388	33442	137979	468011
Total Assets 26	31125	0	187	716	2123	6586	15430	35935	71806	163514	324636	1232812	24608306
Notes and Loans Payable 27	6296	0	524	694	368	2232	3202	8340	17590	47608	108264	492040	2878328
All Other Liabilities 28	13682	0	149	370	492	1632	4223	8860	20585	38807	106250	347380	13134928
Net Worth 29	11147	0	-486	-348	1264	2722	8005	18736	33631	77099	110122	393392	8595050

Selected Financial Ratios (Times to 1)

Current Ratio 30	1.3	•	1.2	1.2	3.0	1.7	2.0	2.3	2.0	2.0	1.9	2.0	1.1
Quick Ratio 31	0.4	•	0.5	0.9	1.9	0.8	1.1	1.3	1.1	1.1	1.1	1.2	0.1
Net Sales to Working Capital 32	5.5	•	33.1	19.8	5.0	6.5	5.0	3.9	4.0	4.6	4.8	4.0	9.5
Coverage Ratio 33	2.2	43.0	•	2.2	10.2	3.0	6.4	3.0	2.5	2.0	1.6	1.2	2.4
Total Asset Turnover 34	0.6	•	4.3	3.0	2.2	1.9	1.8	1.4	1.1	1.1	1.0	0.7	0.2
Inventory Turnover 35	5.3	•	4.7	9.3	5.2	3.3	4.3	3.8	3.9	5.1	5.1	5.3	8.5
Receivables Turnover 36	7.0	•	9.5	10.0	7.1	7.9	6.0	5.3	5.3	6.3	6.8	6.1	9.8
Total Liabilities to Net Worth 37	1.8	•	•	•	0.7	1.4	0.9	0.9	1.1	1.1	1.9	2.1	1.9
Current Assets to Working Capital 38	4.4	•	7.3	5.3	1.5	2.4	2.0	1.8	2.0	2.0	2.1	2.0	16.8
Current Liabilities to Working Capital 39	3.4	•	6.3	4.3	0.5	1.4	1.0	0.8	1.0	1.0	1.1	1.0	15.8
Working Capital to Net Sales 40	0.2	•	0.0	0.1	0.2	0.2	0.2	0.3	0.3	0.2	0.2	0.2	0.1
Inventory to Working Capital 41	0.7	•	3.5	1.3	0.5	1.2	0.7	0.7	0.7	0.7	0.6	0.5	0.8
Total Receipts to Cash Flow 42	9.2	1.9	41.9	3.7	5.2	7.1	9.8	10.4	9.5	13.2	8.8	13.7	9.6
Cost of Goods to Cash Flow 43	6.4	1.3	25.1	2.0	2.9	4.6	7.1	7.3	6.6	9.6	5.8	9.3	7.1
Cash Flow to Total Debt 44	0.1	•	0.0	0.5	1.1	0.4	0.4	0.3	0.2	0.2	0.2	0.1	0.0

Selected Financial Factors (in Percentages)

Debt Ratio 45	64.2	•	359.6	148.6	40.5	58.7	48.1	47.9	53.2	52.8	66.1	68.1	65.1
Return on Total Assets 46	3.7	•	•	16.0	12.2	7.4	9.3	4.4	4.3	4.2	4.0	3.9	2.8
Return on Equity Before Income Taxes 47	5.6	•	27.6	•	18.5	12.0	15.2	5.7	5.5	4.5	4.8	2.2	4.7
Return on Equity After Income Taxes 48	3.7	•	27.7	•	16.8	9.0	12.9	3.7	3.9	2.4	•	•	3.6
Profit Margin (Before Income Tax) 49	3.5	57.9	•	•	5.0	2.7	4.4	2.1	2.3	1.9	0.5	1.0	6.6
Profit Margin (After Income Tax) 50	2.3	47.8	•	2.9	4.5	2.0	3.7	1.3	1.6	1.0	•	•	5.1

Table II

Corporations with Net Income

OTHER ELECTRICAL EQUIPMENT AND COMPONENT

MONEY AMOUNTS AND SIZE OF ASSETS IN THOUSANDS OF DOLLARS

Item Description for Accounting Period 7/08 Through 6/09	Total	Zero Assets	Under 500	500 to 1000	1,000 to 5,000	5,000 to 10,000	10,000 to 25,000	25,000 to 50,000	50,000 to 100,000	100,000 to 250,000	250,000 to 500,000	500,000 to 2,500,000	2,500,000 and over
Number of Enterprises 1	2564	528	391	663	508	177	155	54	34	29	13	10	3
Revenues ($ in Thousands)													
Net Sales 2	54938058	258463	178482	1413385	2558524	2573837	4723538	3131603	3270004	5706907	4225189	8628994	18269133
Interest 3	396196	190	0	13	1371	2825	3210	4067	7869	13297	30942	83587	248825
Rents 4	34123	0	0	138	0	120	2248	0	1402	338	1029	4	28844
Royalties 5	207150	0	7073	0	0	0	939	2493	1959	33276	20086	5121	136202
Other Portfolio Income 6	813729	59120	0	33	60	2686	3454	7442	4112	16591	15941	249340	454951
Other Receipts 7	524619	144709	11554	446	8456	13124	17367	5804	41882	39526	51836	14221	175693
Total Receipts 8	56913875	462482	197109	1414015	2568411	2592592	4750756	3151409	3327228	5809935	4345023	8981267	19313648
Average Total Receipts 9	22197	876	504	2133	5056	14647	30650	58359	97860	200343	334233	898127	6437883
Operating Costs/Operating Income (%)													
Cost of Operations 10	68.7	71.5	56.6	61.0	55.1	56.1	72.9	66.2	70.2	69.1	61.3	68.5	73.7
Salaries and Wages 11	8.1	12.4	14.1	8.2	8.5	9.1	6.1	9.9	7.5	8.6	8.6	8.3	7.9
Taxes Paid 12	1.3	3.4	2.5	2.3	1.7	1.8	1.5	1.3	1.3	1.2	1.4	1.1	1.0
Interest Paid 13	2.6	1.3	1.9	0.0	0.3	1.1	0.7	1.0	0.9	1.7	2.3	3.1	4.6
Depreciation 14	1.9	2.8	1.0	1.6	1.1	0.8	1.5	2.9	1.9	2.2	2.7	2.8	1.5
Amortization and Depletion 15	0.8	1.1	•	•	0.1	0.3	0.1	0.1	0.3	0.8	0.7	1.4	1.1
Pensions and Other Deferred Comp. 16	0.5	0.1	•	0.3	0.3	0.2	0.4	0.5	0.6	0.4	0.5	1.2	0.4
Employee Benefits 17	1.4	1.9	0.0	0.8	1.3	1.1	1.1	1.8	1.5	1.4	1.6	2.3	1.1
Advertising 18	1.2	0.4	1.0	0.1	0.7	0.8	0.4	0.4	0.5	0.7	1.2	0.9	2.2
Other Expenses 19	8.5	25.8	28.8	13.0	16.3	16.1	6.8	8.2	7.8	7.4	10.4	8.2	6.2
Officers' Compensation 20	1.5	2.0	1.8	5.8	6.2	3.8	2.3	1.7	1.6	1.9	0.7	0.9	0.3
Operating Margin 21	3.5	•	•	7.0	8.4	8.9	6.2	6.0	5.7	4.7	8.7	1.3	0.1
Operating Margin Before Officers' Comp. 22	5.0	•	•	12.8	14.5	12.7	8.6	7.7	7.3	6.7	9.3	2.2	0.4

Selected Average Balance Sheet ($ in Thousands)

Net Receivables 23	2646	0	19	277	383	1824	4103	8193	15231	32523	59189	103177	578616
Inventories 24	2662	0	41	135	498	2988	4872	10527	17479	29389	40025	117480	490134
Net Property, Plant and Equipment 25	2045	0	9	37	341	916	2338	6522	11092	23151	34420	126438	468011
Total Assets 26	40751	0	111	696	1986	6999	15664	35087	71038	156122	311175	1259881	24608306
Notes and Loans Payable 27	6438	0	53	111	226	1873	3129	8518	14074	45091	100222	329656	2878328
All Other Liabilities 28	18620	0	104	124	356	1979	4415	7810	18810	37853	92338	363998	13114928
Net Worth 29	15693	0	-46	461	1404	3146	8120	18759	38153	73177	118615	566227	8595050

Selected Financial Ratios (Times to 1)

Current Ratio 30	1.3	•	1.1	2.4	3.2	2.1	2.0	2.3	2.3	1.9	2.0	2.3	1.1
Quick Ratio 31	0.3	•	0.3	1.9	2.2	1.1	1.2	1.1	1.1	1.1	1.1	1.4	0.1
Net Sales to Working Capital 32	5.6	•	70.5	6.7	5.0	5.4	5.1	4.7	4.2	5.1	4.0	4.0	9.5
Coverage Ratio 33	3.9	58.4	2.4	217.3	35.0	9.9	10.7	7.9	9.0	5.0	6.0	2.9	2.4
Total Asset Turnover 34	0.5	•	4.1	3.1	2.5	2.1	1.9	1.7	1.4	1.3	1.0	0.7	0.2
Inventory Turnover 35	5.5	•	6.3	9.6	5.6	2.7	4.6	3.6	3.9	4.6	5.0	5.0	9.2
Receivables Turnover 36	7.6	•	13.7	7.3	8.0	6.7	6.5	5.4	5.3	6.2	•	•	•
Total Liabilities to Net Worth 37	1.6	•	•	0.5	0.4	1.2	0.9	0.9	0.9	1.1	1.6	1.2	1.9
Current Assets to Working Capital 38	4.8	•	15.3	1.7	1.5	1.9	2.0	1.8	1.8	2.1	2.0	1.8	16.8
Current Liabilities to Working Capital 39	3.8	•	14.3	0.7	0.5	0.9	1.0	0.8	0.8	1.1	1.0	0.8	15.8
Working Capital to Net Sales 40	0.2	•	0.0	0.2	0.2	0.2	0.2	0.2	0.2	0.2	0.2	0.3	0.1
Inventory to Working Capital 41	0.7	•	6.6	0.4	0.4	0.8	0.8	0.8	0.7	0.8	0.5	0.5	0.8
Total Receipts to Cash Flow 42	7.5	1.6	4.2	6.5	4.3	4.2	8.2	7.6	7.2	8.0	4.9	10.6	9.6
Cost of Goods to Cash Flow 43	5.1	1.1	2.4	4.0	2.4	2.3	6.0	5.0	5.1	5.5	3.0	7.3	7.1
Cash Flow to Total Debt 44	0.1	•	0.7	1.4	2.0	0.9	0.5	0.5	0.4	0.3	0.3	0.1	0.0

Selected Financial Factors (in Percentages)

Debt Ratio 45	61.5	•	141.1	33.8	29.3	55.0	48.2	46.5	46.3	53.1	61.9	55.1	65.1
Return on Total Assets 46	5.3	•	18.7	21.5	22.9	22.3	14.6	12.6	11.5	10.5	14.6	6.1	2.8
Return on Equity Before Income Taxes 47	10.3	•	•	32.4	31.5	44.7	25.5	20.6	19.1	18.0	31.9	8.8	4.7
Return on Equity After Income Taxes 48	8.3	•	•	32.1	29.5	39.9	22.7	17.4	16.8	15.3	21.7	6.5	3.6
Profit Margin (Before Income Tax) 49	7.5	74.6	2.6	7.0	8.8	9.7	6.8	6.7	7.6	6.7	11.6	5.7	6.6
Profit Margin (After Income Tax) 50	6.1	64.0	2.5	6.9	8.2	8.6	6.0	5.6	6.7	5.7	7.3	4.3	5.1

Table I

Corporations with and without Net Income

MOTOR VEHICLES AND PARTS

MONEY AMOUNTS AND SIZE OF ASSETS IN THOUSANDS OF DOLLARS

Item Description for Accounting Period 7/08 Through 6/09		Total	Zero Assets	Under 500	500 to 1,000	1,000 to 5,000	5,000 to 10,000	10,000 to 25,000	25,000 to 50,000	50,000 to 100,000	100,000 to 250,000	250,000 to 500,000	500,000 to 2,500,000	2,500,000 and over
Number of Enterprises	1	5784	816	2751	299	828	340	268	167	103	95	50	44	23
Revenues ($ in Thousands)														
Net Sales	2	469961860	1649109	1541427	415754	4262208	3977021	7397706	9988711	12646688	21322261	26963866	50795632	329001477
Interest	3	26261381	7970	250	1	9298	3131	6649	14345	18024	35614	105783	451853	25608465
Rents	4	7425382	0	0	0	1842	483	1558	6497	1892	9935	13152	94116	7295906
Royalties	5	8232425	584	0	0	410	0	0	8844	2388	5665	32810	289087	7892637
Other Portfolio Income	6	10049545	8535	5906	80	6228	12984	25285	58659	142614	46436	58690	327033	9357096
Other Receipts	7	20108239	39829	30929	1857	95553	36642	58121	117479	113811	176308	223928	431198	18782581
Total Receipts	8	542038832	1706027	1578512	417692	4375539	4030261	7489319	10194535	12925417	21596219	27398229	52388919	397938162
Average Total Receipts	9	93713	2091	574	1397	5284	11854	27945	61045	125489	227329	547965	1190657	17301659
Operating Costs/Operating Income (%)														
Cost of Operations	10	81.4	82.5	69.3	67.3	71.3	76.2	78.9	82.2	82.6	85.8	84.9	82.2	81.0
Salaries and Wages	11	4.4	8.2	4.2	9.0	9.2	7.4	5.8	5.3	3.9	3.8	3.9	5.5	4.1
Taxes Paid	12	0.7	1.0	1.3	1.9	1.6	1.3	1.1	1.1	0.7	0.7	0.8	0.8	0.7
Interest Paid	13	8.2	1.6	0.8	1.4	2.0	2.2	1.0	1.2	1.2	1.3	1.8	2.8	10.9
Depreciation	14	7.3	2.6	1.3	1.6	3.2	2.8	3.3	3.5	4.0	4.1	3.7	4.3	8.8
Amortization and Depletion	15	1.3	0.1	0.0	0.0	0.1	0.1	0.3	0.2	0.3	0.3	0.5	0.5	1.7
Pensions and Other Deferred Comp.	16	1.5	0.3	0.0	0.2	0.8	0.2	0.3	0.3	0.3	0.2	0.4	0.9	1.9
Employee Benefits	17	1.5	0.5	0.5	1.1	1.5	2.0	1.8	1.8	1.8	1.7	1.6	2.0	1.4
Advertising	18	1.6	0.0	1.8	0.5	0.7	0.4	0.7	0.4	0.4	0.3	0.2	0.5	2.0
Other Expenses	19	13.4	7.7	19.7	21.0	14.0	10.6	8.1	8.1	6.0	5.1	6.4	6.1	16.3
Officers' Compensation	20	0.3	3.0	3.4	3.7	4.1	1.5	1.7	1.0	0.8	0.5	0.6	0.3	0.1
Operating Margin	21	•	•	•	•	•	•	•	•	•	•	•	•	•
Operating Margin Before Officers' Comp.	22	•	•	1.2	•	•	•	•	•	•	•	•	•	•

Selected Average Balance Sheet ($ in Thousands)

Net Receivables **23**	43249	0	32	120	500	1264	2805	6819	13296	23715	60289	205811	10069523
Inventories **24**	7189	0	62	353	677	2213	4128	7130	14542	25578	59735	128740	1092136
Net Property, Plant and Equipment **25**	24088	0	25	132	475	1515	4959	10943	24903	51083	99147	228990	4899950
Total Assets **26**	149577	0	142	665	2288	6678	15912	33797	72025	143105	335980	1021303	33380022
Notes and Loans Payable **27**	60514	0	54	275	1404	4854	5881	11994	26113	47298	147882	390407	13549318
All Other Liabilities **28**	74393	0	66	326	1283	2228	4460	10755	24937	41773	105342	416085	17177741
Net Worth **29**	14670	0	23	64	-399	-404	5570	11049	20974	54035	82756	214811	2652964

Selected Financial Ratios (Times to 1)

Current Ratio **30**	1.2	•	1.3	1.3	1.8	1.6	1.5	1.3	1.2	1.2	1.4	1.1	1.1
Quick Ratio **31**	0.8	•	0.6	0.4	0.8	0.6	0.7	0.6	0.6	0.6	0.7	0.7	0.8
Net Sales to Working Capital **32**	8.8	•	21.5	13.0	7.5	7.0	9.3	15.2	24.5	18.9	12.3	25.8	7.3
Coverage Ratio **33**	0.3	•	1.3	•	•	•	•	1.2	•	•	•	0.1	0.4
Total Asset Turnover **34**	0.5	•	3.9	2.1	2.2	1.8	1.7	1.8	1.7	1.6	1.6	1.1	0.4
Inventory Turnover **35**	9.2	•	6.3	2.7	5.4	4.0	5.3	6.9	7.0	7.5	7.7	7.4	10.6
Receivables Turnover **36**	1.6	•	23.7	4.3	13.0	9.9	9.7	9.0	7.9	8.0	8.1	4.9	1.2
Total Liabilities to Net Worth **37**	9.2	•	5.3	9.3	•	•	1.9	2.1	2.4	1.6	3.1	3.8	11.6
Current Assets to Working Capital **38**	7.6	•	4.1	4.6	2.3	2.8	3.2	4.9	7.0	5.5	3.6	9.6	8.0
Current Liabilities to Working Capital **39**	6.6	•	3.1	3.6	1.3	1.8	2.2	3.9	6.0	4.5	2.6	8.6	7.0
Working Capital to Net Sales **40**	0.1	•	0.0	0.1	0.1	0.1	0.1	0.1	0.0	0.1	0.1	0.0	0.1
Inventory to Working Capital **41**	0.7	•	2.1	2.8	1.2	1.6	1.5	2.1	2.6	2.1	1.4	2.4	0.5
Total Receipts to Cash Flow **42**	19.1	46.0	6.2	25.2	39.3	26.6	20.6	32.1	23.5	84.4	48.4	55.7	15.5
Cost of Goods to Cash Flow **43**	15.5	38.0	4.3	17.0	28.0	20.3	16.2	26.4	19.4	72.4	41.1	45.8	12.6
Cash Flow to Total Debt **44**	0.0	•	0.8	0.1	0.0	0.1	0.1	0.1	0.0	0.0	0.0	0.0	0.0

Selected Financial Factors (in Percentages)

Debt Ratio **45**	90.2	•	84.0	90.3	117.4	106.0	65.0	67.3	70.9	62.2	75.4	79.0	92.1
Return on Total Assets **46**	1.4	•	4.3	•	•	•	•	•	•	•	•	0.3	1.7
Return on Equity Before Income Taxes **47**	•	•	6.3	•	71.8	100.3	1.6	•	•	•	•	•	•
Return on Equity After Income Taxes **48**	•	•	5.9	•	73.6	107.6	•	•	•	•	•	•	•
Profit Margin (Before Income Tax) **49**	•	•	0.3	•	•	•	0.3	0.3	•	•	•	•	•
Profit Margin (After Income Tax) **50**	•	•	0.2	•	•	•	•	•	•	•	•	•	•

Table II

Corporations with Net Income

MOTOR VEHICLES AND PARTS

MONEY AMOUNTS AND SIZE OF ASSETS IN THOUSANDS OF DOLLARS

Item Description for Accounting Period 7/08 Through 6/09	Total	Zero Assets	Under 500	500 to 1,000	1,000 to 5,000	5,000 to 10,000	10,000 to 25,000	25,000 to 50,000	50,000 to 100,000	100,000 to 250,000	250,000 to 500,000	500,000 to 2,500,000	2,500,000 and over
Number of Enterprises **1**	2733	509	1230	127	409	139	134	66	•	•	16	14	•
Revenues ($ in Thousands)													
Net Sales **2**	108455836	457748	1260591	191235	2467987	2578161	4155672	3807657	•	•	10069031	16703672	•
Interest **3**	1250828	5	106	0	898	1847	2169	5222	•	•	16269	54760	•
Rents **4**	388755	0	0	0	1710	414	1106	3846	•	•	2886	1129	•
Royalties **5**	650784	117	0	0	410	0	0	1536	•	•	980	96292	•
Other Portfolio Income **6**	1492823	7940	5627	0	2745	12560	8223	41264	•	•	29374	140565	•
Other Receipts **7**	1335652	708	25564	1553	15640	27421	15451	19851	•	•	84102	135690	•
Total Receipts **8**	113574678	466518	1291888	192788	2489390	2620403	4182621	3879376	•	•	10202642	17132108	•
Average Total Receipts **9**	41557	917	1050	1518	6087	18852	31214	58778	•	•	637665	1223722	•
Operating Costs/Operating Income (%)													
Cost of Operations **10**	80.0	73.9	67.5	74.0	66.3	70.5	74.5	72.4	•	•	83.3	80.8	•
Salaries and Wages **11**	4.5	10.7	3.5	3.4	8.2	7.8	5.2	5.5	•	•	3.3	3.6	•
Taxes Paid **12**	1.6	2.0	1.2	1.8	1.5	1.2	1.1	1.2	•	•	0.8	0.5	•
Interest Paid **13**	2.5	0.1	0.9	1.4	1.4	1.0	0.8	1.0	•	•	1.1	1.2	•
Depreciation **14**	3.3	0.4	0.5	0.8	4.6	2.4	2.4	3.2	•	•	2.9	4.1	•
Amortization and Depletion **15**	0.3	0.0	•	•	0.0	0.1	0.1	0.1	•	•	0.3	0.3	•
Pensions and Other Deferred Comp. **16**	0.9	0.3	•	•	0.2	0.2	0.4	0.3	•	•	0.3	0.5	•
Employee Benefits **17**	1.4	0.4	0.5	0.0	0.7	2.0	1.8	1.6	•	•	1.5	1.4	•
Advertising **18**	0.3	0.0	2.0	0.3	1.0	0.1	0.8	0.7	•	•	0.2	0.2	•
Other Expenses **19**	6.3	6.1	18.3	13.0	8.2	8.6	6.2	9.6	•	•	4.7	4.6	•
Officers' Compensation **20**	0.6	0.6	2.9	4.8	4.6	1.3	2.1	1.1	•	•	0.5	0.3	•
Operating Margin **21**	•	5.5	2.7	0.6	3.3	4.7	4.6	3.5	•	•	1.2	2.6	•
Operating Margin Before Officers' Comp. **22**	•	6.1	5.6	5.4	7.8	6.0	6.7	4.5	•	•	1.7	2.8	•

Selected Average Balance Sheet ($ in Thousands)

Net Receivables 23	7546	0	40	196	580	2234	3039	7528	•	66243	220174
Inventories 24	6656	0	67	452	902	2009	5795	8510	•	102538	99152
Net Property, Plant and Equipment 25	5578	0	8	91	705	1518	3765	9555	•	88214	279726
Total Assets 26	37495	0	155	779	2327	7134	15315	33840	•	330876	1070540
Notes and Loans Payable 27	11631	0	28	195	1910	2315	4387	10286	•	98800	323925
All Other Liabilities 28	15227	0	101	48	820	2563	4040	9943	•	115142	367558
Net Worth 29	10636	0	26	536	-403	2256	6887	13611	•	116934	379057

Selected Financial Ratios (Times to 1)

Current Ratio 30	1.7	•	1.2	9.9	1.5	1.5	2.0	1.5	•	1.4	1.4
Quick Ratio 31	1.0	•	0.4	3.1	0.6	0.9	0.8	0.7	•	0.7	0.9
Net Sales to Working Capital 32	5.3	•	51.4	2.4	11.9	10.9	6.0	8.2	•	11.7	8.9
Coverage Ratio 33	2.6	99.5	6.5	2.0	3.9	7.4	7.4	6.5	•	3.4	5.8
Total Asset Turnover 34	1.1	•	6.6	1.9	2.6	2.6	2.0	1.7	•	1.9	1.1
Inventory Turnover 35	4.8	•	10.3	2.5	4.4	6.5	4.0	4.9	•	5.1	9.7
Receivables Turnover 36	0.9	•	41.7	5.4	11.6	7.9	8.8	6.6	•	5.5	•
Total Liabilities to Net Worth 37	2.5	•	5.0	0.5	•	2.2	1.2	1.5	•	1.8	1.8
Current Assets to Working Capital 38	2.4	•	6.9	1.1	3.0	3.0	2.0	3.0	•	3.4	3.8
Current Liabilities to Working Capital 39	1.4	•	5.9	0.1	2.0	2.0	1.0	2.0	•	2.4	2.8
Working Capital to Net Sales 40	0.2	•	0.0	0.4	0.1	0.1	0.2	0.1	•	0.1	0.1
Inventory to Working Capital 41	0.5	•	4.5	0.8	1.7	1.1	1.1	1.2	•	1.5	0.7
Total Receipts to Cash Flow 42	12.4	8.3	5.0	7.9	10.1	8.4	9.8	8.3	•	16.0	11.3
Cost of Goods to Cash Flow 43	9.9	6.2	3.3	5.8	6.7	5.9	7.3	6.0	•	13.3	9.1
Cash Flow to Total Debt 44	0.1	•	1.6	0.8	0.2	0.5	0.4	0.3	•	0.2	0.2

Selected Financial Factors (in Percentages)

Debt Ratio 45	71.6	•	83.2	31.2	117.3	68.4	55.0	59.8	•	64.7	64.6
Return on Total Assets 46	6.7	•	40.3	5.4	14.4	19.1	12.2	10.8	•	7.1	7.5
Return on Equity Before Income Taxes 47	14.4	•	203.4	4.0	•	52.1	23.4	22.7	•	14.2	17.5
Return on Equity After Income Taxes 48	11.4	•	202.8	3.7	•	49.0	20.9	19.0	•	9.9	13.1
Profit Margin (Before Income Tax) 49	3.9	7.4	5.2	1.4	4.1	6.3	5.2	5.4	•	2.6	5.6
Profit Margin (After Income Tax) 50	3.1	7.2	5.2	1.3	3.9	6.0	4.6	4.5	•	1.8	4.2

Table I
Corporations with and without Net Income

Aerospace Product and Parts

Money Amounts and Size of Assets in Thousands of Dollars

Item Description for Accounting Period 7/08 Through 6/09	Total	Zero Assets	Under 500	500 to 1,000	1,000 to 5,000	5,000 to 10,000	10,000 to 25,000	25,000 to 50,000	50,000 to 100,000	100,000 to 250,000	250,000 to 500,000	500,000 to 2,500,000	2,500,000 and over
Number of Enterprises **1**	2144	301	1175	69	331	58	95	37	19	22	7	16	15
Revenues ($ in Thousands)													
Net Sales **2**	287412269	25221	459504	41097	1573048	575685	2447627	1548896	1420364	3560596	3321715	19753489	252685025
Interest **3**	2165682	254	707	10	1577	64	3630	2246	4414	5860	21628	139019	1986272
Rents **4**	1281128	0	0	0	0	2664	1357	0	640	450	620	39437	1235960
Royalties **5**	1661194	0	0	0	0	0	114	0	0	2437	0	5353	1653291
Other Portfolio Income **6**	1783933	19566	10515	0	245	0	3143	7455	377	5709	355	338955	1397610
Other Receipts **7**	2575675	1002	-3961	1	1004	669	26127	8844	45594	40051	9805	111110	2335434
Total Receipts **8**	296879881	46043	466765	41108	1575874	579082	2481998	1567441	1471389	3615103	3354123	20387363	261293592
Average Total Receipts **9**	138470	153	397	596	4761	9984	26126	42363	77442	164323	479160	1274210	17419573
Operating Costs/Operating Income (%)													
Cost of Operations **10**	74.3	78.1	43.1	35.8	73.6	62.0	65.2	66.6	62.9	71.4	68.8	73.5	74.8
Salaries and Wages **11**	4.3	6.5	14.4	16.3	9.4	8.2	7.1	5.7	13.2	5.7	7.3	7.8	3.8
Taxes Paid **12**	1.4	9.6	2.0	2.8	1.5	1.5	1.6	1.2	1.9	1.0	1.3	2.4	1.4
Interest Paid **13**	1.9	1.8	0.5	0.1	1.5	1.9	2.3	1.6	2.0	2.7	4.3	3.4	1.7
Depreciation **14**	2.6	5.7	2.1	4.0	1.8	2.7	3.1	3.9	3.6	3.1	3.2	2.7	2.6
Amortization and Depletion **15**	0.8	•	•	7.0	0.0	0.2	0.4	0.1	1.4	0.5	2.7	1.0	0.7
Pensions and Other Deferred Comp. **16**	1.8	•	•	0.1	0.7	0.4	0.4	0.5	0.3	0.4	0.8	0.8	1.9
Employee Benefits **17**	2.8	2.2	0.7	2.3	2.7	1.2	2.2	1.7	2.3	1.3	1.9	2.4	2.9
Advertising **18**	0.3	1.8	0.3	0.7	0.1	0.1	0.2	0.2	0.4	0.2	0.5	0.1	0.3
Other Expenses **19**	8.3	153.7	23.0	30.4	8.8	10.7	11.1	9.3	11.4	7.3	6.8	3.9	8.6
Officers' Compensation **20**	0.3	3.0	6.4	14.6	5.0	1.3	2.6	2.7	2.7	1.1	0.9	0.7	0.2
Operating Margin **21**	1.3	•	7.4	•	•	9.5	3.6	6.6	•	5.3	2.0	1.2	1.2
Operating Margin Before Officers' Comp. **22**	1.6	7.4	13.8	0.6	0.5	10.9	6.3	9.3	0.2	6.5	2.8	2.0	1.3

Selected Average Balance Sheet ($ in Thousands)

Net Receivables 23	18576	0	1	47	524	1200	4042	6598	9671	20001	65328	222454	2287386
Inventories 24	20191	0	4	402	484	3004	4834	8847	20567	38887	168959	245501	2385248
Net Property, Plant and Equipment 25	19487	0	9	60	325	1253	3349	7698	12671	33750	66318	226429	2394144
Total Assets 26	154079	0	152	678	2006	6937	16286	35039	74528	162222	360210	1536093	19608400
Notes and Loans Payable 27	34661	0	55	493	1548	3236	6919	12315	19151	53327	307356	482467	4066203
All Other Liabilities 28	84202	0	74	18	333	850	10621	5907	21479	50848	-213023	582030	11313738
Net Worth 29	35216	0	23	167	125	2851	-1255	16817	33898	58047	265878	471596	4228459

Selected Financial Ratios (Times to 1)

Current Ratio 30	1.2	•	2.4	13.5	4.1	3.8	1.2	3.0	1.7	1.8	2.4	1.4	1.1
Quick Ratio 31	0.5	•	2.1	7.2	2.3	1.3	0.6	1.3	0.8	0.6	0.6	0.7	0.5
Net Sales to Working Capital 32	16.0	•	16.0	2.7	3.9	2.5	12.6	2.4	4.8	4.9	2.4	6.9	22.5
Coverage Ratio 33	3.8	•	19.2	•	•	6.4	3.2	5.8	1.5	3.5	1.7	2.3	4.1
Total Asset Turnover 34	0.9	•	2.6	0.9	2.4	1.4	1.6	1.2	1.0	1.0	1.3	0.8	0.9
Inventory Turnover 35	4.9	•	44.5	0.5	7.2	2.1	3.5	3.2	2.3	3.0	1.9	3.7	5.3
Receivables Turnover 36	7.4	•	119.9	9.0	10.1	9.9	7.0	7.2	6.2	9.4	7.3	6.2	7.4
Total Liabilities to Net Worth 37	3.4	•	5.6	3.1	15.0	1.4	•	1.1	1.2	1.8	0.4	2.3	3.6
Current Assets to Working Capital 38	6.4	•	1.7	1.1	1.3	1.4	6.0	1.5	2.4	2.3	1.7	3.5	8.7
Current Liabilities to Working Capital 39	5.4	•	0.7	0.1	0.3	0.4	5.0	0.5	1.4	1.3	0.7	2.5	7.7
Working Capital to Net Sales 40	0.1	•	0.1	0.4	0.3	0.4	0.1	0.4	0.2	0.2	0.4	0.1	0.0
Inventory to Working Capital 41	2.7	•	0.1	0.5	0.5	0.9	2.7	0.6	1.1	1.3	1.2	1.4	3.6
Total Receipts to Cash Flow 42	9.2	1.5	4.1	9.7	101.8	5.3	7.9	7.0	9.6	7.9	11.7	18.6	8.9
Cost of Goods to Cash Flow 43	6.9	1.2	1.8	3.5	74.9	3.3	5.2	4.7	6.0	5.6	8.0	13.7	6.7
Cash Flow to Total Debt 44	0.1	•	0.7	0.1	0.0	0.5	0.2	0.3	0.2	0.2	0.4	0.1	0.1

Selected Financial Factors (in Percentages)

Debt Ratio 45	77.1	•	84.7	75.4	93.8	58.9	107.7	52.0	54.5	64.2	26.2	69.3	78.4
Return on Total Assets 46	6.0	•	24.5	•	•	17.1	11.7	11.3	3.1	9.6	9.6	6.3	5.9
Return on Equity Before Income Taxes 47	19.4	•	152.1	•	•	35.2	•	19.4	2.4	19.2	5.3	11.8	20.7
Return on Equity After Income Taxes 48	12.6	•	152.1	•	•	33.0	•	16.9	0.1	16.7	4.7	7.9	13.3
Profit Margin (Before Income Tax) 49	5.1	•	9.0	•	•	10.1	5.0	7.8	1.1	6.9	3.0	4.5	5.2
Profit Margin (After Income Tax) 50	3.3	•	9.0	•	•	9.5	3.7	6.8	0.0	6.0	2.6	3.0	3.3

Table II

Corporations with Net Income

AEROSPACE PRODUCT AND PARTS

MONEY AMOUNTS AND SIZE OF ASSETS IN THOUSANDS OF DOLLARS

Item Description for Accounting Period 7/08 Through 6/09	Total	Zero Assets	Under 500	500 to 1,000	1,000 to 5,000	5,000 to 10,000	10,000 to 25,000	25,000 to 50,000	50,000 to 100,000	100,000 to 250,000	250,000 to 500,000	500,000 to 2,500,000	2,500,000 and over
Number of Enterprises 1	1035	•	584	6	247	40	70	31	13	14	3	•	•
Revenues ($ in Thousands)													
Net Sales 2	216340240	•	409213	31113	1310326	445140	2054803	1374000	903184	2704603	2377597	•	•
Interest 3	1643676	•	0	0	305	52	3481	1846	3085	2965	2399	•	•
Rents 4	547528	•	0	0	0	1755	1357	0	637	444	0	•	•
Royalties 5	1533920	•	0	0	0	0	114	0	0	2149	0	•	•
Other Portfolio Income 6	1747227	•	8992	0	203	0	374	1494	369	2861	333	•	•
Other Receipts 7	2148537	•	75	0	324	601	14820	8226	37448	40526	5604	•	•
Total Receipts 8	223961128	•	418280	31113	1311158	447548	2074949	1385566	944723	2753548	2385933	•	•
Average Total Receipts 9	216388	•	716	5186	5308	11189	29642	44696	72671	196682	795311	•	•
Operating Costs/Operating Income (%)													
Cost of Operations 10	72.3	•	39.6	11.6	72.7	57.4	62.3	65.0	62.5	70.1	68.5	•	•
Salaries and Wages 11	5.0	•	16.2	15.0	8.7	7.2	6.5	5.8	9.6	4.7	6.8	•	•
Taxes Paid 12	1.3	•	2.2	1.4	1.4	1.5	1.3	1.2	1.7	1.0	1.5	•	•
Interest Paid 13	1.9	•	0.5	0.0	0.3	0.4	2.4	1.1	1.6	1.9	2.6	•	•
Depreciation 14	2.3	•	2.2	0.1	1.3	1.7	2.6	3.6	3.0	3.0	3.0	•	•
Amortization and Depletion 15	0.8	•	•	•	0.0	0.0	0.1	0.1	0.6	0.4	2.2	•	•
Pensions and Other Deferred Comp. 16	2.3	•	•	•	0.2	0.9	0.4	0.4	0.5	0.1	0.4	•	•
Employee Benefits 17	3.2	•	•	•	0.3	1.2	2.0	1.2	1.3	1.2	2.0	•	•
Advertising 18	0.4	•	0.0	•	0.1	0.1	0.2	0.2	0.4	0.1	0.6	•	•
Other Expenses 19	7.0	•	20.7	4.6	5.9	6.0	10.3	8.4	9.6	6.2	6.1	•	•
Officers' Compensation 20	0.4	•	5.9	2.9	5.4	1.3	2.7	2.8	3.6	1.3	1.0	•	•
Operating Margin 21	3.2	•	12.8	64.4	3.6	22.3	9.0	10.3	5.6	10.0	5.4	•	•
Operating Margin Before Officers' Comp. 22	3.5	•	18.8	67.3	9.0	23.6	11.8	13.1	9.2	11.3	6.4	•	•

Selected Average Balance Sheet ($ in Thousands)

Net Receivables 23	32349	0	382	527	1260	4873	6601	9778	23607	98508
Inventories 24	31389	5	3195	411	2384	5100	7650	17024	46142	302552
Net Property, Plant and Equipment 25	26944	16	12	271	1400	3304	7565	9590	36768	89651
Total Assets 26	254141	268	639	1551	6593	16969	35235	73938	159715	390427
Notes and Loans Payable 27	58012	84	0	468	1372	5097	8958	15266	45910	446046
All Other Liabilities 28	122130	134	8	346	766	10800	5850	16712	38317	-626159
Net Worth 29	73999	49	632	736	4455	1072	20428	41961	75488	570540

Selected Financial Ratios (Times to 1)

Current Ratio 30	1.4	176.3	83.6	3.1	6.0	1.4	3.8	2.1	1.8	3.1
Quick Ratio 31	0.7	167.0	83.6	1.9	2.4	0.7	1.7	1.1	0.6	0.7
Net Sales to Working Capital 32	9.2	14.0	8.4	6.0	2.7	7.5	2.3	3.8	5.1	1.9
Coverage Ratio 33	4.8	33.6	10023.0	11.6	66.2	5.1	11.4	7.1	7.3	3.2
Total Asset Turnover 34	0.8	2.6	8.1	3.4	1.7	1.7	1.3	0.9	1.2	2.0
Inventory Turnover 35	4.8	57.0	0.2	9.4	2.7	3.6	3.8	2.6	2.9	1.8
Receivables Turnover 36	6.2	126.2	7.8	9.8	10.0	6.9	7.7	5.5	8.8	7.6
Total Liabilities to Net Worth 37	2.4	4.4	0.0	1.1	0.5	14.8	0.7	0.8	1.1	•
Current Assets to Working Capital 38	3.6	1.0	1.0	1.5	1.2	3.6	1.4	1.9	2.3	1.5
Current Liabilities to Working Capital 39	2.6	0.0	0.0	0.5	0.2	2.6	0.4	0.9	1.3	0.5
Working Capital to Net Sales 40	0.1	0.1	0.1	0.2	0.4	0.1	0.4	0.3	0.2	0.5
Inventory to Working Capital 41	1.3	•	•	0.5	0.7	1.4	0.5	0.8	1.3	1.1
Total Receipts to Cash Flow 42	9.0	3.3	1.5	13.6	3.6	5.9	5.8	5.7	6.0	9.3
Cost of Goods to Cash Flow 43	6.5	1.3	0.2	9.9	2.1	3.7	3.7	3.5	4.2	6.4
Cash Flow to Total Debt 44	0.1	1.0	464.0	0.5	1.4	0.3	0.5	0.4	0.4	•

Selected Financial Factors (in Percentages)

Debt Ratio 45	70.9	81.6	1.2	52.5	32.4	93.7	42.0	43.2	52.7	•
Return on Total Assets 46	7.7	40.6	522.7	13.8	39.1	21.5	15.3	11.1	16.6	16.8
Return on Equity Before Income Taxes 47	20.9	213.5	528.9	26.5	57.0	274.6	24.1	16.7	30.4	7.9
Return on Equity After Income Taxes 48	14.2	213.5	528.9	20.8	54.9	231.2	21.5	14.1	27.3	7.3
Profit Margin (Before Income Tax) 49	7.4	15.0	64.4	3.7	22.8	10.0	11.1	10.1	11.9	5.7
Profit Margin (After Income Tax) 50	5.0	15.0	64.4	2.9	22.0	8.4	9.9	8.5	10.7	5.3

Table I

Corporations with and without Net Income

SHIP AND BOAT BUILDING

MONEY AMOUNTS AND SIZE OF ASSETS IN THOUSANDS OF DOLLARS

Item Description for Accounting Period 7/08 Through 6/09	Total	Zero Assets	Under 500	500 to 1,000	1,000 to 5,000	5,000 to 10,000	10,000 to 25,000	25,000 to 50,000	50,000 to 100,000	100,000 to 250,000	250,000 to 500,000	500,000 to 2,500,000	2,500,000 and over
Number of Enterprises **1**	1668	424	674	12	287	124	81	37	15	9	•	•	•
Revenues ($ in Thousands)													
Net Sales **2**	36542268	220474	1253922	67982	1328608	1198346	2468179	1781685	1561849	1560551	•	•	•
Interest **3**	93222	173	253	240	1369	238	1343	2246	1192	3190	•	•	•
Rents **4**	39686	0	0	0	428	0	273	3066	153	2690	•	•	•
Royalties **5**	3254	145	0	0	0	0	0	3018	0	0			
Other Portfolio Income **6**	142736	675	0	0	496	14	8908	19032	111	2372	•	•	•
Other Receipts **7**	105249	238	0	0	8697	4634	7036	23031	15091	29050	•	•	•
Total Receipts **8**	36926415	221705	1254175	68222	1339598	1203232	2485739	1832078	1578396	1597853	•	•	•
Average Total Receipts **9**	22138	523	1861	5685	4668	9703	30688	49516	105226	177539	•	•	•
Operating Costs/Operating Income (%)													
Cost of Operations **10**	76.2	76.5	56.8	95.6	80.5	72.5	78.7	75.2	78.5	84.6	•	•	•
Salaries and Wages **11**	3.4	3.9	5.9	0.1	4.6	4.2	4.6	5.3	3.8	3.4	•	•	•
Taxes Paid **12**	1.2	0.7	2.9	0.0	1.5	2.0	0.8	1.4	1.1	1.3	•	•	•
Interest Paid **13**	0.7	1.0	0.0	0.1	1.5	0.5	0.9	1.5	2.2	1.4	•	•	•
Depreciation **14**	1.5	2.1	0.2	0.2	2.0	3.5	2.7	3.7	3.1	3.3	•	•	•
Amortization and Depletion **15**	0.7	0.0	0.0	•	0.0	0.0	0.1	0.3	0.6	0.1	•	•	•
Pensions and Other Deferred Comp. **16**	0.8	0.1	0.0	•	0.3	0.2	0.3	0.6	0.5	0.6	•	•	•
Employee Benefits **17**	2.0	2.2	3.6	•	1.6	1.4	1.1	1.2	1.6	1.6	•	•	•
Advertising **18**	0.4	0.9	0.7	•	0.9	0.6	0.8	1.0	1.1	0.4	•	•	•
Other Expenses **19**	6.6	13.1	22.7	0.9	9.4	7.7	8.6	11.2	8.6	2.7	•	•	•
Officers' Compensation **20**	1.2	0.3	5.4	0.2	4.4	1.7	1.8	1.5	1.3	1.1	•	•	•
Operating Margin **21**	5.4	•	1.7	2.9	•	5.6	•	•	•	•	•	•	•
Operating Margin Before Officers' Comp. **22**	6.5	•	7.1	3.1	•	7.4	1.6	•	•	0.6	•	•	•

Selected Average Balance Sheet ($ in Thousands)

Net Receivables 23	1887	0	67	20	318	520	2938	4503	8693	15592	•
Inventories 24	3295	0	19	44	850	3073	2393	5279	16275	17840	•
Net Property, Plant and Equipment 25	2838	0	35	33	883	657	4572	12901	25651	50382	•
Total Assets 26	19547	0	261	926	2491	7916	14807	35436	67895	136767	•
Notes and Loans Payable 27	4471	0	7	55	1122	4060	4868	14288	31879	48668	•
All Other Liabilities 28	7422	0	16	331	605	2300	5019	10150	23998	42550	•
Net Worth 29	7654	0	238	540	764	1556	4920	10997	12018	45550	•

Selected Financial Ratios (Times to 1)

Current Ratio 30	1.3	•	11.6	2.6	1.8	3.0	1.3	1.4	1.0	1.3	•
Quick Ratio 31	0.5	•	10.4	2.6	0.5	0.9	0.6	0.7	0.4	0.5	•
Net Sales to Working Capital 32	11.8	•	9.2	10.3	6.8	2.0	15.1	9.2	110.0	12.1	•
Coverage Ratio 33	10.5	0.9	57.7	62.4	•	13.0	1.6	1.0	0.4	2.3	•
Total Asset Turnover 34	1.1	•	7.1	6.1	1.9	1.2	2.1	1.4	1.5	1.3	•
Inventory Turnover 35	5.1	•	55.1	122.5	4.4	2.3	10.0	6.9	5.0	8.2	•
Receivables Turnover 36	12.3	•	52.5	3.6	15.5	16.3	12.7	8.0	8.9	11.0	•
Total Liabilities to Net Worth 37	1.6	•	0.1	0.7	2.3	4.1	2.0	2.2	4.6	2.0	•
Current Assets to Working Capital 38	4.2	•	1.1	1.6	2.3	1.5	4.1	3.4	35.4	4.1	•
Current Liabilities to Working Capital 39	3.2	•	0.1	0.6	1.3	0.5	3.1	2.4	34.4	3.1	•
Working Capital to Net Sales 40	0.1	•	0.1	0.1	0.1	0.5	0.1	0.1	0.0	0.1	•
Inventory to Working Capital 41	2.1	•	0.1	0.0	1.4	0.9	1.2	1.1	16.2	1.2	•
Total Receipts to Cash Flow 42	9.4	14.1	10.2	26.6	•	8.0	15.7	13.8	17.7	33.3	•
Cost of Goods to Cash Flow 43	7.1	10.8	5.8	25.5	•	5.8	12.3	10.4	13.9	28.1	•
Cash Flow to Total Debt 44	0.2	8.0	8.0	0.6	•	0.2	0.2	0.1	0.1	0.1	•

Selected Financial Factors (in Percentages)

Debt Ratio 45	60.8	•	8.7	41.7	69.3	80.3	66.8	69.0	82.3	66.7	•
Return on Total Assets 46	8.3	•	12.6	20.2	•	8.0	2.9	2.0	1.4	4.0	•
Return on Equity Before Income Taxes 47	19.1	•	13.6	34.1	•	37.6	3.3	•	•	6.9	•
Return on Equity After Income Taxes 48	12.0	•	13.6	27.5	•	33.9	2.6	•	•	2.0	•
Profit Margin (Before Income Tax) 49	6.7	•	1.7	3.2	•	6.0	0.5	•	•	1.8	•
Profit Margin (After Income Tax) 50	4.2	•	1.7	2.6	•	5.5	0.4	•	•	0.5	•

Table II

Corporations with Net Income

SHIP AND BOAT BUILDING

MONEY AMOUNTS AND SIZE OF ASSETS IN THOUSANDS OF DOLLARS

Item Description for Accounting Period 7/08 Through 6/09	Total	Zero Assets	Under 500	500 to 1,000	1,000 to 5,000	5,000 to 10,000	10,000 to 25,000	25,000 to 50,000	50,000 to 100,000	100,000 to 250,000	250,000 to 500,000	500,000 to 2,500,000	2,500,000 and over
Number of Enterprises 1	846	15	581	12	95	66	40	20	8	•	•	0	0
Revenues ($ in Thousands)													
Net Sales 2	31979775	142277	1215503	67982	851328	1058102	1547648	1141502	973309	•	•	0	0
Interest 3	85999	173	0	240	729	112	186	1956	916	•	•	0	0
Rents 4	38741	0	0	0	0	0	0	3066	153	•	•	0	0
Royalties 5	60	0	0	0	0	0	0	0	0	•	•	0	0
Other Portfolio Income 6	128976	667	0	0	395	13	527	18450	97	•	•	0	0
Other Receipts 7	75900	82	0	0	6590	4593	10378	12911	7376	•	•	0	0
Total Receipts 8	32309451	143199	1215503	68222	859042	1062820	1558739	1177885	981851	•	•	0	0
Average Total Receipts 9	38191	9547	2092	5685	9043	16103	38968	58894	122731				
Operating Costs/Operating Income (%)													
Cost of Operations 10	75.6	69.0	56.7	95.6	83.6	71.3	78.8	71.7	78.2	•	•	•	•
Salaries and Wages 11	2.9	3.6	6.1	0.1	2.6	3.8	3.4	4.9	3.2	•	•	•	•
Taxes Paid 12	1.2	0.6	3.0	0.0	0.9	1.9	0.8	1.4	1.4	•	•	•	•
Interest Paid 13	0.5	1.0	0.0	0.1	0.8	0.2	0.3	0.9	0.7	•	•	•	•
Depreciation 14	1.3	2.3	0.2	0.2	1.6	3.8	2.4	2.3	2.8	•	•	•	•
Amortization and Depletion 15	0.8	0.0	•	•	0.0	0.0	0.1	0.4	0.2	•	•	•	•
Pensions and Other Deferred Comp. 16	0.8	0.1	0.0	0.3	0.0	0.2	0.3	0.8	0.6	•	•	•	•
Employee Benefits 17	2.0	3.3	3.6	1.5	1.5	1.6	0.8	1.8	1.7	•	•	•	•
Advertising 18	0.2	0.1	0.7	0.3	0.3	0.1	0.8	0.1	0.8	•	•	•	•
Other Expenses 19	5.7	7.3	22.5	0.9	5.0	6.5	5.5	11.4	6.3	•	•	•	•
Officers' Compensation 20	1.1	0.3	5.3	0.2	3.8	1.2	2.2	1.7	1.7	•	•	•	•
Operating Margin 21	7.8	12.3	2.0	2.9	•	9.3	4.7	2.7	2.4	•	•	•	•
Operating Margin Before Officers' Comp. 22	8.9	12.6	7.3	3.1	3.5	10.5	6.8	4.4	4.1	•	•	•	•

Selected Average Balance Sheet ($ in Thousands)

Net Receivables 23	2768	0	74	20	806	899	3422	6061	12463
Inventories 24	5542	0	10	39	1210	1982	3714	5246	14281
Net Property, Plant and Equipment 25	4278	0	36	33	1065	961	3321	9884	26550
Total Assets 26	32988	0	249	926	2354	6685	13964	35958	70495
Notes and Loans Payable 27	5912	0	8	55	812	729	2203	8235	14294
All Other Liabilities 28	12771	0	7	331	546	3087	4465	11731	29806
Net Worth 29	14305	0	234	540	997	2869	7296	15992	26395

Selected Financial Ratios (Times to 1)

Current Ratio 30	1.3	•	19.7	2.6	2.2	1.8	1.9	1.8	1.2
Quick Ratio 31	0.5	•	19.5	2.6	1.6	1.2	0.9	1.1	0.6
Net Sales to Working Capital 32	13.4	•	10.4	10.3	12.7	6.6	8.4	6.7	23.6
Coverage Ratio 33	20.0	13.6	64.5	62.4	1.7	43.5	16.5	7.5	5.6
Total Asset Turnover 34	1.1	•	8.4	6.1	3.8	2.4	2.8	1.6	1.7
Inventory Turnover 35	5.2	•	115.7	140.1	6.2	5.8	8.2	7.8	6.7
Receivables Turnover 36	12.9	•	53.9	3.9	10.9	15.0	12.1	6.5	•
Total Liabilities to Net Worth 37	1.3	•	0.1	0.7	1.4	1.3	0.9	1.2	1.7
Current Assets to Working Capital 38	4.3	•	1.1	1.6	1.8	2.3	2.1	2.3	7.6
Current Liabilities to Working Capital 39	3.3	•	0.1	0.6	0.8	1.3	1.1	1.3	6.6
Working Capital to Net Sales 40	0.1	•	0.1	0.1	0.1	0.2	0.1	0.2	0.0
Inventory to Working Capital 41	2.2	•	0.0	0.0	0.4	0.3	0.6	0.3	2.8
Total Receipts to Cash Flow 42	8.1	5.7	10.2	26.6	25.0	6.6	10.0	8.0	13.7
Cost of Goods to Cash Flow 43	6.1	3.9	5.8	25.5	20.9	4.7	7.9	5.7	10.7
Cash Flow to Total Debt 44	0.3	•	13.8	0.6	0.3	0.6	0.6	0.4	0.2

Selected Financial Factors (in Percentages)

Debt Ratio 45	56.6	•	6.0	41.7	57.7	57.1	47.8	55.5	62.6
Return on Total Assets 46	11.0	•	17.2	20.2	5.0	23.9	15.9	10.8	6.9
Return on Equity Before Income Taxes 47	24.1	•	18.0	34.1	5.1	54.3	28.6	21.1	15.2
Return on Equity After Income Taxes 48	16.6	•	18.0	27.5	3.9	50.6	27.6	17.7	14.5
Profit Margin (Before Income Tax) 49	9.1	13.0	2.0	3.2	0.6	9.7	5.4	5.9	3.3
Profit Margin (After Income Tax) 50	6.3	9.5	2.0	2.6	0.4	9.0	5.2	5.0	3.2

Table I

Corporations with and without Net Income

OTHER TRANSPORTATION EQUIPMENT AND RAILROAD ROLLING STOCK

MONEY AMOUNTS AND SIZE OF ASSETS IN THOUSANDS OF DOLLARS

Item Description for Accounting Period 7/08 Through 6/09	Total	Zero Assets	Under 500	500 to 1,000	1,000 to 5,000	5,000 to 10,000	10,000 to 25,000	25,000 to 50,000	50,000 to 100,000	100,000 to 250,000	250,000 to 500,000	500,000 to 2,500,000	2,500,000 and over
Number of Enterprises 1	1995	8	1436	63	319	53	58	16	15	11	•	•	•
Revenues ($ in Thousands)													
Net Sales 2	31334411	463232	295747	154373	1545700	1040242	1600029	1189386	1189759	1876677	•	•	•
Interest 3	919158	0	3	0	956	33	962	1626	2828	2100	•	•	•
Rents 4	75046	0	0	0	169	18	0	0	1545	0	•	•	•
Royalties 5	68413	0	0	0	0	0	0	734	264	6032	•	•	•
Other Portfolio Income 6	182224	28778	825	0	2472	0	1517	7296	2319	1068	•	•	•
Other Receipts 7	401707	10522	182	0	5768	2609	28085	5860	14172	2722	•	•	•
Total Receipts 8	32980959	502532	296757	154373	1555065	1042902	1630593	1204902	1210887	1888599	•	•	•
Average Total Receipts 9	16532	62816	207	2450	4875	19677	28114	75306	80726	171691	•	•	•
Operating Costs/Operating Income (%)													
Cost of Operations 10	70.6	56.5	61.1	81.7	79.2	76.0	75.3	79.0	69.6	78.2	•	•	•
Salaries and Wages 11	6.3	13.6	3.0	•	3.2	10.9	7.8	5.7	5.9	5.2	•	•	•
Taxes Paid 12	1.1	1.4	4.8	0.6	1.4	1.0	1.0	0.8	1.3	1.0	•	•	•
Interest Paid 13	2.7	1.9	5.2	1.6	0.4	0.9	0.7	0.8	1.9	1.8	•	•	•
Depreciation 14	5.5	2.7	4.9	0.4	1.6	2.4	1.9	1.2	2.8	3.5	•	•	•
Amortization and Depletion 15	0.7	0.9	0.1	0.1	0.1	0.0	0.1	0.1	0.8	1.0	•	•	•
Pensions and Other Deferred Comp. 16	0.5	0.1	•	•	0.1	0.0	0.2	0.1	0.7	0.3	•	•	•
Employee Benefits 17	1.6	1.6	0.5	•	0.5	2.4	0.9	0.4	1.4	1.2	•	•	•
Advertising 18	0.8	1.9	3.4	0.3	0.3	0.1	0.9	1.0	0.3	1.1	•	•	•
Other Expenses 19	10.4	28.3	32.2	8.2	5.4	4.2	11.6	8.2	4.0	5.4	•	•	•
Officers' Compensation 20	0.9	0.1	8.7	4.2	4.1	0.6	1.9	0.7	1.8	0.7	•	•	•
Operating Margin 21	•	•	•	2.9	3.6	1.5	•	1.9	9.5	0.7	•	•	•
Operating Margin Before Officers' Comp. 22	•	•	•	7.2	7.7	2.1	•	2.5	11.3	1.4	•	•	•

Selected Average Balance Sheet ($ in Thousands)

	•	•	•	•	•	•	•	•	•
Net Receivables 23	3768	0	7	346	536	1964	3261	7311	8135	20426
Inventories 24	2181	0	55	324	495	5195	3959	8828	10099	25292
Net Property, Plant and Equipment 25	3515	0	24	88	258	1708	3140	5911	10624	25451
Total Assets 26	16603	0	95	935	1980	9156	14412	29858	64211	161026
Notes and Loans Payable 27	6282	0	172	166	1048	3824	3959	7771	22313	44426
All Other Liabilities 28	4176	0	14	665	429	2755	4134	8301	11910	61152
Net Worth 29	6145	0	-91	104	503	2577	6319	13785	29989	55449

Selected Financial Ratios (Times to 1)

	•	•	•	•	•	•	•	•	•
Current Ratio 30	1.4	•	0.7	1.1	2.5	2.7	1.7	2.1	1.8	1.3
Quick Ratio 31	0.8	•	0.1	0.5	1.5	0.7	0.8	1.0	0.9	0.5
Net Sales to Working Capital 32	7.1	•	•	44.0	5.1	4.1	7.4	6.4	6.7	8.2
Coverage Ratio 33	2.5	0.4	•	2.9	10.6	3.0	0.7	4.9	6.8	1.7
Total Asset Turnover 34	0.9	•	2.2	2.6	2.4	2.1	1.9	2.5	1.2	1.1
Inventory Turnover 35	5.1	•	2.3	6.2	7.8	2.9	5.2	6.7	5.5	5.3
Receivables Turnover 36	4.7	•	31.3	7.8	8.8	9.2	8.9	11.7	10.4	10.2
Total Liabilities to Net Worth 37	1.7	•	•	8.0	2.9	2.6	1.3	1.2	1.1	1.9
Current Assets to Working Capital 38	3.5	•	•	13.8	1.7	1.6	2.5	1.9	2.2	4.1
Current Liabilities to Working Capital 39	2.5	•	•	12.8	0.7	0.6	1.5	0.9	1.2	3.1
Working Capital to Net Sales 40	0.1	•	•	0.0	0.2	0.2	0.1	0.2	0.1	0.1
Inventory to Working Capital 41	1.0	•	•	6.9	0.6	1.2	1.2	0.8	0.9	1.6
Total Receipts to Cash Flow 42	8.2	3.8	44.9	11.1	12.4	25.3	11.6	10.4	7.3	17.2
Cost of Goods to Cash Flow 43	5.8	2.2	27.4	9.1	9.8	19.3	8.7	8.3	5.1	13.5
Cash Flow to Total Debt 44	0.2	•	0.0	0.3	0.3	0.1	0.3	0.4	0.3	0.1

Selected Financial Factors (in Percentages)

	•	•	•	•	•	•	•	•	•
Debt Ratio 45	63.0	•	195.5	88.8	74.6	71.9	56.2	53.8	53.3	65.6
Return on Total Assets 46	6.6	•	•	11.8	11.4	5.7	1.0	9.9	16.4	3.3
Return on Equity Before Income Taxes 47	10.9	•	53.3	68.8	40.6	13.4	17.0	30.0	•	4.1
Return on Equity After Income Taxes 48	6.2	•	53.3	68.8	36.2	13.4	14.6	27.2	•	1.3
Profit Margin (Before Income Tax) 49	4.3	•	•	2.9	4.2	1.8	•	3.2	11.3	1.3
Profit Margin (After Income Tax) 50	2.4	•	•	2.9	3.8	1.8	•	2.7	10.3	0.4

159

Table II

Corporations with Net Income

OTHER TRANSPORTATION EQUIPMENT AND RAILROAD ROLLING STOCK

MONEY AMOUNTS AND SIZE OF ASSETS IN THOUSANDS OF DOLLARS

Item Description for Accounting Period 7/08 Through 6/09	Total	Zero Assets	Under 500	500 to 1,000	1,000 to 5,000	5,000 to 10,000	10,000 to 25,000	25,000 to 50,000	50,000 to 100,000	100,000 to 250,000	250,000 to 500,000	500,000 to 2,500,000	2,500,000 and over
Number of Enterprises 1	494	•	103	63	192	50	39	13	•	6	•	•	0
Revenues ($ in Thousands)													
Net Sales 2	20323998	•	87672	154373	1294832	1022874	1052830	1057495	•	949524	•	•	0
Interest 3	766991	•	0	0	0	0	411	411	•	1160	•	•	0
Rents 4	66083	•	0	0	0	0	0	0	•	0	•	•	0
Royalties 5	57576	•	0	0	0	0	0	0	•	0	•	•	0
Other Portfolio Income 6	68505	•	0	0	0	0	1397	7194	•	767	•	•	0
Other Receipts 7	164304	•	0	0	5014	1883	1674	4466	•	824	•	•	0
Total Receipts 8	21447457	•	87672	154373	1299846	1024757	1056312	1069566	•	952275	•	•	0
Average Total Receipts 9	43416	•	851	2450	6770	20495	27085	82274	•	158712	•	•	•
Operating Costs/Operating Income (%)													
Cost of Operations 10	71.6	•	54.9	81.7	78.4	75.2	76.5	81.2	•	76.9	•	•	•
Salaries and Wages 11	5.1	•	•	•	2.3	10.1	4.1	4.4	•	4.2	•	•	•
Taxes Paid 12	0.8	•	0.2	0.6	1.4	1.0	0.7	0.6	•	0.8	•	•	•
Interest Paid 13	2.6	•	5.0	1.6	0.2	0.9	0.5	0.3	•	2.1	•	•	•
Depreciation 14	2.8	•	1.2	0.4	1.3	2.3	1.1	1.1	•	4.1	•	•	•
Amortization and Depletion 15	0.8	•	•	0.1	0.0	•	0.1	0.1	•	1.3	•	•	•
Pensions and Other Deferred Comp. 16	0.4	•	•	•	0.1	0.0	0.2	0.1	•	0.3	•	•	•
Employee Benefits 17	1.7	•	1.0	•	0.0	2.4	1.0	0.4	•	1.8	•	•	•
Advertising 18	1.0	•	1.8	0.3	0.1	0.1	0.6	1.0	•	0.1	•	•	•
Other Expenses 19	8.0	•	20.8	8.2	2.4	4.2	9.7	6.7	•	2.4	•	•	•
Officers' Compensation 20	0.9	•	7.8	4.2	4.2	0.6	1.6	0.6	•	1.0	•	•	•
Operating Margin 21	4.4	•	7.3	2.9	9.6	3.2	4.0	3.7	•	5.0	•	•	•
Operating Margin Before Officers' Comp. 22	5.3	•	15.1	7.2	13.7	3.8	5.6	4.2	•	6.0	•	•	•

Selected Average Balance Sheet ($ in Thousands)

Net Receivables 23	13232	29	346	865	2045	3646	7486	15471
Inventories 24	5732	86	385	610	5392	3353	9042	29716
Net Property, Plant and Equipment 25	5572	37	88	161	1714	1504	5920	27907
Total Assets 26	34779	261	935	2267	9218	13165	30489	157626
Notes and Loans Payable 27	14046	347	166	751	2533	2719	5730	54665
All Other Liabilities 28	9780	48	665	463	2709	4400	7181	49234
Net Worth 29	10953	-135	104	1053	3976	6046	17577	53727

Selected Financial Ratios (Times to 1)

Current Ratio 30	1.5	1.2	1.1	2.8	2.8	1.5	2.7	1.4
Quick Ratio 31	1.0	0.2	0.5	1.8	0.8	0.8	1.3	0.6
Net Sales to Working Capital 32	5.7	24.0	44.0	5.0	4.2	8.6	5.5	5.8
Coverage Ratio 33	4.9	2.4	2.9	59.8	4.8	10.1	16.3	3.6
Total Asset Turnover 34	1.2	3.3	2.6	3.0	2.2	2.1	2.7	1.0
Inventory Turnover 35	5.1	5.4	5.2	8.7	2.9	6.2	7.3	4.1
Receivables Turnover 36	3.5	58.7	8.7	7.5	9.1	8.9	13.3	•
Total Liabilities to Net Worth 37	2.2	•	8.0	1.2	1.3	1.2	0.7	1.9
Current Assets to Working Capital 38	3.2	5.6	13.8	1.6	1.6	3.0	1.6	3.3
Current Liabilities to Working Capital 39	2.2	4.6	12.8	0.6	0.6	2.0	0.6	2.3
Working Capital to Net Sales 40	0.2	0.0	0.0	0.2	0.2	0.1	0.2	0.2
Inventory to Working Capital 41	0.7	4.5	6.9	0.6	1.1	1.4	0.7	1.1
Total Receipts to Cash Flow 42	6.1	3.8	11.1	8.9	17.8	8.9	10.3	15.1
Cost of Goods to Cash Flow 43	4.4	2.1	9.1	6.9	13.4	6.8	8.3	11.6
Cash Flow to Total Debt 44	0.3	0.6	0.3	0.6	0.2	0.4	0.6	0.1

Selected Financial Factors (in Percentages)

Debt Ratio 45	68.5	151.9	88.8	53.6	56.9	54.1	42.3	65.9
Return on Total Assets 46	15.0	40.3	11.8	30.1	9.4	9.8	13.6	7.4
Return on Equity Before Income Taxes 47	38.0	•	68.8	63.6	17.3	19.2	22.2	15.7
Return on Equity After Income Taxes 48	27.5	•	68.8	60.2	17.3	16.5	19.9	10.4
Profit Margin (Before Income Tax) 49	10.1	7.3	2.9	9.9	3.4	4.3	4.8	5.3
Profit Margin (After Income Tax) 50	7.3	7.3	2.9	9.4	3.4	3.7	4.3	3.5

Table I

Corporations with and without Net Income

FURNITURE AND RELATED PRODUCT MANUFACTURING

MONEY AMOUNTS AND SIZE OF ASSETS IN THOUSANDS OF DOLLARS

Item Description for Accounting Period 7/08 Through 6/09	Total	Zero Assets	Under 500	500 to 1,000	1,000 to 5,000	5,000 to 10,000	10,000 to 25,000	25,000 to 50,000	50,000 to 100,000	100,000 to 250,000	250,000 to 500,000	500,000 to 2,500,000	2,500,000 and over
Number of Enterprises 1	12058	1185	8156	939	1287	181	167	68	30	24	7	14	0
Revenues ($ in Thousands)													
Net Sales 2	63053477	355547	5290606	1855562	7588808	2889338	5433845	4847005	3478490	4916936	3342853	23054487	0
Interest 3	90357	984	404	1321	7835	2420	2291	4127	2590	9106	11843	47434	0
Rents 4	37332	430	355	0	624	462	257	3402	1317	11570	1376	17539	0
Royalties 5	61899	0	0	0	0	0	0	1222	1738	255	407	58277	0
Other Portfolio Income 6	279406	0	1420	298	1475	705	4561	13015	5738	15683	8831	227676	0
Other Receipts 7	571506	559	14557	3181	26432	24376	28809	18857	20019	54341	-28251	408632	0
Total Receipts 8	64093977	357520	5307342	1860362	7625174	2917301	5469763	4887628	3509892	5007891	3337059	23814045	0
Average Total Receipts 9	5315	302	651	1981	5925	16118	32753	71877	116996	208662	476723	1701003	•
Operating Costs/Operating Income (%)													
Cost of Operations 10	68.3	61.9	55.1	61.4	70.0	72.3	70.3	73.4	73.9	73.7	62.1	68.3	•
Salaries and Wages 11	8.9	13.3	15.4	7.3	8.4	8.9	7.9	7.9	6.4	6.5	10.9	8.7	•
Taxes Paid 12	1.5	2.7	2.9	2.7	2.1	0.9	1.2	1.4	0.9	0.9	1.5	1.3	•
Interest Paid 13	1.3	0.5	0.8	0.4	0.8	1.0	0.9	1.1	2.4	1.3	1.1	1.8	•
Depreciation 14	1.9	2.1	1.3	0.8	1.9	2.6	1.9	1.8	1.9	2.2	2.2	2.0	•
Amortization and Depletion 15	0.4	0.1	0.2	0.1	0.0	0.0	0.1	0.2	0.7	0.6	0.3	0.7	•
Pensions and Other Deferred Comp. 16	0.4	0.2	0.5	0.3	0.2	0.1	0.2	0.4	0.2	0.6	0.3	0.6	•
Employee Benefits 17	2.0	1.3	0.7	3.0	1.4	1.7	2.4	1.9	1.4	3.0	4.9	1.9	•
Advertising 18	2.0	1.3	0.4	0.4	1.2	2.3	0.7	0.9	2.2	1.4	3.9	3.0	•
Other Expenses 19	12.2	26.7	15.2	15.1	11.5	9.2	10.6	10.1	11.5	9.9	13.8	13.0	•
Officers' Compensation 20	2.0	2.1	8.6	4.4	3.8	2.2	1.9	1.1	1.1	0.9	0.4	0.6	•
Operating Margin 21	•	•	•	4.1	•	•	1.8	•	•	•	•	•	•
Operating Margin Before Officers' Comp. 22	0.9	•	7.4	8.5	2.4	0.8	3.8	0.9	•	•	•	•	•

Selected Average Balance Sheet ($ in Thousands)

Net Receivables 23	511	0	24	190	555	1822	3330	8625	15557	22620	54166	157893
Inventories 24	506	0	24	90	538	1588	3604	8731	16796	31648	46170	146921
Net Property, Plant and Equipment 25	628	0	27	131	666	2565	3678	8711	11951	38991	67573	209612
Total Assets 26	2888	0	121	638	2141	6729	14806	34341	66717	131439	307870	1224467
Notes and Loans Payable 27	998	0	57	307	1185	3049	4494	10230	32594	35201	72835	387722
All Other Liabilities 28	935	0	54	159	930	1680	3154	8043	20428	29534	103927	432942
Net Worth 29	954	0	9	172	26	1999	7158	16068	13694	66704	131108	403803

Selected Financial Ratios (Times to 1)

Current Ratio 30	1.5	•	1.1	2.6	1.7	1.8	2.3	1.7	1.7	2.3	1.6	1.1
Quick Ratio 31	0.8	•	0.6	1.8	0.9	1.1	1.2	0.9	0.8	1.1	0.9	0.6
Net Sales to Working Capital 32	12.1	•	125.7	6.9	10.6	9.4	6.3	8.1	7.0	5.4	10.5	33.2
Coverage Ratio 33	1.4	•	•	11.3	•	0.6	3.7	1.5	0.3	1.6	•	1.9
Total Asset Turnover 34	1.8	•	5.4	3.1	2.8	2.4	2.2	2.1	1.7	1.6	1.6	1.3
Inventory Turnover 35	7.1	•	15.0	13.5	7.7	7.3	6.3	6.0	5.1	4.8	6.4	7.7
Receivables Turnover 36	9.6	•	25.7	9.2	10.1	8.6	8.9	8.7	7.5	7.7	8.7	9.4
Total Liabilities to Net Worth 37	2.0	•	11.9	2.7	80.6	2.4	1.1	1.1	3.9	1.0	1.3	2.0
Current Assets to Working Capital 38	3.1	•	12.6	1.6	2.5	2.2	1.8	2.4	2.4	1.8	2.7	9.0
Current Liabilities to Working Capital 39	2.1	•	11.6	0.6	1.5	1.2	0.8	1.4	1.4	0.8	1.7	8.0
Working Capital to Net Sales 40	0.1	•	0.0	0.1	0.1	0.1	0.2	0.1	0.1	0.2	0.1	0.0
Inventory to Working Capital 41	1.1	•	5.0	0.4	0.9	0.7	0.7	1.0	1.0	0.7	0.9	2.7
Total Receipts to Cash Flow 42	10.4	13.5	10.1	7.9	14.7	18.0	9.3	11.6	12.6	11.8	11.8	8.7
Cost of Goods to Cash Flow 43	7.1	8.3	5.6	4.8	10.3	13.0	6.5	8.5	9.3	8.7	7.4	6.0
Cash Flow to Total Debt 44	0.3	•	0.6	0.5	0.2	0.2	0.5	0.3	0.2	0.3	0.2	0.2

Selected Financial Factors (in Percentages)

Debt Ratio 45	67.0	•	92.2	73.1	98.8	70.3	51.7	53.2	79.5	49.3	57.4	67.0
Return on Total Assets 46	3.5	•	•	14.7	•	1.4	7.5	3.5	1.2	3.3	•	4.6
Return on Equity Before Income Taxes 47	3.2	•	•	49.9	•	•	11.3	2.5	•	2.5	•	6.6
Return on Equity After Income Taxes 48	1.6	•	•	48.1	•	•	10.7	1.6	•	1.7	•	4.1
Profit Margin (Before Income Tax) 49	0.6	•	•	4.3	•	•	2.5	0.6	•	0.8	•	1.6
Profit Margin (After Income Tax) 50	0.3	•	•	4.2	•	•	2.3	0.4	•	0.6	•	1.0

Table II

Corporations with Net Income

FURNITURE AND RELATED PRODUCT MANUFACTURING

MONEY AMOUNTS AND SIZE OF ASSETS IN THOUSANDS OF DOLLARS

Item Description for Accounting Period 7/08 Through 6/09		Total	Zero Assets	Under 500	500 to 1,000	1,000 to 5,000	5,000 to 10,000	10,000 to 25,000	25,000 to 50,000	50,000 to 100,000	100,000 to 250,000	250,000 to 500,000	500,000 to 2,500,000	2,500,000 and over
Number of Enterprises	1	6162	391	4139	599	773	77	107	38	13	12	4	9	0
Revenues ($ in Thousands)														
Net Sales	2	38410062	72785	3314770	1225844	4432809	1764229	3580002	3106462	1638373	2492082	2124258	14658447	0
Interest	3	47996	17	221	1146	6885	992	1656	2789	1647	1393	3084	28166	0
Rents	4	13836	430	355	0	624	128	150	2840	753	148	70	8339	0
Royalties	5	40758	0	0	0	0	0	0	1222	1367	0	407	37762	0
Other Portfolio Income	6	152146	0	0	248	494	277	2960	6433	5245	3436	584	132466	0
Other Receipts	7	464316	13	542	7	14945	16031	24890	11764	8687	35819	10847	340773	0
Total Receipts	8	39129114	73245	3315888	1227245	4455757	1781657	3609658	3131510	1656072	2532878	2139250	15205953	0
Average Total Receipts	9	6350	187	801	2049	5764	23138	33735	82408	127390	211073	534812	1689550	•
Operating Costs/Operating Income (%)														
Cost of Operations	10	67.0	50.5	52.4	54.2	68.3	72.0	69.3	69.4	73.7	73.7	65.9	67.6	•
Salaries and Wages	11	8.9	5.3	15.3	6.9	7.3	9.7	7.4	8.1	6.6	5.6	9.8	9.3	•
Taxes Paid	12	1.4	3.1	2.8	2.7	1.7	0.5	1.2	1.6	1.0	0.5	1.0	1.3	•
Interest Paid	13	0.9	0.3	0.5	0.2	0.6	0.4	0.4	0.6	1.6	1.0	1.0	1.2	•
Depreciation	14	1.7	1.6	0.7	0.5	1.2	1.5	1.8	1.8	1.3	2.5	2.0	2.1	•
Amortization and Depletion	15	0.3	0.2	0.2	0.1	0.0	0.0	0.1	0.0	0.8	0.4	0.3	0.4	•
Pensions and Other Deferred Comp.	16	0.5	0.7	0.7	0.2	0.3	0.1	0.3	0.6	0.3	0.4	0.4	0.7	•
Employee Benefits	17	2.2	0.4	0.3	3.5	1.2	1.5	2.1	2.1	1.5	3.8	6.4	2.1	•
Advertising	18	1.7	1.0	0.5	0.5	1.4	2.8	0.6	1.0	1.0	0.9	1.6	2.8	•
Other Expenses	19	10.5	30.8	14.0	17.4	11.0	7.3	8.9	8.8	8.1	6.0	9.7	11.0	•
Officers' Compensation	20	2.2	2.2	9.0	5.5	4.5	1.7	2.1	1.2	1.0	0.9	0.2	0.6	•
Operating Margin	21	2.7	3.8	3.5	8.3	2.4	2.4	5.8	4.8	3.1	4.5	1.7	0.8	•
Operating Margin Before Officers' Comp.	22	4.9	5.9	12.5	13.8	6.9	4.1	7.9	5.9	4.1	5.4	1.9	1.4	•

Selected Average Balance Sheet ($ in Thousands)

Net Receivables 23	645	0	30	196	535	3057	3334	9636	16095	23268	57461	182754
Inventories 24	609	0	24	28	581	2429	3754	9413	17237	38593	33337	150626
Net Property, Plant and Equipment 25	671	0	14	164	444	1259	3350	10319	9350	36754	76238	213671
Total Assets 26	3180	0	139	643	1950	6567	14462	34947	65657	127902	285250	1134864
Notes and Loans Payable 27	759	0	39	245	698	1137	2591	7619	22719	27374	61585	256176
All Other Liabilities 28	1076	0	54	103	614	2523	2950	8502	15168	23753	90863	465576
Net Worth 29	1345	0	47	295	638	2907	8921	18826	27770	76775	132802	413112

Selected Financial Ratios (Times to 1)

Current Ratio 30	1.9	•	1.5	3.3	2.2	1.8	3.0	2.0	2.6	4.0	2.1	1.5
Quick Ratio 31	1.1	•	0.9	2.7	1.2	1.2	1.6	1.1	1.4	2.3	1.3	0.9
Net Sales to Working Capital 32	8.1	•	28.8	7.1	7.5	10.1	5.2	7.7	5.4	4.1	7.8	10.2
Coverage Ratio 33	6.2	15.7	8.7	45.1	5.5	9.1	16.3	10.7	3.7	7.0	3.4	4.7
Total Asset Turnover 34	2.0	•	5.7	3.2	2.9	3.5	2.3	2.3	1.9	1.6	1.9	1.4
Inventory Turnover 35	6.9	•	17.4	39.6	6.7	6.8	6.2	6.0	5.4	4.0	10.5	7.3
Receivables Turnover 36	8.3	•	22.8	•	10.4	6.6	8.0	7.8	7.0	6.4	•	7.6
Total Liabilities to Net Worth 37	1.4	•	2.0	1.2	2.1	1.3	0.6	0.9	1.4	0.7	1.1	1.7
Current Assets to Working Capital 38	2.1	•	2.9	1.4	1.8	2.3	1.5	2.0	1.6	1.3	1.9	2.9
Current Liabilities to Working Capital 39	1.1	•	1.9	0.4	0.8	1.3	0.5	1.0	0.6	0.3	0.9	1.9
Working Capital to Net Sales 40	0.1	•	0.0	0.1	0.1	0.1	0.2	0.1	0.2	0.2	0.1	0.1
Inventory to Working Capital 41	0.6	•	1.1	0.1	0.7	0.6	0.5	0.7	0.7	0.5	0.5	0.6
Total Receipts to Cash Flow 42	8.1	3.2	7.6	5.9	9.6	13.7	7.4	7.7	9.2	8.9	10.6	7.5
Cost of Goods to Cash Flow 43	5.4	1.6	4.0	3.2	6.6	9.8	5.1	5.4	6.8	6.6	7.0	5.1
Cash Flow to Total Debt 44	0.4	•	1.1	1.0	0.5	0.5	0.8	0.7	0.4	0.5	0.3	0.3

Selected Financial Factors (in Percentages)

Debt Ratio 45	57.7	•	66.4	54.2	67.3	55.7	38.3	46.1	57.7	40.0	53.4	63.6
Return on Total Assets 46	10.7	•	22.7	27.5	10.4	13.1	16.3	14.3	11.1	11.4	6.2	8.3
Return on Equity Before Income Taxes 47	21.2	•	59.8	58.6	26.1	26.4	24.8	24.1	19.2	16.3	9.4	17.9
Return on Equity After Income Taxes 48	18.9	•	59.7	57.0	25.6	24.9	24.0	22.7	18.1	15.1	7.8	14.2
Profit Margin (Before Income Tax) 49	4.6	4.4	3.5	8.4	2.9	3.4	6.6	5.5	4.2	6.0	2.4	4.5
Profit Margin (After Income Tax) 50	4.1	3.6	3.5	8.2	2.8	3.2	6.4	5.2	4.0	5.6	2.0	3.6

Table I
Corporations with and without Net Income

MEDICAL EQUIPMENT AND SUPPLIES

MONEY AMOUNTS AND SIZE OF ASSETS IN THOUSANDS OF DOLLARS

Item Description for Accounting Period 7/08 Through 6/09		Total	Zero Assets	Under 500	500 to 1,000	1,000 to 5,000	5,000 to 10,000	10,000 to 25,000	25,000 to 50,000	50,000 to 100,000	100,000 to 250,000	250,000 to 500,000	500,000 to 2,500,000	2,500,000 and over
Number of Enterprises	1	8332	876	5547	397	928	131	154	104	64	40	33	42	16
Revenues ($ in Thousands)														
Net Sales	2	147394273	338886	2048830	792757	5306190	1111444	2948155	4649667	4536466	5529989	7934936	31887684	80309268
Interest	3	3740063	763	1574	794	3083	5763	16710	16306	21993	41362	53423	291463	3286831
Rents	4	786415	0	0	1	0	494	183	585	1870	3918	910	20665	757790
Royalties	5	3538115	0	0	0	0	1742	48	19230	6606	37225	103203	161602	3208459
Other Portfolio Income	6	2083762	6766	6860	14	7666	412	3121	67529	61893	32125	141777	402032	1353567
Other Receipts	7	2912825	3940	1681	480	34777	21682	26640	37723	41889	84472	70955	474870	2113714
Total Receipts	8	160455453	350355	2058945	794046	5351716	1141537	2994857	4791040	4670717	5729091	8305204	33238316	91029629
Average Total Receipts	9	19258	400	371	2000	5767	8714	19447	46068	72980	143227	251673	791388	5689352
Operating Costs/Operating Income (%)														
Cost of Operations	10	55.9	47.8	36.7	49.2	61.1	54.7	55.4	59.2	52.4	50.2	44.8	50.6	59.8
Salaries and Wages	11	16.7	55.8	11.2	8.3	10.5	17.6	20.1	15.5	15.3	16.6	19.1	14.6	17.8
Taxes Paid	12	1.3	3.5	3.4	1.4	1.8	2.9	2.4	1.9	1.6	1.6	1.7	1.5	1.0
Interest Paid	13	5.1	1.1	0.4	2.9	0.9	2.2	1.3	1.9	1.6	2.0	2.6	3.4	7.2
Depreciation	14	3.3	3.2	1.8	1.1	1.8	3.1	2.3	2.8	2.7	3.6	3.4	3.1	3.6
Amortization and Depletion	15	1.3	1.1	0.1	0.1	0.2	0.8	0.5	0.9	1.1	1.3	2.0	1.8	1.2
Pensions and Other Deferred Comp.	16	0.8	0.0	0.4	0.2	0.5	0.3	0.4	0.5	0.4	0.6	0.5	0.7	1.1
Employee Benefits	17	3.0	1.9	2.3	3.5	1.1	2.0	2.1	2.0	2.0	2.7	1.8	2.7	3.5
Advertising	18	1.0	0.5	0.6	1.3	1.8	1.6	2.6	2.3	1.6	1.8	1.2	0.9	0.8
Other Expenses	19	13.7	34.3	21.2	29.8	16.1	29.9	23.9	18.7	18.1	17.6	19.1	16.2	10.2
Officers' Compensation	20	1.5	3.1	17.1	7.9	5.5	8.2	3.9	2.3	2.1	1.8	1.9	1.2	0.7
Operating Margin	21	•	•	4.7	•	•	•	•	•	1.1	0.3	2.0	3.2	•
Operating Margin Before Officers' Comp.	22	•	•	21.8	2.3	4.1	•	•	•	3.2	2.1	3.8	4.4	•

Selected Average Balance Sheet ($ in Thousands)

Net Receivables 23	3563	0	12	353	714	1404	2989	7337	12465	20405	47323	144048	1136325
Inventories 24	2337	0	11	111	587	1557	3522	5613	8999	19177	26234	92021	713605
Net Property, Plant and Equipment 25	2805	0	17	95	304	814	1922	5564	8729	25472	37578	132380	849946
Total Assets 26	31287	0	81	641	2142	6907	15321	35374	69700	155136	358424	1192721	11153854
Notes and Loans Payable 27	9636	0	32	662	656	1922	2972	11396	14137	43595	66293	353102	3604685
All Other Liabilities 28	9302	0	18	248	739	3273	3652	12095	16845	32596	102039	314162	3464298
Net Worth 29	12349	0	31	-269	746	1713	8697	11883	38719	78945	190092	525457	4084871

Selected Financial Ratios (Times to 1)

Current Ratio 30	1.6	•	1.8	1.6	1.8	1.3	2.4	1.9	2.4	1.7	2.4	1.6	1.5
Quick Ratio 31	0.9	•	1.2	1.3	1.1	0.9	1.6	1.2	1.5	1.0	1.4	1.0	0.8
Net Sales to Working Capital 32	5.0	•	18.0	9.7	8.1	7.6	2.8	4.4	3.3	4.9	2.5	5.2	5.5
Coverage Ratio 33	2.2	•	13.7	•	0.4	•	•	•	3.8	3.0	3.7	3.4	2.1
Total Asset Turnover 34	0.6	•	4.6	3.1	2.7	1.2	1.2	1.3	1.0	0.9	0.7	0.6	0.5
Inventory Turnover 35	4.2	•	11.8	8.8	5.9	3.0	3.0	4.7	4.1	3.6	4.1	4.2	4.2
Receivables Turnover 36	4.8	•	26.1	7.0	7.1	6.8	5.6	6.5	5.8	5.1	5.2	5.6	4.1
Total Liabilities to Net Worth 37	1.5	•	1.6	•	1.9	3.0	0.8	2.0	0.8	1.0	0.9	1.3	1.7
Current Assets to Working Capital 38	2.6	•	2.3	2.6	2.3	4.0	1.7	2.1	1.7	2.4	1.7	2.7	2.9
Current Liabilities to Working Capital 39	1.6	•	1.3	1.6	1.3	3.0	0.7	1.1	0.7	1.4	0.7	1.7	1.9
Working Capital to Net Sales 40	0.2	•	0.1	0.1	0.1	0.1	0.4	0.2	0.3	0.2	0.4	0.2	0.2
Inventory to Working Capital 41	0.7	•	0.5	0.5	0.7	1.3	0.4	0.6	0.4	0.6	0.3	0.7	0.8
Total Receipts to Cash Flow 42	6.2	•	4.8	5.0	9.3	18.5	13.6	9.3	5.1	5.2	4.4	4.7	7.1
Cost of Goods to Cash Flow 43	3.5	•	1.7	2.5	5.7	10.1	7.5	5.5	2.7	2.6	2.0	2.4	4.2
Cash Flow to Total Debt 44	0.2	•	1.6	0.4	0.4	0.1	0.2	0.2	0.4	0.3	0.3	0.2	0.1

Selected Financial Factors (in Percentages)

Debt Ratio 45	60.5	•	61.8	141.9	65.2	75.2	43.2	66.4	44.4	49.1	47.0	55.9	63.4
Return on Total Assets 46	6.3	•	25.6	•	0.8	•	•	•	6.2	5.5	6.5	7.5	6.8
Return on Equity Before Income Taxes 47	8.8	•	62.0	40.1	•	•	•	•	8.2	7.2	8.9	12.1	9.7
Return on Equity After Income Taxes 48	5.5	•	61.7	41.0	•	•	•	•	5.0	4.1	6.4	7.8	6.6
Profit Margin (Before Income Tax) 49	6.1	•	5.2	•	•	•	•	•	4.5	4.1	7.0	8.3	7.9
Profit Margin (After Income Tax) 50	3.8	•	5.2	•	•	•	•	•	2.7	2.3	5.1	5.4	5.4

Table II

Corporations with Net Income

MEDICAL EQUIPMENT AND SUPPLIES

MONEY AMOUNTS AND SIZE OF ASSETS IN THOUSANDS OF DOLLARS

Item Description for Accounting Period 7/08 Through 6/09	Total	Zero Assets	Under 500	500 to 1,000	1,000 to 5,000	5,000 to 10,000	10,000 to 25,000	25,000 to 50,000	50,000 to 100,000	100,000 to 250,000	250,000 to 500,000	500,000 to 2,500,000	2,500,000 and over
Number of Enterprises **1**	4800	378	3260	279	591	41	74	52	40	28	20	27	11
Revenues ($ in Thousands)													
Net Sales **2**	115842346	168194	1243230	713747	3610598	602558	2128722	3161353	3552542	4082889	5260013	23883410	67435089
Interest **3**	3441927	494	0	347	1060	610	3236	4334	9203	30912	32086	232969	3126675
Rents **4**	769717	0	0	1	0	11	22	461	1865	2634	892	6521	757308
Royalties **5**	3358895	0	0	0	0	615	0	13494	3083	26259	96840	138023	3080581
Other Portfolio Income **6**	1796257	0	0	3	229	67	1267	29419	48822	17550	139133	373692	1186077
Other Receipts **7**	2545750	3486	1018	32	14637	1715	14381	32393	27896	56873	43662	445015	1904645
Total Receipts **8**	127754892	172174	1244248	714130	3626524	605576	2147628	3241454	3643411	4217117	5572626	25079630	77490375
Average Total Receipts **9**	26616	455	382	2560	6136	14770	29022	62336	91085	150611	278631	928875	7044580
Operating Costs/Operating Income (%)													
Cost of Operations **10**	56.1	61.9	40.7	49.8	53.4	48.5	57.6	62.5	54.0	47.4	43.8	49.9	60.2
Salaries and Wages **11**	16.9	10.3	7.3	5.0	10.3	8.4	10.1	12.0	11.6	16.4	18.6	13.5	19.5
Taxes Paid **12**	1.3	1.2	3.1	1.2	1.9	2.3	1.6	1.5	1.4	1.7	1.8	1.5	1.1
Interest Paid **13**	4.7	0.0	0.3	2.9	0.7	1.1	0.5	1.1	1.4	1.8	2.2	2.2	6.8
Depreciation **14**	3.3	4.0	1.9	0.8	1.8	2.1	1.6	2.4	2.6	3.4	2.8	3.0	3.7
Amortization and Depletion **15**	1.0	1.6	•	0.0	0.1	0.6	0.2	0.3	0.8	1.0	2.0	1.2	1.0
Pensions and Other Deferred Comp. **16**	0.9	0.0	0.2	0.2	0.5	0.2	0.5	0.6	0.5	0.7	0.5	0.7	1.2
Employee Benefits **17**	2.7	1.2	1.9	3.5	1.1	0.4	1.3	1.5	1.7	2.6	1.5	2.6	3.0
Advertising **18**	0.9	0.7	0.6	0.8	2.3	1.3	2.4	1.3	1.4	1.5	1.3	1.0	0.7
Other Expenses **19**	11.1	16.2	17.7	24.7	16.7	14.9	12.4	10.7	14.3	15.5	15.7	15.1	8.2
Officers' Compensation **20**	1.2	1.6	12.9	6.3	4.5	5.5	2.2	1.8	1.8	1.7	1.9	1.3	0.6
Operating Margin **21**	•	1.3	13.5	5.0	6.7	14.9	9.7	4.3	8.5	6.5	7.8	7.9	•
Operating Margin Before Officers' Comp. **22**	1.0	2.9	26.4	11.3	11.2	20.3	11.9	6.1	10.3	8.1	9.8	9.2	•

Selected Average Balance Sheet ($ in Thousands)

Net Receivables 23	4107	0	8	459	745	2154	4093	10140	12990	20564	48725	174077	1039169
Inventories 24	3135	0	11	74	507	2040	4808	5916	10032	20041	27419	108932	863098
Net Property, Plant and Equipment 25	3609	0	14	99	346	942	2172	6329	9207	29104	32213	146588	975592
Total Assets 26	39544	0	65	619	2127	7852	14830	35616	70428	158049	352372	1230956	12488618
Notes and Loans Payable 27	10865	0	15	761	410	1716	2443	8904	12793	43211	64228	293864	3635927
All Other Liabilities 28	12327	0	13	212	544	1762	3204	11094	18840	28165	83340	305509	4218193
Net Worth 29	16353	0	37	-353	1173	4373	9182	15618	38795	86674	204804	631584	4634498

Selected Financial Ratios (Times to 1)

Current Ratio 30	1.7	•	2.2	2.4	2.3	2.7	2.6	1.9	2.3	2.4	3.0	1.9	1.5
Quick Ratio 31	0.9	•	1.8	2.1	1.5	1.7	1.6	1.2	1.3	1.4	1.9	1.2	0.6
Net Sales to Working Capital 32	5.1	•	17.1	8.2	7.0	4.4	4.0	5.8	4.3	3.7	2.6	4.0	6.3
Coverage Ratio 33	3.3	413.9	48.1	2.8	11.6	15.3	23.8	7.4	9.3	6.5	7.5	7.2	2.5
Total Asset Turnover 34	0.6	•	5.9	4.1	2.9	1.9	1.9	1.7	1.3	0.9	0.7	0.7	0.5
Inventory Turnover 35	4.3	•	13.9	17.2	6.4	3.5	3.4	6.4	4.8	3.4	4.2	4.1	4.3
Receivables Turnover 36	5.3	•	47.8	6.8	6.9	7.0	5.4	6.8	6.9	5.0	5.1	5.5	5.0
Total Liabilities to Net Worth 37	1.4	•	0.7	•	0.8	0.8	0.6	1.3	0.8	0.8	0.7	0.9	1.7
Current Assets to Working Capital 38	2.4	•	1.8	1.7	1.8	1.6	1.6	2.1	1.8	1.7	1.5	2.1	3.0
Current Liabilities to Working Capital 39	1.4	•	0.8	0.7	0.8	0.6	0.6	1.1	0.8	0.7	0.5	1.1	2.0
Working Capital to Net Sales 40	0.2	•	0.1	0.1	0.1	0.2	0.3	0.2	0.2	0.3	0.4	0.2	0.2
Inventory to Working Capital 41	0.7	•	0.3	0.2	0.5	0.5	0.6	0.6	0.5	0.4	0.3	0.5	0.9
Total Receipts to Cash Flow 42	5.4	5.6	3.8	3.8	5.2	3.6	4.8	6.6	4.4	4.4	3.8	3.9	6.9
Cost of Goods to Cash Flow 43	3.0	3.5	1.5	1.9	2.8	1.7	2.8	4.1	2.4	2.1	1.7	1.9	4.2
Cash Flow to Total Debt 44	0.2	•	3.6	0.7	1.2	1.2	1.1	0.5	0.6	0.5	0.5	0.4	0.1

Selected Financial Factors (in Percentages)

Debt Ratio 45	58.6	•	42.8	157.1	44.9	44.3	38.1	56.1	44.9	45.2	41.9	48.7	62.9
Return on Total Assets 46	9.6	•	81.5	32.7	22.6	30.8	21.3	13.4	16.3	10.6	12.3	11.5	8.3
Return on Equity Before Income Taxes 47	16.2	•	139.4	•	37.4	51.7	33.0	26.5	26.4	16.3	18.4	19.4	13.4
Return on Equity After Income Taxes 48	11.9	•	138.9	•	35.5	45.0	30.8	23.2	21.4	12.3	14.6	13.9	9.4
Profit Margin (Before Income Tax) 49	11.0	3.7	13.6	5.0	7.2	15.4	10.5	6.8	11.5	9.7	14.3	13.8	10.1
Profit Margin (After Income Tax) 50	8.1	3.6	13.5	4.9	6.8	13.4	9.8	6.0	9.4	7.3	11.4	9.9	7.1

Table I

Corporations with and without Net Income

OTHER MISCELLANEOUS MANUFACTURING

MONEY AMOUNTS AND SIZE OF ASSETS IN THOUSANDS OF DOLLARS

Item Description for Accounting Period 7/08 Through 6/09	Total	Zero Assets	Under 500	500 to 1,000	1,000 to 5,000	5,000 to 10,000	10,000 to 25,000	25,000 to 50,000	50,000 to 100,000	100,000 to 250,000	250,000 to 500,000	500,000 to 2,500,000	2,500,000 and over
Number of Enterprises 1	23532	1409	17673	1599	1799	424	328	122	74	57	21	20	4
Revenues ($ in Thousands)													
Net Sales 2	98074383	270395	6910005	2385835	11755090	5319931	8319882	6856086	6824906	10884791	7181778	20207684	11157998
Interest 3	654453	213	1019	2343	7569	4301	4466	6299	19104	23899	41790	61785	481664
Rents 4	43123	0	3604	2510	4309	3959	2383	1425	143	2512	5991	16200	85
Royalties 5	869993	343	116	0	0	4864	2118	7730	7305	33742	37214	666861	109699
Other Portfolio Income 6	1193526	1284	347	602	45733	24756	51425	22560	19919	39266	27624	291146	668867
Other Receipts 7	2112431	136312	61632	50899	79690	-36393	79239	34507	42946	174547	176820	266482	1045753
Total Receipts 8	102947909	408547	6976723	2442189	11892391	5321418	8459513	6928607	6914323	11158757	7471217	21510158	13464066
Average Total Receipts 9	4375	290	395	1527	6611	12551	25791	56792	93437	195768	355772	1075508	3366016
Operating Costs/Operating Income (%)													
Cost of Operations 10	65.0	69.9	43.9	55.4	64.1	68.7	70.1	68.6	66.0	69.1	60.3	73.9	55.3
Salaries and Wages 11	9.8	12.6	16.7	11.1	9.3	10.9	8.4	8.4	9.6	8.2	13.5	7.6	10.2
Taxes Paid 12	1.5	2.0	3.0	2.6	2.2	1.4	1.4	1.4	1.5	1.1	1.5	1.0	1.4
Interest Paid 13	2.5	2.1	1.1	2.0	0.9	1.3	1.3	1.4	1.7	2.6	3.1	2.6	7.0
Depreciation 14	2.6	2.9	1.3	1.3	2.2	3.2	2.5	2.3	2.8	2.8	3.4	2.5	3.7
Amortization and Depletion 15	0.7	0.4	0.3	0.3	0.1	0.3	0.4	0.5	0.6	1.1	0.9	1.4	0.6
Pensions and Other Deferred Comp. 16	0.5	0.2	0.3	0.1	0.6	0.3	0.4	0.4	0.7	0.4	0.7	0.5	0.7
Employee Benefits 17	1.5	1.4	1.4	1.8	1.5	1.9	1.6	1.5	1.7	1.5	2.1	1.5	1.1
Advertising 18	1.8	0.6	2.2	2.6	1.0	0.7	1.1	2.0	2.3	2.3	1.9	2.3	1.2
Other Expenses 19	13.6	6.8	22.1	17.7	13.2	10.8	10.3	10.2	11.9	9.7	13.9	10.1	25.0
Officers' Compensation 20	2.3	4.4	8.3	4.9	5.2	2.6	3.0	1.8	2.0	1.1	1.0	0.4	0.5
Operating Margin 21	•	•	•	0.2	•	•	•	1.7	•	0.1	•	•	•
Operating Margin Before Officers' Comp. 22	0.5	1.1	7.8	5.1	5.0	0.6	2.6	3.5	1.2	1.2	•	•	•

Selected Average Balance Sheet ($ in Thousands)

Item													
Net Receivables 23	517	0	20	170	677	1469	3813	8714	12411	27463	61081	115823	328811
Inventories 24	578	0	27	223	935	2540	4902	9412	15492	32031	51396	131947	289648
Net Property, Plant and Equipment 25	521	0	20	110	509	1752	2528	7552	12609	29859	66539	118343	483035
Total Assets 26	3341	0	104	708	2640	7084	15720	35866	70838	166923	362788	958786	4203362
Notes and Loans Payable 27	1357	0	86	399	1124	3118	4943	10491	21705	73880	150151	382097	1729468
All Other Liabilities 28	1100	0	54	192	840	1653	4118	12633	22697	48091	99042	368834	1409800
Net Worth 29	884	0	-36	117	676	2313	6659	12743	26437	44951	113595	207855	1064094

Selected Financial Ratios (Times to 1)

Item													
Current Ratio 30	1.4	•	1.0	1.7	1.9	1.7	1.8	1.6	1.6	2.1	1.1	0.9	
Quick Ratio 31	0.7	•	0.6	0.8	1.0	0.8	0.9	0.9	0.7	1.1	0.6	0.4	
Net Sales to Working Capital 32	9.9	•	125.9	7.3	7.4	6.5	5.5	6.9	6.3	7.0	4.1	36.5	•
Coverage Ratio 33	2.5	23.8	1.5	2.3	2.0	•	2.0	3.0	1.4	2.1	1.6	2.3	3.6
Total Asset Turnover 34	1.2	•	3.8	2.1	2.5	1.8	1.6	1.6	1.3	1.1	0.9	1.1	0.7
Inventory Turnover 35	4.7	•	6.5	3.7	4.5	3.4	3.6	4.1	3.9	4.0	5.7	5.3	
Receivables Turnover 36	7.4	•	19.2	7.9	8.5	8.1	6.1	6.0	6.5	5.3	6.1	17.0	
Total Liabilities to Net Worth 37	2.8	•	•	5.1	2.9	2.1	1.4	1.8	1.7	2.2	3.6	3.0	
Current Assets to Working Capital 38	3.5	•	21.9	2.4	2.2	2.5	2.3	2.8	2.6	1.9	10.6	•	
Current Liabilities to Working Capital 39	2.5	•	20.9	1.4	1.2	1.5	1.3	1.8	1.6	0.9	9.6	•	
Working Capital to Net Sales 40	0.1	•	0.0	0.1	0.1	0.2	0.2	0.1	0.2	0.2	0.0	•	
Inventory to Working Capital 41	1.3	•	7.6	1.2	0.9	1.1	1.0	1.0	1.0	0.7	3.3	•	
Total Receipts to Cash Flow 42	7.1	2.0	5.8	6.4	9.7	17.5	11.2	9.1	9.6	7.6	9.2	2.8	
Cost of Goods to Cash Flow 43	4.6	1.4	2.5	3.6	6.2	12.0	7.9	6.2	6.3	4.6	6.8	1.5	
Cash Flow to Total Debt 44	0.2	•	0.5	0.4	0.3	0.2	0.2	0.3	0.2	0.2	0.1	0.3	

Selected Financial Factors (in Percentages)

Item													
Debt Ratio 45	73.5	•	134.2	83.5	74.4	67.4	57.6	64.5	62.7	73.1	78.3	74.7	
Return on Total Assets 46	7.9	•	5.8	9.7	4.7	•	4.1	6.4	3.3	6.3	6.3	16.8	
Return on Equity Before Income Taxes 47	18.0	•	•	33.0	9.1	•	4.9	12.1	2.7	12.1	16.4	48.0	
Return on Equity After Income Taxes 48	12.1	•	•	31.3	7.6	•	3.7	9.3	•	9.3	8.2	34.4	
Profit Margin (Before Income Tax) 49	3.8	47.2	0.5	2.6	0.9	•	1.3	2.7	0.8	2.8	3.4	18.3	
Profit Margin (After Income Tax) 50	2.6	45.7	0.3	2.4	0.8	•	1.0	2.1	•	2.2	1.7	13.1	

Table II

Corporations with Net Income

OTHER MISCELLANEOUS MANUFACTURING

MONEY AMOUNTS AND SIZE OF ASSETS IN THOUSANDS OF DOLLARS

Item Description for Accounting Period 7/08 Through 6/09	Total	Zero Assets	Under 500	500 to 1,000	1,000 to 5,000	5,000 to 10,000	10,000 to 25,000	25,000 to 50,000	50,000 to 100,000	100,000 to 250,000	250,000 to 500,000	500,000 to 2,500,000	2,500,000 and over
Number of Enterprises **1**	12123	509	8647	1146	1218	230	189	•	44	36	15	13	•
Revenues ($ in Thousands)													
Net Sales **2**	72586185	149189	4807821	1913367	7541420	3707424	4970411	•	4560455	7256098	5021066	16897893	•
Interest **3**	595793	12	700	2009	3918	1627	2809	•	11819	11583	29846	46781	•
Rents **4**	33531	0	3596	0	4101	1459	1690	•	103	821	4713	15938	•
Royalties **5**	776952	0	75	0	0	3526	0	•	7301	24413	6678	624399	•
Other Portfolio Income **6**	1118262	0	0	251	38861	21665	13214	•	13812	27897	27612	287931	•
Other Receipts **7**	1857092	151315	56268	9488	65657	23621	62894	•	21747	67788	106771	226874	•
Total Receipts **8**	76967815	300516	4868460	1925115	7653957	3759322	5051018	•	4615237	7388600	5196686	18099816	•
Average Total Receipts **9**	6349	590	563	1680	6284	16345	26725	•	104892	205239	346446	1392294	•
Operating Costs/Operating Income (%)													
Cost of Operations **10**	63.0	69.7	37.9	50.7	62.8	68.9	67.8	•	64.1	65.1	57.1	73.6	•
Salaries and Wages **11**	9.8	12.4	19.1	11.0	8.8	9.0	8.3	•	8.4	8.9	15.0	7.5	•
Taxes Paid **12**	1.5	1.8	2.8	2.7	2.0	1.1	1.5	•	1.6	1.2	1.7	1.1	•
Interest Paid **13**	2.3	1.2	0.5	1.7	0.7	0.7	0.8	•	1.1	2.2	2.7	1.8	•
Depreciation **14**	2.4	3.3	0.7	1.3	1.6	1.5	2.2	•	2.4	2.6	3.7	2.5	•
Amortization and Depletion **15**	0.6	•	0.3	0.3	0.0	0.1	0.3	•	0.2	0.8	0.7	1.3	•
Pensions and Other Deferred Comp. **16**	0.6	0.3	0.4	0.1	0.6	0.3	0.4	•	0.8	0.5	1.0	0.5	•
Employee Benefits **17**	1.4	0.4	1.6	2.0	0.9	1.9	1.6	•	1.5	1.5	2.1	1.5	•
Advertising **18**	1.5	0.3	1.6	3.2	1.2	0.5	0.7	•	1.5	1.7	1.1	2.1	•
Other Expenses **19**	13.1	•	19.3	17.8	12.3	7.7	10.2	•	10.4	8.5	12.7	9.7	•
Officers' Compensation **20**	2.0	0.9	7.4	4.5	4.7	2.5	2.0	•	2.4	1.3	1.1	0.4	•
Operating Margin **21**	1.7	16.1	8.4	4.9	4.5	5.6	4.2	•	5.5	5.8	1.2	•	•
Operating Margin Before Officers' Comp. **22**	3.7	17.1	15.8	9.4	9.2	8.1	6.2	•	8.0	7.0	2.3	•	•

Selected Average Balance Sheet ($ in Thousands)

Net Receivables 23	716	0	25	187	746	1899	4040	•	12412	26917	62040	133373
Inventories 24	762	0	21	156	923	2672	5495	•	16519	36351	45356	156386
Net Property, Plant and Equipment 25	696	0	14	134	400	963	2251	•	12908	28543	74148	145629
Total Assets 26	4702	0	120	725	2516	6860	16365	•	67645	166227	357310	1047318
Notes and Loans Payable 27	1596	0	45	447	756	1545	3878	•	15940	61321	110592	327001
All Other Liabilities 28	1526	0	41	140	829	1600	4523	•	16953	36508	113093	425438
Net Worth 29	1580	0	34	138	931	3714	7963	•	34752	68398	133625	294880

Selected Financial Ratios (Times to 1)

Current Ratio 30	1.5	•	2.2	1.7	2.2	2.2	1.8	•	2.1	2.0	2.0	1.4
Quick Ratio 31	0.8	•	1.4	0.9	1.2	1.2	0.9	•	1.0	0.9	1.1	0.7
Net Sales to Working Capital 32	8.4	•	11.6	8.8	5.9	5.6	5.2	•	5.3	5.1	4.1	14.9
Coverage Ratio 33	4.8	97.1	18.9	4.3	9.3	11.1	8.2	•	7.1	4.6	2.8	4.3
Total Asset Turnover 34	1.3	•	4.6	2.3	2.5	2.3	1.6	•	1.5	1.2	0.9	1.2
Inventory Turnover 35	5.0	•	9.9	5.4	4.2	4.2	3.2	•	4.0	3.6	4.2	6.1
Receivables Turnover 36	7.7	•	21.8	7.8	7.0	7.8	5.1	•	7.1	6.5	5.5	7.1
Total Liabilities to Net Worth 37	2.0	•	2.5	4.2	1.7	0.8	1.1	•	0.9	1.4	1.7	2.6
Current Assets to Working Capital 38	2.8	•	1.8	2.4	1.9	1.8	2.2	•	1.9	2.0	2.0	3.8
Current Liabilities to Working Capital 39	1.8	•	0.8	1.4	0.9	0.8	1.2	•	0.9	1.0	1.0	2.8
Working Capital to Net Sales 40	0.1	•	0.1	0.1	0.2	0.2	0.2	•	0.2	0.2	0.2	0.1
Inventory to Working Capital 41	1.0	•	0.4	1.0	0.8	0.8	1.0	•	0.8	0.8	0.6	1.1
Total Receipts to Cash Flow 42	5.4	0.9	4.1	5.5	6.7	8.0	7.6	•	6.6	7.0	6.5	7.7
Cost of Goods to Cash Flow 43	3.4	0.6	1.5	2.8	4.2	5.5	5.2	•	4.2	4.6	3.7	5.7
Cash Flow to Total Debt 44	0.4	•	1.6	0.5	0.6	0.6	0.4	•	0.5	0.3	0.2	0.2

Selected Financial Factors (in Percentages)

Debt Ratio 45	66.4	•	71.2	80.9	63.0	45.9	51.3	•	48.6	58.9	62.6	71.8
Return on Total Assets 46	13.9	•	47.6	16.5	16.5	18.0	10.7	•	12.3	12.1	7.1	9.6
Return on Equity Before Income Taxes 47	32.8	•	156.5	66.0	39.7	30.3	19.3	•	20.5	22.9	12.2	26.3
Return on Equity After Income Taxes 48	26.5	•	152.8	64.0	38.1	27.8	17.6	•	16.7	20.0	10.2	17.4
Profit Margin (Before Income Tax) 49	8.7	117.6	9.7	5.5	6.0	7.0	5.9	•	6.9	7.8	4.9	6.0
Profit Margin (After Income Tax) 50	7.0	114.7	9.5	5.3	5.7	6.4	5.3	•	5.6	6.8	4.1	4.0

Table I

Corporations with and without Net Income

MOTOR VEHICLE AND MOTOR VEHICLE PARTS AND SUPPLIES

MONEY AMOUNTS AND SIZE OF ASSETS IN THOUSANDS OF DOLLARS

Item Description for Accounting Period 7/08 Through 6/09	Total	Zero Assets	Under 500	500 to 1,000	1,000 to 5,000	5,000 to 10,000	10,000 to 25,000	25,000 to 50,000	50,000 to 100,000	100,000 to 250,000	250,000 to 500,000	500,000 to 2,500,000	2,500,000 and over
Number of Enterprises 1	18890	3129	9798	2294	•	557	323	119	50	29	13	20	8
Revenues ($ in Thousands)													
Net Sales 2	262653311	1587674	9183249	6252987	•	8487050	13168512	9605633	7168968	8253110	11984462	47105660	123139900
Interest 3	2698268	99	1776	1680	•	12768	10436	6549	5532	11069	20860	221507	2389345
Rents 4	796229	0	0	663	•	1516	4082	7987	6366	5340	4698	51879	709778
Royalties 5	60048	0	0	0	•	32	219	34	0	1035	6975	14094	37659
Other Portfolio Income 6	695633	2665	2638	169	•	12587	21086	11388	8951	16426	32538	34671	526038
Other Receipts 7	3389878	18817	26544	3998	•	51632	92391	64578	39008	127549	30989	546110	2271004
Total Receipts 8	270293367	1609255	9214207	6259497	•	8565585	13296726	9696169	7228825	8414529	12080522	47973921	129073724
Average Total Receipts 9	14309	514	940	2729	•	15378	41166	81480	144576	290156	929271	2398696	16134216
Operating Costs/Operating Income (%)													
Cost of Operations 10	81.7	97.6	85.0	84.7	•	79.6	82.2	79.5	78.6	80.2	87.2	85.4	80.1
Salaries and Wages 11	4.2	2.3	4.1	4.4	•	6.4	6.5	7.0	7.2	6.1	2.7	3.8	3.3
Taxes Paid 12	0.7	0.7	1.0	1.1	•	1.1	1.0	1.0	1.1	1.2	0.4	0.7	0.4
Interest Paid 13	1.4	0.2	0.3	0.4	•	1.0	0.8	0.9	1.1	1.0	1.2	0.9	2.1
Depreciation 14	5.3	0.6	0.4	0.5	•	0.9	1.0	1.3	1.7	1.4	1.2	1.4	10.1
Amortization and Depletion 15	0.1	0.1	0.1	0.0	•	0.0	0.1	0.1	0.4	0.3	0.3	0.2	0.1
Pensions and Other Deferred Comp. 16	0.2	•	0.0	0.1	•	0.2	0.1	0.1	0.1	0.2	0.1	0.1	0.3
Employee Benefits 17	0.5	0.2	0.4	0.4	•	0.6	0.6	0.8	0.8	0.7	0.5	0.5	0.5
Advertising 18	2.9	2.7	0.1	0.3	•	0.6	0.4	0.6	0.5	1.1	1.5	2.0	4.8
Other Expenses 19	6.6	9.6	6.7	6.5	•	6.9	6.1	6.6	7.4	8.2	4.3	6.0	6.7
Officers' Compensation 20	0.6	1.3	2.4	2.0	•	2.0	1.2	1.6	0.8	0.8	0.5	0.2	0.1
Operating Margin 21	•	•	•	•	•	0.7	0.0	0.4	0.3	•	0.2	•	•
Operating Margin Before Officers' Comp. 22	•	•	1.9	1.7	•	2.7	1.2	2.1	1.1	•	0.6	•	•

Selected Average Balance Sheet ($ in Thousands)

Net Receivables 23	2581	0	27	141	•	1442	4062	8885	14659	23015	54196	232673	4589362
Inventories 24	1756	0	60	282	•	2905	7767	14368	25079	53340	124878	334702	1593511
Net Property, Plant and Equipment 25	2362	0	11	76	•	947	1693	3813	12377	22052	52498	166704	4634912
Total Assets 26	9383	0	139	699	•	6755	15616	34825	71480	162840	394790	1111568	15017677
Notes and Loans Payable 27	3478	0	79	203	•	2482	5992	11869	19975	50883	194128	380889	5684368
All Other Liabilities 28	3800	0	50	258	•	2085	5112	11811	23633	55446	126583	451124	6462561
Net Worth 29	2105	0	10	238	•	2189	4512	11145	27871	56511	74079	279554	2870748

Selected Financial Ratios (Times to 1)

Current Ratio 30	1.5	•	1.5	1.9	•	1.7	1.5	1.5	1.6	1.4	1.2	1.5	1.4
Quick Ratio 31	0.9	•	0.6	0.9	•	0.7	0.6	0.6	0.7	0.5	0.4	0.6	1.0
Net Sales to Working Capital 32	7.5	•	25.4	9.9	•	6.6	9.1	8.4	8.2	10.7	29.4	10.1	5.9
Coverage Ratio 33	0.1	•	0.6	0.5	•	2.7	2.2	2.5	2.0	1.7	2.0	1.6	•
Total Asset Turnover 34	1.5	•	6.7	3.9	•	2.3	2.6	2.3	2.0	1.7	2.3	2.1	1.0
Inventory Turnover 35	6.5	•	13.3	8.2	•	4.2	4.3	4.5	4.5	4.3	6.4	6.0	7.7
Receivables Turnover 36	5.3	•	38.6	14.6	•	10.3	9.0	9.3	9.1	10.7	12.3	10.1	3.4
Total Liabilities to Net Worth 37	3.5	•	12.9	1.9	•	2.1	2.5	2.1	1.6	1.9	4.3	3.0	4.2
Current Assets to Working Capital 38	3.1	•	2.9	2.1	•	2.4	2.8	2.9	2.8	3.7	6.2	3.2	3.2
Current Liabilities to Working Capital 39	2.1	•	1.9	1.1	•	1.4	1.8	1.9	1.8	2.7	5.2	2.2	2.2
Working Capital to Net Sales 40	0.1	•	0.0	0.1	•	0.2	0.1	0.1	0.1	0.1	0.0	0.1	0.2
Inventory to Working Capital 41	1.0	•	1.6	1.1	•	1.3	1.5	1.6	1.4	1.9	3.5	1.5	0.6
Total Receipts to Cash Flow 42	24.8	•	19.8	22.6	•	15.8	18.3	16.0	15.1	13.8	22.7	18.2	45.8
Cost of Goods to Cash Flow 43	20.3	•	16.8	19.1	•	12.6	15.0	12.7	11.9	11.0	19.8	15.6	36.7
Cash Flow to Total Debt 44	0.1	•	0.4	0.3	•	0.2	0.2	0.2	0.2	0.2	0.1	0.2	0.0

Selected Financial Factors (in Percentages)

Debt Ratio 45	77.6	•	92.8	66.0	•	67.6	71.1	68.0	61.0	65.3	81.2	74.9	80.9
Return on Total Assets 46	0.1	•	1.3	0.6	•	5.9	4.7	5.3	4.5	3.1	5.4	3.0	•
Return on Equity Before Income Taxes 47	•	•	•	•	•	11.4	8.8	9.9	5.8	3.6	14.3	4.7	•
Return on Equity After Income Taxes 48	•	•	•	•	•	8.9	6.9	8.4	4.4	1.4	12.1	1.1	•
Profit Margin (Before Income Tax) 49	•	•	•	•	•	1.6	1.0	1.4	1.1	0.7	1.2	0.6	•
Profit Margin (After Income Tax) 50	•	•	•	•	•	1.3	0.8	1.2	0.8	0.3	1.0	0.1	•

Table II

Corporations with Net Income

MOTOR VEHICLE AND MOTOR VEHICLE PARTS AND SUPPLIES

MONEY AMOUNTS AND SIZE OF ASSETS IN THOUSANDS OF DOLLARS

Item Description for Accounting Period 7/08 Through 6/09		Total	Zero Assets	Under 500	500 to 1,000	1,000 to 5,000	5,000 to 10,000	10,000 to 25,000	25,000 to 50,000	50,000 to 100,000	100,000 to 250,000	250,000 to 500,000	500,000 to 2,500,000	2,500,000 and over
Number of Enterprises	1	10739	814	5484	1822	387	•	222	78	35	18	7	15	0
Revenues ($ in Thousands)														
Net Sales	2	115442588	292599	6397170	5320019	6337779	•	10098886	6281893	4984642	4804941	10122896	48499921	0
Interest	3	259125	0	579	842	11728	•	5709	3447	3451	7312	14288	198584	0
Rents	4	80282	0	0	0	1516	•	3424	6772	5911	775	4427	55989	0
Royalties	5	39124	0	0	0	0	•	0	0	0	11	6975	32138	0
Other Portfolio Income	6	119594	2665	1645	24	11626	•	15942	6991	6306	10518	12208	32216	0
Other Receipts	7	1063975	5835	2044	1445	39277	•	85120	40837	29688	90892	6568	664233	0
Total Receipts	8	117004688	301099	6401438	5322330	6401926	•	10209081	6339940	5029998	4914449	10167362	49483081	•
Average Total Receipts	9	10895	370	1167	2921	16542	•	45987	81281	143714	273025	1452480	3298872	•
Operating Costs/Operating Income (%)														
Cost of Operations	10	82.3	58.0	84.4	86.3	79.4	•	82.5	78.3	79.3	78.0	88.0	82.6	•
Salaries and Wages	11	5.2	7.9	3.5	3.7	6.2	•	6.3	6.7	6.9	6.9	2.2	5.2	•
Taxes Paid	12	0.9	1.4	0.8	0.8	1.1	•	1.0	1.0	1.1	1.6	0.4	0.9	•
Interest Paid	13	0.6	0.2	0.3	0.3	0.6	•	0.7	0.6	0.8	1.0	0.4	0.8	•
Depreciation	14	0.9	0.8	0.4	0.5	0.8	•	0.6	1.0	1.6	0.9	0.7	1.1	•
Amortization and Depletion	15	0.1	0.0	0.1	0.0	0.0	•	0.1	0.1	0.2	0.2	0.1	0.1	•
Pensions and Other Deferred Comp.	16	0.2	•	0.1	0.1	0.2	•	0.2	0.2	0.1	0.3	0.1	0.2	•
Employee Benefits	17	0.5	0.8	0.2	0.3	0.6	•	0.7	0.6	0.8	0.5	0.3	0.6	•
Advertising	18	1.0	2.3	0.1	0.1	0.6	•	0.4	0.4	0.4	0.9	1.7	1.5	•
Other Expenses	19	5.7	10.2	6.1	5.7	6.2	•	5.0	6.5	5.4	6.9	3.5	5.5	•
Officers' Compensation	20	1.0	6.3	2.8	1.4	1.5	•	1.1	1.8	0.9	1.0	0.5	0.3	•
Operating Margin	21	1.6	12.1	1.2	0.8	2.7	•	1.4	2.8	2.5	1.7	2.1	1.1	•
Operating Margin Before Officers' Comp.	22	2.6	18.4	4.0	2.1	4.2	•	2.6	4.7	3.5	2.7	2.6	1.3	•

Selected Average Balance Sheet ($ in Thousands)

Net Receivables 23	926	0	25	158	1757	4657	9326	14347	22097	64681	303620	•
Inventories 24	2004	0	71	285	3238	9222	15915	26350	57331	193965	449764	•
Net Property, Plant and Equipment 25	440	0	12	75	498	1364	3213	12108	11065	48659	168180	•
Total Assets 26	4161	0	137	710	6864	15907	34726	69417	152621	361007	1469371	•
Notes and Loans Payable 27	1189	0	64	189	1676	6168	8827	18148	47682	109632	406411	•
All Other Liabilities 28	1519	0	28	278	2093	4862	11247	21897	39816	162403	619668	•
Net Worth 29	1454	0	45	243	3095	4877	14652	29372	65123	88972	443293	•

Selected Financial Ratios (Times to 1)

Current Ratio 30	1.8	•	2.4	1.9	2.0	1.6	1.7	1.6	1.7	1.2	1.8	•
Quick Ratio 31	0.7	•	1.0	0.9	0.9	0.7	0.7	0.8	0.6	0.4	0.7	•
Net Sales to Working Capital 32	8.2	•	16.5	10.6	5.5	8.5	6.6	8.2	7.2	28.6	7.5	•
Coverage Ratio 33	5.7	65.4	5.8	3.4	6.9	4.6	6.9	5.4	5.1	7.4	5.0	•
Total Asset Turnover 34	2.6	•	8.5	4.1	2.4	2.9	2.3	2.1	1.7	4.0	2.2	•
Inventory Turnover 35	4.4	•	13.9	8.8	4.0	4.1	4.0	4.3	3.6	6.6	5.9	•
Receivables Turnover 36	5.4	•	•	13.9	9.2	8.6	8.2	8.3	9.2	13.2	11.7	•
Total Liabilities to Net Worth 37	1.9	•	2.0	1.9	1.2	2.3	1.4	1.4	1.3	3.1	2.3	•
Current Assets to Working Capital 38	2.3	•	1.7	2.1	2.0	2.6	2.3	2.7	2.5	5.3	2.3	•
Current Liabilities to Working Capital 39	1.3	•	0.7	1.1	1.0	1.6	1.3	1.7	1.5	4.3	1.3	•
Working Capital to Net Sales 40	0.1	•	0.1	0.1	0.2	0.1	0.2	0.1	0.1	0.0	0.1	•
Inventory to Working Capital 41	1.2	•	1.0	1.1	1.1	1.4	1.3	1.3	1.3	3.3	1.2	•
Total Receipts to Cash Flow 42	13.7	4.8	16.4	20.6	12.8	16.3	11.6	13.6	10.8	18.3	13.5	•
Cost of Goods to Cash Flow 43	11.3	2.8	13.8	17.8	10.1	13.5	9.1	10.8	8.4	16.1	11.1	•
Cash Flow to Total Debt 44	0.3	•	0.8	0.3	0.3	0.3	0.3	0.3	0.3	0.3	0.2	•

Selected Financial Factors (in Percentages)

Debt Ratio 45	65.1	•	67.0	65.8	54.9	69.3	57.8	57.7	57.3	75.4	69.8	•
Return on Total Assets 46	9.4	•	12.7	4.8	10.3	9.2	10.2	8.6	8.6	11.8	8.5	•
Return on Equity Before Income Taxes 47	22.1	•	31.9	9.8	19.6	23.6	20.7	16.6	16.2	41.2	22.6	•
Return on Equity After Income Taxes 48	18.1	•	31.3	9.4	17.1	21.1	18.9	14.6	13.1	37.7	15.8	•
Profit Margin (Before Income Tax) 49	3.0	15.0	1.2	0.8	3.7	2.5	3.8	3.4	3.9	2.5	3.1	•
Profit Margin (After Income Tax) 50	2.4	15.0	1.2	0.8	3.2	2.3	3.4	3.0	3.2	2.3	2.2	•

Table I

Corporations with and without Net Income

LUMBER AND OTHER CONSTRUCTION MATERIALS

MONEY AMOUNTS AND SIZE OF ASSETS IN THOUSANDS OF DOLLARS

Item Description for Accounting Period 7/08 Through 6/09	Total	Zero Assets	Under 500	500 to 1,000	1,000 to 5,000	5,000 to 10,000	10,000 to 25,000	25,000 to 50,000	50,000 to 100,000	100,000 to 250,000	250,000 to 500,000	500,000 to 2,500,000	2,500,000 and over
Number of Enterprises 1	16731	1055	8923	1070	3886	1152	471	97	44	23	4	6	0
Revenues ($ in Thousands)													
Net Sales 2	115394579	214138	5970271	2482051	29295364	21884745	20487611	8913739	8096278	6124083	1928947	9997351	0
Interest 3	163490	36	12234	8821	22494	8725	13391	7732	4073	8420	15503	62061	0
Rents 4	35152	0	307	7935	7263	3431	4048	4982	3164	731	1728	1563	0
Royalties 5	13359	0	0	0	0	48	0	81	858	0	0	12371	0
Other Portfolio Income 6	243226	7323	1094	796	16703	14042	19810	18052	1579	106452	4564	52811	0
Other Receipts 7	658232	18623	26825	3793	158141	138434	115079	38490	50271	33783	25185	49609	0
Total Receipts 8	116508038	240120	6010731	2503396	29499965	22049425	20639939	8983076	8156223	6273469	1975927	10175766	0
Average Total Receipts 9	6964	228	674	2340	7591	19140	43822	92609	185369	272760	493982	1695961	•
Operating Costs/Operating Income (%)													
Cost of Operations 10	79.3	81.6	68.0	73.0	76.4	82.6	80.5	82.6	82.7	77.6	71.8	82.7	•
Salaries and Wages 11	7.0	13.4	6.3	5.5	7.5	5.9	7.3	6.0	6.6	8.6	10.7	7.4	•
Taxes Paid 12	1.2	2.7	1.4	2.2	1.5	1.0	1.0	0.8	0.9	1.2	1.7	1.0	•
Interest Paid 13	0.8	1.5	0.6	0.4	0.6	0.9	0.6	0.9	0.6	1.2	2.6	1.8	•
Depreciation 14	1.2	0.9	1.0	0.9	1.0	0.7	1.2	1.0	0.9	2.0	1.5	2.4	•
Amortization and Depletion 15	0.1	0.7	0.1	0.0	0.0	0.0	0.0	0.1	0.1	0.3	0.6	0.4	•
Pensions and Other Deferred Comp. 16	0.3	0.0	0.8	0.5	0.2	0.3	0.2	0.1	0.1	0.3	0.3	0.6	•
Employee Benefits 17	0.7	1.7	0.4	0.4	0.6	0.6	0.8	0.5	0.7	0.9	0.5	1.0	•
Advertising 18	0.4	0.5	1.3	0.8	0.3	0.3	0.4	0.2	0.2	0.4	0.4	0.1	•
Other Expenses 19	7.6	17.6	15.0	12.2	8.3	6.5	6.2	6.1	6.6	9.3	9.4	5.6	•
Officers' Compensation 20	1.7	2.0	4.2	4.7	2.4	1.4	1.3	0.8	0.9	0.6	2.2	0.7	•
Operating Margin 21	•	•	0.9	•	1.2	•	0.4	0.9	•	•	•	•	•
Operating Margin Before Officers' Comp. 22	1.6	•	5.0	4.1	3.6	1.2	1.7	1.7	0.6	0.5	0.7	•	•

Selected Average Balance Sheet ($ in Thousands)

													•
Net Receivables 23	721	0	26	250	767	1930	4317	8304	21020	35673	57916	255515	•
Inventories 24	744	0	23	283	720	2394	4823	13125	20845	43301	46074	122530	•
Net Property, Plant and Equipment 25	484	0	12	53	358	1059	2615	5979	10081	27537	81446	351482	•
Total Assets 26	2627	0	125	708	2364	6831	15438	36809	66508	136354	356585	1113929	•
Notes and Loans Payable 27	879	0	61	134	723	2467	4517	16560	19442	49927	122572	356394	•
All Other Liabilities 28	744	0	49	206	676	1943	3731	7473	16283	43279	92169	393709	•
Net Worth 29	1003	0	15	368	965	2421	7190	12775	30783	43148	141844	363826	•

Selected Financial Ratios (Times to 1)

													•
Current Ratio 30	1.8	•	1.9	2.4	2.0	1.7	1.9	1.7	1.9	1.5	1.6	1.9	•
Quick Ratio 31	0.9	•	1.2	1.6	1.1	0.7	1.0	0.6	1.0	0.7	0.9	1.2	•
Net Sales to Working Capital 32	8.6	•	15.8	6.9	8.0	9.0	8.2	8.5	8.5	9.7	11.3	7.4	•
Coverage Ratio 33	2.1	•	3.7	1.8	4.1	1.6	2.8	2.8	1.7	1.0	1.3	0.5	•
Total Asset Turnover 34	2.6	•	5.3	3.3	3.2	2.8	2.8	2.5	2.8	2.0	1.4	1.5	•
Inventory Turnover 35	7.4	•	19.8	6.0	8.0	6.6	7.3	5.8	7.3	4.8	7.5	11.3	•
Receivables Turnover 36	9.1	•	24.4	9.0	8.9	10.2	9.8	8.9	8.9	6.4	5.8	6.9	•
Total Liabilities to Net Worth 37	1.6	•	7.4	0.9	1.4	1.8	1.1	1.9	1.2	2.2	1.5	2.1	•
Current Assets to Working Capital 38	2.2	•	2.2	1.7	2.0	2.5	2.1	2.4	2.1	3.0	2.6	2.1	•
Current Liabilities to Working Capital 39	1.2	•	1.2	0.7	1.0	1.5	1.1	1.4	1.1	2.0	1.6	1.1	•
Working Capital to Net Sales 40	0.1	•	0.1	0.1	0.1	0.1	0.1	0.1	0.1	0.1	0.1	0.1	•
Inventory to Working Capital 41	0.9	•	0.7	0.5	0.8	1.2	0.9	1.2	0.9	1.4	0.9	0.6	•
Total Receipts to Cash Flow 42	15.8	•	8.3	11.6	12.3	19.1	18.3	16.8	20.1	14.0	14.7	42.4	•
Cost of Goods to Cash Flow 43	12.5	•	5.6	8.4	9.4	15.8	14.8	13.9	16.6	10.8	10.6	35.1	•
Cash Flow to Total Debt 44	0.3	•	0.7	0.6	0.4	0.2	0.3	0.2	0.3	0.2	0.2	0.1	•

Selected Financial Factors (in Percentages)

													•
Debt Ratio 45	61.8	•	88.1	48.1	59.2	64.6	53.4	65.3	53.7	68.4	60.2	67.3	•
Return on Total Assets 46	4.7	•	11.2	2.4	8.2	3.9	4.8	6.3	2.8	2.4	4.5	1.2	•
Return on Equity Before Income Taxes 47	6.5	•	69.2	2.1	15.2	4.1	6.7	11.8	2.5	0.4	2.6	•	•
Return on Equity After Income Taxes 48	5.4	•	66.0	1.0	14.4	3.3	5.7	10.4	2.1	•	0.6	•	•
Profit Margin (Before Income Tax) 49	0.9	•	1.5	0.3	1.9	0.5	1.1	1.6	0.4	0.1	0.8	•	•
Profit Margin (After Income Tax) 50	0.8	•	1.5	0.2	1.8	0.4	0.9	1.4	0.3	•	0.2	•	•

169

Table II

Corporations with Net Income

LUMBER AND OTHER CONSTRUCTION MATERIALS

MONEY AMOUNTS AND SIZE OF ASSETS IN THOUSANDS OF DOLLARS

Item Description for Accounting Period 7/08 Through 6/09		Total	Zero Assets	Under 500	500 to 1,000	1,000 to 5,000	5,000 to 10,000	10,000 to 25,000	25,000 to 50,000	50,000 to 100,000	100,000 to 250,000	250,000 to 500,000	500,000 to 2,500,000	2,500,000 and over
Number of Enterprises	1	10255	659	5157	543	2725	745	319	•	21	13	•	0	0
Revenues ($ in Thousands)														
Net Sales	2	78089012	32771	3776809	1328634	22258396	15716943	15492333	•	3365644	3018409	•	0	0
Interest	3	73384	1	11064	4004	15867	6064	8286	•	1339	2621	•	0	0
Rents	4	19365	0	149	6213	6908	2982	1133	•	0	0	•	0	0
Royalties	5	13311	0	0	0	0	0	0	•	858	0	•	0	0
Other Portfolio Income	6	193843	7318	24	337	7768	5780	11777	•	531	105019	•	0	0
Other Receipts	7	393246	16934	6710	2334	124252	56590	64773	•	13504	17072	•	0	0
Total Receipts	8	78782161	57024	3794756	1341522	22413191	15788359	15578302	•	3381876	3143121	•	0	0
Average Total Receipts	9	7682	87	736	2471	8225	21192	48835	•	161042	241779	•	•	•
Operating Costs/Operating Income (%)														
Cost of Operations	10	78.2	37.9	59.5	67.7	76.9	82.8	81.1	•	78.2	75.6	•	•	•
Salaries and Wages	11	6.6	0.9	4.4	5.3	7.4	5.3	6.5	•	7.3	7.3	•	•	•
Taxes Paid	12	1.1	2.9	1.1	3.0	1.3	0.9	0.9	•	1.1	1.0	•	•	•
Interest Paid	13	0.6	0.5	0.1	0.2	0.4	0.6	0.4	•	0.7	1.0	•	•	•
Depreciation	14	0.9	2.0	1.1	0.7	0.6	0.5	0.9	•	1.1	2.2	•	•	•
Amortization and Depletion	15	0.1	2.1	0.0	0.0	0.0	0.0	0.0	•	0.1	0.3	•	•	•
Pensions and Other Deferred Comp.	16	0.3	•	1.2	0.8	0.2	0.3	0.2	•	0.2	0.3	•	•	•
Employee Benefits	17	0.6	0.7	0.4	0.2	0.5	0.5	0.7	•	0.7	0.9	•	•	•
Advertising	18	0.3	•	1.0	1.1	0.2	0.2	0.4	•	0.2	0.6	•	•	•
Other Expenses	19	6.7	26.0	16.8	12.6	6.5	4.7	5.2	•	6.3	10.1	•	•	•
Officers' Compensation	20	1.8	0.7	4.0	5.9	2.5	1.3	1.2	•	1.3	0.6	•	•	•
Operating Margin	21	2.7	26.2	10.3	2.6	3.4	3.0	2.4	•	2.7	0.0	•	•	•
Operating Margin Before Officers' Comp.	22	4.5	26.9	14.3	8.5	5.8	4.3	3.6	•	4.0	0.7	•	•	•

Selected Average Balance Sheet ($ in Thousands)

Net Receivables 23	812	0	8	296	811	2130	4419	21990	40901
Inventories 24	860	0	14	288	797	2689	5285	29337	48975
Net Property, Plant and Equipment 25	410	0	15	28	261	742	2265	7751	29763
Total Assets 26	2650	0	90	726	2368	6915	15332	66060	140429
Notes and Loans Payable 27	700	0	22	66	532	2207	3779	19928	46768
All Other Liabilities 28	669	0	12	227	669	1416	3422	16336	44401
Net Worth 29	1281	0	56	434	1167	3292	8132	29797	49260

Selected Financial Ratios (Times to 1)

Current Ratio 30	2.1	•	6.5	2.4	2.3	2.0	2.3	1.9	1.6
Quick Ratio 31	1.1	•	5.2	1.7	1.3	0.9	1.2	0.9	0.9
Net Sales to Working Capital 32	7.2	•	12.2	6.8	7.2	7.1	7.3	6.6	7.5
Coverage Ratio 33	7.4	190.8	86.7	17.1	10.3	6.3	8.4	5.5	5.1
Total Asset Turnover 34	2.9	•	8.2	3.4	3.4	3.1	3.2	2.4	1.7
Inventory Turnover 35	6.9	•	31.8	5.8	7.9	6.5	7.5	4.3	3.6
Receivables Turnover 36	8.4	•	52.3	7.7	8.6	9.7	10.0	5.8	4.1
Total Liabilities to Net Worth 37	1.1	•	0.6	0.7	1.0	1.1	0.9	1.2	1.9
Current Assets to Working Capital 38	1.9	•	1.2	1.7	1.8	2.0	1.8	2.2	2.7
Current Liabilities to Working Capital 39	0.9	•	0.2	0.7	0.8	1.0	0.8	1.2	1.7
Working Capital to Net Sales 40	0.1	•	0.1	0.1	0.1	0.1	0.1	0.2	0.1
Inventory to Working Capital 41	0.8	•	0.2	0.4	0.7	0.9	0.7	1.0	1.0
Total Receipts to Cash Flow 42	11.9	1.0	4.5	7.6	11.4	14.6	15.4	13.8	8.3
Cost of Goods to Cash Flow 43	9.3	0.4	2.7	5.1	8.8	12.1	12.5	10.8	6.2
Cash Flow to Total Debt 44	0.5	•	4.8	1.1	0.6	0.4	0.4	0.3	0.3

Selected Financial Factors (in Percentages)

Debt Ratio 45	51.6	•	37.7	40.3	50.7	52.4	47.0	54.9	64.9
Return on Total Assets 46	12.3	•	88.8	12.8	15.5	12.3	10.5	9.3	8.6
Return on Equity Before Income Taxes 47	22.1	•	140.9	20.2	28.3	21.8	17.4	16.9	19.7
Return on Equity After Income Taxes 48	20.7	•	139.4	18.3	27.4	20.8	16.1	16.0	17.3
Profit Margin (Before Income Tax) 49	3.7	100.2	10.8	3.6	4.1	3.4	2.9	3.1	4.2
Profit Margin (After Income Tax) 50	3.5	91.6	10.6	3.2	3.9	3.2	2.7	3.0	3.7

Table I

Corporations with and without Net Income

PROFESSIONAL AND COMMERCIAL EQUIPMENT AND SUPPLIES

MONEY AMOUNTS AND SIZE OF ASSETS IN THOUSANDS OF DOLLARS

Item Description for Accounting Period 7/08 Through 6/09		Total	Zero Assets	Under 500	500 to 1,000	1,000 to 5,000	5,000 to 10,000	10,000 to 25,000	25,000 to 50,000	50,000 to 100,000	100,000 to 250,000	250,000 to 500,000	500,000 to 2,500,000	2,500,000 and over
Number of Enterprises	1	33920	5627	19831	2798	4375	597	372	138	67	59	19	24	13
Revenues ($ in Thousands)														
Net Sales	2	232448347	10623141	11004522	5447164	24525746	19475201	14994362	13832327	8942908	20415309	11787900	39545006	51854761
Interest	3	796081	14747	3106	3729	12288	30523	10805	14062	12583	35018	24494	196419	438307
Rents	4	323740	2995	36	0	7292	2834	1628	679	15821	2019	70243	92625	127567
Royalties	5	250611	16	0	283	335	0	14320	17561	3193	32879	28710	12816	140498
Other Portfolio Income	6	378995	22560	1285	6796	10882	18342	17709	12068	31194	56835	15642	8960	176722
Other Receipts	7	2544738	57125	59403	27205	170867	78746	106933	88735	59868	153278	337088	253415	1152078
Total Receipts	8	236742512	10720584	11068352	5485177	24727410	19605646	15145757	13965432	9065567	20695338	12264077	40109241	53889933
Average Total Receipts	9	6979	1905	558	1960	5652	32840	40714	101199	135307	350768	645478	1671218	4145379
Operating Costs/Operating Income (%)														
Cost of Operations	10	76.8	92.0	63.0	62.0	65.5	82.5	75.4	78.6	75.5	80.4	72.8	80.4	78.2
Salaries and Wages	11	8.5	3.6	8.1	8.8	12.1	7.1	9.2	8.6	9.1	7.3	10.5	8.0	8.5
Taxes Paid	12	1.0	0.4	1.5	1.7	1.6	0.7	1.3	0.9	1.0	0.7	1.3	0.8	1.1
Interest Paid	13	0.9	0.2	0.6	0.7	0.7	0.3	0.5	0.5	1.1	0.7	0.8	1.0	1.4
Depreciation	14	1.5	0.2	0.6	0.7	1.1	0.4	0.9	1.0	2.1	1.0	1.5	1.3	3.1
Amortization and Depletion	15	0.3	0.0	0.0	0.0	0.1	0.0	0.1	0.2	0.6	0.3	0.7	0.5	0.4
Pensions and Other Deferred Comp.	16	0.2	0.1	0.4	0.2	0.3	0.1	0.3	0.2	0.2	0.3	0.3	0.2	0.2
Employee Benefits	17	0.9	0.2	0.7	0.7	1.1	0.7	0.8	0.7	0.8	0.7	0.9	1.0	1.1
Advertising	18	0.8	0.2	0.6	1.2	0.8	0.3	0.9	0.5	0.8	0.6	2.2	1.1	0.7
Other Expenses	19	7.8	3.7	13.4	17.1	11.7	5.5	8.5	7.1	8.9	6.6	9.1	5.0	7.4
Officers' Compensation	20	1.4	1.2	7.0	4.0	3.9	1.4	1.5	1.0	0.8	0.6	0.4	0.3	0.2
Operating Margin	21	0.0	•	4.0	2.8	1.2	0.9	0.6	0.7	•	0.9	•	0.4	•
Operating Margin Before Officers' Comp.	22	1.4	•	11.0	6.8	5.1	2.3	2.1	1.7	0.1	1.5	0.7	•	•

Selected Average Balance Sheet ($ in Thousands)

Item													
Net Receivables 23	840	0	23	192	592	2535	5232	13748	21287	49602	78926	224157	640927
Inventories 24	534	0	27	207	482	1761	4230	7465	14950	32066	46690	138123	318968
Net Property, Plant and Equipment 25	266	0	12	54	293	558	1602	2854	7490	11421	20506	76935	200226
Total Assets 26	3686	0	102	692	1985	6706	15080	35236	69519	152821	338944	1063364	4021137
Notes and Loans Payable 27	960	0	57	265	776	1981	4089	7814	17568	33232	85277	257220	965958
All Other Liabilities 28	1294	0	29	260	803	2955	6958	16500	27582	65894	126401	447888	1041275
Net Worth 29	1433	0	15	166	406	1771	4033	10922	24368	53695	127266	358255	2013904

Selected Financial Ratios (Times to 1)

Item													
Current Ratio 30	1.4	•	2.4	1.9	1.6	1.5	1.5	1.5	1.5	1.4	1.3	1.5	1.1
Quick Ratio 31	0.8	•	1.4	1.0	0.9	1.0	0.9	1.0	0.9	0.9	0.7	0.8	0.7
Net Sales to Working Capital 32	13.5	•	12.2	6.9	10.1	17.3	10.5	10.7	9.8	10.8	14.5	9.3	37.2
Coverage Ratio 33	3.3	•	8.6	6.2	3.7	6.4	4.4	4.3	2.0	4.2	5.4	3.2	2.2
Total Asset Turnover 34	1.9	•	5.5	2.8	2.8	4.9	2.7	2.8	1.9	2.3	1.8	1.5	1.0
Inventory Turnover 35	9.9	•	13.1	5.8	7.6	15.3	7.2	10.6	6.7	8.7	9.7	9.6	9.8
Receivables Turnover 36	8.2	•	20.9	9.4	9.0	12.3	7.1	7.4	6.5	6.8	7.9	7.6	6.6
Total Liabilities to Net Worth 37	1.6	•	5.8	3.2	3.9	2.8	2.7	2.2	1.9	1.8	1.7	2.0	1.0
Current Assets to Working Capital 38	3.6	•	1.7	2.1	2.7	2.9	3.1	2.9	3.2	3.3	4.5	3.0	11.6
Current Liabilities to Working Capital 39	2.6	•	0.7	1.1	1.7	1.9	2.1	1.9	2.2	2.3	3.5	2.0	10.6
Working Capital to Net Sales 40	0.1	•	0.1	0.1	0.1	0.1	0.1	0.1	0.1	0.1	0.1	0.1	0.0
Inventory to Working Capital 41	1.1	•	0.5	0.7	0.9	0.9	1.1	0.8	1.1	1.0	1.3	0.8	3.1
Total Receipts to Cash Flow 42	12.3	53.8	6.7	5.7	9.0	16.7	11.6	13.1	12.2	13.0	9.0	17.3	13.2
Cost of Goods to Cash Flow 43	9.5	49.5	4.2	3.6	5.9	13.7	8.8	10.3	9.2	10.4	6.6	13.9	10.3
Cash Flow to Total Debt 44	0.2	•	1.0	0.6	0.4	0.4	0.3	0.3	0.2	0.3	0.3	0.1	0.2

Selected Financial Factors (in Percentages)

Item													
Debt Ratio 45	61.1	•	85.3	76.0	79.6	73.6	73.3	69.0	64.9	64.9	62.5	66.3	49.9
Return on Total Assets 46	5.3	•	28.5	11.8	7.7	9.1	5.7	6.1	4.0	7.0	7.9	4.9	3.2
Return on Equity Before Income Taxes 47	9.5	•	171.9	41.2	27.5	29.0	16.4	15.1	5.8	15.2	17.2	9.9	3.5
Return on Equity After Income Taxes 48	6.8	•	168.0	39.6	25.7	26.0	12.9	12.2	2.2	11.3	12.2	6.3	1.6
Profit Margin (Before Income Tax) 49	2.0	•	4.6	3.5	2.0	1.6	1.6	1.6	1.1	2.4	3.5	2.2	1.8
Profit Margin (After Income Tax) 50	1.4	•	4.5	3.4	1.9	1.4	1.3	1.3	0.4	1.8	2.5	1.4	0.8

Table II
Corporations with Net Income

PROFESSIONAL AND COMMERCIAL EQUIPMENT AND SUPPLIES

MONEY AMOUNTS AND SIZE OF ASSETS IN THOUSANDS OF DOLLARS

Item Description for Accounting Period 7/08 Through 6/09	Total	Zero Assets	Under 500	500 to 1,000	1,000 to 5,000	5,000 to 10,000	10,000 to 25,000	25,000 to 50,000	50,000 to 100,000	100,000 to 250,000	250,000 to 500,000	500,000 to 2,500,000	2,500,000 and over
Number of Enterprises **1**	22904	3348	13611	2096	2911	452	261	94	44	47	15	17	9
Revenues ($ in Thousands)													
Net Sales **2**	178966033	9542465	8783046	4180750	19977553	17213422	11069287	11552802	6697593	16380869	10375035	32497978	30695233
Interest **3**	453024	13835	2908	2971	6005	6231	7063	7060	7637	25415	23411	93548	256942
Rents **4**	150347	0	0	0	6458	0	346	512	15650	2012	37918	50104	37346
Royalties **5**	203539	0	0	0	324	0	14320	0	3193	19578	28710	7346	130069
Other Portfolio Income **6**	296941	22472	1285	940	5997	18242	17176	10463	20848	56806	4665	7399	130650
Other Receipts **7**	2182719	9482	55271	20128	145221	60594	45350	53793	69965	137860	336083	144599	1104371
Total Receipts **8**	182252603	9588254	8842510	4204789	20141558	17298489	11153542	11624630	6814886	16622540	10805822	32800974	32354611
Average Total Receipts **9**	7957	2864	650	2006	6919	38271	42734	123666	154884	353671	720388	1929469	3594957
Operating Costs/Operating Income (%)													
Cost of Operations **10**	77.8	93.9	62.8	59.1	66.4	83.2	73.5	79.7	78.2	78.8	74.2	81.0	81.8
Salaries and Wages **11**	7.8	1.3	7.0	7.5	11.1	6.4	9.3	7.6	7.6	7.6	9.1	7.8	8.1
Taxes Paid **12**	1.0	0.2	1.4	1.7	1.4	0.6	1.4	0.8	1.0	0.8	1.1	0.7	1.1
Interest Paid **13**	0.6	0.1	0.3	0.4	0.6	0.1	0.5	0.3	0.8	0.5	0.8	0.7	1.3
Depreciation **14**	1.0	0.2	0.5	0.6	0.7	0.3	0.9	0.5	1.4	1.0	1.4	1.3	1.4
Amortization and Depletion **15**	0.2	0.0	0.0	0.0	0.1	0.0	0.1	0.1	0.4	0.2	0.7	0.4	0.3
Pensions and Other Deferred Comp. **16**	0.2	0.0	0.4	0.2	0.4	0.1	0.3	0.2	0.2	0.3	0.3	0.2	0.1
Employee Benefits **17**	0.8	0.1	0.4	0.6	1.0	0.5	0.7	0.6	0.7	0.8	1.0	0.9	0.9
Advertising **18**	0.6	0.1	0.7	1.5	0.6	0.3	0.7	0.4	0.6	0.6	2.1	0.6	0.3
Other Expenses **19**	6.4	1.9	12.0	18.5	10.0	5.1	7.5	5.8	6.2	6.6	8.8	4.1	4.7
Officers' Compensation **20**	1.4	0.5	7.1	3.4	3.6	1.4	1.8	1.0	0.8	0.6	0.3	0.3	0.3
Operating Margin **21**	2.2	1.6	7.3	6.4	4.1	1.8	3.4	3.1	2.2	2.2	0.2	1.9	•
Operating Margin Before Officers' Comp. **22**	3.6	2.2	14.4	9.8	7.7	3.3	5.2	4.1	2.9	2.8	0.5	2.2	•

Selected Average Balance Sheet ($ in Thousands)

Net Receivables 23	884	0	20	174	695	2579	5387	15785	20335	49537	88138	250002	527169
Inventories 24	600	0	23	224	454	1889	4555	9179	17198	34144	45494	160683	248657
Net Property, Plant and Equipment 25	257	0	13	50	322	462	1404	2550	6838	12673	20292	78667	146633
Total Assets 26	3739	0	106	703	2129	6535	14855	34852	68530	148732	340212	1103166	3617528
Notes and Loans Payable 27	683	0	41	168	597	969	3503	5670	15962	32618	77286	174051	527509
All Other Liabilities 28	1366	0	32	183	740	3033	6116	16732	25420	60908	144212	487889	1036905
Net Worth 29	1691	0	33	351	793	2533	5236	12450	27148	55206	118714	441227	2053114

Selected Financial Ratios (Times to 1)

Current Ratio 30	1.5	•	2.3	3.0	1.8	1.6	1.6	1.7	1.5	1.5	1.3	1.7	1.0
Quick Ratio 31	0.9	•	1.4	1.5	1.2	1.1	0.9	1.1	0.9	0.9	0.8	0.9	0.7
Net Sales to Working Capital 32	13.0	•	13.9	4.9	9.2	17.9	9.2	10.6	10.4	10.1	16.2	8.3	813.4
Coverage Ratio 33	7.5	35.6	29.3	16.6	9.3	18.6	9.5	13.9	6.8	8.0	6.6	5.4	4.9
Total Asset Turnover 34	2.1	•	6.1	2.8	3.2	5.8	2.9	3.5	2.2	2.3	2.0	1.7	0.9
Inventory Turnover 35	10.1	•	17.8	5.3	10.0	16.8	6.8	10.7	6.9	8.0	11.3	9.6	11.2
Receivables Turnover 36	8.2	•	•	10.0	9.4	13.8	7.0	7.2	7.3	6.5	9.6	7.8	•
Total Liabilities to Net Worth 37	1.2	•	2.2	1.0	1.7	1.6	1.8	1.8	1.5	1.7	1.9	1.5	0.8
Current Assets to Working Capital 38	3.2	•	1.7	1.5	2.2	2.6	2.6	2.5	3.0	3.2	4.6	2.5	225.8
Current Liabilities to Working Capital 39	2.2	•	0.7	0.5	1.2	1.6	1.6	1.5	2.0	2.2	3.6	1.5	224.8
Working Capital to Net Sales 40	0.1	•	0.1	0.2	0.1	0.1	0.1	0.1	0.1	0.1	0.1	0.1	0.0
Inventory to Working Capital 41	0.9	•	0.5	0.5	0.7	0.8	1.0	0.7	1.1	0.9	1.3	0.7	59.3
Total Receipts to Cash Flow 42	11.0	29.9	5.7	4.5	7.9	15.5	10.0	11.7	11.1	11.1	8.3	17.3	12.3
Cost of Goods to Cash Flow 43	8.6	28.0	3.6	2.7	5.2	12.9	7.3	9.3	8.7	8.7	6.2	14.0	10.1
Cash Flow to Total Debt 44	0.3	•	1.6	1.3	0.7	0.6	0.4	0.5	0.3	0.3	0.4	0.2	0.2

Selected Financial Factors (in Percentages)

Debt Ratio 45	54.8	•	68.5	50.0	62.8	61.2	64.8	64.3	60.4	62.9	65.1	60.0	43.2
Return on Total Assets 46	10.1	•	50.5	21.1	17.8	14.4	13.3	14.2	11.6	10.0	10.6	6.8	6.2
Return on Equity Before Income Taxes 47	19.3	•	154.7	39.7	42.8	35.2	33.9	36.9	24.9	23.5	25.9	13.8	8.6
Return on Equity After Income Taxes 48	16.0	•	152.2	38.6	41.3	32.4	30.0	33.1	20.0	18.9	19.0	9.7	5.9
Profit Margin (Before Income Tax) 49	4.2	2.1	8.0	7.0	4.9	2.3	4.2	3.7	4.4	3.7	4.4	3.2	5.2
Profit Margin (After Income Tax) 50	3.5	2.0	7.9	6.8	4.8	2.2	3.7	3.4	3.6	3.0	3.3	2.2	3.6

Table I

Corporations with and without Net Income

METAL AND MINERAL (EXCEPT PETROLEUM)

MONEY AMOUNTS AND SIZE OF ASSETS IN THOUSANDS OF DOLLARS

Item Description for Accounting Period 7/08 Through 6/09	Total	Zero Assets	Under 500	500 to 1,000	1,000 to 5,000	5,000 to 10,000	10,000 to 25,000	25,000 to 50,000	50,000 to 100,000	100,000 to 250,000	250,000 to 500,000	500,000 to 2,500,000	2,500,000 and over
Number of Enterprises **1**	6513	306	3814	467	1084	292	294	104	65	45	20	19	3
Revenues ($ in Thousands)													
Net Sales **2**	151362738	849856	2759436	1363684	9764115	6420199	18553292	10460480	12677571	18577354	14661740	36301039	18973972
Interest **3**	344089	0	268	1474	3483	3833	7067	4470	6368	21762	39362	55304	200698
Rents **4**	85464	0	0	0	155	427	661	804	694	765	18764	18127	45066
Royalties **5**	82612	0	0	1376	499	0	0	0	0	50	0	0	80688
Other Portfolio Income **6**	188179	26404	42	4765	3208	470	5472	1864	3254	4327	65698	53321	19355
Other Receipts **7**	1238203	-27297	2715	4415	-26306	25323	68286	26470	44120	429412	118173	183961	388931
Total Receipts **8**	153301285	848963	2762461	1375714	9745154	6450252	18634778	10494088	12732007	19033670	14903737	36611752	19708710
Average Total Receipts **9**	23538	2774	724	2946	8990	22090	63384	100905	195877	422970	745187	1926934	6569570
Operating Costs/Operating Income (%)													
Cost of Operations **10**	86.2	79.4	66.6	78.4	83.9	85.2	89.3	88.6	89.1	88.2	88.2	88.6	77.1
Salaries and Wages **11**	3.4	1.8	6.3	3.3	4.0	3.5	2.4	2.7	2.6	2.5	2.5	3.2	6.5
Taxes Paid **12**	0.6	1.1	1.6	1.0	0.8	0.5	0.5	0.4	0.4	0.6	0.6	0.4	0.9
Interest Paid **13**	1.0	0.2	0.4	0.3	0.2	0.7	0.3	0.6	0.6	0.4	0.8	1.4	2.9
Depreciation **14**	0.9	0.3	0.6	0.7	0.3	0.3	0.8	0.9	0.6	0.5	0.6	0.8	2.9
Amortization and Depletion **15**	0.3	0.7	0.0	•	0.0	0.0	0.0	0.0	0.0	0.1	0.1	0.2	1.7
Pensions and Other Deferred Comp. **16**	0.2	0.1	0.4	0.5	0.0	0.2	0.1	0.1	0.2	0.2	0.2	0.2	0.2
Employee Benefits **17**	0.5	0.1	0.4	0.7	0.4	0.4	0.3	0.3	0.3	0.4	0.3	0.7	0.8
Advertising **18**	0.1	0.0	0.3	0.1	0.1	0.2	0.1	0.1	0.1	0.1	0.0	0.0	0.3
Other Expenses **19**	3.7	6.3	7.8	7.2	4.8	3.7	2.4	2.7	2.3	3.8	3.9	2.7	6.8
Officers' Compensation **20**	1.1	2.1	12.8	4.2	3.6	2.2	0.9	1.2	0.8	0.6	0.6	0.3	0.5
Operating Margin **21**	1.9	7.9	2.6	3.5	1.5	3.2	3.0	2.4	3.0	2.7	1.9	1.4	•
Operating Margin Before Officers' Comp. **22**	3.0	10.0	15.4	7.8	5.2	5.4	3.9	3.6	3.7	3.3	2.5	1.7	•

Selected Average Balance Sheet ($ in Thousands)

Net Receivables 23	2499	0	39	140	667	2433	4705	9480	19351	43502	77548	197668	1246144
Inventories 24	2946	0	30	178	757	3206	5203	11612	32213	58986	101530	261021	919192
Net Property, Plant and Equipment 25	1958	0	9	51	122	474	1884	3041	6472	11741	39079	150826	2318620
Total Assets 26	11286	0	166	647	2411	7583	15965	34484	71796	159653	345268	947394	7567772
Notes and Loans Payable 27	3500	0	134	101	364	1850	3552	10715	23065	49183	86136	361921	2277177
All Other Liabilities 28	4759	0	19	80	740	2920	5153	12334	22738	53779	122653	337281	4557490
Net Worth 29	3027	0	14	466	1307	2813	7259	11435	25993	56690	136479	248192	733105

Selected Financial Ratios (Times to 1)

Current Ratio 30	1.7	•	3.6	4.9	2.2	1.6	1.9	1.7	1.6	1.8	1.9	1.9	1.4
Quick Ratio 31	0.8	•	2.5	3.1	1.4	0.7	1.0	0.7	0.6	0.7	0.8	0.8	0.6
Net Sales to Working Capital 32	7.9	•	7.3	6.5	8.2	9.1	10.5	8.6	9.2	7.2	6.3	7.2	7.6
Coverage Ratio 33	4.2	37.2	7.6	15.6	8.1	6.5	12.9	5.3	7.0	12.8	5.3	2.7	2.1
Total Asset Turnover 34	2.1	•	4.3	4.5	3.7	2.9	4.0	2.9	2.7	2.6	2.1	2.0	0.8
Inventory Turnover 35	6.8	•	15.9	12.9	10.0	5.8	10.8	7.7	5.4	6.2	6.4	6.5	5.3
Receivables Turnover 36	8.7	•	18.2	15.0	11.2	8.8	14.0	11.9	9.4	10.3	8.5	9.2	4.1
Total Liabilities to Net Worth 37	2.7	•	10.9	0.4	0.8	1.7	1.2	2.0	1.8	1.8	1.5	2.8	9.3
Current Assets to Working Capital 38	2.4	•	1.4	1.3	1.8	2.8	2.1	2.5	2.8	2.3	2.1	2.1	3.5
Current Liabilities to Working Capital 39	1.4	•	0.4	0.3	0.8	1.8	1.1	1.5	1.8	1.3	1.1	1.1	2.5
Working Capital to Net Sales 40	0.1	•	0.1	0.2	0.1	0.1	0.1	0.1	0.1	0.1	0.2	0.1	0.1
Inventory to Working Capital 41	1.0	•	0.4	0.5	0.6	1.3	0.9	1.2	1.4	1.2	1.0	1.0	1.1
Total Receipts to Cash Flow 42	17.3	7.5	11.5	10.8	19.4	15.2	19.3	22.0	19.8	12.0	15.9	24.7	14.2
Cost of Goods to Cash Flow 43	14.9	5.9	7.7	8.5	16.3	12.9	17.2	19.5	17.7	10.6	14.1	21.9	11.0
Cash Flow to Total Debt 44	0.2	•	0.4	1.5	0.4	0.3	0.4	0.2	0.2	0.3	0.2	0.1	0.1

Selected Financial Factors (in Percentages)

Debt Ratio 45	73.2	•	91.6	28.0	45.8	62.9	54.5	66.8	63.8	64.5	60.5	73.8	90.3
Return on Total Assets 46	8.7	•	13.7	20.8	5.8	12.7	14.6	9.8	10.8	14.6	9.4	7.4	5.2
Return on Equity Before Income Taxes 47	24.7	•	142.3	27.1	9.3	28.8	29.6	24.0	25.5	37.8	19.3	17.6	28.5
Return on Equity After Income Taxes 48	18.7	•	137.0	26.2	8.3	28.0	27.3	21.5	21.4	28.9	13.7	11.9	12.3
Profit Margin (Before Income Tax) 49	3.2	7.8	2.7	4.3	1.4	3.7	3.4	2.7	3.4	5.2	3.6	2.3	3.3
Profit Margin (After Income Tax) 50	2.4	7.8	2.6	4.2	1.2	3.6	3.1	2.4	2.9	4.0	2.6	1.5	1.4

Table II

Corporations with Net Income

METAL AND MINERAL (EXCEPT PETROLEUM)

MONEY AMOUNTS AND SIZE OF ASSETS IN THOUSANDS OF DOLLARS

Item Description for Accounting Period 7/08 Through 6/09	Total	Zero Assets	Under 500	500 to 1,000	1,000 to 5,000	5,000 to 10,000	10,000 to 25,000	25,000 to 50,000	50,000 to 100,000	100,000 to 250,000	250,000 to 500,000	500,000 to 2,500,000	2,500,000 and over
Number of Enterprises **1**	4468	45	2643	344	782	206	244	82	51	39	15	16	0
Revenues ($ in Thousands)													
Net Sales **2**	120615305	588085	2228290	1197038	8126225	5029215	16619456	8459096	10600150	17341418	10757132	39669200	0
Interest **3**	272825	0	268	27	2807	3581	5106	3198	2653	19457	30381	205347	0
Rents **4**	81079	0	0	0	155	0	460	664	635	492	16710	61963	0
Royalties **5**	80338	0	0	0	0	0	0	0	0	50	0	80288	0
Other Portfolio Income **6**	166126	26404	42	1456	1848	431	5286	1447	3148	3970	65029	57066	0
Other Receipts **7**	1100685	6365	1	3800	7506	23839	67156	24934	32332	425635	98184	410933	0
Total Receipts **8**	122316358	620854	2228601	1202321	8138541	5057066	16697464	8489339	10638918	17791022	10967436	40484797	0
Average Total Receipts **9**	27376	13797	843	3495	10407	24549	68432	103529	208606	456180	731162	2530300	•
Operating Costs/Operating Income (%)													
Cost of Operations **10**	85.1	72.7	63.0	82.6	82.7	84.3	89.2	87.1	88.1	88.7	85.2	82.7	•
Salaries and Wages **11**	3.4	2.1	7.2	1.7	3.6	3.8	2.3	2.9	2.6	2.4	2.9	4.5	•
Taxes Paid **12**	0.6	1.4	1.7	0.7	0.7	0.5	0.4	0.4	0.4	0.5	0.7	0.7	•
Interest Paid **13**	0.8	0.3	0.4	0.1	0.1	0.5	0.3	0.5	0.5	0.4	0.8	1.6	•
Depreciation **14**	0.7	0.2	0.4	0.5	0.3	0.3	0.7	0.8	0.6	0.3	0.7	1.1	•
Amortization and Depletion **15**	0.1	1.1	0.0	•	0.0	0.0	0.0	0.0	0.0	0.0	0.2	0.3	•
Pensions and Other Deferred Comp. **16**	0.2	0.1	0.5	0.5	0.4	0.2	0.2	0.1	0.2	0.2	0.3	0.2	•
Employee Benefits **17**	0.5	0.1	0.5	0.2	0.5	0.4	0.3	0.3	0.3	0.4	0.4	0.8	•
Advertising **18**	0.1	0.0	0.1	0.1	0.1	0.2	0.0	0.1	0.1	0.1	0.0	0.2	•
Other Expenses **19**	3.7	8.5	7.1	2.3	4.2	3.4	2.2	2.6	2.2	3.4	4.4	4.7	•
Officers' Compensation **20**	1.2	1.3	14.2	4.3	3.8	1.7	0.9	1.3	0.7	0.5	0.7	0.4	•
Operating Margin **21**	3.5	12.2	4.8	6.9	3.6	4.7	3.5	3.8	4.2	3.1	3.6	2.9	•
Operating Margin Before Officers' Comp. **22**	4.7	13.5	19.0	11.2	7.5	6.3	4.4	5.1	5.0	3.7	4.3	3.3	•

Selected Average Balance Sheet ($ in Thousands)

Net Receivables 23	2752	0	47	147	742	1876	4847	10239	20045	43185	76469	329873
Inventories 24	3470	0	46	183	902	3863	5417	11977	33060	64376	96444	297029
Net Property, Plant and Equipment 25	1168	0	9	43	84	589	1752	2767	6932	9059	43837	185742
Total Assets 26	11775	0	182	580	2391	7592	15872	34521	71687	160610	348727	1665100
Notes and Loans Payable 27	3734	0	42	129	274	1793	2977	8704	21445	42018	90455	650744
All Other Liabilities 28	3637	0	19	56	756	2392	4865	12387	21094	56161	103905	504345
Net Worth 29	4404	0	121	394	1361	3408	8030	13431	29148	62431	154367	510010

Selected Financial Ratios (Times to 1)

Current Ratio 30	1.9	•	3.3	5.6	2.7	1.8	1.9	1.8	1.6	1.8	2.1	1.8
Quick Ratio 31	0.8	•	2.2	3.8	1.8	0.7	1.1	0.8	0.7	0.7	1.0	0.8
Net Sales to Working Capital 32	7.3	•	8.3	8.0	7.4	8.7	11.1	7.8	9.0	7.5	6.1	6.0
Coverage Ratio 33	7.2	65.4	12.6	121.8	42.8	11.3	16.1	9.6	10.6	16.0	7.5	4.2
Total Asset Turnover 34	2.3	•	4.6	6.0	4.3	3.2	4.3	3.0	2.9	2.8	2.1	1.5
Inventory Turnover 35	6.6	•	11.5	15.7	9.5	5.3	11.2	7.5	5.5	6.1	6.3	6.9
Receivables Turnover 36	8.5	•	•	14.4	10.5	9.5	14.1	11.1	9.2	11.1	8.2	9.2
Total Liabilities to Net Worth 37	1.7	•	0.5	0.5	0.8	1.2	1.0	1.6	1.5	1.6	1.3	2.3
Current Assets to Working Capital 38	2.2	•	1.4	1.2	1.6	2.3	2.1	2.3	2.6	2.3	1.9	2.2
Current Liabilities to Working Capital 39	1.2	•	0.4	0.2	0.6	1.3	1.1	1.3	1.6	1.3	0.9	1.2
Working Capital to Net Sales 40	0.1	•	0.1	0.1	0.1	0.1	0.1	0.1	0.1	0.1	0.2	0.2
Inventory to Working Capital 41	1.0	•	0.5	0.4	0.5	1.3	0.9	1.0	1.3	1.3	0.9	0.9
Total Receipts to Cash Flow 42	13.2	3.9	9.7	11.8	14.0	12.8	17.9	17.0	16.1	11.8	11.9	12.3
Cost of Goods to Cash Flow 43	11.2	2.9	6.1	9.7	11.6	10.8	16.0	14.8	14.2	10.4	10.1	10.2
Cash Flow to Total Debt 44	0.3	•	1.4	1.6	0.7	0.5	0.5	0.3	0.3	0.4	0.3	0.2

Selected Financial Factors (in Percentages)

Debt Ratio 45	62.6	•	33.7	32.0	43.1	55.1	49.4	61.1	59.3	61.1	55.7	69.4
Return on Total Assets 46	13.1	•	24.2	44.0	16.8	18.4	18.4	13.9	14.7	16.9	13.1	9.7
Return on Equity Before Income Taxes 47	30.1	•	33.6	64.1	28.8	37.4	34.1	32.0	32.7	40.7	25.7	24.1
Return on Equity After Income Taxes 48	24.2	•	32.7	62.8	27.4	36.4	31.5	29.3	28.2	31.3	19.1	16.5
Profit Margin (Before Income Tax) 49	4.9	17.8	4.8	7.3	3.8	5.2	4.0	4.2	4.6	5.7	5.5	5.0
Profit Margin (After Income Tax) 50	3.9	17.8	4.7	7.1	3.6	5.1	3.7	3.8	3.9	4.4	4.1	3.4

Table I

Corporations with and without Net Income

ELECTRICAL GOODS

MONEY AMOUNTS AND SIZE OF ASSETS IN THOUSANDS OF DOLLARS

Item Description for Accounting Period 7/08 Through 6/09		Total	Zero Assets	Under 500	500 to 1,000	1,000 to 5,000	5,000 to 10,000	10,000 to 25,000	25,000 to 50,000	50,000 to 100,000	100,000 to 250,000	250,000 to 500,000	500,000 to 2,500,000	2,500,000 and over
Number of Enterprises	1	28245	3768	15618	3374	3890	741	427	190	106	71	21	26	11
Revenues ($ in Thousands)														
Net Sales	2	331760682	3426305	11452254	7338278	28343984	13227572	19920501	16178934	18374099	29189126	22549710	64294137	97465782
Interest	3	860035	1646	1802	5885	14986	7993	14112	14889	29281	31940	28150	257398	451952
Rents	4	158005	3068	545	0	976	5270	2000	631	2924	16134	4649	26138	95668
Royalties	5	1298312	870	0	0	0	0	0	13	7712	8521	35380	36902	1208915
Other Portfolio Income	6	329196	1391	2190	16994	4641	3096	3032	2148	41708	25048	11906	45096	171948
Other Receipts	7	3714584	9040	69556	40876	251356	71041	155016	121857	88410	368046	95608	493592	1950187
Total Receipts	8	338120814	3442320	11526347	7402033	28615943	13314972	20094661	16318472	18544134	29638815	22725403	65153263	101344452
Average Total Receipts	9	11971	914	738	2194	7356	17969	47060	85887	174945	417448	1082162	2505895	9213132
Operating Costs/Operating Income (%)														
Cost of Operations	10	82.7	81.9	58.4	72.7	75.4	76.7	83.4	80.4	83.6	84.7	92.5	87.5	83.5
Salaries and Wages	11	6.1	7.2	11.6	7.1	8.3	8.7	6.4	7.5	5.9	6.0	3.5	4.5	5.8
Taxes Paid	12	0.8	1.1	1.9	1.5	1.1	1.1	0.8	0.9	0.8	0.6	0.3	0.8	0.6
Interest Paid	13	0.6	0.5	0.9	0.7	0.4	0.6	0.4	0.5	0.6	0.5	0.1	0.6	0.8
Depreciation	14	1.0	0.4	0.6	0.6	0.6	0.9	0.5	0.6	0.6	0.7	0.4	0.5	1.9
Amortization and Depletion	15	0.9	0.3	0.0	0.0	0.0	0.1	0.1	0.2	0.1	0.2	0.0	0.3	2.8
Pensions and Other Deferred Comp.	16	0.3	0.6	0.5	0.3	0.4	0.2	0.2	0.2	0.4	0.2	0.1	0.3	0.4
Employee Benefits	17	0.6	0.6	1.2	0.4	0.7	0.6	0.5	0.6	0.6	0.6	0.3	0.7	0.7
Advertising	18	0.8	0.2	0.9	0.4	0.7	0.4	0.4	0.5	0.8	0.8	0.3	0.6	1.1
Other Expenses	19	5.8	9.3	13.9	9.8	7.8	7.3	5.6	6.5	4.8	5.4	2.4	4.2	5.6
Officers' Compensation	20	1.0	1.6	6.5	5.9	3.4	2.1	1.2	1.2	0.8	0.4	0.3	0.1	0.1
Operating Margin	21	•	•	3.6	0.7	1.1	1.2	0.6	0.9	1.0	•	•	•	•
Operating Margin Before Officers' Comp.	22	0.3	•	10.1	6.6	4.5	3.3	1.7	2.1	1.8	0.3	0.1	•	•

Selected Average Balance Sheet ($ in Thousands)

Net Receivables 23	1647	0	28	170	695	2135	5437	11794	23312	56650	137688	354328	1641751
Inventories 24	1022	0	21	260	766	2065	4743	9342	21113	34961	74940	221068	663116
Net Property, Plant and Equipment 25	446	0	14	122	227	657	995	1897	5677	11840	15537	74037	555567
Total Assets 26	5939	0	133	750	2359	7233	14697	35072	68726	156520	359200	1166175	7217082
Notes and Loans Payable 27	1420	0	128	282	614	2373	3554	7143	18438	29847	15970	161508	1958738
All Other Liabilities 28	2385	0	77	285	861	2567	7228	13583	27862	73315	198971	463295	2719126
Net Worth 29	2133	0	-71	183	883	2293	3914	14347	22426	53358	144258	541372	2539219

Selected Financial Ratios (Times to 1)

Current Ratio 30	1.3	•	1.4	1.8	1.8	1.7	1.4	1.8	1.7	1.8	1.3	1.4	1.1
Quick Ratio 31	0.8	•	1.0	1.0	1.0	1.0	0.8	1.0	1.0	1.0	0.9	0.9	0.6
Net Sales to Working Capital 32	12.7	•	24.7	8.5	8.1	7.2	13.0	7.2	7.8	7.9	16.0	11.3	40.0
Coverage Ratio 33	3.1	•	5.6	3.5	5.9	4.4	4.4	4.3	4.1	4.1	9.8	3.1	1.8
Total Asset Turnover 34	2.0	•	5.5	2.9	3.1	2.5	3.2	2.4	2.5	2.6	3.0	2.1	1.2
Inventory Turnover 35	9.5	•	20.0	6.1	7.2	6.6	8.2	7.3	6.9	10.0	13.3	9.8	11.2
Receivables Turnover 36	6.9	•	26.1	11.5	9.7	7.8	8.0	7.3	6.5	7.5	8.1	6.4	5.4
Total Liabilities to Net Worth 37	1.8	•	•	3.1	1.7	2.2	2.8	1.4	2.1	1.9	1.5	1.2	1.8
Current Assets to Working Capital 38	3.9	•	3.4	2.2	2.2	2.4	3.4	2.3	2.5	2.3	3.9	3.3	15.7
Current Liabilities to Working Capital 39	2.9	•	2.4	1.2	1.2	1.4	2.4	1.3	1.5	1.3	2.9	2.3	14.7
Working Capital to Net Sales 40	0.1	•	0.0	0.1	0.1	0.1	0.1	0.1	0.1	0.1	0.1	0.1	0.0
Inventory to Working Capital 41	1.1	•	0.9	0.9	0.9	0.9	1.3	0.9	0.9	0.7	0.9	1.0	2.9
Total Receipts to Cash Flow 42	17.2	27.9	6.9	11.5	12.4	12.3	16.9	15.1	17.5	16.8	39.3	21.6	19.8
Cost of Goods to Cash Flow 43	14.2	22.8	4.0	8.4	9.3	9.5	14.1	12.1	14.6	14.2	36.4	18.9	16.5
Cash Flow to Total Debt 44	0.2	•	0.5	0.3	0.4	0.3	0.3	0.3	0.2	0.2	0.1	0.2	0.1

Selected Financial Factors (in Percentages)

Debt Ratio 45	64.1	•	153.0	75.5	62.5	68.3	73.4	59.1	67.4	65.9	59.8	53.6	64.8
Return on Total Assets 46	3.8	•	28.4	6.5	7.6	6.0	5.9	5.6	6.4	5.1	2.1	4.3	1.8
Return on Equity Before Income Taxes 47	7.2	•	•	19.0	16.8	14.6	17.1	10.6	14.9	11.3	4.7	6.3	2.2
Return on Equity After Income Taxes 48	5.4	•	•	15.9	14.9	12.4	13.1	8.8	12.5	8.6	2.8	4.0	1.2
Profit Margin (Before Income Tax) 49	1.3	•	4.2	1.6	2.0	1.9	1.4	1.8	1.9	1.5	0.6	1.4	0.6
Profit Margin (After Income Tax) 50	1.0	•	4.1	1.3	1.8	1.6	1.1	1.5	1.6	1.1	0.4	0.9	0.3

Table II

Corporations with Net Income

ELECTRICAL GOODS

MONEY AMOUNTS AND SIZE OF ASSETS IN THOUSANDS OF DOLLARS

Item Description for Accounting Period 7/08 Through 6/09		Total	Zero Assets	Under 500	500 to 1,000	1,000 to 5,000	5,000 to 10,000	10,000 to 25,000	25,000 to 50,000	50,000 to 100,000	100,000 to 250,000	250,000 to 500,000	500,000 to 2,500,000	2,500,000 and over
Number of Enterprises	1	15983	1996	7983	2148	2718	529	302	142	76	51	13	18	8
Revenues ($ in Thousands)														
Net Sales	2	230477576	1528985	8200879	5877240	21692838	11043542	15300847	12744605	15095229	22338345	20470045	51524729	44660292
Interest	3	525826	4	1445	4988	10359	6394	12455	11105	15372	24023	19376	233942	186364
Rents	4	75061	27	545	0	324	1907	940	502	779	15670	2113	24137	28115
Royalties	5	272772	0	0	0	0	0	0	0	2009	8471	25445	11136	225712
Other Portfolio Income	6	198476	37	2175	16994	2585	2656	2150	844	31383	20670	6320	37357	75303
Other Receipts	7	2636421	5125	63991	34144	222114	62271	114798	51898	61724	227389	72074	359524	1361372
Total Receipts	8	234186132	1534178	8269035	5933366	21928220	11116770	15431190	12808954	15206496	22634568	20595373	52190825	46537158
Average Total Receipts	9	14652	769	1036	2762	8068	21015	51097	90204	200085	443815	1584259	2899490	5817145
Operating Costs/Operating Income (%)														
Cost of Operations	10	82.6	79.9	50.9	73.0	75.7	76.1	82.7	79.8	83.4	84.4	93.4	87.4	83.6
Salaries and Wages	11	6.3	4.8	13.4	6.8	7.5	8.4	6.0	7.1	5.6	5.7	2.9	4.6	7.7
Taxes Paid	12	0.8	0.6	2.2	1.5	1.1	1.1	0.8	0.9	0.7	0.6	0.3	0.9	0.7
Interest Paid	13	0.6	0.0	0.3	0.4	0.4	0.4	0.4	0.4	0.5	0.4	0.1	0.6	1.1
Depreciation	14	0.5	0.2	0.7	0.6	0.4	1.0	0.5	0.4	0.5	0.5	0.3	0.5	0.8
Amortization and Depletion	15	0.2	0.0	0.0	0.0	0.0	0.1	0.1	0.1	0.1	0.2	0.0	0.2	0.4
Pensions and Other Deferred Comp.	16	0.3	0.0	0.6	0.4	0.4	0.2	0.2	0.2	0.4	0.2	0.1	0.3	0.5
Employee Benefits	17	0.6	0.3	1.4	0.4	0.6	0.6	0.5	0.5	0.5	0.6	0.2	0.7	0.8
Advertising	18	0.5	0.2	0.7	0.4	0.4	0.4	0.3	0.4	0.7	0.6	0.1	0.4	0.9
Other Expenses	19	5.0	8.0	13.8	7.6	6.8	6.4	5.2	5.8	4.3	5.0	1.8	3.4	5.0
Officers' Compensation	20	1.2	1.5	7.3	6.4	3.5	2.2	1.2	1.1	0.8	0.4	0.2	0.1	0.3
Operating Margin	21	1.4	4.5	8.6	2.5	3.1	3.0	2.2	3.2	2.5	1.4	0.6	0.9	•
Operating Margin Before Officers' Comp.	22	2.6	5.9	15.9	9.0	6.6	5.2	3.4	4.3	3.3	1.8	0.8	1.0	•

Selected Average Balance Sheet ($ in Thousands)

Net Receivables 23	2016	0	32	140	752	2133	5833	12218	26238	59021	187967	385461	1327140
Inventories 24	1414	0	25	283	814	2126	5273	10364	23614	35825	99711	257440	729634
Net Property, Plant and Equipment 25	379	0	16	133	224	772	1001	1651	5518	9801	18649	79398	186440
Total Assets 26	6600	0	178	746	2365	7277	14788	34730	68425	157030	387126	1178086	5417751
Notes and Loans Payable 27	1106	0	32	189	574	1766	2663	6361	13994	29474	11898	121103	989712
All Other Liabilities 28	2634	0	65	180	801	2753	6414	13476	28184	73717	252169	482482	1980992
Net Worth 29	2859	0	81	378	990	2757	5711	14893	26247	53839	123058	574501	2447047

Selected Financial Ratios (Times to 1)

Current Ratio 30	1.6	•	1.9	2.8	2.0	1.6	1.7	1.9	1.7	1.8	1.3	1.5	1.6
Quick Ratio 31	1.0	•	1.3	1.6	1.2	0.9	1.0	1.0	1.0	1.1	1.0	0.9	1.1
Net Sales to Working Capital 32	9.1	•	15.8	7.4	7.7	9.0	10.0	6.8	8.1	8.1	18.3	11.3	7.1
Coverage Ratio 33	6.5	313.9	30.7	10.4	11.8	9.6	9.7	10.5	7.9	7.9	23.5	4.8	3.3
Total Asset Turnover 34	2.2	•	5.8	3.7	3.4	2.9	3.4	2.6	2.9	2.8	4.1	2.4	1.0
Inventory Turnover 35	8.4	•	20.6	7.0	7.4	7.5	8.0	6.9	7.0	10.3	14.8	9.7	6.4
Receivables Turnover 36	6.0	•	29.8	14.4	8.9	8.2	7.7	6.9	6.6	7.6	8.8	6.6	3.1
Total Liabilities to Net Worth 37	1.3	•	1.2	1.0	1.4	1.6	1.6	1.3	1.6	1.9	2.1	1.1	1.2
Current Assets to Working Capital 38	2.6	•	2.1	1.6	2.0	2.5	2.5	2.2	2.3	2.3	3.9	3.1	2.8
Current Liabilities to Working Capital 39	1.6	•	1.1	0.6	1.0	1.5	1.5	1.2	1.3	1.3	2.9	2.1	1.8
Working Capital to Net Sales 40	0.1	•	0.1	0.1	0.1	0.1	0.1	0.1	0.1	0.1	0.1	0.1	0.1
Inventory to Working Capital 41	0.8	•	0.6	0.6	0.7	0.9	0.9	0.8	0.9	0.7	0.9	1.0	0.7
Total Receipts to Cash Flow 42	14.6	8.7	5.1	11.6	10.6	11.0	13.7	12.5	15.2	14.5	38.2	20.5	16.2
Cost of Goods to Cash Flow 43	12.0	7.0	2.6	8.4	8.0	8.4	11.3	9.9	12.7	12.2	35.7	17.9	13.5
Cash Flow to Total Debt 44	0.3	•	2.1	0.6	0.5	0.4	0.4	0.4	0.3	0.3	0.2	0.2	0.1

Selected Financial Factors (in Percentages)

Debt Ratio 45	56.7	•	54.5	49.4	58.1	62.1	61.4	57.1	61.6	65.7	68.2	51.2	54.8
Return on Total Assets 46	7.9	•	56.2	14.1	15.3	11.8	11.8	10.6	10.7	8.8	5.1	7.3	3.9
Return on Equity Before Income Taxes 47	15.4	•	119.4	25.2	33.5	27.8	27.4	22.4	24.4	22.5	15.5	11.8	6.0
Return on Equity After Income Taxes 48	13.0	•	117.6	22.8	31.1	25.3	23.5	20.1	21.6	18.8	12.1	8.7	4.5
Profit Margin (Before Income Tax) 49	3.1	4.8	9.4	3.5	4.2	3.7	3.1	3.7	3.2	2.8	1.2	2.4	2.6
Profit Margin (After Income Tax) 50	2.6	4.4	9.3	3.2	3.9	3.3	2.6	3.3	2.9	2.3	0.9	1.7	2.0

Table I

Corporations with and without Net Income

HARDWARE, PLUMBING, HEATING EQUIPMENT, AND SUPPLIES

MONEY AMOUNTS AND SIZE OF ASSETS IN THOUSANDS OF DOLLARS

Item Description for Accounting Period 7/08 Through 6/09		Total	Zero Assets	Under 500	500 to 1,000	1,000 to 5,000	5,000 to 10,000	10,000 to 25,000	25,000 to 50,000	50,000 to 100,000	100,000 to 250,000	250,000 to 500,000	500,000 to 2,500,000	2,500,000 and over
Number of Enterprises	1	16507	2696	8087	1696	2946	533	369	95	54	17	5	8	0
Revenues ($ in Thousands)														
Net Sales	2	99674997	378916	2875591	5510302	18981103	9632418	15645780	8139730	7530700	4973695	3204048	22802713	0
Interest	3	223106	162	445	2457	22281	6395	7125	6553	4812	2705	2518	167654	0
Rents	4	9197	0	322	0	2869	674	2851	863	344	1058	16	200	0
Royalties	5	5207	0	0	0	0	4	5191	12	0	0	0	0	0
Other Portfolio Income	6	67200	0	2320	579	7481	7458	35272	6660	3257	656	24	3494	0
Other Receipts	7	819518	296	15221	6981	282568	81285	102935	43178	40920	36184	60907	149043	0
Total Receipts	8	100799225	379374	2893899	5520319	19296302	9728234	15799154	8196996	7580033	5014298	3267513	23123104	0
Average Total Receipts	9	6106	141	358	3255	6550	18252	42816	86284	140371	294959	653503	2890388	•
Operating Costs/Operating Income (%)														
Cost of Operations	10	71.9	52.4	59.3	70.2	72.6	70.3	74.0	77.3	73.6	77.2	72.6	69.3	•
Salaries and Wages	11	10.1	13.1	10.4	8.8	9.0	10.3	10.8	8.3	9.6	8.3	9.9	11.8	•
Taxes Paid	12	1.3	1.9	2.2	1.3	1.3	1.5	1.2	1.0	1.1	1.2	1.4	1.5	•
Interest Paid	13	0.9	1.1	0.8	0.4	0.5	0.6	0.5	0.7	0.9	0.7	0.7	1.8	•
Depreciation	14	0.8	0.3	1.3	0.3	0.5	1.4	0.5	0.7	0.9	1.1	0.8	1.2	•
Amortization and Depletion	15	0.2	•	1.1	0.0	0.1	0.0	0.1	0.1	0.2	0.1	0.4	0.5	•
Pensions and Other Deferred Comp.	16	0.4	•	0.6	0.3	0.4	0.5	0.3	0.4	0.3	0.2	0.6	0.5	•
Employee Benefits	17	1.1	0.0	0.8	0.7	0.9	1.2	0.7	0.7	1.1	0.6	1.5	1.8	•
Advertising	18	0.4	1.4	1.9	0.3	0.4	0.4	0.5	0.8	0.6	0.5	0.1	0.2	•
Other Expenses	19	8.2	21.0	16.7	9.3	8.3	8.8	5.9	6.4	8.3	6.7	9.8	8.6	•
Officers' Compensation	20	2.3	9.6	6.9	5.3	4.4	3.0	2.2	1.1	0.8	0.7	1.0	0.1	•
Operating Margin	21	2.3	•	•	3.1	1.6	2.0	3.3	2.6	2.6	2.8	1.3	2.6	•
Operating Margin Before Officers' Comp.	22	4.6	8.8	4.9	8.4	6.1	5.0	5.5	3.7	3.4	3.5	2.3	2.7	•

Selected Average Balance Sheet ($ in Thousands)

Net Receivables 23	859	0	24	210	711	2020	4785	10262	19053	35665	58596	723254	•
Inventories 24	834	0	15	260	840	2636	6268	14006	25448	57870	86653	362199	•
Net Property, Plant and Equipment 25	273	0	11	44	182	831	1229	2985	8016	21651	29495	210924	•
Total Assets 26	2815	0	87	737	2462	7112	15701	33886	67109	150784	304089	2091868	•
Notes and Loans Payable 27	826	0	76	226	503	2010	3927	10422	19147	32086	68648	714668	•
All Other Liabilities 28	893	0	41	279	832	1780	3989	8802	17328	51782	116344	727937	•
Net Worth 29	1096	0	-30	231	1126	3322	7784	14761	30634	66915	119096	649264	•

Selected Financial Ratios (Times to 1)

Current Ratio 30	1.9	•	1.4	2.0	2.2	2.1	2.1	2.0	2.1	1.9	1.6	1.7	•
Quick Ratio 31	1.0	•	1.1	1.1	1.1	0.9	1.0	0.9	1.0	0.8	0.6	1.1	•
Net Sales to Working Capital 32	6.2	•	21.4	10.2	5.7	5.6	6.3	5.9	5.1	5.7	9.7	6.1	•
Coverage Ratio 33	4.9	0.4	•	10.2	8.2	6.2	8.9	5.4	4.5	6.3	5.9	3.2	•
Total Asset Turnover 34	2.1	•	4.1	4.4	2.6	2.5	2.7	2.5	2.1	1.9	2.1	1.4	•
Inventory Turnover 35	5.2	•	14.4	8.8	5.6	4.8	5.0	4.7	4.0	3.9	5.4	5.5	•
Receivables Turnover 36	7.3	•	14.9	12.7	9.3	10.5	8.6	8.4	6.8	7.7	11.4	4.3	•
Total Liabilities to Net Worth 37	1.6	•	•	2.2	1.2	1.1	1.0	1.3	1.2	1.3	1.6	2.2	•
Current Assets to Working Capital 38	2.1	•	3.5	2.0	1.8	1.9	1.9	2.0	1.9	2.1	2.6	2.5	•
Current Liabilities to Working Capital 39	1.1	•	2.5	1.0	0.8	0.9	0.9	1.0	0.9	1.1	1.6	1.5	•
Working Capital to Net Sales 40	0.2	•	0.0	0.1	0.2	0.2	0.2	0.2	0.2	0.2	0.1	0.2	•
Inventory to Working Capital 41	0.9	•	0.7	0.9	0.8	1.0	0.9	1.0	0.9	1.1	1.4	0.7	•
Total Receipts to Cash Flow 42	10.8	6.1	8.3	9.6	10.9	11.2	12.5	13.1	10.6	12.1	9.2	10.1	•
Cost of Goods to Cash Flow 43	7.8	3.2	5.0	6.7	7.9	7.9	9.2	10.1	7.8	9.3	6.7	7.0	•
Cash Flow to Total Debt 44	0.3	•	0.4	0.7	0.4	0.4	0.4	0.3	0.4	0.3	0.4	0.2	•

Selected Financial Factors (in Percentages)

Debt Ratio 45	61.0	•	133.9	68.6	54.3	53.3	50.4	56.6	54.4	55.6	60.8	69.0	•
Return on Total Assets 46	9.2	•	•	16.2	9.7	9.0	12.9	10.2	8.6	8.3	8.3	7.9	•
Return on Equity Before Income Taxes 47	18.9	•	16.1	46.5	18.7	16.2	23.2	19.1	14.8	15.8	17.6	17.5	•
Return on Equity After Income Taxes 48	15.8	•	16.7	42.0	16.6	14.4	20.7	16.8	13.0	13.3	13.1	12.7	•
Profit Margin (Before Income Tax) 49	3.4	•	•	3.3	3.3	3.0	4.3	3.3	3.2	3.6	3.3	4.0	•
Profit Margin (After Income Tax) 50	2.9	•	•	3.0	2.9	2.7	3.8	2.9	2.9	3.0	2.4	2.9	•

Table II

Corporations with Net Income

HARDWARE, PLUMBING, HEATING EQUIPMENT, AND SUPPLIES

MONEY AMOUNTS AND SIZE OF ASSETS IN THOUSANDS OF DOLLARS

Item Description for Accounting Period 7/08 Through 6/09		Total	Zero Assets	Under 500	500 to 1,000	1,000 to 5,000	5,000 to 10,000	10,000 to 25,000	25,000 to 50,000	50,000 to 100,000	100,000 to 250,000	250,000 to 500,000	500,000 to 2,500,000	2,500,000 and over
Number of Enterprises	1	8367	817	3163	1148	2305	455	334	•	41	13	5	•	0
Revenues ($ in Thousands)														
Net Sales	2	86158984	211197	1435533	4132953	15902984	8221579	14076191	•	5735319	4534529	3204048	•	0
Interest	3	207931	141	264	1823	21122	5431	5946	•	2282	2556	2518	•	0
Rents	4	7294	0	322	0	2276	674	2780	•	308	119	16	•	0
Royalties	5	5191	0	0	0	0	0	5191	•	0	0	0	•	0
Other Portfolio Income	6	56262	0	34	579	7044	7185	28225	•	2521	631	24	•	0
Other Receipts	7	766627	296	4199	5362	275548	74851	92620	•	26219	33234	60907	•	0
Total Receipts	8	87202289	211634	1440352	4140717	16208974	8309720	14210953	•	5766649	4571069	3267513	•	0
Average Total Receipts	9	10422	259	455	3607	7032	18263	42548	•	140650	351621	653503	•	•
Operating Costs/Operating Income (%)														
Cost of Operations	10	71.6	67.1	52.3	69.0	72.6	69.1	73.3	•	72.2	76.7	72.6	•	•
Salaries and Wages	11	10.1	0.9	8.9	8.5	8.8	10.9	11.0	•	9.4	8.5	9.9	•	•
Taxes Paid	12	1.3	0.2	2.0	1.2	1.2	1.6	1.1	•	1.2	1.2	1.4	•	•
Interest Paid	13	0.9	0.1	1.1	0.2	0.4	0.6	0.5	•	0.9	0.5	0.7	•	•
Depreciation	14	0.8	0.5	1.5	0.4	0.4	1.5	0.4	•	0.9	1.0	0.8	•	•
Amortization and Depletion	15	0.2	•	0.2	0.0	0.1	0.0	0.0	•	0.2	0.1	0.4	•	•
Pensions and Other Deferred Comp.	16	0.4	•	1.0	0.4	0.5	0.5	0.3	•	0.4	0.2	0.6	•	•
Employee Benefits	17	1.1	0.0	0.8	0.8	0.9	1.3	0.7	•	1.0	0.5	1.5	•	•
Advertising	18	0.4	1.1	3.1	0.2	0.4	0.3	0.5	•	0.6	0.5	0.1	•	•
Other Expenses	19	7.7	16.6	16.4	8.9	7.7	7.7	5.8	•	7.8	6.4	9.8	•	•
Officers' Compensation	20	2.1	0.1	6.6	5.5	4.4	3.4	2.3	•	0.9	0.7	1.0	•	•
Operating Margin	21	3.4	13.3	6.1	4.9	2.6	3.1	4.1	•	4.5	3.7	1.3	•	•
Operating Margin Before Officers' Comp.	22	5.5	13.5	12.7	10.4	7.1	6.4	6.4	•	5.4	4.5	2.3	•	•

Selected Average Balance Sheet ($ in Thousands)

Item									
Net Receivables 23	1519	19	226	746	2065	4867	19073	40751	58596
Inventories 24	1438	13	308	893	2800	6222	27698	60171	86653
Net Property, Plant and Equipment 25	455	12	33	148	866	1054	8367	23466	29495
Total Assets 26	4826	90	729	2450	7154	15642	67847	152457	304089
Notes and Loans Payable 27	1348	59	119	462	1993	3727	18049	30629	68648
All Other Liabilities 28	1473	42	250	718	1496	3949	15915	44275	116344
Net Worth 29	2005	-11	360	1270	3664	7966	33883	77552	119096

Selected Financial Ratios (Times to 1)

Item									
Current Ratio 30	2.0	2.0	2.2	2.4	2.3	2.1	2.3	2.1	1.6
Quick Ratio 31	1.1	1.7	1.2	1.3	1.0	1.0	1.1	0.9	0.6
Net Sales to Working Capital 32	6.1	11.9	9.8	5.6	5.2	6.1	4.8	5.6	9.7
Coverage Ratio 33	6.3	115.6	7.1	24.5	13.1	8.3	11.0	6.8	5.9
Total Asset Turnover 34	2.1	•	4.9	2.8	2.5	2.7	2.1	2.3	2.1
Inventory Turnover 35	5.1	18.6	8.1	5.6	4.5	5.0	3.6	4.4	5.4
Receivables Turnover 36	6.9	13.9	11.2	9.4	10.0	8.4	6.0	8.7	11.4
Total Liabilities to Net Worth 37	1.4	•	1.0	0.9	1.0	1.0	1.0	1.0	1.6
Current Assets to Working Capital 38	2.0	2.0	1.9	1.7	1.8	1.9	1.8	1.9	2.6
Current Liabilities to Working Capital 39	1.0	1.0	0.9	0.7	0.8	0.9	0.8	0.9	1.6
Working Capital to Net Sales 40	0.2	0.1	0.1	0.2	0.2	0.2	0.2	0.2	0.1
Inventory to Working Capital 41	0.8	0.3	0.7	0.8	0.9	0.9	0.8	1.0	1.4
Total Receipts to Cash Flow 42	10.0	3.5	5.0	8.5	9.9	10.3	11.5	9.1	11.2
Cost of Goods to Cash Flow 43	7.2	2.3	2.6	5.9	7.2	7.1	8.4	6.6	6.7
Cash Flow to Total Debt 44	0.4	0.9	1.1	0.6	0.5	0.5	0.5	0.4	0.4

Selected Financial Factors (in Percentages)

Item									
Debt Ratio 45	58.5	112.1	50.7	48.2	48.8	49.1	50.1	49.1	60.8
Return on Total Assets 46	11.6	37.6	26.1	13.9	11.9	14.9	12.2	11.5	8.3
Return on Equity Before Income Taxes 47	23.5	•	50.7	24.7	20.4	26.5	20.9	20.5	17.6
Return on Equity After Income Taxes 48	20.2	•	46.4	22.3	18.5	23.9	18.9	17.6	13.1
Profit Margin (Before Income Tax) 49	4.6	13.5	5.1	4.5	4.1	5.0	5.1	4.6	3.3
Profit Margin (After Income Tax) 50	3.9	12.5	4.6	4.1	3.8	4.5	4.6	3.9	2.4

Table I

Corporations with and without Net Income

MACHINERY, EQUIPMENT, AND SUPPLIES

MONEY AMOUNTS AND SIZE OF ASSETS IN THOUSANDS OF DOLLARS

Item Description for Accounting Period 7/08 Through 6/09		Total	Zero Assets	Under 500	500 to 1,000	1,000 to 5,000	5,000 to 10,000	10,000 to 25,000	25,000 to 50,000	50,000 to 100,000	100,000 to 250,000	250,000 to 500,000	500,000 to 2,500,000	2,500,000 and over
Number of Enterprises	1	48173	5436	26062	5317	8199	1426	1087	343	147	92	35	22	7
Revenues ($ in Thousands)														
Net Sales	2	267675551	6424047	15209543	10140990	47886288	23140682	37422883	22272899	18049483	19925736	14123257	19820056	33259686
Interest	3	487840	7328	7643	13325	29520	15958	25753	31725	25706	47048	34388	65336	184110
Rents	4	188024	0	1943	6797	26835	16886	17014	17083	7793	39605	35394	12680	5995
Royalties	5	17140	0	100	0	0	20	18	648	489	0	2108	6975	6781
Other Portfolio Income	6	1244742	10511	47589	17728	74240	68091	158577	177247	121843	169898	138091	255087	5843
Other Receipts	7	3399821	53173	160901	119184	291816	163343	315329	1071577	183114	188989	263241	215674	373479
Total Receipts	8	273013118	6495059	15427719	10298024	48308699	23404980	37939574	23571179	18388428	20371276	14596479	20375808	33835894
Average Total Receipts	9	5667	1195	592	1937	5892	16413	34903	68721	125091	221427	417042	926173	4833699
Operating Costs/Operating Income (%)														
Cost of Operations	10	75.6	92.2	68.9	71.8	73.1	75.1	77.4	78.3	77.6	75.4	72.3	64.9	83.3
Salaries and Wages	11	7.2	2.3	5.6	6.9	8.3	8.1	7.7	7.1	7.1	7.3	7.5	9.4	4.7
Taxes Paid	12	1.1	0.4	1.4	1.6	1.2	1.3	1.0	1.0	1.0	1.1	1.0	1.4	0.8
Interest Paid	13	0.9	0.5	0.5	0.7	0.6	0.7	0.7	0.8	1.0	1.4	1.4	1.8	1.1
Depreciation	14	2.1	0.4	0.5	1.3	1.0	1.2	1.7	2.6	3.1	3.7	5.7	5.4	1.0
Amortization and Depletion	15	0.2	0.0	0.0	0.0	0.0	0.1	0.1	0.1	0.1	0.2	0.3	0.8	0.5
Pensions and Other Deferred Comp.	16	0.4	0.2	0.8	0.2	0.3	0.4	0.3	0.2	0.3	0.5	0.2	0.7	0.6
Employee Benefits	17	0.9	0.5	0.5	0.9	0.7	0.9	0.8	0.8	0.8	1.4	1.5	1.8	0.8
Advertising	18	0.5	0.1	0.5	0.6	0.5	0.4	0.4	0.5	0.3	0.6	0.5	0.4	0.7
Other Expenses	19	7.6	4.3	13.3	10.4	8.7	7.6	6.6	6.6	6.8	7.5	9.2	8.2	4.2
Officers' Compensation	20	2.0	1.2	7.3	5.3	3.4	2.4	1.7	1.3	0.9	0.7	0.4	0.8	0.2
Operating Margin	21	1.5	•	0.6	0.3	2.1	1.9	1.6	0.7	1.0	0.2	•	4.4	2.0
Operating Margin Before Officers' Comp.	22	3.5	•	8.0	5.6	5.5	4.2	3.3	1.9	1.8	0.9	0.4	5.2	2.3

Selected Average Balance Sheet ($ in Thousands)

Net Receivables 23	667	0	31	163	561	1620	3777	7473	15331	30336	58396	162854	886321
Inventories 24	937	0	31	215	864	3319	6252	13577	23595	51287	109509	222388	425994
Net Property, Plant and Equipment 25	429	0	12	90	250	852	2027	5332	11730	27882	72858	178497	257995
Total Assets 26	2953	0	123	712	2202	6904	14934	33940	68800	156897	334138	838647	3539591
Notes and Loans Payable 27	941	0	55	300	639	2210	4624	9907	23514	52945	110411	278661	1025574
All Other Liabilities 28	1022	0	33	198	774	2017	5301	12031	21356	54555	98618	246613	1595971
Net Worth 29	990	0	35	214	789	2678	5009	12003	23930	49398	125109	313373	918045

Selected Financial Ratios (Times to 1)

Current Ratio 30	1.7	•	2.5	2.2	1.7	1.8	1.5	1.6	1.7	1.4	1.6	1.7	1.8
Quick Ratio 31	0.7	•	1.5	1.1	0.8	0.7	0.7	0.6	0.7	0.5	0.6	0.7	0.8
Net Sales to Working Capital 32	6.8	•	9.9	6.0	7.7	6.4	8.3	7.1	6.4	7.4	5.3	5.1	5.2
Coverage Ratio 33	4.8	•	5.2	3.5	6.2	5.0	5.2	8.7	3.9	2.7	3.4	5.0	4.4
Total Asset Turnover 34	1.9	•	4.7	2.7	2.7	2.4	2.3	1.9	1.8	1.4	1.2	1.1	1.3
Inventory Turnover 35	4.5	•	12.9	6.4	4.9	3.7	4.3	3.7	4.0	3.2	2.7	2.6	9.3
Receivables Turnover 36	8.5	•	19.4	11.4	10.2	8.8	9.3	8.0	8.2	7.1	6.9	5.5	6.5
Total Liabilities to Net Worth 37	2.0	•	2.5	2.3	1.8	1.6	2.0	1.8	1.9	2.2	1.7	1.7	2.9
Current Assets to Working Capital 38	2.5	•	1.7	1.8	2.4	2.2	2.9	2.8	2.5	3.4	2.6	2.5	2.3
Current Liabilities to Working Capital 39	1.5	•	0.7	0.8	1.4	1.2	1.9	1.8	1.5	2.4	1.6	1.5	1.3
Working Capital to Net Sales 40	0.1	•	0.1	0.2	0.1	0.2	0.1	0.1	0.2	0.1	0.2	0.2	0.2
Inventory to Working Capital 41	1.2	•	0.5	0.8	1.1	1.3	1.5	1.6	1.3	1.8	1.3	1.3	0.5
Total Receipts to Cash Flow 42	10.7	35.8	7.9	10.5	10.2	11.1	12.4	8.5	12.6	12.3	10.3	7.5	13.7
Cost of Goods to Cash Flow 43	8.1	33.0	5.4	7.5	7.4	8.3	9.6	6.6	9.7	9.3	7.5	4.9	11.4
Cash Flow to Total Debt 44	0.3	•	0.8	0.4	0.4	0.3	0.3	0.3	0.2	0.2	0.2	0.2	0.1

Selected Financial Factors (in Percentages)

Debt Ratio 45	66.5	•	71.3	69.9	64.2	61.2	66.5	64.6	65.2	68.5	62.6	62.6	74.1
Return on Total Assets 46	8.3	•	12.2	6.8	9.6	8.8	8.4	14.1	6.8	5.3	5.7	9.8	6.6
Return on Equity Before Income Taxes 47	19.6	•	34.3	16.3	22.4	18.2	20.3	35.2	14.7	10.6	10.9	21.0	19.7
Return on Equity After Income Taxes 48	15.6	•	32.0	14.8	20.3	15.4	17.6	32.1	10.5	8.2	8.0	14.0	12.2
Profit Margin (Before Income Tax) 49	3.5	•	2.1	1.8	3.0	3.0	3.0	6.5	2.9	2.4	3.4	7.3	3.8
Profit Margin (After Income Tax) 50	2.8	•	1.9	1.7	2.7	2.5	2.6	5.9	2.0	1.9	2.5	4.9	2.4

Table II

Corporations with Net Income

MACHINERY, EQUIPMENT, AND SUPPLIES

MONEY AMOUNTS AND SIZE OF ASSETS IN THOUSANDS OF DOLLARS

Item Description for Accounting Period 7/08 Through 6/09		Total	Zero Assets	Under 500	500 to 1,000	1,000 to 5,000	5,000 to 10,000	10,000 to 25,000	25,000 to 50,000	50,000 to 100,000	100,000 to 250,000	250,000 to 500,000	500,000 to 2,500,000	2,500,000 and over
Number of Enterprises	1	30823	1678	17100	3543	6049	1142	865	238	99	63	25	•	•
Revenues ($ in Thousands)														
Net Sales	2	215091590	5937265	10657391	6915479	39728509	19671879	32145761	16851854	12845121	14503409	10152700	•	•
Interest	3	342327	5237	4323	10352	25436	12613	20919	25648	18851	31383	27142	•	•
Rents	4	128736	0	1778	441	26299	16576	16064	15589	6636	8047	30203	•	•
Royalties	5	9635	0	100	0	0	20	18	648	489	0	2108	•	•
Other Portfolio Income	6	758163	5882	25199	14999	47230	33254	111109	81458	61829	84506	64845	•	•
Other Receipts	7	2859047	39167	128238	79413	246731	150444	224240	1035653	157532	143560	205414	•	•
Total Receipts	8	219189498	5987551	10817029	7020684	40074205	19884786	32518111	18010850	13090458	14770905	10482412	•	•
Average Total Receipts	9	7111	3568	633	1982	6625	17412	37593	75676	132227	234459	419296	•	•
Operating Costs/Operating Income (%)														
Cost of Operations	10	75.5	92.5	65.6	71.2	72.5	74.8	77.8	78.5	76.9	75.5	71.5	•	•
Salaries and Wages	11	6.8	2.1	3.7	6.1	8.1	7.9	7.4	6.6	7.0	7.2	6.9	•	•
Taxes Paid	12	1.1	0.3	1.3	1.4	1.2	1.3	1.0	1.0	1.0	1.1	1.0	•	•
Interest Paid	13	0.7	0.5	0.3	0.5	0.5	0.7	0.6	0.6	0.7	1.1	1.0	•	•
Depreciation	14	1.5	0.2	0.5	0.9	0.9	0.9	1.1	1.6	1.8	2.1	4.5	•	•
Amortization and Depletion	15	0.1	0.0	0.0	0.0	0.0	0.1	0.1	0.1	0.1	0.2	0.3	•	•
Pensions and Other Deferred Comp.	16	0.4	0.2	1.1	0.3	0.4	0.4	0.3	0.2	0.4	0.6	0.2	•	•
Employee Benefits	17	0.9	0.3	0.4	1.0	0.7	0.9	0.7	0.7	0.8	1.3	1.4	•	•
Advertising	18	0.4	0.1	0.4	0.5	0.5	0.4	0.4	0.5	0.3	0.7	0.2	•	•
Other Expenses	19	6.8	2.9	12.1	8.7	8.3	6.9	6.2	6.0	6.3	6.8	8.4	•	•
Officers' Compensation	20	2.0	0.7	8.4	5.2	3.3	2.4	1.5	1.2	0.9	0.6	0.4	•	•
Operating Margin	21	3.7	0.4	6.3	4.2	3.7	3.3	3.0	3.0	3.8	2.9	4.0	•	•
Operating Margin Before Officers' Comp.	22	5.7	1.0	14.6	9.3	7.0	5.8	4.6	4.2	4.7	3.5	4.4	•	•

Selected Average Balance Sheet ($ in Thousands)

	•	•	•	•	•	•	•	•	•	•	•
Net Receivables 23	806	0	31	184	600	1666	3978	8255	16524	31704	60091
Inventories 24	1176	0	25	183	921	3627	6512	14398	25299	60804	125360
Net Property, Plant and Equipment 25	427	0	12	91	238	655	1620	4214	9228	20042	63405
Total Assets 26	3391	0	120	699	2217	6953	14817	34061	68400	158716	330844
Notes and Loans Payable 27	958	0	40	201	599	2034	3963	7105	18040	46464	92644
All Other Liabilities 28	1130	0	26	172	741	1945	5531	13252	20424	55563	101913
Net Worth 29	1303	0	54	327	877	2973	5322	13704	29936	56689	136287

Selected Financial Ratios (Times to 1)

		•	•	•	•	•	•	•	•	•	•
Current Ratio 30	1.8	•	3.1	2.6	1.9	1.9	1.5	1.7	1.8	1.5	1.8
Quick Ratio 31	0.8	•	2.1	1.4	0.9	0.7	0.7	0.7	0.8	0.6	0.7
Net Sales to Working Capital 32	6.4	•	9.6	5.6	7.5	6.0	8.5	6.4	6.1	6.5	4.3
Coverage Ratio 33	8.5	3.6	30.6	11.8	9.8	7.6	8.3	16.5	9.3	5.4	8.1
Total Asset Turnover 34	2.1	•	5.2	2.8	3.0	2.5	2.5	2.1	1.9	1.5	1.2
Inventory Turnover 35	4.5	•	16.2	7.6	5.2	3.6	4.4	3.9	3.9	2.9	2.3
Receivables Turnover 36	8.4	•	•	10.1	10.9	8.5	9.3	7.5	7.4	6.4	6.3
Total Liabilities to Net Worth 37	1.6	•	1.2	1.1	1.5	1.3	1.8	1.5	1.3	1.8	1.4
Current Assets to Working Capital 38	2.2	•	1.5	1.6	2.1	2.1	2.8	2.4	2.3	3.1	2.3
Current Liabilities to Working Capital 39	1.2	•	0.5	0.6	1.1	1.1	1.8	1.4	1.3	2.1	1.3
Working Capital to Net Sales 40	0.2	•	0.1	0.2	0.1	0.2	0.1	0.2	0.2	0.2	0.2
Inventory to Working Capital 41	1.0	•	0.4	0.6	1.0	1.2	1.4	1.3	1.1	1.7	1.1
Total Receipts to Cash Flow 42	9.2	26.4	5.7	8.1	9.1	10.2	11.2	6.9	9.6	10.2	7.8
Cost of Goods to Cash Flow 43	7.0	24.5	3.7	5.8	6.6	7.6	8.7	5.4	7.4	7.7	5.6
Cash Flow to Total Debt 44	0.4	•	1.7	0.6	0.5	0.4	0.4	0.5	0.4	0.2	0.3

Selected Financial Factors (in Percentages)

		•	•	•	•	•	•	•	•	•	•
Debt Ratio 45	61.6	•	55.1	53.2	60.5	57.2	64.1	59.8	56.2	64.3	58.8
Return on Total Assets 46	13.1	•	41.7	17.4	15.0	12.5	12.1	21.8	12.2	8.5	10.2
Return on Equity Before Income Taxes 47	30.1	•	89.9	34.0	34.0	25.5	29.5	50.8	24.8	19.3	21.6
Return on Equity After Income Taxes 48	25.3	•	87.6	32.6	31.4	22.4	26.3	46.9	19.9	16.2	18.0
Profit Margin (Before Income Tax) 49	5.6	1.2	7.8	5.7	4.5	4.4	4.2	9.8	5.7	4.7	7.3
Profit Margin (After Income Tax) 50	4.7	1.1	7.6	5.5	4.2	3.9	3.8	9.1	4.6	4.0	6.0

Table I

Corporations with and without Net Income

FURNITURE, SPORTS, TOYS, JEWELRY, OTHER DURABLE GOODS

MONEY AMOUNTS AND SIZE OF ASSETS IN THOUSANDS OF DOLLARS

Item Description for Accounting Period 7/08 Through 6/09	Total	Zero Assets	Under 500	500 to 1,000	1,000 to 5,000	5,000 to 10,000	10,000 to 25,000	25,000 to 50,000	50,000 to 100,000	100,000 to 250,000	250,000 to 500,000	500,000 to 2,500,000	2,500,000 and over
Number of Enterprises **1**	71709	12862	42728	5520	7918	1326	884	248	128	57	21	11	5
Revenues ($ in Thousands)													
Net Sales **2**	259036752	6535601	16966021	9297689	56637620	20372444	32410637	24939646	16373778	19223238	13334681	12787376	30158022
Interest **3**	417171	5575	5380	15598	29377	14545	34261	28619	20493	37496	46311	17247	162267
Rents **4**	102063	490	5812	50	8216	2643	4086	4882	4495	7689	2024	31916	29760
Royalties **5**	336011	1443	0	14591	15460	1077	13535	6131	50571	21536	80582	6932	124153
Other Portfolio Income **6**	480934	16384	17320	12754	71232	20670	38580	22295	44201	18026	15973	156648	46851
Other Receipts **7**	1835992	109257	180521	48841	365104	148375	180182	169444	139142	134544	207536	34822	118227
Total Receipts **8**	262208923	6668750	17175054	9389523	57127009	20559754	32681281	25171017	16632680	19442529	13687107	13034941	30639280
Average Total Receipts **9**	3657	518	402	1701	7215	15505	36970	101496	129943	341097	651767	1184995	6127856
Operating Costs/Operating Income (%)													
Cost of Operations **10**	79.2	84.5	66.9	68.8	77.1	71.2	80.4	83.9	78.3	82.6	83.3	80.2	88.2
Salaries and Wages **11**	5.7	7.9	6.6	7.2	5.7	8.8	6.0	4.7	6.1	4.8	5.1	5.4	3.6
Taxes Paid **12**	0.9	0.7	1.3	1.5	1.0	1.3	1.0	0.7	1.1	0.7	0.8	0.9	0.5
Interest Paid **13**	0.8	1.2	0.5	0.7	0.5	0.8	0.7	0.8	1.1	0.9	0.8	2.2	1.1
Depreciation **14**	0.7	0.4	0.6	0.9	0.7	0.6	0.7	0.7	1.1	0.8	1.3	1.0	0.6
Amortization and Depletion **15**	0.3	0.9	0.1	0.1	0.0	0.1	0.1	0.1	0.3	0.3	0.4	1.3	0.9
Pensions and Other Deferred Comp. **16**	0.2	0.1	0.7	0.2	0.2	0.3	0.1	0.1	0.2	0.2	0.1	0.3	0.2
Employee Benefits **17**	0.4	0.5	0.4	0.4	0.3	0.6	0.5	0.4	0.7	0.6	1.0	0.7	0.2
Advertising **18**	1.3	0.5	0.9	1.4	1.1	0.9	1.0	1.1	1.6	1.9	2.3	1.7	1.8
Other Expenses **19**	8.0	9.8	16.1	14.5	9.1	10.1	7.1	6.0	8.3	6.0	6.3	5.8	2.7
Officers' Compensation **20**	2.0	0.7	7.8	4.2	2.5	3.3	2.0	0.8	1.2	0.6	0.8	0.5	0.3
Operating Margin **21**	0.3	•	•	0.1	1.9	1.9	0.4	0.7	0.1	0.6	•	0.1	•
Operating Margin Before Officers' Comp. **22**	2.3	•	6.0	4.4	4.4	5.3	2.4	1.5	1.3	1.2	•	•	0.2

Selected Average Balance Sheet ($ in Thousands)

Net Receivables 23	358	15	153	559	1808	4263	10888	17878	39296	113183	106321	568977
Inventories 24	465	39	287	797	2922	5738	13717	23356	47093	50585	184235	536424
Net Property, Plant and Equipment 25	126	9	95	207	407	1290	3804	6706	12511	31666	77432	162629
Total Assets 26	1537	104	662	2285	6983	15257	36520	68247	148095	333032	927548	3563514
Notes and Loans Payable 27	482	75	274	619	1971	4732	12396	22839	43236	77213	329551	895158
All Other Liabilities 28	550	30	237	809	2589	5249	14459	24509	54064	137284	208910	1480481
Net Worth 29	504	0	150	857	2422	5276	9665	20899	50795	118535	389087	1187875

Selected Financial Ratios (Times to 1)

Current Ratio 30	1.6	2.1	1.9	1.9	1.6	1.6	1.5	1.6	1.7	1.5	2.1	1.1
Quick Ratio 31	0.7	0.9	0.8	0.9	0.8	0.8	0.7	0.7	0.9	0.9	0.8	0.4
Net Sales to Working Capital 32	8.8	9.4	6.5	8.1	6.9	7.7	10.6	6.8	8.2	7.9	6.5	26.4
Coverage Ratio 33	2.9	•	2.6	6.9	4.6	2.6	3.1	2.5	3.0	2.3	2.1	2.4
Total Asset Turnover 34	2.4	3.8	2.5	3.1	2.2	2.4	2.8	1.9	2.3	1.9	1.3	1.7
Inventory Turnover 35	6.1	6.8	4.0	6.9	3.7	5.1	6.1	4.3	5.9	10.5	5.1	9.9
Receivables Turnover 36	9.3	27.4	10.9	13.3	7.8	7.7	8.3	6.3	7.5	6.2	6.7	9.5
Total Liabilities to Net Worth 37	2.0	3822.8	3.4	1.7	1.9	1.9	2.8	2.3	1.9	1.8	1.4	2.0
Current Assets to Working Capital 38	2.6	1.9	2.1	2.1	2.6	2.6	3.1	2.7	2.4	3.0	1.9	8.5
Current Liabilities to Working Capital 39	1.6	0.9	1.1	1.1	1.6	1.6	2.1	1.7	1.4	2.0	0.9	7.5
Working Capital to Net Sales 40	0.1	0.1	0.2	0.1	0.1	0.1	0.1	0.1	0.1	0.1	0.2	0.0
Inventory to Working Capital 41	1.1	1.0	1.1	1.0	1.2	1.2	1.3	1.1	1.0	0.9	0.8	2.7
Total Receipts to Cash Flow 42	13.7	9.3	9.1	11.0	9.9	15.4	16.5	11.9	16.4	18.8	16.9	29.8
Cost of Goods to Cash Flow 43	10.9	6.2	6.3	8.5	7.1	12.4	13.8	9.3	13.5	15.6	13.5	26.3
Cash Flow to Total Debt 44	0.3	0.4	0.4	0.5	0.3	0.2	0.2	0.2	0.2	0.2	0.1	0.1

Selected Financial Factors (in Percentages)

Debt Ratio 45	67.2	100.0	77.3	62.5	65.3	65.4	73.5	69.4	65.7	64.4	58.1	66.7
Return on Total Assets 46	5.7	•	4.7	10.0	8.0	4.6	6.7	5.3	5.9	3.5	5.8	4.4
Return on Equity Before Income Taxes 47	11.4	•	12.5	22.8	18.1	8.2	17.2	10.3	11.5	5.5	7.4	7.8
Return on Equity After Income Taxes 48	8.6	•	11.2	21.3	16.6	6.6	14.1	6.8	8.3	1.2	2.9	4.3
Profit Margin (Before Income Tax) 49	1.6	•	1.1	2.7	2.9	1.2	1.7	1.7	1.7	1.0	2.5	1.5
Profit Margin (After Income Tax) 50	1.2	•	1.0	2.6	2.6	1.0	1.4	1.1	1.3	0.2	1.0	0.8

Table II

Corporations with Net Income

FURNITURE, SPORTS, TOYS, JEWELRY, OTHER DURABLE GOODS

MONEY AMOUNTS AND SIZE OF ASSETS IN THOUSANDS OF DOLLARS

Item Description for Accounting Period 7/08 Through 6/09	Total	Zero Assets	Under 500	500 to 1,000	1,000 to 5,000	5,000 to 10,000	10,000 to 25,000	25,000 to 50,000	50,000 to 100,000	100,000 to 250,000	250,000 to 500,000	500,000 to 2,500,000	2,500,000 and over
Number of Enterprises **1**	34535	4600	18414	3577	6019	990	624	168	85	36	•	7	•
Revenues ($ in Thousands)													
Net Sales **2**	201632762	1000412	8830703	6977921	49534396	15707905	24523867	19326364	12780313	14422393	•	11588407	•
Interest **3**	309472	4584	3405	11645	25275	9096	9810	19676	12118	12306	•	9966	•
Rents **4**	86132	0	5812	46	5862	2639	2833	3279	1994	1116	•	31916	•
Royalties **5**	266153	0	0	14591	15460	0	12591	6101	50056	8228	•	4511	•
Other Portfolio Income **6**	384906	16232	5374	12730	46358	17004	19773	18979	35227	12929	•	148416	•
Other Receipts **7**	1455970	103535	203922	40281	303294	86896	152704	104012	120526	71785	•	38760	•
Total Receipts **8**	204135395	1124763	9049216	7057214	49930645	15823540	24721578	19478411	13000234	14528757	•	11821976	•
Average Total Receipts **9**	5911	245	491	1973	8296	15983	39618	115943	152944	403577	•	1688854	•
Operating Costs/Operating Income (%)													
Cost of Operations **10**	79.7	69.5	61.1	69.8	77.5	70.3	80.4	84.9	78.6	83.2	•	80.8	•
Salaries and Wages **11**	5.0	8.3	6.8	6.3	5.1	7.9	5.6	4.0	5.4	4.0	•	5.2	•
Taxes Paid **12**	0.9	1.3	1.3	1.4	0.9	1.3	1.0	0.7	0.9	0.6	•	0.9	•
Interest Paid **13**	0.6	0.7	0.3	0.7	0.4	0.7	0.6	0.6	0.7	0.6	•	1.2	•
Depreciation **14**	0.7	0.4	0.6	1.0	0.5	0.6	0.6	0.6	1.0	0.7	•	1.0	•
Amortization and Depletion **15**	0.2	0.0	0.1	0.0	0.0	0.0	0.1	0.0	0.1	0.2	•	0.4	•
Pensions and Other Deferred Comp. **16**	0.2	0.4	0.8	0.2	0.2	0.3	0.1	0.1	0.2	0.1	•	0.2	•
Employee Benefits **17**	0.4	0.2	0.3	0.2	0.2	0.5	0.4	0.3	0.6	0.5	•	0.7	•
Advertising **18**	1.2	1.0	0.4	1.5	1.1	0.6	0.8	0.8	1.5	1.5	•	1.6	•
Other Expenses **19**	6.6	19.1	13.9	12.6	8.5	8.6	5.8	4.6	6.7	5.0	•	5.5	•
Officers' Compensation **20**	1.9	3.1	9.1	3.5	2.4	3.8	1.6	0.8	1.2	0.7	•	0.4	•
Operating Margin **21**	2.8	•	5.3	2.9	3.3	5.2	2.9	2.7	3.0	3.1	•	2.3	•
Operating Margin Before Officers' Comp. **22**	4.7	•	14.3	6.4	9.1	9.1	4.6	3.5	4.2	3.7	•	2.7	•

Selected Average Balance Sheet ($ in Thousands)

	•	•	•	•	•	•	•	•	•	•	•
Net Receivables 23	555	0	21	165	590	1914	4528	10793	19737	46996	145647
Inventories 24	717	0	36	273	834	2996	5863	14905	25594	54005	256898
Net Property, Plant and Equipment 25	183	0	9	97	191	399	1203	3573	6566	12649	110406
Total Assets 26	2262	0	120	670	2356	6981	15340	36034	68291	152186	958504
Notes and Loans Payable 27	600	0	46	231	585	1860	4290	12007	15308	38780	330061
All Other Liabilities 28	799	0	30	200	794	2335	5255	12170	25504	57017	245478
Net Worth 29	862	0	43	239	977	2786	5795	11857	27479	56389	382965

Selected Financial Ratios (Times to 1)

	•	•	•	•	•	•	•	•	•	•	•
Current Ratio 30	1.8	•	2.5	2.2	2.0	1.9	1.7	1.7	1.6	1.9	2.2
Quick Ratio 31	0.8	•	1.4	1.0	1.0	0.9	0.8	0.8	0.8	0.9	0.9
Net Sales to Working Capital 32	8.2	•	8.5	6.5	8.3	5.9	7.9	9.8	7.3	7.8	7.7
Coverage Ratio 33	7.7	13.0	28.0	7.1	10.4	9.8	7.5	6.9	7.7	7.6	5.0
Total Asset Turnover 34	2.6	•	4.0	2.9	3.5	2.3	2.6	3.2	2.2	2.6	1.7
Inventory Turnover 35	6.5	•	8.1	5.0	7.6	3.7	5.4	6.6	4.6	6.2	5.2
Receivables Turnover 36	9.2	•	•	11.3	14.3	7.2	7.5	8.6	6.1	7.2	7.1
Total Liabilities to Net Worth 37	1.6	•	1.8	1.8	1.4	1.5	1.6	2.0	1.5	1.7	1.5
Current Assets to Working Capital 38	2.3	•	1.7	1.8	2.0	2.2	2.5	2.5	2.6	2.2	1.8
Current Liabilities to Working Capital 39	1.3	•	0.7	0.8	1.0	1.2	1.5	1.5	1.6	1.2	0.8
Working Capital to Net Sales 40	0.1	•	0.1	0.2	0.1	0.2	0.1	0.1	0.1	0.1	0.1
Inventory to Working Capital 41	1.0	•	0.6	0.9	0.9	1.0	1.1	1.1	1.1	0.9	0.9
Total Receipts to Cash Flow 42	11.5	4.9	5.6	8.0	9.9	8.4	12.8	14.9	9.8	13.3	12.6
Cost of Goods to Cash Flow 43	9.2	3.4	3.4	5.6	7.6	5.9	10.3	12.6	7.7	11.1	10.2
Cash Flow to Total Debt 44	0.4	•	1.1	0.6	0.6	0.4	0.3	0.3	0.4	0.3	0.2

Selected Financial Factors (in Percentages)

	•	•	•	•	•	•	•	•	•	•	•
Debt Ratio 45	61.9	•	63.9	64.3	58.5	60.1	62.2	67.1	59.8	62.9	60.0
Return on Total Assets 46	12.2	•	32.0	13.6	15.7	15.1	11.0	12.9	12.0	11.6	10.1
Return on Equity Before Income Taxes 47	27.9	•	85.5	32.7	34.2	33.9	25.1	33.6	25.9	27.1	20.2
Return on Equity After Income Taxes 48	24.4	•	84.2	31.4	32.4	32.2	23.1	30.0	21.9	22.6	13.2
Profit Margin (Before Income Tax) 49	4.1	8.4	7.7	4.0	4.1	6.0	3.7	3.5	4.7	3.8	4.7
Profit Margin (After Income Tax) 50	3.6	7.7	7.6	3.9	3.8	5.7	3.4	3.1	4.0	3.2	3.1

Table I

Corporations with and without Net Income

PAPER AND PAPER PRODUCT

MONEY AMOUNTS AND SIZE OF ASSETS IN THOUSANDS OF DOLLARS

Item Description for Accounting Period 7/08 Through 6/09		Total	Zero Assets	Under 500	500 to 1,000	1,000 to 5,000	5,000 to 10,000	10,000 to 25,000	25,000 to 50,000	50,000 to 100,000	100,000 to 250,000	250,000 to 500,000	500,000 to 2,500,000	2,500,000 and over
Number of Enterprises	1	9542	1601	6218	793	587	133	111	56	22	12	5	5	0
Revenues ($ in Thousands)														
Net Sales	2	51792816	413117	1951984	2181991	5264919	3449835	5656853	5744430	4758124	7821958	2179088	12370517	0
Interest	3	29483	33	790	1185	2442	3413	3021	1090	640	3644	542	12683	0
Rents	4	8454	0	0	24	1512	0	408	728	1557	412	526	3287	0
Royalties	5	23326	0	0	0	6509	0	0	0	264	0	8718	7835	0
Other Portfolio Income	6	62870	0	32088	0	7693	289	2605	225	3014	1056	15722	178	0
Other Receipts	7	288094	229	3375	2687	93006	23144	18366	41743	10454	72341	5564	17185	0
Total Receipts	8	52205043	413379	1988237	2185887	5376081	3476681	5681253	5788216	4774053	7899411	2210160	12411685	0
Average Total Receipts	9	5471	258	320	2756	9159	26140	51182	103361	217002	658284	442032	2482337	•
Operating Costs/Operating Income (%)														
Cost of Operations	10	82.8	74.6	60.5	68.8	74.7	82.1	80.3	83.3	84.2	90.7	86.0	87.7	•
Salaries and Wages	11	5.9	1.1	6.8	6.1	10.0	7.5	6.5	7.1	6.0	3.6	4.4	4.4	•
Taxes Paid	12	0.7	0.6	1.8	1.0	1.3	1.1	0.8	0.8	0.6	0.4	0.4	0.5	•
Interest Paid	13	0.8	0.2	0.7	0.1	0.8	0.5	0.4	0.6	0.6	0.6	3.8	1.1	•
Depreciation	14	0.7	0.2	0.5	0.6	0.9	0.4	0.6	0.7	0.9	0.3	2.6	0.6	•
Amortization and Depletion	15	0.2	0.0	0.1	0.0	0.1	0.1	0.0	0.2	0.1	0.1	0.9	0.4	•
Pensions and Other Deferred Comp.	16	0.2	•	0.0	1.1	0.2	0.1	0.2	0.2	0.2	0.1	0.1	0.3	•
Employee Benefits	17	0.4	0.1	0.3	0.3	0.8	0.3	0.4	0.7	0.5	0.2	0.5	0.3	•
Advertising	18	0.2	0.2	0.8	0.2	0.2	0.3	0.9	0.2	0.1	0.0	0.1	0.1	•
Other Expenses	19	5.8	10.1	19.7	8.8	9.6	3.4	5.7	5.5	5.4	4.0	5.7	3.6	•
Officers' Compensation	20	1.2	5.5	5.5	3.3	2.4	1.8	1.9	0.9	0.9	0.3	0.3	0.2	•
Operating Margin	21	0.9	7.5	3.2	9.7	•	2.4	2.2	•	0.6	•	0.5	0.8	•
Operating Margin Before Officers' Comp.	22	2.1	13.0	8.6	13.0	1.4	4.2	4.0	0.9	1.5	•	0.9	0.9	•

Selected Average Balance Sheet ($ in Thousands)

Line Item													
Net Receivables 23	617	0	17	211	838	3813	5786	13508	23040	103561	44767	249060	•
Inventories 24	377	0	22	114	753	1152	3784	9875	21672	37538	21544	154631	•
Net Property, Plant and Equipment 25	194	0	7	90	268	759	1580	3362	10572	12076	71200	75877	•
Total Assets 26	1688	0	86	726	2203	7029	15363	33850	70048	167658	317520	804863	•
Notes and Loans Payable 27	594	0	67	17	692	2295	4003	9902	23876	63665	186295	261567	•
All Other Liabilities 28	684	0	36	270	764	3250	5600	13122	26399	73644	83829	393445	•
Net Worth 29	409	0	-17	438	747	1484	5760	10826	19773	30349	47396	149851	•

Selected Financial Ratios (Times to 1)

Line Item													
Current Ratio 30	1.4	•	1.5	2.1	1.6	1.5	1.7	1.4	1.4	1.9	1.2	1.0	•
Quick Ratio 31	0.9	•	0.8	1.7	0.9	1.1	1.1	0.8	0.7	1.4	0.7	0.6	•
Net Sales to Working Capital 32	15.5	•	16.9	8.8	14.7	12.6	10.0	12.7	12.9	8.9	28.0	2362.6	•
Coverage Ratio 33	3.0	45.4	8.4	194.7	2.4	6.9	7.3	2.6	2.6	2.1	0.1	2.0	•
Total Asset Turnover 34	3.2	•	3.6	3.8	4.1	3.7	3.3	3.0	3.1	3.9	1.4	3.1	•
Inventory Turnover 35	11.9	•	8.7	16.7	8.9	18.5	10.8	8.7	8.4	15.7	17.4	14.0	•
Receivables Turnover 36	8.7	•	11.9	13.1	8.9	9.9	8.5	7.1	9.6	6.6	9.4	9.4	•
Total Liabilities to Net Worth 37	3.1	•	•	0.7	1.9	3.7	1.7	2.1	2.5	4.5	5.7	4.4	•
Current Assets to Working Capital 38	3.4	•	3.2	1.9	2.8	3.0	2.4	3.3	3.2	2.1	6.0	427.8	•
Current Liabilities to Working Capital 39	2.4	•	2.2	0.9	1.8	2.0	1.4	2.3	2.2	1.1	5.0	426.8	•
Working Capital to Net Sales 40	0.1	•	0.1	0.1	0.1	0.1	0.1	0.1	0.1	0.1	0.0	0.0	•
Inventory to Working Capital 41	1.0	•	0.8	0.4	1.0	0.7	0.7	1.2	1.4	0.5	1.6	145.9	•
Total Receipts to Cash Flow 42	17.4	7.8	5.6	5.9	12.7	20.3	14.7	20.6	22.1	27.3	135.9	28.3	•
Cost of Goods to Cash Flow 43	14.4	5.8	3.4	4.1	9.5	16.6	11.8	17.1	18.6	24.7	116.9	24.8	•
Cash Flow to Total Debt 44	0.2	•	0.5	1.6	0.2	0.2	0.4	0.2	0.2	0.0	0.2	0.1	•

Selected Financial Factors (in Percentages)

Line Item													
Debt Ratio 45	75.8	•	120.2	39.7	66.1	78.9	62.5	68.0	71.8	81.9	85.1	81.4	•
Return on Total Assets 46	8.1	•	20.6	37.6	7.7	13.6	10.0	4.6	4.6	5.0	0.6	6.8	•
Return on Equity Before Income Taxes 47	22.3	•	•	62.0	13.3	55.0	23.0	8.9	10.0	14.3	•	18.0	•
Return on Equity After Income Taxes 48	19.1	•	•	62.0	11.8	51.2	20.4	5.5	9.1	11.8	•	10.2	•
Profit Margin (Before Income Tax) 49	1.7	7.6	•	9.9	1.1	3.1	2.6	0.9	0.9	0.8	0.7	1.1	•
Profit Margin (After Income Tax) 50	1.4	7.6	•	9.9	1.0	2.9	2.3	0.6	0.8	0.6	0.6	0.6	•

Table II

Corporations with Net Income

PAPER AND PAPER PRODUCT

MONEY AMOUNTS AND SIZE OF ASSETS IN THOUSANDS OF DOLLARS

Item Description for Accounting Period 7/08 Through 6/09	Total	Zero Assets	Under 500	500 to 1,000	1,000 to 5,000	5,000 to 10,000	10,000 to 25,000	25,000 to 50,000	50,000 to 100,000	100,000 to 250,000	250,000 to 500,000	500,000 to 2,500,000	2,500,000 and over
Number of Enterprises **1**	6506	1091	4126	599	391	129	99	40	18	•	0	•	0

Revenues ($ in Thousands)

Item	Total	Zero Assets	Under 500	500 to 1,000	1,000 to 5,000	5,000 to 10,000	10,000 to 25,000	25,000 to 50,000	50,000 to 100,000	100,000 to 250,000	250,000 to 500,000	500,000 to 2,500,000	2,500,000 and over
Net Sales **2**	39155691	296149	1159970	1785617	3586590	3276771	5330586	4429852	4357279	•	•	•	0
Interest **3**	22739	33	790	1	716	3413	3018	681	574	•	•	•	0
Rents **4**	2575	0	0	24	7	0	408	167	1557	•	•	•	0
Royalties **5**	6337	0	0	0	0	0	0	0	4	•	•	•	0
Other Portfolio Income **6**	59795	0	32088	0	7384	289	2605	36	1310	•	•	•	0
Other Receipts **7**	205447	210	537	63	42321	22447	15850	49260	11374	•	•	•	0
Total Receipts **8**	39452584	296392	1193385	1785705	3637018	3302920	5352467	4479996	4372098	•	•	•	0
Average Total Receipts **9**	6064	272	289	2981	9302	25604	54065	112000	242894	•	•	•	•

Operating Costs/Operating Income (%)

Item	Total	Zero Assets	Under 500	500 to 1,000	1,000 to 5,000	5,000 to 10,000	10,000 to 25,000	25,000 to 50,000	50,000 to 100,000	100,000 to 250,000	250,000 to 500,000	500,000 to 2,500,000	2,500,000 and over
Cost of Operations **10**	82.1	65.7	53.6	65.5	72.4	81.6	80.6	84.5	85.9	•	•	•	•
Salaries and Wages **11**	5.8	0.5	5.8	6.5	10.7	7.7	6.4	6.2	5.5	•	•	•	•
Taxes Paid **12**	0.7	0.8	1.3	1.0	1.3	1.1	0.8	0.8	0.6	•	•	•	•
Interest Paid **13**	0.7	0.2	0.9	0.0	0.5	0.5	0.4	0.4	0.5	•	•	•	•
Depreciation **14**	0.6	0.2	0.5	0.7	0.7	0.4	0.4	0.6	0.5	•	•	•	•
Amortization and Depletion **15**	0.2	0.0	0.0	•	0.1	0.1	0.0	0.2	0.1	•	•	•	•
Pensions and Other Deferred Comp. **16**	0.2	•	•	0.6	0.3	0.1	0.2	0.2	0.2	•	•	•	•
Employee Benefits **17**	0.4	0.1	0.5	0.3	0.9	0.3	0.4	0.6	0.5	•	•	•	•
Advertising **18**	0.2	0.2	1.1	0.2	0.2	0.3	0.8	0.1	0.1	•	•	•	•
Other Expenses **19**	5.3	10.5	22.9	8.9	9.4	3.4	5.2	4.4	4.3	•	•	•	•
Officers' Compensation **20**	1.2	7.5	6.7	2.9	1.8	1.9	1.9	0.8	0.8	•	•	•	•
Operating Margin **21**	2.4	14.4	6.8	13.3	1.7	2.5	2.8	1.1	1.1	•	•	•	•
Operating Margin Before Officers' Comp. **22**	3.6	21.9	13.4	16.2	3.5	4.4	4.8	2.0	1.9	•	•	•	•

Selected Average Balance Sheet ($ in Thousands)

Net Receivables 23	700	0	18	198	849	3764	6016	14571	25923
Inventories 24	399	0	9	111	760	1022	4099	11072	25916
Net Property, Plant and Equipment 25	172	0	4	110	267	776	1122	2518	7014
Total Assets 26	1829	0	59	728	2227	6940	15412	34257	68405
Notes and Loans Payable 27	551	0	20	2	707	2108	3498	9281	23515
All Other Liabilities 28	752	0	21	270	659	3298	5836	14180	26360
Net Worth 29	526	0	19	456	860	1534	6078	10796	18530

Selected Financial Ratios (Times to 1)

Current Ratio 30	1.4	•	1.6	2.1	1.6	1.6	1.7	1.4	1.5
Quick Ratio 31	0.9	•	1.4	1.7	0.9	1.1	1.1	0.8	0.8
Net Sales to Working Capital 32	16.2	•	19.6	9.9	14.6	11.8	9.8	12.6	12.1
Coverage Ratio 33	5.4	78.7	12.0	790.6	6.8	7.4	8.8	6.9	3.7
Total Asset Turnover 34	3.3	•	4.8	4.1	4.1	3.7	3.5	3.2	3.5
Inventory Turnover 35	12.4	•	17.2	17.6	8.7	20.3	10.6	8.5	8.0
Receivables Turnover 36	8.8	•	11.4	13.1	7.9	10.3	8.4	7.3	•
Total Liabilities to Net Worth 37	2.5	•	2.2	0.6	1.6	3.5	1.5	2.2	2.7
Current Assets to Working Capital 38	3.5	•	2.6	1.9	2.7	2.8	2.3	3.2	2.8
Current Liabilities to Working Capital 39	2.5	•	1.6	0.9	1.7	1.8	1.3	2.2	1.8
Working Capital to Net Sales 40	0.1	•	0.1	0.1	0.1	0.1	0.1	0.1	0.1
Inventory to Working Capital 41	1.1	•	0.3	0.3	1.1	0.7	0.7	1.2	1.3
Total Receipts to Cash Flow 42	14.4	4.9	4.0	4.8	10.7	19.5	14.3	17.9	22.2
Cost of Goods to Cash Flow 43	11.8	3.2	2.2	3.2	7.8	15.9	11.5	15.1	19.0
Cash Flow to Total Debt 44	0.3	•	1.7	2.3	0.6	0.2	0.4	0.3	0.2

Selected Financial Factors (in Percentages)

Debt Ratio 45	71.2	•	68.4	37.3	61.4	77.9	60.6	68.5	72.9
Return on Total Assets 46	12.7	•	50.4	54.5	15.0	14.1	12.8	9.5	7.1
Return on Equity Before Income Taxes 47	36.1	•	146.1	86.9	33.1	55.3	28.8	25.8	19.1
Return on Equity After Income Taxes 48	32.5	•	146.0	86.9	31.2	51.5	26.0	21.0	17.9
Profit Margin (Before Income Tax) 49	3.2	14.4	9.6	13.3	3.1	3.3	3.2	2.5	1.5
Profit Margin (After Income Tax) 50	2.8	14.4	9.6	13.3	2.9	3.1	2.9	2.0	1.4

Table I

Corporations with and without Net Income

DRUGS AND DRUGGISTS' SUNDRIES

MONEY AMOUNTS AND SIZE OF ASSETS IN THOUSANDS OF DOLLARS

Item Description for Accounting Period 7/08 Through 6/09		Total	Zero Assets	Under 500	500 to 1,000	1,000 to 5,000	5,000 to 10,000	10,000 to 25,000	25,000 to 50,000	50,000 to 100,000	100,000 to 250,000	250,000 to 500,000	500,000 to 2,500,000	2,500,000 and over
Number of Enterprises	1	5683	1469	2339	588	826	153	144	51	35	32	13	18	14
Revenues ($ in Thousands)														
Net Sales	2	379236298	787178	1305695	858227	5695694	3319795	4609048	4738724	4737108	7070226	13359378	19024515	313730709
Interest	3	541097	99	982	1001	3537	3270	4535	5515	12795	15560	12074	120970	360759
Rents	4	590586	0	0	0	672	0	369	600	203	121	628	4497	583495
Royalties	5	2819397	1702	0	0	33500	157	199	3116	92779	1657	721	127264	2558303
Other Portfolio Income	6	423798	119552	2307	3	10233	3380	12332	2362	20385	8439	1893	76456	166459
Other Receipts	7	4115826	19974	12060	6742	37978	12258	21523	99413	117818	37983	55792	406845	3287440
Total Receipts	8	387727002	928505	1321044	865973	5781614	3338860	4648006	4849730	4981088	7133986	13430486	19760547	320687165
Average Total Receipts	9	68226	632	565	1473	7000	21823	32278	95093	142317	222937	1033114	1097808	22906226
Operating Costs/Operating Income (%)														
Cost of Operations	10	85.5	76.9	64.2	67.8	68.8	75.8	70.2	81.5	68.9	67.4	88.1	51.9	88.9
Salaries and Wages	11	3.8	7.6	8.9	7.9	7.6	7.2	8.8	5.4	8.4	9.4	2.9	10.9	3.0
Taxes Paid	12	0.5	1.2	1.9	1.3	1.2	0.7	1.3	0.6	1.0	1.3	0.4	1.5	0.3
Interest Paid	13	0.6	5.7	0.1	0.6	0.4	0.8	0.6	0.3	0.8	1.0	0.9	1.8	0.5
Depreciation	14	0.6	0.3	0.5	0.6	0.6	0.3	0.7	0.4	1.1	0.8	0.5	1.4	0.5
Amortization and Depletion	15	0.3	0.0	0.2	0.0	0.1	0.0	0.4	0.1	0.7	0.5	0.2	1.2	0.3
Pensions and Other Deferred Comp.	16	0.1	0.1	0.2	0.3	0.1	0.1	0.1	0.1	0.2	0.2	0.3	0.3	0.1
Employee Benefits	17	0.4	0.4	0.1	0.2	0.2	0.4	0.6	0.5	0.7	0.5	0.2	1.6	0.4
Advertising	18	0.8	1.3	1.6	1.2	0.7	0.8	1.9	1.0	3.6	1.6	0.3	3.0	0.6
Other Expenses	19	6.2	28.8	21.0	20.3	16.3	11.8	13.0	8.3	13.6	12.7	4.8	22.3	4.5
Officers' Compensation	20	0.4	2.6	7.2	3.9	3.4	1.5	2.4	1.1	1.3	0.8	0.2	0.5	0.2
Operating Margin	21	0.7	•	•	•	0.6	0.7	0.1	0.8	•	3.8	1.1	3.6	0.6
Operating Margin Before Officers' Comp.	22	1.1	•	1.3	•	4.0	2.2	2.4	2.0	0.8	4.6	1.3	4.1	0.8

Selected Average Balance Sheet ($ in Thousands)

Net Receivables 23	5682	0	11	102	664	2300	4346	9780	17285	23072	110415	159674	1752033
Inventories 24	5393	0	57	176	700	3201	5501	9476	15025	27584	103074	108536	1668957
Net Property, Plant and Equipment 25	1960	0	11	64	207	436	840	1881	7063	19605	27408	61446	591783
Total Assets 26	32461	0	152	763	2341	7990	15891	33786	74859	145907	380747	1112697	10302632
Notes and Loans Payable 27	6450	0	158	130	675	1438	3631	6091	16194	53945	146847	236150	1867807
All Other Liabilities 28	13827	0	42	218	1453	3716	6850	14618	26181	35013	151654	293445	4682915
Net Worth 29	12184	0	-48	415	213	2836	5410	13077	32484	56949	82245	583101	3751911

Selected Financial Ratios (Times to 1)

Current Ratio 30	1.2	•	2.7	1.8	1.3	1.4	1.5	1.6	1.6	1.2	1.7	1.8	1.1
Quick Ratio 31	0.6	•	0.9	1.0	0.6	0.6	0.7	0.9	0.9	0.7	0.9	0.9	0.6
Net Sales to Working Capital 32	29.7	•	7.7	6.8	17.2	13.1	7.2	9.7	7.1	13.6	9.2	4.0	92.8
Coverage Ratio 33	6.0	•	•	•	5.7	2.7	2.5	11.5	6.7	5.6	2.8	5.4	6.6
Total Asset Turnover 34	2.1	•	3.7	1.9	2.9	2.7	2.0	2.8	1.8	1.5	2.7	0.9	2.2
Inventory Turnover 35	10.6	•	6.3	5.6	6.8	5.1	4.1	8.0	6.2	5.4	8.8	5.1	11.9
Receivables Turnover 36	12.0	•	56.6	14.3	11.1	9.9	6.3	10.0	7.4	8.7	9.3	6.7	13.2
Total Liabilities to Net Worth 37	1.7	•	•	0.8	10.0	1.8	1.9	1.6	1.3	1.6	3.6	0.9	1.7
Current Assets to Working Capital 38	6.9	•	1.6	2.2	4.8	3.8	2.9	2.6	2.7	5.4	2.4	2.2	18.5
Current Liabilities to Working Capital 39	5.9	•	0.6	1.2	3.8	2.8	1.9	1.6	1.7	4.4	1.4	1.2	17.5
Working Capital to Net Sales 40	0.0	•	0.1	0.1	0.1	0.1	0.1	0.1	0.1	0.1	0.1	0.2	0.0
Inventory to Working Capital 41	2.4	•	0.9	0.7	2.0	1.8	1.3	1.0	0.8	1.7	0.9	0.4	7.0
Total Receipts to Cash Flow 42	11.8	26.5	18.0	8.3	6.3	8.9	8.6	9.4	6.0	6.1	16.4	3.6	14.5
Cost of Goods to Cash Flow 43	10.1	20.4	11.5	5.6	4.3	6.8	6.0	7.7	4.1	4.1	14.5	1.9	12.9
Cash Flow to Total Debt 44	0.3	•	0.2	0.5	0.5	0.5	0.4	0.5	0.5	0.4	0.2	0.5	0.2

Selected Financial Factors (in Percentages)

Debt Ratio 45	62.5	•	131.6	45.5	90.9	64.5	66.0	61.3	56.6	61.0	78.4	47.6	63.6
Return on Total Assets 46	7.5	•	•	•	7.5	5.6	3.0	9.5	10.2	8.7	6.9	9.1	7.4
Return on Equity Before Income Taxes 47	16.7	•	54.9	•	67.8	9.9	5.3	22.4	20.0	18.4	20.5	14.1	17.3
Return on Equity After Income Taxes 48	11.4	•	57.6	•	55.6	6.2	3.6	20.2	13.5	8.8	15.5	8.0	12.2
Profit Margin (Before Income Tax) 49	3.0	•	•	•	2.1	1.3	0.9	3.2	4.8	4.7	1.6	7.8	2.9
Profit Margin (After Income Tax) 50	2.1	•	•	•	1.7	0.8	0.6	2.8	3.2	2.3	1.2	4.4	2.0

Table II

Corporations with Net Income

DRUGS AND DRUGGISTS' SUNDRIES

MONEY AMOUNTS AND SIZE OF ASSETS IN THOUSANDS OF DOLLARS

Item Description for Accounting Period 7/08 Through 6/09	Total	Zero Assets	Under 500	500 to 1,000	1,000 to 5,000	5,000 to 10,000	10,000 to 25,000	25,000 to 50,000	50,000 to 100,000	100,000 to 250,000	250,000 to 500,000	500,000 to 2,500,000	2,500,000 and over
Number of Enterprises **1**	2154	98	583	•	605	126	89	46	26	22	9	15	•
Revenues ($ in Thousands)													
Net Sales **2**	369440460	374364	923664	•	5054295	3009706	2937629	4609010	3509798	5313383	11735981	17667919	•
Interest **3**	400868	1	202	•	2270	1183	2441	5075	6370	10658	7685	111584	•
Rents **4**	589936	0	0	•	120	0	353	600	125	118	628	4497	•
Royalties **5**	2608499	0	0	•	7008	0	0	2609	11604	839	672	40675	•
Other Portfolio Income **6**	412776	119068	2307	•	10233	2469	10817	2362	20004	5670	1893	71497	•
Other Receipts **7**	4037734	17753	6	•	35124	11569	-1531	89903	117151	37471	35990	405510	•
Total Receipts **8**	377490273	511186	926179	•	5109050	3024927	2949709	4709559	3665052	5368139	11782849	18301682	•
Average Total Receipts **9**	175251	5216	1589	•	8445	24007	33143	102382	140964	244006	1309205	1220112	•
Operating Costs/Operating Income (%)													
Cost of Operations **10**	85.9	71.6	70.4	•	71.3	76.3	71.4	82.7	69.0	60.8	88.8	52.1	•
Salaries and Wages **11**	3.6	6.3	6.3	•	7.1	7.1	6.4	5.0	7.2	11.4	2.5	10.0	•
Taxes Paid **12**	0.4	1.1	0.9	•	1.1	0.7	1.1	0.6	1.0	1.5	0.3	1.5	•
Interest Paid **13**	0.5	11.7	0.0	•	0.2	0.4	0.3	0.2	0.8	0.7	0.8	1.4	•
Depreciation **14**	0.5	0.3	0.3	•	0.5	0.3	0.6	0.4	0.8	0.8	0.5	1.2	•
Amortization and Depletion **15**	0.3	•	0.1	•	0.0	0.0	0.2	0.1	0.7	0.3	0.1	0.9	•
Pensions and Other Deferred Comp. **16**	0.1	0.1	0.3	•	0.1	0.1	0.1	0.1	0.3	0.2	0.1	0.3	•
Employee Benefits **17**	0.4	0.4	0.0	•	0.2	0.3	0.4	0.4	0.7	0.6	0.2	1.6	•
Advertising **18**	0.7	2.4	0.2	•	0.6	0.7	1.9	0.6	4.2	0.8	0.2	2.6	•
Other Expenses **19**	5.8	28.7	13.8	•	12.8	9.3	10.0	7.2	10.0	13.6	4.4	21.1	•
Officers' Compensation **20**	0.3	3.2	3.1	•	2.4	1.3	1.6	1.1	1.3	0.9	0.1	0.5	•
Operating Margin **21**	1.2	•	4.5	•	3.8	3.5	6.0	1.6	4.0	8.5	1.9	6.7	•
Operating Margin Before Officers' Comp. **22**	1.6	•	7.6	•	6.2	4.8	7.6	2.7	5.4	9.4	2.0	7.2	•

Selected Average Balance Sheet ($ in Thousands)

Net Receivables 23	14494	0	0	•	787	2583	4473	10552	17577	29009	139662	179848	•
Inventories 24	13266	0	106	•	803	3048	5914	9542	16310	23612	97340	108174	•
Net Property, Plant and Equipment 25	4853	0	20	•	202	459	466	1999	3645	26405	30628	57336	•
Total Assets 26	80203	0	229	•	2449	8394	14452	33769	71798	147126	389680	1169453	•
Notes and Loans Payable 27	15098	0	33	•	503	1003	1955	3919	18905	51805	150215	218247	•
All Other Liabilities 28	34322	0	48	•	1361	4180	6190	15232	24186	45105	192363	319126	•
Net Worth 29	30784	0	148	•	585	3211	6307	14619	28706	50216	47102	632080	•

Selected Financial Ratios (Times to 1)

Current Ratio 30	1.2	•	3.4	•	1.6	1.3	1.7	1.7	1.6	1.2	1.4	1.9	•
Quick Ratio 31	0.6	•	1.5	•	0.9	0.6	0.8	0.9	0.9	0.7	0.8	0.9	•
Net Sales to Working Capital 32	33.6	•	14.7	•	10.1	14.5	6.5	9.6	7.2	13.1	18.2	4.2	•
Coverage Ratio 33	7.5	1.9	111.0	•	26.5	10.4	22.6	16.1	11.5	15.0	3.8	8.5	•
Total Asset Turnover 34	2.1	•	6.9	•	3.4	2.8	2.3	3.0	1.9	1.6	3.3	1.0	•
Inventory Turnover 35	11.1	•	10.5	•	7.4	6.0	4.0	8.7	5.7	6.2	11.9	5.7	•
Receivables Turnover 36	12.3	•	109.7	•	11.1	11.2	5.6	10.3	6.9	•	9.9	6.8	•
Total Liabilities to Net Worth 37	1.6	•	0.5	•	3.2	1.6	1.3	1.3	1.5	1.9	7.3	0.9	•
Current Assets to Working Capital 38	7.5	•	1.4	•	2.5	4.0	2.5	2.5	2.7	5.0	3.7	2.2	•
Current Liabilities to Working Capital 39	6.5	•	0.4	•	1.5	3.0	1.5	1.5	1.7	4.0	2.7	1.2	•
Working Capital to Net Sales 40	0.0	•	0.1	•	0.1	0.1	0.2	0.1	0.1	0.1	0.1	0.2	•
Inventory to Working Capital 41	2.6	•	0.8	•	1.1	2.0	1.1	0.9	0.9	1.3	1.2	0.4	•
Total Receipts to Cash Flow 42	11.7	15.1	11.4	•	6.4	8.6	6.8	9.8	5.7	4.6	15.8	3.4	•
Cost of Goods to Cash Flow 43	10.1	10.8	8.0	•	4.6	6.5	4.9	8.1	4.0	2.8	14.0	1.8	•
Cash Flow to Total Debt 44	0.3	10.5	1.7	•	0.7	0.5	0.6	0.5	0.5	0.5	0.2	0.6	•

Selected Financial Factors (in Percentages)

Debt Ratio 45	61.6	•	35.2	•	76.1	61.7	56.4	56.7	60.0	65.9	87.9	46.0	•
Return on Total Assets 46	8.6	•	33.3	•	17.2	12.5	15.3	11.8	17.8	16.8	10.4	12.1	•
Return on Equity Before Income Taxes 47	19.5	•	50.9	•	69.5	29.6	33.4	25.6	40.7	46.0	63.1	19.7	•
Return on Equity After Income Taxes 48	13.9	•	47.3	•	63.4	25.7	31.0	23.4	30.8	30.3	50.5	13.0	•
Profit Margin (Before Income Tax) 49	3.5	10.7	4.8	•	4.9	4.0	6.4	3.7	8.7	9.6	2.3	10.6	•
Profit Margin (After Income Tax) 50	2.5	10.5	4.4	•	4.4	3.5	5.9	3.4	6.6	6.3	1.8	7.0	•

Table I

Corporations with and without Net Income

APPAREL, PIECE GOODS, AND NOTIONS

MONEY AMOUNTS AND SIZE OF ASSETS IN THOUSANDS OF DOLLARS

Item Description for Accounting Period 7/08 Through 6/09	Total	Zero Assets	Under 500	500 to 1,000	1,000 to 5,000	5,000 to 10,000	10,000 to 25,000	25,000 to 50,000	50,000 to 100,000	100,000 to 250,000	250,000 to 500,000	500,000 to 2,500,000	2,500,000 and over
Number of Enterprises **1**	19433	2828	12224	1504	2001	465	215	90	47	26	18	11	3
Revenues ($ in Thousands)													
Net Sales **2**	93079240	1209823	7859465	3221619	11419813	8295052	8095300	6593966	5602649	6201670	7316426	11688183	15575275
Interest **3**	124448	1021	3756	180	6811	1657	3576	2562	12641	18324	22663	17071	34186
Rents **4**	49499	0	0	392	2767	338	677	1132	2424	17099	6956	1701	16013
Royalties **5**	1218028	518	0	0	0	389	366	352	47951	24919	75797	264624	803111
Other Portfolio Income **6**	929423	37861	2128	5	13003	90	1191	7755	13962	27306	17885	155137	653100
Other Receipts **7**	1208226	53114	37170	50489	37369	21636	206056	60704	76475	69223	119829	38321	437839
Total Receipts **8**	96608864	1302337	7902519	3272685	11479763	8319162	8307166	6666471	5756102	6358541	7559556	12165037	17519524
Average Total Receipts **9**	4971	461	646	2176	5737	17891	38638	74072	122470	244559	419975	1105912	5839841
Operating Costs/Operating Income (%)													
Cost of Operations **10**	67.0	52.1	68.9	68.2	74.6	72.2	76.4	74.3	71.1	66.2	63.6	63.1	54.2
Salaries and Wages **11**	9.1	9.6	3.9	6.1	6.0	8.0	7.9	7.5	8.1	8.6	10.3	11.7	14.4
Taxes Paid **12**	2.4	1.6	1.9	2.2	2.6	2.2	2.7	2.2	2.1	2.9	1.9	2.4	3.1
Interest Paid **13**	1.1	1.3	0.4	0.5	0.8	1.0	0.7	0.9	0.9	1.9	1.5	1.8	0.8
Depreciation **14**	1.4	1.1	0.3	0.2	0.4	0.4	0.4	0.9	1.1	1.9	2.1	2.4	2.7
Amortization and Depletion **15**	0.3	1.1	0.0	0.0	0.0	0.2	0.1	0.1	0.3	0.3	0.6	1.0	0.4
Pensions and Other Deferred Comp. **16**	0.2	0.3	0.2	0.7	0.2	0.2	0.1	0.1	0.3	0.3	0.3	0.2	0.3
Employee Benefits **17**	0.6	1.3	0.2	0.3	0.4	0.7	0.5	0.4	0.7	0.9	0.7	0.9	0.8
Advertising **18**	2.3	2.7	0.4	2.2	0.7	1.3	1.1	1.3	2.1	2.7	3.6	2.6	5.3
Other Expenses **19**	13.4	32.4	13.9	12.9	10.2	10.6	8.5	9.5	13.5	12.4	12.3	14.0	20.1
Officers' Compensation **20**	2.3	4.8	7.8	4.2	3.1	3.0	2.2	1.5	1.5	1.9	0.9	1.0	0.8
Operating Margin **21**	•	•	2.1	2.4	1.1	0.2	•	1.3	•	0.1	2.1	•	•
Operating Margin Before Officers' Comp. **22**	2.1	•	9.8	6.6	4.2	3.2	1.8	2.8	•	2.0	3.0	•	•

Selected Average Balance Sheet ($ in Thousands)

Net Receivables 23	610	21	176	695	1797	4194	8127	16967	37970	49050	261710	643933
Inventories 24	703	35	389	641	2784	6216	13529	19525	50469	83330	145145	727192
Net Property, Plant and Equipment 25	330	9	15	99	695	823	3901	5640	20103	36313	122864	812175
Total Assets 26	3591	103	733	2111	6718	15095	34619	69680	163112	345022	1172057	9032660
Notes and Loans Payable 27	799	45	395	535	2056	4156	9508	20178	71535	84642	318660	921780
All Other Liabilities 28	964	67	211	857	3647	6852	12509	21162	35149	82237	391701	1300255
Net Worth 29	1828	-8	127	718	1015	4088	12602	28340	56428	178144	461696	6810625

Selected Financial Ratios (Times to 1)

Current Ratio 30	1.6	1.7	2.2	1.8	1.3	1.6	1.7	1.9	2.3	2.2	1.4	1.3
Quick Ratio 31	0.8	1.1	0.8	1.0	0.6	0.7	0.6	0.8	1.1	1.0	0.8	0.7
Net Sales to Working Capital 32	7.1	20.8	6.0	7.5	12.6	7.5	6.2	4.7	4.0	3.8	6.6	10.8
Coverage Ratio 33	5.1	7.4	8.5	3.1	1.5	4.3	3.8	2.2	2.4	4.7	2.8	17.1
Total Asset Turnover 34	1.3	6.2	2.9	2.7	2.7	2.5	2.1	1.7	1.5	1.2	0.9	0.6
Inventory Turnover 35	4.6	12.6	3.8	6.6	4.6	4.6	4.0	4.3	3.1	3.1	4.6	3.9
Receivables Turnover 36	7.9	26.2	13.2	8.8	9.0	8.7	8.3	7.0	6.0	9.1	4.2	8.0
Total Liabilities to Net Worth 37	1.0	•	4.8	1.9	5.6	2.7	1.7	1.5	1.9	0.9	1.5	0.3
Current Assets to Working Capital 38	2.6	2.5	1.9	2.3	4.0	2.6	2.4	2.1	1.8	1.8	3.4	4.3
Current Liabilities to Working Capital 39	1.6	1.5	0.9	1.3	3.0	1.6	1.4	1.1	0.8	0.8	2.4	3.3
Working Capital to Net Sales 40	0.1	0.0	0.2	0.1	0.1	0.1	0.2	0.2	0.2	0.3	0.2	0.1
Inventory to Working Capital 41	1.0	0.8	1.2	0.8	2.0	1.2	1.1	0.8	0.8	0.8	0.9	1.5
Total Receipts to Cash Flow 42	7.5	7.9	8.5	10.8	10.5	11.3	10.3	8.4	8.9	7.6	8.5	3.9
Cost of Goods to Cash Flow 43	5.0	5.4	5.8	8.0	7.6	8.6	7.6	6.0	5.9	4.8	5.3	2.1
Cash Flow to Total Debt 44	0.4	0.7	0.4	0.4	0.3	0.3	0.3	0.3	0.2	0.3	0.2	0.6

Selected Financial Factors (in Percentages)

Debt Ratio 45	49.1	107.7	82.7	66.0	84.9	72.9	63.6	59.3	65.4	48.4	60.6	24.6
Return on Total Assets 46	7.2	18.7	13.3	6.5	4.1	7.4	7.0	3.4	6.8	8.4	4.6	8.3
Return on Equity Before Income Taxes 47	11.3	•	67.9	13.0	9.0	20.9	14.2	4.5	11.5	12.7	7.5	10.3
Return on Equity After Income Taxes 48	7.7	•	67.1	12.2	7.4	18.5	12.9	2.5	6.3	9.2	3.9	6.3
Profit Margin (Before Income Tax) 49	4.3	2.6	4.0	1.6	0.5	2.3	2.4	1.1	2.7	5.6	3.2	13.6
Profit Margin (After Income Tax) 50	3.0	2.6	4.0	1.5	0.4	2.0	2.2	0.6	1.5	4.0	1.7	8.3

Table II

Corporations with Net Income

APPAREL, PIECE GOODS, AND NOTIONS

MONEY AMOUNTS AND SIZE OF ASSETS IN THOUSANDS OF DOLLARS

Item Description for Accounting Period 7/08 Through 6/09	Total	Zero Assets	Under 500	500 to 1,000	1,000 to 5,000	5,000 to 10,000	10,000 to 25,000	25,000 to 50,000	50,000 to 100,000	100,000 to 250,000	250,000 to 500,000	500,000 to 2,500,000	2,500,000 and over
Number of Enterprises **1**	10991	1167	6818	•	1379	218	147	66	27	19	13	•	0
Revenues ($ in Thousands)													
Net Sales **2**	65981311	389135	5121056	•	9218045	3462172	5943433	5213935	33395721	4460767	5615806	•	0
Interest **3**	87111	110	2195	•	4329	1333	2742	1081	7268	11275	15242	•	0
Rents **4**	19264	0	0	•	2591	332	677	1132	1159	5047	6222	•	0
Royalties **5**	997546	0	0	•	0	0	232	70	29736	23251	66928	•	0
Other Portfolio Income **6**	819974	0	1	•	10122	90	1062	7229	11305	13004	17885	•	0
Other Receipts **7**	983029	25904	5666	•	31202	10050	193578	49664	44245	42447	107775	•	0
Total Receipts **8**	68888235	415149	5128918	•	9266289	3473977	6141724	5273111	3489434	4555791	5829858	•	0
Average Total Receipts **9**	6268	356	752	•	6720	15936	41780	79896	129238	239778	448451	•	•
Operating Costs/Operating Income (%)													
Cost of Operations **10**	66.3	44.4	68.5	•	74.7	76.2	76.5	75.2	71.5	65.8	61.2	•	•
Salaries and Wages **11**	8.7	5.8	2.3	•	5.9	3.9	7.1	6.7	6.8	8.2	10.4	•	•
Taxes Paid **12**	2.5	1.1	2.2	•	2.8	1.7	2.7	1.9	1.8	2.9	2.2	•	•
Interest Paid **13**	0.8	0.3	0.5	•	0.9	0.7	0.7	0.6	0.7	1.2	0.7	•	•
Depreciation **14**	1.4	0.4	0.3	•	0.3	0.3	0.3	0.7	0.5	1.4	2.1	•	•
Amortization and Depletion **15**	0.2	0.0	0.0	•	0.0	0.0	0.0	0.1	0.1	0.3	0.3	•	•
Pensions and Other Deferred Comp. **16**	0.2	0.3	0.3	•	0.2	0.1	0.1	0.1	0.2	0.3	0.3	•	•
Employee Benefits **17**	0.5	0.8	0.2	•	0.4	0.3	0.4	0.3	0.7	0.7	0.8	•	•
Advertising **18**	2.3	0.4	0.4	•	0.8	0.3	0.5	1.1	1.4	2.4	3.8	•	•
Other Expenses **19**	12.0	25.8	12.6	•	8.2	9.3	8.0	7.9	11.6	10.4	12.4	•	•
Officers' Compensation **20**	2.1	7.0	5.6	•	2.9	1.9	2.1	1.4	1.7	2.5	1.0	•	•
Operating Margin **21**	3.0	13.6	7.1	•	2.7	5.2	1.6	4.1	3.0	3.9	4.8	•	•
Operating Margin Before Officers' Comp. **22**	5.1	20.6	12.7	•	5.6	7.1	3.7	5.5	4.7	6.3	5.7	•	•

Selected Average Balance Sheet ($ in Thousands)

	•	•	•	•	•	•	•	•	•	•	•
Net Receivables 23	798	0	23	•	840	1965	4461	9087	19161	41996	46984
Inventories 24	884	0	40	•	742	3741	6748	15407	21813	52452	73061
Net Property, Plant and Equipment 25	429	0	7	•	110	1033	765	2483	3251	16144	39215
Total Assets 26	4822	0	103	•	2287	6501	14842	34393	67557	156213	347464
Notes and Loans Payable 27	733	0	35	•	624	1850	4163	8951	16205	43939	54339
All Other Liabilities 28	1166	0	35	•	933	2369	5414	11578	20537	31552	84643
Net Worth 29	2923	0	33	•	729	2282	5264	13865	30816	80722	208481

Selected Financial Ratios (Times to 1)

	•	•	•	•	•	•	•	•	•	•	•
Current Ratio 30	1.8	•	2.2	•	1.7	1.8	1.7	1.9	2.2	2.8	2.3
Quick Ratio 31	0.9	•	1.5	•	1.0	1.0	0.8	0.7	1.0	1.4	1.1
Net Sales to Working Capital 32	6.1	•	18.8	•	7.8	6.8	7.4	5.8	4.2	3.5	3.7
Coverage Ratio 33	12.1	71.3	15.3	•	4.6	9.0	8.1	9.5	9.1	6.0	13.2
Total Asset Turnover 34	1.2	•	7.3	•	2.9	2.4	2.7	2.3	1.9	1.5	1.2
Inventory Turnover 35	4.5	•	12.9	•	6.7	3.2	4.6	3.9	4.1	2.9	3.6
Receivables Turnover 36	7.2	•	27.4	•	8.5	4.9	8.6	7.7	6.2	5.3	10.7
Total Liabilities to Net Worth 37	0.6	•	2.1	•	2.1	1.8	1.8	1.5	1.2	0.9	0.7
Current Assets to Working Capital 38	2.3	•	1.8	•	2.4	2.2	2.5	2.2	1.8	1.6	1.8
Current Liabilities to Working Capital 39	1.3	•	0.8	•	1.4	1.2	1.5	1.2	0.8	0.6	0.8
Working Capital to Net Sales 40	0.2	•	0.1	•	0.1	0.1	0.1	0.2	0.2	0.3	0.3
Inventory to Working Capital 41	0.8	•	0.6	•	0.7	0.9	1.1	1.1	0.7	0.7	0.7
Total Receipts to Cash Flow 42	6.1	2.5	6.0	•	11.2	7.3	8.9	8.6	6.4	7.2	6.1
Cost of Goods to Cash Flow 43	4.1	1.1	4.1	•	8.3	5.5	6.8	6.5	4.6	4.7	3.8
Cash Flow to Total Debt 44	0.5	•	1.8	•	0.4	0.5	0.5	0.4	0.5	0.4	0.5

Selected Financial Factors (in Percentages)

	•	•	•	•	•	•	•	•	•	•	•
Debt Ratio 45	39.4	•	68.2	•	68.1	64.9	64.5	59.7	54.4	48.3	40.0
Return on Total Assets 46	11.5	•	56.5	•	12.1	15.3	15.2	13.5	12.2	11.0	11.8
Return on Equity Before Income Taxes 47	17.3	•	165.9	•	29.8	38.9	37.7	29.9	23.7	17.8	18.2
Return on Equity After Income Taxes 48	13.4	•	165.1	•	28.7	37.4	35.0	28.2	20.5	12.9	14.0
Profit Margin (Before Income Tax) 49	8.4	20.3	7.2	•	3.3	5.6	4.9	5.2	5.8	6.1	8.8
Profit Margin (After Income Tax) 50	6.5	19.9	7.2	•	3.1	5.4	4.6	5.0	5.2	4.4	6.8

Table I

Corporations with and without Net Income

GROCERY AND RELATED PRODUCT

MONEY AMOUNTS AND SIZE OF ASSETS IN THOUSANDS OF DOLLARS

Item Description for Accounting Period 7/08 Through 6/09	Total	Zero Assets	Under 500	500 to 1,000	1,000 to 5,000	5,000 to 10,000	10,000 to 25,000	25,000 to 50,000	50,000 to 100,000	100,000 to 250,000	250,000 to 500,000	500,000 to 2,500,000	2,500,000 and over
Number of Enterprises **1**	32509	3566	18862	2655	5518	874	612	221	110	51	14	21	5
Revenues ($ in Thousands)													
Net Sales **2**	562148888	1318893	20411220	9026135	64351420	33714854	44451766	31172874	30723345	23471192	17862515	76966959	208677715
Interest **3**	5613547	1129	5001	9125	21721	15279	14884	17731	10408	17609	4229	53350	5443082
Rents **4**	1152804	0	1312	3134	17564	3568	7519	20540	4484	7479	1862	49090	1036253
Royalties **5**	657648	0	0	0	0	0	1474	0	70	1302	5485	2919	646398
Other Portfolio Income **6**	5507101	4482	29810	2751	34851	7220	13095	32815	79928	80970	26751	41794	5152634
Other Receipts **7**	4986914	65161	70520	72334	490847	140655	160099	140602	382974	234583	88311	701785	2439040
Total Receipts **8**	580066902	1389665	20517863	9113479	64916403	33881576	44648837	31384562	31201209	23813135	17989153	77815897	223395122
Average Total Receipts **9**	17843	390	1088	3433	11764	38766	72956	142012	283647	466924	1284940	3705519	44679024
Operating Costs/Operating Income (%)													
Cost of Operations **10**	81.4	73.9	81.7	79.4	85.5	88.7	86.9	86.4	86.8	85.6	85.5	85.7	73.9
Salaries and Wages **11**	6.0	4.8	3.8	5.3	4.1	3.2	4.3	4.9	4.6	4.6	3.8	5.0	8.6
Taxes Paid **12**	1.0	0.9	0.8	1.2	0.8	0.6	0.7	0.6	1.0	0.7	0.7	0.7	1.4
Interest Paid **13**	1.2	0.4	0.2	0.4	0.3	0.3	0.3	0.4	0.5	0.8	0.4	0.7	2.4
Depreciation **14**	1.4	0.6	0.6	0.8	0.5	0.3	0.5	0.6	0.8	0.9	1.6	0.8	2.7
Amortization and Depletion **15**	0.2	0.1	0.0	0.1	0.0	0.0	0.0	0.0	0.1	0.2	0.0	0.2	0.5
Pensions and Other Deferred Comp. **16**	0.3	0.2	0.1	0.1	0.2	0.1	0.2	0.2	0.2	0.2	0.1	0.2	0.6
Employee Benefits **17**	0.7	0.6	0.2	0.4	0.5	0.3	0.5	0.4	0.4	0.7	0.4	0.7	1.2
Advertising **18**	0.6	0.7	0.4	0.3	0.2	0.1	0.3	0.3	0.6	1.2	0.7	0.5	0.9
Other Expenses **19**	6.7	18.7	8.8	9.6	5.8	4.6	4.5	4.6	4.2	5.0	5.0	5.5	8.9
Officers' Compensation **20**	0.7	6.2	2.7	2.3	1.6	1.0	1.0	0.6	0.7	0.5	0.3	0.2	0.2
Operating Margin **21**	•	•	0.6	0.1	0.7	0.6	0.9	1.0	0.1	•	1.5	•	•
Operating Margin Before Officers' Comp. **22**	0.5	•	3.3	2.4	2.3	1.6	1.9	1.6	0.8	0.3	1.7	0.1	•

Selected Average Balance Sheet ($ in Thousands)

Net Receivables **23**	1235	0	27	157	756	2859	5442	10949	18576	33988	87618	143235	3760576
Inventories **24**	974	0	22	127	437	1591	3793	9163	20901	45697	101274	211465	2458065
Net Property, Plant and Equipment **25**	1871	0	19	154	299	614	2157	5397	11684	23464	98921	201937	9449135
Total Assets **26**	14969	0	125	672	2036	7059	15750	33771	68049	144837	367976	991807	81426669
Notes and Loans Payable **27**	2948	0	53	299	605	2277	4606	9960	23771	53699	76743	334890	14047494
All Other Liabilities **28**	4083	0	28	267	699	2646	5247	12689	21922	47418	144874	359353	20982112
Net Worth **29**	7938	0	44	106	732	2136	5896	11122	22356	43720	146359	297564	46397063

Selected Financial Ratios (Times to 1)

Current Ratio **30**	1.2	•	2.5	1.4	1.9	1.6	1.6	1.5	1.6	1.5	1.7	1.4	1.0
Quick Ratio **31**	0.7	•	1.6	0.8	1.3	1.0	0.9	0.8	0.8	0.6	0.8	0.5	0.6
Net Sales to Working Capital **32**	26.9	•	21.0	30.4	15.8	18.9	16.3	17.9	16.0	14.4	14.2	28.5	113.1
Coverage Ratio **33**	3.7	•	6.8	3.7	7.2	4.3	5.1	5.0	4.5	2.5	6.4	2.5	3.5
Total Asset Turnover **34**	1.2	•	8.6	5.1	5.7	5.5	4.6	4.2	4.1	3.2	3.5	3.7	0.5
Inventory Turnover **35**	14.4	•	40.8	21.3	22.8	21.5	16.6	13.3	11.6	8.6	10.8	14.9	12.5
Receivables Turnover **36**	13.9	•	39.1	22.5	15.4	15.1	13.0	12.5	14.9	12.6	13.4	25.4	11.0
Total Liabilities to Net Worth **37**	0.9	•	1.9	5.4	1.8	2.3	1.7	2.0	2.0	2.3	1.5	2.3	0.8
Current Assets to Working Capital **38**	6.1	•	1.7	3.8	2.1	2.8	2.6	3.1	2.7	3.0	2.5	3.6	40.8
Current Liabilities to Working Capital **39**	5.1	•	0.7	2.8	1.1	1.8	1.6	2.1	1.7	2.0	1.5	2.6	39.8
Working Capital to Net Sales **40**	0.0	•	0.0	0.0	0.1	0.1	0.1	0.1	0.1	0.1	0.1	0.0	0.0
Inventory to Working Capital **41**	1.6	•	0.4	1.3	0.6	0.9	0.9	1.1	1.2	1.5	1.1	1.6	7.3
Total Receipts to Cash Flow **42**	12.9	6.7	12.4	11.2	17.0	20.1	21.8	19.7	20.5	21.3	16.1	19.7	8.6
Cost of Goods to Cash Flow **43**	10.5	4.9	10.1	8.9	14.5	17.8	19.0	17.0	17.8	18.2	13.7	16.9	6.3
Cash Flow to Total Debt **44**	0.2	•	1.1	0.5	0.5	0.4	0.3	0.3	0.3	0.2	0.4	0.3	0.1

Selected Financial Factors (in Percentages)

Debt Ratio **45**	47.0	•	65.0	84.3	64.1	69.7	62.6	67.1	67.1	69.8	60.2	70.0	43.0
Return on Total Assets **46**	4.9	•	11.8	7.4	10.5	8.1	7.6	8.5	8.7	6.2	8.8	5.9	4.3
Return on Equity Before Income Taxes **47**	6.7	•	28.7	34.2	25.2	20.5	16.4	20.7	20.5	12.3	18.6	11.8	5.5
Return on Equity After Income Taxes **48**	4.9	•	27.7	33.6	23.8	18.7	14.8	18.3	18.2	8.3	15.5	6.9	3.7
Profit Margin (Before Income Tax) **49**	3.1	•	1.2	1.1	1.6	1.1	1.3	1.6	1.6	1.2	2.1	1.0	6.1
Profit Margin (After Income Tax) **50**	2.2	•	1.1	1.0	1.5	1.0	1.2	1.4	1.5	0.8	1.8	0.6	4.1

Table II

Corporations with Net Income

GROCERY AND RELATED PRODUCT

MONEY AMOUNTS AND SIZE OF ASSETS IN THOUSANDS OF DOLLARS

Item Description for Accounting Period 7/08 Through 6/09	Total	Zero Assets	Under 500	500 to 1,000	1,000 to 5,000	5,000 to 10,000	10,000 to 25,000	25,000 to 50,000	50,000 to 100,000	100,000 to 250,000	250,000 to 500,000	500,000 to 2,500,000	2,500,000 and over
Number of Enterprises 1	20354	1866	11031	1843	4056	718	498	190	84	36	•	15	•
Revenues ($ in Thousands)													
Net Sales 2	455971087	840450	12590898	6489087	51374843	30199540	38149372	28276115	24294413	18049937	•	41217237	•
Interest 3	5562116	1071	4379	7545	17480	14555	12446	11637	8733	13642	•	32224	•
Rents 4	1111941	0	1095	875	16355	3068	5564	5225	4458	6993	•	32190	•
Royalties 5	655199	0	0	0	0	0	1468	0	70	1144	•	1183	•
Other Portfolio Income 6	5456915	1457	24325	542	26771	2324	6934	29768	74969	77406	•	33035	•
Other Receipts 7	4277949	62540	66440	46247	353009	125333	149441	120616	321514	192706	•	421274	•
Total Receipts 8	473035207	905518	12687137	6544296	51788458	30344820	38325225	28443361	24704157	18341828	•	41737143	•
Average Total Receipts 9	23240	485	1150	3551	12768	42263	76958	149702	294097	509495	•	2782476	•
Operating Costs/Operating Income (%)													
Cost of Operations 10	80.0	64.3	77.9	80.5	85.0	88.7	87.1	86.0	86.5	85.3	•	82.4	•
Salaries and Wages 11	6.1	5.1	3.4	5.0	3.8	3.0	4.1	4.9	4.9	4.6	•	5.5	•
Taxes Paid 12	1.0	1.0	0.9	1.1	0.7	0.6	0.6	0.6	0.7	0.7	•	0.8	•
Interest Paid 13	1.2	0.5	0.2	0.3	0.2	0.3	0.3	0.4	0.4	0.6	•	0.7	•
Depreciation 14	1.6	0.5	0.6	0.6	0.5	0.3	0.4	0.6	0.7	0.8	•	1.0	•
Amortization and Depletion 15	0.2	0.1	0.1	0.1	0.0	0.0	0.0	0.0	0.1	0.1	•	0.2	•
Pensions and Other Deferred Comp. 16	0.3	0.3	0.1	0.1	0.2	0.1	0.1	0.2	0.2	0.2	•	0.2	•
Employee Benefits 17	0.8	0.8	0.2	0.4	0.4	0.3	0.5	0.4	0.4	0.7	•	0.6	•
Advertising 18	0.6	1.0	0.4	0.1	0.1	0.1	0.2	0.2	0.5	1.2	•	0.9	•
Other Expenses 19	7.0	17.4	9.1	8.0	5.7	4.5	4.0	4.4	4.0	4.8	•	6.3	•
Officers' Compensation 20	0.7	9.6	3.2	2.2	1.6	0.7	1.0	0.6	0.7	0.6	•	0.2	•
Operating Margin 21	0.4	•	3.9	1.6	1.9	1.3	1.6	1.6	0.9	0.5	•	1.2	•
Operating Margin Before Officers' Comp. 22	1.1	9.1	7.1	3.7	3.4	2.0	2.6	2.2	1.6	1.0	•	1.3	•

Selected Average Balance Sheet ($ in Thousands)

Net Receivables **23**	1691	0	26	171	793	3140	5826	11170	18341	35430	126967
Inventories **24**	1295	0	16	149	446	1644	4147	9094	22329	49038	195640
Net Property, Plant and Equipment **25**	2723	0	19	123	307	546	1768	5189	11173	25358	178670
Total Assets **26**	22388	0	128	663	2086	7164	15957	33905	68963	144416	808454
Notes and Loans Payable **27**	4021	0	34	290	516	2234	4022	9364	23033	47021	262169
All Other Liabilities **28**	6001	0	20	277	649	2678	5514	12575	21379	48117	272227
Net Worth **29**	12365	0	75	96	922	2252	6421	11965	24551	49277	274058

Selected Financial Ratios (Times to 1)

Current Ratio **30**	1.2	•	3.5	1.4	2.2	1.5	1.7	1.5	1.6	1.7	1.4
Quick Ratio **31**	0.7	•	2.6	0.8	1.5	1.0	1.0	0.8	0.8	0.8	0.6
Net Sales to Working Capital **32**	25.6	•	20.3	30.4	20.2	15.1	15.1	18.4	15.3	12.3	23.0
Coverage Ratio **33**	4.4	17.1	29.3	8.1	14.3	6.7	8.4	6.8	7.1	4.6	4.5
Total Asset Turnover **34**	1.0	•	8.9	5.3	6.1	5.9	4.8	4.4	4.2	3.5	3.4
Inventory Turnover **35**	13.8	•	55.0	19.1	24.2	22.7	16.1	14.1	11.2	8.7	11.6
Receivables Turnover **36**	13.0	•	38.9	21.0	16.2	14.9	12.6	13.3	15.2	13.2	19.0
Total Liabilities to Net Worth **37**	0.8	•	0.7	5.9	1.3	2.2	1.5	1.8	1.8	1.9	1.9
Current Assets to Working Capital **38**	6.3	•	1.4	3.8	1.9	2.8	2.5	3.0	2.6	2.4	3.3
Current Liabilities to Working Capital **39**	5.3	•	0.4	2.8	0.9	1.8	1.5	2.0	1.6	1.4	2.3
Working Capital to Net Sales **40**	0.0	•	0.0	0.0	0.1	0.0	0.1	0.1	0.1	0.1	0.0
Inventory to Working Capital **41**	1.5	•	0.2	1.4	0.5	0.9	0.8	1.1	1.1	1.2	1.4
Total Receipts to Cash Flow **42**	11.1	4.3	8.3	11.2	14.6	18.2	20.1	18.0	18.2	18.5	14.0
Cost of Goods to Cash Flow **43**	8.9	2.8	6.5	9.0	12.4	16.1	17.5	15.5	15.7	15.8	11.5
Cash Flow to Total Debt **44**	0.2	•	2.6	0.6	0.7	0.5	0.4	0.4	0.4	0.3	0.4

Selected Financial Factors (in Percentages)

Debt Ratio **45**	44.8	•	41.6	85.6	55.8	68.6	59.8	64.7	64.4	65.9	66.1
Return on Total Assets **46**	5.5	•	43.2	14.7	17.4	12.0	11.1	11.3	12.3	9.3	10.4
Return on Equity Before Income Taxes **47**	7.7	•	71.4	89.4	36.7	32.6	24.3	27.2	29.8	21.2	23.9
Return on Equity After Income Taxes **48**	5.8	•	70.4	88.5	35.2	30.6	22.5	24.7	27.1	16.2	16.5
Profit Margin (Before Income Tax) **49**	4.2	7.3	4.7	2.4	2.7	1.7	2.0	2.2	2.5	2.1	2.4
Profit Margin (After Income Tax) **50**	3.2	6.6	4.6	2.4	2.6	1.6	1.9	2.0	2.3	1.6	1.6

Table I

Corporations with and without Net Income

FARM PRODUCT RAW MATERIAL

Money Amounts and Size of Assets in Thousands of Dollars

Item Description for Accounting Period 7/08 Through 6/09		Total	Zero Assets	Under 500	500 to 1,000	1,000 to 5,000	5,000 to 10,000	10,000 to 25,000	25,000 to 50,000	50,000 to 100,000	100,000 to 250,000	250,000 to 500,000	500,000 to 2,500,000	2,500,000 and over
Number of Enterprises	1	4555	18	2186	930	975	170	164	67	19	13	5	6	3
Revenues ($ in Thousands)														
Net Sales	2	156556422	5157	1587425	3768967	8462772	4108563	8876816	10128496	3808534	11645727	9572798	17736848	76854318
Interest	3	474985	0	1357	5185	9833	4514	5719	5037	2259	16489	14452	54470	355671
Rents	4	58583	0	253	2023	14710	3063	4745	1648	2394	2247	69	2002	25430
Royalties	5	67762	0	0	0	0	4057	0	0	0	0	0	189	63516
Other Portfolio Income	6	343926	1	7303	5724	12303	189	10674	19277	2256	11036	2194	47073	225899
Other Receipts	7	2645188	930	75270	115474	109498	19202	96588	65821	34358	81918	85346	65439	1895339
Total Receipts	8	160146866	6088	1671608	3897373	8609116	4139588	8994542	10220279	3849801	11757417	9674859	17906021	79420173
Average Total Receipts	9	35158	338	765	4191	8830	24351	54845	152541	202621	904417	1934972	2984337	26473391
Operating Costs/Operating Income (%)														
Cost of Operations	10	93.6	85.6	82.4	90.9	86.0	93.4	91.9	93.4	91.7	96.8	96.4	94.9	94.1
Salaries and Wages	11	2.2	7.6	1.9	2.9	3.5	1.7	2.0	2.0	2.1	0.7	0.7	1.4	2.7
Taxes Paid	12	0.3	3.4	0.5	0.7	0.6	0.3	0.3	0.3	0.4	0.1	0.1	0.2	0.2
Interest Paid	13	1.1	•	0.5	0.3	1.0	1.0	0.7	0.7	1.1	0.5	0.2	0.6	1.6
Depreciation	14	1.0	3.0	0.8	1.0	0.6	0.6	0.6	0.5	1.2	0.2	0.3	0.6	1.5
Amortization and Depletion	15	0.0	•	0.0	0.0	0.1	0.0	0.0	0.0	0.0	•	0.0	0.0	0.0
Pensions and Other Deferred Comp.	16	0.2	•	•	0.1	0.2	0.0	0.1	0.1	0.1	0.0	0.0	0.4	0.3
Employee Benefits	17	0.5	2.6	0.0	0.1	0.3	0.1	0.1	0.2	0.1	0.1	0.0	0.2	0.8
Advertising	18	0.1	0.1	0.1	0.1	0.2	0.1	0.0	0.0	0.1	0.0	0.2	0.0	0.1
Other Expenses	19	2.5	2.9	13.8	4.3	6.4	3.0	3.1	2.3	3.5	0.6	0.9	1.9	2.2
Officers' Compensation	20	0.7	0.3	2.0	1.8	2.3	0.5	0.6	0.5	0.3	0.2	0.3	0.3	0.6
Operating Margin	21	•	•	•	•	•	•	0.5	•	•	0.7	0.8	•	•
Operating Margin Before Officers' Comp.	22	•	•	•	1.4	•	•	1.1	0.5	•	0.9	1.1	•	•

Selected Average Balance Sheet ($ in Thousands)

Net Receivables 23	3182	0	28	112	477	1641	2974	10978	15963	47997	65469	437180	2827978
Inventories 24	3013	0	9	74	450	1739	4626	13430	23150	55131	139898	249616	2629177
Net Property, Plant and Equipment 25	1721	0	17	220	425	1142	2566	3841	14761	15464	36991	111772	1657662
Total Assets 26	16904	0	147	728	2287	7068	14433	35117	69215	150877	304269	1057719	18900663
Notes and Loans Payable 27	6240	0	162	338	961	2700	4602	12336	25580	47106	108108	353978	7005574
All Other Liabilities 28	4531	0	44	196	692	2977	5628	16821	24368	62328	91288	397341	4337455
Net Worth 29	6133	0	-59	194	634	1392	4203	5960	19268	41442	104872	306400	7557635

Selected Financial Ratios (Times to 1)

Current Ratio 30	1.5	•	1.4	1.3	1.8	1.9	1.4	1.2	1.3	1.3	1.7	1.4	1.5
Quick Ratio 31	0.7	•	1.3	0.9	0.9	0.7	0.6	0.6	0.6	0.6	0.7	0.9	0.7
Net Sales to Working Capital 32	13.1	•	25.5	49.8	11.2	9.0	19.2	27.9	15.9	35.3	20.0	13.2	10.4
Coverage Ratio 33	1.7	•	7.8	4.8	2.4	1.0	3.6	2.3	1.5	4.4	10.9	2.5	1.2
Total Asset Turnover 34	2.0	•	4.9	5.6	3.8	3.4	3.8	4.3	2.9	5.9	6.3	2.8	1.4
Inventory Turnover 35	10.7	•	68.3	49.5	16.6	13.0	10.8	10.5	7.9	15.7	13.2	11.2	9.2
Receivables Turnover 36	11.2	•	15.8	40.5	17.9	13.7	16.4	14.8	11.3	17.7	16.4	9.0	9.3
Total Liabilities to Net Worth 37	1.8	•	•	2.8	2.6	4.1	2.4	4.9	2.6	2.6	1.9	2.5	1.5
Current Assets to Working Capital 38	3.0	•	3.8	4.1	2.2	2.1	3.8	5.4	4.0	4.6	2.5	3.5	2.8
Current Liabilities to Working Capital 39	2.0	•	2.8	3.1	1.2	1.1	2.8	4.4	3.0	3.6	1.5	2.5	1.8
Working Capital to Net Sales 40	0.1	•	0.0	0.0	0.1	0.1	0.1	0.0	0.1	0.0	0.0	0.1	0.1
Inventory to Working Capital 41	1.0	•	0.0	0.7	0.6	0.7	1.8	2.3	1.9	1.9	1.3	0.7	0.9
Total Receipts to Cash Flow 42	50.3	7.1	6.9	21.7	17.0	42.8	23.7	40.4	32.4	48.7	40.9	62.8	125.0
Cost of Goods to Cash Flow 43	47.1	6.1	5.7	19.7	14.6	40.0	21.8	37.7	29.7	47.1	39.4	59.6	117.5
Cash Flow to Total Debt 44	0.1	•	0.5	0.3	0.3	0.1	0.2	0.1	0.1	0.2	0.2	0.1	0.0

Selected Financial Factors (in Percentages)

Debt Ratio 45	63.7	•	140.3	73.4	72.3	80.3	70.9	83.0	72.2	72.5	65.5	71.0	60.0
Return on Total Assets 46	3.7	•	18.0	8.0	5.4	3.2	9.1	6.7	4.7	12.8	12.8	3.9	2.6
Return on Equity Before Income Taxes 47	4.3	•	•	23.8	11.5	•	22.7	22.2	5.7	36.0	33.8	8.1	1.1
Return on Equity After Income Taxes 48	3.3	•	•	23.0	9.5	•	21.3	18.1	1.9	27.3	22.0	3.0	1.0
Profit Margin (Before Income Tax) 49	0.8	12.6	3.2	1.1	0.8	•	1.8	0.9	0.6	1.7	1.9	0.8	0.3
Profit Margin (After Income Tax) 50	0.6	11.0	3.2	1.1	0.7	•	1.7	0.7	0.2	1.3	1.2	0.3	0.3

191

Table II

Corporations with Net Income

FARM PRODUCT RAW MATERIAL

MONEY AMOUNTS AND SIZE OF ASSETS IN THOUSANDS OF DOLLARS

Item Description for Accounting Period 7/08 Through 6/09	Total	Zero Assets	Under 500	500 to 1,000	1,000 to 5,000	5,000 to 10,000	10,000 to 25,000	25,000 to 50,000	50,000 to 100,000	100,000 to 250,000	250,000 to 500,000	500,000 to 2,500,000	2,500,000 and over
Number of Enterprises **1**	3098	18	1251	713	765	117	134	62	16	•	•	•	0
Revenues ($ in Thousands)													
Net Sales **2**	94861978	5157	782128	2603000	7239055	3221305	7895530	9659550	2950254	•	•	•	0
Interest **3**	250786	0	611	3870	4468	1481	3433	4605	1925	•	•	•	0
Rents **4**	23037	0	253	2023	6934	49	4431	1648	2366	•	•	•	0
Royalties **5**	189	0	0	0	0	0	0	0	0	•	•	•	0
Other Portfolio Income **6**	205654	1	1372	4638	12300	98	9358	19191	2256	•	•	•	0
Other Receipts **7**	938182	930	70141	115027	91707	14334	51735	62089	22463	•	•	•	0
Total Receipts **8**	96279826	6088	854505	2728558	7354464	3237267	7964487	9747083	2979264	•	•	•	0
Average Total Receipts **9**	31078	338	683	3827	9614	27669	59436	157211	186204	•	•	•	•
Operating Costs/Operating Income (%)													
Cost of Operations **10**	93.5	85.6	69.4	87.7	86.7	94.4	91.6	92.8	89.4	•	•	•	•
Salaries and Wages **11**	1.5	7.6	3.7	3.9	2.9	0.8	1.8	2.1	2.4	•	•	•	•
Taxes Paid **12**	0.3	3.4	0.9	0.8	0.5	0.3	0.2	0.3	0.5	•	•	•	•
Interest Paid **13**	0.7	•	0.4	0.2	0.4	0.9	0.6	0.6	0.9	•	•	•	•
Depreciation **14**	0.5	3.0	1.2	0.9	0.7	0.5	0.5	0.5	1.4	•	•	•	•
Amortization and Depletion **15**	•	•	0.0	0.0	0.0	•	0.0	0.0	0.0	•	•	•	•
Pensions and Other Deferred Comp. **16**	0.1	•	•	0.1	0.1	0.0	0.1	0.1	0.1	•	•	•	•
Employee Benefits **17**	0.2	2.6	0.0	0.0	0.2	0.1	0.1	0.2	0.1	•	•	•	•
Advertising **18**	0.1	0.1	0.1	0.2	0.2	0.0	0.0	0.0	0.1	•	•	•	•
Other Expenses **19**	2.3	2.9	16.9	5.0	5.9	2.1	2.8	2.2	3.5	•	•	•	•
Officers' Compensation **20**	0.5	0.3	3.8	2.2	1.6	0.5	0.6	0.5	0.4	•	•	•	•
Operating Margin **21**	0.3	3.5	•	0.8	0.3	0.3	1.6	0.7	1.2	•	•	•	•
Operating Margin Before Officers' Comp. **22**	0.8	•	7.3	1.1	2.4	0.7	2.3	1.2	1.7	•	•	•	•

Selected Average Balance Sheet ($ in Thousands)

Net Receivables 23	2368	0	17	116	436	1776	2923	10887	17201
Inventories 24	3436	0	11	85	502	1943	5190	11895	19396
Net Property, Plant and Equipment 25	1086	0	18	218	374	818	1968	3965	15951
Total Assets 26	10495	0	123	708	2378	7380	14246	34849	68315
Notes and Loans Payable 27	4739	0	58	248	796	2543	3779	10549	19915
All Other Liabilities 28	3357	0	-24	80	698	3280	6125	16157	22497
Net Worth 29	2399	0	89	379	884	1557	4342	8143	25903

Selected Financial Ratios (Times to 1)

Current Ratio 30	1.5	•	7.8	1.8	2.0	2.2	1.4	1.4	1.6
Quick Ratio 31	0.6	•	7.5	1.2	1.0	0.9	0.6	0.6	0.8
Net Sales to Working Capital 32	12.8	•	7.8	27.9	10.0	7.8	17.7	20.4	10.4
Coverage Ratio 33	3.7	•	35.7	19.0	6.3	1.9	5.2	3.7	3.6
Total Asset Turnover 34	2.9	•	5.1	5.2	4.0	3.7	4.1	4.5	2.7
Inventory Turnover 35	8.3	•	38.2	37.8	16.3	13.4	10.4	12.2	8.5
Receivables Turnover 36	9.5	•	23.4	37.0	20.8	12.7	18.3	17.4	•
Total Liabilities to Net Worth 37	3.4	•	0.4	0.9	1.7	3.7	2.3	3.3	1.6
Current Assets to Working Capital 38	3.0	•	1.1	2.3	2.0	1.8	3.4	3.8	2.7
Current Liabilities to Working Capital 39	2.0	•	0.1	1.3	1.0	0.8	2.4	2.8	1.7
Working Capital to Net Sales 40	0.1	•	0.1	0.0	0.1	0.1	0.1	0.0	0.1
Inventory to Working Capital 41	0.9	•	0.0	0.5	0.6	0.5	1.7	1.5	1.1
Total Receipts to Cash Flow 42	29.2	7.1	3.7	12.9	14.3	41.0	21.1	32.4	20.8
Cost of Goods to Cash Flow 43	27.3	6.1	2.6	11.3	12.4	38.7	19.3	30.1	18.6
Cash Flow to Total Debt 44	0.1	•	5.0	0.9	0.4	0.1	0.3	0.2	0.2

Selected Financial Factors (in Percentages)

Debt Ratio 45	77.1	•	27.4	46.4	62.8	78.9	69.5	76.6	62.1
Return on Total Assets 46	7.6	•	66.5	20.3	11.2	6.3	12.8	10.1	8.3
Return on Equity Before Income Taxes 47	24.2	•	89.1	35.9	25.3	13.8	33.9	31.4	15.9
Return on Equity After Income Taxes 48	20.2	•	89.0	35.4	23.5	11.6	32.3	28.2	12.5
Profit Margin (Before Income Tax) 49	1.9	12.6	12.7	3.7	2.4	0.8	2.5	1.6	2.2
Profit Margin (After Income Tax) 50	1.6	11.0	12.7	3.7	2.2	0.7	2.4	1.5	1.8

Table I

Corporations with and without Net Income

CHEMICAL AND ALLIED PRODUCTS

MONEY AMOUNTS AND SIZE OF ASSETS IN THOUSANDS OF DOLLARS

Item Description for Accounting Period 7/08 Through 6/09	Total	Zero Assets	Under 500	500 to 1,000	1,000 to 5,000	5,000 to 10,000	10,000 to 25,000	25,000 to 50,000	50,000 to 100,000	100,000 to 250,000	250,000 to 500,000	500,000 to 2,500,000	2,500,000 and over
Number of Enterprises 1	7929	1891	3319	705	1339	276	250	73	41	16	9	7	3
Revenues ($ in Thousands)													
Net Sales 2	85081512	214871	2159364	1410075	9658089	7835493	9209535	7345124	10233904	4021396	4694537	11139618	17159505
Interest 3	184207	436	3513	1221	6981	3318	11223	1865	8409	10135	15044	52768	69294
Rents 4	16697	28	789	1040	177	887	1319	76	1400	7282	638	794	2268
Royalties 5	8356	0	0	0	0	0	33	0	529	291	0	7479	24
Other Portfolio Income 6	119660	403	6840	1398	1285	2900	1157	3171	7582	6938	2111	52913	32960
Other Receipts 7	1021236	913	23342	483	63429	15929	35475	62678	154100	17117	8673	205158	433942
Total Receipts 8	86431668	216651	2193848	1414217	9729961	7858527	9258742	7412914	10405924	4063159	4721003	11458730	17697993
Average Total Receipts 9	10901	115	661	2006	7267	28473	37035	101547	253803	253947	524556	1636961	5899331
Operating Costs/Operating Income (%)													
Cost of Operations 10	79.3	89.9	72.3	62.1	63.4	80.3	79.3	84.7	91.1	83.6	84.0	83.2	76.0
Salaries and Wages 11	6.0	1.6	3.9	8.6	12.2	7.3	5.9	5.2	2.7	4.1	4.1	4.1	6.5
Taxes Paid 12	0.9	1.1	0.9	1.9	1.2	0.7	0.9	0.7	0.5	0.8	0.3	1.0	0.9
Interest Paid 13	1.0	0.0	0.6	0.8	0.6	0.2	0.6	0.5	0.4	0.7	1.3	2.1	1.9
Depreciation 14	1.5	0.1	0.6	1.0	1.0	0.5	1.3	1.1	0.3	0.8	2.8	1.0	3.5
Amortization and Depletion 15	0.5	•	0.0	0.0	0.0	0.0	0.1	0.2	0.1	0.5	0.2	0.5	1.8
Pensions and Other Deferred Comp. 16	0.3	0.0	0.1	1.4	0.4	0.2	0.3	0.6	0.1	0.3	0.1	0.3	0.4
Employee Benefits 17	0.9	0.2	0.4	1.1	0.7	0.2	0.5	0.5	0.3	0.7	0.5	0.6	2.3
Advertising 18	0.2	0.1	0.4	0.4	0.8	0.1	0.3	0.2	0.1	0.1	0.7	0.1	0.0
Other Expenses 19	6.3	12.4	14.3	9.2	11.3	6.0	6.6	5.3	2.9	3.6	6.2	6.3	5.0
Officers' Compensation 20	1.3	•	6.1	11.7	3.0	1.8	1.3	0.9	0.5	0.7	0.5	0.5	0.4
Operating Margin 21	1.8	•	0.6	1.8	5.4	2.6	2.8	0.3	1.1	4.1	•	0.3	1.3
Operating Margin Before Officers' Comp. 22	3.1	•	6.7	13.5	8.4	4.5	4.1	1.2	1.5	4.8	•	0.8	1.7

Selected Average Balance Sheet ($ in Thousands)

Net Receivables 23	1068	0	16	191	693	2632	4832	11190	23044	40612	82640	179651	335126
Inventories 24	867	0	28	65	377	1514	3971	8865	19382	42473	51192	159947	374222
Net Property, Plant and Equipment 25	1032	0	13	123	324	469	2262	4728	6132	19585	81869	201126	1290814
Total Assets 26	5735	0	116	723	2130	6910	14633	33744	74537	161639	342450	1059979	5850101
Notes and Loans Payable 27	2002	0	75	223	623	1559	4266	10171	19324	36816	122099	577143	1956609
All Other Liabilities 28	1961	0	49	238	766	2749	4432	9968	26415	66387	96542	383211	1966022
Net Worth 29	1772	0	-8	262	741	2603	5935	13606	28798	58437	123808	99626	1927470

Selected Financial Ratios (Times to 1)

Current Ratio 30	1.5	•	1.6	2.7	1.6	1.5	1.7	1.6	1.5	1.3	1.5	1.2	1.4
Quick Ratio 31	0.8	•	1.0	2.4	1.1	1.0	0.9	0.9	0.8	0.7	0.8	0.7	0.5
Net Sales to Working Capital 32	11.1	•	17.1	5.5	12.2	13.9	8.5	11.7	13.2	13.4	8.4	20.3	8.4
Coverage Ratio 33	4.3	•	4.9	3.4	11.5	12.8	6.3	3.7	7.5	8.6	0.9	2.6	3.3
Total Asset Turnover 34	1.9	•	5.6	2.8	3.4	4.1	2.5	3.0	3.3	1.6	1.5	1.5	1.0
Inventory Turnover 35	9.8	•	16.8	19.0	12.2	15.1	7.4	9.6	11.7	4.9	8.6	8.3	11.6
Receivables Turnover 36	9.8	•	28.2	9.7	9.8	11.8	8.0	10.0	11.8	4.2	8.7	7.2	16.1
Total Liabilities to Net Worth 37	2.2	•	•	1.8	1.9	1.7	1.5	1.5	1.6	1.8	1.8	9.6	2.0
Current Assets to Working Capital 38	3.1	•	2.6	1.6	2.6	3.0	2.5	2.8	2.9	4.9	2.8	5.1	3.3
Current Liabilities to Working Capital 39	2.1	•	1.6	0.6	1.6	2.0	1.5	1.8	1.9	3.9	1.8	4.1	2.3
Working Capital to Net Sales 40	0.1	•	0.1	0.2	0.1	0.1	0.1	0.1	0.1	0.1	0.1	0.0	0.1
Inventory to Working Capital 41	1.0	•	0.7	0.2	0.7	0.8	1.0	1.1	1.2	1.8	1.1	2.0	0.6
Total Receipts to Cash Flow 42	12.2	13.2	7.0	12.0	6.3	12.4	11.3	18.6	19.9	12.7	20.7	11.6	15.1
Cost of Goods to Cash Flow 43	9.7	11.9	5.0	7.5	4.0	10.0	9.0	15.7	18.1	10.6	17.4	9.7	11.5
Cash Flow to Total Debt 44	0.2	•	0.8	0.4	0.8	0.5	0.4	0.3	0.3	0.2	0.1	0.1	0.1

Selected Financial Factors (in Percentages)

Debt Ratio 45	69.1	•	107.2	63.8	65.2	62.3	59.4	59.7	61.4	63.8	63.8	90.6	67.1
Return on Total Assets 46	8.4	•	15.5	8.0	22.8	12.9	10.0	5.1	10.8	9.2	1.9	8.1	6.2
Return on Equity Before Income Taxes 47	20.7	•	•	15.7	59.9	31.5	20.7	9.3	24.2	22.5	•	52.6	13.2
Return on Equity After Income Taxes 48	16.7	•	•	8.9	58.7	27.9	17.5	7.5	20.4	16.6	•	37.5	9.2
Profit Margin (Before Income Tax) 49	3.4	•	2.2	2.1	6.1	2.9	3.3	1.3	2.8	5.2	•	3.3	4.5
Profit Margin (After Income Tax) 50	2.8	•	2.1	1.2	6.0	2.6	2.8	1.0	2.4	3.9	•	2.3	3.1

Table II

Corporations with Net Income

CHEMICAL AND ALLIED PRODUCTS

MONEY AMOUNTS AND SIZE OF ASSETS IN THOUSANDS OF DOLLARS

Item Description for Accounting Period 7/08 Through 6/09	Total	Zero Assets	Under 500	500 to 1,000	1,000 to 5,000	5,000 to 10,000	10,000 to 25,000	25,000 to 50,000	50,000 to 100,000	100,000 to 250,000	250,000 to 500,000	500,000 to 2,500,000	2,500,000 and over
Number of Enterprises **1**	4129	669	1452	264	1160	263	202	60	32	•	4	•	0
Revenues ($ in Thousands)													
Net Sales **2**	70830464	206630	1700566	680879	8920063	7416147	7587740	7121104	8383634	•	1326048	•	0
Interest **3**	160833	415	990	1214	5329	3259	6099	1204	4678	•	12884	•	0
Rents **4**	14595	28	789	1040	153	887	625	76	1328	•	18	•	0
Royalties **5**	877	0	0	0	0	0	33	0	529	•	0	•	0
Other Portfolio Income **6**	80208	80	6840	1398	585	2869	827	1437	7569	•	1633	•	0
Other Receipts **7**	1007599	914	23137	230	63055	15868	33187	60539	146506	•	23835	•	0
Total Receipts **8**	72094576	208067	1732322	684761	8989185	7439030	7628511	7184360	8544244	•	1364418	•	0
Average Total Receipts **9**	17461	311	1193	2594	7749	28285	37765	119739	267008	•	341104	•	•
Operating Costs/Operating Income (%)													
Cost of Operations **10**	79.9	89.8	70.9	43.7	62.7	79.6	79.2	85.0	89.7	•	78.1	•	•
Salaries and Wages **11**	5.5	1.5	3.4	14.9	12.8	7.5	5.7	5.0	3.0	•	8.6	•	•
Taxes Paid **12**	0.9	0.9	0.8	2.5	1.2	0.6	0.9	0.7	0.5	•	0.5	•	•
Interest Paid **13**	1.0	0.0	0.4	1.2	0.6	0.2	0.5	0.4	0.4	•	2.3	•	•
Depreciation **14**	0.9	0.1	0.6	1.1	0.9	0.5	0.9	0.9	0.3	•	1.5	•	•
Amortization and Depletion **15**	0.5	•	0.0	0.0	0.0	0.0	0.1	0.1	0.1	•	0.3	•	•
Pensions and Other Deferred Comp. **16**	0.4	0.0	0.1	2.6	0.4	0.2	0.4	0.6	0.1	•	0.1	•	•
Employee Benefits **17**	0.7	0.2	0.2	1.7	0.7	0.2	0.5	0.5	0.4	•	0.6	•	•
Advertising **18**	0.2	0.1	0.4	0.4	0.8	0.1	0.2	0.1	0.1	•	0.4	•	•
Other Expenses **19**	5.7	6.5	12.9	10.0	10.8	6.1	5.5	4.0	2.8	•	7.8	•	•
Officers' Compensation **20**	1.4	•	5.3	16.7	3.1	1.9	1.4	0.9	0.5	•	0.2	•	•
Operating Margin **21**	2.9	0.8	5.0	5.2	6.0	3.0	4.6	2.0	2.1	•	•	•	•
Operating Margin Before Officers' Comp. **22**	4.3	0.8	10.3	21.9	9.1	4.9	6.0	2.9	2.6	•	•	•	•

Selected Average Balance Sheet ($ in Thousands)

Net Receivables 23	1722	0	18	193	703	2546	5260	12332	25327	54863	•
Inventories 24	1437	0	43	158	388	1437	4428	9757	21195	66071	•
Net Property, Plant and Equipment 25	1200	0	27	105	313	480	1678	4647	5807	27082	•
Total Assets 26	8580	0	171	689	2138	6826	14594	33881	75329	296401	•
Notes and Loans Payable 27	2948	0	79	347	692	1502	3918	9709	17292	110722	•
All Other Liabilities 28	3053	0	72	332	828	2674	4423	9890	29549	102676	•
Net Worth 29	2579	0	20	11	618	2650	6254	14282	28489	83002	•

Selected Financial Ratios (Times to 1)

Current Ratio 30	1.5	•	1.6	2.1	1.5	1.5	1.7	1.6	1.5	1.3	•
Quick Ratio 31	0.8	•	0.8	1.4	1.0	1.0	1.0	0.9	0.8	0.6	•
Net Sales to Working Capital 32	10.6	•	24.2	9.5	14.9	13.4	7.6	11.9	12.9	10.5	•
Coverage Ratio 33	5.9	73.3	17.5	5.9	12.1	15.3	10.7	9.0	10.0	2.3	•
Total Asset Turnover 34	2.0	•	6.9	3.7	3.6	4.1	2.6	3.5	3.5	1.1	•
Inventory Turnover 35	9.5	•	19.3	7.1	12.4	15.6	6.7	10.3	11.1	3.9	•
Receivables Turnover 36	9.2	•	33.9	•	10.1	12.5	7.2	10.6	11.3	4.8	•
Total Liabilities to Net Worth 37	2.3	•	7.5	63.7	2.5	1.6	1.3	1.4	1.6	2.6	•
Current Assets to Working Capital 38	3.0	•	2.8	1.9	3.0	2.8	2.3	2.6	2.8	4.4	•
Current Liabilities to Working Capital 39	2.0	•	1.8	0.9	2.0	1.8	1.3	1.6	1.8	3.4	•
Working Capital to Net Sales 40	0.1	•	0.0	0.1	0.1	0.1	0.1	0.1	0.1	0.1	•
Inventory to Working Capital 41	0.9	•	0.9	0.6	0.9	0.8	0.9	1.0	1.2	1.9	•
Total Receipts to Cash Flow 42	10.9	12.5	5.6	8.4	6.3	11.6	10.4	17.0	16.4	11.8	•
Cost of Goods to Cash Flow 43	8.7	11.3	3.9	3.7	4.0	9.3	8.3	14.4	14.7	9.2	•
Cash Flow to Total Debt 44	0.3	•	1.4	0.5	0.8	0.6	0.4	0.4	0.3	0.1	•

Selected Financial Factors (in Percentages)

Debt Ratio 45	69.9	•	88.2	98.5	71.1	61.2	57.1	57.8	62.2	72.0	•
Return on Total Assets 46	11.4	•	49.6	25.8	26.5	14.6	14.7	11.5	15.5	5.8	•
Return on Equity Before Income Taxes 47	31.6	•	397.3	1386.9	84.1	35.2	31.0	24.3	36.9	11.5	•
Return on Equity After Income Taxes 48	26.3	•	388.5	942.0	82.4	31.5	27.3	22.3	32.0	8.6	•
Profit Margin (Before Income Tax) 49	4.7	1.5	6.8	5.7	6.8	3.3	5.2	2.9	4.0	2.9	•
Profit Margin (After Income Tax) 50	3.9	1.4	6.7	3.9	3.9	3.0	4.5	2.7	3.5	2.2	•

Table I

Corporations with and without Net Income

PETROLEUM AND PETROLEUM PRODUCTS

MONEY AMOUNTS AND SIZE OF ASSETS IN THOUSANDS OF DOLLARS

Item Description for Accounting Period 7/08 Through 6/09		Total	Zero Assets	Under 500	500 to 1,000	1,000 to 5,000	5,000 to 10,000	10,000 to 25,000	25,000 to 50,000	50,000 to 100,000	100,000 to 250,000	250,000 to 500,000	500,000 to 2,500,000	2,500,000 and over
Number of Enterprises	1	8253	806	3365	637	2127	661	396	138	53	34	13	16	7
Revenues ($ in Thousands)														
Net Sales	2	592733517	45315707	4415172	6205740	58248947	48790623	56671956	41092330	30783963	57336805	39882300	90661464	113328511
Interest	3	533955	11906	3336	2798	12572	20280	16747	8641	8871	24839	11636	66488	345841
Rents	4	385238	0	0	508	25103	24337	40239	11007	8517	10411	16642	85884	162591
Royalties	5	46305	1673	0	0	129	899	28	2	1213	8	1661	151	40542
Other Portfolio Income	6	1919987	36744	20003	1582	57407	54872	40480	44903	25006	11279	56687	56968	1514054
Other Receipts	7	2548590	94324	553	18059	222080	124590	105129	80265	66484	102354	59982	765263	909506
Total Receipts	8	598167592	45460354	4439064	6228687	58566238	49015601	56874579	41237148	30894054	57485696	40028908	91636218	116301045
Average Total Receipts	9	72479	56402	1319	9778	27535	74154	143623	298820	582907	1690756	3079147	5727264	1661435
Operating Costs/Operating Income (%)														
Cost of Operations	10	93.6	99.5	77.0	94.1	93.6	95.1	94.0	95.1	95.1	97.5	97.4	97.6	83.8
Salaries and Wages	11	1.0	0.3	3.2	1.0	1.9	1.4	1.6	1.1	1.2	0.6	0.6	0.5	1.1
Taxes Paid	12	0.4	0.0	1.7	1.2	0.4	0.3	0.5	0.3	0.3	0.3	0.1	0.1	0.9
Interest Paid	13	0.6	0.3	0.7	0.1	0.1	0.2	0.2	0.2	0.3	0.2	0.2	0.6	1.9
Depreciation	14	0.8	0.1	1.3	0.4	0.4	0.3	0.6	0.6	0.5	0.2	0.3	0.3	2.5
Amortization and Depletion	15	0.2	0.0	0.1	0.0	0.0	0.0	0.0	0.0	0.0	0.0	0.0	0.0	0.8
Pensions and Other Deferred Comp.	16	0.1	0.0	0.1	0.1	0.1	0.1	0.0	0.0	0.0	0.0	0.1	0.0	0.1
Employee Benefits	17	0.1	0.0	0.1	0.2	0.1	0.1	0.1	0.1	0.1	0.1	0.1	0.1	0.1
Advertising	18	0.0	0.0	0.1	0.6	0.1	0.0	0.1	0.0	0.0	0.0	0.0	0.0	0.0
Other Expenses	19	2.8	0.8	9.4	1.6	2.8	2.0	2.3	2.1	1.6	0.9	1.6	1.7	6.7
Officers' Compensation	20	0.3	0.0	3.1	1.1	0.7	0.4	0.3	0.2	0.3	0.1	0.1	0.2	0.1
Operating Margin	21	0.2	•	3.2	•	•	0.2	0.3	0.2	0.5	0.1	•	•	1.9
Operating Margin Before Officers' Comp.	22	0.4	•	6.3	0.9	0.5	0.5	0.6	0.4	0.8	0.2	•	•	2.0

Selected Average Balance Sheet ($ in Thousands)

Net Receivables 23	2333	0	32	238	685	2262	4519	8826	24261	52012	95287	209532	770124
Inventories 24	1536	0	33	78	414	849	1981	3646	9061	32418	59555	191955	622627
Net Property, Plant and Equipment 25	9184	0	32	97	497	1420	4917	11009	15330	30162	76821	135557	9308095
Total Assets 26	17889	0	214	726	2412	6733	15870	34472	67439	156214	333552	1066902	13647941
Notes and Loans Payable 27	5616	0	82	157	611	2048	4970	10819	17765	44130	95996	279596	4528144
All Other Liabilities 28	6428	0	34	193	831	2287	5477	11798	27797	74511	152935	475088	4590847
Net Worth 29	5845	0	99	375	970	2398	5424	11856	21877	37574	84621	312218	4528950

Selected Financial Ratios (Times to 1)

Current Ratio 30	1.2	•	4.5	2.0	1.7	1.6	1.3	1.2	1.5	1.2	1.2	1.1	0.9
Quick Ratio 31	0.7	•	3.4	1.7	1.1	1.3	0.9	0.8	1.1	0.7	0.7	0.7	0.5
Net Sales to Working Capital 32	91.9	•	10.7	34.7	42.9	42.5	66.9	88.9	40.0	80.1	80.6	93.6	•
Coverage Ratio 33	2.9	•	6.0	2.7	4.4	4.2	3.6	3.5	4.4	3.1	0.0	0.7	3.5
Total Asset Turnover 34	4.0	•	6.1	13.4	11.4	11.0	9.0	8.6	8.6	10.8	9.2	5.3	1.2
Inventory Turnover 35	43.8	•	30.4	117.9	61.9	82.7	67.9	77.7	61.0	50.7	50.2	28.8	21.8
Receivables Turnover 36	22.2	•	29.7	35.2	35.7	25.9	27.9	29.6	23.4	29.9	25.5	19.2	11.4
Total Liabilities to Net Worth 37	2.1	•	1.2	0.9	1.5	1.8	1.9	1.9	2.1	3.2	2.9	2.4	2.0
Current Assets to Working Capital 38	7.3	•	1.3	2.0	2.5	2.6	4.2	5.4	3.0	5.3	5.5	9.2	•
Current Liabilities to Working Capital 39	6.3	•	0.3	1.0	1.5	1.6	3.2	4.4	2.0	4.3	4.5	8.2	•
Working Capital to Net Sales 40	0.0	•	0.1	0.0	0.0	0.0	0.0	0.0	0.0	0.0	0.0	0.0	•
Inventory to Working Capital 41	1.6	•	0.3	0.2	0.6	0.4	0.9	1.1	0.6	1.7	1.1	2.5	•
Total Receipts to Cash Flow 42	31.4	•	9.0	67.0	40.3	48.6	42.5	48.2	50.4	101.7	98.4	81.1	10.3
Cost of Goods to Cash Flow 43	29.4	•	7.0	63.0	37.7	46.2	39.9	45.8	47.9	99.1	95.8	79.1	8.6
Cash Flow to Total Debt 44	0.2	•	1.3	0.4	0.5	0.4	0.3	0.3	0.3	0.1	0.1	0.1	0.2

Selected Financial Factors (in Percentages)

Debt Ratio 45	67.3	•	54.1	48.3	59.8	64.4	65.8	65.6	67.6	75.9	74.6	70.7	66.8
Return on Total Assets 46	6.8	•	27.6	3.9	6.1	8.8	8.1	6.6	9.7	6.2	0.1	2.3	7.9
Return on Equity Before Income Taxes 47	13.7	•	50.1	4.8	11.7	18.9	17.2	13.7	23.0	17.6	•	•	16.9
Return on Equity After Income Taxes 48	9.3	•	49.5	0.5	10.9	17.7	15.1	12.1	20.1	13.3	•	•	11.1
Profit Margin (Before Income Tax) 49	1.1	•	3.8	0.2	0.4	0.6	0.7	0.5	0.9	0.4	•	•	4.7
Profit Margin (After Income Tax) 50	0.8	•	3.7	0.0	0.4	0.6	0.5	0.5	0.8	0.3	•	•	3.1

Table II

Corporations with Net Income

PETROLEUM AND PETROLEUM PRODUCTS

MONEY AMOUNTS AND SIZE OF ASSETS IN THOUSANDS OF DOLLARS

Item Description for Accounting Period 7/08 Through 6/09	Total	Zero Assets	Under 500	500 to 1,000	1,000 to 5,000	5,000 to 10,000	10,000 to 25,000	25,000 to 50,000	50,000 to 100,000	100,000 to 250,000	250,000 to 500,000	500,000 to 2,500,000	2,500,000 and over
Number of Enterprises **1**	6578	414	3010	•	1596	565	308	97	37	26	7	6	•
Revenues ($ in Thousands)													
Net Sales **2**	414684231	8134897	3920655	•	40662694	42594129	46385472	33801454	24247312	39705985	20485914	45567231	•
Interest **3**	405922	267	2221	•	7090	14377	13524	7371	7852	9348	8772	6491	•
Rents **4**	286602	0	0	•	20515	13072	34107	10936	4066	9804	16318	14732	•
Royalties **5**	42142	0	0	•	0	72	28	2	1213	8	127	151	•
Other Portfolio Income **6**	1859745	21283	19783	•	42379	48832	37628	44589	22346	8115	54457	44946	•
Other Receipts **7**	1757213	58860	552	•	141363	110059	105227	73196	46134	110414	64577	237575	•
Total Receipts **8**	419035855	8215307	3943211	•	40874041	42780541	46575986	33937548	24328923	39843674	20630165	45871126	•
Average Total Receipts **9**	63703	19844	1310	•	25610	75718	151221	349872	657538	1532449	2947166	7645188	•
Operating Costs/Operating Income (%)													
Cost of Operations **10**	92.1	99.9	74.6	•	93.6	95.1	93.9	95.1	95.2	96.8	96.8	97.8	•
Salaries and Wages **11**	1.1	0.1	3.4	•	1.8	1.4	1.6	1.1	1.1	0.7	0.8	0.4	•
Taxes Paid **12**	0.5	0.0	1.8	•	0.3	0.3	0.5	0.2	0.2	0.5	0.2	0.1	•
Interest Paid **13**	0.6	0.0	0.8	•	0.1	0.2	0.2	0.2	0.2	0.2	0.2	0.2	•
Depreciation **14**	0.9	0.0	1.3	•	0.4	0.3	0.6	0.6	0.5	0.3	0.2	0.2	•
Amortization and Depletion **15**	0.2	0.0	0.1	•	0.0	0.0	0.0	0.0	0.0	0.0	0.0	0.0	•
Pensions and Other Deferred Comp. **16**	0.1	0.0	0.1	•	0.1	0.1	0.0	0.0	0.0	0.0	0.0	0.0	•
Employee Benefits **17**	0.1	0.0	0.0	•	0.1	0.1	0.1	0.1	0.1	0.1	0.2	0.1	•
Advertising **18**	0.0	0.0	0.0	•	0.0	0.0	0.1	0.0	0.0	0.0	0.0	0.0	•
Other Expenses **19**	3.0	0.3	10.0	•	2.1	1.8	2.2	2.1	1.4	1.0	1.5	0.5	•
Officers' Compensation **20**	0.3	0.0	3.4	•	0.8	0.4	0.3	0.2	0.3	0.1	0.1	0.3	•
Operating Margin **21**	1.0	•	4.4	•	0.6	0.4	0.6	0.4	0.9	0.4	0.0	0.4	•
Operating Margin Before Officers' Comp. **22**	1.3	•	7.8	•	1.5	0.8	0.8	0.6	1.2	0.5	0.1	0.7	•

Selected Average Balance Sheet ($ in Thousands)

				•								
Net Receivables 23	2237	0	34	•	795	2237	4866	9296	26494	51703	91550	246354
Inventories 24	1497	0	35	•	426	823	2098	3596	10369	33950	53856	362306
Net Property, Plant and Equipment 25	10219	0	33	•	477	1371	4479	1145	14331	34836	47016	142503
Total Assets 26	18464	0	224	•	2547	6633	16155	34456	66535	154428	310269	1191610
Notes and Loans Payable 27	6140	0	79	•	539	1694	4334	10181	13687	36425	79608	393343
All Other Liabilities 28	6231	0	31	•	850	2205	5849	12877	24195	68404	137799	437509
Net Worth 29	6093	0	114	•	1158	2734	5973	11397	28653	49599	92862	360758

Selected Financial Ratios (Times to 1)

				•								
Current Ratio 30	1.2	•	5.4	•	1.8	1.7	1.4	1.2	1.7	1.4	1.3	1.5
Quick Ratio 31	0.8	•	4.1	•	1.3	1.3	1.0	0.8	1.3	0.8	0.8	0.7
Net Sales to Working Capital 32	69.2	•	9.4	•	33.6	41.5	55.5	108.4	33.2	50.4	54.1	38.6
Coverage Ratio 33	4.5	27.1	7.5	•	9.7	5.8	5.3	5.0	8.2	6.0	4.7	7.2
Total Asset Turnover 34	3.4	•	5.8	•	10.0	11.4	9.3	10.1	9.8	9.9	9.4	6.4
Inventory Turnover 35	38.8	•	27.6	•	56.0	87.1	67.4	92.2	60.2	43.5	52.6	20.5
Receivables Turnover 36	18.7	•	27.3	•	30.2	27.4	26.6	33.1	21.4	26.4	22.2	15.6
Total Liabilities to Net Worth 37	2.0	•	1.0	•	1.2	1.4	1.7	2.0	1.3	2.1	2.3	2.3
Current Assets to Working Capital 38	5.9	•	1.2	•	2.3	2.4	3.5	5.9	2.4	3.6	4.0	3.2
Current Liabilities to Working Capital 39	4.9	•	0.2	•	1.3	1.4	2.5	4.9	1.4	2.6	3.0	2.2
Working Capital to Net Sales 40	0.0	•	0.1	•	0.0	0.0	0.0	0.0	0.0	0.0	0.0	0.0
Inventory to Working Capital 41	1.2	•	0.3	•	0.5	0.4	0.8	1.1	0.4	1.2	0.5	1.2
Total Receipts to Cash Flow 42	23.1	127.9	7.8	•	39.2	46.1	38.7	43.4	46.6	67.9	57.0	67.5
Cost of Goods to Cash Flow 43	21.3	127.7	5.9	•	36.7	43.9	36.3	41.3	44.4	65.7	55.1	66.0
Cash Flow to Total Debt 44	0.2	•	1.5	•	0.5	0.4	0.4	0.3	0.4	0.2	0.2	0.1

Selected Financial Factors (in Percentages)

				•								
Debt Ratio 45	67.0	•	49.0	•	54.5	58.8	63.0	66.9	56.9	67.9	70.1	69.7
Return on Total Assets 46	9.2	•	33.4	•	12.5	11.6	11.1	9.9	13.9	9.3	8.3	8.0
Return on Equity Before Income Taxes 47	21.7	•	56.8	•	24.7	23.3	24.3	23.9	28.4	24.2	21.9	22.8
Return on Equity After Income Taxes 48	16.4	•	56.3	•	23.8	22.1	21.8	21.6	25.2	19.9	19.2	21.1
Profit Margin (Before Income Tax) 49	2.1	0.6	5.0	•	1.1	0.8	1.0	0.8	1.2	0.8	0.7	1.1
Profit Margin (After Income Tax) 50	1.6	0.4	4.9	•	1.1	0.8	0.9	0.7	1.1	0.6	0.6	1.0

Table I

Corporations with and without Net Income

BEER, WINE, AND DISTILLED ALCOHOLIC BEVERAGE

MONEY AMOUNTS AND SIZE OF ASSETS IN THOUSANDS OF DOLLARS

Item Description for Accounting Period 7/08 Through 6/09		Total	Zero Assets	Under 500	500 to 1,000	1,000 to 5,000	5,000 to 10,000	10,000 to 25,000	25,000 to 50,000	50,000 to 100,000	100,000 to 250,000	250,000 to 500,000	500,000 to 2,500,000	2,500,000 and over
Number of Enterprises	1	3446	836	543	206	1050	369	258	72	63	28	10	12	0
Revenues ($ in Thousands)														
Net Sales	2	77966074	18094	320747	436732	10785403	7679468	11505968	6797164	8929042	8929908	5603803	16959746	0
Interest	3	104938	1154	15	317	3916	1968	619	2225	1803	3564	6558	82800	0
Rents	4	52804	88	0	0	0	167	0	104	356	11053	14504	26533	0
Royalties	5	73200	0	0	0	0	0	0	302	30719	34626	2646	4907	0
Other Portfolio Income	6	339318	6958	1263	0	80045	50279	10559	7137	50304	53264	29789	49719	0
Other Receipts	7	1255867	3658	7869	74058	94156	63947	107906	90480	130676	305183	103144	274788	0
Total Receipts	8	79792201	29952	329894	511107	10963520	7795829	11625052	6897412	9142900	9337598	5760444	17398493	0
Average Total Receipts	9	23155	36	608	2481	10441	21127	45058	95797	145125	333486	576044	1449874	•
Operating Costs/Operating Income (%)														
Cost of Operations	10	75.8	39.7	20.3	75.8	75.0	74.8	75.4	76.0	76.7	76.4	77.9	76.4	•
Salaries and Wages	11	8.2	•	4.9	13.5	9.2	8.4	8.0	8.5	8.1	7.7	6.2	8.5	•
Taxes Paid	12	2.9	1.9	2.3	2.1	2.9	2.6	3.1	2.1	2.0	2.2	1.8	4.7	•
Interest Paid	13	1.1	55.5	0.5	0.3	0.3	0.5	0.9	0.5	0.7	0.6	1.6	2.5	•
Depreciation	14	0.7	1.8	0.8	0.8	0.6	0.7	0.8	0.7	1.3	0.6	0.5	0.6	•
Amortization and Depletion	15	0.6	11.4	0.1	0.2	0.2	0.3	0.7	0.6	0.7	0.5	2.0	0.7	•
Pensions and Other Deferred Comp.	16	0.4	•	0.7	0.0	0.4	0.8	0.4	0.5	0.2	0.5	0.6	0.3	•
Employee Benefits	17	0.8	•	0.2	0.5	0.9	0.8	0.9	0.8	0.8	0.5	0.9	0.7	•
Advertising	18	1.4	•	1.0	2.2	0.6	0.8	0.7	1.1	1.3	2.9	3.1	1.3	•
Other Expenses	19	6.0	72.3	12.5	18.1	6.8	5.6	5.3	6.8	6.1	6.4	5.2	5.4	•
Officers' Compensation	20	1.3	13.3	13.7	1.3	2.7	1.8	1.4	1.1	0.8	1.3	0.4	0.3	•
Operating Margin	21	0.7	•	42.9	•	0.5	3.1	2.5	1.4	1.2	0.1	•	•	•
Operating Margin Before Officers' Comp.	22	2.0	•	56.6	•	3.1	4.8	3.9	2.5	2.0	1.5	0.2	•	•

Selected Average Balance Sheet ($ in Thousands)

Net Receivables 23	1660	0	38	105	437	926	1656	6134	10700	34755	32613	169573
Inventories 24	2254	0	16	482	604	2019	3075	9122	11779	34975	47911	218959
Net Property, Plant and Equipment 25	1171	0	17	70	353	1085	2409	4095	10362	16544	32994	73031
Total Assets 26	14661	0	179	783	2395	7125	15693	34080	68592	156072	355492	2197434
Notes and Loans Payable 27	5918	0	153	258	509	1568	6133	7966	22054	43513	132699	1087921
All Other Liabilities 28	2633	0	190	44	829	1477	2696	8138	15556	49128	98497	243546
Net Worth 29	6110	0	-163	480	1057	4080	6864	17976	30981	63432	124295	865967

Selected Financial Ratios (Times to 1)

Current Ratio 30	1.6	•	0.4	3.4	1.6	2.3	2.2	1.9	1.7	1.7	1.5	1.4
Quick Ratio 31	0.8	•	0.3	1.2	0.9	1.2	1.1	0.9	0.9	0.9	0.7	0.6
Net Sales to Working Capital 32	11.0	•	•	5.1	17.5	8.8	12.2	9.6	10.5	8.0	14.6	10.7
Coverage Ratio 33	3.8	0.5	94.4	7.6	8.4	10.8	5.0	7.2	5.8	8.5	2.7	1.4
Total Asset Turnover 34	1.5	•	3.3	2.7	4.3	2.9	2.8	2.8	2.1	2.0	1.6	0.6
Inventory Turnover 35	7.6	•	7.4	3.3	12.7	7.7	10.9	7.9	9.2	7.0	9.1	4.9
Receivables Turnover 36	13.6	•	23.2	14.3	24.0	19.7	22.5	14.5	15.7	9.9	17.6	8.2
Total Liabilities to Net Worth 37	1.4	•	•	0.6	1.3	0.7	1.3	0.9	1.2	1.5	1.9	1.5
Current Assets to Working Capital 38	2.5	•	•	1.4	2.7	1.8	1.9	2.1	2.4	2.4	2.9	3.6
Current Liabilities to Working Capital 39	1.5	•	•	0.4	1.7	0.8	0.9	1.1	1.4	1.4	1.9	2.6
Working Capital to Net Sales 40	0.1	•	•	0.2	0.1	0.1	0.1	0.1	0.1	0.1	0.1	0.1
Inventory to Working Capital 41	1.1	•	•	0.9	1.1	0.8	0.8	0.9	0.9	1.0	1.4	1.7
Total Receipts to Cash Flow 42	13.2	•	1.8	5.6	14.1	11.9	13.5	12.7	12.6	10.0	14.4	19.5
Cost of Goods to Cash Flow 43	10.0	•	0.4	4.2	10.6	8.9	10.2	9.6	9.7	7.6	11.2	14.9
Cash Flow to Total Debt 44	0.2	•	1.0	1.3	0.5	0.6	0.4	0.5	0.3	0.3	0.2	0.1

Selected Financial Factors (in Percentages)

Debt Ratio 45	58.3	•	191.3	38.7	55.9	42.7	56.3	47.3	54.8	59.4	65.0	60.6
Return on Total Assets 46	6.4	•	151.6	6.9	10.3	14.8	12.6	9.0	8.8	10.8	6.7	2.3
Return on Equity Before Income Taxes 47	11.4	•	•	9.7	20.5	23.4	23.0	14.8	16.2	23.4	12.0	1.8
Return on Equity After Income Taxes 48	10.3	•	•	7.4	17.6	21.7	22.6	13.7	15.0	21.4	9.1	1.3
Profit Margin (Before Income Tax) 49	3.1	•	45.5	2.2	2.1	4.6	3.5	2.8	3.5	4.7	2.7	1.1
Profit Margin (After Income Tax) 50	2.8	•	45.5	1.7	1.8	4.3	3.5	2.6	3.3	4.2	2.0	0.8

Table II
Corporations with Net Income

BEER, WINE, AND DISTILLED ALCOHOLIC BEVERAGE

MONEY AMOUNTS AND SIZE OF ASSETS IN THOUSANDS OF DOLLARS

Item Description for Accounting Period 7/08 Through 6/09	Total	Zero Assets	Under 500	500 to 1,000	1,000 to 5,000	5,000 to 10,000	10,000 to 25,000	25,000 to 50,000	50,000 to 100,000	100,000 to 250,000	250,000 to 500,000	500,000 to 2,500,000	2,500,000 and over
Number of Enterprises **1**	2465	450	238	179	906	334	208	58	53	25	6	8	0
Revenues ($ in Thousands)													
Net Sales **2**	69285230	11471	320747	430279	9763014	7060144	9694729	5999231	7771055	7884837	4226457	16123268	0
Interest **3**	30576	0	0	317	3319	1826	503	1577	1709	3512	5773	12040	0
Rents **4**	37460	0	0	0	0	167	0	104	356	11053	934	24847	0
Royalties **5**	69027	0	0	0	0	0	0	0	30719	34626	0	3683	0
Other Portfolio Income **6**	319833	6958	1263	0	77540	39817	10425	5719	45594	53264	29553	49699	0
Other Receipts **7**	1078257	-1	7869	74059	90310	61549	105317	80865	126722	297798	101735	132031	0
Total Receipts **8**	70820383	18428	329879	504655	9934183	7163503	9810974	6087496	7976155	8285090	4364452	16345568	0
Average Total Receipts **9**	28730	41	1386	2819	10965	21448	47168	104957	150493	331404	727409	2043196	•
Operating Costs/Operating Income (%)													
Cost of Operations **10**	75.7	10.5	20.3	75.6	73.3	74.4	75.3	75.4	77.7	75.8	80.1	77.0	•
Salaries and Wages **11**	8.3	•	4.9	13.7	9.5	8.5	7.6	8.5	7.9	7.7	5.8	8.8	•
Taxes Paid **12**	3.0	0.3	2.2	2.1	3.1	2.7	3.1	2.2	2.1	2.4	1.3	4.7	•
Interest Paid **13**	0.7	•	0.5	0.3	0.3	0.4	0.8	0.4	0.6	0.5	1.5	0.9	•
Depreciation **14**	0.7	•	0.8	0.8	0.7	0.8	0.8	0.6	1.1	0.6	0.5	0.6	•
Amortization and Depletion **15**	0.5	•	0.1	0.2	0.2	0.2	0.6	0.3	0.6	0.4	1.4	0.7	•
Pensions and Other Deferred Comp. **16**	0.4	•	0.7	0.0	0.3	0.9	0.4	0.5	0.2	0.4	0.3	0.3	•
Employee Benefits **17**	0.8	•	0.2	0.5	1.0	0.8	0.9	0.7	0.7	0.7	1.0	0.8	•
Advertising **18**	1.1	•	0.1	2.2	0.5	0.8	0.7	1.1	1.4	3.1	2.4	0.6	•
Other Expenses **19**	5.7	24.9	8.3	18.3	6.5	5.2	5.0	7.1	5.0	6.5	4.8	5.0	•
Officers' Compensation **20**	1.2	20.9	13.7	1.3	2.7	1.7	1.2	1.0	0.7	1.4	0.4	0.3	•
Operating Margin **21**	1.8	43.4	48.1	•	1.9	3.6	3.6	2.2	1.9	0.5	0.6	0.4	•
Operating Margin Before Officers' Comp. **22**	3.1	64.3	61.9	•	4.6	5.3	4.8	3.2	2.6	1.9	1.0	0.7	•

Selected Average Balance Sheet ($ in Thousands)

Net Receivables 23	1999	0	0	97	421	881	1577	6786	11064	34225	39500	229212
Inventories 24	2814	0	19	344	645	2038	3109	9193	12088	34841	64357	312603
Net Property, Plant and Equipment 25	1255	0	40	80	388	1081	2672	4044	9824	16434	46847	44188
Total Assets 26	11249	0	190	764	2390	7137	15827	33121	67506	152846	378445	1014490
Notes and Loans Payable 27	3320	0	109	160	449	1421	5989	7143	18809	34379	137059	363707
All Other Liabilities 28	3081	0	6	51	803	1326	2754	7867	14610	52274	124691	319424
Net Worth 29	4848	0	75	553	1138	4389	7083	18111	34087	66193	116695	331359

Selected Financial Ratios (Times to 1)

Current Ratio 30	1.9	•	4.5	9.3	1.7	2.5	2.3	1.9	1.7	1.9	1.5	1.9
Quick Ratio 31	0.9	•	2.0	3.6	0.9	1.2	1.2	0.9	0.9	1.0	0.6	0.8
Net Sales to Working Capital 32	9.6	•	26.4	5.0	16.1	8.6	11.9	10.7	11.2	7.2	16.4	7.0
Coverage Ratio 33	7.1	•	105.2	7.6	14.0	13.3	7.0	10.8	8.0	11.0	3.7	3.0
Total Asset Turnover 34	2.5	•	7.1	3.1	4.5	3.0	2.9	3.1	2.2	2.1	1.9	2.0
Inventory Turnover 35	7.6	•	14.5	5.3	12.3	7.7	11.3	8.5	9.4	6.9	8.8	5.0
Receivables Turnover 36	13.7	•	13648.8	22.6	26.0	22.8	24.2	14.5	15.9	9.8	•	2.1
Total Liabilities to Net Worth 37	1.3	•	1.5	0.4	1.1	0.6	1.2	0.8	1.0	1.3	2.2	2.1
Current Assets to Working Capital 38	2.1	•	1.3	1.1	2.4	1.7	1.7	2.1	2.4	2.2	3.1	2.1
Current Liabilities to Working Capital 39	1.1	•	0.3	0.1	1.4	0.7	0.7	1.1	1.4	1.2	2.1	1.1
Working Capital to Net Sales 40	0.1	•	0.0	0.2	0.1	0.1	0.1	0.1	0.1	0.1	0.1	0.1
Inventory to Working Capital 41	1.0	•	0.7	0.6	1.1	0.8	0.7	0.9	0.9	0.8	1.5	1.1
Total Receipts to Cash Flow 42	12.1	1.5	1.8	5.5	12.1	11.6	11.9	11.0	12.6	8.9	13.0	18.7
Cost of Goods to Cash Flow 43	9.2	0.2	0.4	4.2	8.9	8.6	9.0	8.3	9.8	6.8	10.4	14.4
Cash Flow to Total Debt 44	0.4	•	6.6	2.1	0.7	0.7	0.4	0.6	0.3	0.4	0.2	0.2

Selected Financial Factors (in Percentages)

Debt Ratio 45	56.9	•	60.5	27.6	52.4	38.5	55.2	45.3	49.5	56.7	69.2	67.3
Return on Total Assets 46	11.8	•	364.1	8.1	17.5	16.1	16.4	12.6	11.2	12.5	10.0	5.3
Return on Equity Before Income Taxes 47	23.5	•	912.5	9.7	34.2	24.1	31.3	20.9	19.4	26.2	23.6	10.7
Return on Equity After Income Taxes 48	21.6	•	912.4	7.4	31.1	22.5	31.2	19.6	18.0	24.0	18.4	8.8
Profit Margin (Before Income Tax) 49	4.0	104.1	50.7	2.2	3.6	5.0	4.8	3.7	4.5	5.5	3.9	1.8
Profit Margin (After Income Tax) 50	3.7	104.1	50.7	1.7	3.3	4.7	4.7	3.4	4.2	5.0	3.0	1.4

Table I

Corporations with and without Net Income

MISCELLANEOUS NONDURABLE GOODS

MONEY AMOUNTS AND SIZE OF ASSETS IN THOUSANDS OF DOLLARS

Item Description for Accounting Period 7/08 Through 6/09	Total	Zero Assets	Under 500	500 to 1,000	1,000 to 5,000	5,000 to 10,000	10,000 to 25,000	25,000 to 50,000	50,000 to 100,000	100,000 to 250,000	250,000 to 500,000	500,000 to 2,500,000	2,500,000 and over
Number of Enterprises **1**	31090	5646	18082	2906	3387	451	345	150	63	35	11	14	0
Revenues ($ in Thousands)													
Net Sales **2**	156343464	1414485	12157418	7879683	31248997	14134649	17399068	13955420	12997927	13489679	5348261	26317877	0
Interest **3**	132999	6125	4355	2357	11203	14786	11548	11268	5614	18539	3745	43459	0
Rents **4**	19831	0	2	80	5761	654	1262	1937	829	4850	1012	3445	0
Royalties **5**	137425	0	0	0	0	0	366	11731	3982	14288	1030	106029	0
Other Portfolio Income **6**	311472	38799	33782	12167	5425	16179	19815	10982	45045	64917	4912	59448	0
Other Receipts **7**	1314218	103787	16497	169813	92453	37799	209211	120311	122327	116174	112117	213730	0
Total Receipts **8**	158259409	1563196	12212054	8064100	31363839	14204067	17641270	14111649	13175724	13708447	5471077	26743988	0
Average Total Receipts **9**	5090	277	675	2775	9260	31495	51134	94078	209138	391670	497371	1910285	•
Operating Costs/Operating Income (%)													
Cost of Operations **10**	82.0	78.9	79.2	78.3	85.1	86.7	81.7	85.1	83.6	83.9	69.8	77.8	•
Salaries and Wages **11**	5.2	5.7	5.0	6.6	4.1	4.4	6.0	4.7	5.1	4.7	8.6	6.1	•
Taxes Paid **12**	1.0	1.2	1.1	1.9	0.8	0.5	1.8	1.1	0.6	0.8	1.0	0.9	•
Interest Paid **13**	0.7	0.8	0.3	0.6	0.4	0.4	0.5	0.6	0.5	0.8	1.1	1.4	•
Depreciation **14**	0.9	1.2	0.6	0.9	0.5	0.4	0.7	0.7	0.7	1.0	1.4	1.9	•
Amortization and Depletion **15**	0.2	0.0	0.1	0.0	0.1	0.0	0.1	0.1	0.2	0.1	0.6	0.6	•
Pensions and Other Deferred Comp. **16**	0.2	0.1	0.2	0.0	0.1	0.1	0.2	0.2	0.2	0.2	0.3	0.5	•
Employee Benefits **17**	0.5	0.5	0.5	0.4	0.3	0.3	0.5	0.4	0.4	0.5	0.7	1.0	•
Advertising **18**	0.8	0.4	0.2	0.6	0.5	0.4	0.7	0.4	1.3	0.7	3.2	1.1	•
Other Expenses **19**	6.3	14.5	9.4	8.9	5.9	4.5	6.0	4.8	4.8	4.9	7.7	7.4	•
Officers' Compensation **20**	1.3	2.5	3.8	3.4	1.4	0.9	1.4	0.9	0.9	0.5	0.6	0.3	•
Operating Margin **21**	0.9	•	•	•	0.7	1.3	0.5	0.9	1.8	2.0	5.0	1.0	•
Operating Margin Before Officers' Comp. **22**	2.2	•	3.5	1.7	2.1	2.2	1.9	1.8	2.6	2.5	5.6	1.3	•

Selected Average Balance Sheet ($ in Thousands)

Net Receivables 23	430	0	18	298	657	2217	4777	9301	18466	43778	61492	181838	•
Inventories 24	444	0	35	248	627	2239	4353	10570	19678	33336	86767	204376	•
Net Property, Plant and Equipment 25	227	0	14	87	204	495	1692	4268	8316	20904	42979	192438	•
Total Assets 26	1767	0	106	778	2078	7097	14864	34296	70719	147731	323776	1218572	•
Notes and Loans Payable 27	580	0	56	307	651	2145	5182	9173	19771	52796	78100	418203	•
All Other Liabilities 28	666	0	38	230	938	2547	5296	13851	24503	68094	89382	443874	•
Net Worth 29	520	0	12	241	490	2406	4385	11272	26445	26841	156294	356496	•

Selected Financial Ratios (Times to 1)

Current Ratio 30	1.5	•	1.7	2.2	1.5	1.8	1.4	1.5	1.5	1.5	1.6	1.3	•
Quick Ratio 31	0.8	•	0.9	1.3	0.9	1.0	0.8	0.7	0.7	0.8	0.7	0.6	•
Net Sales to Working Capital 32	13.3	•	21.2	8.3	15.4	11.2	14.0	11.2	11.3	12.1	7.8	17.9	•
Coverage Ratio 33	4.2	7.1	1.4	2.3	3.6	5.5	5.0	4.4	7.4	5.5	7.8	2.9	•
Total Asset Turnover 34	2.8	•	6.4	3.5	4.4	4.4	3.4	2.7	2.9	2.6	1.5	1.5	•
Inventory Turnover 35	9.3	•	15.1	8.6	12.5	12.1	9.5	7.5	8.8	9.7	3.9	7.2	•
Receivables Turnover 36	11.2	•	33.0	8.4	14.6	12.1	10.9	9.9	12.2	9.3	6.0	8.9	•
Total Liabilities to Net Worth 37	2.4	•	7.9	2.2	3.2	2.0	2.4	2.0	1.7	4.5	1.1	2.4	•
Current Assets to Working Capital 38	3.0	•	2.4	1.9	2.8	2.2	3.2	3.2	2.8	3.2	2.7	4.5	•
Current Liabilities to Working Capital 39	2.0	•	1.4	0.9	1.8	1.2	2.2	2.2	1.8	2.2	1.7	3.5	•
Working Capital to Net Sales 40	0.1	•	0.0	0.1	0.1	0.1	0.1	0.1	0.1	0.1	0.1	0.1	•
Inventory to Working Capital 41	1.2	•	1.1	0.7	1.1	0.7	1.3	1.4	1.2	1.0	1.2	2.0	•
Total Receipts to Cash Flow 42	14.8	7.1	14.9	13.9	17.4	21.2	15.1	18.0	14.9	14.0	7.5	12.6	•
Cost of Goods to Cash Flow 43	12.1	5.6	11.8	10.9	14.8	18.4	12.4	15.3	12.5	11.8	5.3	9.8	•
Cash Flow to Total Debt 44	0.3	•	0.5	0.4	0.3	0.3	0.3	0.2	0.3	0.2	0.4	0.2	•

Selected Financial Factors (in Percentages)

Debt Ratio 45	70.6	•	88.8	69.1	76.4	66.1	70.5	67.1	62.6	81.8	51.7	70.7	•
Return on Total Assets 46	8.0	•	3.1	4.5	6.7	9.6	8.1	6.9	10.6	11.5	12.5	6.5	•
Return on Equity Before Income Taxes 47	20.8	•	8.1	8.3	20.4	23.1	22.0	16.3	24.5	51.9	22.6	14.8	•
Return on Equity After Income Taxes 48	17.2	•	2.6	6.9	18.9	22.2	19.6	14.0	21.5	40.3	19.9	10.2	•
Profit Margin (Before Income Tax) 49	2.2	4.7	0.1	0.7	1.1	1.8	1.9	2.0	3.1	3.6	7.3	2.8	•
Profit Margin (After Income Tax) 50	1.8	4.1	0.0	0.6	1.0	1.7	1.7	1.7	2.8	2.8	6.4	1.9	•

Table II
Corporations with Net Income

MISCELLANEOUS NONDURABLE GOODS

MONEY AMOUNTS AND SIZE OF ASSETS IN THOUSANDS OF DOLLARS

Item Description for Accounting Period 7/08 Through 6/09	Total	Zero Assets	Under 500	500 to 1,000	1,000 to 5,000	5,000 to 10,000	10,000 to 25,000	25,000 to 50,000	50,000 to 100,000	100,000 to 250,000	250,000 to 500,000	500,000 to 2,500,000	2,500,000 and over
Number of Enterprises **1**	14514	950	8893	1597	2258	348	•	•	48	30	•	•	0

Revenues ($ in Thousands)

Item Description for Accounting Period 7/08 Through 6/09	Total	Zero Assets	Under 500	500 to 1,000	1,000 to 5,000	5,000 to 10,000	10,000 to 25,000	25,000 to 50,000	50,000 to 100,000	100,000 to 250,000	250,000 to 500,000	500,000 to 2,500,000	2,500,000 and over
Net Sales **2**	127858422	866980	9569516	5382572	24376683	11276220	•	•	11221281	12140361	•	•	0
Interest **3**	118237	6046	1440	1647	10459	14003	•	•	5023	17882	•	•	0
Rents **4**	16119	0	2	80	4463	596	•	•	322	4637	•	•	0
Royalties **5**	124164	0	0	0	0	0	•	•	2396	14288	•	•	0
Other Portfolio Income **6**	303058	38769	33752	11230	4160	15530	•	•	42747	63969	•	•	0
Other Receipts **7**	1124437	100537	27055	149718	83140	28562	•	•	103672	114814	•	•	0
Total Receipts **8**	129544437	1012332	9631765	5545247	24478905	11334911	•	•	11375441	12355951	•	•	0
Average Total Receipts **9**	8925	1066	1083	3472	10841	32572	•	•	236988	411865	•	•	•

Operating Costs/Operating Income (%)

Item Description for Accounting Period 7/08 Through 6/09	Total	Zero Assets	Under 500	500 to 1,000	1,000 to 5,000	5,000 to 10,000	10,000 to 25,000	25,000 to 50,000	50,000 to 100,000	100,000 to 250,000	250,000 to 500,000	500,000 to 2,500,000	2,500,000 and over
Cost of Operations **10**	82.0	77.7	81.1	79.3	85.3	87.5	•	•	84.6	84.4	•	•	•
Salaries and Wages **11**	4.9	6.1	3.8	5.3	4.0	3.5	•	•	4.8	4.1	•	•	•
Taxes Paid **12**	1.0	1.3	0.8	2.1	0.7	0.5	•	•	0.6	0.7	•	•	•
Interest Paid **13**	0.6	0.8	0.2	0.5	0.3	0.4	•	•	0.4	0.9	•	•	•
Depreciation **14**	0.8	1.1	0.4	0.7	0.4	0.3	•	•	0.6	0.9	•	•	•
Amortization and Depletion **15**	0.2	0.0	0.1	0.0	0.0	0.0	•	•	0.1	0.1	•	•	•
Pensions and Other Deferred Comp. **16**	0.2	0.1	0.2	0.1	0.1	0.0	•	•	0.2	0.2	•	•	•
Employee Benefits **17**	0.5	0.6	0.6	0.2	0.3	0.3	•	•	0.3	0.4	•	•	•
Advertising **18**	0.8	0.2	0.2	0.7	0.3	0.4	•	•	1.3	0.7	•	•	•
Other Expenses **19**	5.6	10.3	6.6	7.9	5.1	4.1	•	•	3.5	4.6	•	•	•
Officers' Compensation **20**	1.2	3.0	3.6	3.5	1.4	0.8	•	•	0.8	0.5	•	•	•
Operating Margin **21**	2.2	•	2.4	•	2.1	2.2	•	•	2.7	2.4	•	•	•
Operating Margin Before Officers' Comp. **22**	3.4	1.8	6.0	3.1	3.5	3.0	•	•	3.5	3.0	•	•	•

Selected Average Balance Sheet ($ in Thousands)

Net Receivables 23	727	0	19	351	705	2301	•	18187	46086
Inventories 24	766	0	44	305	687	2522	•	21405	33499
Net Property, Plant and Equipment 25	371	0	11	51	165	439	•	7099	20995
Total Assets 26	3011	0	129	784	2188	7388	•	68800	148060
Notes and Loans Payable 27	896	0	35	352	497	2148	•	17768	57718
All Other Liabilities 28	1042	0	36	208	860	2435	•	23294	55563
Net Worth 29	1073	0	58	223	831	2805	•	27739	34779

Selected Financial Ratios (Times to 1)

Current Ratio 30	1.7	•	2.5	2.5	1.9	2.0	•	1.6	1.5
Quick Ratio 31	0.9	•	1.4	1.5	1.1	1.0	•	0.8	0.9
Net Sales to Working Capital 32	11.6	•	17.5	8.2	12.1	10.1	•	11.5	11.7
Coverage Ratio 33	6.7	20.5	14.0	7.0	9.5	7.4	•	10.4	6.0
Total Asset Turnover 34	2.9	•	8.3	4.3	4.9	4.4	•	3.4	2.7
Inventory Turnover 35	9.4	•	20.0	8.8	13.4	11.2	•	9.2	10.2
Receivables Turnover 36	11.1	•	38.9	7.9	16.2	11.2	•	13.1	9.0
Total Liabilities to Net Worth 37	1.8	•	1.2	2.5	1.6	1.6	•	1.5	3.3
Current Assets to Working Capital 38	2.5	•	1.7	1.7	2.1	2.0	•	2.6	2.8
Current Liabilities to Working Capital 39	1.5	•	0.7	0.7	1.1	1.0	•	1.6	1.8
Working Capital to Net Sales 40	0.1	•	0.1	0.1	0.1	0.1	•	0.1	0.1
Inventory to Working Capital 41	1.0	•	0.7	0.6	0.8	0.6	•	1.1	0.9
Total Receipts to Cash Flow 42	13.1	4.6	13.4	11.9	15.1	18.0	•	15.6	13.3
Cost of Goods to Cash Flow 43	10.7	3.6	10.9	9.4	12.9	15.7	•	13.2	11.2
Cash Flow to Total Debt 44	0.3	•	1.1	0.5	0.5	0.4	•	0.4	0.3

Selected Financial Factors (in Percentages)

Debt Ratio 45	64.4	•	54.9	71.5	62.0	62.0	•	59.7	76.5
Return on Total Assets 46	12.3	•	27.5	14.4	13.8	13.8	•	15.3	14.0
Return on Equity Before Income Taxes 47	29.5	•	56.7	43.2	32.4	31.4	•	34.2	49.7
Return on Equity After Income Taxes 48	25.8	•	54.4	40.6	31.0	30.4	•	30.5	39.2
Profit Margin (Before Income Tax) 49	3.6	15.6	3.1	2.9	2.5	2.7	•	4.1	4.3
Profit Margin (After Income Tax) 50	3.1	14.6	2.9	2.7	2.4	2.6	•	3.6	3.4

Table I

Corporations with and without Net Income

WHOLESALE ELECTRONIC MARKETS AND AGENTS AND BROKERS

MONEY AMOUNTS AND SIZE OF ASSETS IN THOUSANDS OF DOLLARS

Item Description for Accounting Period 7/08 Through 6/09	Total	Zero Assets	Under 500	500 to 1,000	1,000 to 5,000	5,000 to 10,000	10,000 to 25,000	25,000 to 50,000	50,000 to 100,000	100,000 to 250,000	250,000 to 500,000	500,000 to 2,500,000	2,500,000 and over
Number of Enterprises **1**	17644	3177	13934	343	167	•	12	•	0	0	0	0	0
Revenues ($ in Thousands)													
Net Sales **2**	6174754	89939	5107619	211621	182279	•	79770	•	0	0	0	0	0
Interest **3**	19325	987	2386	1244	212	•	148	•	0	0	0	0	0
Rents **4**	2876	0	0	0	0	•	0	•	0	0	0	0	0
Royalties **5**	326	0	0	0	0	•	0	•	0	0	0	0	0
Other Portfolio Income **6**	18026	0	0	0	515	•	0	•	0	0	0	0	0
Other Receipts **7**	87585	28585	16005	0	143	•	2416	•	0	0	0	0	0
Total Receipts **8**	6302892	119511	5126010	212865	183149	•	82334	•	0	0	0	0	0
Average Total Receipts **9**	357	38	368	621	1097	•	6861	•	•	•	•	•	•
Operating Costs/Operating Income (%)													
Cost of Operations **10**	1.3	•	•	•	•	•	•	•	•	•	•	•	•
Salaries and Wages **11**	26.4	45.9	24.2	21.4	27.1	•	16.4	•	•	•	•	•	•
Taxes Paid **12**	3.1	1.8	2.9	2.7	4.4	•	1.0	•	•	•	•	•	•
Interest Paid **13**	0.9	5.1	0.4	0.5	3.6	•	2.8	•	•	•	•	•	•
Depreciation **14**	1.4	0.2	0.9	14.5	1.6	•	3.5	•	•	•	•	•	•
Amortization and Depletion **15**	0.3	0.1	0.1	0.3	•	•	3.7	•	•	•	•	•	•
Pensions and Other Deferred Comp. **16**	1.4	0.1	1.4	•	0.1	•	•	•	•	•	•	•	•
Employee Benefits **17**	2.1	0.2	2.0	2.9	0.8	•	1.7	•	•	•	•	•	•
Advertising **18**	0.4	•	0.2	0.2	3.0	•	5.0	•	•	•	•	•	•
Other Expenses **19**	34.2	21.0	35.1	48.5	49.8	•	16.3	•	•	•	•	•	•
Officers' Compensation **20**	20.9	0.1	23.5	16.8	14.9	•	24.9	•	•	•	•	•	•
Operating Margin **21**	7.7	25.4	9.2	•	•	•	24.7	•	•	•	•	•	•
Operating Margin Before Officers' Comp. **22**	28.5	25.5	32.7	9.2	9.5	•	49.6	•	•	•	•	•	•

Selected Average Balance Sheet ($ in Thousands)

Net Receivables 23	12	0	2	0	699	17
Inventories 24	1	0	0	0	119	0
Net Property, Plant and Equipment 25	16	0	9	164	114	341
Total Assets 26	111	0	54	703	1942	16340
Notes and Loans Payable 27	32	0	23	66	279	1379
All Other Liabilities 28	27	0	8	152	488	11198
Net Worth 29	51	0	23	486	1176	3764

Selected Financial Ratios (Times to 1)

Current Ratio 30	1.5	•	1.6	2.7	2.5	0.7
Quick Ratio 31	1.2	•	1.6	2.7	1.9	0.4
Net Sales to Working Capital 32	19.5	•	34.9	4.1	1.8	•
Coverage Ratio 33	11.3	12.5	22.8	•	•	11.0
Total Asset Turnover 34	3.2	•	6.8	0.9	0.6	0.4
Inventory Turnover 35	3.7	•	•	•	•	•
Receivables Turnover 36	20.4	•	76.0	2534.4	1.7	785.9
Total Liabilities to Net Worth 37	1.2	•	1.3	0.4	0.7	3.3
Current Assets to Working Capital 38	2.9	•	2.6	1.6	1.7	•
Current Liabilities to Working Capital 39	1.9	•	1.6	0.6	0.7	•
Working Capital to Net Sales 40	0.1	•	0.0	0.2	0.6	•
Inventory to Working Capital 41	0.0	•	0.0	•	•	•
Total Receipts to Cash Flow 42	2.6	1.3	2.5	2.7	2.8	2.3
Cost of Goods to Cash Flow 43	0.0	•	•	•	•	•
Cash Flow to Total Debt 44	2.3	•	4.8	1.0	0.5	0.2

Selected Financial Factors (in Percentages)

Debt Ratio 45	53.7	•	57.1	30.9	39.4	77.0
Return on Total Assets 46	33.7	•	68.3	•	•	12.5
Return on Equity Before Income Taxes 47	66.3	•	152.4	•	•	49.4
Return on Equity After Income Taxes 48	64.7	•	150.5	•	•	49.4
Profit Margin (Before Income Tax) 49	9.7	58.3	9.5	•	•	28.0
Profit Margin (After Income Tax) 50	9.5	57.5	9.4	•	•	28.0

Table II
Corporations with Net Income

WHOLESALE ELECTRONIC MARKETS AND AGENTS AND BROKERS

MONEY AMOUNTS AND SIZE OF ASSETS IN THOUSANDS OF DOLLARS

Item Description for Accounting Period 7/08 Through 6/09	Total	Zero Assets	Under 500	500 to 1000	1,000 to 5,000	5,000 to 10,000	10,000 to 25,000	25,000 to 50,000	50,000 to 100,000	100,000 to 250,000	250,000 to 500,000	500,000 to 2,500,000	2,500,000 and over
Number of Enterprises **1**	11984	2115	9619	•	44	4	•	•	0	0	0	0	0
Revenues ($ in Thousands)													
Net Sales **2**	5819256	89939	4903358	•	175286	3246	•	•	0	0	0	0	0
Interest **3**	15807	9	1265	•	185	0	•	•	0	0	0	0	0
Rents **4**	2876	0	0	•	0	0	•	•	0	0	0	0	0
Royalties **5**	326	0	0	•	0	0	•	•	0	0	0	0	0
Other Portfolio Income **6**	17817	0	0	•	410	0	•	•	0	0	0	0	0
Other Receipts **7**	76113	22751	10320	•	192	16804	•	•	0	0	0	0	0
Total Receipts **8**	5932195	112699	4914943	•	176073	20050	•	•	0	0	0	0	0
Average Total Receipts **9**	495	53	511	•	4002	5012	•	•	•	•	•	•	•
Operating Costs/Operating Income (%)													
Cost of Operations **10**	1.3	•	•	•	•	•	•	•	•	•	•	•	•
Salaries and Wages **11**	26.1	37.4	24.1	•	24.1	•	•	•	•	•	•	•	•
Taxes Paid **12**	3.0	1.7	2.8	•	3.9	4.7	•	•	•	•	•	•	•
Interest Paid **13**	0.9	0.6	0.4	•	3.7	1.7	•	•	•	•	•	•	•
Depreciation **14**	1.3	0.2	0.8	•	1.3	•	•	•	•	•	•	•	•
Amortization and Depletion **15**	0.2	0.1	0.1	•	•	•	•	•	•	•	•	•	•
Pensions and Other Deferred Comp. **16**	1.4	0.1	1.5	•	0.0	•	•	•	•	•	•	•	•
Employee Benefits **17**	2.0	0.2	1.9	•	0.6	•	•	•	•	•	•	•	•
Advertising **18**	0.2	•	0.2	•	3.0	•	•	•	•	•	•	•	•
Other Expenses **19**	33.1	15.8	34.6	•	46.9	3.7	•	•	•	•	•	•	•
Officers' Compensation **20**	20.3	0.1	23.0	•	12.5	•	•	•	•	•	•	•	•
Operating Margin **21**	10.1	43.7	10.7	•	4.0	90.0	•	•	•	•	•	•	•
Operating Margin Before Officers' Comp. **22**	30.4	43.8	33.7	•	16.5	90.0	•	•	•	•	•	•	•

Selected Average Balance Sheet ($ in Thousands)

Net Receivables 23	11	0	1	•	1530	0
Inventories 24	1	0	0	•	143	0
Net Property, Plant and Equipment 25	18	0	10	•	294	0
Total Assets 26	114	0	58	•	2862	6358
Notes and Loans Payable 27	40	0	26	•	1030	321
All Other Liabilities 28	35	0	10	•	1518	38
Net Worth 29	39	0	22	•	314	5998

Selected Financial Ratios (Times to 1)

Current Ratio 30	1.2	•	1.4	•	1.6	•
Quick Ratio 31	0.9	•	1.4	•	1.1	•
Net Sales to Working Capital 32	50.3	•	55.2	•	4.3	•
Coverage Ratio 33	14.5	113.3	26.3	•	2.2	366.3
Total Asset Turnover 34	4.3	•	8.8	•	1.4	0.1
Inventory Turnover 35	10.5	•	•	•	•	•
Receivables Turnover 36	27.8	•	101.0	•	2.3	0.2
Total Liabilities to Net Worth 37	1.9	•	1.7	•	8.1	0.1
Current Assets to Working Capital 38	5.9	•	3.4	•	2.6	•
Current Liabilities to Working Capital 39	4.9	•	2.4	•	1.6	•
Working Capital to Net Sales 40	0.0	•	0.0	•	0.2	•
Inventory to Working Capital 41	0.0	•	•	•	•	•
Total Receipts to Cash Flow 42	2.5	1.2	2.4	•	2.3	0.2
Cost of Goods to Cash Flow 43	0.0	•	•	•	•	•
Cash Flow to Total Debt 44	2.6	•	5.8	•	0.7	13.8

Selected Financial Factors (in Percentages)

Debt Ratio 45	65.9	•	62.7	•	89.0	5.7
Return on Total Assets 46	55.2	•	100.1	•	11.4	77.8
Return on Equity Before Income Taxes 47	150.6	•	258.2	•	56.5	82.2
Return on Equity After Income Taxes 48	147.5	•	255.3	•	37.6	82.2
Profit Margin (Before Income Tax) 49	12.0	69.0	10.9	•	4.5	607.7
Profit Margin (After Income Tax) 50	11.8	68.2	10.8	•	3.0	607.7

202

Table I

Corporations with and without Net Income

NEW AND USED CAR DEALERS

MONEY AMOUNTS AND SIZE OF ASSETS IN THOUSANDS OF DOLLARS

Item Description for Accounting Period 7/08 Through 6/09	Total	Zero Assets	Under 500	500 to 1,000	1,000 to 5,000	5,000 to 10,000	10,000 to 25,000	25,000 to 50,000	50,000 to 100,000	100,000 to 250,000	250,000 to 500,000	500,000 to 2,500,000	2,500,000 and over
Number of Enterprises **1**	48819	6601	20662	4350	8489	4706	3125	661	150	58	8	9	0
Revenues ($ in Thousands)													
Net Sales **2**	551547534	3700756	18757233	10223565	71507374	115000968	161506856	71526749	27719202	21041668	5483601	45079563	0
Interest **3**	940925	15986	12159	27545	128169	97291	140289	53443	34950	61786	34347	334959	0
Rents **4**	337247	151	8084	10	10193	11357	25667	30009	11773	50318	8622	181063	0
Royalties **5**	132668	0	0	0	0	40	0	75	0	3319	0	129233	0
Other Portfolio Income **6**	529629	26663	57346	4269	90708	65506	79621	42860	62666	51954	5512	42521	0
Other Receipts **7**	10362539	131122	257097	74956	1146633	2019556	3241032	1430373	575608	412209	83285	990673	0
Total Receipts **8**	563850542	3874678	19091919	10330345	72883077	117194718	164993465	73083509	28404199	21621254	5615367	46758012	0
Average Total Receipts **9**	11550	587	924	2375	8586	24903	52798	110565	189361	372780	701921	5195335	•
Operating Costs/Operating Income (%)													
Cost of Operations **10**	87.1	90.1	82.6	84.8	86.1	88.1	87.8	88.2	87.0	86.0	82.4	85.5	•
Salaries and Wages **11**	5.6	5.2	4.1	3.9	5.7	5.3	5.5	5.3	5.8	6.2	7.1	6.7	•
Taxes Paid **12**	1.0	1.2	1.9	1.5	1.0	0.9	0.9	0.8	0.9	0.9	0.9	1.4	•
Interest Paid **13**	0.8	1.1	0.8	0.7	0.9	0.7	0.6	0.7	0.8	1.0	1.2	1.5	•
Depreciation **14**	0.6	0.7	0.3	0.6	0.3	0.4	0.4	0.7	1.1	1.0	1.3	1.3	•
Amortization and Depletion **15**	0.0	1.2	0.0	0.0	0.0	0.1	0.1	0.1	0.1	0.1	0.1	•	•
Pensions and Other Deferred Comp. **16**	0.1	0.1	0.0	0.0	0.0	0.0	0.1	0.1	0.1	0.1	0.1	0.1	•
Employee Benefits **17**	0.5	0.3	0.1	0.2	0.6	0.5	0.5	0.5	0.5	0.5	0.6	0.5	•
Advertising **18**	1.2	1.1	1.0	0.7	1.3	1.3	1.2	1.1	1.1	1.2	1.1	0.9	•
Other Expenses **19**	5.0	9.6	9.7	6.3	5.4	4.5	4.4	4.0	4.6	5.3	7.7	6.0	•
Officers' Compensation **20**	0.7	1.5	2.0	1.6	1.2	0.7	0.6	0.5	0.5	0.4	0.4	0.0	•
Operating Margin **21**	•	•	•	•	0.0	0.7	0.1	0.1	0.1	0.1	0.1	•	•
Operating Margin Before Officers' Comp. **22**	•	•	•	1.2	•	•	•	•	•	•	•	•	•

Selected Average Balance Sheet ($ in Thousands)

Item													
Net Receivables 23	352	0	22	106	341	644	1514	3178	7489	15671	30116	138002	•
Inventories 24	1993	0	74	342	1594	4862	9486	19245	33488	52749	112312	500315	•
Net Property, Plant and Equipment 25	443	0	18	68	170	531	1534	5013	11708	27860	81769	540871	•
Total Assets 26	3481	0	145	667	2555	7007	15056	33529	65992	137581	301160	2211559	•
Notes and Loans Payable 27	2357	0	92	384	1692	5316	11042	22470	43309	84204	186907	1096882	•
All Other Liabilities 28	422	0	61	106	386	659	1354	3315	6950	17902	5963	441706	•
Net Worth 29	702	0	-8	177	477	1032	2660	7744	15733	35474	108291	672970	•

Selected Financial Ratios (Times to 1)

Item													
Current Ratio 30	1.3	•	1.4	2.7	1.4	1.2	1.2	1.2	1.2	1.3	1.1	1.1	•
Quick Ratio 31	0.3	•	0.5	1.0	0.4	0.3	0.3	0.3	0.4	0.4	0.3	0.2	•
Net Sales to Working Capital 32	21.3	•	25.7	6.7	12.3	24.2	22.7	22.1	23.2	20.2	68.0	111.1	•
Coverage Ratio 33	0.8	•	0.1	1.8	0.3	0.2	1.1	1.3	1.2	1.1	0.7	1.4	•
Total Asset Turnover 34	3.2	•	6.3	3.5	3.3	3.5	3.4	3.2	2.8	2.6	2.3	2.3	•
Inventory Turnover 35	4.9	•	10.2	5.8	4.5	4.4	4.8	5.0	4.8	5.9	5.0	8.6	•
Receivables Turnover 36	28.0	•	40.1	22.9	23.4	35.4	31.1	27.0	20.7	19.7	15.2	45.0	•
Total Liabilities to Net Worth 37	4.0	•	•	2.8	4.4	5.8	4.7	3.3	3.2	2.9	1.8	2.3	•
Current Assets to Working Capital 38	4.9	•	3.3	1.6	3.2	5.9	5.4	5.7	5.1	4.9	16.1	20.5	•
Current Liabilities to Working Capital 39	3.9	•	2.3	0.6	2.2	4.9	4.4	4.7	4.1	3.9	15.1	19.5	•
Working Capital to Net Sales 40	0.0	•	0.0	0.1	0.1	0.0	0.0	0.0	0.0	0.0	0.0	0.0	•
Inventory to Working Capital 41	3.5	•	2.1	1.0	2.3	4.5	3.9	3.5	3.7	2.9	9.3	14.4	•
Total Receipts to Cash Flow 42	30.9	•	17.2	18.4	31.6	41.9	32.5	33.0	29.1	25.7	38.7	20.6	•
Cost of Goods to Cash Flow 43	26.9	•	14.2	15.6	27.2	36.9	28.6	29.1	25.3	22.1	31.9	17.6	•
Cash Flow to Total Debt 44	0.1	•	0.3	0.3	0.1	0.1	0.1	0.1	0.1	0.1	0.1	0.2	•

Selected Financial Factors (in Percentages)

Item													
Debt Ratio 45	79.8	•	105.4	73.5	81.3	85.3	82.3	76.9	76.2	74.2	64.0	69.6	•
Return on Total Assets 46	2.0	•	0.7	4.6	0.8	0.4	2.4	2.8	2.7	2.7	1.9	4.6	•
Return on Equity Before Income Taxes 47	•	•	85.7	7.9	•	•	1.7	2.9	2.2	0.7	•	4.2	•
Return on Equity After Income Taxes 48	•	•	91.5	7.8	•	•	1.3	2.6	1.6	0.2	•	1.7	•
Profit Margin (Before Income Tax) 49	•	•	•	0.6	•	•	0.1	0.2	0.2	0.1	•	0.6	•
Profit Margin (After Income Tax) 50	•	•	•	0.6	•	•	0.1	0.2	0.1	0.0	•	0.2	•

Table II

Corporations with Net Income

NEW AND USED CAR DEALERS

MONEY AMOUNTS AND SIZE OF ASSETS IN THOUSANDS OF DOLLARS

Item Description for Accounting Period 7/08 Through 6/09	Total	Zero Assets	Under 500	500 to 1,000	1,000 to 5,000	5,000 to 10,000	10,000 to 25,000	25,000 to 50,000	50,000 to 100,000	100,000 to 250,000	250,000 to 500,000	500,000 to 2,500,000	2,500,000 and over
Number of Enterprises **1**	21671	1688	10447	1885	3643	1953	1570	366	81	32	3	4	0
Revenues ($ in Thousands)													
Net Sales **2**	284665969	556538	10935988	5930671	32088413	52137586	89792969	42093800	15439030	10999648	2157653	22533672	0
Interest **3**	453299	0	9552	21964	89971	53595	67819	30735	23374	21265	33030	101994	0
Rents **4**	91804	96	3697	10	7408	4083	9434	14653	3026	5850	8310	35237	0
Royalties **5**	3922	0	0	0	0	0	0	0	0	3319	0	603	0
Other Portfolio Income **6**	328060	19684	43518	4269	72499	50451	37758	17298	29476	13850	3800	35457	0
Other Receipts **7**	5599854	81731	221190	9338	532624	931752	1921726	911527	291127	237788	39703	421349	0
Total Receipts **8**	291142908	658049	11213945	5966252	32790915	53177467	91829706	43068013	15786033	11281720	2242496	23128312	0
Average Total Receipts **9**	13435	390	1073	3165	9001	27229	58490	117672	194889	352554	747499	5782078	•
Operating Costs/Operating Income (%)													
Cost of Operations **10**	86.6	79.5	80.4	84.0	84.0	88.3	87.5	87.8	87.6	84.8	76.7	85.4	•
Salaries and Wages **11**	5.3	4.9	2.8	2.5	5.9	4.7	5.3	5.3	5.2	6.1	7.6	7.1	°
Taxes Paid **12**	0.9	1.9	1.7	1.2	1.1	0.8	0.8	0.8	0.8	0.9	0.8	1.1	•
Interest Paid **13**	0.6	0.9	0.8	0.3	0.7	0.5	0.5	0.6	0.7	0.9	1.3	1.0	•
Depreciation **14**	0.5	2.5	0.2	0.5	0.3	0.3	0.4	0.5	0.7	0.8	1.3	1.8	•
Amortization and Depletion **15**	0.1	0.1	0.0	0.0	0.0	0.0	0.1	0.1	0.1	0.1	0.0	0.3	•
Pensions and Other Deferred Comp. **16**	0.1	0.0	0.0	0.0	0.1	0.1	0.1	0.1	0.1	0.1	0.1	0.1	•
Employee Benefits **17**	0.5	0.5	0.1	0.1	0.5	0.5	0.5	0.4	0.5	0.5	0.8	0.6	•
Advertising **18**	1.0	0.7	0.9	0.3	1.0	1.0	1.2	1.1	1.0	1.0	1.0	0.8	•
Other Expenses **19**	4.4	12.5	9.3	5.7	5.5	3.8	4.0	3.8	3.9	5.1	13.4	2.5	•
Officers' Compensation **20**	0.7	0.7	1.7	1.6	1.3	0.8	0.7	0.6	0.4	0.6	0.5	0.0	•
Operating Margin **21**	•	•	2.0	3.8	1.3	•	•	•	•	•	•	•	•
Operating Margin Before Officers' Comp. **22**	0.0	•	3.7	5.4	0.9	•	•	•	•	•	•	•	•

Selected Average Balance Sheet ($ in Thousands)

	•	•	•	•	•	•	•	•	•	•	•	•
Net Receivables 23	399	0	27	111	429	712	1519	3303	6683	11884	34031	144421
Inventories 24	2600	0	79	398	1878	5925	11225	21796	41954	64352	89396	660242
Net Property, Plant and Equipment 25	506	0	15	27	172	569	1440	4925	10871	27207	51436	761848
Total Assets 26	3874	0	165	667	2605	7065	15456	33642	65197	131481	293523	2685215
Notes and Loans Payable 27	2386	0	75	217	1508	4658	10694	21926	40973	73051	146279	1249873
All Other Liabilities 28	435	0	55	102	376	674	1354	3471	6084	13474	-13624	425026
Net Worth 29	1054	0	35	347	722	1733	3409	8245	18139	44956	160869	1010316

Selected Financial Ratios (Times to 1)

Current Ratio 30	1.4	•	2.1	4.7	1.7	1.3	1.3	1.3	1.2	1.3	1.3	1.2
Quick Ratio 31	0.4	•	0.7	2.4	0.5	0.3	0.3	0.4	0.4	0.5	0.4	0.3
Net Sales to Working Capital 32	17.0	•	14.5	6.6	9.3	19.2	18.3	21.1	21.9	16.5	17.7	39.0
Coverage Ratio 33	3.5	17.3	6.4	15.2	3.4	3.0	3.6	3.0	3.0	2.8	1.3	3.0
Total Asset Turnover 34	3.4	•	6.3	4.7	3.4	3.8	3.7	3.4	2.9	2.6	2.5	2.1
Inventory Turnover 35	4.4	•	10.7	6.6	3.9	4.0	4.5	4.6	4.0	4.5	6.2	7.3
Receivables Turnover 36	23.9	•	39.9	29.5	17.2	29.1	28.8	24.4	18.7	19.2	•	•
Total Liabilities to Net Worth 37	2.7	•	3.7	0.9	2.6	3.1	3.5	3.1	2.6	1.9	0.8	1.7
Current Assets to Working Capital 38	3.7	•	1.9	1.3	2.4	4.3	4.1	4.7	5.1	3.9	4.3	6.5
Current Liabilities to Working Capital 39	2.7	•	0.9	0.3	1.4	3.3	3.1	3.7	4.1	2.9	3.3	5.5
Working Capital to Net Sales 40	0.1	•	0.1	0.2	0.1	0.1	0.1	0.0	0.0	0.1	0.1	0.0
Inventory to Working Capital 41	2.6	•	1.2	0.6	1.6	3.2	2.9	3.2	3.5	2.4	2.2	4.6
Total Receipts to Cash Flow 42	21.9	5.3	8.8	11.2	17.3	27.5	24.7	25.8	23.8	17.6	34.3	30.0
Cost of Goods to Cash Flow 43	19.0	4.2	7.1	9.4	14.5	24.3	21.6	22.7	20.8	15.0	26.4	25.6
Cash Flow to Total Debt 44	0.2	0.9	0.9	0.9	0.3	0.2	0.2	0.2	0.2	0.2	0.2	0.1

Selected Financial Factors (in Percentages)

Debt Ratio 45	72.8	•	78.9	47.9	72.3	75.5	77.9	75.5	72.2	65.8	45.2	62.4
Return on Total Assets 46	7.5	•	34.3	22.0	8.5	6.2	6.6	5.9	6.1	6.7	4.3	6.3
Return on Equity Before Income Taxes 47	19.6	•	137.5	39.5	21.7	17.0	21.8	15.9	14.7	12.5	2.0	11.1
Return on Equity After Income Taxes 48	18.4	•	134.9	39.3	20.6	16.5	21.1	15.5	13.9	11.8	1.5	7.3
Profit Margin (Before Income Tax) 49	1.6	14.0	4.6	4.4	1.8	1.1	1.3	1.1	1.4	1.6	0.4	2.0
Profit Margin (After Income Tax) 50	1.5	13.2	4.5	4.3	1.7	1.1	1.3	1.1	1.3	1.5	0.3	1.3

Table I

Corporations with and without Net Income

OTHER MOTOR VEHICLE AND PARTS DEALERS

MONEY AMOUNTS AND SIZE OF ASSETS IN THOUSANDS OF DOLLARS

Item Description for Accounting Period 7/08 Through 6/09		Total	Zero Assets	Under 500	500 to 1,000	1,000 to 5,000	5,000 to 10,000	10,000 to 25,000	25,000 to 50,000	50,000 to 100,000	100,000 to 250,000	250,000 to 500,000	500,000 to 2,500,000	2,500,000 and over
Number of Enterprises	1	42586	3164	24889	5341	7361	1208	412	132	45	17	6	9	3
Revenues ($ in Thousands)														
Net Sales	2	149107633	1114337	15204083	8762083	39327817	16761394	11981507	10398706	7143504	4884800	2247400	16252987	15029016
Interest	3	123554	2746	3716	5332	25328	8425	13073	8425	10421	2096	5953	27689	10349
Rents	4	67231	847	1547	2750	9086	6468	4903	1423	27424	1703	354	9866	860
Royalties	5	38409	0	0	11	302	2508	1873	0	632	0	2113	10057	20912
Other Portfolio Income	6	403921	24319	39607	28087	27918	22749	40383	17307	30578	27171	12096	125221	8487
Other Receipts	7	1709972	13234	35420	87308	427040	331243	148296	117875	113829	23349	40402	292207	79770
Total Receipts	8	151450720	1155483	15284373	8885571	39817491	17132787	12190035	10543736	7326388	4939119	2308318	16718027	15149394
Average Total Receipts	9	3556	365	614	1664	5409	14183	29587	79877	162809	290536	384720	1857559	5049798
Operating Costs/Operating Income (%)														
Cost of Operations	10	72.2	75.7	70.4	69.7	74.4	78.0	78.7	79.1	78.4	70.9	63.8	73.7	49.8
Salaries and Wages	11	9.6	5.0	9.0	8.4	8.6	8.0	8.5	8.2	7.6	9.7	11.5	10.4	17.6
Taxes Paid	12	1.8	3.3	2.5	2.3	1.8	1.4	1.2	1.1	1.2	1.5	1.6	1.5	3.1
Interest Paid	13	1.2	1.0	1.0	1.3	1.2	1.6	1.4	1.1	1.2	1.4	1.3	1.1	1.0
Depreciation	14	1.6	0.5	1.0	1.1	1.0	1.4	1.5	1.4	2.3	4.2	7.6	1.5	2.9
Amortization and Depletion	15	0.1	0.1	0.1	0.1	0.1	0.1	0.1	0.1	0.1	0.1	0.3	0.5	0.1
Pensions and Other Deferred Comp.	16	0.1	0.2	0.0	0.1	0.1	0.1	0.1	0.1	0.2	0.4	0.5	0.3	0.1
Employee Benefits	17	0.8	0.3	0.3	0.8	0.7	0.7	0.6	0.7	0.8	1.2	2.1	0.8	1.5
Advertising	18	1.3	1.3	1.4	1.0	1.3	1.4	1.2	0.9	1.3	0.6	1.1	1.3	1.5
Other Expenses	19	10.1	15.9	12.8	12.9	9.2	7.8	7.2	7.4	8.3	8.3	10.8	11.3	14.6
Officers' Compensation	20	1.6	7.0	3.6	4.0	2.1	1.5	1.1	0.7	0.5	0.7	0.5	0.2	0.1
Operating Margin	21	•	•	•	•	•	•	•	•	•	1.1	•	•	7.7
Operating Margin Before Officers' Comp.	22	1.0	•	1.5	2.3	1.5	•	•	•	1.7	1.7	•	•	7.8

Selected Average Balance Sheet ($ in Thousands)

	1	2	3	4	5	6	7	8	9	10	11	12	13
Net Receivables 23	158	0	13	67	202	422	1224	3845	10529	26610	51304	134087	206547
Inventories 24	871	0	67	353	1548	4779	8725	17571	35046	55337	98474	522687	1761025
Net Property, Plant and Equipment 25	315	0	21	122	297	988	2529	5632	16800	36395	75917	202313	1147002
Total Assets 26	1732	0	132	704	2419	7072	14327	33905	73304	152354	307356	1019415	4354192
Notes and Loans Payable 27	742	0	88	405	924	3420	8585	19870	38569	68412	107516	341272	1173854
All Other Liabilities 28	538	0	39	166	809	2368	3051	6686	18112	41862	52376	325751	1768273
Net Worth 29	452	0	4	133	687	1284	2692	7349	16623	42080	147464	352391	1412066

Selected Financial Ratios (Times to 1)

	1	2	3	4	5	6	7	8	9	10	11	12	13
Current Ratio 30	1.5	•	2.1	1.8	1.6	1.4	1.4	1.3	1.3	1.6	1.7	1.8	1.3
Quick Ratio 31	0.3	•	0.7	0.5	0.3	0.2	0.3	0.3	0.4	0.6	0.7	0.6	0.2
Net Sales to Working Capital 32	8.7	•	11.6	7.7	7.0	8.9	8.7	13.6	13.6	9.0	4.6	8.1	10.2
Coverage Ratio 33	1.8	•	•	0.7	1.6	1.1	1.1	1.6	1.4	2.5	2.3	1.3	9.3
Total Asset Turnover 34	2.0	•	4.6	2.3	2.2	2.0	2.0	2.3	2.2	1.9	1.2	1.8	1.2
Inventory Turnover 35	2.9	•	6.4	3.2	2.6	2.3	2.6	3.5	3.6	3.7	2.4	2.5	1.4
Receivables Turnover 36	22.4	•	54.4	21.7	27.7	34.3	21.9	20.7	15.4	10.7	7.3	11.1	48.5
Total Liabilities to Net Worth 37	2.8	•	29.7	4.3	2.5	4.5	4.3	3.6	3.4	2.6	1.1	1.9	2.1
Current Assets to Working Capital 38	2.9	•	1.9	2.3	2.6	3.5	3.3	4.3	4.2	2.8	2.3	2.3	4.3
Current Liabilities to Working Capital 39	1.9	•	0.9	1.3	1.6	2.5	2.3	3.3	3.2	1.8	1.3	1.3	3.3
Working Capital to Net Sales 40	0.1	•	0.1	0.1	0.1	0.1	0.1	0.1	0.1	0.1	0.2	0.1	0.1
Inventory to Working Capital 41	2.2	•	1.3	1.6	2.1	2.8	2.5	3.2	2.9	1.5	1.2	1.3	3.6
Total Receipts to Cash Flow 42	13.0	25.4	14.5	12.5	13.8	18.4	21.0	16.7	15.8	13.1	11.6	14.7	5.8
Cost of Goods to Cash Flow 43	9.4	19.3	10.2	8.7	10.3	14.4	16.5	13.2	12.4	9.3	7.4	10.8	2.9
Cash Flow to Total Debt 44	0.2	•	0.3	0.2	0.2	0.1	0.1	0.2	0.2	0.2	0.2	0.2	0.3

Selected Financial Factors (in Percentages)

	1	2	3	4	5	6	7	8	9	10	11	12	13
Debt Ratio 45	73.9	•	96.7	81.1	71.6	81.8	81.2	78.3	77.3	72.4	52.0	65.4	67.6
Return on Total Assets 46	4.5	•	•	2.1	4.2	3.4	3.2	4.0	3.6	6.8	3.7	2.6	10.9
Return on Equity Before Income Taxes 47	8.0	•	•	•	5.4	1.7	1.7	6.9	4.5	14.8	4.3	1.9	30.1
Return on Equity After Income Taxes 48	4.9	•	•	•	4.7	0.9	•	6.5	2.7	13.8	1.2	1.0	19.7
Profit Margin (Before Income Tax) 49	1.0	•	•	•	0.7	0.2	0.2	0.6	0.5	2.2	1.7	0.4	8.5
Profit Margin (After Income Tax) 50	0.6	•	•	•	0.6	0.1	•	0.6	0.3	2.0	0.5	0.2	5.6

Table II

Corporations with Net Income

OTHER MOTOR VEHICLE AND PARTS DEALERS

MONEY AMOUNTS AND SIZE OF ASSETS IN THOUSANDS OF DOLLARS

Item Description for Accounting Period 7/08 Through 6/09	Total	Zero Assets	Under 500	500 to 1,000	1,000 to 5,000	5,000 to 10,000	10,000 to 25,000	25,000 to 50,000	50,000 to 100,000	100,000 to 250,000	250,000 to 500,000	500,000 to 2,500,000	2,500,000 and over
Number of Enterprises 1	20783	713	11438	2927	4658	669	241	93	23	11	3	4	3
Revenues ($ in Thousands)													
Net Sales 2	95770490	153130	7814988	5162139	27293916	8904509	8475636	7549497	4195722	3474263	1131592	6586084	15029016
Interest 3	72635	2746	2354	3126	16975	4701	10059	2045	9682	1489	5923	3185	10349
Rents 4	42598	847	448	1605	3558	2411	4842	54	26240	125	354	1255	860
Royalties 5	26974	0	0	11	302	2508	1873	0	628	0	306	433	20912
Other Portfolio Income 6	314882	20680	38486	23358	19512	18953	21333	10060	20801	6299	2794	124119	8487
Other Receipts 7	950023	4301	3307	14644	307751	109795	90530	60605	51823	10334	8024	209138	79770
Total Receipts 8	97177602	181704	7859583	5204883	27642014	9042877	8604273	7622261	4304896	3492510	1148993	6924214	15149394
Average Total Receipts 9	4676	255	687	1778	5934	13517	35702	81960	187169	317501	382998	1731054	5049798
Operating Costs/Operating Income (%)													
Cost of Operations 10	68.5	75.2	67.7	68.6	72.7	74.8	77.4	78.3	80.1	67.7	63.8	56.9	49.8
Salaries and Wages 11	10.6	2.0	8.7	7.5	8.8	7.6	8.4	8.4	6.9	11.0	11.2	18.3	17.6
Taxes Paid 12	2.1	4.0	2.9	2.4	2.0	1.5	1.2	1.1	1.2	1.8	1.8	2.5	3.1
Interest Paid 13	1.0	1.2	0.6	1.0	0.9	1.5	1.0	0.9	0.8	0.8	0.5	1.7	1.0
Depreciation 14	1.6	0.2	0.6	0.9	0.8	1.9	1.5	1.4	1.3	2.5	4.9	2.4	2.9
Amortization and Depletion 15	0.1	•	0.1	0.1	0.0	0.2	0.1	0.1	0.1	0.1	0.0	0.5	0.1
Pensions and Other Deferred Comp. 16	0.2	•	0.0	0.1	0.2	0.1	0.1	0.1	0.2	0.5	0.9	0.6	0.1
Employee Benefits 17	0.8	•	0.2	0.7	0.7	0.7	0.6	0.9	0.8	1.4	1.6	0.9	1.5
Advertising 18	1.3	0.1	1.0	1.0	1.3	1.2	1.3	0.8	1.1	0.6	1.0	2.1	1.5
Other Expenses 19	10.1	6.6	11.2	11.6	9.2	7.6	6.4	6.6	7.2	9.6	8.2	16.3	14.6
Officers' Compensation 20	1.5	5.6	3.7	4.3	2.0	1.9	1.1	0.7	0.6	0.6	0.1	0.3	0.1
Operating Margin 21	2.2	4.9	3.4	1.6	1.5	1.0	0.9	0.7	•	3.3	6.1	•	7.7
Operating Margin Before Officers' Comp. 22	3.8	10.6	7.1	5.9	3.5	2.9	2.1	1.4	0.3	4.0	6.2	•	7.8

Selected Average Balance Sheet ($ in Thousands)

Net Receivables 23	228	0	16	77	254	429	1679	3527	12019	30077	83412	162876	206547
Inventories 24	1199	0	72	367	1515	4913	9333	18739	43728	65810	73754	304936	1761025
Net Property, Plant and Equipment 25	458	0	15	152	295	1328	2506	6439	11516	41781	61271	273730	1147002
Total Assets 26	2324	0	131	688	2350	7376	14096	33571	73850	150472	288732	1275178	4354192
Notes and Loans Payable 27	865	0	56	452	797	3122	7081	18896	33289	50145	54647	439039	1173854
All Other Liabilities 28	719	0	23	140	735	2274	3030	6802	18705	46102	59318	385575	1768273
Net Worth 29	740	0	52	96	819	1980	3985	7873	21856	54225	174767	450564	1412066

Selected Financial Ratios (Times to 1)

Current Ratio 30	1.6	•	3.4	1.5	1.8	1.6	1.6	1.3	1.6	1.7	2.3	2.3	1.3
Quick Ratio 31	0.4	•	1.2	0.5	0.4	0.3	0.4	0.3	0.5	0.7	1.4	0.8	0.2
Net Sales to Working Capital 32	7.9	•	9.1	11.8	6.7	6.9	8.8	15.0	9.6	7.9	3.2	5.3	10.2
Coverage Ratio 33	4.7	19.9	7.8	3.4	4.1	2.7	3.5	2.9	3.7	5.8	15.8	2.6	9.3
Total Asset Turnover 34	2.0	•	5.2	2.6	2.5	1.8	2.5	2.4	2.5	2.1	1.3	1.3	1.2
Inventory Turnover 35	2.6	•	6.4	3.3	2.8	2.0	2.9	3.4	3.3	3.2	3.3	3.1	1.4
Receivables Turnover 36	19.5	•	47.3	17.5	25.0	29.1	18.3	20.9	12.8	10.0	•	•	48.5
Total Liabilities to Net Worth 37	2.1	•	1.5	6.1	1.9	2.7	2.5	3.3	2.4	1.8	0.7	1.8	2.1
Current Assets to Working Capital 38	2.6	•	1.4	3.2	2.2	2.7	2.6	4.5	2.8	2.4	1.8	1.8	4.3
Current Liabilities to Working Capital 39	1.6	•	0.4	2.2	1.2	1.7	1.6	3.5	1.8	1.4	0.8	0.8	3.3
Working Capital to Net Sales 40	0.1	•	0.1	0.1	0.1	0.1	0.1	0.1	0.1	0.1	0.3	0.2	0.1
Inventory to Working Capital 41	1.9	•	0.9	2.1	1.7	2.1	1.8	3.3	1.9	1.3	0.6	1.0	3.6
Total Receipts to Cash Flow 42	9.6	5.3	9.2	9.4	10.5	13.2	15.2	15.9	13.7	9.8	7.0	7.9	5.8
Cost of Goods to Cash Flow 43	6.6	4.0	6.2	6.5	7.7	9.9	11.7	12.4	11.0	6.6	4.5	4.5	2.9
Cash Flow to Total Debt 44	0.3	•	1.0	0.3	0.4	0.2	0.2	0.2	0.3	0.3	0.5	0.3	0.3

Selected Financial Factors (in Percentages)

Debt Ratio 45	68.2	•	59.9	86.0	65.2	73.2	71.7	76.5	70.4	64.0	39.5	64.7	67.6
Return on Total Assets 46	9.3	•	23.7	8.9	9.1	7.3	8.6	6.2	7.7	9.7	10.8	5.6	10.9
Return on Equity Before Income Taxes 47	23.1	•	51.7	44.7	19.8	17.2	21.8	17.2	19.1	22.4	16.8	9.7	30.1
Return on Equity After Income Taxes 48	19.2	•	50.6	42.9	18.8	16.4	20.0	16.6	16.5	21.2	11.6	8.1	19.7
Profit Margin (Before Income Tax) 49	3.7	23.6	4.0	2.4	2.8	2.6	2.5	1.7	2.3	3.8	7.8	2.7	8.5
Profit Margin (After Income Tax) 50	3.1	20.5	3.9	2.3	2.6	2.4	2.3	1.6	2.0	3.6	5.4	2.2	5.6

Table I

Corporations with and without Net Income

FURNITURE AND HOME FURNISHINGS STORES

MONEY AMOUNTS AND SIZE OF ASSETS IN THOUSANDS OF DOLLARS

Item Description for Accounting Period 7/08 Through 6/09	Total	Zero Assets	Under 500	500 to 1,000	1,000 to 5,000	5,000 to 10,000	10,000 to 25,000	25,000 to 50,000	50,000 to 100,000	100,000 to 250,000	250,000 to 500,000	500,000 to 2,500,000	2,500,000 and over
Number of Enterprises **1**	39433	3741	27793	4468	2797	402	155	25	22	12	9	9	0
Revenues ($ in Thousands)													
Net Sales **2**	85765542	638758	14680559	9967517	13024012	6954068	6496828	2261770	3259435	3043594	4777028	20661972	0
Interest **3**	270572	0	2568	18498	49476	18068	3620	465	612	34907	131963	10394	0
Rents **4**	29518	0	1597	2885	6558	2159	5389	231	0	1806	2650	6244	0
Royalties **5**	12306	0	0	0	0	0	0	0	0	16	2557	9732	0
Other Portfolio Income **6**	159161	15916	22056	5623	39344	628	1407	213	7072	4645	747	61508	0
Other Receipts **7**	747899	1840	37505	96858	97897	81216	86169	38539	95103	56650	105372	50755	0
Total Receipts **8**	86984998	656514	14744285	10091381	13217287	7056139	6593413	2301218	3362222	3141618	5020317	20800605	0
Average Total Receipts **9**	2206	175	531	2259	4726	17553	42538	92049	152828	261802	557813	2311178	•
Operating Costs/Operating Income (%)													
Cost of Operations **10**	59.2	79.1	59.0	66.2	61.6	63.5	63.6	61.7	54.8	54.0	53.0	53.6	•
Salaries and Wages **11**	12.6	4.3	9.9	9.6	11.8	11.0	14.2	15.6	15.5	15.6	16.3	14.6	•
Taxes Paid **12**	2.4	3.0	2.2	2.7	2.1	1.7	2.0	1.8	2.5	2.8	2.4	3.0	•
Interest Paid **13**	0.9	0.1	0.8	0.8	0.9	0.7	0.6	0.4	1.0	1.1	1.4	1.0	•
Depreciation **14**	1.6	0.5	0.8	0.7	0.8	1.4	0.7	0.9	2.7	2.0	2.2	3.1	•
Amortization and Depletion **15**	0.2	0.0	0.1	0.1	0.2	0.1	0.0	0.1	0.1	0.5	0.3	0.2	•
Pensions and Other Deferred Comp. **16**	0.1	•	0.1	0.1	0.1	0.2	0.1	0.5	0.2	0.1	0.1	0.1	•
Employee Benefits **17**	0.9	0.1	0.7	0.6	0.5	0.9	0.8	1.2	1.2	1.2	1.1	1.4	•
Advertising **18**	3.9	1.6	2.8	2.5	3.4	3.6	3.5	2.0	5.0	6.1	5.8	5.1	•
Other Expenses **19**	17.1	21.7	18.1	14.7	15.7	17.5	13.2	13.9	21.0	20.2	22.5	17.3	•
Officers' Compensation **20**	2.5	1.4	6.1	3.8	3.8	1.5	1.6	0.9	1.0	0.5	0.6	0.3	•
Operating Margin **21**	•	•	•	•	•	•	•	1.1	•	•	•	0.5	•
Operating Margin Before Officers' Comp. **22**	1.3	•	5.3	2.1	2.8	2.1	1.3	1.9	•	•	•	0.9	•

Selected Average Balance Sheet ($ in Thousands)

	•	•	•	•	•	•	•	•	•	•	•	•	•
Net Receivables 23	143	0	18	159	317	878	3296	9711	4821	24987	97994	128979	•
Inventories 24	372	0	57	238	949	2920	6986	10420	28906	48107	82550	543224	•
Net Property, Plant and Equipment 25	280	0	28	153	386	1745	2760	4915	21739	53736	77019	604459	•
Total Assets 26	1032	0	146	734	2112	6926	15867	36152	72367	150130	359589	1628942	•
Notes and Loans Payable 27	358	0	97	296	879	2869	3411	8685	20904	50562	102019	415727	•
All Other Liabilities 28	361	0	53	227	690	2149	6471	12192	26824	48506	107854	610201	•
Net Worth 29	313	0	-5	212	543	1908	5985	15276	24640	51062	149716	603014	•

Selected Financial Ratios (Times to 1)

Current Ratio 30	1.5	•	1.9	1.9	2.0	1.5	1.6	1.7	1.5	1.6	2.1	1.1	•
Quick Ratio 31	0.6	•	0.8	0.9	0.7	0.4	0.6	0.8	0.4	0.8	1.0	0.4	•
Net Sales to Working Capital 32	9.9	•	10.3	9.5	6.3	11.9	9.1	8.8	11.3	8.1	4.8	24.0	•
Coverage Ratio 33	1.2	•	0.7	0.4	1.5	0.1	3.0	7.9	•	0.1	0.5	2.3	•
Total Asset Turnover 34	2.1	•	3.6	3.0	2.2	2.5	2.6	2.5	2.0	1.7	1.5	1.4	•
Inventory Turnover 35	3.5	•	5.5	6.2	3.0	3.8	3.8	5.4	2.8	2.8	3.4	2.3	•
Receivables Turnover 36	14.8	•	26.4	16.4	13.8	19.0	12.5	8.5	29.9	7.7	6.3	16.3	•
Total Liabilities to Net Worth 37	2.3	•	•	2.5	2.9	2.6	1.7	1.4	1.9	1.9	1.4	1.7	•
Current Assets to Working Capital 38	2.9	•	2.1	2.2	2.0	3.2	2.6	2.5	3.1	2.6	1.9	8.5	•
Current Liabilities to Working Capital 39	1.9	•	1.1	1.2	1.0	2.2	1.6	1.5	2.1	1.6	0.9	7.5	•
Working Capital to Net Sales 40	0.1	•	0.1	0.1	0.2	0.1	0.1	0.1	0.1	0.1	0.2	0.0	•
Inventory to Working Capital 41	1.6	•	1.1	1.1	1.3	2.0	1.4	1.0	2.1	1.2	0.9	4.8	•
Total Receipts to Cash Flow 42	9.5	29.6	8.9	10.5	9.6	10.3	11.9	8.6	9.0	8.1	7.8	9.5	•
Cost of Goods to Cash Flow 43	5.6	23.4	5.2	7.0	5.9	6.5	7.6	5.3	4.9	4.4	4.1	5.1	•
Cash Flow to Total Debt 44	0.3	•	0.4	0.4	0.3	0.3	0.4	0.5	0.3	0.3	0.3	0.2	•

Selected Financial Factors (in Percentages)

Debt Ratio 45	69.7	•	103.1	71.1	74.3	72.4	62.3	57.7	66.0	66.0	58.4	63.0	•
Return on Total Assets 46	2.2	•	2.0	1.0	3.2	0.2	4.6	8.1	•	0.1	1.1	3.2	•
Return on Equity Before Income Taxes 47	1.3	•	33.0	•	4.3	•	8.1	16.7	•	•	•	4.8	•
Return on Equity After Income Taxes 48	•	•	40.1	•	3.1	•	7.6	15.7	•	•	•	•	•
Profit Margin (Before Income Tax) 49	0.2	•	•	•	0.5	•	1.2	2.8	•	•	•	1.3	•
Profit Margin (After Income Tax) 50	•	•	•	•	0.4	•	1.1	2.7	•	•	•	•	•

Table II

Corporations with Net Income

FURNITURE AND HOME FURNISHINGS STORES

MONEY AMOUNTS AND SIZE OF ASSETS IN THOUSANDS OF DOLLARS

Item Description for Accounting Period 7/08 Through 6/09	Total	Zero Assets	Under 500	500 to 1,000	1,000 to 5,000	5,000 to 10,000	10,000 to 25,000	25,000 to 50,000	50,000 to 100,000	100,000 to 250,000	250,000 to 500,000	500,000 to 2,500,000	2,500,000 and over
Number of Enterprises 1	19357	264	15057	2070	1585	238	104	16	8	5	5	4	0

Revenues ($ in Thousands)

Item Description for Accounting Period 7/08 Through 6/09	Total	Zero Assets	Under 500	500 to 1,000	1,000 to 5,000	5,000 to 10,000	10,000 to 25,000	25,000 to 50,000	50,000 to 100,000	100,000 to 250,000	250,000 to 500,000	500,000 to 2,500,000	2,500,000 and over
Net Sales 2	54173892	19604	9334194	5364564	8603104	4564807	4517871	1814020	1114933	954564	2691411	15194821	0
Interest 3	182691	0	1440	2979	36159	15554	3291	267	33	13816	104029	5124	0
Rents 4	15256	0	1597	36	78	470	5253	0	0	1745	2307	3771	0
Royalties 5	1737	0	0	0	0	0	0	0	0	0	0	1737	0
Other Portfolio Income 6	96066	11341	15879	5055	27648	100	632	213	5826	4590	741	24040	0
Other Receipts 7	412345	1	22888	44178	30328	50747	65427	33439	33001	20604	90087	21644	0
Total Receipts 8	54881987	30946	9375998	5416812	8697317	4631678	4592474	1847939	1153793	995319	2888575	15251137	0
Average Total Receipts 9	2835	117	623	2617	5487	19461	44158	115496	144224	199064	577715	3812784	•

Operating Costs/Operating Income (%)

Item Description for Accounting Period 7/08 Through 6/09	Total	Zero Assets	Under 500	500 to 1,000	1,000 to 5,000	5,000 to 10,000	10,000 to 25,000	25,000 to 50,000	50,000 to 100,000	100,000 to 250,000	250,000 to 500,000	500,000 to 2,500,000	2,500,000 and over
Cost of Operations 10	59.1	49.3	57.8	71.4	61.1	62.6	62.8	64.7	51.8	56.1	55.6	52.9	•
Salaries and Wages 11	11.6	17.3	8.7	7.9	11.0	9.4	14.4	15.0	15.1	14.9	15.5	13.2	•
Taxes Paid 12	2.3	16.1	1.9	2.2	2.1	1.5	1.8	2.3	2.3	2.8	2.5	2.9	•
Interest Paid 13	0.7	•	0.6	0.5	0.7	0.6	0.4	0.3	1.2	0.6	0.7	0.8	•
Depreciation 14	1.6	•	0.8	0.6	0.5	1.0	0.6	0.8	4.2	1.7	1.9	3.5	•
Amortization and Depletion 15	0.1	•	0.1	0.1	0.1	0.1	0.0	0.1	0.1	0.1	0.2	0.2	•
Pensions and Other Deferred Comp. 16	0.1	•	0.2	0.1	0.1	0.2	0.1	0.6	0.3	0.1	0.1	0.0	•
Employee Benefits 17	0.8	•	0.7	0.5	0.3	0.4	0.9	1.3	1.4	1.0	0.8	1.2	•
Advertising 18	3.6	3.0	2.6	1.7	2.8	4.0	3.7	1.7	3.1	6.0	5.7	4.8	•
Other Expenses 19	14.9	34.7	15.7	8.9	14.5	18.9	11.4	10.1	19.3	15.4	21.3	15.5	•
Officers' Compensation 20	2.5	21.8	6.1	4.2	3.8	1.3	1.7	0.9	1.1	0.8	0.8	0.3	•
Operating Margin 21	2.8	•	4.9	1.8	2.8	•	1.7	2.8	0.3	0.5	•	4.7	•
Operating Margin Before Officers' Comp. 22	5.3	•	11.0	6.0	6.6	1.3	3.4	3.8	1.4	1.3	•	5.0	•

Selected Average Balance Sheet ($ in Thousands)

	•	•	•	•	•	•	•	•	•	•	•	•
Net Receivables 23	171	0	21	144	450	811	4105	12698	8059	31060	113511	94304
Inventories 24	487	0	45	282	1031	3739	6084	10767	44539	58939	89161	936001
Net Property, Plant and Equipment 25	374	0	32	135	376	1419	2629	5074	11948	49636	62023	1133311
Total Assets 26	1282	0	150	714	2278	6706	15952	39766	68570	149899	310315	2682638
Notes and Loans Payable 27	349	0	55	187	564	2644	3103	9627	24309	35206	77257	695094
All Other Liabilities 28	391	0	60	205	664	2193	5928	10257	21963	26791	82984	789871
Net Worth 29	542	0	35	321	1049	1869	6921	19882	22298	87902	150074	1197673

Selected Financial Ratios (Times to 1)

	•	•	•	•	•	•	•	•	•	•	•	•
Current Ratio 30	1.6	•	1.7	2.2	2.5	1.4	1.7	1.8	2.1	2.5	2.4	1.1
Quick Ratio 31	0.6	•	1.0	1.2	1.1	0.4	0.7	1.0	0.6	1.7	1.2	0.2
Net Sales to Working Capital 32	9.8	•	13.7	9.9	5.2	14.8	8.5	9.3	6.7	3.6	3.8	31.0
Coverage Ratio 33	7.1	•	9.3	6.1	6.2	3.6	8.6	16.4	4.2	8.3	4.5	7.5
Total Asset Turnover 34	2.2	•	4.1	3.6	2.4	2.9	2.7	2.9	2.0	1.3	1.7	1.4
Inventory Turnover 35	3.4	•	8.0	6.6	3.2	3.2	4.5	6.8	1.6	1.8	3.4	2.1
Receivables Turnover 36	14.1	•	27.2	15.9	11.0	16.9	10.8	7.6	14.3	3.8	5.5	24.1
Total Liabilities to Net Worth 37	1.4	•	3.3	1.2	1.2	2.6	1.3	1.0	2.1	0.7	1.1	1.2
Current Assets to Working Capital 38	2.8	•	2.4	1.9	1.7	3.8	2.4	2.3	1.9	1.7	1.7	10.4
Current Liabilities to Working Capital 39	1.8	•	1.4	0.9	0.7	2.8	1.4	1.3	0.9	0.7	0.7	9.4
Working Capital to Net Sales 40	0.1	•	0.1	0.1	0.2	0.1	0.1	0.1	0.2	0.3	0.3	0.0
Inventory to Working Capital 41	1.5	•	1.0	0.8	0.9	2.4	1.2	0.9	1.2	0.4	0.8	6.7
Total Receipts to Cash Flow 42	7.4	•	6.4	11.7	7.3	7.6	10.3	9.1	5.9	5.9	6.6	6.7
Cost of Goods to Cash Flow 43	4.4	•	3.7	8.3	4.5	4.8	6.5	5.9	3.0	3.3	3.7	3.6
Cash Flow to Total Debt 44	0.5	•	0.8	0.6	0.6	0.5	0.5	0.6	0.5	0.5	0.5	0.4

Selected Financial Factors (in Percentages)

	•		•	•	•	•	•	•	•	•	•	•
Debt Ratio 45	57.7	•	76.5	55.0	53.9	72.1	56.6	50.0	67.5	41.4	51.6	55.4
Return on Total Assets 46	10.4	•	24.8	12.1	10.9	5.8	10.2	14.3	10.2	6.4	5.2	8.4
Return on Equity Before Income Taxes 47	21.1	•	94.2	22.5	19.9	15.0	20.8	26.8	23.9	9.6	8.3	16.4
Return on Equity After Income Taxes 48	17.6	•	92.5	20.3	18.8	12.3	20.1	25.7	22.1	6.7	6.9	10.6
Profit Margin (Before Income Tax) 49	4.1	15.6	5.4	2.8	3.9	1.5	3.3	4.7	3.8	4.4	2.3	5.2
Profit Margin (After Income Tax) 50	3.4	15.6	5.3	2.5	3.6	1.2	3.2	4.5	3.5	3.1	1.9	3.4

Table I

Corporations with and without Net Income

ELECTRONICS AND APPLIANCE STORES

MONEY AMOUNTS AND SIZE OF ASSETS IN THOUSANDS OF DOLLARS

Item Description for Accounting Period 7/08 Through 6/09		Total	Zero Assets	Under 500	500 to 1,000	1,000 to 5,000	5,000 to 10,000	10,000 to 25,000	25,000 to 50,000	50,000 to 100,000	100,000 to 250,000	250,000 to 500,000	500,000 to 2,500,000	2,500,000 and over
Number of Enterprises	1	30951	5866	21287	1547	1919	167	83	33	21	12	7	11	0
Revenues ($ in Thousands)														
Net Sales	2	117970225	1007421	11507526	4128328	13501057	3295761	2873796	3056544	3559253	4167727	6344903	64527909	0
Interest	3	346888	0	2698	3711	4957	3549	1520	4793	3416	7062	4916	310266	0
Rents	4	58759	0	1435	3284	1754	1152	0	94	352	0	1161	49527	0
Royalties	5	56814	0	0	0	0	0	0	5107	0	5	0	51701	0
Other Portfolio Income	6	131686	43806	2558	2101	5705	6479	9935	0	8837	6264	4796	41205	0
Other Receipts	7	2207092	0	74715	8687	69323	9085	19133	4264	30548	59226	18024	1914087	0
Total Receipts	8	120771464	1051227	11588932	4146111	13582796	3316026	2904384	3070802	3602406	4240284	6373800	66894695	0
Average Total Receipts	9	3902	179	544	2680	7078	19856	34993	93055	171543	353357	910543	6081336	•
Operating Costs/Operating Income (%)														
Cost of Operations	10	70.5	42.8	54.8	45.4	71.3	66.8	68.1	76.2	75.4	75.1	75.1	74.2	•
Salaries and Wages	11	10.6	12.0	15.1	22.9	11.0	15.4	13.0	9.1	8.8	11.9	9.8	8.8	•
Taxes Paid	12	1.7	3.4	2.5	2.6	1.6	1.4	1.4	1.1	1.0	1.4	1.2	1.6	•
Interest Paid	13	0.6	0.6	0.6	0.7	0.5	0.3	0.5	0.5	0.4	0.1	0.9	0.6	•
Depreciation	14	1.2	1.0	1.0	1.0	0.7	0.3	2.4	1.5	2.0	1.3	1.0	1.4	•
Amortization and Depletion	15	0.1	0.3	0.1	0.1	0.0	0.3	0.2	0.2	0.1	0.1	0.7	0.1	•
Pensions and Other Deferred Comp.	16	0.2	0.3	0.2	0.9	0.3	0.2	0.3	0.1	0.2	0.1	0.0	0.1	•
Employee Benefits	17	0.6	0.8	0.6	1.7	0.9	1.0	0.9	0.5	0.5	0.9	0.4	0.4	•
Advertising	18	2.0	0.4	1.6	1.0	2.1	1.6	1.8	1.3	1.0	1.1	1.8	2.4	•
Other Expenses	19	11.2	34.9	17.9	17.6	8.3	8.5	10.0	8.7	6.5	7.3	8.5	10.9	•
Officers' Compensation	20	1.6	7.8	6.2	6.7	2.9	1.7	1.7	0.7	0.9	1.0	0.9	0.2	•
Operating Margin	21	•	•	•	•	0.3	2.5	•	0.2	3.0	•	•	•	•
Operating Margin Before Officers' Comp.	22	1.2	3.6	5.7	6.1	3.2	4.2	1.2	0.9	4.0	0.7	0.5	•	•

Selected Average Balance Sheet ($ in Thousands)

	•	•	•	•	•	•	•	•	•	•	•	•
Net Receivables 23	348655	88282	32496	16919	12938	2580	1711	467	92	16	0	243
Inventories 24	575759	72774	26261	15126	6588	3347	1068	633	205	39	0	340
Net Property, Plant and Equipment 25	453012	38908	16420	8368	4003	1728	265	369	176	17	0	236
Total Assets 26	2515396	377631	161981	69965	36518	13673	6187	2033	701	116	0	1439
Notes and Loans Payable 27	377262	102420	8339	10422	11021	3175	1893	494	315	64	0	288
All Other Liabilities 28	1311892	173847	62207	24671	17459	6295	2226	800	270	73	0	708
Net Worth 29	824242	101364	91436	34872	8038	4204	2068	739	115	-21	0	443

Selected Financial Ratios (Times to 1)

	•	•	•	•	•	•	•	•	•	•	•	•
Current Ratio 30	1.0	1.2	1.6	1.6	1.3	1.4	1.3	1.6	1.2	1.0	•	1.1
Quick Ratio 31	0.4	0.7	0.9	1.0	0.9	0.7	1.0	0.9	0.5	0.5	•	0.5
Net Sales to Working Capital 32	28067.8	31.7	9.3	10.2	16.7	13.2	19.8	12.0	38.3	166.8	•	41.1
Coverage Ratio 33	5.8	1.1	11.7	11.6	2.4	2.0	12.6	2.9	0.8	1.4	1.2	4.5
Total Asset Turnover 34	2.3	2.4	2.1	2.4	2.5	2.5	3.2	3.5	3.8	4.7	•	2.6
Inventory Turnover 35	7.6	9.4	9.9	8.4	10.7	7.1	12.3	7.9	5.9	7.6	•	7.9
Receivables Turnover 36	22.5	10.2	9.9	8.3	8.6	10.0	11.9	16.2	22.6	29.1	•	17.7
Total Liabilities to Net Worth 37	2.1	2.7	0.8	1.0	3.5	2.3	2.0	1.8	5.1	•	•	2.2
Current Assets to Working Capital 38	5710.2	7.1	2.7	2.7	4.5	3.5	4.1	2.5	6.2	25.2	•	8.5
Current Liabilities to Working Capital 39	5709.2	6.1	1.7	1.7	3.5	2.5	3.1	1.5	5.2	24.2	•	7.5
Working Capital to Net Sales 40	0.0	0.0	0.1	0.1	0.1	0.1	0.1	0.1	0.0	0.0	•	0.0
Inventory to Working Capital 41	2471.7	2.0	0.8	0.8	1.0	1.2	0.9	1.0	3.4	11.8	•	3.4
Total Receipts to Cash Flow 42	10.6	19.0	13.9	11.2	13.5	13.1	10.9	14.7	7.1	7.9	4.0	10.7
Cost of Goods to Cash Flow 43	7.9	14.3	10.4	8.4	10.3	8.9	7.3	10.5	3.2	4.4	1.7	7.6
Cash Flow to Total Debt 44	0.3	0.2	0.4	0.4	0.2	0.3	0.4	0.4	0.6	0.5	•	0.4

Selected Financial Factors (in Percentages)

	•	•	•	•	•	•	•	•	•	•	•	•
Debt Ratio 45	67.2	73.2	43.6	50.2	78.0	69.3	66.6	63.6	83.5	118.0	•	69.2
Return on Total Assets 46	8.3	2.4	3.7	11.2	2.9	2.7	10.7	4.9	2.1	3.9	•	7.0
Return on Equity Before Income Taxes 47	21.1	0.5	6.1	20.6	7.7	4.4	29.5	8.8	•	•	•	17.6
Return on Equity After Income Taxes 48	11.3	•	6.0	18.4	4.7	3.9	27.2	8.0	•	•	•	10.7
Profit Margin (Before Income Tax) 49	3.0	0.1	1.6	4.2	0.7	0.5	3.1	0.9	0.2	0.2	0.1	2.0
Profit Margin (After Income Tax) 50	1.6	•	1.6	3.8	0.4	0.5	2.9	0.8	•	0.2	0.1	1.2

Table II

Corporations with Net Income

ELECTRONICS AND APPLIANCE STORES

MONEY AMOUNTS AND SIZE OF ASSETS IN THOUSANDS OF DOLLARS

Item Description for Accounting Period 7/08 Through 6/09	Total	Zero Assets	Under 500	500 to 1,000	1,000 to 5,000	5,000 to 10,000	10,000 to 25,000	25,000 to 50,000	50,000 to 100,000	100,000 to 250,000	250,000 to 500,000	500,000 to 2,500,000	2,500,000 and over
Number of Enterprises **1**	14206	1674	9964	968	1389	99	49	21	18	8	•	•	0
Revenues ($ in Thousands)													
Net Sales **2**	93236364	516632	6580185	3031175	10322507	1003725	1640600	2342111	3420443	3470608	•	•	0
Interest **3**	326189	0	1361	998	3359	2897	856	2883	3042	1590	•	•	0
Rents **4**	37596	0	146	2836	1202	1152	0	94	352	0	•	•	0
Royalties **5**	51707	0	0	0	0	0	0	0	0	5	•	•	0
Other Portfolio Income **6**	122979	43806	882	1483	4233	6474	9245	0	8059	5482	•	•	0
Other Receipts **7**	1127198	0	24582	4848	21993	7898	15936	3420	30347	42982	•	•	0
Total Receipts **8**	94902033	560438	6607156	3041340	10353294	1022146	1666637	2348508	3462243	3520667	•	•	0
Average Total Receipts **9**	6680	335	663	3142	7454	10325	34013	111834	192347	440083	•	•	•
Operating Costs/Operating Income (%)													
Cost of Operations **10**	70.6	27.7	52.7	37.2	73.7	34.8	70.4	81.1	76.8	79.7	•	•	•
Salaries and Wages **11**	9.8	13.4	13.0	26.2	9.7	19.8	10.7	8.1	8.5	10.0	•	•	•
Taxes Paid **12**	1.6	3.6	1.9	2.8	1.5	2.6	1.3	1.0	1.0	1.1	•	•	•
Interest Paid **13**	0.6	0.2	0.2	0.4	0.3	0.8	0.4	0.4	0.4	0.1	•	•	•
Depreciation **14**	1.1	0.5	0.8	0.6	0.5	0.8	0.9	0.4	0.9	0.9	•	•	•
Amortization and Depletion **15**	0.2	•	0.0	0.1	0.0	1.1	0.2	0.1	0.1	0.0	•	•	•
Pensions and Other Deferred Comp. **16**	0.2	•	0.3	1.2	0.3	0.5	0.2	0.0	0.2	0.1	•	•	•
Employee Benefits **17**	0.5	1.2	0.5	2.0	0.8	2.5	0.6	0.4	0.5	0.6	•	•	•
Advertising **18**	1.8	0.2	1.4	1.0	1.8	2.0	1.9	0.7	1.1	0.6	•	•	•
Other Expenses **19**	9.5	31.9	16.1	19.0	5.9	13.3	8.3	5.4	6.3	5.5	•	•	•
Officers' Compensation **20**	1.5	8.1	7.2	7.6	2.8	4.9	1.7	0.8	0.8	0.9	•	•	•
Operating Margin **21**	2.6	13.2	5.9	2.0	2.5	16.9	3.4	1.6	3.5	0.9	•	•	•
Operating Margin Before Officers' Comp. **22**	4.0	21.3	13.0	9.5	5.4	21.8	5.1	2.4	4.3	1.4	•	•	•

Selected Average Balance Sheet ($ in Thousands)

Net Receivables 23	434	0	23	92	531	540	3097	17426	19064	41503
Inventories 24	595	0	48	160	679	1334	3844	5886	16605	38272
Net Property, Plant and Equipment 25	407	0	13	127	319	317	1534	1643	8491	14538
Total Assets 26	2580	0	126	661	1961	6216	13623	37343	68771	157674
Notes and Loans Payable 27	446	0	26	242	364	1004	2005	11589	9681	7798
All Other Liabilities 28	1237	0	59	232	739	1736	5689	16812	27677	68429
Net Worth 29	897	0	41	187	857	3476	5929	8942	31413	81446

Selected Financial Ratios (Times to 1)

Current Ratio 30	1.2	•	1.5	1.3	2.0	1.6	1.6	1.5	1.5	1.5
Quick Ratio 31	0.5	•	0.8	0.6	1.2	1.2	0.8	1.1	1.0	0.9
Net Sales to Working Capital 32	35.6	•	19.3	38.9	9.7	8.8	9.0	10.7	10.7	11.5
Coverage Ratio 33	8.9	145.8	30.6	7.2	9.3	25.7	12.7	5.4	13.9	15.7
Total Asset Turnover 34	2.5	•	5.2	4.7	3.8	1.6	2.5	3.0	2.8	2.8
Inventory Turnover 35	7.8	•	7.3	7.3	8.1	2.6	6.1	15.4	8.8	9.0
Receivables Turnover 36	17.9	•	28.6	23.5	15.0	7.7	9.0	•	8.9	•
Total Liabilities to Net Worth 37	1.9	•	2.1	2.5	1.3	0.8	1.3	3.2	1.2	0.9
Current Assets to Working Capital 38	7.5	•	3.0	4.9	2.0	2.6	2.7	3.0	2.8	2.9
Current Liabilities to Working Capital 39	6.5	•	2.0	3.9	1.0	1.6	1.7	2.0	1.8	1.9
Working Capital to Net Sales 40	0.0	•	0.1	0.0	0.1	0.1	0.1	0.1	0.1	0.1
Inventory to Working Capital 41	3.1	•	1.3	2.3	0.8	0.4	0.8	0.6	0.8	1.0
Total Receipts to Cash Flow 42	9.2	2.0	5.8	5.5	14.3	3.5	9.5	16.8	11.0	16.5
Cost of Goods to Cash Flow 43	6.5	0.5	3.1	2.1	10.6	1.2	6.7	13.6	8.4	13.2
Cash Flow to Total Debt 44	0.4	•	1.3	1.2	0.5	1.1	0.5	0.2	0.5	0.3

Selected Financial Factors (in Percentages)

Debt Ratio 45	65.2	•	67.3	71.8	56.3	44.1	56.5	76.1	54.3	48.3
Return on Total Assets 46	12.6	•	34.0	12.6	11.9	31.9	13.3	7.0	13.9	6.1
Return on Equity Before Income Taxes 47	32.1	•	100.5	38.4	24.2	54.9	28.2	23.8	28.2	11.0
Return on Equity After Income Taxes 48	24.6	•	99.8	37.3	23.3	52.5	27.6	19.6	25.4	10.9
Profit Margin (Before Income Tax) 49	4.4	21.7	6.3	2.3	2.8	18.8	5.0	1.9	4.7	2.1
Profit Margin (After Income Tax) 50	3.4	21.7	6.2	2.2	2.7	18.0	4.9	1.6	4.2	2.1

Table I
Corporations with and without Net Income

HOMES CENTERS; PAINT AND WALLPAPER STORES

MONEY AMOUNTS AND SIZE OF ASSETS IN THOUSANDS OF DOLLARS

Item Description for Accounting Period 7/08 Through 6/09	Total	Zero Assets	Under 500	500 to 1,000	1,000 to 5,000	5,000 to 10,000	10,000 to 25,000	25,000 to 50,000	50,000 to 100,000	100,000 to 250,000	250,000 to 500,000	500,000 to 2,500,000	2,500,000 and over
Number of Enterprises **1**	3366	504	1844	433	438	83	47	8	6	0	0	0	3
Revenues ($ in Thousands)													
Net Sales **2**	130232430	15236	1991852	505781	2696012	1208997	1185337	774379	1041373	0	0	0	120813462
Interest **3**	45497	0	954	928	3425	2919	1417	350	487	0	0	0	35017
Rents **4**	388413	0	0	26	932	5002	22	0	0	0	0	0	382432
Royalties **5**	216686	0	0	0	0	0	0	0	0	0	0	0	216686
Other Portfolio Income **6**	47744	0	135	44	5871	3531	1843	97	1165	0	0	0	35058
Other Receipts **7**	3630667	6	97	1403	9430	3172	14171	7555	10540	0	0	0	3584293
Total Receipts **8**	134561437	15242	1993038	508182	2715670	1223621	1202790	782381	1053565	0	0	0	125066948
Average Total Receipts **9**	39977	30	1081	1174	6200	14742	25591	97798	175594	•	•	•	41688983
Operating Costs/Operating Income (%)													
Cost of Operations **10**	66.4	577.3	62.9	66.8	68.3	72.7	65.9	71.4	71.4	•	•	•	66.2
Salaries and Wages **11**	12.7	17.8	11.8	6.5	13.4	9.6	15.5	12.7	11.2	•	•	•	12.7
Taxes Paid **12**	2.2	1.5	7.6	1.5	2.6	1.7	2.2	1.4	1.7	•	•	•	2.2
Interest Paid **13**	1.0	1.9	0.6	2.7	0.6	0.5	0.7	0.7	1.0	•	•	•	1.0
Depreciation **14**	3.2	15.9	0.4	1.8	0.8	0.9	1.3	2.0	2.0	•	•	•	3.3
Amortization and Depletion **15**	0.0	49.0	0.0	0.0	0.1	0.0	0.1	0.1	0.1	•	•	•	0.0
Pensions and Other Deferred Comp. **16**	0.2	•	0.0	0.1	0.5	0.3	0.2	0.2	0.8	•	•	•	0.2
Employee Benefits **17**	1.1	•	0.4	0.8	0.9	0.8	1.3	1.1	1.3	•	•	•	1.1
Advertising **18**	1.6	0.7	0.5	1.2	0.6	0.6	1.2	0.5	2.2	•	•	•	1.7
Other Expenses **19**	9.1	47.7	13.5	11.1	9.2	5.6	11.6	8.0	8.3	•	•	•	9.0
Officers' Compensation **20**	0.2	•	3.5	8.5	2.4	2.2	1.3	1.7	0.5	•	•	•	0.1
Operating Margin **21**	2.3	•	•	•	0.7	5.2	•	0.2	•	•	•	•	2.5
Operating Margin Before Officers' Comp. **22**	2.5	•	2.4	7.5	3.1	7.4	•	1.9	0.0	•	•	•	2.5

Selected Average Balance Sheet ($ in Thousands)

Item													
Net Receivables 23	1033	0	42	73	573	856	3208	8509	10900	•	•	•	921129
Inventories 24	6056	0	119	255	727	1919	4850	13736	33424	•	•	•	6345623
Net Property, Plant and Equipment 25	12400	0	20	413	191	1232	2847	11545	28038	•	•	•	13647569
Total Assets 26	32648	0	201	774	2386	7091	13856	39288	83814	•	•	•	35361467
Notes and Loans Payable 27	12839	0	128	565	603	1117	4850	12140	21138	•	•	•	13975560
All Other Liabilities 28	8832	0	86	115	513	1070	2241	8734	18426	•	•	•	9639772
Net Worth 29	10977	0	-12	94	1269	4904	6765	18413	44250	•	•	•	1746135

Selected Financial Ratios (Times to 1)

Item													
Current Ratio 30	1.2	•	2.1	1.9	3.4	4.0	2.1	2.9	2.9	•	•	•	1.2
Quick Ratio 31	0.2	•	0.6	0.6	2.0	2.6	1.0	1.1	0.8	•	•	•	0.1
Net Sales to Working Capital 32	19.8	•	11.7	7.7	4.2	3.6	5.1	6.1	5.5	•	•	•	25.1
Coverage Ratio 33	6.8	•	•	0.8	3.4	14.5	1.1	2.7	1.6	•	•	•	7.1
Total Asset Turnover 34	1.2	•	5.4	1.5	2.6	2.1	1.8	2.5	2.1	•	•	•	1.1
Inventory Turnover 35	4.2	•	5.7	3.1	5.8	5.5	3.4	5.0	3.7	•	•	•	4.2
Receivables Turnover 36	8.8	•	25.8	14.7	11.2	15.0	7.0	11.1	14.2	•	•	•	8.6
Total Liabilities to Net Worth 37	2.0	•	•	7.3	0.9	0.4	1.0	1.1	0.9	•	•	•	2.0
Current Assets to Working Capital 38	5.4	•	1.9	2.1	1.4	1.3	1.9	1.5	1.5	•	•	•	6.8
Current Liabilities to Working Capital 39	4.4	•	0.9	1.1	0.4	0.3	0.9	0.5	0.5	•	•	•	5.8
Working Capital to Net Sales 40	0.1	•	0.1	0.1	0.2	0.3	0.2	0.2	0.2	•	•	•	0.0
Inventory to Working Capital 41	3.1	•	1.3	1.4	0.5	0.4	0.9	0.9	1.0	•	•	•	3.9
Total Receipts to Cash Flow 42	8.4	•	14.2	13.0	12.5	9.5	12.7	14.3	16.3	•	•	•	8.2
Cost of Goods to Cash Flow 43	5.6	•	8.9	8.7	8.6	6.9	8.4	10.2	11.6	•	•	•	5.4
Cash Flow to Total Debt 44	0.2	•	0.4	0.1	0.4	0.7	0.3	0.3	0.3	•	•	•	0.2

Selected Financial Factors (in Percentages)

Item													
Debt Ratio 45	66.4	•	106.2	87.9	46.8	30.8	51.2	53.1	47.2	•	•	•	66.8
Return on Total Assets 46	8.0	•	•	3.2	5.1	13.5	1.4	4.7	3.4	•	•	•	8.2
Return on Equity Before Income Taxes 47	20.3	•	98.2	•	6.8	18.2	0.2	6.3	2.5	•	•	•	21.3
Return on Equity After Income Taxes 48	13.8	•	115.9	•	6.2	17.0	•	6.3	2.0	•	•	•	14.5
Profit Margin (Before Income Tax) 49	5.8	•	•	•	1.4	6.1	0.0	1.2	0.6	•	•	•	6.2
Profit Margin (After Income Tax) 50	3.9	•	•	•	1.3	5.7	•	1.2	0.5	•	•	•	4.2

Table II

Corporations with Net Income

HOMES CENTERS; PAINT AND WALLPAPER STORES

MONEY AMOUNTS AND SIZE OF ASSETS IN THOUSANDS OF DOLLARS

Item Description for Accounting Period 7/08 Through 6/09		Total	Zero Assets	Under 500	500 to 1,000	1,000 to 5,000	5,000 to 10,000	10,000 to 25,000	25,000 to 50,000	50,000 to 100,000	100,000 to 250,000	250,000 to 500,000	500,000 to 2,500,000	2,500,000 and over
Number of Enterprises	1	1630	426	621	118	357	78	20	5	3	0	0	0	3
Revenues ($ in Thousands)														
Net Sales	2	127418325	9562	1633913	129490	2353681	1119160	485062	434575	439419	0	0	0	120813462
Interest	3	42581	0	429	537	3417	2333	361	0	487	0	0	0	35017
Rents	4	387366	0	0	26	932	3975	2	0	0	0	0	0	382432
Royalties	5	216686	0	0	0	0	0	0	0	0	0	0	0	216686
Other Portfolio Income	6	45341	0	86	44	5871	3531	635	35	81	0	0	0	35058
Other Receipts	7	3610847	5	52	127	6111	3084	6938	7113	3124	0	0	0	3584293
Total Receipts	8	131721146	9567	1634480	130224	2370012	1132083	492998	441723	443111	0	0	0	125066948
Average Total Receipts	9	80811	22	2632	1104	6639	14514	24650	88345	147704	•	•	•	41688983
Operating Costs/Operating Income (%)														
Cost of Operations	10	66.3	60.8	64.2	67.3	68.6	72.6	64.9	68.4	75.1	•	•	•	66.2
Salaries and Wages	11	12.7	•	11.6	8.5	13.4	9.3	14.0	14.9	7.8	•	•	•	12.7
Taxes Paid	12	2.2	0.2	7.9	1.6	1.9	1.7	2.2	1.6	1.6	•	•	•	2.2
Interest Paid	13	1.0	3.1	0.1	3.6	0.5	0.4	0.7	0.4	0.8	•	•	•	1.0
Depreciation	14	3.2	3.5	0.3	2.4	0.7	0.9	1.5	2.0	1.8	•	•	•	3.3
Amortization and Depletion	15	0.0	•	0.0	0.0	0.1	0.0	0.0	0.1	0.1	•	•	•	0.0
Pensions and Other Deferred Comp.	16	0.2	•	•	0.2	0.6	0.3	0.4	0.4	1.0	•	•	•	0.2
Employee Benefits	17	1.1	•	0.3	1.9	0.8	0.8	1.3	1.3	1.7	•	•	•	1.1
Advertising	18	1.6	1.0	0.3	1.5	0.7	0.6	1.5	0.6	0.6	•	•	•	1.7
Other Expenses	19	9.0	24.6	10.6	6.4	9.2	5.3	9.5	7.5	5.5	•	•	•	9.0
Officers' Compensation	20	0.2	•	2.7	6.2	2.2	2.2	1.2	1.6	0.7	•	•	•	0.1
Operating Margin	21	2.5	6.9	1.9	0.2	1.4	5.9	2.9	1.2	3.5	•	•	•	2.5
Operating Margin Before Officers' Comp.	22	2.7	6.9	4.7	6.5	3.6	8.2	4.1	2.7	4.2	•	•	•	2.5

Selected Average Balance Sheet ($ in Thousands)

Net Receivables 23	1998	0	98	69	639	797	2596	9281	11868	921129
Inventories 24	12209	0	166	352	681	1864	7999	12695	31479	6345623
Net Property, Plant and Equipment 25	25358	0	43	381	134	1151	2765	10605	24370	13647569
Total Assets 26	66560	0	349	780	2415	7014	14442	38578	69243	35361467
Notes and Loans Payable 27	26031	0	39	576	473	1031	3649	7878	16446	13975560
All Other Liabilities 28	18055	0	161	113	574	912	2377	8090	10972	9639772
Net Worth 29	22474	0	148	91	1368	5071	8416	22610	41825	11746135

Selected Financial Ratios (Times to 1)

Current Ratio 30	1.2	•	1.8	1.7	3.7	4.6	2.0	3.1	3.3	1.2
Quick Ratio 31	0.2	•	0.8	0.5	2.4	3.0	0.9	1.2	1.2	0.1
Net Sales to Working Capital 32	21.0	•	19.8	6.6	4.1	3.4	4.6	5.4	5.2	25.1
Coverage Ratio 33	7.1	3.3	19.9	1.2	5.5	19.7	7.6	7.8	6.7	7.1
Total Asset Turnover 34	1.2	•	7.5	1.4	2.7	2.0	1.7	2.3	2.1	1.1
Inventory Turnover 35	4.2	•	10.1	2.1	6.6	5.6	2.0	4.7	3.5	4.2
Receivables Turnover 36	8.7	•	•	10.5	11.4	15.4	4.2	•	11.4	8.6
Total Liabilities to Net Worth 37	2.0	•	1.4	7.6	0.8	0.4	0.7	0.7	0.7	2.0
Current Assets to Working Capital 38	5.7	•	2.2	2.4	1.4	1.3	2.0	1.5	1.4	6.8
Current Liabilities to Working Capital 39	4.7	•	1.2	1.4	0.4	0.3	1.0	0.5	0.4	5.8
Working Capital to Net Sales 40	0.0	•	0.1	0.2	0.2	0.3	0.2	0.2	0.2	0.0
Inventory to Working Capital 41	3.2	•	1.3	1.7	0.4	0.4	1.0	0.8	0.8	3.9
Total Receipts to Cash Flow 42	8.3	3.3	12.8	16.1	11.8	9.0	9.2	11.2	12.5	8.2
Cost of Goods to Cash Flow 43	5.5	2.0	8.2	10.8	8.1	6.5	6.0	7.7	9.4	5.4
Cash Flow to Total Debt 44	0.2	•	1.0	0.1	0.5	0.8	0.4	0.5	0.4	0.2

Selected Financial Factors (in Percentages)

Debt Ratio 45	66.2	•	57.6	88.3	43.4	27.7	41.7	41.4	39.6	66.8
Return on Total Assets 46	8.3	•	15.7	6.2	7.1	14.7	9.0	7.2	10.7	8.2
Return on Equity Before Income Taxes 47	21.1	•	35.2	9.8	10.2	19.3	13.4	10.8	15.1	21.3
Return on Equity After Income Taxes 48	14.5	•	30.8	9.7	9.5	18.1	11.9	10.8	14.0	14.5
Profit Margin (Before Income Tax) 49	6.1	6.9	2.0	0.8	2.1	6.8	4.7	2.8	4.3	6.2
Profit Margin (After Income Tax) 50	4.2	6.9	1.7	0.8	2.0	6.4	4.1	2.8	4.0	4.2

Table I

Corporations with and without Net Income

HARDWARE STORES

MONEY AMOUNTS AND SIZE OF ASSETS IN THOUSANDS OF DOLLARS

Item Description for Accounting Period 7/08 Through 6/09	Total	Zero Assets	Under 500	500 to 1,000	1,000 to 5,000	5,000 to 10,000	10,000 to 25,000	25,000 to 50,000	50,000 to 100,000	100,000 to 250,000	250,000 to 500,000	500,000 to 2,500,000	2,500,000 and over
Number of Enterprises 1	8529	1324	2392	2479	2200	79	•	11	•	•	0	•	0
Revenues ($ in Thousands)													
Net Sales 2	19175713	100850	2294539	4233552	8319300	802204	•	934920	•	•	0	•	0
Interest 3	20359	894	1300	3212	11469	1955	•	220	•	•	0	•	0
Rents 4	25256	0	1115	11799	10541	0	•	863	•	•	0	•	0
Royalties 5	24	0	0	23	1	0	•	0	•	•	0	•	0
Other Portfolio Income 6	41206	862	75	5385	17326	15878	•	1477	•	•	0	•	0
Other Receipts 7	181864	6225	22380	51331	71127	6707	•	3848	•	•	0	•	0
Total Receipts 8	19444422	108831	2319409	4305302	8429764	826744	•	941328	•	•	0	•	0
Average Total Receipts 9	2280	82	970	1737	3832	10465	•	85575	•	•	•	•	•
Operating Costs/Operating Income (%)													
Cost of Operations 10	63.1	64.1	59.6	61.7	64.5	60.7	•	65.4	•	•	•	•	•
Salaries and Wages 11	12.8	2.2	11.2	12.0	12.9	14.8	•	15.2	•	•	•	•	•
Taxes Paid 12	2.4	3.6	2.3	2.2	2.4	2.5	•	3.0	•	•	•	•	•
Interest Paid 13	1.0	3.0	0.6	0.9	0.9	0.4	•	1.0	•	•	•	•	•
Depreciation 14	1.4	3.3	0.5	1.0	1.8	1.3	•	1.3	•	•	•	•	•
Amortization and Depletion 15	0.1	•	0.0	0.0	0.0	•	•	0.1	•	•	•	•	•
Pensions and Other Deferred Comp. 16	0.2	•	0.1	0.3	0.3	0.3	•	0.2	•	•	•	•	•
Employee Benefits 17	1.1	0.2	1.1	1.0	1.1	0.8	•	1.4	•	•	•	•	•
Advertising 18	1.6	0.0	1.2	2.2	1.3	1.4	•	1.6	•	•	•	•	•
Other Expenses 19	12.0	20.5	13.9	14.0	11.0	10.3	•	10.9	•	•	•	•	•
Officers' Compensation 20	3.7	0.0	8.0	4.4	3.2	4.7	•	0.9	•	•	•	•	•
Operating Margin 21	0.7	3.1	1.3	0.3	0.4	2.8	•	•	•	•	•	•	•
Operating Margin Before Officers' Comp. 22	4.4	3.1	9.3	4.7	3.6	7.5	•	•	•	•	•	•	•

Selected Average Balance Sheet ($ in Thousands)

Net Receivables 23	101	0	36	61	197	568	2929
Inventories 24	475	0	196	391	781	1907	19442
Net Property, Plant and Equipment 25	207	0	17	81	324	2758	12058
Total Assets 26	1079	0	337	749	1895	6681	34486
Notes and Loans Payable 27	407	0	87	312	727	649	17078
All Other Liabilities 28	192	0	105	93	293	904	6090
Net Worth 29	480	0	145	345	874	5128	11317

Selected Financial Ratios (Times to 1)

Current Ratio 30	2.7	•	2.0	4.4	3.1	2.9	1.7
Quick Ratio 31	0.8	•	0.5	0.9	1.0	1.3	0.3
Net Sales to Working Capital 32	5.1	•	7.4	3.9	4.5	4.7	10.5
Coverage Ratio 33	3.2	4.6	4.8	3.2	2.9	13.9	0.8
Total Asset Turnover 34	2.1	•	2.8	2.3	2.0	1.5	2.5
Inventory Turnover 35	3.0	•	2.9	2.7	3.1	3.2	2.9
Receivables Turnover 36	20.4	•	28.1	25.3	17.5	15.0	25.3
Total Liabilities to Net Worth 37	1.3	•	1.3	1.2	1.2	0.3	2.0
Current Assets to Working Capital 38	1.6	•	2.0	1.3	1.5	1.5	2.5
Current Liabilities to Working Capital 39	0.6	•	1.0	0.3	0.5	0.5	1.5
Working Capital to Net Sales 40	0.2	•	0.1	0.3	0.2	0.2	0.1
Inventory to Working Capital 41	1.1	•	1.4	1.0	0.9	0.8	1.9
Total Receipts to Cash Flow 42	10.9	3.6	9.2	10.6	11.3	9.1	16.2
Cost of Goods to Cash Flow 43	6.9	2.3	5.5	6.5	7.3	5.5	10.6
Cash Flow to Total Debt 44	0.3	•	0.5	0.4	0.3	0.7	0.2

Selected Financial Factors (in Percentages)

Debt Ratio 45	55.6	•	57.0	54.0	53.9	23.3	67.2
Return on Total Assets 46	6.4	•	8.7	6.7	5.3	9.5	2.0
Return on Equity Before Income Taxes 47	10.0	•	16.0	10.1	7.5	11.5	•
Return on Equity After Income Taxes 48	8.7	•	15.5	9.7	6.7	8.6	•
Profit Margin (Before Income Tax) 49	2.1	11.0	2.4	2.0	1.7	5.8	•
Profit Margin (After Income Tax) 50	1.9	11.0	2.3	2.0	1.6	4.3	•

Table II

Corporations with Net Income

HARDWARE STORES

MONEY AMOUNTS AND SIZE OF ASSETS IN THOUSANDS OF DOLLARS

Item Description for Accounting Period 7/08 Through 6/09	Total	Zero Assets	Under 500	500 to 1,000	1,000 to 5,000	5,000 to 10,000	10,000 to 25,000	25,000 to 50,000	50,000 to 100,000	100,000 to 250,000	250,000 to 500,000	500,000 to 2,500,000	2,500,000 and over
Number of Enterprises 1	5449	628	1619	1882	1221	61	•	5	•	•	0	•	0

Revenues ($ in Thousands)

Item	Total	Zero Assets	Under 500	500 to 1,000	1,000 to 5,000	5,000 to 10,000	10,000 to 25,000	25,000 to 50,000	50,000 to 100,000	100,000 to 250,000	250,000 to 500,000	500,000 to 2,500,000	2,500,000 and over
Net Sales 2	14367835	91551	1879839	3390812	5604088	622846	•	492153	•	•	0	•	0
Interest 3	9449	0	781	416	7056	446	•	0	•	•	0	•	0
Rents 4	16194	0	1110	11780	2417	0	•	0	•	•	0	•	0
Royalties 5	1	0	0	0	1	0	•	0	•	•	0	•	0
Other Portfolio Income 6	27149	862	0	4027	6286	15844	•	0	•	•	0	•	0
Other Receipts 7	149535	6226	22297	46407	56092	2774	•	546	•	•	0	•	0
Total Receipts 8	14570163	98639	1904027	3453442	5675940	641910	•	492699	•	•	0	•	0
Average Total Receipts 9	2674	157	1176	1835	4649	10523	•	98540	•	•	•	•	•

Operating Costs/Operating Income (%)

Item	Total	Zero Assets	Under 500	500 to 1,000	1,000 to 5,000	5,000 to 10,000	10,000 to 25,000	25,000 to 50,000	50,000 to 100,000	100,000 to 250,000	250,000 to 500,000	500,000 to 2,500,000	2,500,000 and over
Cost of Operations 10	62.4	63.5	59.2	61.4	63.4	60.1	•	70.7	•	•	•	•	•
Salaries and Wages 11	12.5	2.4	11.9	11.9	12.3	13.1	•	14.2	•	•	•	•	•
Taxes Paid 12	2.2	3.2	2.2	1.9	2.3	2.7	•	1.5	•	•	•	•	•
Interest Paid 13	0.9	3.3	0.4	0.9	0.7	0.5	•	0.8	•	•	•	•	•
Depreciation 14	1.3	1.8	0.3	1.0	1.9	1.1	•	1.0	•	•	•	•	•
Amortization and Depletion 15	0.0	•	0.0	0.0	0.1	•	•	0.1	•	•	•	•	•
Pensions and Other Deferred Comp. 16	0.3	•	0.2	0.3	0.3	0.3	•	0.1	•	•	•	•	•
Employee Benefits 17	1.0	0.3	1.0	0.8	1.0	0.0	•	1.4	•	•	•	•	•
Advertising 18	1.5	0.0	1.3	2.1	1.0	1.3	•	1.2	•	•	•	•	•
Other Expenses 19	11.8	13.0	14.0	13.0	11.4	9.9	•	6.9	•	•	•	•	•
Officers' Compensation 20	3.6	0.0	7.1	4.5	3.0	5.8	•	0.9	•	•	•	•	•
Operating Margin 21	2.6	12.4	2.4	2.1	2.5	5.0	•	1.1	•	•	•	•	•
Operating Margin Before Officers' Comp. 22	6.2	12.4	9.5	6.6	5.5	10.8	•	2.0	•	•	•	•	•

Selected Average Balance Sheet ($ in Thousands)

Net Receivables 23	107	0	29	54	235	423	•	5070
Inventories 24	554	0	189	423	932	2315	•	33545
Net Property, Plant and Equipment 25	221	0	13	82	331	3060	•	9134
Total Assets 26	1159	0	380	775	1963	6800	•	33073
Notes and Loans Payable 27	345	0	57	308	445	699	•	16212
All Other Liabilities 28	210	0	131	99	257	852	•	5606
Net Worth 29	604	0	191	368	1261	5249	•	11256

Selected Financial Ratios (Times to 1)

Current Ratio 30	2.9	•	1.8	4.2	4.9	2.8	•	1.4
Quick Ratio 31	0.9	•	0.4	0.9	1.9	1.1	•	0.4
Net Sales to Working Capital 32	5.1	•	9.5	3.9	4.0	5.0	•	16.2
Coverage Ratio 33	5.6	7.0	9.9	5.4	6.1	17.4	•	2.6
Total Asset Turnover 34	2.3	•	3.1	2.3	2.3	1.5	•	3.0
Inventory Turnover 35	3.0	•	3.6	2.6	3.1	2.7	•	2.1
Receivables Turnover 36	20.1	•	43.0	25.2	15.9	14.2	•	14.7
Total Liabilities to Net Worth 37	0.9	•	1.0	1.1	0.6	0.3	•	1.9
Current Assets to Working Capital 38	1.5	•	2.3	1.3	1.3	1.6	•	3.4
Current Liabilities to Working Capital 39	0.5	•	1.3	0.3	0.3	0.6	•	2.4
Working Capital to Net Sales 40	0.2	•	0.1	0.3	0.3	0.2	•	0.1
Inventory to Working Capital 41	1.0	•	1.7	1.0	0.7	0.9	•	2.4
Total Receipts to Cash Flow 42	9.2	3.4	8.7	8.7	9.0	8.2	•	20.1
Cost of Goods to Cash Flow 43	5.8	2.2	5.1	5.4	5.7	4.9	•	14.2
Cash Flow to Total Debt 44	0.5	•	0.7	0.5	0.7	0.8	•	0.2

Selected Financial Factors (in Percentages)

Debt Ratio 45	47.9	•	49.7	52.6	35.7	22.8	•	66.0
Return on Total Assets 46	11.0	•	12.6	11.4	10.6	12.9	•	6.1
Return on Equity Before Income Taxes 47	17.3	•	22.5	19.5	13.8	15.7	•	11.0
Return on Equity After Income Taxes 48	15.8	•	22.0	19.0	12.9	12.0	•	11.0
Profit Margin (Before Income Tax) 49	4.0	20.1	3.7	4.0	3.8	8.1	•	1.3
Profit Margin (After Income Tax) 50	3.6	20.1	3.6	3.9	3.5	6.2	•	1.3

Table I

Corporations with and without Net Income

OTHER BUILDING MATERIAL DEALERS

MONEY AMOUNTS AND SIZE OF ASSETS IN THOUSANDS OF DOLLARS

Item Description for Accounting Period 7/08 Through 6/09	Total	Zero Assets	Under 500	500 to 1,000	1,000 to 5,000	5,000 to 10,000	10,000 to 25,000	25,000 to 50,000	50,000 to 100,000	100,000 to 250,000	250,000 to 500,000	500,000 to 2,500,000	2,500,000 and over
Number of Enterprises **1**	20010	1411	11497	3307	3076	439	199	47	19	•	0	•	0
Revenues ($ in Thousands)													
Net Sales **2**	65494131	615724	6433315	7564774	18134138	7785698	6378822	2998912	2770510	•	0	•	0
Interest **3**	453146	2715	200	7196	19968	5680	7593	5740	3308	•	0	•	0
Rents **4**	36797	7536	3406	2356	6484	30	4815	5497	2364	•	0	•	0
Royalties **5**	15561	0	3213	0	0	0	249	0	0	•	0	•	0
Other Portfolio Income **6**	125690	15457	1791	3918	25455	2832	6801	7947	6623	•	0	•	0
Other Receipts **7**	687985	10785	70498	76834	119022	20352	53614	18843	19248	•	0	•	0
Total Receipts **8**	66813310	652217	6512423	7655078	18305067	7814592	6451894	3036939	2802053	•	0	•	0
Average Total Receipts **9**	3339	462	566	2315	5951	17801	32422	64616	147476	•	•	•	•
Operating Costs/Operating Income (%)													
Cost of Operations **10**	73.1	82.5	65.1	70.2	71.5	78.8	73.9	72.8	75.1	•	•	•	•
Salaries and Wages **11**	10.3	3.2	6.4	9.4	10.1	8.5	11.2	12.8	10.4	•	•	•	•
Taxes Paid **12**	1.6	1.2	1.8	2.2	1.7	1.5	1.5	1.7	1.4	•	•	•	•
Interest Paid **13**	1.7	2.9	0.8	0.4	0.5	0.7	0.7	0.6	1.1	•	•	•	•
Depreciation **14**	1.4	4.2	2.0	0.7	1.2	0.9	1.3	1.8	1.9	•	•	•	•
Amortization and Depletion **15**	0.4	2.4	0.1	0.0	0.0	0.1	0.1	0.1	0.2	•	•	•	•
Pensions and Other Deferred Comp. **16**	0.3	0.0	0.1	0.3	0.3	0.2	0.4	0.4	0.5	•	•	•	•
Employee Benefits **17**	1.2	0.1	0.6	0.8	1.1	0.6	1.0	1.0	0.9	•	•	•	•
Advertising **18**	0.9	1.0	2.3	0.8	0.9	0.4	0.7	0.5	0.5	•	•	•	•
Other Expenses **19**	9.7	15.0	16.8	9.5	8.8	7.0	8.3	9.1	8.3	•	•	•	•
Officers' Compensation **20**	2.2	0.5	5.0	4.6	2.7	1.7	1.2	1.0	0.7	•	•	•	•
Operating Margin **21**	•	•	•	1.1	1.1	•	•	•	•	•	•	•	•
Operating Margin Before Officers' Comp. **22**	•	•	4.0	5.7	3.8	1.4	0.8	•	•	•	•	•	•

Selected Average Balance Sheet ($ in Thousands)

Net Receivables 23	282	0	19	178	453	1760	3696	5873	16319
Inventories 24	434	0	47	250	895	2192	5047	10131	17082
Net Property, Plant and Equipment 25	279	0	35	64	309	1201	2997	7828	19106
Total Assets 26	1722	0	148	732	2172	7347	15078	35348	71723
Notes and Loans Payable 27	803	0	92	199	604	2011	3885	8048	25276
All Other Liabilities 28	377	0	39	165	490	1168	3202	4399	14866
Net Worth 29	542	0	18	368	1077	4167	7991	22901	31582

Selected Financial Ratios (Times to 1)

Current Ratio 30	2.2	•	1.7	2.8	2.6	2.2	2.2	2.8	1.9
Quick Ratio 31	1.1	•	0.7	1.4	1.2	1.2	1.1	1.3	1.0
Net Sales to Working Capital 32	6.1	•	13.8	5.7	5.6	5.7	5.6	4.6	7.3
Coverage Ratio 33	0.5	•	1.3	6.4	4.7	1.2	2.0	0.1	1.2
Total Asset Turnover 34	1.9	•	3.8	3.1	2.7	2.4	2.1	1.8	2.0
Inventory Turnover 35	5.5	•	7.7	6.4	4.7	6.4	4.7	4.6	6.4
Receivables Turnover 36	8.0	•	23.7	13.2	11.1	9.0	8.0	8.3	9.6
Total Liabilities to Net Worth 37	2.2	•	7.4	1.0	1.0	0.8	0.9	0.5	1.3
Current Assets to Working Capital 38	1.8	•	2.3	1.6	1.6	1.8	1.8	1.5	2.1
Current Liabilities to Working Capital 39	0.8	•	1.3	0.6	0.6	0.8	0.8	0.5	1.1
Working Capital to Net Sales 40	0.2	•	0.1	0.2	0.2	0.2	0.2	0.2	0.1
Inventory to Working Capital 41	0.8	•	1.1	0.7	0.8	0.7	0.9	0.6	0.9
Total Receipts to Cash Flow 42	17.3	•	7.9	11.5	13.0	19.3	16.0	17.2	17.5
Cost of Goods to Cash Flow 43	12.7	•	5.1	8.0	9.3	15.2	11.8	12.5	13.2
Cash Flow to Total Debt 44	0.2	•	0.5	0.5	0.4	0.3	0.3	0.3	0.2

Selected Financial Factors (in Percentages)

Debt Ratio 45	68.5	•	88.1	49.7	50.4	43.3	47.0	35.2	56.0
Return on Total Assets 46	1.7	•	3.8	8.5	7.0	1.9	3.1	0.1	2.5
Return on Equity Before Income Taxes 47	•	•	6.9	14.2	11.1	0.5	3.0	•	0.8
Return on Equity After Income Taxes 48	•	•	4.8	13.9	10.4	0.4	1.4	•	0.7
Profit Margin (Before Income Tax) 49	•	•	0.2	2.3	2.0	0.1	0.7	•	0.2
Profit Margin (After Income Tax) 50	•	•	0.2	2.2	1.9	0.1	0.4	•	0.1

Table II

Corporations with Net Income

OTHER BUILDING MATERIAL DEALERS

MONEY AMOUNTS AND SIZE OF ASSETS IN THOUSANDS OF DOLLARS

Item Description for Accounting Period 7/08 Through 6/09	Total	Zero Assets	Under 500	500 to 1,000	1,000 to 5,000	5,000 to 10,000	10,000 to 25,000	25,000 to 50,000	50,000 to 100,000	100,000 to 250,000	250,000 to 500,000	500,000 to 2,500,000	2,500,000 and over
Number of Enterprises **1**	11678	666	6662	1934	2039	218	•	24	7	•	0	0	0
Revenues ($ in Thousands)													
Net Sales **2**	34630712	15709	3450548	5178756	11787396	4559095	•	1577242	1062921	•	0	0	0
Interest **3**	38837	0	80	5964	12622	3932	•	3920	54	•	0	0	0
Rents **4**	15489	0	3406	2356	5859	0	•	702	0	•	0	0	0
Royalties **5**	3462	0	3213	0	0	0	•	0	0	•	0	0	0
Other Portfolio Income **6**	83890	14396	1745	988	21945	1467	•	4229	451	•	0	0	0
Other Receipts **7**	285172	11	69592	62688	75445	2070	•	6336	8782	•	0	0	0
Total Receipts **8**	35057562	30116	3528584	5250752	11903267	4566564	•	1592429	1072208	•	0	0	0
Average Total Receipts **9**	3002	45	530	2715	5838	20948	•	66351	153173	•	•	•	•
Operating Costs/Operating Income (%)													
Cost of Operations **10**	72.6	58.9	63.7	71.3	71.9	81.8	•	72.2	74.8	•	•	•	•
Salaries and Wages **11**	7.9	0.0	5.0	8.1	8.0	6.1	•	11.6	9.5	•	•	•	•
Taxes Paid **12**	1.5	8.7	1.9	2.0	1.4	0.9	•	1.6	1.0	•	•	•	•
Interest Paid **13**	0.5	•	1.0	0.4	0.4	0.6	•	0.2	0.6	•	•	•	•
Depreciation **14**	1.0	0.7	1.7	0.3	1.0	0.6	•	1.4	1.4	•	•	•	•
Amortization and Depletion **15**	0.0	•	0.0	0.0	0.0	0.0	•	0.1	0.1	•	•	•	•
Pensions and Other Deferred Comp. **16**	0.3	•	0.2	0.2	0.4	0.2	•	0.3	0.7	•	•	•	•
Employee Benefits **17**	0.9	•	0.8	0.7	1.0	0.5	•	1.3	1.1	•	•	•	•
Advertising **18**	1.0	•	2.6	0.6	1.0	0.1	•	0.4	0.4	•	•	•	•
Other Expenses **19**	8.1	36.9	15.5	7.5	8.0	5.1	•	7.1	3.6	•	•	•	•
Officers' Compensation **20**	2.6	0.2	5.1	4.8	2.8	1.5	•	1.1	0.7	•	•	•	•
Operating Margin **21**	3.5	•	2.4	4.1	4.0	2.5	•	2.9	5.9	•	•	•	•
Operating Margin Before Officers' Comp. **22**	6.1	7.6	7.6	8.9	6.7	4.0	•	4.0	6.6	•	•	•	•

Selected Average Balance Sheet ($ in Thousands)

Net Receivables 23	267	0	20	211	399	2197	5696	18566
Inventories 24	462	0	23	252	987	2336	7718	24813
Net Property, Plant and Equipment 25	198	0	34	73	285	595	6879	17133
Total Assets 26	1206	0	126	733	2197	7637	37006	77707
Notes and Loans Payable 27	284	0	66	148	455	2418	2161	13945
All Other Liabilities 28	255	0	33	137	425	1033	4112	15546
Net Worth 29	668	0	27	448	1317	4187	30732	48216

Selected Financial Ratios (Times to 1)

Current Ratio 30	2.8	•	1.6	3.7	4.0	2.4	5.7	2.8
Quick Ratio 31	1.4	•	0.8	2.2	1.8	1.4	2.9	1.7
Net Sales to Working Capital 32	5.1	•	18.1	6.1	4.5	5.4	3.2	4.6
Coverage Ratio 33	9.7	•	5.8	15.5	12.7	5.2	18.3	12.8
Total Asset Turnover 34	2.5	•	4.1	3.7	2.6	2.7	1.8	2.0
Inventory Turnover 35	4.7	•	14.5	7.6	4.2	7.3	6.1	4.6
Receivables Turnover 36	8.8	•	•	11.8	10.2	10.1	•	6.6
Total Liabilities to Net Worth 37	0.8	•	3.7	0.6	0.7	0.8	0.2	0.6
Current Assets to Working Capital 38	1.5	•	2.6	1.4	1.3	1.7	1.2	1.5
Current Liabilities to Working Capital 39	0.5	•	1.6	0.4	0.3	0.7	0.2	0.5
Working Capital to Net Sales 40	0.2	•	0.1	0.2	0.2	0.2	0.3	0.2
Inventory to Working Capital 41	0.7	•	0.8	0.5	0.7	0.6	0.4	0.6
Total Receipts to Cash Flow 42	9.6	1.6	6.1	9.0	10.1	14.5	11.2	10.6
Cost of Goods to Cash Flow 43	7.0	1.0	3.9	6.4	7.2	11.9	8.1	7.9
Cash Flow to Total Debt 44	0.6	•	0.9	1.0	0.7	0.4	0.9	0.5

Selected Financial Factors (in Percentages)

Debt Ratio 45	44.7	•	78.5	38.9	40.1	45.2	17.0	38.0
Return on Total Assets 46	12.9	•	23.4	21.5	14.1	9.1	7.1	14.3
Return on Equity Before Income Taxes 47	20.9	•	90.2	32.8	21.7	13.4	8.1	21.3
Return on Equity After Income Taxes 48	19.8	•	88.0	32.4	20.8	13.1	7.1	21.2
Profit Margin (Before Income Tax) 49	4.7	86.2	4.7	5.5	4.9	2.7	3.8	6.8
Profit Margin (After Income Tax) 50	4.5	78.7	4.6	5.4	4.8	2.6	3.3	6.7

Table I

Corporations with and without Net Income

LAWN AND GARDEN EQUIPMENT AND SUPPLIES STORES

MONEY AMOUNTS AND SIZE OF ASSETS IN THOUSANDS OF DOLLARS

Item Description for Accounting Period 7/08 Through 6/09	Total	Zero Assets	Under 500	500 to 1,000	1,000 to 5,000	5,000 to 10,000	10,000 to 25,000	25,000 to 50,000	50,000 to 100,000	100,000 to 250,000	250,000 to 500,000	500,000 to 2,500,000	2,500,000 and over
Number of Enterprises **1**	8205	968	4381	1539	1136	118	•	19	•	0	0	0	0
Revenues ($ in Thousands)													
Net Sales **2**	16560238	99361	2401408	3253580	4940663	1879483	•	1181194	•	0	0	0	0
Interest **3**	17584	0	383	827	10030	3283	•	1933	•	0	0	0	0
Rents **4**	5218	0	93	121	4661	0	•	161	•	0	0	0	0
Royalties **5**	0	0	0	0	0	0	•	0	•	0	0	0	0
Other Portfolio Income **6**	28015	0	4487	1048	4986	1269	•	15478	•	0	0	0	0
Other Receipts **7**	90229	0	2804	1703	27744	16710	•	3371	•	0	0	0	0
Total Receipts **8**	16701284	99361	2409175	3257279	4988084	1900745	•	1202137	•	0	0	0	0
Average Total Receipts **9**	2036	103	550	2116	4391	16108	•	63270	•	•	•	•	•
Operating Costs/Operating Income (%)													
Cost of Operations **10**	73.5	109.2	68.1	69.2	74.7	79.1	•	69.2	•	•	•	•	•
Salaries and Wages **11**	8.8	13.3	8.2	10.8	8.9	6.4	•	11.5	•	•	•	•	•
Taxes Paid **12**	1.7	1.7	2.9	2.2	1.5	1.0	•	1.5	•	•	•	•	•
Interest Paid **13**	0.9	0.8	0.9	0.6	1.0	1.1	•	1.0	•	•	•	•	•
Depreciation **14**	1.4	1.0	2.0	0.8	1.3	0.6	•	4.4	•	•	•	•	•
Amortization and Depletion **15**	0.0	•	0.0	0.0	0.0	0.0	•	0.0	•	•	•	•	•
Pensions and Other Deferred Comp. **16**	0.1	•	0.0	0.1	0.1	0.1	•	0.2	•	•	•	•	•
Employee Benefits **17**	0.6	•	0.4	0.8	0.7	0.4	•	0.2	•	•	•	•	•
Advertising **18**	1.0	0.7	1.2	0.9	1.4	0.7	•	0.7	•	•	•	•	•
Other Expenses **19**	10.3	30.2	13.9	9.5	10.0	9.3	•	10.9	•	•	•	•	•
Officers' Compensation **20**	2.7	5.8	5.6	3.5	2.5	1.7	•	1.2	•	•	•	•	•
Operating Margin **21**	•	•	•	1.7	•	•	•	•	•	•	•	•	•
Operating Margin Before Officers' Comp. **22**	1.6	•	2.2	5.2	0.5	1.4	•	0.2	•	•	•	•	•

Selected Average Balance Sheet ($ in Thousands)

Item							
Net Receivables 23	118	0	26	66	189	746	7471
Inventories 24	420	0	104	359	1008	4527	10002
Net Property, Plant and Equipment 25	173	0	62	153	498	514	8884
Total Assets 26	915	0	245	716	2145	6549	33751
Notes and Loans Payable 27	376	0	97	267	790	3066	14477
All Other Liabilities 28	290	0	102	127	615	2546	8522
Net Worth 29	248	0	45	321	741	937	10752

Selected Financial Ratios (Times to 1)

Item							
Current Ratio 30	1.7		1.8	3.4	1.8	1.5	1.3
Quick Ratio 31	0.5		0.5	1.3	0.4	0.2	0.5
Net Sales to Working Capital 32	7.8		9.1	5.5	6.2	8.3	14.5
Coverage Ratio 33	0.7			3.9		1.7	1.8
Total Asset Turnover 34	2.2		2.2	3.0	2.0	2.4	1.8
Inventory Turnover 35	3.5		3.6	4.1	3.2	2.8	4.3
Receivables Turnover 36	17.4		27.5	24.1	21.8	25.1	11.3
Total Liabilities to Net Worth 37	2.7		4.4	1.2	1.9	6.0	2.1
Current Assets to Working Capital 38	2.5		2.3	1.4	2.3	3.0	4.9
Current Liabilities to Working Capital 39	1.5		1.3	0.4	1.3	2.0	3.9
Working Capital to Net Sales 40	0.1		0.1	0.2	0.2	0.1	0.1
Inventory to Working Capital 41	1.6		1.6	0.9	1.5	2.4	2.6
Total Receipts to Cash Flow 42	13.6		15.0	12.8	14.8	12.2	11.3
Cost of Goods to Cash Flow 43	10.0		10.2	8.8	11.1	9.6	7.8
Cash Flow to Total Debt 44	0.2		0.2	0.4	0.2	0.2	0.2

Selected Financial Factors (in Percentages)

Item							
Debt Ratio 45	72.9		81.5	55.1	65.5	85.7	68.1
Return on Total Assets 46	1.5			7.3		4.6	3.4
Return on Equity Before Income Taxes 47				12.0		13.6	4.7
Return on Equity After Income Taxes 48				11.4		12.2	4.6
Profit Margin (Before Income Tax) 49				1.8		0.8	0.8
Profit Margin (After Income Tax) 50				1.7		0.7	0.8

Table II

Corporations with Net Income

LAWN AND GARDEN EQUIPMENT AND SUPPLIES STORES

MONEY AMOUNTS AND SIZE OF ASSETS IN THOUSANDS OF DOLLARS

Item Description for Accounting Period 7/08 Through 6/09	Total	Zero Assets	Under 500	500 to 1,000	1,000 to 5,000	5,000 to 10,000	10,000 to 25,000	25,000 to 50,000	50,000 to 100,000	100,000 to 250,000	250,000 to 500,000	500,000 to 2,500,000	2,500,000 and over
Number of Enterprises 1	3969	265	1965	818	767	103	32	15	4	0	0	0	0
Revenues ($ in Thousands)													
Net Sales 2	10854579	64973	1038422	2221306	3227276	1523954	1381620	951155	445873	0	0	0	0
Interest 3	12861	0	381	666	8856	1985	0	374	598	0	0	0	0
Rents 4	4311	0	93	121	3754	0	0	161	182	0	0	0	0
Royalties 5	0	0	0	0	0	0	0	0	0	0	0	0	0
Other Portfolio Income 6	14097	0	3827	1048	1101	1269	281	6368	203	0	0	0	0
Other Receipts 7	76662	0	1835	1060	22506	15998	17535	3107	14621	0	0	0	0
Total Receipts 8	10962510	64973	1044558	2224201	3263493	1543206	1399436	961165	461477	0	0	0	0
Average Total Receipts 9	2762	245	532	2719	4255	14983	43732	64078	115369	•	•	•	•
Operating Costs/Operating Income (%)													
Cost of Operations 10	72.5	45.0	59.0	68.7	74.1	83.2	71.4	69.6	87.5	•	•	•	•
Salaries and Wages 11	8.5	15.1	9.8	11.2	7.8	5.3	8.0	11.2	4.7	•	•	•	•
Taxes Paid 12	1.5	2.1	2.4	2.2	1.2	0.9	1.4	1.5	0.7	•	•	•	•
Interest Paid 13	0.8	1.2	0.8	0.3	0.7	1.2	0.8	0.9	1.3	•	•	•	•
Depreciation 14	1.3	•	2.6	0.7	1.1	0.7	1.0	3.5	1.4	•	•	•	•
Amortization and Depletion 15	0.0	•	0.0	0.0	0.0	0.0	0.1	0.0	0.0	•	•	•	•
Pensions and Other Deferred Comp. 16	0.1	•	0.0	0.2	0.1	0.1	0.3	0.2	0.1	•	•	•	•
Employee Benefits 17	0.6	•	0.0	0.6	0.8	0.5	0.7	0.3	0.6	•	•	•	•
Advertising 18	1.0	0.4	1.1	0.5	1.4	0.8	1.1	0.8	0.2	•	•	•	•
Other Expenses 19	9.6	12.7	15.7	8.3	9.9	5.7	11.1	10.5	5.2	•	•	•	•
Officers' Compensation 20	2.2	8.8	4.1	2.7	2.4	1.6	0.9	1.1	0.2	•	•	•	•
Operating Margin 21	1.9	14.6	4.4	4.6	0.4	0.0	3.2	0.4	•	•	•	•	•
Operating Margin Before Officers' Comp. 22	4.1	23.5	8.5	7.2	2.8	1.6	4.1	1.5	•	•	•	•	•

Selected Average Balance Sheet ($ in Thousands)

Net Receivables 23	153	0	25	90	196	736	1610	7948	21281
Inventories 24	613	0	130	386	1103	3722	11847	14500	18292
Net Property, Plant and Equipment 25	175	0	62	125	312	391	2003	6598	7273
Total Assets 26	1136	0	202	740	2147	6292	16210	31386	55486
Notes and Loans Payable 27	399	0	78	198	654	2668	6852	14197	14635
All Other Liabilities 28	335	0	37	158	617	2700	4314	9168	24592
Net Worth 29	403	0	86	385	876	923	5044	8021	16258

Selected Financial Ratios (Times to 1)

Current Ratio 30	1.9	•	3.0	2.8	1.9	1.6	2.0	1.3	1.5
Quick Ratio 31	0.5	•	1.0	1.4	0.4	0.3	0.2	0.5	0.7
Net Sales to Working Capital 32	6.4	•	5.7	7.2	5.1	6.7	6.6	14.3	7.2
Coverage Ratio 33	4.8	13.0	7.4	14.9	3.0	2.1	6.8	2.6	2.2
Total Asset Turnover 34	2.4	•	2.6	3.7	2.0	2.4	2.7	2.0	2.0
Inventory Turnover 35	3.2	•	2.4	4.8	2.8	3.3	2.6	3.0	5.3
Receivables Turnover 36	17.5	•	31.9	25.0	20.0	30.0	21.1	5.3	10.5
Total Liabilities to Net Worth 37	1.8	•	1.3	0.9	1.4	5.8	2.2	2.9	2.4
Current Assets to Working Capital 38	2.2	•	1.5	1.6	2.1	2.6	2.0	5.0	3.0
Current Liabilities to Working Capital 39	1.2	•	0.5	0.6	1.1	1.6	1.0	4.0	2.0
Working Capital to Net Sales 40	0.2	•	0.2	0.1	0.2	0.2	0.2	0.1	0.1
Inventory to Working Capital 41	1.4	•	1.0	0.8	1.4	2.1	1.7	2.6	1.2
Total Receipts to Cash Flow 42	9.9	4.2	5.8	9.5	11.2	18.7	7.5	10.7	18.5
Cost of Goods to Cash Flow 43	7.2	1.9	3.4	6.5	8.3	15.5	5.4	7.4	16.2
Cash Flow to Total Debt 44	0.4	•	0.8	0.8	0.3	0.1	0.5	0.3	0.2

Selected Financial Factors (in Percentages)

Debt Ratio 45	64.6	•	57.4	48.0	59.2	85.3	68.9	74.4	70.7
Return on Total Assets 46	8.8	•	15.1	18.4	4.4	5.8	14.0	4.7	5.7
Return on Equity Before Income Taxes 47	19.8	•	30.7	33.1	7.2	20.5	38.4	11.4	10.6
Return on Equity After Income Taxes 48	18.8	•	29.4	32.2	5.9	18.8	38.4	11.1	10.5
Profit Margin (Before Income Tax) 49	2.9	14.6	5.0	4.7	1.5	1.3	4.5	1.4	1.5
Profit Margin (After Income Tax) 50	2.8	14.6	4.8	4.6	1.2	1.2	4.5	1.4	1.5

RETAIL TRADE
45115

Table I
Corporations with and without Net Income

FOOD AND BEVERAGE STORES

MONEY AMOUNTS AND SIZE OF ASSETS IN THOUSANDS OF DOLLARS

Item Description for Accounting Period 7/08 Through 6/09	Total	Zero Assets	Under 500	500 to 1,000	1,000 to 5,000	5,000 to 10,000	10,000 to 25,000	25,000 to 50,000	50,000 to 100,000	100,000 to 250,000	250,000 to 500,000	500,000 to 2,500,000	2,500,000 and over
Number of Enterprises **1**	72031	11796	50352	4489	4446	542	202	67	50	42	12	24	11
Revenues ($ in Thousands)													
Net Sales **2**	486632048	1892220	34945304	13904740	38209995	14180764	16553280	11264845	13670298	25411040	11063268	89080372	216455924
Interest **3**	730370	282	1809	3632	11000	4135	2038	4212	7421	9724	8680	82342	595095
Rents **4**	653857	101	1415	7651	12080	16345	16987	7887	12375	18218	14570	194590	351640
Royalties **5**	1682548	2287	0	0	48	272	3928	353	3383	15524	0	56965	1599788
Other Portfolio Income **6**	644507	30681	47395	45481	122261	10214	22134	11640	33070	159294	40633	21348	100357
Other Receipts **7**	4568014	63058	518603	55854	384031	118533	157199	77677	180384	178730	135445	1447281	1251216
Total Receipts **8**	494911344	1988629	35514526	14017358	38739415	14330263	16755566	11366614	13906931	25792530	11262596	90882898	220354020
Average Total Receipts **9**	6871	169	705	3123	8713	26440	82948	169651	278139	614108	938550	3786787	20032184
Operating Costs/Operating Income (%)													
Cost of Operations **10**	73.5	63.0	70.2	77.8	76.2	76.0	78.4	80.0	72.3	74.4	74.6	74.6	72.0
Salaries and Wages **11**	9.5	9.0	7.7	6.9	8.5	9.7	8.2	7.6	11.3	10.5	11.3	10.4	9.7
Taxes Paid **12**	1.5	2.8	2.4	1.1	1.4	1.4	1.2	1.2	2.1	1.5	1.3	1.4	1.5
Interest Paid **13**	0.7	0.6	0.6	0.6	0.5	0.5	0.3	0.4	0.5	0.5	0.6	0.7	0.9
Depreciation **14**	2.0	2.1	1.1	0.5	1.0	1.3	1.3	1.4	1.9	1.9	2.1	2.2	2.6
Amortization and Depletion **15**	0.1	1.1	0.3	0.2	0.1	0.1	0.1	0.1	0.1	0.2	0.1	0.2	0.1
Pensions and Other Deferred Comp. **16**	0.4	0.0	0.1	0.0	0.1	0.1	0.1	0.2	0.5	0.3	0.3	0.5	0.6
Employee Benefits **17**	1.2	0.2	0.3	0.3	0.4	1.0	1.0	0.7	1.6	1.2	1.2	1.6	1.3
Advertising **18**	0.7	0.9	0.6	0.5	1.1	0.9	0.7	0.7	0.8	0.8	0.8	0.8	0.6
Other Expenses **19**	10.2	33.6	14.6	9.6	9.9	7.8	8.8	7.7	9.3	9.3	7.8	8.6	10.8
Officers' Compensation **20**	0.5	4.6	3.1	1.4	0.9	1.0	0.4	0.3	0.5	0.3	0.3	0.2	0.0
Operating Margin **21**	•	•	•	1.1	•	0.3	•	•	•	•	•	•	•
Operating Margin Before Officers' Comp. **22**	0.0	•	2.3	2.5	0.9	1.3	•	•	•	•	•	•	•

Selected Average Balance Sheet ($ in Thousands)

Net Receivables 23	164	0	5	38	220	473	1543	2352	5355	7647	19257	48428	703971
Inventories 24	345	0	33	148	415	1331	3918	7752	11622	25565	50306	190485	1076181
Net Property, Plant and Equipment 25	1051	0	49	184	700	2724	5828	15322	26942	69165	139112	616155	4082020
Total Assets 26	2397	0	139	673	1996	6480	16085	36179	70162	151818	368421	1237547	9145895
Notes and Loans Payable 27	666	0	98	304	716	2246	4471	12619	22961	39467	84924	346906	2122491
All Other Liabilities 28	979	0	16	144	538	1555	5837	11850	22008	56551	113359	414443	4459639
Net Worth 29	753	0	25	226	742	2678	5777	11710	25193	55800	170138	476197	2563766

Selected Financial Ratios (Times to 1)

Current Ratio 30	1.0	•	3.0	2.3	2.0	1.7	1.2	1.3	1.1	1.2	0.9	1.0	0.8
Quick Ratio 31	0.4	•	1.2	0.9	1.0	0.7	0.5	0.6	0.5	0.4	0.4	0.3	0.4
Net Sales to Working Capital 32	•	•	16.6	17.8	17.1	23.3	58.4	43.9	82.7	88.2	•	367.3	•
Coverage Ratio 33	2.8	•	2.4	4.5	3.9	4.0	3.8	2.1	2.8	2.3	3.7	2.3	2.8
Total Asset Turnover 34	2.8	•	5.0	4.6	4.3	4.0	5.1	4.6	3.9	4.0	2.5	3.0	2.2
Inventory Turnover 35	14.4	•	14.6	16.2	15.8	14.9	16.4	17.3	17.0	17.6	13.7	14.5	13.2
Receivables Turnover 36	39.9	•	131.2	81.8	42.9	56.5	48.7	69.9	59.0	83.3	39.6	76.4	26.6
Total Liabilities to Net Worth 37	2.2	•	4.6	2.0	1.7	1.4	1.8	2.1	1.8	1.7	1.2	1.6	2.6
Current Assets to Working Capital 38	•	•	1.5	1.8	2.1	2.5	5.6	4.3	8.1	7.7	•	33.4	•
Current Liabilities to Working Capital 39	•	•	0.5	0.8	1.1	1.5	4.6	3.3	7.1	6.7	•	32.4	•
Working Capital to Net Sales 40	•	•	0.1	0.1	0.1	0.0	0.0	0.0	0.0	0.0	•	0.0	•
Inventory to Working Capital 41	•	18.4	0.8	0.9	0.8	1.2	2.7	1.9	3.7	3.9	•	19.0	•
Total Receipts to Cash Flow 42	12.3	10.8	12.6	12.8	14.9	16.0	18.7	15.0	15.6	15.8	14.8	10.7	
Cost of Goods to Cash Flow 43	9.0	11.6	9.8	9.8	11.3	12.5	15.0	10.8	11.6	11.8	11.0	7.7	
Cash Flow to Total Debt 44	0.3	•	0.6	0.6	0.5	0.5	0.4	0.4	0.4	0.3	0.3	0.3	

Selected Financial Factors (in Percentages)

Debt Ratio 45	68.6	•	82.2	66.5	62.8	58.7	64.1	67.6	64.1	63.2	53.8	61.5	72.0
Return on Total Assets 46	5.4	•	6.6	11.3	7.5	7.3	5.2	4.3	5.1	4.8	5.1	4.8	5.4
Return on Equity Before Income Taxes 47	11.0	•	21.6	26.1	15.0	13.3	10.6	7.1	9.1	7.5	8.0	7.2	12.5
Return on Equity After Income Taxes 48	7.4	•	20.6	25.8	13.9	11.6	9.5	4.9	7.0	6.5	5.9	4.3	7.5
Profit Margin (Before Income Tax) 49	1.2	•	0.8	1.9	1.3	1.4	0.7	0.5	0.8	0.7	1.5	0.9	1.6
Profit Margin (After Income Tax) 50	0.8	•	0.7	1.9	1.2	1.2	0.7	0.3	0.6	0.6	1.1	0.6	1.0

Table II

Corporations with Net Income

FOOD AND BEVERAGE STORES

MONEY AMOUNTS AND SIZE OF ASSETS IN THOUSANDS OF DOLLARS

Item Description for Accounting Period 7/08 Through 6/09	Total	Zero Assets	Under 500	500 to 1,000	1,000 to 5,000	5,000 to 10,000	10,000 to 25,000	25,000 to 50,000	50,000 to 100,000	100,000 to 250,000	250,000 to 500,000	500,000 to 2,500,000	2,500,000 and over
Number of Enterprises **1**	39700	2932	29640	3468	3024	356	•	47	•	28	9	16	8
Revenues ($ in Thousands)													
Net Sales **2**	372092525	621874	26481114	11407681	29058347	9545218	•	7305794	•	17711286	8052340	63013569	178585299
Interest **3**	645150	245	1498	1135	9890	3986	•	4083	•	4857	7469	75827	529620
Rents **4**	320499	101	25	7651	10281	7843	•	6151	•	5973	14487	165653	80662
Royalties **5**	1675892	0	0	0	48	0	•	24	•	15524	0	56965	1599788
Other Portfolio Income **6**	470374	30539	30817	18083	110642	5838	•	8529	•	120016	37211	19429	60773
Other Receipts **7**	3446259	8455	329977	46659	336477	93667	•	67912	•	106616	118261	1042303	1029711
Total Receipts **8**	378650699	661214	26843431	11481209	29525685	9656552	•	7392493	•	17364272	8229768	64373746	181885853
Average Total Receipts **9**	9538	226	906	3311	9764	27125	•	157287	•	620153	914419	4023359	22735732
Operating Costs/Operating Income (%)													
Cost of Operations **10**	74.0	57.0	71.9	78.2	76.6	75.6	•	79.6	•	75.3	75.3	75.5	72.3
Salaries and Wages **11**	9.1	11.6	6.7	6.2	8.1	9.5	•	7.6	•	10.0	9.9	9.9	9.3
Taxes Paid **12**	1.4	4.0	2.1	1.0	1.2	1.3	•	1.4	•	1.3	1.4	1.4	1.5
Interest Paid **13**	0.5	0.4	0.3	0.4	0.3	0.3	•	0.4	•	0.4	0.4	0.6	0.7
Depreciation **14**	2.0	0.3	0.8	0.4	0.8	0.9	•	1.3	•	1.9	2.2	2.2	2.6
Amortization and Depletion **15**	0.1	0.3	0.1	0.2	0.1	0.1	•	0.0	•	0.1	0.1	0.2	0.1
Pensions and Other Deferred Comp. **16**	0.5	0.0	0.1	0.0	0.1	0.1	•	0.2	•	0.2	0.4	0.6	0.6
Employee Benefits **17**	1.1	0.1	0.2	0.2	0.4	1.2	•	0.8	•	0.9	1.7	1.3	1.3
Advertising **18**	0.6	0.3	0.4	0.4	1.0	1.1	•	0.8	•	0.8	0.7	0.6	0.5
Other Expenses **19**	9.7	18.5	12.6	9.3	9.1	7.1	•	6.9	•	8.3	7.0	7.8	10.7
Officers' Compensation **20**	0.5	4.0	3.1	1.3	0.9	1.1	•	0.4	•	0.3	0.4	0.2	0.0
Operating Margin **21**	0.6	3.5	1.7	2.4	1.3	1.7	•	0.6	•	0.6	0.4	•	0.5
Operating Margin Before Officers' Comp. **22**	1.1	7.6	4.8	3.7	2.2	2.8	•	1.0	•	0.8	0.8	0.0	0.5

Selected Average Balance Sheet ($ in Thousands)

Net Receivables 23	250	0	7	12	198	609	2003	7112	12032	52356	902205
Inventories 24	515	0	40	152	443	1614	8677	26005	50464	201309	1381765
Net Property, Plant and Equipment 25	1387	0	40	186	634	1941	15534	70557	150233	665302	4309629
Total Assets 26	3326	0	138	662	2023	6504	37418	147941	361558	1222536	10502589
Notes and Loans Payable 27	812	0	63	245	514	1746	10490	33265	63747	333180	2372180
All Other Liabilities 28	1265	0	16	122	484	1445	11168	42000	100860	379020	4653293
Net Worth 29	1248	0	58	296	1024	3313	15760	72676	196951	510335	3477116

Selected Financial Ratios (Times to 1)

Current Ratio 30	1.0	•	4.0	2.5	2.4	2.2	•	•	1.7	•	•	1.3	•	0.9	1.1	0.8
Quick Ratio 31	0.4	•	1.8	0.9	1.2	1.0	•	•	0.8	•	•	0.5	•	0.3	0.4	0.4
Net Sales to Working Capital 32	4053.9	•	15.0	18.5	15.1	14.4	•	•	21.9	•	62.2	•	•	147.4	•	
Coverage Ratio 33	5.3	24.3	10.2	8.2	10.2	9.5	•	5.8	•	6.5	•	7.1	4.2	4.5		
Total Asset Turnover 34	2.8	•	6.5	5.0	4.8	4.1	•	4.2	•	4.1	•	2.5	3.2	2.1		
Inventory Turnover 35	13.5	•	16.1	17.0	16.6	12.6	•	14.3	•	17.7	•	13.3	14.8	11.7		
Receivables Turnover 36	35.0	•	114.0	156.0	62.0	43.5	•	68.8	•	79.1	•	58.0	71.2	22.7		
Total Liabilities to Net Worth 37	1.7	•	1.4	1.2	1.0	1.0	•	1.4	•	1.0	•	0.8	1.4	2.0		
Current Assets to Working Capital 38	472.4	•	1.3	1.7	1.7	1.8	•	2.5	•	5.0	•	12.4	•			
Current Liabilities to Working Capital 39	471.4	•	0.3	0.7	0.7	0.8	•	1.5	•	4.0	•	11.4	•			
Working Capital to Net Sales 40	0.0	•	0.1	0.1	0.1	0.1	•	0.0	•	0.0	•	0.0	•			
Inventory to Working Capital 41	210.9	•	0.6	0.9	0.7	0.8	•	1.1	•	2.6	•	6.7	•			
Total Receipts to Cash Flow 42	10.9	5.6	9.3	11.1	11.3	12.9	•	15.3	•	14.0	14.2	13.5	9.7			
Cost of Goods to Cash Flow 43	8.1	3.2	6.7	8.6	8.7	9.8	•	12.2	•	10.5	10.7	10.2	7.0			
Cash Flow to Total Debt 44	0.4	•	1.2	0.8	0.9	0.6	•	0.5	•	0.6	0.4	0.4	0.3			

Selected Financial Factors (in Percentages)

Debt Ratio 45	62.5	•	57.5	55.3	49.4	49.1	•	•	57.9	•	50.9	•	•	45.5	58.3	66.9
Return on Total Assets 46	8.2	•	22.1	17.0	15.3	13.3	•	•	9.1	•	10.0	•	•	7.6	8.6	6.3
Return on Equity Before Income Taxes 47	17.8	•	47.0	33.3	27.2	23.4	•	•	18.0	•	17.2	•	•	12.0	15.6	14.7
Return on Equity After Income Taxes 48	13.9	•	46.2	33.1	26.1	21.4	•	•	15.7	•	16.0	•	•	9.6	11.7	9.6
Profit Margin (Before Income Tax) 49	2.4	9.9	3.1	3.0	2.9	2.9	•	1.8	•	2.0	•	2.6	2.0	2.3		
Profit Margin (After Income Tax) 50	1.8	9.6	3.0	3.0	2.8	2.6	•	1.6	•	1.9	•	2.1	1.5	1.5		

Table I

Corporations with and without Net Income

BEER, WINE, AND LIQUOR STORES

MONEY AMOUNTS AND SIZE OF ASSETS IN THOUSANDS OF DOLLARS

Item Description for Accounting Period 7/08 Through 6/09	Total	Zero Assets	Under 500	500 to 1,000	1,000 to 5,000	5,000 to 10,000	10,000 to 25,000	25,000 to 50,000	50,000 to 100,000	100,000 to 250,000	250,000 to 500,000	500,000 to 2,500,000	2,500,000 and over
Number of Enterprises **1**	21880	1935	16241	2617	1014	46	10	10	3	3	0	0	0
Revenues ($ in Thousands)													
Net Sales **2**	28469687	344502	13887289	4513025	5872144	612743	251618	1003828	532709	1451829	0	0	0
Interest **3**	8269	0	2248	1009	3014	497	1179	0	0	322	0	0	0
Rents **4**	857	0	0	0	0	0	0	0	0	857	0	0	0
Royalties **5**	0	0	0	0	0	0	0	0	0	0	0	0	0
Other Portfolio Income **6**	13736	9210	3087	708	24	0	4	0	0	703	0	0	0
Other Receipts **7**	542315	1347	368563	87668	22729	7724	38889	5121	1078	9197	0	0	0
Total Receipts **8**	29034864	355059	14261187	4602410	5897911	620964	291690	1008949	533787	1462908	0	0	0
Average Total Receipts **9**	1327	183	878	1759	5816	13499	29169	100895	177929	487636	•	•	•
Operating Costs/Operating Income (%)													
Cost of Operations **10**	78.8	89.3	77.2	79.5	81.0	88.6	78.9	77.2	75.1	78.0	•	•	•
Salaries and Wages **11**	5.6	0.5	6.0	4.8	4.5	3.8	12.2	7.4	9.0	7.1	•	•	•
Taxes Paid **12**	2.1	1.1	2.9	2.2	1.0	0.5	1.8	1.5	1.6	1.1	•	•	•
Interest Paid **13**	0.8	1.3	0.7	0.9	0.7	0.2	3.1	0.7	1.2	1.4	•	•	•
Depreciation **14**	0.6	0.8	0.6	0.6	0.3	0.2	1.4	1.0	0.9	1.7	•	•	•
Amortization and Depletion **15**	0.4	1.7	0.5	0.6	0.2	0.1	0.1	0.1	0.2	0.1	•	•	•
Pensions and Other Deferred Comp. **16**	0.1	•	0.0	0.0	0.1	0.2	0.0	0.1	0.1	0.1	•	•	•
Employee Benefits **17**	0.2	0.0	0.2	0.2	0.2	0.2	0.7	0.1	0.8	0.9	•	•	•
Advertising **18**	0.6	0.1	0.4	0.5	0.6	0.1	3.3	0.6	1.3	1.2	•	•	•
Other Expenses **19**	9.0	10.9	9.8	9.4	7.2	3.5	17.7	8.5	8.1	8.4	•	•	•
Officers' Compensation **20**	2.5	5.3	3.2	2.6	1.7	0.9	1.9	1.4	0.9	0.5	•	•	•
Operating Margin **21**	•	•	•	•	2.6	1.8	•	1.6	0.7	•	•	•	•
Operating Margin Before Officers' Comp. **22**	1.8	•	1.6	1.5	4.3	2.7	•	3.0	1.7	0.1	•	•	•

Selected Average Balance Sheet ($ in Thousands)

Net Receivables 23	14	0	1	9	42	2856	5096	1378	1293	6432
Inventories 24	162	0	90	254	813	2367	3027	20460	56448	62126
Net Property, Plant and Equipment 25	68	0	35	94	278	878	6788	3612	8711	75973
Total Assets 26	396	0	208	702	1690	7715	21115	35117	67498	205189
Notes and Loans Payable 27	212	0	120	435	765	3350	9917	13319	32705	93039
All Other Liabilities 28	65	0	28	78	317	1298	5037	12140	16603	51341
Net Worth 29	120	0	60	189	608	3067	6161	9658	18191	60810

Selected Financial Ratios (Times to 1)

Current Ratio 30	2.7	•	3.7	4.2	2.4	2.0	1.4	1.5	1.8	1.5
Quick Ratio 31	0.8	•	1.0	1.3	0.6	1.2	0.6	0.2	0.2	0.2
Net Sales to Working Capital 32	8.2	•	9.0	5.9	8.0	4.0	6.6	10.0	8.5	20.0
Coverage Ratio 33	2.7	•	2.5	2.0	5.5	14.8	•	4.0	1.8	1.3
Total Asset Turnover 34	3.3	•	4.1	2.5	3.4	1.7	1.2	2.9	2.6	2.4
Inventory Turnover 35	6.3	•	7.4	5.4	5.8	5.0	6.6	3.8	2.4	6.1
Receivables Turnover 36	95.7	•	697.8	225.9	100.0	5.0	8.0	82.3	22.7	150.5
Total Liabilities to Net Worth 37	2.3	•	2.5	2.7	1.8	1.5	2.4	2.6	2.7	2.4
Current Assets to Working Capital 38	1.6	•	1.4	1.3	1.7	2.0	3.2	3.0	2.3	3.1
Current Liabilities to Working Capital 39	0.6	•	0.4	0.3	0.7	1.0	2.2	2.0	1.3	2.1
Working Capital to Net Sales 40	0.1	•	0.1	0.2	0.1	0.3	0.2	0.1	0.1	0.1
Inventory to Working Capital 41	1.1	•	1.0	0.9	1.2	0.7	1.0	2.2	1.4	2.6
Total Receipts to Cash Flow 42	15.0	•	13.9	15.5	14.3	17.7	12.3	16.0	22.8	22.8
Cost of Goods to Cash Flow 43	11.8	•	10.7	12.3	11.6	15.6	9.7	12.4	17.1	17.7
Cash Flow to Total Debt 44	0.3	•	0.4	0.2	0.4	0.2	0.1	0.2	0.2	0.1

Selected Financial Factors (in Percentages)

Debt Ratio 45	69.8	•	71.3	73.1	64.0	60.3	70.8	72.5	73.1	70.4
Return on Total Assets 46	6.8	•	6.9	4.3	12.6	5.8	•	8.2	5.6	4.3
Return on Equity Before Income Taxes 47	14.1	•	14.6	8.1	28.6	13.7	•	22.4	9.2	3.5
Return on Equity After Income Taxes 48	13.0	•	13.7	7.7	26.6	13.0	•	22.4	9.2	1.1
Profit Margin (Before Income Tax) 49	1.3	•	1.0	0.9	3.0	3.1	•	2.2	0.9	0.4
Profit Margin (After Income Tax) 50	1.2	•	1.0	0.8	2.8	3.0	•	2.2	0.9	0.1

Table II

Corporations with Net Income

BEER, WINE, AND LIQUOR STORES

MONEY AMOUNTS AND SIZE OF ASSETS IN THOUSANDS OF DOLLARS

Item Description for Accounting Period 7/08 Through 6/09	Total	Zero Assets	Under 500	500 to 1,000	1,000 to 5,000	5,000 to 10,000	10,000 to 25,000	25,000 to 50,000	50,000 to 100,000	100,000 to 250,000	250,000 to 500,000	500,000 to 2,500,000	2,500,000 and over
Number of Enterprises 1	13814	84	11120	1785	762	46	•	10	•	0	0	0	0
Revenues ($ in Thousands)													
Net Sales 2	21890122	50379	10581523	3206947	5091262	612743	•	1003828	•	0	0	0	0
Interest 3	7356	0	1433	950	2976	497	•	0	•	0	0	0	0
Rents 4	857	0	0	0	0	0	•	0	•	0	0	0	0
Royalties 5	0	0	0	0	0	0	•	0	•	0	0	0	0
Other Portfolio Income 6	3434	0	1999	708	24	0	•	0	•	0	0	0	0
Other Receipts 7	463895	0	304973	78794	18413	7724	•	5121	•	0	0	0	0
Total Receipts 8	22365664	50379	10889928	3287399	5112675	620964	•	1008949	•	0	0	0	0
Average Total Receipts 9	1619	600	979	1842	6710	13499	•	100895	•	•	•	•	•
Operating Costs/Operating Income (%)													
Cost of Operations 10	78.7	82.1	77.0	79.4	81.1	88.6	•	77.2	•	•	•	•	•
Salaries and Wages 11	5.5	3.5	5.7	4.6	4.6	3.8	•	7.4	•	•	•	•	•
Taxes Paid 12	1.7	0.8	2.3	1.1	1.0	0.5	•	1.5	•	•	•	•	•
Interest Paid 13	0.5	1.9	0.5	0.6	0.5	0.2	•	0.7	•	•	•	•	•
Depreciation 14	0.5	0.3	0.5	0.5	0.2	0.2	•	1.0	•	•	•	•	•
Amortization and Depletion 15	0.3	1.7	0.3	0.4	0.1	0.1	•	0.1	•	•	•	•	•
Pensions and Other Deferred Comp. 16	0.1	•	0.1	0.0	0.1	0.2	•	0.0	•	•	•	•	•
Employee Benefits 17	0.2	0.2	0.1	0.3	0.1	0.2	•	0.1	•	•	•	•	•
Advertising 18	0.6	0.0	0.5	0.5	0.7	0.1	•	0.6	•	•	•	•	•
Other Expenses 19	8.5	8.1	9.4	9.3	6.8	3.5	•	8.5	•	•	•	•	•
Officers' Compensation 20	2.7	•	3.6	3.3	1.5	0.9	•	1.4	•	•	•	•	•
Operating Margin 21	0.8	1.2	•	0.1	3.2	1.8	•	1.6	•	•	•	•	•
Operating Margin Before Officers' Comp. 22	3.5	1.2	3.6	3.4	4.7	2.7	•	3.0	•	•	•	•	•

Selected Average Balance Sheet ($ in Thousands)

Net Receivables 23	16	0	1	7	28	2856	1378
Inventories 24	189	0	94	249	824	2367	20460
Net Property, Plant and Equipment 25	69	0	33	70	237	878	3612
Total Assets 26	461	0	223	738	1717	7715	35117
Notes and Loans Payable 27	213	0	109	385	712	3350	13319
All Other Liabilities 28	74	0	29	62	366	1298	12140
Net Worth 29	173	0	85	292	639	3067	9658

Selected Financial Ratios (Times to 1)

Current Ratio 30	2.8	•	4.5	4.6	2.2	2.0	1.5
Quick Ratio 31	0.9	•	1.4	1.7	0.6	1.2	0.2
Net Sales to Working Capital 32	8.0	•	8.8	5.6	9.0	4.0	10.0
Coverage Ratio 33	6.5	1.6	6.7	5.3	8.8	14.8	4.0
Total Asset Turnover 34	3.4	•	4.3	2.4	3.9	1.7	2.9
Inventory Turnover 35	6.6	•	7.8	5.7	6.6	5.0	3.8
Receivables Turnover 36	108.9	•	1047.8	435.7	195.4	5.0	82.3
Total Liabilities to Net Worth 37	1.7	•	1.6	1.5	1.7	1.5	2.6
Current Assets to Working Capital 38	1.6	•	1.3	1.3	1.9	2.0	3.0
Current Liabilities to Working Capital 39	0.6	•	0.3	0.3	0.9	1.0	2.0
Working Capital to Net Sales 40	0.1	•	0.1	0.2	0.1	0.3	0.1
Inventory to Working Capital 41	1.0	•	0.9	0.8	1.3	0.7	2.2
Total Receipts to Cash Flow 42	12.6	25.9	11.6	12.4	13.3	17.7	16.0
Cost of Goods to Cash Flow 43	9.9	21.3	9.0	9.8	10.8	15.6	12.4
Cash Flow to Total Debt 44	0.4	•	0.6	0.3	0.5	0.2	0.2

Selected Financial Factors (in Percentages)

Debt Ratio 45	62.4	•	62.1	60.5	62.8	60.3	72.5
Return on Total Assets 46	12.0	•	14.5	7.7	15.7	5.8	8.2
Return on Equity Before Income Taxes 47	26.9	•	32.6	15.8	37.4	13.7	22.4
Return on Equity After Income Taxes 48	25.6	•	31.6	15.3	34.8	13.0	22.4
Profit Margin (Before Income Tax) 49	2.9	1.2	2.9	2.6	3.6	3.1	2.2
Profit Margin (After Income Tax) 50	2.8	1.1	2.8	2.5	3.3	3.0	2.2

Table I

Corporations with and without Net Income

HEALTH AND PERSONAL CARE STORES

MONEY AMOUNTS AND SIZE OF ASSETS IN THOUSANDS OF DOLLARS

Item Description for Accounting Period 7/08 Through 6/09		Total	Zero Assets	Under 500	500 to 1,000	1,000 to 5,000	5,000 to 10,000	10,000 to 25,000	25,000 to 50,000	50,000 to 100,000	100,000 to 250,000	250,000 to 500,000	500,000 to 2,500,000	2,500,000 and over
Number of Enterprises	1	40683	3108	29641	4424	3233	128	86	18	14	13	8	3	6
Revenues ($ in Thousands)														
Net Sales	2	305557878	4042790	25814554	16652338	20415273	3115361	2652400	1106523	1753698	4948267	3625444	4591383	216839847
Interest	3	249410	685	2400	4061	8399	3360	6523	473	383	3035	1911	4438	213743
Rents	4	144571	5227	10	1385	2223	769	583	2490	15	7837	4861	67	119104
Royalties	5	75034	0	0	0	22	0	1563	0	8655	2111	831	35967	25885
Other Portfolio Income	6	122860	9	8955	30826	26900	158	212	51	2119	35665	4125	0	13840
Other Receipts	7	4004063	67188	34712	84044	65731	60042	77618	65967	6936	35238	60517	29065	3417003
Total Receipts	8	310153816	4115899	25860631	16772654	20518548	3179690	2738899	1175504	1771806	5032153	3697689	4660920	220629422
Average Total Receipts	9	7624	1324	872	3791	6347	24841	31848	65306	126558	387089	462211	1553640	36771570
Operating Costs/Operating Income (%)														
Cost of Operations	10	73.5	68.1	69.9	73.9	72.6	72.5	65.8	58.3	59.8	74.4	54.5	57.5	75.0
Salaries and Wages	11	9.5	13.2	7.0	8.7	10.3	11.3	15.4	16.8	18.3	11.0	14.1	15.3	9.3
Taxes Paid	12	1.1	1.8	1.5	1.7	1.4	1.3	1.5	2.8	1.8	1.3	2.1	2.1	1.0
Interest Paid	13	0.8	0.3	0.2	0.2	0.6	0.4	2.2	2.3	1.0	1.3	3.2	2.2	0.8
Depreciation	14	1.2	1.7	0.5	0.3	0.8	1.5	2.0	2.3	1.5	1.1	2.6	3.4	1.3
Amortization and Depletion	15	0.3	0.3	0.1	0.1	0.2	0.2	0.5	0.3	0.4	0.4	1.5	1.3	0.3
Pensions and Other Deferred Comp.	16	0.3	0.3	0.2	0.5	0.3	0.2	0.4	0.2	0.3	0.1	0.2	0.2	0.2
Employee Benefits	17	0.5	0.9	0.4	0.3	0.4	1.1	1.2	0.8	1.1	1.4	1.2	1.1	0.5
Advertising	18	0.8	0.8	0.8	0.4	0.7	2.5	0.8	1.6	1.5	0.8	1.3	2.1	0.8
Other Expenses	19	9.0	10.2	10.3	6.4	7.7	8.3	11.3	18.3	13.9	8.4	14.9	16.0	8.9
Officers' Compensation	20	1.1	3.0	5.7	4.7	3.0	1.6	1.6	0.9	1.4	0.4	1.0	0.5	0.1
Operating Margin	21	1.8	•	3.4	2.8	2.0	•	•	•	•	•	3.4	•	1.9
Operating Margin Before Officers' Comp.	22	2.9	2.4	9.0	7.5	5.0	0.8	•	•	0.5	•	4.4	•	1.9

Selected Average Balance Sheet ($ in Thousands)

Net Receivables 23	517	0	19	88	420	2261	3798	4982	15204	26926	39205	78897	2815578
Inventories 24	672	0	60	234	426	1699	2468	8716	9994	47358	57745	251940	3429406
Net Property, Plant and Equipment 25	554	0	19	73	284	1225	1365	9029	11102	23680	56916	177761	3139648
Total Assets 26	3580	0	156	750	1798	6783	14657	34208	77227	152896	336275	1169929	19984231
Notes and Loans Payable 27	988	0	61	227	636	2477	8004	14978	21427	69913	188291	474079	4983390
All Other Liabilities 28	1070	0	54	207	511	2865	16044	15707	29979	51724	62973	287367	5809247
Net Worth 29	1523	0	40	315	651	1440	-9392	3522	25821	31259	85010	408483	9191594

Selected Financial Ratios (Times to 1)

Current Ratio 30	1.4	•	2.2	2.5	1.9	1.1	0.6	1.3	1.2	1.6	2.3	2.3	1.3
Quick Ratio 31	0.6	•	1.0	1.2	1.1	0.7	0.4	0.6	0.7	0.8	1.2	0.7	0.6
Net Sales to Working Capital 32	19.8	•	13.3	11.0	10.4	45.0	•	15.7	18.0	11.5	7.0	7.9	24.6
Coverage Ratio 33	5.3	4.4	15.3	16.7	5.2	4.2	1.2	1.6	1.2	1.8	2.7	1.0	5.6
Total Asset Turnover 34	2.1	•	5.6	5.0	3.5	3.6	2.1	1.8	1.6	2.5	1.3	1.3	1.8
Inventory Turnover 35	8.2	•	10.2	11.9	10.8	10.4	8.2	4.1	7.5	6.0	4.3	3.5	7.9
Receivables Turnover 36	15.2	•	48.2	39.3	16.5	11.2	11.0	8.7	10.1	13.6	14.6	11.8	13.5
Total Liabilities to Net Worth 37	1.4	•	2.9	1.4	1.8	3.7	•	8.7	2.0	3.9	3.0	1.9	1.2
Current Assets to Working Capital 38	3.7	•	1.8	1.7	2.1	8.5	•	4.3	5.1	2.6	1.8	1.8	4.8
Current Liabilities to Working Capital 39	2.7	•	0.8	0.7	1.1	7.5	•	3.3	4.1	1.6	0.8	0.8	3.8
Working Capital to Net Sales 40	0.1	•	0.1	0.1	0.1	0.0	•	0.1	0.1	0.1	0.1	0.1	0.0
Inventory to Working Capital 41	1.8	•	1.0	0.7	0.8	2.9	•	2.1	1.2	1.1	0.7	1.1	2.4
Total Receipts to Cash Flow 42	10.8	13.7	10.2	13.5	12.0	12.8	10.9	7.5	10.1	17.9	6.7	10.8	10.6
Cost of Goods to Cash Flow 43	8.0	9.3	7.1	10.0	8.8	9.3	7.1	4.4	6.0	13.3	3.6	6.2	8.0
Cash Flow to Total Debt 44	0.3	•	0.7	0.6	0.5	0.4	0.1	0.3	0.2	0.2	0.3	0.2	0.3

Selected Financial Factors (in Percentages)

Debt Ratio 45	57.5	•	74.1	58.0	63.8	78.8	164.1	89.7	66.6	79.6	74.7	65.1	54.0
Return on Total Assets 46	8.6	•	21.1	18.9	11.0	5.6	5.7	6.8	1.9	5.9	11.4	2.8	7.9
Return on Equity Before Income Taxes 47	16.4	•	76.1	42.4	24.6	20.2	•	25.3	0.8	13.0	28.0	•	14.2
Return on Equity After Income Taxes 48	11.5	•	75.0	41.2	22.9	11.8	•	21.6	•	8.3	19.7	•	8.9
Profit Margin (Before Income Tax) 49	3.3	1.2	3.5	3.5	2.5	1.2	0.5	1.4	0.2	1.1	5.2	•	3.6
Profit Margin (After Income Tax) 50	2.3	0.7	3.5	3.4	2.4	0.7	0.5	1.2	•	0.7	3.7	•	2.3

Table II

Corporations with Net Income

HEALTH AND PERSONAL CARE STORES

MONEY AMOUNTS AND SIZE OF ASSETS IN THOUSANDS OF DOLLARS

Item Description for Accounting Period 7/08 Through 6/09		Total	Zero Assets	Under 500	500 to 1,000	1,000 to 5,000	5,000 to 10,000	10,000 to 25,000	25,000 to 50,000	50,000 to 100,000	100,000 to 250,000	250,000 to 500,000	500,000 to 2,500,000	2,500,000 and over
Number of Enterprises	1	27183	1013	20302	3312	2386	73	57	11	•	9	8	0	•
Revenues ($ in Thousands)														
Net Sales	2	262334763	3843535	21734400	14550126	16709746	1400137	1942769	452399	•	4063679	5664085	0	•
Interest	3	237156	685	898	3316	7027	3282	874	293	•	2121	5060	0	•
Rents	4	102277	5227	0	1287	2211	769	583	2490	•	7837	4927	0	•
Royalties	5	63548	0	0	0	0	0	0	0	•	864	36798	0	•
Other Portfolio Income	6	119133	9	8431	29815	26091	158	175	51	•	34319	4125	0	•
Other Receipts	7	3182059	64018	25186	67364	49397	51937	61884	65509	•	29864	88930	0	•
Total Receipts	8	266038936	3913474	21768915	14651908	16794472	1456283	2006285	520742	•	4138684	5803925	0	•
Average Total Receipts	9	9787	3863	1072	4424	7039	19949	35198	47340	•	459854	725491	•	•
Operating Costs/Operating Income (%)														
Cost of Operations	10	73.5	68.5	70.1	74.0	72.9	56.1	66.0	61.8	•	72.9	53.1	•	•
Salaries and Wages	11	9.1	13.7	6.6	8.3	10.5	15.1	14.7	17.2	•	12.4	14.8	•	•
Taxes Paid	12	1.0	1.6	1.4	1.6	1.4	2.0	1.4	2.2	•	1.3	2.4	•	•
Interest Paid	13	0.6	0.3	0.2	0.1	0.5	0.7	0.5	0.7	•	0.8	2.6	•	•
Depreciation	14	1.2	1.7	0.4	0.3	0.6	2.4	2.2	2.6	•	1.1	3.8	•	•
Amortization and Depletion	15	0.3	0.2	0.1	0.1	0.2	0.3	0.3	0.5	•	0.3	0.6	•	•
Pensions and Other Deferred Comp.	16	0.3	0.3	0.2	0.5	0.3	0.3	0.5	0.4	•	0.2	0.1	•	•
Employee Benefits	17	0.4	0.9	0.4	0.3	0.4	1.1	1.4	1.0	•	1.5	1.2	•	•
Advertising	18	0.7	0.5	0.8	0.4	0.6	5.1	0.5	1.2	•	0.8	2.3	•	•
Other Expenses	19	8.9	8.9	9.3	6.0	6.0	12.3	8.3	16.3	•	8.1	16.4	•	•
Officers' Compensation	20	1.0	2.7	5.0	4.7	2.7	2.4	1.9	1.4	•	0.3	0.8	•	•
Operating Margin	21	3.0	0.6	5.5	3.9	3.9	2.3	2.4	•	•	0.3	1.9	•	•
Operating Margin Before Officers' Comp.	22	4.0	3.3	10.6	8.5	6.5	4.7	4.3	•	•	0.6	2.7	•	•

Selected Average Balance Sheet ($ in Thousands)

Net Receivables 23	699	0	22	72	462	1835	3997	2728	•	25269	19130
Inventories 24	818	0	65	265	452	2342	2430	6841	•	58240	87809
Net Property, Plant and Equipment 25	695	0	19	49	261	986	1506	7739	•	28292	112457
Total Assets 26	4805	0	174	767	1878	7093	13930	32881	•	153811	596854
Notes and Loans Payable 27	1103	0	49	136	553	2172	3448	9616	•	73206	243640
All Other Liabilities 28	1350	0	57	207	529	2135	4156	6253	•	47170	143974
Net Worth 29	2352	0	69	423	796	2786	6326	17012	•	33436	209241

Selected Financial Ratios (Times to 1)

Current Ratio 30	1.4	•	2.3	2.8	2.0	1.9	1.9	2.0	•	1.7	1.9
Quick Ratio 31	0.7	•	1.1	1.3	1.2	1.0	1.2	0.8	•	0.7	0.4
Net Sales to Working Capital 32	20.4	•	14.2	11.4	10.3	8.9	7.5	6.8	•	12.6	9.5
Coverage Ratio 33	8.2	9.2	24.9	32.4	9.2	10.5	13.0	14.2	•	3.7	2.7
Total Asset Turnover 34	2.0	•	6.1	5.7	3.7	2.7	2.4	1.3	•	2.9	1.2
Inventory Turnover 35	8.7	•	11.5	12.2	11.3	4.6	9.2	3.7	•	5.7	4.3
Receivables Turnover 36	14.7	•	52.4	50.0	16.8	7.5	11.3	7.6	•	16.3	50.5
Total Liabilities to Net Worth 37	1.0	•	1.5	0.8	1.4	1.5	1.2	0.9	•	3.6	1.9
Current Assets to Working Capital 38	3.8	•	1.8	1.6	2.0	2.1	2.1	2.0	•	2.4	2.1
Current Liabilities to Working Capital 39	2.8	•	0.8	0.6	1.0	1.1	1.1	1.0	•	1.4	1.1
Working Capital to Net Sales 40	0.0	•	0.1	0.1	0.1	0.1	0.1	0.1	•	0.1	0.1
Inventory to Working Capital 41	1.8	•	0.9	0.7	0.7	0.9	0.7	1.0	•	1.3	1.5
Total Receipts to Cash Flow 42	9.6	12.9	8.9	12.4	11.4	6.2	8.6	4.7	•	16.5	7.8
Cost of Goods to Cash Flow 43	7.1	8.8	6.2	9.2	8.3	3.5	5.7	2.9	•	12.0	4.1
Cash Flow to Total Debt 44	0.4	•	1.1	1.0	0.6	0.7	0.5	0.6	•	0.2	0.2

Selected Financial Factors (in Percentages)

Debt Ratio 45	51.0	•	60.7	44.8	57.6	60.7	54.6	48.3	•	78.3	64.9
Return on Total Assets 46	10.1	•	36.4	27.0	18.2	18.8	15.0	13.0	•	8.5	8.2
Return on Equity Before Income Taxes 47	18.1	•	89.0	47.5	38.4	43.3	30.4	23.4	•	28.3	14.6
Return on Equity After Income Taxes 48	13.4	•	88.0	46.3	36.6	35.7	29.9	22.2	•	22.0	11.2
Profit Margin (Before Income Tax) 49	4.4	2.4	5.7	4.6	4.4	6.3	5.7	9.7	•	2.1	4.3
Profit Margin (After Income Tax) 50	3.3	1.9	5.6	4.5	4.2	5.2	5.6	9.2	•	1.6	3.3

Table I

Corporations with and without Net Income

GASOLINE STATIONS

MONEY AMOUNTS AND SIZE OF ASSETS IN THOUSANDS OF DOLLARS

Item Description for Accounting Period 7/08 Through 6/09		Total	Zero Assets	Under 500	500 to 1,000	1,000 to 5,000	5,000 to 10,000	10,000 to 25,000	25,000 to 50,000	50,000 to 100,000	100,000 to 250,000	250,000 to 500,000	500,000 to 2,500,000	2,500,000 and over
Number of Enterprises	1	40942	2770	27485	5008	4984	385	179	64	37	15	3	8	3
Revenues ($ in Thousands)														
Net Sales	2	338307916	2392132	60713708	27618047	59184733	17999529	19021374	19238668	14316746	19124100	5940790	47093458	45664630
Interest	3	68715	0	2334	2458	7131	2254	4309	4222	2350	724	2575	16061	24297
Rents	4	117750	0	2236	7035	7968	6267	9501	10446	8155	1945	2946	328	60924
Royalties	5	20673	0	7	33	0	0	0	2	0	0	0	0	20631
Other Portfolio Income	6	239326	32492	19210	1311	18867	13622	22681	24800	21569	3416	22377	7043	51935
Other Receipts	7	1684615	5447	441147	35903	255557	51029	171767	72627	58421	109817	166360	194547	121997
Total Receipts	8	340438995	2430071	61178642	27664787	59474256	18072701	19229632	19350765	14407241	19240002	6135048	47311437	45944414
Average Total Receipts	9	8315	877	2226	5524	11933	46942	107428	302356	389385	1282667	2045016	5913930	15314805
Operating Costs/Operating Income (%)														
Cost of Operations	10	91.6	94.0	90.2	90.0	91.9	92.2	88.7	92.9	92.3	92.8	87.3	90.9	94.7
Salaries and Wages	11	2.5	1.7	2.1	2.3	2.4	2.5	4.1	2.3	2.4	2.5	4.9	2.7	1.9
Taxes Paid	12	0.7	0.8	0.8	1.3	0.9	0.6	0.8	0.5	0.5	0.4	0.6	0.5	0.2
Interest Paid	13	0.4	0.6	0.2	0.4	0.5	0.4	0.4	0.3	0.4	0.2	0.2	0.4	0.3
Depreciation	14	1.0	0.2	0.5	0.8	0.7	0.8	1.0	0.9	0.8	1.1	1.2	1.4	2.0
Amortization and Depletion	15	0.1	0.0	0.1	0.1	0.1	0.1	0.0	0.0	0.0	0.0	0.0	0.1	0.1
Pensions and Other Deferred Comp.	16	0.0	•	0.0	0.0	0.0	0.0	0.0	0.0	0.0	0.0	0.5	0.1	0.0
Employee Benefits	17	0.1	0.0	0.0	0.1	0.1	0.1	0.1	0.1	0.1	0.2	0.3	0.3	0.1
Advertising	18	0.1	0.3	0.1	0.0	0.1	0.0	0.2	0.1	0.1	0.1	0.2	0.1	0.1
Other Expenses	19	3.7	9.8	5.4	4.8	3.4	2.9	4.8	3.0	3.3	2.3	4.1	2.9	2.5
Officers' Compensation	20	0.3	0.1	0.9	0.5	0.4	0.3	0.2	0.2	0.2	0.1	0.1	0.1	0.0
Operating Margin	21	•	•	•	•	•	0.0	•	•	•	0.2	0.8	0.8	•
Operating Margin Before Officers' Comp.	22	•	•	0.6	0.2	•	0.4	•	•	•	0.3	0.8	0.6	•

Selected Average Balance Sheet ($ in Thousands)

Net Receivables **23**	177862	82984	53702	15222	5183	2562	1257	455	66	34	10	0	76
Inventories **24**	252408	90427	38530	19432	5457	4058	1948	706	179	99	49	0	139
Net Property, Plant and Equipment **25**	1781089	568639	128526	93089	35533	18186	7781	4186	1048	369	63	0	634
Total Assets **26**	2971601	978505	457191	171712	67461	34454	16422	7607	1697	716	197	0	1190
Notes and Loans Payable **27**	787001	353016	51518	52423	26241	14328	6839	3742	1430	477	112	0	568
All Other Liabilities **28**	1101697	289696	131713	57093	16682	10688	4940	2354	333	101	39	0	322
Net Worth **29**	1082903	335794	273960	62195	24538	9438	4643	1512	-66	138	47	0	299

Selected Financial Ratios (Times to 1)

Current Ratio **30**	0.9	1.2	2.0	1.0	1.3	1.2	1.1	1.5	1.4	1.9	2.1	•	1.3
Quick Ratio **31**	0.5	0.7	1.6	0.6	0.8	0.7	0.6	0.9	0.7	0.9	0.9	•	0.7
Net Sales to Working Capital **32**	•	126.1	16.0	1254.6	70.7	135.5	335.4	68.5	101.5	45.6	45.6	•	92.8
Coverage Ratio **33**	•	3.7	21.2	4.2	2.1	2.3	2.5	2.0	1.0	0.6	2.9	•	1.6
Total Asset Turnover **34**	5.1	6.0	4.3	7.4	5.7	8.7	6.5	6.1	7.0	7.7	11.2	•	6.9
Inventory Turnover **35**	57.1	59.2	44.9	60.9	65.5	68.8	48.4	61.0	60.8	50.3	40.5	•	54.3
Receivables Turnover **36**	58.5	60.5	26.2	67.9	51.7	96.6	76.0	73.0	151.8	141.7	185.6	•	85.6
Total Liabilities to Net Worth **37**	1.7	1.9	0.7	1.8	1.7	2.7	2.5	4.0	•	4.2	3.2	•	3.0
Current Assets to Working Capital **38**	•	5.9	2.0	48.6	4.1	5.9	16.7	2.8	3.7	2.1	1.9	•	4.1
Current Liabilities to Working Capital **39**	•	4.9	1.0	47.6	3.1	4.9	15.7	1.8	2.7	1.1	0.9	•	3.1
Working Capital to Net Sales **40**	•	0.0	0.1	0.0	0.0	0.0	0.0	0.0	0.0	0.0	0.0	•	0.0
Inventory to Working Capital **41**	1.8	1.8	0.2	17.4	1.0	1.5	6.1	0.9	1.5	0.7	0.9	•	1.4
Total Receipts to Cash Flow **42**	217.7	34.1	14.7	42.4	36.7	41.9	26.0	41.5	42.8	33.9	28.8	•	38.7
Cost of Goods to Cash Flow **43**	206.2	31.0	12.9	39.3	33.9	38.9	23.1	38.3	39.3	30.6	25.9	•	35.5
Cash Flow to Total Debt **44**	0.0	0.3	0.7	0.3	0.2	0.3	0.3	0.2	0.2	0.3	0.5	•	0.2

Selected Financial Factors (in Percentages)

Debt Ratio **45**	63.6	65.7	40.1	63.8	63.6	72.6	71.7	80.1	103.9	80.7	76.3	•	74.8
Return on Total Assets **46**	•	8.4	18.1	7.8	4.7	5.6	6.5	5.3	3.8	1.7	6.8	•	3.8
Return on Equity Before Income Taxes **47**	•	17.9	28.8	16.4	6.7	11.5	13.8	13.1	1.0	•	18.6	•	5.4
Return on Equity After Income Taxes **48**	•	15.3	25.8	15.1	5.9	9.7	12.2	12.7	5.4	•	18.2	•	4.0
Profit Margin (Before Income Tax) **49**	•	1.0	4.0	0.8	0.4	0.4	0.6	0.4	•	•	0.4	•	0.2
Profit Margin (After Income Tax) **50**	•	0.9	3.6	0.7	0.4	0.3	0.5	0.4	•	•	0.4	•	0.1

Table II

Corporations with Net Income

GASOLINE STATIONS

MONEY AMOUNTS AND SIZE OF ASSETS IN THOUSANDS OF DOLLARS

Item Description for Accounting Period 7/08 Through 6/09	Total	Zero Assets	Under 500	500 to 1,000	1,000 to 5,000	5,000 to 10,000	10,000 to 25,000	25,000 to 50,000	50,000 to 100,000	100,000 to 250,000	250,000 to 500,000	500,000 to 2,500,000	2,500,000 and over
Number of Enterprises **1**	22224	586	16064	2467	2709	205	106	39	24	•	3	•	0
Revenues ($ in Thousands)													
Net Sales **2**	209078925	25356	39285330	13783802	29253249	14158565	12622423	13774167	10538968	•	5940790	•	0
Interest **3**	54722	0	1405	1253	3312	1543	3650	2832	1493	•	2575	•	0
Rents **4**	51460	0	2236	561	7049	1181	7169	5000	6112	•	2946	•	0
Royalties **5**	18625	0	7	0	0	0	0	2	0	•	0	•	0
Other Portfolio Income **6**	138303	2777	18887	335	14306	12686	13319	18383	16605	•	22377	•	0
Other Receipts **7**	1263337	0	312913	20085	182458	28318	128870	49200	46087	•	166360	•	0
Total Receipts **8**	210605372	28133	39620778	13806036	29460374	14202293	12775431	13849584	10609265	•	6135048	•	0
Average Total Receipts **9**	9476	48	2466	5596	10875	69279	120523	355118	442053	•	2045016	•	•
Operating Costs/Operating Income (%)													
Cost of Operations **10**	90.6	•	90.0	89.5	90.4	92.2	88.0	93.2	92.7	•	87.3	•	•
Salaries and Wages **11**	2.6	0.1	2.0	1.8	2.7	2.5	4.4	2.2	2.2	•	4.9	•	•
Taxes Paid **12**	0.7	8.3	0.5	2.0	0.8	0.6	1.0	0.5	0.5	•	0.6	•	•
Interest Paid **13**	0.3	14.8	0.1	0.3	0.5	0.2	0.3	0.2	0.3	•	0.2	•	•
Depreciation **14**	0.8	0.1	0.3	0.5	0.7	0.7	1.0	0.6	0.7	•	1.2	•	•
Amortization and Depletion **15**	0.1	•	0.1	0.1	0.1	0.0	0.0	0.0	0.0	•	0.0	•	•
Pensions and Other Deferred Comp. **16**	0.0	•	0.0	0.0	0.0	0.0	0.0	0.0	0.0	•	0.5	•	•
Employee Benefits **17**	0.1	•	0.0	0.0	0.1	0.2	0.1	0.0	0.1	•	0.3	•	•
Advertising **18**	0.1	•	0.1	0.1	0.1	0.0	0.1	0.0	0.1	•	0.2	•	•
Other Expenses **19**	3.7	70.8	4.9	4.1	3.7	2.7	4.7	2.5	2.9	•	4.1	•	•
Officers' Compensation **20**	0.4	•	1.0	0.5	0.5	0.4	0.2	0.2	0.2	•	0.1	•	•
Operating Margin **21**	0.5	17.5	0.8	1.0	0.6	0.4	•	0.5	0.3	•	0.8	•	•
Operating Margin Before Officers' Comp. **22**	0.9	17.5	1.8	1.5	1.1	0.8	0.2	0.7	0.4	•	0.8	•	•

Selected Average Balance Sheet ($ in Thousands)

Item											
Net Receivables 23	96	0	9	42	84	765	1129	2979	6209	•	53702
Inventories 24	175	0	45	112	184	975	2215	4737	5671	•	38530
Net Property, Plant and Equipment 25	621	0	53	310	989	2918	7813	15416	32976	•	128526
Total Assets 26	1295	0	201	684	1750	7575	16522	34398	69111	•	457191
Notes and Loans Payable 27	541	0	83	403	1314	2986	6164	10503	22096	•	51518
All Other Liabilities 28	378	0	37	75	468	1826	5360	11388	16164	•	131713
Net Worth 29	376	0	80	206	-31	2763	4998	12507	30852	•	273960

Selected Financial Ratios (Times to 1)

Item											
Current Ratio 30	1.4	•	2.2	2.8	1.2	1.7	1.1	1.3	1.5	•	2.0
Quick Ratio 31	0.8	•	1.1	1.2	0.6	1.0	0.6	0.8	1.0	•	1.6
Net Sales to Working Capital 32	72.4	•	43.4	28.6	150.6	55.6	355.4	90.4	49.6	•	16.0
Coverage Ratio 33	4.9	2.9	12.9	4.7	3.4	4.0	4.8	6.9	4.7	•	21.2
Total Asset Turnover 34	7.3	•	12.2	8.2	6.2	9.1	7.2	10.3	6.4	•	4.3
Inventory Turnover 35	48.6	•	49.0	44.5	53.2	65.3	47.3	69.5	71.8	•	44.9
Receivables Turnover 36	69.4	•	•	114.5	98.6	76.0	75.3	88.2	56.8	•	26.2
Total Liabilities to Net Worth 37	2.4	•	1.5	2.3	•	1.7	2.3	1.8	1.2	•	0.7
Current Assets to Working Capital 38	3.5	•	1.8	1.6	6.8	2.5	16.2	4.0	3.1	•	2.0
Current Liabilities to Working Capital 39	2.5	•	0.8	0.6	5.8	1.5	15.2	3.0	2.1	•	1.0
Working Capital to Net Sales 40	0.0	•	0.0	0.0	0.0	0.0	0.0	0.0	0.0	•	0.1
Inventory to Working Capital 41	1.1	•	0.8	0.5	2.2	0.7	6.0	0.9	0.7	•	0.2
Total Receipts to Cash Flow 42	27.2	1.5	22.3	25.2	26.4	38.6	22.2	36.0	34.8	•	14.7
Cost of Goods to Cash Flow 43	24.6	•	20.0	22.6	23.8	35.6	19.5	33.5	32.3	•	12.9
Cash Flow to Total Debt 44	0.4	•	0.9	0.5	0.2	0.4	0.5	0.4	0.3	•	0.7

Selected Financial Factors (in Percentages)

Item											
Debt Ratio 45	71.0	•	60.1	69.9	101.8	63.5	69.8	63.6	55.4	•	40.1
Return on Total Assets 46	11.5	•	22.0	12.1	11.2	8.9	10.7	12.1	7.4	•	18.1
Return on Equity Before Income Taxes 47	31.6	•	50.8	31.6	•	18.4	28.1	28.5	13.1	•	28.8
Return on Equity After Income Taxes 48	29.5	•	50.4	31.1	•	18.0	25.6	26.3	12.1	•	25.8
Profit Margin (Before Income Tax) 49	1.3	28.5	1.7	1.2	1.3	0.7	1.2	1.0	0.9	•	4.0
Profit Margin (After Income Tax) 50	1.2	26.6	1.7	1.1	1.2	0.7	1.1	0.9	0.9	•	3.6

Table I

Corporations with and without Net Income

CLOTHING AND CLOTHING ACCESSORIES STORES

MONEY AMOUNTS AND SIZE OF ASSETS IN THOUSANDS OF DOLLARS

Item Description for Accounting Period 7/08 Through 6/09	Total	Zero Assets	Under 500	500 to 1,000	1,000 to 5,000	5,000 to 10,000	10,000 to 25,000	25,000 to 50,000	50,000 to 100,000	100,000 to 250,000	250,000 to 500,000	500,000 to 2,500,000	2,500,000 and over
Number of Enterprises **1**	50174	8173	35195	3953	2190	358	145	39	34	26	16	35	9
Revenues ($ in Thousands)													
Net Sales **2**	183701991	2860688	11977091	5260982	7432334	4376620	4385739	2925864	4755140	7800904	12385705	63313670	56227254
Interest **3**	731645	4609	3833	4325	8552	1133	14396	9802	10169	12432	38141	170485	453770
Rents **4**	157110	1854	0	2648	7200	1278	1310	1524	5675	9766	1419	52806	71631
Royalties **5**	819181	16721	0	0	0	0	126	0	3048	11483	41358	492247	254198
Other Portfolio Income **6**	546482	6795	964	5686	6523	10233	1383	1692	4550	13610	12709	163473	318862
Other Receipts **7**	3109327	196660	120811	61966	46638	43413	41849	75570	61623	25752	236472	1053163	1145409
Total Receipts **8**	189065736	3087327	12102699	5335607	7501247	4432677	4444803	3014452	4840205	7873947	12715804	65245844	58471124
Average Total Receipts **9**	3768	378	344	1350	3425	12382	30654	77294	142359	302844	794738	1864167	6496792
Operating Costs/Operating Income (%)													
Cost of Operations **10**	54.5	47.8	52.2	60.6	58.7	66.3	59.9	59.7	55.8	53.7	55.4	53.8	53.3
Salaries and Wages **11**	14.0	14.0	9.0	12.6	12.7	10.5	14.7	14.7	15.4	15.1	15.2	14.0	15.1
Taxes Paid **12**	2.1	1.9	2.1	2.3	2.0	1.6	3.2	2.8	3.5	2.1	2.3	1.9	2.2
Interest Paid **13**	1.0	0.8	0.7	1.1	1.0	1.0	1.1	1.0	1.8	1.1	0.9	0.9	1.2
Depreciation **14**	3.2	5.1	0.8	0.8	1.0	1.2	1.6	2.3	2.0	3.3	3.0	3.9	3.8
Amortization and Depletion **15**	0.2	0.2	0.3	0.1	0.1	0.0	0.5	0.2	0.3	0.4	0.1	•	0.7
Pensions and Other Deferred Comp. **16**	0.2	0.1	0.2	0.3	0.3	0.5	0.1	0.1	0.1	0.1	0.1	0.3	0.2
Employee Benefits **17**	1.2	1.0	0.4	0.6	0.7	0.5	0.7	0.8	1.3	1.2	0.8	1.5	1.3
Advertising **18**	2.5	2.6	2.1	3.3	3.4	2.8	2.4	4.2	2.7	1.9	3.4	2.4	2.2
Other Expenses **19**	20.3	32.6	25.9	16.4	17.0	13.7	20.5	22.9	28.5	23.1	19.0	21.5	17.7
Officers' Compensation **20**	1.4	2.1	7.3	5.3	4.7	2.1	1.6	1.0	0.9	0.7	0.5	0.7	0.4
Operating Margin **21**	•	•	•	•	•	•	•	•	•	•	•	•	2.0
Operating Margin Before Officers' Comp. **22**	0.6	•	6.2	2.0	3.1	2.0	1.6	1.0	•	0.7	•	•	2.4

Selected Average Balance Sheet ($ in Thousands)

Net Receivables 23	151	0	5	32	107	430	1986	2784	5950	9583	9235	52886	452025
Inventories 24	682	0	80	433	1263	3351	6659	17966	27690	63941	140523	272903	1070735
Net Property, Plant and Equipment 25	559	0	10	84	276	855	3013	6365	14404	47872	118331	332123	1169136
Total Assets 26	2240	0	130	676	1955	6449	16254	35660	71955	163054	370812	1118515	4780989
Notes and Loans Payable 27	539	0	64	264	682	2176	5515	9578	19021	41928	54841	193609	1210848
All Other Liabilities 28	896	0	43	197	513	2214	8066	14467	39108	61978	141128	427105	2100406
Net Worth 29	805	0	22	216	761	2159	2674	11615	13827	59148	174844	497802	1469735

Selected Financial Ratios (Times to 1)

Current Ratio 30	1.7	•	2.2	2.4	2.2	1.5	1.1	1.6	1.3	1.4	2.0	1.7	1.7
Quick Ratio 31	0.6	•	0.6	0.5	0.4	0.3	0.4	0.4	0.3	0.4	0.7	0.5	0.8
Net Sales to Working Capital 32	7.4	•	5.8	4.3	4.1	7.1	34.1	8.1	14.2	11.7	7.2	8.2	6.8
Coverage Ratio 33	3.3	1.3	0.8	•	0.3	2.1	•	•	•	•	3.1	3.5	6.6
Total Asset Turnover 34	1.6	•	2.6	2.0	1.7	1.9	1.9	2.1	1.9	1.8	2.1	1.6	1.3
Inventory Turnover 35	2.9	•	2.2	1.9	1.6	2.4	2.7	2.5	2.8	2.5	3.1	3.6	3.1
Receivables Turnover 36	21.6	•	88.0	38.5	30.2	26.9	17.6	23.6	24.9	30.5	59.6	24.7	13.3
Total Liabilities to Net Worth 37	1.8	•	4.9	2.1	1.6	2.0	5.1	2.1	4.2	1.8	1.1	1.2	2.3
Current Assets to Working Capital 38	2.4	•	1.9	1.7	1.9	2.9	13.0	2.8	4.6	3.3	2.0	2.4	2.4
Current Liabilities to Working Capital 39	1.4	•	0.9	0.7	0.9	1.9	12.0	1.8	3.6	2.3	1.0	1.4	1.4
Working Capital to Net Sales 40	0.1	•	0.2	0.2	0.2	0.1	0.0	0.1	0.1	0.1	0.1	0.1	0.1
Inventory to Working Capital 41	1.3	•	1.3	1.3	1.4	1.8	7.4	1.9	2.7	2.1	1.2	1.3	1.1
Total Receipts to Cash Flow 42	7.9	5.3	7.0	14.2	10.7	11.8	15.4	15.5	147.2	10.0	10.2	7.6	6.3
Cost of Goods to Cash Flow 43	4.3	2.6	3.7	8.6	6.3	7.8	9.2	9.3	82.1	5.4	5.7	4.1	3.4
Cash Flow to Total Debt 44	0.3	•	0.5	0.2	0.3	0.2	0.1	0.2	0.0	0.3	0.4	0.4	0.3

Selected Financial Factors (in Percentages)

Debt Ratio 45	64.1	•	82.9	68.1	61.1	66.5	83.6	67.4	80.8	63.7	52.8	55.5	69.3
Return on Total Assets 46	5.5	•	1.6	•	0.5	4.0	•	•	•	•	5.5	5.2	10.2
Return on Equity Before Income Taxes 47	10.5	•	•	•	•	6.3	•	•	•	•	8.0	8.3	28.2
Return on Equity After Income Taxes 48	4.8	•	•	•	•	5.3	•	•	•	•	3.9	3.4	19.0
Profit Margin (Before Income Tax) 49	2.3	0.2	•	•	1.1	1.1	•	•	•	•	1.8	2.3	6.6
Profit Margin (After Income Tax) 50	1.1	•	•	•	0.9	0.9	•	•	•	•	0.9	0.9	4.5

Table II

Corporations with Net Income

CLOTHING AND CLOTHING ACCESSORIES STORES

MONEY AMOUNTS AND SIZE OF ASSETS IN THOUSANDS OF DOLLARS

Item Description for Accounting Period 7/08 Through 6/09	Total	Zero Assets	Under 500	500 to 1,000	1,000 to 5,000	5,000 to 10,000	10,000 to 25,000	25,000 to 50,000	50,000 to 100,000	100,000 to 250,000	250,000 to 500,000	500,000 to 2,500,000	2,500,000 and over
Number of Enterprises **1**	26037	3402	18167	2689	1355	279	71	19	•	6	9	20	•
Revenues ($ in Thousands)													
Net Sales **2**	129754264	2126717	8035457	3498301	4953505	3163529	1901026	1333827	•	2235620	6961819	39229171	•
Interest **3**	602401	1602	3234	3562	7079	687	858	2238	•	1159	19788	102297	•
Rents **4**	106600	100	0	2648	7138	1140	798	1489	•	280	0	21353	•
Royalties **5**	739167	7396	0	0	0	0	126	0	•	0	31448	445999	•
Other Portfolio Income **6**	511794	6136	184	4508	5637	10233	905	1664	•	4086	10843	150556	•
Other Receipts **7**	1971924	71420	104519	45949	14402	41468	10293	7930	•	6224	52974	492352	•
Total Receipts **8**	133686150	2213371	8143394	3554968	4987761	3217057	1914006	1347148	•	2247369	7076872	40441728	•
Average Total Receipts **9**	5134	651	448	1322	3681	11531	26958	70903	•	374562	786319	2022086	•
Operating Costs/Operating Income (%)													
Cost of Operations **10**	53.4	47.7	48.9	59.6	60.4	62.6	57.9	58.9	•	54.9	53.6	52.0	•
Salaries and Wages **11**	13.6	11.7	8.7	10.6	10.7	10.2	11.6	13.0	•	13.4	14.8	13.5	•
Taxes Paid **12**	2.1	1.9	1.9	2.3	1.9	1.8	3.1	2.2	•	1.8	2.7	1.9	•
Interest Paid **13**	0.8	0.5	0.5	0.9	0.8	0.6	0.9	0.6	•	0.2	0.1	0.9	•
Depreciation **14**	3.4	4.8	0.4	0.6	1.0	1.0	1.3	1.6	•	4.4	3.5	4.2	•
Amortization and Depletion **15**	0.4	0.2	0.1	0.0	0.0	0.0	0.2	0.0	•	0.1	0.0	0.2	•
Pensions and Other Deferred Comp. **16**	0.2	0.2	0.2	0.2	0.3	0.7	0.2	0.0	•	0.0	0.1	0.2	•
Employee Benefits **17**	1.2	0.9	0.2	0.7	0.6	0.5	0.5	0.8	•	0.7	0.7	1.6	•
Advertising **18**	2.2	2.4	1.9	4.0	2.8	3.1	2.9	3.4	•	1.2	1.7	2.1	•
Other Expenses **19**	18.4	23.8	25.3	13.2	14.6	14.2	15.7	15.9	•	16.6	18.1	19.3	•
Officers' Compensation **20**	1.3	1.9	6.9	4.9	4.9	2.3	1.5	0.9	•	0.6	0.6	0.8	•
Operating Margin **21**	3.1	4.4	5.0	2.9	2.0	3.0	4.3	2.6	•	6.0	4.1	3.3	•
Operating Margin Before Officers' Comp. **22**	4.4	6.2	11.9	7.8	6.9	5.3	5.8	3.4	•	6.7	4.8	4.0	•

Selected Average Balance Sheet ($ in Thousands)

Net Receivables 23	230	0	7	39	114	115	1519	3721	5182	7956	55439
Inventories 24	963	0	79	464	1552	3299	9090	23005	105544	159270	331829
Net Property, Plant and Equipment 25	802	0	9	75	261	816	3180	4843	65294	134702	376130
Total Assets 26	3120	0	147	695	2028	6108	15480	35707	193321	380826	1221085
Notes and Loans Payable 27	603	0	50	249	585	1405	4153	5112	19235	6265	202034
All Other Liabilities 28	1265	0	49	151	543	1724	4431	15633	65389	129052	455301
Net Worth 29	1251	0	49	296	900	2979	6895	14962	108697	245509	563750

Selected Financial Ratios (Times to 1)

Current Ratio 30	1.8	•	2.4	3.4	2.5	2.0	1.8	1.7	1.8	2.3	1.7
Quick Ratio 31	0.7	•	0.8	0.7	0.5	0.2	0.4	0.5	0.6	1.0	0.6
Net Sales to Working Capital 32	6.5	•	6.0	3.2	3.7	4.9	5.2	5.9	7.4	6.1	8.1
Coverage Ratio 33	8.9	17.6	14.6	5.9	4.2	8.7	6.7	6.4	32.9	111.3	7.8
Total Asset Turnover 34	1.6	•	3.0	1.9	1.8	1.9	1.7	2.0	1.9	2.0	1.6
Inventory Turnover 35	2.8	•	2.7	1.7	1.4	2.1	1.7	1.8	1.9	2.6	3.1
Receivables Turnover 36	18.2	•	•	33.1	24.8	81.6	14.2	16.1	33.9	63.0	18.3
Total Liabilities to Net Worth 37	1.5	•	2.0	1.4	1.3	1.1	1.2	1.4	0.8	0.6	1.2
Current Assets to Working Capital 38	2.2	•	1.7	1.4	1.6	2.0	2.2	2.5	2.2	1.8	2.3
Current Liabilities to Working Capital 39	1.2	•	0.7	0.4	0.6	1.0	1.2	1.5	1.2	0.8	1.3
Working Capital to Net Sales 40	0.2	•	0.2	0.3	0.3	0.2	0.2	0.2	0.1	0.2	0.1
Inventory to Working Capital 41	1.1	•	1.1	1.0	1.3	1.4	1.6	1.6	1.2	0.9	1.1
Total Receipts to Cash Flow 42	6.3	4.5	4.7	8.3	8.7	8.3	7.5	9.1	6.4	7.9	6.1
Cost of Goods to Cash Flow 43	3.3	2.1	2.3	4.9	5.3	5.2	4.3	5.3	3.5	4.2	3.2
Cash Flow to Total Debt 44	0.4	•	1.0	0.4	0.4	0.4	0.4	0.4	0.7	0.7	0.5

Selected Financial Factors (in Percentages)

Debt Ratio 45	59.9	•	66.9	57.5	55.6	51.2	55.5	58.1	43.8	35.5	53.8
Return on Total Assets 46	11.4	•	20.4	10.2	6.3	9.8	10.1	8.0	12.7	11.6	11.8
Return on Equity Before Income Taxes 47	25.1	•	57.2	19.9	10.8	17.7	19.3	16.1	21.9	17.8	22.2
Return on Equity After Income Taxes 48	18.1	•	56.5	19.2	9.2	16.8	18.0	12.5	15.3	12.6	14.7
Profit Margin (Before Income Tax) 49	6.3	8.4	6.3	4.5	2.7	4.7	5.0	3.4	6.4	5.6	6.4
Profit Margin (After Income Tax) 50	4.5	7.0	6.2	4.4	2.3	4.4	4.6	2.7	4.5	4.0	4.2

Table I

Corporations with and without Net Income

SPORTING GOODS, HOBBY, BOOK, AND MUSIC STORES

MONEY AMOUNTS AND SIZE OF ASSETS IN THOUSANDS OF DOLLARS

Item Description for Accounting Period 7/08 Through 6/09	Total	Zero Assets	Under 500	500 to 1,000	1,000 to 5,000	5,000 to 10,000	10,000 to 25,000	25,000 to 50,000	50,000 to 100,000	100,000 to 250,000	250,000 to 500,000	500,000 to 2,500,000	2,500,000 and over
Number of Enterprises **1**	29155	4921	19738	2530	1720	106	78	12	6	14	11	18	0
Revenues ($ in Thousands)													
Net Sales **2**	82488720	636884	7436483	3651132	6879642	1286372	2479862	608333	874046	3999633	6747169	47889164	0
Interest **3**	551856	567	3061	1471	9006	4375	2106	1357	2	1715	4992	523204	0
Rents **4**	398847	6179	0	0	2823	0	9325	5776	0	3123	19	371603	0
Royalties **5**	180899	0	0	11	0	0	0	0	0	265	15775	164847	0
Other Portfolio Income **6**	131699	14169	2961	7002	2424	363	1038	602	11	33560	3865	65706	0
Other Receipts **7**	1156928	19889	99564	5160	31126	13884	22270	21498	14094	57212	47279	824949	0
Total Receipts **8**	84908949	677688	7542069	3664776	6925021	1304994	2514601	637566	888153	4095508	6819099	49839473	0
Average Total Receipts **9**	2912	138	382	1449	4026	12311	32238	53130	148026	292536	619918	2768860	•
Operating Costs/Operating Income (%)													
Cost of Operations **10**	61.7	55.3	60.8	60.6	61.9	70.8	69.3	65.4	61.3	58.9	64.7	61.2	•
Salaries and Wages **11**	12.1	9.2	9.4	14.2	12.0	12.7	10.0	9.4	14.2	13.0	11.7	12.5	•
Taxes Paid **12**	2.2	2.7	2.8	1.8	2.3	1.7	1.9	1.6	2.2	2.1	1.7	2.2	•
Interest Paid **13**	2.2	5.1	1.0	0.9	0.9	1.1	1.3	0.8	1.7	1.5	1.3	2.9	•
Depreciation **14**	2.3	1.8	1.1	0.7	1.4	1.3	1.0	1.0	1.7	2.0	2.7	2.9	•
Amortization and Depletion **15**	0.3	6.2	0.1	0.2	0.1	0.1	0.3	0.7	0.3	0.4	0.5	0.2	•
Pensions and Other Deferred Comp. **16**	0.2	•	0.1	0.0	0.3	0.0	0.4	0.2	0.1	0.1	0.1	0.2	•
Employee Benefits **17**	0.7	0.5	0.8	0.4	0.5	1.0	0.6	1.0	1.3	1.3	0.9	0.7	•
Advertising **18**	2.5	1.1	1.6	2.0	1.9	1.7	2.6	6.2	2.6	4.1	3.0	2.6	•
Other Expenses **19**	16.4	27.7	19.9	15.5	13.2	11.2	14.2	14.4	16.1	15.7	13.8	16.9	•
Officers' Compensation **20**	1.4	3.5	5.2	4.2	3.9	1.2	1.5	1.4	0.6	0.8	0.3	0.3	•
Operating Margin **21**	•	•	•	•	1.6	•	•	•	•	0.0	•	•	•
Operating Margin Before Officers' Comp. **22**	•	•	2.5	3.7	5.5	•	•	•	•	0.9	•	•	•

Selected Average Balance Sheet ($ in Thousands)

Net Receivables 23	88	0	5	43	113	709	1242	5060	6020	18817	37958	68222
Inventories 24	663	0	79	488	978	4031	6636	12588	40220	71504	141246	511622
Net Property, Plant and Equipment 25	415	0	21	101	290	927	2079	5356	10043	28991	80822	514085
Total Assets 26	1608	0	135	753	1946	6692	15359	34718	69141	159033	329278	1687107
Notes and Loans Payable 27	686	0	81	327	565	2535	5024	5953	30001	59194	116625	753551
All Other Liabilities 28	663	0	47	196	525	1975	6619	12686	31650	68993	113993	760956
Net Worth 29	259	0	6	231	856	2181	3716	16079	7490	30846	98660	172601

Selected Financial Ratios (Times to 1)

Current Ratio 30	1.5	•	1.8	2.7	2.5	1.6	1.2	1.8	1.1	1.7	1.6	1.3
Quick Ratio 31	0.3	•	0.5	0.5	0.7	0.4	0.4	0.8	0.2	0.4	0.4	0.3
Net Sales to Working Capital 32	9.8	•	8.5	3.9	4.7	7.4	22.0	4.8	42.2	6.8	7.7	14.8
Coverage Ratio 33	1.5	•	•	0.7	3.6	•	•	4.4	0.7	2.6	1.3	1.6
Total Asset Turnover 34	1.8	•	2.8	1.9	2.1	1.8	2.1	1.5	2.1	1.8	1.9	1.6
Inventory Turnover 35	2.6	•	2.9	1.8	2.5	2.1	3.3	2.6	2.2	2.4	2.8	3.2
Receivables Turnover 36	32.0	•	98.1	31.5	32.8	17.6	19.7	10.2	27.5	12.5	18.6	47.6
Total Liabilities to Net Worth 37	5.2	•	21.7	2.3	1.3	2.1	3.1	1.2	8.2	4.2	2.3	8.8
Current Assets to Working Capital 38	3.1	•	2.2	1.6	1.7	2.7	7.3	2.3	13.9	2.4	2.8	4.5
Current Liabilities to Working Capital 39	2.1	•	1.2	0.6	0.7	1.7	6.3	1.3	12.9	1.4	1.8	3.5
Working Capital to Net Sales 40	0.1	•	0.1	0.3	0.2	0.1	0.0	0.2	0.0	0.1	0.1	0.1
Inventory to Working Capital 41	2.2	•	1.6	1.3	1.2	2.0	4.5	1.0	11.3	1.7	1.9	3.2
Total Receipts to Cash Flow 42	10.4	13.3	9.9	12.1	10.0	23.7	16.8	7.2	13.2	9.8	11.9	10.0
Cost of Goods to Cash Flow 43	6.4	7.4	6.0	7.3	6.2	16.8	11.6	4.7	8.1	5.7	7.7	6.1
Cash Flow to Total Debt 44	0.2	•	0.3	0.2	0.4	0.1	0.2	0.4	0.2	0.2	0.2	0.2

Selected Financial Factors (in Percentages)

Debt Ratio 45	83.9	•	95.6	69.4	56.0	67.4	75.8	53.7	89.2	80.6	70.0	89.8
Return on Total Assets 46	5.8	•	•	1.2	6.4	•	•	5.3	2.5	7.1	3.2	7.3
Return on Equity Before Income Taxes 47	12.0	•	•	•	10.5	•	•	8.8	•	22.5	2.4	26.5
Return on Equity After Income Taxes 48	7.4	•	•	•	9.7	•	•	6.1	•	19.7	0.5	17.5
Profit Margin (Before Income Tax) 49	1.1	•	•	•	2.3	•	•	2.8	•	2.4	0.4	1.7
Profit Margin (After Income Tax) 50	0.7	•	•	2.1	•	•	1.9	•	2.1	0.1	0.4	1.1

Table II

Corporations with Net Income

SPORTING GOODS, HOBBY, BOOK, AND MUSIC STORES

MONEY AMOUNTS AND SIZE OF ASSETS IN THOUSANDS OF DOLLARS

Item Description for Accounting Period 7/08 Through 6/09	Total	Zero Assets	Under 500	500 to 1,000	1,000 to 5,000	5,000 to 10,000	10,000 to 25,000	25,000 to 50,000	50,000 to 100,000	100,000 to 250,000	250,000 to 500,000	500,000 to 2,500,000	2,500,000 and over
Number of Enterprises **1**	13492	2232	8763	1049	1311	53	43	9	•	•	7	14	0
Revenues ($ in Thousands)													
Net Sales **2**	61552931	322513	3872734	1693034	6045771	676651	1325790	459393	•	•	4200038	40015593	0
Interest **3**	479072	3	1066	817	7655	2470	958	1211	•	•	678	463051	0
Rents **4**	374332	0	0	0	2783	0	69	2982	•	•	19	368480	0
Royalties **5**	126925	0	0	11	0	0	0	0	•	•	11141	115772	0
Other Portfolio Income **6**	118997	13990	0	17	2400	363	1027	102	•	•	2091	65637	0
Other Receipts **7**	974662	736	38881	4754	29689	6074	7888	19055	•	•	44406	780654	0
Total Receipts **8**	63626919	337242	3912681	1698633	6088298	685558	1335732	482743	•	•	4258373	41809187	0
Average Total Receipts **9**	4716	151	447	1619	4644	12935	31064	53638	•	•	608339	2986370	•
Operating Costs/Operating Income (%)													
Cost of Operations **10**	61.5	54.7	58.7	59.2	63.0	61.3	71.2	65.2	•	•	63.9	61.4	•
Salaries and Wages **11**	11.9	4.7	8.2	13.1	11.5	14.8	9.4	8.4	•	•	12.0	12.4	•
Taxes Paid **12**	2.1	3.6	2.5	1.8	2.3	2.0	1.1	1.6	•	•	1.9	2.2	•
Interest Paid **13**	2.2	0.1	0.7	0.3	0.7	0.8	1.0	1.0	•	•	0.4	2.9	•
Depreciation **14**	2.3	1.5	1.1	0.6	0.7	1.0	1.0	1.0	•	•	3.1	2.8	•
Amortization and Depletion **15**	0.2	0.3	0.2	0.1	0.1	0.2	0.1	0.9	•	•	0.4	0.2	•
Pensions and Other Deferred Comp. **16**	0.2	•	0.1	0.1	0.4	0.0	0.6	0.2	•	•	0.2	0.2	•
Employee Benefits **17**	0.7	•	0.8	0.7	0.5	1.4	0.5	1.0	•	•	0.9	0.6	•
Advertising **18**	2.7	1.1	0.9	2.2	1.9	2.0	1.7	8.0	•	•	3.6	2.8	•
Other Expenses **19**	15.3	21.9	18.5	12.3	12.0	14.3	9.8	12.6	•	•	11.6	16.2	•
Officers' Compensation **20**	1.2	6.5	4.3	5.6	4.0	2.2	0.8	1.5	•	•	0.4	0.4	•
Operating Margin **21**	•	5.5	4.1	4.2	2.8	0.0	2.9	•	•	•	1.6	•	•
Operating Margin Before Officers' Comp. **22**	0.9	12.0	8.4	9.8	6.8	2.2	3.6	0.2	•	•	2.0	•	•

Selected Average Balance Sheet ($ in Thousands)

Net Receivables 23	145	0	4	32	137	656	1554	1810	•	43645	79767
Inventories 24	993	0	90	583	1054	3134	6003	9144	•	150852	570157
Net Property, Plant and Equipment 25	727	0	19	120	213	1251	1950	4665	•	79782	590085
Total Assets 26	2620	0	129	748	2107	7126	14415	33655	•	321012	1831415
Notes and Loans Payable 27	1086	0	61	144	555	1156	4916	7059	•	57361	857865
All Other Liabilities 28	1079	0	38	219	547	2215	4420	7281	•	103734	822495
Net Worth 29	454	0	30	385	1005	3755	5078	19316	•	159917	151055

Selected Financial Ratios (Times to 1)

Current Ratio 30	1.5	•	2.1	2.5	2.7	1.7	1.3	2.8	•	1.9	1.3
Quick Ratio 31	0.4	•	0.6	0.6	0.8	0.6	0.4	0.9	•	0.5	0.3
Net Sales to Working Capital 32	9.7	•	8.6	4.6	4.5	8.3	14.1	3.6	•	5.7	15.1
Coverage Ratio 33	2.5	110.9	8.3	18.1	5.9	2.6	4.8	4.7	•	8.2	1.9
Total Asset Turnover 34	1.7	•	3.4	2.2	2.2	1.8	2.1	1.5	•	1.9	1.6
Inventory Turnover 35	2.8	•	2.9	1.6	2.8	2.5	3.7	3.6	•	2.5	3.1
Receivables Turnover 36	30.0	•	100.2	29.6	32.8	14.2	17.7	14.3	•	•	11.1
Total Liabilities to Net Worth 37	4.8	•	3.3	0.9	1.1	0.9	1.8	0.7	•	1.0	11.1
Current Assets to Working Capital 38	3.0	•	1.9	1.7	1.6	2.5	4.3	1.6	•	2.1	4.4
Current Liabilities to Working Capital 39	2.0	•	0.9	0.7	0.6	1.5	3.3	0.6	•	1.1	3.4
Working Capital to Net Sales 40	0.1	•	0.1	0.2	0.2	0.1	0.1	0.3	•	0.2	0.1
Inventory to Working Capital 41	2.0	•	1.4	1.2	1.1	1.5	2.8	0.8	•	1.4	3.0
Total Receipts to Cash Flow 42	8.7	4.8	6.5	8.2	9.3	11.5	10.6	7.4	•	9.9	9.0
Cost of Goods to Cash Flow 43	5.3	2.6	3.8	4.9	5.9	7.1	7.6	4.8	•	6.3	5.5
Cash Flow to Total Debt 44	0.2	•	0.7	0.5	0.4	0.3	0.3	0.5	•	0.4	0.2

Selected Financial Factors (in Percentages)

Debt Ratio 45	82.7	•	76.7	48.5	52.3	47.3	64.8	42.6	•	50.2	91.8
Return on Total Assets 46	9.3	•	20.0	10.5	9.2	3.8	9.8	7.3	•	6.4	8.7
Return on Equity Before Income Taxes 47	32.3	•	75.5	19.2	16.0	4.4	22.1	10.0	•	11.3	49.8
Return on Equity After Income Taxes 48	26.7	•	73.1	18.5	15.1	3.7	20.0	7.0	•	9.5	36.7
Profit Margin (Before Income Tax) 49	3.2	10.1	5.1	4.6	3.5	1.3	3.6	3.8	•	3.0	2.6
Profit Margin (After Income Tax) 50	2.7	10.1	5.0	4.4	3.3	1.1	3.3	2.7	•	2.5	1.9

Table I

Corporations with and without Net Income

GENERAL MERCHANDISE STORES

MONEY AMOUNTS AND SIZE OF ASSETS IN THOUSANDS OF DOLLARS

Item Description for Accounting Period 7/08 Through 6/09	Total	Zero Assets	Under 500	500 to 1,000	1,000 to 5,000	5,000 to 10,000	10,000 to 25,000	25,000 to 50,000	50,000 to 100,000	100,000 to 250,000	250,000 to 500,000	500,000 to 2,500,000	2,500,000 and over
Number of Enterprises **1**	10430	2380	6907	635	384	44	22	13	7	9	7	8	13
Revenues ($ in Thousands)													
Net Sales **2**	612097868	435824	3633268	800059	2489118	1116219	474005	1599326	1204289	3382444	4195038	32053231	560715046
Interest **3**	3083194	10	2562	1490	1738	1224	811	411	13779	11357	20176	50990	2978647
Rents **4**	895579	0	143	651	0	359	1001	5336	7445	4547	1764	45779	828553
Royalties **5**	1805819	0	0	0	228	0	0	0	382	8769	391	107981	1688067
Other Portfolio Income **6**	706318	456	0	1119	189	161	19486	152	5026	2380	14450	5548	657354
Other Receipts **7**	24342028	1616	75934	13535	35261	1944	8156	43357	9971	64240	36180	557151	23494681
Total Receipts **8**	642930806	437906	3711907	816854	2526534	1119907	503459	1648582	1240892	3473737	4267999	32820680	590362348
Average Total Receipts **9**	61642	184	537	1286	6580	25452	22884	126814	177270	385971	609714	4102585	45412488
Operating Costs/Operating Income (%)													
Cost of Operations **10**	75.5	64.7	65.8	81.7	69.1	64.6	73.7	74.6	65.5	67.0	70.5	73.3	75.9
Salaries and Wages **11**	11.1	13.7	9.1	6.4	11.9	12.8	8.0	13.7	13.1	12.6	12.8	10.5	11.1
Taxes Paid **12**	1.8	2.7	1.5	1.3	2.1	2.4	2.1	2.2	1.9	1.6	1.6	1.8	1.8
Interest Paid **13**	1.1	2.0	0.5	1.2	1.1	0.1	1.4	1.2	0.2	1.0	0.6	0.7	1.1
Depreciation **14**	2.2	1.9	1.2	0.4	0.5	0.7	1.0	0.8	1.8	1.7	1.7	2.2	2.3
Amortization and Depletion **15**	0.0	0.0	0.0	0.2	0.1	0.0	0.0	0.3	0.0	0.1	0.2	0.1	0.0
Pensions and Other Deferred Comp. **16**	0.5	0.1	0.0	0.1	0.7	0.3	0.2	0.1	0.1	0.1	0.1	0.2	0.5
Employee Benefits **17**	0.9	0.7	0.1	0.5	0.7	1.3	0.7	1.0	1.4	1.0	1.8	1.1	0.8
Advertising **18**	1.4	2.2	1.6	0.2	1.3	1.1	1.0	1.8	2.2	2.0	1.6	1.2	1.4
Other Expenses **19**	7.2	24.6	17.6	12.6	10.6	16.1	8.2	22.4	14.4	13.3	8.6	9.6	6.8
Officers' Compensation **20**	0.1	1.8	5.2	1.6	2.0	0.7	0.3	0.3	0.2	1.1	0.7	0.3	0.1
Operating Margin **21**	•	•	•	•	•	•	3.3	•	•	•	•	•	•
Operating Margin Before Officers' Comp. **22**	•	•	2.5	•	1.8	0.5	3.5	•	•	•	0.5	•	•

Selected Average Balance Sheet ($ in Thousands)

Net Receivables 23	1194	0	0	85	131	372	938	977	9524	14002	26061	40099	892305
Inventories 24	6844	0	61	125	1121	3545	6618	13473	28086	63259	122412	597637	4890412
Net Property, Plant and Equipment 25	10237	0	31	52	304	1434	2635	3510	15776	44774	75944	514267	7775882
Total Assets 26	33920	0	113	654	2089	6572	16031	33609	72526	180877	320335	1463626	25740134
Notes and Loans Payable 27	8647	0	66	289	796	625	2490	33207	5767	61558	49624	310459	6562096
All Other Liabilities 28	14205	0	25	77	471	3269	5185	65229	16957	68116	106414	512704	10851637
Net Worth 29	11067	0	22	288	821	2678	8355	-64827	49802	51202	164298	640462	8326400

Selected Financial Ratios (Times to 1)

Current Ratio 30	0.8	•	2.5	3.0	3.1	1.8	1.7	0.3	2.9	1.3	1.5	1.8	0.7
Quick Ratio 31	0.2	•	0.5	1.3	0.9	0.7	0.7	0.1	0.8	0.4	0.4	0.3	0.2
Net Sales to Working Capital 32	•	•	11.2	4.9	6.3	12.9	6.4	•	5.1	16.0	12.2	11.3	•
Coverage Ratio 33	4.0	•	0.0	•	2.2	2.4	7.6	•	9.8	2.3	3.4	3.3	4.1
Total Asset Turnover 34	1.7	•	4.7	1.9	3.1	3.9	1.3	3.7	2.4	2.1	1.9	2.7	1.7
Inventory Turnover 35	6.5	•	5.7	8.2	4.0	4.6	2.4	6.8	4.0	4.0	3.4	4.9	6.7
Receivables Turnover 36	49.1	•	197.6	21.7	54.0	53.8	23.1	72.6	17.4	28.0	17.9	101.7	48.5
Total Liabilities to Net Worth 37	2.1	•	4.2	1.3	1.5	1.5	0.9	•	0.5	2.5	0.9	1.3	2.1
Current Assets to Working Capital 38	•	•	1.7	1.5	1.5	2.3	2.5	•	1.5	4.1	3.0	2.2	•
Current Liabilities to Working Capital 39	•	•	0.7	0.5	0.5	1.3	1.5	•	0.5	3.1	2.0	1.2	•
Working Capital to Net Sales 40	•	•	0.1	0.2	0.2	0.1	0.2	•	0.2	0.1	0.1	0.1	•
Inventory to Working Capital 41	•	•	1.2	0.7	1.0	1.2	1.3	•	0.8	2.8	2.1	1.7	•
Total Receipts to Cash Flow 42	12.5	•	11.2	30.9	12.5	11.4	8.7	•	9.6	10.1	15.0	14.5	12.4
Cost of Goods to Cash Flow 43	9.5	•	7.4	25.2	8.7	7.4	6.4	•	6.3	6.8	10.6	10.6	9.4
Cash Flow to Total Debt 44	0.2	•	0.5	0.1	0.4	0.6	0.3	•	0.8	0.3	0.3	0.3	0.2

Selected Financial Factors (in Percentages)

Debt Ratio 45	67.4	•	80.9	56.0	60.7	59.3	47.9	292.9	31.3	71.7	48.7	56.2	67.7
Return on Total Assets 46	7.8	•	0.0	•	7.5	1.2	14.5	•	5.8	4.7	4.0	6.2	8.0
Return on Equity Before Income Taxes 47	17.9	•	•	•	10.2	1.7	24.1	29.4	7.5	9.5	5.5	9.8	18.8
Return on Equity After Income Taxes 48	11.2	•	•	•	8.2	1.6	21.4	29.6	5.5	8.2	4.5	4.1	11.9
Profit Margin (Before Income Tax) 49	3.4	•	•	•	1.3	0.2	9.3	•	2.2	1.3	1.5	1.6	3.6
Profit Margin (After Income Tax) 50	2.1	•	•	•	1.0	0.2	8.3	•	1.6	1.1	1.2	0.7	2.3

Table II

Corporations with Net Income

GENERAL MERCHANDISE STORES

MONEY AMOUNTS AND SIZE OF ASSETS IN THOUSANDS OF DOLLARS

Item Description for Accounting Period 7/08 Through 6/09	Total	Zero Assets	Under 500	500 to 1,000	1,000 to 5,000	5,000 to 10,000	10,000 to 25,000	25,000 to 50,000	50,000 to 100,000	100,000 to 250,000	250,000 to 500,000	500,000 to 2,500,000	2,500,000 and over
Number of Enterprises **1**	4379	614	2935	427	324	18	17	10	•	•	•	5	10
Revenues ($ in Thousands)													
Net Sales **2**	545610351	36399	2281870	615109	2229673	344087	452789	887303	•	•	•	24016922	508356621
Interest **3**	3044656	0	6	1381	1473	249	246	32	•	•	•	50382	2967004
Rents **4**	782469	0	0	0	0	0	485	12	•	•	•	11748	757870
Royalties **5**	1706636	0	0	0	228	0	0	0	•	•	•	38520	1658346
Other Portfolio Income **6**	647184	0	0	434	118	4	19485	127	•	•	•	4359	609997
Other Receipts **7**	22971208	1144	53872	13112	34401	1118	6083	3932	•	•	•	427304	22353150
Total Receipts **8**	574762504	37543	2335748	630036	2265893	345458	479088	891406	•	•	•	24549235	536702988
Average Total Receipts **9**	131254	61	796	1475	6993	19192	28182	89141	•	•	•	4909847	53670299
Operating Costs/Operating Income (%)													
Cost of Operations **10**	76.4	70.3	72.7	82.5	70.8	41.2	74.0	72.6	•	•	•	75.7	76.7
Salaries and Wages **11**	10.6	4.5	4.1	4.4	11.1	26.1	7.3	10.4	•	•	•	8.5	10.7
Taxes Paid **12**	1.7	0.5	1.0	1.0	2.1	4.3	1.9	1.3	•	•	•	1.5	1.7
Interest Paid **13**	1.2	0.3	0.2	1.0	1.2	0.0	0.5	0.6	•	•	•	0.3	1.2
Depreciation **14**	2.2	•	0.4	0.0	0.4	1.0	0.3	0.9	•	•	•	1.9	2.3
Amortization and Depletion **15**	0.0	•	0.0	0.3	0.1	0.0	0.0	0.1	•	•	•	0.0	0.0
Pensions and Other Deferred Comp. **16**	0.5	•	0.0	•	0.7	0.1	0.1	0.2	•	•	•	0.2	0.5
Employee Benefits **17**	0.9	•	0.1	0.3	0.6	0.5	0.6	0.5	•	•	•	1.0	0.8
Advertising **18**	1.2	•	2.1	0.1	1.2	0.9	0.8	1.2	•	•	•	0.9	1.2
Other Expenses **19**	6.6	17.0	9.9	10.5	10.4	20.0	5.7	7.5	•	•	•	8.4	6.4
Officers' Compensation **20**	0.1	6.2	5.6	1.2	1.5	1.5	0.3	0.6	•	•	•	0.3	0.1
Operating Margin **21**	•	1.2	4.0	•	•	4.3	8.4	4.0	•	•	•	1.3	•
Operating Margin Before Officers' Comp. **22**	•	7.4	9.6	•	1.4	5.8	8.7	4.6	•	•	•	1.6	•

Selected Average Balance Sheet ($ in Thousands)

Net Receivables 23	2635	0	0	27	152	138	1136	1190	•	46147	1090395
Inventories 24	14468	0	73	131	894	4021	7462	19586	•	633876	5236441
Net Property, Plant and Equipment 25	21326	0	42	20	338	1713	628	4109	•	451342	9002620
Total Assets 26	71668	0	123	671	2027	6723	16313	33099	•	1437698	30128756
Notes and Loans Payable 27	17779	0	30	312	905	343	1640	9509	•	81862	7627561
All Other Liabilities 28	30109	0	6	97	459	1271	1211	4722	•	554657	12778834
Net Worth 29	23779	0	87	262	663	5109	13462	18868	•	801179	9722362

Selected Financial Ratios (Times to 1)

Current Ratio 30	0.7	•	7.4	2.2	3.2	3.9	12.1	3.1	•	1.7	0.7
Quick Ratio 31	0.2	•	1.6	0.8	1.0	2.6	5.3	0.4	•	0.3	0.2
Net Sales to Working Capital 32	•	•	11.2	7.3	6.9	6.3	3.1	5.7	•	14.3	•
Coverage Ratio 33	4.6	15.8	36.9	2.0	2.2	107.7	27.3	8.2	•	12.3	4.4
Total Asset Turnover 34	1.7	•	6.3	2.1	3.4	2.8	1.6	2.7	•	3.3	1.7
Inventory Turnover 35	6.6	•	7.7	9.1	5.5	2.0	2.6	3.3	•	5.7	7.4
Receivables Turnover 36	46.0	•	498.9	41.7	50.9	28.1	24.3	•	•	•	•
Total Liabilities to Net Worth 37	2.0	•	0.4	1.6	2.1	0.3	0.2	0.8	•	0.8	2.1
Current Assets to Working Capital 38	•	•	1.2	1.9	1.5	1.3	1.1	1.5	•	2.5	•
Current Liabilities to Working Capital 39	•	•	0.2	0.9	0.5	0.3	0.1	0.5	•	1.5	•
Working Capital to Net Sales 40	•	•	0.1	0.1	0.1	0.2	0.3	0.2	•	0.1	•
Inventory to Working Capital 41	•	•	0.8	0.9	0.9	0.4	0.5	1.2	•	1.9	•
Total Receipts to Cash Flow 42	12.1	7.5	8.3	14.2	12.3	6.6	6.7	11.4	•	12.5	12.1
Cost of Goods to Cash Flow 43	9.2	5.3	6.0	11.7	8.7	2.7	5.0	8.3	•	9.5	9.3
Cash Flow to Total Debt 44	0.2	•	2.7	0.2	0.4	1.8	1.4	0.5	•	0.6	0.2

Selected Financial Factors (in Percentages)

Debt Ratio 45	66.8	•	28.8	60.9	67.3	24.0	17.5	43.0	•	44.3	67.7
Return on Total Assets 46	9.2	•	41.4	4.5	9.2	13.4	23.9	13.8	•	12.8	9.0
Return on Equity Before Income Taxes 47	21.6	•	56.5	5.9	15.6	17.5	27.9	21.2	•	21.1	21.7
Return on Equity After Income Taxes 48	14.2	•	56.5	5.4	12.7	17.4	25.7	20.5	•	13.7	14.1
Profit Margin (Before Income Tax) 49	4.1	4.3	6.4	1.1	1.5	4.7	14.1	4.5	•	3.5	4.2
Profit Margin (After Income Tax) 50	2.7	4.1	6.4	1.0	1.2	4.7	13.0	4.4	•	2.3	2.7

Table I

Corporations with and without Net Income

MISCELLANEOUS STORE RETAILERS

MONEY AMOUNTS AND SIZE OF ASSETS IN THOUSANDS OF DOLLARS

Item Description for Accounting Period 7/08 Through 6/09		Total	Zero Assets	Under 500	500 to 1,000	1,000 to 5,000	5,000 to 10,000	10,000 to 25,000	25,000 to 50,000	50,000 to 100,000	100,000 to 250,000	250,000 to 500,000	500,000 to 2,500,000	2,500,000 and over
Number of Enterprises	1	84139	15841	60066	4011	3503	385	212	58	29	15	7	8	4
Revenues ($ in Thousands)														
Net Sales	2	120633347	1470031	27902984	6802932	14112017	4432410	5938659	3467826	3233261	4306702	2543709	11488880	34933936
Interest	3	590502	2187	8013	2009	36003	3959	7696	1361	2805	7686	7505	27544	483734
Rents	4	65598	542	834	5124	18229	0	11112	929	5095	1360	4165	2310	15898
Royalties	5	374475	0	0	0	3589	0	35850	0	31121	0	1325	41196	261394
Other Portfolio Income	6	258905	36996	6691	9895	22058	2835	5936	45481	2556	3231	482	8965	113777
Other Receipts	7	1217969	7323	223730	70874	225455	46429	70759	103190	69077	5592	9090	291794	94657
Total Receipts	8	123140796	1517079	28142252	6890834	14417351	4485633	6070012	3618787	3343915	4324571	2566276	11860689	35903396
Average Total Receipts	9	1464	96	469	1718	4116	11651	28632	62393	115307	288305	366611	1482586	8975849
Operating Costs/Operating Income (%)														
Cost of Operations	10	63.0	61.8	57.9	66.7	65.6	70.3	66.4	68.0	62.0	59.6	58.4	50.5	68.4
Salaries and Wages	11	11.2	7.9	11.0	10.1	11.5	9.5	11.6	10.1	11.9	13.5	12.5	16.2	9.8
Taxes Paid	12	1.9	1.9	2.4	2.2	2.1	1.3	1.7	1.7	1.6	1.8	1.8	2.5	1.3
Interest Paid	13	2.1	1.9	0.7	1.7	1.0	1.1	0.8	1.4	1.8	3.4	2.4	2.2	3.8
Depreciation	14	1.7	1.0	1.1	1.2	1.1	0.8	1.7	2.6	2.9	1.7	2.4	3.7	1.8
Amortization and Depletion	15	0.3	3.6	0.1	0.1	0.1	0.1	0.1	0.2	0.5	0.2	0.5	0.3	0.4
Pensions and Other Deferred Comp.	16	0.2	0.0	0.1	0.1	0.3	0.3	0.2	0.2	0.4	0.0	0.1	0.1	0.2
Employee Benefits	17	0.9	0.2	0.6	0.5	0.7	0.7	0.6	0.7	0.9	1.5	1.3	1.4	1.2
Advertising	18	1.9	0.9	1.6	1.4	0.8	0.8	1.1	1.0	3.7	3.1	5.1	2.3	2.4
Other Expenses	19	16.1	30.5	20.6	14.3	13.1	12.3	12.1	12.7	16.3	12.1	16.5	21.1	13.9
Officers' Compensation	20	2.3	1.8	4.9	4.1	4.3	3.0	2.8	1.3	1.6	0.5	0.5	0.5	0.1
Operating Margin	21	•	•	•	•	•	•	0.9	•	•	2.3	•	•	•
Operating Margin Before Officers' Comp.	22	0.7	•	3.9	1.9	3.7	2.7	3.7	1.2	2.9	•	•	•	•

Selected Average Balance Sheet ($ in Thousands)

Net Receivables 23	76	0	10	94	310	1180	2126	6175	9553	18174	14316	114571	366356
Inventories 24	216	0	43	347	800	3648	5952	10990	20790	46855	116529	269377	957834
Net Property, Plant and Equipment 25	133	0	22	146	393	717	2418	5464	16458	27427	44811	283821	831668
Total Assets 26	778	0	111	725	2088	6813	14518	33630	69740	173577	341011	1292030	5892630
Notes and Loans Payable 27	326	0	69	377	714	2368	4868	12306	26978	120816	147574	483918	2288998
All Other Liabilities 28	213	0	32	182	482	1857	4385	8839	21011	56145	74204	388116	1574569
Net Worth 29	239	0	9	166	893	2588	5266	12486	21751	-3384	119234	419996	2029063

Selected Financial Ratios (Times to 1)

Current Ratio 30	1.7	•	1.9	2.0	2.0	1.9	1.8	1.7	1.2	1.5	2.3	1.4	1.6
Quick Ratio 31	0.5	•	0.7	0.7	0.9	0.5	0.7	0.7	0.5	0.5	0.8	0.5	0.3
Net Sales to Working Capital 32	8.4	•	13.5	6.8	5.6	4.4	5.9	6.2	15.3	9.8	4.3	10.6	8.9
Coverage Ratio 33	1.3	•	0.7	0.5	2.5	1.8	4.7	4.0	0.9	1.8	0.7	2.2	1.0
Total Asset Turnover 34	1.8	•	4.2	2.3	1.9	1.7	1.9	1.8	1.6	1.7	1.1	1.1	1.5
Inventory Turnover 35	4.2	•	6.2	3.3	3.3	2.2	3.1	3.7	3.3	3.7	1.8	2.7	6.2
Receivables Turnover 36	17.2	•	41.5	18.4	12.6	10.4	11.6	10.0	10.8	16.0	18.1	7.8	24.8
Total Liabilities to Net Worth 37	2.3	•	10.7	3.4	1.3	1.6	1.8	1.7	2.2	•	1.9	2.1	1.9
Current Assets to Working Capital 38	2.4	•	2.2	2.0	2.0	2.1	2.2	2.4	5.1	3.1	1.8	3.7	2.7
Current Liabilities to Working Capital 39	1.4	•	1.2	1.0	1.0	1.1	1.2	1.4	4.1	2.1	0.8	2.7	1.7
Working Capital to Net Sales 40	0.1	•	0.1	0.1	0.2	0.2	0.2	0.2	0.1	0.1	0.2	0.1	0.1
Inventory to Working Capital 41	1.2	•	1.3	1.3	1.0	1.3	1.3	1.2	2.6	1.7	1.0	1.7	1.0
Total Receipts to Cash Flow 42	9.6	15.6	8.3	12.9	9.1	10.8	9.5	8.5	8.6	12.2	15.5	6.7	11.6
Cost of Goods to Cash Flow 43	6.0	9.7	4.8	8.6	6.0	7.6	6.3	5.8	5.3	7.3	9.0	3.4	8.0
Cash Flow to Total Debt 44	0.3	•	0.6	0.2	0.4	0.3	0.3	0.3	0.3	0.1	0.1	0.2	0.2

Selected Financial Factors (in Percentages)

Debt Ratio 45	69.3	•	91.4	77.1	57.2	62.0	63.7	62.9	68.8	101.9	65.0	67.5	65.6
Return on Total Assets 46	5.0	•	2.3	1.8	5.0	3.4	7.7	10.2	2.6	10.2	1.9	5.4	5.7
Return on Equity Before Income Taxes 47	3.9	•	•	•	7.1	4.0	16.8	20.6	•	•	•	9.1	0.3
Return on Equity After Income Taxes 48	2.2	•	•	•	6.2	3.2	15.4	19.1	•	•	•	6.0	•
Profit Margin (Before Income Tax) 49	0.6	•	•	•	1.6	0.9	3.2	4.3	•	2.7	•	2.6	0.1
Profit Margin (After Income Tax) 50	0.4	•	•	•	1.4	0.7	2.9	4.0	•	1.7	•	1.8	•

Table II

Corporations with Net Income

MISCELLANEOUS STORE RETAILERS

MONEY AMOUNTS AND SIZE OF ASSETS IN THOUSANDS OF DOLLARS

Item Description for Accounting Period 7/08 Through 6/09	Total	Zero Assets	Under 500	500 to 1,000	1,000 to 5,000	5,000 to 10,000	10,000 to 25,000	25,000 to 50,000	50,000 to 100,000	100,000 to 250,000	250,000 to 500,000	500,000 to 2,500,000	2,500,000 and over
Number of Enterprises **1**	38360	5219	28405	1999	2251	264	150	37	13	10	•	•	0
Revenues ($ in Thousands)													
Net Sales **2**	75434234	534793	17061672	3212124	11217798	3584678	4403392	2580878	1697563	3638298	•	•	0
Interest **3**	94643	2113	4927	1253	27761	3741	5945	813	1790	7519	•	•	0
Rents **4**	42610	384	834	3675	15338	0	7307	10	401	112	•	•	0
Royalties **5**	183034	0	0	0	3589	0	35850	0	30309	0	•	•	0
Other Portfolio Income **6**	192291	35551	5132	9066	18179	2765	3787	40624	757	707	•	•	0
Other Receipts **7**	958527	5470	147612	60529	198744	35734	74822	89710	29408	17455	•	•	0
Total Receipts **8**	76905339	578311	17220177	3286647	11481409	3626918	4531103	2712035	1760228	3664091	•	•	0
Average Total Receipts **9**	2005	111	606	1644	5101	13738	30207	73298	135402	366409	•	•	•
Operating Costs/Operating Income (%)													
Cost of Operations **10**	59.9	55.9	53.9	63.4	64.7	73.5	63.7	70.3	53.2	61.1	•	•	•
Salaries and Wages **11**	12.0	5.2	12.0	11.6	11.8	7.1	11.7	8.2	12.1	12.7	•	•	•
Taxes Paid **12**	1.9	2.3	2.6	2.2	1.9	1.1	1.8	1.6	1.6	1.8	•	•	•
Interest Paid **13**	1.1	0.2	0.6	1.1	0.8	0.8	0.7	0.9	0.9	2.8	•	•	•
Depreciation **14**	1.8	0.6	0.9	1.1	0.9	0.6	1.6	1.4	3.2	1.3	•	•	•
Amortization and Depletion **15**	0.2	3.9	0.1	0.0	0.1	0.1	0.1	0.0	0.3	0.1	•	•	•
Pensions and Other Deferred Comp. **16**	0.1	0.0	0.1	0.1	0.3	0.1	0.3	0.2	0.6	0.0	•	•	•
Employee Benefits **17**	1.0	0.0	0.7	0.6	0.7	0.3	0.6	0.7	1.0	1.4	•	•	•
Advertising **18**	1.8	1.0	1.5	1.2	0.7	0.7	0.9	0.5	4.9	3.1	•	•	•
Other Expenses **19**	15.0	26.4	18.9	13.3	11.7	10.8	11.7	11.6	18.4	10.2	•	•	•
Officers' Compensation **20**	2.5	1.6	5.0	4.8	4.4	2.6	3.4	1.4	2.5	0.5	•	•	•
Operating Margin **21**	2.6	2.8	3.6	0.4	2.0	2.3	3.5	3.1	1.3	4.8	•	•	•
Operating Margin Before Officers' Comp. **22**	5.1	4.4	8.7	5.2	6.4	4.9	6.9	4.5	3.8	5.4	•	•	•

Selected Average Balance Sheet ($ in Thousands)

Net Receivables 23	91	0	14	105	391	1323	2561	6776	10616	17540
Inventories 24	325	0	48	368	858	4344	5947	9908	24486	59697
Net Property, Plant and Equipment 25	170	0	27	159	294	392	2062	3766	13834	19211
Total Assets 26	1050	0	138	712	2183	6745	15016	34196	66192	178672
Notes and Loans Payable 27	412	0	59	317	600	2343	4044	10349	14114	135978
All Other Liabilities 28	227	0	33	165	517	2256	4928	9656	24489	49259
Net Worth 29	411	0	46	230	1065	2145	6044	14192	27589	-6565

Selected Financial Ratios (Times to 1)

Current Ratio 30	1.8	•	2.0	2.3	2.2	1.8	1.8	2.1	1.3	1.7
Quick Ratio 31	0.6	•	0.9	1.1	1.0	0.5	0.7	0.8	0.6	0.5
Net Sales to Working Capital 32	7.4	•	13.0	6.2	5.7	5.3	5.9	5.5	15.2	8.9
Coverage Ratio 33	5.5	56.3	8.9	3.4	6.3	5.5	9.6	9.7	6.4	2.9
Total Asset Turnover 34	1.9	•	4.4	2.3	2.3	2.0	2.0	2.0	2.0	2.0
Inventory Turnover 35	3.6	•	6.8	2.8	3.8	2.3	3.1	4.9	2.8	3.7
Receivables Turnover 36	15.2	•	35.5	12.8	12.4	10.1	10.1	10.2	9.5	•
Total Liabilities to Net Worth 37	1.6	•	2.0	2.1	1.0	2.1	1.5	1.4	1.4	•
Current Assets to Working Capital 38	2.2	•	2.0	1.8	1.9	2.2	2.2	1.9	4.5	2.5
Current Liabilities to Working Capital 39	1.2	•	1.0	0.8	0.9	1.2	1.2	0.9	3.5	1.5
Working Capital to Net Sales 40	0.1	•	0.1	0.2	0.2	0.2	0.2	0.2	0.1	0.1
Inventory to Working Capital 41	1.0	•	1.1	0.9	0.9	1.4	1.2	0.9	2.1	1.5
Total Receipts to Cash Flow 42	7.2	5.0	6.3	9.7	7.5	9.1	7.3	6.7	5.1	9.3
Cost of Goods to Cash Flow 43	4.3	2.8	3.4	6.2	4.9	6.7	4.7	4.7	2.7	5.7
Cash Flow to Total Debt 44	0.4	•	1.0	0.3	0.6	0.3	0.4	0.5	0.7	0.2

Selected Financial Factors (in Percentages)

Debt Ratio 45	60.8	•	66.4	67.7	51.2	68.2	59.7	58.5	58.3	103.7
Return on Total Assets 46	11.0	•	22.5	8.7	11.8	8.5	13.9	18.7	11.7	17.0
Return on Equity Before Income Taxes 47	22.9	•	59.4	18.9	20.4	21.8	31.0	40.4	23.6	•
Return on Equity After Income Taxes 48	20.8	•	58.7	17.7	19.2	20.3	29.3	38.3	21.1	•
Profit Margin (Before Income Tax) 49	4.8	11.0	4.6	2.7	4.4	3.4	6.4	8.2	5.0	5.5
Profit Margin (After Income Tax) 50	4.3	9.6	4.5	2.5	4.1	3.2	6.0	7.8	4.4	4.3

Table I

Corporations with and without Net Income

NONSTORE RETAILERS

MONEY AMOUNTS AND SIZE OF ASSETS IN THOUSANDS OF DOLLARS

Item Description for Accounting Period 7/08 Through 6/09		Total	Zero Assets	Under 500	500 to 1,000	1,000 to 5,000	5,000 to 10,000	10,000 to 25,000	25,000 to 50,000	50,000 to 100,000	100,000 to 250,000	250,000 to 500,000	500,000 to 2,500,000	2,500,000 and over
Number of Enterprises	1	53768	15383	32362	3336	1905	400	179	79	49	37	13	14	10
Revenues ($ in Thousands)														
Net Sales	2	168020717	776114	16928840	13462412	17856667	6446970	8703142	6883910	7925169	14895502	10209033	14472021	49460937
Interest	3	1413372	1020	2944	6983	7140	4933	6148	10288	33630	28644	190813	129098	991730
Rents	4	102812	0	0	8402	987	4040	5773	5540	8574	2385	3869	48734	14507
Royalties	5	697005	0	0	0	16771	0	1563	0	5636	230	500	62990	609315
Other Portfolio Income	6	623952	48164	19724	2519	16781	6372	10051	32051	12992	92120	7222	130750	245207
Other Receipts	7	4679125	8889	43342	79620	187899	117063	102297	28948	108398	133247	44884	418357	3406182
Total Receipts	8	175536983	834187	16994850	13559936	18086245	6579378	8828974	6960737	8094399	15152128	10456321	15261950	54727878
Average Total Receipts	9	3265	54	525	4065	9494	16448	49324	88111	165192	409517	804332	1090139	5472788
Operating Costs/Operating Income (%)														
Cost of Operations	10	70.5	43.3	67.1	75.2	74.0	62.9	68.8	70.9	66.4	75.5	76.9	70.0	68.7
Salaries and Wages	11	8.2	12.2	6.7	6.4	7.6	10.7	9.6	8.6	7.3	7.3	5.9	9.4	9.3
Taxes Paid	12	1.2	2.9	1.4	1.4	1.7	1.4	1.1	1.1	1.0	0.9	0.6	1.0	1.1
Interest Paid	13	1.9	2.8	0.4	0.3	0.7	1.1	0.5	0.6	0.9	0.8	1.4	2.3	4.2
Depreciation	14	1.5	3.7	1.2	0.8	1.0	2.7	1.3	2.1	1.5	1.2	0.8	1.7	2.0
Amortization and Depletion	15	0.5	0.3	0.2	0.0	0.2	0.2	0.2	0.2	0.4	0.5	0.5	0.9	0.8
Pensions and Other Deferred Comp.	16	0.2	0.1	0.2	0.1	0.1	0.3	0.3	0.1	0.2	0.1	0.1	0.5	0.1
Employee Benefits	17	0.8	0.2	0.6	0.4	0.6	0.9	0.7	1.1	0.8	0.8	0.7	1.2	0.9
Advertising	18	2.7	2.4	2.6	2.1	2.0	3.1	4.3	2.6	4.2	1.6	4.7	3.1	2.5
Other Expenses	19	13.5	44.6	14.9	9.9	10.4	14.7	14.9	11.9	16.5	10.6	8.2	15.1	15.6
Officers' Compensation	20	1.4	8.4	4.6	2.7	1.9	2.9	1.1	1.0	1.0	0.6	0.6	0.3	0.4
Operating Margin	21	•	•	0.1	0.5	•	•	•	•	•	0.3	•	•	•
Operating Margin Before Officers' Comp.	22	•	•	4.7	3.2	1.7	2.0	•	0.9	0.8	0.9	0.3	•	•

Selected Average Balance Sheet ($ in Thousands)

Net Receivables 23	287	0	6	124	699	1625	2403	7610	13055	27452	100291	126242	706267
Inventories 24	186	0	23	120	508	1098	2946	7126	13144	34223	66386	81771	244098
Net Property, Plant and Equipment 25	192	0	22	143	403	1764	2317	5417	10277	17396	20756	91119	415887
Total Assets 26	2586	0	80	730	2321	6989	14837	34839	71613	156980	372259	990211	9336645
Notes and Loans Payable 27	816	0	41	280	851	2788	3476	8820	21857	46314	91996	293055	2948539
All Other Liabilities 28	804	0	31	203	991	2829	7346	12905	24206	53558	119669	355176	2649638
Net Worth 29	965	0	7	247	479	1372	4014	13114	25551	57108	160594	341981	3738468

Selected Financial Ratios (Times to 1)

Current Ratio 30	1.3	•	1.6	1.9	1.4	1.1	1.3	1.6	1.7	1.5	1.6	1.1	1.2
Quick Ratio 31	0.7	•	0.8	1.3	0.9	0.7	0.7	0.9	1.0	0.8	1.0	0.7	0.6
Net Sales to Working Capital 32	14.9	•	26.8	16.9	21.6	51.8	22.6	9.7	8.7	14.5	10.1	29.8	11.4
Coverage Ratio 33	2.2	•	2.4	4.6	2.6	2.1	•	2.9	3.0	3.6	2.5	1.2	2.3
Total Asset Turnover 34	1.2	•	6.6	5.5	4.0	2.3	3.3	2.5	2.3	2.6	2.1	1.0	0.5
Inventory Turnover 35	11.8	•	15.3	25.3	13.7	9.2	11.3	8.7	8.2	8.9	9.1	8.8	13.9
Receivables Turnover 36	10.5	•	61.2	33.0	13.1	10.7	17.3	11.4	11.4	15.3	7.7	9.9	6.4
Total Liabilities to Net Worth 37	1.7	•	10.0	2.0	3.8	4.1	2.7	1.7	1.8	1.7	1.3	1.9	1.5
Current Assets to Working Capital 38	4.4	•	2.7	2.1	3.7	12.6	4.5	2.7	2.3	3.2	2.7	9.1	5.8
Current Liabilities to Working Capital 39	3.4	•	1.7	1.1	2.7	11.6	3.5	1.7	1.3	2.2	1.7	8.1	4.8
Working Capital to Net Sales 40	0.1	•	0.0	0.1	0.0	0.0	0.0	0.1	0.1	0.1	0.1	0.0	0.1
Inventory to Working Capital 41	0.9	•	1.2	0.6	1.1	3.4	1.2	0.9	0.7	1.1	0.8	2.1	0.6
Total Receipts to Cash Flow 42	7.2	6.6	7.6	10.5	10.4	7.2	9.2	8.9	5.9	9.5	10.5	7.6	5.2
Cost of Goods to Cash Flow 43	5.1	2.9	5.1	7.9	7.7	4.5	6.4	6.3	3.9	7.2	8.1	5.3	3.6
Cash Flow to Total Debt 44	0.3	•	0.9	0.8	0.5	0.4	0.5	0.5	0.6	0.4	0.4	0.2	0.2

Selected Financial Factors (in Percentages)

Debt Ratio 45	62.7	•	90.9	66.2	79.4	80.4	72.9	62.4	64.3	63.6	56.9	65.5	60.0
Return on Total Assets 46	5.1	•	5.7	8.9	7.0	5.2	•	4.1	6.4	7.4	7.4	2.9	5.2
Return on Equity Before Income Taxes 47	7.5	•	37.1	20.6	21.1	13.6	•	7.2	12.1	14.7	10.2	1.3	7.4
Return on Equity After Income Taxes 48	5.0	•	34.3	19.4	18.4	12.2	•	5.0	6.4	10.8	7.8	•	5.0
Profit Margin (Before Income Tax) 49	2.3	•	0.5	1.3	1.1	1.2	•	1.1	1.9	2.1	2.1	0.4	5.6
Profit Margin (After Income Tax) 50	1.6	•	0.5	1.2	0.9	1.0	•	0.7	1.0	1.5	1.6	•	3.8

Table II

Corporations with Net Income

NONSTORE RETAILERS

MONEY AMOUNTS AND SIZE OF ASSETS IN THOUSANDS OF DOLLARS

Item Description for Accounting Period 7/08 Through 6/09	Total	Zero Assets	Under 500	500 to 1,000	1,000 to 5,000	5,000 to 10,000	10,000 to 25,000	25,000 to 50,000	50,000 to 100,000	100,000 to 250,000	250,000 to 500,000	500,000 to 2,500,000	2,500,000 and over
Number of Enterprises **1**	23869	4749	15044	2310	1312	239	89	46	29	•	10	8	•
Revenues ($ in Thousands)													
Net Sales **2**	132435097	326410	11653171	11064749	13640288	4175353	4396725	4490566	5781758	•	9451023	11093016	•
Interest **3**	1308867	682	1871	1936	3934	2865	2225	6969	30133	•	137138	120621	•
Rents **4**	88758	0	0	7812	105	3424	45	5540	8065	•	3787	43086	•
Royalties **5**	667486	0	0	0	0	0	0	0	4963	•	500	52477	•
Other Portfolio Income **6**	558794	45488	17594	1518	5106	4636	5505	1241	10853	•	1858	130681	•
Other Receipts **7**	4144840	5528	31479	52944	110305	104647	27398	19956	83943	•	23666	204736	•
Total Receipts **8**	139203842	378108	11704115	11128959	13759738	4290925	4431898	4524272	5919715	•	9617972	11644617	•
Average Total Receipts **9**	5832	80	778	4818	10488	17954	49797	98354	204128	•	961797	1455577	•
Operating Costs/Operating Income (%)													
Cost of Operations **10**	70.9	29.3	68.8	75.4	76.9	63.0	69.7	70.1	68.4	•	79.8	71.4	•
Salaries and Wages **11**	7.7	6.0	4.5	6.0	6.2	12.1	7.2	8.2	5.2	•	5.3	9.0	•
Taxes Paid **12**	1.1	1.8	1.3	1.4	1.5	1.4	0.9	1.1	0.7	•	0.6	1.0	•
Interest Paid **13**	2.0	2.2	0.4	0.3	0.4	1.0	0.3	0.5	0.6	•	1.0	1.8	•
Depreciation **14**	1.2	1.1	0.7	0.5	0.5	1.7	0.7	1.7	0.8	•	0.7	1.2	•
Amortization and Depletion **15**	0.5	0.1	0.2	0.0	0.1	0.2	0.1	0.2	0.3	•	0.5	0.7	•
Pensions and Other Deferred Comp. **16**	0.2	•	0.3	0.1	0.1	0.3	0.1	0.2	0.2	•	0.1	0.5	•
Employee Benefits **17**	0.7	0.0	0.5	0.4	0.5	0.9	0.5	1.0	0.6	•	0.6	1.2	•
Advertising **18**	2.6	0.6	1.8	2.2	1.4	3.5	5.1	1.5	4.2	•	4.0	2.6	•
Other Expenses **19**	12.1	39.7	12.0	8.2	7.2	10.3	11.0	10.8	15.1	•	6.3	12.6	•
Officers' Compensation **20**	1.3	11.4	4.7	2.3	1.8	3.1	1.1	1.0	0.9	•	0.5	0.2	•
Operating Margin **21**	•	7.8	4.8	3.2	3.3	2.7	3.3	3.8	3.0	•	0.8	•	•
Operating Margin Before Officers' Comp. **22**	1.0	19.3	9.5	5.6	5.1	5.7	4.3	4.8	3.9	•	1.3	•	•

Selected Average Balance Sheet ($ in Thousands)

Net Receivables 23	555	0	9	120	825	2017	2774	7992	17104	92124	188784
Inventories 24	317	0	32	135	466	1148	2939	8564	9491	78297	121285
Net Property, Plant and Equipment 25	294	0	19	102	260	1524	1831	6359	7706	23866	87612
Total Assets 26	4808	0	112	716	2299	7402	14424	36047	74481	354316	925516
Notes and Loans Payable 27	1452	0	36	156	629	2588	2352	6936	15108	58487	275850
All Other Liabilities 28	1496	0	41	202	765	2318	6686	12461	25329	134146	362554
Net Worth 29	1860	0	35	358	906	2497	5386	16650	34043	161683	287111

Selected Financial Ratios (Times to 1)

Current Ratio 30	1.3	•	2.3	2.1	1.7	1.4	1.4	1.9	1.9	1.7	1.2
Quick Ratio 31	0.8	•	1.2	1.4	1.2	0.9	0.8	1.0	1.3	0.9	0.8
Net Sales to Working Capital 32	14.2	•	18.3	17.3	14.3	13.3	18.5	9.0	8.8	11.4	22.1
Coverage Ratio 33	3.6	11.8	15.8	16.1	11.5	6.5	16.2	11.2	10.4	3.6	2.8
Total Asset Turnover 34	1.2	•	6.9	6.7	4.5	2.4	3.4	2.7	2.7	2.7	1.5
Inventory Turnover 35	12.4	•	16.7	26.8	17.2	9.6	11.7	8.0	14.4	9.6	8.2
Receivables Turnover 36	9.9	•	54.8	37.4	12.4	11.4	13.2	•	•	•	8.9
Total Liabilities to Net Worth 37	1.6	•	2.2	1.0	1.5	2.0	1.7	1.2	1.2	1.2	2.2
Current Assets to Working Capital 38	4.3	•	1.8	1.9	2.4	3.3	3.5	2.2	2.1	2.5	6.6
Current Liabilities to Working Capital 39	3.3	•	0.8	0.9	1.4	2.3	2.5	1.2	1.1	1.5	5.6
Working Capital to Net Sales 40	0.1	•	0.1	0.1	0.1	0.1	0.1	0.1	0.1	0.1	0.0
Inventory to Working Capital 41	0.8	•	0.7	0.6	0.6	0.8	1.0	0.8	0.4	0.9	1.5
Total Receipts to Cash Flow 42	6.4	2.0	6.4	9.5	9.9	7.1	7.2	7.0	5.1	12.3	7.2
Cost of Goods to Cash Flow 43	4.6	0.6	4.4	7.1	7.6	4.5	5.0	4.9	3.5	9.8	5.2
Cash Flow to Total Debt 44	0.3	•	1.6	1.4	0.8	0.5	0.8	0.7	1.0	0.4	0.3

Selected Financial Factors (in Percentages)

Debt Ratio 45	61.3	•	69.1	50.0	60.6	66.3	62.7	53.8	54.3	54.4	69.0
Return on Total Assets 46	8.3	•	38.7	27.0	20.5	15.1	14.7	14.0	16.2	9.3	7.7
Return on Equity Before Income Taxes 47	15.4	•	117.2	50.7	47.6	37.8	36.9	27.7	32.1	14.7	16.1
Return on Equity After Income Taxes 48	12.6	•	115.9	49.5	45.5	36.5	33.7	24.7	24.9	11.5	13.5
Profit Margin (Before Income Tax) 49	5.2	23.7	5.2	3.8	4.1	5.4	4.0	4.7	5.5	2.5	3.3
Profit Margin (After Income Tax) 50	4.2	23.5	5.2	3.7	4.0	5.2	3.7	4.2	4.3	2.0	2.8

Table I

Corporations with and without Net Income

AIR TRANSPORTATION

MONEY AMOUNTS AND SIZE OF ASSETS IN THOUSANDS OF DOLLARS

Item Description for Accounting Period 7/08 Through 6/09	Total	Zero Assets	Under 500	500 to 1,000	1,000 to 5,000	5,000 to 10,000	10,000 to 25,000	25,000 to 50,000	50,000 to 100,000	100,000 to 250,000	250,000 to 500,000	500,000 to 2,500,000	2,500,000 and over
1 Number of Enterprises	7442	1403	3880	953	752	187	143	58	19	11	8	17	11
Revenues ($ in Thousands)													
2 Net Sales	167276656	1240915	458616	1236597	1582590	542875	3758332	1000677	3268890	2051371	4556908	17473761	130105124
3 Interest	899768	9772	1	318	6642	274	2390	2179	3700	3234	33703	83538	754018
4 Rents	213365	0	0	0	995	567	0	323	50	164	0	74426	136842
5 Royalties	31	0	0	0	0	0	0	0	0	0	0	19	12
6 Other Portfolio Income	2167640	33524	13370	278	34823	33767	27366	9269	17194	2981	17729	515918	1461424
7 Other Receipts	3466091	-4709	41177	1625	2150	39032	57172	6429	51578	74422	75972	176108	2945130
8 Total Receipts	174023551	1279502	513164	1238818	1627200	616515	3845260	1018877	3341412	2132172	4684312	18323770	135402550
9 Average Total Receipts	23384	912	132	1300	2164	3297	26890	17567	175864	193834	585539	1077869	12309323
Operating Costs/Operating Income (%)													
10 Cost of Operations	32.6	3.9	46.9	69.8	59.0	52.9	65.5	41.2	36.4	27.6	37.0	33.6	30.7
11 Salaries and Wages	15.2	6.9	2.3	6.1	13.4	8.7	8.1	13.3	10.5	15.9	15.9	16.6	15.5
12 Taxes Paid	2.1	0.1	1.8	1.2	1.7	2.0	1.3	1.9	1.3	2.0	1.7	2.4	2.2
13 Interest Paid	2.6	0.1	1.8	0.5	1.2	6.0	1.7	3.0	0.9	3.5	2.0	3.5	2.6
14 Depreciation	5.6	3.2	20.5	12.9	4.4	30.6	6.7	12.4	3.8	5.7	6.1	7.3	5.2
15 Amortization and Depletion	0.7	•	0.0	0.0	0.1	0.1	0.1	0.1	0.2	0.1	2.2	0.6	0.7
16 Pensions and Other Deferred Comp.	1.2	0.0	•	0.1	0.1	0.3	0.1	0.2	0.1	0.3	0.4	1.2	1.4
17 Employee Benefits	2.3	0.1	0.0	0.2	1.0	0.9	0.8	1.3	0.7	2.9	1.5	2.2	2.5
18 Advertising	0.6	0.1	•	0.5	0.4	0.0	0.3	0.3	0.3	0.3	1.6	0.3	0.6
19 Other Expenses	44.1	132.7	42.1	19.9	22.7	38.9	22.8	32.5	51.0	46.4	48.2	39.0	44.8
20 Officers' Compensation	0.3	2.6	1.1	4.6	1.3	2.3	1.0	1.1	0.2	0.7	0.3	0.5	0.2
21 Operating Margin	•	•	•	•	•	•	•	•	•	•	•	•	•
22 Operating Margin Before Officers' Comp.	•	•	•	•	•	•	•	•	•	•	•	•	•

Selected Average Balance Sheet ($ in Thousands)

Net Receivables 23	1466	0	23	70	85	554	3306	2599	18639	15033	19800	84088	713731
Inventories 24	404	0	20	5	5	38	380	1169	5764	6960	8153	29836	185355
Net Property, Plant and Equipment 25	14022	0	87	355	1439	3675	7975	13496	19524	58769	183462	512063	8072277
Total Assets 26	26345	0	152	661	2266	6062	15234	32048	73001	163975	366410	1113877	14809775
Notes and Loans Payable 27	11243	0	159	355	708	4973	8231	14428	41802	82028	188572	552235	6058510
All Other Liabilities 28	13603	0	33	48	1280	1284	5388	3079	28167	51263	146174	369738	8214132
Net Worth 29	1499	0	-40	257	278	-196	1615	14541	3032	30685	31663	191904	537133

Selected Financial Ratios (Times to 1)

Current Ratio 30	0.9	•	1.8	3.1	1.7	1.5	1.2	2.0	1.1	1.0	1.2	1.3	0.8
Quick Ratio 31	0.6	•	1.3	2.9	0.7	1.2	1.0	1.2	0.8	0.6	0.8	0.8	0.6
Net Sales to Working Capital 32	•	•	4.0	6.3	7.7	4.4	32.2	4.3	66.9	•	27.8	15.1	•
Coverage Ratio 33	•	•	•	•	•	•	•	•	•	0.6	•	0.4	0.1
Total Asset Turnover 34	0.9	•	0.8	2.0	0.9	0.5	1.7	0.5	2.4	1.1	1.6	0.9	0.8
Inventory Turnover 35	18.1	•	2.8	184.8	240.9	40.3	45.3	6.1	10.9	7.4	25.9	11.6	19.6
Receivables Turnover 36	17.3	•	7.6	11.4	11.4	4.8	8.0	5.2	11.9	10.8	31.9	12.9	19.6
Total Liabilities to Net Worth 37	16.6	•	•	1.6	7.2	•	8.4	1.2	23.1	4.3	10.6	4.8	26.6
Current Assets to Working Capital 38	•	•	2.2	1.5	2.4	3.2	6.8	2.0	15.3	•	6.0	4.9	•
Current Liabilities to Working Capital 39	•	•	1.2	0.5	1.4	2.2	5.8	1.0	14.3	•	5.0	3.9	•
Working Capital to Net Sales 40	•	•	0.2	0.2	0.1	0.2	0.0	0.2	0.0	•	0.0	0.1	•
Inventory to Working Capital 41	•	•	0.7	0.0	0.0	0.0	0.3	0.3	2.5	•	0.7	0.4	•
Total Receipts to Cash Flow 42	3.6	1.2	5.5	•	6.2	•	9.8	8.7	3.0	3.9	6.3	4.6	3.3
Cost of Goods to Cash Flow 43	1.2	0.0	2.6	•	3.6	•	6.4	3.6	1.1	1.1	2.4	1.5	1.0
Cash Flow to Total Debt 44	0.3	•	0.1	•	0.2	•	0.2	0.1	0.8	0.4	0.3	0.2	0.2

Selected Financial Factors (in Percentages)

Debt Ratio 45	94.3	•	126.1	61.1	87.7	103.2	89.4	54.6	95.8	81.3	91.4	82.8	96.4
Return on Total Assets 46	•	•	•	•	•	•	•	•	•	2.4	•	1.2	0.3
Return on Equity Before Income Taxes 47	•	•	14.1	•	431.0	•	•	•	•	•	•	•	•
Return on Equity After Income Taxes 48	•	•	15.7	•	444.0	•	•	•	•	•	•	•	•
Profit Margin (Before Income Tax) 49	•	•	•	•	•	•	•	•	•	•	•	•	•
Profit Margin (After Income Tax) 50	•	•	•	•	•	•	•	•	•	•	•	•	•

Table II
Corporations with Net Income

AIR TRANSPORTATION

MONEY AMOUNTS AND SIZE OF ASSETS IN THOUSANDS OF DOLLARS

Item Description for Accounting Period 7/08 Through 6/09	Total	Zero Assets	Under 500	500 to 1,000	1,000 to 5,000	5,000 to 10,000	10,000 to 25,000	25,000 to 50,000	50,000 to 100,000	100,000 to 250,000	250,000 to 500,000	500,000 to 2,500,000	2,500,000 and over
Number of Enterprises 1	2587	459	1858	60	128	•	37	11	7	5	0	0	6
Revenues ($ in Thousands)													
Net Sales 2	67422621	8589	110363	379147	863682	•	2381708	558857	1544077	1930820	0	0	5617999
Interest 3	351701	0	1	98	5647	•	391	935	736	7342	0	0	44379
Rents 4	15553	0	0	0	0	•	0	323	50	164	0	0	58
Royalties 5	0	0	0	0	0	•	0	0	0	0	0	0	0
Other Portfolio Income 6	1729504	32996	13370	0	28812	•	14061	5751	330	1356	0	0	357891
Other Receipts 7	708321	0	41177	20	1958	•	38131	-444	12185	83785	0	0	74744
Total Receipts 8	70227700	41585	164911	379265	900099	•	2434291	565422	1557378	2023467	0	0	6095071
Average Total Receipts 9	27146	91	89	6321	7032	•	65792	51402	222483	404693	•	•	1015845
Operating Costs/Operating Income (%)													
Cost of Operations 10	39.6	•	0.0	92.0	59.1	•	75.3	40.2	60.3	28.4	•	•	41.3
Salaries and Wages 11	18.6	•	0.1	4.8	13.9	•	7.2	13.0	8.0	14.8	•	•	18.3
Taxes Paid 12	2.4	3.3	0.1	0.5	1.6	•	1.3	1.8	0.7	1.5	•	•	2.2
Interest Paid 13	2.0	•	0.6	•	1.2	•	0.3	0.8	0.5	2.5	•	•	3.6
Depreciation 14	5.3	1.2	10.5	0.1	1.2	•	1.1	3.5	1.7	5.2	•	•	9.6
Amortization and Depletion 15	0.2	•	•	•	0.0	•	0.0	0.0	0.0	0.0	•	•	•
Pensions and Other Deferred Comp. 16	0.9	•	•	•	0.1	•	0.1	0.3	0.1	0.2	•	•	1.7
Employee Benefits 17	2.4	•	0.0	•	0.9	•	0.7	1.2	0.7	3.7	•	•	2.8
Advertising 18	0.8	•	•	0.0	0.2	•	0.1	0.4	0.0	0.6	•	•	0.3
Other Expenses 19	30.2	60.7	22.0	2.3	16.8	•	10.0	32.4	22.4	42.4	•	•	24.8
Officers' Compensation 20	0.2	34.1	4.6	•	0.8	•	0.9	1.0	0.1	0.8	•	•	0.5
Operating Margin 21	•	0.6	62.0	0.3	4.1	•	3.0	5.5	5.4	•	•	•	•
Operating Margin Before Officers' Comp. 22	•	34.8	66.7	0.3	4.9	•	3.9	6.5	5.6	0.5	•	•	•

Selected Average Balance Sheet ($ in Thousands)

	1	2	3	4	5	6	7	8	9
Net Receivables 23	987	15	247	442	7910	6399	26186	10257	55024
Inventories 24	689	0	0	16	652	1727	3760	15012	24626
Net Property, Plant and Equipment 25	16249	22	6	277	2919	11724	15339	100550	610849
Total Assets 26	26525	57	668	3680	16522	32482	68071	232269	1188418
Notes and Loans Payable 27	10926	192	0	1025	4214	7680	20272	99048	530204
All Other Liabilities 28	13646	1	380	5945	9071	9955	25296	89663	379349
Net Worth 29	1953	-136	288	-3290	3236	14847	22503	43557	278865

Selected Financial Ratios (Times to 1)

	1	2	3	4	5	6	7	8	9
Current Ratio 30	0.9	5.5	1.7	3.5	1.3	1.7	1.5	0.8	1.3
Quick Ratio 31	0.5	5.5	1.7	1.2	1.1	1.3	1.1	0.5	1.1
Net Sales to Working Capital 32	•	2.1	22.4	3.0	26.0	7.4	15.9	•	11.4
Coverage Ratio 33	1.8	194.7	•	7.8	19.0	9.5	12.5	2.8	2.1
Total Asset Turnover 34	1.0	1.0	9.5	1.8	3.9	1.6	3.2	1.7	0.8
Inventory Turnover 35	15.0	0.1	•	242.3	74.3	11.8	35.4	7.3	15.7
Receivables Turnover 36	17.0	7.9	18.8	6.7	8.5	5.6	9.4	15.3	•
Total Liabilities to Net Worth 37	12.6	•	1.3	•	4.1	1.2	2.0	4.3	3.3
Current Assets to Working Capital 38	•	1.2	2.3	1.4	4.9	2.4	3.2	•	3.9
Current Liabilities to Working Capital 39	•	0.2	1.3	0.4	3.9	1.4	2.2	•	2.9
Working Capital to Net Sales 40	•	0.5	0.0	0.3	0.0	0.1	0.1	•	0.1
Inventory to Working Capital 41	•	•	•	•	0.1	0.4	0.4	•	0.3
Total Receipts to Cash Flow 42	5.6	0.8	46.7	4.3	7.6	4.7	4.9	3.1	6.6
Cost of Goods to Cash Flow 43	2.2	0.0	42.9	2.6	5.7	1.9	2.9	0.9	2.7
Cash Flow to Total Debt 44	0.2	0.4	0.4	0.2	0.6	0.6	1.0	0.7	0.2

Selected Financial Factors (in Percentages)

	1	2	3	4	5	6	7	8	9
Debt Ratio 45	92.6	340.8	56.9	189.4	80.4	54.3	66.9	81.2	76.5
Return on Total Assets 46	3.6	117.5	3.2	17.5	21.5	11.6	22.2	11.7	6.0
Return on Equity Before Income Taxes 47	21.9	•	7.5	•	103.8	22.8	61.7	39.9	13.7
Return on Equity After Income Taxes 48	19.0	•	7.5	•	95.2	21.2	59.6	27.0	11.6
Profit Margin (Before Income Tax) 49	1.6	384.8	111.5	0.3	8.3	5.2	6.7	6.3	4.5
Profit Margin (After Income Tax) 50	1.4	365.6	109.3	0.3	6.6	4.8	6.2	6.1	3.0

Table I

Corporations with and without Net Income

RAIL TRANSPORTATION

MONEY AMOUNTS AND SIZE OF ASSETS IN THOUSANDS OF DOLLARS

Item Description for Accounting Period 7/08 Through 6/09	Total	Zero Assets	Under 500	500 to 1,000	1,000 to 5,000	5,000 to 10,000	10,000 to 25,000	25,000 to 50,000	50,000 to 100,000	100,000 to 250,000	250,000 to 500,000	500,000 to 2,500,000	2,500,000 and over
Number of Enterprises 1	551	292	108	0	71	18	18	12	8	7	4	4	8
Revenues ($ in Thousands)													
Net Sales 2	68691317	10119	222	0	409237	56427	199945	350008	195470	470126	812304	1265892	64921566
Interest 3	1286557	0	857	0	107	1577	42	843	1745	1913	1261	62021	1216191
Rents 4	506568	0	89	0	2681	887	0	4497	1313	3629	8380	22395	462696
Royalties 5	53836	0	0	0	314	0	0	0	22	346	0	0	53156
Other Portfolio Income 6	399516	79	22267	0	7154	11354	0	3571	945	6056	4028	7413	336648
Other Receipts 7	1578951	-19025	1252	0	13529	1694	2894	18734	5037	3558	5857	98590	1446832
Total Receipts 8	72516745	-8827	24687	0	433022	71939	202881	377653	204532	485628	831830	1456311	68437089
Average Total Receipts 9	131609	-30	229	•	6099	3997	11271	31471	25566	69375	207958	364078	8554636
Operating Costs/Operating Income (%)													
Cost of Operations 10	23.2	•	176.6	•	3.8	56.4	8.4	52.7	4.9	34.9	28.9	3.9	23.5
Salaries and Wages 11	18.8	1.7	•	•	9.5	1.2	13.7	9.2	19.1	17.7	12.3	23.1	19.0
Taxes Paid 12	4.9	•	349.1	•	2.7	2.2	3.5	3.1	6.2	3.7	3.1	5.4	4.9
Interest Paid 13	5.6	•	•	•	1.1	0.6	1.4	1.6	5.0	3.0	1.6	13.4	5.6
Depreciation 14	12.0	8.9	67.1	•	9.7	4.5	4.3	9.1	23.0	9.5	8.6	16.1	12.0
Amortization and Depletion 15	0.1	•	•	•	0.0	0.0	0.1	0.0	0.0	0.1	0.1	0.9	0.1
Pensions and Other Deferred Comp. 16	1.5	•	•	•	0.1	1.8	•	0.3	0.7	1.7	0.0	0.2	1.5
Employee Benefits 17	4.1	•	•	•	0.9	1.4	2.7	0.9	4.3	3.0	1.4	5.7	4.2
Advertising 18	0.2	•	•	•	0.3	•	0.2	0.0	0.1	0.0	0.0	0.0	0.2
Other Expenses 19	26.5	42.9	481.5	•	69.5	18.6	38.8	18.0	44.0	27.1	34.0	45.2	25.7
Officers' Compensation 20	0.7	•	•	•	4.8	•	0.6	1.4	0.9	1.2	0.5	1.4	0.7
Operating Margin 21	2.3	46.6	•	•	•	13.3	26.3	3.7	•	•	9.4	•	2.5
Operating Margin Before Officers' Comp. 22	3.0	46.6	•	•	2.5	13.3	26.9	5.1	•	•	10.0	•	3.2

Selected Average Balance Sheet ($ in Thousands)

Net Receivables 23	9372	0	2	•	284	477	1056	4559	3248	7383	36490	142778	533340
Inventories 24	2296	0	1	•	6	9	107	684	853	1557	8644	1191	149698
Net Property, Plant and Equipment 25	252222	0	105	•	1935	1348	5947	21917	48609	104177	229132	716155	16691510
Total Assets 26	325063	0	308	•	3367	6435	15561	35321	71125	134838	346786	1475886	21151789
Notes and Loans Payable 27	71418	0	186	•	1517	421	2311	7357	22278	28214	117655	467046	4546424
All Other Liabilities 28	145142	0	23	•	442	709	1712	10844	17634	53911	112737	321697	9668673
Net Worth 29	108504	0	99	•	1409	5305	11538	17120	31213	52713	116394	687143	6916692

Selected Financial Ratios (Times to 1)

Current Ratio 30	0.8	•	8.9	•	0.6	12.0	1.2	1.1	3.0	1.1	0.8	0.7	0.8
Quick Ratio 31	0.5	•	8.9	•	0.6	11.7	1.0	0.9	2.3	0.8	0.6	0.6	0.5
Net Sales to Working Capital 32	•	•	0.0	•	•	0.8	33.6	44.0	2.7	42.1	•	•	•
Coverage Ratio 33	2.4	•	•	•	4.3	64.0	20.7	8.3	0.3	1.5	8.6	1.0	2.4
Total Asset Turnover 34	0.4	•	0.0	•	1.7	0.5	0.7	0.8	0.3	0.5	0.6	0.2	0.4
Inventory Turnover 35	12.6	•	3.1	•	35.6	188.1	8.7	22.4	1.4	15.1	6.8	10.3	12.7
Receivables Turnover 36	12.6	•	0.2	•	33.0	3.6	8.6	5.7	6.1	4.3	6.8	2.2	14.4
Total Liabilities to Net Worth 37	2.0	•	2.1	•	1.4	0.2	0.3	1.1	1.3	1.6	2.0	1.1	2.1
Current Assets to Working Capital 38	•	•	1.1	•	•	1.1	5.1	15.6	1.5	13.2	•	•	•
Current Liabilities to Working Capital 39	•	•	0.1	•	•	0.1	4.1	14.6	0.5	12.2	•	•	•
Working Capital to Net Sales 40	•	•	87.4	•	•	1.3	0.0	0.0	0.4	0.0	•	•	•
Inventory to Working Capital 41	•	•	•	•	•	0.0	0.4	1.3	0.2	0.4	•	•	•
Total Receipts to Cash Flow 42	3.8	•	0.0	•	2.2	1.7	1.9	4.6	3.0	5.4	2.8	3.0	3.9
Cost of Goods to Cash Flow 43	0.9	•	0.1	•	0.1	1.0	0.2	2.4	0.1	1.9	0.8	0.1	0.9
Cash Flow to Total Debt 44	0.2	•	0.2	•	1.4	1.6	1.4	0.3	0.2	0.2	0.3	0.1	0.1

Selected Financial Factors (in Percentages)

Debt Ratio 45	66.6	•	67.9	•	58.2	17.6	25.9	51.5	56.1	60.9	66.4	53.4	67.3
Return on Total Assets 46	5.2	•	67.1	•	7.9	20.2	20.9	10.9	0.5	2.2	7.8	2.8	5.2
Return on Equity Before Income Taxes 47	9.1	•	209.0	•	14.5	24.1	26.8	19.7	•	1.7	20.6	•	9.4
Return on Equity After Income Taxes 48	5.6	•	197.7	•	11.0	22.5	26.6	14.4	•	1.2	15.9	•	5.8
Profit Margin (Before Income Tax) 49	7.9	•	10045.0	•	3.5	40.8	27.8	11.6	•	1.4	11.8	•	8.0
Profit Margin (After Income Tax) 50	4.9	•	9500.0	•	2.7	38.1	27.7	8.5	•	1.0	9.1	•	4.9

Table II
Corporations with Net Income

RAIL TRANSPORTATION

MONEY AMOUNTS AND SIZE OF ASSETS IN THOUSANDS OF DOLLARS

Item Description for Accounting Period 7/08 Through 6/09	Total	Zero Assets	Under 500	500 to 1,000	1,000 to 5,000	5,000 to 10,000	10,000 to 25,000	25,000 to 50,000	50,000 to 100,000	100,000 to 250,000	250,000 to 500,000	500,000 to 2,500,000	2,500,000 and over
Number of Enterprises **1**	503	284	108	0	66	8	14	6	3	4	•	0	•
Revenues ($ in Thousands)													
Net Sales **2**	64155492	10119	222	0	403371	56427	199945	121470	49961	219459	•	0	•
Interest **3**	1167606	0	857	0	107	396	28	843	1491	1121	•	0	•
Rents **4**	429220	0	89	0	2681	887	0	4497	80	1080	•	0	•
Royalties **5**	52698	0	0	0	314	0	0	0	0	27	•	0	•
Other Portfolio Income **6**	366771	79	22267	0	3883	11354	0	3471	50	3823	•	0	•
Other Receipts **7**	599962	1	1252	0	13410	1689	2894	1031	3250	1313	•	0	•
Total Receipts **8**	66771749	10199	24687	0	423766	70753	202867	131312	54832	226823	•	0	•
Average Total Receipts **9**	132747	36	229	•	6421	8844	14490	21885	18277	56706	•	•	•
Operating Costs/Operating Income (%)													
Cost of Operations **10**	23.9	•	176.6	•	3.6	56.4	8.4	16.0	•	9.8	•	•	•
Salaries and Wages **11**	17.6	1.7	•	•	9.2	•	13.7	14.1	11.2	23.1	•	•	•
Taxes Paid **12**	4.7	•	349.1	•	2.5	2.2	3.5	5.9	6.1	4.7	•	•	•
Interest Paid **13**	5.2	•	•	•	1.0	0.6	1.4	3.1	3.6	1.8	•	•	•
Depreciation **14**	12.1	8.9	67.1	•	9.8	4.5	4.3	7.4	28.2	9.8	•	•	•
Amortization and Depletion **15**	0.1	•	•	•	0.0	0.0	0.1	0.0	•	0.1	•	•	•
Pensions and Other Deferred Comp. **16**	1.4	•	•	•	0.1	•	•	0.6	1.2	1.8	•	•	•
Employee Benefits **17**	4.0	•	•	•	0.8	1.2	2.7	2.0	2.8	3.6	•	•	•
Advertising **18**	0.0	•	•	•	0.1	•	0.2	0.1	0.2	0.0	•	•	•
Other Expenses **19**	24.9	42.9	481.5	•	69.7	16.8	38.0	19.7	37.2	36.6	•	•	•
Officers' Compensation **20**	0.7	•	•	•	1.2	•	0.6	2.4	0.2	1.3	•	•	•
Operating Margin **21**	5.5	46.6	•	•	2.0	18.4	27.1	28.7	9.4	7.4	•	•	•
Operating Margin Before Officers' Comp. **22**	6.2	46.6	•	•	3.2	18.4	27.7	31.1	9.6	8.7	•	•	•

Selected Average Balance Sheet ($ in Thousands)

Net Receivables 23	9359	0	2	•	305	1074	1357	2900	1765	4537
Inventories 24	2388	0	1	•	0	21	138	461	288	548
Net Property, Plant and Equipment 25	250208	0	105	•	2046	3018	7646	19090	36952	104855
Total Assets 26	319941	0	308	•	3471	7284	16479	37379	62570	132334
Notes and Loans Payable 27	71448	0	186	•	1577	947	2971	7117	20288	22714
All Other Liabilities 28	144247	0	23	•	401	659	1405	7182	9582	62358
Net Worth 29	104245	0	99	•	1494	5678	12102	23080	32701	47262

Selected Financial Ratios (Times to 1)

Current Ratio 30	0.8	•	8.9	•	0.6	4.4	1.2	2.5	7.6	0.9
Quick Ratio 31	0.5	•	8.9	•	0.6	4.1	1.0	2.3	6.3	0.7
Net Sales to Working Capital 32	•	•	0.0	•		3.7	33.3	2.8	0.9	•
Coverage Ratio 33	2.8	•	•		7.7	68.7	21.3	12.9	6.3	6.8
Total Asset Turnover 34	0.4	•	0.0	•	1.8	1.0	0.9	0.5	0.3	0.4
Inventory Turnover 35	12.7	•	3.1	•	4851.3	188.1	8.7	7.0	•	9.8
Receivables Turnover 36	12.8	•	0.2	•	32.6	3.6	8.6	•	3.7	7.6
Total Liabilities to Net Worth 37	2.1	•	2.1	•	1.3	0.3	0.4	0.6	0.9	1.8
Current Assets to Working Capital 38	•	•	1.1	•	•	1.3	5.0	1.6	1.2	•
Current Liabilities to Working Capital 39	•	•	0.1	•	•	0.3	4.0	0.6	0.2	•
Working Capital to Net Sales 40	•	•	87.4	•	•	0.3	0.0	0.4	1.1	•
Inventory to Working Capital 41	•	•	•	•	•	0.0	0.4	0.1	•	•
Total Receipts to Cash Flow 42	3.8	1.2	0.0	•	2.0	1.7	1.9	2.0	2.0	3.0
Cost of Goods to Cash Flow 43	0.9	•	0.1	•	0.1	0.9	0.2	0.3	•	0.3
Cash Flow to Total Debt 44	0.2	•	0.2	•	1.5	2.6	1.7	0.7	0.3	0.2

Selected Financial Factors (in Percentages)

Debt Ratio 45	67.4	•	67.9	•	57.0	22.0	26.6	38.3	47.7	64.3
Return on Total Assets 46	5.9	•	67.1	•	14.2	43.0	26.0	21.6	6.0	5.2
Return on Equity Before Income Taxes 47	11.8	•	209.0	•	28.8	54.4	33.7	32.3	9.7	12.5
Return on Equity After Income Taxes 48	7.8	•	197.7	•	25.4	51.1	33.5	24.4	7.1	11.5
Profit Margin (Before Income Tax) 49	9.6	47.3	10045.0	•	7.0	43.8	28.6	36.8	19.1	10.7
Profit Margin (After Income Tax) 50	6.4	41.3	9500.0	•	6.2	41.1	28.4	27.8	13.9	9.9

Table I

Corporations with and without Net Income

WATER TRANSPORTATION

MONEY AMOUNTS AND SIZE OF ASSETS IN THOUSANDS OF DOLLARS

Item Description for Accounting Period 7/08 Through 6/09		Total	Zero Assets	Under 500	500 to 1,000	1,000 to 5,000	5,000 to 10,000	10,000 to 25,000	25,000 to 50,000	50,000 to 100,000	100,000 to 250,000	250,000 to 500,000	500,000 to 2,500,000	2,500,000 and over
Number of Enterprises	1	4918	436	2890	684	456	253	99	28	22	26	7	18	0
Revenues ($ in Thousands)														
Net Sales	2	31340425	1503920	2270414	1771116	561644	1140450	2001958	686594	1220476	2303463	873673	17006716	0
Interest	3	122454	18404	77	1200	698	438	2497	1264	3569	3534	3615	87157	0
Rents	4	207997	56	0	0	0	399	367	1166	1451	1230	0	203327	0
Royalties	5	534	518	0	0	0	0	0	0	0	16	0	0	0
Other Portfolio Income	6	487053	34760	0	5292	181948	415	56566	8263	26268	12403	6142	154996	0
Other Receipts	7	804922	118845	151981	894	9449	2811	16633	37323	-3681	29004	635571	-193906	0
Total Receipts	8	32963385	1676503	2422472	1778502	753739	1144513	2078021	734610	1248083	2349650	1519001	17258290	0
Average Total Receipts	9	6703	3845	838	2600	1653	4524	20990	26236	56731	90371	217000	958794	•
Operating Costs/Operating Income (%)														
Cost of Operations	10	35.8	25.2	58.1	4.8	20.6	26.1	35.0	38.3	43.4	35.7	46.7	37.0	•
Salaries and Wages	11	10.9	11.2	11.3	27.7	12.5	27.1	9.8	8.3	11.0	8.1	6.1	8.8	•
Taxes Paid	12	1.6	0.8	1.7	1.9	3.1	3.0	1.5	2.2	1.6	1.6	0.7	1.6	•
Interest Paid	13	2.4	6.1	0.6	2.6	1.6	1.5	1.4	3.3	3.0	4.5	2.0	2.1	•
Depreciation	14	7.7	6.8	1.4	6.0	9.2	15.3	3.3	12.0	8.4	12.9	15.1	7.5	•
Amortization and Depletion	15	0.2	0.6	0.0	0.0	0.0	0.2	0.0	0.1	0.4	0.4	0.2	0.3	•
Pensions and Other Deferred Comp.	16	0.8	0.4	0.5	0.4	0.2	0.4	0.2	1.1	0.7	0.6	0.4	1.0	•
Employee Benefits	17	1.8	1.2	0.1	0.3	0.8	1.8	1.2	2.1	1.4	1.8	1.8	2.3	•
Advertising	18	0.4	2.0	0.1	1.3	0.4	0.2	0.2	1.1	0.4	0.2	0.1	0.3	•
Other Expenses	19	37.9	58.5	21.9	50.2	37.2	23.6	45.8	36.6	27.7	37.8	86.4	35.4	•
Officers' Compensation	20	1.5	1.4	5.8	3.2	4.0	3.7	1.1	1.5	1.5	0.6	1.6	0.8	•
Operating Margin	21	•	•	•	1.6	10.5	•	0.4	•	0.5	•	•	2.9	•
Operating Margin Before Officers' Comp.	22	0.4	•	4.5	4.8	14.5	0.7	1.5	•	2.1	•	•	3.7	•

Selected Average Balance Sheet ($ in Thousands)

Item												
Net Receivables 23	738	0	0	0	64	291	4114	1771	6993	11211	73056	117485
Inventories 24	88	0	4	0	0	76	404	490	408	1934	20491	
Net Property, Plant and Equipment 25	4200	68	420	1299	3681	4619	16367	41135	102707	149637	728396	
Total Assets 26	7799	184	804	2815	6190	13197	32306	71465	150994	323001	1358474	
Notes and Loans Payable 27	2912	151	242	640	3114	4496	16686	30826	79769	79388	467682	
All Other Liabilities 28	1877	33	515	886	415	3369	6459	17284	24945	60096	350673	
Net Worth 29	3010	1	47	1289	2661	5332	9162	23355	46280	183517	540118	

Selected Financial Ratios (Times to 1)

Item												
Current Ratio 30	1.0	•	1.3	0.5	1.0	1.1	1.7	1.0	1.1	0.9	1.9	0.9
Quick Ratio 31	0.7	•	1.2	0.2	0.9	0.4	1.5	0.6	0.7	0.7	1.7	0.7
Net Sales to Working Capital 32	163.7	•	72.4	•	61.6	41.4	6.8	•	58.3	•	2.6	•
Coverage Ratio 33	2.9	1.2	10.0	1.8	29.2	•	4.0	1.1	1.9	0.5	7.6	3.3
Total Asset Turnover 34	0.8	•	4.3	3.2	0.4	0.7	1.5	0.8	0.8	0.6	0.4	0.7
Inventory Turnover 35	25.9	•	125.9	•	1094.2	92.6	23.2	49.1	77.6	30.1	17.1	
Receivables Turnover 36	8.8	•	17737.6	92.9	9.3	7.6	7.9	8.0	7.4	1.5	8.8	
Total Liabilities to Net Worth 37	1.6	•	351.4	16.2	1.3	1.5	2.5	2.1	2.3	0.8	1.5	
Current Assets to Working Capital 38	39.7	•	4.9	•	21.1	2.4	•	19.1	•	2.1	•	
Current Liabilities to Working Capital 39	38.7	•	3.9	•	20.1	1.4	18.1	•	1.1	•		
Working Capital to Net Sales 40	0.0	•	0.0	•	0.0	0.1	0.0	•	0.4	•		
Inventory to Working Capital 41	2.3	•	•	•	0.0	0.0	0.2	•	0.0	•		
Total Receipts to Cash Flow 42	3.0	1.8	4.2	3.8	1.4	5.4	5.1	4.6	4.2	3.6	1.1	3.1
Cost of Goods to Cash Flow 43	1.1	0.5	2.5	0.2	0.3	1.4	1.8	1.8	1.8	1.3	0.5	1.1
Cash Flow to Total Debt 44	0.4	•	1.0	•	0.6	0.2	0.5	0.2	0.3	0.2	0.8	0.4

Selected Financial Factors (in Percentages)

Item												
Debt Ratio 45	61.4	•	99.7	94.2	57.0	54.2	59.6	71.6	67.3	69.3	43.2	60.2
Return on Total Assets 46	5.6	•	25.8	14.8	•	20.2	8.6	2.7	4.5	1.4	5.8	4.8
Return on Equity Before Income Taxes 47	9.4	•	8173.5	113.7	•	42.7	16.0	0.5	6.7	•	8.9	8.3
Return on Equity After Income Taxes 48	7.1	•	7920.4	110.6	41.0	15.0	•	4.9	•	6.9	5.7	
Profit Margin (Before Income Tax) 49	4.5	1.5	5.4	2.0	44.7	4.2	2.8	•	13.2	4.8		
Profit Margin (After Income Tax) 50	3.3	0.5	5.3	2.0	42.9	4.0	2.1	•	10.2	3.3		

Table II
Corporations with Net Income

WATER TRANSPORTATION

MONEY AMOUNTS AND SIZE OF ASSETS IN THOUSANDS OF DOLLARS

Item Description for Accounting Period 7/08 Through 6/09	Total	Zero Assets	Under 500	500 to 1,000	1,000 to 5,000	5,000 to 10,000	10,000 to 25,000	25,000 to 50,000	50,000 to 100,000	100,000 to 250,000	250,000 to 500,000	500,000 to 2,500,000	2,500,000 and over
Number of Enterprises **1**	2680	24	1788	381	345	•	52	13	9	14	•	13	0
Revenues ($ in Thousands)													
Net Sales **2**	21963163	1276742	1943669	1657753	497884	•	1204873	369615	783546	1381950	•	11715036	0
Interest **3**	80761	2810	0	1200	694	•	2497	1232	1647	1060	•	65876	0
Rents **4**	116921	56	0	0	0	•	367	1166	1367	0	•	113566	0
Royalties **5**	518	518	0	0	0	•	0	0	0	0	•	0	0
Other Portfolio Income **6**	438703	19910	0	5292	181463	•	56494	8067	19431	8148	•	137907	0
Other Receipts **7**	974014	88178	151982	481	9426	•	15598	23803	-8080	26773	•	29082	0
Total Receipts **8**	23574080	1388214	2095651	1664726	689467	•	1279829	403883	797911	1417931	•	12061467	0
Average Total Receipts **9**	8796	57842	1172	4369	1998	•	24612	31068	88657	101281	•	927805	•
Operating Costs/Operating Income (%)													
Cost of Operations **10**	37.4	23.2	67.8	5.1	23.2	•	32.8	37.8	42.9	45.9	•	38.2	•
Salaries and Wages **11**	10.5	5.4	8.4	27.6	10.9	•	7.8	4.5	8.8	7.8	•	9.9	•
Taxes Paid **12**	1.6	0.3	1.6	1.7	2.9	•	1.1	1.5	1.5	1.7	•	1.8	•
Interest Paid **13**	1.9	1.5	0.4	0.2	1.7	•	0.4	1.6	2.5	2.7	•	2.5	•
Depreciation **14**	7.7	4.1	1.4	4.8	9.9	•	1.9	7.1	8.2	11.7	•	9.3	•
Amortization and Depletion **15**	0.2	0.4	0.0	0.0	0.0	•	0.1	0.0	0.2	0.2	•	0.3	•
Pensions and Other Deferred Comp. **16**	0.8	0.2	0.5	0.5	0.1	•	0.2	0.3	0.6	0.7	•	1.1	•
Employee Benefits **17**	2.1	0.4	0.1	0.2	0.3	•	0.7	1.6	1.1	2.1	•	3.1	•
Advertising **18**	0.3	2.2	0.0	1.3	0.4	•	0.3	0.3	0.6	0.1	•	0.1	•
Other Expenses **19**	34.0	58.2	13.8	48.0	35.8	•	48.1	45.9	27.6	23.3	•	28.6	•
Officers' Compensation **20**	1.8	0.4	6.7	3.3	2.6	•	1.2	1.4	1.6	0.9	•	1.0	•
Operating Margin **21**	1.6	3.7	•	7.3	12.1	•	5.4	•	4.6	2.9	•	4.1	•
Operating Margin Before Officers' Comp. **22**	3.4	4.1	5.9	10.6	14.7	•	6.6	•	6.1	3.8	•	5.1	•

Selected Average Balance Sheet ($ in Thousands)

	1	2	3	4	5	6	7	8	9	10
Net Receivables 23	986	0	0	0	9	4968	3293	10807	12146	121982
Inventories 24	147	0	6	0	0	140	671	706	211	28937
Net Property, Plant and Equipment 25	5238	0	52	422	1015	1940	17798	43189	85894	805376
Total Assets 26	10071	0	136	883	2920	12629	37116	78160	147106	1481586
Notes and Loans Payable 27	3587	0	75	200	828	2928	9858	38611	60070	545131
All Other Liabilities 28	2147	0	20	145	1127	4782	9206	20479	26653	305257
Net Worth 29	4336	0	42	538	965	4919	18053	19069	60383	631197

Selected Financial Ratios (Times to 1)

	1	2	3	4	5	6	7	8	9	10
Current Ratio 30	1.6	•	1.9	1.5	1.0	1.7	0.9	1.5	1.2	1.7
Quick Ratio 31	1.1	•	1.9	0.3	0.8	1.4	0.7	0.9	0.9	1.1
Net Sales to Working Capital 32	10.9	•	33.9	36.3	•	5.8	•	8.6	19.9	9.1
Coverage Ratio 33	5.8	9.3	17.6	33.3	29.9	5.7	3.6	3.6	3.0	4.0
Total Asset Turnover 34	0.8	•	8.0	4.9	0.5	1.8	0.8	1.1	0.7	0.6
Inventory Turnover 35	20.8	•	125.9	•	•	54.2	16.0	52.9	214.9	11.9
Receivables Turnover 36	7.9	•	19436.7	157.4	17.7	7.1	•	8.5	7.7	•
Total Liabilities to Net Worth 37	1.3	•	2.3	0.6	2.0	1.6	1.1	3.1	1.4	1.3
Current Assets to Working Capital 38	2.8	•	2.1	2.9	•	2.4	•	2.9	6.0	2.5
Current Liabilities to Working Capital 39	1.8	•	1.1	1.9	•	1.4	•	1.9	5.0	1.5
Working Capital to Net Sales 40	0.1	•	0.0	0.0	•	0.2	•	0.1	0.1	0.1
Inventory to Working Capital 41	0.2	•	•	•	•	0.0	•	0.0	0.0	0.3
Total Receipts to Cash Flow 42	3.1	1.4	5.0	3.3	1.3	5.6	3.0	3.9	4.4	3.8
Cost of Goods to Cash Flow 43	1.2	0.3	3.4	0.2	0.3	1.9	1.1	1.7	2.0	1.4
Cash Flow to Total Debt 44	0.5	•	2.3	3.8	0.6	0.5	0.5	0.4	0.3	0.3

Selected Financial Factors (in Percentages)

	1	2	3	4	5	6	7	8	9	10
Debt Ratio 45	56.9	•	69.5	39.1	67.0	61.0	51.4	75.6	59.0	57.4
Return on Total Assets 46	9.0	•	59.0	39.3	25.9	22.0	6.9	9.9	5.5	6.1
Return on Equity Before Income Taxes 47	17.4	•	182.3	62.6	75.7	54.7	11.8	29.1	9.0	10.8
Return on Equity After Income Taxes 48	14.4	•	177.1	62.1	72.6	52.8	8.9	23.8	7.6	7.7
Profit Margin (Before Income Tax) 49	9.2	12.5	7.0	7.7	50.6	11.6	7.5	6.4	5.5	7.6
Profit Margin (After Income Tax) 50	7.6	11.3	6.8	7.7	48.5	11.2	5.6	5.2	4.6	5.4

Table I
Corporations with and without Net Income

TRUCK TRANSPORTATION

MONEY AMOUNTS AND SIZE OF ASSETS IN THOUSANDS OF DOLLARS

Item Description for Accounting Period 7/08 Through 6/09	Total	Zero Assets	Under 500	500 to 1,000	1,000 to 5,000	5,000 to 10,000	10,000 to 25,000	25,000 to 50,000	50,000 to 100,000	100,000 to 250,000	250,000 to 500,000	500,000 to 2,500,000	2,500,000 and over
Number of Enterprises **1**	106781	28553	66151	4952	5586	846	426	111	66	42	22	22	3
Revenues ($ in Thousands)													
Net Sales **2**	244875900	6829231	48688254	16854419	41902235	17743476	16785470	11045079	9224232	11150149	12587295	33862657	18203404
Interest **3**	458116	65718	3780	6731	19089	8563	7936	8076	5526	17998	8787	87475	218436
Rents **4**	227491	1415	967	4856	33421	3082	27305	22618	8355	18732	9616	67002	30121
Royalties **5**	90296	0	0	0	0	0	12	9	0	1717	0	884	87675
Other Portfolio Income **6**	1420018	163996	303663	45879	126613	123948	159094	45682	52192	74510	72648	183631	68165
Other Receipts **7**	4378676	227513	506935	25587	722200	190944	145254	77346	68944	497311	324232	1290303	302103
Total Receipts **8**	251450497	7287873	49503599	16937472	42803558	18070013	17125071	11198810	9359249	11760417	13002578	35491952	18909904
Average Total Receipts **9**	2355	255	748	3420	7663	21359	40200	100890	141807	280010	591026	1613271	6303301
Operating Costs/Operating Income (%)													
Cost of Operations **10**	32.9	42.3	27.9	36.8	41.4	36.3	43.2	47.1	27.3	24.6	27.2	30.9	13.9
Salaries and Wages **11**	15.7	6.9	10.8	14.2	10.8	15.8	14.7	12.9	20.0	21.9	18.8	19.6	31.6
Taxes Paid **12**	3.0	1.7	2.4	2.7	2.4	2.7	3.0	2.2	3.9	3.3	3.1	3.7	5.0
Interest Paid **13**	1.3	2.0	0.8	0.8	1.0	0.9	1.1	1.0	1.7	2.0	1.6	1.0	3.4
Depreciation **14**	4.7	2.3	3.4	3.3	4.5	4.6	5.4	4.5	6.4	7.2	7.2	5.8	4.6
Amortization and Depletion **15**	0.1	0.4	0.0	0.0	0.1	0.1	0.1	0.2	0.1	0.3	0.4	0.2	0.1
Pensions and Other Deferred Comp. **16**	0.4	0.1	0.1	0.2	0.2	0.2	0.2	0.3	0.2	0.5	0.5	0.7	1.1
Employee Benefits **17**	2.4	0.7	0.7	2.0	1.6	1.7	1.9	1.4	3.5	2.4	2.4	3.1	9.0
Advertising **18**	0.2	0.2	0.4	0.1	0.3	0.2	0.2	0.2	0.2	0.2	0.1	0.2	0.1
Other Expenses **19**	38.0	43.2	45.0	35.5	36.2	36.7	29.4	29.6	37.2	43.1	41.6	36.0	36.8
Officers' Compensation **20**	2.5	3.7	7.6	3.0	1.8	1.5	1.6	0.8	0.8	0.6	0.5	0.3	0.2
Operating Margin **21**	•	•	0.8	1.3	•	•	•	•	•	•	•	•	•
Operating Margin Before Officers' Comp. **22**	1.4	0.3	8.4	4.3	1.5	0.9	0.7	0.7	•	•	•	•	•

Selected Average Balance Sheet ($ in Thousands)

Item												
Net Receivables 23	162	0	145	504	1768	3670	9466	14810	26778	63654	165800	622357
Inventories 24	11	0	11	32	118	226	625	1172	1881	5062	13703	14806
Net Property, Plant and Equipment 25	387	42	337	912	2907	7137	16300	37455	80973	180377	431150	1713652
Total Assets 26	875	85	711	2133	6760	15170	36338	71687	158596	346628	921102	5627845
Notes and Loans Payable 27	384	81	464	1148	3277	6896	14588	35225	68713	129233	234912	2130563
All Other Liabilities 28	249	17	130	399	1521	3208	8407	18774	39505	87318	296535	2560141
Net Worth 29	242	-13	117	586	1961	5066	13343	17687	50377	130077	389654	937140

Selected Financial Ratios (Times to 1)

Item												
Current Ratio 30	1.2	•	1.4	1.5	1.2	1.2	1.3	1.0	1.1	1.4	1.8	0.8
Quick Ratio 31	0.9	•	1.2	1.1	1.0	1.0	1.1	0.8	0.8	1.1	1.3	0.3
Net Sales to Working Capital 32	41.3	•	45.0	24.7	37.3	33.1	28.4	253.3	42.5	20.1	10.9	•
Coverage Ratio 33	2.2	2.7	3.1	2.8	2.4	2.0	2.2	1.1	0.7	0.9	4.2	0.4
Total Asset Turnover 34	2.6	•	4.8	3.5	3.1	2.6	2.7	1.9	1.7	1.7	1.7	1.1
Inventory Turnover 35	68.1	•	110.6	97.8	64.4	75.5	74.9	32.6	34.7	30.7	34.7	57.1
Receivables Turnover 36	12.4	•	27.0	12.8	10.3	10.0	10.1	9.1	9.0	8.3	9.2	5.8
Total Liabilities to Net Worth 37	2.6	•	5.1	2.6	2.4	2.0	1.7	3.1	2.1	1.7	1.4	5.0
Current Assets to Working Capital 38	5.8	11.0	3.7	3.2	6.0	5.2	4.4	45.2	7.8	3.7	2.2	•
Current Liabilities to Working Capital 39	4.8	10.0	2.7	2.2	5.0	4.2	3.4	44.2	6.8	2.7	1.2	•
Working Capital to Net Sales 40	0.0	•	0.0	0.0	0.0	0.0	0.0	0.0	0.0	0.0	0.1	•
Inventory to Working Capital 41	0.2	•	0.1	0.1	0.3	0.2	0.2	2.5	0.2	0.2	0.1	•
Total Receipts to Cash Flow 42	3.1	2.5	3.4	3.3	3.6	4.3	5.4	3.5	3.2	3.2	2.8	3.4
Cost of Goods to Cash Flow 43	1.0	1.1	1.3	1.4	1.3	1.9	2.5	1.0	0.8	0.9	0.9	0.5
Cash Flow to Total Debt 44	1.2	•	1.7	1.5	1.2	0.9	0.8	0.7	0.8	0.8	1.0	0.4

Selected Financial Factors (in Percentages)

Item												
Debt Ratio 45	72.4	•	115.2	72.5	71.0	66.6	63.3	75.3	68.2	62.5	57.7	83.3
Return on Total Assets 46	7.3	•	28.0	10.0	6.7	5.9	6.1	3.7	2.4	2.5	7.2	1.6
Return on Equity Before Income Taxes 47	14.5	•	51.2	23.5	13.4	8.7	8.9	1.4	•	•	13.0	•
Return on Equity After Income Taxes 48	12.2	•	48.8	22.4	11.9	6.7	7.4	0.7	•	•	8.9	•
Profit Margin (Before Income Tax) 49	1.5	3.4	1.8	1.8	1.3	1.1	1.2	0.2	0.2	0.9	3.3	•
Profit Margin (After Income Tax) 50	1.3	3.2	1.7	1.7	1.1	0.9	1.0	0.1	0.2	0.8	2.3	•

Table II

Corporations with Net Income

TRUCK TRANSPORTATION

MONEY AMOUNTS AND SIZE OF ASSETS IN THOUSANDS OF DOLLARS

Item Description for Accounting Period 7/08 Through 6/09		Total	Zero Assets	Under 500	500 to 1,000	1,000 to 5,000	5,000 to 10,000	10,000 to 25,000	25,000 to 50,000	50,000 to 100,000	100,000 to 250,000	250,000 to 500,000	500,000 to 2,500,000	2,500,000 and over
Number of Enterprises	1	66456	16377	42502	3614	3021	549	243	59	•	20	11	•	0
Revenues ($ in Thousands)														
Net Sales	2	158050936	2989143	32692764	13401535	23267235	12906292	10852914	6779934	•	5762331	6529351	•	0
Interest	3	184651	1264	1035	6592	15104	6566	5888	4586	•	10456	2773	•	0
Rents	4	142778	0	159	4856	26234	1264	6817	7819	•	14802	0	•	0
Royalties	5	2534	0	0	0	0	0	12	9	•	1	0	•	0
Other Portfolio Income	6	974052	151821	226632	38233	72962	82101	92708	19774	•	33628	41198	•	0
Other Receipts	7	3611813	18525	480104	18416	570008	169293	134124	59313	•	472496	262654	•	0
Total Receipts	8	162966764	3160753	33400694	13469632	23951543	13165516	11092463	6871435	•	6293714	6835976	•	0
Average Total Receipts	9	2452	193	786	3727	7928	23981	45648	116465	•	314686	621452	•	•
Operating Costs/Operating Income (%)														
Cost of Operations	10	34.7	6.7	32.8	33.2	38.2	35.6	47.8	56.9	•	30.8	20.6	•	•
Salaries and Wages	11	14.5	8.9	9.2	14.7	11.4	15.6	12.7	10.7	•	20.1	21.4	•	•
Taxes Paid	12	2.8	2.9	2.2	2.5	2.3	2.5	2.9	2.0	•	3.1	3.6	•	•
Interest Paid	13	0.9	1.0	0.7	0.6	1.0	0.8	0.8	0.5	•	1.6	0.5	•	•
Depreciation	14	4.4	3.0	2.8	2.6	4.6	3.9	3.9	2.8	•	5.8	8.8	•	•
Amortization and Depletion	15	0.1	0.1	0.0	0.0	0.1	0.1	0.0	0.2	•	0.2	0.1	•	•
Pensions and Other Deferred Comp.	16	0.3	0.0	0.1	0.2	0.3	0.2	0.2	0.3	•	0.2	0.5	•	•
Employee Benefits	17	1.8	0.7	0.6	2.0	1.4	1.8	1.6	1.2	•	2.6	2.5	•	•
Advertising	18	0.2	0.3	0.2	0.2	0.3	0.2	0.1	0.1	•	0.2	0.2	•	•
Other Expenses	19	35.7	63.8	37.4	37.9	35.1	37.1	26.8	22.0	•	40.5	42.5	•	•
Officers' Compensation	20	3.2	4.1	10.1	3.1	2.5	1.4	1.9	0.9	•	0.5	0.5	•	•
Operating Margin	21	1.3	8.6	3.8	3.0	2.7	0.8	1.2	2.4	•	•	•	•	•
Operating Margin Before Officers' Comp.	22	4.5	12.7	13.8	6.1	5.3	2.1	3.1	3.3	•	•	•	•	•

Selected Average Balance Sheet ($ in Thousands)

Net Receivables 23	174	0	7	169	508	1981	4044	9559	•	30430	75670
Inventories 24	12	0	1	14	47	143	203	683	•	1286	3838
Net Property, Plant and Equipment 25	374	0	39	281	959	2731	6328	11669	•	76092	224199
Total Assets 26	824	0	86	688	2278	6552	15177	34652	•	158489	360426
Notes and Loans Payable 27	296	0	64	393	1055	3028	5355	10477	•	55856	59595
All Other Liabilities 28	215	0	12	132	312	1760	3485	8440	•	29946	92905
Net Worth 29	313	0	10	163	911	1763	6337	15735	•	72686	207925

Selected Financial Ratios (Times to 1)

Current Ratio 30	1.5	•	1.6	1.7	1.9	1.1	1.4	1.6	•	1.6	1.6
Quick Ratio 31	1.2	•	1.2	1.5	1.6	0.9	1.2	1.2	•	1.2	1.4
Net Sales to Working Capital 32	21.5	•	61.9	30.3	15.5	63.1	22.9	17.6	•	15.5	15.2
Coverage Ratio 33	5.8	15.8	9.5	6.9	6.7	4.4	5.1	7.9	•	3.2	7.9
Total Asset Turnover 34	2.9	•	9.0	5.4	3.4	3.6	2.9	3.3	•	1.8	1.6
Inventory Turnover 35	71.6	•	169.9	90.8	62.8	58.5	105.2	95.7	•	69.0	31.8
Receivables Turnover 36	11.8	•	99.1	29.7	11.5	12.6	10.2	11.2	•	•	7.6
Total Liabilities to Net Worth 37	1.6	•	7.9	3.2	1.5	2.7	1.4	1.2	•	1.2	0.7
Current Assets to Working Capital 38	2.9	•	2.6	2.5	2.1	9.1	3.6	2.7	•	2.8	2.8
Current Liabilities to Working Capital 39	1.9	•	1.6	1.5	1.1	8.1	2.6	1.7	•	1.8	1.8
Working Capital to Net Sales 40	0.0	•	0.0	0.0	0.1	0.0	0.0	0.1	•	0.1	0.1
Inventory to Working Capital 41	0.1	•	0.2	0.1	0.1	0.5	0.1	0.1	•	0.1	0.0
Total Receipts to Cash Flow 42	3.0	1.5	2.8	3.0	2.9	3.3	4.4	5.8	•	2.9	3.2
Cost of Goods to Cash Flow 43	1.1	0.1	0.9	1.0	1.1	1.2	2.1	3.3	•	0.9	0.7
Cash Flow to Total Debt 44	1.5	•	3.6	2.3	2.0	1.5	1.1	1.0	•	1.2	1.2

Selected Financial Factors (in Percentages)

Debt Ratio 45	62.0	•	88.8	76.4	60.0	73.1	58.2	54.6	•	54.1	42.3
Return on Total Assets 46	15.4	•	59.1	22.1	22.5	12.9	12.3	14.3	•	9.3	6.5
Return on Equity Before Income Taxes 47	33.5	•	470.6	79.9	47.8	37.2	23.7	27.5	•	14.0	9.9
Return on Equity After Income Taxes 48	30.6	•	467.6	77.5	46.4	34.6	20.9	25.3	•	12.3	8.8
Profit Margin (Before Income Tax) 49	4.4	14.3	5.9	3.5	5.7	2.8	3.4	3.8	•	3.5	3.5
Profit Margin (After Income Tax) 50	4.0	14.0	5.9	3.4	5.5	2.6	3.0	3.5	•	3.1	3.1

Table I

Corporations with and without Net Income

TRANSIT AND GROUND PASSENGER TRANSPORTATION

MONEY AMOUNTS AND SIZE OF ASSETS IN THOUSANDS OF DOLLARS

Item Description for Accounting Period 7/08 Through 6/09	Total	Zero Assets	Under 500	500 to 1,000	1,000 to 5,000	5,000 to 10,000	10,000 to 25,000	25,000 to 50,000	50,000 to 100,000	100,000 to 250,000	250,000 to 500,000	500,000 to 2,500,000	2,500,000 and over
Number of Enterprises **1**	27763	7127	16689	2151	1511	171	84	10	9	8	0	4	0
Revenues ($ in Thousands)													
Net Sales **2**	25437117	1164785	3925381	698523	6038841	2332489	2039619	580298	660494	2041290	0	5955396	0
Interest **3**	79891	892	835	529	2268	300	2888	261	725	2191	0	69000	0
Rents **4**	36016	0	38	2724	56	1122	300	0	108	1615	0	30054	0
Royalties **5**	0	0	0	0	0	0	0	0	0	0	0	0	0
Other Portfolio Income **6**	217652	12464	11105	2088	14946	112032	20394	660	929	2018	0	41017	0
Other Receipts **7**	420546	1	48227	11614	40270	9535	49572	3229	-554	33257	0	225395	0
Total Receipts **8**	26191222	1178142	3985586	715478	6096381	2455478	2112773	584448	661702	2080371	0	6320862	0
Average Total Receipts **9**	943	165	239	333	4035	14360	25152	58445	73522	260046	•	1580216	•
Operating Costs/Operating Income (%)													
Cost of Operations **10**	32.8	57.4	8.2	16.6	44.1	53.6	46.5	44.8	60.9	33.5	•	17.4	•
Salaries and Wages **11**	21.9	1.2	29.1	22.9	13.3	6.9	12.9	21.0	7.2	26.2	•	38.8	•
Taxes Paid **12**	3.8	1.5	3.2	4.4	3.2	6.5	2.6	2.8	2.5	3.7	•	4.9	•
Interest Paid **13**	3.0	0.6	2.9	9.2	1.4	1.9	1.5	2.3	3.0	4.3	•	5.1	•
Depreciation **14**	7.4	2.8	2.7	7.3	7.1	17.8	10.5	11.8	7.2	5.5	•	7.0	•
Amortization and Depletion **15**	0.7	0.4	0.4	3.6	0.3	0.0	0.1	0.0	0.2	0.9	•	1.4	•
Pensions and Other Deferred Comp. **16**	0.3	•	0.0	0.1	0.3	0.2	0.6	0.1	0.2	0.7	•	0.6	•
Employee Benefits **17**	1.7	1.3	0.3	0.4	1.1	0.8	2.2	2.1	1.9	5.3	•	2.2	•
Advertising **18**	0.5	0.4	0.9	0.4	0.8	0.2	0.4	0.3	0.8	0.4	•	0.3	•
Other Expenses **19**	28.6	29.3	46.5	31.6	24.2	19.4	21.5	18.0	16.7	21.2	•	31.9	•
Officers' Compensation **20**	2.2	4.4	4.5	4.5	3.7	0.9	1.5	1.0	1.7	0.2	•	0.1	•
Operating Margin **21**	•	0.8	1.3	•	0.5	•	•	•	•	•	•	•	•
Operating Margin Before Officers' Comp. **22**	•	5.2	5.7	3.5	4.1	•	1.4	•	•	•	•	•	•

Selected Average Balance Sheet ($ in Thousands)

	1	2	3	4	5	6	7	8	9	10	11
Net Receivables 23	75	0	4	2	371	1341	1619	5738	11156	31295	170264
Inventories 24	5	0	0	1	4	42	107	210	2108	1287	20043
Net Property, Plant and Equipment 25	242	0	20	100	813	5169	7967	18633	21135	67143	617102
Total Assets 26	690	0	107	694	1906	7587	15726	38677	70192	224969	1892611
Notes and Loans Payable 27	423	0	69	588	1269	5804	5830	28954	33711	132931	1062772
All Other Liabilities 28	127	0	18	38	251	757	2972	5740	10306	75252	410759
Net Worth 29	140	0	19	68	386	1027	6924	3984	26176	16785	419080

Selected Financial Ratios (Times to 1)

	1	2	3	4	5	6	7	8	9	10	11
Current Ratio 30	1.1	•	1.2	1.4	0.7	1.5	1.3	1.3	1.6	1.3	0.8
Quick Ratio 31	0.8	•	0.4	1.2	0.5	1.2	0.8	0.8	0.8	1.0	0.6
Net Sales to Working Capital 32	120.0	•	48.7	84.0	23.9	•	14.8	22.7	6.5	•	21.0
Coverage Ratio 33	1.0	4.3	2.0	2.0	•	3.2	•	•	0.3	1.1	0.3
Total Asset Turnover 34	1.3	•	2.2	2.1	1.8	1.5	1.5	1.5	1.0	1.1	0.8
Inventory Turnover 35	57.7	•	233.8	57.9	441.5	173.9	105.5	123.9	21.2	66.5	12.9
Receivables Turnover 36	12.3	•	48.2	47.4	12.1	10.6	•	•	9.5	9.9	8.7
Total Liabilities to Net Worth 37	3.9	•	4.5	9.2	3.9	6.4	1.3	8.7	1.7	12.4	3.5
Current Assets to Working Capital 38	20.2	•	5.7	12.8	3.8	•	3.2	4.2	2.8	4.1	•
Current Liabilities to Working Capital 39	19.2	•	4.7	11.8	2.8	•	2.2	3.2	1.8	3.1	•
Working Capital to Net Sales 40	0.0	•	0.0	0.0	0.0	•	0.1	0.0	0.2	0.0	0.3
Inventory to Working Capital 41	0.6	•	0.0	0.1	0.0	0.1	0.1	0.1	0.2	0.1	•
Total Receipts to Cash Flow 42	4.7	5.4	2.3	4.3	5.8	13.3	5.0	9.8	14.2	6.4	4.5
Cost of Goods to Cash Flow 43	1.5	3.1	0.2	0.7	2.6	7.1	2.3	4.4	8.7	2.2	0.8
Cash Flow to Total Debt 44	0.4	1.2	1.2	0.5	0.2	0.2	0.6	0.2	0.1	0.2	0.2

Selected Financial Factors (in Percentages)

	1	2	3	4	5	6	7	8	9	10	11
Debt Ratio 45	79.7	•	81.7	90.2	79.8	86.5	56.0	89.7	62.7	92.5	77.9
Return on Total Assets 46	4.0	•	12.5	5.0	6.1	•	7.5	•	0.8	5.2	1.2
Return on Equity Before Income Taxes 47	•	•	33.9	6.9	15.5	•	11.8	•	•	4.3	•
Return on Equity After Income Taxes 48	•	•	33.1	5.4	13.3	•	9.0	•	•	13.3	•
Profit Margin (Before Income Tax) 49	•	1.9	2.8	1.4	1.5	•	3.4	•	•	0.3	•
Profit Margin (After Income Tax) 50	•	1.9	2.7	1.1	1.3	•	2.6	•	•	•	•

Table II

Corporations with Net Income

TRANSIT AND GROUND PASSENGER TRANSPORTATION

MONEY AMOUNTS AND SIZE OF ASSETS IN THOUSANDS OF DOLLARS

Item Description for Accounting Period 7/08 Through 6/09	Total	Zero Assets	Under 500	500 to 1,000	1,000 to 5,000	5,000 to 10,000	10,000 to 25,000	25,000 to 50,000	50,000 to 100,000	100,000 to 250,000	250,000 to 500,000	500,000 to 2,500,000	2,500,000 and over
Number of Enterprises 1	14291	3241	8912	1161	870	50	50	0	•	•	•	•	0
Revenues ($ in Thousands)													
Net Sales 2	11720544	1000181	2325737	393049	3691539	965501	1595473	0	•	•	•	•	0
Interest 3	11579	818	391	371	1946	0	2227	0	•	•	•	•	0
Rents 4	3245	0	38	2724	56	0	133	0	•	•	•	•	0
Royalties 5	0	0	0	0	0	0	0	0	•	•	•	•	0
Other Portfolio Income 6	55647	0	11105	2088	9662	193	5741	0	•	•	•	•	0
Other Receipts 7	112209	-1	1849	10599	32297	4594	44772	0	•	•	•	•	0
Total Receipts 8	11903224	1000998	2339120	408831	3735500	970288	1648346	0	•	•	•	•	0
Average Total Receipts 9	833	309	262	352	4294	19406	32967	•	•	•	•	•	•
Operating Costs/Operating Income (%)													
Cost of Operations 10	38.0	57.3	13.0	29.5	48.8	58.0	51.5	•	•	•	•	•	•
Salaries and Wages 11	17.5	1.0	23.0	21.1	13.0	10.3	13.4	•	•	•	•	•	•
Taxes Paid 12	3.2	1.2	3.3	4.1	3.4	2.5	2.6	•	•	•	•	•	•
Interest Paid 13	1.8	0.4	2.1	8.2	1.5	0.8	0.8	•	•	•	•	•	•
Depreciation 14	5.2	2.8	3.2	9.0	7.6	0.8	5.8	•	•	•	•	•	•
Amortization and Depletion 15	0.2	•	0.0	0.3	0.1	0.0	0.1	•	•	•	•	•	•
Pensions and Other Deferred Comp. 16	0.2	•	0.0	0.2	0.2	0.2	0.7	•	•	•	•	•	•
Employee Benefits 17	1.5	1.5	0.2	0.7	1.4	1.0	2.3	•	•	•	•	•	•
Advertising 18	0.7	0.3	1.0	0.5	0.8	0.2	0.4	•	•	•	•	•	•
Other Expenses 19	24.9	26.9	40.1	18.0	17.4	19.7	17.7	•	•	•	•	•	•
Officers' Compensation 20	2.8	4.0	6.7	4.3	2.1	•	1.5	•	•	•	•	•	•
Operating Margin 21	4.0	4.6	7.4	4.1	3.5	6.5	3.3	•	•	•	•	•	•
Operating Margin Before Officers' Comp. 22	6.8	8.6	14.1	8.4	5.6	6.5	4.7	•	•	•	•	•	•

Selected Average Balance Sheet ($ in Thousands)

Net Receivables 23	66	0	7	1	449	3749	2231
Inventories 24	3	0	0	2	2	0	133
Net Property, Plant and Equipment 25	154	0	28	171	989	698	6819
Total Assets 26	440	0	125	699	1961	6002	16297
Notes and Loans Payable 27	220	0	55	530	1229	3511	3953
All Other Liabilities 28	91	0	31	32	287	1153	4082
Net Worth 29	128	0	39	137	444	1337	8261

Selected Financial Ratios (Times to 1)

Current Ratio 30	1.3	•	1.3	1.2	1.2	1.1	1.6
Quick Ratio 31	0.9	•	0.5	1.1	1.2	0.9	1.2
Net Sales to Working Capital 32	26.8	•	30.1	50.0	32.4	46.9	12.9
Coverage Ratio 33	4.0	13.6	4.8	2.0	4.1	10.3	9.0
Total Asset Turnover 34	1.9	•	2.1	0.5	2.2	3.2	2.0
Inventory Turnover 35	89.5	•	218.2	57.9	999.1	•	123.7
Receivables Turnover 36	10.7	•	38.5	30.9	9.7	5.5	12.5
Total Liabilities to Net Worth 37	2.4	•	2.2	4.1	3.4	3.5	1.0
Current Assets to Working Capital 38	4.6	•	4.3	7.6	5.1	11.9	2.6
Current Liabilities to Working Capital 39	3.6	•	3.3	6.6	4.1	10.9	1.6
Working Capital to Net Sales 40	0.0	•	0.0	0.0	0.0	0.0	0.1
Inventory to Working Capital 41	0.1	•	0.0	0.1	0.0	•	0.0
Total Receipts to Cash Flow 42	4.3	5.0	2.4	5.4	6.1	8.1	4.9
Cost of Goods to Cash Flow 43	1.6	2.9	0.3	1.6	3.0	4.7	2.5
Cash Flow to Total Debt 44	0.6	•	1.3	0.1	0.5	0.5	0.8

Selected Financial Factors (in Percentages)

Debt Ratio 45	70.9	•	68.7	80.4	77.3	77.7	49.3
Return on Total Assets 46	13.9	•	21.0	7.9	13.5	25.1	14.5
Return on Equity Before Income Taxes 47	35.9	•	53.1	19.9	44.8	101.6	25.4
Return on Equity After Income Taxes 48	33.5	•	52.4	18.5	41.6	101.6	21.3
Profit Margin (Before Income Tax) 49	5.6	4.6	8.0	8.1	4.7	7.0	6.6
Profit Margin (After Income Tax) 50	5.2	4.6	7.9	7.5	4.4	7.0	5.5

Table I

Corporations with and without Net Income

PIPELINE TRANSPORTATION

MONEY AMOUNTS AND SIZE OF ASSETS IN THOUSANDS OF DOLLARS

Item Description for Accounting Period 7/08 Through 6/09	Total	Zero Assets	Under 500	500 to 1,000	1,000 to 5,000	5,000 to 10,000	10,000 to 25,000	25,000 to 50,000	50,000 to 100,000	100,000 to 250,000	250,000 to 500,000	500,000 to 2,500,000	2,500,000 and over
Number of Enterprises **1**	503	0	268	0	123	61	22	11	6	3	3	7	0
Revenues ($ in Thousands)													
Net Sales **2**	11366007	0	253361	0	474151	130486	542721	941488	602038	178644	263115	7980002	0
Interest **3**	54110	0	9	0	782	99	577	1439	1410	422	1138	48235	0
Rents **4**	6483	0	0	0	0	0	1153	721	268	0	0	4342	0
Royalties **5**	778	0	0	0	704	0	0	0	0	0	0	74	0
Other Portfolio Income **6**	11623	0	0	0	11	378	2067	3	125	6	216	8817	0
Other Receipts **7**	298229	0	0	0	41151	-20877	7647	256	4998	1969	55722	207360	0
Total Receipts **8**	11737230	0	253370	0	516799	110086	554165	943907	608839	181041	320191	8248830	0
Average Total Receipts **9**	23334	•	945	•	4202	1805	25189	85810	101473	60347	106730	1178404	•
Operating Costs/Operating Income (%)													
Cost of Operations **10**	63.5	•	12.1	•	40.9	39.7	63.4	82.4	51.1	3.6	76.8	66.5	•
Salaries and Wages **11**	3.3	•	•	•	24.7	6.4	2.7	0.5	15.0	10.5	•	1.5	•
Taxes Paid **12**	2.3	•	1.0	•	2.9	2.2	1.5	1.4	3.9	5.0	4.2	2.2	•
Interest Paid **13**	6.9	•	0.5	•	0.0	2.1	0.2	1.4	0.7	7.2	3.4	9.2	•
Depreciation **14**	5.9	•	2.8	•	0.4	13.2	2.0	1.5	4.2	12.2	15.1	6.7	•
Amortization and Depletion **15**	0.3	•	0.3	•	0.9	•	0.3	0.0	0.1	•	0.6	0.3	•
Pensions and Other Deferred Comp. **16**	0.3	•	•	•	•	1.8	0.1	0.0	0.7	0.8	•	0.3	•
Employee Benefits **17**	0.6	•	•	•	•	1.4	0.4	0.2	2.7	2.3	0.3	0.4	•
Advertising **18**	0.0	•	0.3	•	0.8	•	0.0	•	0.0	•	0.0	0.0	•
Other Expenses **19**	12.8	•	48.7	•	18.1	14.4	14.9	3.5	17.4	40.9	1.5	11.7	•
Officers' Compensation **20**	0.2	•	•	•	2.0	1.0	0.6	0.0	0.3	•	•	0.1	•
Operating Margin **21**	3.9	•	34.3	•	9.4	17.7	14.0	9.1	3.8	17.5	•	1.0	•
Operating Margin Before Officers' Comp. **22**	4.1	•	34.3	•	11.4	18.7	14.6	9.1	4.1	17.5	•	1.1	•

Selected Average Balance Sheet ($ in Thousands)

Net Receivables 23	3290	0	239	991	3282	5477	8710	4599	136283	136794
Inventories 24	564	0	186	83	161	353	428	458	1150	33658
Net Property, Plant and Equipment 25	19429	63	59	1317	4506	25385	36449	135713	128163	1182844
Total Assets 26	40378	273	1911	5668	12282	38239	68681	167645	310269	2445673
Notes and Loans Payable 27	20818	37	4	3009	213	20686	12952	51611	57665	1377149
All Other Liabilities 28	9012	31	27	668	4227	12206	27271	29842	167857	499562
Net Worth 29	10547	205	1881	1992	7843	5347	28458	86192	84747	568961

Selected Financial Ratios (Times to 1)

Current Ratio 30	1.1	3.3	43.0	3.2	1.6	0.6	1.7	1.2	1.1	1.0
Quick Ratio 31	0.9	3.3	20.7	2.8	1.4	0.6	1.3	0.9	1.0	0.7
Net Sales to Working Capital 32	41.1	9.7	3.2	1.8	12.0	•	9.0	19.3	9.6	•
Coverage Ratio 33	2.0	75.7	4851.2	2.0	97.7	7.5	8.3	3.6	6.8	1.5
Total Asset Turnover 34	0.6	3.5	2.0	0.4	2.0	2.2	1.5	0.4	0.3	0.5
Inventory Turnover 35	25.4	•	8.5	10.3	96.9	199.8	119.8	4.6	58.5	22.5
Receivables Turnover 36	6.6	•	5.7	3.5	•	•	10.7	12.5	0.6	7.9
Total Liabilities to Net Worth 37	2.8	0.3	0.0	1.8	0.6	6.2	1.4	0.9	2.7	3.3
Current Assets to Working Capital 38	9.7	1.4	1.0	1.5	2.7	•	2.4	5.6	17.1	•
Current Liabilities to Working Capital 39	8.7	0.4	0.0	0.5	1.7	•	1.4	4.6	16.1	•
Working Capital to Net Sales 40	0.0	0.1	0.3	0.5	0.1	•	0.1	0.1	0.1	•
Inventory to Working Capital 41	1.0	•	0.2	0.1	0.1	•	0.1	0.3	0.1	•
Total Receipts to Cash Flow 42	5.8	1.8	2.9	8.0	3.5	8.3	5.9	1.8	5.0	7.1
Cost of Goods to Cash Flow 43	3.7	0.2	1.2	3.2	2.2	6.8	3.0	0.1	3.8	4.7
Cash Flow to Total Debt 44	0.1	7.8	44.0	0.1	1.6	0.3	0.4	0.4	0.1	0.1

Selected Financial Factors (in Percentages)

Debt Ratio 45	73.9	24.9	1.6	64.9	36.1	86.0	58.6	48.6	72.7	76.7
Return on Total Assets 46	7.9	120.6	37.1	1.6	32.6	24.1	8.2	9.2	6.6	6.3
Return on Equity Before Income Taxes 47	15.4	158.5	37.7	2.2	50.6	149.2	17.4	13.0	20.5	8.8
Return on Equity After Income Taxes 48	11.2	156.5	34.7	•	37.4	91.6	10.9	8.6	14.1	5.9
Profit Margin (Before Income Tax) 49	7.2	34.3	18.4	2.1	16.1	9.3	4.9	18.8	19.8	4.4
Profit Margin (After Income Tax) 50	5.2	33.9	17.0	•	11.9	5.7	3.1	12.4	13.6	2.9

Table II

Corporations with Net Income

PIPELINE TRANSPORTATION

MONEY AMOUNTS AND SIZE OF ASSETS IN THOUSANDS OF DOLLARS

Item Description for Accounting Period 7/08 Through 6/09	Total	Zero Assets	Under 500	500 to 1,000	1,000 to 5,000	5,000 to 10,000	10,000 to 25,000	25,000 to 50,000	50,000 to 100,000	100,000 to 250,000	250,000 to 500,000	500,000 to 2,500,000	2,500,000 and over
Number of Enterprises 1	448	0	268	0	123	14	22	8	•	•	0	4	0
Revenues ($ in Thousands)													
Net Sales 2	8989794	0	253361	0	474151	97176	542721	237728	•	•	0	6391929	0
Interest 3	47969	0	9	0	782	99	577	543	•	•	0	43568	0
Rents 4	2446	0	0	0	0	0	1153	721	•	•	0	305	0
Royalties 5	704	0	0	0	704	0	0	0	•	•	0	0	0
Other Portfolio Income 6	11455	0	0	0	11	378	2067	0	•	•	0	8652	0
Other Receipts 7	317195	0	0	0	41151	120	7647	256	•	•	0	205330	0
Total Receipts 8	9369563	0	253370	0	516799	97773	554165	239248	•	•	0	6649784	0
Average Total Receipts 9	20914	•	945	•	4202	6984	25189	29906	•	•	•	1662446	•
Operating Costs/Operating Income (%)													
Cost of Operations 10	66.6	•	12.1	•	40.9	41.2	63.4	32.1	•	•	•	75.6	•
Salaries and Wages 11	3.8	•	•	•	24.7	8.3	2.7	1.3	•	•	•	1.4	•
Taxes Paid 12	2.1	•	1.0	•	2.9	2.7	1.5	5.6	•	•	•	1.6	•
Interest Paid 13	3.3	•	0.5	•	0.0	0.0	0.2	1.1	•	•	•	4.1	•
Depreciation 14	5.6	•	2.8	•	0.4	9.4	2.0	5.4	•	•	•	6.0	•
Amortization and Depletion 15	0.3	•	0.3	•	0.9	•	0.3	•	•	•	•	0.2	•
Pensions and Other Deferred Comp. 16	0.4	•	•	•	•	2.4	0.1	•	•	•	•	0.4	•
Employee Benefits 17	0.5	•	•	•	•	1.8	0.4	0.7	•	•	•	0.3	•
Advertising 18	0.1	•	0.3	•	0.8	•	0.0	•	•	•	•	•	•
Other Expenses 19	11.0	•	48.7	•	18.1	6.1	14.9	13.1	•	•	•	7.5	•
Officers' Compensation 20	0.2	•	•	•	2.0	0.7	0.6	•	•	•	•	0.1	•
Operating Margin 21	6.3	•	34.3	•	9.4	27.3	14.0	40.7	•	•	•	2.8	•
Operating Margin Before Officers' Comp. 22	6.5	•	34.3	•	11.4	28.0	14.6	40.7	•	•	•	2.9	•

Selected Average Balance Sheet ($ in Thousands)

Item							
Net Receivables 23	2481	0	239	559	3282	3155	219358
Inventories 24	445	0	186	330	161	263	29366
Net Property, Plant and Equipment 25	15763	63	59	2411	4506	34210	1409394
Total Assets 26	24843	273	1911	5946	12282	41241	2179506
Notes and Loans Payable 27	9980	37	4	0	213	12774	987072
All Other Liabilities 28	5876	31	27	2880	4227	10141	513866
Net Worth 29	8987	205	1881	3066	7843	18325	678568

Selected Financial Ratios (Times to 1)

Item							
Current Ratio 30	1.3	3.3	43.0	1.7	1.6	0.5	1.1
Quick Ratio 31	1.0	3.3	20.7	1.3	1.4	0.4	0.9
Net Sales to Working Capital 32	23.9	9.7	3.2	4.6	12.0		52.7
Coverage Ratio 33	4.2	75.7	4851.2	1181.9	97.7	38.2	2.7
Total Asset Turnover 34	0.8	3.5	2.0	1.2	2.0	0.7	0.7
Inventory Turnover 35	30.0		8.5	8.7	96.9	36.2	41.1
Receivables Turnover 36	10.4		12.4	8.6			
Total Liabilities to Net Worth 37	1.8	0.3	0.0	0.9	0.6	1.3	2.2
Current Assets to Working Capital 38	4.9	1.4	1.0	2.3	2.7		9.4
Current Liabilities to Working Capital 39	3.9	0.4	0.0	1.3	1.7		8.4
Working Capital to Net Sales 40	0.0	0.1	0.3	0.2	0.1		0.0
Inventory to Working Capital 41	0.4		0.2	0.3	0.1		1.0
Total Receipts to Cash Flow 42	5.3	1.8	2.9	3.4	3.5	1.9	7.8
Cost of Goods to Cash Flow 43	3.5	0.2	1.2	1.4	2.2	0.6	5.9
Cash Flow to Total Debt 44	0.2	7.8	44.0	0.7	1.6	0.7	0.1

Selected Financial Factors (in Percentages)

Item							
Debt Ratio 45	63.8	24.9	1.6	48.4	36.1	55.6	68.9
Return on Total Assets 46	11.1	120.6	37.1	32.7	32.6	30.6	8.0
Return on Equity Before Income Taxes 47	23.4	158.5	37.7	63.3	50.6	67.0	16.1
Return on Equity After Income Taxes 48	17.9	156.5	34.7	54.7	37.4	43.9	11.8
Profit Margin (Before Income Tax) 49	10.5	34.3	18.4	27.9	16.1	41.3	6.8
Profit Margin (After Income Tax) 50	8.0	33.9	17.0	24.2	11.9	27.1	5.0

Table I

Corporations with and without Net Income

OTHER TRANSPORTATION AND SUPPORT ACTIVITIES

MONEY AMOUNTS AND SIZE OF ASSETS IN THOUSANDS OF DOLLARS

Item Description for Accounting Period 7/08 Through 6/09		Total	Zero Assets	Under 500	500 to 1,000	1,000 to 5,000	5,000 to 10,000	10,000 to 25,000	25,000 to 50,000	50,000 to 100,000	100,000 to 250,000	250,000 to 500,000	500,000 to 2,500,000	2,500,000 and over
Number of Enterprises	1	42699	8072	28168	2836	2784	385	251	75	60	35	9	18	6
Revenues ($ in Thousands)														
Net Sales	2	226279675	1024637	23798421	8715696	21781748	6509896	10670448	6420126	9205317	6016339	2572648	12372941	117191459
Interest	3	1058416	1423	2204	4670	8705	3833	8118	8374	12236	16513	40658	168719	782963
Rents	4	221829	11	2	265	1133	4548	3522	215	9855	36796	7373	32339	125769
Royalties	5	1810146	0	0	0	0	0	3814	0	22	1803	0	0	1804507
Other Portfolio Income	6	743040	31353	47082	3575	60265	28020	9209	15901	27752	11355	1806	194267	312456
Other Receipts	7	2866922	950	38348	61954	101273	45501	46873	114088	166450	76281	125811	208503	1880889
Total Receipts	8	232980028	1058374	23886057	8786160	21953124	6591798	10741984	6558704	9421632	6159087	2748296	12976769	122098043
Average Total Receipts	9	5456	131	848	3098	7885	17122	42797	87449	157027	175974	305366	720932	20349674
Operating Costs/Operating Income (%)														
Cost of Operations	10	40.6	5.8	60.4	45.6	63.6	67.7	63.7	72.6	64.7	55.9	16.9	50.3	23.7
Salaries and Wages	11	16.7	15.6	8.5	11.2	12.9	12.1	10.0	9.7	11.5	13.3	28.6	17.8	21.0
Taxes Paid	12	2.9	2.4	2.6	6.2	4.1	1.3	1.4	1.4	3.2	1.8	3.7	2.4	2.9
Interest Paid	13	1.1	0.8	0.6	0.3	0.6	0.7	0.8	0.7	1.1	1.6	1.6	4.0	1.2
Depreciation	14	3.4	2.5	1.3	1.8	2.1	1.3	1.2	2.1	2.1	4.5	4.0	2.4	4.6
Amortization and Depletion	15	0.3	0.0	0.1	0.0	0.3	0.2	0.2	0.3	0.5	0.8	0.6	1.5	0.3
Pensions and Other Deferred Comp.	16	1.5	0.0	0.2	0.2	0.2	1.1	0.2	0.4	0.2	0.5	0.5	0.7	2.5
Employee Benefits	17	3.9	0.2	0.5	0.6	1.0	1.3	1.0	1.7	1.3	2.6	4.5	4.4	6.1
Advertising	18	0.4	0.3	0.2	0.3	0.2	0.2	0.1	0.1	0.3	0.2	0.2	0.2	0.5
Other Expenses	19	28.1	72.4	18.9	26.0	10.6	11.1	18.0	9.4	14.8	16.6	41.0	18.1	38.3
Officers' Compensation	20	1.4	2.1	4.1	5.5	2.9	2.5	2.2	0.7	0.7	1.6	1.3	0.8	0.3
Operating Margin	21	•	•	2.7	2.4	1.3	0.5	1.3	0.8	•	0.5	•	•	•
Operating Margin Before Officers' Comp.	22	1.0	•	6.7	7.9	4.2	2.9	3.6	1.6	0.2	2.1	•	•	•

Selected Average Balance Sheet ($ in Thousands)

Net Receivables 23	644	0	19	154	759	1779	5755	10288	17570	35251	50185	169217	2617012
Inventories 24	42	0	2	19	63	246	295	1290	2965	4485	1398	7185	126397
Net Property, Plant and Equipment 25	1002	0	32	163	563	1598	4331	10598	19121	48841	89903	108187	5293500
Total Assets 26	3129	0	98	635	2117	6294	15983	34987	70474	162281	325913	1048931	13728288
Notes and Loans Payable 27	1035	0	69	231	1022	2141	5118	10460	31489	45217	78914	361795	4191995
All Other Liabilities 28	1099	0	29	195	611	2242	6763	13086	21069	57674	79691	357422	4976076
Net Worth 29	995	0	-0	208	484	1912	4101	11440	17917	59390	167309	329714	4560217

Selected Financial Ratios (Times to 1)

Current Ratio 30	1.2	•	1.3	1.4	1.7	1.4	1.2	1.2	1.4	1.1	2.0	1.2	1.1
Quick Ratio 31	1.0	•	1.1	1.1	1.4	1.2	1.0	0.9	1.1	0.8	1.6	1.0	0.9
Net Sales to Working Capital 32	29.6	•	71.7	31.0	14.9	18.4	32.4	32.6	15.0	30.9	5.1	14.6	46.4
Coverage Ratio 33	3.4	2.3	6.2	11.7	4.6	3.3	3.6	5.4	2.7	2.8	3.4	1.7	3.4
Total Asset Turnover 34	1.7	•	8.6	4.8	3.7	2.7	2.7	2.4	2.2	1.1	0.9	0.7	1.4
Inventory Turnover 35	51.1	•	211.9	72.3	79.6	46.5	91.6	48.2	33.5	21.4	34.6	48.1	36.7
Receivables Turnover 36	8.0	•	39.3	16.3	10.2	7.8	8.1	7.9	9.0	4.3	4.3	3.8	7.5
Total Liabilities to Net Worth 37	2.1	•	•	2.0	3.4	2.3	2.9	2.1	2.9	1.7	0.9	2.2	2.0
Current Assets to Working Capital 38	5.8	•	4.6	3.6	2.5	3.5	7.3	7.1	3.3	11.1	2.0	6.3	9.1
Current Liabilities to Working Capital 39	4.8	•	3.6	2.6	1.5	2.5	6.3	6.1	2.3	10.1	1.0	5.3	8.1
Working Capital to Net Sales 40	0.0	•	0.0	0.0	0.1	0.1	0.0	0.0	0.0	0.0	0.2	0.1	0.0
Inventory to Working Capital 41	0.2	•	0.1	0.1	0.1	0.3	0.1	0.3	0.3	0.8	0.0	0.0	0.3
Total Receipts to Cash Flow 42	3.9	1.7	5.7	3.9	10.1	9.7	6.1	11.7	8.0	7.4	2.6	6.1	2.9
Cost of Goods to Cash Flow 43	1.6	0.1	3.5	1.8	6.4	6.6	3.9	8.5	5.2	4.2	0.4	3.1	0.7
Cash Flow to Total Debt 44	0.6	•	1.5	1.9	0.5	0.4	0.6	0.3	0.4	0.2	0.7	0.2	0.7

Selected Financial Factors (in Percentages)

Debt Ratio 45	68.2	•	100.5	67.2	77.1	69.6	74.3	67.3	74.6	63.4	48.7	68.6	66.8
Return on Total Assets 46	6.5	•	31.1	17.2	9.8	6.6	7.4	8.9	6.4	4.8	4.8	4.4	5.7
Return on Equity Before Income Taxes 47	14.4	•	•	48.0	33.5	15.1	20.9	22.3	15.9	8.6	6.6	5.9	12.2
Return on Equity After Income Taxes 48	8.7	•	•	46.8	29.4	13.8	17.2	19.1	9.3	6.3	3.9	•	5.9
Profit Margin (Before Income Tax) 49	2.7	1.1	3.0	3.2	2.1	1.7	2.0	3.0	1.9	3.0	3.9	2.8	2.9
Profit Margin (After Income Tax) 50	1.6	1.1	3.0	3.2	1.8	1.6	1.7	2.5	1.1	2.2	2.3	•	1.4

Table II
Corporations with Net Income

OTHER TRANSPORTATION AND SUPPORT ACTIVITIES

MONEY AMOUNTS AND SIZE OF ASSETS IN THOUSANDS OF DOLLARS

Item Description for Accounting Period 7/08 Through 6/09	Total	Zero Assets	Under 500	500 to 1,000	1,000 to 5,000	5,000 to 10,000	10,000 to 25,000	25,000 to 50,000	50,000 to 100,000	100,000 to 250,000	250,000 to 500,000	500,000 to 2,500,000	2,500,000 and over
Number of Enterprises **1**	23060	4223	14816	1857	1625	219	182	60	37	•	•	•	3
Revenues ($ in Thousands)													
Net Sales **2**	178604718	500765	14358005	5718600	16077015	4873611	8225601	5630007	6487811	•	•	•	100746854
Interest **3**	745786	1	703	3235	7446	3208	4799	5818	8432	•	•	•	592382
Rents **4**	190434	0	0	265	1133	4548	1838	0	8678	•	•	•	125712
Royalties **5**	1806318	0	0	0	0	0	0	0	8	•	•	•	1804507
Other Portfolio Income **6**	680179	31353	46310	817	55575	27952	8450	15881	26843	•	•	•	265791
Other Receipts **7**	907919	269	34715	38155	46388	33371	46345	105016	129214	•	•	•	265243
Total Receipts **8**	182935354	532388	14439733	5761072	16187557	4942690	8287033	5756722	6660986	•	•	•	103800489
Average Total Receipts **9**	7933	126	975	3102	9962	22569	45533	95945	180027	•	•	•	34600163
Operating Costs/Operating Income (%)													
Cost of Operations **10**	37.9	3.9	50.3	45.6	65.5	73.3	61.4	74.9	64.6	•	•	•	21.9
Salaries and Wages **11**	17.4	5.9	10.4	11.4	13.2	8.5	9.2	9.0	11.5	•	•	•	21.6
Taxes Paid **12**	2.9	1.6	3.5	2.9	4.4	1.1	1.3	1.4	2.7	•	•	•	3.0
Interest Paid **13**	0.8	0.8	0.6	0.3	0.3	0.3	0.5	0.5	0.5	•	•	•	1.1
Depreciation **14**	3.5	3.3	1.4	1.6	0.9	0.6	1.2	2.0	1.8	•	•	•	4.9
Amortization and Depletion **15**	0.2	0.0	0.0	0.0	0.0	0.1	0.0	0.2	0.2	•	•	•	0.2
Pensions and Other Deferred Comp. **16**	1.8	0.0	0.4	0.3	0.3	1.0	0.3	0.4	0.2	•	•	•	2.9
Employee Benefits **17**	3.7	•	0.6	0.6	0.9	1.4	1.0	1.7	1.3	•	•	•	5.5
Advertising **18**	0.4	0.1	0.2	0.3	0.1	0.1	0.1	0.1	0.2	•	•	•	0.5
Other Expenses **19**	27.2	73.2	21.4	24.3	8.2	8.2	19.6	7.2	14.6	•	•	•	36.3
Officers' Compensation **20**	1.3	2.1	4.3	7.6	2.3	2.2	2.2	0.7	0.7	•	•	•	0.3
Operating Margin **21**	2.9	9.0	6.9	5.2	3.9	3.1	3.1	1.8	1.8	•	•	•	1.8
Operating Margin Before Officers' Comp. **22**	4.1	11.1	11.2	12.7	6.2	5.3	5.4	2.5	2.5	•	•	•	2.0

Selected Average Balance Sheet ($ in Thousands)

Net Receivables 23	875	0	14	147	741	1916	7047	10834	20028	•	3850918
Inventories 24	61	0	4	26	32	383	159	1307	3737	•	215393
Net Property, Plant and Equipment 25	1541	0	40	114	278	949	3521	9002	16696	•	9776046
Total Assets 26	4060	0	109	628	1907	6168	15806	33769	67998	•	21303563
Notes and Loans Payable 27	1148	0	58	232	451	1216	3814	10328	14562	•	6473654
All Other Liabilities 28	1216	0	33	187	654	2199	6948	12004	20498	•	6070288
Net Worth 29	1695	0	18	208	801	2753	5044	11437	32937	•	8759621

Selected Financial Ratios (Times to 1)

Current Ratio 30	1.3	•	2.0	1.3	1.8	1.5	1.3	1.2	1.7	•	1.2
Quick Ratio 31	1.1	•	1.6	0.9	1.4	1.3	1.1	0.9	1.3	•	1.1
Net Sales to Working Capital 32	21.4	•	36.4	36.9	16.0	18.0	16.4	24.2	11.7	•	30.0
Coverage Ratio 33	7.4	20.1	13.7	19.5	18.1	15.8	8.8	8.5	10.5	•	5.6
Total Asset Turnover 34	1.9	•	8.9	4.9	5.2	3.6	2.9	2.8	2.6	•	1.6
Inventory Turnover 35	48.5	•	137.9	53.8	202.8	42.6	174.3	53.8	30.3	•	34.2
Receivables Turnover 36	8.7	•	60.4	13.6	12.9	8.2	•	8.6	8.4	•	•
Total Liabilities to Net Worth 37	1.4	•	5.1	2.0	1.4	1.2	2.1	2.0	1.1	•	1.4
Current Assets to Working Capital 38	4.0	•	2.0	4.5	2.3	3.0	4.0	5.2	2.5	•	5.2
Current Liabilities to Working Capital 39	3.0	•	1.0	3.5	1.3	2.0	3.0	4.2	1.5	•	4.2
Working Capital to Net Sales 40	0.0	•	0.0	0.0	0.1	0.1	0.1	0.0	0.1	•	0.0
Inventory to Working Capital 41	0.1	•	0.1	0.2	0.0	0.3	0.1	0.2	0.2	•	0.2
Total Receipts to Cash Flow 42	3.6	1.3	4.2	3.7	9.5	9.6	5.0	13.0	6.7	•	2.9
Cost of Goods to Cash Flow 43	1.4	0.1	2.1	1.7	6.2	7.0	3.1	9.8	4.3	•	0.6
Cash Flow to Total Debt 44	0.9	•	2.5	2.0	0.9	0.7	0.8	0.3	0.7	•	0.9

Selected Financial Factors (in Percentages)

Debt Ratio 45	58.2	•	83.7	66.8	58.0	55.4	68.1	66.1	51.6	•	58.9
Return on Total Assets 46	11.9	•	71.3	30.6	24.8	17.3	12.5	12.8	12.6	•	9.5
Return on Equity Before Income Taxes 47	24.7	•	404.4	87.5	55.8	36.3	34.8	33.5	23.6	•	18.9
Return on Equity After Income Taxes 48	18.5	•	401.6	85.7	51.5	34.7	30.6	29.4	17.8	•	12.3
Profit Margin (Before Income Tax) 49	5.4	15.3	7.4	5.9	4.5	4.5	3.9	4.1	4.4	•	4.9
Profit Margin (After Income Tax) 50	4.1	15.3	7.4	5.8	4.2	4.3	3.4	3.6	3.3	•	3.2

Table I

Corporations with and without Net Income

WAREHOUSING AND STORAGE

MONEY AMOUNTS AND SIZE OF ASSETS IN THOUSANDS OF DOLLARS

Item Description for Accounting Period 7/08 Through 6/09		Total	Zero Assets	Under 500	500 to 1,000	1,000 to 5,000	5,000 to 10,000	10,000 to 25,000	25,000 to 50,000	50,000 to 100,000	100,000 to 250,000	250,000 to 500,000	500,000 to 2,500,000	2,500,000 and over
Number of Enterprises	1	4571	273	1986	854	1026	147	204	37	17	15	6	7	0
Revenues ($ in Thousands)														
Net Sales	2	19510404	81870	176593	1418744	2516218	1947911	3554982	633667	874939	2393588	769973	5141919	0
Interest	3	69805	0	34	3407	3193	2930	5209	1794	5122	7422	10839	29855	0
Rents	4	29616	0	0	0	2783	1637	1120	1964	6244	4325	6951	4591	0
Royalties	5	29094	0	0	0	720	0	0	0	0	1411	341	26621	0
Other Portfolio Income	6	33718	0	1	4571	1751	2519	12832	1416	1472	4511	631	4014	0
Other Receipts	7	493268	-20084	367	780	74264	32325	62403	12614	4519	95770	154951	75361	0
Total Receipts	8	20165905	61786	176995	1427502	2598929	1987322	3636546	651455	892296	2507027	943686	5282361	0
Average Total Receipts	9	4412	226	89	1672	2533	13519	17826	17607	52488	167135	157281	754623	•
Operating Costs/Operating Income (%)														
Cost of Operations	10	32.7	33.6	2.0	22.1	53.8	56.4	42.5	22.0	47.6	22.3	0.9	18.9	•
Salaries and Wages	11	18.6	33.4	5.6	23.7	12.1	8.7	13.0	21.1	12.2	31.7	21.4	22.7	•
Taxes Paid	12	3.3	0.7	5.1	2.2	3.0	1.9	2.8	4.1	2.7	3.7	4.7	4.1	•
Interest Paid	13	3.9	0.7	0.2	1.3	2.2	1.4	1.7	3.8	3.1	1.6	10.8	8.2	•
Depreciation	14	5.4	2.0	6.3	1.5	3.4	2.7	4.8	6.7	5.3	3.9	11.4	8.6	•
Amortization and Depletion	15	0.8	•	•	0.0	0.2	0.1	0.1	0.5	0.9	0.4	0.1	2.4	•
Pensions and Other Deferred Comp.	16	0.5	•	0.0	0.4	0.5	0.3	0.9	0.4	0.7	0.8	0.6	0.3	•
Employee Benefits	17	2.1	1.2	0.3	2.4	1.6	1.4	1.7	1.8	2.8	4.1	4.1	1.7	•
Advertising	18	0.3	0.2	0.8	1.3	0.1	0.2	0.2	0.2	0.1	0.1	0.1	0.4	•
Other Expenses	19	31.1	27.1	110.7	37.4	22.3	19.8	28.9	35.8	20.4	32.5	50.7	34.6	•
Officers' Compensation	20	1.8	•	0.2	3.7	2.7	3.4	2.4	1.9	2.0	0.7	1.2	0.3	•
Operating Margin	21	•	1.1	•	4.1	•	3.7	1.1	1.8	2.1	•	•	•	•
Operating Margin Before Officers' Comp.	22	1.2	1.1	•	7.8	0.9	7.0	3.4	3.7	4.1	•	0.3	•	•

Selected Average Balance Sheet ($ in Thousands)

Net Receivables 23	624	0	1	142	190	1122	1839	2177	9387	30677	12372	174413	•
Inventories 24	122	0	1	18	153	268	396	331	4357	6635	2983	3043	•
Net Property, Plant and Equipment 25	2109	0	99	256	1039	3315	6644	18826	32392	51012	182511	458515	•
Total Assets 26	6366	0	123	654	1848	7246	15685	32833	66800	139315	370875	2209683	•
Notes and Loans Payable 27	2673	0	179	522	851	2916	4959	18901	22219	33882	144424	950349	•
All Other Liabilities 28	1156	0	6	143	319	1046	2789	4398	8840	44285	113881	348592	•
Net Worth 29	2537	0	-61	-11	678	3284	7937	9535	35741	61148	112570	910742	•

Selected Financial Ratios (Times to 1)

Current Ratio 30	1.5	•	5.1	1.6	1.6	2.1	1.6	2.6	1.5	1.6	0.7	1.3	•
Quick Ratio 31	1.2	•	2.5	1.4	1.1	1.6	1.2	2.0	1.1	1.2	0.5	1.2	•
Net Sales to Working Capital 32	10.6	•	4.7	16.2	11.1	7.5	10.7	4.0	7.7	8.6	•	13.0	•
Coverage Ratio 33	1.7	•	•	4.5	1.6	4.9	3.0	2.2	2.3	2.8	2.5	1.1	•
Total Asset Turnover 34	0.7	•	0.7	2.5	1.3	1.8	1.1	0.5	0.8	1.1	0.3	0.3	•
Inventory Turnover 35	11.5	•	3.0	20.8	8.7	27.9	18.7	11.4	5.6	5.4	5.4	45.5	•
Receivables Turnover 36	6.7	•	19.4	12.0	8.1	10.6	•	•	5.4	4.9	6.9	5.0	•
Total Liabilities to Net Worth 37	1.5	•	•	•	1.7	1.2	1.0	2.4	0.9	1.3	2.3	1.4	•
Current Assets to Working Capital 38	3.0	•	1.2	2.7	2.8	1.9	2.8	1.6	3.1	2.8	•	4.3	•
Current Liabilities to Working Capital 39	2.0	•	0.2	1.7	1.8	0.9	1.8	0.6	2.1	1.8	•	3.3	•
Working Capital to Net Sales 40	0.1	•	0.2	0.1	0.1	0.1	0.1	0.3	0.1	0.1	•	0.1	•
Inventory to Working Capital 41	0.3	•	0.1	0.1	0.7	0.2	0.2	0.1	0.2	0.5	•	0.1	•
Total Receipts to Cash Flow 42	4.4	•	•	3.7	6.1	7.4	4.7	3.5	5.4	3.9	1.6	4.2	•
Cost of Goods to Cash Flow 43	1.4	•	•	0.8	3.3	4.2	2.0	0.8	2.6	0.9	0.0	0.8	•
Cash Flow to Total Debt 44	0.3	•	•	0.7	0.3	0.4	0.5	0.2	0.3	0.5	0.3	0.1	•

Selected Financial Factors (in Percentages)

Debt Ratio 45	60.2	•	149.7	101.7	63.3	54.7	49.4	71.0	46.5	56.1	69.6	58.8	•
Return on Total Assets 46	4.5	•	•	15.2	4.7	13.0	5.5	4.4	5.5	5.2	9.4	2.9	•
Return on Equity Before Income Taxes 47	4.7	•	45.0	•	5.0	22.9	7.3	8.3	5.8	7.6	18.8	0.5	•
Return on Equity After Income Taxes 48	3.8	•	46.9	•	3.9	20.3	6.3	7.6	4.5	5.3	15.3	0.2	•
Profit Margin (Before Income Tax) 49	2.8	•	•	4.7	1.4	5.7	3.3	4.6	4.0	2.9	16.5	0.6	•
Profit Margin (After Income Tax) 50	2.2	•	•	4.7	1.1	5.0	2.9	4.2	3.1	2.0	13.4	0.2	•

Table II

Corporations with Net Income

WAREHOUSING AND STORAGE

MONEY AMOUNTS AND SIZE OF ASSETS IN THOUSANDS OF DOLLARS

Item Description for Accounting Period 7/08 Through 6/09	Total	Zero Assets	Under 500	500 to 1000	1,000 to 5,000	5,000 to 10,000	10,000 to 25,000	25,000 to 50,000	50,000 to 100,000	100,000 to 250,000	250,000 to 500,000	500,000 to 2,500,000	2,500,000 and over
Number of Enterprises **1**	2359	268	651	368	802	92	123	24	10	12	6	4	0
Revenues ($ in Thousands)													
Net Sales **2**	13960268	81870	50067	1046573	1340210	1668876	2222481	540027	677417	2150278	769973	3412495	0
Interest **3**	34322	0	2	0	2257	2554	2134	1740	4473	7188	10839	3134	0
Rents **4**	25354	0	0	0	1954	1637	165	1964	6244	4325	6951	2114	0
Royalties **5**	29094	0	0	0	720	0	0	0	0	1411	341	26621	0
Other Portfolio Income **6**	25810	0	1	4560	458	1220	9125	1245	1452	4167	631	2951	0
Other Receipts **7**	425395	462	-1	180	34146	26792	57109	13385	3521	91337	154951	43515	0
Total Receipts **8**	14500243	82332	50069	1051313	1379745	1701079	2291014	558361	693107	2258706	943686	3490830	0
Average Total Receipts **9**	6147	307	77	2857	1720	18490	18626	23265	69311	188226	157281	872708	•
Operating Costs/Operating Income (%)													
Cost of Operations **10**	32.3	33.6	0.5	29.5	38.4	59.7	52.9	25.8	48.9	18.0	0.9	18.4	•
Salaries and Wages **11**	19.4	33.4	4.3	20.6	13.0	7.0	9.3	20.4	12.1	35.0	21.4	25.0	•
Taxes Paid **12**	3.3	0.5	7.1	1.5	3.9	1.7	1.9	4.1	2.5	4.0	4.7	4.3	•
Interest Paid **13**	3.8	0.7	0.3	0.7	3.0	1.1	1.3	2.9	1.2	1.5	10.8	8.7	•
Depreciation **14**	5.7	2.0	6.0	1.4	4.0	1.4	3.8	5.8	5.3	3.3	11.4	11.5	•
Amortization and Depletion **15**	0.7	•	•	0.0	0.3	0.0	0.1	0.4	0.1	0.3	0.1	2.5	•
Pensions and Other Deferred Comp. **16**	0.5	•	0.0	0.5	0.8	0.1	0.7	0.4	0.7	0.7	0.6	0.3	•
Employee Benefits **17**	2.4	1.2	0.1	2.3	1.8	1.5	1.3	1.7	3.3	3.9	4.1	2.4	•
Advertising **18**	0.2	0.2	0.1	0.7	0.2	0.0	0.2	0.2	0.1	0.1	0.1	0.4	•
Other Expenses **19**	27.3	27.1	51.0	30.1	26.5	19.6	21.2	32.8	18.2	33.4	50.7	25.9	•
Officers' Compensation **20**	1.8	•	0.8	4.1	3.4	2.9	2.4	2.0	2.2	0.7	1.2	0.4	•
Operating Margin **21**	2.5	1.3	29.8	8.6	4.8	4.9	5.0	3.5	5.5	•	•	0.2	•
Operating Margin Before Officers' Comp. **22**	4.4	1.3	30.6	12.7	8.2	7.8	7.4	5.5	7.7	•	•	0.5	•

Selected Average Balance Sheet ($ in Thousands)

		1	2	3	4	5	6	7	8	9	10	11	
Net Receivables	23	952	0	1	247	156	1457	1727	2901	12065	36088	12372	246238
Inventories	24	158	0	0	30	45	317	580	1503	7296	8305	93	3828
Net Property, Plant and Equipment	25	3274	0	217	240	1175	3435	6003	15408	38345	52753	182511	754093
Total Assets	26	7947	0	252	774	1784	7633	15122	30547	70130	142518	370875	2233705
Notes and Loans Payable	27	3420	0	223	706	869	2971	4581	12143	13004	30335	144424	1119416
All Other Liabilities	28	1646	0	0	301	160	1326	3051	5199	9881	49505	113881	411485
Net Worth	29	2881	0	30	-232	755	3337	7489	13204	47245	62677	112570	702804

Selected Financial Ratios (Times to 1)

Current Ratio	30	1.5	•	47.8	1.3	2.4	1.8	1.4	3.3	1.9	1.6	0.7	1.3
Quick Ratio	31	1.2	•	4.1	1.2	2.0	1.3	1.0	2.5	1.2	1.3	0.5	1.2
Net Sales to Working Capital	32	9.4	•	2.2	22.8	6.0	10.7	12.1	3.5	5.4	7.5	•	9.8
Coverage Ratio	33	2.7	3.7	105.3	13.2	3.6	7.0	7.0	3.4	7.3	3.7	2.5	1.3
Total Asset Turnover	34	0.7	•	0.3	3.7	0.9	2.4	1.2	0.7	1.0	1.3	0.3	0.4
Inventory Turnover	35	12.1	•	•	27.8	14.3	34.1	16.5	3.9	4.5	3.9	12.4	41.0
Receivables Turnover	36	6.7	•	9.5	16.7	7.0	10.3	9.8	5.5	5.6	5.4	20.7	4.4
Total Liabilities to Net Worth	37	1.8	•	7.5	•	1.4	1.3	1.0	1.3	0.5	1.3	2.3	2.2
Current Assets to Working Capital	38	2.9	•	1.0	4.1	1.7	2.2	3.3	1.4	2.1	2.5	•	4.0
Current Liabilities to Working Capital	39	1.9	•	0.0	3.1	0.7	1.2	2.3	0.4	1.1	1.5	•	3.0
Working Capital to Net Sales	40	0.1	•	0.4	0.0	0.2	0.1	0.1	0.3	0.2	0.1	•	0.1
Inventory to Working Capital	41	0.2	•	•	0.1	0.2	0.2	0.4	0.1	0.2	0.5	•	0.1
Total Receipts to Cash Flow	42	4.2	4.6	2.1	3.5	4.1	7.7	4.9	3.4	4.5	3.7	1.6	5.5
Cost of Goods to Cash Flow	43	1.4	1.5	0.0	1.0	1.6	4.6	2.6	0.9	2.2	0.7	0.0	1.0
Cash Flow to Total Debt	44	0.3	•	0.2	0.8	0.4	0.5	0.4	0.7	0.6	0.3	•	0.1

Selected Financial Factors (in Percentages)

Debt Ratio	45	63.7	•	88.2	130.0	57.7	56.3	50.5	56.8	32.6	56.0	69.6	68.5
Return on Total Assets	46	7.6	•	9.2	36.0	10.1	18.9	11.2	7.2	8.6	6.9	9.4	4.3
Return on Equity Before Income Taxes	47	13.2	•	76.9	•	17.2	37.1	19.3	11.8	11.0	11.4	18.8	3.1
Return on Equity After Income Taxes	48	11.5	•	65.0	•	15.8	33.0	17.6	11.0	9.4	8.6	15.3	2.4
Profit Margin (Before Income Tax)	49	6.4	1.9	29.8	9.1	7.8	6.8	8.0	6.9	7.7	4.0	16.5	2.6
Profit Margin (After Income Tax)	50	5.6	1.8	25.2	9.1	7.2	6.1	7.3	6.5	6.6	3.0	13.4	2.0

Table I

Corporations with and without Net Income

NEWSPAPER PUBLISHERS

MONEY AMOUNTS AND SIZE OF ASSETS IN THOUSANDS OF DOLLARS

Item Description for Accounting Period 7/08 Through 6/09		Total	Zero Assets	Under 500	500 to 1,000	1,000 to 5,000	5,000 to 10,000	10,000 to 25,000	25,000 to 50,000	50,000 to 100,000	100,000 to 250,000	250,000 to 500,000	500,000 to 2,500,000	2,500,000 and over
Number of Enterprises	1	5432	300	3905	640	358	41	90	27	27	13	12	11	8
Revenues ($ in Thousands)														
Net Sales	2	41466586	78109	2189274	771711	1717949	262684	1417749	887765	1368154	1989994	3778188	6241355	20763655
Interest	3	180830	83	104	602	314	1919	3952	1549	7185	4566	24785	10870	124900
Rents	4	115811	0	11	0	0	1151	1039	3671	4236	4052	19908	23500	58244
Royalties	5	117767	0	0	0	0	0	0	0	77	21	1300	409	115960
Other Portfolio Income	6	1328950	4802	12900	0	30239	25954	2784	3671	3630	46016	464957	264324	469672
Other Receipts	7	2608274	-5520	41895	79	74011	4758	-7251	10863	40677	16346	30437	71717	2330261
Total Receipts	8	45818218	77474	2244184	772392	1822513	296466	1418273	907519	1423959	2060995	4319575	6612175	23862692
Average Total Receipts	9	8435	258	575	1207	5091	7231	15759	33612	52739	158538	359965	601107	2982836
Operating Costs/Operating Income (%)														
Cost of Operations	10	27.0	11.5	44.1	51.1	24.1	35.1	36.6	19.9	31.0	28.9	15.1	19.7	28.0
Salaries and Wages	11	25.7	11.3	21.7	14.7	35.6	29.0	24.8	29.7	29.3	26.3	26.6	27.8	24.6
Taxes Paid	12	3.5	2.5	2.6	2.3	4.7	2.2	3.9	3.5	3.4	3.2	3.7	3.6	3.5
Interest Paid	13	6.0	3.3	0.8	1.5	2.0	2.7	1.2	2.1	3.2	2.4	4.8	7.7	7.7
Depreciation	14	4.6	1.9	0.5	0.9	2.5	2.6	4.0	3.2	6.0	5.4	6.7	5.0	4.7
Amortization and Depletion	15	4.3	0.1	0.0	2.8	0.3	2.4	0.7	2.7	1.9	3.6	3.7	7.2	5.0
Pensions and Other Deferred Comp.	16	1.2	0.3	0.1	0.1	0.2	0.4	0.8	1.1	1.6	1.1	2.1	2.3	1.0
Employee Benefits	17	3.3	0.6	1.7	4.2	3.2	1.4	3.3	3.6	3.7	4.3	4.0	3.8	3.0
Advertising	18	1.8	0.0	1.3	0.3	0.7	2.4	0.5	1.9	1.4	1.8	1.8	1.1	2.4
Other Expenses	19	26.7	93.6	26.2	28.0	32.2	28.2	22.0	32.3	23.9	28.6	32.1	32.1	23.5
Officers' Compensation	20	2.0	23.5	4.3	3.8	4.0	2.0	3.0	1.9	2.7	2.3	2.1	1.2	1.5
Operating Margin	21	•	•	•	•	•	•	•	0.1	•	•	•	•	•
Operating Margin Before Officers' Comp.	22	•	0.9	•	•	•	•	2.1	•	•	•	•	•	•

Selected Average Balance Sheet ($ in Thousands)

Net Receivables 23	1660	0	47	149	556	663	1724	3753	7428	17158	34474	85796	809158
Inventories 24	118	0	3	6	31	145	259	475	865	2331	3731	9943	45336
Net Property, Plant and Equipment 25	2634	0	22	56	1384	1231	4662	8812	20613	49272	112828	214652	1008637
Total Assets 26	13759	0	111	642	3249	6953	16020	35360	61694	173247	369476	940645	6419192
Notes and Loans Payable 27	6892	0	203	347	1622	2189	3902	12906	34160	84052	195752	625926	2975554
All Other Liabilities 28	4485	0	72	659	701	1387	2714	7621	17815	42283	121759	298314	2141075
Net Worth 29	2382	0	-164	-364	925	3377	9404	14833	9719	46912	51964	16405	1302563

Selected Financial Ratios (Times to 1)

Current Ratio 30	0.9	•	1.7	0.3	1.2	3.0	1.9	1.4	0.9	1.1	1.5	0.5	1.0
Quick Ratio 31	0.7	•	1.6	0.3	0.9	1.9	1.2	1.0	0.7	0.8	1.0	0.4	0.7
Net Sales to Working Capital 32	•	•	17.4	•	39.3	4.8	5.3	14.2	•	47.0	10.5	•	•
Coverage Ratio 33	1.7	•	•	•	2.6	•	0.2	1.1	•	•	3.4	0.3	2.3
Total Asset Turnover 34	0.6	•	5.1	1.9	1.5	0.9	1.0	0.9	0.8	0.9	0.9	0.6	0.4
Inventory Turnover 35	17.5	•	87.0	107.7	37.3	15.5	22.3	13.7	18.2	19.0	12.8	11.2	16.0
Receivables Turnover 36	4.3	•	17.9	7.3	8.2	7.7	8.8	7.1	6.2	9.0	8.2	6.6	2.9
Total Liabilities to Net Worth 37	4.8	•	•	•	2.5	1.1	0.7	1.4	5.3	2.7	6.1	56.3	3.9
Current Assets to Working Capital 38	•	•	2.4	•	7.2	1.5	2.1	3.7	•	14.9	3.2	•	•
Current Liabilities to Working Capital 39	•	•	1.4	•	6.2	0.5	1.1	2.7	•	13.9	2.2	•	•
Working Capital to Net Sales 40	•	•	0.1	•	0.0	0.2	0.2	0.1	•	0.0	0.1	•	•
Inventory to Working Capital 41	•	•	0.1	•	0.3	0.1	0.1	0.2	•	0.7	0.1	•	•
Total Receipts to Cash Flow 42	3.9	2.5	4.9	6.5	4.1	4.9	5.8	3.3	6.2	5.3	3.5	4.8	3.4
Cost of Goods to Cash Flow 43	1.0	0.3	2.2	3.3	1.0	1.7	2.1	0.7	1.9	1.5	0.5	0.9	0.9
Cash Flow to Total Debt 44	0.2	•	0.4	0.2	0.5	0.4	0.4	0.5	0.2	0.2	0.3	0.1	0.1

Selected Financial Factors (in Percentages)

Debt Ratio 45	82.7	•	248.8	156.7	71.5	51.4	41.3	58.1	84.2	72.9	85.9	98.3	79.7
Return on Total Assets 46	5.7	•	•	•	6.5	2.2	0.2	2.2	•	•	14.0	1.2	7.1
Return on Equity Before Income Taxes 47	14.0	•	3.1	31.7	8.3	0.6	•	•	•	•	70.1	•	19.8
Return on Equity After Income Taxes 48	8.3	•	3.2	31.7	3.4	•	•	•	•	•	38.7	•	15.3
Profit Margin (Before Income Tax) 49	4.4	•	•	•	4.4	0.3	•	•	•	•	11.6	•	9.9
Profit Margin (After Income Tax) 50	2.6	•	•	•	1.8	•	•	•	•	•	6.4	•	7.7

Table II

Corporations with Net Income

NEWSPAPER PUBLISHERS

MONEY AMOUNTS AND SIZE OF ASSETS IN THOUSANDS OF DOLLARS

Item Description for Accounting Period 7/08 Through 6/09	Total	Zero Assets	Under 500	500 to 1,000	1,000 to 5,000	5,000 to 10,000	10,000 to 25,000	25,000 to 50,000	50,000 to 100,000	100,000 to 250,000	250,000 to 500,000	500,000 to 2,500,000	2,500,000 and over
Number of Enterprises **1**	2959	10	2458	203	173	30	43	•	8	4	5	•	•
Revenues ($ in Thousands)													
Net Sales **2**	29822183	17146	1214534	456472	564697	164187	786173	•	473490	632543	1629647	•	•
Interest **3**	99803	83	102	0	270	1307	3301	•	541	2890	9681	•	•
Rents **4**	85163	0	11	0	0	1151	0	•	645	3923	3073	•	•
Royalties **5**	116602	0	0	0	0	0	0	•	0	6	227	•	•
Other Portfolio Income **6**	1142420	0	12899	0	30205	25954	1498	•	2387	440	460446	•	•
Other Receipts **7**	2537063	10	41892	0	68261	4623	22542	•	10771	3863	32085	•	•
Total Receipts **8**	33803234	17239	1269438	456472	663433	197222	813514	•	487834	643665	2135159	•	•
Average Total Receipts **9**	11424	1724	516	2249	3835	6574	18919	•	60979	160916	427032	•	•
Operating Costs/Operating Income (%)													
Cost of Operations **10**	27.0	0.4	43.3	63.2	37.2	30.0	42.5	•	21.8	37.7	10.6	•	•
Salaries and Wages **11**	24.8	0.4	20.4	2.8	16.6	26.6	19.4	•	28.2	18.1	29.4	•	•
Taxes Paid **12**	3.5	0.4	2.6	1.4	4.6	2.2	3.7	•	3.5	3.0	3.2	•	•
Interest Paid **13**	6.0	0.1	0.7	0.3	1.8	3.0	0.9	•	1.3	1.2	1.7	•	•
Depreciation **14**	4.4	0.5	0.5	1.1	2.7	2.8	3.5	•	3.9	3.2	4.3	•	•
Amortization and Depletion **15**	4.5	•	0.0	1.4	0.1	2.3	0.2	•	1.1	3.4	4.2	•	•
Pensions and Other Deferred Comp. **16**	1.0	•	0.2	0.0	0.2	0.4	0.3	•	1.9	0.6	1.3	•	•
Employee Benefits **17**	2.9	•	0.9	4.8	1.4	1.4	2.5	•	2.9	2.2	3.6	•	•
Advertising **18**	1.9	0.0	0.2	0.4	1.1	3.8	0.3	•	1.6	1.1	1.5	•	•
Other Expenses **19**	24.2	88.7	21.8	12.9	33.3	17.4	19.8	•	24.1	21.3	31.9	•	•
Officers' Compensation **20**	2.1	0.0	6.2	6.2	8.0	2.6	2.6	•	3.0	3.6	2.7	•	•
Operating Margin **21**	•	9.4	3.3	5.6	•	7.5	4.3	•	6.7	4.6	5.6	•	•
Operating Margin Before Officers' Comp. **22**	•	9.5	9.6	11.7	0.9	10.0	6.9	•	9.7	8.2	8.3	•	•

Selected Average Balance Sheet ($ in Thousands)

Net Receivables 23	1754	0	49	162	402	667	1949	•	7325	16363	38531
Inventories 24	171	0	0	22	8	193	349	•	1529	2876	5039
Net Property, Plant and Equipment 25	3602	0	18	126	1170	1116	4540	•	15787	37958	84246
Total Assets 26	19807	0	120	578	2726	6324	16362	•	66398	191333	390217
Notes and Loans Payable 27	9534	0	16	143	1327	2353	2373	•	14179	73980	117070
All Other Liabilities 28	5487	0	76	9	331	1603	3533	•	27859	42304	81393
Net Worth 29	4786	0	28	426	1068	2368	10455	•	24360	75048	191754

Selected Financial Ratios (Times to 1)

Current Ratio 30	1.0	•	2.5	28.0	1.4	3.2	2.9	•	0.8	1.4	1.6
Quick Ratio 31	0.7	•	2.5	24.8	1.3	1.9	2.1	•	0.6	1.0	1.2
Net Sales to Working Capital 32	72.4	114.9	9.1	9.4	23.3	3.6	3.7	•	•	7.3	12.3
Coverage Ratio 33	2.8	•	13.0	19.8	6.7	10.1	9.7	•	8.1	6.3	22.2
Total Asset Turnover 34	0.5	•	4.1	3.9	1.2	0.9	1.1	•	0.9	0.8	0.8
Inventory Turnover 35	15.9	•	1810.2	65.4	159.0	8.5	22.2	•	8.4	20.7	6.8
Receivables Turnover 36	4.9	•	16.5	•	7.8	5.4	7.4	•	4.1	7.2	5.1
Total Liabilities to Net Worth 37	3.1	•	3.3	0.4	1.6	1.7	0.6	•	1.7	1.5	1.0
Current Assets to Working Capital 38	26.6	•	1.7	1.0	3.8	1.4	1.5	•	•	3.5	2.7
Current Liabilities to Working Capital 39	25.6	•	0.7	0.0	2.8	0.4	0.5	•	•	2.5	1.7
Working Capital to Net Sales 40	0.0	•	0.1	0.1	0.0	0.3	0.3	•	•	0.1	0.1
Inventory to Working Capital 41	1.1	•	0.0	0.1	0.0	0.1	0.0	•	•	0.1	0.2
Total Receipts to Cash Flow 42	3.4	1.0	4.0	6.4	2.7	3.6	4.0	•	3.2	4.0	2.6
Cost of Goods to Cash Flow 43	0.9	0.0	1.7	4.0	1.0	1.1	1.7	•	0.7	1.5	0.3
Cash Flow to Total Debt 44	0.2	•	1.3	2.3	0.7	0.4	0.8	•	0.4	0.3	0.6

Selected Financial Factors (in Percentages)

Debt Ratio 45	75.8	•	76.7	26.3	60.8	62.6	36.1	•	63.3	60.8	50.9
Return on Total Assets 46	8.7	•	34.9	22.9	14.7	26.5	9.5	•	9.8	6.3	32.1
Return on Equity Before Income Taxes 47	23.3	•	138.3	29.5	32.0	63.7	13.3	•	23.4	13.4	62.3
Return on Equity After Income Taxes 48	18.1	•	137.0	29.2	29.2	54.2	12.8	•	21.0	11.5	41.8
Profit Margin (Before Income Tax) 49	11.1	10.0	7.9	5.6	10.5	27.6	7.6	•	9.6	6.4	36.7
Profit Margin (After Income Tax) 50	8.6	6.9	7.8	5.6	9.6	23.4	7.3	•	8.6	5.4	24.6

Table I

Corporations with and without Net Income

PERIODICAL PUBLISHERS

MONEY AMOUNTS AND SIZE OF ASSETS IN THOUSANDS OF DOLLARS

Item Description for Accounting Period 7/08 Through 6/09	Total	Zero Assets	Under 500	500 to 1,000	1,000 to 5,000	5,000 to 10,000	10,000 to 25,000	25,000 to 50,000	50,000 to 100,000	100,000 to 250,000	250,000 to 500,000	500,000 to 2,500,000	2,500,000 and over
Number of Enterprises **1**	6819	1332	4664	335	180	161	61	28	17	12	13	11	3
Revenues ($ in Thousands)													
Net Sales **2**	28137350	513979	1749712	754080	1046167	1896206	1614822	1293131	1263503	1479881	2223159	4748374	9554336
Interest **3**	181428	11521	2408	26	990	4118	765	1983	2551	3773	10142	31551	111601
Rents **4**	74156	469	0	65	0	1590	11	0	1633	5889	2193	12807	49500
Royalties **5**	331824	97403	0	0	0	1730	0	10	613	3453	102439	91203	34972
Other Portfolio Income **6**	862990	4777	2	0	100	1594	1278	17139	2927	5076	24812	162563	642722
Other Receipts **7**	683513	47561	6226	2802	41940	25227	-6214	-655	20078	66174	122821	196090	161461
Total Receipts **8**	30271261	675710	1758348	756973	1089197	1930465	1610662	1311608	1291305	1564246	2485566	5242588	10554592
Average Total Receipts **9**	4439	507	377	2260	6051	11990	26404	46843	75959	130354	191197	476599	3518197
Operating Costs/Operating Income (%)													
Cost of Operations **10**	34.5	45.5	34.7	36.5	61.7	54.8	49.0	48.6	28.4	42.4	31.6	38.6	20.4
Salaries and Wages **11**	21.6	31.4	19.7	7.3	11.1	18.0	15.0	18.0	20.5	19.3	19.6	20.5	27.4
Taxes Paid **12**	2.5	2.8	3.4	2.4	2.4	2.7	1.7	3.7	1.6	2.0	2.6	1.9	2.7
Interest Paid **13**	5.9	0.9	0.7	2.1	2.5	0.6	1.0	1.4	3.2	5.8	5.6	10.9	8.2
Depreciation **14**	2.5	3.7	1.1	1.1	1.2	1.2	2.5	2.3	2.6	2.3	3.6	1.6	3.5
Amortization and Depletion **15**	3.6	1.2	0.2	2.2	0.1	0.4	0.8	1.0	2.3	3.9	5.2	7.5	4.2
Pensions and Other Deferred Comp. **16**	1.3	0.1	0.5	1.2	0.5	1.1	0.5	0.3	0.6	0.6	1.1	0.9	2.4
Employee Benefits **17**	1.9	3.2	2.4	2.0	0.7	1.7	1.9	1.8	2.7	1.6	3.3	2.2	1.5
Advertising **18**	2.1	6.2	2.2	2.2	0.1	1.6	1.3	1.1	2.1	2.9	3.3	3.7	1.2
Other Expenses **19**	38.9	33.2	35.2	37.4	20.8	16.7	23.4	18.2	30.2	29.3	33.2	19.4	65.6
Officers' Compensation **20**	3.2	5.9	17.0	6.0	3.5	2.8	2.6	3.2	1.5	2.0	2.5	2.5	1.5
Operating Margin **21**	•	•	•	•	•	•	0.4	0.4	4.4	•	•	•	•
Operating Margin Before Officers' Comp. **22**	•	5.7	•	5.7	1.4	1.4	2.9	3.6	5.9	•	•	•	•

Selected Average Balance Sheet ($ in Thousands)

Net Receivables 23	615	0	32	226	1315	1395	2999	6717	13693	22223	31723	56318	535038
Inventories 24	96	0	4	27	15	193	1550	1591	2202	4515	2678	22325	55867
Net Property, Plant and Equipment 25	420	0	19	31	203	678	5048	8695	8634	17579	23055	20805	394691
Total Assets 26	7144	0	140	778	2523	6097	16091	35972	68587	146988	325988	886985	9151782
Notes and Loans Payable 27	4277	0	122	592	325	1069	4866	12429	27739	68350	132904	720329	5525880
All Other Liabilities 28	2287	0	53	320	3028	2869	7797	11877	39189	54766	105262	211848	2801531
Net Worth 29	580	0	-35	-133	-830	2159	3428	11666	1659	23872	87823	-45191	824371

Selected Financial Ratios (Times to 1)

Current Ratio 30	1.1	•	1.8	1.0	2.1	1.4	1.5	1.1	0.8	1.0	1.5	0.8	1.0
Quick Ratio 31	0.8	•	1.3	0.9	1.9	1.3	0.8	0.8	0.5	0.8	1.3	0.5	0.6
Net Sales to Working Capital 32	47.4	•	8.5	•	6.0	8.8	10.4	29.5	•	66.9	5.7	•	•
Coverage Ratio 33	•	•	•	1.0	0.8	1.7	1.1	2.2	3.0	•	0.9	1.1	•
Total Asset Turnover 34	0.6	•	2.7	2.9	2.3	1.9	1.6	1.3	1.1	0.8	0.5	0.5	0.3
Inventory Turnover 35	14.8	•	32.2	30.2	231.4	33.4	8.4	14.1	9.6	11.6	20.2	7.5	11.7
Receivables Turnover 36	6.9	•	15.2	6.9	3.1	11.4	8.1	4.9	5.5	6.7	5.2	4.0	11.9
Total Liabilities to Net Worth 37	11.3	•	•	•	•	1.8	3.7	2.1	40.3	5.2	2.7	•	10.1
Current Assets to Working Capital 38	15.4	•	2.3	•	2.0	3.3	3.1	10.3	•	23.5	3.2	•	•
Current Liabilities to Working Capital 39	14.4	•	1.3	•	1.0	2.3	2.1	9.3	•	22.5	2.2	•	•
Working Capital to Net Sales 40	0.0	•	0.1	•	0.2	0.1	0.1	0.0	•	0.0	0.2	•	•
Inventory to Working Capital 41	1.0	•	0.1	•	0.0	0.2	0.6	1.0	•	2.2	0.1	•	•
Total Receipts to Cash Flow 42	8.2	4.1	7.1	3.1	5.8	7.0	4.7	6.0	2.9	6.1	3.9	7.1	•
Cost of Goods to Cash Flow 43	2.8	1.9	2.5	1.1	3.6	3.8	2.3	2.9	0.8	2.6	1.2	2.7	•
Cash Flow to Total Debt 44	0.1	•	0.3	0.8	0.3	0.4	0.4	0.3	0.4	0.2	0.2	0.1	•

Selected Financial Factors (in Percentages)

Debt Ratio 45	91.9	•	125.1	117.1	132.9	64.6	78.7	67.6	97.6	83.8	73.1	105.1	91.0
Return on Total Assets 46	•	•	•	6.3	4.5	1.9	1.9	3.9	10.4	•	2.7	6.0	•
Return on Equity Before Income Taxes 47	•	•	177.7	•	4.0	2.3	0.7	6.7	287.7	•	•	•	•
Return on Equity After Income Taxes 48	•	•	178.0	•	4.0	1.8	•	4.9	249.0	•	•	•	•
Profit Margin (Before Income Tax) 49	•	•	•	0.1	•	0.4	0.1	1.7	6.4	•	•	1.5	•
Profit Margin (After Income Tax) 50	•	•	•	0.1	•	0.3	•	1.2	5.6	•	•	0.0	•

Table II

Corporations with Net Income

PERIODICAL PUBLISHERS

MONEY AMOUNTS AND SIZE OF ASSETS IN THOUSANDS OF DOLLARS

Item Description for Accounting Period 7/08 Through 6/09		Total	Zero Assets	Under 500	500 to 1,000	1,000 to 5,000	5,000 to 10,000	10,000 to 25,000	25,000 to 50,000	50,000 to 100,000	100,000 to 250,000	250,000 to 500,000	500,000 to 2,500,000	2,500,000 and over
Number of Enterprises	1	2738	235	1954	316	122	47	23	14	9	5	6	7	0
Revenues ($ in Thousands)														
Net Sales	2	13791906	164576	599310	692756	835367	569249	668667	679119	854692	777027	1036810	6914332	0
Interest	3	60236	11419	2026	0	92	3224	389	1846	2244	1661	4658	32677	0
Rents	4	9024	0	0	0	0	0	3	0	0	52	2193	6777	0
Royalties	5	191356	96716	0	0	0	1730	0	10	0	0	54707	38194	0
Other Portfolio Income	6	581189	4777	0	0	0	529	720	233	2641	1594	23648	547049	0
Other Receipts	7	349838	37158	0	2803	41617	16149	2420	4093	13885	58390	4787	168532	0
Total Receipts	8	14983549	314646	601336	695559	877076	590881	672199	685301	873462	838724	1126803	7707561	0
Average Total Receipts	9	5472	1339	308	2201	7189	12572	29226	48950	97051	167745	187800	1101080	•
Operating Costs/Operating Income (%)														
Cost of Operations	10	33.7	30.1	25.0	35.6	62.9	32.0	31.4	43.9	17.3	39.9	36.5	31.1	•
Salaries and Wages	11	19.9	38.5	8.1	6.0	7.5	27.0	18.6	11.7	22.3	23.3	19.5	23.0	•
Taxes Paid	12	2.6	3.8	2.1	2.3	2.2	3.2	2.2	4.6	1.9	2.1	2.6	2.6	•
Interest Paid	13	6.3	0.0	0.9	0.8	3.1	0.1	0.9	0.4	1.4	1.0	0.8	11.4	•
Depreciation	14	2.5	8.5	0.5	1.0	1.1	0.6	2.3	1.1	2.0	2.6	1.9	3.2	•
Amortization and Depletion	15	3.0	0.4	0.1	2.1	0.1	0.2	1.5	1.2	1.1	0.2	2.5	5.0	•
Pensions and Other Deferred Comp.	16	1.3	•	0.3	1.3	0.4	2.9	0.4	0.3	0.8	0.9	2.1	1.7	•
Employee Benefits	17	2.2	3.1	0.9	1.9	0.5	2.5	2.5	1.4	3.0	1.7	4.0	2.2	•
Advertising	18	2.0	5.2	1.4	2.3	0.1	1.8	2.6	0.8	3.0	3.4	2.3	1.9	•
Other Expenses	19	23.3	63.6	32.8	36.0	16.7	15.4	27.7	19.5	35.7	21.9	19.8	20.8	•
Officers' Compensation	20	2.9	15.7	11.7	5.7	3.5	4.0	1.8	4.2	1.2	2.7	2.8	1.6	•
Operating Margin	21	0.4	•	15.9	5.1	1.9	10.3	8.1	10.8	10.3	0.3	5.3	•	•
Operating Margin Before Officers' Comp.	22	3.3	•	27.7	10.8	5.3	14.3	9.9	15.0	11.6	3.0	8.1	•	•

Selected Average Balance Sheet ($ in Thousands)

Net Receivables **23**	826	0	39	208	1519	1030	2663	6788	13876	23292	39018	179358
Inventories **24**	133	0	5	10	20	559	1989	1723	3322	8184	3338	23303
Net Property, Plant and Equipment **25**	410	0	17	30	250	684	5590	6015	9514	22514	27859	62610
Total Assets **26**	7755	0	109	782	2252	7273	16618	34410	67651	142251	327128	2287234
Notes and Loans Payable **27**	6505	0	33	226	74	173	5145	4306	17048	18039	24896	2440974
All Other Liabilities **28**	1998	0	38	210	3862	2869	11406	8037	41658	72097	134960	400657
Net Worth **29**	-749	0	37	346	-1684	4232	67	22067	8945	52115	167272	-554397

Selected Financial Ratios (Times to 1)

Current Ratio **30**	1.2	•	2.8	1.4	2.7	1.8	1.4	2.6	0.9	1.0	1.9	1.0
Quick Ratio **31**	0.9	•	2.5	1.3	2.6	1.5	0.7	2.1	0.4	0.8	1.8	0.7
Net Sales to Working Capital **32**	16.0	•	6.8	28.9	5.4	5.5	14.7	4.5	•	132.1	2.4	•
Coverage Ratio **33**	2.4	10743.7	18.9	8.0	3.2	147.3	10.8	27.7	9.7	9.3	17.8	1.6
Total Asset Turnover **34**	0.6	•	2.8	2.8	3.0	1.7	1.7	1.4	1.4	1.1	0.5	0.4
Inventory Turnover **35**	12.7	•	14.1	80.0	218.1	6.9	4.6	12.4	4.9	7.6	18.9	13.2
Receivables Turnover **36**	5.2	•	7.7	13.6	3.1	8.8	6.7	3.4	5.2	5.8	4.0	5.3
Total Liabilities to Net Worth **37**	•	•	1.9	1.3	•	0.7	245.9	0.6	6.6	1.7	1.0	•
Current Assets to Working Capital **38**	5.7	•	1.6	3.4	1.6	2.3	3.6	1.6	•	39.7	2.1	•
Current Liabilities to Working Capital **39**	4.7	•	0.6	2.4	0.6	1.3	2.6	0.6	•	38.7	1.1	•
Working Capital to Net Sales **40**	0.1	•	0.1	0.0	0.2	0.2	0.1	0.2	•	0.0	0.4	•
Inventory to Working Capital **41**	0.3	•	0.1	0.1	0.0	0.3	0.9	0.1	•	4.2	0.1	•
Total Receipts to Cash Flow **42**	4.0	1.3	2.3	2.7	4.8	3.7	2.9	3.5	2.2	3.8	3.4	5.9
Cost of Goods to Cash Flow **43**	1.3	0.4	0.6	1.0	3.0	1.2	0.9	1.5	0.4	1.5	1.2	1.8
Cash Flow to Total Debt **44**	0.1	•	1.9	1.9	0.4	1.1	0.6	1.1	0.7	0.5	0.3	0.1

Selected Financial Factors (in Percentages)

Debt Ratio **45**	109.7	•	65.7	55.8	174.8	41.8	99.6	35.9	86.8	63.4	48.9	124.2
Return on Total Assets **46**	9.9	•	48.6	17.5	30.3	23.5	16.6	17.1	19.2	9.9	7.1	8.0
Return on Equity Before Income Taxes **47**	•	•	134.2	34.7	•	40.1	3727.2	25.7	130.4	24.2	13.1	•
Return on Equity After Income Taxes **48**	•	•	133.5	34.7	•	39.2	3626.1	24.1	116.9	22.9	9.0	•
Profit Margin (Before Income Tax) **49**	8.9	19.6	16.3	5.5	6.9	14.0	8.6	11.7	12.3	8.1	12.7	7.1
Profit Margin (After Income Tax) **50**	7.3	14.6	16.2	5.5	6.9	13.7	8.4	11.0	11.0	7.7	8.7	4.9

Table I

Corporations with and without Net Income

BOOK PUBLISHERS

MONEY AMOUNTS AND SIZE OF ASSETS IN THOUSANDS OF DOLLARS

Item Description for Accounting Period 7/08 Through 6/09	Total	Zero Assets	Under 500	500 to 1,000	1,000 to 5,000	5,000 to 10,000	10,000 to 25,000	25,000 to 50,000	50,000 to 100,000	100,000 to 250,000	250,000 to 500,000	500,000 to 2,500,000	2,500,000 and over
Number of Enterprises **1**	5857	1046	3873	591	208	37	52	18	8	10	0	5	8
Revenues ($ in Thousands)													
Net Sales **2**	36784331	23126	133351	933914	841742	246750	962281	546454	490274	1679827	0	3680608	27246003
Interest **3**	785934	1	456	2817	1542	5	1039	1814	309	16533	0	15796	745622
Rents **4**	74929	168	0	0	94	0	0	652	1106	0	0	5384	67525
Royalties **5**	927662	17	0	0	1722	0	3424	889	8759	3104	0	38513	871234
Other Portfolio Income **6**	1029923	0	0	0	28452	0	17435	3588	207	35265	0	19694	925282
Other Receipts **7**	984287	95	11	10673	1523	3949	-22239	11102	3136	111973	0	198569	665495
Total Receipts **8**	40587066	23407	133818	947404	875075	250704	961940	564499	503791	1846702	0	3958564	30521161
Average Total Receipts **9**	6930	22	35	1603	4207	6776	18499	31361	62974	184670	•	791713	3815145
Operating Costs/Operating Income (%)													
Cost of Operations **10**	35.1	45.8	10.7	48.9	34.8	50.7	38.8	46.2	44.9	35.3	•	46.1	32.5
Salaries and Wages **11**	20.3	18.3	41.6	9.1	8.7	14.8	18.1	18.8	17.3	19.8	•	21.3	21.0
Taxes Paid **12**	2.3	1.7	3.4	1.4	1.2	1.3	2.2	1.8	1.7	2.1	•	2.3	2.4
Interest Paid **13**	9.7	1.4	0.3	3.3	0.4	1.2	3.1	1.9	2.1	5.3	•	5.4	11.6
Depreciation **14**	4.5	1.7	1.2	0.6	0.4	0.2	1.9	1.5	1.2	1.8	•	3.5	5.3
Amortization and Depletion **15**	3.9	0.1	0.9	0.0	0.1	•	0.4	2.2	1.8	4.1	•	3.7	4.5
Pensions and Other Deferred Comp. **16**	1.1	•	•	4.8	1.8	0.3	0.5	0.4	0.5	0.7	•	1.4	1.0
Employee Benefits **17**	2.2	9.4	•	0.4	0.9	1.4	3.0	4.4	2.0	1.7	•	2.9	2.2
Advertising **18**	1.8	5.4	10.1	0.3	1.6	2.5	3.3	4.7	4.6	3.3	•	2.8	1.4
Other Expenses **19**	25.1	30.7	20.3	18.6	29.3	26.9	21.2	23.0	21.3	33.3	•	16.7	26.1
Officers' Compensation **20**	1.5	2.1	7.8	14.4	7.3	1.7	2.8	4.9	2.1	2.5	•	0.8	0.8
Operating Margin **21**	•	•	3.7	•	13.6	•	4.9	•	0.5	•	•	•	•
Operating Margin Before Officers' Comp. **22**	•	•	11.5	12.5	20.8	0.7	7.8	2.6	•	•	•	•	•

Selected Average Balance Sheet ($ in Thousands)

Net Receivables 23	1067	0	2	122	535	1141	2620	5231	11580	33854	•	158788	570119
Inventories 24	610	0	20	185	579	1668	2859	9965	14450	17569	•	69424	275204
Net Property, Plant and Equipment 25	645	0	9	200	47	209	1938	2588	5833	12699	•	83234	358744
Total Assets 26	12596	0	55	663	2572	6318	15169	34605	63955	207099	•	1379600	7688164
Notes and Loans Payable 27	5214	0	35	1003	537	1673	3293	4615	55234	104490	•	601106	311207
All Other Liabilities 28	5423	0	10	317	803	1823	7298	17009	22108	67735	•	491239	3413238
Net Worth 29	1958	0	10	-657	1232	2823	4577	12980	-13386	34874	•	287256	1163719

Selected Financial Ratios (Times to 1)

Current Ratio 30	0.9	•	1.5	1.0	2.5	1.6	1.8	2.2	1.6	1.5	•	0.9	0.9
Quick Ratio 31	0.4	•	0.6	0.5	1.6	0.7	1.0	0.8	0.6	0.8	•	0.5	0.4
Net Sales to Working Capital 32	•	•	2.9	188.2	3.0	4.1	4.7	2.4	4.5	5.6	•	•	•
Coverage Ratio 33	1.3	•	14.7	0.9	48.0	1.5	2.5	•	2.6	1.0	•	1.1	1.3
Total Asset Turnover 34	0.5	•	0.6	2.4	1.6	1.1	1.2	0.9	1.0	0.8	•	0.5	0.4
Inventory Turnover 35	3.6	•	0.2	4.2	2.4	2.0	2.5	1.4	1.9	3.4	•	4.9	4.0
Receivables Turnover 36	6.1	•	16.9	15.8	7.3	4.1	8.8	5.1	4.8	6.7	•	4.4	6.4
Total Liabilities to Net Worth 37	5.4	•	4.7	•	1.1	1.2	2.3	1.7	•	4.9	•	3.8	5.6
Current Assets to Working Capital 38	•	•	2.9	43.6	1.7	2.6	2.2	1.8	2.8	2.8	•	•	•
Current Liabilities to Working Capital 39	•	•	1.9	42.6	0.7	1.6	1.2	0.8	1.8	1.8	•	•	•
Working Capital to Net Sales 40	•	•	0.4	0.0	0.3	0.2	0.2	0.4	0.2	0.2	•	•	•
Inventory to Working Capital 41	•	•	1.7	23.0	0.5	1.0	0.7	0.6	1.0	0.7	•	•	•
Total Receipts to Cash Flow 42	4.8	10.5	4.3	9.0	2.4	4.0	4.7	7.8	4.6	3.4	•	7.8	4.7
Cost of Goods to Cash Flow 43	1.7	4.8	0.5	4.4	0.8	2.0	1.8	3.6	2.1	1.2	•	3.6	1.5
Cash Flow to Total Debt 44	0.1	•	0.2	0.1	1.2	0.5	0.4	0.2	0.2	0.3	•	0.1	0.1

Selected Financial Factors (in Percentages)

Debt Ratio 45	84.5	•	82.6	199.1	52.1	55.3	69.8	62.5	120.9	83.2	•	79.2	84.9
Return on Total Assets 46	6.3	•	2.7	6.8	28.2	2.0	9.5	•	5.1	4.4	•	3.3	6.7
Return on Equity Before Income Taxes 47	9.8	•	14.5	1.2	57.6	1.6	19.0	•	•	0.3	•	1.8	10.0
Return on Equity After Income Taxes 48	5.1	•	14.5	1.2	57.5	1.3	15.8	•	•	•	•	•	4.9
Profit Margin (Before Income Tax) 49	3.1	•	4.1	•	17.5	0.7	4.7	•	3.3	0.1	•	0.7	3.4
Profit Margin (After Income Tax) 50	1.6	•	4.1	•	17.5	0.5	3.9	•	2.4	•	•	•	1.7

Table II

Corporations with Net Income

BOOK PUBLISHERS

MONEY AMOUNTS AND SIZE OF ASSETS IN THOUSANDS OF DOLLARS

Item Description for Accounting Period 7/08 Through 6/09	Total	Zero Assets	Under 500	500 to 1,000	1,000 to 5,000	5,000 to 10,000	10,000 to 25,000	25,000 to 50,000	50,000 to 100,000	100,000 to 250,000	250,000 to 500,000	500,000 to 2,500,000	2,500,000 and over
Number of Enterprises 1	1599	263	818	263	175	16	38	•	•	5	•	0	5

Revenues ($ in Thousands)

Item Description for Accounting Period 7/08 Through 6/09	Total	Zero Assets	Under 500	500 to 1,000	1,000 to 5,000	5,000 to 10,000	10,000 to 25,000	25,000 to 50,000	50,000 to 100,000	100,000 to 250,000	250,000 to 500,000	500,000 to 2,500,000	2,500,000 and over
Net Sales 2	28793370	5482	98514	741715	834868	102973	770696	•	•	614379	•	0	22863035
Interest 3	427420	0	456	0	1542	0	530	•	•	12641	•	0	397906
Rents 4	67367	0	0	0	94	0	0	•	•	0	•	0	66167
Royalties 5	752106	0	0	0	1722	0	3424	•	•	0	•	0	711194
Other Portfolio Income 6	999724	0	0	0	28424	0	17435	•	•	27596	•	0	925151
Other Receipts 7	730921	0	11	9569	1347	5	3596	•	•	42941	•	0	476604
Total Receipts 8	31770908	5482	98981	751284	867997	102978	795681	•	•	697557	•	0	25440057
Average Total Receipts 9	19869	21	121	2857	4960	6436	20939	•	•	139511	•	•	5088011

Operating Costs/Operating Income (%)

Item Description for Accounting Period 7/08 Through 6/09	Total	Zero Assets	Under 500	500 to 1,000	1,000 to 5,000	5,000 to 10,000	10,000 to 25,000	25,000 to 50,000	50,000 to 100,000	100,000 to 250,000	250,000 to 500,000	500,000 to 2,500,000	2,500,000 and over
Cost of Operations 10	31.6	•	2.3	50.7	34.5	33.2	36.4	•	•	48.2	•	•	29.6
Salaries and Wages 11	21.6	26.3	42.3	6.5	8.8	18.7	20.1	•	•	16.3	•	•	22.9
Taxes Paid 12	2.3	0.1	2.4	1.2	1.2	1.7	2.7	•	•	1.8	•	•	2.4
Interest Paid 13	8.3	•	•	0.2	0.4	0.7	0.8	•	•	6.9	•	•	9.8
Depreciation 14	4.4	0.1	•	0.7	0.3	0.3	2.2	•	•	1.2	•	•	5.1
Amortization and Depletion 15	4.2	•	•	0.0	0.1	•	0.2	•	•	7.1	•	•	4.7
Pensions and Other Deferred Comp. 16	1.2	•	•	6.0	1.8	0.5	0.5	•	•	0.7	•	•	1.1
Employee Benefits 17	2.3	26.6	•	0.2	0.9	0.5	3.0	•	•	2.1	•	•	2.3
Advertising 18	1.5	5.2	7.2	0.2	1.6	1.4	3.3	•	•	3.5	•	•	1.1
Other Expenses 19	23.4	27.3	11.0	16.1	29.5	20.5	20.8	•	•	16.7	•	•	23.8
Officers' Compensation 20	1.5	•	9.2	14.1	7.3	2.0	3.1	•	•	3.1	•	•	0.6
Operating Margin 21	•	14.6	25.6	3.8	13.7	20.6	6.8	•	•	•	•	•	•
Operating Margin Before Officers' Comp. 22	•	14.6	34.8	18.0	21.0	22.6	10.0	•	•	•	•	•	•

Selected Average Balance Sheet ($ in Thousands)

Net Receivables 23	3150	0	0	154	629	1614	2207	•	23102	•	794613
Inventories 24	1602	0	41	1	687	1814	2928	•	22035	•	369994
Net Property, Plant and Equipment 25	1770	0	0	449	49	435	2553	•	5581	•	479495
Total Assets 26	30160	0	58	613	2845	5226	16153	•	165307	•	8325138
Notes and Loans Payable 27	8801	0	0	0	630	766	2392	•	71515	•	235149
All Other Liabilities 28	16701	0	0	386	934	1191	3162	•	56731	•	4878236
Net Worth 29	4657	0	58	227	1281	3270	10599	•	37061	•	1095753

Selected Financial Ratios (Times to 1)

Current Ratio 30	0.9	•	492.6	0.4	2.5	2.9	2.7	•	2.3	•	0.8
Quick Ratio 31	0.5	•	492.6	0.4	1.6	1.6	1.6	•	1.2	•	0.5
Net Sales to Working Capital 32	•	•	5.6	•	3.1	2.0	3.7	•	2.9	•	1.8
Coverage Ratio 33	2.0	•	•	22.6	49.3	31.3	12.9	•	1.9	•	•
Total Asset Turnover 34	0.6	•	2.1	4.6	1.7	1.2	1.3	•	0.7	•	0.5
Inventory Turnover 35	3.6	•	0.1	1529.0	2.4	1.2	2.5	•	2.7	•	3.7
Receivables Turnover 36	5.9	•	22.9	36.4	7.3	2.1	10.8	•	2.3	•	•
Total Liabilities to Net Worth 37	5.5	•	0.0	1.7	1.2	0.6	0.5	•	3.5	•	6.6
Current Assets to Working Capital 38	•	•	1.0	•	1.7	1.5	1.6	•	1.8	•	•
Current Liabilities to Working Capital 39	•	•	0.0	•	0.7	0.5	0.6	•	0.8	•	•
Working Capital to Net Sales 40	•	•	0.2	•	0.3	0.5	0.3	•	0.3	•	•
Inventory to Working Capital 41	•	•	•	•	0.5	0.6	0.4	•	0.4	•	•
Total Receipts to Cash Flow 42	4.0	2.9	2.8	7.7	2.4	2.5	3.9	•	5.1	•	4.1
Cost of Goods to Cash Flow 43	1.3	•	0.1	3.9	0.8	0.8	1.4	•	2.5	•	1.2
Cash Flow to Total Debt 44	0.2	•	989.6	1.0	1.3	1.3	0.9	•	0.2	•	0.2

Selected Financial Factors (in Percentages)

Debt Ratio 45	84.6	•	0.1	63.0	55.0	37.4	34.4	•	77.6	•	86.8
Return on Total Assets 46	9.9	•	54.5	24.7	30.3	26.2	13.4	•	9.5	•	9.8
Return on Equity Before Income Taxes 47	31.9	•	54.6	63.7	65.9	40.5	18.8	•	19.7	•	33.5
Return on Equity After Income Taxes 48	24.6	•	54.5	63.7	65.8	39.9	16.9	•	16.5	•	24.9
Profit Margin (Before Income Tax) 49	8.3	14.6	26.1	5.1	17.7	20.6	9.8	•	5.9	•	8.0
Profit Margin (After Income Tax) 50	6.4	12.4	26.1	5.1	17.7	20.3	8.8	•	5.0	•	6.0

Table I

Corporations with and without Net Income

DATABASE, DIRECTORY, AND OTHER PUBLISHERS

MONEY AMOUNTS AND SIZE OF ASSETS IN THOUSANDS OF DOLLARS

Item Description for Accounting Period 7/08 Through 6/09		Total	Zero Assets	Under 500	500 to 1,000	1,000 to 5,000	5,000 to 10,000	10,000 to 25,000	25,000 to 50,000	50,000 to 100,000	100,000 to 250,000	250,000 to 500,000	500,000 to 2,500,000	2,500,000 and over
Number of Enterprises	1	4319	567	3078	321	199	69	42	10	9	10	3	6	4
Revenues ($ in Thousands)														
Net Sales	2	22981099	375316	1249494	700079	1631744	516327	842853	369627	684566	1019077	339117	6036230	9216669
Interest	3	400782	468	120	809	4705	292	2189	376	2036	3300	521	20572	365396
Rents	4	51177	0	0	0	52	254	0	146	704	0	99	1432	48490
Royalties	5	105352	0	0	0	1416	0	0	3049	7	3409	893	38905	57674
Other Portfolio Income	6	611299	17116	20353	0	101	6162	28729	2471	2797	7780	6	63457	462325
Other Receipts	7	587955	-13475	459	88055	-5357	273	4528	4350	24223	23402	29463	284897	147135
Total Receipts	8	24737664	379425	1270426	788943	1632661	523308	878299	380019	714333	1056968	370099	6445493	10297689
Average Total Receipts	9	5728	669	413	2458	8204	7584	20912	38002	79370	105697	123366	1074249	2574422
Operating Costs/Operating Income (%)														
Cost of Operations	10	30.8	62.2	64.0	42.9	31.4	13.9	53.2	24.6	37.1	23.5	49.4	22.4	28.3
Salaries and Wages	11	18.8	30.6	16.3	35.9	19.1	43.6	16.7	17.9	20.9	20.9	16.2	24.1	12.4
Taxes Paid	12	3.2	1.3	1.5	3.8	2.1	4.8	1.7	2.8	2.5	2.5	1.3	2.9	4.3
Interest Paid	13	11.9	9.7	0.1	0.6	0.3	1.5	2.3	0.5	2.7	7.5	7.4	14.3	18.2
Depreciation	14	2.3	1.0	0.0	1.4	2.0	0.5	1.8	1.3	2.7	3.3	2.2	3.1	2.4
Amortization and Depletion	15	5.7	27.0	0.0	0.0	0.3	0.6	0.9	0.3	1.4	5.0	6.1	3.1	10.0
Pensions and Other Deferred Comp.	16	0.4	0.1	•	0.3	0.4	0.6	0.2	0.1	1.3	0.1	0.1	0.7	0.3
Employee Benefits	17	1.9	1.4	•	0.5	0.8	3.2	1.1	2.2	2.0	3.0	1.6	3.9	1.1
Advertising	18	2.8	1.0	1.1	0.0	2.0	3.9	3.2	4.8	3.7	2.7	2.3	3.3	3.0
Other Expenses	19	24.2	19.1	16.3	23.6	15.7	19.7	15.3	22.5	19.3	38.6	19.1	21.4	29.0
Officers' Compensation	20	3.2	0.8	0.2	10.4	26.2	7.3	2.8	8.3	1.4	2.3	0.9	0.8	0.7
Operating Margin	21	•	•	0.5	•	•	0.4	0.9	14.6	5.1	•	•	0.0	•
Operating Margin Before Officers' Comp.	22	•	•	0.7	•	26.0	7.7	3.7	22.9	6.5	•	•	0.8	0.8

Selected Average Balance Sheet ($ in Thousands)

Net Receivables 23	1159	0	9	273	1230	3890	3220	5873	13263	22442	29739	286407	507754
Inventories 24	306	0	33	0	19	127	651	234	486	2872	8701	32208	230881
Net Property, Plant and Equipment 25	437	0	1	41	330	51	1303	2554	10822	12919	3696	100006	220604
Total Assets 26	9709	0	65	632	2408	6944	15498	37395	76132	153584	330422	1408737	6970722
Notes and Loans Payable 27	7543	0	106	218	359	863	4398	2291	16467	101900	108363	2232982	4237700
All Other Liabilities 28	2742	0	25	756	894	5470	6527	14473	29176	42618	117074	437952	1720187
Net Worth 29	-576	0	-66	-342	1155	611	4572	20632	30489	9066	104984	-1262197	1012834

Selected Financial Ratios (Times to 1)

Current Ratio 30	0.9	•	2.4	0.6	1.7	1.1	1.4	3.3	1.8	0.7	1.1	1.1	0.8
Quick Ratio 31	0.5	•	0.5	0.4	1.3	1.0	1.1	3.0	1.5	0.4	0.6	0.8	0.3
Net Sales to Working Capital 32	•	•	11.1	•	10.4	15.8	8.9	2.0	5.5	•	23.6	35.3	•
Coverage Ratio 33	1.2	•	25.7	•	0.5	2.2	3.3	35.8	4.5	0.4	1.3	1.5	1.2
Total Asset Turnover 34	0.5	•	6.2	3.4	3.4	1.1	1.3	1.0	1.0	0.7	0.3	0.7	0.3
Inventory Turnover 35	5.4	•	7.8	•	137.4	8.2	16.4	38.8	58.1	8.3	6.4	7.0	2.8
Receivables Turnover 36	4.4	•	42.4	7.7	7.6	1.8	6.3	4.7	7.5	4.1	3.8	3.4	4.2
Total Liabilities to Net Worth 37	•	•	•	•	1.1	10.4	2.4	0.8	1.5	15.9	2.1	•	5.9
Current Assets to Working Capital 38	•	•	1.7	•	2.5	10.2	3.3	1.4	2.3	•	14.6	18.4	•
Current Liabilities to Working Capital 39	•	•	0.7	•	1.5	9.2	2.3	0.4	1.3	•	13.6	17.4	•
Working Capital to Net Sales 40	•	•	0.1	•	0.1	0.1	0.1	0.5	0.2	•	0.0	0.0	•
Inventory to Working Capital 41	•	•	1.2	•	0.0	0.1	0.3	0.0	0.0	•	1.8	1.1	•
Total Receipts to Cash Flow 42	5.1	•	6.7	10.5	8.5	6.6	7.0	2.8	3.8	3.5	5.3	4.0	5.1
Cost of Goods to Cash Flow 43	1.6	•	4.3	4.5	2.7	0.9	3.7	0.7	1.4	0.8	2.6	0.9	1.4
Cash Flow to Total Debt 44	0.1	•	0.5	0.2	0.8	0.2	0.3	0.8	0.4	0.2	0.1	0.1	0.1

Selected Financial Factors (in Percentages)

Debt Ratio 45	105.9	•	202.1	154.1	52.0	91.2	70.5	44.8	60.0	94.1	68.2	189.6	85.5
Return on Total Assets 46	8.1	•	13.9	•	0.5	3.5	9.5	17.8	11.9	1.8	3.4	15.3	7.2
Return on Equity Before Income Taxes 47	•	•	•	•	•	43.7	22.0	22.4	31.4	23.1	2.6	•	7.9
Return on Equity After Income Taxes 48	•	•	•	•	•	43.7	9.5	18.1	31.2	17.9	2.5	•	3.6
Profit Margin (Before Income Tax) 49	2.9	•	2.1	•	1.8	5.1	17.5	9.3	•	2.4	7.1	•	3.5
Profit Margin (After Income Tax) 50	1.1	•	1.7	•	0.8	4.1	17.4	7.2	•	2.3	3.7	•	1.6

Table II

Corporations with Net Income

DATABASE, DIRECTORY, AND OTHER PUBLISHERS

MONEY AMOUNTS AND SIZE OF ASSETS IN THOUSANDS OF DOLLARS

Item Description for Accounting Period 7/08 Through 6/09	Total	Zero Assets	Under 500	500 to 1,000	1,000 to 5,000	5,000 to 10,000	10,000 to 25,000	25,000 to 50,000	50,000 to 100,000	100,000 to 250,000	250,000 to 500,000	500,000 to 2,500,000	2,500,000 and over
Number of Enterprises **1**	2128	5	1878	0	162	43	14	10	5	3	0	•	•
Revenues ($ in Thousands)													
Net Sales **2**	16851022	22418	1201065	0	1282892	410669	194735	369627	527337	420908	0	•	•
Interest **3**	293080	0	106	0	377	165	2148	376	1028	1808	0	•	•
Rents **4**	49305	0	0	0	52	0	0	146	0	0	0	•	•
Royalties **5**	102650	0	0	0	1416	0	0	3049	0	1606	0	•	•
Other Portfolio Income **6**	594707	15035	20353	0	29	0	28584	2471	1160	1306	0	•	•
Other Receipts **7**	435882	1	451	0	2286	273	3359	4350	16557	31228	0	•	•
Total Receipts **8**	18326646	37454	1221975	0	1287052	411107	228826	380019	546082	456856	0	•	•
Average Total Receipts **9**	8612	7491	651	•	7945	9561	16345	38002	109216	152285	•	•	•
Operating Costs/Operating Income (%)													
Cost of Operations **10**	32.8	75.2	65.9	•	34.8	1.5	25.6	24.6	39.7	45.1	•	•	•
Salaries and Wages **11**	19.3	0.1	13.7	•	18.7	51.7	28.1	17.9	19.9	15.5	•	•	•
Taxes Paid **12**	3.7	4.7	1.3	•	1.7	5.7	2.2	2.8	2.4	1.5	•	•	•
Interest Paid **13**	9.1	1.5	•	•	0.1	0.6	2.1	0.5	0.7	1.8	•	•	•
Depreciation **14**	2.3	1.2	0.0	•	1.9	0.3	1.5	1.3	2.5	1.7	•	•	•
Amortization and Depletion **15**	2.1	•	0.0	•	0.1	0.0	0.5	0.3	0.3	1.7	•	•	•
Pensions and Other Deferred Comp. **16**	0.5	0.2	•	•	0.2	0.8	0.4	0.1	0.8	0.1	•	•	•
Employee Benefits **17**	2.0	2.0	•	•	0.1	3.5	1.6	2.2	1.7	2.4	•	•	•
Advertising **18**	3.2	0.0	1.1	•	1.7	4.9	1.3	4.8	4.4	3.8	•	•	•
Other Expenses **19**	21.5	11.4	12.6	•	8.1	18.8	15.1	22.5	14.9	15.3	•	•	•
Officers' Compensation **20**	3.1	5.5	0.3	•	26.7	7.3	3.5	8.3	1.3	3.8	•	•	•
Operating Margin **21**	0.4	•	5.1	•	6.0	4.9	18.0	14.6	11.6	7.4	•	•	•
Operating Margin Before Officers' Comp. **22**	3.6	3.6	5.3	•	32.7	12.2	21.6	22.9	12.8	11.1	•	•	•

Selected Average Balance Sheet ($ in Thousands)

Net Receivables 23	1687	0	15	•	1320	5984	4327	5873	•	19417	34373
Inventories 24	592	0	53	•	15	0	312	234	•	264	13548
Net Property, Plant and Equipment 25	643	0	0	•	316	14	815	2554	•	11913	13673
Total Assets 26	10883	0	102	•	2405	6649	13330	37395	•	72728	171596
Notes and Loans Payable 27	8460	0	13	•	30	305	4053	2291	•	7776	22818
All Other Liabilities 28	3163	0	39	•	878	5663	6381	14473	•	31183	69664
Net Worth 29	-740	0	50	•	1497	681	2896	20632	•	33769	79114

Selected Financial Ratios (Times to 1)

Current Ratio 30	1.0	•	2.6	•	2.3	1.1	1.4	3.3	•	1.9	5.8
Quick Ratio 31	0.6	•	0.5	•	1.8	1.1	1.2	3.0	•	1.8	2.2
Net Sales to Working Capital 32	44.8	•	10.2	•	6.9	12.3	5.6	2.0	•	4.8	1.8
Coverage Ratio 33	2.1	43.9	•	•	93.1	10.0	17.9	35.8	•	22.5	10.0
Total Asset Turnover 34	0.7	•	6.3	•	3.3	1.4	1.0	1.0	•	1.5	0.8
Inventory Turnover 35	4.4	•	7.9	•	182.0	•	11.4	38.8	•	158.9	4.7
Receivables Turnover 36	4.5	•	47.9	•	6.5	1.6	2.8	4.7	•	9.2	2.7
Total Liabilities to Net Worth 37	•	•	1.1	•	0.6	8.8	3.6	0.8	•	1.2	1.2
Current Assets to Working Capital 38	22.8	•	1.6	•	1.8	8.3	3.3	1.4	•	2.1	1.2
Current Liabilities to Working Capital 39	21.8	•	0.6	•	0.8	7.3	2.3	0.4	•	1.1	0.2
Working Capital to Net Sales 40	0.0	•	0.1	•	0.1	0.1	0.2	0.5	•	0.2	0.5
Inventory to Working Capital 41	3.2	•	1.1	•	0.0	•	0.2	0.0	•	0.0	0.1
Total Receipts to Cash Flow 42	4.4	1.4	6.2	•	7.6	5.2	3.0	2.8	•	3.6	3.4
Cost of Goods to Cash Flow 43	1.5	1.0	4.1	•	2.7	0.1	0.8	0.7	•	1.4	1.5
Cash Flow to Total Debt 44	0.2	•	2.0	•	1.1	0.3	0.4	0.8	•	0.8	0.4

Selected Financial Factors (in Percentages)

Debt Ratio 45	106.8	•	51.4	•	37.7	89.8	78.3	44.8	•	53.6	53.9
Return on Total Assets 46	13.9	•	42.8	•	21.0	8.1	39.2	17.8	•	22.6	14.4
Return on Equity Before Income Taxes 47	•	•	88.1	•	33.4	70.9	170.6	31.4	•	46.5	28.1
Return on Equity After Income Taxes 48	•	•	82.1	•	32.4	52.8	150.3	31.2	•	38.0	26.6
Profit Margin (Before Income Tax) 49	10.0	65.1	6.8	•	6.3	5.1	35.5	17.5	•	14.9	15.9
Profit Margin (After Income Tax) 50	7.5	65.1	6.4	•	6.1	3.8	31.3	17.4	•	12.2	15.0

Table I

Corporations with and without Net Income

SOFTWARE PUBLISHERS

MONEY AMOUNTS AND SIZE OF ASSETS IN THOUSANDS OF DOLLARS

Item Description for Accounting Period 7/08 Through 6/09	Total	Zero Assets	Under 500	500 to 1,000	1,000 to 5,000	5,000 to 10,000	10,000 to 25,000	25,000 to 50,000	50,000 to 100,000	100,000 to 250,000	250,000 to 500,000	500,000 to 2,500,000	2,500,000 and over
Number of Enterprises **1**	8988	1672	5316	372	1015	198	167	69	46	52	20	46	15
Revenues ($ in Thousands)													
Net Sales **2**	114665363	1398568	1391782	690615	3040481	1529395	3354729	1648026	2717200	5234738	3921941	21336340	68401548
Interest **3**	2077598	2598	1506	2212	10641	7853	17143	22271	24961	70836	40032	252657	1624889
Rents **4**	183893	0	0	0	4	531	416	387	154	1436	8607	20094	152262
Royalties **5**	8323547	5650	0	0	4268	0	50157	25533	48846	95355	110995	1902606	6080137
Other Portfolio Income **6**	1857934	3358	130	61675	22597	299	8527	11818	4981	17207	20553	492214	1214574
Other Receipts **7**	24465399	81783	803	149137	131219	40385	26944	52213	144150	36148	13395	475847	23313378
Total Receipts **8**	151573734	1491957	1394221	903639	3209210	1578463	3457916	1760248	2940292	5455720	4115523	24479758	100786788
Average Total Receipts **9**	16864	892	262	2429	3162	7972	20706	25511	63919	104918	205776	532169	6719119
Operating Costs/Operating Income (%)													
Cost of Operations **10**	30.3	54.2	2.2	3.5	28.6	20.3	30.1	20.6	34.9	22.5	14.4	30.3	32.5
Salaries and Wages **11**	35.0	10.8	43.0	73.8	39.1	49.1	37.3	38.9	29.7	33.0	33.0	33.8	35.1
Taxes Paid **12**	3.6	3.8	4.9	7.0	4.2	4.4	3.5	6.7	3.4	3.1	3.5	2.7	3.7
Interest Paid **13**	5.2	1.4	0.9	1.7	2.5	2.8	1.0	1.8	2.1	2.9	2.5	4.0	6.7
Depreciation **14**	3.4	0.7	1.3	3.1	2.3	2.8	2.8	3.0	2.0	2.5	3.1	3.1	3.8
Amortization and Depletion **15**	2.0	0.5	0.7	0.8	1.7	2.1	1.1	1.1	2.5	3.2	3.1	2.6	1.8
Pensions and Other Deferred Comp. **16**	0.4	0.0	1.5	0.7	1.0	0.2	0.8	0.5	0.5	0.3	0.6	0.6	0.3
Employee Benefits **17**	3.6	1.0	3.1	3.5	3.4	4.4	3.8	2.5	2.9	3.0	3.6	3.6	3.7
Advertising **18**	5.2	1.0	1.5	0.9	2.1	3.3	2.6	3.6	1.3	3.4	2.7	2.8	6.9
Other Expenses **19**	29.5	28.9	43.0	27.6	37.0	33.2	27.7	30.0	23.3	29.9	31.9	23.8	30.7
Officers' Compensation **20**	1.8	1.4	15.6	11.2	8.2	5.4	3.5	3.4	2.1	2.2	2.1	1.3	1.0
Operating Margin **21**	•	•	•	•	•	•	•	•	•	•	•	•	•
Operating Margin Before Officers' Comp. **22**	•	•	•	•	•	•	•	•	•	•	1.5	•	•

Selected Average Balance Sheet ($ in Thousands)

Net Receivables 23	2795	0	7	58	488	1439	3837	6653	12445	28547	52118	121604	966023
Inventories 24	232	0	3	2	52	90	391	171	767	809	1588	18574	63422
Net Property, Plant and Equipment 25	1648	0	8	49	252	563	1543	2817	3011	6730	22055	56593	693086
Total Assets 26	28120	0	69	609	2206	7147	16623	34654	68215	161443	376503	1068006	11675997
Notes and Loans Payable 27	4638	0	165	479	1494	1611	4393	8128	11758	32183	65254	238210	1534808
All Other Liabilities 28	13557	0	108	317	1597	4880	11259	19304	31079	54394	112054	346354	6194973
Net Worth 29	9926	0	-204	-187	-885	656	971	7223	25378	74866	199194	483442	3946216

Selected Financial Ratios (Times to 1)

Current Ratio 30	0.7	•	0.2	1.0	0.9	1.2	1.1	1.4	1.3	1.4	1.5	1.2	0.5
Quick Ratio 31	0.5	•	0.2	0.8	0.7	0.9	0.9	1.1	1.0	1.0	1.1	1.0	0.4
Net Sales to Working Capital 32	•	•	•	88.1	•	8.4	21.9	4.8	7.8	4.5	3.7	7.4	•
Coverage Ratio 33	3.9	3.1	•	•	•	•	•	•	2.8	0.4	2.7	2.8	4.8
Total Asset Turnover 34	0.5	•	3.8	3.0	1.4	1.1	1.2	0.7	0.9	0.6	0.5	0.4	0.4
Inventory Turnover 35	16.7	•	1.7	26.4	16.4	17.3	15.5	28.7	-26.9	28.0	17.8	7.6	23.4
Receivables Turnover 36	4.2	•	25.5	18.0	6.2	5.1	4.8	3.0	4.0	3.2	3.9	3.4	4.4
Total Liabilities to Net Worth 37	1.8	•	•	•	•	9.9	16.1	3.8	1.7	1.2	0.9	1.2	2.0
Current Assets to Working Capital 38	•	•	•	21.6	•	5.6	10.7	3.8	4.3	3.6	2.9	5.1	•
Current Liabilities to Working Capital 39	•	•	•	20.6	•	4.6	9.7	2.8	3.3	2.6	1.9	4.1	•
Working Capital to Net Sales 40	•	•	•	0.0	•	0.1	0.0	0.2	0.1	0.2	0.3	0.1	•
Inventory to Working Capital 41	•	•	•	0.2	•	0.1	0.5	0.0	0.1	0.0	0.0	0.3	•
Total Receipts to Cash Flow 42	2.7	3.3	5.1	6.6	13.0	24.2	7.8	5.2	4.2	4.2	3.1	3.9	2.1
Cost of Goods to Cash Flow 43	0.8	1.8	0.1	0.2	3.7	4.9	2.3	1.1	1.5	0.9	0.4	1.2	0.7
Cash Flow to Total Debt 44	0.3	•	0.2	0.4	0.1	0.0	0.2	0.2	0.3	0.3	0.4	0.2	0.3

Selected Financial Factors (in Percentages)

Debt Ratio 45	64.7	•	395.7	130.6	140.1	90.8	94.2	79.2	62.8	53.6	47.1	54.7	66.2
Return on Total Assets 46	9.1	•	•	•	•	•	•	•	5.1	0.8	3.6	4.8	12.4
Return on Equity Before Income Taxes 47	19.2	•	22.4	29.1	83.1	•	•	•	8.8	•	4.3	6.8	29.1
Return on Equity After Income Taxes 48	12.0	•	22.6	30.5	85.7	•	•	•	4.9	•	0.9	5.0	19.5
Profit Margin (Before Income Tax) 49	14.9	3.0	•	•	•	•	•	•	3.8	•	4.3	7.1	25.2
Profit Margin (After Income Tax) 50	9.3	1.3	•	•	•	•	•	•	2.1	•	0.9	5.2	16.9

Table II

Corporations with Net Income

SOFTWARE PUBLISHERS

MONEY AMOUNTS AND SIZE OF ASSETS IN THOUSANDS OF DOLLARS

Item Description for Accounting Period 7/08 Through 6/09		Total	Zero Assets	Under 500	500 to 1,000	1,000 to 5,000	5,000 to 10,000	10,000 to 25,000	25,000 to 50,000	50,000 to 100,000	100,000 to 250,000	250,000 to 500,000	500,000 to 2,500,000	2,500,000 and over
Number of Enterprises	1	3641	677	1907	251	518	80	65	31	•	30	•	•	34
Revenues ($ in Thousands)														
Net Sales	2	95765059	1172988	895730	547761	1883851	677018	1746092	1011304	•	3526555	•	•	14685212
Interest	3	1897453	423	367	1600	2644	2792	6515	11114	•	37504	•	•	215447
Rents	4	173254	0	0	0	0	531	0	0	•	1436	•	•	10415
Royalties	5	7407091	327	0	0	2807	0	14251	24774	•	28658	•	•	1286386
Other Portfolio Income	6	1823468	2363	1	61672	20991	159	0	11144	•	16561	•	•	481935
Other Receipts	7	24163938	31663	333	143131	54932	36110	14151	47490	•	8730	•	•	424720
Total Receipts	8	131230263	1207764	896431	754164	1965225	716610	1781009	1105826	•	3619444	•	•	17104115
Average Total Receipts	9	36042	1784	470	3005	3794	8958	27400	35672	•	120648	•	•	503062
Operating Costs/Operating Income (%)														
Cost of Operations	10	27.4	58.3	0.1	3.4	23.1	20.3	27.9	21.0	•	18.9	•	•	14.3
Salaries and Wages	11	35.1	5.9	32.6	72.1	21.9	28.3	29.7	32.2	•	29.8	•	•	39.5
Taxes Paid	12	3.7	3.8	3.6	5.2	3.1	3.0	3.1	8.2	•	3.0	•	•	3.4
Interest Paid	13	5.4	1.2	0.3	0.3	1.1	1.7	0.7	1.0	•	1.2	•	•	2.9
Depreciation	14	3.5	0.3	0.6	2.8	1.5	3.0	2.7	3.3	•	2.1	•	•	3.7
Amortization and Depletion	15	1.8	0.0	0.1	0.1	0.9	1.9	0.8	0.3	•	1.6	•	•	2.4
Pensions and Other Deferred Comp.	16	0.5	•	2.1	0.9	1.5	0.4	0.7	0.7	•	0.4	•	•	0.9
Employee Benefits	17	3.7	0.7	3.3	3.9	2.9	4.0	3.6	1.9	•	2.7	•	•	4.1
Advertising	18	5.4	0.2	0.9	0.3	1.7	5.2	2.2	3.6	•	2.1	•	•	2.6
Other Expenses	19	29.0	20.1	30.5	17.7	26.7	22.8	20.8	21.2	•	25.9	•	•	25.2
Officers' Compensation	20	1.5	0.1	13.8	6.4	7.4	5.6	3.2	2.8	•	2.0	•	•	1.4
Operating Margin	21	•	9.5	12.0	•	8.1	3.8	4.6	3.8	•	10.2	•	•	1.4
Operating Margin Before Officers' Comp.	22	•	9.5	25.7	•	15.5	9.4	7.8	6.6	•	12.2	•	•	1.1

Selected Average Balance Sheet ($ in Thousands)

	•	•	•	•	•	•	•	•	•	•
Net Receivables 23	5785	0	4	30	664	1275	5045	7102	27113	124103
Inventories 24	297	0	0	7	62	64	384	199	430	3933
Net Property, Plant and Equipment 25	3718	0	11	59	270	770	1148	4960	5948	65899
Total Assets 26	60730	0	101	595	1862	6952	15825	36696	164715	1082915
Notes and Loans Payable 27	8293	0	22	244	1161	1838	2591	5099	24688	142127
All Other Liabilities 28	30000	0	14	66	889	2942	9054	18609	48511	364044
Net Worth 29	22437	0	66	285	-188	2172	4180	12988	91517	576745

Selected Financial Ratios (Times to 1)

	•	•	•	•	•	•	•	•	•	•
Current Ratio 30	0.6	•	4.1	3.3	1.3	2.0	1.4	1.6	1.8	1.4
Quick Ratio 31	0.5	•	3.7	2.8	1.1	1.7	1.2	1.4	1.4	1.2
Net Sales to Working Capital 32	•	•	8.5	7.6	11.0	3.9	9.0	4.6	3.5	4.2
Coverage Ratio 33	5.3	11.7	37.0	92.3	12.0	6.6	9.8	13.5	11.6	6.9
Total Asset Turnover 34	0.4	•	4.6	3.7	2.0	1.2	1.7	0.9	0.7	0.4
Inventory Turnover 35	24.3	•	7.1	10.3	13.5	26.6	19.5	34.4	51.8	15.7
Receivables Turnover 36	4.2	•	34.4	•	6.9	4.6	5.3	4.5	3.7	3.1
Total Liabilities to Net Worth 37	1.7	•	0.5	1.1	•	2.2	2.8	1.8	0.8	0.9
Current Assets to Working Capital 38	•	•	1.3	1.4	3.9	2.0	3.8	2.8	2.3	3.3
Current Liabilities to Working Capital 39	•	•	0.3	0.4	2.9	1.0	2.8	1.8	1.3	2.3
Working Capital to Net Sales 40	•	•	0.1	0.1	0.1	0.3	0.1	0.2	0.3	0.2
Inventory to Working Capital 41	•	•	•	0.0	0.2	0.0	0.0	0.0	0.0	0.0
Total Receipts to Cash Flow 42	2.2	3.1	2.5	3.1	2.8	3.5	4.2	3.4	2.8	2.7
Cost of Goods to Cash Flow 43	0.6	1.8	0.0	0.1	0.7	0.7	1.2	0.7	0.5	0.4
Cash Flow to Total Debt 44	0.3	•	5.4	2.3	0.6	0.5	0.6	0.4	0.6	0.3

Selected Financial Factors (in Percentages)

	•	•	•	•	•	•	•	•	•	•
Debt Ratio 45	63.1	•	35.2	52.1	110.1	68.8	73.6	64.6	44.4	46.7
Return on Total Assets 46	12.3	•	57.3	90.8	26.6	13.8	12.5	12.6	10.0	8.1
Return on Equity Before Income Taxes 47	27.1	•	86.1	187.5	•	37.6	42.3	32.9	16.4	12.9
Return on Equity After Income Taxes 48	19.2	•	84.1	186.1	•	26.5	39.4	28.5	12.3	10.9
Profit Margin (Before Income Tax) 49	23.1	12.4	12.0	24.5	12.5	9.6	6.6	13.1	12.8	17.3
Profit Margin (After Income Tax) 50	16.4	10.5	11.8	24.3	11.2	6.8	6.1	11.4	9.6	14.6

Table I

Corporations with and without Net Income

MOTION PICTURE AND VIDEO INDUSTRIES (EXCEPT VIDEO RENTAL)

MONEY AMOUNTS AND SIZE OF ASSETS IN THOUSANDS OF DOLLARS

Item Description for Accounting Period 7/08 Through 6/09	Total	Zero Assets	Under 500	500 to 1,000	1,000 to 5,000	5,000 to 10,000	10,000 to 25,000	25,000 to 50,000	50,000 to 100,000	100,000 to 250,000	250,000 to 500,000	500,000 to 2,500,000	2,500,000 and over
Number of Enterprises 1	25323	5212	18107	731	906	147	132	27	20	12	11	9	9
Revenues ($ in Thousands)													
Net Sales 2	68178218	550201	4866733	1537014	3237597	1435206	2840299	572025	1041315	1438083	1579459	3707707	45372578
Interest 3	920591	2057	5332	4164	10424	2230	1181	1182	6588	5365	12656	56793	812620
Rents 4	233307	0	0	3451	0	0	0	217	310	200	5527	4754	218848
Royalties 5	689775	104555	20282	0	3	0	0	170	447	3119	11972	0	549227
Other Portfolio Income 6	906683	29	120	6178	994	14900	16905	1481	9226	128	7680	18276	830762
Other Receipts 7	3219239	60368	217465	4507	6087	393451	23862	7118	203877	28547	33427	266117	1974417
Total Receipts 8	74147813	717210	5109932	1555314	3255105	1845787	2882247	582193	1261763	1475442	1638749	4065619	49758452
Average Total Receipts 9	2928	138	282	2128	3593	12556	21835	21563	63088	122954	148977	451735	5528717
Operating Costs/Operating Income (%)													
Cost of Operations 10	30.7	43.3	33.3	10.8	22.8	20.5	57.1	24.2	42.1	45.1	28.0	39.5	28.9
Salaries and Wages 11	10.6	10.6	5.1	30.2	16.8	21.0	10.6	19.3	10.8	4.6	8.4	8.4	10.1
Taxes Paid 12	2.8	3.1	2.1	3.0	2.4	3.4	2.2	2.3	4.1	1.0	2.1	1.3	3.1
Interest Paid 13	5.2	1.9	1.8	1.1	1.0	2.4	1.9	4.5	4.2	2.0	6.1	2.8	6.6
Depreciation 14	7.7	1.5	2.0	3.6	1.1	6.6	5.3	11.0	4.4	1.6	17.9	2.4	9.5
Amortization and Depletion 15	11.8	0.1	0.1	0.1	4.1	1.3	1.1	10.4	5.1	18.3	2.6	18.4	14.8
Pensions and Other Deferred Comp. 16	0.7	0.0	0.2	0.2	0.3	0.1	0.2	0.4	0.3	0.1	0.1	0.3	0.7
Employee Benefits 17	1.1	0.4	1.7	2.4	0.3	0.9	0.8	1.3	1.2	0.2	0.9	0.9	1.2
Advertising 18	4.8	1.2	0.3	2.7	0.9	2.2	0.8	1.0	2.5	0.2	0.3	2.8	6.6
Other Expenses 19	25.3	110.1	27.7	38.7	43.0	45.6	17.4	37.3	46.7	15.3	24.3	16.7	22.5
Officers' Compensation 20	3.8	0.7	23.8	9.2	9.9	26.7	3.8	2.8	1.3	3.7	8.3	1.1	0.4
Operating Margin 21	•	•	0.1	•	•	•	•	•	•	7.8	1.0	5.5	•
Operating Margin Before Officers' Comp. 22	•	•	23.9	7.1	7.3	•	2.7	•	•	11.5	9.4	6.5	•

Selected Average Balance Sheet ($ in Thousands)

Item													
Net Receivables 23	519	0	5	72	129	329	3416	4089	12640	24785	70751	132425	1083818
Inventories 24	193	0	1	80	69	224	918	316	1934	9426	6277	7449	477382
Net Property, Plant and Equipment 25	577	0	10	342	600	1836	3937	11589	11281	24874	82533	92994	1141102
Total Assets 26	5959	0	42	708	1966	7206	15113	33997	65864	146307	345363	1108240	14115413
Notes and Loans Payable 27	2659	0	73	621	1226	2200	6571	22766	29576	35504	155304	249468	6408966
All Other Liabilities 28	1543	0	20	195	511	2329	6002	8974	26707	58448	110740	356925	3451724
Net Worth 29	1757	0	-51	-108	229	2678	2540	2257	9581	52354	79319	501846	4254723

Selected Financial Ratios (Times to 1)

Item													
Current Ratio 30	1.2	•	1.1	1.2	2.0	1.3	1.2	0.6	1.7	0.9	1.3	1.6	1.1
Quick Ratio 31	0.7	•	0.9	0.5	1.4	1.0	0.8	0.5	1.0	0.5	0.9	1.0	0.7
Net Sales to Working Capital 32	12.5	•	135.6	33.0	7.5	9.7	23.8	•	3.4	•	4.9	3.3	14.3
Coverage Ratio 33	1.9	•	3.8	0.2	•	1.2	1.2	•	0.6	6.2	1.8	6.3	1.8
Total Asset Turnover 34	0.5	•	6.4	3.0	1.8	1.4	1.4	0.6	0.8	0.8	0.4	0.4	0.4
Inventory Turnover 35	4.3	•	70.1	2.9	11.8	9.0	13.4	16.2	11.3	5.7	6.4	21.8	3.1
Receivables Turnover 36	5.6	•	51.6	29.3	21.9	17.9	5.9	4.6	4.7	4.9	3.0	4.0	4.9
Total Liabilities to Net Worth 37	2.4	•	•	•	7.6	1.7	4.9	14.1	5.9	1.8	3.4	1.2	2.3
Current Assets to Working Capital 38	6.6	•	12.3	5.8	2.0	3.9	7.4	•	2.4	•	4.8	2.8	8.4
Current Liabilities to Working Capital 39	5.6	•	11.3	4.8	1.0	2.9	6.4	•	1.4	•	3.8	1.8	7.4
Working Capital to Net Sales 40	0.1	•	0.0	0.0	0.1	0.1	0.0	•	0.3	•	0.2	0.3	0.1
Inventory to Working Capital 41	0.9	•	0.2	2.2	0.1	0.0	0.6	•	0.2	•	0.0	0.1	1.3
Total Receipts to Cash Flow 42	5.0	1.9	3.6	3.7	5.1	2.7	11.8	6.6	2.8	5.4	4.7	3.6	5.7
Cost of Goods to Cash Flow 43	1.5	0.8	1.2	0.4	1.2	0.6	6.8	1.6	1.2	2.4	1.3	1.4	1.6
Cash Flow to Total Debt 44	0.1	•	0.8	0.7	0.4	0.8	0.1	0.1	0.3	0.2	0.1	0.2	0.1

Selected Financial Factors (in Percentages)

Item													
Debt Ratio 45	70.5	•	222.1	115.2	88.4	62.8	83.2	93.4	85.5	64.2	77.0	54.7	69.9
Return on Total Assets 46	4.4	•	•	0.7	•	•	3.1	•	2.1	10.2	4.5	6.5	4.3
Return on Equity Before Income Taxes 47	6.8	•	•	17.0	•	•	3.0	•	•	23.9	8.4	12.1	6.4
Return on Equity After Income Taxes 48	3.9	•	•	23.0	•	•	2.7	•	•	19.8	8.4	8.8	3.5
Profit Margin (Before Income Tax) 49	4.4	•	5.1	•	•	•	0.4	•	•	10.5	4.6	14.8	5.4
Profit Margin (After Income Tax) 50	2.5	•	5.0	•	•	•	0.3	•	•	8.6	4.6	10.7	3.0

Table II
Corporations with Net Income

MOTION PICTURE AND VIDEO INDUSTRIES (EXCEPT VIDEO RENTAL)

MONEY AMOUNTS AND SIZE OF ASSETS IN THOUSANDS OF DOLLARS

Item Description for Accounting Period 7/08 Through 6/09		Total	Zero Assets	Under 500	500 to 1,000	1,000 to 5,000	5,000 to 10,000	10,000 to 25,000	25,000 to 50,000	50,000 to 100,000	100,000 to 250,000	250,000 to 500,000	500,000 to 2,500,000	2,500,000 and over
Number of Enterprises	1	12150	2166	9291	143	391	•	81	•	•	7	4	5	•
Revenues ($ in Thousands)														
Net Sales	2	54531020	278465	3181286	431980	1522107	•	2131525	•	•	1212251	564178	2561243	•
Interest	3	631393	47	3637	256	8859	•	651	•	•	5158	635	48024	•
Rents	4	169395	0	0	3451	0	•	0	•	•	0	0	1	•
Royalties	5	219794	0	20282	0	3	•	0	•	•	3119	0	9157	•
Other Portfolio Income	6	553620	0	83	735	268	•	13787	•	•	70	6756	15876	•
Other Receipts	7	3102295	1425	222180	190	5363	•	10259	•	•	22914	10235	251563	•
Total Receipts	8	59207517	279937	3427468	436612	1536600	•	2156222	•	•	1243512	581804	2885864	•
Average Total Receipts	9	4873	129	369	3053	3930	•	26620	•	•	177645	145451	577173	•
Operating Costs/Operating Income (%)														
Cost of Operations	10	30.4	55.9	23.1	22.3	15.1	•	63.1	•	•	52.5	30.1	41.7	•
Salaries and Wages	11	9.8	3.0	4.9	3.5	20.2	•	10.4	•	•	3.3	5.1	8.4	•
Taxes Paid	12	2.6	0.6	2.2	1.4	1.7	•	1.3	•	•	0.5	1.4	1.3	•
Interest Paid	13	4.4	0.1	2.5	0.2	0.5	•	0.8	•	•	1.0	4.4	2.7	•
Depreciation	14	7.0	1.2	1.5	4.3	0.4	•	2.7	•	•	0.3	3.1	2.2	•
Amortization and Depletion	15	13.4	•	0.1	0.0	0.0	•	0.1	•	•	21.2	1.5	13.0	•
Pensions and Other Deferred Comp.	16	0.7	0.0	1.8	0.8	0.7	•	0.2	•	•	0.1	0.1	0.4	•
Employee Benefits	17	1.1	0.4	1.1	0.6	0.2	•	0.7	•	•	0.1	0.2	1.1	•
Advertising	18	5.5	0.2	0.3	0.1	0.2	•	0.5	•	•	0.0	0.1	3.5	•
Other Expenses	19	19.9	26.7	24.6	28.1	30.0	•	9.4	•	•	5.7	11.5	10.2	•
Officers' Compensation	20	3.9	•	27.8	21.1	19.6	•	4.3	•	•	4.1	21.8	1.2	•
Operating Margin	21	1.2	11.8	10.1	17.7	11.2	•	6.7	•	•	11.1	20.8	14.2	•
Operating Margin Before Officers' Comp.	22	5.1	11.8	37.9	38.8	30.9	•	10.9	•	•	15.2	42.7	15.4	•

Selected Average Balance Sheet ($ in Thousands)

Item									
Net Receivables 23	792	0	16	106	4350		29071	104372	181634
Inventories 24	371	0	38	52	148		15897	16361	8648
Net Property, Plant and Equipment 25	694	0	11	241	545	3308	8956	11656	45928
Total Assets 26	9639	0	50	738	2096	14094	151993	358515	1226438
Notes and Loans Payable 27	4000	0	59	222	547	3541	17749	77553	169695
All Other Liabilities 28	2283	0	20	221	225	5628	69955	102801	342620
Net Worth 29	3356	0	-29	295	1323	4925	64289	178161	714123

Selected Financial Ratios (Times to 1)

Item									
Current Ratio 30	1.5		1.4	1.6	5.8	1.4	1.2	1.4	1.8
Quick Ratio 31	1.0		1.3	1.3	4.6	1.2	0.7	1.3	1.4
Net Sales to Working Capital 32	7.3		41.8	19.2	3.5	13.9	9.5	4.0	3.5
Coverage Ratio 33	3.3	187.2	8.2	77.2	24.3	10.7	14.7	6.4	10.7
Total Asset Turnover 34	0.5		6.8	4.1	1.9	1.9	1.1	0.4	0.4
Inventory Turnover 35	3.7	648.3	17.9	11.2	112.6		5.7	2.6	24.7
Receivables Turnover 36	5.6		63.5	56.8	19.3	6.5	6.3	2.0	3.5
Total Liabilities to Net Worth 37	1.9			1.5	0.6	1.9	1.4	1.0	0.7
Current Assets to Working Capital 38	3.2		3.6	2.7	1.2	3.7	5.3	3.7	2.2
Current Liabilities to Working Capital 39	2.2		2.6	1.7	0.2	2.7	4.3	2.7	1.2
Working Capital to Net Sales 40	0.1		0.0	0.1	0.3	0.1	0.1	0.3	0.3
Inventory to Working Capital 41	0.6		0.0		0.0	0.1	1.1	0.0	0.1
Total Receipts to Cash Flow 42	4.3	2.7	2.6	2.8	2.8	7.3	5.4	2.9	2.9
Cost of Goods to Cash Flow 43	1.3	1.5	0.6	0.6	0.4	4.6	2.8	0.9	1.2
Cash Flow to Total Debt 44	0.2		1.6	2.4	1.8	0.4	0.4	0.3	0.3

Selected Financial Factors (in Percentages)

Item									
Debt Ratio 45	65.2		157.9	60.0	36.9	65.1	57.7	50.3	41.8
Return on Total Assets 46	6.7		138.8	77.8	23.6	16.1	16.8	11.0	12.2
Return on Equity Before Income Taxes 47	13.4			192.0	35.8	41.7	37.0	18.7	18.9
Return on Equity After Income Taxes 48	10.1			180.7	34.6	41.4	31.2	18.6	14.7
Profit Margin (Before Income Tax) 49	10.0	12.4	17.8	18.7	12.2	7.8	13.7	23.6	26.4
Profit Margin (After Income Tax) 50	7.6	12.1	17.6	17.6	11.8	7.8	11.6	23.5	20.4

Table I

Corporations with and without Net Income

SOUND RECORDING INDUSTRIES

MONEY AMOUNTS AND SIZE OF ASSETS IN THOUSANDS OF DOLLARS

Item Description for Accounting Period 7/08 Through 6/09		Total	Zero Assets	Under 500	500 to 1,000	1,000 to 5,000	5,000 to 10,000	10,000 to 25,000	25,000 to 50,000	50,000 to 100,000	100,000 to 250,000	250,000 to 500,000	500,000 to 2,500,000	2,500,000 and over
Number of Enterprises	1	7536	1253	5966	0	223	56	16	15	0	3	0	3	0
Revenues ($ in Thousands)														
Net Sales	2	6676845	49565	842038	0	211760	193690	25197	430790	0	132405	0	4791401	0
Interest	3	74318	0	0	0	873	1396	263	3602	0	872	0	67312	0
Rents	4	7797	0	0	0	0	0	0	7787	0	1	0	10	0
Royalties	5	2517873	0	0	0	20170	0	314	99343	0	3370	0	2394677	0
Other Portfolio Income	6	37345	0	10146	0	0	87	0	739	0	0	0	26373	0
Other Receipts	7	806921	0	261	0	24692	3250	267169	17705	0	7819	0	486022	0
Total Receipts	8	10121099	49565	852445	0	257495	198423	292943	559966	0	144467	0	7765795	0
Average Total Receipts	9	1343	40	143	•	1155	3543	18309	37331	•	48156	•	2588598	•
Operating Costs/Operating Income (%)														
Cost of Operations	10	34.6	37.8	14.7	•	7.0	49.2	9.7	53.7	•	55.7	•	36.5	•
Salaries and Wages	11	15.9	•	2.9	•	15.0	6.0	107.6	15.6	•	12.6	•	18.5	•
Taxes Paid	12	2.8	0.1	3.0	•	3.0	1.3	10.0	1.5	•	1.2	•	2.9	•
Interest Paid	13	7.7	•	0.7	•	1.4	1.2	9.5	3.2	•	11.3	•	9.8	•
Depreciation	14	6.6	3.6	3.1	•	3.3	1.8	7.5	3.1	•	1.8	•	8.0	•
Amortization and Depletion	15	4.6	•	•	•	0.0	0.2	19.5	4.4	•	25.0	•	5.2	•
Pensions and Other Deferred Comp.	16	0.5	•	1.7	•	1.7	0.0	2.3	0.5	•	0.1	•	0.3	•
Employee Benefits	17	1.5	7.9	1.6	•	0.3	0.2	8.0	2.3	•	1.5	•	1.4	•
Advertising	18	2.7	3.2	0.6	•	•	0.2	0.1	3.1	•	6.1	•	3.2	•
Other Expenses	19	68.5	25.7	49.3	•	16.0	18.4	1009.0	29.9	•	15.7	•	76.6	•
Officers' Compensation	20	4.2	9.6	22.1	•	6.6	0.8	57.9	4.4	•	6.0	•	0.7	•
Operating Margin	21	•	12.0	0.2	•	45.7	20.6	•	•	•	•	•	•	•
Operating Margin Before Officers' Comp.	22	•	21.6	22.3	•	52.3	21.4	•	•	•	•	•	•	•

Selected Average Balance Sheet ($ in Thousands)

Item													
Net Receivables **23**	506	0	1	•	•	277	1030	42	5789	•	3319	•	1194931
Inventories **24**	66	0	0	•	•	17	623	58	2943	•	1328	•	134618
Net Property, Plant and Equipment **25**	75	0	9	•	•	122	1622	480	6199	•	2575	•	95698
Total Assets **26**	3220	0	26	•	•	1832	6269	20023	45121	•	217604	•	7234803
Notes and Loans Payable **27**	710	0	53	•	•	610	1360	4988	16807	•	121164	•	1375877
All Other Liabilities **28**	829	0	12	•	•	67	1144	21039	15240	•	45479	•	1798994
Net Worth **29**	1680	0	-40	•	•	1155	3765	-6004	13073	•	50962	•	4059932

Selected Financial Ratios (Times to 1)

Item													
Current Ratio **30**	1.1	•	0.6	0.7	•	16.3	4.0	0.7	1.4	•	0.5	•	1.0
Quick Ratio **31**	0.8	•	0.6	0.3	•	13.3	1.6	0.3	0.7	•	0.3	•	0.8
Net Sales to Working Capital **32**	13.3	•	•	•	•	1.0	1.0	•	3.5	•	•	•	29.6
Coverage Ratio **33**	1.6	•	3.1	•	•	48.7	20.5	•	4.1	•	0.2	•	1.2
Total Asset Turnover **34**	0.3	•	5.5	0.1	•	0.5	0.6	0.1	0.6	•	0.2	•	0.2
Inventory Turnover **35**	4.6	•	•	2.6	•	3.8	2.7	2.6	5.2	•	18.5	•	4.3
Receivables Turnover **36**	0.9	•	92.0	2.0	•	3.7	5.8	2.0	7.1	•	14.9	•	0.7
Total Liabilities to Net Worth **37**	0.9	•	•	•	•	0.6	0.7	•	2.5	•	3.3	•	0.8
Current Assets to Working Capital **38**	12.5	•	•	•	•	1.1	1.3	•	3.3	•	•	•	31.0
Current Liabilities to Working Capital **39**	11.5	•	•	•	•	0.1	0.3	•	2.3	•	•	•	30.0
Working Capital to Net Sales **40**	0.1	•	•	•	•	1.0	1.0	•	0.3	•	•	•	0.0
Inventory to Working Capital **41**	1.0	•	•	•	•	0.0	0.2	•	0.4	•	•	•	2.5
Total Receipts to Cash Flow **42**	1.5	3.3	2.6	0.1	•	1.3	2.6	0.1	2.9	•	1.3	•	1.4
Cost of Goods to Cash Flow **43**	0.5	1.2	0.4	0.0	•	0.1	1.3	0.0	1.5	•	0.1	•	0.5
Cash Flow to Total Debt **44**	0.4	•	0.8	0.6	•	1.1	0.5	0.6	0.3	•	1.1	•	0.4

Selected Financial Factors (in Percentages)

Item													
Debt Ratio **45**	47.8	•	255.4	130.0	•	37.0	39.9	•	71.0	•	76.6	•	43.9
Return on Total Assets **46**	3.3	•	11.8	20.6	•	35.6	13.3	•	8.2	•	•	•	2.6
Return on Equity Before Income Taxes **47**	2.2	•	•	20.6	•	55.4	21.1	•	21.2	•	•	•	0.8
Return on Equity After Income Taxes **48**	2.1	•	•	20.6	•	54.4	19.0	•	15.3	•	•	•	0.8
Profit Margin (Before Income Tax) **49**	4.3	12.0	1.4	•	•	67.3	23.0	•	9.7	•	•	•	2.0
Profit Margin (After Income Tax) **50**	4.0	12.0	1.4	•	•	66.2	20.6	•	7.0	•	•	•	2.0

Table II
Corporations with Net Income

SOUND RECORDING INDUSTRIES

MONEY AMOUNTS AND SIZE OF ASSETS IN THOUSANDS OF DOLLARS

Item Description for Accounting Period 7/08 Through 6/09	Total	Zero Assets	Under 500	500 to 1,000	1,000 to 5,000	5,000 to 10,000	10,000 to 25,000	25,000 to 50,000	50,000 to 100,000	100,000 to 250,000	250,000 to 500,000	500,000 to 2,500,000	2,500,000 and over
1 Number of Enterprises	2713	437	1979	0	223	•	4	•	•	0	0	0	•
Revenues ($ in Thousands)													
2 Net Sales	4137785	49565	672989	0	211760	•	9495	•	•	0	0	0	•
3 Interest	43408	0	0	0	873	•	0	•	•	0	0	0	•
4 Rents	330	0	0	0	0	•	0	•	•	0	0	0	•
5 Royalties	1563770	0	0	0	20170	•	0	•	•	0	0	0	•
6 Other Portfolio Income	20651	0	7626	0	0	•	0	•	•	0	0	0	•
7 Other Receipts	150310	0	261	0	24692	•	-158	•	•	0	0	0	•
8 Total Receipts	5916254	49565	680876	0	257495	•	9337	•	•	0	0	0	•
9 Average Total Receipts	2181	113	344	•	1155	•	2334	•	•	•	•	•	•
Operating Costs/Operating Income (%)													
10 Cost of Operations	34.5	37.8	18.4	•	7.0	•	5.2	•	•	•	•	•	•
11 Salaries and Wages	16.6	•	3.7	•	15.0	•	19.8	•	•	•	•	•	•
12 Taxes Paid	1.5	0.0	1.6	•	3.0	•	0.2	•	•	•	•	•	•
13 Interest Paid	5.7	•	0.1	•	1.4	•	5.6	•	•	•	•	•	•
14 Depreciation	1.3	3.6	0.2	•	3.3	•	0.3	•	•	•	•	•	•
15 Amortization and Depletion	3.6	•	•	•	0.0	•	•	•	•	•	•	•	•
16 Pensions and Other Deferred Comp.	0.8	•	2.1	•	1.7	•	•	•	•	•	•	•	•
17 Employee Benefits	1.9	7.9	1.9	•	0.3	•	•	•	•	•	•	•	•
18 Advertising	1.9	2.7	0.0	•	•	•	•	•	•	•	•	•	•
19 Other Expenses	62.0	23.6	33.2	•	16.0	•	45.3	•	•	•	•	•	•
20 Officers' Compensation	5.2	9.6	26.1	•	6.6	•	•	•	•	•	•	•	•
21 Operating Margin	•	14.6	12.7	•	45.7	•	23.7	•	•	•	•	•	•
22 Operating Margin Before Officers' Comp.	•	24.3	38.7	•	52.3	•	23.7	•	•	•	•	•	•

Selected Average Balance Sheet ($ in Thousands)

Net Receivables 23	173	0	4	•	277	•	54
Inventories 24	171	0	0	•	17	•	0
Net Property, Plant and Equipment 25	97	0	3	•	122	•	7
Total Assets 26	5644	0	44	•	1832	•	19056
Notes and Loans Payable 27	281	0	56	•	610	•	0
All Other Liabilities 28	444	0	32	•	67	•	22012
Net Worth 29	4920	0	-44	•	1155	•	-2956

Selected Financial Ratios (Times to 1)

Current Ratio 30	1.9	•	0.5	•	16.3	•	0.7
Quick Ratio 31	0.8	•	0.5	•	13.3	•	0.0
Net Sales to Working Capital 32	4.4	•	•	•	1.0	•	•
Coverage Ratio 33	3.0	•	111.2	•	48.7	•	5.0
Total Asset Turnover 34	0.3	•	7.8	•	0.5	•	0.1
Inventory Turnover 35	3.1	•	•	•	3.8	•	•
Receivables Turnover 36	0.8	•	73.5	•	3.7	•	87.5
Total Liabilities to Net Worth 37	0.1	•	•	•	0.6	•	•
Current Assets to Working Capital 38	2.1	•	•	•	1.1	•	•
Current Liabilities to Working Capital 39	1.1	•	0.1	•	0.1	•	•
Working Capital to Net Sales 40	0.2	•	•	•	1.0	•	•
Inventory to Working Capital 41	0.5	•	•	•	0.0	•	•
Total Receipts to Cash Flow 42	1.5	3.2	2.4	•	1.3	•	1.5
Cost of Goods to Cash Flow 43	0.5	1.2	0.4	•	0.1	•	0.1
Cash Flow to Total Debt 44	1.4	•	1.6	•	1.1	•	0.1

Selected Financial Factors (in Percentages)

Debt Ratio 45	12.8	•	201.8	•	37.0	•	115.5
Return on Total Assets 46	4.6	•	109.0	•	35.6	•	3.4
Return on Equity Before Income Taxes 47	3.5	•	•	•	55.4	•	•
Return on Equity After Income Taxes 48	3.4	•	•	•	54.4	•	•
Profit Margin (Before Income Tax) 49	11.4	14.6	13.8	•	67.3	•	22.0
Profit Margin (After Income Tax) 50	10.9	14.6	13.8	•	66.2	•	21.9

Table I
Corporations with and without Net Income

BROADCASTING (EXCEPT INTERNET)

MONEY AMOUNTS AND SIZE OF ASSETS IN THOUSANDS OF DOLLARS

Item Description for Accounting Period 7/08 Through 6/09		Total	Zero Assets	Under 500	500 to 1,000	1,000 to 5,000	5,000 to 10,000	10,000 to 25,000	25,000 to 50,000	50,000 to 100,000	100,000 to 250,000	250,000 to 500,000	500,000 to 2,500,000	2,500,000 and over
Number of Enterprises	1	6466	988	3479	841	666	195	134	46	32	26	15	30	14
Revenues ($ in Thousands)														
Net Sales	2	113498968	3054961	480088	920025	1623774	1041364	1521150	811123	1337659	1695278	3811581	10891703	86310263
Interest	3	2880680	42040	0	1805	3955	5873	6684	12297	3901	12025	181991	163039	2447070
Rents	4	327949	18919	0	0	5876	648	764	2507	896	2504	24778	19031	252026
Royalties	5	5196869	0	0	0	58522	4442	0	9	0	64098	35819	155112	4878866
Other Portfolio Income	6	1124481	51344	5849	41799	3619	3820	32488	59636	21346	23709	156582	170036	554256
Other Receipts	7	4188985	-209718	1593	4154	7173	38586	16770	11663	30928	105749	95098	569857	3517129
Total Receipts	8	127217932	2957546	487530	967783	1702919	1094733	1577856	897235	1394730	1903363	4305849	11968778	97959610
Average Total Receipts	9	19675	2993	140	1151	2557	5614	11775	19505	43585	73206	287057	398959	6997115
Operating Costs/Operating Income (%)														
Cost of Operations	10	16.4	0.5	5.3	13.3	16.3	18.4	31.9	16.4	13.0	22.6	58.0	10.0	15.7
Salaries and Wages	11	14.0	25.8	10.7	36.6	33.8	17.8	24.9	22.6	23.4	21.5	11.1	23.6	11.3
Taxes Paid	12	2.3	5.0	2.2	4.1	5.2	2.9	3.2	3.0	2.9	3.5	1.6	4.5	1.8
Interest Paid	13	7.3	11.2	0.6	1.8	3.3	6.2	4.1	5.5	8.6	8.4	7.3	11.9	6.9
Depreciation	14	5.9	6.6	2.7	1.7	4.3	6.7	3.6	11.2	4.6	5.3	5.6	7.7	5.7
Amortization and Depletion	15	7.7	9.1	•	1.0	1.1	2.4	5.9	9.5	8.0	10.9	5.2	12.7	7.4
Pensions and Other Deferred Comp.	16	0.8	0.2	•	0.4	0.4	0.1	0.5	0.9	0.4	0.1	0.4	0.7	0.9
Employee Benefits	17	2.5	2.3	0.8	2.5	2.2	1.1	1.5	2.0	1.6	1.4	0.9	2.0	2.8
Advertising	18	3.3	1.5	0.2	1.6	1.6	1.1	2.3	2.8	3.6	2.0	0.9	2.6	3.8
Other Expenses	19	45.3	42.7	68.6	24.1	36.5	44.0	24.2	37.1	37.9	35.9	43.7	31.7	48.2
Officers' Compensation	20	1.4	0.9	2.8	10.7	6.0	8.7	2.2	2.7	3.0	2.2	1.0	1.3	1.1
Operating Margin	21	•	•	6.2	2.7	•	•	•	•	•	•	•	•	•
Operating Margin Before Officers' Comp.	22	•	•	9.0	13.4	•	•	•	•	•	•	•	•	•

Selected Average Balance Sheet ($ in Thousands)

Net Receivables 23	3512	0	2	135	332	671	1735	2338	8323	20179	37489	81601	1292472
Inventories 24	204	0	0	3	33	8	64	92	461	4291	715	1434	78483
Net Property, Plant and Equipment 25	5944	0	8	118	675	913	2207	7404	10907	19138	65234	128210	2240754
Total Assets 26	43084	0	23	760	2233	6488	14826	36548	73585	148412	308984	1076132	16307931
Notes and Loans Payable 27	17433	0	44	560	1665	8291	5912	16901	44038	74715	188393	593457	5987245
All Other Liabilities 28	15016	0	0	514	716	1643	1640	7539	20196	48416	805023	281849	5204344
Net Worth 29	10635	0	-22	-314	-148	-3446	7274	12108	9350	25280	-684432	200826	5116343

Selected Financial Ratios (Times to 1)

Current Ratio 30	0.9	•	4.7	0.7	0.5	3.1	1.5	1.1	1.2	1.1	1.4	1.1	0.8
Quick Ratio 31	0.6	•	4.2	0.5	0.4	2.6	1.4	0.5	0.9	0.8	1.2	0.9	0.5
Net Sales to Working Capital 32	•	•	13.9	•	•	2.2	6.0	30.3	12.7	13.8	13.9	35.2	•
Coverage Ratio 33	1.7	0.2	12.2	5.4	•	0.3	0.9	0.4	0.7	0.8	•	1.1	2.2
Total Asset Turnover 34	0.4	•	6.0	1.4	1.1	0.8	0.8	0.5	0.6	0.4	0.8	0.3	0.4
Inventory Turnover 35	14.1	•	•	44.8	12.0	115.5	56.8	31.3	11.8	3.4	206.2	25.3	12.3
Receivables Turnover 36	4.0	•	18.4	12.2	6.3	9.7	5.7	8.6	4.7	3.3	4.5	4.6	3.7
Total Liabilities to Net Worth 37	3.1	•	•	•	•	•	1.0	2.0	6.9	4.9	•	4.4	2.2
Current Assets to Working Capital 38	•	•	1.3	•	•	1.5	2.8	16.1	5.9	8.9	3.8	15.2	•
Current Liabilities to Working Capital 39	•	•	0.3	•	•	0.5	1.8	15.1	4.9	7.9	2.8	14.2	•
Working Capital to Net Sales 40	•	•	0.1	•	•	0.5	0.2	0.0	0.1	0.1	0.1	0.0	•
Inventory to Working Capital 41	•	•	•	•	•	0.0	0.1	0.3	0.1	0.9	0.0	0.2	•
Total Receipts to Cash Flow 42	2.1	4.4	5.3	3.9	5.0	2.9	5.0	4.4	3.3	3.4	6.8	3.5	1.9
Cost of Goods to Cash Flow 43	0.4	0.0	0.7	0.6	0.5	0.5	1.6	0.7	0.4	0.8	4.0	0.4	0.3
Cash Flow to Total Debt 44	0.3	•	2.2	0.2	0.3	0.2	0.3	0.2	0.2	0.2	0.0	0.1	0.3

Selected Financial Factors (in Percentages)

Debt Ratio 45	75.3	•	193.4	141.3	106.6	153.1	50.9	66.9	87.3	83.0	321.5	81.3	68.6
Return on Total Assets 46	5.1	•	42.6	13.9	•	1.5	2.8	1.1	3.2	3.0	•	4.4	5.7
Return on Equity Before Income Taxes 47	8.6	•	•	•	98.7	6.7	•	•	•	•	8.5	1.8	9.9
Return on Equity After Income Taxes 48	4.1	•	•	•	107.6	8.7	•	•	•	•	9.0	•	6.0
Profit Margin (Before Income Tax) 49	5.2	•	6.6	7.9	•	•	•	•	•	•	•	1.0	8.2
Profit Margin (After Income Tax) 50	2.5	•	6.6	7.8	•	•	•	•	•	•	•	•	5.0

Table II
Corporations with Net Income

BROADCASTING (EXCEPT INTERNET)

MONEY AMOUNTS AND SIZE OF ASSETS IN THOUSANDS OF DOLLARS

Item Description for Accounting Period 7/08 Through 6/09		Total	Zero Assets	Under 500	500 to 1,000	1,000 to 5,000	5,000 to 10,000	10,000 to 25,000	25,000 to 50,000	50,000 to 100,000	100,000 to 250,000	250,000 to 500,000	500,000 to 2,500,000	2,500,000 and over
Number of Enterprises	1	2097	268	873	537	221	59	77	17	13	11	5	10	6
Revenues ($ in Thousands)														
Net Sales	2	93278239	2993201	320065	902293	633213	465653	1187559	375700	778705	821567	2352353	5038394	77409536
Interest	3	2317445	42026	0	1792	368	4627	5274	6334	1665	11298	9390	57854	2176817
Rents	4	290987	18919	0	0	2142	328	761	1571	260	2074	22806	10301	231824
Royalties	5	5034940	0	0	0	58522	4442	0	1	0	0	92	93033	4878849
Other Portfolio Income	6	772242	51344	5849	41799	453	3820	31311	59418	19839	9903	154468	42272	351766
Other Receipts	7	4037832	9707	-3991	4154	5561	34784	9801	9260	22575	24804	50818	475291	3395069
Total Receipts	8	105731685	3115197	321923	950038	700259	513654	1234706	452284	823044	869646	2589927	5717145	88443861
Average Total Receipts	9	50420	11624	369	1769	3169	8706	16035	26605	63311	79059	517985	571714	14740644
Operating Costs/Operating Income (%)														
Cost of Operations	10	17.0	0.3	0.2	13.6	23.3	27.0	39.5	21.2	22.0	18.7	86.3	7.0	15.7
Salaries and Wages	11	12.2	26.0	2.7	37.2	29.3	7.4	20.1	17.0	16.0	20.5	4.7	24.6	10.4
Taxes Paid	12	1.8	5.1	0.5	4.0	4.9	3.1	3.0	2.1	2.2	3.4	0.7	4.2	1.5
Interest Paid	13	5.5	7.3	0.0	1.5	0.9	9.0	1.8	3.9	1.6	4.2	0.7	8.2	5.6
Depreciation	14	5.3	6.7	0.9	0.7	2.7	3.5	2.7	12.7	2.8	5.0	1.2	6.0	5.5
Amortization and Depletion	15	7.0	9.2	•	0.2	0.1	0.8	1.3	5.0	2.3	7.8	1.6	10.5	7.2
Pensions and Other Deferred Comp.	16	0.9	0.1	•	•	0.9	0.2	0.2	0.8	0.7	0.1	0.3	1.3	0.9
Employee Benefits	17	2.7	2.2	0.1	2.4	3.4	0.5	1.2	2.4	1.3	1.6	0.3	2.4	2.9
Advertising	18	3.6	1.5	0.3	1.6	0.6	1.7	1.6	3.4	4.4	2.7	0.6	3.3	3.9
Other Expenses	19	45.2	42.6	71.1	21.6	23.1	21.9	16.9	30.2	33.6	28.5	5.8	31.1	48.7
Officers' Compensation	20	1.4	0.1	0.2	10.9	10.6	14.8	2.1	3.0	3.1	2.5	0.4	1.6	1.2
Operating Margin	21	•	•	24.0	6.1	0.2	10.1	9.4	•	10.2	5.0	•	•	•
Operating Margin Before Officers' Comp.	22	•	•	24.2	17.0	10.9	24.9	11.5	1.3	13.3	7.6	•	1.5	•

Selected Average Balance Sheet ($ in Thousands)

Net Receivables 23	8408	0	0	194	529	952	2293	2338	13681	17203	44408	110304	2574368
Inventories 24	537	0	0	2	45	26	40	23	480	5007	1944	1076	171416
Net Property, Plant and Equipment 25	12837	0	0	107	229	995	2628	6892	10782	19233	51379	161107	4035617
Total Assets 26	89392	22	0	749	1493	6437	14071	39630	72670	142401	297260	1180464	28127550
Notes and Loans Payable 27	25098	0	0	410	369	8137	3267	10831	15388	41768	36887	548223	7514520
All Other Liabilities 28	26564	0	0	173	1455	1122	2975	5428	27819	31763	139236	338595	8351574
Net Worth 29	37730	22	0	167	-331	-2821	7829	23371	29462	68869	121137	293647	12261456

Selected Financial Ratios (Times to 1)

Current Ratio 30	1.1	•	92.8	2.3	0.6	2.9	2.2	1.0	1.5	2.3	1.0	1.4	1.0
Quick Ratio 31	0.7	•	88.2	2.2	0.5	2.8	2.0	0.5	1.1	1.2	0.9	1.2	0.6
Net Sales to Working Capital 32	39.2	•	16.9	8.2	•	3.5	3.9	•	6.0	2.4	142.0	7.4	96.4
Coverage Ratio 33	3.0	1.4	7289.7	8.4	13.3	3.3	8.5	5.8	11.0	3.5	10.9	2.6	2.9
Total Asset Turnover 34	0.5	•	16.7	2.2	1.9	1.2	1.1	0.6	0.8	0.5	1.6	0.4	0.5
Inventory Turnover 35	14.0	•	•	129.5	14.9	82.6	153.4	204.6	27.4	2.8	208.9	32.8	11.8
Receivables Turnover 36	3.9	•	28.2	15.1	3.7	8.2	7.1	8.7	4.2	3.7	6.5	6.8	3.5
Total Liabilities to Net Worth 37	1.4	•	0.0	3.5	•	•	0.8	0.7	1.5	1.1	1.5	3.0	1.3
Current Assets to Working Capital 38	15.6	•	1.0	1.8	•	1.5	1.8	•	3.2	1.7	29.4	3.5	40.0
Current Liabilities to Working Capital 39	14.6	•	0.0	0.8	•	0.5	0.8	•	2.2	0.7	28.4	2.5	39.0
Working Capital to Net Sales 40	0.0	•	0.1	0.1	•	0.3	0.3	•	0.2	0.4	0.0	0.1	0.0
Inventory to Working Capital 41	0.6	•	•	0.0	•	0.0	0.0	•	0.0	0.3	0.2	0.0	1.6
Total Receipts to Cash Flow 42	1.9	2.9	1.0	4.9	3.2	2.5	3.7	3.3	2.2	2.8	16.9	2.4	1.8
Cost of Goods to Cash Flow 43	0.3	0.0	0.0	0.7	0.8	0.7	1.5	0.7	0.5	0.5	14.6	0.2	0.3
Cash Flow to Total Debt 44	0.5	•	1488.7	0.6	0.5	0.3	0.7	0.4	0.6	0.4	0.2	0.2	0.5

Selected Financial Factors (in Percentages)

Debt Ratio 45	57.8	•	1.1	77.7	122.1	143.8	44.4	41.0	59.5	51.6	59.2	75.1	56.4
Return on Total Assets 46	8.1	•	380.9	29.1	22.3	36.0	16.6	12.5	14.3	7.8	12.9	8.9	7.6
Return on Equity Before Income Taxes 47	12.8	•	385.0	115.1	•	26.3	17.5	32.2	11.6	28.6	21.9		11.5
Return on Equity After Income Taxes 48	8.9	•	385.0	113.9	•	23.2	17.0	27.8	8.7	19.8	16.8		7.7
Profit Margin (Before Income Tax) 49	10.9	2.9	22.8	11.4	10.8	20.4	13.4	18.5	15.8	10.7	7.4	12.7	10.9
Profit Margin (After Income Tax) 50	7.5	1.9	22.8	11.3	9.4	17.6	11.8	18.0	13.7	8.1	5.1	9.8	7.3

Table I

Corporations with and without Net Income

TELECOMMUNICATIONS (WIRED, WIRELESS, SATELLITE, INTERNET PROVIDERS)

MONEY AMOUNTS AND SIZE OF ASSETS IN THOUSANDS OF DOLLARS

Item Description for Accounting Period 7/08 Through 6/09	Total	Zero Assets	Under 500	500 to 1,000	1,000 to 5,000	5,000 to 10,000	10,000 to 25,000	25,000 to 50,000	50,000 to 100,000	100,000 to 250,000	250,000 to 500,000	500,000 to 2,500,000	2,500,000 and over
Number of Enterprises **1**	17543	3442	10294	1058	1447	391	387	186	129	88	40	46	33
Revenues ($ in Thousands)													
Net Sales **2**	459119836	2501217	10848323	9792899	7433602	3993315	6174095	4879698	5520210	10478456	10229022	25282319	361986680
Interest **3**	16211598	7259	2844	2350	24167	21399	52382	27117	42855	74955	108462	274585	15573224
Rents **4**	10180097	1241	600	2203	2774	2395	14564	8188	9407	19098	16813	48518	10054297
Royalties **5**	11726110	114	0	0	10201	0	326	75	20246	292899	43981	103	11358167
Other Portfolio Income **6**	3638637	70	22818	136	132794	20273	73043	156024	76590	121939	14096	210078	2810776
Other Receipts **7**	24248285	-334448	91611	43681	196434	81379	187850	243537	218480	322094	208480	1133048	21856135
Total Receipts **8**	525124563	2175453	10966196	9841269	7799972	4118761	6502260	5314639	5887788	11309441	10620854	26948651	423639279
Average Total Receipts **9**	29934	632	1065	9302	5390	10534	16802	28573	45642	128516	265521	585840	12837554
Operating Costs/Operating Income (%)													
Cost of Operations **10**	20.9	31.9	70.6	77.8	65.6	65.9	45.0	46.9	41.9	48.4	43.1	42.8	12.4
Salaries and Wages **11**	13.5	15.5	6.8	9.0	12.8	10.4	15.4	14.4	10.7	10.8	12.4	15.4	13.9
Taxes Paid **12**	2.5	1.7	0.9	1.6	1.7	1.5	2.4	2.2	2.5	2.1	2.4	2.8	2.7
Interest Paid **13**	8.4	7.5	0.2	0.6	0.9	1.0	2.0	3.2	2.5	2.9	5.5	6.7	9.7
Depreciation **14**	12.4	8.0	0.7	0.9	2.8	4.5	7.6	9.6	12.5	9.5	9.3	13.2	13.6
Amortization and Depletion **15**	2.6	6.2	0.1	0.0	0.3	0.5	0.6	1.4	1.1	2.1	1.6	2.9	2.8
Pensions and Other Deferred Comp. **16**	0.7	0.9	0.5	0.0	0.1	0.1	0.3	0.2	0.4	0.2	0.5	0.5	0.8
Employee Benefits **17**	1.8	1.9	0.6	0.2	1.3	0.7	1.3	1.4	1.5	1.3	1.7	1.9	1.9
Advertising **18**	2.4	10.4	0.3	0.3	0.5	1.1	1.5	1.1	1.3	1.2	3.0	1.7	2.6
Other Expenses **19**	44.2	41.9	12.5	8.5	18.8	19.2	30.9	26.9	30.2	26.5	25.7	20.1	50.3
Officers' Compensation **20**	0.6	2.5	5.2	0.8	3.1	2.2	2.7	1.8	1.7	1.0	0.8	0.8	0.3
Operating Margin **21**	•	•	1.6	0.2	•	•	•	•	•	•	•	•	•
Operating Margin Before Officers' Comp. **22**	•	•	6.8	1.0	•	•	•	•	•	•	•	•	•

Selected Average Balance Sheet ($ in Thousands)

Item													
Net Receivables 23	6959	0	21	100	600	1120	2173	3847	7203	16963	36199	107539	3335651
Inventories 24	822	0	9	59	127	136	350	904	2053	5248	3761	16209	366780
Net Property, Plant and Equipment 25	17184	0	11	123	490	1904	5423	11444	28277	52574	113418	312498	8131863
Total Assets 26	77493	0	110	687	2278	6956	15655	35692	69123	158847	346380	983994	38087239
Notes and Loans Payable 27	26259	0	29	886	792	2885	3825	10249	18299	49953	145583	427763	12773163
All Other Liabilities 28	23333	0	32	889	1112	3077	3502	8285	14982	65545	128555	348905	11316930
Net Worth 29	27901	0	49	-1088	375	993	8328	17158	35842	43349	72242	207326	13997146

Selected Financial Ratios (Times to 1)

Item													
Current Ratio 30	0.8	•	0.5	1.2	1.4	1.9	1.5	1.6	1.2	1.4			0.8
Quick Ratio 31	0.7	•	0.2	0.9	1.0	1.3	1.1	1.1	0.7	1.1			0.6
Net Sales to Working Capital 32	•	•	31.8	28.3	9.5	4.6	6.0	6.5	16.0	7.8			•
Coverage Ratio 33	1.5	•	2.1	•	•	0.9	1.1	1.7	0.6	0.7			1.6
Total Asset Turnover 34	0.3	•	13.5	2.3	1.5	0.7	0.6	0.7	0.7	0.6			0.3
Inventory Turnover 35	6.7	•	122.1	26.6	49.4	13.6	8.7	11.0	29.3	14.5			3.7
Receivables Turnover 36	3.7	•	69.8	9.1	6.6	5.5	5.9	6.7	7.3	4.7			3.2
Total Liabilities to Net Worth 37	1.8	•	•	5.1	6.0	1.1	0.9	2.7	3.8	3.7			1.7
Current Assets to Working Capital 38	•	•	•	7.5	3.7	2.2	2.9	2.6	7.0	3.7			•
Current Liabilities to Working Capital 39	•	•	•	6.5	2.7	1.2	1.9	1.6	6.0	2.7			•
Working Capital to Net Sales 40	•	•	•	0.0	0.1	0.2	0.2	0.2	0.1	0.1			•
Inventory to Working Capital 41	•	•	•	0.8	0.2	0.1	0.3	0.3	0.2	0.2			•
Total Receipts to Cash Flow 42	2.3	•	13.0	8.7	7.9	5.2	4.2	4.2	5.0	7.9			2.0
Cost of Goods to Cash Flow 43	0.5	•	10.1	5.7	5.2	2.4	1.7	2.0	2.1	3.4			0.2
Cash Flow to Total Debt 44	0.2	•	0.4	0.3	0.2	0.3	0.3	0.2	0.2	0.1			0.2

Selected Financial Factors (in Percentages)

Item													
Debt Ratio 45	64.0	•	55.3	258.3	83.6	85.7	46.8	51.9	48.1	72.7	79.1	78.9	63.2
Return on Total Assets 46	4.3	•	26.9	17.0	•	•	•	2.2	1.8	3.8	2.5	2.6	4.6
Return on Equity Before Income Taxes 47	4.2	•	56.9	•	•	•	•	•	0.4	5.8	•	•	4.8
Return on Equity After Income Taxes 48	2.8	•	52.3	•	•	•	•	•	•	2.3	•	•	3.5
Profit Margin (Before Income Tax) 49	4.5	•	2.6	0.7	•	•	•	0.3	•	2.1	•	•	6.2
Profit Margin (After Income Tax) 50	3.0	•	2.4	0.6	•	•	•	•	0.8	•	•	•	4.5

Table II

Corporations with Net Income

TELECOMMUNICATIONS (WIRED, WIRELESS, SATELLITE, INTERNET PROVIDERS)

MONEY AMOUNTS AND SIZE OF ASSETS IN THOUSANDS OF DOLLARS

Item Description for Accounting Period 7/08 Through 6/09	Total	Zero Assets	Under 500	500 to 1,000	1,000 to 5,000	5,000 to 10,000	10,000 to 25,000	25,000 to 50,000	50,000 to 100,000	100,000 to 250,000	250,000 to 500,000	500,000 to 2,500,000	2,500,000 and over
Number of Enterprises 1	8794	945	5844	477	771	266	193	106	71	58	19	20	23
Revenues ($ in Thousands)													
Net Sales 2	384373049	120685	7569664	9051632	4636758	3538551	3540517	2770052	3445932	7040953	3714409	12081415	326862481
Interest 3	10408068	282	2666	465	6439	11190	25339	17107	26687	57175	51040	112842	10096838
Rents 4	9654665	12	600	0	553	2395	14056	5885	7534	15689	15636	11754	9580552
Royalties 5	11655775	114	0	0	0	0	0	75	20039	290392	582	92	11344483
Other Portfolio Income 6	3454304	0	12889	0	125030	14656	68555	151941	67407	110962	9413	141352	2752102
Other Receipts 7	23060106	51634	87418	46623	46974	82084	143481	191181	145535	264297	144081	818644	21038146
Total Receipts 8	442605967	172727	7673237	9098720	4815754	3648876	3791948	3136241	3713134	7779468	3935161	13166099	381674602
Average Total Receipts 9	50330	183	1313	19075	6246	13718	19647	29587	52298	134129	207114	658305	16594548
Operating Costs/Operating Income (%)													
Cost of Operations 10	18.7	33.8	69.5	79.6	70.1	68.9	52.1	44.9	40.9	49.7	39.2	38.9	12.1
Salaries and Wages 11	13.3	5.3	5.6	8.0	8.1	6.3	8.9	11.7	8.6	10.0	12.5	13.4	14.0
Taxes Paid 12	2.6	4.3	0.7	1.3	1.2	1.2	1.6	2.1	2.7	1.9	1.9	2.7	2.7
Interest Paid 13	7.7	4.3	0.1	0.4	0.2	0.6	0.7	2.3	2.0	2.5	3.4	6.0	8.7
Depreciation 14	12.7	1.5	0.7	0.7	1.7	3.4	6.2	7.8	10.3	9.1	11.4	10.2	13.8
Amortization and Depletion 15	2.6	1.0	0.1	0.0	0.1	0.3	0.2	1.0	0.9	0.9	1.3	2.7	2.8
Pensions and Other Deferred Comp. 16	0.8	•	0.3	0.0	0.0	0.1	0.4	0.1	0.3	0.2	0.6	0.6	0.9
Employee Benefits 17	1.7	0.8	0.4	0.1	0.8	0.2	0.5	1.1	1.3	1.4	2.2	1.8	1.9
Advertising 18	2.1	0.5	0.2	0.1	0.4	0.9	0.4	0.7	1.5	1.3	0.7	1.8	2.3
Other Expenses 19	45.0	25.1	11.3	7.2	10.5	13.7	25.1	24.0	27.0	24.6	25.8	19.3	49.9
Officers' Compensation 20	0.5	19.6	5.3	0.3	2.5	1.3	2.7	1.3	1.3	1.0	0.7	0.8	0.3
Operating Margin 21	•	3.8	5.8	2.4	4.3	3.1	1.4	3.1	3.2	•	0.4	1.9	•
Operating Margin Before Officers' Comp. 22	•	23.4	11.1	2.7	6.7	4.4	4.0	4.4	4.5	•	1.1	2.6	•

Selected Average Balance Sheet ($ in Thousands)

Net Receivables 23	12710	0	19	67	585	1061	1975	3926	8168	17384	32253	125176	4582306
Inventories 24	1449	0	11	19	120	148	341	1179	2253	5695	4783	16222	497638
Net Property, Plant and Equipment 25	28685	0	16	120	288	2048	5430	10767	28031	55181	125880	286852	10253419
Total Assets 26	136929	0	121	707	2063	6830	15799	35328	69386	163635	354776	1011528	50066133
Notes and Loans Payable 27	45173	0	24	1460	236	1297	2573	8428	14485	45104	105960	426012	16535554
All Other Liabilities 28	40765	0	13	614	835	2449	-579	6845	12470	41505	91437	411537	14910979
Net Worth 29	50991	0	84	-1367	991	3084	13805	20055	42430	77026	157379	173979	18619601

Selected Financial Ratios (Times to 1)

Current Ratio 30	0.8	•	3.6	0.9	1.6	1.5	2.1	2.5	1.9	2.0	1.9	1.8	0.7
Quick Ratio 31	0.6	•	3.1	0.4	1.2	0.9	1.6	1.6	1.4	1.4	1.1	1.3	0.6
Net Sales to Working Capital 32	•	•	23.1	•	11.7	11.3	5.6	3.4	4.3	4.8	4.0	4.3	•
Coverage Ratio 33	2.0	13.4	100.1	8.5	34.3	11.8	13.4	8.1	6.5	4.4	2.9	2.8	1.8
Total Asset Turnover 34	0.3	•	10.7	26.8	2.9	1.9	1.2	0.7	0.7	0.7	0.6	0.6	0.3
Inventory Turnover 35	5.6	•	82.0	796.7	35.1	62.1	28.0	9.9	8.8	10.6	16.0	14.5	3.4
Receivables Turnover 36	3.3	•	97.6	221.6	9.5	8.0	8.2	4.5	5.6	6.9	6.3	4.6	3.0
Total Liabilities to Net Worth 37	1.7	•	0.4	•	1.1	1.2	0.1	0.8	0.6	1.1	1.3	4.8	1.7
Current Assets to Working Capital 38	•	•	1.4	•	2.6	3.1	1.9	1.7	2.1	2.1	2.1	2.3	•
Current Liabilities to Working Capital 39	•	•	0.4	•	1.6	2.1	0.9	0.7	1.1	1.1	1.1	1.3	•
Working Capital to Net Sales 40	•	•	0.0	•	0.1	0.1	0.2	0.3	0.2	0.2	0.2	0.2	•
Inventory to Working Capital 41	•	•	0.2	•	0.2	0.1	0.1	0.1	0.2	0.2	0.1	0.2	•
Total Receipts to Cash Flow 42	2.1	1.4	5.9	11.4	6.7	5.5	3.4	3.3	3.2	3.5	3.7	3.9	1.9
Cost of Goods to Cash Flow 43	0.4	0.5	4.1	9.1	4.7	3.8	1.8	1.5	1.3	1.7	1.4	1.5	0.2
Cash Flow to Total Debt 44	0.2	•	5.9	0.8	0.8	0.6	2.7	0.5	0.6	0.4	0.3	0.2	0.2

Selected Financial Factors (in Percentages)

Debt Ratio 45	62.8	•	30.6	293.4	52.0	54.9	12.6	43.2	38.8	52.9	55.6	82.8	62.8
Return on Total Assets 46	4.9	•	78.2	88.2	24.9	13.3	10.5	13.7	9.0	8.1	5.4	10.1	4.6
Return on Equity Before Income Taxes 47	6.4	•	111.5	•	50.3	27.0	11.2	21.2	12.4	13.3	7.9	38.3	5.6
Return on Equity After Income Taxes 48	4.9	•	106.7	•	42.4	22.5	9.2	16.8	9.0	10.4	5.9	30.5	4.2
Profit Margin (Before Income Tax) 49	7.5	53.5	7.2	2.9	8.3	6.3	8.4	16.3	10.9	8.4	6.3	11.0	7.4
Profit Margin (After Income Tax) 50	5.7	52.4	6.9	2.9	7.0	5.2	6.9	12.9	7.9	6.6	4.7	8.8	5.5

Table I

Corporations with and without Net Income

DATA PROCESSING, HOSTING AND RELATED SERVICES

MONEY AMOUNTS AND SIZE OF ASSETS IN THOUSANDS OF DOLLARS

Item Description for Accounting Period 7/08 Through 6/09	Total	Zero Assets	Under 500	500 to 1,000	1,000 to 5,000	5,000 to 10,000	10,000 to 25,000	25,000 to 50,000	50,000 to 100,000	100,000 to 250,000	250,000 to 500,000	500,000 to 2,500,000	2,500,000 and over
Number of Enterprises **1**	8927	2297	5504	343	530	102	61	31	16	21	7	9	6
Revenues ($ in Thousands)													
Net Sales **2**	40235055	6795787	2597533	620861	3232339	691259	888260	1074337	908271	1721504	1414112	3602259	16688533
Interest **3**	925874	58615	278	1069	2274	3431	3812	9705	1441	16014	11444	40913	776877
Rents **4**	160575	33244	4574	0	0	386	261	1088	0	23	1	815	120183
Royalties **5**	1449266	1089734	0	0	0	1	520	0	719	2440	0	18245	337607
Other Portfolio Income **6**	1454922	249117	1659	193	2670	17099	1960	12911	7454	6767	7350	12815	1134926
Other Receipts **7**	2946393	46472	34283	38629	41367	11142	10829	24916	5702	110347	7558	39315	2575838
Total Receipts **8**	47172085	8272969	2638327	660752	3278650	723318	905642	1122957	923587	1857095	1440465	3714362	21633964
Average Total Receipts **9**	5284	3602	479	1926	6186	7091	14847	36224	57724	88433	205781	412707	3605661
Operating Costs/Operating Income (%)													
Cost of Operations **10**	17.8	0.2	29.7	44.1	27.8	61.7	28.6	41.9	29.6	34.6	26.3	19.1	13.0
Salaries and Wages **11**	29.9	35.9	12.6	23.5	29.8	22.5	24.2	29.6	17.5	23.2	24.0	30.8	32.7
Taxes Paid **12**	3.5	4.0	2.4	2.8	2.3	1.5	3.7	3.0	2.3	2.3	2.4	3.6	4.1
Interest Paid **13**	4.8	3.1	0.8	0.6	0.7	2.1	4.5	2.8	3.4	5.6	2.7	4.9	7.3
Depreciation **14**	6.6	5.1	0.9	2.6	3.1	2.4	3.7	4.2	5.9	6.0	5.4	9.7	8.9
Amortization and Depletion **15**	2.9	2.9	0.0	0.1	0.6	2.6	3.5	2.4	2.0	4.9	1.6	5.8	3.1
Pensions and Other Deferred Comp. **16**	1.0	0.9	0.1	2.3	0.7	0.4	0.7	0.4	0.2	0.6	0.1	0.5	1.6
Employee Benefits **17**	2.4	3.2	0.4	0.7	1.7	1.3	2.5	2.6	1.5	2.6	2.2	2.8	2.6
Advertising **18**	1.0	0.3	0.5	6.4	1.5	1.5	2.1	1.0	1.4	1.4	6.3	1.4	0.4
Other Expenses **19**	35.9	46.8	46.1	16.1	33.5	22.1	33.5	24.4	32.1	26.8	22.3	24.9	37.2
Officers' Compensation **20**	2.5	1.3	8.5	11.8	7.9	8.2	3.4	3.4	2.2	3.2	1.5	1.4	0.5
Operating Margin **21**	•	•	•	•	•	•	•	•	1.9	•	5.1	•	•
Operating Margin Before Officers' Comp. **22**	•	•	6.4	0.8	•	•	•	•	4.0	•	6.6	•	•

Selected Average Balance Sheet ($ in Thousands)

Net Receivables 23	627	0	14	85	394	1586	1854	9578	5604	19115	44575	92356	512452
Inventories 24	19	0	1	33	21	97	144	403	256	264	24	4298	10583
Net Property, Plant and Equipment 25	1110	0	11	67	360	443	2760	3932	13343	16451	24711	112218	1259799
Total Assets 26	10220	0	74	706	2069	7123	14465	36039	74289	145217	383445	828280	12063323
Notes and Loans Payable 27	2588	0	150	369	641	2580	4252	10026	23954	61357	65974	311505	2672914
All Other Liabilities 28	5460	0	60	189	1330	1997	5711	13479	22810	38758	180497	190716	7085068
Net Worth 29	2172	0	-136	148	99	2546	4502	12535	27525	45102	136975	326059	2305341

Selected Financial Ratios (Times to 1)

Current Ratio 30	0.8	•	•	2.0	0.9	1.7	1.5	1.9	1.2	1.1	1.4	1.9	0.6
Quick Ratio 31	0.5	•	0.3	1.7	0.8	1.5	1.2	1.5	0.7	0.8	0.8	1.7	0.3
Net Sales to Working Capital 32	•	•	•	7.5	•	3.6	7.2	3.8	15.4	22.7	4.5	3.1	•
Coverage Ratio 33	2.9	6.8	0.3	•	2.9	•	•	•	2.0	0.4	3.5	0.6	3.5
Total Asset Turnover 34	0.4	•	6.4	2.6	2.9	1.0	1.0	1.0	0.8	0.6	0.5	0.5	0.2
Inventory Turnover 35	41.9	•	143.9	23.9	80.5	43.0	28.9	36.1	65.4	107.3	2171.8	17.8	34.1
Receivables Turnover 36	6.4	•	24.8	16.6	20.7	6.0	5.4	5.0	5.4	4.5	4.1	5.0	4.3
Total Liabilities to Net Worth 37	3.7	•	•	3.8	19.9	1.8	2.2	1.9	1.7	2.2	1.8	1.5	4.2
Current Assets to Working Capital 38	•	•	•	2.0	•	2.4	3.2	2.1	6.5	11.1	3.4	2.1	•
Current Liabilities to Working Capital 39	•	•	•	1.0	•	1.4	2.2	1.1	5.5	10.1	2.4	1.1	•
Working Capital to Net Sales 40	•	•	•	0.1	•	0.3	0.1	0.3	0.1	0.0	0.2	0.3	•
Inventory to Working Capital 41	•	•	•	0.2	•	0.1	0.1	0.0	0.0	0.1	0.0	0.0	•
Total Receipts to Cash Flow 42	2.8	1.9	2.5	11.5	5.0	•	4.8	11.9	3.3	5.4	3.7	6.0	2.3
Cost of Goods to Cash Flow 43	0.5	0.0	0.7	5.1	1.4	•	1.4	5.0	1.0	1.9	1.0	1.2	0.3
Cash Flow to Total Debt 44	0.2	•	0.9	0.3	0.6	•	0.3	0.1	0.4	0.2	0.2	0.1	0.1

Selected Financial Factors (in Percentages)

Debt Ratio 45	78.7	•	283.6	79.1	95.2	64.3	68.9	65.2	62.9	68.9	64.3	60.6	80.9
Return on Total Assets 46	6.1	•	1.7	•	•	•	•	•	5.2	1.3	5.0	1.5	6.0
Return on Equity Before Income Taxes 47	18.9	•	2.0	•	•	•	•	•	7.1	•	10.1	•	22.3
Return on Equity After Income Taxes 48	10.1	•	2.0	•	•	•	•	•	5.9	•	8.1	•	13.5
Profit Margin (Before Income Tax) 49	9.1	18.0	•	•	•	•	•	•	3.5	•	6.8	•	18.5
Profit Margin (After Income Tax) 50	4.9	12.0	•	•	•	•	•	•	2.9	•	5.5	•	11.2

271

Table II

Corporations with Net Income

DATA PROCESSING, HOSTING AND RELATED SERVICES

MONEY AMOUNTS AND SIZE OF ASSETS IN THOUSANDS OF DOLLARS

Item Description for Accounting Period 7/08 Through 6/09		Total	Zero Assets	Under 500	500 to 1,000	1,000 to 5,000	5,000 to 10,000	10,000 to 25,000	25,000 to 50,000	50,000 to 100,000	100,000 to 250,000	250,000 to 500,000	500,000 to 2,500,000	2,500,000 and over
Number of Enterprises	1	5108	2276	2380	183	187	13	26	11	10	8	•	4	•
Revenues ($ in Thousands)														
Net Sales	2	28508440	6766648	1942758	569738	1844274	285989	589164	449533	665863	905612	•	1339076	•
Interest	3	856317	57866	22	272	1039	667	1816	5640	887	2206	•	24711	•
Rents	4	156060	33244	3739	0	0	0	261	1088	0	0	•	815	•
Royalties	5	1445971	1089734	0	0	0	0	24	0	719	2440	•	18245	•
Other Portfolio Income	6	1314205	248892	1636	0	25	931	1919	12186	1967	3717	•	11236	•
Other Receipts	7	2512574	46111	1	11945	33462	8983	10336	20631	4179	5213	•	27931	•
Total Receipts	8	34793567	8242495	1948156	581955	1878800	296570	603520	489078	673615	919188	•	1422014	•
Average Total Receipts	9	6812	3621	819	3180	10047	22813	23212	44462	67362	114898	•	355504	•
Operating Costs/Operating Income (%)														
Cost of Operations	10	11.0	0.2	25.1	41.0	21.6	67.4	29.2	33.2	35.1	35.9	•	9.9	•
Salaries and Wages	11	32.6	35.8	10.4	19.6	33.3	11.2	14.8	28.7	14.0	17.5	•	37.5	•
Taxes Paid	12	3.6	4.0	2.0	2.1	1.7	1.2	2.8	2.9	1.8	1.5	•	2.5	•
Interest Paid	13	3.4	3.1	0.5	0.6	0.4	0.1	2.6	1.0	2.0	4.9	•	2.0	•
Depreciation	14	4.2	5.1	0.6	0.8	3.7	0.8	3.4	3.2	3.0	4.0	•	3.9	•
Amortization and Depletion	15	2.4	2.9	0.0	0.0	0.4	•	1.6	0.4	1.6	2.4	•	5.6	•
Pensions and Other Deferred Comp.	16	1.2	0.9	0.2	•	0.3	0.7	0.9	1.0	0.1	0.8	•	0.5	•
Employee Benefits	17	2.6	3.2	0.4	0.5	1.3	0.3	2.0	3.7	1.3	1.9	•	2.7	•
Advertising	18	1.0	0.2	0.4	6.5	2.4	0.0	1.9	0.4	1.6	1.8	•	0.6	•
Other Expenses	19	38.6	46.7	47.5	12.7	23.8	5.0	29.3	23.3	29.9	20.5	•	29.1	•
Officers' Compensation	20	2.0	1.3	7.5	8.7	4.6	9.4	2.3	4.5	1.8	1.0	•	2.8	•
Operating Margin	21	•	•	5.4	7.5	6.5	3.8	9.0	•	7.9	7.8	•	2.8	•
Operating Margin Before Officers' Comp.	22	•	•	12.8	16.1	11.1	13.2	11.4	2.2	9.7	8.8	•	5.6	•

Selected Average Balance Sheet ($ in Thousands)

Net Receivables 23	770	0	18	158	330	2961	2688	14288	6881	18784	84869	•
Inventories 24	19	0	1	58	3	445	171	285	226	464	98	•
Net Property, Plant and Equipment 25	425	0	14	92	641	248	1614	4113	8048	16853	27713	•
Total Assets 26	13487	0	115	734	1754	6624	14596	33287	76044	143824	795422	•
Notes and Loans Payable 27	2328	0	148	551	701	261	4344	9495	17092	75306	133236	•
All Other Liabilities 28	7993	0	38	262	434	3799	5018	10195	28465	36240	198780	•
Net Worth 29	3166	0	-71	-79	620	2564	5235	13597	30487	32278	463406	•

Selected Financial Ratios (Times to 1)

Current Ratio 30	0.7	•	0.9	1.5	1.3	1.2	1.5	3.1	1.4	1.0	1.4	•
Quick Ratio 31	0.3	•	0.5	1.1	1.1	1.0	1.2	2.6	0.8	0.8	1.2	•
Net Sales to Working Capital 32	•	•	•	19.4	74.7	23.8	8.4	2.6	7.3	•	4.5	•
Coverage Ratio 33	6.7	6.9	11.3	17.3	21.7	113.2	5.3	7.7	5.5	2.9	5.5	•
Total Asset Turnover 34	0.4	•	7.1	4.2	5.6	3.3	1.6	1.2	0.9	0.8	0.4	•
Inventory Turnover 35	32.7	•	192.9	22.1	625.8	33.3	38.8	47.7	103.7	87.7	335.9	•
Receivables Turnover 36	6.1	•	40.9	36.4	33.0	6.1	5.8	3.9	6.0	•	4.9	•
Total Liabilities to Net Worth 37	3.3	•	•	1.8	1.6	1.8	1.4	1.5	•	3.5	0.7	•
Current Assets to Working Capital 38	•	•	•	3.2	4.8	5.3	2.9	1.5	3.2	•	3.3	•
Current Liabilities to Working Capital 39	•	•	•	2.2	3.8	4.3	1.9	0.5	2.2	•	2.3	•
Working Capital to Net Sales 40	•	•	•	0.1	0.0	0.0	0.1	0.4	0.1	•	0.2	•
Inventory to Working Capital 41	•	•	•	0.7	0.0	0.0	0.4	0.1	0.0	0.0	0.0	•
Total Receipts to Cash Flow 42	2.1	1.9	2.0	5.0	3.5	9.1	2.7	4.0	2.7	4.1	3.5	•
Cost of Goods to Cash Flow 43	0.2	0.0	0.5	2.1	0.8	6.1	0.8	1.3	0.9	1.5	0.3	•
Cash Flow to Total Debt 44	0.3	•	2.2	0.8	2.5	0.6	0.9	0.5	0.5	0.2	0.3	•

Selected Financial Factors (in Percentages)

Debt Ratio 45	76.5	•	161.7	110.8	64.7	61.3	64.1	59.2	59.9	77.6	41.7	•
Return on Total Assets 46	9.5	•	43.8	43.4	49.3	25.1	21.8	9.8	9.6	11.1	4.7	•
Return on Equity Before Income Taxes 47	34.5	•	•	•	133.2	64.3	49.5	20.8	19.6	32.3	6.6	•
Return on Equity After Income Taxes 48	24.0	•	•	•	130.1	45.7	40.9	15.4	17.8	26.3	6.5	•
Profit Margin (Before Income Tax) 49	19.6	18.3	5.6	9.6	8.4	7.5	11.4	6.9	9.0	9.2	9.1	•
Profit Margin (After Income Tax) 50	13.6	12.3	5.6	7.9	8.2	5.3	9.4	5.1	8.1	7.5	9.0	•

Table I

Corporations with and without Net Income

OTHER INFORMATION SERVICES, INTERNET PUBLISHING, WEB PORTALS

MONEY AMOUNTS AND SIZE OF ASSETS IN THOUSANDS OF DOLLARS

Item Description for Accounting Period 7/08 Through 6/09		Total	Zero Assets	Under 500	500 to 1,000	1,000 to 5,000	5,000 to 10,000	10,000 to 25,000	25,000 to 50,000	50,000 to 100,000	100,000 to 250,000	250,000 to 500,000	500,000 to 2,500,000	2,500,000 and over
Number of Enterprises	1	21069	4095	15148	752	702	175	102	35	15	18	11	14	3
Revenues ($ in Thousands)														
Net Sales	2	43344393	1028122	4946767	1088007	2916626	2526049	1058132	1232780	990793	1894177	2175042	5330890	18157010
Interest	3	384956	1749	2958	1086	9508	6525	9595	10810	6129	10889	42719	62300	220689
Rents	4	24898	1	809	0	1415	1657	109	1892	0	0	173	8553	10290
Royalties	5	1265326	0	28	0	0	0	0	191	135	12193	198	695847	556734
Other Portfolio Income	6	1108433	100012	59064	38	652	136	14534	694	1752	9718	1547	603623	316664
Other Receipts	7	3208079	2116	83115	800	28859	7159	69962	13353	3526	12244	1063753	126866	1796319
Total Receipts	8	49336085	1132000	5092741	1089931	2957060	2541526	1152332	1259720	1002335	1939221	3283432	6828079	21057706
Average Total Receipts	9	2342	276	336	1449	4212	14523	11297	35992	66822	107734	298494	487720	7019235
Operating Costs/Operating Income (%)														
Cost of Operations	10	23.4	12.6	30.0	60.2	33.3	54.9	32.2	34.7	24.7	18.2	9.1	34.6	11.7
Salaries and Wages	11	25.1	41.7	14.3	15.0	36.1	18.2	41.2	21.5	23.1	24.8	28.3	26.9	25.5
Taxes Paid	12	2.9	2.2	2.5	3.5	3.1	3.4	5.9	2.3	2.3	3.0	3.1	3.1	2.6
Interest Paid	13	1.9	1.8	1.2	0.8	2.8	0.9	2.7	1.8	1.7	1.4	0.8	6.1	1.1
Depreciation	14	4.7	3.1	2.4	1.0	2.3	1.7	5.9	4.9	4.2	2.8	3.0	3.5	7.1
Amortization and Depletion	15	1.8	4.6	0.1	1.0	1.0	0.3	4.6	2.0	2.4	2.0	2.9	4.7	1.3
Pensions and Other Deferred Comp.	16	0.6	0.0	0.8	0.1	0.1	1.3	0.1	0.2	0.9	1.2	1.3	0.8	0.5
Employee Benefits	17	1.9	3.2	0.9	1.3	1.9	2.1	2.4	1.7	3.5	2.3	2.7	2.7	1.6
Advertising	18	2.5	1.7	0.7	2.4	5.8	2.9	3.1	4.5	0.9	9.1	4.4	3.2	1.2
Other Expenses	19	35.5	42.3	29.9	30.2	34.3	17.2	40.1	31.2	38.5	25.2	83.0	24.4	38.3
Officers' Compensation	20	3.2	2.9	13.7	5.9	4.9	3.0	6.8	3.1	1.7	2.0	1.5	2.6	0.5
Operating Margin	21	•	•	3.6	•	•	•	•	•	•	8.0	•	8.5	•
Operating Margin Before Officers' Comp.	22	•	•	17.2	•	•	•	•	•	•	10.0	•	9.0	•

Selected Average Balance Sheet ($ in Thousands)

Net Receivables 23	408	0	8	44	318	1827	1653	7878	11022	12262	41152	62507	1916568
Inventories 24	29	0	1	9	8	32	67	64	4946	537	1287	19010	69073
Net Property, Plant and Equipment 25	372	0	12	46	214	642	2017	3468	6069	10928	23538	54132	1910154
Total Assets 26	3422	0	50	597	2291	7135	15369	34783	75758	163849	367535	1018427	14289311
Notes and Loans Payable 27	547	0	90	210	1533	1437	5102	5958	11105	17711	16262	334801	867295
All Other Liabilities 28	1047	0	92	260	733	1902	5676	15788	36856	47317	161356	344118	3499729
Net Worth 29	1828	0	-133	127	26	3796	4591	13037	27797	99421	189917	339509	9922287

Selected Financial Ratios (Times to 1)

Current Ratio 30	1.8	•	0.3	1.2	1.3	2.5	1.6	1.7	2.0	1.7	1.1	1.0	2.9
Quick Ratio 31	1.0	•	0.3	1.0	1.2	2.3	1.3	1.4	1.4	1.3	0.8	0.4	1.2
Net Sales to Working Capital 32	2.9	•	•	29.0	15.7	4.8	3.5	4.3	2.9	4.0	19.2	100.4	1.3
Coverage Ratio 33	6.4	6.3	•	•	•	•	•	•	•	8.6	14.7	3.7	23.5
Total Asset Turnover 34	0.6	•	6.5	2.4	1.8	2.0	0.7	1.0	0.9	0.6	0.5	0.4	0.4
Inventory Turnover 35	16.7	•	177.4	97.8	167.2	245.9	50.1	189.3	3.3	35.6	14.0	6.9	10.3
Receivables Turnover 36	4.8	•	53.4	24.1	17.2	7.6	5.3	4.3	5.0	7.6	5.4	2.3	3.8
Total Liabilities to Net Worth 37	0.9	•	•	3.7	88.3	0.9	2.3	1.7	1.7	0.6	0.9	2.0	0.4
Current Assets to Working Capital 38	2.2	•	•	6.3	4.3	1.7	2.8	2.5	2.0	2.4	14.7	75.8	1.5
Current Liabilities to Working Capital 39	1.2	•	•	5.3	3.3	0.7	1.8	1.5	1.0	1.4	13.7	74.8	0.5
Working Capital to Net Sales 40	0.3	•	•	0.0	0.1	0.2	0.3	0.2	0.3	0.2	0.1	0.0	0.8
Inventory to Working Capital 41	0.1	•	•	0.3	0.1	0.0	0.0	0.0	0.2	0.0	0.2	4.8	0.0
Total Receipts to Cash Flow 42	2.5	4.1	3.2	21.7	22.7	10.8	1139.0	4.5	3.2	3.0	1.1	3.9	1.7
Cost of Goods to Cash Flow 43	0.6	0.5	1.0	13.1	7.6	5.9	366.9	1.6	0.8	0.6	0.1	1.3	0.2
Cash Flow to Total Debt 44	0.5	•	0.6	0.1	0.1	0.4	0.0	0.4	0.4	0.5	1.0	0.1	0.8

Selected Financial Factors (in Percentages)

Debt Ratio 45	46.6	•	363.9	78.8	98.9	46.8	70.1	62.5	63.3	39.3	48.3	66.7	30.6
Return on Total Assets 46	7.4	•	50.3	•	•	•	•	•	•	7.6	6.4	8.6	10.8
Return on Equity Before Income Taxes 47	11.7	•	•	•	•	•	•	•	•	11.1	11.5	18.9	15.0
Return on Equity After Income Taxes 48	7.5	•	•	•	•	•	•	•	•	7.0	7.0	16.0	10.8
Profit Margin (Before Income Tax) 49	10.4	6.5	•	•	•	•	•	•	•	10.5	11.0	16.8	24.5
Profit Margin (After Income Tax) 50	6.6	6.2	•	•	•	•	•	•	•	6.6	6.8	14.3	17.6

Table II
Corporations with Net Income

OTHER INFORMATION SERVICES, INTERNET PUBLISHING, WEB PORTALS

MONEY AMOUNTS AND SIZE OF ASSETS IN THOUSANDS OF DOLLARS

Item Description for Accounting Period 7/08 Through 6/09	Total	Zero Assets	Under 500	500 to 1,000	1,000 to 5,000	5,000 to 10,000	10,000 to 25,000	25,000 to 50,000	50,000 to 100,000	100,000 to 250,000	250,000 to 500,000	500,000 to 2,500,000	2,500,000 and over
Number of Enterprises **1**	11486	1664	8980	382	303	89	20	10	7	11	•	•	8
Revenues ($ in Thousands)													
Net Sales **2**	36066651	239507	3663469	890388	2171237	1723360	335511	724155	763325	1510711	•	•	4182259
Interest **3**	330438	108	1151	158	1136	2427	1281	5094	4062	9196	•	•	50602
Rents **4**	18569	0	295	0	0	751	0	0	0	0	•	•	7060
Royalties **5**	1259691	0	28	0	0	0	0	191	135	8787	•	•	693618
Other Portfolio Income **6**	1076483	83142	59030	0	196	105	7358	0	1417	9281	•	•	597785
Other Receipts **7**	3131531	16	81254	108	4730	5547	68271	10459	1939	7875	•	•	92027
Total Receipts **8**	41883363	322773	3805227	890654	2177299	1732190	412421	739899	770878	1545850	•	•	5623351
Average Total Receipts **9**	3646	194	424	2332	7186	19463	20621	73990	110125	140532	•	•	702919
Operating Costs/Operating Income (%)													
Cost of Operations **10**	21.9	42.4	16.3	72.1	36.5	59.8	19.1	48.5	15.7	19.7	•	•	39.1
Salaries and Wages **11**	23.3	8.9	14.1	5.3	26.3	11.5	41.7	13.7	20.5	23.3	•	•	29.1
Taxes Paid **12**	2.7	2.1	2.4	3.1	1.8	3.8	3.4	1.4	2.3	2.8	•	•	3.6
Interest Paid **13**	1.3	0.0	0.5	0.1	2.4	0.2	0.7	1.2	0.7	1.2	•	•	3.5
Depreciation **14**	4.8	0.1	2.1	0.1	1.4	1.1	4.9	2.0	4.4	2.3	•	•	3.6
Amortization and Depletion **15**	1.3	0.3	0.0	0.0	0.3	0.0	0.7	0.3	1.2	2.1	•	•	2.9
Pensions and Other Deferred Comp. **16**	0.7	0.1	0.8	0.1	0.0	1.9	0.1	0.1	1.1	0.5	•	•	1.0
Employee Benefits **17**	1.6	0.9	0.7	0.5	1.0	2.0	1.8	1.0	3.6	2.1	•	•	2.6
Advertising **18**	2.0	1.4	0.5	1.6	4.7	0.2	2.0	2.8	0.3	9.4	•	•	2.1
Other Expenses **19**	33.7	22.8	28.9	10.6	18.0	8.0	33.0	18.0	41.5	21.8	•	•	23.2
Officers' Compensation **20**	2.9	10.6	17.4	2.7	2.2	1.9	3.6	1.7	1.3	1.2	•	•	3.1
Operating Margin **21**	3.9	10.5	16.5	3.7	5.5	9.6	•	9.1	7.2	13.6	•	•	•
Operating Margin Before Officers' Comp. **22**	6.8	21.1	33.8	6.4	7.7	11.5	•	10.8	8.6	14.8	•	•	•

Selected Average Balance Sheet ($ in Thousands)

Net Receivables 23	•	675	0	8	47	486	2518	2090	5492	16066	16799	91445 •
Inventories 24	•	43	0	0	32	15	11	179	173	177	43	32759 •
Net Property, Plant and Equipment 25	•	605	0	11	16	192	576	1368	2301	9845	8346	72561 •
Total Assets 26	•	5211	0	46	593	2298	7319	16748	35247	78749	156928	1120795 •
Notes and Loans Payable 27	•	528	0	49	131	1167	324	2190	2887	5757	20456	269361 •
All Other Liabilities 28	•	1509	0	116	80	613	1941	9553	20125	57099	42299	371615 •
Net Worth 29	•	3174	0	-119	382	519	5054	5004	12235	15893	94173	479818 •

Selected Financial Ratios (Times to 1)

Current Ratio 30	•	2.1	•	0.2	5.8	2.0	2.7	1.2	1.6	1.2	1.8	1.2 •
Quick Ratio 31	•	1.0	•	0.2	5.1	1.8	2.5	1.1	1.5	1.1	1.4	0.5 •
Net Sales to Working Capital 32	•	2.4	•	•	6.1	12.2	5.9	17.0	8.1	13.4	4.1	10.1 •
Coverage Ratio 33	•	16.9	15496.3	44.7	43.6	3.4	57.4	17.5	10.1	12.2	14.1	7.5 •
Total Asset Turnover 34	•	0.6	•	8.8	3.9	3.1	2.6	1.0	2.1	1.4	0.9	0.5 •
Inventory Turnover 35	•	16.0	•	4274.7	52.0	172.8	1085.4	17.8	203.4	96.7	627.6	6.2 •
Receivables Turnover 36	•	4.4	•	63.9	52.8	20.6	6.6	3.5	6.2	7.6	7.5	1.9 •
Total Liabilities to Net Worth 37	•	0.6	•	•	0.6	3.4	0.4	2.3	1.9	4.0	0.7	1.3 •
Current Assets to Working Capital 38	•	1.9	•	•	1.2	2.0	1.6	6.1	2.6	5.6	2.2	7.6 •
Current Liabilities to Working Capital 39	•	0.9	•	•	0.2	1.0	0.6	5.1	1.6	4.6	1.2	6.6 •
Working Capital to Net Sales 40	•	0.4	•	•	0.2	0.1	0.2	0.1	0.1	0.1	0.2	0.1 •
Inventory to Working Capital 41	•	0.0	•	•	0.1	0.0	0.0	0.1	0.0	0.0	0.0	0.6 •
Total Receipts to Cash Flow 42	•	2.1	2.3	2.2	10.0	5.0	5.9	2.4	3.5	2.2	2.9	3.7 •
Cost of Goods to Cash Flow 43	•	0.4	1.0	0.4	7.2	1.8	3.5	0.5	1.7	0.3	0.6	1.4 •
Cash Flow to Total Debt 44	•	0.8	•	1.1	1.1	0.8	1.4	0.6	0.9	0.8	0.8	0.2 •

Selected Financial Factors (in Percentages)

Debt Ratio 45	•	39.1	•	358.4	35.6	77.4	31.0	70.1	65.3	79.8	40.0	57.2 •
Return on Total Assets 46	•	13.0	•	183.5	15.1	25.6	27.2	12.8	25.8	12.3	15.1	12.1 •
Return on Equity Before Income Taxes 47	•	20.0	•	•	23.0	80.3	38.7	40.4	66.9	56.1	23.3	24.5 •
Return on Equity After Income Taxes 48	•	15.6	•	•	22.0	73.4	36.1	39.6	63.9	39.3	16.3	21.0 •
Profit Margin (Before Income Tax) 49	•	20.3	45.3	20.3	3.8	5.8	10.1	12.0	11.3	8.2	16.0	22.5 •
Profit Margin (After Income Tax) 50	•	15.8	43.0	19.9	3.6	5.3	9.4	11.8	10.8	5.7	11.2	19.3 •

274

Table I

Corporations with and without Net Income

CREDIT INTERMEDIATION

MONEY AMOUNTS AND SIZE OF ASSETS IN THOUSANDS OF DOLLARS

Item Description for Accounting Period 7/08 Through 6/09	Total	Zero Assets	Under 500	500 to 1,000	1,000 to 5,000	5,000 to 10,000	10,000 to 25,000	25,000 to 50,000	50,000 to 100,000	100,000 to 250,000	250,000 to 500,000	500,000 to 2,500,000	2,500,000 and over
Number of Enterprises **1**	55179	12223	28549	4514	4644	1176	891	682	737	863	390	380	131
Revenues ($ in Thousands)													
Net Sales **2**	538328169	49069118	6003790	2401905	5381931	3788008	4455587	3887331	5842370	13236770	12011718	38369800	393879841
Interest **3**	382777695	60462700	109829	53320	270944	148758	490001	631900	1850833	6351520	6015429	20317511	286074950
Rents **4**	1066846	336819	6450	4	3665	486	3566	6871	7574	20540	29529	124121	527222
Royalties **5**	653610	6664	0	122	0	0	0	161	235	281	1006	20342	624799
Other Portfolio Income **6**	12415594	3359182	3643	14431	37868	7591	26462	44328	100004	303034	231524	1329544	6957977
Other Receipts **7**	141414424	-15096247	5883868	2334028	5069454	3631173	3935558	3204071	3883724	6561395	5734230	16578282	99694893
Total Receipts **8**	538328169	49069118	6003790	2401905	5381931	3788008	4455587	3887331	5842370	13236770	12011718	38369800	393879841
Average Total Receipts **9**	9756	4014	210	532	1159	3221	5001	5700	7927	15338	30799	100973	3006716
Operating Costs/Operating Income (%)													
Cost of Operations **10**	0.5	0.6	•	•	0.3	3.7	1.4	0.1	0.8	0.3	2.0	0.8	0.4
Salaries and Wages **11**	8.4	8.0	34.8	31.2	27.3	28.3	28.7	28.2	20.2	18.9	15.7	15.4	5.7
Taxes Paid **12**	1.2	1.9	4.0	4.1	3.2	3.1	3.0	3.7	2.8	2.7	2.3	2.0	0.7
Interest Paid **13**	56.8	99.6	3.7	3.0	6.7	7.0	13.0	16.7	21.9	31.0	30.7	28.5	59.6
Depreciation **14**	2.9	5.1	1.8	1.3	1.6	3.2	1.7	3.2	2.5	2.9	3.4	2.6	2.7
Amortization and Depletion **15**	1.8	0.1	0.2	1.1	0.4	0.6	0.5	0.4	0.7	0.8	1.3	1.5	2.2
Pensions and Other Deferred Comp. **16**	0.4	0.4	0.4	0.3	0.3	0.1	0.3	0.5	0.8	0.8	0.8	0.9	0.4
Employee Benefits **17**	0.8	0.6	1.2	1.0	1.2	0.8	1.5	1.8	2.2	2.0	2.0	1.8	0.6
Advertising **18**	1.3	0.3	3.5	2.2	1.7	3.7	2.3	2.4	1.8	1.4	1.2	1.3	1.3
Other Expenses **19**	37.7	63.8	42.1	41.3	43.3	52.7	48.2	39.6	40.0	61.6	30.1	38.2	33.3
Officers' Compensation **20**	0.9	0.7	9.9	6.8	5.7	2.9	5.0	5.6	5.9	4.3	3.1	1.5	0.3
Operating Margin **21**	•	•	•	7.8	8.4	•	•	•	0.2	•	7.3	5.4	•
Operating Margin Before Officers' Comp. **22**	•	•	8.4	14.6	14.1	•	•	3.3	6.2	•	10.4	6.9	•

Selected Average Balance Sheet ($ in Thousands)

Line Item													
Net Receivables 23	13236	0	171	12	966	2600	6922	16512	33530	69211	103924	258427	3672352
Inventories 24	•	•	•	•	•	•	•	•	•	•	•	•	•
Net Property, Plant and Equipment 25	1030	0	74	15	145	691	522	921	1720	3498	6790	15629	309755
Total Assets 26	84925	0	739	100	2305	7018	16248	36683	72368	160729	357720	1006459	29827552
Notes and Loans Payable 27	50052	0	373	43	926	4091	8417	10306	1119	25621	54442	208487	19981862
All Other Liabilities 28	30635	0	97	68	1071	2183	5890	19816	51319	118246	260185	672681	8891372
Net Worth 29	4237	0	269	-11	308	744	1942	6562	9930	16862	43093	125291	1054318

Selected Financial Ratios (Times to 1)

Line Item													
Current Ratio 30	0.5	•	2.8	1.8	1.2	1.4	1.2	1.0	0.9	0.8	0.6	0.6	0.4
Quick Ratio 31	0.4	•	2.2	1.3	1.1	1.2	1.0	0.9	0.8	0.7	0.5	0.5	0.3
Net Sales to Working Capital 32	7.7	•	1.9	7.7	4.3	2.8	2.6	14.8	•	•	•	•	•
Coverage Ratio 33	0.8	0.2	3.6	0.6	2.2	0.1	0.6	0.8	1.0	0.1	1.2	1.2	0.9
Total Asset Turnover 34	0.1	•	0.7	2.1	0.5	0.5	0.3	0.2	0.1	0.1	0.1	0.1	0.1
Inventory Turnover 35	•	•	•	•	•	•	•	•	•	•	•	•	•
Receivables Turnover 36	•	•	•	•	•	•	•	•	•	•	•	•	•
Total Liabilities to Net Worth 37	19.0	•	1.7	•	6.5	8.4	7.4	4.6	6.3	8.5	7.3	7.0	27.3
Current Assets to Working Capital 38	•	•	1.6	2.2	5.5	3.4	5.5	64.0	•	•	•	•	•
Current Liabilities to Working Capital 39	•	•	0.6	1.2	4.5	2.4	4.5	63.0	•	•	•	•	•
Working Capital to Net Sales 40	•	•	0.5	0.1	0.2	0.4	0.4	0.1	•	•	•	•	•
Inventory to Working Capital 41	•	•	•	•	0.0	0.0	0.0	0.0	•	•	•	•	•
Total Receipts to Cash Flow 42	6.9	•	2.6	3.2	2.3	2.9	2.7	3.1	2.8	16.0	3.0	2.7	6.6
Cost of Goods to Cash Flow 43	0.0	•	•	•	0.0	0.1	0.0	0.0	0.0	0.1	0.1	0.0	0.0
Cash Flow to Total Debt 44	0.0	•	0.4	0.6	0.3	0.2	0.1	0.1	0.0	0.0	0.0	0.0	0.0

Selected Financial Factors (in Percentages)

Line Item													
Debt Ratio 45	95.0	•	63.6	111.2	86.6	89.4	88.0	82.1	86.3	89.5	88.0	87.6	96.5
Return on Total Assets 46	5.0	•	7.7	4.6	7.6	0.4	2.2	2.2	2.3	0.4	3.2	3.4	5.3
Return on Equity Before Income Taxes 47	•	•	15.3	28.6	31.4	•	•	•	•	•	4.6	4.0	•
Return on Equity After Income Taxes 48	•	•	14.7	31.4	28.9	•	•	•	•	•	2.2	1.1	•
Profit Margin (Before Income Tax) 49	•	•	7.7	•	8.4	•	•	•	•	•	6.4	5.0	•
Profit Margin (After Income Tax) 50	•	•	7.4	•	7.7	•	•	•	•	•	3.0	1.3	•

Table II

Corporations with Net Income

CREDIT INTERMEDIATION

MONEY AMOUNTS AND SIZE OF ASSETS IN THOUSANDS OF DOLLARS

Item Description for Accounting Period 7/08 Through 6/09		Total	Zero Assets	Under 500	500 to 1,000	1,000 to 5,000	5,000 to 10,000	10,000 to 25,000	25,000 to 50,000	50,000 to 100,000	100,000 to 250,000	250,000 to 500,000	500,000 to 2,500,000	2,500,000 and over
Number of Enterprises	1	26800	3177	15006	2642	2680	671	516	421	450	567	303	281	86
Revenues ($ in Thousands)														
Net Sales	2	255888432	23816941	4202983	1486868	3753064	2839990	2951695	2755367	3996436	8337048	9262570	26335442	166150028
Interest	3	13682637	15610747	86663	37664	122475	76361	167803	394996	1167959	3850249	4582052	13084547	97701123
Rents	4	480826	58450	5734	4	3136	46	2463	2028	3753	12874	19188	71769	301381
Royalties	5	626414	0	0	0	0	0	0	136	30	96	6	1347	624799
Other Portfolio Income	6	8805670	1944354	66	9170	28355	2734	17103	24753	63275	226061	195109	1068606	5226082
Other Receipts	7	109092885	6203390	4110520	1440030	3599098	2760849	2764326	2333454	2761419	4247768	4466215	12109173	62296643
Total Receipts	8	255888432	23816941	4202983	1486868	3753064	2839990	2951695	2755367	3996436	8337048	9262570	26335442	166150028
Average Total Receipts	9	9548	7497	280	563	1400	4232	5720	6545	8881	14704	30570	93720	1931977
Operating Costs/Operating Income (%)														
Cost of Operations	10	0.2	0.6	•	•	0.4	0.7	0.6	•	0.1	0.0	0.5	1.0	0.1
Salaries and Wages	11	9.3	3.8	25.3	18.1	19.5	26.8	28.5	26.5	17.7	18.2	15.4	14.1	6.7
Taxes Paid	12	1.5	1.8	2.7	3.0	2.9	3.2	3.2	3.6	2.5	2.7	2.4	2.0	1.1
Interest Paid	13	36.6	44.1	3.1	2.0	5.0	5.6	10.5	13.9	18.8	26.5	28.1	27.5	41.6
Depreciation	14	1.9	8.3	1.0	1.5	1.2	3.4	1.6	1.3	1.7	2.7	3.2	2.4	0.8
Amortization and Depletion	15	0.6	0.1	0.2	0.0	0.1	0.6	0.4	0.1	0.4	0.3	0.7	1.7	0.5
Pensions and Other Deferred Comp.	16	0.6	0.2	0.4	0.1	0.3	0.1	0.3	0.5	0.8	0.8	0.9	0.9	0.6
Employee Benefits	17	1.0	0.4	0.5	0.1	0.8	0.8	1.6	1.6	1.8	2.0	2.1	1.9	0.8
Advertising	18	2.1	0.0	4.1	1.6	1.3	4.2	2.3	2.2	1.9	1.6	1.3	1.4	2.6
Other Expenses	19	31.2	20.0	36.6	39.4	41.7	40.1	32.5	30.1	32.4	27.1	25.9	27.7	33.2
Officers' Compensation	20	1.3	0.5	10.2	6.9	5.4	2.3	5.2	4.9	5.1	4.7	3.2	1.7	0.5
Operating Margin	21	13.7	20.3	15.9	27.3	21.3	12.2	13.4	15.3	16.9	13.3	16.2	17.8	11.5
Operating Margin Before Officers' Comp.	22	15.0	20.8	26.1	34.2	26.7	14.6	18.6	20.2	22.0	18.0	19.3	19.5	12.0

Selected Average Balance Sheet ($ in Thousands)

Net Receivables 23	17097	0	11	215	1241	2855	8618	16840	31396	67275	103940	237078	3375767
Inventories 24	•	•	•	•	•	•	•	•	•	•	•	•	•
Net Property, Plant and Equipment 25	717	0	16	109	153	528	506	527	1363	3277	6666	15400	100106
Total Assets 26	98884	0	112	751	2403	6581	16377	36735	71950	162293	359182	1004367	24374283
Notes and Loans Payable 27	53253	0	30	284	844	3258	8137	9287	10600	20367	41342	171048	15540768
All Other Liabilities 28	38207	0	18	131	570	2286	4945	20266	49962	121044	271556	678406	7502024
Net Worth 29	7424	0	65	336	989	1037	3295	7182	11388	20881	46283	154914	1331491

Selected Financial Ratios (Times to 1)

Current Ratio 30	0.6	•	4.6	2.7	2.6	1.9	1.3	1.0	0.9	0.8	0.6	0.5	0.5
Quick Ratio 31	0.5	•	3.2	2.1	2.4	1.6	1.2	0.9	0.8	0.7	0.5	0.5	0.4
Net Sales to Working Capital 32	•	•	4.7	1.7	1.3	1.9	1.9	6.3	1.8	1.5	1.5	1.6	•
Coverage Ratio 33	1.4	1.5	6.2	14.7	5.2	3.2	2.3	2.1	1.8	1.5	1.5	1.6	1.3
Total Asset Turnover 34	0.1	•	2.5	0.7	0.6	0.6	0.3	0.2	0.1	0.1	0.1	0.1	0.1
Inventory Turnover 35	•	•	•	•	•	•	•	•	•	•	•	•	•
Receivables Turnover 36	•	•	•	•	•	•	•	•	•	•	•	•	•
Total Liabilities to Net Worth 37	12.3	•	0.7	1.2	1.4	5.3	4.0	4.1	5.3	6.8	6.8	5.5	17.3
Current Assets to Working Capital 38	•	•	1.3	1.6	1.6	2.1	3.9	25.2	•	•	•	•	•
Current Liabilities to Working Capital 39	•	•	0.3	0.6	0.6	1.1	2.9	24.2	•	•	•	•	•
Working Capital to Net Sales 40	•	•	0.2	0.6	0.8	0.5	0.5	0.2	•	•	•	•	•
Inventory to Working Capital 41	•	•	•	•	0.0	0.0	0.0	0.0	0.0	•	•	•	•
Total Receipts to Cash Flow 42	2.4	2.7	2.2	1.7	1.7	2.2	2.4	2.4	2.2	2.8	2.6	2.5	2.3
Cost of Goods to Cash Flow 43	0.0	0.0	•	0.0	0.0	0.0	0.0	•	0.0	0.0	0.0	0.0	0.0
Cash Flow to Total Debt 44	0.0	•	2.6	0.8	0.6	0.3	0.2	0.1	0.1	0.0	0.0	0.0	0.0

Selected Financial Factors (in Percentages)

Debt Ratio 45	92.5	•	42.3	55.3	58.8	84.2	79.9	80.4	84.2	87.1	87.1	84.6	94.5
Return on Total Assets 46	4.8	•	47.7	22.0	15.3	11.4	8.3	5.1	4.3	3.6	3.7	4.2	4.2
Return on Equity Before Income Taxes 47	17.2	•	69.2	45.8	30.1	49.6	23.2	13.5	12.5	9.4	10.0	10.5	16.4
Return on Equity After Income Taxes 48	12.8	•	67.2	45.0	29.1	48.1	21.3	12.1	10.3	7.3	7.1	7.3	11.8
Profit Margin (Before Income Tax) 49	13.4	19.9	15.9	27.3	21.3	12.2	13.4	14.8	16.0	13.4	15.2	17.4	11.3
Profit Margin (After Income Tax) 50	10.0	15.0	15.5	26.9	20.6	11.8	12.3	13.3	13.3	10.4	10.8	12.0	8.1

Table I

Corporations with and without Net Income

COMMERCIAL BANKING

Money Amounts and Size of Assets in Thousands of Dollars

Item Description for Accounting Period 7/08 Through 6/09		Total	Zero Assets	Under 500	500 to 1,000	1,000 to 5,000	5,000 to 10,000	10,000 to 25,000	25,000 to 50,000	50,000 to 100,000	100,000 to 250,000	250,000 to 500,000	500,000 to 2,500,000	2,500,000 and over
Number of Enterprises	1	1684	214	0	0	6	19	133	257	404	455	125	61	9
Revenues ($ in Thousands)														
Net Sales	2	55201094	39165148	0	0	22836	18722	170167	579090	1692853	4399722	2807794	4185393	2159369
Interest	3	66684232	56832447	0	0	4756	3295	101686	291849	1009076	2661379	1679406	2541757	1558582
Rents	4	194621	113284	0	0	0	1	344	533	1279	4801	12650	8416	53312
Royalties	5	6897	6664	0	0	0	0	0	0	14	99	6	0	114
Other Portfolio Income	6	1779396	1349480	0	0	0	4	4068	22028	48573	128170	71242	104817	51013
Other Receipts	7	-13464052	-19136727	0	0	18080	15422	64069	264680	633911	1605273	1044490	1530403	496348
Total Receipts	8	55201094	39165148	0	0	22836	18722	170167	579090	1692853	4399722	2807794	4185393	2159369
Average Total Receipts	9	32780	183015	•	•	3806	985	1279	2253	4190	9670	22462	68613	239930
Operating Costs/Operating Income (%)														
Cost of Operations	10	0.1	•	•	•	•	•	•	•	•	•	1.2	•	•
Salaries and Wages	11	10.5	8.9	•	•	4.3	4.0	13.5	16.4	16.0	15.2	15.3	14.2	9.8
Taxes Paid	12	2.4	2.3	•	•	0.1	0.6	3.1	2.8	3.0	2.6	2.7	2.4	2.5
Interest Paid	13	94.6	118.8	•	•	9.8	1.4	33.1	32.6	35.2	36.7	35.1	36.1	35.2
Depreciation	14	2.0	1.2	•	•	•	0.5	5.0	3.9	4.0	3.1	2.9	2.5	8.9
Amortization and Depletion	15	0.3	0.1	•	•	0.0	•	0.6	0.7	0.6	0.9	0.4	0.8	0.5
Pensions and Other Deferred Comp.	16	0.5	0.5	•	•	•	•	0.7	1.0	0.7	0.7	0.6	0.7	0.8
Employee Benefits	17	1.2	0.7	•	•	0.0	0.8	3.8	3.4	2.9	2.4	2.0	1.9	1.9
Advertising	18	0.4	0.2	•	•	0.1	0.1	1.1	1.2	1.2	0.9	0.9	0.6	0.5
Other Expenses	19	59.0	72.2	•	•	167.5	174.5	51.9	32.4	27.0	28.2	26.8	25.7	20.0
Officers' Compensation	20	2.3	0.7	•	•	•	1.6	15.3	12.5	10.3	6.6	5.2	3.4	6.0
Operating Margin	21	•	•	•	•	•	•	•	•	•	2.6	7.0	11.7	14.0
Operating Margin Before Officers' Comp.	22	•	•	•	•	•	•	•	5.6	9.4	9.2	12.1	15.1	20.0

Selected Average Balance Sheet ($ in Thousands)

Net Receivables 23	88246	0	•	•	0	1501	9140	23371	45799	98682	209529	580976	1813606
Inventories 24	•	•	•	•	•	•	•	•	•	•	•	•	•
Net Property, Plant and Equipment 25	2498	0	•	•	340	45	554	695	1480	3093	5794	13779	42324
Total Assets 26	154244	0	•	•	2551	6960	18817	38611	73001	154320	352271	1036345	4468310
Notes and Loans Payable 27	8628	0	•	•	0	0	777	738	2011	7506	20027	68238	371437
All Other Liabilities 28	128837	0	•	•	7336	48274	15071	31779	61210	130766	295765	858555	3584407
Net Worth 29	16779	0	•	•	-4785	-41313	2969	6093	9781	16049	36479	109552	512467

Selected Financial Ratios (Times to 1)

Current Ratio 30	1.0	•	•	•	0.5	2.0	1.2	1.1	1.0	1.0	0.9	0.9	1.0
Quick Ratio 31	0.9	•	•	•	0.4	1.9	1.1	1.1	1.0	0.9	0.9	0.9	0.8
Net Sales to Working Capital 32	•	•	•	•	0.3	•	0.5	0.7	1.6	•	•	•	•
Coverage Ratio 33	0.2	0.1	•	•	•	0.1	0.1	0.7	0.9	1.0	1.1	1.3	1.4
Total Asset Turnover 34	0.2	•	•	•	1.5	0.1	0.1	0.1	0.1	0.1	0.1	0.1	0.1
Inventory Turnover 35	•	•	•	•	•	•	•	•	•	•	•	•	•
Receivables Turnover 36	•	•	•	•	•	•	•	•	•	•	•	•	•
Total Liabilities to Net Worth 37	8.2	•	•	•	•	•	5.3	5.3	6.5	8.6	8.7	8.5	7.7
Current Assets to Working Capital 38	•	•	•	•	2.0	6.3	10.7	24.2	8.7	•	•	•	•
Current Liabilities to Working Capital 39	•	•	•	•	1.0	5.3	9.7	23.2	•	•	•	•	•
Working Capital to Net Sales 40	•	•	•	•	2.9	2.1	1.4	0.6	•	•	•	•	•
Inventory to Working Capital 41	•	•	•	•	•	•	•	•	•	•	•	•	•
Total Receipts to Cash Flow 42	3.1	•	•	•	•	•	19.3	4.8	4.5	3.7	3.4	3.0	3.4
Cost of Goods to Cash Flow 43	•	•	•	•	•	•	•	0.0	0.0	0.0	•	•	•
Cash Flow to Total Debt 44	0.2	•	•	•	•	•	0.0	0.0	0.0	0.0	0.0	0.0	0.0

Selected Financial Factors (in Percentages)

Debt Ratio 45	89.1	•	•	287.6	693.6	84.2	84.2	86.6	89.6	89.6	84.2	89.4	88.5
Return on Total Assets 46	4.3	•	•	•	•	1.4	0.2	•	1.8	2.4	2.6	3.1	2.6
Return on Equity Before Income Taxes 47	65.1	•	•	2.0	•	•	•	•	•	0.5	3.2	6.3	6.4
Return on Equity After Income Taxes 48	65.1	•	•	2.0	•	•	•	•	•	1.5	•	4.3	4.1
Profit Margin (Before Income Tax) 49	•	•	•	•	•	•	•	•	0.8	5.2	0.8	10.0	13.6
Profit Margin (After Income Tax) 50	•	•	•	•	•	•	•	•	•	•	2.5	6.8	8.7

277

Table II

Corporations with Net Income

COMMERCIAL BANKING

MONEY AMOUNTS AND SIZE OF ASSETS IN THOUSANDS OF DOLLARS

Item Description for Accounting Period 7/08 Through 6/09	Total	Zero Assets	Under 500	500 to 1,000	1,000 to 5,000	5,000 to 10,000	10,000 to 25,000	25,000 to 50,000	50,000 to 100,000	100,000 to 250,000	250,000 to 500,000	500,000 to 2,500,000	2,500,000 and over
Number of Enterprises **1**	1014	96	0	0	0	•	74	160	227	291	95	46	•
Revenues ($ in Thousands)													
Net Sales **2**	28226244	16555424	0	0	0	0	101428	385838	1036070	2883040	2124994	3212248	•
Interest **3**	20358590	13393290	0	0	0	0	69045	165574	518590	1655376	1195683	1922947	•
Rents **4**	127651	56489	0	0	0	0	56	190	763	4097	6092	6651	•
Royalties **5**	230	0	0	0	0	0	0	0	14	96	6	0	•
Other Portfolio Income **6**	492464	161413	0	0	0	0	2236	16651	37949	85536	59805	81955	•
Other Receipts **7**	7247309	2944232	0	0	0	0	30091	203423	478754	1137935	863408	1200695	•
Total Receipts **8**	28226244	16555424	0	0	0	0	101428	385838	1036070	2883040	2124994	3212248	•
Average Total Receipts **9**	27837	172452	•	•	•	•	1371	2411	4564	9907	22368	69831	•
Operating Costs/Operating Income (%)													
Cost of Operations **10**	•	•	•	•	•	•	•	•	•	•	•	•	•
Salaries and Wages **11**	8.3	5.1	•	•	•	•	9.6	10.5	12.3	13.6	14.4	13.2	•
Taxes Paid **12**	2.5	2.3	•	•	•	•	2.5	2.5	2.7	2.7	2.8	2.5	•
Interest Paid **13**	46.5	54.7	•	•	•	•	39.8	31.3	32.6	35.1	33.3	35.5	•
Depreciation **14**	1.7	0.9	•	•	•	•	2.1	2.0	2.6	2.7	2.8	2.3	•
Amortization and Depletion **15**	0.2	0.1	•	•	•	•	0.0	0.2	0.3	0.3	0.4	0.2	•
Pensions and Other Deferred Comp. **16**	0.5	0.3	•	•	•	•	0.9	1.2	0.8	0.7	0.6	0.7	•
Employee Benefits **17**	1.2	0.6	•	•	•	•	4.1	3.3	2.8	2.4	2.1	1.6	•
Advertising **18**	0.3	0.0	•	•	•	•	0.8	0.8	0.8	0.9	0.8	0.6	•
Other Expenses **19**	19.8	19.9	•	•	•	•	16.5	18.3	19.2	18.9	19.5	21.0	•
Officers' Compensation **20**	2.7	0.5	•	•	•	•	11.4	11.5	8.6	6.8	5.6	3.6	•
Operating Margin **21**	16.3	15.7	•	•	•	•	12.3	18.5	17.2	15.8	17.7	18.8	•
Operating Margin Before Officers' Comp. **22**	19.1	16.2	•	•	•	•	23.7	30.0	25.9	22.6	23.2	22.4	•

Selected Average Balance Sheet ($ in Thousands)

Net Receivables 23	102811	0	9257	22398	42642	97914	216399	555719
Inventories 24	•	•	•	•	•	•	•	•
Net Property, Plant and Equipment 25	2716	0	194	497	1207	2977	5440	13603
Total Assets 26	184569	0	19107	38430	72265	157727	359843	1028871
Notes and Loans Payable 27	10555	0	407	648	2045	7596	18675	69329
All Other Liabilities 28	154318	0	16119	32580	61327	132880	302211	851940
Net Worth 29	19696	0	2581	5202	8893	17251	38957	107602

Selected Financial Ratios (Times to 1)

Current Ratio 30	1.0	•	1.2	1.1	1.0	1.0	1.0	0.9
Quick Ratio 31	0.9	•	1.1	1.1	1.0	0.9	0.9	0.9
Net Sales to Working Capital 32	•	1.3	0.6	0.8	1.8	1.4	•	1.5
Coverage Ratio 33	1.3	•	1.3	1.5	1.4	1.4	1.5	1.5
Total Asset Turnover 34	0.2	•	0.1	0.1	0.1	0.1	0.1	0.1
Inventory Turnover 35	•	•	•	•	•	•	•	•
Receivables Turnover 36	•	•	•	•	•	•	•	•
Total Liabilities to Net Worth 37	8.4	•	6.4	6.4	7.1	8.1	8.2	8.6
Current Assets to Working Capital 38	•	•	7.3	11.9	26.0	•	•	•
Current Liabilities to Working Capital 39	•	•	6.3	10.9	25.0	•	•	•
Working Capital to Net Sales 40	•	•	1.7	1.3	0.5	•	•	•
Inventory to Working Capital 41	•	•	•	•	•	•	•	•
Total Receipts to Cash Flow 42	3.1	3.1	3.8	3.0	2.9	3.2	3.0	2.7
Cost of Goods to Cash Flow 43	•	•	•	•	•	•	•	•
Cash Flow to Total Debt 44	0.1	•	0.0	0.0	0.0	0.0	0.0	0.0

Selected Financial Factors (in Percentages)

Debt Ratio 45	89.3	•	86.5	86.5	87.7	89.1	89.2	89.5
Return on Total Assets 46	9.3	•	3.6	2.9	3.0	3.1	3.0	3.6
Return on Equity Before Income Taxes 47	21.6	•	5.4	7.3	7.3	7.8	9.0	11.1
Return on Equity After Income Taxes 48	16.9	•	4.5	6.3	6.1	6.2	6.9	8.4
Profit Margin (Before Income Tax) 49	15.3	15.2	10.3	15.7	14.3	13.5	15.7	17.2
Profit Margin (After Income Tax) 50	12.0	12.1	8.4	13.5	12.0	10.9	12.0	13.0

Table I

Corporations with and without Net Income

SAVINGS INSTITUTIONS AND OTHER DEPOSITORY CREDIT

MONEY AMOUNTS AND SIZE OF ASSETS IN THOUSANDS OF DOLLARS

Item Description for Accounting Period 7/08 Through 6/09	Total	Zero Assets	Under 500	500 to 1,000	1,000 to 5,000	5,000 to 10,000	10,000 to 25,000	25,000 to 50,000	50,000 to 100,000	100,000 to 250,000	250,000 to 500,000	500,000 to 2,500,000	2,500,000 and over
Number of Enterprises 1	1591	22	407	0	49	9	56	123	151	274	214	228	58
Revenues ($ in Thousands)													
Net Sales 2	91241574	1691625	10196	0	139378	3421	90124	294642	645076	3913306	4659976	13550014	66243817
Interest 3	6667875	889416	16	0	74678	3357	48826	208738	558381	2906270	3670219	10543288	47764685
Rents 4	498413	221671	0	0	170	22	121	1280	1551	10297	10617	62912	189772
Royalties 5	8952	0	0	0	0	0	0	38	48	0	0	1367	7499
Other Portfolio Income 6	2437223	205477	0	0	0	0	160	8709	11928	91583	147995	462071	1509300
Other Receipts 7	21629111	375061	10180	0	64530	42	41017	75877	73168	905156	831145	2480376	16772561
Total Receipts 8	91241574	1691625	10196	0	139378	3421	90124	294642	645076	3913306	4659976	13550014	66243817
Average Total Receipts 9	57349	76892	25	•	2844	380	1609	2395	4272	14282	21776	59430	1142135
Operating Costs/Operating Income (%)													
Cost of Operations 10	0.2	•	•	•	•	•	3.2	•	•	•	•	0.2	0.3
Salaries and Wages 11	12.8	2.8	•	•	20.9	15.2	20.8	18.6	13.4	18.2	14.7	15.3	12.1
Taxes Paid 12	1.6	0.6	•	•	3.2	1.3	2.7	2.9	2.8	2.9	2.6	2.3	1.3
Interest Paid 13	44.2	38.1	322.9	•	41.7	61.0	34.0	36.6	43.8	38.1	41.4	42.7	45.3
Depreciation 14	2.0	10.7	7.8	•	2.0	1.1	2.9	2.5	2.7	2.2	4.3	2.6	1.5
Amortization and Depletion 15	0.7	0.0	11.2	•	0.4	•	0.1	0.3	0.1	0.1	0.2	0.4	0.8
Pensions and Other Deferred Comp. 16	0.8	0.8	•	•	1.2	•	0.7	1.5	1.9	1.4	1.6	1.3	0.6
Employee Benefits 17	1.8	0.4	•	•	1.5	•	1.9	3.0	2.7	2.1	2.6	2.5	1.6
Advertising 18	1.4	2.1	•	•	0.4	0.5	2.1	1.0	1.1	1.0	1.1	1.2	1.5
Other Expenses 19	69.9	32.7	63.8	•	27.6	22.9	74.9	23.0	23.9	117.8	20.9	24.7	81.5
Officers' Compensation 20	1.1	0.4	•	•	0.8	•	4.2	9.1	7.3	4.0	3.6	2.1	0.5
Operating Margin 21	•	11.4	•	•	0.1	•	•	1.5	0.2	•	7.0	4.8	•
Operating Margin Before Officers' Comp. 22	•	11.8	•	•	1.0	•	•	10.6	7.5	•	10.6	6.9	•

Selected Average Balance Sheet ($ in Thousands)

Net Receivables 23	67786	0	3	254	-35	509	3370	8438	19104	29586	73120	1342750
Inventories 24	•	•	•	•	•	•	•	•	•	•	•	•
Net Property, Plant and Equipment 25	9478	0	12	32	35	296	761	1563	3149	6911	15589	152250
Total Assets 26	894551	0	115	1743	7161	17517	38628	75346	167837	360760	969929	18303277
Notes and Loans Payable 27	165214	0	20	11	0	2961	2198	4973	16114	39550	109421	3859182
All Other Liabilities 28	665397	0	2599	48315	6567	14850	28606	59502	133331	280332	767491	13281297
Net Worth 29	63940	0	-2503	-46582	594	-294	7824	10870	18393	40878	93018	1162799

Selected Financial Ratios (Times to 1)

Current Ratio 30	0.3	•	1.3	0.0	0.0	0.3	0.3	0.3	0.3	0.3	0.2	0.3
Quick Ratio 31	0.2	•	1.3	0.0	0.0	0.3	0.3	0.3	0.3	0.2	0.2	0.2
Net Sales to Working Capital 32	•	•	2.2	•	•	•	•	•	•	•	•	•
Coverage Ratio 33	0.2	1.3	0.1	1.0	1.0	1.0	1.0	1.0	1.0	1.1	1.1	1.1
Total Asset Turnover 34	0.1	•	0.2	1.6	0.1	0.1	0.1	0.1	0.1	0.1	0.1	0.1
Inventory Turnover 35	•	•	•	•	•	•	•	•	•	•	•	•
Receivables Turnover 36	•	•	•	•	•	•	•	•	•	•	•	•
Total Liabilities to Net Worth 37	13.0	•	•	•	11.1	•	3.9	5.9	8.1	7.8	9.4	14.7
Current Assets to Working Capital 38	•	•	4.3	•	•	•	•	•	•	•	•	•
Current Liabilities to Working Capital 39	•	•	3.3	•	•	•	•	•	•	•	•	•
Working Capital to Net Sales 40	•	•	0.5	•	•	•	•	•	•	•	•	•
Inventory to Working Capital 41	•	•	•	•	•	•	•	•	•	•	•	•
Total Receipts to Cash Flow 42	•	2.3	•	4.7	5.0	3.9	4.7	5.2	4.3	4.0	4.0	4.0
Cost of Goods to Cash Flow 43	•	•	•	•	•	0.1	•	•	•	0.0	0.0	0.0
Cash Flow to Total Debt 44	•	•	•	0.0	0.0	0.0	0.0	0.0	0.0	0.0	0.0	0.0

Selected Financial Factors (in Percentages)

Debt Ratio 45	92.9	2269.7	2772.3	91.7	101.7	79.7	85.6	89.0	88.7	90.4	•	93.6
Return on Total Assets 46	0.5	3.7	68.2	3.1	•	2.3	2.4	•	2.8	2.9	•	•
Return on Equity Before Income Taxes 47	•	3.1	•	•	259.4	0.1	•	•	3.1	2.6	•	•
Return on Equity After Income Taxes 48	•	3.1	0.4	•	262.2	•	•	•	1.6	0.7	•	•
Profit Margin (Before Income Tax) 49	11.3	•	0.1	•	•	0.3	•	•	5.8	4.0	•	•
Profit Margin (After Income Tax) 50	10.9	•	•	•	•	•	•	•	2.9	1.1	•	•

Table II

Corporations with Net Income

SAVINGS INSTITUTIONS AND OTHER DEPOSITORY CREDIT

MONEY AMOUNTS AND SIZE OF ASSETS IN THOUSANDS OF DOLLARS

Item Description for Accounting Period 7/08 Through 6/09	Total	Zero Assets	Under 500	500 to 1,000	1,000 to 5,000	5,000 to 10,000	10,000 to 25,000	25,000 to 50,000	50,000 to 100,000	100,000 to 250,000	250,000 to 500,000	500,000 to 2,500,000	2,500,000 and over
Number of Enterprises 1	1245	13	•	•	0	0	31	81	108	204	179	181	•
Revenues ($ in Thousands)													
Net Sales 2	46460190	275446	•	•	0	0	44001	217770	477081	2412523	3937919	10392580	•
Interest 3	34548154	25052	•	•	0	0	27523	138733	418370	1696785	3104058	8332707	•
Rents 4	218565	96	•	•	0	0	97	419	909	5433	8282	46712	•
Royalties 5	8885	0	•	•	0	0	0	38	0	0	0	1347	•
Other Portfolio Income 6	1450021	128	•	•	0	0	31	7234	9383	62958	125446	314837	•
Other Receipts 7	10234565	250170	•	•	0	0	16350	71346	48419	647347	700133	1696977	•
Total Receipts 8	46460190	275446	•	•	0	0	44001	217770	477081	2412523	3937919	10392580	•
Average Total Receipts 9	37317	21188	•	•	•	•	1419	2689	4417	11826	22000	57418	•
Operating Costs/Operating Income (%)													
Cost of Operations 10	0.0	•	•	•	•	•	•	•	•	•	•	0.0	•
Salaries and Wages 11	12.0	0.7	•	•	•	•	22.3	19.4	12.0	20.0	14.0	15.0	•
Taxes Paid 12	2.1	0.3	•	•	•	•	2.8	2.8	2.8	2.7	2.6	2.3	•
Interest Paid 13	44.9	4.8	•	•	•	•	39.7	33.5	43.4	34.8	40.8	41.8	•
Depreciation 14	2.2	0.2	•	•	•	•	0.9	2.1	2.1	2.4	4.6	2.6	•
Amortization and Depletion 15	1.0	•	•	•	•	•	0.0	0.1	0.0	0.1	0.2	0.5	•
Pensions and Other Deferred Comp. 16	1.2	0.0	•	•	•	•	0.6	1.5	1.4	1.6	1.6	1.4	•
Employee Benefits 17	1.8	0.2	•	•	•	•	1.4	2.7	2.7	2.3	2.7	2.5	•
Advertising 18	1.5	0.1	•	•	•	•	0.7	0.8	0.9	1.1	1.1	1.2	•
Other Expenses 19	16.3	1.7	•	•	•	•	18.1	19.2	16.2	18.6	16.4	17.7	•
Officers' Compensation 20	1.6	0.5	•	•	•	•	3.7	7.8	6.5	4.9	3.7	2.1	•
Operating Margin 21	15.4	91.5	•	•	•	•	9.8	10.3	11.9	11.5	12.4	12.8	•
Operating Margin Before Officers' Comp. 22	17.0	92.0	•	•	•	•	13.5	18.1	18.4	16.4	16.1	14.9	•

Selected Average Balance Sheet ($ in Thousands)

Net Receivables 23	43617	0	700	3630	7957	17530	29636	67154
Inventories 24	•	•	•	•	•	•	•	•
Net Property, Plant and Equipment 25	7135	0	186	679	1388	3048	6813	14850
Total Assets 26	609930	0	18006	38463	76221	167032	359549	954139
Notes and Loans Payable 27	89305	0	5149	2377	4341	15826	39107	104396
All Other Liabilities 28	466302	0	10967	28641	60798	130362	280763	744364
Net Worth 29	54323	0	1890	7444	11082	20843	39680	105379

Selected Financial Ratios (Times to 1)

Current Ratio 30	0.2	•	0.2	0.3	0.3	0.3	0.3	0.2
Quick Ratio 31	0.2	•	0.2	0.3	0.3	0.2	0.2	0.2
Net Sales to Working Capital 32	•	•	•	•	•	•	•	•
Coverage Ratio 33	1.3	20.2	1.2	1.3	1.2	1.3	1.3	1.3
Total Asset Turnover 34	0.1	•	0.1	0.1	0.1	0.1	0.1	0.1
Inventory Turnover 35	•	•	•	•	•	•	•	•
Receivables Turnover 36	•	•	•	•	•	•	•	•
Total Liabilities to Net Worth 37	10.2	•	8.5	4.2	5.9	7.0	8.1	8.1
Current Assets to Working Capital 38	•	•	•	•	•	•	•	•
Current Liabilities to Working Capital 39	•	•	•	•	•	•	•	•
Working Capital to Net Sales 40	•	•	•	•	•	•	•	•
Inventory to Working Capital 41	•	•	•	•	•	•	•	•
Total Receipts to Cash Flow 42	3.6	1.1	3.8	3.6	3.9	3.7	3.9	3.7
Cost of Goods to Cash Flow 43	0.0	•	•	•	•	•	•	0.0
Cash Flow to Total Debt 44	0.0	•	0.0	0.0	0.0	0.0	0.0	0.0

Selected Financial Factors (in Percentages)

Debt Ratio 45	91.1	•	89.5	80.6	85.5	87.5	89.0	89.0
Return on Total Assets 46	3.7	•	3.9	3.0	3.1	3.2	3.2	3.2
Return on Equity Before Income Taxes 47	10.2	•	7.3	3.3	4.3	6.0	6.2	6.6
Return on Equity After Income Taxes 48	7.4	•	6.5	2.7	3.0	4.2	4.3	4.5
Profit Margin (Before Income Tax) 49	14.9	91.5	9.7	9.2	10.7	10.5	11.2	12.0
Profit Margin (After Income Tax) 50	10.7	89.1	8.7	7.5	7.5	7.4	7.8	8.2

Table I
Corporations with and without Net Income

CREDIT CARD ISSUING AND OTHER CONSUMER CREDIT

MONEY AMOUNTS AND SIZE OF ASSETS IN THOUSANDS OF DOLLARS

Item Description for Accounting Period 7/08 Through 6/09	Total	Zero Assets	Under 500	500 to 1,000	1,000 to 5,000	5,000 to 10,000	10,000 to 25,000	25,000 to 50,000	50,000 to 100,000	100,000 to 250,000	250,000 to 500,000	500,000 to 2,500,000	2,500,000 and over
Number of Enterprises **1**	9224	1818	3610	1400	1535	331	270	90	49	50	23	30	17
Revenues ($ in Thousands)													
Net Sales **2**	102758916	1707712	256815	512649	1698527	2006496	1917785	911784	1151276	2365958	2321342	8140386	79768187
Interest **3**	32492471	873741	6192	14520	92368	88316	222871	52983	130975	415726	276689	3674370	26643721
Rents **4**	6675	0	0	4	408	25	372	628	479	559	8	4193	0
Royalties **5**	293287	0	0	0	0	0	0	0	0	0	0	11767	281520
Other Portfolio Income **6**	3341989	229565	121	3655	14304	3164	5315	3669	8942	4288	4022	18229	3046712
Other Receipts **7**	6624494	604406	250502	494470	1591447	1914991	1689227	854504	1010880	1945385	2040623	4431827	49796234
Total Receipts **8**	102758916	1707712	256815	512649	1698527	2006496	1917785	911784	1151276	2365958	2321342	8140386	79768187
Average Total Receipts **9**	11140	939	71	366	1107	6062	7103	10131	23495	47319	100928	271346	4692246
Operating Costs/Operating Income (%)													
Cost of Operations **10**	0.4	•	•	•	0.7	•	0.2	•	3.9	0.0	0.2	0.0	0.5
Salaries and Wages **11**	10.0	17.2	55.7	20.7	14.1	22.3	23.9	18.1	19.3	18.4	16.7	16.8	7.6
Taxes Paid **12**	1.5	1.4	6.9	3.3	2.1	3.3	2.2	2.5	2.4	2.4	2.3	1.8	1.3
Interest Paid **13**	21.8	13.0	7.3	4.0	7.8	6.8	12.1	12.7	9.5	23.7	16.5	18.5	23.7
Depreciation **14**	8.7	3.4	2.2	0.2	1.4	3.9	1.0	5.0	1.8	3.3	3.2	2.9	10.4
Amortization and Depletion **15**	0.5	0.0	•	2.5	0.3	0.9	0.8	0.5	0.7	1.1	1.5	1.1	0.4
Pensions and Other Deferred Comp. **16**	0.5	0.1	0.6	0.0	0.1	0.0	0.3	0.2	1.1	0.2	0.1	0.1	0.5
Employee Benefits **17**	0.7	0.8	1.3	0.2	1.4	0.3	1.2	1.0	1.7	1.1	1.6	0.8	0.6
Advertising **18**	2.5	0.9	2.5	2.1	1.4	5.5	2.4	1.8	3.9	1.4	1.5	1.0	2.7
Other Expenses **19**	47.8	37.8	68.0	55.1	50.8	52.9	48.4	56.1	43.3	49.2	43.8	54.1	47.1
Officers' Compensation **20**	0.5	0.5	8.5	3.4	7.0	1.5	4.3	2.9	4.1	2.3	1.0	0.5	0.1
Operating Margin **21**	5.1	24.9	•	8.5	12.9	2.5	3.2	•	8.3	•	11.6	2.4	5.1
Operating Margin Before Officers' Comp. **22**	5.6	25.4	•	11.9	19.9	4.1	7.5	2.0	12.4	•	12.5	2.9	5.2

Selected Average Balance Sheet ($ in Thousands)

	Col 1	Col 2	Col 3	Col 4	Col 5	Col 6	Col 7	Col 8	Col 9	Col 10	Col 11	Col 12	Col 13
Net Receivables 23	34964	0	42	411	1913	4522	11604	23297	43036	103776	213680	666384	16465548
Inventories 24	•	•	•	•	•	•	•	•	•	•	•	•	•
Net Property, Plant and Equipment 25	3063	0	19	5	37	345	940	3161	3628	5423	7649	•	1589338
Total Assets 26	62610	150	782	2501	7617	15952	34250	66268	166556	368245	1107477	•	29933282
Notes and Loans Payable 27	34571	0	96	266	1101	4458	9997	22968	37948	131672	204486	753016	16147034
All Other Liabilities 28	20342	0	120	102	320	631	2704	4708	13413	33513	69425	206983	10297901
Net Worth 29	7697	0	-66	413	1080	2527	3250	6574	14907	1371	94334	147478	3488347

Selected Financial Ratios (Times to 1)

	Col 1	Col 2	Col 3	Col 4	Col 5	Col 6	Col 7	Col 8	Col 9	Col 10	Col 11	Col 12	Col 13
Current Ratio 30	1.9	•	1.2	4.5	3.4	3.0	2.1	1.9	2.1	1.6	1.5	1.6	1.9
Quick Ratio 31	1.8	•	0.6	3.6	3.2	2.5	1.9	1.6	1.8	1.4	1.4	1.5	1.8
Net Sales to Working Capital 32	0.6	•	3.7	0.7	0.7	1.6	1.0	0.8	0.8	0.9	1.2	0.9	0.5
Coverage Ratio 33	1.2	2.9	•	3.1	2.7	1.4	1.3	0.9	1.9	0.9	1.7	1.1	1.2
Total Asset Turnover 34	0.2	•	0.5	0.5	0.4	0.8	0.4	0.3	0.4	0.3	0.3	0.2	0.2
Inventory Turnover 35	•	•	•	•	•	•	•	•	•	•	•	•	•
Receivables Turnover 36	•	•	•	•	•	•	•	•	•	•	120.5	•	•
Total Liabilities to Net Worth 37	7.1	•	•	0.9	1.3	2.0	3.9	4.2	3.4	2.9	2.9	6.5	7.6
Current Assets to Working Capital 38	2.2	•	5.9	1.3	1.4	1.5	1.9	2.1	1.9	2.6	2.9	2.7	2.2
Current Liabilities to Working Capital 39	1.2	•	4.9	0.3	0.4	0.5	0.9	1.1	0.9	1.6	1.9	1.7	1.2
Working Capital to Net Sales 40	1.7	•	0.3	1.4	1.4	0.6	1.0	1.3	1.2	1.1	0.8	1.1	1.9
Inventory to Working Capital 41	0.0	•	•	0.0	0.0	0.0	0.0	0.0	0.0	0.0	0.0	0.0	0.0
Total Receipts to Cash Flow 42	2.1	1.9	150.4	1.7	1.7	2.2	2.1	2.0	2.1	2.6	2.0	1.8	2.1
Cost of Goods to Cash Flow 43	0.0	•	•	0.0	0.0	•	0.0	0.1	0.0	0.0	0.0	0.0	0.0
Cash Flow to Total Debt 44	0.1	•	0.0	0.5	0.6	0.6	0.3	0.2	0.2	0.1	0.2	0.2	0.1

Selected Financial Factors (in Percentages)

	Col 1	Col 2	Col 3	Col 4	Col 5	Col 6	Col 7	Col 8	Col 9	Col 10	Col 11	Col 12	Col 13
Debt Ratio 45	87.7	•	144.0	47.1	56.8	66.8	79.6	80.8	77.5	99.2	74.4	86.7	88.3
Return on Total Assets 46	4.8	•	•	5.9	9.2	7.5	6.8	3.5	6.3	5.8	7.7	5.1	4.5
Return on Equity Before Income Taxes 47	7.4	•	57.3	7.5	13.2	6.1	7.0	13.1	•	•	12.4	4.3	7.0
Return on Equity After Income Taxes 48	4.0	•	57.4	7.1	12.5	5.5	5.4	9.7	•	•	6.9	1.1	3.9
Profit Margin (Before Income Tax) 49	5.1	24.9	•	8.5	12.9	2.5	3.2	8.3	•	•	11.6	2.3	5.2
Profit Margin (After Income Tax) 50	2.7	9.2	•	8.0	12.2	2.3	2.5	6.1	•	•	6.5	0.6	2.9

Table II
Corporations with Net Income

CREDIT CARD ISSUING AND OTHER CONSUMER CREDIT

MONEY AMOUNTS AND SIZE OF ASSETS IN THOUSANDS OF DOLLARS

Item Description for Accounting Period 7/08 Through 6/09		Total	Zero Assets	Under 500	500 to 1,000	1,000 to 5,000	5,000 to 10,000	10,000 to 25,000	25,000 to 50,000	50,000 to 100,000	100,000 to 250,000	250,000 to 500,000	500,000 to 2,500,000	2,500,000 and over
Number of Enterprises	1	4214	684	933	931	1105	209	193	55	33	29	14	18	9
Revenues ($ in Thousands)														
Net Sales	2	72944087	999858	89824	355115	1384112	1705641	1335710	645222	915512	1375757	1955669	3389136	58792529
Interest	3	22460867	415594	5	11688	49337	45655	19658	45112	120044	250747	84157	1183955	20234915
Rents	4	1326	0	0	4	354	13	372	483	92	0	8	0	0
Royalties	5	281520	0	0	0	0	0	0	0	0	0	0	0	281520
Other Portfolio Income	6	3259951	209019	0	1821	8916	1014	5315	336	7358	1452	3260	11520	3009939
Other Receipts	7	46940423	375245	89819	341602	1325505	1658959	1310365	599291	788018	1123558	1868244	2193661	35266155
Total Receipts	8	72944087	999858	89824	355115	1384112	1705641	1335710	645222	915512	1375757	1955669	3389136	58792529
Average Total Receipts	9	17310	1462	96	381	1253	8161	6921	11731	27743	47440	139691	188285	6532503
Operating Costs/Operating Income (%)														
Cost of Operations	10	0.2	•	•	•	0.9	•	0.3	•	•	0.0	0.2	•	0.2
Salaries and Wages	11	9.4	3.1	4.4	6.5	12.2	23.1	22.9	14.9	19.5	17.6	18.1	9.6	8.0
Taxes Paid	12	1.3	1.5	2.9	1.7	1.9	3.6	2.5	2.6	2.5	2.7	2.3	1.3	1.1
Interest Paid	13	16.0	3.1	2.3	4.1	6.4	5.7	9.6	9.8	7.4	12.9	7.7	20.0	17.4
Depreciation	14	0.9	5.1	0.2	0.2	1.0	4.5	1.0	1.2	1.8	3.4	2.0	2.1	0.5
Amortization and Depletion	15	0.5	0.0	•	0.0	0.3	1.0	0.6	0.1	0.1	0.6	1.1	2.1	0.4
Pensions and Other Deferred Comp.	16	0.4	•	•	0.0	0.1	0.0	0.4	0.2	1.3	0.2	0.2	0.2	0.5
Employee Benefits	17	0.8	0.5	0.7	0.0	0.6	0.3	1.2	0.6	1.7	1.3	1.8	1.1	0.7
Advertising	18	3.3	0.0	4.4	0.7	0.6	6.2	2.0	1.4	4.5	1.9	1.7	0.8	3.6
Other Expenses	19	51.9	7.2	59.3	56.8	46.7	46.4	37.0	50.4	41.0	44.1	45.6	44.3	54.3
Officers' Compensation	20	0.5	0.4	9.2	4.8	7.0	1.3	4.9	1.9	3.5	2.5	0.9	0.8	0.1
Operating Margin	21	14.8	79.2	16.6	25.2	22.4	8.0	17.4	17.0	16.8	12.9	18.4	17.8	13.3
Operating Margin Before Officers' Comp.	22	15.3	79.5	25.8	29.9	29.4	9.3	22.3	18.9	20.3	15.3	19.3	18.6	13.4

Selected Average Balance Sheet ($ in Thousands)

Item													
Net Receivables 23	47455	0	41	481	2161	3586	13301	22143	45848	106377	230038	807330	18912864
Inventories 24	•	•	•	•	•	•	•	•	•	•	•	•	•
Net Property, Plant and Equipment 25	547	0	3	6	27	1102	271	290	2210	3951	8300	7284	170415
Total Assets 26	84869	262	823	2605	7543	15829	33625	64992	157426	362373	1122311		35031662
Notes and Loans Payable 27	32359	0	117	245	1014	3488	9231	21014	39080	86665	136346	609619	12727881
All Other Liabilities 28	38556	0	47	149	324	451	2332	5643	10722	33957	97459	253866	17089695
Net Worth 29	13955	0	97	429	1267	3603	4266	6968	15190	36804	128568	258825	5214086

Selected Financial Ratios (Times to 1)

Item													
Current Ratio 30	2.0	•	32.9	3.6	4.2	3.5	2.5	1.8	2.4	2.4	1.7	2.2	1.9
Quick Ratio 31	1.9	•	6.8	2.7	4.1	2.5	2.4	1.5	2.1	2.1	1.6	2.1	1.9
Net Sales to Working Capital 32	0.6	•	0.4	0.7	0.7	2.1	0.8	0.9	0.8	0.6	1.3	0.4	0.6
Coverage Ratio 33	1.9	26.5	8.3	7.1	4.5	2.4	2.8	2.7	3.3	2.0	3.4	1.9	1.8
Total Asset Turnover 34	0.2	•	0.4	0.5	0.5	1.1	0.4	0.3	0.4	0.3	0.4	0.2	0.2
Inventory Turnover 35	•	•	•	•	•	•	•	•	•	•	•	•	•
Receivables Turnover 36	•	•	•	•	•	•	•	•	•	•	•	•	•
Total Liabilities to Net Worth 37	5.1	•	1.7	0.9	1.1	1.1	2.7	3.8	3.3	3.3	1.8	3.3	5.7
Current Assets to Working Capital 38	2.0	•	1.0	1.4	1.3	1.4	1.7	2.2	1.7	1.7	2.4	1.8	2.1
Current Liabilities to Working Capital 39	1.0	•	0.0	0.4	0.3	0.4	0.7	1.2	0.7	0.7	1.4	0.8	1.1
Working Capital to Net Sales 40	1.6	•	2.4	1.5	1.5	0.5	1.2	1.1	1.2	1.6	0.7	2.7	1.6
Inventory to Working Capital 41	0.0	•	•	•	•	•	0.0	•	•	0.0	0.0	0.0	0.0
Total Receipts to Cash Flow 42	1.6	1.2	1.4	1.3	1.5	2.3	2.0	1.6	1.8	2.0	1.7	1.6	1.5
Cost of Goods to Cash Flow 43	0.0	•	•	•	0.0	•	0.0	•	•	0.0	0.0	•	0.0
Cash Flow to Total Debt 44	0.2	•	0.4	0.8	0.6	0.9	0.3	0.3	0.3	0.2	0.3	0.1	0.1

Selected Financial Factors (in Percentages)

Item													
Debt Ratio 45	83.6	•	62.8	47.8	51.4	52.2	73.0	79.3	76.6	76.6	64.5	76.9	85.1
Return on Total Assets 46	6.3	•	6.9	13.6	13.8	14.8	11.8	9.3	10.3	7.8	10.0	6.3	5.7
Return on Equity Before Income Taxes 47	18.3	•	16.4	22.4	22.1	18.0	28.2	28.5	30.6	16.6	19.9	12.9	16.6
Return on Equity After Income Taxes 48	14.1	•	16.0	21.8	21.3	17.4	26.5	25.9	25.7	15.0	13.3	9.8	12.7
Profit Margin (Before Income Tax) 49	14.8	79.2	16.6	25.2	22.4	8.0	17.4	17.0	16.8	12.9	18.4	17.7	13.3
Profit Margin (After Income Tax) 50	11.4	52.3	16.2	24.5	21.5	7.7	16.3	15.4	14.1	11.6	12.3	13.5	10.1

Table I

Corporations with and without Net Income

REAL ESTATE CREDIT INCL. MORTGAGE BANKERS AND ORIGINATORS

MONEY AMOUNTS AND SIZE OF ASSETS IN THOUSANDS OF DOLLARS

Item Description for Accounting Period 7/08 Through 6/09	Total	Zero Assets	Under 500	500 to 1,000	1,000 to 5,000	5,000 to 10,000	10,000 to 25,000	25,000 to 50,000	50,000 to 100,000	100,000 to 250,000	250,000 to 500,000	500,000 to 2,500,000	2,500,000 and over
Number of Enterprises **1**	13164	3117	7436	576	1187	384	235	106	61	34	10	11	8
Revenues ($ in Thousands)													
Net Sales **2**	23036521	149837	1610213	327836	1154983	417704	992180	1146460	893555	735704	768586	1912883	12926580
Interest **3**	9390865	74738	5182	5587	58640	28443	68281	24830	20026	136538	189441	1245450	7553708
Rents **4**	39266	0	4783	0	618	217	2048	3460	3599	1731	3797	8020	10992
Royalties **5**	1182	0	0	0	0	0	0	0	0	182	1000	0	0
Other Portfolio Income **6**	381250	2	1493	453	8806	3701	11842	3920	24162	15750	4920	231084	75117
Other Receipts **7**	13223958	75097	1598755	321796	1086919	385343	910009	1114250	845768	581503	569428	428329	5306763
Total Receipts **8**	23036521	149837	1610213	327836	1154983	417704	992180	1146460	893555	735704	768586	1912883	12926580
Average Total Receipts **9**	1750	48	217	569	973	1088	4222	10816	14648	21638	76859	173898	1615822
Operating Costs/Operating Income (%)													
Cost of Operations **10**	2.3	0.8	•	•	•	•	•	•	•	0.0	4.9	0.0	3.9
Salaries and Wages **11**	24.5	25.7	41.3	29.0	40.6	28.3	37.6	43.8	36.3	36.8	18.4	17.5	17.8
Taxes Paid **12**	2.8	2.9	5.1	4.9	4.3	4.0	4.0	5.4	4.3	3.6	1.7	2.1	2.0
Interest Paid **13**	29.6	23.1	1.7	3.6	9.0	13.5	15.0	10.6	13.6	25.9	28.5	22.6	41.4
Depreciation **14**	1.7	1.7	2.2	0.8	1.2	1.6	1.0	1.0	1.5	3.1	1.4	3.3	1.6
Amortization and Depletion **15**	1.6	0.0	0.1	•	0.1	0.1	•	0.1	0.2	1.5	2.4	0.3	2.6
Pensions and Other Deferred Comp. **16**	0.4	0.4	0.2	0.3	0.5	0.1	0.2	0.3	0.2	0.4	0.2	1.3	0.3
Employee Benefits **17**	1.5	0.6	1.5	0.4	1.0	1.5	1.6	1.9	1.4	2.3	1.6	2.5	1.3
Advertising **18**	1.9	1.0	4.4	0.3	1.5	3.9	3.1	4.0	2.0	1.9	0.5	4.0	1.1
Other Expenses **19**	64.0	129.6	46.9	49.0	34.4	68.8	54.9	40.0	49.1	43.2	49.2	94.3	69.7
Officers' Compensation **20**	2.2	7.8	10.1	7.6	6.1	6.8	4.3	3.4	4.1	3.4	3.5	1.1	0.2
Operating Margin **21**	•	•	•	4.2	1.5	•	•	•	•	•	•	•	•
Operating Margin Before Officers' Comp. **22**	•	•	•	11.8	7.6	•	•	•	•	•	•	•	•

Selected Average Balance Sheet ($ in Thousands)

Net Receivables 23	1631	0	4	89	256	1668	3661	8365	10189	20445	32948	549555	1375247
Inventories 24	•	•	•	•	•	•	•	•	•	•	•	•	•
Net Property, Plant and Equipment 25	143	0	3	15	312	272	351	1383	1975	9250	6471	22723	49099
Total Assets 26	7387	0	97	714	2438	6677	15240	33894	67273	176303	380848	957419	7381010
Notes and Loans Payable 27	3146	0	27	379	895	3018	11533	24169	36362	98042	261394	303695	2750188
All Other Liabilities 28	2718	0	5	36	760	1757	4762	7231	37305	58989	114108	541654	2609751
Net Worth 29	1523	0	65	299	783	1901	-1055	2494	-6394	19272	5345	112070	2021071

Selected Financial Ratios (Times to 1)

Current Ratio 30	1.0	•	4.3	6.1	0.8	0.8	0.7	0.9	0.4	0.5	0.5	1.2	1.1
Quick Ratio 31	0.9	•	3.5	3.2	0.7	0.7	0.5	0.6	0.3	0.4	0.4	1.2	1.1
Net Sales to Working Capital 32	•	•	5.3	1.7	•	•	•	•	•	•	•	1.5	6.3
Coverage Ratio 33	•	•	•	2.2	1.2	•	0.3	•	0.1	0.1	0.6	•	0.2
Total Asset Turnover 34	0.2	•	2.2	0.8	0.4	0.3	0.3	0.3	0.2	0.1	0.2	0.2	0.2
Inventory Turnover 35	•	•	•	•	•	•	•	•	•	•	•	•	•
Receivables Turnover 36	•	•	•	•	•	•	•	•	•	•	•	•	•
Total Liabilities to Net Worth 37	3.8	•	0.5	1.4	2.1	2.5	•	12.6	8.1	•	70.3	7.5	2.7
Current Assets to Working Capital 38	•	•	1.3	1.2	•	•	•	•	•	•	•	5.6	7.7
Current Liabilities to Working Capital 39	•	•	0.3	0.2	•	•	•	•	•	•	•	•	6.7
Working Capital to Net Sales 40	•	•	0.2	0.6	•	•	•	•	•	•	•	0.7	0.2
Inventory to Working Capital 41	•	•	•	•	•	•	•	•	•	•	•	0.0	0.0
Total Receipts to Cash Flow 42	6.5	6.3	4.6	2.1	3.5	3.3	3.9	4.7	3.3	7.3	3.1	13.6	10.0
Cost of Goods to Cash Flow 43	0.2	0.1	•	•	•	•	•	•	•	0.0	0.2	0.0	0.4
Cash Flow to Total Debt 44	0.0	1.5	0.7	0.2	0.2	0.1	0.1	0.1	0.1	0.0	0.1	0.0	0.0

Selected Financial Factors (in Percentages)

Debt Ratio 45	79.4	•	32.6	58.1	67.9	71.5	106.9	92.6	109.5	89.1	98.6	88.3	72.6
Return on Total Assets 46	•	•	6.2	4.2	•	•	•	•	0.2	0.4	•	3.3	•
Return on Equity Before Income Taxes 47	•	•	7.9	•	1.8	•	86.9	•	29.1	•	•	•	•
Return on Equity After Income Taxes 48	•	•	7.7	•	1.2	•	88.1	•	30.6	•	•	•	•
Profit Margin (Before Income Tax) 49	•	•	4.2	•	1.5	•	•	•	•	•	•	•	•
Profit Margin (After Income Tax) 50	•	•	4.0	•	0.9	•	•	•	•	•	•	•	•

Table II

Corporations with Net Income

REAL ESTATE CREDIT INCL. MORTGAGE BANKERS AND ORIGINATORS

MONEY AMOUNTS AND SIZE OF ASSETS IN THOUSANDS OF DOLLARS

Item Description for Accounting Period 7/08 Through 6/09	Total	Zero Assets	Under 500	500 to 1,000	1,000 to 5,000	5,000 to 10,000	10,000 to 25,000	25,000 to 50,000	50,000 to 100,000	100,000 to 250,000	250,000 to 500,000	500,000 to 2,500,000	2,500,000 and over
Number of Enterprises **1**	5626	716	3490	275	690	227	118	52	33	14	•	4	•
Revenues ($ in Thousands)													
Net Sales **2**	6170908	75286	637049	199526	689391	278802	662045	801207	530126	311192	•	687271	•
Interest **3**	1187791	27608	1316	3055	52540	22188	27424	2979	7935	62411	•	163389	•
Rents **4**	29324	0	4573	0	383	32	1489	6	1322	246	•	7936	•
Royalties **5**	0	0	0	0	0	0	0	0	0	0	•	0	•
Other Portfolio Income **6**	220341	0	66	51	7778	1716	8833	484	7417	12995	•	173784	•
Other Receipts **7**	4733452	47678	631094	196420	628690	254866	624299	797738	513452	235540	•	342162	•
Total Receipts **8**	6170908	75286	637049	199526	689391	278802	662045	801207	530126	311192	•	687271	•
Average Total Receipts **9**	1097	105	183	726	999	1228	5611	15408	16064	22228	•	171818	•
Operating Costs/Operating Income (%)													
Cost of Operations **10**	0.6	•	•	•	•	•	•	•	•	0.1	•	•	•
Salaries and Wages **11**	25.3	10.3	12.1	28.1	26.7	14.5	42.9	43.7	34.2	31.4	•	27.4	•
Taxes Paid **12**	3.3	2.4	2.5	4.2	3.6	2.9	4.7	5.5	3.7	3.5	•	3.6	•
Interest Paid **13**	13.3	8.2	1.0	4.0	10.7	14.6	8.7	5.5	8.9	15.7	•	12.1	•
Depreciation **14**	1.2	1.3	0.2	0.3	1.8	1.5	0.8	0.7	0.9	1.3	•	3.3	•
Amortization and Depletion **15**	0.2	•	0.1	•	0.1	0.1	0.1	0.2	0.2	0.2	•	0.0	•
Pensions and Other Deferred Comp. **16**	0.2	0.7	•	0.5	0.6	0.1	0.3	0.1	0.2	0.2	•	0.1	•
Employee Benefits **17**	1.3	1.0	•	0.1	1.1	1.1	1.4	1.9	1.2	1.2	•	3.5	•
Advertising **18**	3.5	0.6	8.4	0.2	1.8	1.5	3.8	3.6	2.4	1.4	•	10.2	•
Other Expenses **19**	32.3	56.5	51.3	37.8	35.8	38.3	26.1	29.3	29.4	25.1	•	27.0	•
Officers' Compensation **20**	4.1	8.4	11.0	10.4	4.8	6.9	4.7	2.8	4.7	3.3	•	0.8	•
Operating Margin **21**	14.7	10.5	13.3	14.4	12.9	18.6	6.7	6.5	14.1	16.5	•	12.0	•
Operating Margin Before Officers' Comp. **22**	18.8	19.0	24.3	24.7	17.7	25.5	11.3	9.4	18.8	19.8	•	12.8	•

Selected Average Balance Sheet ($ in Thousands)

Net Receivables 23	2065	0	5	25	237	2585	4649	11536	14310	32617	591216
Inventories 24	•	•	•	•	•	•	•	•	•	•	•
Net Property, Plant and Equipment 25	113	0	3	14	319	140	258	544	971	4243	24884
Total Assets 26	6218	0	92	796	2409	5887	16356	35228	68158	163812	895474
Notes and Loans Payable 27	2128	0	3	478	1008	3642	11490	22405	28265	72265	426534
All Other Liabilities 28	1337	0	3	32	651	1009	2178	6700	28349	68030	133538
Net Worth 29	2753	0	86	286	750	1236	2687	6123	11543	23518	335402

Selected Financial Ratios (Times to 1)

Current Ratio 30	1.0	•	14.9	4.1	1.1	1.1	0.8	1.2	0.6	0.5	1.4
Quick Ratio 31	0.9	•	11.9	2.7	0.8	1.1	0.6	0.8	0.5	0.5	1.4
Net Sales to Working Capital 32	•	•	3.3	2.4	25.0	3.5	•	4.7	•	•	1.0
Coverage Ratio 33	2.1	2.3	13.9	4.6	2.2	2.2	1.8	2.2	2.6	2.0	2.0
Total Asset Turnover 34	0.2	•	2.0	0.9	0.4	0.2	0.3	0.4	0.2	0.1	0.2
Inventory Turnover 35	•	•	•	•	•	•	•	•	•	•	•
Receivables Turnover 36	•	•	•	•	•	•	•	•	•	•	•
Total Liabilities to Net Worth 37	1.3	•	0.1	1.8	2.2	3.8	5.1	4.8	4.9	6.0	1.7
Current Assets to Working Capital 38	•	•	1.1	1.3	16.2	9.7	•	6.3	•	•	3.5
Current Liabilities to Working Capital 39	•	•	0.1	0.3	15.2	8.7	•	5.3	•	•	2.5
Working Capital to Net Sales 40	•	•	0.3	0.4	0.0	0.3	•	0.2	•	•	1.0
Inventory to Working Capital 41	•	•	•	•	•	•	•	•	•	•	0.0
Total Receipts to Cash Flow 42	2.4	1.6	1.8	2.1	2.3	1.9	3.7	3.6	2.6	3.0	2.9
Cost of Goods to Cash Flow 43	0.0	•	•	•	•	•	•	•	•	0.0	•
Cash Flow to Total Debt 44	0.1	•	18.0	0.7	0.3	0.1	0.1	0.1	0.1	0.1	0.1

Selected Financial Factors (in Percentages)

Debt Ratio 45	55.7	•	6.2	64.1	68.9	79.0	83.6	82.6	83.1	85.6	62.5
Return on Total Assets 46	4.9	•	28.4	16.7	9.8	6.8	5.3	5.3	5.4	4.3	4.6
Return on Equity Before Income Taxes 47	5.8	•	28.1	36.4	17.2	17.8	13.9	16.4	19.6	15.3	6.1
Return on Equity After Income Taxes 48	4.8	•	27.1	35.8	16.0	17.6	12.9	16.2	18.0	13.4	4.0
Profit Margin (Before Income Tax) 49	14.6	10.5	13.3	14.4	12.9	18.0	6.7	6.5	14.1	16.1	12.0
Profit Margin (After Income Tax) 50	12.1	10.2	12.8	14.1	12.0	17.7	6.2	6.5	13.0	14.1	7.8

Table I

Corporations with and without Net Income

INTL. TRADE, SECONDARY FINANCING, OTHER NONDEPOSITORY CREDIT

MONEY AMOUNTS AND SIZE OF ASSETS IN THOUSANDS OF DOLLARS

Item Description for Accounting Period 7/08 Through 6/09	Total	Zero Assets	Under 500	500 to 1,000	1,000 to 5,000	5,000 to 10,000	10,000 to 25,000	25,000 to 50,000	50,000 to 100,000	100,000 to 250,000	250,000 to 500,000	500,000 to 2,500,000	2,500,000 and over
Number of Enterprises **1**	6545	1553	3053	668	774	202	110	50	39	25	11	27	33
Revenues ($ in Thousands)													
Net Sales **2**	219170780	2668528	788788	172042	517584	468588	503345	390502	413109	533257	671202	3334285	208709549
Interest **3**	204168639	407445	86880	29010	29484	14214	14188	38955	104245	215450	167676	1747895	201313198
Rents **4**	121517	1864	466	0	1780	0	0	570	89	1474	1270	28022	85982
Royalties **5**	6009	0	0	122	0	0	0	122	16	0	0	5749	0
Other Portfolio Income **6**	2275710	541531	0	1525	13794	18	3972	4993	4606	4435	3307	6353	1691175
Other Receipts **7**	12598905	1717688	701442	141385	472526	454356	485185	345862	304153	311898	498949	1546266	5619194
Total Receipts **8**	219170780	2668528	788788	172042	517584	468588	503345	390502	413109	533257	671202	3334285	208709549
Average Total Receipts **9**	33487	1718	258	258	669	2320	4576	7810	10593	21330	61018	123492	6324532
Operating Costs/Operating Income (%)													
Cost of Operations **10**	0.3	4.9	•	•	0.9	•	8.3	1.4	•	•	23.4	7.4	•
Salaries and Wages **11**	1.6	0.6	24.5	31.8	26.7	31.3	23.6	16.5	20.7	12.1	10.6	10.8	1.0
Taxes Paid **12**	0.2	0.3	3.6	6.0	3.7	3.1	3.2	3.0	1.4	1.5	0.6	1.5	0.1
Interest Paid **13**	82.1	25.3	11.8	10.9	6.0	7.0	13.2	19.3	18.5	37.2	12.8	32.4	85.0
Depreciation **14**	1.0	59.9	0.3	3.2	3.8	1.3	1.8	5.5	1.2	1.2	1.8	2.5	0.2
Amortization and Depletion **15**	3.2	0.1	0.2	0.6	1.8	0.3	0.2	0.6	0.6	0.3	3.7	1.2	3.3
Pensions and Other Deferred Comp. **16**	0.1	•	1.9	0.0	0.1	0.5	0.0	0.5	0.1	0.3	0.0	0.2	0.1
Employee Benefits **17**	0.2	•	0.0	0.4	1.2	1.5	1.4	1.2	1.1	0.9	0.3	0.7	0.2
Advertising **18**	0.1	0.0	2.7	5.0	4.3	2.3	1.7	0.7	0.7	0.8	0.7	1.0	0.0
Other Expenses **19**	9.8	7.7	38.2	88.4	46.7	36.4	44.1	28.6	41.2	44.9	36.8	27.5	8.9
Officers' Compensation **20**	0.3	0.7	4.5	10.3	7.8	4.2	6.3	5.8	3.9	2.0	0.6	1.0	0.2
Operating Margin **21**	1.3	0.5	12.1	•	•	12.2	•	17.0	10.6	•	8.7	13.9	1.0
Operating Margin Before Officers' Comp. **22**	1.6	1.1	16.7	•	4.8	16.4	2.4	22.8	14.5	0.7	9.3	14.8	1.2

Selected Average Balance Sheet ($ in Thousands)

Net Receivables 23	17153	0	25	143	951	1916	5782	23202	40652	115187	173310	540731	2672843
Inventories 24	•	•	•	•	•	•	•	•	•	•	•	•	•
Net Property, Plant and Equipment 25	429	0	5	16	108	1408	842	965	704	1944	4092	13038	54642
Total Assets 26	334333	0	113	709	1650	6292	15417	33540	70702	171712	328046	1106693	64876740
Notes and Loans Payable 27	315978	0	30	588	747	4276	9113	18619	30909	130340	163832	630968	61845944
All Other Liabilities 28	21818	0	7	31	369	832	2028	1864	17301	30873	95583	218039	4048580
Net Worth 29	-3464	0	76	90	533	1183	4275	13057	22492	10499	68631	257686	-1017784

Selected Financial Ratios (Times to 1)

Current Ratio 30	0.3	•	5.9	3.5	2.2	1.7	2.0	2.0	1.7	1.4	1.3	1.1	0.3
Quick Ratio 31	0.2	•	3.3	2.7	2.1	1.3	1.4	1.9	1.4	1.2	1.0	1.0	0.2
Net Sales to Working Capital 32	•	•	3.1	0.8	0.9	1.7	0.9	0.5	0.5	0.5	1.0	1.8	1.0
Coverage Ratio 33	1.0	1.0	2.0	•	0.5	2.7	0.7	1.9	1.6	1.0	1.7	1.4	1.0
Total Asset Turnover 34	0.1	•	2.3	0.4	0.4	0.4	0.3	0.2	0.1	0.1	0.2	0.1	0.1
Inventory Turnover 35	•	•	•	•	•	•	•	•	•	•	•	•	•
Receivables Turnover 36	•	•	•	•	•	•	•	•	•	•	•	•	•
Total Liabilities to Net Worth 37	•	•	0.5	6.8	2.1	4.3	2.6	1.6	2.1	15.4	3.8	3.3	•
Current Assets to Working Capital 38	•	•	1.2	1.4	1.8	2.5	2.0	2.0	2.5	3.6	4.0	9.6	•
Current Liabilities to Working Capital 39	•	•	0.2	0.4	0.8	1.5	1.0	1.0	1.5	2.6	3.0	8.6	•
Working Capital to Net Sales 40	•	•	0.3	1.2	1.2	0.6	1.1	1.8	2.0	1.9	1.0	0.5	•
Inventory to Working Capital 41	•	•	•	0.0	0.0	•	0.0	0.0	0.0	0.0	0.0	0.0	•
Total Receipts to Cash Flow 42	9.4	13.4	2.3	2.6	2.6	2.3	3.2	2.4	2.1	2.4	2.4	2.6	10.3
Cost of Goods to Cash Flow 43	0.0	0.7	•	0.0	0.0	•	0.3	0.0	•	•	0.6	0.2	•
Cash Flow to Total Debt 44	0.0	•	3.0	0.2	0.2	0.2	0.1	0.2	0.1	0.1	0.1	0.1	0.0

Selected Financial Factors (in Percentages)

Debt Ratio 45	101.0	•	33.0	87.2	67.7	81.2	72.3	61.1	68.2	93.9	79.1	76.7	101.6
Return on Total Assets 46	8.3	•	55.0	•	1.2	7.1	2.8	8.5	4.5	4.5	4.0	5.2	8.3
Return on Equity Before Income Taxes 47	•	•	41.6	•	•	23.9	•	10.2	5.3	•	7.7	6.6	•
Return on Equity After Income Taxes 48	0.2	•	40.0	•	21.8	•	9.1	2.2	1.3	•	3.8	1.2	•
Profit Margin (Before Income Tax) 49	0.6	0.5	12.1	•	12.2	•	17.0	11.3	8.7	•	13.9	0.3	•
Profit Margin (After Income Tax) 50	•	0.2	11.7	•	11.1	•	15.2	4.6	1.4	•	7.9	•	•

Table II

Corporations with Net Income

INTL. TRADE, SECONDARY FINANCING, OTHER NONDEPOSITORY CREDIT

MONEY AMOUNTS AND SIZE OF ASSETS IN THOUSANDS OF DOLLARS

Item Description for Accounting Period 7/08 Through 6/09		Total	Zero Assets	Under 500	500 to 1,000	1,000 to 5,000	5,000 to 10,000	10,000 to 25,000	25,000 to 50,000	50,000 to 100,000	100,000 to 250,000	250,000 to 500,000	500,000 to 2,500,000	2,500,000 and over
Number of Enterprises	1	3526	465	•	268	379	•	59	36	29	18	6	18	20
Revenues ($ in Thousands)														
Net Sales	2	67626302	2633081	•	121064	341099	•	331778	267102	338847	375876	167554	2467296	59560057
Interest	3	55652920	385794	•	21830	19363	•	6795	29035	87945	173923	120767	1235980	53557633
Rents	4	51595	1864	•	0	1780	•	0	570	89	1419	1270	2946	41190
Royalties	5	113	0	•	0	0	•	0	97	16	0	0	0	0
Other Portfolio Income	6	1412437	541467	•	0	11326	•	97	0	882	4435	3303	3223	847704
Other Receipts	7	10509237	1703956	•	99234	308630	•	324886	237400	249915	196099	42214	1225147	5113530
Total Receipts	8	67626302	2633081	•	121064	341099	•	331778	267102	338847	375876	167554	2467296	59560057
Average Total Receipts	9	19179	5663	•	452	900	•	5623	7420	11684	20882	27926	137072	2978003
Operating Costs/Operating Income (%)														
Cost of Operations	10	0.6	5.0	•	•	1.3	•	•	•	•	•	10.0	•	•
Salaries and Wages	11	3.1	0.4	•	29.7	17.0	•	22.6	17.1	17.1	11.9	1.9	9.6	2.1
Taxes Paid	12	0.3	0.3	•	5.3	2.8	•	3.0	3.3	1.3	1.4	0.2	1.4	0.2
Interest Paid	13	67.0	24.9	•	0.6	4.2	•	13.8	18.0	16.3	29.9	18.3	27.4	73.2
Depreciation	14	2.6	60.7	•	3.3	1.9	•	1.6	1.0	1.2	1.1	0.4	1.4	0.2
Amortization and Depletion	15	0.2	•	•	0.2	0.4	•	0.1	•	0.5	0.1	0.2	1.1	0.1
Pensions and Other Deferred Comp.	16	0.1	•	•	•	0.1	•	0.0	0.7	0.1	0.4	•	0.2	0.0
Employee Benefits	17	0.4	•	•	0.0	0.4	•	1.8	0.8	0.9	0.7	0.1	0.5	0.4
Advertising	18	0.1	0.0	•	2.6	1.3	•	1.3	0.5	0.7	0.5	0.0	1.3	0.0
Other Expenses	19	17.4	6.8	•	38.5	38.1	•	37.2	19.8	26.2	36.7	12.0	22.8	17.0
Officers' Compensation	20	0.6	0.6	•	7.2	4.8	•	8.0	3.7	3.6	1.9	0.5	0.7	0.4
Operating Margin	21	7.5	1.3	•	12.5	27.6	•	10.7	35.4	32.1	15.5	66.4	23.8	6.2
Operating Margin Before Officers' Comp.	22	8.1	2.0	•	19.7	32.4	•	18.7	39.2	35.7	17.3	66.9	24.5	6.6

Selected Average Balance Sheet ($ in Thousands)

Net Receivables 23	22898	0	•	284	1013	•	8223	24828	41708	119476	216586	600082	3152411
Inventories 24	•	•	•	•	•	•	•	•	•	•	•	•	•
Net Property, Plant and Equipment 25	457	0	•	19	156	•	1232	519	834	2340	34	10347	57049
Total Assets 26	348227	0	•	710	1550	•	15167	32411	68581	176190	346122	1172912	59785167
Notes and Loans Payable 27	322635	0	•	87	586	•	9334	18594	29483	115912	166323	595957	56057245
All Other Liabilities 28	24089	0	•	18	246	•	2729	921	17103	33673	76398	187854	3978561
Net Worth 29	1502	0	•	605	718	•	3104	12896	21995	26605	103401	389101	-250639

Selected Financial Ratios (Times to 1)

Current Ratio 30	0.4	•	•	3.1	•	•	1.9	2.0	1.9	1.5	1.2	1.4	0.4
Quick Ratio 31	0.3	•	•	2.9	•	•	1.7	1.9	1.6	1.3	1.0	1.2	0.3
Net Sales to Working Capital 32	•	•	•	1.1	•	•	1.1	0.5	0.5	0.4	0.6	0.7	0.4
Coverage Ratio 33	1.1	1.1	•	7.5	•	•	1.8	3.0	3.0	1.5	4.6	1.9	1.1
Total Asset Turnover 34	0.1	•	•	0.6	•	•	0.4	0.2	0.2	0.1	0.1	0.1	0.0
Inventory Turnover 35	•	•	•	•	•	•	•	•	•	•	•	•	•
Receivables Turnover 36	•	•	•	•	•	•	•	•	•	•	•	•	•
Total Liabilities to Net Worth 37	230.8	•	•	1.2	1.5	•	3.9	2.1	2.1	5.6	2.3	2.0	2.0
Current Assets to Working Capital 38	•	•	•	1.5	1.1	•	2.1	2.1	2.9	5.5	4.5	5.5	3.8
Current Liabilities to Working Capital 39	•	•	•	0.5	0.1	•	1.1	1.1	1.9	1.9	4.5	4.5	2.8
Working Capital to Net Sales 40	•	•	•	0.9	1.3	•	0.9	1.9	2.2	2.3	1.8	1.4	1.4
Inventory to Working Capital 41	•	•	•	0.0	0.0	•	0.0	0.0	0.0	0.0	0.0	0.0	0.0
Total Receipts to Cash Flow 42	4.1	13.3	•	1.7	2.7	•	2.3	1.8	1.9	2.0	1.3	2.3	4.4
Cost of Goods to Cash Flow 43	0.0	0.7	•	0.0	0.0	•	0.0	0.0	0.0	0.0	0.0	0.2	0.2
Cash Flow to Total Debt 44	0.0	•	•	0.7	1.6	•	0.2	0.1	0.1	0.1	0.1	0.1	0.0

Selected Financial Factors (in Percentages)

Debt Ratio 45	99.6	•	•	14.7	53.7	•	79.5	60.2	67.9	84.9	70.1	66.8	100.4
Return on Total Assets 46	4.1	•	•	8.3	18.5	•	9.1	12.2	8.2	5.4	6.8	6.0	3.9
Return on Equity Before Income Taxes 47	83.9	•	•	9.4	34.6	•	19.4	20.4	17.1	12.1	17.9	8.4	•
Return on Equity After Income Taxes 48	58.3	•	•	7.4	33.0	•	17.8	18.8	12.7	8.8	10.1	5.5	•
Profit Margin (Before Income Tax) 49	6.6	1.3	•	12.5	27.6	•	10.7	35.4	32.1	15.5	66.4	23.8	5.2
Profit Margin (After Income Tax) 50	4.6	1.1	•	9.8	26.3	•	9.8	32.7	24.0	11.3	37.3	15.7	3.5

Table I

Corporations with and without Net Income

ACTIVITIES RELATED TO CREDIT INTERMEDIATION

MONEY AMOUNTS AND SIZE OF ASSETS IN THOUSANDS OF DOLLARS

Item Description for Accounting Period 7/08 Through 6/09	Total	Zero Assets	Under 500	500 to 1,000	1,000 to 5,000	5,000 to 10,000	10,000 to 25,000	25,000 to 50,000	50,000 to 100,000	100,000 to 250,000	250,000 to 500,000	500,000 to 2,500,000	2,500,000 and over
Number of Enterprises 1	22971	5498	14043	1869	1093	229	88	56	33	25	7	23	6
Revenues ($ in Thousands)													
Net Sales 2	46919284	3686270	3337778	1389379	1848623	873077	781985	564852	1046501	1288823	782817	7246839	24072340
Interest 3	3373612	1384912	11558	4203	11017	11133	34149	14545	28129	16158	31999	564750	1261057
Rents 4	206355	0	1200	0	688	221	681	399	577	1679	1187	12557	187164
Royalties 5	337282	0	0	0	0	0	0	0	157	0	0	1458	335667
Other Portfolio Income 6	2200027	1033130	2029	8798	963	704	1105	1009	1792	58806	41	506989	584658
Other Receipts 7	40802008	1268228	3322991	1376378	1835955	861019	746050	548899	1015846	1212180	749590	6161085	21703794
Total Receipts 8	46919284	3686270	3337778	1389379	1848623	873077	781985	564852	1046501	1288823	782817	7246839	24072340
Average Total Receipts 9	2043	670	238	743	1691	3813	8886	10087	31712	51553	111831	315080	4012057
Operating Costs/Operating Income (%)													
Cost of Operations 10	1.7	3.8	•	•	•	16.2	1.7	•	0.2	3.5	0.7	0.5	1.8
Salaries and Wages 11	18.2	1.9	32.5	35.6	32.0	41.1	36.6	38.2	18.4	26.7	22.4	16.4	14.7
Taxes Paid 12	2.3	0.7	3.3	4.0	3.4	2.1	3.3	3.8	2.1	2.9	2.1	1.9	2.2
Interest Paid 13	8.5	20.7	1.5	1.5	1.8	4.3	6.0	7.1	9.2	4.0	11.3	8.4	8.9
Depreciation 14	2.6	5.0	1.8	1.5	1.3	3.4	3.4	2.6	2.3	4.2	4.3	2.3	2.3
Amortization and Depletion 15	1.8	0.1	0.2	0.9	0.3	0.2	0.9	0.2	1.6	1.6	6.6	4.6	1.7
Pensions and Other Deferred Comp. 16	1.2	0.0	0.2	0.4	0.4	0.2	0.3	0.3	1.0	0.5	0.1	1.7	1.6
Employee Benefits 17	1.5	0.1	1.3	1.6	1.1	1.1	1.7	1.0	2.0	2.4	0.8	2.1	1.6
Advertising 18	4.5	1.0	3.4	2.3	1.5	0.4	1.7	3.4	1.5	3.9	3.1	1.6	7.0
Other Expenses 19	45.3	39.1	38.7	28.5	40.6	51.0	38.1	35.6	59.2	45.5	32.1	43.0	49.3
Officers' Compensation 20	1.9	0.4	11.1	7.4	4.3	3.6	4.9	5.7	2.4	2.9	0.9	0.9	0.5
Operating Margin 21	10.4	27.2	6.0	16.3	13.4	•	1.4	2.0	0.1	1.9	15.6	16.7	8.4
Operating Margin Before Officers' Comp. 22	12.3	27.6	17.1	23.7	17.7	•	6.3	7.6	2.5	4.8	16.5	17.6	8.8

Selected Average Balance Sheet ($ in Thousands)

	1	2	3	4	5	6	7	8	9	10	11	12	13
Net Receivables 23	768	0	5	27	455	2205	3337	12438	18764	33233	122474	237167	1292669
Inventories 24	•	0	•	•	•	•	•	•	•	•	•	•	•
Net Property, Plant and Equipment 25	199	0	24	166	145	804	1213	1371	3971	8174	30057	30988	358633
Total Assets 26	6099	0	85	725	2375	7426	16016	35560	71431	155661	341122	1063341	16126355
Notes and Loans Payable 27	2441	0	41	374	887	5732	9299	18006	40859	44215	163718	310748	6655206
All Other Liabilities 28	2116	0	29	137	810	2353	3857	9736	15169	62489	103051	443672	5441567
Net Worth 29	1543	0	16	215	677	-659	2861	7819	15403	48957	74353	308920	4029582

Selected Financial Ratios (Times to 1)

	1	2	3	4	5	6	7	8	9	10	11	12	13
Current Ratio 30	1.2	•	1.3	1.4	1.4	1.1	1.2	1.0	0.9	1.2	1.0	1.6	1.2
Quick Ratio 31	0.8	•	1.2	1.2	1.2	1.0	0.7	0.8	0.7	1.0	1.0	1.2	0.7
Net Sales to Working Capital 32	4.8	•	23.0	9.7	4.4	16.5	6.5	•	•	3.5	24.6	2.1	4.5
Coverage Ratio 33	2.3	2.3	4.9	11.9	8.3	•	1.2	1.3	1.0	3.4	2.4	3.0	2.1
Total Asset Turnover 34	0.3	•	2.8	1.0	0.7	0.5	0.6	0.3	0.4	0.3	0.3	0.3	0.2
Inventory Turnover 35	•	•	•	•	•	•	•	•	•	•	•	•	•
Receivables Turnover 36	•	•	•	•	•	•	•	•	•	•	•	•	•
Total Liabilities to Net Worth 37	3.0	•	4.4	2.4	2.5	•	4.6	3.5	3.6	2.2	3.6	2.4	3.0
Current Assets to Working Capital 38	5.0	•	4.2	3.7	3.6	17.0	6.5	•	•	5.5	40.2	2.8	5.7
Current Liabilities to Working Capital 39	4.0	•	3.2	2.7	2.6	16.0	5.5	•	•	4.5	39.2	1.8	4.7
Working Capital to Net Sales 40	0.2	•	0.0	0.1	0.2	0.1	0.2	•	•	0.3	0.0	0.5	0.2
Inventory to Working Capital 41	0.0	•	•	•	•	0.1	0.0	•	•	0.0	0.3	0.0	0.0
Total Receipts to Cash Flow 42	2.0	1.5	2.8	2.7	2.3	29.1	3.0	3.0	1.8	2.6	2.3	2.1	1.8
Cost of Goods to Cash Flow 43	0.0	0.1	•	•	•	4.7	0.1	•	0.0	0.1	0.0	0.0	0.0
Cash Flow to Total Debt 44	0.2	1.2	1.2	0.5	0.4	0.0	0.2	0.1	0.3	0.2	0.2	0.2	0.2

Selected Financial Factors (in Percentages)

	1	2	3	4	5	6	7	8	9	10	11	12	13
Debt Ratio 45	74.7	•	81.4	70.3	71.5	108.9	82.1	78.0	78.4	68.5	78.2	70.9	75.0
Return on Total Assets 46	6.7	•	21.0	18.2	10.8	•	4.1	2.5	4.1	4.5	8.8	7.6	4.7
Return on Income Before Income Taxes 47	15.1	•	90.1	56.1	33.5	136.1	4.2	2.3	0.0	10.1	23.4	17.6	9.9
Return on Equity After Income Taxes 48	9.6	•	89.3	56.0	32.9	136.1	0.8	0.8	•	5.5	18.9	10.2	6.1
Profit Margin (Before Income Tax) 49	11.4	26.9	6.0	16.2	13.4	•	1.4	1.8	0.0	9.6	15.6	17.2	9.9
Profit Margin (After Income Tax) 50	7.3	16.4	6.0	16.2	13.2	•	0.2	•	•	5.2	12.5	10.0	6.1

Table II
Corporations with Net Income

ACTIVITIES RELATED TO CREDIT INTERMEDIATION

MONEY AMOUNTS AND SIZE OF ASSETS IN THOUSANDS OF DOLLARS

Item Description for Accounting Period 7/08 Through 6/09	Total	Zero Assets	Under 500	500 to 1,000	1,000 to 5,000	5,000 to 10,000	10,000 to 25,000	25,000 to 50,000	50,000 to 100,000	100,000 to 250,000	250,000 to 500,000	500,000 to 2,500,000	2,500,000 and over
Number of Enterprises 1	11175	1203	8058	1167	506	108	41	37	20	12	•	•	14
Revenues ($ in Thousands)													
Net Sales 2	34460701	3277847	2749951	811163	1338462	441063	476732	438228	698800	978660	•	6186911	•
Interest 3	2674315	1363408	3254	1092	1235	247	17358	13562	15075	11006	•	245570	•
Rents 4	52366	0	525	0	619	0	448	360	577	1679	•	7525	•
Royalties 5	335667	0	0	0	0	0	0	0	0	0	•	0	•
Other Portfolio Income 6	1970458	1032327	0	7298	336	0	591	48	284	58685	•	483288	•
Other Receipts 7	29427895	882112	2746172	802773	1336272	440816	458335	424258	682864	907290	•	5450528	•
Total Receipts 8	34460701	3277847	2749951	811163	1338462	441063	476732	438228	698800	978660	•	6186911	•
Average Total Receipts 9	3084	2725	341	695	2645	4084	11628	11844	34940	81555	•	441922	•
Operating Costs/Operating Income (%)													
Cost of Operations 10	0.2	•	•	•	•	4.2	2.8	•	0.3	0.3	•	0.2	•
Salaries and Wages 11	15.8	0.2	29.7	19.1	24.0	47.8	32.7	35.5	14.7	26.5	•	15.6	•
Taxes Paid 12	2.5	0.5	2.4	2.9	3.6	2.1	3.3	3.4	1.7	3.3	•	1.7	•
Interest Paid 13	5.2	22.5	1.1	0.8	0.9	1.8	3.9	7.6	5.3	1.8	•	5.1	•
Depreciation 14	2.3	5.4	1.3	2.1	0.9	2.6	4.2	1.6	1.0	3.3	•	2.4	•
Amortization and Depletion 15	1.6	0.0	0.2	0.0	0.0	0.0	0.5	0.3	1.2	0.5	•	5.0	•
Pensions and Other Deferred Comp. 16	1.2	0.0	0.0	0.1	0.0	•	0.3	0.3	0.3	0.6	•	1.0	•
Employee Benefits 17	1.1	0.0	0.7	0.1	1.0	1.9	2.3	1.0	0.7	1.6	•	1.7	•
Advertising 18	5.8	0.2	3.4	2.2	1.6	0.2	2.0	4.0	0.8	4.8	•	1.6	•
Other Expenses 19	43.5	36.0	33.8	32.2	40.4	27.2	30.1	23.5	57.0	45.4	•	41.1	•
Officers' Compensation 20	2.0	0.3	11.3	6.9	4.3	2.7	3.6	6.6	2.0	3.0	•	0.9	•
Operating Margin 21	18.8	34.9	16.0	33.7	22.8	9.5	14.2	16.3	14.8	8.9	•	23.9	•
Operating Margin Before Officers' Comp. 22	20.8	35.1	27.4	40.6	27.1	12.3	17.8	22.9	16.8	11.9	•	24.8	•

Selected Average Balance Sheet ($ in Thousands)

	•	•	•	•	•	•	•	•	•	•	•
Net Receivables 23	655	0	4	31	771	2179	3396	13526	19725	31987	85899
Inventories 24	•	•	•	•	•	•	•	•	•	•	•
Net Property, Plant and Equipment 25	270	0	27	233	201	337	2085	661	3019	12816	42631
Total Assets 26	7436	0	96	694	2593	6594	14600	36573	67937	168061	1236006
Notes and Loans Payable 27	1730	0	33	316	441	3186	7823	16853	37967	41496	183796
All Other Liabilities 28	2863	0	22	166	1240	2969	3675	8306	10511	68885	587699
Net Worth 29	2842	0	41	212	912	439	3101	11414	19459	57679	464511

Selected Financial Ratios (Times to 1)

	•	•	•	•	•	•	•	•	•	•	•
Current Ratio 30	1.3	•	2.2	1.5	1.9	1.8	1.0	1.2	1.1	1.2	1.2
Quick Ratio 31	0.8	•	2.1	1.3	1.5	1.7	0.6	0.9	0.9	0.9	0.7
Net Sales to Working Capital 32	5.8	•	11.5	6.0	2.4	1.9	88.9	3.4	18.5	4.1	7.1
Coverage Ratio 33	4.9	2.5	15.6	43.6	26.6	6.3	4.6	3.2	3.8	11.4	5.9
Total Asset Turnover 34	0.4	•	3.5	1.0	1.0	0.6	0.8	0.3	0.5	0.5	0.4
Inventory Turnover 35	•	•	•	•	•	•	•	•	•	•	•
Receivables Turnover 36	•	•	•	•	•	•	•	•	•	•	•
Total Liabilities to Net Worth 37	1.6	•	1.4	2.3	1.8	14.0	3.7	2.2	2.5	1.9	1.7
Current Assets to Working Capital 38	5.0	•	1.8	3.2	2.1	2.3	58.7	6.4	18.3	5.6	5.0
Current Liabilities to Working Capital 39	4.0	•	0.8	2.2	1.1	1.3	57.7	5.4	17.3	4.6	4.0
Working Capital to Net Sales 40	0.2	•	0.1	0.2	0.4	0.5	0.0	0.3	0.1	0.2	0.1
Inventory to Working Capital 41	0.0	•	•	•	0.0	0.0	0.3	0.0	0.0	0.0	0.0
Total Receipts to Cash Flow 42	1.7	1.4	2.4	1.8	1.8	3.1	2.6	2.8	1.4	2.2	1.9
Cost of Goods to Cash Flow 43	0.0	•	•	•	•	0.1	0.1	•	0.0	0.0	0.0
Cash Flow to Total Debt 44	0.4	•	2.6	0.8	0.9	0.2	0.4	0.2	0.5	0.3	0.3

Selected Financial Factors (in Percentages)

	•	•	•	•	•	•	•	•	•	•	•
Debt Ratio 45	61.8	•	57.7	69.4	64.8	93.3	78.8	68.8	71.4	65.7	62.4
Return on Total Assets 46	10.5	•	60.8	34.5	24.2	7.0	14.4	7.7	10.3	10.1	10.6
Return on Equity Before Income Taxes 47	21.7	•	134.4	110.4	66.1	88.7	53.2	16.9	26.5	26.8	23.3
Return on Equity After Income Taxes 48	15.6	•	133.8	110.1	65.2	88.7	46.4	13.9	23.4	18.8	15.3
Profit Margin (Before Income Tax) 49	20.0	34.5	16.0	33.7	22.8	9.5	14.2	16.3	14.8	19.0	24.5
Profit Margin (After Income Tax) 50	14.4	22.7	16.0	33.6	22.5	9.5	12.4	13.4	13.0	13.3	16.1

Table I

Corporations with and without Net Income

INVESTMENT BANKING AND SECURITIES DEALING

MONEY AMOUNTS AND SIZE OF ASSETS IN THOUSANDS OF DOLLARS

Item Description for Accounting Period 7/08 Through 6/09	Total	Zero Assets	Under 500	500 to 1,000	1,000 to 5,000	5,000 to 10,000	10,000 to 25,000	25,000 to 50,000	50,000 to 100,000	100,000 to 250,000	250,000 to 500,000	500,000 to 2,500,000	2,500,000 and over
Number of Enterprises **1**	3081	1196	1220	289	227	24	34	26	17	12	7	14	14
Revenues ($ in Thousands)													
Net Sales **2**	175070734	11055595	518104	-4761	237603	35235	92271	334712	270075	410771	575155	2938595	158607378
Interest **3**	155723525	5482033	250	209	77411	2231	6459	15766	7062	73597	28884	398403	149631221
Rents **4**	187024	8070	6	0	7098	0	0	0	0	0	0	7	171843
Royalties **5**	144052	19738	0	0	0	0	0	0	0	0	17602	37	106674
Other Portfolio Income **6**	8410204	1057136	2231	339	1145	287	2808	1221	19555	15563	2156	195450	7112316
Other Receipts **7**	10605929	4488618	515617	-5309	151949	32717	83004	317725	243458	321611	526513	2344698	1585324
Total Receipts **8**	175070734	11055595	518104	-4761	237603	35235	92271	334712	270075	410771	575155	2938595	158607378
Average Total Receipts **9**	56823	9244	425	-16	1047	1468	2714	12874	15887	34231	82165	209900	11329098
Operating Costs/Operating Income (%)													
Cost of Operations **10**	1.3	5.7	•	•	•	•	•	•	•	•	•	•	1.0
Salaries and Wages **11**	17.8	35.7	7.5	•	7.3	105.7	17.0	58.8	35.6	47.3	31.2	21.0	16.3
Taxes Paid **12**	1.3	0.6	1.3	•	2.1	4.0	2.8	3.5	3.5	1.1	5.7	2.5	1.3
Interest Paid **13**	84.3	48.1	0.0	•	29.4	5.3	5.0	3.9	2.2	18.4	8.9	8.5	89.4
Depreciation **14**	0.9	0.6	0.2	•	0.5	7.5	0.2	4.1	1.5	0.8	1.8	0.8	0.9
Amortization and Depletion **15**	0.6	0.7	•	•	0.1	3.6	0.1	0.5	0.4	2.7	0.8	0.5	0.6
Pensions and Other Deferred Comp. **16**	0.6	1.1	0.8	•	•	3.0	0.2	1.0	1.3	1.2	0.1	0.2	0.6
Employee Benefits **17**	1.3	0.4	0.2	•	1.0	3.5	1.8	2.6	1.0	0.8	1.3	0.9	1.4
Advertising **18**	0.1	0.1	•	•	0.0	1.3	0.0	1.6	0.4	0.1	5.3	0.2	0.1
Other Expenses **19**	27.1	43.2	69.9	•	39.1	74.4	52.9	52.1	43.1	37.4	37.9	59.2	25.0
Officers' Compensation **20**	0.7	0.2	9.4	•	3.7	55.8	21.5	2.6	8.5	0.7	3.8	3.0	0.6
Operating Margin **21**	•	•	10.7	187.4	16.9	•	•	•	2.6	•	3.2	3.1	3.1
Operating Margin Before Officers' Comp. **22**	•	•	20.1	187.4	20.6	•	19.9	•	11.1	•	7.0	•	6.1

Selected Average Balance Sheet ($ in Thousands)

Net Receivables 23	355434	0	0	37	45	88	1692	1935	8057	5475	100686	215578	77931006
Inventories 24	•	•	•	•	•	•	•	•	•	•	•	•	•
Net Property, Plant and Equipment 25	2957	•	6	0	126	191	59	2902	972	963	18714	6181	624729
Total Assets 26	1489556	•	662	124	2047	8090	15620	35350	72369	154383	352185	1031477	326205751
Notes and Loans Payable 27	253318	0	2	470	531	483	1365	6772	8129	23026	21985	106440	55565726
All Other Liabilities 28	1120741	0	25	16	245	884	4432	3063	16400	61577	183875	520062	245933891
Net Worth 29	115497	0	97	175	1272	6724	9822	25515	47840	69779	146325	404976	24706134

Selected Financial Ratios (Times to 1)

Current Ratio 30	1.0	•	4.5	32.1	5.4	4.3	2.9	4.4	2.3	1.3	1.2	1.6	1.0
Quick Ratio 31	0.6	•	2.3	10.7	3.7	4.2	2.0	1.5	1.4	0.5	1.0	1.0	0.5
Net Sales to Working Capital 32	14.8	•	7.6	•	1.0	0.4	0.4	1.2	0.7	1.5	2.8	1.1	21.8
Coverage Ratio 33	0.6	0.3	668.1	•	1.6	•	0.1	•	0.4	0.4	1.3	1.2	0.6
Total Asset Turnover 34	0.0	•	3.4	•	0.5	0.2	0.2	0.4	0.2	0.2	0.2	0.2	0.0
Inventory Turnover 35	•	•	•	•	•	•	•	•	•	•	•	•	•
Receivables Turnover 36	•	•	•	•	•	•	•	•	•	•	•	•	•
Total Liabilities to Net Worth 37	11.9	•	0.3	2.8	0.6	0.2	0.6	0.4	0.5	1.2	1.4	1.5	12.2
Current Assets to Working Capital 38	229.7	•	1.3	1.0	1.2	1.3	1.5	1.3	1.8	4.4	6.4	2.8	372.2
Current Liabilities to Working Capital 39	228.7	•	0.3	0.0	0.2	0.3	0.5	0.3	0.8	3.4	5.4	1.8	371.2
Working Capital to Net Sales 40	0.1	•	0.1	•	1.0	2.5	2.3	0.9	1.3	0.7	0.4	0.9	0.0
Inventory to Working Capital 41	0.0	•	0.0	•	•	•	•	•	•	•	•	•	0.0
Total Receipts to Cash Flow 42	•	97.1	•	0.9	2.0	•	5.3	7.6	2.6	5.0	2.9	2.0	•
Cost of Goods to Cash Flow 43	•	5.5	•	•	•	•	•	•	•	•	•	•	•
Cash Flow to Total Debt 44	•	•	11.6	0.7	•	0.1	0.1	0.2	0.3	0.1	0.1	0.2	•

Selected Financial Factors (in Percentages)

Debt Ratio 45	92.2	•	21.5	73.6	37.9	16.9	37.1	27.8	33.9	54.8	58.5	60.7	92.4
Return on Total Assets 46	1.9	•	36.7	•	23.6	•	0.1	•	0.2	1.7	2.8	2.1	1.9
Return on Equity Before Income Taxes 47	•	•	46.7	•	13.7	•	•	•	•	•	•	1.0	•
Return on Equity After Income Taxes 48	•	•	46.1	•	13.7	•	•	•	•	•	•	•	•
Profit Margin (Before Income Tax) 49	•	•	10.7	187.5	16.7	•	•	•	•	•	3.0	•	•
Profit Margin (After Income Tax) 50	•	•	10.5	187.7	16.7	•	•	•	•	•	2.0	•	•

Table II

Corporations with Net Income

INVESTMENT BANKING AND SECURITIES DEALING

MONEY AMOUNTS AND SIZE OF ASSETS IN THOUSANDS OF DOLLARS

Item Description for Accounting Period 7/08 Through 6/09	Total	Zero Assets	Under 500	500 to 1,000	1,000 to 5,000	5,000 to 10,000	10,000 to 25,000	25,000 to 50,000	50,000 to 100,000	100,000 to 250,000	250,000 to 500,000	500,000 to 2,500,000	2,500,000 and over
Number of Enterprises **1**	694	269	258	0	115	5	16	5	7	5	4	6	4
Revenues ($ in Thousands)													
Net Sales **2**	10860974	4523912	188235	0	166572	34022	80965	34978	150247	143653	293600	1252764	3992026
Interest **3**	5237531	1823299	96	0	72732	539	3783	9019	3064	21603	4496	150066	3148834
Rents **4**	15334	8070	6	0	7098	0	0	0	0	0	0	1	159
Royalties **5**	19871	19738	0	0	0	0	0	0	0	0	0	0	133
Other Portfolio Income **6**	1196209	714631	2247	0	656	279	2248	11	5204	12609	691	161589	296045
Other Receipts **7**	4392029	1958174	185886	0	86086	33204	74934	25948	141979	109441	288413	941108	546855
Total Receipts **8**	10860974	4523912	188235	0	166572	34022	80965	34978	150247	143653	293600	1252764	3992026
Average Total Receipts **9**	15650	16818	730	•	1448	6804	5060	6996	21464	28731	73400	208794	998006
Operating Costs/Operating Income (%)													
Cost of Operations **10**	•	•	•	•	•	•	•	•	•	•	•	•	•
Salaries and Wages **11**	8.6	4.7	•	•	2.7	6.6	16.7	19.2	40.2	41.7	27.3	16.5	7.2
Taxes Paid **12**	1.4	0.6	1.8	•	1.8	1.5	2.5	4.8	3.0	0.9	4.7	3.1	1.4
Interest Paid **13**	41.5	31.1	•	•	40.5	0.7	2.1	22.0	1.1	13.5	2.8	7.5	72.6
Depreciation **14**	0.7	1.1	0.0	•	0.1	1.6	0.1	0.7	0.8	0.5	1.8	0.5	0.2
Amortization and Depletion **15**	0.7	1.0	•	•	0.1	•	0.1	•	0.0	0.0	1.6	0.6	0.4
Pensions and Other Deferred Comp. **16**	0.2	0.2	2.1	•	•	3.1	•	•	1.3	•	0.2	0.1	0.1
Employee Benefits **17**	0.4	0.4	0.6	•	0.1	1.9	1.7	1.5	1.6	•	0.6	0.3	0.4
Advertising **18**	0.3	0.1	•	•	0.0	0.1	0.0	0.0	0.1	•	10.1	0.1	0.0
Other Expenses **19**	33.0	57.8	10.0	•	6.9	17.9	20.3	21.4	28.3	36.6	21.9	33.3	8.4
Officers' Compensation **20**	1.7	0.1	25.8	•	•	21.6	18.1	6.7	12.1	•	5.8	4.9	0.3
Operating Margin **21**	11.5	3.0	59.7	•	47.8	44.9	38.3	23.6	11.5	6.8	23.3	33.0	9.1
Operating Margin Before Officers' Comp. **22**	13.2	3.1	85.5	•	47.8	66.5	56.3	30.3	23.6	6.8	29.0	37.9	9.3

Selected Average Balance Sheet ($ in Thousands)

Item	1	2	3	4	5	6	7	8	9	10	11	12	13
Net Receivables 23	15779	0	2	•	74	146	3428	3415	6950	9742	148270	118213	2367286
Inventories 24	•	•	•	•	•	•	•	•	•	•	•	•	•
Net Property, Plant and Equipment 25	274	0	0	•	228	486	112	232	543	242	20294	6073	8976
Total Assets 26	126051	0	336	•	2888	5862	17970	27791	73695	158039	339570	1089936	19350258
Notes and Loans Payable 27	16023	0	0	•	105	998	481	2051	12002	19637	31643	58168	2606788
All Other Liabilities 28	100623	0	68	•	410	1606	9245	1427	16263	44400	216652	521180	16318813
Net Worth 29	9405	0	268	•	2373	3259	8243	24313	45429	94003	91275	510587	424657

Selected Financial Ratios (Times to 1)

Item	1	2	3	4	5	6	7	8	9	10	11	12	13
Current Ratio 30	1.2	•	4.9	•	•	0.8	1.5	7.1	2.5	2.1	1.3	1.0	1.2
Quick Ratio 31	0.4	•	2.5	•	•	0.8	1.3	3.1	1.4	0.7	1.1	0.5	0.3
Net Sales to Working Capital 32	0.9	•	2.8	•	•	•	1.5	0.6	0.8	0.4	1.3	292.3	0.4
Coverage Ratio 33	1.4	•	•	•	2.2	60.9	18.2	2.1	8.4	1.5	9.3	5.4	1.1
Total Asset Turnover 34	0.1	1.4	2.2	•	•	0.5	0.3	0.3	0.3	0.2	0.2	0.2	0.1
Inventory Turnover 35	•	•	•	•	•	•	•	•	•	•	•	•	•
Receivables Turnover 36	•	•	•	•	•	•	•	•	•	•	•	•	•
Total Liabilities to Net Worth 37	12.4	•	0.3	•	•	0.2	1.2	0.1	0.6	0.7	2.7	1.1	44.6
Current Assets to Working Capital 38	6.9	•	1.3	•	•	1.3	2.8	1.2	1.7	2.0	4.2	730.1	7.1
Current Liabilities to Working Capital 39	5.9	•	0.3	•	•	0.3	1.8	0.2	0.7	1.0	3.2	729.1	6.1
Working Capital to Net Sales 40	1.1	•	0.4	•	•	1.0	0.7	1.8	1.2	2.3	0.7	0.0	2.7
Inventory to Working Capital 41	•	•	•	•	•	•	•	•	•	•	•	•	•
Total Receipts to Cash Flow 42	2.6	1.8	1.5	•	•	1.9	1.7	1.8	2.5	3.0	2.3	1.9	8.3
Cost of Goods to Cash Flow 43	•	•	•	•	•	•	•	•	•	•	•	•	•
Cash Flow to Total Debt 44	0.1	•	7.0	•	•	1.5	0.3	0.8	0.3	0.2	0.1	0.2	0.0

Selected Financial Factors (in Percentages)

Item	1	2	3	4	5	6	7	8	9	10	11	12	13
Debt Ratio 45	92.5	•	20.2	•	17.8	44.4	54.1	12.5	38.4	40.5	73.1	53.2	97.8
Return on Total Assets 46	7.1	•	129.3	•	44.2	53.0	10.6	11.5	2.6	3.7	5.6	7.8	4.2
Return on Equity Before Income Taxes 47	25.9	•	162.1	•	29.1	93.8	21.9	6.8	3.8	2.1	18.5	13.5	19.4
Return on Equity After Income Taxes 48	18.5	•	161.0	•	29.1	90.9	21.0	4.5	3.7	1.4	12.2	8.9	12.8
Profit Margin (Before Income Tax) 49	15.6	13.5	59.6	•	47.6	44.9	35.7	23.6	8.0	6.8	23.0	33.0	8.3
Profit Margin (After Income Tax) 50	11.1	9.3	59.2	•	47.6	43.5	34.2	15.6	7.8	4.5	15.1	21.7	5.5

Table I

Corporations with and without Net Income

SECURITIES BROKERAGE

MONEY AMOUNTS AND SIZE OF ASSETS IN THOUSANDS OF DOLLARS

Item Description for Accounting Period 7/08 Through 6/09	Total	Zero Assets	Under 500	500 to 1,000	1,000 to 5,000	5,000 to 10,000	10,000 to 25,000	25,000 to 50,000	50,000 to 100,000	100,000 to 250,000	250,000 to 500,000	500,000 to 2,500,000	2,500,000 and over
Number of Enterprises **1**	7437	884	5103	459	672	93	102	35	21	18	7	17	26
Revenues ($ in Thousands)													
Net Sales **2**	182495948	5877048	2193291	925713	2252201	784179	2279776	1112498	1221029	2606912	1103615	5724802	156414884
Interest **3**	117036559	1899882	1082	1415	8063	14128	22296	13052	171687	69714	37381	353630	114444230
Rents **4**	819032	0	0	0	804	1088	657	1710	0	2980	272	18572	792949
Royalties **5**	58957	0	0	0	0	0	9658	0	0	856	0	3528	44915
Other Portfolio Income **6**	4380294	398542	2173	0	23942	3520	24001	16348	32909	49416	3421	47250	3778774
Other Receipts **7**	60201106	3578624	2190036	924298	2219392	765443	2223164	1081388	1016433	2483946	1062541	5301822	37354016
Total Receipts **8**	182495948	5877048	2193291	925713	2252201	784179	2279776	1112498	1221029	2606912	1103615	5724802	156414884
Average Total Receipts **9**	24539	6648	430	2017	3351	8432	22351	31786	58144	144828	157659	336753	6015957
Operating Costs/Operating Income (%)													
Cost of Operations **10**	0.1	•	•	•	•	•	2.9	0.4	•	2.2	•	0.6	0.0
Salaries and Wages **11**	17.2	13.5	25.1	39.9	38.9	28.4	24.9	44.2	36.8	26.6	39.9	40.7	15.1
Taxes Paid **12**	1.4	1.0	2.1	2.7	3.5	2.4	2.1	2.8	2.4	2.1	10.3	3.3	1.1
Interest Paid **13**	56.7	45.7	0.7	0.0	0.7	0.0	0.9	1.6	13.8	1.0	2.5	4.8	64.1
Depreciation **14**	1.1	1.0	1.3	0.2	0.4	0.6	1.0	0.9	0.9	1.2	1.8	2.0	1.1
Amortization and Depletion **15**	0.8	0.5	0.0	0.1	0.1	0.1	0.1	0.1	0.7	0.5	0.0	1.4	0.8
Pensions and Other Deferred Comp. **16**	0.6	•	0.8	0.3	0.4	0.3	1.2	0.4	1.1	0.3	2.1	0.4	0.6
Employee Benefits **17**	0.9	0.0	0.6	2.7	1.9	2.2	1.1	1.4	1.2	1.3	1.8	1.4	0.9
Advertising **18**	0.5	0.1	1.5	0.0	0.4	0.3	0.2	0.4	1.2	0.5	0.7	1.5	0.5
Other Expenses **19**	47.5	124.9	45.5	29.1	37.4	46.3	56.5	36.1	28.1	61.7	17.2	30.2	45.6
Officers' Compensation **20**	2.4	11.1	9.9	15.4	12.8	10.5	5.7	10.7	7.1	0.9	1.4	2.0	1.6
Operating Margin **21**	•	•	12.4	9.5	3.5	8.7	3.5	1.2	6.7	1.9	22.2	11.7	•
Operating Margin Before Officers' Comp. **22**	•	•	22.3	24.9	16.3	19.3	9.2	11.9	13.8	2.8	23.6	13.6	•

Selected Average Balance Sheet ($ in Thousands)

	1	2	3	4	5	6	7	8	9	10	11	12
Net Receivables 23	89498	1	134	199	626	1351	1229	12299	21891	44438	329910	25530345
Inventories 24	•	•	•	•	•	•	•	•	•	•	•	•
Net Property, Plant and Equipment 25	958	14	17	88	153	811	1168	1553	6269	11011	21614	240608
Total Assets 26	327616	91	695	2180	8541	15086	36168	69004	152125	309920	1105646	9251428
Notes and Loans Payable 27	64945	52	159	315	24	1751	2990	14980	11211	23703	109456	18446749
All Other Liabilities 28	230176	18	181	650	3053	5315	12752	24404	47513	129057	630512	65267250
Net Worth 29	32495	21	355	1215	5464	8020	20425	29619	93401	157161	365678	8804429

Selected Financial Ratios (Times to 1)

	1	2	3	4	5	6	7	8	9	10	11	12
Current Ratio 30	1.1	•	2.0	4.1	3.6	4.6	2.2	2.0	1.4	2.3	1.8	1.1
Quick Ratio 31	0.6	•	1.6	3.7	2.3	3.8	1.6	1.1	0.9	1.6	1.4	1.0
Net Sales to Working Capital 32	1.8	•	21.3	4.7	3.3	1.8	3.8	3.1	5.2	2.9	1.6	1.6
Coverage Ratio 33	0.5	•	17.7	191.8	5.6	273.8	4.6	1.7	1.4	2.9	9.7	3.4
Total Asset Turnover 34	0.1	•	4.7	2.9	1.5	1.0	1.5	0.9	0.8	1.0	0.5	0.3
Inventory Turnover 35	•	•	•	•	•	•	•	•	•	•	•	•
Receivables Turnover 36	•	•	•	•	•	•	•	•	•	•	•	9.5
Total Liabilities to Net Worth 37	9.1	•	3.3	1.0	0.8	0.6	0.9	0.8	1.3	0.6	1.0	2.0
Current Assets to Working Capital 38	15.4	2.0	1.3	1.4	1.3	1.9	2.0	3.8	1.8	2.2	8.5	16.0
Current Liabilities to Working Capital 39	14.4	1.0	0.3	0.4	0.3	0.9	1.0	2.8	0.8	1.2	7.5	15.0
Working Capital to Net Sales 40	0.6	0.0	0.2	0.3	0.6	0.3	0.3	0.2	0.3	0.6	0.2	0.6
Inventory to Working Capital 41	0.0	•	0.0	0.0	•	•	0.0	0.0	0.1	0.1	0.0	0.1
Total Receipts to Cash Flow 42	6.8	10.3	2.1	2.9	2.0	1.8	3.0	3.1	1.7	2.9	2.6	8.8
Cost of Goods to Cash Flow 43	0.0	•	•	•	•	•	0.0	0.0	0.0	0.0	0.0	0.0
Cash Flow to Total Debt 44	0.0	•	3.0	2.0	1.2	1.4	1.8	0.7	0.5	1.5	0.4	0.0

Selected Financial Factors (in Percentages)

	1	2	3	4	5	6	7	8	9	10	11	12
Debt Ratio 45	90.1	76.8	48.9	44.3	36.0	46.8	43.5	57.1	38.6	49.3	66.9	90.5
Return on Total Assets 46	2.1	2.4	5.7	8.3	6.2	8.4	6.6	16.4	2.7	12.5	4.9	2.2
Return on Equity Before Income Taxes 47	•	251.5	54.0	27.7	13.0	9.1	1.7	11.2	2.9	22.2	10.5	•
Return on Equity After Income Taxes 48	•	250.6	52.7	6.6	12.0	6.4	8.4	8.1	3.0	14.4	6.9	•
Profit Margin (Before Income Tax) 49	•	12.4	9.5	3.0	8.4	3.3	1.1	5.7	1.9	22.1	11.4	•
Profit Margin (After Income Tax) 50	•	12.3	9.3	2.4	7.7	2.3	•	4.1	1.0	14.3	7.5	•

Table II
Corporations with Net Income

SECURITIES BROKERAGE

Item Description for Accounting Period 7/08 Through 6/09

MONEY AMOUNTS AND SIZE OF ASSETS IN THOUSANDS OF DOLLARS

Item		Total	Zero Assets	Under 500	500 to 1,000	1,000 to 5,000	5,000 to 10,000	10,000 to 25,000	25,000 to 50,000	50,000 to 100,000	100,000 to 250,000	250,000 to 500,000	500,000 to 2,500,000	2,500,000 and over
Number of Enterprises	1	4878	•	3448	391	455	55	53	25	16	•	•	•	13
Revenues ($ in Thousands)														
Net Sales	2	35404680	•	1304240	852241	1579438	527254	1634984	692561	805368	•	•	•	21120650
Interest	3	6608032	•	51	750	7440	11977	7713	6651	8576	•	•	•	6239867
Rents	4	20732	•	0	0	0	0	0	0	0	•	•	•	747
Royalties	5	19220	•	0	0	0	0	9658	0	0	•	•	•	6696
Other Portfolio Income	6	384778	•	0	0	478	2484	18216	6157	30772	•	•	•	237439
Other Receipts	7	28371918	•	1304189	851491	1571520	512793	1599397	679753	766020	•	•	•	14635901
Total Receipts	8	35404680	•	1304240	852241	1579438	527254	1634984	692561	805368	•	•	•	21120650
Average Total Receipts	9	7258	•	378	2180	3471	9586	30849	27702	50336	•	•	•	1624665
Operating Costs/Operating Income (%)														
Cost of Operations	10	0.3	•	•	•	•	•	4.1	0.6	•	•	•	•	•
Salaries and Wages	11	22.4	•	18.6	40.8	26.5	20.8	21.4	41.9	40.1	•	•	•	17.6
Taxes Paid	12	2.8	•	1.9	2.6	2.9	1.9	1.8	2.9	2.9	•	•	•	2.6
Interest Paid	13	12.2	•	0.3	0.0	0.4	0.0	0.7	0.4	1.2	•	•	•	19.0
Depreciation	14	1.3	•	0.5	0.0	0.3	0.3	0.6	0.6	1.0	•	•	•	1.5
Amortization and Depletion	15	0.8	•	0.0	0.0	0.1	0.2	0.0	0.0	0.6	•	•	•	1.0
Pensions and Other Deferred Comp.	16	0.7	•	0.6	0.2	0.5	0.4	1.5	0.5	1.6	•	•	•	0.6
Employee Benefits	17	1.3	•	0.6	2.8	1.1	1.3	0.8	1.2	1.2	•	•	•	1.4
Advertising	18	2.1	•	1.7	0.0	0.1	0.4	0.2	0.3	1.5	•	•	•	3.0
Other Expenses	19	34.6	•	39.8	25.6	38.3	50.4	53.3	24.2	28.9	•	•	•	32.6
Officers' Compensation	20	3.6	•	9.7	14.5	15.9	6.3	5.2	15.1	7.4	•	•	•	1.8
Operating Margin	21	17.8	•	26.4	13.5	13.9	18.1	10.4	12.3	13.6	•	•	•	19.0
Operating Margin Before Officers' Comp.	22	21.4	•	36.1	27.9	29.8	24.4	15.6	27.4	20.9	•	•	•	20.8

Selected Average Balance Sheet ($ in Thousands)

Item												
Net Receivables 23	8998	•	0	138	249	725	1563	1219	15667	•	•	2939138
Inventories 24	•	•	•	•	•	•	•	•	•	•	•	•
Net Property, Plant and Equipment 25	359	•	7	15	94	34	786	949	1354	•	•	94361
Total Assets 26	39747	•	85	684	2047	8773	15339	36471	69873	•	•	13130538
Notes and Loans Payable 27	3793	•	20	68	128	0	2177	1080	14428	•	•	1240924
All Other Liabilities 28	29764	•	9	163	684	4051	5660	13129	28742	•	•	10303441
Net Worth 29	6190	•	56	453	1234	4722	7502	22261	26703	•	•	1586172

Selected Financial Ratios (Times to 1)

Item									
Current Ratio 30	0.9	•	2.3	5.4	3.7	5.7	1.9	2.0	1.2
Quick Ratio 31	0.7	•	1.8	4.7	2.9	5.1	1.4	1.0	0.9
Net Sales to Working Capital 32	•	•	20.7	4.5	3.2	1.9	5.5	2.6	9.0
Coverage Ratio 33	2.5	•	93.2	1224.4	36.3	3322.1	15.2	29.3	10.8
Total Asset Turnover 34	0.2	•	4.4	3.2	1.7	1.1	2.0	0.8	0.7
Inventory Turnover 35	•	•	•	•	•	•	•	•	•
Receivables Turnover 36	•	•	•	•	•	•	•	•	•
Total Liabilities to Net Worth 37	5.4	•	0.5	0.5	0.7	0.9	1.0	0.6	1.6
Current Assets to Working Capital 38	•	•	1.8	1.2	1.4	1.2	2.1	2.0	7.5
Current Liabilities to Working Capital 39	•	•	0.8	0.2	0.4	0.2	1.1	1.0	6.5
Working Capital to Net Sales 40	•	•	0.0	0.2	0.3	0.5	0.2	0.4	0.1
Inventory to Working Capital 41	•	•	•	•	•	•	•	•	0.0
Total Receipts to Cash Flow 42	2.1	•	1.8	2.9	2.1	1.5	1.6	3.0	2.5
Cost of Goods to Cash Flow 43	0.0	•	•	•	•	•	0.1	0.0	•
Cash Flow to Total Debt 44	0.1	•	7.2	3.3	2.0	1.6	2.4	0.7	0.5

Selected Financial Factors (in Percentages)

Item									
Debt Ratio 45	84.4	•	34.8	33.8	39.7	46.2	51.1	39.0	61.8
Return on Total Assets 46	5.5	•	118.2	43.1	24.3	19.3	21.6	9.7	9.6
Return on Equity Before Income Taxes 47	20.8	•	179.5	64.9	39.1	35.8	41.3	15.3	22.9
Return on Equity After Income Taxes 48	15.2	•	179.0	63.8	36.6	33.8	35.8	13.1	18.3
Profit Margin (Before Income Tax) 49	17.7	•	26.4	13.5	13.9	17.6	10.1	12.3	12.1
Profit Margin (After Income Tax) 50	13.0	•	26.3	13.3	13.0	16.6	8.7	10.5	9.7

Table I

Corporations with and without Net Income

COMMODITY CONTRACTS DEALING AND BROKERAGE

MONEY AMOUNTS AND SIZE OF ASSETS IN THOUSANDS OF DOLLARS

Item Description for Accounting Period 7/08 Through 6/09		Total	Zero Assets	Under 500	500 to 1,000	1,000 to 5,000	5,000 to 10,000	10,000 to 25,000	25,000 to 50,000	50,000 to 100,000	100,000 to 250,000	250,000 to 500,000	500,000 to 2,500,000	2,500,000 and over
Number of Enterprises	1	1370	12	787	264	182	14	61	12	11	12	3	7	6
Revenues ($ in Thousands)														
Net Sales	2	6886268	120663	119136	81812	82228	112178	702277	206232	27501	167957	103162	869982	4293139
Interest	3	1863170	2741	0	333	957	55	6258	1443	6066	16110	14568	93570	1721069
Rents	4	27155	0	0	0	0	0	0	184	0	8558	0	1220	17193
Royalties	5	36	0	0	0	0	0	0	0	0	0	0	0	36
Other Portfolio Income	6	450531	0	0	0	52	296	14216	0	16555	27978	0	19420	372016
Other Receipts	7	4545376	117922	119136	81479	81219	111827	681803	204605	4880	115311	88594	755772	2182825
Total Receipts	8	6886268	120663	119136	81812	82228	112178	702277	206232	27501	167957	103162	869982	4293139
Average Total Receipts	9	5026	10055	151	310	452	8013	11513	17186	2500	13996	34387	124283	715523
Operating Costs/Operating Income (%)														
Cost of Operations	10	0.4	20.1	•	•	•	•	•	•	•	•	•	•	0.0
Salaries and Wages	11	20.2	15.0	0.5	74.6	33.5	34.3	25.1	43.0	157.6	21.9	35.1	16.3	16.8
Taxes Paid	12	2.2	0.9	2.2	5.2	5.1	3.0	3.7	4.8	19.3	7.4	1.7	2.1	1.5
Interest Paid	13	21.2	23.9	0.5	10.8	20.5	1.7	1.2	4.6	18.0	9.3	8.2	9.9	29.5
Depreciation	14	1.3	0.2	0.2	1.0	4.0	0.9	0.7	2.2	4.5	1.5	1.3	0.8	1.4
Amortization and Depletion	15	2.2	•	•	•	7.9	•	0.4	0.1	2.1	0.2	0.3	1.3	3.0
Pensions and Other Deferred Comp.	16	0.6	0.4	0.5	5.5	12.8	0.8	0.7	2.7	2.5	0.8	0.0	0.6	0.1
Employee Benefits	17	1.4	0.2	3.9	3.3	2.4	1.7	2.1	3.1	6.2	1.9	1.3	2.3	0.9
Advertising	18	0.4	•	1.5	0.0	0.4	0.8	0.7	1.8	1.0	0.2	3.1	0.2	0.2
Other Expenses	19	46.3	23.3	52.1	30.7	40.8	17.6	24.1	41.5	257.6	47.4	25.8	43.8	51.3
Officers' Compensation	20	6.9	4.9	27.3	27.9	37.3	15.7	26.8	5.8	17.4	26.9	0.9	5.0	1.6
Operating Margin	21	•	11.1	11.3	•	•	23.3	14.6	•	•	•	22.3	17.7	•
Operating Margin Before Officers' Comp.	22	4.0	16.0	38.6	•	39.1	•	41.4	•	•	9.4	23.1	22.7	•

Selected Average Balance Sheet ($ in Thousands)

Line Item												
Net Receivables 23	20722	0	71	731	1101	2429	6043	18689	10925	32792	476298	4038680
Inventories 24	•	•	•	•	•	•	•	•	•	•	•	•
Net Property, Plant and Equipment 25	314	2	2	62	278	406	2198	343	4536	1203	18480	28457
Total Assets 26	78814	774	2167	6651	15644	32652	61645	154204	304264	1130123	15763056	
Notes and Loans Payable 27	5700	3	2	912	72	1347	11331	9958	19563	60	93784	1069879
All Other Liabilities 28	68785	1	36	918	948	8501	16781	22581	68108	211744	943343	14170073
Net Worth 29	4330	5	735	337	5631	5796	4540	29106	66534	92460	92996	523104

Selected Financial Ratios (Times to 1)

Line Item													
Current Ratio 30	1.2	•	1.7	6.5	1.5	4.0	2.1	1.1	1.2	1.0	1.4	1.0	1.2
Quick Ratio 31	0.7	•	0.5	4.2	1.4	1.8	1.4	0.8	0.9	0.5	1.3	0.6	0.7
Net Sales to Working Capital 32	0.4	•	53.8	1.5	0.9	2.2	9.5	0.4	5.2	0.4	0.3	•	0.3
Coverage Ratio 33	0.9	1.5	23.2	•	14.4	13.4	•	0.0	•	3.7	2.8	•	0.8
Total Asset Turnover 34	0.1	•	16.3	0.4	0.2	1.2	0.7	0.5	0.0	0.1	0.1	•	0.0
Inventory Turnover 35	•	•	•	•	•	•	•	•	•	•	•	•	•
Receivables Turnover 36	•	•	•	•	•	•	•	•	•	•	•	•	•
Total Liabilities to Net Worth 37	17.2	•	0.8	0.1	5.4	0.2	1.7	6.2	1.1	1.3	2.3	11.2	29.1
Current Assets to Working Capital 38	6.0	•	2.5	1.2	2.9	1.3	1.9	9.3	6.3	33.2	3.4	•	5.6
Current Liabilities to Working Capital 39	5.0	•	1.5	0.2	1.9	0.3	0.9	8.3	5.3	32.2	2.4	•	4.6
Working Capital to Net Sales 40	2.4	•	0.0	0.7	1.1	0.3	0.4	0.1	2.2	0.2	2.5	•	3.6
Inventory to Working Capital 41	0.0	•	•	•	•	•	•	•	0.0	•	•	•	0.0
Total Receipts to Cash Flow 42	2.7	2.9	1.8	•	2.6	•	2.9	5.3	•	14.0	2.2	1.7	2.5
Cost of Goods to Cash Flow 43	0.0	0.6	•	•	•	•	•	•	•	•	•	•	0.0
Cash Flow to Total Debt 44	0.0	•	19.8	•	3.1	•	0.4	0.1	0.1	0.0	0.1	•	0.0

Selected Financial Factors (in Percentages)

Line Item													
Debt Ratio 45	94.5	•	45.7	5.0	84.4	15.3	63.0	86.1	52.8	56.9	69.6	91.8	96.7
Return on Total Assets 46	1.2	•	192.7	•	•	29.9	11.8	•	•	•	3.4	3.0	1.1
Return on Equity Before Income Taxes 47	•	•	339.3	•	•	32.8	29.4	•	•	8.3	8.3	23.6	•
Return on Equity After Income Taxes 48	•	•	339.3	•	•	32.8	29.3	•	•	5.5	5.5	13.6	•
Profit Margin (Before Income Tax) 49	•	11.1	11.3	•	23.1	14.8	14.8	•	•	22.3	22.3	17.7	•
Profit Margin (After Income Tax) 50	•	10.2	11.3	•	23.1	14.8	14.8	•	•	14.8	22.3	17.7	10.2

Table II

Corporations with Net Income

COMMODITY CONTRACTS DEALING AND BROKERAGE

MONEY AMOUNTS AND SIZE OF ASSETS IN THOUSANDS OF DOLLARS

Item Description for Accounting Period 7/08 Through 6/09	Total	Zero Assets	Under 500	500 to 1,000	1,000 to 5,000	5,000 to 10,000	10,000 to 25,000	25,000 to 50,000	50,000 to 100,000	100,000 to 250,000	250,000 to 500,000	500,000 to 2,500,000	2,500,000 and over
Number of Enterprises 1	206	•	5	55	66	7	33	6	3	•	0	•	•
Revenues ($ in Thousands)													
Net Sales 2	6171749	•	29248	49271	67345	102427	638003	154593	45157	•	0	•	•
Interest 3	1794776	•	0	310	956	0	2145	1426	869	•	0	•	•
Rents 4	26971	•	0	0	0	0	0	0	0	•	0	•	•
Royalties 5	36	•	0	0	0	0	0	0	0	•	0	•	•
Other Portfolio Income 6	443127	•	0	0	37	296	8256	0	16427	•	0	•	•
Other Receipts 7	3906839	•	29248	48961	66352	102131	627602	153167	27861	•	0	•	•
Total Receipts 8	6171749	•	29248	49271	67345	102427	638003	154593	45157	•	0	•	•
Average Total Receipts 9	29960	•	5850	896	1020	14632	19333	25766	15052	•	•	•	•
Operating Costs/Operating Income (%)													
Cost of Operations 10	0.4	•	•	•	•	•	•	•	•	•	•	•	•
Salaries and Wages 11	17.9	•	2.1	0.7	5.2	30.7	21.5	34.9	28.3	•	•	•	•
Taxes Paid 12	2.0	•	1.4	0.7	1.7	2.6	3.5	3.4	2.7	•	•	•	•
Interest Paid 13	21.7	•	0.3	•	16.3	0.1	0.4	4.1	4.9	•	•	•	•
Depreciation 14	1.2	•	•	0.5	0.1	0.9	0.3	1.9	0.8	•	•	•	•
Amortization and Depletion 15	0.5	•	•	•	9.6	•	•	0.2	0.3	•	•	•	•
Pensions and Other Deferred Comp. 16	0.4	•	2.0	•	1.4	0.9	0.2	3.6	1.1	•	•	•	•
Employee Benefits 17	1.1	•	•	•	2.2	1.4	2.0	1.7	1.0	•	•	•	•
Advertising 18	0.2	•	•	0.1	•	0.8	0.1	0.0	0.4	•	•	•	•
Other Expenses 19	31.1	•	11.9	14.3	11.6	3.7	11.1	25.2	44.5	•	•	•	•
Officers' Compensation 20	5.7	•	17.6	2.0	16.9	17.0	27.5	5.6	4.3	•	•	•	•
Operating Margin 21	17.8	•	64.8	81.8	35.0	42.0	33.2	19.6	11.7	•	•	•	•
Operating Margin Before Officers' Comp. 22	23.5	•	82.4	83.7	51.9	59.0	60.7	25.2	15.9	•	•	•	•

Selected Average Balance Sheet ($ in Thousands)

Net Receivables 23	105635	•	0	343	1043	2200	1202	6164	41094
Inventories 24	•	•	•	•	•	•	•	•	•
Net Property, Plant and Equipment 25	1821	•	0	2	1	510	420	1892	342
Total Assets 26	463871	•	365	567	2490	7718	15256	29801	54502
Notes and Loans Payable 27	31277	•	0	11	1167	48	947	12550	14801
All Other Liabilities 28	411191	•	118	30	1093	800	3761	23108	30794
Net Worth 29	21404	•	247	526	230	6869	10547	-5856	8907

Selected Financial Ratios (Times to 1)

Current Ratio 30	1.2	•	3.1	10.9	1.4	3.3	1.9	1.0	1.1
Quick Ratio 31	0.7	•	3.1	8.5	1.4	3.3	1.2	0.8	1.1
Net Sales to Working Capital 32	0.4	•	23.6	2.2	2.3	7.9	5.2	•	2.7
Coverage Ratio 33	1.8	•	247.2	•	3.1	475.6	77.7	5.8	3.4
Total Asset Turnover 34	0.1	•	16.0	1.6	0.4	1.9	1.3	0.9	0.3
Inventory Turnover 35	•	•	•	•	•	•	•	•	•
Receivables Turnover 36	•	•	•	•	•	•	•	•	•
Total Liabilities to Net Worth 37	20.7	•	0.5	0.1	9.8	0.1	0.4	•	5.1
Current Assets to Working Capital 38	5.1	•	1.5	1.1	3.7	1.4	2.1	•	8.8
Current Liabilities to Working Capital 39	4.1	•	0.5	0.1	2.7	0.4	1.1	•	7.8
Working Capital to Net Sales 40	2.8	•	0.0	0.4	0.4	0.1	0.2	•	0.4
Inventory to Working Capital 41	0.0	•	•	•	•	•	•	•	•
Total Receipts to Cash Flow 42	2.3	•	1.3	1.1	2.2	2.2	2.4	2.4	5.5
Cost of Goods to Cash Flow 43	0.0	•	•	•	•	•	•	•	•
Cash Flow to Total Debt 44	0.0	•	37.9	19.8	0.2	7.8	1.7	0.3	0.1

Selected Financial Factors (in Percentages)

Debt Ratio 45	95.4	•	32.3	7.2	90.8	11.0	30.9	119.7	83.7
Return on Total Assets 46	2.6	•	1042.5	129.3	21.0	79.2	42.6	20.4	4.6
Return on Equity Before Income Taxes 47	25.4	•	1532.7	139.2	155.2	88.8	60.8	•	19.7
Return on Equity After Income Taxes 48	19.5	•	1532.7	134.5	154.2	88.8	60.8	•	15.4
Profit Margin (Before Income Tax) 49	18.1	•	64.8	81.8	35.0	41.7	33.2	19.6	11.7
Profit Margin (After Income Tax) 50	13.9	•	64.8	79.0	34.8	41.7	33.2	16.3	9.1

Table I

Corporations with and without Net Income

SECURITIES & COMMODITY EXCHANGES, OTHER FINANCIAL INVESTMENT

MONEY AMOUNTS AND SIZE OF ASSETS IN THOUSANDS OF DOLLARS

Item Description for Accounting Period 7/08 Through 6/09	Total	Zero Assets	Under 500	500 to 1,000	1,000 to 5,000	5,000 to 10,000	10,000 to 25,000	25,000 to 50,000	50,000 to 100,000	100,000 to 250,000	250,000 to 500,000	500,000 to 2,500,000	2,500,000 and over
Number of Enterprises 1	44979	8142	29717	1944	2992	873	620	273	168	101	58	55	35
Revenues ($ in Thousands)													
Net Sales 2	140462706	2469404	9811159	1513880	10539569	4612529	3593042	4532135	4532828	4657369	2525609	12919258	78755923
Interest 3	16036231	61241	71739	7894	35170	21223	49902	115764	135343	161955	339413	1010085	14026502
Rents 4	135193	5762	7272	0	211	854	4015	1092	6788	4288	9467	42409	53036
Royalties 5	133768	142	11851	129	0	15	145	4181	1546	2442	273	21	113023
Other Portfolio Income 6	4644672	90996	96755	32048	59219	77080	149946	127389	190000	154025	205940		3218817
Other Receipts 7	119512842	2311263	9623542	1473809	10444969	4513357	3389034	4283709	4199151	4246225	2022431	11660803	61344545
Total Receipts 8	140462706	2469404	9811159	1513880	10539569	4612529	3593042	4532135	4532828	4657369	2525609	12919258	78755923
Average Total Receipts 9	3123	303	330	779	3523	5284	5795	16601	26981	46113	43545	234896	2250169
Operating Costs/Operating Income (%)													
Cost of Operations 10	0.8	0.5	•	1.8	•	•	0.5	7.2	1.1	0.0	0.0	1.4	0.6
Salaries and Wages 11	19.0	12.8	15.9	15.3	18.6	30.1	32.9	25.0	23.5	25.8	17.0	22.3	17.0
Taxes Paid 12	2.3	6.6	2.6	2.4	2.6	3.4	2.4	2.4	2.9	2.7	4.3	2.2	1.8
Interest Paid 13	11.2	2.4	0.9	1.0	0.5	1.2	3.1	5.2	5.1	4.7	11.9	8.5	16.8
Depreciation 14	1.5	1.1	0.9	0.9	0.7	1.2	1.5	1.6	1.7	2.8	3.0	1.6	1.5
Amortization and Depletion 15	1.2	0.7	0.4	0.3	0.1	0.8	0.7	1.0	0.4	2.2	2.2	2.5	1.2
Pensions and Other Deferred Comp. 16	1.2	2.2	2.3	4.2	0.8	0.8	1.1	0.7	0.6	0.8	0.6	0.6	1.3
Employee Benefits 17	1.5	1.4	1.7	1.4	1.3	1.6	1.4	1.3	1.1	1.4	1.3	1.8	1.5
Advertising 18	1.0	0.4	1.2	0.3	0.2	0.3	0.4	0.4	0.9	2.1	0.4	0.8	1.2
Other Expenses 19	40.1	48.0	35.2	22.4	23.9	38.2	36.7	26.7	43.5	27.1	46.8	40.7	44.3
Officers' Compensation 20	9.6	21.0	26.6	32.1	41.8	12.4	9.9	18.4	13.4	16.1	4.3	6.2	1.9
Operating Margin 21	10.6	2.9	12.2	18.0	9.5	10.1	9.2	10.2	5.7	14.2	8.3	11.3	10.8
Operating Margin Before Officers' Comp. 22	20.3	24.0	38.8	50.1	51.4	22.6	19.1	28.6	19.1	30.4	12.6	17.5	12.7

Selected Average Balance Sheet ($ in Thousands)

Item												
Net Receivables 23	953	0	4	106	219	545	1417	3823	5867	16293	13456	119038	844261
Inventories 24	•	•	•	•	•	•	•	•	•	•	•	•	•
Net Property, Plant and Equipment 25	333	0	12	43	407	523	970	1607	4538	7410	14177	27565	227798
Total Assets 26	14366	0	73	696	2348	6732	15554	34236	68887	157315	363105	1044277	14422005
Notes and Loans Payable 27	3235	0	24	217	734	1789	4692	9980	15844	33314	100416	288448	3064895
All Other Liabilities 28	7064	0	26	110	514	1322	2133	5552	15101	37796	64820	347875	8056052
Net Worth 29	4066	0	23	369	1101	3621	8729	18703	37942	86204	197869	407954	3301058

Selected Financial Ratios (Times to 1)

Item												
Current Ratio 30	1.0	•	1.6	1.6	2.4	1.7	1.7	1.7	1.9	2.1	1.9	1.5	0.9
Quick Ratio 31	0.5	•	1.4	1.2	1.8	1.0	1.3	1.2	1.3	1.3	1.1	0.9	0.4
Net Sales to Working Capital 32	•	•	22.6	5.8	7.2	5.7	3.2	3.4	2.2	1.3	0.9	1.7	•
Coverage Ratio 33	2.0	2.2	14.1	19.1	19.9	9.2	3.7	3.0	2.1	3.9	1.7	2.3	1.7
Total Asset Turnover 34	0.2	2.2	4.5	1.1	1.5	0.8	0.4	0.5	0.4	0.3	0.1	0.2	0.2
Inventory Turnover 35	•	•	•	•	•	•	•	•	•	•	•	•	•
Receivables Turnover 36	•	•	•	•	•	•	•	•	•	•	•	•	•
Total Liabilities to Net Worth 37	2.5	•	2.2	0.9	1.1	0.9	0.8	0.8	0.8	0.8	0.8	1.6	3.4
Current Assets to Working Capital 38	•	•	2.7	2.7	1.7	2.3	2.5	2.4	2.1	1.9	2.1	2.9	•
Current Liabilities to Working Capital 39	•	•	1.7	1.7	0.7	1.3	1.5	1.4	1.1	0.9	1.1	1.9	•
Working Capital to Net Sales 40	•	•	0.0	0.2	0.1	0.2	0.3	0.3	0.5	0.8	1.2	0.6	•
Inventory to Working Capital 41	•	•	•	0.0	0.0	0.0	0.0	0.0	0.0	0.0	0.0	0.1	•
Total Receipts to Cash Flow 42	2.1	2.3	2.4	2.8	3.4	2.3	2.6	3.0	2.3	2.9	2.0	2.0	1.9
Cost of Goods to Cash Flow 43	0.0	0.0	0.0	0.0	0.0	•	0.0	0.2	0.0	0.0	0.0	0.0	0.0
Cash Flow to Total Debt 44	0.1	•	2.7	0.8	0.8	0.7	0.3	0.4	0.4	0.2	0.1	0.2	0.1

Selected Financial Factors (in Percentages)

Item												
Debt Ratio 45	71.7	•	68.8	47.0	53.1	46.2	43.9	45.4	44.9	45.2	45.5	60.9	77.1
Return on Total Assets 46	4.8	•	59.1	21.2	15.0	8.9	4.3	7.5	4.2	5.5	2.5	4.5	4.5
Return on Equity Before Income Taxes 47	8.5	•	176.1	37.9	30.5	14.8	5.5	9.1	3.9	7.4	1.9	6.5	8.0
Return on Equity After Income Taxes 48	5.9	•	173.3	36.4	29.0	13.5	4.1	7.7	1.7	5.6	0.1	3.6	5.1
Profit Margin (Before Income Tax) 49	11.1	2.8	12.2	18.0	9.5	10.1	8.4	10.2	5.5	13.9	8.6	11.4	11.7
Profit Margin (After Income Tax) 50	7.6	•	12.0	17.2	9.1	9.2	6.2	8.6	2.4	10.5	6.3		7.5

Table II
Corporations with Net Income

SECURITIES & COMMODITY EXCHANGES, OTHER FINANCIAL INVESTMENT

MONEY AMOUNTS AND SIZE OF ASSETS IN THOUSANDS OF DOLLARS

Item Description for Accounting Period 7/08 Through 6/09		Total	Zero Assets	Under 500	500 to 1,000	1,000 to 5,000	5,000 to 10,000	10,000 to 25,000	25,000 to 50,000	50,000 to 100,000	100,000 to 250,000	250,000 to 500,000	500,000 to 2,500,000	2,500,000 and over
Number of Enterprises	1	26680	3412	19340	1309	1508	469	311	117	76	52	•	33	•
Revenues ($ in Thousands)														
Net Sales	2	116964110	1792240	7955692	1437584	8605579	4085061	2879976	3396834	3352130	4329666	•	11379081	•
Interest	3	3984343	18092	57361	6906	21751	11319	34291	74064	67691	120469	•	442719	•
Rents	4	118759	5762	4220	0	211	46	1903	19	6517	2275	•	35366	•
Royalties	5	120425	142	0	129	0	0	145	4168	848	1695	•	21	•
Other Portfolio Income	6	1944377	64128	58675	31072	53565	62743	79891	118093	168353	194018	•	195922	•
Other Receipts	7	110796206	1704116	7835436	1399477	8530052	4010953	2763746	3200490	3108721	4011209	•	10705053	•
Total Receipts	8	116964110	1792240	7955692	1437584	8605579	4085061	2879976	3396834	3352130	4329666	•	11379081	•
Average Total Receipts	9	4384	525	411	1098	5707	8710	9260	29033	44107	83263	•	344821	•
Operating Costs/Operating Income (%)														
Cost of Operations	10	0.8	0.7	•	•	•	•	0.0	7.9	1.5	•	•	1.6	•
Salaries and Wages	11	19.2	8.1	14.7	15.6	15.5	29.7	26.9	19.2	16.9	22.9	•	21.4	•
Taxes Paid	12	2.4	8.0	2.6	2.1	2.5	3.2	2.1	2.1	2.9	2.6	•	2.1	•
Interest Paid	13	3.2	0.8	0.8	0.6	0.2	0.4	1.4	2.1	1.1	3.6	•	5.1	•
Depreciation	14	1.5	0.8	0.7	0.7	0.5	0.8	1.3	1.1	1.2	2.5	•	1.3	•
Amortization and Depletion	15	1.0	0.8	0.5	0.2	0.1	0.4	0.6	0.7	0.3	0.4	•	2.2	•
Pensions and Other Deferred Comp.	16	1.2	1.6	1.6	4.4	0.7	0.8	1.3	0.7	0.7	0.6	•	0.6	•
Employee Benefits	17	1.5	0.8	1.4	1.5	1.1	1.3	1.3	1.2	1.1	1.0	•	1.7	•
Advertising	18	1.1	0.2	1.2	0.3	0.1	0.3	0.4	0.3	1.2	2.2	•	0.9	•
Other Expenses	19	39.5	35.7	34.8	14.5	19.5	33.0	23.8	18.6	35.8	17.6	•	27.2	•
Officers' Compensation	20	8.8	6.7	23.0	33.8	43.5	10.8	8.5	16.2	12.9	15.1	•	4.5	•
Operating Margin	21	19.7	36.0	18.5	26.4	16.2	19.2	32.4	29.7	24.5	31.7	•	31.4	•
Operating Margin Before Officers' Comp.	22	28.5	42.7	41.6	60.1	59.7	30.0	40.9	45.9	37.4	46.8	•	35.8	•

Selected Average Balance Sheet ($ in Thousands)

Net Receivables 23	1172	0	4	90	266	498	2020	3869	6615	21804	93793
Inventories 24	•	•	•	•	•	•	•	•	•	•	•
Net Property, Plant and Equipment 25	428	0	11	54	235	638	823	2395	3695	7345	39248
Total Assets 26	15041	0	82	700	2228	6726	15214	33876	67606	160319	1054523
Notes and Loans Payable 27	2250	0	21	219	449	1510	3867	7563	11493	39154	223570
All Other Liabilities 28	7609	0	17	122	485	1242	2198	5654	14023	41966	245020
Net Worth 29	5182	0	44	360	1295	3974	9149	20659	42089	79199	585933

Selected Financial Ratios (Times to 1)

Current Ratio 30	1.3	•	2.6	1.7	2.6	2.2	2.2	1.7	2.6	2.6	2.1
Quick Ratio 31	0.8	•	2.3	1.2	1.9	1.3	1.7	1.2	1.9	1.8	1.4
Net Sales to Working Capital 32	3.9	•	14.5	7.5	9.0	6.1	3.0	5.4	2.6	1.9	2.0
Coverage Ratio 33	7.3	45.5	23.4	47.9	68.6	48.9	24.3	15.1	23.2	9.7	7.1
Total Asset Turnover 34	0.3	•	5.0	1.6	2.6	1.3	0.6	0.9	0.7	0.5	0.3
Inventory Turnover 35	•	•	•	•	•	•	•	•	•	•	•
Receivables Turnover 36	•	•	•	•	•	•	•	•	•	•	•
Total Liabilities to Net Worth 37	1.9	•	0.9	0.9	0.7	0.7	0.7	0.6	0.6	1.0	0.8
Current Assets to Working Capital 38	4.8	•	1.6	2.4	1.6	1.8	1.8	2.5	1.6	1.6	1.9
Current Liabilities to Working Capital 39	3.8	•	0.6	1.4	0.6	0.8	0.8	1.5	0.6	0.6	0.9
Working Capital to Net Sales 40	0.3	•	0.1	0.1	0.1	0.2	0.3	0.2	0.4	0.5	0.5
Inventory to Working Capital 41	0.0	•	•	•	•	•	0.0	•	0.0	0.0	0.1
Total Receipts to Cash Flow 42	1.8	1.5	2.1	2.7	3.1	2.0	1.9	2.3	1.8	2.3	1.8
Cost of Goods to Cash Flow 43	0.0	0.0	•	•	•	•	0.0	0.2	0.0	0.0	0.0
Cash Flow to Total Debt 44	0.2	•	5.3	1.2	2.0	1.5	0.8	1.0	0.9	0.5	0.4

Selected Financial Factors (in Percentages)

Debt Ratio 45	65.5	•	46.1	48.6	41.9	40.9	39.9	39.0	37.7	50.6	44.4
Return on Total Assets 46	6.9	6.9	97.7	42.1	42.1	25.4	20.4	27.2	16.6	18.3	11.9
Return on Equity Before Income Taxes 47	17.2	•	173.4	80.3	71.4	42.1	32.6	41.7	25.6	33.2	18.5
Return on Equity After Income Taxes 48	13.7	13.7	171.2	78.0	69.0	39.9	29.8	38.7	21.6	29.4	15.1
Profit Margin (Before Income Tax) 49	20.3	35.9	18.5	26.3	16.2	19.2	32.2	29.6	24.4	31.5	31.4
Profit Margin (After Income Tax) 50	16.2	28.2	18.3	25.6	15.7	18.2	29.5	27.5	20.6	27.9	25.6

Table I

Corporations with and without Net Income

LIFE INSURANCE

MONEY AMOUNTS AND SIZE OF ASSETS IN THOUSANDS OF DOLLARS

Item Description for Accounting Period 7/08 Through 6/09	Total	Zero Assets	Under 500	500 to 1,000	1,000 to 5,000	5,000 to 10,000	10,000 to 25,000	25,000 to 50,000	50,000 to 100,000	100,000 to 250,000	250,000 to 500,000	500,000 to 2,500,000	2,500,000 and over
Number of Enterprises **1**	945	48	217	78	150	53	69	61	36	39	39	63	92
Revenues ($ in Thousands)													
Net Sales **2**	1076878477	19079190	42280	27741	163119	101381	546762	1072282	1023387	2284067	4102790	22902129	102553347
Interest **3**	181508973	37075	1354	1929	13663	12199	38770	87100	94971	238220	520718	3628549	176834425
Rents **4**	8378577	0	0	0	80	265	2396	3481	5933	9444	11772	25351	8319854
Royalties **5**	47973	0	0	0	0	0	0	0	0	1557	606	227	45583
Other Portfolio Income **6**	20171369	4956	88	338	1170	3695	10268	14308	29657	10387	93673	176104	19826726
Other Receipts **7**	866771585	19037159	40838	25474	148206	85222	495328	967393	892826	2024459	3476021	19071898	820506759
Total Receipts **8**	1076878477	19079190	42280	27741	163119	101381	546762	1072282	1023387	2284067	4102790	22902129	102553347
Average Total Receipts **9**	1139554	397483	195	356	1087	1913	7924	17578	28427	58566	105200	363526	11147102
Operating Costs/Operating Income (%)													
Cost of Operations **10**	56.5	0.4	26.6	23.5	16.8	30.9	43.5	45.2	36.7	43.1	41.1	49.6	57.8
Salaries and Wages **11**	2.1	•	•	•	•	•	0.4	0.7	1.8	0.6	1.9	0.5	2.2
Taxes Paid **12**	0.7	0.0	0.7	0.5	0.7	1.1	2.0	1.7	1.7	1.6	1.5	0.8	0.7
Interest Paid **13**	3.8	0.0	0.2	0.3	0.1	0.2	0.2	0.3	0.2	4.1	0.9	0.5	3.9
Depreciation **14**	0.7	0.0	0.0	0.0	0.0	0.3	0.2	0.8	0.7	0.3	0.4	0.3	0.7
Amortization and Depletion **15**	0.9	0.0	0.3	0.6	1.7	0.9	2.2	2.5	2.3	2.7	2.3	1.4	0.9
Pensions and Other Deferred Comp. **16**	0.3	0.0	0.0	•	0.2	0.1	0.7	0.6	1.8	0.8	0.8	0.5	0.3
Employee Benefits **17**	0.2	•	•	•	0.1	0.1	0.2	0.3	0.4	0.2	0.2	0.1	0.2
Advertising **18**	0.2	0.0	•	•	0.1	0.2	0.2	0.4	0.7	0.1	0.5	0.5	0.2
Other Expenses **19**	38.4	99.0	63.5	41.6	112.2	45.1	45.0	45.3	47.6	48.6	43.6	51.0	36.9
Officers' Compensation **20**	0.1	•	0.0	•	0.3	•	•	0.1	0.2	0.1	0.2	0.2	0.1
Operating Margin **21**	•	0.6	8.8	33.5	•	21.0	5.5	2.2	5.9	•	6.6	•	•
Operating Margin Before Officers' Comp. **22**	•	0.6	8.8	33.5	•	21.0	5.5	2.3	6.0	•	6.8	•	•

Selected Average Balance Sheet ($ in Thousands)

Item	1	2	3	4	5	6	7	8	9	10	11	12	13	14
Net Receivables 23	112767	0	0	7	32	40	417	1263	1469	1049	7022	4121	8839	1144852
Inventories 24	•	•	•	•	•	•	•	•	•	•	•	•	•	•
Net Property, Plant and Equipment 25	60547	0	0	1	69	221	237	945	477	1830	3616	•	•	617737
Total Assets 26	5894179	0	207	760	2353	6413	16751	37375	71548	162430	358577	1205332	•	59423215
Notes and Loans Payable 27	38168	0	0	0	0	0	0	77	120	1164	6959	2544	•	3909973
All Other Liabilities 28	4776149	0	241	406	1254	3224	10085	23869	51450	138871	277156	1028624	•	48130279
Net Worth 29	736862	0	-34	354	1099	3189	6666	13429	19978	22395	74462	174165	•	7382963

Selected Financial Ratios (Times to 1)

Item	1	2	3	4	5	6	7	8	9	10	11	12	13	14
Current Ratio 30	0.4	•	4.4	15.9	9.6	4.1	2.2	1.3	1.9	1.0	1.1	1.3	•	0.4
Quick Ratio 31	0.2	•	3.1	13.4	7.1	3.1	1.6	0.9	1.4	0.8	0.8	1.0	•	0.2
Net Sales to Working Capital 32	•	•	1.6	0.6	0.8	0.8	1.7	4.2	2.1	40.0	6.8	4.1	•	0.4
Coverage Ratio 33	•	208.3	39.0	118.8	•	88.4	26.5	7.2	26.3	0.4	8.3	•	•	0.2
Total Asset Turnover 34	0.2	•	0.9	0.5	0.5	0.3	0.5	0.5	0.4	0.4	0.3	0.3	•	0.2
Inventory Turnover 35	•	•	•	•	•	•	•	•	•	•	•	•	•	•
Receivables Turnover 36	•	•	•	•	•	•	•	•	•	•	•	•	•	•
Total Liabilities to Net Worth 37	7.0	•	•	1.1	1.1	1.0	1.5	1.8	2.6	6.3	3.8	5.9	•	7.0
Current Assets to Working Capital 38	•	•	1.3	1.1	1.1	1.3	1.8	3.9	2.1	39.4	8.9	4.1	•	•
Current Liabilities to Working Capital 39	•	•	0.3	0.1	0.1	0.3	0.8	2.9	1.1	38.4	7.9	3.1	•	•
Working Capital to Net Sales 40	•	•	0.6	1.6	1.3	1.3	0.6	0.2	0.5	0.0	0.1	0.2	•	•
Inventory to Working Capital 41	•	•	•	•	•	•	•	•	•	0.0	0.0	0.0	•	•
Total Receipts to Cash Flow 42	3.0	1.0	1.4	1.3	1.3	1.6	2.1	2.2	2.0	2.2	2.0	2.2	•	3.1
Cost of Goods to Cash Flow 43	1.7	0.0	0.4	0.3	0.2	0.5	0.9	1.0	0.7	0.9	0.8	1.1	•	1.8
Cash Flow to Total Debt 44	0.1	•	0.6	0.7	0.7	0.4	0.4	0.3	0.3	0.2	0.2	0.2	•	0.1

Selected Financial Factors (in Percentages)

Item	1	2	3	4	5	6	7	8	9	10	11	12	13	14
Debt Ratio 45	87.5	•	116.6	53.4	53.3	50.3	60.2	64.1	72.1	86.2	79.2	85.6	•	87.6
Return on Total Assets 46	•	8.4	•	15.6	•	6.3	2.7	1.1	2.4	0.6	2.1	•	•	•
Return on Equity Before Income Taxes 47	•	•	•	33.3	•	12.5	6.5	2.6	8.2	•	9.1	•	•	•
Return on Equity After Income Taxes 48	•	•	•	29.7	•	10.3	4.7	0.1	5.0	•	4.6	•	•	•
Profit Margin (Before Income Tax) 49	0.6	8.7	•	33.1	•	20.9	5.5	2.0	5.8	•	6.4	•	•	•
Profit Margin (After Income Tax) 50	0.3	7.5	•	29.6	•	17.2	3.9	0.1	3.5	•	3.3	•	•	•

Table II

Corporations with Net Income

LIFE INSURANCE

MONEY AMOUNTS AND SIZE OF ASSETS IN THOUSANDS OF DOLLARS

Item Description for Accounting Period 7/08 Through 6/09	Total	Zero Assets	Under 500	500 to 1,000	1,000 to 5,000	5,000 to 10,000	10,000 to 25,000	25,000 to 50,000	50,000 to 100,000	100,000 to 250,000	250,000 to 500,000	500,000 to 2,500,000	2,500,000 and over
Number of Enterprises **1**	661	24	148	71	101	43	58	43	27	25	28	46	47
Revenues ($ in Thousands)													
Net Sales **2**	404894210	18495319	23534	26896	62607	87972	381076	696757	761891	1601168	3213077	17718638	361825275
Interest **3**	62338193	421	1149	1792	7513	9145	34074	67259	78444	159471	423483	2593758	58961684
Rents **4**	755393	0	0	0	80	195	1948	894	2903	7691	5634	24275	711775
Royalties **5**	8893	0	0	0	0	0	0	0	0	0	606	223	8064
Other Portfolio Income **6**	6146417	3601	79	338	979	3299	9884	10604	26799	5048	58752	118032	5909003
Other Receipts **7**	335645314	18491297	22306	24766	54035	75333	335170	618000	653745	1428958	2724602	14982350	296234749
Total Receipts **8**	404894210	18495319	23534	26896	62607	87972	381076	696757	761891	1601168	3213077	17718638	361825275
Average Total Receipts **9**	612548	770638	159	379	620	2046	6570	16204	28218	64047	114753	385188	7698410
Operating Costs/Operating Income (%)													
Cost of Operations **10**	49.9	0.1	22.4	23.9	24.7	26.9	33.0	48.4	32.0	51.1	45.2	55.9	52.3
Salaries and Wages **11**	2.3	•	•	•	•	•	0.5	0.5	2.4	0.5	2.3	0.6	2.5
Taxes Paid **12**	0.8	0.0	0.9	0.5	0.8	0.7	2.0	1.2	1.5	1.9	1.7	0.9	0.8
Interest Paid **13**	1.5	•	0.2	•	0.2	0.0	0.3	0.1	0.2	0.6	0.9	0.4	1.7
Depreciation **14**	0.4	0.0	•	0.0	0.0	0.2	0.3	0.5	0.6	0.4	0.4	0.3	0.5
Amortization and Depletion **15**	1.0	0.0	0.3	0.6	1.2	0.9	1.6	1.7	1.8	2.9	2.4	1.4	1.0
Pensions and Other Deferred Comp. **16**	0.4	0.0	•	0.1	0.1	0.1	0.6	0.8	2.0	0.9	0.9	0.5	0.4
Employee Benefits **17**	0.3	•	•	0.1	0.1	0.1	0.3	0.3	0.6	0.2	0.2	0.2	0.3
Advertising **18**	0.2	0.0	•	0.0	0.0	0.2	0.1	0.4	0.9	0.1	0.4	0.5	0.2
Other Expenses **19**	39.0	99.0	37.0	40.1	36.3	44.1	46.9	33.5	46.4	33.9	31.5	34.2	36.3
Officers' Compensation **20**	0.0	•	•	•	•	•	•	0.1	0.1	0.1	0.2	0.3	0.0
Operating Margin **21**	4.0	0.9	39.2	34.9	36.6	26.9	14.4	12.5	11.5	7.3	14.1	4.8	4.0
Operating Margin Before Officers' Comp. **22**	4.1	0.9	39.2	34.9	36.6	26.9	14.4	12.6	11.6	7.4	14.2	5.1	4.0

Selected Average Balance Sheet ($ in Thousands)

Net Receivables 23	27588	0	10	36	23	511	1501	1788	1155	10827	3189	10763	365042
Inventories 24	•	•	•	•	•	•	•	•	•	•	•	•	•
Net Property, Plant and Equipment 25	3150	0	•	0	0	49	252	254	750	570	1495	4070	38101
Total Assets 26	2680371	0	239	765	2362	6392	16734	38359	70941	162044	362776	1236201	36074738
Notes and Loans Payable 27	31063	0	0	0	0	0	0	95	160	1078	9207	3212	427482
All Other Liabilities 28	2317272	0	189	418	1105	2772	9196	24003	50377	134066	276152	1008241	31298710
Net Worth 29	332037	0	50	347	1258	3620	7537	14262	20403	26900	77417	224748	4348545

Selected Financial Ratios (Times to 1)

Current Ratio 30	0.4	•	4.7	16.7	9.6	6.0	3.1	1.4	2.3	1.3	1.3	1.9	0.3
Quick Ratio 31	0.2	•	3.4	14.3	7.3	4.4	2.2	1.0	1.7	1.1	0.9	1.4	0.2
Net Sales to Working Capital 32	•	•	1.0	0.6	0.4	0.8	1.1	3.1	1.8	3.9	3.6	2.3	•
Coverage Ratio 33	3.6	•	171.3	•	195.9	2942.0	53.5	119.6	47.0	12.4	16.5	13.0	3.3
Total Asset Turnover 34	0.2	•	0.7	0.5	0.3	0.3	0.4	0.4	0.4	0.4	0.3	0.3	0.2
Inventory Turnover 35	•	•	•	•	•	•	•	•	•	•	•	•	•
Receivables Turnover 36	•	•	•	•	•	•	•	•	•	•	•	•	•
Total Liabilities to Net Worth 37	7.1	•	3.8	1.2	0.9	0.8	1.2	1.7	2.5	5.0	3.7	4.5	7.3
Current Assets to Working Capital 38	•	•	1.3	1.1	1.1	1.2	1.5	3.4	1.8	4.2	4.5	2.2	•
Current Liabilities to Working Capital 39	•	•	0.3	0.1	0.1	0.2	0.5	2.4	0.8	3.2	3.5	1.2	•
Working Capital to Net Sales 40	•	•	1.0	1.6	2.3	1.3	0.9	0.3	0.6	0.3	0.3	0.4	•
Inventory to Working Capital 41	•	•	•	•	•	•	•	•	•	•	0.0	0.0	•
Total Receipts to Cash Flow 42	2.4	1.0	1.3	1.3	1.4	1.5	1.7	2.2	1.9	2.5	2.3	2.6	2.6
Cost of Goods to Cash Flow 43	1.2	0.0	0.3	0.3	0.3	0.4	0.6	1.1	0.6	1.3	1.0	1.5	1.3
Cash Flow to Total Debt 44	0.1	•	0.6	0.7	0.4	0.5	0.4	0.3	0.3	0.2	0.2	0.1	0.1

Selected Financial Factors (in Percentages)

Debt Ratio 45	87.6	•	79.2	54.6	46.8	43.4	55.0	62.8	71.2	83.4	78.7	81.8	87.9
Return on Total Assets 46	1.3	•	26.2	17.1	9.6	8.6	5.7	5.2	4.6	3.1	4.7	1.6	1.2
Return on Equity Before Income Taxes 47	7.3	•	125.1	37.6	18.0	15.1	12.5	13.8	15.8	17.2	20.7	8.0	6.9
Return on Equity After Income Taxes 48	5.0		118.4	33.6	15.7	12.7	10.6	10.4	11.6	11.7	14.7	5.4	4.8
Profit Margin (Before Income Tax) 49	4.0	0.9	39.1	34.5	36.4	26.7	14.4	12.2	11.4	7.2	13.9	4.7	3.9
Profit Margin (After Income Tax) 50	2.7	0.6	37.0	30.8	31.8	22.5	12.2	9.2	8.4	4.9	9.9	3.1	2.7

Table I

Corporations with and without Net Income

LIFE INSURANCE, STOCK COMPANIES (FORM 1120L)

MONEY AMOUNTS AND SIZE OF ASSETS IN THOUSANDS OF DOLLARS

Item Description for Accounting Period 7/08 Through 6/09	Total	Zero Assets	Under 500	500 to 1,000	1,000 to 5,000	5,000 to 10,000	10,000 to 25,000	25,000 to 50,000	50,000 to 100,000	100,000 to 250,000	250,000 to 500,000	500,000 to 2,500,000	2,500,000 and over
Number of Enterprises **1**	890	46	211	75	142	53	65	55	36	36	34	53	84
Revenues ($ in Thousands)													
Net Sales **2**	970403248	19079120	42197	27658	159673	101381	519581	965826	1023387	2132278	3578979	19924460	922848706
Interest **3**	160719023	37069	1297	1861	12599	12199	36790	72884	94971	209325	447936	2878285	156913807
Rents **4**	8071046	0	0	0	0	265	2396	2910	5933	8027	9229	19690	8022596
Royalties **5**	32325	0	0	0	0	0	0	0	0	0	606	218	31500
Other Portfolio Income **6**	19467257	4956	88	338	1080	3695	9508	13766	29657	8031	88745	155906	19151483
Other Receipts **7**	782113597	19037095	40812	25459	145994	85222	470887	876266	892826	1906895	3032463	16870361	738729320
Total Receipts **8**	970403248	19079120	42197	27658	159673	101381	519581	965826	1023387	2132278	3578979	19924460	922848706
Average Total Receipts **9**	1090341	414763	200	369	1124	1913	7994	17560	28427	59230	105264	375933	10986294
Operating Costs/Operating Income (%)													
Cost of Operations **10**	57.1	0.4	26.6	23.4	16.5	30.9	45.6	43.1	36.7	42.6	41.6	49.9	58.6
Salaries and Wages **11**	2.3	•	•	•	•	•	0.4	0.8	1.8	0.6	2.1	0.6	2.4
Taxes Paid **12**	0.7	0.0	0.7	0.5	0.7	1.1	2.0	1.7	1.7	1.6	1.4	0.7	0.7
Interest Paid **13**	4.2	0.0	0.2	•	0.1	0.2	0.2	0.3	0.2	4.4	1.0	0.4	4.4
Depreciation **14**	0.8	0.0	0.0	0.0	0.0	0.3	0.2	0.6	0.7	0.3	0.4	0.3	0.8
Amortization and Depletion **15**	0.9	0.0	0.3	0.6	1.7	0.9	1.6	2.6	2.3	2.7	2.2	1.2	0.9
Pensions and Other Deferred Comp. **16**	0.4	0.0	0.0	•	0.2	0.1	0.7	0.4	1.8	0.8	0.8	0.4	0.4
Employee Benefits **17**	0.2	•	•	•	0.1	0.1	0.2	0.3	0.4	0.2	0.2	0.2	0.3
Advertising **18**	0.3	0.0	•	•	0.1	0.2	0.2	0.4	0.7	0.1	0.6	0.5	0.3
Other Expenses **19**	37.6	99.0	63.3	41.5	113.2	45.1	41.0	47.1	47.6	48.7	42.4	52.6	35.9
Officers' Compensation **20**	0.1	•	•	•	•	•	•	0.1	0.2	0.1	0.2	0.2	0.1
Operating Margin **21**	•	0.6	8.9	33.8	•	21.0	7.9	2.7	5.9	7.2	7.2	•	•
Operating Margin Before Officers' Comp. **22**	•	0.6	8.9	33.8	•	21.0	7.9	2.7	6.0	7.4	7.4	•	•

Selected Average Balance Sheet ($ in Thousands)

Net Receivables 23	118705	0	8	34	42	417	1341	1627	1049	7585	4178	10313	1243328
Inventories 24	•	•	•	•	•	•	•	•	•	•	•	•	•
Net Property, Plant and Equipment 25	63578	0	0	0	1	69	88	255	945	436	1895	2875	670172
Total Assets 26	5611598	0	206	756	2343	6413	17028	36473	71548	158812	364960	1172596	58423657
Notes and Loans Payable 27	404544	0	0	0	0	0	0	86	120	1262	7983	2985	4280475
All Other Liabilities 28	4468027	0	241	415	1226	3224	10076	22287	51450	134979	278122	986566	46497393
Net Worth 29	739027	0	-35	341	1116	3189	6952	14100	19978	22572	78855	183044	7645790

Selected Financial Ratios (Times to 1)

Current Ratio 30	0.4	•	4.2	15.9	12.5	4.1	2.2	1.4	1.9	1.0	1.0	1.1	0.4
Quick Ratio 31	0.3	•	2.9	13.5	9.3	3.1	1.5	1.0	1.4	0.8	0.7	0.8	0.3
Net Sales to Working Capital 32	•	•	1.7	0.6	0.7	0.8	1.7	3.5	2.1	120.3	112.4	10.0	•
Coverage Ratio 33	•	208.4	39.4	•	•	88.4	36.1	8.6	26.3	0.5	8.1	•	•
Total Asset Turnover 34	0.2	•	1.0	0.5	0.5	0.3	0.5	0.5	0.4	0.4	0.3	0.3	0.2
Inventory Turnover 35	•	•	•	•	•	•	•	•	•	•	•	•	•
Receivables Turnover 36	•	•	•	•	•	•	•	•	•	•	•	•	•
Total Liabilities to Net Worth 37	6.6	•	•	1.2	1.1	1.0	1.4	1.6	2.6	6.0	3.6	5.4	6.6
Current Assets to Working Capital 38	•	•	1.3	1.1	1.1	1.3	1.8	3.3	2.1	115.2	148.4	9.4	•
Current Liabilities to Working Capital 39	•	•	0.3	0.1	0.1	0.3	0.8	2.3	1.1	114.2	147.4	8.4	•
Working Capital to Net Sales 40	•	•	0.6	1.6	1.4	1.3	0.6	0.3	0.5	0.0	0.0	0.1	•
Inventory to Working Capital 41	•	•	•	•	•	•	•	•	•	•	•	•	•
Total Receipts to Cash Flow 42	3.1	1.0	1.4	1.3	1.2	1.6	2.1	2.1	2.0	2.2	2.1	2.2	3.1
Cost of Goods to Cash Flow 43	1.8	0.0	0.4	0.3	0.2	0.5	1.0	0.9	0.7	0.9	0.9	1.1	1.8
Cash Flow to Total Debt 44	0.1	•	0.6	0.7	0.7	0.4	0.4	0.4	0.3	0.2	0.2	0.2	0.1

Selected Financial Factors (in Percentages)

Debt Ratio 45	86.8	•	117.1	54.9	52.4	50.3	59.2	61.3	72.1	85.8	78.4	84.4	86.9
Return on Total Assets 46	•	•	8.8	16.3	•	6.3	3.8	1.3	2.4	0.8	2.3	•	•
Return on Equity Before Income Taxes 47	•	•	•	36.2	•	12.5	9.1	3.0	8.2	•	9.3	•	•
Return on Equity After Income Taxes 48	•	•	•	32.4	•	10.3	7.3	0.4	5.0	•	4.5	•	•
Profit Margin (Before Income Tax) 49	•	0.6	8.8	33.4	•	20.9	7.9	2.4	5.8	•	7.0	•	•
Profit Margin (After Income Tax) 50	•	0.3	7.7	29.9	•	17.2	6.4	0.3	3.5	•	3.4	•	•

Table II

Corporations with Net Income

LIFE INSURANCE, STOCK COMPANIES (FORM 1120L)

MONEY AMOUNTS AND SIZE OF ASSETS IN THOUSANDS OF DOLLARS

Item Description for Accounting Period 7/08 Through 6/09	Total	Zero Assets	Under 500	500 to 1,000	1,000 to 5,000	5,000 to 10,000	10,000 to 25,000	25,000 to 50,000	50,000 to 100,000	100,000 to 250,000	250,000 to 500,000	500,000 to 2,500,000	2,500,000 and over
Number of Enterprises **1**	632	24	146	71	98	43	•	•	•	•	•	•	43
Revenues ($ in Thousands)													
Net Sales **2**	335572150	18495319	23461	26896	61684	87972	•	•	•	•	•	•	295732480
Interest **3**	48557603	421	1102	1792	6865	9145	•	•	•	•	•	•	45901105
Rents **4**	703839	0	0	0	0	195	•	•	•	•	•	•	666339
Royalties **5**	6934	0	0	0	0	0	•	•	•	•	•	•	6109
Other Portfolio Income **6**	5706455	3601	79	338	965	3299	•	•	•	•	•	•	5491838
Other Receipts **7**	280597319	18491297	22280	24766	53854	75333	•	•	•	•	•	•	243667089
Total Receipts **8**	335572150	18495319	23461	26896	61684	87972	•	•	•	•	•	•	295732480
Average Total Receipts **9**	530969	770638	161	379	629	2046	•	•	•	•	•	•	6877500
Operating Costs/Operating Income (%)													
Cost of Operations **10**	50.4	0.1	22.4	23.9	24.9	26.9	•	•	•	•	•	•	53.3
Salaries and Wages **11**	2.7	•	•	•	•	•	•	•	•	•	•	•	3.0
Taxes Paid **12**	0.9	0.0	0.8	0.5	0.7	0.7	•	•	•	•	•	•	0.9
Interest Paid **13**	1.8	•	0.2	•	0.2	0.0	•	•	•	•	•	•	2.1
Depreciation **14**	0.5	0.0	•	0.0	0.0	0.2	•	•	•	•	•	•	0.5
Amortization and Depletion **15**	0.9	0.0	0.3	0.6	1.2	0.9	•	•	•	•	•	•	0.9
Pensions and Other Deferred Comp. **16**	0.5	0.0	•	0.0	0.0	0.1	•	•	•	•	•	•	0.5
Employee Benefits **17**	0.3	•	•	•	•	0.1	•	•	•	•	•	•	0.4
Advertising **18**	0.3	0.0	•	•	0.0	0.2	•	•	•	•	•	•	0.3
Other Expenses **19**	36.9	99.0	36.9	40.1	35.9	44.1	•	•	•	•	•	•	33.3
Officers' Compensation **20**	0.1	•	•	•	•	•	•	•	•	•	•	•	0.0
Operating Margin **21**	4.7	0.9	39.3	34.9	37.0	26.9	•	•	•	•	•	•	4.8
Operating Margin Before Officers' Comp. **22**	4.8	0.9	39.3	34.9	37.0	26.9	•	•	•	•	•	•	4.8

Selected Average Balance Sheet ($ in Thousands)

	1	2	3	4	5	6	7	8	9	10	11
Net Receivables 23	28366	0	10	36	23	511	•	•	•	•	392484
Inventories 24	•	0	•	•	•	•	•	•	•	•	•
Net Property, Plant and Equipment 25	2885	0	•	0	0	49	•	•	•	•	37367
Total Assets 26	2200025	0	234	765	2363	6392	•	•	•	•	30872047
Notes and Loans Payable 27	32476	0	0	0	0	0	•	•	•	•	467070
All Other Liabilities 28	1849232	0	183	418	1066	2772	•	•	•	•	26052868
Net Worth 29	318318	0	50	347	1296	3620	•	•	•	•	4352110

Selected Financial Ratios (Times to 1)

	1	2	3	4	5	6	7	8	9	10	11
Current Ratio 30	0.4	•	4.5	16.7	10.5	6.0	•	•	•	•	0.4
Quick Ratio 31	0.3	•	3.2	14.3	7.9	4.4	•	•	•	•	0.3
Net Sales to Working Capital 32	•	•	1.1	0.6	0.4	0.8	•	•	•	•	•
Coverage Ratio 33	3.5	•	170.9	•	198.1	2942.0	•	•	•	•	3.3
Total Asset Turnover 34	0.2	•	0.7	0.5	0.3	0.3	•	•	•	•	0.2
Inventory Turnover 35	•	•	•	•	•	•	•	•	•	•	•
Receivables Turnover 36	•	•	•	•	•	•	•	•	•	•	6.1
Total Liabilities to Net Worth 37	5.9	•	3.6	1.2	0.8	0.8	•	•	•	•	•
Current Assets to Working Capital 38	•	•	1.3	1.1	1.1	1.2	•	•	•	•	•
Current Liabilities to Working Capital 39	•	•	0.3	0.1	0.1	0.2	•	•	•	•	•
Working Capital to Net Sales 40	•	•	0.9	1.6	2.4	1.3	•	•	•	•	•
Inventory to Working Capital 41	•	•	•	•	•	•	•	•	•	•	•
Total Receipts to Cash Flow 42	2.5	1.0	1.3	1.3	1.4	1.5	•	•	•	•	2.7
Cost of Goods to Cash Flow 43	1.2	0.0	0.3	0.3	0.3	0.4	•	•	•	•	1.5
Cash Flow to Total Debt 44	0.1	•	0.7	0.7	0.4	0.5	•	•	•	•	0.1

Selected Financial Factors (in Percentages)

	1	2	3	4	5	6	7	8	9	10	11
Debt Ratio 45	85.5	•	78.5	54.6	45.1	43.4	•	•	•	•	85.9
Return on Total Assets 46	1.6	•	27.0	17.1	9.8	8.6	•	•	•	•	1.5
Return on Equity Before Income Taxes 47	7.7	•	124.9	37.6	17.8	15.1	•	•	•	•	7.4
Return on Equity After Income Taxes 48	5.3	•	118.2	33.6	15.6	12.7	•	•	•	•	5.1
Profit Margin (Before Income Tax) 49	4.6	0.9	39.1	34.5	36.8	26.7	•	•	•	•	4.7
Profit Margin (After Income Tax) 50	3.2	0.6	37.0	30.8	32.0	22.5	•	•	•	•	3.2

Table I

Corporations with and without Net Income

LIFE INSURANCE, MUTUAL COMPANIES (FORM 1120L)

MONEY AMOUNTS AND SIZE OF ASSETS IN THOUSANDS OF DOLLARS

Item Description for Accounting Period 7/08 Through 6/09	Total	Zero Assets	Under 500	500 to 1,000	1,000 to 5,000	5,000 to 10,000	10,000 to 25,000	25,000 to 50,000	50,000 to 100,000	100,000 to 250,000	250,000 to 500,000	500,000 to 2,500,000	2,500,000 and over
Number of Enterprises **1**	55	3	6	3	8	0	4	5	0	3	5	10	8
Revenues ($ in Thousands)													
Net Sales **2**	106475229	70	83	83	3446	0	27180	106456	0	151789	523811	2977669	102684641
Interest **3**	20789950	6	56	69	1063	0	1980	14216	0	28895	72782	750264	19920618
Rents **4**	307532	0	0	0	80	0	0	571	0	1417	2543	5662	297259
Royalties **5**	15648	0	0	0	0	0	0	0	0	1557	0	9	14082
Other Portfolio Income **6**	704112	0	0	0	91	0	760	541	0	2355	4926	20198	675243
Other Receipts **7**	84657987	64	27	14	2212	0	24440	91128	0	117565	443560	2201536	81777439
Total Receipts **8**	106475229	70	83	83	3446	0	27180	106456	0	151789	523811	2977669	102684641
Average Total Receipts **9**	193913	23	14	28	431	•	6795	21291	•	50596	104762	297767	12835580
Operating Costs/Operating Income (%)													
Cost of Operations **10**	51.2	127.1	19.3	33.7	30.0	•	3.4	64.6	•	49.2	37.8	47.8	51.3
Salaries and Wages **11**	0.7	•	•	•	•	•	•	•	•	•	0.0	0.1	0.7
Taxes Paid **12**	0.4	12.9	3.6	•	3.3	•	3.3	1.9	•	1.5	2.4	1.6	0.4
Interest Paid **13**	0.0	•	•	94.0	0.1	•	•	0.3	•	0.1	0.2	0.7	0.0
Depreciation **14**	0.2	•	•	•	0.1	•	0.6	2.2	•	0.2	0.4	0.4	0.2
Amortization and Depletion **15**	1.5	•	•	•	1.7	•	13.2	2.0	•	2.6	3.3	2.7	1.5
Pensions and Other Deferred Comp. **16**	0.2	•	•	•	1.3	•	•	2.2	•	1.7	0.7	1.0	0.2
Employee Benefits **17**	0.1	•	•	•	1.9	•	•	0.2	•	0.3	0.3	0.0	0.1
Advertising **18**	0.1	•	•	•	•	•	•	0.1	•	0.3	0.1	0.3	0.1
Other Expenses **19**	45.5	10.0	125.3	45.8	66.2	•	120.9	28.4	•	47.1	51.9	40.2	45.6
Officers' Compensation **20**	0.0	•	4.8	•	16.0	•	•	•	•	•	•	0.5	•
Operating Margin **21**	0.0	•	•	•	•	•	•	•	•	•	2.9	4.7	•
Operating Margin Before Officers' Comp. **22**	0.1	•	•	•	•	•	•	•	•	•	2.9	5.1	•

Selected Average Balance Sheet ($ in Thousands)

Line Item											
Net Receivables 23	16667	0	0	0	30	•	•	268	3732	1025	110856
Inventories 24	•	•	•	•	•	•	•	•	•	•	•
Net Property, Plant and Equipment 25	11502	0	0	2389	89	•	•	967	1390	7545	67160
Total Assets 26	10466863	235	863	12246	54774	•	•	205841	315174	1378836	69918574
Notes and Loans Payable 27	2904	0	0	0	0	•	•	0	0	205	19708
All Other Liabilities 28	9762120	235	1741	10228	46043	•	•	185572	270582	1251530	65275581
Net Worth 29	701840	0	794	2018	8731	•	•	20269	44592	127101	4623284

Selected Financial Ratios (Times to 1)

Line Item											
Current Ratio 30	0.2	•	19.7	0.7	2.5	0.8	•	1.2	8.7	7.5	0.2
Quick Ratio 31	0.1	•	•	0.3	2.3	0.6	•	0.9	7.0	5.9	0.1
Net Sales to Working Capital 32	•	0.1	0.3	•	1.8	•	•	3.9	0.9	0.8	•
Coverage Ratio 33	0.3	•	0.2	•	•	•	•	16.0	7.3	•	•
Total Asset Turnover 34	0.2	0.1	0.0	0.2	0.6	0.4	•	0.2	0.3	0.2	0.2
Inventory Turnover 35	•	•	•	•	•	•	•	•	•	•	•
Receivables Turnover 36	•	•	•	•	•	•	•	•	•	•	•
Total Liabilities to Net Worth 37	13.9	•	0.3	2.2	5.1	5.3	•	9.2	6.1	9.8	14.1
Current Assets to Working Capital 38	•	1.0	1.1	•	1.7	•	•	5.3	1.1	1.2	•
Current Liabilities to Working Capital 39	•	0.1	0.1	•	0.7	•	•	4.3	0.1	0.2	•
Working Capital to Net Sales 40	16.0	3.4	•	•	0.6	•	•	0.3	1.1	1.2	•
Inventory to Working Capital 41	•	•	•	•	•	•	•	•	•	0.0	•
Total Receipts to Cash Flow 42	2.2	1.4	2.2	•	1.3	3.9	•	2.3	1.9	2.3	2.2
Cost of Goods to Cash Flow 43	1.1	0.3	0.7	•	0.0	2.5	•	1.1	0.7	1.1	1.1
Cash Flow to Total Debt 44	0.1	0.0	0.1	•	0.5	0.1	•	0.1	0.2	0.1	0.1

Selected Financial Factors (in Percentages)

Line Item											
Debt Ratio 45	93.3	100.0	20.9	68.7	83.5	84.1	•	90.2	85.9	90.8	93.4
Return on Total Assets 46	0.0	0.7	•	•	•	•	•	•	•	1.0	1.2
Return on Equity Before Income Taxes 47	•	•	•	•	•	•	•	•	6.5	•	10.9
Return on Equity After Income Taxes 48	•	•	•	•	•	•	•	•	5.9	•	7.0
Profit Margin (Before Income Tax) 49	•	•	•	•	•	•	•	•	2.8	•	4.7
Profit Margin (After Income Tax) 50	•	•	•	•	•	•	•	•	2.5	•	3.0

Table II

Corporations with Net Income

LIFE INSURANCE, MUTUAL COMPANIES (FORM 1120L)

MONEY AMOUNTS AND SIZE OF ASSETS IN THOUSANDS OF DOLLARS

Item Description for Accounting Period 7/08 Through 6/09	Total	Zero Assets	Under 500	500 to 1000	1,000 to 5,000	5,000 to 10,000	10,000 to 25,000	25,000 to 50,000	50,000 to 100,000	100,000 to 250,000	250,000 to 500,000	500,000 to 2,500,000	2,500,000 and over
Number of Enterprises **1**	29	0	3	0	3	0	•	•	•	•	•	•	4
Revenues ($ in Thousands)													
Net Sales **2**	69322060	0	73	0	923	0	•	•	•	•	•	•	66092795
Interest **3**	13780590	0	47	0	649	0	•	•	•	•	•	•	13060579
Rents **4**	51554	0	0	0	80	0	•	•	•	•	•	•	45436
Royalties **5**	1959	0	0	0	0	0	•	•	•	•	•	•	1954
Other Portfolio Income **6**	439963	0	0	0	15	0	•	•	•	•	•	•	417165
Other Receipts **7**	55047994	0	26	0	179	0	•	•	•	•	•	•	52567661
Total Receipts **8**	69322060	0	73	0	923	0	•	•	•	•	•	•	66092795
Average Total Receipts **9**	2390416	•	24	•	308	•	•	•	•	•	•	•	16523199
Operating Costs/Operating Income (%)													
Cost of Operations **10**	47.6	•	15.1	•	7.7	•	•	•	•	•	•	•	47.6
Salaries and Wages **11**	0.3	•	•	•	•	•	•	•	•	•	•	•	0.3
Taxes Paid **12**	0.2	•	4.1	•	4.3	•	•	•	•	•	•	•	0.1
Interest Paid **13**	0.1	•	•	•	0.2	•	•	•	•	•	•	•	0.0
Depreciation **14**	0.1	•	•	•	0.5	•	•	•	•	•	•	•	0.1
Amortization and Depletion **15**	1.5	•	•	•	1.5	•	•	•	•	•	•	•	1.5
Pensions and Other Deferred Comp. **16**	0.1	•	•	•	4.8	•	•	•	•	•	•	•	0.0
Employee Benefits **17**	0.0	•	•	•	7.3	•	•	•	•	•	•	•	0.0
Advertising **18**	0.0	•	•	•	•	•	•	•	•	•	•	•	0.0
Other Expenses **19**	49.3	•	56.2	•	58.8	•	•	•	•	•	•	•	49.7
Officers' Compensation **20**	0.0	•	•	•	•	•	•	•	•	•	•	•	•
Operating Margin **21**	0.8	•	24.7	•	14.8	•	•	•	•	•	•	•	0.6
Operating Margin Before Officers' Comp. **22**	0.9	•	24.7	•	14.8	•	•	•	•	•	•	•	0.6

Selected Average Balance Sheet ($ in Thousands)

Net Receivables 23	10615	0	0	70047
Inventories 24				
Net Property, Plant and Equipment 25	8924	0	0	45996
Total Assets 26	13148591	393	2362	92003664
Notes and Loans Payable 27	264	0	0	1917
All Other Liabilities 28	12517313	393	2361	87691518
Net Worth 29	631013	0	0	430229

Selected Financial Ratios (Times to 1)

Current Ratio 30	0.2			0.1
Quick Ratio 31	0.1			0.1
Net Sales to Working Capital 32		0.1		
Coverage Ratio 33	15.3		69.0	25.7
Total Asset Turnover 34	0.2		0.1	0.2
Inventory Turnover 35				
Receivables Turnover 36				
Total Liabilities to Net Worth 37	19.8			20.3
Current Assets to Working Capital 38		1.0		
Current Liabilities to Working Capital 39				
Working Capital to Net Sales 40		16.2		
Inventory to Working Capital 41				
Total Receipts to Cash Flow 42	2.0	1.2	1.4	2.0
Cost of Goods to Cash Flow 43	1.0	0.2	0.2	1.0
Cash Flow to Total Debt 44	0.1	0.1	0.1	0.1

Selected Financial Factors (in Percentages)

Debt Ratio 45	95.2	100.0	100.0	95.3
Return on Total Assets 46	0.2	1.5	1.9	0.1
Return on Equity Before Income Taxes 47	3.0			2.3
Return on Equity After Income Taxes 48	2.3			1.8
Profit Margin (Before Income Tax) 49	0.8	24.7	14.7	0.6
Profit Margin (After Income Tax) 50	0.6	23.3	13.9	0.5

Table I

Corporations with and without Net Income

MUTUAL PROPERTY AND CASUALTY COMPANIES (FORM 1120-PC)

MONEY AMOUNTS AND SIZE OF ASSETS IN THOUSANDS OF DOLLARS

Item Description for Accounting Period 7/08 Through 6/09		Total	Zero Assets	Under 500	500 to 1,000	1,000 to 5,000	5,000 to 10,000	10,000 to 25,000	25,000 to 50,000	50,000 to 100,000	100,000 to 250,000	250,000 to 500,000	500,000 to 2,500,000	2,500,000 and over
Number of Enterprises	1	1503	47	105	21	514	157	226	119	92	78	53	67	25
Revenues ($ in Thousands)														
Net Sales	2	256118431	20543	3957	244	500993	465553	1353377	1900045	2385739	6943333	8750586	45892225	187901837
Interest	3	13845614	1493	406	244	44487	28769	101660	108521	188489	340363	451937	2015064	10564182
Rents	4	514115	0	50	0	1170	643	1869	2406	3843	10677	15328	72686	405443
Royalties	5	1035	0	0	0	0	0	1	0	2	1	5	752	273
Other Portfolio Income	6	9450946	1931	309	0	7444	10808	26371	30899	56120	159382	278683	1145946	7733051
Other Receipts	7	232306721	17119	3192	0	447892	425333	1223476	1758219	2137285	6432910	8004633	42657777	169198888
Total Receipts	8	256118431	20543	3957	244	500993	465553	1353377	1900045	2385739	6943333	8750586	45892225	187901837
Average Total Receipts	9	170405	437	38	12	975	2965	5988	15967	25932	89017	165105	684959	7516073
Operating Costs/Operating Income (%)														
Cost of Operations	10	62.3	43.5	77.3	•	53.2	51.6	60.1	61.8	48.4	57.3	58.1	66.1	62.0
Salaries and Wages	11	12.4	7.1	•	459.0	15.0	10.2	10.3	10.6	16.6	17.3	14.1	13.0	11.9
Taxes Paid	12	2.1	5.2	0.3	0.4	3.3	2.7	4.2	3.7	3.2	2.4	2.3	2.0	2.1
Interest Paid	13	0.4	0.1	•	•	0.1	0.1	0.2	0.2	0.5	0.3	0.2	0.3	0.4
Depreciation	14	1.1	0.2	0.1	3.3	0.4	0.3	0.4	0.6	0.8	1.2	1.3	1.1	1.2
Amortization and Depletion	15	0.2	•	•	•	0.0	0.0	1.3	0.0	0.0	0.1	0.1	0.0	0.2
Pensions and Other Deferred Comp.	16	0.4	0.2	•	•	0.2	0.3	0.2	0.4	0.4	0.6	1.1	0.6	0.3
Employee Benefits	17	1.2	0.7	•	•	1.4	0.5	0.7	1.3	1.3	2.0	2.2	1.7	1.1
Advertising	18	0.6	0.6	•	•	0.4	0.2	0.2	0.4	0.6	0.4	0.2	0.4	0.7
Other Expenses	19	16.2	20.0	109.1	•	26.8	28.9	27.4	17.7	21.7	13.3	14.4	11.4	17.3
Officers' Compensation	20	0.2	2.9	•	•	2.1	1.3	0.8	1.1	1.2	0.7	0.7	0.3	0.1
Operating Margin	21	2.9	19.6	•	86.1	•	3.9	•	2.1	5.4	4.5	5.2	3.3	2.6
Operating Margin Before Officers' Comp.	22	3.1	22.5	•	86.1	•	5.2	•	3.2	6.5	5.1	5.9	3.6	2.8

Selected Average Balance Sheet ($ in Thousands)

Item	1	2	3	4	5	6	7	8	9	10	11	12	13
Net Receivables 23	31317	0	•	77	209	1330	2215	4650	14733	37095	122957	•	1386082
Inventories 24	•	•	•	•	•	•	•	•	•	•	•	•	•
Net Property, Plant and Equipment 25	5672	0	2	29	63	82	118	279	945	3865	5565	29389	230642
Total Assets 26	410940	0	189	880	2743	7163	16179	34946	71905	163315	337203	1217383	19358599
Notes and Loans Payable 27	8351	0	10	0	7	245	145	12	667	1288	1000	13408	454728
All Other Liabilities 28	255659	0	99	176	1034	3542	11171	24591	47406	93797	220292	727823	12223405
Net Worth 29	146931	0	80	704	1701	3376	4864	10344	23832	68518	115622	476152	6860467

Selected Financial Ratios (Times to 1)

Item	1	2	3	4	5	6	7	8	9	10	11	12	13
Current Ratio 30	0.8	•	1.5	4.9	1.9	1.6	1.0	0.9	0.9	1.0	0.9	0.8	0.8
Quick Ratio 31	0.7	•	1.5	3.9	1.8	1.3	0.9	0.8	0.7	0.9	0.9	0.8	0.7
Net Sales to Working Capital 32	0.8	•	0.8	0.0	1.2	1.6	13.4	•	•	•	23.7	•	•
Coverage Ratio 33	3.6	•	223.2	•	30.7	8.6	•	8.9	13.0	17.3	•	8.5	2.5
Total Asset Turnover 34	0.4	•	0.2	0.0	0.4	0.4	0.4	0.5	0.4	0.5	0.5	0.6	0.4
Inventory Turnover 35	•	•	•	•	•	•	•	•	•	•	•	•	•
Receivables Turnover 36	•	•	•	•	•	•	•	•	•	•	•	•	•
Total Liabilities to Net Worth 37	1.8	•	1.4	0.3	0.6	1.1	2.3	2.4	2.0	1.4	1.9	1.6	1.8
Current Assets to Working Capital 38	•	•	3.0	1.3	2.1	2.8	24.7	•	•	•	24.3	•	•
Current Liabilities to Working Capital 39	•	•	2.0	0.3	1.1	1.8	23.7	•	•	•	23.3	•	•
Working Capital to Net Sales 40	•	•	1.3	58.2	0.4	0.8	0.6	0.1	•	•	0.5	0.0	•
Inventory to Working Capital 41	•	•	•	•	•	•	•	•	•	•	•	•	•
Total Receipts to Cash Flow 42	5.7	3.2	•	5.0	4.4	3.1	4.8	5.3	3.9	5.9	5.5	7.4	5.5
Cost of Goods to Cash Flow 43	3.6	1.4	•	3.8	2.3	1.6	2.9	3.3	1.9	3.4	3.2	4.9	3.4
Cash Flow to Total Debt 44	0.1	•	0.1	0.2	0.2	0.3	0.1	0.1	0.1	0.2	0.1	0.1	0.1

Selected Financial Factors (in Percentages)

Item	1	2	3	4	5	6	7	8	9	10	11	12	13
Debt Ratio 45	64.2	•	57.8	20.0	38.0	52.9	69.9	70.4	66.9	58.0	65.7	60.9	64.9
Return on Total Assets 46	0.6	•	•	1.1	•	1.1	•	0.7	1.7	1.8	1.7	1.2	0.4
Return on Equity Before Income Taxes 47	1.2	•	•	1.4	•	2.3	•	1.9	4.6	4.0	4.5	2.8	0.7
Return on Equity After Income Taxes 48	•	•	•	1.2	•	1.0	•	•	2.2	1.9	2.1	1.1	•
Profit Margin (Before Income Tax) 49	1.0	18.4	•	86.1	•	2.6	•	1.3	4.3	3.1	3.2	1.9	0.6
Profit Margin (After Income Tax) 50	•	16.2	•	72.1	•	1.1	•	•	2.1	1.5	1.5	0.8	•

Table II
Corporations with Net Income

MUTUAL PROPERTY AND CASUALTY COMPANIES (FORM 1120-PC)

MONEY AMOUNTS AND SIZE OF ASSETS IN THOUSANDS OF DOLLARS

Item Description for Accounting Period 7/08 Through 6/09	Total	Zero Assets	Under 500	500 to 1,000	1,000 to 5,000	5,000 to 10,000	10,000 to 25,000	25,000 to 50,000	50,000 to 100,000	100,000 to 250,000	250,000 to 500,000	500,000 to 2,500,000	2,500,000 and over
Number of Enterprises **1**	981	36	63	21	330	95	142	•	64	56	36	45	•
Revenues ($ in Thousands)													
Net Sales **2**	139407263	20268	3613	244	232823	254426	876232	•	1661981	3768827	5033295	27616434	•
Interest **3**	7579538	1472	386	244	28120	16380	62527	•	128365	249343	313645	1473505	•
Rents **4**	254296	0	50	0	532	149	554	•	2499	8414	10929	38507	•
Royalties **5**	725	0	0	0	0	0	1	•	2	0	5	716	•
Other Portfolio Income **6**	4191419	1931	309	0	4547	7245	16979	•	41925	123039	209634	758355	•
Other Receipts **7**	127381285	16865	2868	0	199624	230652	796171	•	1489190	3388031	4499082	25345351	•
Total Receipts **8**	139407263	20268	3613	244	232823	254426	876232	•	1661981	3768827	5033295	27616434	•
Average Total Receipts **9**	142107	563	57	12	706	2678	6171	•	25968	67300	139814	613699	•
Operating Costs/Operating Income (%)													
Cost of Operations **10**	59.7	44.1	71.2	•	36.6	43.3	47.4	•	43.4	42.6	46.4	60.4	•
Salaries and Wages **11**	12.5	7.2	•	459.0	12.8	9.4	10.9	•	16.8	20.7	14.5	13.5	•
Taxes Paid **12**	2.4	5.3	0.3	0.4	2.4	3.3	2.0	•	3.5	2.8	2.7	2.4	•
Interest Paid **13**	0.5	0.1	•	•	0.1	0.0	0.1	•	0.4	0.2	0.3	0.3	•
Depreciation **14**	1.0	0.2	0.1	3.3	0.6	0.4	0.4	•	0.8	1.3	1.7	1.2	•
Amortization and Depletion **15**	0.2	•	•	•	0.1	0.0	0.0	•	0.1	0.1	0.1	0.1	•
Pensions and Other Deferred Comp. **16**	0.5	0.2	•	•	0.0	0.0	0.3	•	0.4	0.8	1.3	0.8	•
Employee Benefits **17**	1.5	0.7	•	•	2.2	0.5	0.8	•	1.2	2.8	2.2	1.9	•
Advertising **18**	0.5	0.6	•	•	0.6	0.3	0.3	•	0.4	0.6	0.3	0.4	•
Other Expenses **19**	14.2	18.7	17.0	•	23.9	27.8	24.7	•	19.9	16.0	17.0	11.5	•
Officers' Compensation **20**	0.3	3.0	•	•	2.3	2.0	0.9	•	1.3	0.9	0.7	0.4	•
Operating Margin **21**	6.5	20.0	11.4	86.1	18.5	12.8	12.3	•	11.8	11.3	12.9	7.2	•
Operating Margin Before Officers' Comp. **22**	6.8	23.0	11.4	86.1	20.8	14.8	13.1	•	13.1	12.1	13.6	7.6	•

Selected Average Balance Sheet ($ in Thousands)

Net Receivables 23	29592	•	5	0	46	265	1288	•	4438	14642	32282	123307
Inventories 24	•	•	•	•	•	•	•	•	•	•	•	•
Net Property, Plant and Equipment 25	4671	•	3	29	45	72	135	•	932	3205	4495	26023
Total Assets 26	330961	•	236	880	2641	7037	16385	•	71628	167986	336079	1248210
Notes and Loans Payable 27	6737	•	0	0	1	0	137	•	407	995	992	13507
All Other Liabilities 28	199762	•	73	176	714	3174	9890	•	46380	95607	224148	761390
Net Worth 29	124461	•	163	704	1926	3863	6358	•	24841	71384	110939	473313

Selected Financial Ratios (Times to 1)

Current Ratio 30	0.9	•	2.3	4.9	2.7	1.8	1.1	•	0.9	1.0	1.0	0.9
Quick Ratio 31	0.8	•	2.3	3.9	2.6	1.5	1.0	•	0.7	0.9	0.9	0.8
Net Sales to Working Capital 32	•	•	0.6	0.0	0.7	1.3	4.4	•	15.2	•	•	•
Coverage Ratio 33	10.1	225.8	•	274.0	•	4762.8	93.6	•	27.0	39.1	40.3	18.2
Total Asset Turnover 34	0.4	•	0.2	0.0	0.3	0.4	0.4	•	0.4	0.4	0.4	0.5
Inventory Turnover 35	•	•	•	•	•	•	•	•	•	•	•	•
Receivables Turnover 36	•	•	•	•	•	•	•	•	•	•	•	•
Total Liabilities to Net Worth 37	1.7	•	0.4	0.3	0.4	0.8	1.6	•	1.9	1.4	2.0	1.6
Current Assets to Working Capital 38	•	•	1.8	1.3	1.6	2.3	7.7	•	21.1	•	•	•
Current Liabilities to Working Capital 39	•	•	0.8	0.3	0.6	1.3	6.7	•	20.1	•	•	•
Working Capital to Net Sales 40	•	•	1.6	58.2	1.4	0.8	0.2	•	0.1	•	•	•
Inventory to Working Capital 41	•	•	•	•	•	•	•	•	•	•	•	•
Total Receipts to Cash Flow 42	5.2	3.3	3.9	•	2.4	2.5	2.8	•	3.3	3.8	3.5	5.8
Cost of Goods to Cash Flow 43	3.1	1.5	2.7	•	0.9	1.1	1.3	•	1.4	1.6	1.6	3.5
Cash Flow to Total Debt 44	0.1	0.2	0.2	•	0.4	0.3	0.2	•	0.2	0.2	0.2	0.1

Selected Financial Factors (in Percentages)

Debt Ratio 45	62.4	•	30.8	20.0	27.1	45.1	61.2	•	65.3	57.5	67.0	62.1
Return on Total Assets 46	2.4	•	2.8	1.1	4.7	4.3	4.2	•	4.0	3.9	4.4	3.1
Return on Equity Before Income Taxes 47	5.7	•	4.0	1.4	6.5	7.8	10.8	•	11.1	8.8	12.9	7.7
Return on Equity After Income Taxes 48	3.8	•	3.7	1.2	4.9	6.0	7.9	•	7.8	6.1	9.2	5.3
Profit Margin (Before Income Tax) 49	5.0	18.9	11.4	86.1	17.7	11.2	11.1	•	10.6	9.4	10.2	5.9
Profit Margin (After Income Tax) 50	3.3	16.6	10.6	72.1	13.3	8.6	8.1	•	7.5	6.4	7.3	4.1

Table I

Corporations with and without Net Income

STOCK PROPERTY AND CASUALTY COMPANIES (FORM 1120-PC)

MONEY AMOUNTS AND SIZE OF ASSETS IN THOUSANDS OF DOLLARS

Item Description for Accounting Period 7/08 Through 6/09	Total	Zero Assets	Under 500	500 to 1,000	1,000 to 5,000	5,000 to 10,000	10,000 to 25,000	25,000 to 50,000	50,000 to 100,000	100,000 to 250,000	250,000 to 500,000	500,000 to 2,500,000	2,500,000 and over
Number of Enterprises **1**	6167	228	2304	743	1488	404	340	165	135	111	61	110	78
Revenues ($ in Thousands)													
Net Sales **2**	670042465	1923144	61080	69953	664184	1044170	3145256	3984494	8040443	13309897	13250397	73487656	551061790
Interest **3**	41206660	189100	12102	14708	80095	70575	142719	121829	216931	460490	524832	2546113	36827165
Rents **4**	1110950	0	0	0	3585	2632	2026	985	2495	18912	8714	60184	1011418
Royalties **5**	310250	0	0	0	0	206	3	0	0	7924	5796	36462	259859
Other Portfolio Income **6**	17937722	24695	3628	4189	18409	15437	35323	49897	56093	113629	206603	1428000	15981818
Other Receipts **7**	609476883	1709349	45350	51056	562095	955320	2965185	3811783	7764924	12708942	12504452	69416897	496981530
Total Receipts **8**	670042465	1923144	61080	69953	664184	1044170	3145256	3984494	8040443	13309897	13250397	73487656	551061790
Average Total Receipts **9**	108650	8435	27	94	446	2585	9251	24148	59559	119909	217220	668070	7064895
Operating Costs/Operating Income (%)													
Cost of Operations **10**	64.0	54.6	65.5	62.2	67.3	79.0	55.7	61.2	69.9	63.6	59.4	65.1	64.0
Salaries and Wages **11**	12.3	10.0	12.4	4.8	11.6	8.5	12.8	11.0	9.8	13.5	12.5	12.7	12.3
Taxes Paid **12**	2.0	2.4	1.1	0.8	1.0	2.2	2.2	2.1	1.5	2.0	2.0	2.1	2.0
Interest Paid **13**	2.1	3.7	0.6	0.1	0.2	0.3	0.3	0.2	0.3	1.2	0.5	0.8	2.4
Depreciation **14**	0.9	1.5	•	•	0.5	0.2	0.4	0.4	0.5	0.8	0.8	1.0	0.9
Amortization and Depletion **15**	0.3	0.6	0.8	•	0.0	0.1	0.1	0.1	0.1	0.1	0.2	0.2	0.3
Pensions and Other Deferred Comp. **16**	0.4	0.0	•	•	0.0	0.2	0.1	0.1	0.1	0.1	0.3	0.6	0.4
Employee Benefits **17**	1.0	0.2	1.0	•	0.5	0.6	0.4	0.4	0.8	0.8	1.1	1.1	1.0
Advertising **18**	0.6	1.3	•	0.0	0.1	0.5	0.3	0.4	0.4	0.4	0.9	0.3	0.6
Other Expenses **19**	11.1	30.2	14.8	16.9	17.1	13.9	24.3	18.7	11.6	12.0	17.4	12.1	10.6
Officers' Compensation **20**	0.4	0.4	•	•	0.4	1.0	0.9	0.8	1.3	0.6	0.5	0.5	0.3
Operating Margin **21**	4.9	•	3.9	15.2	1.3	•	2.6	4.6	3.6	4.8	4.3	3.5	5.2
Operating Margin Before Officers' Comp. **22**	5.3	•	3.9	15.2	1.6	3.5	3.5	5.5	4.9	5.4	4.8	4.1	5.5

Selected Average Balance Sheet ($ in Thousands)

Net Receivables 23	19859	0	24	131	389	1222	2420	7481	13513	28659	111773	1342688
Inventories 24	•	•	•	•	•	•	•	•	•	•	•	•
Net Property, Plant and Equipment 25	4305	0	0	18	78	94	397	752	3168	6554	18084	301952
Total Assets 26	288712	214	743	2306	7094	15787	35295	72156	159442	335973	1140474	20366298
Notes and Loans Payable 27	23998	2	5	11	130	415	410	1792	8332	13266	82151	1752534
All Other Liabilities 28	172566	223	839	2272	5179	12495	24402	75182	108451	207985	685340	12039330
Net Worth 29	92148	-12	-100	23	1785	2876	10483	-4817	42659	114722	372983	6574434

Selected Financial Ratios (Times to 1)

Current Ratio 30	0.7	•	0.5	1.1	0.9	1.1	1.0	0.7	1.0	1.1	0.9	0.7
Quick Ratio 31	0.6	•	0.5	0.9	0.8	0.8	0.8	0.6	0.9	1.0	0.8	0.6
Net Sales to Working Capital 32	•	•	•	2.6	•	15.6	89.6	•	•	23.1	•	•
Coverage Ratio 33	2.8	7.2	211.8	4.6	•	7.6	17.8	13.3	4.5	8.0	4.4	2.6
Total Asset Turnover 34	0.4	0.1	0.1	0.2	0.4	0.6	0.7	0.8	0.8	0.6	0.6	0.3
Inventory Turnover 35	•	•	•	•	•	•	•	•	•	•	•	•
Receivables Turnover 36	•	•	•	•	•	•	•	•	•	•	•	•
Total Liabilities to Net Worth 37	2.1	•	•	•	3.0	4.5	2.4	•	2.7	1.9	2.1	2.1
Current Assets to Working Capital 38	•	•	•	8.0	•	18.5	82.3	•	•	19.9	•	•
Current Liabilities to Working Capital 39	•	•	•	7.0	•	17.5	81.3	•	•	18.9	•	•
Working Capital to Net Sales 40	•	•	•	0.4	•	0.1	0.0	•	•	0.0	•	•
Inventory to Working Capital 41	•	•	•	•	•	0.0	0.0	•	•	0.0	•	•
Total Receipts to Cash Flow 42	6.9	4.6	3.3	5.9	15.2	3.8	4.5	7.0	6.4	4.9	7.1	7.1
Cost of Goods to Cash Flow 43	4.4	2.5	2.0	4.0	12.0	2.1	2.7	4.9	4.1	2.9	4.6	4.5
Cash Flow to Total Debt 44	0.1	0.0	0.0	0.0	0.0	0.2	0.2	0.1	0.2	0.2	0.1	0.1

Selected Financial Factors (in Percentages)

Debt Ratio 45	68.1	105.4	113.5	99.0	74.8	81.8	70.3	106.7	73.2	65.9	67.3	67.7
Return on Total Assets 46	2.2	0.5	1.7	0.2	•	1.3	3.0	2.9	4.2	2.5	2.1	2.2
Return on Equity Before Income Taxes 47	4.4	•	•	13.9	•	6.2	9.5	•	12.1	6.4	5.0	4.3
Return on Equity After Income Taxes 48	2.3	•	•	•	•	•	5.1	•	6.9	3.1	2.1	2.2
Profit Margin (Before Income Tax) 49	3.8	3.8	13.3	0.7	•	1.9	4.1	3.2	4.3	3.4	2.8	4.0
Profit Margin (After Income Tax) 50	1.9	0.2	10.2	•	•	2.2	2.2	1.6	2.5	1.6	1.2	2.1

Table II
Corporations with Net Income

STOCK PROPERTY AND CASUALTY COMPANIES (FORM 1120-PC)

MONEY AMOUNTS AND SIZE OF ASSETS IN THOUSANDS OF DOLLARS

Item Description for Accounting Period 7/08 Through 6/09	Total	Zero Assets	Under 500	500 to 1,000	1,000 to 5,000	5,000 to 10,000	10,000 to 25,000	25,000 to 50,000	50,000 to 100,000	100,000 to 250,000	250,000 to 500,000	500,000 to 2,500,000	2,500,000 and over
Number of Enterprises 1	5217	203	2043	681	1305	283	226	116	93	88	46	77	58
Revenues ($ in Thousands)													
Net Sales 2	546470149	1709768	19165	26281	568984	733707	1804285	2860007	5940134	9275825	9693218	52584582	461254191
Interest 3	32705228	148902	11206	13231	71771	54484	84515	85804	150259	355530	386799	1877179	29465548
Rents 4	883818	0	0	0	154	577	214	342	2310	9176	8071	37091	825881
Royalties 5	309847	0	0	0	0	206	3	0	0	7924	5796	36059	259859
Other Portfolio Income 6	15333187	18282	3522	4127	17024	13224	18838	33188	47281	85456	177792	1075992	13838460
Other Receipts 7	497238069	1542584	4437	8923	480035	665216	1700715	2740673	5740284	8817739	9114760	49558261	416864443
Total Receipts 8	546470149	1709768	19165	26281	568984	733707	1804285	2860007	5940134	9275825	9693218	52584582	461254191
Average Total Receipts 9	104748	8423	9	39	436	2593	7984	24655	63872	105407	210722	682917	7952658
Operating Costs/Operating Income (%)													
Cost of Operations 10	63.7	42.6	1.7	9.2	53.4	54.2	45.7	55.6	67.4	58.7	58.4	60.9	64.4
Salaries and Wages 11	11.6	10.8	4.9	9.4	8.2	8.4	12.2	10.3	8.9	12.3	11.7	12.5	11.5
Taxes Paid 12	2.0	2.6	0.2	0.2	0.8	2.2	2.3	2.3	1.6	2.3	2.4	2.1	2.0
Interest Paid 13	2.0	3.5	0.2	0.2	0.2	0.3	0.2	0.2	0.2	1.5	0.5	0.7	2.2
Depreciation 14	0.8	1.7	•	•	0.4	0.1	0.3	0.4	0.5	0.7	1.0	0.9	0.8
Amortization and Depletion 15	0.2	0.7	0.1	•	0.0	0.1	0.0	0.0	0.1	0.1	0.2	0.2	0.2
Pensions and Other Deferred Comp. 16	0.4	•	•	•	0.0	0.1	0.0	0.0	0.1	0.2	0.3	0.6	0.4
Employee Benefits 17	0.9	0.2	•	•	0.5	0.3	0.1	0.3	0.8	0.8	1.1	1.1	0.9
Advertising 18	0.5	1.4	•	•	0.1	0.3	0.4	0.3	0.3	0.4	1.2	0.3	0.6
Other Expenses 19	9.5	28.7	11.8	13.5	14.2	12.1	22.1	19.5	10.6	12.4	14.2	12.0	8.9
Officers' Compensation 20	0.4	0.4	•	•	0.4	0.5	0.8	0.8	1.6	0.7	0.5	0.5	0.4
Operating Margin 21	8.0	7.4	81.1	67.6	21.8	21.5	15.6	10.2	7.9	9.9	8.7	8.2	7.8
Operating Margin Before Officers' Comp. 22	8.4	7.8	81.1	67.6	22.2	22.0	16.5	11.0	9.5	10.6	9.2	8.7	8.2

Selected Average Balance Sheet ($ in Thousands)

	Total												
Net Receivables 23	15607	0	2	15	127	346	1261	2673	7789	14275	28715	120255	1172190
Inventories 24	•	•	•	•	•	•	•	•	•	•	•	•	•
Net Property, Plant and Equipment 25	4527	0	0	0	12	18	73	393	788	2492	7724	15432	374070
Total Assets 26	259206	221	732	2296	7128	15697	36034	71907	159402	337413	1165670	•	20906766
Notes and Loans Payable 27	20767	0	5	10	73	199	428	1308	9657	12158	66217	•	1751386
All Other Liabilities 28	144658	176	487	1241	3707	10447	22734	74911	102466	196509	654820	•	11566863
Net Worth 29	93781	45	240	1045	3348	5051	12871	-4312	47279	128746	444633	•	7588517

Selected Financial Ratios (Times to 1)

Current Ratio 30	0.7	•	0.7	0.9	1.1	1.2	1.1	1.1	0.7	1.0	1.1	1.1	0.6
Quick Ratio 31	0.5	•	0.6	0.8	0.9	1.0	0.9	0.9	0.6	0.8	1.0	0.9	0.5
Net Sales to Working Capital 32	•	•	•	•	2.5	3.6	6.7	11.4	•	•	10.7	19.3	•
Coverage Ratio 33	4.5	3.0	409.9	374.2	98.6	64.9	74.4	53.7	42.4	7.2	17.6	12.0	4.1
Total Asset Turnover 34	0.4	•	0.0	0.1	0.2	0.4	0.5	0.7	0.9	0.7	0.6	0.6	0.4
Inventory Turnover 35	•	•	•	•	•	•	•	•	•	•	•	•	•
Receivables Turnover 36	•	•	•	•	•	•	•	•	•	•	•	•	•
Total Liabilities to Net Worth 37	1.8	3.9	•	2.1	1.2	2.1	1.1	1.8	2.4	1.6	1.6	•	1.8
Current Assets to Working Capital 38	•	•	•	•	7.8	6.0	9.0	10.5	•	•	9.7	17.3	•
Current Liabilities to Working Capital 39	•	•	•	•	6.8	5.0	8.0	9.5	•	•	8.7	16.3	•
Working Capital to Net Sales 40	•	•	•	•	0.4	0.3	0.2	0.1	•	•	0.1	0.1	•
Inventory to Working Capital 41	•	•	•	•	•	•	•	0.0	•	•	0.0	0.0	•
Total Receipts to Cash Flow 42	6.3	3.1	1.1	1.3	2.9	3.1	2.7	3.5	5.6	4.7	4.6	5.4	6.6
Cost of Goods to Cash Flow 43	4.0	1.3	0.0	0.1	1.5	1.7	1.2	1.9	3.8	2.8	2.7	3.3	4.3
Cash Flow to Total Debt 44	0.1	•	0.0	0.1	0.1	0.2	0.3	0.3	0.1	0.2	0.2	0.1	0.1

Selected Financial Factors (in Percentages)

Debt Ratio 45	63.8	79.6	67.2	54.5	53.0	67.8	64.3	106.0	70.3	61.8	61.9	•	63.7
Return on Total Assets 46	3.6	3.4	3.3	4.1	7.7	7.8	6.8	6.9	7.2	5.0	4.7	•	3.4
Return on Equity Before Income Taxes 47	7.7	16.9	10.1	8.8	16.1	23.8	18.8	•	20.9	12.3	11.4	•	7.0
Return on Equity After Income Taxes 48	5.2	14.5	8.7	6.9	12.3	17.2	13.7	•	15.0	8.4	7.9	•	4.7
Profit Margin (Before Income Tax) 49	6.9	81.1	62.5	21.2	20.8	15.1	9.8	7.5	9.4	7.5	7.4	•	6.7
Profit Margin (After Income Tax) 50	4.6	69.6	54.3	16.5	15.9	10.9	7.2	5.4	6.7	5.1	7.4	•	4.5

Table I

Corporations with and without Net Income

INSURANCE AGENCIES AND BROKERAGES

MONEY AMOUNTS AND SIZE OF ASSETS IN THOUSANDS OF DOLLARS

Item Description for Accounting Period 7/08 Through 6/09	Total	Zero Assets	Under 500	500 to 1,000	1,000 to 5,000	5,000 to 10,000	10,000 to 25,000	25,000 to 50,000	50,000 to 100,000	100,000 to 250,000	250,000 to 500,000	500,000 to 2,500,000	2,500,000 and over
Number of Enterprises **1**	91398	17942	63544	5303	3816	410	218	73	36	31	10	12	3
Revenues ($ in Thousands)													
Net Sales **2**	70317701	2710884	20933653	6236181	10542263	3154811	3450892	2303235	1924621	2436093	1636199	6589125	8399743
Interest **3**	687144	24167	16295	12802	23561	14334	19148	14149	17029	28539	34278	102344	380499
Rents **4**	52115	14	4552	4437	8063	9569	4565	5969	2127	542	1167	6197	4913
Royalties **5**	22056	0	0	7465	0	1	5	3997	53	0	0	0	10535
Other Portfolio Income **6**	853080	51691	97809	25956	29589	28032	11691	31839	9270	6494	21748	400989	137973
Other Receipts **7**	68703306	2635012	20814997	6185521	10481050	3102875	3415483	2247281	1896142	2400518	1579006	6079595	7865823
Total Receipts **8**	70317701	2710884	20933653	6236181	10542263	3154811	3450892	2303235	1924621	2436093	1636199	6589125	8399743
Average Total Receipts **9**	769	151	329	1176	2763	7695	15830	31551	53462	78584	163620	549094	2799914
Operating Costs/Operating Income (%)													
Cost of Operations **10**	2.5	16.3	•	•	4.4	1.2	4.4	4.4	12.0	9.2	5.8	•	•
Salaries and Wages **11**	31.9	19.3	26.7	27.9	36.0	38.3	33.3	32.2	36.2	32.9	18.7	31.4	45.6
Taxes Paid **12**	3.4	3.1	3.3	3.9	3.4	3.5	3.2	3.0	3.1	3.0	3.5	2.9	4.1
Interest Paid **13**	2.7	3.7	0.8	1.6	1.0	0.8	1.2	1.4	1.4	4.7	3.1	6.5	8.7
Depreciation **14**	1.3	1.4	0.9	0.9	1.1	1.3	1.5	1.8	1.7	1.5	1.5	1.8	2.2
Amortization and Depletion **15**	1.4	0.3	0.5	1.2	1.4	0.7	0.7	0.8	2.0	2.9	0.8	4.5	2.0
Pensions and Other Deferred Comp. **16**	1.3	0.8	1.0	1.6	1.1	0.9	1.5	1.3	1.5	0.5	0.8	0.8	3.4
Employee Benefits **17**	2.4	1.6	1.5	2.9	2.6	2.0	2.1	2.4	3.0	3.0	2.4	3.1	3.2
Advertising **18**	1.5	2.9	2.1	1.3	1.2	1.4	1.6	0.6	4.0	2.0	1.8	0.6	0.5
Other Expenses **19**	30.9	36.9	31.9	28.1	27.2	26.7	31.1	35.4	23.9	29.8	46.4	34.9	28.9
Officers' Compensation **20**	12.1	14.4	16.2	18.0	15.0	14.4	11.5	10.5	7.3	3.6	2.0	2.9	5.7
Operating Margin **21**	8.6	•	15.2	12.7	5.6	8.9	7.9	6.1	4.1	6.8	13.5	10.6	•
Operating Margin Before Officers' Comp. **22**	20.7	13.6	31.3	30.6	20.7	23.3	19.4	16.7	11.4	10.4	15.5	13.4	1.3

Selected Average Balance Sheet ($ in Thousands)

Line Item												
Net Receivables 23	254	0	•	64	319	1315	2982	9924	13027	21189	55467	168590
	5237087											
Inventories 24	•	•	•	•	•	•	•	•	•	•	•	•
Net Property, Plant and Equipment 25	45	0	•	97	127	848	952	2543	3039	4531	8853	31031
	280999											
Total Assets 26	1157	80	677	2057	7571	14273	32931	67414	155752	343770	1415101	17649688
Notes and Loans Payable 27	217	40	247	517	1078	3506	6688	16197	51179	70634	436795	1401760
All Other Liabilities 28	479	18	213	1053	3926	7284	18281	34316	67045	198508	453721	7399395
Net Worth 29	461	22	217	487	2568	3483	7961	16902	37529	74627	524585	8848534

Selected Financial Ratios (Times to 1)

Line Item													
Current Ratio 30	1.1	•	1.6	1.2	1.1	1.4	1.2	1.2	1.1	1.1	1.0	1.0	
Quick Ratio 31	0.9	•	1.4	1.1	1.0	1.2	1.1	1.0	0.7	0.9	0.7	0.9	
Net Sales to Working Capital 32	18.9	•	10.0	12.3	17.8	6.3	8.3	7.5	14.2	15.0	•	•	
Coverage Ratio 33	4.2	0.8	9.0	6.8	11.7	7.4	5.5	4.0	2.4	5.2	2.6	0.6	
Total Asset Turnover 34	0.7	•	1.7	1.3	1.0	1.1	1.0	0.8	0.5	0.5	0.4	0.2	
Inventory Turnover 35	•	•	•	•	•	•	•	•	•	•	•	•	
Receivables Turnover 36	•	•	•	•	•	•	•	•	•	•	•	•	
Total Liabilities to Net Worth 37	1.5	•	2.1	3.2	1.9	3.1	3.1	3.0	3.2	3.6	1.7	1.0	
Current Assets to Working Capital 38	11.8	•	2.7	5.2	10.0	3.7	5.7	5.7	13.9	16.3	•	•	
Current Liabilities to Working Capital 39	10.8	•	1.7	4.2	9.0	2.7	4.7	4.7	12.9	15.3	•	•	
Working Capital to Net Sales 40	0.1	•	0.1	0.1	0.1	0.2	0.1	0.1	0.1	0.1	•	•	
Inventory to Working Capital 41	0.0	•	•	•	0.0	0.0	0.0	•	0.0	0.0	•	•	
Total Receipts to Cash Flow 42	3.0	3.7	2.9	3.7	3.3	2.8	2.7	4.3	3.0	1.8	2.7	5.8	
Cost of Goods to Cash Flow 43	0.1	0.6	•	0.2	0.0	0.1	0.1	0.5	0.3	0.1	•	•	
Cash Flow to Total Debt 44	0.4	•	0.9	0.5	0.5	0.5	0.5	0.2	0.2	0.3	0.2	0.1	

Selected Financial Factors (in Percentages)

Line Item													
Debt Ratio 45	60.2	•	72.8	67.9	76.3	66.1	75.6	75.8	74.9	75.9	78.3	62.9	49.9
Return on Total Assets 46	7.6	•	65.6	24.8	8.9	9.7	7.3	4.3	5.7	7.6	6.6	0.9	
Return on Equity Before Income Taxes 47	14.5	•	228.9	68.6	32.0	26.2	35.8	24.8	13.0	14.0	28.2	10.9	
Return on Equity After Income Taxes 48	13.0	•	225.8	67.6	30.4	24.1	30.5	20.2	9.9	9.9	16.3	6.9	
Profit Margin (Before Income Tax) 49	8.7	•	15.1	12.7	5.6	8.8	7.9	6.2	4.1	6.7	12.9	10.4	
Profit Margin (After Income Tax) 50	7.8	•	14.9	12.5	5.4	8.1	6.7	5.1	3.1	4.7	7.4	6.6	

Table II

Corporations with Net Income

INSURANCE AGENCIES AND BROKERAGES

MONEY AMOUNTS AND SIZE OF ASSETS IN THOUSANDS OF DOLLARS

Item Description for Accounting Period 7/08 Through 6/09		Total	Zero Assets	Under 500	500 to 1,000	1,000 to 5,000	5,000 to 10,000	10,000 to 25,000	25,000 to 50,000	50,000 to 100,000	100,000 to 250,000	250,000 to 500,000	500,000 to 2,500,000	2,500,000 and over
Number of Enterprises	1	66647	10708	47965	4377	2998	332	154	•	26	17	•	9	0
Revenues ($ in Thousands)														
Net Sales	2	50034657	1419413	17607652	5126831	7891902	2685978	2739518	•	1246688	1568435	•	6602570	0
Interest	3	228055	18430	13012	9897	17352	10851	8815	•	8562	15509	•	107687	0
Rents	4	30968	0	2737	4276	1414	7888	1586	•	1300	102	•	5772	0
Royalties	5	7524	0	0	7465	0	0	5	•	53	0	•	0	0
Other Portfolio Income	6	655396	27156	86262	25623	26365	26942	8920	•	6978	1604	•	399156	0
Other Receipts	7	49112714	1373827	17505641	5079570	7846771	2640297	2720192	•	1229795	1551220	•	6089955	0
Total Receipts	8	50034657	1419413	17607652	5126831	7891902	2685978	2739518	•	1246688	1568435	•	6602570	0
Average Total Receipts	9	751	133	367	1171	2632	8090	17789	•	47950	92261	•	733619	•
Operating Costs/Operating Income (%)														
Cost of Operations	10	2.3	17.1	•	•	5.8	1.3	4.8	•	1.3	10.3	•	•	•
Salaries and Wages	11	29.3	9.2	25.3	26.8	32.7	40.0	35.2	•	40.9	35.3	•	32.8	•
Taxes Paid	12	3.2	2.6	3.0	3.7	3.0	3.6	3.2	•	3.5	3.1	•	3.3	•
Interest Paid	13	1.4	0.3	0.8	1.5	0.9	0.7	1.0	•	1.0	2.5	•	3.8	•
Depreciation	14	1.1	0.8	0.8	0.8	0.7	1.1	1.2	•	1.8	1.7	•	1.8	•
Amortization and Depletion	15	1.3	0.3	0.5	1.2	1.3	0.4	0.6	•	1.5	1.8	•	4.0	•
Pensions and Other Deferred Comp.	16	1.1	0.8	0.9	1.6	1.1	1.0	1.7	•	2.0	0.7	•	0.9	•
Employee Benefits	17	2.1	1.3	1.5	2.7	2.2	1.9	2.2	•	3.1	3.5	•	2.6	•
Advertising	18	1.3	1.3	2.0	1.3	0.8	0.6	1.2	•	0.8	2.0	•	0.4	•
Other Expenses	19	28.2	29.3	29.5	27.4	22.4	20.4	23.8	•	21.7	22.6	•	35.2	•
Officers' Compensation	20	12.7	13.1	15.6	16.4	16.1	15.6	12.4	•	9.8	3.4	•	2.5	•
Operating Margin	21	16.2	24.1	20.1	16.6	12.9	13.5	12.7	•	12.6	13.1	•	12.8	•
Operating Margin Before Officers' Comp.	22	29.0	37.2	35.7	33.0	29.0	29.1	25.2	•	22.4	16.6	•	15.3	•

Selected Average Balance Sheet ($ in Thousands)

Line	Item	1	2	3	4	5	6	7	8	9	10
23	Net Receivables	91	0	5	65	360	1332	3121	14912	22992	203005
24	Inventories	•	•	•	•	•	•	•	•	•	•
25	Net Property, Plant and Equipment	38	0	14	100	79	941	946	3308	5777	35809
26	Total Assets	618	0	85	680	1985	7680	14226	64010	159317	1663177
27	Notes and Loans Payable	147	0	34	210	389	980	3022	9142	36104	395950
28	All Other Liabilities	251	0	16	211	963	3938	7104	35733	78574	562274
29	Net Worth	220	0	36	259	633	2761	4099	19135	44639	704952

Selected Financial Ratios (Times to 1)

Line	Item	1	2	3	4	5	6	7	8	9	10
30	Current Ratio	1.2	•	2.0	1.7	1.3	1.2	1.5	1.2	1.1	1.0
31	Quick Ratio	1.0	•	1.8	1.4	1.1	1.1	1.3	1.0	0.7	0.7
32	Net Sales to Working Capital	13.9	•	18.3	8.5	10.0	11.4	6.0	6.0	12.3	1.0
33	Coverage Ratio	12.8	86.5	27.5	12.0	16.1	21.4	14.1	13.1	6.3	4.3
34	Total Asset Turnover	1.2	•	4.3	1.7	1.3	1.1	1.3	0.7	0.6	0.4
35	Inventory Turnover	•	•	•	•	•	•	•	•	•	•
36	Receivables Turnover	•	•	•	•	•	•	•	•	•	•
37	Total Liabilities to Net Worth	1.8	•	1.4	1.6	2.1	1.8	2.5	2.3	2.6	1.4
38	Current Assets to Working Capital	5.5	•	2.0	2.4	4.6	6.5	3.2	5.1	12.6	1.4
39	Current Liabilities to Working Capital	4.5	•	1.0	1.4	3.6	5.5	2.2	4.1	11.6	0.3
40	Working Capital to Net Sales	0.1	•	0.1	0.1	0.1	0.1	0.2	0.2	0.1	0.1
41	Inventory to Working Capital	0.0	•	•	•	0.0	0.0	0.0	0.0	0.1	0.0
42	Total Receipts to Cash Flow	2.6	2.1	2.3	2.6	3.3	3.5	3.0	3.5	3.1	2.6
43	Cost of Goods to Cash Flow	0.1	0.4	•	0.2	0.2	0.0	0.1	0.0	0.3	0.3
44	Cash Flow to Total Debt	0.7	•	3.2	1.1	0.6	0.5	0.6	0.3	0.3	0.3

Selected Financial Factors (in Percentages)

Line	Item	1	2	3	4	5	6	7	8	9	10
45	Debt Ratio	64.4	•	58.2	62.0	68.1	64.0	71.2	70.1	72.0	57.6
46	Return on Total Assets	21.4	89.7	31.2	18.3	14.8	17.1	10.2	9.0	7.3	
47	Return on Equity Before Income Taxes	55.2	207.1	75.2	53.8	39.2	55.2	31.4	27.1	13.2	
48	Return on Equity After Income Taxes	51.1	204.6	74.1	52.2	36.7	48.8	27.7	20.8	8.8	
49	Profit Margin (Before Income Tax)	16.2	24.0	20.1	16.6	12.9	13.4	12.7	12.5	13.1	12.7
50	Profit Margin (After Income Tax)	15.0	23.9	19.9	16.4	12.6	12.5	11.3	11.1	10.1	

Table I

Corporations with and without Net Income

OTHER INSURANCE RELATED ACTIVITIES

MONEY AMOUNTS AND SIZE OF ASSETS IN THOUSANDS OF DOLLARS

Item Description for Accounting Period 7/08 Through 6/09		Total	Zero Assets	Under 500	500 to 1,000	1,000 to 5,000	5,000 to 10,000	10,000 to 25,000	25,000 to 50,000	50,000 to 100,000	100,000 to 250,000	250,000 to 500,000	500,000 to 2,500,000	2,500,000 and over
Number of Enterprises	1	14878	3392	9735	593	752	139	123	43	34	35	12	16	4
Revenues ($ in Thousands)														
Net Sales	2	44793634	542923	2408833	221778	2960479	1942963	1449396	1155724	1813670	6434966	2131827	6239548	17491527
Interest	3	1397177	839	1955	2251	8528	6064	24321	13838	25408	64703	141312	139001	968958
Rents	4	103501	0	0	0	10127	841	1271	6131	1525	2489	13651	2629	64838
Royalties	5	15009	0	0	0	0	0	0	0	0	0	0	14942	68
Other Portfolio Income	6	1250482	11848	643	164	5489	3395	8994	8036	1876	19928	224285	62321	903503
Other Receipts	7	42027465	530236	2406235	219363	2936335	1932663	1414810	1127719	1784861	6347846	1752579	6020655	15554160
Total Receipts	8	44793634	542923	2408833	221778	2960479	1942963	1449396	1155724	1813670	6434966	2131827	6239548	17491527
Average Total Receipts	9	3011	160	247	374	3937	13978	11784	26877	53343	183856	177652	389972	4372882
Operating Costs/Operating Income (%)														
Cost of Operations	10	14.3	0.4	•	0.7	•	0.0	0.3	12.3	16.3	10.9	8.1	24.5	20.3
Salaries and Wages	11	20.2	55.1	22.5	25.3	16.9	32.8	39.4	33.4	23.8	22.2	17.4	31.0	10.7
Taxes Paid	12	2.3	1.9	2.5	2.5	2.0	3.0	4.0	1.6	4.6	2.3	2.6	3.2	1.4
Interest Paid	13	3.2	0.1	1.2	2.2	0.6	0.7	0.8	0.8	2.8	1.5	9.9	3.5	4.5
Depreciation	14	1.3	0.2	0.8	1.4	1.4	0.6	1.9	1.9	1.9	1.1	2.0	2.3	1.1
Amortization and Depletion	15	0.9	0.0	0.0	0.1	0.3	0.1	0.5	0.6	2.3	0.8	2.2	2.0	0.6
Pensions and Other Deferred Comp.	16	0.8	0.0	4.3	•	3.2	0.3	1.2	1.2	0.4	0.4	0.3	0.8	0.3
Employee Benefits	17	2.7	0.4	1.7	0.8	1.6	1.3	13.7	2.6	11.6	2.2	2.2	4.1	1.2
Advertising	18	0.9	0.8	1.5	0.9	1.0	1.0	1.5	2.0	0.4	0.3	0.3	2.4	0.4
Other Expenses	19	50.8	22.5	46.2	75.7	61.1	46.6	32.9	33.2	30.8	57.1	52.1	20.2	63.9
Officers' Compensation	20	2.5	3.0	13.7	3.2	8.4	6.5	2.4	4.3	2.1	1.1	3.5	1.3	0.3
Operating Margin	21	0.1	15.4	5.6	•	3.4	7.2	1.5	6.1	3.1	•	•	4.8	•
Operating Margin Before Officers' Comp.	22	2.6	18.5	19.3	•	11.8	13.6	3.9	10.4	5.1	1.1	2.8	6.1	•

Selected Average Balance Sheet ($ in Thousands)

Net Receivables 23	484	0	4	188	207	1527	1844	5201	8790	23113	25820	172047	514592
Inventories 24	•	•	•	•	•	•	•	•	•	•	•	•	•
Net Property, Plant and Equipment 25	170	0	8	27	342	364	926	3198	4259	9974	15308	31520	173188
Total Assets 26	5006	0	51	613	1899	7458	14900	37144	67227	162189	340429	848605	10525925
Notes and Loans Payable 27	1161	0	69	166	773	1952	1624	5257	19563	33212	209595	228612	1805538
All Other Liabilities 28	2572	0	11	190	895	4431	6646	18726	28961	84838	70266	270850	6500767
Net Worth 29	1273	0	-29	257	231	1075	6630	13161	18703	44139	60568	349144	2219620

Selected Financial Ratios (Times to 1)

Current Ratio 30	0.8	•	2.1	1.6	1.4	1.3	1.8	1.2	1.1	1.1	0.9	0.9	0.5
Quick Ratio 31	0.6	•	1.7	0.9	1.1	1.0	1.4	0.8	0.8	0.8	0.6	0.9	0.4
Net Sales to Working Capital 32	•	•	13.0	1.9	13.0	10.9	3.1	10.0	25.5	26.3	•	•	•
Coverage Ratio 33	0.8	133.8	5.7	•	6.2	11.7	2.6	8.1	2.1	1.0	0.9	2.3	•
Total Asset Turnover 34	0.6	•	4.9	0.6	2.1	1.9	0.8	0.7	0.8	1.1	0.5	0.5	0.4
Inventory Turnover 35	•	•	•	•	•	•	•	•	•	•	•	•	•
Receivables Turnover 36	•	•	•	•	•	•	•	•	•	•	•	•	•
Total Liabilities to Net Worth 37	2.9	•	•	1.4	7.2	5.9	1.2	1.8	2.6	2.7	4.6	1.4	3.7
Current Assets to Working Capital 38	•	•	1.9	2.6	3.4	4.4	2.3	6.1	12.7	10.9	•	•	•
Current Liabilities to Working Capital 39	•	•	0.9	1.6	2.4	3.4	1.3	5.1	11.7	9.9	•	•	•
Working Capital to Net Sales 40	•	•	0.1	0.5	0.1	0.1	0.3	0.1	0.0	0.0	•	•	•
Inventory to Working Capital 41	•	•	•	•	0.0	0.0	•	0.0	0.0	0.0	•	•	•
Total Receipts to Cash Flow 42	2.1	3.4	2.0	1.8	1.7	1.9	3.4	2.8	3.4	1.8	2.1	4.9	1.8
Cost of Goods to Cash Flow 43	0.3	0.0	•	0.0	•	0.0	0.0	0.3	0.6	0.2	0.2	1.2	0.4
Cash Flow to Total Debt 44	0.4	•	1.5	0.6	1.4	1.1	0.4	0.4	0.3	0.8	0.3	0.2	0.3

Selected Financial Factors (in Percentages)

Debt Ratio 45	74.6	•	157.6	58.1	87.8	85.6	55.5	64.6	72.2	72.8	82.2	58.9	78.9
Return on Total Assets 46	1.6	•	33.2	•	8.2	14.6	1.7	4.9	4.6	1.6	4.8	3.7	•
Return on Equity Before Income Taxes 47	•	•	•	•	56.7	92.8	2.3	12.0	8.6	•	•	5.1	•
Return on Equity After Income Taxes 48	•	•	•	•	55.4	80.9	1.0	8.5	4.4	•	•	2.1	•
Profit Margin (Before Income Tax) 49	•	15.4	5.6	3.3	3.3	7.1	1.3	5.9	3.0	•	•	4.5	•
Profit Margin (After Income Tax) 50	•	14.1	5.6	3.3	3.3	6.2	0.6	4.1	1.6	•	•	1.9	•

Table II

Corporations with Net Income

OTHER INSURANCE RELATED ACTIVITIES

MONEY AMOUNTS AND SIZE OF ASSETS IN THOUSANDS OF DOLLARS

Item Description for Accounting Period 7/08 Through 6/09		Total	Zero Assets	Under 500	500 to 1,000	1,000 to 5,000	5,000 to 10,000	10,000 to 25,000	25,000 to 50,000	50,000 to 100,000	100,000 to 250,000	250,000 to 500,000	500,000 to 2,500,000	2,500,000 and over
Number of Enterprises	1	10350	2511	6899	273	415	96	78	24	21	18	•	•	9
Revenues ($ in Thousands)														
Net Sales	2	33205763	522734	1805767	75898	2150936	1151550	648013	796804	999176	2190133	•	•	3862681
Interest	3	663789	696	26	2222	5444	2592	17399	8494	16606	36894	•	•	27695
Rents	4	81647	0	0	0	7639	572	396	6131	1093	979	•	•	0
Royalties	5	13643	0	0	0	0	0	0	0	0	0	•	•	13575
Other Portfolio Income	6	38219	11787	643	0	2188	895	5096	5898	811	15988	•	•	26697
Other Receipts	7	32064565	510251	1805098	73676	2135665	1147491	625122	776281	980666	2136272	•	•	3794714
Total Receipts	8	33205763	522734	1805767	75898	2150936	1151550	648013	796804	999176	2190133	•	•	3862681
Average Total Receipts	9	3208	208	262	278	5183	11995	8308	33200	47580	121674	•	•	429187
Operating Costs/Operating Income (%)														
Cost of Operations	10	11.6	0.4	•	•	•	•	0.5	0.1	1.6	21.6	•	•	35.2
Salaries and Wages	11	16.2	55.8	13.3	36.8	14.1	29.6	44.3	34.6	29.5	23.7	•	•	23.5
Taxes Paid	12	1.8	1.8	2.5	3.6	1.3	3.1	5.1	1.5	6.6	2.5	•	•	1.9
Interest Paid	13	2.0	0.0	0.4	3.5	0.2	0.8	0.8	1.0	3.0	2.6	•	•	2.9
Depreciation	14	1.2	0.0	0.9	2.2	0.5	0.7	2.0	1.7	1.7	2.1	•	•	2.1
Amortization and Depletion	15	0.7	0.0	0.0	•	0.2	0.1	0.1	0.4	1.6	1.9	•	•	1.7
Pensions and Other Deferred Comp.	16	0.8	0.0	5.4	•	3.0	0.3	1.4	1.0	0.6	0.3	•	•	0.7
Employee Benefits	17	1.7	0.1	0.6	•	1.4	2.0	4.0	3.5	2.4	2.0	•	•	4.1
Advertising	18	0.6	0.8	0.7	0.4	1.2	1.6	0.3	2.8	0.3	0.7	•	•	0.7
Other Expenses	19	48.7	18.3	38.2	33.5	65.5	36.5	25.3	34.4	35.3	34.6	•	•	13.0
Officers' Compensation	20	2.1	3.1	14.8	3.5	4.4	6.7	3.0	4.9	2.4	1.2	•	•	0.5
Operating Margin	21	12.6	19.6	23.0	16.5	8.3	18.6	13.2	14.1	15.1	6.8	•	•	13.7
Operating Margin Before Officers' Comp.	22	14.6	22.6	37.8	20.0	12.6	25.2	16.2	19.1	17.5	8.0	•	•	14.2

Selected Average Balance Sheet ($ in Thousands)

Line Item												
Net Receivables 23	539	0	1	267	166	1638	2186	6995	9966	24719	245052
Inventories 24	•	•	•	•	•	•	•	•	•	•	•
Net Property, Plant and Equipment 25	144	0	10	52	135	386	883	3727	3694	11190	17834
Total Assets 26	4454	0	41	618	1870	7230	15206	37625	66076	161741	773782
Notes and Loans Payable 27	875	0	22	248	524	1477	1420	5137	15224	33125	270305
All Other Liabilities 28	1869	0	13	41	1136	3920	6821	18451	30736	75569	227021
Net Worth 29	1709	0	6	330	211	1833	6965	14037	20016	53048	276456

Selected Financial Ratios (Times to 1)

Line Item												
Current Ratio 30	1.0	•	1.8	1.4	1.2	1.9	2.2	1.9	1.2	1.3	1.1
Quick Ratio 31	0.8	•	1.8	1.4	0.9	1.4	2.0	1.4	1.0	1.1	1.0
Net Sales to Working Capital 32	•	•	20.7	2.4	31.2	3.8	1.6	3.7	10.5	6.8	29.4
Coverage Ratio 33	7.4	480.8	56.4	5.8	35.9	22.9	16.1	14.8	6.0	3.5	5.7
Total Asset Turnover 34	0.7	•	6.3	0.4	2.8	1.7	0.5	0.9	0.7	0.8	0.6
Inventory Turnover 35	•	•	•	•	•	•	•	•	•	•	•
Receivables Turnover 36	•	•	•	•	•	•	•	•	•	•	•
Total Liabilities to Net Worth 37	1.6	•	6.1	0.9	7.9	2.9	1.2	1.7	2.3	2.0	1.8
Current Assets to Working Capital 38	•	•	2.2	3.5	6.9	2.1	1.8	2.1	6.3	3.9	20.1
Current Liabilities to Working Capital 39	•	•	1.2	2.5	5.9	1.1	0.8	1.1	5.3	2.9	19.1
Working Capital to Net Sales 40	•	•	0.0	0.4	0.0	0.3	0.6	0.3	0.1	0.1	0.0
Inventory to Working Capital 41	•	•	•	•	•	0.0	•	0.0	•	0.0	0.0
Total Receipts to Cash Flow 42	1.7	3.3	1.7	2.1	1.4	1.9	2.9	2.3	2.1	2.6	4.2
Cost of Goods to Cash Flow 43	0.2	0.0	•	•	•	•	0.0	0.0	0.0	0.6	1.5
Cash Flow to Total Debt 44	0.7	•	4.3	0.5	2.2	1.2	0.3	0.6	0.5	0.4	0.2

Selected Financial Factors (in Percentages)

Line Item												
Debt Ratio 45	61.6	•	85.9	46.7	88.7	74.7	54.2	62.7	69.6	67.2	64.3
Return on Total Assets 46	10.6	•	148.0	9.0	23.4	32.2	7.4	13.3	13.1	7.0	9.2
Return on Equity Before Income Taxes 47	23.8	•	1034.0	13.9	201.5	121.4	15.3	33.2	35.8	15.3	21.1
Return on Equity After Income Taxes 48	18.2	•	1032.2	11.9	198.9	111.3	13.3	27.3	29.5	10.6	14.4
Profit Margin (Before Income Tax) 49	12.7	19.6	23.0	16.5	8.2	18.6	12.8	14.1	15.1	6.7	13.6
Profit Margin (After Income Tax) 50	9.7	18.2	22.9	14.2	8.1	17.0	11.1	11.5	12.5	4.6	9.3

Table I

Corporations with and without Net Income

OPEN-END INVESTMENT FUNDS (FORM 1120-RIC)

MONEY AMOUNTS AND SIZE OF ASSETS IN THOUSANDS OF DOLLARS

Item Description for Accounting Period 7/08 Through 6/09	Total	Zero Assets	Under 500	500 to 1,000	1,000 to 5,000	5,000 to 10,000	10,000 to 25,000	25,000 to 50,000	50,000 to 100,000	100,000 to 250,000	250,000 to 500,000	500,000 to 2,500,000	2,500,000 and over
Number of Enterprises 1	13140	1103	84	180	986	696	1091	1028	1411	2078	1488	2161	834

Revenues ($ in Thousands)

Net Sales 2	436864480	2092475	3638	2450	146476	246448	832043	1774472	4230714	14960316	21897422	99834257	290843770
Interest 3	201991939	522473	1233	364	19888	53104	193989	568943	1273935	5085037	7523083	36452846	150297043
Rents 4	0	0	0	0	0	0	0	0	0	0	0	0	0
Royalties 5	0	0	0	0	0	0	0	0	0	0	0	0	0
Other Portfolio Income 6	51900253	781751	0	14	16361	84722	195862	360548	870054	3354970	4115012	18886352	23234605
Other Receipts 7	182972288	788251	2405	2072	110227	108622	442192	844981	2086725	6520309	10259327	44495059	117312122
Total Receipts 8	436864480	2092475	3638	2450	146476	246448	832043	1774472	4230714	14960316	21897422	99834257	290843770
Average Total Receipts 9	33247	1897	43	14	149	354	763	1726	2998	7199	14716	46198	348734

Operating Costs/Operating Income (%)

Cost of Operations 10	•	•	•	•	•	•	•	•	•	•	•	•	•
Salaries and Wages 11	0.0	0.1	27.0	•	0.0	0.0	0.2	0.1	0.1	0.1	0.1	0.0	0.0
Taxes Paid 12	0.3	0.1	0.2	0.1	0.3	0.4	0.5	0.7	0.7	0.5	0.6	0.5	0.2
Interest Paid 13	1.9	0.1	•	•	0.0	•	0.5	1.2	1.8	1.5	1.0	2.1	2.0
Depreciation 14	0.0	•	•	•	•	•	0.0	•	•	0.0	0.0	0.0	0.0
Amortization and Depletion 15	0.0	0.6	1.5	17.2	3.5	1.0	0.6	0.2	0.1	0.0	0.0	0.0	0.0
Pensions and Other Deferred Comp. 16	•	•	•	•	•	•	•	•	•	•	•	•	•
Employee Benefits 17	•	•	•	•	•	•	•	•	•	•	•	•	•
Advertising 18	0.0	•	•	•	•	0.0	0.0	0.0	0.0	0.0	0.0	0.0	0.0
Other Expenses 19	18.9	18.0	82.3	53.4	22.4	20.3	34.6	28.9	29.7	26.1	26.2	21.9	16.6
Officers' Compensation 20	0.0	•	•	•	•	•	0.7	0.0	0.0	0.0	0.0	0.0	0.0
Operating Margin 21	78.8	81.2	29.3	73.8	73.8	78.2	62.7	68.8	67.6	71.8	72.0	75.5	81.1
Operating Margin Before Officers' Comp. 22	78.8	81.2	29.3	73.8	78.2	78.2	63.4	68.8	67.6	71.8	72.0	75.5	81.1

Selected Average Balance Sheet ($ in Thousands)

Net Receivables 23	13397	0	12	7	19	43	362	661	1266	2836	5687	22664	131647
Inventories 24	•	•	•	•	•	•	•	•	•	•	•	•	•
Net Property, Plant and Equipment 25	1	0	0	0	0	1	0	0	0	0	1	4	2
Total Assets 26	921958	0	265	725	2898	7137	17060	36941	72736	164440	358011	1099263	10428528
Notes and Loans Payable 27	1355	0	0	0	2	1	44	9	198	701	1361	3353	8079
All Other Liabilities 28	51772	0	36	25	81	249	616	1616	3635	10245	22995	79394	534148
Net Worth 29	868831	0	230	700	2815	6886	16400	35317	68903	153494	333654	1016516	9886302

Selected Financial Ratios (Times to 1)

Current Ratio 30	3.4	•	1.2	0.9	2.0	1.5	3.9	3.2	3.5	3.1	2.9	2.6	3.8
Quick Ratio 31	3.1	•	0.9	0.5	1.0	1.0	3.4	2.8	3.0	2.7	2.6	2.4	3.5
Net Sales to Working Capital 32	0.3	•	8.6	•	1.8	2.7	0.4	0.5	0.3	0.3	0.3	0.4	0.2
Coverage Ratio 33	37.5	1102.3	•	•	1463.0	1520.2	105.9	50.7	31.2	39.9	58.2	31.8	38.3
Total Asset Turnover 34	0.0	•	0.2	0.0	0.1	0.0	0.0	0.0	0.0	0.0	0.0	0.0	0.0
Inventory Turnover 35	•	•	•	•	•	•	•	•	•	•	•	•	•
Receivables Turnover 36	•	•	•	•	•	•	•	•	•	•	•	•	•
Total Liabilities to Net Worth 37	0.1	•	0.2	0.0	0.0	0.0	0.0	0.0	0.1	0.1	0.1	0.1	0.1
Current Assets to Working Capital 38	1.4	•	7.5	•	2.0	2.9	1.3	1.4	1.4	1.5	1.5	1.6	1.4
Current Liabilities to Working Capital 39	0.4	•	6.5	•	1.0	1.9	0.3	0.4	0.4	0.5	0.5	0.6	0.4
Working Capital to Net Sales 40	3.8	•	0.1	•	0.6	0.4	2.4	2.1	3.0	2.9	3.0	2.8	4.3
Inventory to Working Capital 41	•	•	•	•	•	•	•	•	•	•	•	•	•
Total Receipts to Cash Flow 42	1.1	1.1	1.4	1.2	1.1	1.5	1.3	1.1	1.1	1.1	1.1	1.1	1.1
Cost of Goods to Cash Flow 43	•	•	•	•	•	•	•	•	•	•	•	•	•
Cash Flow to Total Debt 44	0.6	•	0.9	0.5	1.7	1.0	0.9	0.9	0.7	0.6	0.6	0.5	0.6

Selected Financial Factors (in Percentages)

Debt Ratio 45	5.8	•	13.5	3.4	2.8	3.5	3.9	4.4	5.3	6.7	6.8	7.5	5.2
Return on Total Assets 46	2.6	•	•	0.5	3.3	3.7	2.5	2.8	2.3	2.5	2.4	2.8	2.6
Return on Equity Before Income Taxes 47	2.7	•	•	0.6	3.4	3.8	2.6	2.8	2.3	2.7	2.5	2.9	2.7
Return on Equity After Income Taxes 48	2.7	•	•	0.6	3.4	3.8	2.6	2.8	2.3	2.7	2.5	2.9	2.7
Profit Margin (Before Income Tax) 49	71.0	57.2	•	29.2	63.9	74.0	56.3	57.9	53.8	56.6	57.4	63.5	75.8
Profit Margin (After Income Tax) 50	71.0	57.2	•	29.2	63.9	74.0	56.3	57.9	53.8	56.5	57.4	63.5	75.8

Table II

Corporations with Net Income

OPEN-END INVESTMENT FUNDS (FORM 1120-RIC)

MONEY AMOUNTS AND SIZE OF ASSETS IN THOUSANDS OF DOLLARS

Item Description for Accounting Period 7/08 Through 6/09		Total	Zero Assets	Under 500	500 to 1,000	1,000 to 5,000	5,000 to 10,000	10,000 to 25,000	25,000 to 50,000	50,000 to 100,000	100,000 to 250,000	250,000 to 500,000	500,000 to 2,500,000	2,500,000 and over
Number of Enterprises	1	10740	789	39	103	728	561	844	811	1130	1769	1267	1919	779
Revenues ($ in Thousands)														
Net Sales	2	421901101	1846867	2250	1964	126059	225766	750915	1579836	3832964	14187967	20616901	95190740	283538872
Interest	3	200268705	520369	1	351	18938	50542	185772	540457	1223449	4954914	7386270	35586864	149800779
Rents	4	0	0	0	0	0	0	0	0	0	0	0	0	0
Royalties	5	0	0	0	0	0	0	0	0	0	0	0	0	0
Other Portfolio Income	6	42127336	593182	0	14	2934	74205	169247	259523	627209	2900371	3419789	16060947	18019913
Other Receipts	7	179505060	733316	2249	1599	104187	101019	395896	779856	1982306	6332682	9810842	43542929	115718180
Total Receipts	8	421901101	1846867	2250	1964	126059	225766	750915	1579836	3832964	14187967	20616901	95190740	283538872
Average Total Receipts	9	39283	2341	58	19	173	402	890	1948	3392	8020	16272	49604	363978
Operating Costs/Operating Income (%)														
Cost of Operations	10	•	•	•	•	•	•	•	•	•	•	•	•	•
Salaries and Wages	11	0.0	0.1	32.4	•	0.0	0.0	0.1	0.1	0.1	0.1	0.1	0.0	0.0
Taxes Paid	12	0.3	0.1	•	0.1	0.2	0.4	0.4	0.7	0.6	0.5	0.5	0.4	0.2
Interest Paid	13	1.6	0.0	•	•	0.0	0.0	0.0	0.2	1.0	0.7	1.0	0.7	2.1
Depreciation	14	0.0	•	•	•	•	•	•	•	•	0.0	0.0	0.0	0.0
Amortization and Depletion	15	0.0	0.5	•	5.3	3.2	0.8	0.5	0.2	0.0	0.0	0.0	0.0	0.0
Pensions and Other Deferred Comp.	16	•	•	•	•	•	•	•	•	•	•	•	•	•
Employee Benefits	17	•	•	•	•	•	•	•	•	•	•	•	•	•
Advertising	18	0.0	•	•	•	•	•	•	•	0.0	0.0	0.0	0.0	0.0
Other Expenses	19	17.2	14.9	36.8	39.1	19.6	15.9	26.4	24.4	24.3	21.6	21.8	19.2	15.9
Officers' Compensation	20	0.0	•	•	•	0.0	•	0.0	0.0	0.0	0.0	0.0	0.0	0.0
Operating Margin	21	80.8	84.4	30.8	55.5	76.9	82.8	72.5	74.4	74.0	77.1	76.5	79.6	81.8
Operating Margin Before Officers' Comp.	22	80.8	84.4	30.8	55.5	76.9	82.8	72.5	74.4	74.0	77.1	76.5	79.6	81.9

Selected Average Balance Sheet ($ in Thousands)

Line item	1	2	3	4	5	6	7	8	9	10	11	12
Net Receivables 23	15496	19	3	16	44	271	612	1232	2855	5798	23609	136804
Inventories 24	•	•	•	•	•	•	•	•	•	•	•	•
Net Property, Plant and Equipment 25	1	0	0	0	2	0	0	0	0	1	2	2
Total Assets 26	1058284	285	748	2863	7228	16925	36899	72537	164720	359459	1107490	10733597
Notes and Loans Payable 27	1630	0	0	3	1	1	4	241	765	1507	3767	8649
All Other Liabilities 28	59746	26	26	72	251	628	1521	3533	10392	23295	79839	557909
Net Worth 29	996908	259	722	2788	6976	16295	35374	68763	153563	334658	1023884	10167040

Selected Financial Ratios (Times to 1)

Line item	1	2	3	4	5	6	7	8	9	10	11	12
Current Ratio 30	3.3	1.0	0.6	2.6	1.6	3.2	2.4	3.1	3.0	2.8	2.6	3.6
Quick Ratio 31	3.0	0.9	0.3	1.3	1.2	2.9	2.0	2.6	2.7	2.5	2.4	3.3
Net Sales to Working Capital 32	0.3	59.2	•	1.4	2.7	0.6	0.9	0.5	0.4	0.4	0.4	0.2
Coverage Ratio 33	46.5	1360.9	•	2230.9	1927.7	1495.4	416.0	66.3	87.5	63.5	96.8	38.6
Total Asset Turnover 34	0.0	0.2	0.0	0.1	0.1	0.1	0.1	0.0	0.0	0.0	0.0	0.0
Inventory Turnover 35	•	•	•	•	•	•	•	•	•	•	•	•
Receivables Turnover 36	•	•	•	•	•	•	•	•	•	•	•	•
Total Liabilities to Net Worth 37	0.1	0.0	0.0	0.0	0.0	0.0	0.0	0.1	0.1	0.1	0.1	0.1
Current Assets to Working Capital 38	1.4	23.8	•	1.6	2.7	1.4	1.7	1.5	1.5	1.6	1.6	1.4
Current Liabilities to Working Capital 39	0.4	22.8	•	0.6	1.7	0.4	0.7	0.5	0.5	0.6	0.6	0.4
Working Capital to Net Sales 40	3.5	0.0	•	0.7	0.4	1.6	1.1	2.2	2.6	2.6	2.6	4.0
Inventory to Working Capital 41	•	•	•	•	•	•	•	•	•	•	•	•
Total Receipts to Cash Flow 42	1.1	1.5	1.1	1.1	1.5	1.2	1.1	1.1	1.1	1.1	1.1	1.1
Cost of Goods to Cash Flow 43	•	•	•	•	•	•	•	•	•	•	•	•
Cash Flow to Total Debt 44	0.6	1.5	0.7	2.2	1.1	1.1	1.1	0.8	0.7	0.6	0.6	0.6

Selected Financial Factors (in Percentages)

Line item	1	2	3	4	5	6	7	8	9	10	11	12
Debt Ratio 45	5.8	9.1	3.5	2.6	3.5	3.7	4.1	5.2	6.8	6.9	6.9	5.3
Return on Total Assets 46	2.8	6.2	1.4	4.6	4.7	3.6	3.6	3.1	3.2	3.2	3.0	2.7
Return on Equity Before Income Taxes 47	3.0	6.9	1.5	4.7	4.8	3.8	3.8	3.2	3.4	3.4	3.1	2.8
Return on Equity After Income Taxes 48	3.0	6.9	1.5	4.7	4.8	3.8	3.8	3.2	3.4	3.4	3.1	2.8
Profit Margin (Before Income Tax) 49	74.9	30.8	55.5	76.1	82.8	68.2	68.9	65.0	64.2	64.3	69.8	78.2
Profit Margin (After Income Tax) 50	74.9	30.8	55.5	76.1	82.8	68.2	68.9	65.0	64.2	64.3	69.8	78.2

Table I

Corporations with and without Net Income

OTHER FINANCIAL VEHICLES

MONEY AMOUNTS AND SIZE OF ASSETS IN THOUSANDS OF DOLLARS

Item Description for Accounting Period 7/08 Through 6/09		Total	Zero Assets	Under 500	500 to 1,000	1,000 to 5,000	5,000 to 10,000	10,000 to 25,000	25,000 to 50,000	50,000 to 100,000	100,000 to 250,000	250,000 to 500,000	500,000 to 2,500,000	2,500,000 and over
Number of Enterprises	1	14014	3003	7741	620	1422	248	223	128	117	118	106	173	115
Revenues ($ in Thousands)														
Net Sales	2	77221957	11613829	820024	75319	397163	852514	600426	709894	516386	1243999	2715817	11357745	46318842
Interest	3	61586454	10745907	46210	22401	25884	131444	357773	364834	317009	842422	2191117	8883573	37657881
Rents	4	2986748	3060	0	835	1444	2397	5617	80253	34221	168154	137944	893119	1659704
Royalties	5	8429	90	0	0	735	5960	0	1142	27	111	149	0	215
Other Portfolio Income	6	2051970	204102	54344	475	37242	51849	79948	38322	56198	91891	70769	153242	1213587
Other Receipts	7	10588356	660670	719470	51608	331858	660864	157088	225343	108931	141421	315838	1427811	5787455
Total Receipts	8	77221957	11613829	820024	75319	397163	852514	600426	709894	516386	1243999	2715817	11357745	46318842
Average Total Receipts	9	5510	3867	106	121	279	3438	2692	5546	4414	10542	25621	65652	402773
Operating Costs/Operating Income (%)														
Cost of Operations	10	0.3	•	•	•	•	15.4	0.1	•	•	•	•	•	0.8
Salaries and Wages	11	0.8	0.0	4.0	•	6.9	2.7	2.5	4.4	1.1	1.5	1.2	0.4	0.8
Taxes Paid	12	0.5	0.1	2.1	7.3	2.8	1.0	1.1	2.0	1.1	2.6	0.9	0.8	0.3
Interest Paid	13	37.7	75.2	4.7	20.8	7.5	10.9	36.9	44.5	24.3	31.5	38.9	31.7	31.3
Depreciation	14	0.9	0.0	0.3	3.4	1.3	0.2	0.2	1.7	1.8	2.9	2.1	0.6	1.0
Amortization and Depletion	15	0.4	0.0	1.2	•	3.5	0.8	0.9	3.1	0.7	0.6	1.1	0.7	0.3
Pensions and Other Deferred Comp.	16	0.0	0.0	0.0	•	0.8	0.0	0.3	0.0	0.0	0.1	•	•	0.0
Employee Benefits	17	0.0	0.0	0.1	•	0.5	0.1	0.2	0.2	0.1	0.1	0.0	0.0	0.0
Advertising	18	0.0	•	0.1	•	0.0	0.0	0.0	0.0	0.1	0.1	0.3	0.0	0.0
Other Expenses	19	24.4	11.4	56.7	79.3	74.0	66.4	48.6	46.3	40.5	48.6	31.6	41.3	19.7
Officers' Compensation	20	0.5	0.1	23.0	10.2	4.2	0.7	0.4	2.9	0.2	0.4	0.1	0.6	0.2
Operating Margin	21	34.5	12.3	8.1	•	•	2.0	8.7	•	30.1	11.7	23.7	23.8	46.3
Operating Margin Before Officers' Comp.	22	35.0	12.5	31.0	•	2.6	2.6	9.2	•	30.4	12.1	23.8	24.4	46.5

Selected Average Balance Sheet ($ in Thousands)

	1	2	3	4	5	6	7	8	9	10	11	12	13
Net Receivables 23	3818	0	•	5	253	502	901	1242	3379	7788	15137	69446	327969
Inventories 24	•	•	•	•	•	•	•	•	•	•	•	•	•
Net Property, Plant and Equipment 25	1680	0	1	10	4	387	1065	2504	1876	11508	8768	32740	127841
Total Assets 26	82899	0	86	748	2127	7010	15903	35541	70961	165373	360139	1141130	7689981
Notes and Loans Payable 27	23753	0	26	1981	668	1642	4146	8536	9965	38452	58615	325852	2258941
All Other Liabilities 28	12398	0	23	316	636	2040	2540	6851	6563	16600	46870	191301	1128097
Net Worth 29	46748	0	37	-1549	823	3328	9218	20154	54433	110322	254654	623977	4302944

Selected Financial Ratios (Times to 1)

	1	2	3	4	5	6	7	8	9	10	11	12	13
Current Ratio 30	0.8	•	2.0	8.2	4.0	2.6	1.4	1.5	1.8	1.7	2.2	0.9	0.7
Quick Ratio 31	0.6	•	0.9	6.1	3.3	2.0	1.0	0.9	1.4	1.2	1.7	0.7	0.5
Net Sales to Working Capital 32	•	•	8.6	0.7	0.6	2.6	2.2	1.6	0.7	0.8	0.8	•	•
Coverage Ratio 33	1.9	1.2	2.7	•	0.7	1.1	1.2	0.9	2.2	1.3	1.6	1.8	2.5
Total Asset Turnover 34	0.1	•	1.2	0.2	0.1	0.5	0.2	0.2	0.1	0.1	0.1	0.1	0.1
Inventory Turnover 35	•	•	•	•	•	•	•	•	•	•	•	•	•
Receivables Turnover 36	•	•	•	•	•	•	•	•	•	•	•	•	•
Total Liabilities to Net Worth 37	0.8	•	1.3	•	1.6	1.1	0.7	0.8	0.3	0.5	0.4	0.8	0.8
Current Assets to Working Capital 38	•	•	2.0	1.1	1.3	1.6	3.3	2.8	2.3	2.5	1.9	•	•
Current Liabilities to Working Capital 39	•	•	1.0	0.1	0.3	0.6	2.3	1.8	1.3	1.5	0.9	•	•
Working Capital to Net Sales 40	•	•	0.1	1.5	1.7	0.4	0.4	0.6	1.3	1.3	1.3	•	•
Inventory to Working Capital 41	•	•	0.2	•	•	•	•	•	0.0	•	•	•	•
Total Receipts to Cash Flow 42	1.8	4.3	1.8	1.9	1.5	1.6	2.3	2.8	1.8	1.9	1.8	1.6	1.6
Cost of Goods to Cash Flow 43	0.0	0.0	•	•	•	0.2	0.0	•	•	•	•	0.0	•
Cash Flow to Total Debt 44	0.1	•	1.2	0.0	0.1	0.6	0.2	0.1	0.2	0.1	0.1	0.1	0.1

Selected Financial Factors (in Percentages)

	1	2	3	4	5	6	7	8	9	10	11	12	13
Debt Ratio 45	43.6	•	56.9	307.0	61.3	52.5	42.0	43.3	23.3	33.3	29.3	45.3	44.0
Return on Total Assets 46	4.8	•	15.5	•	0.7	6.1	7.6	6.1	3.4	2.7	4.4	3.2	4.0
Return on Equity Before Income Taxes 47	4.0	•	22.7	1.6	•	1.6	2.4	•	2.4	1.0	2.4	2.5	4.3
Return on Equity After Income Taxes 48	3.7	•	20.9	1.7	•	•	0.9	•	2.2	0.8	2.2	1.9	4.1
Profit Margin (Before Income Tax) 49	34.3	12.3	8.0	•	1.6	1.6	8.3	•	29.9	10.6	23.4	23.9	46.0
Profit Margin (After Income Tax) 50	31.4	10.3	7.4	•	•	•	3.3	•	27.3	8.0	21.6	18.0	43.7

Table II
Corporations with Net Income

OTHER FINANCIAL VEHICLES

MONEY AMOUNTS AND SIZE OF ASSETS IN THOUSANDS OF DOLLARS

Item Description for Accounting Period 7/08 Through 6/09		Total	Zero Assets	Under 500	500 to 1,000	1,000 to 5,000	5,000 to 10,000	10,000 to 25,000	25,000 to 50,000	50,000 to 100,000	100,000 to 250,000	250,000 to 500,000	500,000 to 2,500,000	2,500,000 and over
Number of Enterprises	1	6504	1375	3702	168	567	103	91	59	73	70	74	135	88
Revenues ($ in Thousands)														
Net Sales	2	63472220	10989565	506992	62956	349206	485871	501699	568036	478217	867017	1977355	9306901	37378406
Interest	3	50533623	10288134	8887	20015	17887	127735	298564	325958	266632	567896	1582525	7302319	29727071
Rents	4	2613636	2365	0	835	1444	24	5606	52547	33967	103936	101890	656372	1654650
Royalties	5	8071	15	0	0	735	5960	0	1142	0	70	149	0	0
Other Portfolio Income	6	1896507	185784	53846	1	29916	48551	74080	35462	50697	59216	56651	92188	1210917
Other Receipts	7	8420383	513267	444259	42105	300024	303601	123449	152927	126921	135899	236140	1256022	4785768
Total Receipts	8	63472220	10989565	506992	62956	349206	485871	501699	568036	478217	867017	1977355	9306901	37378406
Average Total Receipts	9	9759	7992	137	375	616	4717	5513	9628	6551	12386	26721	68940	424755
Operating Costs/Operating Income (%)														
Cost of Operations	10	0.3	0.4	•	•	•	26.9	•	•	•	•	•	0.0	•
Salaries and Wages	11	0.8	0.0	5.2	•	7.8	4.7	0.1	0.9	1.7	1.7	0.1	0.1	1.0
Taxes Paid	12	0.5	0.0	2.8	1.5	2.8	1.2	0.7	1.7	0.9	2.5	0.6	0.5	0.4
Interest Paid	13	29.8	75.3	0.4	23.7	4.7	15.9	34.6	44.7	17.8	12.7	19.3	20.3	20.5
Depreciation	14	0.9	0.0	0.0	0.3	1.3	0.4	0.2	0.6	1.9	2.2	1.3	0.4	1.2
Amortization and Depletion	15	0.2	0.0	0.1	•	4.0	1.3	0.9	0.3	0.2	0.5	0.7	0.4	0.2
Pensions and Other Deferred Comp.	16	0.0	0.0	0.1	•	0.2	0.0	0.1	•	0.0	0.1	•	•	0.0
Employee Benefits	17	0.0	0.0	0.0	•	0.5	0.1	•	0.1	0.0	0.1	0.0	0.0	0.0
Advertising	18	0.0	•	•	•	0.0	0.1	0.0	•	0.1	0.1	0.4	0.0	0.1
Other Expenses	19	14.3	6.1	12.4	32.2	30.4	15.7	22.7	13.5	16.7	17.9	14.6	17.6	15.5
Officers' Compensation	20	0.4	0.0	35.2	•	0.9	1.1	•	0.1	0.1	0.4	0.2	0.0	0.2
Operating Margin	21	52.7	18.1	43.7	42.3	47.3	32.5	40.8	39.2	61.2	61.8	61.2	60.6	60.9
Operating Margin Before Officers' Comp.	22	53.1	18.1	79.0	42.3	48.2	33.6	40.8	39.2	61.3	62.2	61.4	60.6	61.1

Selected Average Balance Sheet ($ in Thousands)

Net Receivables **23**	6460	0	0	0	240	33	880	1133	3344	10188	12603	66030	351467
Inventories **24**	•	•	•	•	•	•	•	•	•	•	•	•	•
Net Property, Plant and Equipment **25**	3197	0	0	21	5	932	0	2659	2071	11075	8420	31850	166887
Total Assets **26**	141302	0	100	770	2055	6971	15871	35319	70662	167548	356802	1131967	8147899
Notes and Loans Payable **27**	27629	0	19	7236	371	1301	1777	4767	5274	19306	51773	231820	1599568
All Other Liabilities **28**	16236	0	1	42	1318	3745	437	4811	4440	11881	20205	133122	948931
Net Worth **29**	97438	0	79	-6508	366	1925	13657	25741	60948	136361	284824	767025	5599401

Selected Financial Ratios (Times to 1)

Current Ratio **30**	1.5	•	22.1	10.0	9.4	4.4	2.6	3.0	3.2	2.4	3.1	1.4	1.5
Quick Ratio **31**	1.1	•	9.2	10.0	6.9	3.3	2.4	2.3	2.7	1.7	2.5	1.0	1.1
Net Sales to Working Capital **32**	1.1	•	4.7	0.9	1.2	2.3	4.9	1.7	0.7	0.6	0.6	1.2	0.9
Coverage Ratio **33**	2.8	1.2	100.0	2.8	11.0	3.0	2.2	1.9	4.5	5.9	4.2	4.0	3.9
Total Asset Turnover **34**	0.1	•	1.4	0.5	0.3	0.7	0.3	0.3	0.1	0.1	0.1	0.1	0.1
Inventory Turnover **35**	•	•	•	•	•	•	•	•	•	•	•	•	•
Receivables Turnover **36**	•	•	•	•	•	•	•	•	•	•	•	•	•
Total Liabilities to Net Worth **37**	0.5	•	0.3	•	4.6	2.6	0.2	0.4	0.2	0.2	0.3	0.5	0.5
Current Assets to Working Capital **38**	2.9	•	1.0	1.1	1.1	1.3	1.6	1.5	1.5	1.7	1.5	3.6	2.9
Current Liabilities to Working Capital **39**	1.9	•	0.0	0.1	0.1	0.3	0.6	0.5	0.5	0.7	0.5	2.6	1.9
Working Capital to Net Sales **40**	0.9	0.2	0.2	1.2	0.9	0.4	0.2	0.6	1.5	1.5	1.6	0.9	1.1
Inventory to Working Capital **41**	0.0	•	•	•	•	•	•	•	0.0	0.0	•	•	•
Total Receipts to Cash Flow **42**	1.5	4.2	2.3	1.4	1.4	2.6	2.1	2.2	1.5	1.3	1.3	1.3	1.4
Cost of Goods to Cash Flow **43**	0.0	0.0	•	•	•	0.7	•	•	•	•	•	0.0	•
Cash Flow to Total Debt **44**	0.1	•	2.9	0.0	0.3	0.4	1.2	0.5	0.5	0.3	0.3	0.1	0.1

Selected Financial Factors (in Percentages)

Debt Ratio **45**	31.0	•	20.8	944.7	82.2	72.4	14.0	27.1	13.7	18.6	20.2	32.2	31.3
Return on Total Assets **46**	5.7	•	60.5	32.1	15.5	32.8	26.2	22.9	7.4	5.5	6.0	4.9	4.2
Return on Equity Before Income Taxes **47**	5.3	•	75.7	•	79.3	79.7	16.5	14.6	6.6	5.6	5.7	5.4	4.6
Return on Equity After Income Taxes **48**	4.9	•	73.9	•	71.7	65.9	14.0	12.9	6.3	5.3	5.5	4.8	4.4
Profit Margin (Before Income Tax) **49**	52.4	18.2	43.7	42.3	47.1	32.5	40.8	39.2	61.5	61.7	61.2	60.5	60.5
Profit Margin (After Income Tax) **50**	49.1	16.1	42.7	41.9	42.6	26.9	34.8	34.4	58.7	58.0	58.7	53.6	57.6

Table I

Corporations with and without Net Income

LESSORS OF BUILDINGS

MONEY AMOUNTS AND SIZE OF ASSETS IN THOUSANDS OF DOLLARS

Item Description for Accounting Period 7/08 Through 6/09		Total	Zero Assets	Under 500	500 to 1,000	1,000 to 5,000	5,000 to 10,000	10,000 to 25,000	25,000 to 50,000	50,000 to 100,000	100,000 to 250,000	250,000 to 500,000	500,000 to 2,500,000	2,500,000 and over
Number of Enterprises	1	218612	26191	107673	36833	40039	4464	2151	602	267	186	83	86	37
Revenues ($ in Thousands)														
Net Sales	2	67793180	2340064	2784712	3265436	7407876	2842409	2749351	2466447	2717268	3374455	3792078	10668049	23385034
Interest	3	2688800	47965	29079	38861	134213	48133	40529	69448	67897	103566	237475	530247	1341387
Rents	4	26977192	102290	37531	30654	234522	96620	178531	229086	375696	1322624	1696047	5244754	17428837
Royalties	5	46681	3	8313	21984	8063	6089	1	1562	362	303	0	0	0
Other Portfolio Income	6	4723812	454425	152515	120651	463315	178282	110634	50784	120077	194204	89410	1567455	1222064
Other Receipts	7	33356695	1735381	2557274	3053286	6567763	2513285	2419656	2115567	2153236	1753758	1769146	3325593	3392746
Total Receipts	8	67793180	2340064	2784712	3265436	7407876	2842409	2749351	2466447	2717268	3374455	3792078	10668049	23385034
Average Total Receipts	9	310	89	26	89	185	637	1278	4097	10177	18142	45688	124047	632028
Operating Costs/Operating Income (%)														
Cost of Operations	10	7.4	15.6	4.4	8.5	17.0	2.2	9.6	20.6	23.1	5.0	17.8	1.4	2.2
Salaries and Wages	11	5.7	1.2	6.6	14.5	6.7	18.3	14.8	9.1	8.7	5.1	3.6	5.4	1.7
Taxes Paid	12	7.0	8.0	12.4	9.3	11.1	10.0	10.0	8.2	7.4	6.4	6.1	6.2	4.3
Interest Paid	13	13.0	15.9	9.2	6.6	12.1	12.0	16.4	14.8	13.1	17.2	16.2	17.8	10.5
Depreciation	14	12.2	9.4	7.9	7.0	8.8	11.5	11.9	10.5	10.0	12.0	9.0	13.6	15.1
Amortization and Depletion	15	1.0	0.3	0.1	0.6	0.5	0.6	0.8	0.8	0.8	2.2	1.5	1.5	1.1
Pensions and Other Deferred Comp.	16	0.2	0.1	0.0	0.6	0.5	2.2	0.5	0.3	0.4	0.1	0.0	0.0	0.0
Employee Benefits	17	0.4	0.1	0.5	0.8	0.9	1.5	0.8	0.8	0.6	0.5	0.4	0.3	0.0
Advertising	18	0.4	0.3	0.3	0.8	0.3	0.6	0.3	0.5	0.5	0.5	0.5	0.4	0.2
Other Expenses	19	32.7	38.5	55.4	36.3	36.3	33.3	33.0	32.3	28.3	43.2	42.6	30.4	26.2
Officers' Compensation	20	2.0	1.7	4.4	9.6	4.2	4.7	3.4	2.8	1.4	1.6	0.5	1.2	0.3
Operating Margin	21	18.1	8.8	•	5.4	1.6	3.0	•	•	5.5	6.2	1.7	21.8	38.5
Operating Margin Before Officers' Comp.	22	20.1	10.6	3.1	15.0	5.8	7.8	1.8	2.2	7.0	7.8	2.2	23.0	38.7

Selected Average Balance Sheet ($ in Thousands)

Net Receivables 23	67	0	4	23	44	187	439	677	2477	5399	7879	24392	132467
Inventories 24	•	•	•	•	•	•	•	•	•	•	•	•	•
Net Property, Plant and Equipment 25	1949	0	138	487	1484	4629	9542	20064	40947	87258	191351	657116	4894887
Total Assets 26	2894	0	186	697	2102	6798	14804	34801	70001	150294	348096	1121569	6692462
Notes and Loans Payable 27	1429	0	128	467	1463	4510	9571	20057	37708	79416	169278	525844	2325735
All Other Liabilities 28	239	0	7	67	157	405	1129	2950	7086	12649	30816	108947	555719
Net Worth 29	1225	0	51	164	482	1883	4104	11794	25206	58229	148003	486778	3811007

Selected Financial Ratios (Times to 1)

Current Ratio 30	1.3	•	2.3	2.2	1.7	1.7	1.8	3.4	1.8	2.1	1.7	1.3	0.6
Quick Ratio 31	0.8	•	1.8	1.6	1.1	1.2	1.2	2.2	1.2	1.4	1.2	0.8	0.4
Net Sales to Working Capital 32	5.6	•	1.5	1.4	1.5	1.9	1.5	0.9	2.1	1.7	4.2	6.6	•
Coverage Ratio 33	2.4	1.6	0.8	1.8	1.1	1.2	0.9	0.9	1.4	1.4	1.1	2.2	4.7
Total Asset Turnover 34	0.1	•	0.1	0.1	0.1	0.1	0.1	0.1	0.1	0.1	0.1	0.1	0.1
Inventory Turnover 35	•	•	•	•	•	•	•	•	•	•	•	•	•
Receivables Turnover 36	•	•	•	•	•	•	•	•	•	•	•	•	•
Total Liabilities to Net Worth 37	1.4	•	2.7	3.3	3.4	2.6	2.6	2.0	1.8	1.6	1.4	1.3	0.8
Current Assets to Working Capital 38	4.9	•	1.7	1.8	2.3	2.4	2.3	1.4	2.2	1.9	2.4	4.2	•
Current Liabilities to Working Capital 39	3.9	•	0.7	0.8	1.3	1.4	1.3	0.4	1.2	0.9	1.4	3.2	•
Working Capital to Net Sales 40	0.2	•	0.6	0.7	0.7	0.5	0.7	1.1	0.5	0.6	0.2	0.2	•
Inventory to Working Capital 41	0.0	•	•	0.0	0.0	0.0	0.0	0.0	0.0	0.0	0.0	0.0	•
Total Receipts to Cash Flow 42	2.7	4.5	2.9	4.0	4.4	4.4	4.9	4.1	4.0	3.4	3.2	3.1	1.8
Cost of Goods to Cash Flow 43	0.2	0.7	0.1	0.3	0.7	0.1	0.5	0.8	0.9	0.2	0.6	0.0	0.0
Cash Flow to Total Debt 44	0.1	•	0.1	0.0	0.0	0.0	0.0	0.0	0.1	0.1	0.1	0.1	0.1

Selected Financial Factors (in Percentages)

Debt Ratio 45	57.7	•	72.6	76.5	77.1	72.3	72.3	66.1	64.0	61.3	57.5	56.6	43.1
Return on Total Assets 46	3.3	•	1.1	1.5	1.2	1.4	1.2	1.6	2.7	2.8	2.3	4.4	4.6
Return on Equity Before Income Taxes 47	4.5	•	•	2.9	0.5	0.8	•	•	2.1	1.9	0.5	5.5	6.4
Return on Equity After Income Taxes 48	4.3	•	•	2.4	0.2	0.2	•	•	1.2	1.5	•	5.5	6.4
Profit Margin (Before Income Tax) 49	17.9	8.8	5.3	5.3	1.4	2.5	•	•	5.3	6.1	1.7	21.8	38.3
Profit Margin (After Income Tax) 50	16.8	4.0	4.4	•	0.5	•	•	•	3.0	5.0	•	21.6	38.3

Table II

Corporations with Net Income

LESSORS OF BUILDINGS

MONEY AMOUNTS AND SIZE OF ASSETS IN THOUSANDS OF DOLLARS

Item Description for Accounting Period 7/08 Through 6/09		Total	Zero Assets	Under 500	500 to 1,000	1,000 to 5,000	5,000 to 10,000	10,000 to 25,000	25,000 to 50,000	50,000 to 100,000	100,000 to 250,000	250,000 to 500,000	500,000 to 2,500,000	2,500,000 and over
Number of Enterprises	1	43788	4406	20132	8446	8515	1182	568	224	113	77	45	•	•
Revenues ($ in Thousands)														
Net Sales	2	50234656	1610876	1645780	2621995	4277213	1380108	1594915	1417987	1660131	2123027	2603015	•	•
Interest	3	2199402	40370	19775	26410	98812	28344	23787	52831	53377	56241	145289	•	•
Rents	4	23188160	87914	21067	19953	74044	24274	76384	108012	225377	831231	1110857	•	•
Royalties	5	37523	0	8313	21832	6090	587	0	337	362	1	0	•	•
Other Portfolio Income	6	4333323	440595	129442	112779	373019	155024	98180	39136	100155	164572	48184	•	•
Other Receipts	7	20476248	1041997	1467183	2441021	3725248	1171879	1396564	1217671	1280860	1070982	1298685	•	•
Total Receipts	8	50234656	1610876	1645780	2621995	4277213	1380108	1594915	1417987	1660131	2123027	2603015	•	•
Average Total Receipts	9	1147	366	82	310	502	1168	2808	6330	14691	27572	57845	•	•
Operating Costs/Operating Income (%)														
Cost of Operations	10	5.8	19.8	0.2	9.9	22.4	1.7	4.6	18.5	17.3	3.6	25.0	•	•
Salaries and Wages	11	4.2	0.7	5.4	15.1	4.0	8.2	18.0	6.0	7.5	3.9	2.9	•	•
Taxes Paid	12	5.9	5.0	9.2	6.2	8.7	10.1	9.3	7.6	7.9	4.8	5.8	•	•
Interest Paid	13	9.9	7.8	5.3	3.6	8.9	10.9	11.1	10.1	10.4	9.8	12.6	•	•
Depreciation	14	11.0	4.1	5.4	4.5	5.9	8.7	8.3	8.8	7.3	8.2	7.4	•	•
Amortization and Depletion	15	0.8	0.2	0.0	0.3	0.4	0.6	0.5	0.7	0.7	0.7	0.6	•	•
Pensions and Other Deferred Comp.	16	0.2	0.0	•	0.7	0.7	4.1	0.3	0.4	0.2	0.1	0.0	•	•
Employee Benefits	17	0.2	0.1	0.4	0.7	0.7	0.7	0.6	0.6	0.6	0.4	0.5	•	•
Advertising	18	0.3	0.4	0.2	1.0	0.1	0.7	0.2	0.5	0.5	0.1	0.6	•	•
Other Expenses	19	25.7	26.3	44.9	31.5	20.5	25.6	23.8	26.2	24.4	33.9	22.9	•	•
Officers' Compensation	20	1.7	1.2	3.6	10.9	4.6	4.5	2.5	2.7	1.3	1.9	0.5	•	•
Operating Margin	21	34.0	34.4	25.4	15.7	23.1	24.2	20.9	17.9	21.8	32.4	21.4	•	•
Operating Margin Before Officers' Comp.	22	35.8	35.6	29.0	26.6	27.7	28.7	23.3	20.6	23.2	34.4	21.9	•	•

Selected Average Balance Sheet ($ in Thousands)

Net Receivables 23	166	0	13	20	83	105	372	1118	2639	4058	5708
Inventories 24	•	•	•	•	•	•	•	•	•	•	•
Net Property, Plant and Equipment 25	5544	0	97	401	1350	4691	9384	19466	39478	86115	187987
Total Assets 26	8242	0	173	688	2156	7029	15448	34638	71001	153839	367694
Notes and Loans Payable 27	3030	0	123	381	1140	3951	8014	15587	34441	61351	159196
All Other Liabilities 28	734	0	8	70	221	353	1117	3478	8295	15851	35009
Net Worth 29	4479	0	41	236	795	2725	6317	15573	28265	76638	173489

Selected Financial Ratios (Times to 1)

Current Ratio 30	0.8	•	4.8	2.4	2.8	2.4	1.4	3.5	2.2	1.9	1.4
Quick Ratio 31	0.6	•	4.3	1.7	2.2	1.7	1.0	2.5	1.3	1.2	0.9
Net Sales to Working Capital 32	•	•	2.1	3.0	1.9	2.2	4.4	1.3	2.2	3.0	7.4
Coverage Ratio 33	4.4	5.4	5.7	5.3	3.6	3.2	2.8	2.7	3.1	4.3	2.7
Total Asset Turnover 34	0.1	•	0.5	0.5	0.2	0.2	0.2	0.2	0.2	0.2	0.2
Inventory Turnover 35	•	•	•	•	•	•	•	•	•	•	•
Receivables Turnover 36	•	•	•	•	•	•	•	•	•	•	•
Total Liabilities to Net Worth 37	0.8	•	3.2	1.9	1.7	1.6	1.4	1.2	1.5	1.0	1.1
Current Assets to Working Capital 38	•	•	1.3	1.7	1.5	1.7	3.5	1.4	1.9	2.2	3.6
Current Liabilities to Working Capital 39	•	•	0.3	0.7	0.5	0.7	2.5	0.4	0.9	1.2	2.6
Working Capital to Net Sales 40	•	•	0.5	0.3	0.5	0.4	0.2	0.8	0.5	0.3	0.1
Inventory to Working Capital 41	•	•	•	•	0.0	•	0.0	0.0	0.0	0.0	0.0
Total Receipts to Cash Flow 42	2.2	3.1	1.8	3.3	3.1	3.2	2.9	2.7	2.8	2.4	3.3
Cost of Goods to Cash Flow 43	0.1	0.6	0.0	0.3	0.7	0.1	0.1	0.5	0.5	0.1	0.8
Cash Flow to Total Debt 44	0.1	•	0.3	0.2	0.1	0.1	0.1	0.1	0.0	0.2	0.1

Selected Financial Factors (in Percentages)

Debt Ratio 45	45.7	•	76.2	65.6	63.1	61.2	59.1	55.0	60.2	50.2	52.8
Return on Total Assets 46	6.1	•	14.5	8.7	7.4	5.8	5.7	5.0	6.6	7.6	5.3
Return on Equity Before Income Taxes 47	8.7	•	50.2	20.5	14.5	10.3	9.1	7.1	11.3	11.6	7.1
Return on Equity After Income Taxes 48	8.3	•	45.2	19.0	12.1	8.6	7.1	5.5	9.3	11.0	6.2
Profit Margin (Before Income Tax) 49	33.9	34.4	25.3	15.6	23.0	24.0	20.4	17.4	21.7	32.3	21.4
Profit Margin (After Income Tax) 50	32.5	27.5	22.7	14.5	19.2	20.1	16.0	13.6	17.9	30.5	18.6

Table I

Corporations with and without Net Income

LESSORS OF MINIWAREHOUSES, SELF-STORAGE, OTHER REAL ESTATE

MONEY AMOUNTS AND SIZE OF ASSETS IN THOUSANDS OF DOLLARS

Item Description for Accounting Period 7/08 Through 6/09	Total	Zero Assets	Under 500	500 to 1,000	1,000 to 5,000	5,000 to 10,000	10,000 to 25,000	25,000 to 50,000	50,000 to 100,000	100,000 to 250,000	250,000 to 500,000	500,000 to 2,500,000	2,500,000 and over
Number of Enterprises 1	83279	12938	48928	7862	10285	1525	883	294	195	159	83	94	33
Revenues ($ in Thousands)													
Net Sales 2	43239283	1391344	3828069	636395	1911754	879498	1428961	827187	1460919	3515850	2185913	9668217	15505175
Interest 3	2963966	122029	13907	13940	88165	30288	70993	61656	78241	201561	164233	658557	1460395
Rents 4	17947158	209715	7252	395	8394	35082	300452	243229	594808	1337827	1007077	6105553	8097375
Royalties 5	92898	175	748	39	35234	3908	12672	10932	14425	1252	0	13514	0
Other Portfolio Income 6	5557256	536152	160502	53797	205717	90642	150404	83656	296147	938381	515182	804766	1761908
Other Receipts 7	16638005	523273	3645660	568224	1574244	719578	894440	427714	477298	1036829	499421	2085827	4185497
Total Receipts 8	43239283	1391344	3828069	636395	1911754	879498	1428961	827187	1460919	3515850	2185913	9668217	15505175
Average Total Receipts 9	519	108	78	81	186	577	1618	2814	7492	22112	26336	102853	469854
Operating Costs/Operating Income (%)													
Cost of Operations 10	0.7	0.9	•	•	2.3	•	1.0	0.2	0.0	0.3	2.5	0.9	0.7
Salaries and Wages 11	4.9	2.2	17.7	6.5	10.3	6.6	11.6	9.2	4.0	4.6	6.1	2.0	2.2
Taxes Paid 12	5.5	6.9	5.9	11.7	7.3	8.4	7.0	6.4	4.8	3.8	5.6	4.6	5.3
Interest Paid 13	15.0	12.1	2.2	14.1	15.0	21.6	15.6	20.6	11.8	16.0	17.9	14.6	17.6
Depreciation 14	9.8	9.5	3.2	8.2	17.9	10.4	7.9	7.9	7.6	8.3	8.9	10.2	11.2
Amortization and Depletion 15	1.2	2.8	0.0	0.2	0.9	0.4	0.8	1.1	0.9	0.9	1.4	1.3	1.4
Pensions and Other Deferred Comp. 16	0.2	0.0	1.6	0.1	0.2	0.4	0.4	0.8	0.1	0.1	0.2	•	0.0
Employee Benefits 17	0.4	0.1	1.7	3.0	0.5	0.5	0.9	1.0	1.7	0.2	0.3	0.0	0.0
Advertising 18	0.6	0.7	2.7	0.7	0.5	0.4	0.7	0.9	0.2	0.5	0.2	0.2	0.4
Other Expenses 19	36.6	49.4	53.2	36.2	49.0	50.6	57.0	55.4	64.2	54.4	65.5	36.9	15.4
Officers' Compensation 20	2.1	1.3	10.1	5.7	3.2	5.5	4.2	8.3	3.5	0.8	1.9	0.2	0.7
Operating Margin 21	22.9	14.1	1.8	13.5	•	•	•	•	1.1	10.2	•	29.1	45.1
Operating Margin Before Officers' Comp. 22	25.1	15.4	11.8	19.2	0.6	•	•	•	4.7	10.9	•	29.3	45.8

Selected Average Balance Sheet ($ in Thousands)

Net Receivables 23	96	0	4	13	80	612	835	597	2688	3570	5386	21215	43844
Inventories 24	•	•	•	•	•	•	•	•	•	•	•	•	•
Net Property, Plant and Equipment 25	2363	0	74	409	1027	2968	5558	10633	21417	51094	115577	526531	2892273
Total Assets 26	5073	0	144	707	2088	6851	15722	34412	68419	160775	362349	1108274	5478686
Notes and Loans Payable 27	1838	0	74	352	1158	3273	7219	12296	24498	51452	107559	299241	2115310
All Other Liabilities 28	352	0	29	55	224	1246	2968	3884	7445	13634	19295	53245	281208
Net Worth 29	2883	0	42	300	707	2333	5535	18232	36477	95689	235494	755788	3082168

Selected Financial Ratios (Times to 1)

Current Ratio 30	1.9	•	1.3	3.6	2.7	1.4	2.1	2.6	1.9	1.7	1.1	1.1	2.9
Quick Ratio 31	1.2	•	0.8	2.9	1.7	0.9	1.1	1.6	1.3	1.1	0.8	0.8	2.0
Net Sales to Working Capital 32	2.4	•	9.8	1.0	0.7	1.2	0.8	0.9	1.6	3.4	11.4	23.8	1.8
Coverage Ratio 33	2.5	2.0	1.8	2.0	0.5	0.7	0.5	0.4	1.1	1.6	0.4	3.0	3.6
Total Asset Turnover 34	0.1	•	0.5	0.1	0.1	0.1	0.1	0.1	0.1	0.1	0.1	0.1	0.1
Inventory Turnover 35	•	•	•	•	•	•	•	•	•	•	•	•	•
Receivables Turnover 36	•	•	•	•	•	•	•	•	•	•	•	•	•
Total Liabilities to Net Worth 37	0.8	•	2.4	1.4	2.0	1.9	1.8	0.9	0.9	0.7	0.5	0.5	0.8
Current Assets to Working Capital 38	2.1	•	4.8	1.4	1.6	3.5	1.9	1.6	2.1	2.4	8.6	13.1	1.5
Current Liabilities to Working Capital 39	1.1	•	3.8	0.4	0.6	2.5	0.9	0.6	1.1	1.4	7.6	12.1	0.5
Working Capital to Net Sales 40	0.4	•	0.1	1.0	1.4	0.8	1.3	1.1	0.6	0.3	0.1	0.0	0.6
Inventory to Working Capital 41	0.0	•	•	0.0	0.0	•	0.0	0.0	0.0	0.0	0.1	0.0	•
Total Receipts to Cash Flow 42	2.4	5.0	2.4	3.3	3.8	3.2	2.6	3.7	2.5	2.9	4.0	2.0	2.2
Cost of Goods to Cash Flow 43	0.0	0.0	•	•	0.1	•	0.0	0.0	0.0	0.0	0.1	0.0	0.0
Cash Flow to Total Debt 44	0.1	•	0.3	0.1	0.0	0.0	0.1	0.0	0.0	0.1	0.1	0.1	0.1

Selected Financial Factors (in Percentages)

Debt Ratio 45	43.2	•	70.8	57.6	66.2	66.0	64.8	47.0	46.7	40.5	35.0	31.8	43.7
Return on Total Assets 46	3.9	•	2.1	3.2	0.7	1.3	0.9	0.7	1.4	3.6	0.5	4.1	5.4
Return on Equity Before Income Taxes 47	4.1	•	3.1	3.6	•	•	•	•	0.2	2.4	•	4.0	6.9
Return on Equity After Income Taxes 48	3.9	•	1.6	2.5	•	•	•	•	•	2.0	•	3.9	6.9
Profit Margin (Before Income Tax) 49	22.8	11.8	1.7	13.5	•	•	•	•	0.9	10.4	•	29.1	45.1
Profit Margin (After Income Tax) 50	21.6	3.0	0.9	9.3	•	•	•	•	•	8.7	•	29.0	45.1

Table II

Corporations with Net Income

LESSORS OF MINIWAREHOUSES, SELF-STORAGE, OTHER REAL ESTATE

MONEY AMOUNTS AND SIZE OF ASSETS IN THOUSANDS OF DOLLARS

Item Description for Accounting Period 7/08 Through 6/09	Total	Zero Assets	Under 500	500 to 1,000	1,000 to 5,000	5,000 to 10,000	10,000 to 25,000	25,000 to 50,000	50,000 to 100,000	100,000 to 250,000	250,000 to 500,000	500,000 to 2,500,000	2,500,000 and over
Number of Enterprises **1**	23151	3738	13534	2109	2488	597	322	93	66	74	39	61	30
Revenues ($ in Thousands)													
Net Sales **2**	34646111	1298262	2742563	559919	1165587	595693	1048681	544426	899650	2421821	1533232	7348053	14448222
Interest **3**	2458182	87408	9354	12629	47163	16590	51191	41732	31817	72942	69698	565473	1452187
Rents **4**	14401927	191194	7169	0	6821	7534	154575	84723	287400	729340	579546	4741318	7612308
Royalties **5**	77956	88	748	39	35234	3908	11454	10932	14316	1237	0	0	0
Other Portfolio Income **6**	4995523	514021	151099	52698	158110	83762	142461	77868	267553	777482	415847	592708	1761908
Other Receipts **7**	12712523	505551	2574193	494553	918259	483899	689000	329171	298564	840820	468141	1448554	3661819
Total Receipts **8**	34646111	1298262	2742563	559919	1165587	595693	1048681	544426	899650	2421821	1533232	7348053	14448222
Average Total Receipts **9**	1497	347	203	265	468	998	3257	5854	13631	32727	39314	120460	482941
Operating Costs/Operating Income (%)													
Cost of Operations **10**	0.1	•	•	•	0.2	•	0.6	0.0	0.0	0.4	0.6	•	•
Salaries and Wages **11**	4.3	1.7	18.1	6.7	8.8	2.9	10.8	6.1	2.2	4.9	5.5	1.8	2.2
Taxes Paid **12**	4.8	4.8	5.3	8.5	6.0	6.5	6.2	5.1	3.5	3.2	2.8	3.9	5.3
Interest Paid **13**	11.1	3.3	1.3	9.4	5.5	18.3	8.0	6.9	4.0	8.2	8.0	10.6	15.8
Depreciation **14**	8.2	7.5	2.4	4.3	5.9	6.4	6.2	4.7	4.3	5.8	4.7	9.2	10.4
Amortization and Depletion **15**	0.9	2.6	0.0	0.1	0.7	0.4	0.7	0.8	1.0	0.6	0.8	1.3	0.9
Pensions and Other Deferred Comp. **16**	0.2	0.0	2.2	0.0	0.0	0.5	0.2	0.8	0.1	0.2	0.2	•	•
Employee Benefits **17**	0.3	0.0	1.6	3.1	0.3	0.3	0.8	0.8	2.2	0.2	0.3	•	•
Advertising **18**	0.6	0.6	3.5	0.7	0.2	0.4	0.6	0.2	0.2	0.4	0.1	•	0.4
Other Expenses **19**	22.8	16.3	34.5	19.8	26.5	29.5	30.0	19.5	31.7	35.2	28.5	26.3	15.3
Officers' Compensation **20**	1.7	1.1	9.5	6.3	1.6	5.1	4.5	9.9	1.5	0.4	0.4	0.2	0.7
Operating Margin **21**	44.9	62.1	21.5	41.0	44.3	29.6	31.4	45.4	49.3	40.6	48.1	46.6	48.9
Operating Margin Before Officers' Comp. **22**	46.7	63.2	31.0	47.3	45.9	34.7	35.9	55.2	50.8	41.0	48.5	46.8	49.6

Selected Average Balance Sheet ($ in Thousands)

Net Receivables 23	208	0	10	39	132	149	844	1009	2211	4638	6269	27514	46587
Inventories 24	•	•	•	•	•	•	•	•	•	•	•	•	•
Net Property, Plant and Equipment 25	5790	0	77	295	1002	3324	6068	8760	19481	53723	98115	557292	2735046
Total Assets 26	12491	0	160	662	2274	6899	15852	36114	67704	161376	366170	1197439	5454953
Notes and Loans Payable 27	3708	0	51	351	816	3559	5633	7390	11968	39467	80075	242195	1871676
All Other Liabilities 28	681	0	18	96	217	502	3083	3337	7346	12352	16847	55158	258704
Net Worth 29	8102	0	91	215	1241	2837	7136	25387	48391	109557	269247	900087	3324573

Selected Financial Ratios (Times to 1)

Current Ratio 30	2.3	•	2.3	3.9	3.6	1.4	2.3	4.9	2.1	2.2	1.8	1.3	3.0
Quick Ratio 31	1.7	•	1.6	3.1	2.7	0.8	1.5	3.3	1.7	1.7	1.6	1.1	2.0
Net Sales to Working Capital 32	2.5	•	6.0	2.3	1.1	3.3	1.3	1.1	2.5	3.5	4.8	10.1	1.7
Coverage Ratio 33	5.0	18.9	17.8	5.4	9.0	2.6	4.9	7.5	13.3	6.0	7.0	5.4	4.1
Total Asset Turnover 34	0.1	•	1.3	0.4	0.2	0.1	0.2	0.2	0.2	0.2	0.1	0.1	0.1
Inventory Turnover 35	•	•	•	•	•	•	•	•	•	•	•	•	•
Receivables Turnover 36	•	•	•	•	•	•	•	•	•	•	•	•	•
Total Liabilities to Net Worth 37	0.5	•	0.8	2.1	0.8	1.4	1.2	0.4	0.4	0.5	0.4	0.3	0.6
Current Assets to Working Capital 38	1.8	•	1.8	1.3	1.4	3.6	1.8	1.3	1.9	1.9	2.2	4.9	1.5
Current Liabilities to Working Capital 39	0.8	•	0.8	0.3	0.4	2.6	0.8	0.3	0.9	0.9	1.2	3.9	0.5
Working Capital to Net Sales 40	0.4	•	0.2	0.4	0.9	0.3	0.7	1.0	0.4	0.3	0.2	0.1	0.6
Inventory to Working Capital 41	0.0	•	•	0.0	0.0	•	0.0	•	0.0	0.0	0.0	0.0	•
Total Receipts to Cash Flow 42	2.0	2.2	2.5	2.3	1.8	2.3	1.9	2.0	2.0	2.5	2.1	1.8	2.0
Cost of Goods to Cash Flow 43	0.0	•	•	•	0.0	•	0.0	0.0	0.0	0.0	0.0	•	•
Cash Flow to Total Debt 44	0.2	•	1.2	0.3	0.2	0.1	0.2	0.3	0.3	0.3	0.2	0.2	0.1

Selected Financial Factors (in Percentages)

Debt Ratio 45	35.1	•	43.3	67.6	45.4	58.9	55.0	29.7	28.5	32.1	26.5	24.8	39.1
Return on Total Assets 46	6.7	•	28.7	20.2	10.2	6.8	8.0	8.3	10.7	10.0	6.0	5.8	5.7
Return on Equity Before Income Taxes 47	8.3	•	47.8	50.7	16.7	10.2	14.2	10.3	13.9	12.2	7.0	6.2	7.1
Return on Equity After Income Taxes 48	8.0	•	45.3	44.9	14.4	7.6	12.1	9.3	12.4	11.5	6.8	6.2	7.1
Profit Margin (Before Income Tax) 49	44.8	59.7	21.4	41.0	44.2	29.0	31.1	44.6	49.2	40.9	48.0	46.6	48.9
Profit Margin (After Income Tax) 50	43.4	50.4	20.3	36.3	38.2	21.6	26.6	40.1	44.0	38.5	46.6	46.4	48.9

Table I

Corporations with and without Net Income

OFFICES OF REAL ESTATE AGENTS AND BROKERS

MONEY AMOUNTS AND SIZE OF ASSETS IN THOUSANDS OF DOLLARS

Item Description for Accounting Period 7/08 Through 6/09	Total	Zero Assets	Under 500	500 to 1,000	1,000 to 5,000	5,000 to 10,000	10,000 to 25,000	25,000 to 50,000	50,000 to 100,000	100,000 to 250,000	250,000 to 500,000	500,000 to 2,500,000	2,500,000 and over
Number of Enterprises 1	127192	31751	89840	2939	2184	271	135	28	20	11	3	6	3
Revenues ($ in Thousands)													
Net Sales 2	47093463	2386124	20969071	4196644	3943229	476959	1899263	499312	378840	380696	1949002	1564754	8449570
Interest 3	312009	1217	21506	4666	22187	12546	3897	5229	7238	19018	7075	61960	145470
Rents 4	365287	13388	22993	14461	30694	29788	5836	762	36015	24509	4533	27588	154720
Royalties 5	609374	0	6	0	1791	6	2078	304	0	0	963	14283	589943
Other Portfolio Income 6	206117	1370	57036	2836	15383	8108	16587	3753	15963	64264	2885	1660	16271
Other Receipts 7	45600676	2370149	20867530	4174681	3873174	426511	1870865	489264	319624	272905	1933546	1459263	7543166
Total Receipts 8	47093463	2386124	20969071	4196644	3943229	476959	1899263	499312	378840	380696	1949002	1564754	8449570
Average Total Receipts 9	370	75	233	1428	1806	1760	14069	17833	18942	34609	649667	260792	2816523
Operating Costs/Operating Income (%)													
Cost of Operations 10	5.9	6.5	0.0	•	•	1.1	1.5	•	•	•	•	3.3	29.9
Salaries and Wages 11	38.0	30.4	38.7	36.3	46.9	39.5	56.4	37.6	49.0	27.0	6.0	56.4	34.9
Taxes Paid 12	2.4	2.4	2.0	2.0	1.8	5.7	2.7	2.3	7.7	4.4	0.8	3.8	3.1
Interest Paid 13	3.2	1.4	0.8	0.8	1.9	12.9	2.5	5.3	8.0	10.0	3.3	4.2	10.2
Depreciation 14	1.7	1.4	1.1	2.0	2.6	3.7	3.1	2.5	6.3	4.1	0.9	3.5	1.9
Amortization and Depletion 15	0.8	0.4	0.1	0.4	0.2	0.2	0.3	0.3	4.7	0.5	1.7	0.0	3.1
Pensions and Other Deferred Comp. 16	0.5	0.1	0.6	1.8	0.3	0.7	0.1	0.0	0.9	0.1	0.0	0.2	0.3
Employee Benefits 17	1.2	0.6	0.8	1.1	0.9	1.3	1.1	2.7	4.7	1.2	0.4	3.1	2.3
Advertising 18	4.5	4.0	4.7	3.3	10.4	1.4	4.6	16.4	12.2	2.1	0.8	1.7	2.6
Other Expenses 19	33.8	38.9	33.9	38.1	33.5	40.1	29.0	29.1	50.4	35.9	86.5	31.2	18.8
Officers' Compensation 20	7.6	8.5	11.7	13.0	2.5	4.7	4.1	2.5	9.2	7.3	0.4	3.0	0.4
Operating Margin 21	0.3	5.4	5.6	1.0	•	•	•	1.3	•	7.2	•	•	•
Operating Margin Before Officers' Comp. 22	7.9	13.9	17.3	14.0	1.3	•	•	3.8	•	14.6	•	•	•

Selected Average Balance Sheet ($ in Thousands)

	1	2	3	4	5	6	7	8	9	10	11	12
Net Receivables 23	20	•	28	204	172	1634	3372	5773	14499	48700	54846	250853
Inventories 24	•	•	•	•	•	•	•	•	•	•	•	•
Net Property, Plant and Equipment 25	75	16	225	655	1754	5134	5905	16834	44035	21260	170270	931950
Total Assets 26	339	57	755	1928	7168	15106	32573	70470	150633	348151	943153	5627012
Notes and Loans Payable 27	155	33	373	1197	4383	9161	15521	47627	66298	66685	393010	1974293
All Other Liabilities 28	134	14	169	292	1717	3512	8646	7442	35565	101709	272090	3676413
Net Worth 29	50	10	214	439	1067	2433	8407	15402	48770	179757	278052	-23695

Selected Financial Ratios (Times to 1)

	1	2	3	4	5	6	7	8	9	10	11	12
Current Ratio 30	1.2	1.7	1.9	2.1	2.8	1.0	1.3	1.1	1.3	3.3	1.5	0.7
Quick Ratio 31	0.6	1.3	0.8	1.0	1.0	0.5	0.7	0.4	0.5	2.4	0.7	0.4
Net Sales to Working Capital 32	19.8	21.2	11.1	4.4	1.3	5.6	4.9	2.3	4.3	3.5	•	•
Coverage Ratio 33	1.1	7.8	2.2	0.4	0.1	1.2	•	•	1.9	0.7	•	0.3
Total Asset Turnover 34	1.1	4.1	1.9	0.9	0.2	0.5	0.3	0.2	0.2	0.2	0.3	0.5
Inventory Turnover 35	•	•	•	•	•	•	•	•	•	•	•	•
Receivables Turnover 36	•	•	•	•	•	•	•	•	•	•	•	•
Total Liabilities to Net Worth 37	5.8	4.8	2.5	3.4	5.7	2.9	3.6	2.1	5.0	0.9	2.4	•
Current Assets to Working Capital 38	5.8	2.5	2.1	1.9	1.6	4.7	7.7	5.0	4.0	1.4	2.8	•
Current Liabilities to Working Capital 39	4.8	1.5	1.1	0.9	0.6	3.7	6.7	4.0	4.0	0.4	1.8	•
Working Capital to Net Sales 40	0.1	0.0	0.1	0.2	0.8	0.2	0.2	0.4	0.2	0.4	0.3	0.2
Inventory to Working Capital 41	0.2	•	•	•	•	•	0.0	0.6	•	•	1.0	•
Total Receipts to Cash Flow 42	4.0	2.6	3.0	2.9	4.0	5.1	4.8	•	4.5	18.4	7.9	15.3
Cost of Goods to Cash Flow 43	0.2	0.0	•	•	0.1	0.2	•	•	•	•	0.3	4.6
Cash Flow to Total Debt 44	0.3	1.6	0.9	0.3	0.1	0.2	•	0.1	0.2	0.2	0.0	0.0

Selected Financial Factors (in Percentages)

	1	2	3	4	5	6	7	8	9	10	11	12
Debt Ratio 45	85.4	82.8	71.7	77.2	85.1	83.9	74.2	78.1	67.6	48.4	70.5	100.4
Return on Total Assets 46	3.9	26.2	3.4	0.6	0.3	3.6	•	4.0	4.0	4.4	•	1.5
Return on Equity Before Income Taxes 47	2.9	132.9	6.7	•	•	2.7	•	5.1	•	•	•	859.4
Return on Equity After Income Taxes 48	1.6	131.1	6.4	•	•	2.4	•	0.4	•	•	•	882.2
Profit Margin (Before Income Tax) 49	0.4	5.6	1.0	•	•	1.3	•	7.2	•	•	•	•
Profit Margin (After Income Tax) 50	0.2	5.5	1.0	•	•	1.1	•	•	•	•	•	•

319

Table II

Corporations with Net Income

OFFICES OF REAL ESTATE AGENTS AND BROKERS

MONEY AMOUNTS AND SIZE OF ASSETS IN THOUSANDS OF DOLLARS

Item Description for Accounting Period 7/08 Through 6/09	Total	Zero Assets	Under 500	500 to 1,000	1,000 to 5,000	5,000 to 10,000	10,000 to 25,000	25,000 to 50,000	50,000 to 100,000	100,000 to 250,000	250,000 to 500,000	500,000 to 2,500,000	2,500,000 and over
Number of Enterprises 1	64770	16481	45924	1202	1026	72	38	•	7	6	•	•	•
Revenues ($ in Thousands)													
Net Sales 2	23305127	1332554	14563576	2022685	1212825	222893	390344	•	229236	269814	•	•	•
Interest 3	99289	1216	14931	2852	11859	9207	219	•	435	7578	•	•	•
Rents 4	247769	11739	6150	0	5336	22933	0	•	22378	23901	•	•	•
Royalties 5	14295	0	6	0	6	0	0	•	0	0	•	•	•
Other Portfolio Income 6	123767	1370	38190	564	3859	6274	174	•	15401	54681	•	•	•
Other Receipts 7	22820007	1318229	14504299	2019269	1191765	184479	389951	•	191022	183654	•	•	•
Total Receipts 8	23305127	1332554	14563576	2022685	1212825	222893	390344	•	229236	269814	•	•	•
Average Total Receipts 9	360	81	317	1683	1182	3096	10272	•	32748	44969	•	•	•
Operating Costs/Operating Income (%)													
Cost of Operations 10	0.2	1.8	0.0	•	•	•	•	•	•	•	•	•	•
Salaries and Wages 11	33.6	11.2	37.8	40.5	26.7	19.6	43.1	•	26.1	21.0	•	•	•
Taxes Paid 12	2.0	2.9	1.7	2.6	2.2	6.5	2.2	•	4.7	5.4	•	•	•
Interest Paid 13	1.3	1.3	0.6	0.2	1.9	2.4	3.9	•	5.1	6.6	•	•	•
Depreciation 14	1.1	1.4	0.8	0.4	2.1	2.2	0.5	•	5.3	3.5	•	•	•
Amortization and Depletion 15	0.1	•	0.0	0.7	0.2	0.2	0.2	•	0.1	0.5	•	•	•
Pensions and Other Deferred Comp. 16	0.9	•	0.8	3.5	0.2	0.8	0.2	•	0.6	0.2	•	•	•
Employee Benefits 17	1.0	0.6	0.7	2.2	1.1	0.8	0.3	•	4.0	1.5	•	•	•
Advertising 18	4.0	3.1	4.6	2.3	6.4	0.2	0.8	•	11.7	1.0	•	•	•
Other Expenses 19	31.5	40.7	26.8	14.4	35.3	38.5	31.2	•	25.3	22.9	•	•	•
Officers' Compensation 20	10.6	11.4	11.3	25.4	3.8	5.5	6.3	•	4.6	8.5	•	•	•
Operating Margin 21	13.7	25.7	14.8	7.8	20.0	23.2	11.4	•	12.5	28.9	•	•	•
Operating Margin Before Officers' Comp. 22	24.3	37.1	26.1	33.2	23.8	28.7	17.8	•	17.1	37.4	•	•	•

Selected Average Balance Sheet ($ in Thousands)

Net Receivables 23	10	•	•	3	124	300	1661	•	720	8005
Inventories 24	•	0	•	•	•	•	•	•	•	•
Net Property, Plant and Equipment 25	53	0	10	98	574	817	2843	•	25219	42479
Total Assets 26	205	0	58	792	1888	7344	13682	•	73461	143800
Notes and Loans Payable 27	64	0	17	174	927	1567	7399	•	36754	29646
All Other Liabilities 28	57	0	12	179	257	3037	4130	•	11288	51689
Net Worth 29	84	0	29	438	704	2740	2153	•	25419	62465

Selected Financial Ratios (Times to 1)

Current Ratio 30	1.4	•	2.3	1.3	4.1	3.5	1.0	•	1.3	1.2
Quick Ratio 31	0.9	•	1.9	0.6	1.8	3.0	0.4	•	0.1	0.4
Net Sales to Working Capital 32	15.4	•	18.6	28.2	2.5	1.9	•	•	6.1	4.7
Coverage Ratio 33	11.7	20.1	24.8	35.6	11.3	10.4	3.9	•	3.4	5.4
Total Asset Turnover 34	1.8	•	5.4	2.1	0.6	0.4	0.8	•	0.4	0.3
Inventory Turnover 35	•	•	•	•	•	•	•	•	•	•
Receivables Turnover 36	•	•	•	•	•	•	•	•	•	•
Total Liabilities to Net Worth 37	1.4	•	1.0	0.8	1.7	1.7	5.4	•	1.9	1.3
Current Assets to Working Capital 38	3.2	•	1.8	4.6	1.3	1.4	•	•	4.2	6.1
Current Liabilities to Working Capital 39	2.2	•	0.8	3.6	0.3	0.4	•	•	3.2	5.1
Working Capital to Net Sales 40	0.1	•	0.1	0.0	0.4	0.5	•	•	0.2	0.2
Inventory to Working Capital 41	0.0	•	•	•	•	•	•	•	0.1	•
Total Receipts to Cash Flow 42	3.0	1.6	2.7	5.6	2.1	1.8	2.6	•	3.0	3.7
Cost of Goods to Cash Flow 43	0.0	0.0	0.0	•	•	•	•	•	•	•
Cash Flow to Total Debt 44	1.0	•	4.0	0.8	0.5	0.4	0.3	•	0.2	0.1

Selected Financial Factors (in Percentages)

Debt Ratio 45	58.9	•	49.4	44.7	62.7	62.7	84.3	•	65.4	56.6
Return on Total Assets 46	26.3	•	84.1	17.0	13.7	10.6	11.5	•	7.9	11.1
Return on Equity Before Income Taxes 47	58.4	•	159.6	29.9	33.5	25.6	54.3	•	16.1	20.8
Return on Equity After Income Taxes 48	57.0	•	158.4	29.6	32.8	24.0	52.6	•	15.8	14.1
Profit Margin (Before Income Tax) 49	13.7	25.7	14.8	7.8	20.0	22.7	11.4	•	12.5	28.9
Profit Margin (After Income Tax) 50	13.4	25.2	14.7	7.7	19.5	21.3	11.0	•	12.2	19.6

Table I

Corporations with and without Net Income

OTHER REAL ESTATE ACTIVITIES

MONEY AMOUNTS AND SIZE OF ASSETS IN THOUSANDS OF DOLLARS

Item Description for Accounting Period 7/08 Through 6/09	Total	Zero Assets	Under 500	500 to 1,000	1,000 to 5,000	5,000 to 10,000	10,000 to 25,000	25,000 to 50,000	50,000 to 100,000	100,000 to 250,000	250,000 to 500,000	500,000 to 2,500,000	2,500,000 and over
Number of Enterprises **1**	172420	36909	112179	8366	11768	1392	1163	338	171	86	33	11	4
Revenues ($ in Thousands)													
Net Sales **2**	50077645	2191874	19431385	1872308	8161318	2391671	2351125	2459150	1926072	1777346	2248828	1295090	3971478
Interest **3**	1508884	33109	61394	18156	90607	51182	52516	66432	47529	161140	120099	27314	779405
Rents **4**	2064840	319809	77733	168248	156745	117804	188263	120880	183158	263065	226309	119505	123323
Royalties **5**	429842	528	3908	902	0	23144	28217	0	3	6654	0	0	366487
Other Portfolio Income **6**	2694925	343112	95431	17015	161921	89556	94019	130627	200988	107974	57671	304803	1091811
Other Receipts **7**	43379154	1495316	19192919	1667987	7752045	2109985	1988110	2141211	1494394	1238513	1844749	843468	1610452
Total Receipts **8**	50077645	2191874	19431385	1872308	8161318	2391671	2351125	2459150	1926072	1777346	2248828	1295090	3971478
Average Total Receipts **9**	290	59	173	224	694	1718	2022	7276	11264	20667	68146	117735	992870
Operating Costs/Operating Income (%)													
Cost of Operations **10**	1.3	20.8	0.0	•	•	0.8	1.8	1.6	2.9	0.1	0.9	0.1	0.5
Salaries and Wages **11**	30.7	14.9	28.2	23.7	53.4	34.4	28.3	9.5	12.6	27.8	38.8	28.6	27.0
Taxes Paid **12**	4.3	3.7	3.4	5.6	5.8	6.5	5.8	2.8	5.2	5.0	4.0	4.6	2.5
Interest Paid **13**	5.6	5.6	0.6	7.3	4.3	7.2	11.7	7.5	11.2	16.6	11.9	10.8	13.6
Depreciation **14**	2.7	2.5	1.0	2.1	2.7	3.4	4.3	2.1	6.6	7.7	4.8	4.9	3.9
Amortization and Depletion **15**	0.6	0.1	0.1	0.0	0.2	0.4	0.6	2.1	0.7	1.4	2.1	1.1	2.2
Pensions and Other Deferred Comp. **16**	0.8	1.3	1.2	0.0	0.4	0.8	0.9	0.1	0.2	0.2	0.4	2.6	0.5
Employee Benefits **17**	2.2	0.8	1.6	2.8	4.4	2.3	1.7	0.9	1.6	1.5	2.3	1.3	3.5
Advertising **18**	1.3	0.8	1.3	1.4	0.5	0.7	0.7	1.1	1.1	1.0	1.9	2.1	2.7
Other Expenses **19**	43.8	53.1	41.6	58.6	30.3	40.0	45.5	73.9	54.4	55.1	37.1	52.0	44.1
Officers' Compensation **20**	9.3	5.9	16.1	10.7	7.1	4.3	8.0	2.7	2.4	1.9	3.2	4.5	0.9
Operating Margin **21**	•	•	4.8	•	•	•	•	•	1.1	•	•	•	•
Operating Margin Before Officers' Comp. **22**	6.7	•	20.9	•	3.4	•	•	•	3.5	•	•	•	•

Selected Average Balance Sheet ($ in Thousands)

Line Item													
Net Receivables 23	119	0	3	41	155	717	1057	2694	3194	7647	38183	107953	2810430
Inventories 24	•	•	•	•	•	•	•	•	•	•	•	•	•
Net Property, Plant and Equipment 25	240	0	18	266	655	2418	4699	9159	25627	50762	111226	278572	529472
Total Assets 26	876	0	68	722	2000	7210	15076	34384	71369	148651	346345	947449	6966625
Notes and Loans Payable 27	451	0	46	425	1168	3692	8156	16466	37788	83538	199259	426523	2558835
All Other Liabilities 28	202	0	19	194	266	1081	2441	8010	12228	24650	77598	335076	2621288
Net Worth 29	223	0	3	103	566	2438	4478	9908	21353	40463	69488	185850	1786503

Selected Financial Ratios (Times to 1)

Line Item													
Current Ratio 30	1.9	•	1.7	1.4	2.7	2.3	1.7	1.7	1.5	1.6	1.3	1.2	2.5
Quick Ratio 31	1.1	•	1.3	0.7	1.5	1.6	0.8	0.9	0.7	0.9	0.7	0.6	1.6
Net Sales to Working Capital 32	1.8	•	13.2	2.6	1.4	1.6	1.0	1.7	2.1	1.7	3.1	1.7	0.4
Coverage Ratio 33	0.5	•	9.3	•	•	0.8	0.2	0.4	1.1	•	0.4	0.9	0.9
Total Asset Turnover 34	0.3	•	2.5	0.3	0.3	0.2	0.1	0.2	0.2	0.1	0.2	0.1	0.1
Inventory Turnover 35	•	•	•	•	•	•	•	•	•	•	•	•	•
Receivables Turnover 36	•	•	•	•	•	•	•	•	•	•	•	•	•
Total Liabilities to Net Worth 37	2.9	•	20.0	6.0	2.5	2.0	2.4	2.5	2.3	2.7	4.0	4.1	2.9
Current Assets to Working Capital 38	2.1	•	2.4	3.4	1.6	1.8	2.5	2.4	3.0	2.7	4.6	5.3	1.7
Current Liabilities to Working Capital 39	1.1	•	1.4	2.4	0.6	0.8	1.5	1.4	2.0	1.7	3.6	4.3	0.7
Working Capital to Net Sales 40	0.6	•	0.1	0.4	0.7	0.6	1.0	0.6	0.5	0.6	0.3	0.6	2.7
Inventory to Working Capital 41	0.0	•	•	•	•	0.0	0.0	0.0	0.0	0.3	0.0	0.2	•
Total Receipts to Cash Flow 42	3.1	5.9	2.6	2.9	6.9	3.3	3.7	1.6	3.6	4.8	4.5	3.1	2.6
Cost of Goods to Cash Flow 43	0.0	1.2	0.0	•	•	0.0	0.1	0.0	0.1	0.0	0.0	0.0	0.0
Cash Flow to Total Debt 44	0.1	•	1.0	0.1	0.1	0.1	0.1	0.2	0.1	0.0	0.1	0.0	0.1

Selected Financial Factors (in Percentages)

Line Item													
Debt Ratio 45	74.6	•	95.2	85.7	71.7	66.2	70.3	71.2	70.1	72.8	79.9	80.4	74.4
Return on Total Assets 46	1.0	•	13.7	•	•	1.4	0.3	0.7	1.9	•	0.9	•	1.8
Return on Equity Before Income Taxes 47	•	•	256.4	•	•	•	•	•	0.5	•	•	•	•
Return on Equity After Income Taxes 48	•	•	247.4	•	•	•	•	•	•	•	•	•	•
Profit Margin (Before Income Tax) 49	•	•	4.8	•	•	•	•	•	0.9	•	•	•	•
Profit Margin (After Income Tax) 50	•	•	4.6	•	•	•	•	•	•	•	•	•	•

Table II
Corporations with Net Income

OTHER REAL ESTATE ACTIVITIES

MONEY AMOUNTS AND SIZE OF ASSETS IN THOUSANDS OF DOLLARS

Item Description for Accounting Period 7/08 Through 6/09		Total	Zero Assets	Under 500	500 to 1,000	1,000 to 5,000	5,000 to 10,000	10,000 to 25,000	25,000 to 50,000	50,000 to 100,000	100,000 to 250,000	250,000 to 500,000	500,000 to 2,500,000	2,500,000 and over
Number of Enterprises	1	72756	11906	54556	2243	3000	582	286	•	51	27	•	8	0
Revenues ($ in Thousands)														
Net Sales	2	33071619	1267018	13433820	1048844	4992916	1426947	1581065	•	1142180	1215259	•	3697570	0
Interest	3	965952	10994	36731	14818	46662	23941	24010	•	26061	82773	•	605995	0
Rents	4	646123	48139	29786	43076	103799	74378	82057	•	47257	98495	•	34529	0
Royalties	5	418058	0	3908	0	0	23144	21561	•	3	2955	•	366487	0
Other Portfolio Income	6	2336865	310748	87528	14566	79027	69880	86756	•	175757	80244	•	1298823	0
Other Receipts	7	28704621	897137	13275867	976384	4763428	1235604	1366681	•	893102	950792	•	1391736	0
Total Receipts	8	33071619	1267018	13433820	1048844	4992916	1426947	1581065	•	1142180	1215259	•	3697570	0
Average Total Receipts	9	455	106	246	468	1664	2452	5528	•	22396	45010	•	462196	•
Operating Costs/Operating Income (%)														
Cost of Operations	10	0.5	5.1	•	•	•	1.1	2.2	•	3.7	•	•	0.1	•
Salaries and Wages	11	28.1	7.4	25.6	19.0	53.6	28.3	21.2	•	6.9	32.1	•	28.8	•
Taxes Paid	12	3.2	2.4	2.8	3.1	4.7	6.3	4.3	•	3.1	3.8	•	2.4	•
Interest Paid	13	2.9	4.6	0.4	2.3	1.9	3.3	3.6	•	5.2	6.7	•	9.9	•
Depreciation	14	1.5	1.5	0.9	0.8	1.3	2.5	2.7	•	2.9	2.6	•	3.1	•
Amortization and Depletion	15	0.5	0.0	0.1	0.0	0.0	0.4	0.3	•	0.4	0.9	•	1.9	•
Pensions and Other Deferred Comp.	16	0.9	0.1	1.3	0.0	0.5	1.0	0.6	•	0.1	0.2	•	1.4	•
Employee Benefits	17	2.0	0.6	1.1	4.3	5.2	1.6	1.2	•	0.8	1.8	•	2.5	•
Advertising	18	0.9	0.7	1.0	0.1	0.3	0.4	0.4	•	0.4	0.7	•	2.7	•
Other Expenses	19	33.3	26.5	32.5	38.2	17.6	25.1	27.8	•	47.0	33.8	•	42.9	•
Officers' Compensation	20	9.0	3.7	16.8	12.0	4.8	3.3	5.8	•	1.5	1.7	•	1.7	•
Operating Margin	21	17.1	47.3	17.5	20.2	10.0	26.9	29.8	•	28.1	15.8	•	2.7	•
Operating Margin Before Officers' Comp.	22	26.1	51.0	34.3	32.2	14.8	30.2	35.6	•	29.6	17.5	•	4.4	•

Selected Average Balance Sheet ($ in Thousands)

Net Receivables 23	142	0	3	52	150	898	1982	•	2912	17253	899461
Inventories 24	•	•	•	•	•	•	•	•	•	•	•
Net Property, Plant and Equipment 25	135	0	13	169	589	1843	4442	•	18030	33033	209640
Total Assets 26	756	0	68	722	1972	6779	15535	•	72988	149755	2641438
Notes and Loans Payable 27	308	0	18	216	917	2450	5568	•	32342	73559	1108782
All Other Liabilities 28	182	0	16	191	271	795	2337	•	9577	20685	929911
Net Worth 29	266	0	35	314	783	3534	7630	•	31069	55511	602745

Selected Financial Ratios (Times to 1)

Current Ratio 30	2.3	•	2.2	3.0	2.9	2.5	1.9	•	1.8	2.0	2.6
Quick Ratio 31	1.3	•	1.9	2.0	1.8	1.8	1.2	•	1.0	1.2	1.3
Net Sales to Working Capital 32	2.0	11.3	13.2	2.0	2.4	1.8	1.9	•	2.6	1.5	0.4
Coverage Ratio 33	6.8	•	44.0	9.6	6.3	8.9	9.2	•	6.4	3.4	1.3
Total Asset Turnover 34	0.6	•	3.6	0.6	0.8	0.4	0.4	•	0.3	0.3	0.2
Inventory Turnover 35	•	•	•	•	•	•	•	•	•	•	•
Receivables Turnover 36	•	•	•	•	•	•	•	•	•	•	•
Total Liabilities to Net Worth 37	1.8	•	1.0	1.3	1.5	0.9	1.0	•	1.3	1.7	3.4
Current Assets to Working Capital 38	1.8	•	1.9	1.5	1.5	1.7	2.1	•	2.2	2.0	1.6
Current Liabilities to Working Capital 39	0.8	•	0.9	0.5	0.5	0.7	1.1	•	1.2	1.0	0.6
Working Capital to Net Sales 40	0.5	•	0.1	0.5	0.4	0.6	0.5	•	0.4	0.7	2.6
Inventory to Working Capital 41	0.0	•	•	•	0.0	0.0	0.0	•	0.0	0.2	0.0
Total Receipts to Cash Flow 42	2.3	1.8	2.2	1.9	4.3	2.2	2.0	•	2.7	2.7	2.4
Cost of Goods to Cash Flow 43	0.0	0.1	•	•	•	0.0	0.0	•	0.1	0.0	0.0
Cash Flow to Total Debt 44	0.4	•	3.3	0.6	0.3	0.3	0.4	•	0.2	0.2	0.1

Selected Financial Factors (in Percentages)

Debt Ratio 45	64.8	•	49.3	56.5	60.3	47.9	50.9	•	57.4	62.9	77.2
Return on Total Assets 46	12.0	•	64.5	14.6	10.1	10.7	11.8	•	10.1	6.7	2.2
Return on Equity Before Income Taxes 47	29.1	•	124.3	30.0	21.3	18.1	21.4	•	20.1	12.8	2.2
Return on Equity After Income Taxes 48	26.9	•	122.6	28.6	19.9	16.5	19.8	•	17.9	10.4	0.8
Profit Margin (Before Income Tax) 49	17.0	47.3	17.5	20.2	10.0	26.2	29.6	•	27.9	15.7	2.8
Profit Margin (After Income Tax) 50	15.8	43.7	17.3	19.2	9.4	23.8	27.3	•	24.9	12.9	1.0

Table I

Corporations with and without Net Income

AUTOMOTIVE EQUIPMENT RENTAL AND LEASING

MONEY AMOUNTS AND SIZE OF ASSETS IN THOUSANDS OF DOLLARS

Item Description for Accounting Period 7/08 Through 6/09	Total	Zero Assets	Under 500	500 to 1,000	1,000 to 5,000	5,000 to 10,000	10,000 to 25,000	25,000 to 50,000	50,000 to 100,000	100,000 to 250,000	250,000 to 500,000	500,000 to 2,500,000	2,500,000 and over
Number of Enterprises 1	7282	344	4776	1016	580	300	156	51	29	19	0	4	7
Revenues ($ in Thousands)													
Net Sales 2	52912464	7774	1167526	564979	1091619	1611880	1681457	1317141	1189041	1735186	0	2053059	40492801
Interest 3	946524	0	737	2	3051	410	1234	1179	3200	6406	0	20981	909326
Rents 4	172652	0	0	0	1096	0	1695	22	1193	22	0	0	168623
Royalties 5	239386	0	0	0	182	0	0	0	0	0	0	75693	163511
Other Portfolio Income 6	1874271	0	32547	17151	135575	79256	89460	39050	40405	101735	0	81	1339011
Other Receipts 7	49679631	7774	1134242	547826	951715	1532214	1589068	1276890	1144243	1627023	0	1956304	37912330
Total Receipts 8	52912464	7774	1167526	564979	1091619	1611880	1681457	1317141	1189041	1735186	0	2053059	40492801
Average Total Receipts 9	7266	23	244	556	1882	5373	10779	25826	41001	91326	•	513265	5784686
Operating Costs/Operating Income (%)													
Cost of Operations 10	19.0	•	27.8	14.9	14.9	48.0	34.0	53.4	40.8	24.0	•	1.6	16.1
Salaries and Wages 11	12.0	91.7	3.6	11.3	7.1	5.1	7.5	5.9	7.6	6.1	•	4.5	13.8
Taxes Paid 12	2.7	1.5	1.7	3.0	2.2	2.2	2.0	1.5	1.7	2.0	•	0.7	3.0
Interest Paid 13	6.7	•	3.1	6.7	4.9	3.6	5.9	5.7	5.2	6.0	•	7.0	7.1
Depreciation 14	31.2	•	14.2	29.4	25.7	18.4	36.3	31.7	34.7	40.0	•	91.5	28.6
Amortization and Depletion 15	0.2	3.5	0.1	0.8	0.0	0.0	0.1	0.1	0.1	0.1	•	0.2	0.3
Pensions and Other Deferred Comp. 16	0.3	•	0.3	0.4	0.0	0.1	0.3	0.1	0.3	0.2	•	0.0	0.3
Employee Benefits 17	1.6	0.0	0.9	0.5	0.5	0.6	0.5	0.7	0.8	1.0	•	0.3	1.9
Advertising 18	1.4	0.6	0.3	1.0	0.6	0.9	0.9	0.5	0.5	0.3	•	0.2	1.6
Other Expenses 19	27.0	180.9	45.7	22.6	39.2	19.6	15.9	9.4	14.4	25.6	•	9.0	28.9
Officers' Compensation 20	0.7	1.1	4.6	3.9	2.1	2.4	1.6	1.2	1.2	1.3	•	0.3	0.4
Operating Margin 21	•	•	•	5.3	2.8	•	•	•	•	•	•	•	•
Operating Margin Before Officers' Comp. 22	•	•	2.3	9.2	5.0	1.6	•	•	•	•	•	•	•

Selected Average Balance Sheet ($ in Thousands)

Net Receivables 23	1341	0	19	55	76	1067	1335	5498	5247	8173	70273	1168096
Inventories 24	•	•	•	•	•	•	•	•	•	•	•	•
Net Property, Plant and Equipment 25	6325	0	73	457	1320	3645	9601	20125	39041	116855	583604	5025254
Total Assets 26	10722	0	160	744	2069	6716	15923	35838	62856	155770	1188368	8499152
Notes and Loans Payable 27	6091	0	184	328	1658	4151	10862	25559	42193	101354	1007740	4393853
All Other Liabilities 28	3003	0	9	33	88	581	1692	4491	7357	24595	217234	2789055
Net Worth 29	1628	0	-33	383	323	1985	3370	5788	13307	29821	-36606	1316244

Selected Financial Ratios (Times to 1)

Current Ratio 30	0.6	•	1.4	2.9	1.5	4.4	0.7	1.0	1.1	0.5	0.1	0.6
Quick Ratio 31	0.5	•	0.8	2.2	1.1	2.0	0.4	0.6	0.7	0.3	0.1	0.5
Net Sales to Working Capital 32	•	•	19.6	3.8	13.5	2.4	•	65.4	36.0	•	•	•
Coverage Ratio 33	0.6	•	0.2	1.8	1.6	0.8	0.2	•	•	•	•	0.7
Total Asset Turnover 34	0.7	•	1.5	0.7	0.9	0.8	0.7	0.7	0.7	0.6	0.4	0.7
Inventory Turnover 35	•	•	•	•	•	•	•	•	•	•	•	•
Receivables Turnover 36	•	•	•	•	•	•	•	•	•	•	•	•
Total Liabilities to Net Worth 37	5.6	•	•	0.9	5.4	2.4	3.7	5.2	3.7	4.2	•	5.5
Current Assets to Working Capital 38	•	•	3.3	1.5	3.0	1.3	•	30.2	13.4	•	•	•
Current Liabilities to Working Capital 39	•	•	2.3	0.5	2.0	0.3	•	29.2	12.4	•	•	•
Working Capital to Net Sales 40	•	•	0.1	0.3	0.1	0.4	•	0.0	0.0	•	•	•
Inventory to Working Capital 41	•	•	0.3	•	0.1	0.2	•	4.8	1.6	•	•	•
Total Receipts to Cash Flow 42	6.5	•	3.1	5.1	8.2	19.1	18.4	•	321.4	10.5	•	5.5
Cost of Goods to Cash Flow 43	1.2	•	0.9	0.8	1.2	9.2	6.2	•	131.3	2.5	•	0.9
Cash Flow to Total Debt 44	0.1	•	0.4	0.3	0.1	0.1	0.0	0.0	0.0	0.1	•	0.1

Selected Financial Factors (in Percentages)

Debt Ratio 45	84.8	•	120.5	48.5	84.4	70.5	78.8	83.8	78.8	80.9	103.1	84.5
Return on Total Assets 46	2.6	•	1.1	9.0	7.0	2.3	0.6	•	•	•	•	3.4
Return on Equity Before Income Taxes 47	•	•	17.3	7.7	16.5	•	•	•	•	•	206.4	•
Return on Equity After Income Taxes 48	•	•	17.6	7.6	13.9	•	•	•	•	•	222.1	•
Profit Margin (Before Income Tax) 49	•	•	•	5.3	2.8	•	•	•	•	•	•	•
Profit Margin (After Income Tax) 50	•	•	•	5.2	2.4	•	•	•	•	•	•	•

Table II

Corporations with Net Income

AUTOMOTIVE EQUIPMENT RENTAL AND LEASING

MONEY AMOUNTS AND SIZE OF ASSETS IN THOUSANDS OF DOLLARS

Item Description for Accounting Period 7/08 Through 6/09	Total	Zero Assets	Under 500	500 to 1,000	1,000 to 5,000	5,000 to 10,000	10,000 to 25,000	25,000 to 50,000	50,000 to 100,000	100,000 to 250,000	250,000 to 500,000	500,000 to 2,500,000	2,500,000 and over
Number of Enterprises **1**	2884	•	1545	596	505	139	66	•	•	7	0	0	0
Revenues ($ in Thousands)													
Net Sales **2**	7429159	•	591198	367498	942307	969349	562685	•	•	776866	0	0	0
Interest **3**	41433	•	15	2	2969	191	925	•	•	5214	0	0	0
Rents **4**	16196	•	0	0	0	0	1633	•	•	0	0	0	0
Royalties **5**	75876	•	0	0	182	0	0	•	•	0	0	0	0
Other Portfolio Income **6**	688490	•	22140	15959	126572	49192	25254	•	•	38771	0	0	0
Other Receipts **7**	6607164	•	569043	351537	812584	919966	534873	•	•	732881	0	0	0
Total Receipts **8**	7429159	•	591198	367498	942307	969349	562685	•	•	776866	0	0	0
Average Total Receipts **9**	2576	•	383	617	1866	6974	8526	•	•	110981	•	•	•
Operating Costs/Operating Income (%)													
Cost of Operations **10**	22.2	•	1.3	19.2	9.1	57.3	24.6	•	•	36.4	•	•	•
Salaries and Wages **11**	6.8	•	0.2	6.0	7.4	3.3	6.5	•	•	7.4	•	•	•
Taxes Paid **12**	1.8	•	2.0	2.6	1.8	1.4	2.1	•	•	2.4	•	•	•
Interest Paid **13**	5.1	•	1.8	6.5	4.8	2.8	6.9	•	•	3.7	•	•	•
Depreciation **14**	29.7	•	16.1	31.9	22.7	11.2	32.4	•	•	20.4	•	•	•
Amortization and Depletion **15**	0.1	•	•	0.0	0.0	0.0	0.1	•	•	0.1	•	•	•
Pensions and Other Deferred Comp. **16**	0.1	•	0.0	0.7	0.0	0.1	0.6	•	•	0.2	•	•	•
Employee Benefits **17**	0.9	•	0.1	0.3	0.5	0.7	0.5	•	•	1.5	•	•	•
Advertising **18**	0.4	•	0.3	0.6	0.6	0.5	0.8	•	•	0.1	•	•	•
Other Expenses **19**	25.7	•	74.3	21.0	43.0	14.8	16.7	•	•	23.6	•	•	•
Officers' Compensation **20**	1.3	•	0.2	1.7	2.3	2.6	1.8	•	•	1.7	•	•	•
Operating Margin **21**	5.8	•	3.5	9.6	8.0	5.3	7.1	•	•	2.7	•	•	•
Operating Margin Before Officers' Comp. **22**	7.1	•	3.7	11.3	10.2	7.8	8.8	•	•	4.3	•	•	•

Selected Average Balance Sheet ($ in Thousands)

Net Receivables 23	399	7	91	84	1874	1971	9565
Inventories 24	•	•	•	•	•	•	•
Net Property, Plant and Equipment 25	1850	100	435	1254	3179	9042	102384
Total Assets 26	3852	137	796	2070	7040	16043	145522
Notes and Loans Payable 27	2535	90	323	1629	3291	9923	96554
All Other Liabilities 28	523	2	44	91	782	1401	20359
Net Worth 29	794	44	429	350	2968	4719	28609

Selected Financial Ratios (Times to 1)

Current Ratio 30	0.8	1.7	3.0	1.5	6.4	0.9	0.6
Quick Ratio 31	0.7	1.5	2.4	1.1	4.1	0.7	0.4
Net Sales to Working Capital 32	•	61.4	2.7	12.6	2.2	•	1.7
Coverage Ratio 33	2.2	2.9	2.5	2.7	2.9	2.0	•
Total Asset Turnover 34	0.7	2.8	0.8	0.9	1.0	0.5	0.8
Inventory Turnover 35	•	•	•	•	•	•	•
Receivables Turnover 36	•	•	•	•	•	•	•
Total Liabilities to Net Worth 37	3.9	2.1	0.9	4.9	1.4	2.4	4.1
Current Assets to Working Capital 38	•	2.4	1.5	3.1	1.2	1.5	•
Current Liabilities to Working Capital 39	•	1.4	0.5	2.1	0.2	0.5	•
Working Capital to Net Sales 40	•	0.0	0.4	0.1	0.4	0.4	•
Inventory to Working Capital 41	•	0.0	•	0.0	0.2	•	•
Total Receipts to Cash Flow 42	5.0	1.7	4.1	5.8	10.8	5.4	9.0
Cost of Goods to Cash Flow 43	1.1	0.0	0.8	0.5	6.2	1.3	3.3
Cash Flow to Total Debt 44	0.2	2.5	0.4	0.2	0.2	0.1	0.1

Selected Financial Factors (in Percentages)

Debt Ratio 45	79.4	68.0	46.2	83.1	57.8	70.6	80.3
Return on Total Assets 46	7.4	14.8	12.4	11.5	8.0	7.4	4.9
Return on Equity Before Income Taxes 47	19.2	30.3	13.7	42.5	12.4	12.8	10.3
Return on Equity After Income Taxes 48	17.5	29.6	13.6	39.7	11.7	12.3	7.4
Profit Margin (Before Income Tax) 49	5.9	3.5	9.6	8.0	5.3	7.1	2.7
Profit Margin (After Income Tax) 50	5.4	3.4	9.5	7.4	5.0	6.8	1.9

Table I

Corporations with and without Net Income

OTHER CONSUMER GOODS AND GENERAL RENTAL CENTERS

MONEY AMOUNTS AND SIZE OF ASSETS IN THOUSANDS OF DOLLARS

Item Description for Accounting Period 7/08 Through 6/09	Total	Zero Assets	Under 500	500 to 1,000	1,000 to 5,000	5,000 to 10,000	10,000 to 25,000	25,000 to 50,000	50,000 to 100,000	100,000 to 250,000	250,000 to 500,000	500,000 to 2,500,000	2,500,000 and over
Number of Enterprises 1	11162	802	8551	1139	469	129	44	19	0	5	0	5	0
Revenues ($ in Thousands)													
Net Sales 2	21504079	189114	3312391	1506159	1227980	1104460	949803	601370	0	810609	0	11802192	0
Interest 3	30761	83	115	1632	1330	0	348	614	0	2597	0	24041	0
Rents 4	5461	0	0	0	1399	0	0	0	0	3484	0	578	0
Royalties 5	109819	0	0	0	0	0	0	0	0	0	0	109819	0
Other Portfolio Income 6	180648	63408	5981	29656	14576	119	21622	19714	0	5164	0	20410	0
Other Receipts 7	21177390	125623	3306295	1474871	1210675	1104341	927833	581042	0	799364	0	11647344	0
Total Receipts 8	21504079	189114	3312391	1506159	1227980	1104460	949803	601370	0	810609	0	11802192	0
Average Total Receipts 9	1927	236	387	1322	2618	8562	21586	31651	•	162122	•	2360438	•
Operating Costs/Operating Income (%)													
Cost of Operations 10	26.0	36.5	25.6	25.7	26.9	16.3	30.8	29.5	•	27.2	•	26.2	•
Salaries and Wages 11	19.5	9.9	17.5	25.9	17.1	21.0	24.3	17.1	•	16.9	•	19.5	•
Taxes Paid 12	3.6	2.3	5.0	4.1	4.7	3.6	2.5	3.0	•	3.6	•	3.2	•
Interest Paid 13	2.3	0.4	1.5	1.8	3.9	1.8	2.3	2.8	•	6.9	•	2.1	•
Depreciation 14	15.3	14.0	6.9	7.0	14.9	27.6	20.5	16.3	•	11.6	•	17.5	•
Amortization and Depletion 15	1.2	0.1	0.2	0.0	0.4	0.1	0.2	1.0	•	12.9	•	1.1	•
Pensions and Other Deferred Comp. 16	0.1	0.1	0.0	0.1	0.1	0.5	0.1	0.1	•	0.1	•	0.1	•
Employee Benefits 17	1.1	0.3	0.9	0.7	1.2	2.0	0.9	1.6	•	1.1	•	1.1	•
Advertising 18	2.9	2.4	1.8	3.2	2.6	3.3	2.1	4.1	•	0.7	•	3.4	•
Other Expenses 19	25.7	19.2	33.5	23.3	25.1	21.2	17.7	25.9	•	19.2	•	25.5	•
Officers' Compensation 20	2.1	1.5	5.7	6.3	1.5	3.4	1.7	2.0	•	1.5	•	0.5	•
Operating Margin 21	0.1	13.3	1.2	2.0	1.6	•	•	•	•	•	•	•	•
Operating Margin Before Officers' Comp. 22	2.2	14.7	7.0	8.3	3.2	2.5	•	•	•	•	•	0.4	•

Selected Average Balance Sheet ($ in Thousands)

Item	1	2	3	4	5	6	7	8	9	10	11
Net Receivables 23	51	0	3	57	87	461	2842	1129		6613	41016
Inventories 24											
Net Property, Plant and Equipment 25	565	0	62	339	1283	3582	7333	21947		100147	617793
Total Assets 26	1335	0	125	697	1809	5471	14758	35829		205970	1824868
Notes and Loans Payable 27	664	0	83	535	1816	2909	9815	14631		129206	703426
All Other Liabilities 28	377	0	24	98	260	715	2003	4450		36994	663379
Net Worth 29	294	0	18	65	-268	1847	2940	16748		39770	458064

Selected Financial Ratios (Times to 1)

Item	1	2	3	4	5	6	7	8	9	10	11
Current Ratio 30	0.7		1.3	3.6	1.4	2.5	1.7	1.0		0.3	0.4
Quick Ratio 31	0.3		0.6	2.1	0.7	0.9	1.3	0.6		0.2	0.2
Net Sales to Working Capital 32			44.2	5.5	22.2	7.9	10.2				
Coverage Ratio 33	1.1	36.4	1.8	2.1	1.4	0.5				0.8	1.0
Total Asset Turnover 34	1.4		3.1	1.9	1.4	1.6	1.5	0.9		0.8	1.3
Inventory Turnover 35											
Receivables Turnover 36											
Total Liabilities to Net Worth 37	3.5		5.9	9.8		2.0	4.0	1.1		4.2	3.0
Current Assets to Working Capital 38			4.8	3.4	1.4	2.5	1.7	1.5			
Current Liabilities to Working Capital 39			3.8	0.4	2.4	0.7	1.5				
Working Capital to Net Sales 40					0.0	0.2	0.0	0.1		0.3	0.1
Inventory to Working Capital 41			1.8	0.6	1.4	0.5	0.3			1.8	
Total Receipts to Cash Flow 42	6.6	5.1	4.6	6.9	6.2	9.4	9.9	6.2		15.3	6.9
Cost of Goods to Cash Flow 43	1.7	1.9	1.2	1.8	1.7	1.5	3.1	1.8		4.2	1.8
Cash Flow to Total Debt 44	0.3		0.8	0.2	0.2	0.3	0.2	0.3		0.1	0.3

Selected Financial Factors (in Percentages)

Item	1	2	3	4	5	6	7	8	9	10	11
Debt Ratio 45	78.0		85.6	90.7	114.8	66.2	80.1	53.3		80.7	74.9
Return on Total Assets 46	3.5		8.3	7.1	8.0	1.4				4.1	2.6
Return on Equity Before Income Taxes 47	0.9		26.1	40.8							
Return on Equity After Income Taxes 48			24.0	40.6							
Profit Margin (Before Income Tax) 49	0.1	13.3	1.2	2.0	1.6					2.0	1.6
Profit Margin (After Income Tax) 50		13.1	1.1	2.0	1.5					2.0	1.5

OTHER CONSUMER GOODS AND GENERAL RENTAL CENTERS

Table II		
Corporations with Net Income		

MONEY AMOUNTS AND SIZE OF ASSETS IN THOUSANDS OF DOLLARS

Item Description for Accounting Period 7/08 Through 6/09	Total	Zero Assets	Under 500	500 to 1,000	1,000 to 5,000	5,000 to 10,000	10,000 to 25,000	25,000 to 50,000	50,000 to 100,000	100,000 to 250,000	250,000 to 500,000	500,000 to 2,500,000	2,500,000 and over
Number of Enterprises 1	6538	•	4748	514	371	85	10	•	0	0	0	•	0
Revenues ($ in Thousands)													
Net Sales 2	14280129	•	2216884	1351615	820323	573174	282811	•	0	0	0	•	0
Interest 3	25616	•	9	1243	914	0	0	•	0	0	0	•	0
Rents 4	5461	•	0	0	1399	0	0	•	0	0	0	•	0
Royalties 5	63940	•	0	0	0	0	0	•	0	0	0	•	0
Other Portfolio Income 6	114481	•	4377	28331	14575	62	0	•	0	0	0	•	0
Other Receipts 7	14070631	•	2212498	1322041	803435	573112	282811	•	0	0	0	•	0
Total Receipts 8	14280129	•	2216884	1351615	820323	573174	282811	•	0	0	0	•	0
Average Total Receipts 9	2184	•	467	2630	2211	6743	28281	•	•	•	•	•	•
Operating Costs/Operating Income (%)													
Cost of Operations 10	23.8	•	18.8	27.7	14.7	20.0	14.4	•	•	•	•	•	•
Salaries and Wages 11	20.2	•	16.0	27.0	19.4	22.6	41.6	•	•	•	•	•	•
Taxes Paid 12	3.6	•	4.4	3.9	5.3	2.2	2.8	•	•	•	•	•	•
Interest Paid 13	1.9	•	1.5	1.1	5.2	2.4	0.5	•	•	•	•	•	•
Depreciation 14	11.9	•	8.0	5.1	18.6	14.3	4.9	•	•	•	•	•	•
Amortization and Depletion 15	1.2	•	0.0	0.0	0.4	0.0	0.0	•	•	•	•	•	•
Pensions and Other Deferred Comp. 16	0.1	•	0.0	0.0	0.0	0.0	0.0	•	•	•	•	•	•
Employee Benefits 17	1.0	•	0.8	0.7	1.1	2.0	0.2	•	•	•	•	•	•
Advertising 18	3.3	•	1.9	3.4	2.7	3.3	1.4	•	•	•	•	•	•
Other Expenses 19	26.8	•	35.8	21.4	23.6	21.7	23.7	•	•	•	•	•	•
Officers' Compensation 20	2.0	•	5.0	5.2	0.8	4.1	1.3	•	•	•	•	•	•
Operating Margin 21	4.3	•	7.6	4.3	8.1	6.4	9.0	•	•	•	•	•	•
Operating Margin Before Officers' Comp. 22	6.3	•	12.5	9.6	8.9	10.6	10.4	•	•	•	•	•	•

Selected Average Balance Sheet ($ in Thousands)

Net Receivables 23	49	3	104	52	681	2205
Inventories 24	•	•	•	•	•	•
Net Property, Plant and Equipment 25	572	86	336	1213	2963	4856
Total Assets 26	1477	145	699	1632	5399	13170
Notes and Loans Payable 27	714	94	425	2011	2657	780
All Other Liabilities 28	481	27	144	175	366	1343
Net Worth 29	282	25	130	-555	2376	11047

Selected Financial Ratios (Times to 1)

Current Ratio 30	0.6	1.0	2.4	1.8	6.6	3.8
Quick Ratio 31	0.3	0.8	1.3	0.7	2.0	3.4
Net Sales to Working Capital 32	•	256.9	12.9	15.7	3.3	7.5
Coverage Ratio 33	3.3	6.0	4.8	2.6	3.6	20.1
Total Asset Turnover 34	1.5	3.2	3.8	1.4	1.2	2.1
Inventory Turnover 35	•	•	•	•	•	•
Receivables Turnover 36	•	•	•	•	•	•
Total Liabilities to Net Worth 37	4.2	4.8	4.4	•	1.3	0.2
Current Assets to Working Capital 38	•	23.7	1.7	2.3	1.2	1.4
Current Liabilities to Working Capital 39	•	22.7	0.7	1.3	0.2	0.4
Working Capital to Net Sales 40	•	0.0	0.1	0.1	0.3	0.1
Inventory to Working Capital 41	•	4.5	0.7	1.2	0.4	0.0
Total Receipts to Cash Flow 42	4.8	3.3	6.2	4.5	6.0	3.6
Cost of Goods to Cash Flow 43	1.1	0.6	1.7	0.7	1.2	0.5
Cash Flow to Total Debt 44	0.4	1.2	0.7	0.2	0.4	3.7

Selected Financial Factors (in Percentages)

Debt Ratio 45	80.9	82.8	81.4	134.0	56.0	16.1
Return on Total Assets 46	9.1	29.2	20.6	18.0	11.1	20.4
Return on Equity Before Income Taxes 47	33.4	142.0	88.1	•	18.2	23.1
Return on Equity After Income Taxes 48	30.3	139.4	87.8	•	18.2	23.1
Profit Margin (Before Income Tax) 49	4.3	7.6	4.3	8.1	6.4	9.0
Profit Margin (After Income Tax) 50	3.9	7.4	4.3	7.8	6.4	9.0

COMMERCIAL AND INDUSTRIAL MACHINERY AND EQUIPMENT RENTAL

Table I
Corporations with and without Net Income

MONEY AMOUNTS AND SIZE OF ASSETS IN THOUSANDS OF DOLLARS

Item Description for Accounting Period 7/08 Through 6/09	Total	Zero Assets	Under 500	500 to 1,000	1,000 to 5,000	5,000 to 10,000	10,000 to 25,000	25,000 to 50,000	50,000 to 100,000	100,000 to 250,000	250,000 to 500,000	500,000 to 2,500,000	2,500,000 and over
Number of Enterprises 1	26447	3728	15417	2548	3533	600	345	117	59	49	15	30	7
Revenues ($ in Thousands)													
Net Sales 2	50535974	937252	4214965	2073513	5246827	4696256	2875169	2896251	2082540	3562638	1646622	11414738	8889201
Interest 3	1160082	3357	8118	5070	11656	7903	9070	39333	22133	110766	62026	355429	525219
Rents 4	2040146	0	1186	31	21211	0	180	29354	8018	6170	2399	1971597	0
Royalties 5	4515	0	0	2	2756	0	0	0	0	1007	0	750	0
Other Portfolio Income 6	1872042	152072	62967	26197	225942	97430	107035	91032	51089	57762	71472	493561	435486
Other Receipts 7	45459189	781823	4142694	2042213	4985262	4590923	2758884	2736532	2001300	3386933	1510725	8593401	7928496
Total Receipts 8	50535974	937252	4214965	2073513	5246827	4696256	2875169	2896251	2082540	3562638	1646622	11414738	8889201
Average Total Receipts 9	1911	251	273	814	1485	7827	8334	24754	35297	72707	109775	380491	1269886
Operating Costs/Operating Income (%)													
Cost of Operations 10	29.8	28.5	38.7	50.5	26.7	47.3	36.9	44.5	33.6	29.6	39.4	22.8	12.7
Salaries and Wages 11	10.5	6.0	9.5	10.2	12.2	8.5	9.9	9.0	10.2	10.8	7.8	12.0	10.6
Taxes Paid 12	2.0	1.4	2.3	2.1	2.6	2.6	2.0	1.9	2.0	1.4	2.2	1.8	1.5
Interest Paid 13	7.7	6.2	1.4	1.2	3.2	2.0	4.2	4.4	6.4	10.5	8.4	11.7	14.1
Depreciation 14	27.0	26.2	9.6	12.6	20.9	16.9	25.5	23.4	29.3	26.4	26.6	34.4	39.7
Amortization and Depletion 15	0.7	0.2	0.0	0.1	0.2	0.0	0.1	0.8	0.5	1.0	1.4	1.0	1.6
Pensions and Other Deferred Comp. 16	0.6	0.0	0.3	0.1	2.0	0.5	0.2	0.8	0.4	0.2	0.2	0.2	1.0
Employee Benefits 17	1.3	0.6	1.3	1.7	1.1	0.6	1.1	1.3	1.1	1.1	0.8	2.1	1.1
Advertising 18	0.4	0.8	0.4	0.7	0.5	0.3	0.4	0.4	0.4	0.5	0.3	0.4	0.3
Other Expenses 19	20.1	47.6	21.8	19.3	25.9	15.5	19.8	16.0	17.5	21.7	10.9	16.2	23.7
Officers' Compensation 20	2.6	1.8	11.4	2.3	3.2	3.6	2.2	1.8	2.2	3.4	1.4	0.7	0.3
Operating Margin 21	•	•	3.3	•	1.5	2.2	•	•	•	•	0.6	•	•
Operating Margin Before Officers' Comp. 22	•	•	14.7	1.5	4.7	5.8	•	•	•	2.1	•	•	•

Selected Average Balance Sheet ($ in Thousands)

Line Item													
Net Receivables 23	756	•	19	47	170	852	1826	4621	9845	31095	74172	102424	1572213
Inventories 24	•	•	•	•	•	•	•	•	•	•	•	•	•
Net Property, Plant and Equipment 25	2033	0	65	338	1248	3958	7163	15125	30869	54433	156120	567711	2430821
Total Assets 26	4076	0	161	687	2165	7297	15442	34981	69344	153472	339810	1077034	4728452
Notes and Loans Payable 27	2254	0	113	310	1122	3765	7086	17953	37732	83737	175767	545976	2993939
All Other Liabilities 28	982	0	18	117	423	635	2670	5666	10101	26820	84417	328287	1270099
Net Worth 29	840	0	29	260	619	2896	5686	11361	21511	42916	79625	202770	464414

Selected Financial Ratios (Times to 1)

Line Item													
Current Ratio 30	1.6	•	2.2	1.8	1.1	1.6	1.4	1.4	1.9	1.4	2.5	1.0	3.1
Quick Ratio 31	1.3	•	1.8	1.4	0.7	0.9	0.7	0.7	1.1	0.9	1.9	0.7	3.0
Net Sales to Working Capital 32	4.0	•	7.1	8.4	23.7	7.8	5.9	6.9	3.5	4.5	1.6	1.1	1.1
Coverage Ratio 33	0.7	•	3.4	0.1	1.5	2.1	0.4	0.1	0.4	0.4	1.1	0.7	0.5
Total Asset Turnover 34	0.5	•	1.7	1.2	0.7	1.1	0.4	0.7	0.5	0.5	0.3	0.4	0.3
Inventory Turnover 35	•	•	•	•	•	•	•	•	•	•	•	•	•
Receivables Turnover 36	•	•	•	•	•	•	•	•	•	•	•	•	•
Total Liabilities to Net Worth 37	3.8	•	4.5	1.6	2.5	1.5	1.7	2.1	2.2	2.6	3.3	4.3	9.2
Current Assets to Working Capital 38	2.6	•	1.8	2.2	9.7	2.6	2.4	3.6	3.4	2.2	3.4	1.7	1.5
Current Liabilities to Working Capital 39	1.6	•	0.8	1.2	8.7	1.6	1.6	2.6	1.2	1.2	2.4	0.7	0.5
Working Capital to Net Sales 40	0.3	•	0.1	0.1	0.0	0.1	0.2	0.2	0.3	0.2	0.7	0.6	0.9
Inventory to Working Capital 41	0.2	•	0.0	0.3	0.8	0.6	1.0	0.2	0.3	0.4	0.4	0.1	0.0
Total Receipts to Cash Flow 42	11.8	5.0	5.3	8.7	5.6	9.0	16.2	14.2	15.1	18.0	11.1	21.1	41.7
Cost of Goods to Cash Flow 43	3.5	1.4	2.0	4.4	1.5	4.3	6.0	6.3	5.1	5.3	4.4	4.8	5.3
Cash Flow to Total Debt 44	0.1	0.4	0.2	0.2	0.2	0.1	0.1	0.0	0.0	0.0	0.0	0.0	0.0

Selected Financial Factors (in Percentages)

Line Item													
Debt Ratio 45	79.4	•	81.9	62.2	71.4	60.3	63.2	67.5	69.0	72.0	76.6	81.2	90.2
Return on Total Assets 46	2.4	•	8.1	0.2	3.2	4.4	0.9	0.4	1.4	1.7	2.9	3.1	2.0
Return on Equity Before Income Taxes 47	•	•	31.3	3.7	5.9	•	0.4	•	•	•	0.9	•	•
Return on Equity After Income Taxes 48	•	•	29.1	2.4	5.4	•	•	•	•	•	•	•	•
Profit Margin (Before Income Tax) 49	•	•	3.3	1.5	2.2	•	•	•	•	•	0.7	•	•
Profit Margin (After Income Tax) 50	•	•	3.1	1.0	2.0	•	•	•	•	•	•	•	•

Table II
Corporations with Net Income

COMMERCIAL AND INDUSTRIAL MACHINERY AND EQUIPMENT RENTAL

MONEY AMOUNTS AND SIZE OF ASSETS IN THOUSANDS OF DOLLARS

Item Description for Accounting Period 7/08 Through 6/09		Total	Zero Assets	Under 500	500 to 1,000	1,000 to 5,000	5,000 to 10,000	10,000 to 25,000	25,000 to 50,000	50,000 to 100,000	100,000 to 250,000	250,000 to 500,000	500,000 to 2,500,000	2,500,000 and over
Number of Enterprises	1	10329	951	6537	1017	1288	293	126	53	22	21	8	14	0
Revenues ($ in Thousands)														
Net Sales	2	22211011	334976	2340950	681735	2930885	3658720	1435083	1639458	1024180	1735399	802655	5626972	0
Interest	3	338263	395	5811	3025	7237	3450	3351	29396	4635	59277	30740	190948	0
Rents	4	33917	0	0	31	11272	0	18	4986	7505	0	2399	7707	0
Royalties	5	3763	0	0	0	2756	0	0	0	0	1007	0	0	0
Other Portfolio Income	6	1107443	138010	58197	18322	190660	77179	69243	45781	30739	35270	63018	381026	0
Other Receipts	7	20727625	196571	2276942	660357	2718960	3578091	1362471	1559295	981301	1639845	706498	5047291	0
Total Receipts	8	22211011	334976	2340950	681735	2930885	3658720	1435083	1639458	1024180	1735399	802655	5626972	0
Average Total Receipts	9	2150	352	358	670	2276	12487	11390	30933	46554	82638	100332	401927	•
Operating Costs/Operating Income (%)														
Cost of Operations	10	27.9	0.0	21.3	12.0	30.4	46.9	33.4	46.9	38.8	29.6	18.8	12.6	•
Salaries and Wages	11	9.7	8.2	9.5	6.7	10.2	8.5	11.0	7.3	10.4	10.3	10.7	10.7	•
Taxes Paid	12	2.3	0.6	2.5	2.4	2.2	2.6	2.5	2.0	2.3	1.5	2.3	2.5	•
Interest Paid	13	4.9	1.5	1.6	1.8	2.6	1.6	1.9	3.7	3.8	5.5	6.7	11.0	•
Depreciation	14	19.2	28.5	9.9	16.4	14.8	14.3	18.7	18.0	13.4	14.2	31.1	29.7	•
Amortization and Depletion	15	0.4	0.1	0.1	•	0.3	0.0	0.0	0.6	0.1	0.5	1.3	1.0	•
Pensions and Other Deferred Comp.	16	0.3	0.0	0.0	0.3	0.5	0.5	0.2	0.2	0.2	0.3	0.3	0.3	•
Employee Benefits	17	1.2	0.9	0.2	2.0	1.3	0.6	1.3	1.3	1.2	1.3	1.0	1.6	•
Advertising	18	0.4	0.6	0.4	0.1	0.6	0.2	0.4	0.2	0.5	0.7	0.5	0.2	•
Other Expenses	19	18.5	34.8	23.3	23.3	17.5	14.8	15.9	13.0	15.9	22.6	13.1	20.2	•
Officers' Compensation	20	3.7	0.4	14.9	3.1	3.5	3.4	2.1	1.9	2.4	5.1	2.3	0.4	•
Operating Margin	21	11.5	24.4	16.3	32.0	16.2	6.6	12.6	4.9	10.9	8.4	11.8	9.8	•
Operating Margin Before Officers' Comp.	22	15.2	24.8	31.2	35.0	19.7	10.0	14.7	6.8	13.3	13.5	14.1	10.2	•

Selected Average Balance Sheet ($ in Thousands)

	•	•	•	•	•	•	•	•	•	•	•	•
Net Receivables 23	399	0	27	35	157	915	2041	3497	15280	30019	62351	109181
Inventories 24	•	•	•	•	•	•	•	•	•	•	•	•
Net Property, Plant and Equipment 25	1545	•	74	355	1086	4259	6549	11203	28959	50646	179608	565376
Total Assets 26	3326	•	203	686	2052	7681	14075	34909	66924	143889	358792	1174595
Notes and Loans Payable 27	1473	•	95	217	832	3001	4785	15257	31115	59157	127827	575940
All Other Liabilities 28	873	•	12	42	307	923	1731	8041	12576	31198	96961	419637
Net Worth 29	980	•	96	427	913	3757	7559	11611	23233	53534	134004	179018

Selected Financial Ratios (Times to 1)

	•	•	•	•	•	•	•	•	•	•	•	•
Current Ratio 30	1.4	•	•	4.7	3.0	1.5	1.3	1.6	1.2	2.0	1.6	1.2
Quick Ratio 31	1.1	•	•	3.9	2.5	1.0	1.0	1.1	0.5	1.4	1.1	1.0
Net Sales to Working Capital 32	7.2	•	•	4.7	4.4	10.3	20.7	5.1	13.8	3.4	4.3	10.4
Coverage Ratio 33	3.4	17.8	11.2	18.6	7.3	5.0	7.5	2.3	3.9	2.5	2.8	1.9
Total Asset Turnover 34	0.6	•	•	1.8	1.0	1.1	1.6	0.8	0.9	0.7	0.6	0.3
Inventory Turnover 35	•	•	•	•	•	•	•	•	•	•	•	•
Receivables Turnover 36	•	•	•	•	•	•	•	•	•	•	•	•
Total Liabilities to Net Worth 37	2.4	•	•	1.1	0.6	1.2	1.0	0.9	2.0	1.9	1.7	5.6
Current Assets to Working Capital 38	3.2	•	•	1.3	1.5	2.9	4.0	2.6	5.5	2.0	2.7	6.8
Current Liabilities to Working Capital 39	2.2	•	•	0.3	0.5	1.9	3.0	1.6	4.5	1.0	1.7	5.8
Working Capital to Net Sales 40	0.1	•	•	0.2	0.2	0.1	0.0	0.2	0.1	0.3	0.2	0.1
Inventory to Working Capital 41	0.4	•	•	0.0	0.0	0.4	0.3	0.4	2.3	0.3	0.4	0.5
Total Receipts to Cash Flow 42	4.7	2.1	3.1	2.3	3.8	6.8	5.0	7.4	5.2	5.3	4.5	5.4
Cost of Goods to Cash Flow 43	1.3	0.0	0.7	0.3	1.2	3.2	1.7	3.5	2.0	1.6	0.9	0.7
Cash Flow to Total Debt 44	0.2	•	•	1.1	1.1	0.5	0.5	0.4	0.2	0.2	0.2	0.1

Selected Financial Factors (in Percentages)

	•	•	•	•	•	•	•	•	•	•	•	•
Debt Ratio 45	70.5	•	52.8	37.7	55.5	51.1	46.3	66.7	65.3	62.8	62.7	84.8
Return on Total Assets 46	10.6	•	31.5	33.0	20.8	13.4	11.7	7.6	10.2	8.0	5.2	7.1
Return on Equity Before Income Taxes 47	25.3	•	60.9	50.1	40.4	21.9	18.9	13.0	21.9	13.0	8.9	22.0
Return on Equity After Income Taxes 48	22.4	•	59.3	47.9	38.0	17.6	21.2	10.6	18.7	11.5	6.1	16.1
Profit Margin (Before Income Tax) 49	11.5	24.4	16.3	31.9	16.2	6.6	12.6	4.9	10.9	8.4	11.9	9.8
Profit Margin (After Income Tax) 50	10.2	23.0	15.9	30.6	15.2	6.4	11.7	4.0	9.3	7.4	8.2	7.2

Table I

Corporations with and without Net Income

LESSORS OF NONFINAN. INTANGIBLE ASSETS (EX. COPYRIGHTED WORKS)

MONEY AMOUNTS AND SIZE OF ASSETS IN THOUSANDS OF DOLLARS

Item Description for Accounting Period 7/08 Through 6/09	Total	Zero Assets	Under 500	500 to 1,000	1,000 to 5,000	5,000 to 10,000	10,000 to 25,000	25,000 to 50,000	50,000 to 100,000	100,000 to 250,000	250,000 to 500,000	500,000 to 2,500,000	2,500,000 and over
Number of Enterprises 1	2184	6	1634	445	19	32	13	11	7	9	0	8	0
Revenues ($ in Thousands)													
Net Sales 2	5563629	147765	222022	377536	72900	169686	184918	337350	164202	754863	0	3132387	0
Interest 3	227159	4726	0	36	565	3634	1121	2479	2481	18370	0	193746	0
Rents 4	5997	0	0	0	0	0	0	1351	105	4359	0	182	0
Royalties 5	1967503	10665	43205	0	0	71296	40435	310	15486	397097	0	1389009	0
Other Portfolio Income 6	60478	0	0	1874	0	1559	978	0	1950	1809	0	52307	0
Other Receipts 7	3302492	132374	178817	375626	72335	93197	142384	333210	144180	333228	0	1497143	0
Total Receipts 8	5563629	147765	222022	377536	72900	169686	184918	337350	164202	754863	0	3132387	0
Average Total Receipts 9	2547	24628	136	848	3837	5303	14224	30668	23457	83874	•	391548	•
Operating Costs/Operating Income (%)													
Cost of Operations 10	4.4	•	•	4.2	•	0.8	3.0	13.8	10.7	0.1	•	5.1	•
Salaries and Wages 11	15.7	2.4	0.2	16.6	26.4	24.4	18.3	18.7	13.4	14.0	•	16.7	•
Taxes Paid 12	1.9	0.6	0.6	1.8	4.8	2.3	1.8	4.1	3.0	0.8	•	2.0	°
Interest Paid 13	8.8	0.2	0.2	0.2	0.4	0.0	2.1	2.1	2.1	0.7	•	15.0	•
Depreciation 14	3.4	0.4	•	0.2	1.0	2.0	3.5	2.0	0.9	1.8	•	5.0	*
Amortization and Depletion 15	3.8	0.2	0.4	0.6	1.6	1.2	0.9	2.7	1.9	6.7	•	4.6	•
Pensions and Other Deferred Comp. 16	0.6	•	•	•	•	1.4	1.2	0.3	•	2.2	•	0.4	•
Employee Benefits 17	1.4	0.0	•	1.1	3.0	0.7	1.6	0.5	1.1	1.4	•	1.6	•
Advertising 18	1.8	1.3	2.9	6.6	3.3	0.6	6.1	1.1	1.5	0.9	•	1.3	•
Other Expenses 19	36.2	72.5	32.5	41.0	56.1	57.2	47.0	25.6	23.5	38.7	•	33.2	•
Officers' Compensation 20	3.0	0.1	•	4.6	19.8	11.0	4.0	5.7	4.6	1.3	•	2.2	•
Operating Margin 21	18.9	22.1	63.2	23.2	•	•	10.5	23.6	37.3	31.4	•	13.0	•
Operating Margin Before Officers' Comp. 22	21.8	22.2	63.2	27.8	3.3	9.5	14.6	29.3	41.9	32.8	•	15.2	•

Selected Average Balance Sheet ($ in Thousands)

Net Receivables 23	475	0	4	34	2001	423	1965	3463	1484	7875	102498
Inventories 24											
Net Property, Plant and Equipment 25	488	0	21	703	123	329	3059	2863	1795	8810	106795
Total Assets 26	9154	0	63		2896	7544	16582	34800	68636	190222	2061208
Notes and Loans Payable 27	2494	0	160	227	134	306	5870	5495	3467	24086	586644
All Other Liabilities 28	2058	0	2	54	552	1536	2844	6381	10434	38300	485347
Net Worth 29	4602	0	-99	422	2210	5701	7869	22924	54734	127835	989217

Selected Financial Ratios (Times to 1)

Current Ratio 30	1.2		12.8	8.0	4.2	2.1	1.8	1.7	3.6	4.5	1.0
Quick Ratio 31	0.8		4.6	7.4	3.7	1.8	1.1	1.2	0.5	2.5	0.6
Net Sales to Working Capital 32	8.5		4.7	2.7	1.9	3.0	5.0	6.2	2.0	2.2	
Coverage Ratio 33	3.1	136.2	268.7	140.2			6.1	12.4	18.1	46.8	1.8
Total Asset Turnover 34	0.3		2.2	1.2	1.3	0.7	0.9	0.9	0.3	0.4	0.2
Inventory Turnover 35											
Receivables Turnover 36											1.1
Total Liabilities to Net Worth 37	1.0			0.7	0.3	0.3	1.1	0.5	0.3	0.5	
Current Assets to Working Capital 38	6.4		1.1	1.1	1.3	1.9	2.2	2.4	1.4	1.3	
Current Liabilities to Working Capital 39	5.4		0.1	0.1	0.3	0.9	1.2	1.4	0.4	0.3	
Working Capital to Net Sales 40	0.1		0.2	0.4	0.5	0.3	0.2	0.2	0.5	0.5	
Inventory to Working Capital 41	0.1		0.0	0.0	0.0	0.0	0.1	0.0	0.0	0.0	
Total Receipts to Cash Flow 42	2.0	1.1	1.0	1.8	2.7	1.9	1.9	2.2	1.7	1.5	2.4
Cost of Goods to Cash Flow 43	0.1			0.1		0.0	0.1	0.3	0.2	0.0	0.1
Cash Flow to Total Debt 44	0.3		0.8	1.7	2.0	1.5	0.9	1.2	1.0	0.9	0.1

Selected Financial Factors (in Percentages)

Debt Ratio 45	49.7		258.4	40.0	23.7	24.4	52.5	34.1	20.3	32.8	52.0
Return on Total Assets 46	7.6		137.4	28.2			10.7	22.6	13.3	14.1	5.2
Return on Equity Before Income Taxes 47	10.3			46.7			18.8	31.5	15.8	20.5	5.0
Return on Equity After Income Taxes 48	7.7			46.2			18.8	23.6	13.2	16.1	2.9
Profit Margin (Before Income Tax) 49	18.6	22.1	63.2	23.2			10.4	23.6	36.8	31.2	12.6
Profit Margin (After Income Tax) 50	14.0	14.5	63.2	23.0			10.4	17.6	30.8	24.6	7.4

Table II

Corporations with Net Income

LESSORS OF NONFINAN. INTANGIBLE ASSETS (EX. COPYRIGHTED WORKS)

MONEY AMOUNTS AND SIZE OF ASSETS IN THOUSANDS OF DOLLARS

Item Description for Accounting Period 7/08 Through 6/09		Total	Zero Assets	Under 500	500 to 1,000	1,000 to 5,000	5,000 to 10,000	10,000 to 25,000	25,000 to 50,000	50,000 to 100,000	100,000 to 250,000	250,000 to 500,000	500,000 to 2,500,000	2,500,000 and over
Number of Enterprises	1	1105	6	781	264	0	18	8	11	•	5	0	•	0
Revenues ($ in Thousands)														
Net Sales	2	4360195	147765	222022	378555	0	146384	122446	337350	•	543153	0	•	0
Interest	3	74175	4726	0	36	0	2117	0	2479	•	12909	0	•	0
Rents	4	1638	0	0	0	0	0	0	1351	•	0	0	•	0
Royalties	5	1872952	10665	43205	0	0	71296	0	310	•	343997	0	•	0
Other Portfolio Income	6	32408	0	0	1874	0	6	0	0	•	2	0	•	0
Other Receipts	7	2379022	132374	178817	376645	0	72965	122446	333210	•	186245	0	•	0
Total Receipts	8	4360195	147765	222022	378555	0	146384	122446	337350	•	543153	0	•	0
Average Total Receipts	9	3946	24628	284	1434	•	8132	15306	30668	•	108631	•	•	•
Operating Costs/Operating Income (%)														
Cost of Operations	10	4.6	•	•	4.2	•	0.9	0.0	13.8	•	•	•	•	•
Salaries and Wages	11	14.4	2.4	0.2	16.6	•	28.2	20.9	18.7	•	15.5	•	•	•
Taxes Paid	12	1.9	0.6	0.5	1.8	•	2.5	1.9	4.1	•	0.5	•	•	•
Interest Paid	13	6.0	0.2	0.2	0.2	•	0.0	2.4	2.1	•	0.7	•	•	•
Depreciation	14	3.9	0.4	•	0.2	•	2.3	3.0	2.0	•	2.1	•	•	•
Amortization and Depletion	15	2.9	0.2	0.4	0.6	•	0.3	0.4	2.7	•	3.1	•	•	•
Pensions and Other Deferred Comp.	16	0.3	•	•	•	•	1.6	1.5	0.3	•	0.1	•	•	•
Employee Benefits	17	1.2	0.0	•	1.1	•	0.7	1.3	0.5	•	1.7	•	•	•
Advertising	18	1.8	1.3	2.9	6.5	•	0.7	6.5	1.1	•	0.2	•	•	•
Other Expenses	19	31.5	72.5	32.4	40.9	•	41.2	22.4	25.6	•	22.5	•	•	•
Officers' Compensation	20	3.0	0.1	•	4.6	•	11.3	5.4	5.7	•	1.1	•	•	•
Operating Margin	21	28.4	22.1	63.4	23.4	•	10.2	34.4	23.6	•	52.6	•	•	•
Operating Margin Before Officers' Comp.	22	31.4	22.2	63.4	28.0	•	21.5	39.8	29.3	•	53.7	•	•	•

Selected Average Balance Sheet ($ in Thousands)

Net Receivables 23	752	0	8	57	598	1982	3463	7223
Inventories 24	•	•	•	•	•	•	•	•
Net Property, Plant and Equipment 25	836	0	10	7	359	4209	2863	4199
Total Assets 26	9989	0	95	737	6618	19746	34800	226235
Notes and Loans Payable 27	3695	0	334	382	46	9363	5495	10240
All Other Liabilities 28	2230	0	4	88	2106	3334	6381	70932
Net Worth 29	4064	0	-244	266	4466	7049	22924	145063

Selected Financial Ratios (Times to 1)

Current Ratio 30	2.7	•	12.2	8.3	1.3	1.4	1.7	7.9
Quick Ratio 31	2.0	•	4.2	7.7	0.9	0.7	1.2	3.9
Net Sales to Working Capital 32	2.3	•	4.9	2.6	12.1	7.9	6.2	2.1
Coverage Ratio 33	5.7	136.2	269.7	142.0	246.4	15.4	12.4	75.8
Total Asset Turnover 34	0.4	•	3.0	1.9	1.2	0.8	0.9	0.5
Inventory Turnover 35	•	•	•	•	•	•	•	•
Receivables Turnover 36	•	•	•	•	•	•	•	•
Total Liabilities to Net Worth 37	1.5	•	•	1.8	0.5	1.8	0.5	0.6
Current Assets to Working Capital 38	1.6	•	1.1	1.1	4.1	3.4	2.4	1.1
Current Liabilities to Working Capital 39	0.6	•	0.1	0.1	3.1	2.4	1.4	0.1
Working Capital to Net Sales 40	0.4	•	0.2	0.4	0.1	0.1	0.2	0.5
Inventory to Working Capital 41	0.0	•	0.0	0.0	0.0	0.0	0.0	0.0
Total Receipts to Cash Flow 42	1.8	1.1	1.0	1.8	2.1	1.8	2.2	1.4
Cost of Goods to Cash Flow 43	0.1	•	•	0.1	0.0	0.0	0.3	•
Cash Flow to Total Debt 44	0.4	•	0.8	1.7	1.8	0.7	1.2	1.0

Selected Financial Factors (in Percentages)

Debt Ratio 45	59.3	•	356.6	63.9	32.5	64.3	34.1	35.9
Return on Total Assets 46	13.5	•	190.6	45.9	12.6	28.5	22.6	25.6
Return on Equity Before Income Taxes 47	27.3	•	•	126.2	18.6	74.6	31.5	39.4
Return on Equity After Income Taxes 48	21.6	•	•	125.1	12.3	74.6	23.6	32.5
Profit Margin (Before Income Tax) 49	28.1	22.1	63.4	23.4	10.2	34.4	23.6	52.6
Profit Margin (After Income Tax) 50	22.2	14.5	63.4	23.2	6.7	34.4	17.6	43.4

Table I

Corporations with and without Net Income

LEGAL SERVICES

MONEY AMOUNTS AND SIZE OF ASSETS IN THOUSANDS OF DOLLARS

Item Description for Accounting Period 7/08 Through 6/09	Total	Zero Assets	Under 500	500 to 1,000	1,000 to 5,000	5,000 to 10,000	10,000 to 25,000	25,000 to 50,000	50,000 to 100,000	100,000 to 250,000	250,000 to 500,000	500,000 to 2,500,000	2,500,000 and over
Number of Enterprises **1**	112775	19119	87207	3250	2810	206	131	•	16	•	•	•	0
Revenues ($ in Thousands)													
Net Sales **2**	96314187	2142640	45630623	9325793	17308972	4284056	7702214	•	3638824	•	•	•	0
Interest **3**	63916	731	17203	6128	8537	7241	4957	•	9057	•	•	•	0
Rents **4**	67194	0	41498	11910	5257	2196	286	•	875	•	•	•	0
Royalties **5**	3579	0	2393	742	0	0	0	•	426	•	•	•	0
Other Portfolio Income **6**	68645	45	14411	19944	10691	4534	2228	•	862	•	•	•	0
Other Receipts **7**	3190314	181182	1628611	107531	663748	44258	309502	•	54358	•	•	•	0
Total Receipts **8**	99707835	2324598	47334739	9472048	17997205	4342285	8019187	•	3704402	•	•	•	0
Average Total Receipts **9**	884	122	543	2914	6405	21079	61215	•	231525	•	•	•	•
Operating Costs/Operating Income (%)													
Cost of Operations **10**	4.4	2.2	4.0	5.8	4.6	5.6	1.8	•	1.5	•	•	•	•
Salaries and Wages **11**	31.2	11.5	25.0	25.7	32.5	48.6	54.7	•	49.8	•	•	•	•
Taxes Paid **12**	3.5	2.8	3.6	3.3	3.6	3.7	3.4	•	3.1	•	•	•	•
Interest Paid **13**	0.6	0.4	0.4	0.7	0.6	0.6	0.5	•	0.6	•	•	•	•
Depreciation **14**	1.0	0.8	0.7	0.7	1.4	0.9	1.6	•	1.5	•	•	•	•
Amortization and Depletion **15**	0.1	0.0	0.0	0.0	0.1	0.0	0.0	•	0.2	•	•	•	•
Pensions and Other Deferred Comp. **16**	2.0	3.7	1.9	1.7	2.0	1.4	3.7	•	3.0	•	•	•	•
Employee Benefits **17**	2.0	0.9	2.0	2.3	1.8	2.7	2.4	•	2.7	•	•	•	•
Advertising **18**	2.5	5.6	2.4	2.4	4.6	1.0	1.1	•	0.7	•	•	•	•
Other Expenses **19**	26.7	41.8	28.2	22.7	22.4	21.4	21.2	•	34.0	•	•	•	•
Officers' Compensation **20**	20.1	19.9	23.3	30.5	21.2	11.8	11.2	•	6.1	•	•	•	•
Operating Margin **21**	5.9	10.5	8.4	4.1	5.2	2.3	•	•	•	•	•	•	•
Operating Margin Before Officers' Comp. **22**	26.0	30.4	31.7	34.6	26.4	14.1	9.5	•	3.0	•	•	•	•

Selected Average Balance Sheet ($ in Thousands)

Net Receivables 23	14	0	5	14	89	409	1214	6072
Inventories 24	1	0	0	0	3	0	51	3437
Net Property, Plant and Equipment 25	34	0	14	118	324	820	3823	13695
Total Assets 26	209	0	81	692	1920	7314	16234	65805
Notes and Loans Payable 27	84	0	38	333	638	1706	4760	22739
All Other Liabilities 28	89	0	38	334	741	4762	6917	24846
Net Worth 29	36	0	6	24	541	847	4557	18219

Selected Financial Ratios (Times to 1)

Current Ratio 30	1.2	•	1.1	0.9	1.2	1.3	1.2	1.6
Quick Ratio 31	0.8	•	0.8	0.5	0.8	0.9	0.6	0.8
Net Sales to Working Capital 32	46.5	•	188.3	•	27.4	15.4	38.5	13.3
Coverage Ratio 33	17.8	48.7	27.9	9.3	16.8	7.6	5.6	•
Total Asset Turnover 34	4.1	•	6.4	4.1	3.2	2.8	3.6	3.5
Inventory Turnover 35	50.5	•	774.5	•	103.4	5640.9	20.3	1.0
Receivables Turnover 36	69.3	•	150.6	189.6	55.2	77.2	54.5	41.4
Total Liabilities to Net Worth 37	4.8	•	13.1	27.9	2.5	7.6	2.6	2.6
Current Assets to Working Capital 38	6.7	•	16.8	•	5.3	4.3	6.2	2.6
Current Liabilities to Working Capital 39	5.7	•	15.8	•	4.3	3.3	5.2	1.6
Working Capital to Net Sales 40	0.0	•	0.0	•	0.0	0.1	0.0	0.1
Inventory to Working Capital 41	0.0	•	0.0	•	0.0	•	0.1	0.2
Total Receipts to Cash Flow 42	3.4	1.9	3.0	4.3	3.9	5.3	6.0	4.1
Cost of Goods to Cash Flow 43	0.1	0.0	0.1	0.3	0.2	0.3	0.1	0.1
Cash Flow to Total Debt 44	1.5	•	2.3	1.0	1.2	0.6	0.8	1.2

Selected Financial Factors (in Percentages)

Debt Ratio 45	82.8	•	92.9	96.5	71.8	88.4	71.9	72.3
Return on Total Assets 46	40.8	•	80.7	26.3	31.4	12.1	10.7	•
Return on Equity Before Income Taxes 47	223.1	•	1095.2	678.9	104.8	90.4	31.2	•
Return on Equity After Income Taxes 48	217.7	•	1085.5	646.4	104.0	84.4	28.0	•
Profit Margin (Before Income Tax) 49	9.4	19.0	12.1	5.7	9.2	3.7	2.4	•
Profit Margin (After Income Tax) 50	9.2	18.8	12.0	5.4	9.1	3.4	2.2	•

Table II
Corporations with Net Income

LEGAL SERVICES

MONEY AMOUNTS AND SIZE OF ASSETS IN THOUSANDS OF DOLLARS

Item Description for Accounting Period 7/08 Through 6/09	Total	Zero Assets	Under 500	500 to 1,000	1,000 to 5,000	5,000 to 10,000	10,000 to 25,000	25,000 to 50,000	50,000 to 100,000	100,000 to 250,000	250,000 to 500,000	500,000 to 2,500,000	2,500,000 and over
Number of Enterprises **1**	79208	12430	62095	2245	2163	141	96	•	10	•	•	•	0
Revenues ($ in Thousands)													
Net Sales **2**	76342479	1758566	38571461	7608235	11301588	3107283	5661565	•	2516236	•	•	•	0
Interest **3**	36088	18	8676	4995	2663	6181	3630	•	1481	•	•	•	0
Rents **4**	34769	0	17053	10373	1593	24	92	•	461	•	•	•	0
Royalties **5**	445	0	0	0	0	0	0	•	426	•	•	•	0
Other Portfolio Income **6**	60549	0	11747	19598	7137	4534	1890	•	345	•	•	•	0
Other Receipts **7**	2708470	189994	1553033	53029	588256	41086	86354	•	7148	•	•	•	0
Total Receipts **8**	79182800	1948578	40161970	7696230	11901237	3159108	5753531	•	2526097	•	•	•	0
Average Total Receipts **9**	1000	157	647	3428	5502	22405	59933	•	252610	•	•	•	•
Operating Costs/Operating Income (%)													
Cost of Operations **10**	4.7	1.3	4.5	5.7	4.8	7.7	0.9	•	0.8	•	•	•	•
Salaries and Wages **11**	28.5	8.2	24.8	22.7	26.5	46.0	51.1	•	43.5	•	•	•	•
Taxes Paid **12**	3.3	2.4	3.5	3.2	3.2	3.7	3.2	•	2.7	•	•	•	•
Interest Paid **13**	0.5	0.3	0.4	0.4	0.6	0.6	0.5	•	0.3	•	•	•	•
Depreciation **14**	0.9	0.4	0.6	0.7	1.3	0.8	1.4	•	1.2	•	•	•	•
Amortization and Depletion **15**	0.1	•	0.0	0.0	0.0	0.0	0.0	•	0.1	•	•	•	•
Pensions and Other Deferred Comp. **16**	1.9	3.8	1.7	1.7	1.9	1.4	3.7	•	2.8	•	•	•	•
Employee Benefits **17**	1.9	0.8	1.9	1.8	1.4	2.9	2.4	•	2.6	•	•	•	•
Advertising **18**	2.5	6.2	2.0	2.8	6.2	0.8	1.1	•	0.8	•	•	•	•
Other Expenses **19**	25.9	39.0	26.9	21.6	21.3	17.7	20.8	•	32.4	•	•	•	•
Officers' Compensation **20**	19.7	18.5	21.6	32.1	22.2	13.0	10.9	•	8.6	•	•	•	•
Operating Margin **21**	10.2	19.2	12.0	7.4	10.7	5.5	4.0	•	4.1	•	•	•	•
Operating Margin Before Officers' Comp. **22**	29.9	37.7	33.6	39.4	32.9	18.6	14.8	•	12.7	•	•	•	•

Selected Average Balance Sheet ($ in Thousands)

Net Receivables 23	16	0	5	19	65	597	1413	•	3621
Inventories 24	0	0	0	0	4	0	139	•	0
Net Property, Plant and Equipment 25	34	0	14	102	290	880	3527	•	13188
Total Assets 26	232	0	92	713	1864	7159	16387	•	63039
Notes and Loans Payable 27	80	0	29	260	619	1634	4116	•	10575
All Other Liabilities 28	94	0	44	369	628	3775	6724	•	28013
Net Worth 29	58	0	19	84	618	1750	5547	•	24451

Selected Financial Ratios (Times to 1)

Current Ratio 30	1.3	•	1.2	1.0	1.4	1.4	1.4	•	1.9
Quick Ratio 31	0.9	•	1.0	0.6	1.0	1.0	0.8	•	0.7
Net Sales to Working Capital 32	31.2	•	70.6	•	14.6	15.9	20.3	•	12.2
Coverage Ratio 33	28.6	109.2	42.4	20.5	26.5	14.0	11.8	•	14.4
Total Asset Turnover 34	4.2	•	6.8	4.8	2.8	3.1	3.6	•	4.0
Inventory Turnover 35	213.4	•	736.9	•	69.7	5640.9	3.7	•	•
Receivables Turnover 36	69.9	•	154.0	201.8	50.3	60.4	45.9	•	•
Total Liabilities to Net Worth 37	3.0	•	3.8	7.5	2.0	3.1	2.0	•	1.6
Current Assets to Working Capital 38	4.5	•	6.1	•	3.4	3.9	3.6	•	2.2
Current Liabilities to Working Capital 39	3.5	•	5.1	•	2.4	2.9	2.6	•	1.2
Working Capital to Net Sales 40	0.0	•	0.0	•	0.1	0.1	0.0	•	0.1
Inventory to Working Capital 41	0.0	•	0.0	•	0.0	•	0.0	•	•
Total Receipts to Cash Flow 42	2.9	1.6	2.7	4.0	3.0	5.2	4.9	•	3.3
Cost of Goods to Cash Flow 43	0.1	0.0	0.1	0.2	0.1	0.4	0.0	•	0.0
Cash Flow to Total Debt 44	1.9	•	3.1	1.4	1.4	0.8	1.1	•	2.0

Selected Financial Factors (in Percentages)

Debt Ratio 45	75.2	•	79.2	88.2	66.9	75.6	66.1	•	61.2
Return on Total Assets 46	59.9	•	111.9	42.5	46.5	23.9	21.9	•	19.1
Return on Equity Before Income Taxes 47	232.5	•	524.5	341.9	135.0	90.6	59.2	•	45.9
Return on Equity After Income Taxes 48	227.6	•	520.3	328.5	134.1	86.4	55.7	•	44.4
Profit Margin (Before Income Tax) 49	13.9	30.0	16.1	8.5	16.0	7.2	5.6	•	4.5
Profit Margin (After Income Tax) 50	13.6	29.8	16.0	8.2	15.9	6.9	5.2	•	4.3

Table I

Corporations with and without Net Income

ACCOUNTING, TAX PREPARATION, BOOKKEEPING, AND PAYROLL SERVICES

MONEY AMOUNTS AND SIZE OF ASSETS IN THOUSANDS OF DOLLARS

Item Description for Accounting Period 7/08 Through 6/09		Total	Zero Assets	Under 500	500 to 1,000	1,000 to 5,000	5,000 to 10,000	10,000 to 25,000	25,000 to 50,000	50,000 to 100,000	100,000 to 250,000	250,000 to 500,000	500,000 to 2,500,000	2,500,000 and over
Number of Enterprises	1	79729	15336	61754	975	1453	104	70	15	8	8	3	3	0
Revenues ($ in Thousands)														
Net Sales	2	36958334	1174950	16784272	2395256	4313024	2893330	2672532	305561	261471	680004	248875	5229059	0
Interest	3	227453	282	9033	3486	7301	1655	5445	1635	2599	12866	6255	176897	0
Rents	4	19652	0	3481	9175	1767	0	4698	6	0	0	0	525	0
Royalties	5	172852	0	7572	0	0	0	1048	0	0	19344	0	144888	0
Other Portfolio Income	6	210188	18622	171758	97	6079	3123	439	1856	4	3044	0	5165	0
Other Receipts	7	644092	55830	111301	18917	12000	-2321	17328	5949	279	-3000	20574	407236	0
Total Receipts	8	38232571	1249684	17087417	2426931	4340171	2895787	2701490	315007	264353	712258	275704	5963770	0
Average Total Receipts	9	480	81	277	2489	2987	27844	38593	21000	33044	89032	91901	1987923	•
Operating Costs/Operating Income (%)														
Cost of Operations	10	14.2	0.5	5.6	0.3	9.9	73.1	55.5	9.8	52.7	1.0	10.4	1.7	
Salaries and Wages	11	30.5	16.9	31.3	37.4	34.9	7.7	17.4	39.2	21.1	45.3	53.0	40.4	
Taxes Paid	12	3.9	4.9	4.8	3.8	3.1	0.6	1.6	4.5	2.6	1.9	2.9	5.3	
Interest Paid	13	2.0	1.1	0.7	0.7	1.2	0.1	0.4	1.2	3.2	4.9	8.3	9.0	
Depreciation	14	1.4	1.8	0.8	2.1	1.0	0.4	1.4	2.2	1.6	3.0	3.6	3.5	
Amortization and Depletion	15	0.7	1.5	0.4	0.2	0.5	0.1	0.1	0.2	1.0	2.3	5.1	2.3	
Pensions and Other Deferred Comp.	16	1.6	1.0	2.6	1.2	1.0	0.4	0.3	0.9	0.2	0.2	•	1.0	
Employee Benefits	17	1.9	2.3	1.8	3.2	2.3	0.5	1.5	4.1	1.4	2.1	5.2	2.4	
Advertising	18	1.5	1.7	1.1	0.5	1.0	0.3	4.6	0.3	0.9	2.5	0.6	3.0	
Other Expenses	19	23.9	55.3	19.9	22.6	28.4	10.8	11.7	27.5	12.9	32.5	22.0	39.4	
Officers' Compensation	20	14.7	17.0	22.8	23.2	11.6	3.2	6.1	22.9	1.3	1.6	2.4	0.4	
Operating Margin	21	3.4	•	8.3	4.7	5.3	2.6	•	•	1.1	2.7	•	•	
Operating Margin Before Officers' Comp.	22	18.1	12.9	31.1	27.9	16.9	5.8	5.3	10.1	2.4	4.3	•	•	

Selected Average Balance Sheet ($ in Thousands)

	•	•	•	•	•	•	•	•	•	•	•	•
Net Receivables 23	78	0	8	35	216	1183	3414	4680	3184	17292	87735	1503140
Inventories 24	0	0	0	5	1	0	6	49	228	444	0	3111
Net Property, Plant and Equipment 25	25	0	11	257	169	527	2099	875	1738	8851	9076	153520
Total Assets 26	375	54	659	1986	5942	15880	32952	60470	143742	307035		6086177
Notes and Loans Payable 27	129	27	352	574	605	5815	4359	23797	38188	69539		2074086
All Other Liabilities 28	183	11	194	876	1328	7988	28791	27189	67680	78550		3438551
Net Worth 29	63	16	113	536	4009	2076	-197	9484	37874	158946		573539

Selected Financial Ratios (Times to 1)

	•	•	•	•	•	•	•	•	•	•	•	•
Current Ratio 30	1.4	1.7	•	•	1.1	3.2	1.3	1.0	1.3	1.2	2.2	1.5
Quick Ratio 31	1.2	1.5	•	0.5	1.0	2.5	0.7	0.6	0.9	0.6	1.3	1.3
Net Sales to Working Capital 32	9.6	23.5	•	•	25.6	8.5	16.4	•	4.1	7.2	0.9	2.4
Coverage Ratio 33	4.4	15.9	3.0	9.3	6.0	20.3	1.6	•	1.7	2.5	0.7	1.6
Total Asset Turnover 34	1.2	5.0	•	3.7	1.5	4.7	2.4	0.6	0.5	0.6	0.3	0.3
Inventory Turnover 35	236.9	1584.6	•	1.4	348.8	•	3261.7	40.3	75.7	1.8	•	9.4
Receivables Turnover 36	4.4	41.5	•	23.9	21.7	23.7	11.4	6.8	9.0	2.1	1.9	0.8
Total Liabilities to Net Worth 37	5.0	2.4	•	4.8	2.7	0.5	6.6	•	5.4	2.8	0.9	9.6
Current Assets to Working Capital 38	3.3	2.4	•	•	9.9	1.4	4.6	•	3.9	6.0	1.8	2.9
Current Liabilities to Working Capital 39	2.3	1.4	•	•	8.9	0.4	3.6	•	2.9	5.0	0.8	1.9
Working Capital to Net Sales 40	0.1	0.0	•	•	0.0	0.1	0.1	•	0.2	0.1	1.1	0.4
Inventory to Working Capital 41	0.0	0.0	•	•	0.0	•	0.0	•	0.0	0.0	•	0.0
Total Receipts to Cash Flow 42	4.3	4.4	2.5	4.2	3.5	11.9	11.1	7.2	8.2	2.8	6.2	3.0
Cost of Goods to Cash Flow 43	0.6	0.2	0.0	0.0	0.3	8.7	6.2	0.7	4.3	0.0	0.6	0.1
Cash Flow to Total Debt 44	0.3	1.6	•	1.1	0.6	1.2	0.2	0.1	0.1	0.3	0.1	0.1

Selected Financial Factors (in Percentages)

	•	•	•	•	•	•	•	•	•	•	•	•
Debt Ratio 45	83.2	70.2	•	82.9	73.0	32.5	86.9	100.6	84.3	73.7	48.2	90.6
Return on Total Assets 46	10.9	54.1	•	25.3	10.6	13.2	1.5	•	2.9	7.3	1.5	4.2
Return on Equity Before Income Taxes 47	50.2	169.9	•	131.8	32.8	18.7	4.3	1008.3	7.6	16.7	•	17.0
Return on Equity After Income Taxes 48	46.6	166.5	•	129.7	31.5	18.1	2.4	1029.8	5.8	11.1	•	11.1
Profit Margin (Before Income Tax) 49	6.8	10.1	2.2	6.1	5.9	2.7	0.2	•	2.2	7.4	•	5.6
Profit Margin (After Income Tax) 50	6.3	9.9	1.6	6.0	5.7	2.6	0.1	•	1.7	4.9	•	3.7

Table II

Corporations with Net Income

ACCOUNTING, TAX PREPARATION, BOOKKEEPING, AND PAYROLL SERVICES

MONEY AMOUNTS AND SIZE OF ASSETS IN THOUSANDS OF DOLLARS

Item Description for Accounting Period 7/08 Through 6/09		Total	Zero Assets	Under 500	500 to 1,000	1,000 to 5,000	5,000 to 10,000	10,000 to 25,000	25,000 to 50,000	50,000 to 100,000	100,000 to 250,000	250,000 to 500,000	500,000 to 2,500,000	2,500,000 and over
Number of Enterprises	1	58357	8334	47907	804	1186	•	32	•	5	•	0	3	0
Revenues ($ in Thousands)														
Net Sales	2	30010614	810166	14076457	1476738	3936898	•	1857004	•	206555	•	0	5229059	0
Interest	3	211296	99	6775	2641	4362	•	4858	•	1483	•	0	176897	0
Rents	4	14538	0	3480	9175	1180	•	171	•	0	•	0	525	0
Royalties	5	171804	0	7572	0	0	•	0	•	0	•	0	144888	0
Other Portfolio Income	6	197396	18622	162402	46	5313	•	0	•	4	•	0	5165	0
Other Receipts	7	513863	-4366	68619	18916	9258	•	363	•	22	•	0	407236	0
Total Receipts	8	31119511	824521	14325305	1507516	3957011	•	1862396	•	208064	•	0	5963770	0
Average Total Receipts	9	533	99	299	1875	3336	•	58200	•	41613	•	•	1987923	•
Operating Costs/Operating Income (%)														
Cost of Operations	10	14.1	0.5	5.8	0.3	10.8	•	79.6	•	64.8	•	•	1.7	•
Salaries and Wages	11	29.9	15.7	31.7	33.1	33.8	•	3.3	•	12.7	•	•	40.4	•
Taxes Paid	12	4.0	3.1	4.8	3.7	3.1	•	0.5	•	2.2	•	•	5.3	•
Interest Paid	13	2.3	1.3	0.7	1.1	0.9	•	0.3	•	2.5	•	•	9.0	•
Depreciation	14	1.3	1.6	0.8	1.6	0.6	•	0.2	•	1.8	•	•	3.5	•
Amortization and Depletion	15	0.8	1.5	0.4	0.3	0.5	•	0.1	•	0.6	•	•	2.3	•
Pensions and Other Deferred Comp.	16	1.7	1.2	2.7	1.6	1.0	•	0.0	•	0.2	•	•	1.0	•
Employee Benefits	17	1.8	1.9	1.6	3.5	2.2	•	0.9	•	0.9	•	•	2.4	•
Advertising	18	1.7	0.7	1.1	0.7	0.8	•	6.4	•	0.5	•	•	3.0	•
Other Expenses	19	22.2	33.3	17.4	24.0	26.9	•	5.3	•	9.8	•	•	39.4	•
Officers' Compensation	20	13.5	16.5	21.5	20.9	11.9	•	0.5	•	1.6	•	•	0.4	•
Operating Margin	21	6.7	22.8	11.6	9.1	7.6	•	2.9	•	2.3	•	•	•	•
Operating Margin Before Officers' Comp.	22	20.2	39.3	33.2	30.0	19.5	•	3.5	•	3.9	•	•	•	•

Selected Average Balance Sheet ($ in Thousands)

Net Receivables 23	99	0	9	35	240	7224	3490	1503140
Inventories 24	0	0	0	0	1	0	345	2854
Net Property, Plant and Equipment 25	26	0	12	277	105	335	2018	153520
Total Assets 26	457	0	60	656	1942	18778	62432	6086177
Notes and Loans Payable 27	152	0	24	368	524	2678	11547	2074086
All Other Liabilities 28	225	0	11	119	809	12428	38571	3438551
Net Worth 29	79	0	24	169	609	3671	12314	573539

Selected Financial Ratios (Times to 1)

Current Ratio 30	1.5	•	1.8	0.5	1.5	1.4	1.1	1.5
Quick Ratio 31	1.3	•	1.6	0.4	1.4	0.8	1.0	1.3
Net Sales to Working Capital 32	8.0	•	21.7	•	7.3	13.4	18.2	2.4
Coverage Ratio 33	5.5	20.6	19.6	10.8	9.7	13.3	2.2	1.6
Total Asset Turnover 34	1.1	•	4.9	2.8	1.7	3.1	0.7	0.3
Inventory Turnover 35	420.2	•	134961.5	26.6	689.8	•	77.5	10.2
Receivables Turnover 36	8.9	•	44.9	27.0	21.5	8.6	8.3	2.3
Total Liabilities to Net Worth 37	4.8	•	1.5	2.9	2.2	4.1	4.1	9.6
Current Assets to Working Capital 38	2.9	•	2.2	2.2	3.0	3.8	11.5	2.9
Current Liabilities to Working Capital 39	1.9	•	1.2	2.0	2.0	2.8	10.5	1.9
Working Capital to Net Sales 40	0.1	•	0.0	•	0.1	0.1	0.1	0.4
Inventory to Working Capital 41	0.0	•	0.0	•	•	•	0.2	0.0
Total Receipts to Cash Flow 42	3.9	2.4	4.3	3.3	3.4	12.7	9.5	3.0
Cost of Goods to Cash Flow 43	0.6	0.0	0.2	0.0	0.4	10.1	6.2	0.1
Cash Flow to Total Debt 44	0.3	•	2.0	1.1	0.7	0.3	0.1	0.1

Selected Financial Factors (in Percentages)

Debt Ratio 45	82.7	•	59.4	74.3	68.6	80.4	80.3	90.6
Return on Total Assets 46	14.3	•	69.5	34.3	15.5	10.7	3.7	4.2
Return on Equity Before Income Taxes 47	67.3	•	162.3	121.1	44.2	50.6	10.3	17.0
Return on Equity After Income Taxes 48	63.4	•	159.4	119.4	42.9	48.2	8.0	11.1
Profit Margin (Before Income Tax) 49	10.4	24.6	13.4	11.1	8.1	3.2	3.1	5.6
Profit Margin (After Income Tax) 50	9.8	23.7	13.2	11.0	7.9	3.1	2.4	3.7

Table I

Corporations with and without Net Income

ARCHITECTURAL, ENGINEERING, AND RELATED SERVICES

MONEY AMOUNTS AND SIZE OF ASSETS IN THOUSANDS OF DOLLARS

Item Description for Accounting Period 7/08 Through 6/09		Total	Zero Assets	Under 500	500 to 1,000	1,000 to 5,000	5,000 to 10,000	10,000 to 25,000	25,000 to 50,000	50,000 to 100,000	100,000 to 250,000	250,000 to 500,000	500,000 to 2,500,000	2,500,000 and over
Number of Enterprises	1	100557	14811	76288	4192	3943	630	370	135	70	57	25	27	9
Revenues ($ in Thousands)														
Net Sales	2	235552615	1762516	54084246	11932268	24788382	10690961	12172295	8672453	8371957	13379396	13276261	21957651	54464230
Interest	3	693426	17207	34032	5673	18971	18300	22118	12466	17301	38826	52262	202500	255769
Rents	4	240307	0	31024	40	25789	183	1783	9432	4962	19889	11564	15575	120066
Royalties	5	73739	0	0	0	0	15	1731	1519	177	14223	1545	28876	25654
Other Portfolio Income	6	625870	118142	36330	14289	33592	2569	37021	10045	6159	76106	4860	46319	240440
Other Receipts	7	1953073	39597	74158	98413	188935	97282	173804	91182	234680	92352	161040	167039	534589
Total Receipts	8	239139030	1937462	54259790	12050683	25055669	10809310	12408752	8797097	8635236	13618792	13507532	22417960	55640748
Average Total Receipts	9	2378	131	711	2875	6354	17158	33537	65164	123361	238926	540301	830295	6182305
Operating Costs/Operating Income (%)														
Cost of Operations	10	43.2	21.7	13.4	43.0	40.3	32.2	30.8	38.8	56.3	42.4	59.1	39.9	76.1
Salaries and Wages	11	18.5	23.7	23.7	18.2	18.2	25.4	25.8	22.7	17.4	20.7	13.4	16.1	11.6
Taxes Paid	12	2.7	3.4	3.8	2.7	3.4	3.2	3.2	3.2	2.2	2.6	2.0	1.9	1.4
Interest Paid	13	0.8	1.2	0.5	0.8	0.6	0.5	0.5	0.7	0.7	0.8	1.3	2.3	0.8
Depreciation	14	1.6	1.0	1.0	1.9	2.0	2.4	2.1	2.4	1.8	2.0	2.9	1.6	1.0
Amortization and Depletion	15	0.4	0.3	0.0	0.1	0.1	0.1	0.4	0.3	0.2	0.6	1.1	1.0	0.6
Pensions and Other Deferred Comp.	16	1.1	0.8	1.1	0.7	1.6	1.3	1.3	1.4	0.9	1.3	0.9	0.6	1.0
Employee Benefits	17	2.1	1.8	1.8	1.4	2.2	2.5	2.9	2.5	2.5	2.9	2.2	2.2	2.0
Advertising	18	0.3	0.6	0.5	0.7	0.4	0.3	0.4	0.5	0.2	0.2	0.2	0.2	0.1
Other Expenses	19	19.0	36.5	27.9	19.3	19.5	21.7	23.9	21.6	16.0	21.4	11.9	31.6	3.6
Officers' Compensation	20	7.4	17.5	21.2	6.3	7.3	6.0	5.5	3.6	2.8	2.4	1.2	1.1	0.9
Operating Margin	21	3.0	•	5.1	5.1	4.5	4.4	3.1	2.4	•	2.7	3.8	1.5	0.9
Operating Margin Before Officers' Comp.	22	10.3	9.2	26.3	11.3	11.8	10.4	8.7	6.0	1.9	5.1	4.9	2.6	1.8

Selected Average Balance Sheet ($ in Thousands)

Net Receivables 23	309	0	9	206	842	2041	5956	12513	24698	47093	113553	220763	870720
Inventories 24	35	0	0	35	72	376	616	1388	1690	6249	13642	17316	121395
Net Property, Plant and Equipment 25	139	0	23	171	415	1481	2600	5650	7148	21256	41204	80961	258783
Total Assets 26	1193	0	73	747	2262	6885	15746	33974	68926	153197	350412	912405	4516821
Notes and Loans Payable 27	310	0	56	313	599	1715	3384	8932	14233	31808	80616	209831	1018102
All Other Liabilities 28	439	0	17	254	701	2039	4954	14330	28355	54750	136871	387373	1669968
Net Worth 29	444	0	-0	180	962	3131	7408	10712	26338	66638	132924	315200	1828751

Selected Financial Ratios (Times to 1)

Current Ratio 30	1.4	•	1.3	1.4	1.8	2.2	1.9	1.3	1.6	1.6	1.6	1.3	1.3
Quick Ratio 31	1.1	•	1.2	1.0	1.5	1.6	1.4	1.0	1.2	1.2	1.2	1.0	0.8
Net Sales to Working Capital 32	12.7	•	77.4	20.7	9.0	6.8	6.3	11.4	7.3	6.9	7.9	11.1	15.3
Coverage Ratio 33	6.4	2.3	11.7	8.8	10.7	11.8	11.9	6.2	4.3	7.1	5.2	2.7	5.1
Total Asset Turnover 34	2.0	•	9.8	3.8	2.8	2.5	2.1	1.9	1.7	1.5	1.5	0.9	1.3
Inventory Turnover 35	29.2	•	282.5	34.8	35.4	14.6	16.4	17.9	39.8	15.9	23.0	18.7	38.0
Receivables Turnover 36	8.0	•	73.3	15.6	8.8	7.3	5.3	4.9	5.1	5.1	5.3	3.5	8.1
Total Liabilities to Net Worth 37	1.7	•	•	3.1	1.4	1.2	1.1	2.2	1.6	1.3	1.6	1.9	1.5
Current Assets to Working Capital 38	3.2	•	3.9	3.5	2.2	1.9	2.1	3.9	2.8	2.6	2.8	4.5	5.0
Current Liabilities to Working Capital 39	2.2	•	2.9	2.5	1.2	0.9	1.1	2.9	1.8	1.6	1.8	3.5	4.0
Working Capital to Net Sales 40	0.1	•	0.0	0.0	0.1	0.1	0.2	0.1	0.1	0.1	0.1	0.1	0.1
Inventory to Working Capital 41	0.2	•	0.0	0.3	0.1	0.2	0.1	0.3	0.1	0.2	0.2	0.2	0.2
Total Receipts to Cash Flow 42	5.1	3.1	3.5	4.5	4.7	4.3	4.0	4.6	6.8	4.6	7.3	3.1	25.7
Cost of Goods to Cash Flow 43	2.2	0.7	0.5	1.9	1.9	1.4	1.2	1.8	3.8	1.9	4.3	1.2	19.5
Cash Flow to Total Debt 44	0.6	•	2.8	1.1	1.0	1.1	1.0	0.6	0.4	0.6	0.3	0.4	0.1

Selected Financial Factors (in Percentages)

Debt Ratio 45	62.8	•	100.6	75.8	57.5	54.5	53.0	68.5	61.8	56.5	62.1	65.5	59.5
Return on Total Assets 46	10.6	•	57.5	26.0	17.0	15.0	11.6	8.7	5.2	8.4	10.4	5.5	5.4
Return on Equity Before Income Taxes 47	24.1	•	•	95.4	36.3	30.2	22.5	23.1	10.4	16.7	22.2	9.9	10.8
Return on Equity After Income Taxes 48	20.7	•	•	92.4	33.8	26.9	18.7	18.0	8.0	10.9	16.3	7.9	7.8
Profit Margin (Before Income Tax) 49	4.6	1.6	5.4	6.1	5.5	5.6	5.1	3.9	2.3	4.7	5.6	3.8	3.3
Profit Margin (After Income Tax) 50	3.9	0.7	5.3	5.9	5.2	5.0	4.2	3.0	1.8	3.1	4.1	3.1	2.3

Table II
Corporations with Net Income

ARCHITECTURAL, ENGINEERING, AND RELATED SERVICES

MONEY AMOUNTS AND SIZE OF ASSETS IN THOUSANDS OF DOLLARS

Item Description for Accounting Period 7/08 Through 6/09		Total	Zero Assets	Under 500	500 to 1,000	1,000 to 5,000	5,000 to 10,000	10,000 to 25,000	25,000 to 50,000	50,000 to 100,000	100,000 to 250,000	250,000 to 500,000	500,000 to 2,500,000	2,500,000 and over
Number of Enterprises	1	62631	8336	47679	2806	2790	497	284	97	50	46	18	19	9
Revenues ($ in Thousands)														
Net Sales	2	198393685	990840	40643532	9583994	18241814	8604037	9661215	6821394	6967020	12516680	11279411	18619519	54464230
Interest	3	546215	83	28721	3479	15357	16780	18807	7535	7916	33889	46557	111322	255769
Rents	4	219027	0	27335	23	18654	114	1165	5708	4865	14156	11558	15383	120066
Royalties	5	66287	0	0	0	0	15	21	789	138	14223	1545	23902	25654
Other Portfolio Income	6	583162	105645	33203	11220	27378	2018	36203	8863	6043	71982	3474	36694	240440
Other Receipts	7	1972118	36800	116255	96620	171599	86866	170881	80206	221442	121866	157199	177795	534589
Total Receipts	8	201780494	1133368	40849046	9695336	18474802	8709830	9888292	6924495	7207424	12772296	11499744	18984615	55640748
Average Total Receipts	9	3222	136	857	3455	6622	17525	34818	71387	144148	277669	638875	999190	6182305
Operating Costs/Operating Income (%)														
Cost of Operations	10	45.2	12.1	13.7	42.8	34.6	30.8	30.1	41.8	55.4	42.5	62.0	40.0	76.1
Salaries and Wages	11	17.5	13.9	22.6	17.9	20.2	22.9	24.7	20.3	17.6	21.0	11.9	15.0	11.6
Taxes Paid	12	2.5	3.1	3.7	2.4	3.6	3.2	3.2	3.1	2.2	2.7	2.0	1.8	1.4
Interest Paid	13	0.7	1.0	0.5	0.7	0.5	0.5	0.3	0.5	0.4	0.5	0.9	1.4	0.8
Depreciation	14	1.4	0.4	0.9	1.2	2.0	2.4	1.9	2.1	1.4	1.8	2.4	1.7	1.0
Amortization and Depletion	15	0.3	0.1	0.0	0.1	0.1	0.0	0.1	0.1	0.1	0.4	1.0	0.6	0.6
Pensions and Other Deferred Comp.	16	1.0	1.0	1.1	0.9	1.1	1.5	1.3	1.5	1.0	1.4	0.9	0.6	1.0
Employee Benefits	17	2.0	2.5	1.4	1.5	1.9	2.7	2.8	2.2	2.5	2.9	1.7	1.8	2.0
Advertising	18	0.3	0.5	0.4	0.7	0.3	0.3	0.3	0.3	0.1	0.2	0.2	0.2	0.1
Other Expenses	19	17.7	33.3	27.9	16.1	19.3	21.6	24.1	19.4	15.0	20.7	10.3	32.9	3.6
Officers' Compensation	20	6.4	16.6	19.1	6.9	7.7	6.3	5.8	3.8	2.9	2.5	1.2	1.0	0.9
Operating Margin	21	5.0	15.5	8.6	8.9	8.6	7.7	5.5	4.8	1.4	3.6	5.6	3.0	0.9
Operating Margin Before Officers' Comp.	22	11.3	32.0	27.7	15.8	16.3	14.1	11.2	8.7	4.3	6.0	6.8	4.0	1.8

Selected Average Balance Sheet ($ in Thousands)

Net Receivables 23	424	0	9	179	869	2006	6256	12808	27539	52869	126930	276009	870720
Inventories 24	45	0	0	42	69	294	599	1357	1449	6278	16507	20240	94730
Net Property, Plant and Equipment 25	178	0	23	174	433	1607	2435	5578	6974	19934	38011	106832	258783
Total Assets 26	1590	0	79	753	2295	6851	15951	33391	67981	151310	359142	983135	4516821
Notes and Loans Payable 27	355	0	53	325	485	1636	2633	5914	10747	22112	58666	185328	1018102
All Other Liabilities 28	594	0	18	195	588	1915	5044	14299	29469	57680	139131	459676	1669968
Net Worth 29	641	0	7	234	1222	3300	8275	13178	27765	71518	161345	338131	1828751

Selected Financial Ratios (Times to 1)

Current Ratio 30	1.5	•	1.5	1.5	2.3	2.3	2.0	1.5	1.6	1.7	1.5	1.3	1.3
Quick Ratio 31	1.1	•	1.4	1.3	2.0	1.8	1.6	1.2	1.3	1.4	1.2	1.1	0.8
Net Sales to Working Capital 32	11.8	•	58.5	21.9	7.4	6.6	5.9	9.1	7.6	7.0	8.4	9.8	15.3
Coverage Ratio 33	10.8	31.4	20.0	16.0	20.6	19.3	23.8	13.0	12.9	12.3	9.5	4.7	5.1
Total Asset Turnover 34	2.0	•	10.8	4.5	2.8	2.5	2.1	2.1	2.0	1.8	1.7	1.0	1.3
Inventory Turnover 35	32.1	•	445.9	34.8	32.9	18.1	17.1	21.7	53.2	18.4	23.5	19.4	48.6
Receivables Turnover 36	7.9	•	88.5	20.4	8.5	6.9	5.4	4.8	5.2	5.3	•	3.5	•
Total Liabilities to Net Worth 37	1.5	•	9.5	2.2	0.9	1.1	0.9	1.5	1.4	1.1	1.2	1.9	1.5
Current Assets to Working Capital 38	3.1	•	2.9	2.9	1.8	1.7	2.0	2.9	2.6	2.5	2.8	4.0	5.0
Current Liabilities to Working Capital 39	2.1	•	1.9	1.9	0.8	0.7	1.0	1.9	1.6	1.5	1.8	3.0	4.0
Working Capital to Net Sales 40	0.1	•	0.0	0.0	0.1	0.2	0.2	0.1	0.1	0.1	0.1	0.1	0.1
Inventory to Working Capital 41	0.2	•	0.0	0.3	0.1	0.2	0.1	0.1	0.1	0.1	0.2	0.2	0.2
Total Receipts to Cash Flow 42	4.8	1.7	3.1	4.3	3.9	3.7	3.6	4.5	6.1	4.4	7.1	2.8	25.7
Cost of Goods to Cash Flow 43	2.2	0.2	0.4	1.8	1.4	1.1	1.1	1.9	3.4	1.9	4.4	1.1	19.5
Cash Flow to Total Debt 44	0.7	•	3.9	1.5	1.5	1.3	1.2	0.8	0.6	0.8	0.4	0.5	0.1

Selected Financial Factors (in Percentages)

Debt Ratio 45	59.7	•	90.5	69.0	46.7	51.8	48.1	60.5	59.2	52.7	55.1	65.6	59.5
Return on Total Assets 46	14.8	•	104.1	48.7	29.3	24.0	17.4	14.4	10.8	11.5	14.7	6.6	5.4
Return on Equity Before Income Taxes 47	33.3	•	1038.7	147.3	52.4	47.3	32.1	33.8	24.4	22.3	29.2	15.1	10.8
Return on Equity After Income Taxes 48	29.5	•	1026.9	143.7	49.7	43.4	27.6	28.0	21.2	15.7	22.4	12.5	7.8
Profit Margin (Before Income Tax) 49	6.7	29.8	9.1	10.1	9.8	9.0	7.8	6.3	4.9	5.9	7.5	5.2	3.3
Profit Margin (After Income Tax) 50	6.0	28.3	9.0	9.8	9.3	8.3	6.7	5.2	4.2	4.1	5.8	4.3	2.3

Table I

Corporations with and without Net Income

SPECIALIZED DESIGN SERVICES

MONEY AMOUNTS AND SIZE OF ASSETS IN THOUSANDS OF DOLLARS

Item Description for Accounting Period 7/08 Through 6/09	Total	Zero Assets	Under 500	500 to 1,000	1,000 to 5,000	5,000 to 10,000	10,000 to 25,000	25,000 to 50,000	50,000 to 100,000	100,000 to 250,000	250,000 to 500,000	500,000 to 2,500,000	2,500,000 and over
Number of Enterprises **1**	35934	8573	25565	971	733	40	36	•	0	•	0	0	0

Revenues ($ in Thousands)

	Total	Zero Assets	Under 500	500 to 1,000	1,000 to 5,000	5,000 to 10,000	10,000 to 25,000	25,000 to 50,000	50,000 to 100,000	100,000 to 250,000	250,000 to 500,000	500,000 to 2,500,000	2,500,000 and over
Net Sales **2**	17161494	638628	9587531	1254919	2171860	605168	612189	•	•	•	0	0	0
Interest **3**	15303	0	6079	483	2763	2867	354	•	•	•	0	0	0
Rents **4**	3747	1261	2110	0	376	0	0	•	•	•	0	0	0
Royalties **5**	15906	0	645	0	0	0	0	•	•	•	0	0	0
Other Portfolio Income **6**	11899	0	2242	1110	4538	356	0	•	•	•	0	0	0
Other Receipts **7**	131905	7142	71847	22632	-321	10604	3658	•	•	•	0	0	0
Total Receipts **8**	17340254	647031	9670454	1279144	2179216	618995	616201	•	•	•	0	0	0
Average Total Receipts **9**	483	75	378	1317	2973	15475	17117	•	•	•	•	•	•

Operating Costs/Operating Income (%)

	Total	Zero Assets	Under 500	500 to 1,000	1,000 to 5,000	5,000 to 10,000	10,000 to 25,000	25,000 to 50,000	50,000 to 100,000	100,000 to 250,000	250,000 to 500,000	500,000 to 2,500,000	2,500,000 and over
Cost of Operations **10**	43.7	43.7	43.2	48.9	59.8	52.4	62.7	•	•	•	•	•	•
Salaries and Wages **11**	14.8	4.1	12.7	11.3	13.6	14.5	14.0	•	•	•	•	•	•
Taxes Paid **12**	2.2	1.7	2.0	2.6	1.8	3.4	1.6	•	•	•	•	•	•
Interest Paid **13**	0.6	1.3	0.5	0.9	0.2	1.2	0.3	•	•	•	•	•	•
Depreciation **14**	1.2	1.1	0.8	1.1	0.6	2.8	0.6	•	•	•	•	•	•
Amortization and Depletion **15**	0.1	0.1	0.1	0.0	0.1	0.2	0.0	•	•	•	•	•	•
Pensions and Other Deferred Comp. **16**	0.5	•	0.5	1.3	0.2	0.5	0.2	•	•	•	•	•	•
Employee Benefits **17**	1.3	0.1	0.9	0.8	0.4	2.5	1.3	•	•	•	•	•	•
Advertising **18**	0.8	1.8	0.8	0.2	1.3	0.3	0.8	•	•	•	•	•	•
Other Expenses **19**	26.6	48.6	27.9	18.3	16.5	22.8	11.3	•	•	•	•	•	•
Officers' Compensation **20**	7.9	8.9	9.7	13.0	5.4	2.2	3.4	•	•	•	•	•	•
Operating Margin **21**	0.2	•	0.9	1.6	0.2	•	3.9	•	•	•	•	•	•
Operating Margin Before Officers' Comp. **22**	8.2	•	10.6	14.6	5.6	•	7.2	•	•	•	•	•	•

Selected Average Balance Sheet ($ in Thousands)

Net Receivables	23	27	0	7	247	212	1405	2424
Inventories	24	26	0	6	83	643	1420	1858
Net Property, Plant and Equipment	25	23	0	11	66	97	1000	774
Total Assets	26	153	0	56	579	1783	6982	14367
Notes and Loans Payable	27	61	0	48	168	648	1834	1507
All Other Liabilities	28	77	0	21	241	1427	4731	8673
Net Worth	29	16	0	-14	170	-292	417	4187

Selected Financial Ratios (Times to 1)

Current Ratio	30	1.3	•	1.3	2.2	0.9	1.5	1.3
Quick Ratio	31	0.8	•	1.0	1.7	0.3	0.9	0.5
Net Sales to Working Capital	32	21.3	•	41.2	5.8	•	10.4	7.6
Coverage Ratio	33	3.2	•	4.3	4.8	3.3	0.7	17.1
Total Asset Turnover	34	3.1	•	6.7	2.2	1.7	2.2	1.2
Inventory Turnover	35	7.9	•	27.9	7.6	2.8	5.6	5.7
Receivables Turnover	36	11.7	•	36.5	4.5	11.1	5.5	6.1
Total Liabilities to Net Worth	37	8.9	•	•	2.4	•	15.7	2.4
Current Assets to Working Capital	38	4.4	•	3.9	1.9	•	3.2	4.8
Current Liabilities to Working Capital	39	3.4	•	2.9	0.9	•	2.2	3.8
Working Capital to Net Sales	40	0.0	•	0.0	0.2	•	0.1	0.1
Inventory to Working Capital	41	1.1	•	0.6	0.3	•	0.5	1.3
Total Receipts to Cash Flow	42	4.5	3.0	4.3	5.7	8.9	6.7	7.5
Cost of Goods to Cash Flow	43	2.0	1.3	1.8	2.8	5.3	3.5	4.7
Cash Flow to Total Debt	44	0.8	•	1.3	0.6	0.2	0.3	0.2

Selected Financial Factors (in Percentages)

Debt Ratio	45	89.9	•	124.6	70.6	116.4	94.0	70.9
Return on Total Assets	46	5.7	•	15.2	9.8	1.0	1.8	5.7
Return on Equity Before Income Taxes	47	38.8	•	•	26.4	•	•	18.4
Return on Equity After Income Taxes	48	33.1	•	•	26.3	•	•	18.4
Profit Margin (Before Income Tax)	49	1.3	•	1.7	3.5	0.4	•	4.5
Profit Margin (After Income Tax)	50	1.1	•	1.6	3.5	0.2	•	4.5

Table II
Corporations with Net Income

SPECIALIZED DESIGN SERVICES

MONEY AMOUNTS AND SIZE OF ASSETS IN THOUSANDS OF DOLLARS

Item Description for Accounting Period 7/08 Through 6/09	Total	Zero Assets	Under 500	500 to 1,000	1,000 to 5,000	5,000 to 10,000	10,000 to 25,000	25,000 to 50,000	50,000 to 100,000	100,000 to 250,000	250,000 to 500,000	500,000 to 2,500,000	2,500,000 and over
Number of Enterprises **1**	21124	3918	16004	693	448	•	17	•	0	•	0	•	0
Revenues ($ in Thousands)													
Net Sales **2**	11828971	357771	6546288	820023	1220554	•	340129	•	•	•	•	•	•
Interest **3**	7644	0	3210	0	1953	•	354	•	•	•	•	•	•
Rents **4**	2485	0	2110	0	376	•	0	•	•	•	•	•	•
Royalties **5**	15906	0	645	0	0	•	0	•	•	•	•	•	•
Other Portfolio Income **6**	5719	0	0	892	817	•	0	•	•	•	•	•	•
Other Receipts **7**	77674	7142	27818	22199	525	•	-590	•	•	•	•	•	•
Total Receipts **8**	11938399	364913	6580071	843114	1224225	•	339893	•	•	•	•	•	•
Average Total Receipts **9**	565	93	411	1217	2733	•	19994	•	•	•	•	•	•
Operating Costs/Operating Income (%)													
Cost of Operations **10**	37.8	24.6	39.4	54.8	52.6	•	51.7	•	•	•	•	•	•
Salaries and Wages **11**	14.7	3.8	11.1	6.8	13.0	•	18.8	•	•	•	•	•	•
Taxes Paid **12**	2.4	2.5	2.2	1.7	1.6	•	1.9	•	•	•	•	•	•
Interest Paid **13**	0.3	0.0	0.3	0.4	0.1	•	0.1	•	•	•	•	•	•
Depreciation **14**	1.2	1.0	0.6	1.4	0.7	•	0.7	•	•	•	•	•	•
Amortization and Depletion **15**	0.1	0.0	0.1	0.0	0.0	•	0.0	•	•	•	•	•	•
Pensions and Other Deferred Comp. **16**	0.6	•	0.6	1.2	0.2	•	0.3	•	•	•	•	•	•
Employee Benefits **17**	1.4	•	1.0	0.0	0.3	•	2.1	•	•	•	•	•	•
Advertising **18**	0.5	1.1	0.4	0.1	1.8	•	1.1	•	•	•	•	•	•
Other Expenses **19**	24.8	30.0	24.8	15.6	16.9	•	7.8	•	•	•	•	•	•
Officers' Compensation **20**	8.6	15.9	11.0	10.7	6.1	•	4.7	•	•	•	•	•	•
Operating Margin **21**	7.5	21.2	8.6	7.4	6.6	•	10.8	•	•	•	•	•	•
Operating Margin Before Officers' Comp. **22**	16.1	37.0	19.6	18.1	12.7	•	15.5	•	•	•	•	•	•

Selected Average Balance Sheet ($ in Thousands)

Net Receivables 23	26	0	6	180	166	1842
Inventories 24	24	0	6	41	551	870
Net Property, Plant and Equipment 25	27	0	11	74	103	1423
Total Assets 26	156	0	55	542	1458	14304
Notes and Loans Payable 27	36	0	10	166	542	985
All Other Liabilities 28	71	0	19	227	1134	8456
Net Worth 29	50	0	25	148	-218	4864

Selected Financial Ratios (Times to 1)

Current Ratio 30	1.5	•	1.8	2.5	1.1	1.1
Quick Ratio 31	0.9	•	1.5	1.7	0.4	0.6
Net Sales to Working Capital 32	16.9	•	28.0	5.6	23.2	25.6
Coverage Ratio 33	27.6	697.8	36.9	28.1	65.9	135.3
Total Asset Turnover 34	3.6	•	7.5	2.2	1.9	1.4
Inventory Turnover 35	8.8	•	25.8	15.7	2.6	11.9
Receivables Turnover 36	14.3	•	50.1	4.3	11.0	5.0
Total Liabilities to Net Worth 37	2.1	•	1.2	2.6	•	1.9
Current Assets to Working Capital 38	3.0	•	2.3	1.7	10.6	12.5
Current Liabilities to Working Capital 39	2.0	•	1.3	0.7	9.6	11.5
Working Capital to Net Sales 40	0.1	•	0.0	0.2	0.0	0.0
Inventory to Working Capital 41	0.8	•	0.3	0.4	6.3	0.3
Total Receipts to Cash Flow 42	3.6	2.0	3.5	4.3	5.7	6.4
Cost of Goods to Cash Flow 43	1.3	0.5	1.4	2.4	3.0	3.3
Cash Flow to Total Debt 44	1.5	•	4.0	0.7	0.3	0.3

Selected Financial Factors (in Percentages)

Debt Ratio 45	68.2	•	54.0	72.6	114.9	66.0
Return on Total Assets 46	31.3	•	70.2	23.0	13.2	15.1
Return on Equity Before Income Taxes 47	94.9	•	148.5	80.9	•	44.0
Return on Equity After Income Taxes 48	91.9	•	146.0	80.9	•	44.0
Profit Margin (Before Income Tax) 49	8.4	23.2	9.1	10.2	6.9	10.7
Profit Margin (After Income Tax) 50	8.1	23.2	9.0	10.1	6.6	10.7

Table I

Corporations with and without Net Income

COMPUTER SYSTEMS DESIGN AND RELATED SERVICES

MONEY AMOUNTS AND SIZE OF ASSETS IN THOUSANDS OF DOLLARS

Item Description for Accounting Period 7/08 Through 6/09	Total	Zero Assets	Under 500	500 to 1,000	1,000 to 5,000	5,000 to 10,000	10,000 to 25,000	25,000 to 50,000	50,000 to 100,000	100,000 to 250,000	250,000 to 500,000	500,000 to 2,500,000	2,500,000 and over
Number of Enterprises **1**	130649	31563	87906	3233	5747	895	764	230	128	99	31	43	9
Revenues ($ in Thousands)													
Net Sales **2**	209597814	8726720	28718845	5713660	32460274	11270915	21303419	9784853	9192152	12186990	6649876	32402891	31187219
Interest **3**	1461846	12613	14915	7907	50135	50101	56033	55231	44830	98382	53862	234842	782994
Rents **4**	71486	0	9858	20	6290	1639	1019	7606	2077	8890	1091	22659	10337
Royalties **5**	1110889	123740	2514	940	16140	465	3462	25415	78035	23760	150099	303424	382896
Other Portfolio Income **6**	1117361	43608	87102	57458	229004	100817	54664	110590	43769	78393	36568	87982	187408
Other Receipts **7**	2264253	82117	204798	23456	265224	58697	205052	131317	224944	126587	148637	321033	472390
Total Receipts **8**	215623649	8988798	29038032	5803441	33027067	11482634	21623649	10115012	9585807	12523002	7040133	33372831	33023244
Average Total Receipts **9**	1650	285	330	1795	5747	12830	28303	43978	74889	126495	227101	776112	3669249
Operating Costs/Operating Income (%)													
Cost of Operations **10**	30.6	13.5	20.2	32.5	39.0	43.8	54.4	30.1	42.5	35.4	42.7	28.3	9.2
Salaries and Wages **11**	26.0	42.3	21.0	26.9	25.6	28.7	21.5	27.0	25.0	29.1	22.8	23.7	30.5
Taxes Paid **12**	3.4	3.9	3.2	2.7	2.8	2.7	2.4	2.8	2.6	2.7	2.0	2.8	7.0
Interest Paid **13**	1.9	0.5	0.6	1.3	0.9	1.0	0.8	1.5	1.3	1.9	2.9	2.4	5.5
Depreciation **14**	1.9	0.9	0.9	1.1	0.8	1.5	1.6	2.1	2.2	2.3	3.3	2.4	3.4
Amortization and Depletion **15**	1.5	0.4	0.2	0.6	0.3	0.7	0.8	1.3	1.5	1.9	3.2	2.1	3.8
Pensions and Other Deferred Comp. **16**	0.7	0.3	1.1	0.2	0.7	0.6	0.6	0.5	0.4	0.4	0.3	0.9	0.6
Employee Benefits **17**	2.4	1.4	1.3	2.2	2.0	2.7	1.8	2.6	2.2	2.6	2.3	3.2	3.7
Advertising **18**	0.8	0.4	0.8	0.6	0.8	1.1	1.2	1.2	1.9	0.8	1.4	0.6	0.3
Other Expenses **19**	26.8	31.0	31.8	28.2	20.2	21.5	18.2	31.9	22.4	22.1	19.9	29.6	35.5
Officers' Compensation **20**	5.0	6.7	16.2	9.6	7.3	4.7	2.7	2.6	2.5	1.7	1.2	0.7	0.6
Operating Margin **21**	•	•	2.6	•	•	•	•	•	•	•	•	3.3	•
Operating Margin Before Officers' Comp. **22**	4.0	5.4	18.8	3.8	6.8	•	•	•	•	0.9	•	4.0	0.5

Selected Average Balance Sheet ($ in Thousands)

Net Receivables 23	423	0	10	169	911	1834	5137	9166	14852	29075	65903	156381	3037039
Inventories 24	16	0	2	41	57	171	331	522	1191	1665	5143	6146	14500
Net Property, Plant and Equipment 25	99	0	10	65	131	410	1207	2217	3191	7325	25019	62209	514207
Total Assets 26	1693	0	59	693	2285	7076	16092	35218	67432	155532	345785	1060030	10398501
Notes and Loans Payable 27	446	0	51	380	733	1364	3368	7231	15670	29340	86261	210223	2925451
All Other Liabilities 28	648	0	24	192	969	3131	7974	15937	23140	54642	148806	306926	4174447
Net Worth 29	599	0	-16	120	584	2581	4750	12049	28622	71550	110719	542882	3298604

Selected Financial Ratios (Times to 1)

Current Ratio 30	1.3	•	1.3	1.5	1.7	1.6	1.4	1.4	1.5	1.4	1.2	1.8	1.1
Quick Ratio 31	1.1	•	1.1	1.3	1.5	1.4	1.2	1.1	1.1	1.1	1.0	1.4	1.0
Net Sales to Working Capital 32	8.0	•	36.2	12.1	7.4	6.8	9.2	8.0	6.7	7.0	10.1	4.8	6.5
Coverage Ratio 33	2.0	4.9	6.8	•	2.0	•	•	0.9	0.9	2.1	2.4	3.7	2.2
Total Asset Turnover 34	0.9	•	5.6	2.6	2.5	1.8	1.7	1.2	1.1	0.8	0.6	0.7	0.3
Inventory Turnover 35	31.5	•	33.4	14.0	38.6	32.2	45.8	24.6	25.6	26.2	17.8	34.8	22.1
Receivables Turnover 36	4.0	•	29.8	8.0	7.0	5.3	5.8	4.7	4.8	4.0	3.7	3.9	1.4
Total Liabilities to Net Worth 37	1.8	•	•	4.8	2.9	1.7	2.4	1.9	1.4	1.2	2.1	1.0	2.2
Current Assets to Working Capital 38	3.9	•	4.5	3.0	2.4	2.8	3.5	3.8	3.2	3.6	5.9	2.3	8.1
Current Liabilities to Working Capital 39	2.9	•	3.5	2.0	1.4	1.8	2.5	2.8	2.2	2.6	4.9	1.3	7.1
Working Capital to Net Sales 40	0.1	•	0.0	0.1	0.1	0.1	0.1	0.1	0.1	0.1	0.1	0.2	0.2
Inventory to Working Capital 41	0.1	•	0.2	0.2	0.1	0.1	0.1	0.1	0.1	0.1	0.3	0.0	0.0
Total Receipts to Cash Flow 42	3.9	3.3	3.1	5.6	5.5	8.7	8.8	3.5	5.0	5.0	4.8	3.0	2.7
Cost of Goods to Cash Flow 43	1.2	0.4	0.6	1.8	2.1	3.8	4.8	1.1	2.1	1.8	2.0	0.8	0.2
Cash Flow to Total Debt 44	0.4	•	1.4	0.5	0.6	0.3	0.3	0.5	0.4	0.3	0.2	0.5	0.2

Selected Financial Factors (in Percentages)

Debt Ratio 45	64.6	•	127.9	82.6	74.5	63.5	70.5	65.8	57.6	54.0	68.0	48.8	68.3
Return on Total Assets 46	3.7	•	23.9	•	4.3	•	•	1.7	1.3	3.2	4.3	6.2	4.0
Return on Equity Before Income Taxes 47	5.2	•	•	8.4	•	•	•	•	•	3.7	7.9	8.9	6.7
Return on Equity After Income Taxes 48	2.4	•	•	5.2	•	•	•	•	•	2.3	4.6	6.5	3.9
Profit Margin (Before Income Tax) 49	2.0	1.8	3.7	0.9	•	•	•	•	•	2.1	4.1	6.4	6.4
Profit Margin (After Income Tax) 50	0.9	0.7	3.6	0.5	•	•	•	•	•	1.3	2.4	4.7	3.7

Table II
Corporations with Net Income

COMPUTER SYSTEMS DESIGN AND RELATED SERVICES

MONEY AMOUNTS AND SIZE OF ASSETS IN THOUSANDS OF DOLLARS

Item Description for Accounting Period 7/08 Through 6/09	Total	Zero Assets	Under 500	500 to 1,000	1,000 to 5,000	5,000 to 10,000	10,000 to 25,000	25,000 to 50,000	50,000 to 100,000	100,000 to 250,000	250,000 to 500,000	500,000 to 2,500,000	2,500,000 and over
Number of Enterprises **1**	77715	15416	55145	2276	3826	398	367	103	65	59	20	35	6
Revenues ($ in Thousands)													
Net Sales **2**	159014555	7021953	21545901	4740095	26559535	7826385	12069459	5943450	5499236	8260789	4158100	29242162	26147491
Interest **3**	729418	2752	8186	2004	25713	15711	15719	21919	23693	42403	43948	217043	310327
Rents **4**	47069	0	913	14	381	518	461	5161	1490	5665	1089	22157	9218
Royalties **5**	633426	0	2514	0	5774	232	422	22578	74419	16878	150085	156011	204513
Other Portfolio Income **6**	969233	43294	80340	54358	211668	90558	30594	101746	39460	74711	33972	71120	137413
Other Receipts **7**	1803982	74940	192683	20343	128474	30477	95676	93348	218662	54451	28277	313108	553541
Total Receipts **8**	163197683	7142939	21830537	4816814	26931545	7963881	12212331	6188202	5856960	8454897	4415471	30021601	27362503
Average Total Receipts **9**	2100	463	396	2116	7039	20010	33276	60080	90107	143303	220774	857760	4560417
Operating Costs/Operating Income (%)													
Cost of Operations **10**	27.9	15.2	19.1	33.3	41.0	43.5	51.8	24.2	44.6	36.6	35.8	27.5	2.3
Salaries and Wages **11**	23.6	33.6	17.5	24.1	20.7	22.5	17.5	23.3	20.3	27.1	25.0	22.8	32.4
Taxes Paid **12**	3.5	3.7	2.7	2.2	2.4	2.4	2.1	2.8	2.2	2.5	2.1	2.9	8.0
Interest Paid **13**	1.4	0.2	0.3	0.9	0.5	0.4	0.5	0.9	1.0	1.3	2.1	1.8	3.9
Depreciation **14**	1.5	0.5	0.6	0.7	0.5	0.9	1.2	1.6	1.4	1.6	2.6	2.2	3.3
Amortization and Depletion **15**	1.0	0.2	0.0	0.3	0.2	0.1	0.4	0.7	0.8	1.5	2.9	1.9	2.4
Pensions and Other Deferred Comp. **16**	0.8	0.2	1.3	0.2	0.8	0.8	0.7	0.6	0.3	0.4	0.3	0.9	0.6
Employee Benefits **17**	2.4	1.3	1.2	1.8	1.7	2.2	1.8	2.3	1.7	2.4	2.9	3.2	3.7
Advertising **18**	0.6	0.4	0.7	0.4	0.6	0.4	0.7	0.7	2.5	0.8	1.9	0.6	0.2
Other Expenses **19**	25.9	28.4	29.4	21.0	16.5	15.4	16.1	32.9	21.1	19.3	19.7	30.3	38.2
Officers' Compensation **20**	4.7	6.0	15.9	8.5	6.7	3.6	2.4	2.4	1.9	1.4	1.5	0.6	0.7
Operating Margin **21**	6.7	10.4	11.3	6.6	8.4	7.8	4.9	7.6	2.1	5.1	3.2	5.3	4.3
Operating Margin Before Officers' Comp. **22**	11.4	16.4	27.2	15.1	15.1	11.4	7.4	10.0	4.1	6.5	4.7	5.9	5.0

Selected Average Balance Sheet ($ in Thousands)

Net Receivables 23	489	0	12	169	1062	2625	6461	10838	15761	29561	74263	164010	3064759
Inventories 24	14	0	2	45	39	105	449	580	1550	737	3548	5028	1679
Net Property, Plant and Equipment 25	115	0	8	52	103	415	1018	2538	3213	5194	17265	68854	653177
Total Assets 26	2056	0	62	683	2304	7144	16491	35625	67229	156136	338139	1084074	12520078
Notes and Loans Payable 27	436	0	24	247	540	941	2960	7635	14588	26291	63280	185965	2906256
All Other Liabilities 28	782	0	18	168	944	3004	7699	15658	21675	54112	114714	317625	5357386
Net Worth 29	838	0	21	267	819	3199	5831	12332	30966	75732	160145	580485	4256436

Selected Financial Ratios (Times to 1)

Current Ratio 30	1.4	•	2.2	1.7	2.0	1.7	1.5	1.4	1.5	1.5	1.3	1.8	1.2
Quick Ratio 31	1.2	•	2.0	1.5	1.7	1.5	1.3	1.2	1.2	1.2	1.1	1.4	1.0
Net Sales to Working Capital 32	7.4	•	14.7	11.9	7.2	8.9	8.0	10.6	7.0	6.7	6.6	4.8	6.3
Coverage Ratio 33	7.8	64.9	41.6	10.4	18.8	26.4	13.4	13.9	10.1	6.7	5.6	5.6	3.4
Total Asset Turnover 34	1.0	•	6.3	3.1	3.0	2.8	2.0	1.6	1.3	0.9	0.6	0.8	0.3
Inventory Turnover 35	40.9	•	33.5	15.3	73.8	81.2	37.9	24.1	24.3	69.4	21.0	45.7	59.6
Receivables Turnover 36	4.5	•	30.5	9.3	7.7	5.7	4.9	5.1	•	•	3.6	4.1	•
Total Liabilities to Net Worth 37	1.5	•	2.0	1.6	1.8	1.2	1.8	1.9	1.2	1.1	1.1	0.9	1.9
Current Assets to Working Capital 38	3.3	•	1.8	2.4	2.0	2.4	2.9	3.8	2.9	3.1	4.7	2.2	6.7
Current Liabilities to Working Capital 39	2.3	•	0.8	1.4	1.0	1.4	1.9	2.8	1.9	2.1	3.7	1.2	5.7
Working Capital to Net Sales 40	0.1	•	0.1	0.1	0.1	0.1	0.1	0.1	0.1	0.1	0.2	0.2	0.2
Inventory to Working Capital 41	0.1	•	0.1	0.2	0.0	0.1	0.1	0.1	0.0	0.2	0.2	0.0	0.0
Total Receipts to Cash Flow 42	3.1	2.6	2.6	4.0	4.2	4.5	4.9	2.4	3.6	4.4	3.8	2.8	2.3
Cost of Goods to Cash Flow 43	0.9	0.4	0.5	1.3	1.7	2.0	2.5	0.6	1.6	1.6	1.4	0.8	0.1
Cash Flow to Total Debt 44	0.5	3.7	3.7	1.2	1.1	1.1	0.6	1.0	0.7	0.4	0.3	0.6	0.2

Selected Financial Factors (in Percentages)

Debt Ratio 45	59.2	•	66.5	60.8	64.4	55.2	64.6	65.4	53.9	51.5	52.6	46.5	66.0
Return on Total Assets 46	10.8	•	81.5	27.8	29.9	27.3	13.3	20.7	12.2	8.0	7.4	7.5	4.6
Return on Equity Before Income Taxes 47	23.0	•	237.6	64.3	79.7	58.6	34.9	55.4	23.9	14.0	12.8	11.5	9.6
Return on Equity After Income Taxes 48	19.7	•	235.9	62.7	76.3	51.8	30.0	48.7	20.2	11.8	9.2	8.8	6.3
Profit Margin (Before Income Tax) 49	9.4	12.1	12.7	8.2	9.4	9.5	6.2	11.8	8.8	7.6	9.8	8.0	9.4
Profit Margin (After Income Tax) 50	8.1	10.7	12.6	8.0	9.0	8.4	5.3	10.4	7.4	6.4	7.1	6.1	6.2

Table I

Corporations with and without Net Income

MANAGEMENT, SCIENTIFIC, AND TECHNICAL CONSULTING SERVICES

MONEY AMOUNTS AND SIZE OF ASSETS IN THOUSANDS OF DOLLARS

Item Description for Accounting Period 7/08 Through 6/09		Total	Zero Assets	Under 500	500 to 1,000	1,000 to 5,000	5,000 to 10,000	10,000 to 25,000	25,000 to 50,000	50,000 to 100,000	100,000 to 250,000	250,000 to 500,000	500,000 to 2,500,000	2,500,000 and over
Number of Enterprises	1	230374	49179	168212	6466	4887	686	521	184	97	74	31	27	8
Revenues ($ in Thousands)														
Net Sales	2	212325863	5393854	55346623	16694829	25997169	10064184	13019935	5762737	7488181	10662663	11347892	20770438	29777358
Interest	3	821159	13508	26966	15801	36890	23704	22353	43733	28027	44187	94053	231940	239995
Rents	4	81990	323	2792	2304	7176	2262	3112	7604	3205	14251	770	13152	25039
Royalties	5	453260	0	2935	19	1157	0	9900	883	16691	67900	438	26292	327046
Other Portfolio Income	6	747407	48334	16574	35239	102602	56664	7620	23462	74585	65729	58122	234765	23709
Other Receipts	7	4882971	441833	1005575	437953	556231	223935	293526	480537	224139	174681	215449	308209	520905
Total Receipts	8	219312650	5897852	56401465	17186145	26701225	10370749	13356446	6318956	7834828	11029411	11716724	21584796	30914052
Average Total Receipts	9	952	120	335	2658	5464	15118	25636	34342	80771	149046	377959	799437	3864256
Operating Costs/Operating Income (%)														
Cost of Operations	10	35.5	26.8	27.8	52.9	49.5	40.1	46.2	38.5	27.5	38.1	37.9	23.8	30.8
Salaries and Wages	11	21.9	15.7	15.7	16.4	17.2	19.5	19.8	27.7	29.7	25.5	17.4	38.3	29.2
Taxes Paid	12	2.9	3.6	3.2	2.4	2.1	2.7	2.2	3.3	2.7	2.3	2.7	3.5	3.7
Interest Paid	13	1.0	1.2	0.4	0.3	0.5	0.8	0.9	1.6	0.9	2.0	2.2	1.6	1.9
Depreciation	14	1.3	1.0	0.9	0.7	0.6	0.7	1.7	2.1	2.1	2.2	1.5	1.7	1.9
Amortization and Depletion	15	0.4	0.4	0.0	0.0	0.1	0.1	0.3	0.8	0.6	1.4	1.2	1.2	0.6
Pensions and Other Deferred Comp.	16	1.3	1.4	1.4	0.6	0.6	0.9	1.0	1.2	0.9	0.8	0.3	1.5	2.6
Employee Benefits	17	1.9	2.7	1.8	1.6	1.1	1.6	1.6	3.1	2.3	2.2	1.6	3.0	1.6
Advertising	18	0.6	1.8	1.0	0.4	0.5	0.2	0.3	0.5	1.1	0.8	0.1	0.4	0.4
Other Expenses	19	23.5	32.3	25.7	16.7	18.9	19.5	17.7	23.8	27.0	23.4	22.1	24.8	28.3
Officers' Compensation	20	7.3	16.0	14.5	6.4	6.5	9.8	2.9	3.8	4.5	1.8	5.2	4.3	0.8
Operating Margin	21	2.4	•	7.4	1.7	2.5	4.2	5.4	•	0.6	•	7.8	•	•
Operating Margin Before Officers' Comp.	22	9.7	13.2	21.9	8.0	9.0	14.0	8.3	•	5.2	1.3	13.0	0.2	•

Selected Average Balance Sheet ($ in Thousands)

Net Receivables 23	138	0	5	134	428	2236	3571	7622	17488	37977	70664	250010	1226241
Inventories 24	12	0	1	9	59	81	487	452	1024	3254	4557	39891	38073
Net Property, Plant and Equipment 25	54	0	10	117	277	502	1875	4362	7840	15390	36091	56558	260422
Total Assets 26	567	0	52	709	2065	6846	15747	33932	70026	155688	358005	1123057	3528480
Notes and Loans Payable 27	180	0	43	319	620	2121	5398	10956	16923	47179	102644	199780	1154215
All Other Liabilities 28	221	0	15	192	626	2715	5010	9755	24748	50361	219106	508923	1410966
Net Worth 29	165	0	-5	198	818	2010	5339	13221	28355	58149	36255	414354	963298

Selected Financial Ratios (Times to 1)

Current Ratio 30	1.4	•	1.9	1.5	2.0	1.6	1.3	1.3	1.5	1.5	1.2	1.2	1.5
Quick Ratio 31	1.1	•	1.6	1.1	1.5	1.3	1.0	0.9	1.1	1.2	0.9	0.8	1.2
Net Sales to Working Capital 32	10.8	•	23.0	18.5	9.4	9.1	13.5	9.2	6.4	5.9	17.8	8.9	5.9
Coverage Ratio 33	6.6	6.3	24.8	15.9	12.3	10.3	9.7	3.0	6.7	2.5	6.1	1.0	2.2
Total Asset Turnover 34	1.6	•	6.3	3.6	2.6	2.1	1.6	0.9	1.1	0.9	1.0	0.7	1.1
Inventory Turnover 35	26.7	•	69.0	156.4	44.9	72.3	23.7	26.7	20.7	16.9	30.5	4.6	30.1
Receivables Turnover 36	6.9	•	57.1	16.7	12.1	7.5	5.9	4.5	4.3	4.0	5.1	3.0	3.5
Total Liabilities to Net Worth 37	2.4	•	•	2.6	1.5	2.4	1.9	1.6	1.5	1.7	8.9	1.7	2.7
Current Assets to Working Capital 38	3.3	•	2.1	3.2	2.0	2.7	4.1	4.8	3.1	2.9	6.8	5.8	3.0
Current Liabilities to Working Capital 39	2.3	•	1.1	2.2	1.0	1.7	3.1	3.8	2.1	1.9	5.8	4.8	2.0
Working Capital to Net Sales 40	0.1	•	0.0	0.1	0.1	0.1	0.1	0.1	0.2	0.2	0.1	0.1	0.2
Inventory to Working Capital 41	0.2	•	0.1	0.1	0.1	0.1	0.2	0.2	0.1	0.1	0.3	0.5	0.1
Total Receipts to Cash Flow 42	3.8	•	3.2	5.5	4.5	4.2	4.6	4.4	3.5	4.3	3.3	4.8	3.7
Cost of Goods to Cash Flow 43	1.4	•	0.9	2.9	2.2	1.7	2.1	1.7	1.0	1.6	1.3	1.2	1.1
Cash Flow to Total Debt 44	0.6	•	1.8	0.9	1.0	0.7	0.5	0.3	0.5	0.3	0.3	0.2	0.4

Selected Financial Factors (in Percentages)

Debt Ratio 45	70.9	•	110.5	72.1	60.4	70.6	66.1	61.0	59.5	62.7	89.9	63.1	72.7
Return on Total Assets 46	11.0	•	61.3	17.9	14.6	16.9	14.1	4.4	6.9	4.5	13.6	1.1	4.2
Return on Equity Before Income Taxes 47	32.0	•	•	60.0	33.7	51.9	37.3	7.7	14.4	7.2	112.4	8.3	8.3
Return on Equity After Income Taxes 48	28.6	•	•	58.2	32.1	48.6	35.0	4.2	11.9	4.3	97.4	4.4	4.4
Profit Margin (Before Income Tax) 49	5.7	6.5	9.3	4.6	5.2	7.1	8.0	3.2	5.3	2.9	11.1	2.2	2.2
Profit Margin (After Income Tax) 50	5.1	5.8	9.2	4.5	4.9	6.7	7.5	1.8	4.4	1.8	9.6	•	1.1

Table II
Corporations with Net Income

MANAGEMENT, SCIENTIFIC, AND TECHNICAL CONSULTING SERVICES

MONEY AMOUNTS AND SIZE OF ASSETS IN THOUSANDS OF DOLLARS

Item Description for Accounting Period 7/08 Through 6/09		Total	Zero Assets	Under 500	500 to 1,000	1,000 to 5,000	5,000 to 10,000	10,000 to 25,000	25,000 to 50,000	50,000 to 100,000	100,000 to 250,000	250,000 to 500,000	500,000 to 2,500,000	2,500,000 and over
Number of Enterprises	1	135082	19183	107855	3810	3184	499	309	103	57	•	19	16	•
Revenues ($ in Thousands)														
Net Sales	2	153449833	3239570	43734595	8766841	21936226	8349209	10666171	3676671	5261306	•	9966533	12328321	•
Interest	3	424544	1999	16388	8928	21698	13551	11472	27411	14881	•	23939	112458	•
Rents	4	26735	102	29	2304	349	1812	1158	4152	1424	•	770	748	•
Royalties	5	409529	0	0	19	0	0	0	879	12662	•	425	1024	•
Other Portfolio Income	6	453835	45211	12651	33305	97709	33291	3760	19256	68704	•	34375	22658	•
Other Receipts	7	3973987	356870	903230	411027	552333	194654	327544	441714	203787	•	123598	138072	•
Total Receipts	8	158738463	3643752	44666893	9222424	22608315	8592517	11010105	4170083	5562764	•	10149640	12603281	•
Average Total Receipts	9	1175	190	414	2421	7101	17219	35631	40486	97592	•	534192	787705	•
Operating Costs/Operating Income (%)														
Cost of Operations	10	35.7	14.5	26.9	34.7	53.0	41.0	44.5	35.0	31.4	•	39.1	31.2	•
Salaries and Wages	11	18.9	14.0	14.5	19.6	14.2	19.2	18.8	28.4	26.2	•	15.6	32.6	•
Taxes Paid	12	2.7	2.6	2.9	2.2	2.0	2.9	2.0	3.5	2.5	•	2.5	3.1	•
Interest Paid	13	0.8	0.4	0.3	0.2	0.3	0.4	0.5	1.4	1.0	•	1.2	1.6	•
Depreciation	14	1.0	1.1	0.8	0.5	0.4	0.5	1.1	1.5	1.6	•	1.2	1.6	•
Amortization and Depletion	15	0.4	0.4	0.0	0.0	0.1	0.0	0.2	0.7	0.4	•	0.7	1.6	•
Pensions and Other Deferred Comp.	16	1.3	1.6	1.5	0.9	0.5	0.9	1.0	1.6	0.8	•	0.3	0.9	•
Employee Benefits	17	1.8	1.0	1.9	1.6	0.8	1.7	1.5	4.0	2.1	•	1.6	3.2	•
Advertising	18	0.6	1.8	0.8	0.6	0.4	0.1	0.2	0.3	1.3	•	0.1	0.4	•
Other Expenses	19	20.9	31.7	22.6	22.0	15.3	13.7	16.5	19.7	23.2	•	18.7	18.4	•
Officers' Compensation	20	7.6	16.3	14.6	9.8	6.6	10.1	2.9	4.3	3.2	•	5.7	0.7	•
Operating Margin	21	8.4	14.6	13.1	7.8	6.5	9.5	10.4	•	6.1	•	13.1	4.6	•
Operating Margin Before Officers' Comp.	22	16.0	30.9	27.7	17.6	13.1	19.6	13.3	3.8	9.4	•	18.8	5.3	•

Selected Average Balance Sheet ($ in Thousands)

Net Receivables 23	165	0	6	140	383	2696	4398	9359	19892	95639	254987	•
Inventories 24	13	0	1	11	70	75	589	557	929	6600	20738	•
Net Property, Plant and Equipment 25	49	0	10	36	243	324	1617	4965	7127	24913	52495	•
Total Assets 26	580	0	57	697	2092	6838	15275	34974	71589	368571	1021855	•
Notes and Loans Payable 27	148	0	23	96	478	1420	3957	11894	14691	74061	162062	•
All Other Liabilities 28	210	0	14	218	470	2021	5221	10172	30208	137174	425376	•
Net Worth 29	222	0	20	384	1144	3397	6097	12908	26691	157336	434417	•

Selected Financial Ratios (Times to 1)

Current Ratio 30	1.6	•	2.4	2.3	2.6	2.2	1.5	1.3	1.4	1.3	1.3	•
Quick Ratio 31	1.2	•	2.1	2.0	1.8	1.9	1.1	1.0	1.1	1.0	1.0	•
Net Sales to Working Capital 32	9.8	•	19.3	8.3	8.8	6.7	11.4	9.2	7.1	13.6	7.4	•
Coverage Ratio 33	15.8	61.4	60.8	60.9	32.8	29.1	26.3	10.0	13.4	13.4	5.3	•
Total Asset Turnover 34	2.0	•	7.1	3.3	3.3	2.4	2.3	1.0	1.3	1.4	0.8	•
Inventory Turnover 35	30.8	•	85.5	70.0	52.4	90.8	26.1	22.4	31.2	31.1	11.6	•
Receivables Turnover 36	6.6	•	59.8	15.5	16.9	7.7	6.2	4.1	4.4	•	1.4	•
Total Liabilities to Net Worth 37	1.6	•	1.8	0.8	0.8	1.0	1.5	1.7	1.7	1.3	1.4	•
Current Assets to Working Capital 38	2.8	•	1.7	1.7	1.6	1.9	3.0	4.5	3.4	4.4	4.3	•
Current Liabilities to Working Capital 39	1.8	•	0.7	0.7	0.6	0.9	2.0	3.5	2.4	3.4	3.3	•
Working Capital to Net Sales 40	0.1	•	0.1	0.1	0.1	0.1	0.1	0.1	0.1	0.1	0.1	•
Inventory to Working Capital 41	0.1	•	0.0	0.0	0.1	0.0	0.2	0.1	0.1	0.2	0.2	•
Total Receipts to Cash Flow 42	3.4	1.8	2.9	3.2	4.2	4.3	3.8	3.5	3.2	3.2	4.5	•
Cost of Goods to Cash Flow 43	1.2	0.3	0.8	1.1	2.2	1.8	1.7	1.2	1.0	1.2	1.4	•
Cash Flow to Total Debt 44	0.9	•	3.8	2.3	1.7	1.1	1.0	0.5	0.6	0.8	0.3	•

Selected Financial Factors (in Percentages)

Debt Ratio 45	61.7	•	64.7	44.9	45.3	50.3	60.1	63.1	62.7	57.3	57.5	•
Return on Total Assets 46	24.9	•	109.7	43.6	32.4	31.4	32.0	14.6	16.5	23.2	6.6	•
Return on Equity Before Income Taxes 47	60.8	•	305.9	77.9	57.5	61.1	77.1	35.7	41.1	50.2	12.6	•
Return on Equity After Income Taxes 48	56.5	•	303.5	76.4	55.7	58.5	74.5	29.3	36.5	44.6	8.7	•
Profit Margin (Before Income Tax) 49	11.9	27.1	15.2	13.0	9.6	12.4	13.6	12.9	11.9	15.1	7.1	•
Profit Margin (After Income Tax) 50	11.1	25.9	15.1	12.7	9.3	11.9	13.2	10.6	10.6	13.4	4.9	•

Table I

Corporations with and without Net Income

SCIENTIFIC RESEARCH AND DEVELOPMENT SERVICES

MONEY AMOUNTS AND SIZE OF ASSETS IN THOUSANDS OF DOLLARS

Item Description for Accounting Period 7/08 Through 6/09	Total	Zero Assets	Under 500	500 to 1,000	1,000 to 5,000	5,000 to 10,000	10,000 to 25,000	25,000 to 50,000	50,000 to 100,000	100,000 to 250,000	250,000 to 500,000	500,000 to 2,500,000	2,500,000 and over
Number of Enterprises **1**	14182	2381	7713	1045	1775	472	409	149	110	74	22	32	0
Revenues ($ in Thousands)													
Net Sales **2**	38988125	902377	3761992	1381355	5449030	2511000	2378291	2294979	2932035	3136472	3810675	10429918	0
Interest **3**	1143410	33730	2837	4399	39105	36171	90870	78592	138460	175997	110121	433129	0
Rents **4**	27672	10	0	0	2692	1191	9808	627	2403	4864	364	5713	0
Royalties **5**	2284885	341016	0	0	7301	25596	38336	85232	41509	425832	121605	1198459	0
Other Portfolio Income **6**	974494	31802	25142	1615	54729	20953	26021	9076	63566	333479	50226	357887	0
Other Receipts **7**	5098650	96442	124187	15662	217201	110600	338781	127059	145879	444957	400064	3077815	0
Total Receipts **8**	48517236	1405377	3914158	1403031	5770058	2705511	2882107	2595565	3323852	4521601	4493055	15502921	0
Average Total Receipts **9**	3421	590	507	1343	3251	5732	7047	17420	30217	61103	204230	484466	•
Operating Costs/Operating Income (%)													
Cost of Operations **10**	27.9	40.5	18.7	24.6	30.0	35.4	25.1	42.3	29.3	26.5	36.0	22.2	•
Salaries and Wages **11**	35.4	62.1	26.2	16.4	29.5	34.6	57.4	37.4	35.4	46.8	31.7	34.5	•
Taxes Paid **12**	3.8	5.3	2.4	3.5	3.8	4.0	6.3	5.0	4.8	4.9	2.5	3.1	•
Interest Paid **13**	4.6	3.8	0.6	1.4	2.7	2.9	3.7	3.6	5.5	5.9	2.8	8.4	•
Depreciation **14**	4.4	4.5	0.6	1.0	2.8	4.2	7.9	5.6	4.7	6.8	3.9	5.2	•
Amortization and Depletion **15**	3.0	2.2	0.2	1.3	0.7	1.5	6.3	4.3	5.6	6.6	1.1	3.5	•
Pensions and Other Deferred Comp. **16**	2.0	1.1	2.3	2.4	0.6	1.8	1.3	0.9	0.6	0.9	0.6	4.3	•
Employee Benefits **17**	4.1	6.7	1.7	2.3	3.0	3.9	5.5	4.7	4.5	4.4	4.0	4.9	•
Advertising **18**	1.5	1.3	3.3	0.3	0.9	2.1	2.4	1.1	1.3	1.7	1.1	1.4	•
Other Expenses **19**	54.2	65.0	35.2	60.5	54.0	49.9	108.4	59.1	83.4	78.3	32.9	39.5	•
Officers' Compensation **20**	7.5	18.4	12.2	7.7	10.8	10.1	11.2	8.2	6.7	7.0	2.7	3.5	•
Operating Margin **21**	•	•		•	•	•	•	•	•	•	•	•	•
Operating Margin Before Officers' Comp. **22**	•	•	8.8	•	•	•	•	•	•	•	•	•	•

Selected Average Balance Sheet ($ in Thousands)

Item												
Net Receivables 23	554	0	2	138	592	977	1339	3848	4875	12614	36857	86994
Inventories 24	179	0	1	19	74	336	414	904	1443	3278	9360	30993
Net Property, Plant and Equipment 25	674	0	14	91	339	778	1778	4287	7570	17200	35116	129317
Total Assets 26	6089	0	91	703	2245	6965	16346	34705	71845	152667	372402	1199529
Notes and Loans Payable 27	1969	0	154	407	1082	2153	3225	8391	11909	28663	77095	489892
All Other Liabilities 28	1746	0	45	960	831	1953	4283	11038	31799	60561	110759	225228
Net Worth 29	2373	0	-108	-664	333	2858	8837	15276	28136	63443	184548	484409

Selected Financial Ratios (Times to 1)

Item												
Current Ratio 30	2.3	•	0.6	0.4	1.7	2.5	2.8	2.3	2.4	2.4	2.6	2.6
Quick Ratio 31	1.5	•	0.6	0.4	1.5	2.1	2.2	1.7	1.8	1.6	1.7	1.2
Net Sales to Working Capital 32	1.5	•	•	•	4.6	1.9	0.8	1.2	0.9	0.8	1.5	1.0
Coverage Ratio 33	•	•	2.0	•	•	•	•	•	•	•	0.7	3.2
Total Asset Turnover 34	0.5	•	5.3	1.9	1.4	0.8	0.4	0.4	0.4	0.3	0.5	0.3
Inventory Turnover 35	4.3	•	169.4	16.7	12.5	5.6	3.5	7.2	5.4	3.4	6.7	2.3
Receivables Turnover 36	4.7	•	188.4	11.6	6.1	4.5	4.3	4.0	5.0	3.8	5.2	4.0
Total Liabilities to Net Worth 37	1.6	•	•	•	5.7	1.4	0.8	1.3	1.6	1.4	1.0	1.5
Current Assets to Working Capital 38	1.8	•	•	•	2.4	1.7	1.6	1.8	1.7	1.7	1.6	1.6
Current Liabilities to Working Capital 39	0.8	•	•	•	1.4	0.7	0.6	0.8	0.7	0.7	0.6	0.6
Working Capital to Net Sales 40	0.7	•	•	•	0.2	0.5	1.2	0.8	1.1	1.2	0.7	1.0
Inventory to Working Capital 41	0.1	•	•	•	0.1	0.1	0.1	0.1	0.0	0.1	0.1	0.1
Total Receipts to Cash Flow 42	4.7	90.1	3.4	3.0	8.0	•	•	•	21.3	6.9	3.8	2.0
Cost of Goods to Cash Flow 43	1.3	36.5	0.6	0.7	2.4	•	•	•	6.2	1.8	1.4	0.5
Cash Flow to Total Debt 44	0.2	•	0.7	0.3	0.2	•	•	•	0.0	0.1	0.2	0.2

Selected Financial Factors (in Percentages)

Item												
Debt Ratio 45	61.0	•	217.8	194.5	85.2	59.0	45.9	56.0	60.8	58.4	50.4	59.6
Return on Total Assets 46	•	•	5.9	•	•	•	•	•	•	•	1.0	7.4
Return on Equity Before Income Taxes 47	•	•	•	39.8	•	•	•	•	•	•	•	12.7
Return on Equity After Income Taxes 48	•	•	•	39.9	•	•	•	•	•	•	•	7.4
Profit Margin (Before Income Tax) 49	•	•	0.6	•	•	•	•	•	•	•	•	18.8
Profit Margin (After Income Tax) 50	•	•	0.5	•	•	•	•	•	•	•	•	11.0

Table II
Corporations with Net Income

SCIENTIFIC RESEARCH AND DEVELOPMENT SERVICES

MONEY AMOUNTS AND SIZE OF ASSETS IN THOUSANDS OF DOLLARS

Item Description for Accounting Period 7/08 Through 6/09	Total	Zero Assets	Under 500	500 to 1,000	1,000 to 5,000	5,000 to 10,000	10,000 to 25,000	25,000 to 50,000	50,000 to 100,000	100,000 to 250,000	250,000 to 500,000	500,000 to 2,500,000	2,500,000 and over
Number of Enterprises **1**	5421	453	3516	364	753	165	80	25	14	20	11	20	0
Revenues ($ in Thousands)													
Net Sales **2**	23224438	478666	2419668	726569	3782419	1833803	1133350	1347002	1190743	1207059	1961625	7153534	0
Interest **3**	494922	1532	392	41	5564	5260	12568	6559	13610	43379	57734	348283	0
Rents **4**	4270	0	0	0	2622	1039	292	155	92	0	0	70	0
Royalties **5**	1631710	1464	0	0	0	9159	15453	20465	15982	405023	118840	1045325	0
Other Portfolio Income **6**	617298	31776	24380	198	43159	14014	14449	4036	43423	236632	45678	159555	0
Other Receipts **7**	4154661	15365	88420	13271	72594	17918	212038	124540	54401	253476	388724	2913910	0
Total Receipts **8**	30137299	528803	2532860	740079	3906358	1881193	1388150	1502757	1318251	2145569	2572601	11620677	0
Average Total Receipts **9**	5559	1167	720	2033	5188	11401	17352	60110	94161	107278	233873	581034	•
Operating Costs/Operating Income (%)													
Cost of Operations **10**	27.2	29.8	26.6	1.7	17.9	31.3	21.6	46.6	47.6	26.3	21.7	29.1	•
Salaries and Wages **11**	25.0	10.8	21.2	10.0	21.0	17.2	29.7	17.3	14.7	34.2	36.7	30.6	•
Taxes Paid **12**	2.8	3.4	1.4	2.8	3.0	2.6	3.9	3.3	2.3	4.7	2.8	2.8	•
Interest Paid **13**	3.1	3.2	0.1	0.7	0.6	0.7	0.5	0.6	0.6	2.2	2.9	7.8	•
Depreciation **14**	3.2	0.6	0.5	0.1	1.6	2.1	3.5	2.5	1.7	5.7	4.6	5.3	•
Amortization and Depletion **15**	1.4	0.3	0.0	•	0.1	0.2	1.2	0.1	0.7	2.4	0.8	3.6	•
Pensions and Other Deferred Comp. **16**	2.7	1.5	2.7	3.9	0.5	2.0	2.2	1.2	0.8	1.3	0.9	5.2	•
Employee Benefits **17**	3.3	5.4	1.8	0.4	2.1	2.8	2.3	2.6	3.2	3.3	4.4	4.8	•
Advertising **18**	1.2	1.4	2.9	0.0	0.5	1.2	0.6	0.1	1.4	0.5	0.6	1.7	•
Other Expenses **19**	29.4	24.6	18.3	60.8	37.3	16.5	39.1	16.6	24.8	39.5	37.3	27.4	•
Officers' Compensation **20**	5.1	10.6	7.7	5.1	8.0	5.7	4.6	2.4	2.8	4.3	2.6	3.8	•
Operating Margin **21**	•	8.4	16.8	14.6	7.3	17.6	•	6.7	•	•	•	•	•
Operating Margin Before Officers' Comp. **22**	0.5	19.0	24.5	19.7	15.4	23.3	•	9.2	2.2	•	•	•	•

Selected Average Balance Sheet ($ in Thousands)

Net Receivables 23	791	0	2	294	746	1910	3315	8630	11720	23150	35630	89882
Inventories 24	305	0	1	43	67	530	305	1303	3948	4244	13146	57650
Net Property, Plant and Equipment 25	904	0	14	131	317	883	2191	6122	7562	13432	47319	159807
Total Assets 26	8000	0	133	689	2020	6976	16578	35245	74016	150353	384069	1475247
Notes and Loans Payable 27	2307	0	102	6	446	1194	1054	2598	9572	10202	68319	518717
All Other Liabilities 28	1799	0	23	339	627	1957	4956	12061	35412	69926	126051	238549
Net Worth 29	3894	0	7	344	947	3826	10568	20586	29032	70225	189699	717981

Selected Financial Ratios (Times to 1)

Current Ratio 30	2.9	•	2.1	1.7	2.1	3.7	2.6	2.9	2.1	3.5	2.7	3.1
Quick Ratio 31	1.5	•	2.0	1.5	2.0	3.0	2.2	2.0	1.5	2.6	1.6	1.2
Net Sales to Working Capital 32	1.6	•	20.0	8.9	6.7	2.9	2.7	3.5	3.2	1.0	1.6	0.8
Coverage Ratio 33	9.2	6.9	246.3	25.7	19.5	28.8	29.5	34.0	18.6	25.3	6.8	6.2
Total Asset Turnover 34	0.5	•	5.2	2.9	2.5	1.6	0.9	1.5	1.1	0.4	0.5	0.2
Inventory Turnover 35	3.8	•	215.2	0.8	13.4	6.6	10.0	19.3	10.3	3.7	2.9	1.8
Receivables Turnover 36	4.5	•	676.2	7.9	7.2	4.2	4.0	5.1	4.6	2.8	4.0	3.0
Total Liabilities to Net Worth 37	1.1	•	18.1	1.0	1.1	0.8	0.6	0.7	1.5	1.1	1.0	1.1
Current Assets to Working Capital 38	1.5	•	1.9	2.5	1.9	1.4	1.6	1.5	1.9	1.4	1.6	1.5
Current Liabilities to Working Capital 39	0.5	•	0.9	1.5	0.9	0.4	0.6	0.5	0.9	0.4	0.6	0.5
Working Capital to Net Sales 40	0.6	•	0.1	0.1	0.2	0.3	0.4	0.3	0.3	1.0	0.6	1.3
Inventory to Working Capital 41	0.1	•	0.0	0.2	0.1	0.2	0.0	0.1	0.1	0.1	0.1	0.2
Total Receipts to Cash Flow 42	2.1	2.7	2.8	1.4	2.4	3.4	2.2	3.3	3.5	1.4	2.1	1.6
Cost of Goods to Cash Flow 43	0.6	0.8	0.8	0.0	0.4	1.1	0.5	1.5	1.7	0.4	0.5	0.5
Cash Flow to Total Debt 44	0.5	•	1.9	4.2	1.9	1.1	1.1	1.1	0.5	0.5	0.4	0.3

Selected Financial Factors (in Percentages)

Debt Ratio 45	51.3	•	94.8	50.0	53.1	45.2	36.3	41.6	60.8	53.3	50.6	51.3
Return on Total Assets 46	15.3	•	111.7	49.5	27.8	33.3	11.7	28.7	12.2	22.2	9.3	11.8
Return on Equity Before Income Taxes 47	28.0	•	2120.3	95.2	56.4	58.7	17.7	47.6	29.5	45.7	16.0	20.3
Return on Equity After Income Taxes 48	23.1	•	2111.5	95.0	52.9	55.6	14.7	43.7	28.6	41.0	13.5	14.6
Profit Margin (Before Income Tax) 49	25.4	18.9	21.4	16.4	10.6	20.2	13.2	18.2	10.1	53.2	17.1	40.7
Profit Margin (After Income Tax) 50	21.0	17.1	21.3	16.4	10.0	19.1	11.0	16.7	9.8	47.7	14.4	29.4

Table I

Corporations with and without Net Income

ADVERTISING AND RELATED SERVICES

MONEY AMOUNTS AND SIZE OF ASSETS IN THOUSANDS OF DOLLARS

Item Description for Accounting Period 7/08 Through 6/09		Total	Zero Assets	Under 500	500 to 1,000	1,000 to 5,000	5,000 to 10,000	10,000 to 25,000	25,000 to 50,000	50,000 to 100,000	100,000 to 250,000	250,000 to 500,000	500,000 to 2,500,000	2,500,000 and over
Number of Enterprises	1	49563	7720	37388	1877	1884	391	160	64	30	28	6	10	5
Revenues ($ in Thousands)														
Net Sales	2	83317410	794032	18550652	2695570	9917929	6271127	4258435	4027060	2660018	6483654	1479671	7591931	18587329
Interest	3	1188169	110	10647	7302	16402	9030	13697	9283	7703	17721	8322	26528	1061425
Rents	4	100843	0	117	304	2964	345	599	1351	0	612	301	1975	92276
Royalties	5	54656	0	0	0	48	0	0	37363	0	0	2903	4951	9391
Other Portfolio Income	6	547264	28639	12096	2366	23274	7597	52177	1701	11602	84475	68	31296	291971
Other Receipts	7	1291006	16192	165371	61941	39481	47644	121471	81261	20878	97818	35846	189054	414050
Total Receipts	8	86499348	838973	18738883	2767483	10000098	6335743	4446379	4158019	2700201	6684280	1527111	7845735	20456442
Average Total Receipts	9	1745	109	501	1474	5308	16204	27790	64969	90007	238724	254518	784574	4091288
Operating Costs/Operating Income (%)														
Cost of Operations	10	43.3	38.8	56.5	41.4	55.3	57.8	59.8	52.9	53.1	68.8	57.4	37.5	4.5
Salaries and Wages	11	20.8	2.8	8.6	15.2	15.2	14.3	15.4	15.3	20.2	11.5	21.4	27.8	42.5
Taxes Paid	12	2.3	1.2	1.8	2.2	1.9	1.4	1.5	1.5	1.7	1.2	2.0	2.6	4.0
Interest Paid	13	3.8	1.0	0.6	0.5	0.8	0.8	0.3	0.8	2.5	1.8	3.2	5.5	11.8
Depreciation	14	1.8	4.1	0.5	2.9	0.8	1.3	1.0	1.4	2.1	1.5	0.9	3.7	3.2
Amortization and Depletion	15	1.1	0.4	0.1	0.0	0.2	0.3	0.2	1.1	1.8	1.2	0.8	1.9	2.6
Pensions and Other Deferred Comp.	16	0.5	0.2	0.3	1.7	0.7	0.3	0.2	0.4	0.4	0.5	0.5	0.3	0.9
Employee Benefits	17	1.3	0.5	0.9	1.1	1.1	0.6	1.0	1.3	1.1	1.0	1.1	2.7	1.9
Advertising	18	2.3	2.3	1.7	10.9	0.6	3.3	5.6	9.7	0.9	0.4	0.5	4.1	0.3
Other Expenses	19	20.1	35.3	18.3	17.6	16.3	16.1	12.2	16.1	18.1	11.8	14.0	18.8	31.9
Officers' Compensation	20	3.9	1.7	7.5	7.2	5.2	2.2	3.4	2.4	1.7	1.2	1.3	0.6	3.1
Operating Margin	21	•	11.5	3.1	•	2.0	1.7	•	•	•	•	•	•	•
Operating Margin Before Officers' Comp.	22	2.7	13.2	10.6	6.5	7.2	3.9	2.7	•	•	0.4	•	•	•

Selected Average Balance Sheet ($ in Thousands)

Line Item													
Net Receivables 23	383	0	10	86	577	2428	6371	10835	17931	37538	64615	193364	2164130
Inventories 24	37	0	2	7	159	206	181	1134	828	1816	5072	11561	207074
Net Property, Plant and Equipment 25	150	0	12	273	327	514	1247	5044	9144	11118	9298	149186	596173
Total Assets 26	2411	0	63	728	2179	6742	15681	36152	69447	158768	309092	1254459	16659405
Notes and Loans Payable 27	490	0	84	319	780	1306	1579	10380	24117	42209	77348	501488	2050608
All Other Liabilities 28	995	0	32	291	1473	2761	9886	15888	31423	62606	129717	410410	6704545
Net Worth 29	927	0	-53	119	-73	2674	4215	9884	13906	53953	102027	342562	7904252

Selected Financial Ratios (Times to 1)

Line Item													
Current Ratio 30	0.8	•	1.0	1.2	1.2	2.1	1.3	1.4	1.0	1.2	1.0	0.9	0.7
Quick Ratio 31	0.7	•	0.8	0.9	0.9	1.9	1.2	1.1	0.8	0.9	0.8	0.7	0.5
Net Sales to Working Capital 32	•	•	25.9	19.1	6.2	10.0	10.8	1322.1	19.8	•	•	•	•
Coverage Ratio 33	1.8	18.6	7.8	5.2	4.5	4.3	11.8	1.3	0.2	2.4	1.1	0.7	1.4
Total Asset Turnover 34	0.7	•	7.9	2.0	2.4	1.7	1.7	1.3	1.5	0.8	0.6	•	0.2
Inventory Turnover 35	19.8	141.2	91.1	18.2	45.0	87.9	29.4	56.9	87.8	27.9	24.6	•	0.8
Receivables Turnover 36	3.2	44.5	12.7	7.7	6.1	3.6	5.6	4.5	6.4	3.1	3.9	•	1.1
Total Liabilities to Net Worth 37	1.6	•	5.1	1.5	2.7	2.7	4.0	1.9	2.0	2.7	•	•	1.1
Current Assets to Working Capital 38	•	•	6.9	5.2	1.9	3.6	3.8	597.8	5.6	•	•	•	•
Current Liabilities to Working Capital 39	•	•	5.9	4.2	0.9	2.8	2.8	596.8	4.6	•	•	•	•
Working Capital to Net Sales 40	•	•	0.0	0.1	0.2	0.1	0.1	0.0	0.1	•	•	•	•
Inventory to Working Capital 41	•	•	0.2	0.5	0.1	0.1	0.2	9.1	0.2	•	•	•	•
Total Receipts to Cash Flow 42	5.4	2.0	5.3	7.1	6.2	6.7	8.1	7.0	7.7	8.5	8.5	8.0	3.6
Cost of Goods to Cash Flow 43	2.4	0.8	3.0	2.9	3.4	3.9	4.9	3.7	4.1	5.8	4.9	3.0	0.2
Cash Flow to Total Debt 44	0.2	•	0.8	0.3	0.4	0.6	0.3	0.3	0.2	0.1	0.1	0.1	0.1

Selected Financial Factors (in Percentages)

Line Item													
Debt Ratio 45	61.6	•	184.8	83.7	103.4	60.3	73.1	72.7	80.0	66.0	67.0	72.7	52.6
Return on Total Assets 46	4.7	•	37.2	4.9	8.8	8.0	6.9	1.7	0.6	6.2	2.7	2.2	3.7
Return on Equity Before Income Taxes 47	5.3	•	•	24.4	15.5	23.4	•	10.7	•	•	0.5	1.5	2.3
Return on Equity After Income Taxes 48	4.3	•	•	22.8	13.9	19.4	•	8.1	•	•	•	•	1.7
Profit Margin (Before Income Tax) 49	2.9	17.2	4.1	2.0	2.8	3.7	2.6	0.2	2.5	0.6	0.2	2.2	4.9
Profit Margin (After Income Tax) 50	2.4	16.9	4.1	1.9	2.6	3.1	2.3	0.2	1.9	•	•	1.9	3.5

Table II
Corporations with Net Income

ADVERTISING AND RELATED SERVICES

MONEY AMOUNTS AND SIZE OF ASSETS IN THOUSANDS OF DOLLARS

Item Description for Accounting Period 7/08 Through 6/09		Total	Zero Assets	Under 500	500 to 1,000	1,000 to 5,000	5,000 to 10,000	10,000 to 25,000	25,000 to 50,000	50,000 to 100,000	100,000 to 250,000	250,000 to 500,000	500,000 to 2,500,000	2,500,000 and over
Number of Enterprises	1	29548	3042	23815	780	1445	281	110	36	11	•	3	6	•
Revenues ($ in Thousands)														
Net Sales	2	58642751	391602	13066393	2266279	9183713	4436230	3595238	2901922	1016833	•	849106	4943922	•
Interest	3	1080403	0	9055	6608	14409	2818	7271	5330	2086	•	3479	17008	•
Rents	4	78330	0	0	304	2132	0	90	297	0	•	301	1751	•
Royalties	5	40493	0	0	0	48	0	0	37363	0	•	2903	133	•
Other Portfolio Income	6	401131	14908	10301	2154	17008	7224	49445	15	465	•	67	17806	•
Other Receipts	7	772716	3824	15965	42194	46689	42448	22504	48414	13319	•	1421	65667	•
Total Receipts	8	61015824	410334	13101714	2317539	9263999	4488720	3674548	2993341	1032703	•	857277	5046287	•
Average Total Receipts	9	2065	135	550	2971	6411	15974	33405	83148	93882	•	285759	841048	•
Operating Costs/Operating Income (%)														
Cost of Operations	10	42.3	7.3	56.6	41.3	57.1	65.7	62.8	53.1	33.6	•	49.8	33.1	•
Salaries and Wages	11	20.0	1.3	6.8	14.6	13.1	10.2	12.3	12.1	27.7	•	25.9	28.3	•
Taxes Paid	12	2.2	1.8	1.5	1.8	1.6	1.1	1.3	1.4	1.5	•	2.7	2.6	•
Interest Paid	13	3.2	0.6	0.3	0.3	0.3	0.1	0.1	0.4	1.1	•	2.4	3.7	•
Depreciation	14	1.1	6.8	0.4	0.9	0.6	0.9	0.7	0.9	1.8	•	1.0	2.1	•
Amortization and Depletion	15	0.8	0.4	0.0	0.0	0.1	0.0	0.0	0.1	0.4	•	0.8	2.1	•
Pensions and Other Deferred Comp.	16	0.6	0.4	0.4	1.5	0.7	0.3	0.3	0.5	0.8	•	0.5	0.3	•
Employee Benefits	17	1.3	0.5	0.8	1.1	1.0	0.4	0.7	1.4	1.0	•	1.3	3.4	•
Advertising	18	1.8	1.0	0.9	9.3	0.4	0.5	3.6	12.9	0.5	•	0.2	2.4	•
Other Expenses	19	19.0	27.6	15.9	12.1	14.9	11.8	9.6	12.6	23.4	•	12.6	17.8	•
Officers' Compensation	20	4.0	3.2	7.1	7.7	4.8	1.7	3.2	2.2	1.6	•	1.1	0.6	•
Operating Margin	21	3.6	49.1	9.2	9.3	5.4	7.2	5.3	2.5	6.5	•	1.7	3.6	•
Operating Margin Before Officers' Comp.	22	7.6	52.4	16.2	17.0	10.2	8.9	8.5	4.6	8.1	•	2.8	4.1	•

Selected Average Balance Sheet ($ in Thousands)

Net Receivables 23	475	0	10	159	599	2793	6770	12668	25603	67720	212477
Inventories 24	48	0	1	3	198	276	174	1332	1653	5399	10174
Net Property, Plant and Equipment 25	93	0	11	79	261	376	824	6687	4889	13426	50480
Total Assets 26	1964	0	64	782	2116	6614	15369	35691	72523	269362	1072417
Notes and Loans Payable 27	400	0	24	72	376	370	796	7957	14551	68896	456941
All Other Liabilities 28	1053	0	21	261	1101	2468	10433	16454	50255	89190	398776
Net Worth 29	510	0	19	448	639	3776	4140	11280	7717	111275	216700

Selected Financial Ratios (Times to 1)

Current Ratio 30	1.0	•	1.5	2.0	1.4	2.7	1.3	1.5	1.1	1.1	0.9
Quick Ratio 31	0.9	•	1.4	1.9	1.0	2.4	1.2	1.2	0.8	1.0	0.8
Net Sales to Working Capital 32	60.1	•	41.8	10.0	15.3	4.5	12.9	9.7	15.6	22.4	•
Coverage Ratio 33	3.5	91.9	30.3	34.0	19.7	60.7	64.9	14.8	8.2	2.2	2.6
Total Asset Turnover 34	1.0	•	8.5	3.7	3.0	2.4	2.1	2.3	1.3	1.1	0.8
Inventory Turnover 35	17.5	•	485.3	344.1	18.3	37.5	117.8	32.1	18.8	26.1	26.8
Receivables Turnover 36	2.6	•	51.9	20.3	8.9	5.3	3.8	6.3	2.5	•	3.9
Total Liabilities to Net Worth 37	2.8	•	2.3	0.7	2.3	0.8	2.7	2.2	8.4	1.4	•
Current Assets to Working Capital 38	24.3	•	3.1	2.0	3.7	1.6	4.9	2.9	9.7	7.8	•
Current Liabilities to Working Capital 39	23.3	•	2.1	1.0	2.7	0.6	3.9	1.9	8.7	6.8	•
Working Capital to Net Sales 40	0.0	•	0.0	0.1	0.1	0.2	0.1	0.1	0.1	0.0	•
Inventory to Working Capital 41	1.2	•	0.1	0.0	0.4	0.1	0.0	0.2	0.1	0.4	•
Total Receipts to Cash Flow 42	4.4	1.3	4.5	4.8	5.5	6.4	7.4	6.1	3.5	8.1	5.1
Cost of Goods to Cash Flow 43	1.9	0.1	2.6	2.0	3.1	4.2	4.6	3.2	1.2	4.1	1.7
Cash Flow to Total Debt 44	0.3	•	2.7	1.8	0.8	0.9	0.4	0.5	0.4	0.2	0.2

Selected Financial Factors (in Percentages)

Debt Ratio 45	74.0	•	69.7	42.6	69.8	42.9	73.1	68.4	89.4	58.7	79.8
Return on Total Assets 46	11.5	•	83.2	44.2	19.9	20.0	16.2	13.7	11.7	5.6	7.3
Return on Equity Before Income Taxes 47	31.6	•	265.6	74.8	62.6	34.4	59.1	40.3	96.5	7.5	21.9
Return on Equity After Income Taxes 48	28.5	•	264.2	73.8	60.3	32.9	53.3	37.3	88.7	4.9	15.8
Profit Margin (Before Income Tax) 49	8.1	53.9	9.4	11.5	6.3	8.2	7.5	5.6	8.1	2.9	5.8
Profit Margin (After Income Tax) 50	7.3	53.5	9.4	11.4	6.1	7.9	6.8	5.2	7.4	1.9	4.2

Table I

Corporations with and without Net Income

OTHER PROFESSIONAL, SCIENTIFIC, AND TECHNICAL SERVICES

MONEY AMOUNTS AND SIZE OF ASSETS IN THOUSANDS OF DOLLARS

Item Description for Accounting Period 7/08 Through 6/09		Total	Zero Assets	Under 500	500 to 1,000	1,000 to 5,000	5,000 to 10,000	10,000 to 25,000	25,000 to 50,000	50,000 to 100,000	100,000 to 250,000	250,000 to 500,000	500,000 to 2,500,000	2,500,000 and over
Number of Enterprises	1	91592	19190	65592	3578	2431	321	280	78	66	32	•	•	0
Revenues ($ in Thousands)														
Net Sales	2	82846113	4453620	28378813	6801602	8076865	4326632	6600630	3776088	5633179	5014720	•	•	0
Interest	3	692194	3799	7449	7470	21732	6094	33475	10607	23304	24569	•	•	0
Rents	4	34994	0	1118	3375	1857	256	949	1788	1150	5800	•	•	0
Royalties	5	213579	563	0	806	0	0	390	629	2355	11167	•	•	0
Other Portfolio Income	6	431596	49160	74084	11848	32923	735	28940	48795	10748	50913	•	•	0
Other Receipts	7	1492258	-30557	298788	61306	128880	104903	489951	61123	133552	95455	•	•	0
Total Receipts	8	85710734	4476585	28760252	6886407	8262257	4438620	7154335	3899030	5804288	5202624	•	•	0
Average Total Receipts	9	936	233	438	1925	3399	13827	25551	49988	87944	162582	•	•	•
Operating Costs/Operating Income (%)														
Cost of Operations	10	29.5	14.9	18.5	28.6	37.5	53.5	47.9	38.6	39.6	41.1	•	•	•
Salaries and Wages	11	20.6	6.7	20.5	20.4	19.8	17.5	20.3	24.0	15.2	24.3	•	•	•
Taxes Paid	12	3.0	1.1	3.3	3.5	2.5	2.4	2.7	2.9	2.0	2.1	•	•	•
Interest Paid	13	2.2	0.7	0.9	0.8	0.7	0.7	1.4	1.1	1.9	2.9	•	•	•
Depreciation	14	1.9	1.9	1.4	0.8	1.9	1.1	2.3	2.7	1.8	3.4	•	•	•
Amortization and Depletion	15	0.7	0.2	0.2	0.3	0.3	0.3	0.4	1.2	1.1	1.4	•	•	•
Pensions and Other Deferred Comp.	16	1.2	0.1	1.3	2.2	0.7	1.1	0.7	0.6	0.6	0.4	•	•	•
Employee Benefits	17	1.7	0.7	1.1	2.1	1.2	3.4	2.4	2.2	1.3	1.7	•	•	•
Advertising	18	0.9	0.9	1.0	0.9	1.1	0.7	0.8	0.7	1.2	1.3	•	•	•
Other Expenses	19	29.6	65.0	29.7	26.0	26.0	19.6	28.2	23.5	38.8	21.0	•	•	•
Officers' Compensation	20	7.5	6.3	12.3	12.9	8.2	3.6	4.3	3.0	1.8	2.4	•	•	•
Operating Margin	21	1.0	1.5	9.7	1.3	0.2	•	•	•	•	•	•	•	•
Operating Margin Before Officers' Comp.	22	8.6	7.8	22.0	14.2	8.3	•	•	2.6	•	0.4	•	•	•

Selected Average Balance Sheet ($ in Thousands)

Net Receivables 23	91	0	6	144	398	2476	3268	8833	14761	21383
Inventories 24	14	0	3	42	81	320	433	668	1129	8078
Net Property, Plant and Equipment 25	74	0	24	136	284	598	2759	5010	6369	19318
Total Assets 26	634	0	90	672	1936	7030	15658	36162	70321	171862
Notes and Loans Payable 27	274	0	75	318	600	2689	4768	9636	20451	63307
All Other Liabilities 28	211	0	25	147	727	2344	5154	13447	25791	53823
Net Worth 29	149	0	-11	207	609	1996	5736	13079	24080	54733

Selected Financial Ratios (Times to 1)

Current Ratio 30	1.2	•	1.2	1.9	1.8	1.8	1.4	1.5	1.2	1.0
Quick Ratio 31	1.0	•	1.0	1.4	1.6	1.4	1.1	1.1	0.9	0.6
Net Sales to Working Capital 32	21.5	•	78.0	11.8	6.6	6.6	9.3	7.1	21.5	9756.3
Coverage Ratio 33	3.1	4.0	13.1	4.0	4.3	•	•	4.3	•	1.6
Total Asset Turnover 34	1.4	•	4.8	2.8	1.7	1.9	1.5	1.3	1.2	0.9
Inventory Turnover 35	18.9	•	24.6	12.9	15.4	22.5	26.1	28.0	30.0	8.0
Receivables Turnover 36	9.8	•	67.2	14.1	8.9	5.4	6.6	5.4	6.9	5.9
Total Liabilities to Net Worth 37	3.3	•	•	2.2	2.2	2.5	1.7	1.8	1.9	2.1
Current Assets to Working Capital 38	5.2	•	6.9	2.2	2.3	2.3	3.2	3.2	7.6	3560.8
Current Liabilities to Working Capital 39	4.2	•	5.9	1.2	1.3	1.3	2.2	2.2	6.6	3559.8
Working Capital to Net Sales 40	0.0	•	0.0	0.1	0.2	0.2	0.1	0.1	0.0	0.0
Inventory to Working Capital 41	0.3	•	0.6	0.2	0.1	0.2	0.2	0.1	0.2	477.5
Total Receipts to Cash Flow 42	3.5	1.6	3.0	4.6	4.4	6.6	4.6	4.3	3.0	5.4
Cost of Goods to Cash Flow 43	1.0	0.2	0.6	1.3	1.7	3.5	2.2	1.7	1.2	2.2
Cash Flow to Total Debt 44	0.5	•	1.4	0.9	0.6	0.4	0.5	0.5	0.6	0.2

Selected Financial Factors (in Percentages)

Debt Ratio 45	76.6	•	112.2	69.2	68.5	71.6	63.4	63.8	65.8	68.2
Return on Total Assets 46	9.7	•	57.8	9.5	5.5	•	•	6.1	•	4.3
Return on Equity Before Income Taxes 47	27.8	•	•	23.0	13.5	•	•	12.8	•	5.0
Return on Equity After Income Taxes 48	25.1	•	•	22.4	11.7	•	•	8.8	•	2.0
Profit Margin (Before Income Tax) 49	4.6	2.0	11.0	2.5	2.5	•	•	3.5	•	1.8
Profit Margin (After Income Tax) 50	4.1	1.8	10.9	2.4	2.1	•	•	2.4	•	0.7

Table II
Corporations with Net Income

OTHER PROFESSIONAL, SCIENTIFIC, AND TECHNICAL SERVICES

MONEY AMOUNTS AND SIZE OF ASSETS IN THOUSANDS OF DOLLARS

Item Description for Accounting Period 7/08 Through 6/09	Total	Zero Assets	Under 500	500 to 1,000	1,000 to 5,000	5,000 to 10,000	10,000 to 25,000	25,000 to 50,000	50,000 to 100,000	100,000 to 250,000	250,000 to 500,000	500,000 to 2,500,000	2,500,000 and over
Number of Enterprises **1**	58525	11678	42760	2373	1309	136	160	47	26	20	•	•	0
Revenues ($ in Thousands)													
Net Sales **2**	57289490	1470090	22271756	5042097	6081462	1810697	5052823	2546328	2329660	2860499	•	•	0
Interest **3**	561637	1113	3735	3749	12911	3122	9479	6638	9448	19990	•	•	0
Rents **4**	17984	0	0	0	1857	256	532	449	1118	391	•	•	0
Royalties **5**	198746	0	0	0	0	0	0	0	0	1089	•	•	0
Other Portfolio Income **6**	283624	44610	18544	4575	32493	728	4560	48739	8875	11949	•	•	0
Other Receipts **7**	1211448	39052	289195	54664	75751	70831	439010	23769	17947	73474	•	•	0
Total Receipts **8**	59562929	1554865	22583230	5105085	6204474	1885634	5506404	2625923	2367048	2967392	•	•	0
Average Total Receipts **9**	1018	133	528	2151	4740	13865	34415	55871	91040	148370	•	•	•
Operating Costs/Operating Income (%)													
Cost of Operations **10**	25.8	19.2	18.3	21.4	34.3	38.0	49.8	39.6	26.7	23.0	•	•	•
Salaries and Wages **11**	20.0	13.4	18.5	21.0	16.6	17.6	17.6	22.7	20.1	27.8	•	•	•
Taxes Paid **12**	3.0	2.5	3.1	3.8	2.1	2.6	2.3	2.2	2.8	2.5	•	•	•
Interest Paid **13**	2.2	0.4	0.6	0.7	0.4	0.6	0.6	0.7	1.8	2.9	•	•	•
Depreciation **14**	1.6	0.8	1.0	0.7	1.3	0.7	1.5	2.0	1.9	2.5	•	•	•
Amortization and Depletion **15**	0.7	0.1	0.2	0.3	0.1	0.0	0.3	1.1	0.8	1.3	•	•	•
Pensions and Other Deferred Comp. **16**	1.4	0.2	1.3	2.8	0.5	2.2	0.6	0.6	1.1	0.5	•	•	•
Employee Benefits **17**	1.6	1.6	0.9	2.4	0.7	1.8	2.2	2.1	1.4	2.0	•	•	•
Advertising **18**	0.9	0.9	1.0	0.5	0.7	1.2	0.8	0.6	2.5	0.5	•	•	•
Other Expenses **19**	26.6	33.0	27.7	27.1	25.4	22.5	24.3	18.0	34.3	28.1	•	•	•
Officers' Compensation **20**	8.3	13.6	12.4	15.1	8.5	3.3	2.7	2.9	2.5	2.6	•	•	•
Operating Margin **21**	7.9	14.4	14.9	4.3	9.4	9.4	•	7.5	4.3	6.3	•	•	•
Operating Margin Before Officers' Comp. **22**	16.2	28.0	27.3	19.4	17.9	12.7	0.1	10.3	6.8	8.8	•	•	•

Selected Average Balance Sheet ($ in Thousands)

Item										
Net Receivables 23	84	0	6	135	440	1465	3788	8507	14250	25616
Inventories 24	11	0	4	52	38	518	629	614	1471	297
Net Property, Plant and Equipment 25	70	0	23	146	300	400	2688	3348	7508	14020
Total Assets 26	660	0	97	662	1803	7001	15291	35605	68380	173921
Notes and Loans Payable 27	271	0	41	279	497	3546	3359	6445	19700	51343
All Other Liabilities 28	193	0	29	130	730	1280	5433	16050	23417	46701
Net Worth 29	196	0	27	253	577	2175	6500	13110	25263	75877

Selected Financial Ratios (Times to 1)

Item										
Current Ratio 30	1.5	•	1.3	2.2	1.6	2.2	1.7	1.5	1.5	1.2
Quick Ratio 31	1.1	•	1.1	1.7	1.4	1.4	1.2	1.2	1.2	0.8
Net Sales to Working Capital 32	14.7	•	59.8	11.6	11.8	5.7	8.6	7.1	8.7	16.5
Coverage Ratio 33	6.5	50.4	29.4	9.1	26.7	24.4	11.1	16.8	4.4	4.5
Total Asset Turnover 34	1.5	•	5.4	3.2	2.6	1.9	2.1	1.5	1.3	0.8
Inventory Turnover 35	23.5	•	26.3	8.8	41.8	9.8	25.0	34.9	16.3	111.0
Receivables Turnover 36	11.5	•	73.9	13.5	12.1	5.6	7.2	5.6	5.9	5.9
Total Liabilities to Net Worth 37	2.4	•	2.6	1.6	2.1	2.2	1.4	1.7	1.7	1.3
Current Assets to Working Capital 38	3.1	•	4.9	1.9	2.6	1.8	2.5	3.0	3.0	6.6
Current Liabilities to Working Capital 39	2.1	•	3.9	0.9	1.6	0.8	1.5	2.0	2.0	5.6
Working Capital to Net Sales 40	0.1	•	0.0	0.1	0.1	0.2	0.1	0.1	0.1	0.1
Inventory to Working Capital 41	0.2	•	0.5	0.2	0.1	0.3	0.2	0.1	0.0	0.0
Total Receipts to Cash Flow 42	3.0	2.2	2.6	4.1	3.2	3.0	3.6	4.0	2.7	2.9
Cost of Goods to Cash Flow 43	0.8	0.4	0.5	0.9	1.1	1.2	1.8	1.6	0.7	0.7
Cash Flow to Total Debt 44	0.7	•	2.8	1.3	1.2	0.9	1.0	0.6	0.8	0.5

Selected Financial Factors (in Percentages)

Item										
Debt Ratio 45	70.3	•	72.0	61.8	68.0	68.9	57.5	63.2	63.1	56.4
Return on Total Assets 46	21.0	•	90.3	20.1	30.6	26.9	14.3	18.5	10.0	10.6
Return on Equity Before Income Taxes 47	59.9	•	311.6	46.8	92.0	83.0	30.6	47.2	20.9	18.9
Return on Equity After Income Taxes 48	56.7	•	309.1	46.1	88.5	78.5	26.6	40.5	15.3	15.4
Profit Margin (Before Income Tax) 49	12.0	20.1	16.3	5.6	11.4	13.6	6.3	11.4	5.9	10.0
Profit Margin (After Income Tax) 50	11.4	19.7	16.2	5.5	11.0	12.8	5.5	9.8	4.3	8.2

Table I
Corporations with and without Net Income

OFFICES OF BANK HOLDING COMPANIES

MONEY AMOUNTS AND SIZE OF ASSETS IN THOUSANDS OF DOLLARS

Item Description for Accounting Period 7/08 Through 6/09	Total	Zero Assets	Under 500	500 to 1,000	1,000 to 5,000	5,000 to 10,000	10,000 to 25,000	25,000 to 50,000	50,000 to 100,000	100,000 to 250,000	250,000 to 500,000	500,000 to 2,500,000	2,500,000 and over
Number of Enterprises **1**	4917	75	0	•	•	•	191	520	889	1490	826	699	181
Revenues ($ in Thousands)													
Net Sales **2**	172633278	180382	0	•	•	•	21341	345073	1107607	3907738	3890852	8055788	155106212
Interest **3**	660666291	2236533	0	•	74838	•	128526	448370	1698204	7501840	10424023	28457306	609696466
Rents **4**	19471485	16931	0	•	0	•	132	1265	8008	26743	41502	204203	19172700
Royalties **5**	343174	0	0	•	0	•	10	15	445	514	732	12218	329239
Other Portfolio Income **6**	36643111	89989	0	•	3374	•	9219	64308	166153	585726	738035	1564930	33417514
Other Receipts **7**	117245422	309200	0	•	6729	•	39741	435827	1213159	3871161	3699598	7838344	99830576
Total Receipts **8**	1007002761	2833035	0	•	97563	•	198969	1294858	4193576	15893722	18794742	46132789	917552707
Average Total Receipts **9**	204800	37774	•	•	10840	•	1042	2490	4717	10667	22754	65998	5069352
Operating Costs/Operating Income (%)													
Cost of Operations **10**	3.4	•	•	•	•	•	•	•	0.2	0.0	0.6	0.1	3.8
Salaries and Wages **11**	76.2	246.3	•	•	136.1	•	118.1	48.0	50.4	56.5	73.1	88.2	76.2
Taxes Paid **12**	8.4	23.7	•	•	22.1	•	28.7	10.8	10.3	10.6	12.6	14.2	7.9
Interest Paid **13**	225.7	928.1	•	•	393.4	•	292.8	119.4	127.8	144.1	176.4	204.1	230.2
Depreciation **14**	20.2	29.0	•	•	9.4	•	29.1	9.3	11.7	12.4	14.9	19.5	20.6
Amortization and Depletion **15**	3.8	1.8	•	•	2.1	•	3.6	1.4	1.6	1.2	1.6	2.9	4.0
Pensions and Other Deferred Comp. **16**	5.7	11.7	•	•	1.3	•	17.2	3.3	3.7	3.7	4.5	5.9	5.7
Employee Benefits **17**	10.0	16.2	•	•	17.5	•	32.2	11.6	10.9	10.3	10.9	11.3	9.9
Advertising **18**	5.8	7.8	•	•	6.1	•	6.4	3.2	3.6	4.9	4.5	5.9	5.9
Other Expenses **19**	206.3	513.3	•	•	1515.4	•	212.4	92.9	87.0	97.5	122.0	157.5	214.4
Officers' Compensation **20**	4.4	35.6	•	•	7.0	•	134.2	39.3	34.0	27.6	25.0	21.0	2.1
Operating Margin **21**	•	•			•			•	•			•	•
Operating Margin Before Officers' Comp. **22**	•	•			•			•	•			•	•

Selected Average Balance Sheet ($ in Thousands)

Net Receivables 23	1344378	0	•	236	•	9127	•	22865	•	46684	105794	231715	621423	31888142
Inventories 24	18	0	•	0	•	0	•	0	•	0	1	0	8	448
Net Property, Plant and Equipment 25	25967	0	•	100	•	208	•	603	•	1485	3639	7504	19685	555936
Total Assets 26	3745935	0	•	2387	•	18927	•	37665	•	74079	163391	351599	990653	94491989
Notes and Loans Payable 27	612689	0	•	7873	•	315	•	730	•	3002	9709	24117	83837	16112814
All Other Liabilities 28	2564675	0	•	1195	•	15170	•	31771	•	62876	138826	297488	829018	63553158
Net Worth 29	568570	0	•	-6681	•	3442	•	5164	•	8201	14855	29994	77799	14826017

Selected Financial Ratios (Times to 1)

Current Ratio 30	0.8	•	•	1.4	•	1.0	•	1.0	•	1.0	1.0	1.0	0.9	0.7
Quick Ratio 31	0.7	•	•	1.3	•	0.9	•	1.0	•	1.0	1.0	1.0	0.9	0.7
Net Sales to Working Capital 32	•	•	•	3.6	•	•	•	0.4	•	0.6	•	•	•	•
Coverage Ratio 33	1.1	0.7	•	•	•	1.1	•	1.2	•	1.2	1.1	1.1	1.1	1.0
Total Asset Turnover 34	0.0	•	•	0.6	•	0.0	•	0.0	•	0.0	0.0	0.0	0.0	0.0
Inventory Turnover 35	66.4	•	•	•	•	•	•	•	•	7.3	0.6	107.3	1.9	71.7
Receivables Turnover 36	0.0	•	•	2.9	•	0.0	•	0.0	•	0.0	0.0	0.0	0.0	0.0
Total Liabilities to Net Worth 37	5.6	•	•	3.6	•	4.5	•	6.3	•	8.0	10.0	10.7	11.7	5.4
Current Assets to Working Capital 38	•	•	•	3.6	•	22.4	•	31.1	•	•	•	•	•	•
Current Liabilities to Working Capital 39	•	•	•	2.6	•	21.4	•	30.1	•	•	•	•	•	•
Working Capital to Net Sales 40	•	•	•	0.3	•	2.2	•	1.7	•	•	•	•	•	•
Inventory to Working Capital 41	•	•	•	•	•	•	•	0.0	•	0.0	•	•	•	•
Total Receipts to Cash Flow 42	0.5	0.6	•	•	•	0.4	•	0.9	•	0.9	0.8	0.7	0.6	0.5
Cost of Goods to Cash Flow 43	0.0	•	•	•	•	•	•	•	•	0.0	0.0	0.0	0.0	0.0
Cash Flow to Total Debt 44	0.0	•	•	0.0	•	0.0	•	0.0	•	0.0	0.0	0.0	0.0	0.0

Selected Financial Factors (in Percentages)

Debt Ratio 45	84.8	•	•	379.9	•	81.8	•	86.3	•	88.9	90.9	91.5	92.1	84.3
Return on Total Assets 46	2.2	•	•	•	•	1.9	•	2.6	•	2.6	2.7	2.7	2.7	2.2
Return on Equity Before Income Taxes 47	0.7	•	•	281.7	•	1.0	•	3.3	•	4.0	4.7	3.6	4.4	0.6
Return on Equity After Income Taxes 48	0.0	•	•	283.8	•	0.4	•	2.8	•	3.1	3.3	2.0	2.1	•
Profit Margin (Before Income Tax) 49	12.0	•	•	32.2	•	32.2	•	26.0	•	26.2	26.5	23.2	29.8	10.8
Profit Margin (After Income Tax) 50	0.0	•	•	•	•	11.7	•	21.4	•	20.4	18.5	12.5	14.3	•

Table II
Corporations with Net Income

OFFICES OF BANK HOLDING COMPANIES

MONEY AMOUNTS AND SIZE OF ASSETS IN THOUSANDS OF DOLLARS

Item Description for Accounting Period 7/08 Through 6/09		Total	Zero Assets	Under 500	500 to 1,000	1,000 to 5,000	5,000 to 10,000	10,000 to 25,000	25,000 to 50,000	50,000 to 100,000	100,000 to 250,000	250,000 to 500,000	500,000 to 2,500,000	2,500,000 and over
Number of Enterprises	1	3740	17	0	•	•	•	126	391	706	1182	619	537	141
Revenues ($ in Thousands)														
Net Sales	2	146198009	12840	0	•	6	•	16466	266190	947379	3251388	3184690	6813498	131697568
Interest	3	422606422	74837	0	•	313	•	93900	329038	1260999	5666184	7510200	21245279	386425511
Rents	4	17283776	298	0	•	0	•	95	608	5585	17236	29843	154688	17075423
Royalties	5	318004	0	0	•	0	•	0	0	414	511	245	9822	307012
Other Portfolio Income	6	26846185	15850	0	•	2661	•	7095	48431	142014	484037	549240	1250994	24342073
Other Receipts	7	88621828	9410	0	•	4268	•	37437	358749	1034891	3266562	2823188	6366270	74721052
Total Receipts	8	701874224	113235	0	•	9585	•	154993	1003016	3391282	12685918	14097406	35840551	634568639
Average Total Receipts	9	187667	6661	•	•	1598	•	1230	2565	4804	10733	22774	66742	4500487
Operating Costs/Operating Income (%)														
Cost of Operations	10	3.4	•	•	•	•	•	•	•	0.2	0.0	0.7	0.0	3.8
Salaries and Wages	11	64.6	124.0	•	•	27.2	•	89.7	45.4	43.6	50.7	63.8	80.4	64.3
Taxes Paid	12	8.4	31.4	•	•	20.3	•	25.2	10.9	9.6	10.2	11.8	13.5	7.9
Interest Paid	13	160.9	213.5	•	•	107.9	•	301.0	112.9	116.4	131.6	151.8	175.4	161.5
Depreciation	14	19.6	29.8	•	•	1.1	•	19.4	7.9	9.6	11.4	13.2	17.4	20.2
Amortization and Depletion	15	1.9	0.5	•	•	8.0	•	2.9	1.2	1.1	1.0	1.5	2.7	1.9
Pensions and Other Deferred Comp.	16	4.9	5.7	•	•	0.8	•	11.4	3.8	3.4	3.7	4.6	5.9	4.8
Employee Benefits	17	7.7	21.0	•	•	6.8	•	29.9	11.0	9.9	10.0	10.3	10.6	7.4
Advertising	18	5.0	8.4	•	•	1.7	•	6.0	3.0	3.1	4.8	4.0	5.6	5.0
Other Expenses	19	150.0	163.7	•	•	45.8	•	158.3	70.7	66.1	72.7	82.7	110.6	156.4
Officers' Compensation	20	4.0	61.7	•	•	20.4	•	122.1	38.5	31.2	26.9	23.8	19.4	1.9
Operating Margin	21	•	•			•	•	•					•	•
Operating Margin Before Officers' Comp.	22	•	•			•	•	•					•	•

Selected Average Balance Sheet ($ in Thousands)

Item									
Net Receivables 23	1323813	355	10312	22918	46302	105179	231385	629356	30514869
Inventories 24	22	0	0	0	0	1	0	10	543
Net Property, Plant and Equipment 25	26848	143	182	530	1331	3477	7141	19889	567588
Total Assets 26	3487268	2070	19721	37890	74416	163197	349948	993226	85315980
Notes and Loans Payable 27	457980	0	376	710	2597	9358	23373	80905	11643350
All Other Liabilities 28	2407274	1171	17981	32071	63734	138175	294551	824915	57835233
Net Worth 29	622014	899	1364	5109	8086	15664	32024	87407	15837396

Selected Financial Ratios (Times to 1)

Item									
Current Ratio 30	0.8	1.7	1.0	1.0	1.0	1.0	1.0	0.9	0.8
Quick Ratio 31	0.8	1.5	0.9	1.0	1.0	1.0	1.0	0.9	0.7
Net Sales to Working Capital 32	•	0.5	•	0.4	0.6	2.3	•	•	•
Coverage Ratio 33	1.3	2.3	1.5	1.5	1.4	1.4	1.4	1.4	1.3
Total Asset Turnover 34	0.0	0.2	0.0	0.0	0.0	0.0	0.0	0.0	0.0
Inventory Turnover 35	60.3	•	•	•	10.6	0.7	107.3	0.0	65.1
Receivables Turnover 36	0.0	•	0.0	0.0	0.0	0.0	0.0	0.0	0.0
Total Liabilities to Net Worth 37	4.6	1.3	13.5	6.4	8.2	9.4	9.9	10.4	4.4
Current Assets to Working Capital 38	•	•	2.5	21.0	29.2	119.9	•	•	•
Current Liabilities to Working Capital 39	•	•	1.5	20.0	28.2	118.9	•	•	•
Working Capital to Net Sales 40	•	1.9	1.9	2.4	1.7	0.4	•	•	•
Inventory to Working Capital 41	•	•	•	•	0.0	0.0	•	•	•
Total Receipts to Cash Flow 42	0.6	0.5	0.3	0.7	0.8	0.8	0.7	0.6	0.5
Cost of Goods to Cash Flow 43	0.0	•	•	•	0.0	0.0	0.0	0.0	0.0
Cash Flow to Total Debt 44	0.0	0.7	0.0	0.0	0.0	0.0	0.0	0.0	0.0

Selected Financial Factors (in Percentages)

Item										
Debt Ratio 45	82.2	56.6	93.1	86.5	89.1	90.4	90.8	91.2	81.4	
Return on Total Assets 46	2.3	47.6	3.0	3.1	3.0	3.2	3.1	3.2	2.3	
Return on Equity Before Income Taxes 47	2.9	62.8	14.6	8.2	8.7	9.7	9.9	10.5	2.6	
Return on Equity After Income Taxes 48	2.0	39.3	12.1	7.4	7.5	8.0	7.8	7.9	1.8	
Profit Margin (Before Income Tax) 49	46.4	200.4	144.6	152.4	61.2	52.2	55.4	61.3	72.5	44.3
Profit Margin (After Income Tax) 50	32.6	162.6	90.5	126.0	55.3	45.4	45.8	48.4	54.2	30.6

Table I

Corporations with and without Net Income

OFFICES OF OTHER HOLDING COMPANIES

MONEY AMOUNTS AND SIZE OF ASSETS IN THOUSANDS OF DOLLARS

Item Description for Accounting Period 7/08 Through 6/09	Total	Zero Assets	Under 500	500 to 1,000	1,000 to 5,000	5,000 to 10,000	10,000 to 25,000	25,000 to 50,000	50,000 to 100,000	100,000 to 250,000	250,000 to 500,000	500,000 to 2,500,000	2,500,000 and over
Number of Enterprises 1	40808	9907	19597	•	4679	•	972	493	265	237	84	71	24
Revenues ($ in Thousands)													
Net Sales 2	1968188	5692	54992	•	83463	•	51400	252393	159974	263927	115303	255070	648239
Interest 3	5354390	579871	277735	•	59643	•	110853	103643	172824	440139	459881	1700465	1341604
Rents 4	205031	36410	3434	•	13381	•	11428	10267	51906	9711	6585	34370	4038
Royalties 5	107298	4135	2879	•	672	•	225	14825	17610	22627	755	14196	17826
Other Portfolio Income 6	5593107	415425	149107	•	462585	•	374183	316317	249821	340274	1273561	658438	1073423
Other Receipts 7	7633130	-1231114	108639	•	772902	•	925558	403918	543898	438076	327134	2207741	2584416
Total Receipts 8	20861144	-189581	596786	•	1392646	•	1473647	1101363	1196033	1514754	2183219	4870280	5669546
Average Total Receipts 9	511	-19	30	•	298	•	1516	2234	4513	6391	25991	68595	236231
Operating Costs/Operating Income (%)													
Cost of Operations 10	22.6	0.4	•	•	9.0	•	1.5	64.5	68.0	10.8	51.2	3.2	10.8
Salaries and Wages 11	49.7	239.7	4.3	•	51.9	•	80.7	28.2	64.5	158.4	37.2	23.9	17.0
Taxes Paid 12	42.7	1665.8	25.1	•	71.6	•	66.2	12.7	24.5	25.3	35.1	47.1	46.5
Interest Paid 13	282.4	11698.4	509.3	•	52.2	•	385.5	58.0	102.3	176.5	746.1	502.3	214.9
Depreciation 14	13.7	105.7	2.9	•	13.3	•	59.8	6.7	21.0	6.8	21.0	28.7	7.5
Amortization and Depletion 15	34.2	1100.4	1.2	•	30.8	•	23.3	25.4	21.6	21.8	20.4	80.7	24.0
Pensions and Other Deferred Comp. 16	4.7	33.9	0.4	•	11.3	•	3.3	2.8	1.4	0.5	1.6	2.0	9.0
Employee Benefits 17	5.0	8.2	22.4	•	18.9	•	7.7	1.5	5.4	11.2	3.8	2.6	1.1
Advertising 18	1.1	0.2	0.0	•	0.7	•	0.9	1.9	0.3	1.0	0.6	0.3	1.5
Other Expenses 19	819.7	55602.0	478.6	•	738.7	•	1199.9	236.7	915.7	787.5	4814.8	272.7	81.8
Officers' Compensation 20	23.2	54.9	9.1	•	165.8	•	80.6	9.9	15.8	13.6	9.6	19.7	11.5
Operating Margin 21	•	•	•	•	•	•	•	•	•	•	•	•	•
Operating Margin Before Officers' Comp. 22	•	•	•	•	•	•	•	•	•	•	•	•	•

Selected Average Balance Sheet ($ in Thousands)

Item	1	2	3	4	5	6	7	8	9	10	11	12	13
Net Receivables 23	486	0	2	•	129	•	646	1243	3290	8469	19290	29504	464994
Inventories 24	4	0	0	•	0	•	0	78	72	99	326	204	1864
Net Property, Plant and Equipment 25	150	0	1	•	95	•	365	1182	1702	3258	13554	28031	8964
Total Assets 26	8750	0	113	•	2232	•	16303	34660	70371	150725	353628	1156966	5657977
Notes and Loans Payable 27	1922	0	42	•	500	•	2572	5800	12177	27337	126796	311614	1059800
All Other Liabilities 28	1064	0	8	•	202	•	2299	2801	10563	19096	69730	115407	689869
Net Worth 29	5764	0	63	•	1529	•	11432	26058	47631	104292	157101	729945	3908309

Selected Financial Ratios (Times to 1)

Item	1	2	3	4	5	6	7	8	9	10	11	12	13
Current Ratio 30	2.0	•	1.9	•	4.8	•	2.1	2.7	3.7	1.7	2.0	1.4	2.2
Quick Ratio 31	1.5	•	1.5	•	3.3	•	1.5	1.8	2.2	1.2	1.3	0.7	2.0
Net Sales to Working Capital 32	0.1	•	0.1	•	0.0	•	0.0	0.1	0.0	0.1	0.0	0.1	0.1
Coverage Ratio 33	0.7	•	1.0	•	10.3	•	3.8	0.6	•	•	•	2.9	4.8
Total Asset Turnover 34	0.0	•	0.0	•	0.0	•	0.0	0.0	0.0	0.0	0.0	0.0	0.0
Inventory Turnover 35	3.0	•	•	•	6.0	•	1.9	4.2	5.7	1.2	2.2	0.6	1.6
Receivables Turnover 36	0.1	•	0.5	•	0.2	•	0.1	0.4	0.2	0.2	0.1	0.1	0.0
Total Liabilities to Net Worth 37	0.5	•	0.8	•	0.5	•	0.4	0.3	0.5	0.4	1.3	0.6	0.4
Current Assets to Working Capital 38	2.0	•	2.1	•	1.3	•	1.9	1.6	1.4	2.5	2.0	3.3	1.8
Current Liabilities to Working Capital 39	1.0	•	1.1	•	0.3	•	0.9	0.6	0.4	1.5	1.0	2.3	0.8
Working Capital to Net Sales 40	16.2	•	7.0	•	26.4	•	35.8	9.5	21.0	9.3	25.4	14.6	16.6
Inventory to Working Capital 41	0.0	•	•	•	0.0	•	0.0	0.0	0.0	0.0	0.0	0.0	0.0
Total Receipts to Cash Flow 42	0.2	•	0.4	•	0.1	•	0.1	0.6	0.4	1.4	0.2	0.1	0.2
Cost of Goods to Cash Flow 43	0.1	•	•	•	0.0	•	0.0	0.4	0.2	0.1	0.1	0.0	0.0
Cash Flow to Total Debt 44	0.1	•	0.2	•	0.2	•	0.2	0.1	0.1	0.0	0.0	0.1	0.1

Selected Financial Factors (in Percentages)

Item	1	2	3	4	5	6	7	8	9	10	11	12	13
Debt Ratio 45	34.1	•	44.6	•	31.5	•	29.9	24.8	32.3	30.8	55.6	36.9	30.9
Return on Total Assets 46	1.0	•	13.2	•	4.3	•	4.7	0.5	•	•	•	4.5	4.9
Return on Equity Before Income Taxes 47	•	•	0.9	•	4.9	•	5.7	•	•	•	•	4.7	5.7
Return on Equity After Income Taxes 48	•	•	4.1	•	3.3	•	4.1	•	•	•	•	3.3	3.9
Profit Margin (Before Income Tax) 49	20.7	•	485.0	•	1065.4	•	•	•	•	•	•	949.1	821.2
Profit Margin (After Income Tax) 50	•	•	348.7	•	706.6	•	•	•	•	•	•	673.7	568.5

Table II

Corporations with Net Income

OFFICES OF OTHER HOLDING COMPANIES

MONEY AMOUNTS AND SIZE OF ASSETS IN THOUSANDS OF DOLLARS

Item Description for Accounting Period 7/08 Through 6/09	Total	Zero Assets	Under 500	500 to 1000	1,000 to 5,000	5,000 to 10,000	10,000 to 25,000	25,000 to 50,000	50,000 to 100,000	100,000 to 250,000	250,000 to 500,000	500,000 to 2,500,000	2,500,000 and over
Number of Enterprises **1**	14144	2947	5915	•	2116	•	427	188	103	98	44	46	15
Revenues ($ in Thousands)													
Net Sales **2**	1132792	4491	11	•	79220	•	35983	30523	40231	35278	100950	190888	610130
Interest **3**	3522315	125312	13108	•	42000	•	63483	62138	83485	237362	350354	1459946	1041130
Rents **4**	123355	8008	3332	•	13376	•	4894	5809	51716	329	5976	7397	222
Royalties **5**	83060	627	1395	•	597	•	225	14822	4987	21647	0	14196	13184
Other Portfolio Income **6**	5040813	324122	143583	•	433927	•	336084	280020	170566	256190	1236956	602424	996621
Other Receipts **7**	14220288	1386289	204562	•	918003	•	1032455	803100	738368	1367819	1032900	3490864	2570056
Total Receipts **8**	24122623	1848849	365991	•	1487123	•	1473124	1196412	1089353	1918625	2727136	5765715	5231343
Average Total Receipts **9**	1706	627	62	•	703	•	3450	6364	10576	19578	61980	125342	348756
Operating Costs/Operating Income (%)													
Cost of Operations **10**	15.8	0.6	•	•	8.8	•	0.2	0.3	26.6	79.3	58.5	2.0	11.5
Salaries and Wages **11**	36.3	238.7	21690.9	•	27.5	•	64.5	61.5	119.7	345.7	28.0	16.0	16.1
Taxes Paid **12**	63.1	1654.0	80145.5	•	66.9	•	73.8	65.0	57.4	115.7	33.2	56.6	49.0
Interest Paid **13**	202.7	1691.9	44809.1	•	31.4	•	157.5	167.3	121.0	304.4	381.4	368.6	134.2
Depreciation **14**	15.1	37.9	6654.5	•	10.4	•	33.2	23.3	9.5	2.6	21.7	32.7	7.9
Amortization and Depletion **15**	40.7	629.6	3118.2	•	6.7	•	22.7	29.2	36.3	38.9	21.2	103.9	25.5
Pensions and Other Deferred Comp. **16**	6.2	42.1	209.1	•	2.5	•	2.3	3.1	2.1	2.1	0.2	2.3	9.5
Employee Benefits **17**	2.2	0.5	5681.8	•	4.2	•	6.3	1.8	5.1	4.9	2.5	2.6	0.8
Advertising **18**	1.1	0.1	109.1	•	0.7	•	0.4	0.2	0.3	1.0	0.4	0.2	1.6
Other Expenses **19**	164.6	2864.5	116545.5	•	143.4	•	306.7	418.7	409.3	384.3	225.0	176.5	63.9
Officers' Compensation **20**	24.8	1.4	18681.8	•	115.9	•	75.2	54.5	21.5	75.2	1.6	8.0	12.0
Operating Margin **21**	•	•	•	•	•	•	•	•	•	•	•	•	•
Operating Margin Before Officers' Comp. **22**	•	•	•	•	•	•	•	•	•	•	•	•	•

Selected Average Balance Sheet ($ in Thousands)

Item												
Net Receivables 23	1138	0	1	151	745	840	3389	12891	28982	36548	709101
Inventories 24	5	0	0	1	0	44	99	619	252	2926	
Net Property, Plant and Equipment 25	211	0	1	11	467	890	582	1236	21008	25595	14331
Total Assets 26	14625	0	116	2186	16663	34048	70832	150132	352977	1232260	6020004
Notes and Loans Payable 27	2757	0	33	223	1886	4211	8738	20822	78760	290140	1109846
All Other Liabilities 28	1602	0	3	147	1435	3292	8235	15179	61824	109509	713964
Net Worth 29	10265	0	80	1816	13342	26545	53859	114131	212393	832612	4196195

Selected Financial Ratios (Times to 1)

Item												
Current Ratio 30	2.9	2.1	6.3	4.1	2.5	5.1	3.4	3.9	2.9	2.4	
Quick Ratio 31	2.3	1.7	4.2	3.0	1.6	3.2	2.7	2.4	1.6	2.4	
Net Sales to Working Capital 32	0.0	0.0	0.1	0.0	0.0	0.0	0.0	0.0	0.0	0.1	
Coverage Ratio 33	10.0	21.5	67.7	47.2	23.6	19.4	16.5	14.8	7.1	7.2	7.8
Total Asset Turnover 34	0.0	0.0	0.0	0.0	0.0	0.0	0.0	0.0	0.0		
Inventory Turnover 35	2.3	4.2	0.2	0.5	2.4	2.9	2.2	0.3	1.6		
Receivables Turnover 36	0.1	0.0	0.1	0.1	0.1	0.0	0.1	0.1	0.0		
Total Liabilities to Net Worth 37	0.4	0.5	0.2	0.3	0.3	0.3	0.7	0.5	0.4		
Current Assets to Working Capital 38	1.5	1.9	1.2	1.7	1.2	1.4	1.3	1.5	1.7		
Current Liabilities to Working Capital 39	0.5	0.9	0.2	0.7	0.2	0.4	0.3	0.5	0.7		
Working Capital to Net Sales 40	24.6	14046.3	16.4	32.2	32.8	42.5	65.9	24.7	31.3	18.0	
Inventory to Working Capital 41	0.0	0.0	0.0	0.0	0.0	0.0	0.0	0.0			
Total Receipts to Cash Flow 42	0.1	0.0	0.1	0.0	0.0	0.0	0.1	0.0	0.2		
Cost of Goods to Cash Flow 43	0.0	0.0	0.0	0.0	0.0	0.0	0.0	0.0	0.0		
Cash Flow to Total Debt 44	0.3	1.2	1.2	0.8	0.7	0.5	0.4	0.3	0.7	0.1	

Selected Financial Factors (in Percentages)

Item												
Debt Ratio 45	29.8	31.3	16.9	19.9	22.0	24.0	24.0	39.8	32.4	30.3	
Return on Total Assets 46	11.1	48.7	25.3	18.8	15.4	11.0	10.8	17.7	8.9	7.1	
Return on Equity Before Income Taxes 47	14.2	69.9	29.9	22.4	18.8	13.6	13.2	25.3	11.3	8.9	
Return on Equity After Income Taxes 48	11.2	61.4	26.9	19.2	17.3	11.8	10.4	18.1	9.5	6.3	
Profit Margin (Before Income Tax) 49	1820.4	34626.2	2989263.6	1448.1	3551.2	3072.5	1873.4	4195.3	2344.6	2274.9	918.1
Profit Margin (After Income Tax) 50	1437.0	25667.8	2626000.0	1304.6	3047.5	2826.5	1633.2	3303.7	1676.5	1906.8	649.5

Table I

Corporations with and without Net Income

EMPLOYMENT SERVICES

MONEY AMOUNTS AND SIZE OF ASSETS IN THOUSANDS OF DOLLARS

Item Description for Accounting Period 7/08 Through 6/09		Total	Zero Assets	Under 500	500 to 1,000	1,000 to 5,000	5,000 to 10,000	10,000 to 25,000	25,000 to 50,000	50,000 to 100,000	100,000 to 250,000	250,000 to 500,000	500,000 to 2,500,000	2,500,000 and over
Number of Enterprises	1	30969	6068	21510	1519	1513	135	136	20	21	13	17	14	3
Revenues ($ in Thousands)														
Net Sales	2	157157797	442958	35719077	6551161	22218614	1721879	9363972	2805327	7099759	7831522	13195940	39983751	6241836
Interest	3	193604	136	2324	2947	10880	3147	6799	1434	2904	6401	21275	104691	30664
Rents	4	9275	0	5504	0	299	0	6	0	3	769	44	2616	35
Royalties	5	344113	0	0	0	0	0	0	0	1261	8082	64822	46907	223042
Other Portfolio Income	6	429748	1177	1917	45618	22397	13945	7859	19185	7245	21897	5523	200482	82502
Other Receipts	7	946688	34262	62123	17269	29440	15887	39818	15128	83510	-2308	118783	-350325	883101
Total Receipts	8	159081225	460533	35790945	6616995	22281630	1754858	9418454	2841074	7194682	7866363	13406387	39988122	7461180
Average Total Receipts	9	5137	735	1664	4356	14727	12999	69253	142054	342604	605105	788611	2856294	2487060
Operating Costs/Operating Income (%)														
Cost of Operations	10	49.7	22.4	30.2	56.5	53.6	20.8	56.7	44.0	60.7	52.7	55.6	58.7	73.9
Salaries and Wages	11	25.2	52.8	24.4	17.1	25.9	57.1	24.7	41.3	28.8	36.0	23.7	21.2	12.6
Taxes Paid	12	3.0	8.2	3.5	2.5	2.0	5.6	3.0	3.6	3.4	3.5	2.5	2.2	4.3
Interest Paid	13	0.5	0.3	0.3	0.2	0.2	1.0	0.3	1.0	0.8	0.8	0.8	0.4	1.7
Depreciation	14	0.4	0.1	0.2	0.3	0.2	0.4	0.4	0.5	0.4	0.5	0.5	0.6	1.0
Amortization and Depletion	15	0.4	0.6	0.0	0.2	0.1	0.5	0.2	0.4	0.3	1.0	1.0	0.6	0.8
Pensions and Other Deferred Comp.	16	0.2	0.1	0.4	0.6	0.1	0.2	0.1	0.1	0.1	0.1	0.8	0.1	0.3
Employee Benefits	17	2.1	1.5	1.1	0.3	2.4	3.2	2.9	2.5	1.4	1.9	1.8	3.3	1.6
Advertising	18	0.4	0.6	0.6	0.5	0.3	1.4	0.4	0.4	0.2	0.2	0.3	0.3	0.2
Other Expenses	19	15.1	12.3	33.6	17.9	11.7	11.7	9.0	6.9	4.1	3.7	10.1	9.6	7.7
Officers' Compensation	20	1.7	0.6	4.8	2.3	1.5	2.9	1.5	0.4	0.6	0.3	0.7	0.3	0.7
Operating Margin	21	1.2	0.7	0.9	1.8	2.0	•	0.9	•	•	•	2.3	2.7	•
Operating Margin Before Officers' Comp.	22	2.9	1.2	5.7	4.0	3.5	•	2.4	•	•	•	3.0	3.0	•

Selected Average Balance Sheet ($ in Thousands)

Net Receivables 23	437	0	19	225	716	3026	5509	12787	25668	51669	99303	407732	557469
Inventories 24	3	0	0	0	0	0	102	56	488	21	141	3797	591
Net Property, Plant and Equipment 25	115	0	11	56	129	222	906	2057	8990	7584	12578	68820	462699
Total Assets 26	1460	98	699	2095	6946	14465	36324	71031	173092	352380	996328		3852122
Notes and Loans Payable 27	381	57	160	652	1926	3424	12274	22147	59813	83541	241259		772218
All Other Liabilities 28	485	32	205	748	1501	4975	16939	37054	58628	122682	308135		1244979
Net Worth 29	594	8	334	695	3519	6067	7111	11830	54651	146157	446934		1834925

Selected Financial Ratios (Times to 1)

Current Ratio 30	1.3	•	1.2	2.1	1.2	1.6	1.6	1.5	1.4	1.3	1.6	1.3	0.8
Quick Ratio 31	1.1	•	1.0	1.6	0.9	1.3	1.2	1.1	1.0	1.2	1.4	1.1	0.7
Net Sales to Working Capital 32	35.3	•	165.1	16.9	66.5	7.7	19.0	18.1	29.7	31.1	12.8	21.3	•
Coverage Ratio 33	6.6	6.0	5.3	16.0	10.5	•	5.4	1.2	1.7	0.8	6.1	7.7	12.6
Total Asset Turnover 34	3.5	•	16.9	6.2	7.0	1.8	4.8	3.9	4.8	3.5	2.2	2.9	0.5
Inventory Turnover 35	881.2	•	33189.6	1790.5	•	•	383.3	1104.0	420.4	153577.4	3055.0	441.8	2602.2
Receivables Turnover 36	12.2	•	90.2	15.8	20.1	3.3	12.9	8.9	12.0	12.1	7.6	7.1	7.5
Total Liabilities to Net Worth 37	1.5	•	10.6	1.1	2.0	1.0	1.4	4.1	5.0	2.2	1.4	1.2	1.1
Current Assets to Working Capital 38	4.9	•	6.5	1.9	6.3	2.7	2.7	3.1	3.6	4.0	2.6	4.3	•
Current Liabilities to Working Capital 39	3.9	•	5.5	0.9	5.3	1.7	1.7	2.1	2.6	3.0	1.6	3.3	•
Working Capital to Net Sales 40	0.0	•	0.0	0.1	0.0	0.1	0.1	0.1	0.0	0.0	0.1	0.0	•
Inventory to Working Capital 41	0.0	•	•	•	0.0	•	0.0	0.0	0.0	•	•	0.0	•
Total Receipts to Cash Flow 42	6.2	8.4	3.0	5.3	7.7	15.3	10.7	19.2	26.8	35.9	8.3	9.5	4.9
Cost of Goods to Cash Flow 43	3.1	1.9	0.9	3.0	4.1	3.2	6.1	8.5	16.3	18.9	4.6	5.6	3.6
Cash Flow to Total Debt 44	0.9	•	6.1	2.2	1.4	0.2	0.8	0.2	0.2	0.1	0.5	0.5	0.2

Selected Financial Factors (in Percentages)

Debt Ratio 45	59.3	•	91.4	52.2	66.8	49.3	58.1	80.4	83.3	68.4	58.5	55.1	52.4
Return on Total Assets 46	10.8	•	23.5	18.4	17.8	•	8.4	4.6	6.6	2.2	10.3	9.1	11.7
Return on Equity Before Income Taxes 47	22.5	•	221.3	36.0	48.6	•	16.3	4.3	16.4	•	20.7	17.6	22.6
Return on Equity After Income Taxes 48	17.6	•	216.0	34.2	46.5	•	14.4	•	13.3	•	16.7	13.0	14.7
Profit Margin (Before Income Tax) 49	2.6	1.4	1.1	2.8	2.3	•	1.4	0.2	0.6	•	3.9	2.8	19.9
Profit Margin (After Income Tax) 50	2.1	1.3	1.1	2.6	2.2	•	1.3	•	0.5	•	3.1	2.0	13.0

353

Table II

Corporations with Net Income

EMPLOYMENT SERVICES

MONEY AMOUNTS AND SIZE OF ASSETS IN THOUSANDS OF DOLLARS

Item Description for Accounting Period 7/08 Through 6/09	Total	Zero Assets	Under 500	500 to 1,000	1,000 to 5,000	5,000 to 10,000	10,000 to 25,000	25,000 to 50,000	50,000 to 100,000	100,000 to 250,000	250,000 to 500,000	500,000 to 2,500,000	2,500,000 and over
Number of Enterprises **1**	15003	387	12225	1070	1104	64	93	•	13	6	•	10	3
Revenues ($ in Thousands)													
Net Sales **2**	112495127	3713527	22541383	3732390	14141493	1097557	6347472	•	3352388	4682120	•	32665049	6241836
Interest **3**	150734	132	614	2318	10039	2351	5034	•	242	923	•	83240	30664
Rents **4**	9243	0	5504	0	299	0	6	•	0	769	•	2587	35
Royalties **5**	327597	0	0	0	0	0	0	•	0	0	•	39734	223042
Other Portfolio Income **6**	308161	0	1761	103	22397	13943	5499	•	1092	2882	•	172064	82502
Other Receipts **7**	853196	34299	45136	15161	19121	7536	27157	•	78457	2645	•	-382962	883101
Total Receipts **8**	114144058	3747958	22594398	3749972	14193349	1121387	6385168	•	3432179	4689339	•	32579712	7461180
Average Total Receipts **9**	7608	9685	1848	3505	12856	17522	68658	•	264014	781556	•	3257971	2487060
Operating Costs/Operating Income (%)													
Cost of Operations **10**	43.8	24.4	13.4	40.0	39.9	13.5	66.1	•	41.0	66.2	•	54.4	73.9
Salaries and Wages **11**	26.4	50.4	23.1	19.8	36.2	65.0	13.7	•	43.3	24.7	•	23.7	12.6
Taxes Paid **12**	3.3	8.1	3.7	3.5	2.8	6.4	2.3	•	6.2	2.6	•	2.5	4.3
Interest Paid **13**	0.4	0.2	0.1	0.2	0.3	0.5	0.3	•	0.8	0.6	•	0.3	1.7
Depreciation **14**	0.4	0.1	0.1	0.3	0.3	0.2	0.3	•	0.4	0.5	•	0.6	1.0
Amortization and Depletion **15**	0.3	0.2	0.1	0.3	0.1	0.0	0.1	•	0.2	0.5	•	0.3	0.8
Pensions and Other Deferred Comp. **16**	0.3	0.1	0.7	0.3	0.1	0.0	0.2	•	0.1	0.1	•	0.1	0.3
Employee Benefits **17**	2.1	1.0	1.0	0.3	1.2	1.2	3.5	•	1.3	1.3	•	3.8	1.6
Advertising **18**	0.3	0.6	0.4	0.5	0.4	0.1	0.2	•	0.3	0.2	•	0.3	0.2
Other Expenses **19**	18.0	11.9	49.0	25.5	13.3	8.6	8.8	•	4.4	2.4	•	9.6	7.7
Officers' Compensation **20**	1.7	0.3	5.0	2.4	1.8	4.0	1.6	•	0.8	0.3	•	0.3	0.7
Operating Margin **21**	3.0	2.7	3.5	6.9	3.7	0.7	2.9	•	1.1	0.7	•	4.1	•
Operating Margin Before Officers' Comp. **22**	4.7	3.0	8.5	9.4	5.5	4.7	4.6	•	2.0	1.0	•	4.4	•

Selected Average Balance Sheet ($ in Thousands)

Net Receivables 23	722	•	22	317	712	3770	6032	27282	51808	•	463697	557469
Inventories 24	4	0	0	0	0	0	149	309	0	•	2750	591
Net Property, Plant and Equipment 25	189	0	14	54	160	209	752	7386	9854	•	58637	462699
Total Assets 26	2379	0	115	717	2038	7173	14536	68645	187756	•	1006579	3852122
Notes and Loans Payable 27	550	0	34	179	732	1875	2761	22413	45713	•	237649	772218
All Other Liabilities 28	780	0	29	176	564	2168	4800	32801	69562	•	322249	1244979
Net Worth 29	1049	0	52	362	742	3130	6974	13430	72481	•	446681	1834925

Selected Financial Ratios (Times to 1)

Current Ratio 30	1.3	•	2.0	2.5	1.3	2.0	1.9	1.6	1.5	•	1.2	0.8
Quick Ratio 31	1.1	•	1.8	2.3	1.0	1.5	1.4	1.2	1.2	•	1.1	0.7
Net Sales to Working Capital 32	31.7	•	45.5	10.8	42.7	5.7	14.7	15.2	28.9	•	32.6	•
Coverage Ratio 33	12.6	17.4	26.8	33.2	15.8	6.9	13.7	5.4	2.5	•	13.4	12.6
Total Asset Turnover 34	3.2	•	16.1	4.9	6.3	2.4	4.7	3.8	4.2	•	3.2	0.5
Inventory Turnover 35	767.5	•	•	13375.7	22614.0	•	303.1	342.0	14.6	•	646.1	2602.2
Receivables Turnover 36	10.5	•	77.4	9.8	17.1	•	11.1	7.6	1.6	•	•	7.5
Total Liabilities to Net Worth 37	1.3	•	1.2	1.0	1.7	1.3	1.1	4.1	3.1	•	1.3	1.1
Current Assets to Working Capital 38	4.8	•	2.0	1.7	4.6	2.0	2.2	2.7	2.1	•	6.3	•
Current Liabilities to Working Capital 39	3.8	•	1.0	0.7	3.6	1.0	1.2	1.7	0.0	•	5.3	•
Working Capital to Net Sales 40	0.0	•	0.0	0.1	0.0	0.2	0.1	0.1	0.0	•	0.0	•
Inventory to Working Capital 41	0.0	•	•	•	0.0	•	0.0	0.0	•	•	0.0	•
Total Receipts to Cash Flow 42	4.8	7.4	2.0	3.2	6.2	11.1	8.7	14.5	36.4	•	8.5	4.9
Cost of Goods to Cash Flow 43	2.1	1.8	0.3	1.3	2.5	1.5	5.7	6.0	24.1	•	4.6	3.6
Cash Flow to Total Debt 44	1.2	•	15.0	3.1	1.6	0.4	1.0	0.3	0.2	•	0.7	0.2

Selected Financial Factors (in Percentages)

Debt Ratio 45	55.9	•	55.0	49.5	63.6	56.4	52.0	80.4	61.4	•	55.6	52.4
Return on Total Assets 46	16.2	•	61.7	37.2	27.2	8.0	17.9	16.2	5.7	•	13.9	11.7
Return on Equity Before Income Taxes 47	33.9	•	132.0	71.4	69.8	15.7	34.6	67.4	8.9	•	28.9	22.6
Return on Equity After Income Taxes 48	28.2	•	130.5	69.0	67.2	14.9	32.1	63.0	6.4	•	22.5	14.7
Profit Margin (Before Income Tax) 49	4.7	3.6	3.7	7.4	4.0	2.9	3.5	3.5	0.8	•	4.0	19.9
Profit Margin (After Income Tax) 50	3.9	3.5	3.7	7.2	3.9	2.7	3.3	3.3	0.6	•	3.1	13.0

Table I

Corporations with and without Net Income

TRAVEL ARRANGEMENT AND RESERVATION SERVICES

MONEY AMOUNTS AND SIZE OF ASSETS IN THOUSANDS OF DOLLARS

Item Description for Accounting Period 7/08 Through 6/09	Total	Zero Assets	Under 500	500 to 1,000	1,000 to 5,000	5,000 to 10,000	10,000 to 25,000	25,000 to 50,000	50,000 to 100,000	100,000 to 250,000	250,000 to 500,000	500,000 to 2,500,000	2,500,000 and over
Number of Enterprises 1	23219	5988	16234	385	407	62	57	26	20	20	10	10	0
Revenues ($ in Thousands)													
Net Sales 2	38955330	1472507	14449004	1556387	1722909	278929	2088135	1426211	1559579	3120798	2936205	8344664	0
Interest 3	232744	242	2243	1009	3649	331	3773	4472	11107	30886	31599	143432	0
Rents 4	53913	45	3570	1909	6	0	323	182	3332	5308	2894	36343	0
Royalties 5	87218	0	0	0	0	0	0	0	1001	0	53609	32607	0
Other Portfolio Income 6	177327	3504	6332	4196	5	11088	4326	11055	24873	13997	11005	86946	0
Other Receipts 7	1925022	5700	40907	2764	99390	4847	15372	114739	105339	78757	935769	521444	0
Total Receipts 8	41431554	1481998	14502056	1566265	1825959	295195	2211929	1556659	1705231	3249746	3971081	9165436	0
Average Total Receipts 9	1784	247	893	4068	4486	4761	37051	59872	85262	162487	397108	916544	•
Operating Costs/Operating Income (%)													
Cost of Operations 10	51.9	69.8	69.4	72.8	53.6	33.8	62.8	54.7	59.5	45.0	49.6	13.7	•
Salaries and Wages 11	13.9	5.2	6.5	8.1	20.3	25.9	17.6	19.5	17.3	14.1	28.2	20.1	•
Taxes Paid 12	1.7	1.2	1.1	1.1	2.0	2.9	1.8	2.6	1.9	1.9	2.5	2.3	•
Interest Paid 13	1.7	2.0	0.2	0.3	0.3	0.1	0.1	1.1	1.4	0.5	2.1	5.5	•
Depreciation 14	1.2	1.1	0.4	0.3	1.3	2.0	0.9	1.6	2.1	1.6	1.8	2.1	•
Amortization and Depletion 15	0.6	0.3	0.0	0.0	0.3	0.2	0.1	0.5	1.1	0.8	1.0	1.5	•
Pensions and Other Deferred Comp. 16	0.6	0.0	0.3	•	0.4	0.1	0.3	0.4	0.4	0.7	1.9	1.0	•
Employee Benefits 17	1.3	0.4	0.4	1.2	1.3	0.6	1.3	1.6	2.2	1.7	2.8	2.4	•
Advertising 18	3.5	0.9	0.6	0.3	1.2	0.2	3.6	2.8	3.3	2.1	3.3	10.7	•
Other Expenses 19	25.8	23.0	16.9	11.1	18.3	28.3	11.0	21.0	20.5	31.7	38.8	44.7	•
Officers' Compensation 20	1.9	2.6	2.6	4.7	4.2	0.7	1.6	1.8	1.2	0.9	0.6	0.8	•
Operating Margin 21	•	•	1.5	0.1	•	5.2	•	•	•	•	•	•	•
Operating Margin Before Officers' Comp. 22	•	•	4.1	4.8	1.0	5.9	0.6	•	•	•	•	•	•

Selected Average Balance Sheet ($ in Thousands)

Net Receivables 23	112	0	4	93	353	1636	2303	10528	10575	23037	8904	107893	•
Inventories 24	6	0	1	0	81	103	133	184	939	282	1885	2001	•
Net Property, Plant and Equipment 25	105	0	11	121	216	120	1399	3238	10401	23876	24180	102760	•
Total Assets 26	1406	0	74	629	1819	6153	15538	35619	71564	145848	371025	2019966	•
Notes and Loans Payable 27	450	0	46	127	318	620	816	8035	24753	12427	101000	746748	•
All Other Liabilities 28	542	0	29	167	1123	4777	12170	25441	37472	74251	156888	613222	•
Net Worth 29	414	0	-1	335	378	756	2552	2142	9339	59170	113138	659997	•

Selected Financial Ratios (Times to 1)

Current Ratio 30	0.8	•	2.0	2.7	1.4	1.1	0.8	0.9	1.0	0.9	0.8	0.5	•
Quick Ratio 31	0.5	•	1.6	2.7	1.1	1.0	0.5	0.7	0.7	0.7	0.3	0.4	•
Net Sales to Working Capital 32	•	•	31.9	13.9	11.0	14.9	•	•	•	•	•	•	•
Coverage Ratio 33	2.4	•	10.3	3.1	10.4	197.7	1.4	2.5	1.1	6.5	2.3	2.0	•
Total Asset Turnover 34	1.2	•	12.0	6.4	2.3	0.7	2.4	1.5	1.1	1.1	0.8	0.4	•
Inventory Turnover 35	147.2	•	556.5	•	27.9	14.7	173.3	163.3	49.4	248.7	77.3	56.9	•
Receivables Turnover 36	13.4	•	161.5	44.0	11.1	3.8	11.2	6.1	6.3	6.4	33.0	12.2	•
Total Liabilities to Net Worth 37	2.4	•	•	0.9	3.8	7.1	5.1	15.6	6.7	1.5	2.3	2.1	•
Current Assets to Working Capital 38	•	•	2.0	1.6	3.4	16.7	•	•	•	•	•	•	•
Current Liabilities to Working Capital 39	•	•	1.0	0.6	2.4	15.7	•	•	•	•	•	•	•
Working Capital to Net Sales 40	•	•	0.0	0.1	0.1	0.1	•	•	•	•	•	•	•
Inventory to Working Capital 41	•	•	0.0	0.2	0.2	0.2	•	•	•	•	•	•	•
Total Receipts to Cash Flow 42	3.9	8.7	6.0	9.8	5.6	2.7	10.4	5.4	6.1	3.1	2.7	2.1	•
Cost of Goods to Cash Flow 43	2.0	6.1	4.2	7.2	3.0	0.9	6.5	2.9	3.6	1.4	1.3	0.3	•
Cash Flow to Total Debt 44	0.4	•	2.0	1.4	0.5	0.3	0.3	0.3	0.2	0.6	0.4	0.3	•

Selected Financial Factors (in Percentages)

Debt Ratio 45	70.5	•	101.4	46.7	79.2	87.7	83.6	94.0	86.9	59.4	69.5	67.3	•
Return on Total Assets 46	4.8	•	24.7	6.6	7.2	8.0	0.2	4.3	•	3.7	3.8	4.6	•
Return on Equity Before Income Taxes 47	9.5	•	•	8.4	31.3	64.6	0.4	42.2	•	7.7	6.9	7.2	•
Return on Equity After Income Taxes 48	6.1	•	•	6.8	27.0	60.5	•	24.9	•	4.8	5.4	3.5	•
Profit Margin (Before Income Tax) 49	2.4	•	1.9	0.7	2.8	10.9	0.0	1.6	•	2.9	2.7	5.7	•
Profit Margin (After Income Tax) 50	1.5	•	1.9	0.6	2.4	10.2	•	1.0	•	1.8	2.1	2.8	•

Table II

Corporations with Net Income

TRAVEL ARRANGEMENT AND RESERVATION SERVICES

MONEY AMOUNTS AND SIZE OF ASSETS IN THOUSANDS OF DOLLARS

Item Description for Accounting Period 7/08 Through 6/09	Total	Zero Assets	Under 500	500 to 1,000	1,000 to 5,000	5,000 to 10,000	10,000 to 25,000	25,000 to 50,000	50,000 to 100,000	100,000 to 250,000	250,000 to 500,000	500,000 to 2,500,000	2,500,000 and over
Number of Enterprises **1**	12129	1721	9701	•	277	58	25	•	9	15	7	4	0
Revenues ($ in Thousands)													
Net Sales **2**	23304420	285960	8447964	•	985557	278929	850624	•	977171	3049060	2532619	3603938	0
Interest **3**	10105	8	392	•	2339	331	718	•	6215	9292	25959	51510	0
Rents **4**	15598	45	3570	•	6	0	323	•	1694	5308	864	3772	0
Royalties **5**	53831	0	0	•	0	0	0	•	0	0	53609	222	0
Other Portfolio Income **6**	132305	2812	6332	•	5	11088	3349	•	1914	13638	9763	78688	0
Other Receipts **7**	1796031	3109	11683	•	61928	5718	20944	•	65326	77945	934743	500012	0
Total Receipts **8**	25403290	291934	8469941	•	1049835	296066	875958	•	1052320	3155243	3557557	4238142	0
Average Total Receipts **9**	2094	170	873	•	3790	5105	35038	•	116924	210350	508222	1059536	•
Operating Costs/Operating Income (%)													
Cost of Operations **10**	54.1	33.8	66.3	•	54.3	33.8	66.4	•	74.8	45.8	52.0	18.3	•
Salaries and Wages **11**	12.2	0.6	4.1	•	19.5	25.9	13.9	•	9.9	13.6	28.4	17.3	•
Taxes Paid **12**	1.6	2.1	1.2	•	1.9	2.9	1.6	•	1.0	1.8	2.6	2.1	•
Interest Paid **13**	0.8	0.2	0.1	•	0.0	0.1	0.1	•	0.7	0.2	1.6	3.1	•
Depreciation **14**	1.1	1.7	0.4	•	1.3	2.0	1.2	•	0.9	1.3	1.6	2.6	•
Amortization and Depletion **15**	0.5	0.4	0.0	•	0.0	0.2	0.3	•	0.7	0.8	0.9	1.7	•
Pensions and Other Deferred Comp. **16**	0.6	0.0	0.4	•	0.8	0.1	0.3	•	0.4	0.7	1.9	0.4	•
Employee Benefits **17**	1.1	0.2	0.3	•	1.0	0.6	1.2	•	1.2	1.6	2.9	1.6	•
Advertising **18**	3.8	0.6	0.9	•	1.1	0.2	1.3	•	3.3	2.0	3.3	16.7	•
Other Expenses **19**	23.9	40.9	18.6	•	14.7	28.3	10.7	•	10.7	29.0	40.8	34.9	•
Officers' Compensation **20**	2.3	2.4	3.5	•	5.1	0.7	2.0	•	1.4	1.0	0.5	0.6	•
Operating Margin **21**	•	17.1	4.2	•	0.3	5.2	1.3	•	•	2.3	•	0.6	•
Operating Margin Before Officers' Comp. **22**	0.2	19.5	7.7	•	5.4	5.9	3.3	•	•	3.2	•	1.2	•

Selected Average Balance Sheet ($ in Thousands)

Net Receivables 23	118	0	4	•	369	1748	2517	•	15245	30070	7357	85385	•
Inventories 24	6	0	1	•	35	58	245	•	509	354	1450	4090	•
Net Property, Plant and Equipment 25	94	0	10	•	166	128	2200	•	4957	17059	24686	100339	•
Total Assets 26	1391	0	80	•	1729	5895	16627	•	75348	141183	375472	2196665	•
Notes and Loans Payable 27	345	0	33	•	143	510	236	•	28266	7411	69710	709882	•
All Other Liabilities 28	619	0	23	•	1133	5107	12286	•	43161	74505	188176	791696	•
Net Worth 29	427	0	23	•	453	278	4105	•	3921	59266	117586	695086	•

Selected Financial Ratios (Times to 1)

Current Ratio 30	0.8	•	2.7	•	2.4	1.1	0.9	•	0.9	1.1	0.8	0.4	•
Quick Ratio 31	0.6	•	2.2	•	1.9	1.0	0.6	•	0.6	0.9	0.4	0.4	•
Net Sales to Working Capital 32	•	•	22.3	•	4.0	13.8	•	•	•	35.9	•	•	•
Coverage Ratio 33	9.5	83.3	30.9	•	369.2	203.3	43.8	•	4.9	31.6	3.3	7.3	•
Total Asset Turnover 34	1.4	•	10.9	•	2.1	0.8	2.0	•	1.4	1.4	1.0	0.4	•
Inventory Turnover 35	181.3	•	460.9	•	55.1	28.0	92.0	•	159.4	263.4	129.9	40.3	•
Receivables Turnover 36	14.5	•	167.8	•	9.9	•	5.6	•	7.3	8.0	51.4	•	•
Total Liabilities to Net Worth 37	2.3	•	2.4	•	2.8	20.2	3.1	•	18.2	1.4	2.2	2.2	•
Current Assets to Working Capital 38	•	•	1.6	•	1.7	15.5	•	•	•	11.8	•	•	•
Current Liabilities to Working Capital 39	•	•	0.6	•	0.7	14.5	•	•	•	10.8	•	•	•
Working Capital to Net Sales 40	•	•	0.0	•	0.3	0.1	•	•	•	0.0	•	•	•
Inventory to Working Capital 41	•	•	0.0	•	0.0	0.2	•	•	•	0.1	•	•	•
Total Receipts to Cash Flow 42	3.5	1.8	4.7	•	5.3	2.7	7.3	•	8.3	3.1	2.5	2.0	•
Cost of Goods to Cash Flow 43	1.9	0.6	3.1	•	2.9	0.9	4.8	•	6.2	1.4	1.3	0.4	•
Cash Flow to Total Debt 44	0.6	•	3.2	•	0.5	0.3	0.4	•	0.2	0.8	0.6	0.3	•

Selected Financial Factors (in Percentages)

Debt Ratio 45	69.3	•	70.9	•	73.8	95.3	75.3	•	94.8	58.0	68.7	68.4	•
Return on Total Assets 46	10.9	•	50.4	•	14.0	9.2	8.7	•	4.8	8.3	5.3	9.3	•
Return on Equity Before Income Taxes 47	31.7	•	167.7	•	53.4	193.3	34.4	•	73.5	19.2	11.8	25.4	•
Return on Equity After Income Taxes 48	25.3	•	166.9	•	48.0	181.2	30.5	•	58.6	15.3	9.7	16.6	•
Profit Margin (Before Income Tax) 49	7.0	19.2	4.5	•	6.8	11.2	4.2	•	2.7	5.6	3.8	19.6	•
Profit Margin (After Income Tax) 50	5.6	17.4	4.5	•	6.1	10.5	3.7	•	2.1	4.5	3.1	12.8	•

OTHER ADMINISTRATIVE AND SUPPORT SERVICES

Table I
Corporations with and without Net Income

MONEY AMOUNTS AND SIZE OF ASSETS IN THOUSANDS OF DOLLARS

Item Description for Accounting Period 7/08 Through 6/09	Total	Zero Assets	Under 500	500 to 1,000	1,000 to 5,000	5,000 to 10,000	10,000 to 25,000	25,000 to 50,000	50,000 to 100,000	100,000 to 250,000	250,000 to 500,000	500,000 to 2,500,000	2,500,000 and over
Number of Enterprises **1**	207292	52045	142174	5972	5799	609	344	121	91	63	26	40	7
Revenues ($ in Thousands)													
Net Sales **2**	227400148	6996659	63970497	10895225	32668886	11394573	9897650	7561937	7061524	8572771	12381965	40903547	15095913
Interest **3**	810233	8160	13874	7146	22539	12826	8799	16440	21096	62681	80039	338306	218327
Rents **4**	93063	0	3376	7931	8472	1128	7195	2570	4364	6168	16005	26120	9734
Royalties **5**	206666	0	2101	0	3	0	13	0	6156	8913	5577	113246	70658
Other Portfolio Income **6**	671363	21200	125553	36234	57721	23675	18782	18630	9559	26095	33877	187284	112752
Other Receipts **7**	4638939	141924	226298	47750	284126	275531	395027	135359	338863	617766	302889	1025822	847583
Total Receipts **8**	233821412	7167943	64341699	10994286	33041747	11707733	10327466	7734936	7441562	9294394	12820352	42594325	16354967
Average Total Receipts **9**	1128	138	453	1841	5698	19225	30022	63925	81775	147530	493090	1064858	2336424
Operating Costs/Operating Income (%)													
Cost of Operations **10**	41.7	40.8	32.3	49.4	57.2	61.2	45.3	42.1	45.8	33.2	58.0	43.0	11.7
Salaries and Wages **11**	19.2	13.6	19.7	13.4	13.8	15.1	25.9	14.3	21.8	26.1	14.9	21.9	27.1
Taxes Paid **12**	2.9	4.4	3.4	2.7	2.4	1.7	3.1	1.9	2.3	3.1	4.3	2.4	3.3
Interest Paid **13**	2.1	0.8	0.8	1.0	1.1	0.6	1.0	1.1	2.6	2.9	2.5	3.4	8.8
Depreciation **14**	2.3	1.7	2.1	2.5	2.1	1.3	2.3	2.0	2.6	2.8	2.0	2.7	4.2
Amortization and Depletion **15**	1.1	0.3	0.2	0.1	0.1	0.3	0.3	0.7	1.2	2.1	1.3	2.1	6.0
Pensions and Other Deferred Comp. **16**	0.5	0.1	0.3	0.4	0.3	0.3	0.5	0.3	0.2	0.3	0.3	1.1	0.6
Employee Benefits **17**	2.0	3.0	1.0	1.4	1.7	1.1	2.5	1.9	2.1	2.3	4.9	2.5	3.8
Advertising **18**	1.3	2.8	1.5	1.5	0.7	0.2	1.1	0.8	1.5	1.9	0.8	1.5	1.3
Other Expenses **19**	22.4	28.3	25.6	19.8	15.5	15.6	18.4	33.5	22.2	29.4	12.0	20.5	35.2
Officers' Compensation **20**	3.9	5.9	8.1	6.7	3.5	2.1	2.1	1.6	2.1	2.4	0.4	0.7	0.5
Operating Margin **21**	0.7	•	5.2	1.2	1.6	0.4	•	•	•	•	•	•	•
Operating Margin Before Officers' Comp. **22**	4.5	4.3	13.3	7.8	5.1	2.6	•	1.3	•	•	•	•	•

Selected Average Balance Sheet ($ in Thousands)

Net Receivables 23	123	0	9	120	544	1954	4574	6730	15884	27211	64304	241962	330956
Inventories 24	11	0	3	30	71	263	496	496	3014	3132	3367	4800	20580
Net Property, Plant and Equipment 25	113	0	24	233	508	1280	2403	4105	10754	14075	61532	114356	789254
Total Assets 26	688	0	85	699	2058	6875	15405	36284	69526	155822	348858	992069	5099803
Notes and Loans Payable 27	287	0	55	332	985	2215	5552	12063	23937	52232	124254	397322	2104092
All Other Liabilities 28	187	0	-0	184	547	2443	4955	13097	24853	50326	99712	252685	1674137
Net Worth 29	214	0	30	184	526	2217	4898	11124	20737	53265	124892	342062	1321574

Selected Financial Ratios (Times to 1)

Current Ratio 30	1.4	•	1.1	1.7	1.5	1.6	1.3	1.2	1.4	1.5	1.3	1.6	1.2
Quick Ratio 31	1.1	•	0.9	1.3	1.1	1.3	1.0	0.9	1.0	0.9	0.9	1.3	0.7
Net Sales to Working Capital 32	15.2	•	93.2	12.5	15.0	9.9	16.2	19.2	8.9	6.4	16.7	7.6	18.6
Coverage Ratio 33	2.7	2.1	8.4	3.1	3.6	6.4	2.7	2.9	1.4	1.7	1.9	1.7	1.8
Total Asset Turnover 34	1.6	•	5.3	2.6	2.7	2.7	1.9	1.7	1.1	0.9	1.4	1.0	0.4
Inventory Turnover 35	41.6	•	51.8	29.6	45.4	43.6	26.3	53.1	11.8	14.4	82.0	91.7	12.2
Receivables Turnover 36	9.5	•	48.6	14.7	9.9	8.9	6.0	8.7	4.9	4.6	7.5	5.0	9.7
Total Liabilities to Net Worth 37	2.2	•	1.8	2.8	2.9	2.1	2.1	2.3	2.4	1.9	1.8	1.9	2.9
Current Assets to Working Capital 38	3.4	•	7.8	2.4	3.1	2.5	4.7	5.1	3.7	3.1	4.6	2.6	5.9
Current Liabilities to Working Capital 39	2.4	•	6.8	1.4	2.1	1.5	3.7	4.1	2.7	2.1	3.6	1.6	4.9
Working Capital to Net Sales 40	0.1	•	0.0	0.1	0.1	0.1	0.1	0.1	0.1	0.2	0.1	0.1	0.1
Inventory to Working Capital 41	0.2	•	0.6	0.2	0.2	0.2	0.3	0.2	0.3	0.1	0.2	0.0	0.2
Total Receipts to Cash Flow 42	4.5	4.0	3.7	5.9	7.1	6.3	6.0	3.1	5.0	3.6	9.0	5.1	2.6
Cost of Goods to Cash Flow 43	1.9	1.6	1.2	2.9	4.1	3.9	2.7	1.3	2.3	1.2	5.2	2.2	0.3
Cash Flow to Total Debt 44	0.5	•	2.2	0.6	0.5	0.6	0.5	0.8	0.3	0.4	0.2	0.3	0.2

Selected Financial Factors (in Percentages)

Debt Ratio 45	69.0	•	64.1	73.7	74.4	67.8	68.2	69.3	70.2	65.8	64.2	65.5	74.1
Return on Total Assets 46	9.0	•	35.0	7.9	10.4	10.3	5.2	5.4	4.0	4.3	6.4	6.0	6.6
Return on Equity Before Income Taxes 47	18.3	•	85.6	20.5	29.2	26.9	10.3	11.4	3.5	5.1	8.5	7.2	11.3
Return on Equity After Income Taxes 48	15.6	•	84.6	20.2	28.0	24.3	9.0	9.7	0.9	3.2	5.5	4.1	7.2
Profit Margin (Before Income Tax) 49	3.6	0.8	5.8	2.1	2.7	3.2	1.8	2.0	0.9	2.0	2.2	2.4	6.9
Profit Margin (After Income Tax) 50	3.0	0.3	5.7	2.0	2.6	2.9	1.5	1.7	0.2	1.2	1.4	1.4	4.4

Table II

Corporations with Net Income

OTHER ADMINISTRATIVE AND SUPPORT SERVICES

MONEY AMOUNTS AND SIZE OF ASSETS IN THOUSANDS OF DOLLARS

Item Description for Accounting Period 7/08 Through 6/09		Total	Zero Assets	Under 500	500 to 1,000	1,000 to 5,000	5,000 to 10,000	10,000 to 25,000	25,000 to 50,000	50,000 to 100,000	100,000 to 250,000	250,000 to 500,000	500,000 to 2,500,000	2,500,000 and over
Number of Enterprises	1	131202	29378	93270	3634	4068	441	216	•	47	29	•	•	27
Revenues ($ in Thousands)														
Net Sales	2	164424303	5151968	45244801	6669509	23592148	9490329	7165963	•	4589824	4833960	•	•	28499621
Interest	3	568505	3925	7568	4478	15208	10672	3352	•	15091	20595	•	•	237517
Rents	4	64820	0	420	7931	6561	1128	7064	•	4045	4419	•	•	7556
Royalties	5	128439	0	2101	0	0	0	13	•	1	0	•	•	55648
Other Portfolio Income	6	509913	14722	62751	30362	46811	21085	8829	•	7391	11708	•	•	149486
Other Receipts	7	4065960	173621	169657	27524	255114	271030	333679	•	291491	320951	•	•	1026656
Total Receipts	8	169761940	5344236	45487298	6739804	23915842	9794244	7518900	•	4907843	5191633	•	•	29976484
Average Total Receipts	9	1294	182	488	1855	5879	22209	34810	•	104422	179022	•	•	1110240
Operating Costs/Operating Income (%)														
Cost of Operations	10	43.7	50.4	30.6	50.8	58.4	58.7	50.8	•	52.8	38.6	•	•	49.0
Salaries and Wages	11	17.2	9.1	18.4	10.0	12.1	15.5	22.1	•	13.4	22.0	•	•	20.8
Taxes Paid	12	2.8	4.5	3.2	2.5	2.3	1.7	3.0	•	1.6	2.7	•	•	2.1
Interest Paid	13	1.9	0.4	0.6	0.9	0.9	0.6	0.8	•	2.0	1.5	•	•	2.4
Depreciation	14	2.0	0.8	1.6	2.2	1.7	1.3	1.8	•	2.1	1.9	•	•	2.2
Amortization and Depletion	15	1.0	0.2	0.1	0.1	0.1	0.1	0.2	•	0.5	1.4	•	•	1.3
Pensions and Other Deferred Comp.	16	0.4	0.1	0.3	0.4	0.3	0.2	0.4	•	0.3	0.2	•	•	0.7
Employee Benefits	17	1.7	3.3	0.8	1.2	1.1	0.9	2.0	•	2.2	2.5	•	•	1.5
Advertising	18	1.1	0.4	1.6	1.0	0.7	0.2	0.5	•	1.0	3.0	•	•	1.1
Other Expenses	19	20.0	18.1	24.0	17.6	13.3	16.1	15.1	•	22.0	20.7	•	•	18.0
Officers' Compensation	20	3.7	3.7	8.0	6.5	4.0	2.0	2.0	•	2.2	1.6	•	•	0.7
Operating Margin	21	4.6	9.0	10.8	6.9	5.0	2.8	1.2	•	•	3.9	•	•	0.1
Operating Margin Before Officers' Comp.	22	8.3	12.7	18.8	13.4	9.0	4.8	3.2	•	2.0	5.5	•	•	0.8

Selected Average Balance Sheet ($ in Thousands)

Item											
Net Receivables 23	140	0	9	114	567	1915	4880	•	19590	28714	267576
Inventories 24	12	0	3	19	65	178	592	•	3711	4210	5802
Net Property, Plant and Equipment 25	127	0	22	264	483	1492	2605	•	10678	15157	110601
Total Assets 26	773	0	88	726	1965	6893	14935	•	69660	154090	995400
Notes and Loans Payable 27	292	0	41	236	813	2305	4301	•	23127	46692	327742
All Other Liabilities 28	193	0	-15	152	510	2122	4479	•	25381	43773	216761
Net Worth 29	288	0	62	339	642	2466	6155	•	21152	63625	450897

Selected Financial Ratios (Times to 1)

Item											
Current Ratio 30	1.6	•	1.6	2.1	1.8	1.7	1.6	•	1.6	1.5	1.9
Quick Ratio 31	1.3	•	1.3	1.5	1.5	1.4	1.2	•	1.1	1.0	1.6
Net Sales to Working Capital 32	12.3	•	33.2	10.1	11.5	11.7	10.5	•	6.8	7.6	6.3
Coverage Ratio 33	5.3	32.3	21.3	10.0	8.5	11.0	9.1	•	4.3	8.6	3.2
Total Asset Turnover 34	1.6	•	5.5	2.5	3.0	3.1	2.2	•	1.4	1.1	1.1
Inventory Turnover 35	47.6	•	52.6	49.4	51.9	70.8	28.4	•	13.9	15.3	89.1
Receivables Turnover 36	9.7	•	50.0	13.3	9.8	10.0	6.3	•	4.6	•	4.8
Total Liabilities to Net Worth 37	1.7	0.4	1.1	2.1	1.8	1.4	•	•	2.3	•	1.2
Current Assets to Working Capital 38	2.6	•	2.8	1.9	2.3	2.4	2.7	•	2.7	3.1	2.2
Current Liabilities to Working Capital 39	1.6	•	1.8	0.9	1.3	1.4	1.7	•	1.7	2.1	1.2
Working Capital to Net Sales 40	0.1	•	0.0	0.1	0.1	0.1	0.1	•	0.1	0.1	0.2
Inventory to Working Capital 41	0.1	•	0.2	0.1	0.1	0.1	0.2	•	0.2	0.2	0.0
Total Receipts to Cash Flow 42	4.1	3.5	3.2	4.6	6.2	5.2	5.4	•	3.8	3.4	4.9
Cost of Goods to Cash Flow 43	1.8	1.8	1.0	2.4	3.6	3.1	2.8	•	2.0	1.3	2.4
Cash Flow to Total Debt 44	0.6	•	5.8	1.0	0.7	0.9	0.7	•	0.5	0.5	0.4

Selected Financial Factors (in Percentages)

Item											
Debt Ratio 45	62.7	•	29.8	53.4	67.3	64.2	58.8	•	69.6	58.7	54.7
Return on Total Assets 46	15.9	•	65.6	22.3	21.4	20.6	15.2	•	12.3	14.1	8.4
Return on Equity Before Income Taxes 47	34.7	•	89.0	43.1	57.9	52.4	32.9	•	30.9	30.1	12.8
Return on Equity After Income Taxes 48	31.5	•	88.2	42.8	56.5	49.3	31.9	•	25.9	26.5	9.3
Profit Margin (Before Income Tax) 49	8.0	12.7	11.3	7.9	6.4	6.0	6.1	•	6.7	11.5	5.5
Profit Margin (After Income Tax) 50	7.3	12.0	11.2	7.9	6.2	5.6	5.9	•	5.6	10.1	4.0

Table I

Corporations with and without Net Income

WASTE MANAGEMENT AND REMEDIATION SERVICES

MONEY AMOUNTS AND SIZE OF ASSETS IN THOUSANDS OF DOLLARS

Item Description for Accounting Period 7/08 Through 6/09		Total	Zero Assets	Under 500	500 to 1,000	1,000 to 5,000	5,000 to 10,000	10,000 to 25,000	25,000 to 50,000	50,000 to 100,000	100,000 to 250,000	250,000 to 500,000	500,000 to 2,500,000	2,500,000 and over
Number of Enterprises	1	14863	2026	9431	909	2003	214	148	52	32	20	10	15	4
Revenues ($ in Thousands)														
Net Sales	2	61649449	710245	6033958	795988	10221905	3317863	3077307	2087130	2244666	2371455	2054972	8703335	20030625
Interest	3	170228	110	1578	1597	5581	469	4425	6331	4385	10261	14682	24702	96107
Rents	4	25627	5	0	171	1011	0	600	4626	2558	1030	249	1623	13754
Royalties	5	12869	0	0	0	0	0	0	0	407	0	762	10967	733
Other Portfolio Income	6	308423	13896	43268	11927	29273	20196	29801	53115	6911	3147	6206	31905	58781
Other Receipts	7	807490	5615	4536	18058	120349	55196	34571	40487	10536	19451	81376	92178	325133
Total Receipts	8	62974086	729871	6083340	827741	10378119	3393724	3146704	2191689	2269463	2405344	2158247	8864710	20525133
Average Total Receipts	9	4237	360	645	911	5181	15859	21262	42148	70921	120267	215825	590981	5131283
Operating Costs/Operating Income (%)														
Cost of Operations	10	39.7	42.9	34.8	12.4	47.3	67.5	50.3	59.5	46.9	51.1	36.1	31.2	32.0
Salaries and Wages	11	14.5	11.0	13.4	15.4	8.6	5.7	9.0	8.3	12.1	12.7	19.5	17.4	19.5
Taxes Paid	12	2.9	3.0	2.9	3.5	2.3	1.2	2.1	2.1	2.0	2.3	2.2	2.9	3.9
Interest Paid	13	2.6	1.3	1.2	1.4	1.1	0.8	1.3	1.7	2.1	3.5	7.2	4.3	3.3
Depreciation	14	6.6	2.8	3.5	3.3	5.3	3.7	7.1	4.5	6.6	7.2	9.3	6.3	8.9
Amortization and Depletion	15	1.5	1.6	0.1	0.4	0.1	0.2	0.2	0.6	1.1	1.4	3.7	3.8	2.2
Pensions and Other Deferred Comp.	16	0.4	0.4	0.4	0.6	0.2	0.3	0.7	0.3	0.4	0.6	0.2	0.8	0.3
Employee Benefits	17	2.1	2.0	1.0	2.0	1.4	0.5	1.8	1.7	2.2	2.6	3.6	2.2	2.8
Advertising	18	0.5	0.7	1.3	1.9	0.4	0.2	0.5	0.3	0.3	0.2	0.3	0.3	0.3
Other Expenses	19	25.1	24.2	27.2	39.9	29.7	16.4	24.1	20.3	24.5	16.6	26.0	30.8	22.2
Officers' Compensation	20	2.0	6.4	6.9	7.4	2.5	2.9	3.2	2.3	1.4	1.5	1.5	0.7	0.2
Operating Margin	21	2.0	3.7	7.2	12.0	1.1	0.7	•	•	0.4	0.4	•	•	4.3
Operating Margin Before Officers' Comp.	22	4.0	10.1	14.0	19.3	3.6	3.6	2.8	0.9	1.8	1.9	•	•	4.5

Selected Average Balance Sheet ($ in Thousands)

Net Receivables 23	636	0	14	129	451	2696	2568	6349	11140	21712	37545	137372	945885
Inventories 24	45	0	4	50	31	205	390	905	1674	1270	1779	6965	43560
Net Property, Plant and Equipment 25	1839	0	62	158	1016	2241	6350	9086	22969	49163	93223	283362	3942462
Total Assets 26	4700	0	133	643	2102	6635	15317	34288	70036	161548	327003	994175	8670601
Notes and Loans Payable 27	1936	0	88	233	966	2682	6797	12395	31047	65870	189897	424279	3248976
All Other Liabilities 28	1366	0	29	47	599	2089	3697	14735	20006	40516	82961	237565	2797369
Net Worth 29	1398	0	16	364	536	1865	4823	7158	18984	55161	54145	332331	2624256

Selected Financial Ratios (Times to 1)

Current Ratio 30	1.1	•	1.4	8.6	1.2	1.7	1.7	1.3	1.4	1.4	1.3	0.9	1.0
Quick Ratio 31	0.9	•	1.3	4.9	0.9	1.3	1.4	1.0	1.1	1.0	1.1	0.7	0.8
Net Sales to Working Capital 32	31.2	•	45.2	2.4	39.9	9.1	7.6	12.7	10.3	8.9	12.7	•	387.3
Coverage Ratio 33	2.6	6.1	7.5	12.2	3.3	4.9	2.3	3.1	1.7	1.5	0.4	1.3	3.1
Total Asset Turnover 34	0.9	•	4.8	1.4	2.4	2.3	1.4	1.2	1.0	0.7	0.6	0.6	0.6
Inventory Turnover 35	36.6	•	54.4	2.2	77.6	51.1	26.9	26.4	19.6	47.7	41.7	26.0	36.8
Receivables Turnover 36	6.9	•	52.6	4.7	11.9	6.0	7.9	7.9	5.6	5.6	5.6	4.8	5.5
Total Liabilities to Net Worth 37	2.4	•	7.5	0.8	2.9	2.6	2.2	3.8	2.7	1.9	5.0	2.0	2.3
Current Assets to Working Capital 38	8.6	•	3.3	1.1	7.0	2.4	2.3	3.9	3.4	3.3	4.0	•	115.3
Current Liabilities to Working Capital 39	7.6	•	2.3	0.1	6.0	1.4	1.3	2.9	2.4	2.3	3.0	•	114.3
Working Capital to Net Sales 40	0.0	•	0.0	0.4	0.0	0.1	0.1	0.1	0.1	0.1	0.1	•	0.0
Inventory to Working Capital 41	0.4	•	0.3	0.2	0.3	0.1	0.1	0.4	0.2	0.2	0.1	•	3.5
Total Receipts to Cash Flow 42	4.1	3.6	3.4	1.9	3.7	5.9	4.7	4.8	4.6	7.1	5.8	3.6	4.4
Cost of Goods to Cash Flow 43	1.6	1.6	1.2	0.2	1.8	4.0	2.4	2.9	2.2	3.6	2.1	1.1	1.4
Cash Flow to Total Debt 44	0.3	•	1.6	1.6	0.9	0.5	0.4	0.3	0.3	0.2	0.1	0.2	0.2

Selected Financial Factors (in Percentages)

Debt Ratio 45	70.3	•	88.3	43.4	74.5	71.9	68.5	79.1	72.9	65.9	83.4	66.6	69.7
Return on Total Assets 46	6.1	•	44.4	23.6	9.1	8.9	4.1	6.0	3.7	3.9	1.7	3.3	5.8
Return on Equity Before Income Taxes 47	12.6	•	327.8	38.4	24.6	25.2	7.5	19.5	5.7	3.9	•	2.4	12.9
Return on Equity After Income Taxes 48	8.9	•	326.0	38.1	22.4	23.5	5.9	12.2	4.4	1.6	•	0.8	7.5
Profit Margin (Before Income Tax) 49	4.2	6.5	8.0	15.9	2.6	3.0	1.7	3.5	1.5	1.8	•	1.4	6.8
Profit Margin (After Income Tax) 50	3.0	6.2	7.9	15.8	2.4	2.8	1.4	2.2	1.2	0.8	•	0.5	3.9

Table II
Corporations with Net Income

WASTE MANAGEMENT AND REMEDIATION SERVICES

MONEY AMOUNTS AND SIZE OF ASSETS IN THOUSANDS OF DOLLARS

Item Description for Accounting Period 7/08 Through 6/09	Total	Zero Assets	Under 500	500 to 1,000	1,000 to 5,000	5,000 to 10,000	10,000 to 25,000	25,000 to 50,000	50,000 to 100,000	100,000 to 250,000	250,000 to 500,000	500,000 to 2,500,000	2,500,000 and over
Number of Enterprises 1	9207	950	6045	•	1149	153	87	31	20	13	0	•	•
Revenues ($ in Thousands)													
Net Sales 2	48220351	555658	4473574	•	6272820	2930579	2128174	1582680	1758975	2175859	0	•	•
Interest 3	122089	98	248	•	4966	223	2763	3808	1907	17147	0	•	•
Rents 4	22754	0	0	•	1011	0	459	4626	520	673	0	•	•
Royalties 5	11700	0	0	•	0	0	0	0	0	0	0	•	•
Other Portfolio Income 6	248822	13831	22058	•	20052	20193	28761	48016	4836	1897	0	•	•
Other Receipts 7	518057	5448	1887	•	110277	54539	31153	40529	2529	2116	0	•	•
Total Receipts 8	49143773	575035	4497767	•	6409126	3005534	2191310	1679659	1768767	2216692	0	•	•
Average Total Receipts 9	5338	605	744	•	5578	19644	25187	54183	88438	170515	•	•	•
Operating Costs/Operating Income (%)													
Cost of Operations 10	38.3	39.1	28.8	•	45.4	68.5	49.5	56.6	53.0	57.9	•	•	•
Salaries and Wages 11	14.9	11.4	15.0	•	6.6	5.0	9.1	8.6	9.6	9.1	•	•	•
Taxes Paid 12	3.0	2.7	3.2	•	2.1	1.1	2.0	2.1	1.9	2.0	•	•	•
Interest Paid 13	2.2	1.4	1.4	•	0.8	0.6	0.7	1.1	1.3	2.5	•	•	•
Depreciation 14	6.3	2.7	2.6	•	4.3	3.6	6.0	3.1	5.2	6.2	•	•	•
Amortization and Depletion 15	1.4	1.7	0.1	•	0.1	0.0	0.2	0.3	0.5	1.4	•	•	•
Pensions and Other Deferred Comp. 16	0.4	0.5	0.4	•	0.1	0.3	0.7	0.3	0.5	0.4	•	•	•
Employee Benefits 17	2.1	2.3	1.0	•	1.1	0.2	1.6	1.5	2.2	2.8	•	•	•
Advertising 18	0.4	0.3	0.9	•	0.4	0.2	0.6	0.2	0.2	0.2	•	•	•
Other Expenses 19	22.7	21.2	27.3	•	31.7	14.8	20.1	21.9	17.7	12.2	•	•	•
Officers' Compensation 20	1.9	6.9	7.2	•	2.5	2.9	3.5	2.4	1.4	1.5	•	•	•
Operating Margin 21	6.4	9.7	12.1	•	4.8	2.8	6.1	1.9	6.4	3.9	•	•	•
Operating Margin Before Officers' Comp. 22	8.3	16.6	19.4	•	7.3	5.7	9.7	4.3	7.8	5.4	•	•	•

Selected Average Balance Sheet ($ in Thousands)

Net Receivables 23	811	0	20	•	415	2072	2501	6032	12485	27903
Inventories 24	59	0	5	•	29	120	295	1446	2591	3091
Net Property, Plant and Equipment 25	2167	0	56	•	928	2660	5776	7784	23050	46308
Total Assets 26	5572	0	145	•	2171	6809	14373	34710	69756	171759
Notes and Loans Payable 27	2132	0	93	•	822	1802	3585	10021	22834	65796
All Other Liabilities 28	1732	0	23	•	654	2174	3063	15079	23225	34500
Net Worth 29	1709	0	29	•	695	2833	7724	9611	23697	71462

Selected Financial Ratios (Times to 1)

Current Ratio 30	1.2	•	2.4	•	1.3	1.5	2.1	1.6	1.4	1.7
Quick Ratio 31	0.9	•	2.2	•	1.1	1.0	1.8	1.2	1.0	1.1
Net Sales to Working Capital 32	25.3	•	21.4	•	22.5	15.2	7.2	9.8	11.2	6.7
Coverage Ratio 33	4.8	10.2	10.2	•	9.5	9.8	13.5	8.5	6.2	3.3
Total Asset Turnover 34	0.9	•	5.1	•	2.5	2.8	1.7	1.5	1.3	1.0
Inventory Turnover 35	33.9	•	41.1	•	86.1	109.0	40.9	20.0	18.0	31.4
Receivables Turnover 36	6.6	•	49.1	•	11.5	10.5	8.8	8.4	5.6	•
Total Liabilities to Net Worth 37	2.3	•	4.0	•	2.1	1.4	0.9	2.6	1.9	1.4
Current Assets to Working Capital 38	6.9	•	1.7	•	3.9	3.1	1.9	2.6	3.3	2.5
Current Liabilities to Working Capital 39	5.9	•	0.7	•	2.9	2.1	0.9	1.6	2.3	1.5
Working Capital to Net Sales 40	0.0	•	0.0	•	0.0	0.1	0.1	0.1	0.1	0.1
Inventory to Working Capital 41	0.3	•	0.1	•	0.1	0.2	0.1	0.4	0.3	0.1
Total Receipts to Cash Flow 42	3.8	3.1	2.8	•	3.1	5.3	4.1	3.8	4.8	6.8
Cost of Goods to Cash Flow 43	1.5	1.2	0.8	•	1.4	3.6	2.0	2.1	2.5	3.9
Cash Flow to Total Debt 44	0.4	•	2.2	•	1.2	0.9	0.9	0.5	0.4	0.2

Selected Financial Factors (in Percentages)

Debt Ratio 45	69.3	•	80.0	•	68.0	58.4	46.3	72.3	66.0	58.4
Return on Total Assets 46	9.9	•	71.6	•	19.7	16.8	16.6	13.5	10.5	8.0
Return on Equity Before Income Taxes 47	25.7	•	323.0	•	55.0	36.3	28.6	42.9	25.9	13.5
Return on Equity After Income Taxes 48	20.9	•	321.5	•	52.0	34.8	26.9	33.8	24.2	10.4
Profit Margin (Before Income Tax) 49	8.4	13.2	12.7	•	7.0	5.4	9.0	8.1	7.0	5.8
Profit Margin (After Income Tax) 50	6.8	12.8	12.6	•	6.6	5.1	8.5	6.4	6.5	4.5

Table I

Corporations with and without Net Income

EDUCATIONAL SERVICES

MONEY AMOUNTS AND SIZE OF ASSETS IN THOUSANDS OF DOLLARS

Item Description for Accounting Period 7/08 Through 6/09	Total	Zero Assets	Under 500	500 to 1,000	1,000 to 5,000	5,000 to 10,000	10,000 to 25,000	25,000 to 50,000	50,000 to 100,000	100,000 to 250,000	250,000 to 500,000	500,000 to 2,500,000	2,500,000 and over
Number of Enterprises **1**	52484	11814	37667	1162	1428	179	104	46	33	31	10	7	3
Revenues ($ in Thousands)													
Net Sales **2**	46497719	1148193	9228887	2997527	5248540	1662776	2110947	2145362	2612696	4870734	2562434	8758246	3151378
Interest **3**	280531	2938	3397	1393	5799	1408	7329	5641	7350	16704	7459	97347	123764
Rents **4**	26815	0	0	18	18	697	0	163	4189	13495	57	5789	2389
Royalties **5**	99245	0	0	0	0	640	35	0	1158	7831	39447	39443	10690
Other Portfolio Income **6**	274701	0	2308	0	8367	1083	1	5094	12212	8769	193977	39709	3181
Other Receipts **7**	552427	17824	60315	4768	64955	10184	120479	44852	53280	17343	31310	174459	47340
Total Receipts **8**	47731438	1168955	9294907	3003706	5327679	1676788	2238791	2201112	2690885	4934876	2834684	9114993	3244062
Average Total Receipts **9**	909	99	247	2585	3731	9368	21527	47850	81542	159190	283468	1302142	1081354
Operating Costs/Operating Income (%)													
Cost of Operations **10**	13.6	30.9	11.3	29.6	10.7	15.3	22.4	25.0	9.0	17.5	7.3	6.8	11.4
Salaries and Wages **11**	29.7	7.6	25.3	29.0	33.5	38.1	28.4	27.4	33.7	30.8	24.3	33.3	31.6
Taxes Paid **12**	3.2	2.1	3.8	3.1	3.5	6.3	3.6	3.2	3.8	2.9	3.1	2.4	2.7
Interest Paid **13**	2.3	0.8	1.0	0.6	0.6	0.5	1.4	1.5	2.2	2.0	4.4	1.0	15.4
Depreciation **14**	2.7	2.7	1.7	1.7	1.9	1.7	2.4	4.2	4.3	3.5	3.1	2.7	5.0
Amortization and Depletion **15**	0.9	0.1	0.3	0.0	0.4	0.2	0.8	0.7	1.1	2.3	1.6	0.8	2.7
Pensions and Other Deferred Comp. **16**	0.4	0.0	0.5	0.6	0.6	0.8	0.3	0.6	0.5	0.4	0.4	0.3	0.5
Employee Benefits **17**	2.2	0.5	1.6	2.3	0.8	1.6	2.5	3.2	2.0	2.2	2.8	3.1	3.8
Advertising **18**	5.4	1.7	2.1	1.5	3.6	5.9	4.0	5.8	7.1	3.8	5.0	11.5	8.3
Other Expenses **19**	31.1	49.6	40.5	22.7	33.2	19.9	29.4	24.7	30.1	30.0	43.6	25.8	19.6
Officers' Compensation **20**	4.3	4.9	9.4	7.7	7.2	4.0	4.4	1.4	1.4	1.7	3.4	0.6	1.3
Operating Margin **21**	4.0	•	2.6	1.2	4.1	5.8	0.3	2.2	4.9	3.0	0.9	11.7	•
Operating Margin Before Officers' Comp. **22**	8.4	4.0	11.9	8.9	11.3	9.8	4.7	3.7	6.2	4.7	4.3	12.3	•

Selected Average Balance Sheet ($ in Thousands)

Net Receivables 23	82	0	5	64	476	1107	3068	5847	7693	20518	67309	83520	136293
Inventories 24	10	0	3	5	32	239	315	1369	1345	2506	2621	2895	14249
Net Property, Plant and Equipment 25	127	0	20	260	506	848	2745	8766	19182	27351	56832	187653	233356
Total Assets 26	751	0	66	654	2097	6339	16217	32784	72025	154546	308003	950779	3981263
Notes and Loans Payable 27	230	0	52	294	415	916	3978	11408	23039	38319	97103	113044	1455711
All Other Liabilities 28	260	0	24	227	1177	3107	6847	12037	24953	50713	119621	278963	1155967
Net Worth 29	260	0	-10	134	505	2316	5393	9339	24033	65513	91278	558773	1369585

Selected Financial Ratios (Times to 1)

Current Ratio 30	1.3	•	1.2	1.5	1.1	1.8	1.2	1.4	1.2	1.1	1.0	1.4	1.7
Quick Ratio 31	1.0	•	0.9	1.4	1.0	1.5	1.0	1.1	0.9	0.9	0.9	1.1	1.3
Net Sales to Working Capital 32	16.1	•	59.9	21.3	26.7	6.1	13.8	11.0	22.2	25.4	62.6	10.1	5.5
Coverage Ratio 33	3.9	2.0	4.3	3.2	10.6	14.6	5.4	4.2	4.6	3.1	3.6	15.9	1.0
Total Asset Turnover 34	1.2	•	3.7	3.9	1.8	1.5	1.3	1.4	1.1	1.0	0.8	1.3	0.3
Inventory Turnover 35	12.5	•	9.8	157.4	12.3	6.0	14.5	8.5	5.3	11.0	7.1	29.3	8.4
Receivables Turnover 36	9.2	•	45.9	28.8	9.5	7.3	6.6	9.6	8.2	8.1	3.4	16.2	2.6
Total Liabilities to Net Worth 37	1.9	•	•	3.9	3.2	1.7	2.0	2.5	2.0	1.4	2.4	0.7	1.9
Current Assets to Working Capital 38	4.6	•	6.5	3.0	9.3	2.2	5.3	3.6	7.5	8.5	25.1	3.5	2.4
Current Liabilities to Working Capital 39	3.6	•	5.5	2.0	8.3	1.2	4.3	2.6	6.5	7.5	24.1	2.5	1.4
Working Capital to Net Sales 40	0.1	•	0.0	0.0	0.0	0.2	0.1	0.1	0.0	0.0	0.0	0.1	0.2
Inventory to Working Capital 41	0.2	•	0.7	0.0	0.3	0.2	0.1	0.5	0.3	0.4	0.7	0.0	0.1
Total Receipts to Cash Flow 42	3.5	2.7	3.2	5.5	3.5	5.1	3.3	4.6	3.4	3.6	2.4	2.9	7.6
Cost of Goods to Cash Flow 43	0.5	0.8	0.4	1.6	0.4	0.8	0.7	1.1	0.3	0.6	0.2	0.2	0.9
Cash Flow to Total Debt 44	0.5	•	1.0	0.9	0.7	0.5	0.6	0.4	0.5	0.5	0.5	1.1	0.1

Selected Financial Factors (in Percentages)

Debt Ratio 45	65.3	•	115.3	79.6	75.9	63.5	66.7	71.5	66.6	57.6	70.4	41.2	65.6
Return on Total Assets 46	10.5	•	15.9	7.8	10.8	10.4	9.7	9.0	11.0	6.4	13.2	21.8	4.2
Return on Equity Before Income Taxes 47	22.5	•	•	26.2	40.8	26.5	23.8	24.2	25.7	10.2	32.1	34.7	0.5
Return on Equity After Income Taxes 48	17.0	•	•	21.7	39.9	25.9	21.9	19.0	21.1	7.2	28.0	22.6	•
Profit Margin (Before Income Tax) 49	6.6	0.8	3.3	1.4	5.6	6.6	6.3	4.8	7.8	4.3	11.4	15.5	0.7
Profit Margin (After Income Tax) 50	5.0	0.2	3.2	1.1	5.5	6.4	5.8	3.8	6.4	3.0	10.0	10.1	•

Table II
Corporations with Net Income

EDUCATIONAL SERVICES

MONEY AMOUNTS AND SIZE OF ASSETS IN THOUSANDS OF DOLLARS

Item Description for Accounting Period 7/08 Through 6/09		Total	Zero Assets	Under 500	500 to 1,000	1,000 to 5,000	5,000 to 10,000	10,000 to 25,000	25,000 to 50,000	50,000 to 100,000	100,000 to 250,000	250,000 to 500,000	500,000 to 2,500,000	2,500,000 and over
Number of Enterprises	1	27981	6162	19512	848	1187	114	65	35	•	21	•	•	0
Revenues ($ in Thousands)														
Net Sales	2	36530470	792185	5250006	2285065	4667345	1369919	1490400	1681622	•	3580672	•	•	0
Interest	3	219015	2873	1233	1121	1715	693	6507	4166	•	12765	•	•	0
Rents	4	20687	0	0	6	18	697	0	163	•	8100	•	•	0
Royalties	5	92183	0	0	0	0	0	34	0	•	3505	•	•	0
Other Portfolio Income	6	270234	0	2206	0	8234	1055	1	3573	•	8499	•	•	0
Other Receipts	7	414596	15860	51308	1893	32408	7045	16177	44959	•	17452	•	•	0
Total Receipts	8	37547185	810918	5304753	2288085	4709720	1379409	1513119	1734483	•	3630993	•	•	0
Average Total Receipts	9	1342	132	272	2698	3968	12100	23279	49557	•	172904	•	•	•
Operating Costs/Operating Income (%)														
Cost of Operations	10	13.6	44.4	10.6	38.2	9.9	11.4	28.1	29.5	•	16.0	•	•	•
Salaries and Wages	11	28.2	5.6	22.3	18.6	31.7	39.2	21.1	25.5	•	28.8	•	•	•
Taxes Paid	12	2.9	1.3	3.3	2.5	3.3	4.3	3.2	3.1	•	2.9	•	•	•
Interest Paid	13	1.8	0.2	0.3	0.4	0.4	0.4	0.7	1.5	•	1.6	•	•	•
Depreciation	14	2.5	1.7	1.1	1.3	1.4	1.5	2.3	3.6	•	3.6	•	•	•
Amortization and Depletion	15	0.6	0.1	0.2	0.0	0.1	0.1	0.3	0.3	•	1.0	•	•	•
Pensions and Other Deferred Comp.	16	0.4	0.0	0.2	0.6	0.6	0.9	0.4	0.6	•	0.1	•	•	•
Employee Benefits	17	2.2	0.4	1.6	1.4	0.7	1.8	1.7	3.0	•	1.9	•	•	•
Advertising	18	5.8	1.3	1.7	0.7	3.7	4.4	3.7	5.6	•	4.5	•	•	•
Other Expenses	19	28.4	35.2	37.3	15.6	32.0	19.5	22.9	18.0	•	31.0	•	•	•
Officers' Compensation	20	4.0	3.1	9.7	9.1	6.9	3.9	5.0	1.5	•	1.6	•	•	•
Operating Margin	21	9.6	6.8	11.7	11.7	9.1	12.5	10.7	7.7	•	6.9	•	•	•
Operating Margin Before Officers' Comp.	22	13.5	9.8	21.4	20.7	16.0	16.4	15.7	9.2	•	8.6	•	•	•

Selected Average Balance Sheet ($ in Thousands)

Net Receivables 23	120	0	7	21	504	1347	3264	6581	20003
Inventories 24	12	0	3	1	27	287	378	1646	443
Net Property, Plant and Equipment 25	183	0	15	276	438	1173	3333	9069	30977
Total Assets 26	970	0	64	633	2056	6210	15803	32242	148535
Notes and Loans Payable 27	221	0	22	237	398	744	2267	11971	30551
All Other Liabilities 28	370	0	18	200	1216	2056	6866	12232	55046
Net Worth 29	378	0	24	196	442	3409	6669	8039	62937

Selected Financial Ratios (Times to 1)

Current Ratio 30	1.3	•	1.9	1.8	1.1	1.8	1.5	1.5	1.0
Quick Ratio 31	1.0	•	1.4	1.7	1.0	1.5	1.2	1.1	0.8
Net Sales to Working Capital 32	15.8	•	17.3	18.4	34.4	6.7	7.4	9.5	•
Coverage Ratio 33	7.9	55.4	43.8	28.5	22.6	35.7	18.9	8.1	6.3
Total Asset Turnover 34	1.3	•	4.2	4.3	1.9	1.9	1.5	1.5	1.1
Inventory Turnover 35	14.4	•	9.2	812.8	14.6	4.8	17.0	8.6	61.7
Receivables Turnover 36	9.3	•	41.1	34.8	10.2	7.6	6.4	8.5	•
Total Liabilities to Net Worth 37	1.6	•	1.7	2.2	3.7	0.8	1.4	3.0	1.4
Current Assets to Working Capital 38	4.6	•	2.1	2.3	11.6	2.2	2.9	3.2	•
Current Liabilities to Working Capital 39	3.6	•	1.1	1.3	10.6	1.2	1.9	2.2	•
Working Capital to Net Sales 40	0.1	•	0.1	0.1	0.0	0.1	0.1	0.1	•
Inventory to Working Capital 41	0.1	•	0.2	0.0	0.3	0.2	0.0	0.5	•
Total Receipts to Cash Flow 42	3.1	3.0	2.6	4.5	3.1	3.9	3.4	4.4	3.1
Cost of Goods to Cash Flow 43	0.4	1.3	0.3	1.7	0.3	0.4	0.9	1.3	0.5
Cash Flow to Total Debt 44	0.7	•	2.6	1.4	0.8	1.1	0.7	0.4	0.6

Selected Financial Factors (in Percentages)

Debt Ratio 45	61.0	•	62.4	69.0	78.5	45.1	57.8	75.1	57.6
Return on Total Assets 46	18.9	•	54.9	52.0	20.1	26.1	18.7	18.5	11.3
Return on Equity Before Income Taxes 47	42.2	•	142.9	162.0	89.3	46.1	42.1	65.1	22.4
Return on Equity After Income Taxes 48	35.2	•	141.2	157.7	88.0	45.5	39.6	57.2	17.7
Profit Margin (Before Income Tax) 49	12.2	9.1	12.8	11.8	10.0	13.1	12.2	10.9	8.3
Profit Margin (After Income Tax) 50	10.2	8.2	12.6	11.5	9.9	12.9	11.5	9.6	6.5

Table I

Corporations with and without Net Income

OFFICES OF PHYSICIANS

MONEY AMOUNTS AND SIZE OF ASSETS IN THOUSANDS OF DOLLARS

Item Description for Accounting Period 7/08 Through 6/09		Total	Zero Assets	Under 500	500 to 1,000	1,000 to 5,000	5,000 to 10,000	10,000 to 25,000	25,000 to 50,000	50,000 to 100,000	100,000 to 250,000	250,000 to 500,000	500,000 to 2,500,000	2,500,000 and over
Number of Enterprises	1	149558	15836	125469	3681	3951	360	164	46	27	16	3	6	0
Revenues ($ in Thousands)														
Net Sales	2	233206958	3430789	136952103	14200556	38168392	9107602	8311197	4898379	3578767	3276917	1181637	10100620	0
Interest	3	141002	2321	50425	4932	17035	6424	8673	8294	10405	8277	4387	19828	0
Rents	4	130197	10058	44693	5498	21184	8525	9904	4417	7364	14075	904	3574	0
Royalties	5	901	0	254	0	0	0	648	0	0	0	0	0	0
Other Portfolio Income	6	298734	20204	78572	4070	60532	31016	8931	1801	6641	6356	653	79958	0
Other Receipts	7	6310730	298716	4198180	157494	579056	74758	159870	120984	238285	43267	11373	428745	0
Total Receipts	8	240088522	3762088	141324227	14372550	38846199	9228325	8499223	5033875	3841462	3348892	1198954	10632725	0
Average Total Receipts	9	1605	238	1126	3905	9832	25634	51825	109432	142276	209306	399651	1772121	•
Operating Costs/Operating Income (%)														
Cost of Operations	10	4.8	0.5	2.8	7.2	7.6	5.4	11.0	15.4	11.5	12.3	4.2	4.0	•
Salaries and Wages	11	29.3	16.6	25.2	30.2	31.9	40.8	42.3	38.4	35.6	42.4	23.3	46.4	•
Taxes Paid	12	3.1	2.7	3.1	3.2	3.0	3.3	2.8	2.4	2.3	2.8	1.9	3.0	•
Interest Paid	13	0.5	0.2	0.3	0.6	0.7	0.5	0.6	0.6	1.1	1.2	2.3	1.3	•
Depreciation	14	1.4	0.7	0.9	1.8	2.3	3.6	2.6	1.4	2.0	3.2	2.4	0.6	•
Amortization and Depletion	15	0.1	0.1	0.0	0.1	0.0	0.2	0.2	0.2	0.2	0.3	0.5	0.6	•
Pensions and Other Deferred Comp.	16	3.3	1.3	3.6	3.0	2.9	1.9	2.4	2.7	1.7	1.8	1.1	6.7	•
Employee Benefits	17	2.2	0.9	1.8	1.5	2.4	2.8	3.0	3.4	2.1	3.8	2.3	5.4	•
Advertising	18	0.6	0.1	0.6	0.4	0.7	0.8	0.4	0.2	0.3	1.9	0.2	0.1	•
Other Expenses	19	31.5	51.4	31.1	26.8	27.3	35.1	35.3	37.5	47.6	31.4	62.4	33.5	•
Officers' Compensation	20	21.0	25.2	27.6	17.2	18.2	6.4	2.4	1.2	0.9	1.2	0.6	0.3	•
Operating Margin	21	2.4	0.3	3.1	8.0	3.0	•	•	•	•	•	•	•	•
Operating Margin Before Officers' Comp.	22	23.4	25.5	30.7	25.2	21.2	5.6	•	•	•	•	•	•	•

Selected Average Balance Sheet ($ in Thousands)

	•	•	•	•	•	•	•	•	•	•	•	•
Net Receivables 23	30	0	2	59	271	1295	2555	8647	14363	27676	139506	80809
Inventories 24	2	0	0	9	9	24	146	421	395	765	993	8128
Net Property, Plant and Equipment 25	75	0	27	209	828	2240	5098	11686	17148	37830	44867	59484
Total Assets 26	274		94	677	1944	6890	14601	37168	68424	140810	363669	1219338
Notes and Loans Payable 27	124	0	50	427	1079	3637	9523	10626	16120	37092	135321	285871
All Other Liabilities 28	123	0	35	190	537	2745	4981	14083	29204	58153	157043	1085538
Net Worth 29	27	0	9	60	328	507	97	12460	23100	45565	71304	-152070

Selected Financial Ratios (Times to 1)

	•	•	•	•	•	•	•	•	•	•	•	•
Current Ratio 30	1.1	•	1.1	1.3	0.9	0.9	0.9	1.1	1.1	1.2	1.1	1.5
Quick Ratio 31	0.9	•	0.9	1.1	0.8	0.8	0.6	0.8	0.8	0.9	1.0	1.2
Net Sales to Working Capital 32	184.1	•	263.6	54.8	•	•	•	76.4	34.2	22.4	26.4	16.5
Coverage Ratio 33	12.0	58.0	20.8	17.5	8.2	2.1	5.0	•	2.9	2.9	1.1	3.5
Total Asset Turnover 34	5.7	•	11.7	5.7	5.0	3.5	3.5	2.9	1.9	1.5	1.1	1.4
Inventory Turnover 35	44.6	•	66.6	31.2	80.8	57.7	38.2	38.9	38.5	33.0	16.8	8.3
Receivables Turnover 36	55.5	•	467.2	78.9	36.0	22.8	21.5	11.4	8.8	6.7	5.6	29.1
Total Liabilities to Net Worth 37	9.1	•	9.5	10.3	4.9	12.6	149.8	2.0	2.0	2.1	4.1	•
Current Assets to Working Capital 38	12.8	•	10.9	4.1	•	•	•	11.5	8.1	5.9	12.2	2.9
Current Liabilities to Working Capital 39	11.8	•	9.9	3.1	•	•	•	10.5	7.1	4.9	11.2	1.9
Working Capital to Net Sales 40	0.0	•	0.0	0.0	•	•	•	0.0	0.0	0.0	0.0	0.1
Inventory to Working Capital 41	0.2	•	0.1	0.1	•	•	•	0.3	0.1	0.1	0.1	0.1
Total Receipts to Cash Flow 42	3.2	1.8	3.1	3.5	3.9	3.5	3.5	2.9	2.1	3.7	1.7	3.2
Cost of Goods to Cash Flow 43	0.2	0.0	0.1	0.2	0.3	0.2	0.4	0.4	0.2	0.5	0.1	0.1
Cash Flow to Total Debt 44	2.0	•	4.1	1.8	1.5	1.1	1.0	1.5	1.4	0.6	0.8	0.4

Selected Financial Factors (in Percentages)

	•	•	•	•	•	•	•	•	•	•	•	•
Debt Ratio 45	90.1	•	90.5	91.2	83.1	92.6	99.3	66.5	66.2	67.6	80.4	112.5
Return on Total Assets 46	33.0	•	76.6	55.7	27.2	4.0	•	•	6.0	1.5	2.7	6.3
Return on Equity Before Income Taxes 47	305.9	•	766.3	594.0	141.5	28.5	•	•	11.6	•	0.9	•
Return on Equity After Income Taxes 48	297.9	•	758.2	588.5	140.5	26.4	•	•	6.9	•	•	•
Profit Margin (Before Income Tax) 49	5.3	10.0	6.3	9.2	4.8	0.6	•	2.0	2.0	•	0.2	3.2
Profit Margin (After Income Tax) 50	5.2	9.9	6.2	9.1	4.8	0.5	•	1.2	1.2	•	•	2.0

Table II

Corporations with Net Income

OFFICES OF PHYSICIANS

MONEY AMOUNTS AND SIZE OF ASSETS IN THOUSANDS OF DOLLARS

Item Description for Accounting Period 7/08 Through 6/09		Total	Zero Assets	Under 500	500 to 1,000	1,000 to 5,000	5,000 to 10,000	10,000 to 25,000	25,000 to 50,000	50,000 to 100,000	100,000 to 250,000	250,000 to 500,000	500,000 to 2,500,000	2,500,000 and over
Number of Enterprises	1	99037	7263	85719	2855	2897	•	81	20	17	12	0	•	0
Revenues ($ in Thousands)														
Net Sales	2	154445764	1651085	89406686	8574513	25898697	•	5435191	2428122	2477504	3302988	•	•	•
Interest	3	88806	2006	25316	848	10897	•	6052	3949	7785	9662	•	•	•
Rents	4	58947	0	38993	137	10719	•	828	105	1477	5252	•	•	•
Royalties	5	707	0	59	0	0	•	648	0	0	0	0	•	0
Other Portfolio Income	6	233116	19598	70742	3945	27194	•	7156	283	4324	6057	•	•	•
Other Receipts	7	4891165	196646	3346848	148921	404940	•	79180	40114	186395	33428	•	•	0
Total Receipts	8	159718505	1869335	92888644	8728364	26352447	•	5529055	2472573	2677485	3357387	•	•	0
Average Total Receipts	9	1613	257	1084	3057	9096	•	68260	123629	157499	279782	•	•	•
Operating Costs/Operating Income (%)														
Cost of Operations	10	5.3	1.0	3.4	10.3	8.6	•	8.9	17.1	13.9	12.1	•	•	•
Salaries and Wages	11	28.0	6.2	24.3	24.1	28.9	•	41.2	38.6	34.8	36.7	•	•	•
Taxes Paid	12	2.9	2.0	3.0	2.9	2.9	•	2.6	2.6	2.2	2.4	•	•	•
Interest Paid	13	0.5	0.4	0.3	0.5	0.6	•	0.3	0.8	1.1	1.7	•	•	•
Depreciation	14	1.2	0.4	0.9	2.1	1.8	•	1.5	1.0	2.3	2.3	•	•	•
Amortization and Depletion	15	0.1	•	0.0	0.1	0.0	•	0.1	0.2	0.3	0.3	•	•	•
Pensions and Other Deferred Comp.	16	3.2	1.4	3.3	2.6	2.7	•	2.7	5.1	2.0	1.4	•	•	•
Employee Benefits	17	2.0	0.8	1.6	1.2	2.0	•	2.7	3.4	2.2	3.2	•	•	•
Advertising	18	0.4	0.2	0.4	0.5	0.6	•	0.3	0.1	0.4	0.3	•	•	•
Other Expenses	19	30.4	50.6	29.9	24.1	26.9	•	35.5	28.8	43.7	37.4	•	•	•
Officers' Compensation	20	19.7	23.5	26.1	16.2	18.3	•	2.6	1.2	1.0	0.7	•	•	•
Operating Margin	21	6.1	13.6	6.8	15.3	6.7	•	1.6	0.9	•	1.4	•	•	•
Operating Margin Before Officers' Comp.	22	25.8	37.1	32.9	31.5	25.0	•	4.2	2.1	•	2.2	•	•	•

Selected Average Balance Sheet ($ in Thousands)

Net Receivables 23	23	0	1	47	202	•	2410	9019	14675	38692
Inventories 24	2	0	1	10	4	•	137	415	315	1088
Net Property, Plant and Equipment 25	69	0	27	203	673	•	4429	13836	18679	36229
Total Assets 26	271	0	97	661	1812	•	14425	37109	70441	169203
Notes and Loans Payable 27	106	0	41	363	810	•	6520	18772	13650	55307
All Other Liabilities 28	111	0	24	110	351	•	4382	13851	27696	64310
Net Worth 29	54	0	31	187	652	•	3523	4487	29095	49586

Selected Financial Ratios (Times to 1)

Current Ratio 30	1.3	•	1.4	1.9	1.1	•	1.0	0.8	1.4	1.8
Quick Ratio 31	1.1	•	1.3	1.6	1.0	•	0.8	0.7	1.0	1.7
Net Sales to Working Capital 32	58.9	•	78.5	23.1	202.4	•	215.4	•	15.3	9.4
Coverage Ratio 33	21.3	76.6	33.7	38.6	15.6	•	12.7	4.3	4.9	2.7
Total Asset Turnover 34	5.7	•	10.8	4.5	4.9	•	4.7	3.3	2.1	1.6
Inventory Turnover 35	46.0	•	65.6	29.8	175.6	•	43.6	50.1	64.4	30.6
Receivables Turnover 36	64.0	•	691.1	75.4	38.7	•	28.9	12.4	9.1	•
Total Liabilities to Net Worth 37	4.0	•	2.1	2.5	1.8	•	3.1	7.3	1.4	2.4
Current Assets to Working Capital 38	4.1	•	3.5	2.1	13.8	•	22.5	•	3.5	2.2
Current Liabilities to Working Capital 39	3.1	•	2.5	1.1	12.8	•	21.5	•	2.5	1.2
Working Capital to Net Sales 40	0.0	•	0.0	0.0	0.0	•	0.0	•	0.1	0.1
Inventory to Working Capital 41	0.1	•	0.0	0.1	0.0	•	0.4	•	0.0	0.0
Total Receipts to Cash Flow 42	2.9	1.4	2.9	2.9	3.4	•	3.0	3.5	2.2	2.7
Cost of Goods to Cash Flow 43	0.2	0.0	0.1	0.3	0.3	•	0.3	0.6	0.3	0.3
Cash Flow to Total Debt 44	2.4	•	5.5	2.2	2.2	•	2.0	1.1	1.6	0.9

Selected Financial Factors (in Percentages)

Debt Ratio 45	80.2	•	67.5	71.7	64.0	•	75.6	87.9	58.7	70.7
Return on Total Assets 46	57.4	•	118.5	79.8	44.5	•	16.7	11.6	10.9	7.8
Return on Equity Before Income Taxes 47	276.4	•	354.4	274.3	115.9	•	62.9	73.9	21.1	16.8
Return on Equity After Income Taxes 48	270.3	•	351.0	272.1	115.2	•	57.2	67.9	15.2	12.8
Profit Margin (Before Income Tax) 49	9.5	26.8	10.7	17.1	8.5	•	3.3	2.7	4.2	3.0
Profit Margin (After Income Tax) 50	9.3	26.7	10.6	17.0	8.4	•	3.0	2.5	3.3	2.3

364

Table I

Corporations with and without Net Income

OFFICES OF DENTISTS

MONEY AMOUNTS AND SIZE OF ASSETS IN THOUSANDS OF DOLLARS

Item Description for Accounting Period 7/08 Through 6/09		Total	Zero Assets	Under 500	500 to 1,000	1,000 to 5,000	5,000 to 10,000	10,000 to 25,000	25,000 to 50,000	50,000 to 100,000	100,000 to 250,000	250,000 to 500,000	500,000 to 2,500,000	2,500,000 and over
Number of Enterprises	1	73315	3827	62450	5852	1151	22	•	3	0	4	•	0	0
Revenues ($ in Thousands)														
Net Sales	2	62917269	1991002	46121541	9491353	2359097	890570	•	223321	0	564448	•	0	0
Interest	3	12471	0	8944	1754	1114	0	•	127	0	122	•	0	0
Rents	4	808	0	802	0	6	0	•	0	0	0	•	0	0
Royalties	5	0	0	0	0	0	0	•	0	0	0	•	0	0
Other Portfolio Income	6	53263	4705	46607	452	722	0	•	289	0	85	•	0	0
Other Receipts	7	1243238	1896	902091	268219	64018	3332	•	6	0	1021	•	0	0
Total Receipts	8	64227049	1997603	47079985	9761778	2424957	893902	•	223743	0	565676	•	0	0
Average Total Receipts	9	876	522	754	1668	2107	40632	•	74581	•	141419	•	•	•
Operating Costs/Operating Income (%)														
Cost of Operations	10	5.7	1.8	4.9	8.9	12.7	•	•	9.5	•	14.7	•	•	•
Salaries and Wages	11	24.6	42.5	22.8	24.4	28.5	32.8	•	44.6	•	29.7	•	•	•
Taxes Paid	12	3.6	4.5	3.6	3.2	4.1	1.9	•	2.8	•	3.2	•	•	•
Interest Paid	13	1.2	0.3	0.9	2.1	2.6	0.2	•	3.7	•	4.5	•	•	•
Depreciation	14	2.1	2.2	1.8	2.7	4.5	0.8	•	3.0	•	3.8	•	•	•
Amortization and Depletion	15	0.5	0.2	0.3	1.0	1.1	•	•	0.4	•	2.7	•	•	•
Pensions and Other Deferred Comp.	16	2.2	1.7	2.3	2.1	1.1	1.9	•	0.1	•	0.1	•	•	•
Employee Benefits	17	1.2	0.1	1.2	1.4	1.2	0.8	•	0.9	•	2.1	•	•	•
Advertising	18	1.7	5.9	1.6	1.2	1.3	1.3	•	2.2	•	3.9	•	•	•
Other Expenses	19	32.0	34.9	33.5	23.7	25.5	57.8	•	22.2	•	36.5	•	•	•
Officers' Compensation	20	18.6	3.7	20.4	19.7	13.8	0.6	•	1.4	•	0.6	•	•	•
Operating Margin	21	6.6	2.3	6.6	9.7	3.7	1.9	•	9.2	•	•	•	•	•
Operating Margin Before Officers' Comp.	22	25.2	6.1	27.1	29.4	17.5	2.5	•	10.6	•	•	•	•	•

Selected Average Balance Sheet ($ in Thousands)

Net Receivables 23	11	0	2	38	48	3129	22051	•	5437
Inventories 24	1	0	1	2	1	8	2330	•	1406
Net Property, Plant and Equipment 25	77	0	55	236	450	570	10343	•	21608
Total Assets 26	223	0	136	684	1554	6395	53902	•	138980
Notes and Loans Payable 27	150	0	98	479	1010	830	28390	•	69861
All Other Liabilities 28	49	0	27	201	129	4558	25806	•	29638
Net Worth 29	24	0	11	4	415	1006	-294	•	39482

Selected Financial Ratios (Times to 1)

Current Ratio 30	1.1	•	1.1	0.8	1.5	0.9	2.0	•	0.8
Quick Ratio 31	0.9	•	1.0	0.6	1.5	0.8	1.7	•	0.5
Net Sales to Working Capital 32	224.6	•	162.2	•	19.8	•	5.1	•	•
Coverage Ratio 33	8.0	9.9	10.5	7.1	3.4	15.4	3.5	•	0.6
Total Asset Turnover 34	3.8	•	5.4	2.4	1.3	6.3	1.4	•	1.0
Inventory Turnover 35	44.0	•	42.9	59.7	291.5	•	3.0	•	14.8
Receivables Turnover 36	80.8	•	384.1	37.6	46.2	13.9	3.2	•	6.0
Total Liabilities to Net Worth 37	8.1	•	11.3	181.1	2.7	5.4	•	•	2.5
Current Assets to Working Capital 38	15.9	•	8.9	•	3.0	•	2.0	•	•
Current Liabilities to Working Capital 39	14.9	•	7.9	•	2.0	•	1.0	•	•
Working Capital to Net Sales 40	0.0	•	0.0	•	0.1	•	0.2	•	•
Inventory to Working Capital 41	0.3	•	0.2	•	0.0	•	0.1	•	•
Total Receipts to Cash Flow 42	2.9	3.2	2.8	3.3	4.0	1.7	3.8	•	3.4
Cost of Goods to Cash Flow 43	0.2	0.1	0.1	0.3	0.5	•	0.4	•	0.5
Cash Flow to Total Debt 44	1.5	•	2.1	0.7	0.5	4.4	0.4	•	0.4

Selected Financial Factors (in Percentages)

Debt Ratio 45	89.0	•	91.9	99.5	73.3	84.3	100.5	•	71.6
Return on Total Assets 46	38.0	•	52.0	34.6	12.0	15.5	18.1	•	2.9
Return on Equity Before Income Taxes 47	303.1	•	580.7	5411.1	32.0	92.1	•	•	•
Return on Equity After Income Taxes 48	301.1	•	578.5	5396.4	31.8	91.7	•	•	•
Profit Margin (Before Income Tax) 49	8.6	2.7	8.7	12.5	6.5	2.3	9.4	•	•
Profit Margin (After Income Tax) 50	8.6	2.6	8.6	12.5	6.4	2.3	5.4	•	•

Table II

Corporations with Net Income

OFFICES OF DENTISTS

MONEY AMOUNTS AND SIZE OF ASSETS IN THOUSANDS OF DOLLARS

Item Description for Accounting Period 7/08 Through 6/09		Total	Zero Assets	Under 500	500 to 1,000	1,000 to 5,000	5,000 to 10,000	10,000 to 25,000	25,000 to 50,000	50,000 to 100,000	100,000 to 250,000	250,000 to 500,000	500,000 to 2,500,000	2,500,000 and over
Number of Enterprises	1	57604	2226	50369	4452	525	•	•	0	0	4	0	0	0
Revenues ($ in Thousands)														
Net Sales	2	47222713	1762621	35630516	7028169	1195637	•	•	0	0	522913	0	0	0
Interest	3	9296	0	7572	587	1013	•	•	0	0	76	0	0	0
Rents	4	6	0	0	0	6	•	•	0	0	0	0	0	0
Royalties	5	0	0	0	0	0	•	•	0	0	0	0	0	0
Other Portfolio Income	6	49446	4705	43801	452	0	•	•	0	0	85	0	0	0
Other Receipts	7	1122739	1741	806720	251430	57287	•	•	0	0	830	0	0	0
Total Receipts	8	48404200	1769067	36488609	7280638	1253943	•	•	0	0	523904	0	0	0
Average Total Receipts	9	840	795	724	1635	2388	•	•	•	•	130976	•	•	•
Operating Costs/Operating Income (%)														
Cost of Operations	10	6.4	0.0	5.5	11.4	15.7	•	•	•	•	17.1	•	•	•
Salaries and Wages	11	23.8	44.4	22.0	24.0	27.8	•	•	•	•	30.7	•	•	•
Taxes Paid	12	3.5	4.6	3.5	3.3	4.2	•	•	•	•	4.0	•	•	•
Interest Paid	13	1.1	0.3	0.9	2.2	1.5	•	•	•	•	4.0	•	•	•
Depreciation	14	1.7	0.3	1.7	2.2	2.6	•	•	•	•	6.1	•	•	•
Amortization and Depletion	15	0.5	0.3	0.4	1.1	0.5	•	•	•	•	3.1	•	•	•
Pensions and Other Deferred Comp.	16	1.9	1.9	2.0	1.8	1.0	•	•	•	•	0.5	•	•	•
Employee Benefits	17	1.1	0.0	1.2	1.0	0.9	•	•	•	•	2.3	•	•	•
Advertising	18	1.8	1.8	1.8	1.0	1.1	•	•	•	•	4.7	•	•	•
Other Expenses	19	30.9	32.6	32.6	21.6	20.0	•	•	•	•	23.2	•	•	•
Officers' Compensation	20	17.1	3.6	18.9	16.2	11.7	•	•	•	•	1.0	•	•	•
Operating Margin	21	10.1	5.5	9.7	14.1	13.0	•	•	•	•	3.3	•	•	•
Operating Margin Before Officers' Comp.	22	27.2	9.1	28.6	30.3	24.7	•	•	•	•	4.3	•	•	•

Selected Average Balance Sheet ($ in Thousands)

Net Receivables 23	9	0	3	41	59	…	8423
Inventories 24	1	0	1	0	0	…	1517
Net Property, Plant and Equipment 25	65	0	50	224	202	…	29652
Total Assets 26	202	0	134	695	1521	…	192031
Notes and Loans Payable 27	115	0	83	434	394	…	80486
All Other Liabilities 28	32	0	25	69	54	…	33525
Net Worth 29	54	0	26	191	1073	…	78020

Selected Financial Ratios (Times to 1)

Current Ratio 30	1.6	•	1.3	2.9	4.7	…	1.1
Quick Ratio 31	1.4	•	1.2	2.5	4.6	…	0.7
Net Sales to Working Capital 32	35.7	•	65.6	13.3	5.4	…	71.1
Coverage Ratio 33	12.8	20.4	15.2	9.1	12.8	…	1.9
Total Asset Turnover 34	4.0	•	5.3	2.3	1.5	…	0.7
Inventory Turnover 35	70.3	•	54.7	488.7	3411.7	…	14.7
Receivables Turnover 36	99.1	•	318.6	30.8	33.6	…	31.0
Total Liabilities to Net Worth 37	2.7	•	4.1	2.6	0.4	…	1.5
Current Assets to Working Capital 38	2.7	•	4.0	1.5	1.3	…	11.5
Current Liabilities to Working Capital 39	1.7	•	3.0	0.5	0.3	…	10.5
Working Capital to Net Sales 40	0.0	•	0.0	0.1	0.2	…	0.0
Inventory to Working Capital 41	0.0	•	0.1	0.0	0.0	…	0.8
Total Receipts to Cash Flow 42	2.7	3.1	2.6	3.0	3.2	…	5.6
Cost of Goods to Cash Flow 43	0.2	0.0	0.1	0.3	0.5	…	1.0
Cash Flow to Total Debt 44	2.0	•	2.5	1.1	1.6	…	0.2

Selected Financial Factors (in Percentages)

Debt Ratio 45	73.1	•	80.3	72.5	29.4	…	59.4
Return on Total Assets 46	55.1	•	68.1	45.2	29.0	…	5.1
Return on Equity Before Income Taxes 47	189.0	•	322.5	146.1	37.9	…	5.9
Return on Equity After Income Taxes 48	187.9	•	321.3	145.7	37.8	…	3.9
Profit Margin (Before Income Tax) 49	12.6	5.8	12.1	17.7	17.9	…	3.5
Profit Margin (After Income Tax) 50	12.5	5.8	12.0	17.7	17.8	…	2.3

Table I
Corporations with and without Net Income

OFFICES OF OTHER HEALTH PRACTITIONERS

MONEY AMOUNTS AND SIZE OF ASSETS IN THOUSANDS OF DOLLARS

Item Description for Accounting Period 7/08 Through 6/09	Total	Zero Assets	Under 500	500 to 1,000	1,000 to 5,000	5,000 to 10,000	10,000 to 25,000	25,000 to 50,000	50,000 to 100,000	100,000 to 250,000	250,000 to 500,000	500,000 to 2,500,000	2,500,000 and over
Number of Enterprises 1	105275	18457	83917	1774	917	106	•	25	16	12	•	•	•
Revenues ($ in Thousands)													
Net Sales 2	61849017	1590844	35061447	3608845	6039120	2381125	•	1131039	1707934	2740807	•	•	•
Interest 3	124802	4378	3753	419	2511	63	•	3111	3802	11258	•	•	•
Rents 4	30954	0	5014	0	2191	0	•	7140	2437	3699	•	•	•
Royalties 5	10112	1280	0	0	0	0	•	0	0	0	•	•	•
Other Portfolio Income 6	46105	7138	23191	14	305	81	•	307	489	317	•	•	•
Other Receipts 7	1361562	21256	173047	67	11445	-1933	•	18473	618616	142218	•	•	•
Total Receipts 8	63422552	1624896	35266452	3609345	6055572	2379336	•	1160070	2333278	2898299	•	•	•
Average Total Receipts 9	602	88	420	2035	6604	22447	•	46403	145830	241525	•	•	•
Operating Costs/Operating Income (%)													
Cost of Operations 10	18.5	9.6	12.3	24.0	37.0	16.1	•	34.7	20.6	36.6	•	•	•
Salaries and Wages 11	18.8	10.2	16.8	16.1	17.7	46.7	•	29.8	19.0	34.2	•	•	•
Taxes Paid 12	2.7	3.0	3.1	3.0	1.8	4.0	•	4.3	1.9	2.2	•	•	•
Interest Paid 13	0.9	1.3	0.6	0.8	0.5	1.2	•	1.6	1.9	1.8	•	•	•
Depreciation 14	1.2	1.6	1.3	1.2	0.6	0.9	•	2.0	1.9	1.5	•	•	•
Amortization and Depletion 15	0.3	0.1	0.1	0.3	0.3	0.1	•	0.5	0.8	1.1	•	•	•
Pensions and Other Deferred Comp. 16	0.7	1.4	0.6	2.0	1.1	0.5	•	0.7	0.3	0.2	•	•	•
Employee Benefits 17	1.6	0.9	1.1	2.2	1.9	3.1	•	3.3	1.7	4.6	•	•	•
Advertising 18	1.2	2.3	1.4	0.8	1.3	0.3	•	0.4	0.6	0.6	•	•	•
Other Expenses 19	41.2	40.4	42.6	22.0	30.2	20.6	•	25.2	87.1	23.4	•	•	•
Officers' Compensation 20	8.8	19.0	11.9	16.6	2.8	3.2	•	3.4	0.5	0.3	•	•	•
Operating Margin 21	4.3	10.1	8.3	11.1	4.8	3.4	•	•	•	•	•	•	•
Operating Margin Before Officers' Comp. 22	13.0	29.1	20.2	27.7	7.6	6.6	•	•	•	•	•	•	•

Selected Average Balance Sheet ($ in Thousands)

Net Receivables 23	25	0	7	48	278	2280	10718	10559	26519
Inventories 24	3	0	2	18	42	2	561	950	670
Net Property, Plant and Equipment 25	34	0	24	179	323	1085	5515	15498	13214
Total Assets 26	174	0	74	665	1568	5998	34869	71133	143539
Notes and Loans Payable 27	76	0	41	333	691	3498	8911	24665	68145
All Other Liabilities 28	42	0	16	102	205	2843	11479	22794	49173
Net Worth 29	56	0	17	231	672	-343	14479	23674	26221

Selected Financial Ratios (Times to 1)

Current Ratio 30	1.5	•	1.4	2.1	2.6	1.2	1.6	1.1	1.0
Quick Ratio 31	1.2	•	1.2	1.9	1.9	1.0	1.2	0.7	0.7
Net Sales to Working Capital 32	26.9	•	44.1	12.1	13.2	48.2	7.0	32.9	108.5
Coverage Ratio 33	8.4	10.2	16.5	15.6	11.9	3.7	•	1.1	0.5
Total Asset Turnover 34	3.4	•	5.6	3.1	4.2	3.7	1.3	1.5	1.6
Inventory Turnover 35	32.0	•	22.6	27.6	57.9	1901.4	28.0	23.2	124.6
Receivables Turnover 36	24.7	•	74.1	23.7	20.8	12.3	4.6	7.6	9.0
Total Liabilities to Net Worth 37	2.1	•	3.3	1.9	1.3	•	1.4	2.0	4.5
Current Assets to Working Capital 38	3.2	•	3.3	1.9	1.6	6.4	2.7	8.6	25.6
Current Liabilities to Working Capital 39	2.2	•	2.3	0.9	0.6	5.4	1.7	7.6	24.6
Working Capital to Net Sales 40	0.0	•	0.0	0.1	0.1	0.0	0.1	0.0	0.0
Inventory to Working Capital 41	0.2	•	0.2	0.1	0.1	0.0	0.1	0.4	0.4
Total Receipts to Cash Flow 42	2.4	2.5	2.3	3.6	3.3	5.2	5.6	1.2	5.6
Cost of Goods to Cash Flow 43	0.4	0.2	0.3	0.9	1.2	0.8	1.9	0.2	2.0
Cash Flow to Total Debt 44	2.0	•	3.2	1.3	2.2	0.7	0.4	1.9	0.3

Selected Financial Factors (in Percentages)

Debt Ratio 45	67.9	•	76.7	65.3	57.2	105.7	58.5	66.7	81.7
Return on Total Assets 46	25.9	•	53.3	36.2	23.4	17.1	•	3.3	1.6
Return on Equity Before Income Taxes 47	71.2	•	214.9	97.7	49.9	•	•	1.2	•
Return on Equity After Income Taxes 48	69.5	•	214.5	96.1	49.7	•	•	0.7	•
Profit Margin (Before Income Tax) 49	6.8	12.2	8.9	11.1	5.1	3.3	•	0.3	•
Profit Margin (After Income Tax) 50	6.6	12.2	8.9	10.9	5.1	3.3	•	0.1	•

367

Table II
Corporations with Net Income

OFFICES OF OTHER HEALTH PRACTITIONERS

MONEY AMOUNTS AND SIZE OF ASSETS IN THOUSANDS OF DOLLARS

Item Description for Accounting Period 7/08 Through 6/09	Total	Zero Assets	Under 500	500 to 1,000	1,000 to 5,000	5,000 to 10,000	10,000 to 25,000	25,000 to 50,000	50,000 to 100,000	100,000 to 250,000	250,000 to 500,000	500,000 to 2,500,000	2,500,000 and over
Number of Enterprises 1	79332	13599	63288	1667	637	83	33	•	8	7	•	•	•
Revenues ($ in Thousands)													
Net Sales 2	47085165	1264390	25119357	3436604	4947781	1617186	1536720	•	869291	2051866	•	•	•
Interest 3	98636	4378	280	419	251	0	1696	•	2735	7252	•	•	•
Rents 4	22107	0	5014	0	2191	0	58	•	372	507	•	•	•
Royalties 5	10112	1280	0	0	0	0	0	•	0	0	•	•	•
Other Portfolio Income 6	31381	7138	9023	14	305	72	60	•	399	168	•	•	•
Other Receipts 7	1161669	21183	135086	67	10820	916	13147	•	522048	132724	•	•	•
Total Receipts 8	48409070	1298369	25268760	3437104	4961348	1618174	1551681	•	1394845	2192517	•	•	•
Average Total Receipts 9	610	95	399	2062	7789	19496	47021	•	174356	313217	•	•	•
Operating Costs/Operating Income (%)													
Cost of Operations 10	20.1	11.3	12.2	25.2	43.5	23.8	50.2	•	2.0	44.6	•	•	•
Salaries and Wages 11	17.9	8.0	16.8	16.9	19.2	44.5	21.0	•	18.8	30.1	•	•	•
Taxes Paid 12	2.8	2.6	3.3	3.2	2.0	4.2	2.0	•	2.0	1.2	•	•	•
Interest Paid 13	0.9	1.3	0.6	0.8	0.4	1.5	0.5	•	1.8	0.9	•	•	•
Depreciation 14	1.1	1.4	1.3	1.2	0.5	0.8	1.4	•	1.8	1.1	•	•	•
Amortization and Depletion 15	0.3	0.0	0.2	0.3	0.2	0.1	0.2	•	0.4	1.0	•	•	•
Pensions and Other Deferred Comp. 16	0.7	0.5	0.7	2.1	1.3	0.2	0.1	•	0.1	0.2	•	•	•
Employee Benefits 17	1.5	0.2	1.1	2.3	2.0	3.4	1.7	•	1.5	4.9	•	•	•
Advertising 18	1.0	1.2	1.2	0.8	1.5	0.3	1.6	•	0.3	0.2	•	•	•
Other Expenses 19	36.7	36.6	36.7	18.1	18.9	11.8	16.3	•	126.7	20.2	•	•	•
Officers' Compensation 20	9.0	16.5	12.5	17.4	3.1	3.3	1.7	•	0.9	0.3	•	•	•
Operating Margin 21	8.0	20.3	13.6	11.6	7.3	6.2	3.5	•	•	•	•	•	•
Operating Margin Before Officers' Comp. 22	17.0	36.8	26.0	29.1	10.5	9.5	5.1	•	•	•	•	•	•

Selected Average Balance Sheet ($ in Thousands)

Net Receivables 23	23	0	6	24	280	2618	3132	13344	28433
Inventories 24	3	0	2	18	49	2	404	681	419
Net Property, Plant and Equipment 25	32	0	23	190	324	790	3297	15667	9644
Total Assets 26	174	0	76	659	1553	5982	13990	72922	129378
Notes and Loans Payable 27	61	0	32	307	438	2899	5122	24438	26287
All Other Liabilities 28	38	0	11	104	197	3336	3338	29304	59881
Net Worth 29	75	0	33	248	918	-253	5530	19179	43211

Selected Financial Ratios (Times to 1)

Current Ratio 30	1.7	•	2.0	2.3	3.5	1.4	1.1	0.9	1.1
Quick Ratio 31	1.4	•	1.7	2.1	2.3	1.3	0.9	0.7	0.9
Net Sales to Working Capital 32	20.2	•	23.9	11.5	12.2	23.5	49.5	•	80.3
Coverage Ratio 33	13.4	18.8	25.5	15.6	18.5	5.1	9.1	3.3	3.3
Total Asset Turnover 34	3.4	•	5.2	3.1	5.0	3.3	3.3	1.5	2.3
Inventory Turnover 35	34.6	•	21.0	28.3	68.6	1901.4	57.8	3.2	312.1
Receivables Turnover 36	27.7	•	84.7	56.4	23.0	9.5	23.4	6.3	•
Total Liabilities to Net Worth 37	1.3	•	1.3	1.7	0.7	•	1.5	2.8	2.0
Current Assets to Working Capital 38	2.4	•	2.0	1.7	1.4	3.7	8.1	•	14.8
Current Liabilities to Working Capital 39	1.4	•	1.0	0.7	0.4	2.7	7.1	•	13.8
Working Capital to Net Sales 40	0.0	•	0.0	0.1	0.1	0.0	0.0	•	0.0
Inventory to Working Capital 41	0.1	•	0.1	0.1	0.1	0.0	0.7	•	0.1
Total Receipts to Cash Flow 42	2.5	2.1	2.4	4.1	4.9	6.4	6.1	0.8	5.0
Cost of Goods to Cash Flow 43	0.5	0.2	0.3	1.0	2.1	1.5	3.0	0.0	2.2
Cash Flow to Total Debt 44	2.4	•	3.8	1.2	2.5	0.5	0.9	2.6	0.7

Selected Financial Factors (in Percentages)

Debt Ratio 45	56.8	•	56.4	62.4	40.9	104.2	60.5	73.7	66.6
Return on Total Assets 46	39.9	•	76.6	38.9	40.2	25.4	16.7	8.8	6.9
Return on Equity Before Income Taxes 47	85.5	•	168.9	96.8	64.3	•	37.5	23.4	14.4
Return on Equity After Income Taxes 48	83.8	•	168.6	95.1	64.0	•	30.8	22.0	10.6
Profit Margin (Before Income Tax) 49	10.8	23.0	14.2	11.6	7.6	6.3	4.5	4.1	2.1
Profit Margin (After Income Tax) 50	10.6	23.0	14.2	11.4	7.6	6.3	3.7	3.9	1.6

Table I

Corporations with and without Net Income

OUTPATIENT CARE CENTERS

MONEY AMOUNTS AND SIZE OF ASSETS IN THOUSANDS OF DOLLARS

Item Description for Accounting Period 7/08 Through 6/09		Total	Zero Assets	Under 500	500 to 1,000	1,000 to 5,000	5,000 to 10,000	10,000 to 25,000	25,000 to 50,000	50,000 to 100,000	100,000 to 250,000	250,000 to 500,000	500,000 to 2,500,000	2,500,000 and over
Number of Enterprises	1	7792	2084	4658	365	565	50	23	9	11	7	5	•	•
Revenues ($ in Thousands)														
Net Sales	2	35332857	477002	2352723	755731	6212994	486326	533353	1581764	1211085	834821	2240876	•	•
Interest	3	214867	127	200	5004	3133	4383	3784	4477	6092	6458	19921	•	•
Rents	4	19815	589	0	0	93	60	288	0	518	748	2808	•	•
Royalties	5	0	0	0	0	0	0	0	0	0	0	0	•	•
Other Portfolio Income	6	66434	5340	0	1022	5895	33	11313	5111	1732	1418	2985	•	•
Other Receipts	7	2056465	3230	-581	2850	10701	5465	3496	18953	324877	41684	915245	•	•
Total Receipts	8	37690438	486288	2352342	764607	6232816	496267	552234	1610305	1544304	885129	3181835	•	•
Average Total Receipts	9	4837	233	505	2095	11032	9925	24010	178923	140391	126447	636367	•	•
Operating Costs/Operating Income (%)														
Cost of Operations	10	30.5	5.1	2.1	20.1	15.5	6.0	3.9	68.4	27.9	6.9	52.5	•	•
Salaries and Wages	11	24.1	22.2	22.3	28.2	35.1	40.7	40.8	5.3	21.1	23.0	24.0	•	•
Taxes Paid	12	3.2	3.0	2.9	3.8	3.0	3.6	3.5	0.5	2.1	2.8	2.2	•	•
Interest Paid	13	3.8	2.0	0.7	1.5	0.5	2.2	2.1	0.5	2.2	3.3	1.3	•	•
Depreciation	14	2.8	3.0	1.3	4.2	1.1	2.8	2.3	0.2	2.8	4.0	1.2	•	•
Amortization and Depletion	15	1.5	0.4	0.1	0.1	0.0	1.6	0.9	0.3	0.6	2.3	0.5	•	•
Pensions and Other Deferred Comp.	16	0.9	0.3	0.4	0.3	3.4	0.5	1.2	0.1	0.5	0.3	0.1	•	•
Employee Benefits	17	5.6	2.6	0.8	3.1	3.4	2.8	4.7	0.4	22.0	1.0	34.1	•	•
Advertising	18	0.4	0.5	0.6	0.4	0.3	0.6	0.2	0.5	0.9	3.6	0.3	•	•
Other Expenses	19	28.4	53.5	48.9	26.3	30.4	52.6	49.1	23.8	45.3	62.4	19.3	•	•
Officers' Compensation	20	2.0	2.9	11.0	5.9	3.8	3.7	2.4	0.2	1.6	0.5	0.7	•	•
Operating Margin	21	•	4.6	8.9	6.1	3.6	•	•	0.0	•	•	•	•	•
Operating Margin Before Officers' Comp.	22	•	7.5	20.0	12.0	7.4	•	•	0.2	•	•	•	•	•

Selected Average Balance Sheet ($ in Thousands)

Item											
Net Receivables 23	566	0	3	157	797	2468	3089	3108	10799	7346	35814
Inventories 24	56	0	2	7	112	52	87	135	844	1096	907
Net Property, Plant and Equipment 25	637	0	24	341	525	913	2826	1827	16754	15510	53266
Total Assets 26	7050	0	104	840	2369	7619	14306	40256	73908	158033	357636
Notes and Loans Payable 27	3656	0	112	763	872	3753	5773	6364	29467	75183	72136
All Other Liabilities 28	1498	0	21	33	996	2847	4414	20421	31383	49341	97489
Net Worth 29	1896	0	-29	44	502	1019	4119	13471	13058	33509	188010

Selected Financial Ratios (Times to 1)

Item											
Current Ratio 30	1.0	•	0.3	2.0	1.1	1.1	2.3	0.9	•	0.5	1.3
Quick Ratio 31	0.8	•	0.3	1.5	0.8	0.9	2.0	0.7	•	0.4	0.8
Net Sales to Working Capital 32	•	•	•	10.1	122.3	44.3	34.6	13.1	•	•	17.0
Coverage Ratio 33	1.9	4.3	13.6	6.0	9.2	•	4.3	4.4	1.1	•	5.7
Total Asset Turnover 34	0.6	•	4.8	2.5	4.6	1.3	1.6	4.4	1.5	0.8	1.3
Inventory Turnover 35	24.5	•	5.0	63.1	15.2	11.2	10.4	888.1	36.3	7.5	259.3
Receivables Turnover 36	8.6	113.5	15.8	15.6	5.6	7.1	55.0	10.6	•	19.9	9.4
Total Liabilities to Net Worth 37	2.7	•	18.0	3.7	6.5	2.5	2.0	4.7	3.7	•	0.9
Current Assets to Working Capital 38	•	•	2.0	18.5	16.4	9.9	1.8	•	•	•	4.2
Current Liabilities to Working Capital 39	•	•	1.0	17.5	15.4	8.9	0.8	•	•	•	3.2
Working Capital to Net Sales 40	•	•	0.1	0.0	0.0	0.0	0.1	•	•	•	0.1
Inventory to Working Capital 41	•	•	•	1.1	0.0	0.1	0.0	•	•	•	0.0
Total Receipts to Cash Flow 42	3.8	2.3	2.2	3.6	3.1	3.6	2.9	4.1	2.3	1.9	4.5
Cost of Goods to Cash Flow 43	1.2	0.1	0.0	0.7	0.5	0.2	0.1	2.8	0.7	0.1	2.4
Cash Flow to Total Debt 44	0.2	•	1.7	0.7	1.9	0.4	0.8	1.6	0.8	0.5	0.6

Selected Financial Factors (in Percentages)

Item											
Debt Ratio 45	73.1	•	127.3	94.7	78.8	86.6	71.2	66.5	82.3	78.8	47.4
Return on Total Assets 46	4.6	•	46.6	21.6	20.5	•	•	10.3	3.8	•	9.0
Return on Equity Before Income Taxes 47	8.0	•	•	341.8	86.0	•	•	23.6	2.6	•	14.1
Return on Equity After Income Taxes 48	4.7	•	•	341.1	79.2	•	•	17.1	•	•	9.7
Profit Margin (Before Income Tax) 49	3.4	6.5	8.9	7.3	3.9	•	•	1.8	0.3	•	5.9
Profit Margin (After Income Tax) 50	2.0	4.1	8.9	7.3	3.6	•	•	1.3	•	•	4.1

HEALTH CARE AND SOCIAL ASSISTANCE
621415

Table II
Corporations with Net Income

OUTPATIENT CARE CENTERS

MONEY AMOUNTS AND SIZE OF ASSETS IN THOUSANDS OF DOLLARS

Item Description for Accounting Period 7/08 Through 6/09	Total	Zero Assets	Under 500	500 to 1,000	1,000 to 5,000	5,000 to 10,000	10,000 to 25,000	25,000 to 50,000	50,000 to 100,000	100,000 to 250,000	250,000 to 500,000	500,000 to 2,500,000	2,500,000 and over
Number of Enterprises **1**	4231	1031	2583	156	423	7	•	•	7	0	•	•	0

Revenues ($ in Thousands)

Net Sales **2**	30057017	448710	1822180	431558	5765603	113098	•	•	1300606	0	•	•	0
Interest **3**	149262	127	101	4043	2524	92	•	•	7388	0	•	•	0
Rents **4**	4797	0	0	0	93	24	•	•	1264	0	•	•	0
Royalties **5**	0	0	0	0	0	0	•	•	0	0	•	•	0
Other Portfolio Income **6**	38905	328	0	0	2417	32	•	•	1708	0	•	•	0
Other Receipts **7**	1439646	3215	20196	2664	18580	234	•	•	11874	0	•	•	0
Total Receipts **8**	31689627	452380	1842477	438265	5789217	113480	•	•	1322840	0	•	•	0
Average Total Receipts **9**	7490	439	713	2809	13686	16211	•	•	188977	•	•	•	•

Operating Costs/Operating Income (%)

Cost of Operations **10**	33.8	5.4	2.2	35.2	13.8	0.7	•	•	17.1	•	•	•	•
Salaries and Wages **11**	21.3	21.6	16.4	17.8	35.8	37.8	•	•	12.9	•	•	•	•
Taxes Paid **12**	3.1	2.5	1.9	2.4	3.0	3.9	•	•	1.8	•	•	•	•
Interest Paid **13**	2.7	2.0	0.3	1.0	0.4	1.5	•	•	0.4	•	•	•	•
Depreciation **14**	2.6	2.2	0.8	1.5	1.0	6.8	•	•	1.5	•	•	•	•
Amortization and Depletion **15**	1.3	0.4	0.1	0.2	0.0	0.0	•	•	0.0	•	•	•	•
Pensions and Other Deferred Comp. **16**	1.0	0.3	0.5	•	3.6	0.5	•	•	0.5	•	•	•	•
Employee Benefits **17**	6.1	2.7	0.6	1.9	3.6	1.8	•	•	19.0	•	•	•	•
Advertising **18**	0.3	0.5	0.4	0.4	0.3	0.1	•	•	0.5	•	•	•	•
Other Expenses **19**	24.2	40.8	45.9	20.8	30.6	30.6	•	•	42.6	•	•	•	•
Officers' Compensation **20**	1.9	3.0	13.7	0.4	3.8	2.8	•	•	1.2	•	•	•	•
Operating Margin **21**	1.8	18.6	17.3	18.4	4.1	13.5	•	•	2.7	•	•	•	•
Operating Margin Before Officers' Comp. **22**	3.8	21.7	31.0	18.8	7.8	16.3	•	•	3.9	•	•	•	•

Selected Average Balance Sheet ($ in Thousands)

Net Receivables **23**	749	0	0	737	486	•	10845
Inventories **24**	98	0	4	147	374	•	381
Net Property, Plant and Equipment **25**	924	0	22	606	3884	•	21038
Total Assets **26**	10287	0	122	2552	6576	•	79536
Notes and Loans Payable **27**	5225	0	49	813	4483	•	20937
All Other Liabilities **28**	1559	0	3	1141	698	•	40299
Net Worth **29**	3504	0	69	597	1394	•	18300

Selected Financial Ratios (Times to 1)

Current Ratio **30**	1.2	•	1.0	1.1	1.1	2.1	0.8
Quick Ratio **31**	0.9	•	0.9	0.7	0.7	1.7	0.7
Net Sales to Working Capital **32**	23.9	•	•	101.6	71.2	13.5	•
Coverage Ratio **33**	3.7	10.6	56.5	20.1	12.1	10.3	11.3
Total Asset Turnover **34**	0.7	•	5.8	3.0	5.3	2.5	2.3
Inventory Turnover **35**	24.6	•	4.0	63.1	12.8	0.3	83.1
Receivables Turnover **36**	9.9	•	455545.0	22.5	21.6	6.1	19.8
Total Liabilities to Net Worth **37**	1.9	•	0.8	0.5	3.3	3.7	3.3
Current Assets to Working Capital **38**	5.5	•	•	8.1	9.2	1.9	•
Current Liabilities to Working Capital **39**	4.5	•	•	7.1	8.2	0.9	•
Working Capital to Net Sales **40**	0.0	•	•	0.0	0.0	0.1	•
Inventory to Working Capital **41**	0.3	•	•	0.7	0.7	0.0	•
Total Receipts to Cash Flow **42**	3.7	1.8	1.9	2.9	3.0	2.8	2.2
Cost of Goods to Cash Flow **43**	1.2	0.1	0.0	1.0	0.4	0.0	0.4
Cash Flow to Total Debt **44**	0.3	•	6.9	3.3	2.3	1.1	1.4

Selected Financial Factors (in Percentages)

Debt Ratio **45**	65.9	•	43.4	32.2	76.6	78.8	77.0
Return on Total Assets **46**	6.9	•	108.8	63.6	26.1	37.6	10.9
Return on Equity Before Income Taxes **47**	14.7	•	188.7	89.2	102.3	160.0	43.3
Return on Equity After Income Taxes **48**	11.4	•	188.3	89.0	94.7	159.1	30.5
Profit Margin (Before Income Tax) **49**	7.3	19.4	18.4	19.9	4.5	13.8	4.3
Profit Margin (After Income Tax) **50**	5.6	16.9	18.4	19.9	4.1	13.7	3.0

Table I

Corporations with and without Net Income

MISC. HEALTH CARE AND SOCIAL ASSISTANCE

MONEY AMOUNTS AND SIZE OF ASSETS IN THOUSANDS OF DOLLARS

Item Description for Accounting Period 7/08 Through 6/09		Total	Zero Assets	Under 500	500 to 1,000	1,000 to 5,000	5,000 to 10,000	10,000 to 25,000	25,000 to 50,000	50,000 to 100,000	100,000 to 250,000	250,000 to 500,000	500,000 to 2,500,000	2,500,000 and over
Number of Enterprises	1	61810	14801	41805	2497	2075	332	123	59	45	37	19	15	0
Revenues ($ in Thousands)														
Net Sales	2	98109640	2539135	27365308	5307254	8932965	6052854	3637853	3065596	3627153	5992983	6884930	24703609	0
Interest	3	198115	550	1798	1126	5294	23103	7515	6556	12537	28238	25233	86164	0
Rents	4	26697	0	9708	0	4254	3498	148	12	1493	3007	3833	745	0
Royalties	5	75144	0	0	0	10967	0	0	0	34339	20035	2707	7094	0
Other Portfolio Income	6	236774	21386	16255	3103	36854	46299	14636	286	4495	4684	22155	66625	0
Other Receipts	7	1672480	14577	177509	22980	149816	197743	29731	-4523	56912	121733	242343	663657	0
Total Receipts	8	100318850	2575648	27570578	5334463	9140150	6323497	3689883	3067927	3736929	6170680	7181201	25527894	0
Average Total Receipts	9	1623	174	660	2136	4405	19047	29999	51999	83043	166775	377958	1701860	•
Operating Costs/Operating Income (%)														
Cost of Operations	10	17.9	17.6	7.6	10.8	16.2	43.9	26.1	27.2	30.9	26.2	10.2	21.0	•
Salaries and Wages	11	30.7	27.3	33.7	32.6	38.0	21.1	24.4	33.4	31.3	26.8	34.3	27.3	•
Taxes Paid	12	3.8	3.6	4.8	4.0	4.3	2.4	3.1	3.5	3.3	3.4	3.5	3.3	•
Interest Paid	13	2.0	0.4	0.5	2.3	1.5	0.9	0.9	1.6	2.5	3.3	4.3	3.6	•
Depreciation	14	2.6	1.4	1.0	2.1	1.8	4.0	2.3	2.1	2.6	3.7	4.6	4.0	•
Amortization and Depletion	15	0.8	0.8	0.1	0.4	0.1	0.1	0.4	0.8	1.4	2.0	1.5	1.6	•
Pensions and Other Deferred Comp.	16	0.5	0.4	0.6	0.3	0.4	0.3	0.3	0.4	0.5	0.2	0.4	0.6	•
Employee Benefits	17	2.3	1.6	1.2	1.7	2.4	2.6	1.5	2.6	2.9	2.1	2.5	3.8	•
Advertising	18	0.6	0.3	0.8	0.8	0.6	0.5	0.8	0.5	0.6	0.4	0.4	0.5	•
Other Expenses	19	31.9	37.1	31.8	36.2	30.1	23.8	38.9	25.6	28.3	30.1	46.6	29.7	•
Officers' Compensation	20	5.0	8.7	12.1	5.9	4.2	2.3	2.3	2.3	1.6	1.1	1.1	0.7	•
Operating Margin	21	1.8	0.7	5.7	2.9	0.3	•	•	•	•	0.8	•	4.0	•
Operating Margin Before Officers' Comp.	22	6.8	9.4	17.9	8.9	4.6	0.4	1.3	2.3	•	1.9	•	4.7	•

Selected Average Balance Sheet ($ in Thousands)

Net Receivables 23	138	0	9	134	384	1292	3342	8341	12289	27292	65469	191094
Inventories 24	12	0	1	6	26	182	442	918	1493	2892	4178	15834
Net Property, Plant and Equipment 25	178	0	32	207	740	1912	2339	5465	7201	18531	85050	251331
Total Assets 26	984	0	87	676	1853	6913	16594	34139	66922	160370	357068	1971383
Notes and Loans Payable 27	426	0	59	413	986	2388	6520	10803	27646	68933	192447	739666
All Other Liabilities 28	273	0	17	181	385	2233	4553	12481	19820	41842	113838	553061
Net Worth 29	285	0	11	82	482	2292	5521	10854	19455	49595	50783	678655

Selected Financial Ratios (Times to 1)

Current Ratio 30	1.5	•	2.1	1.2	2.0	1.6	1.3	1.0	1.1	1.3	1.9	1.5
Quick Ratio 31	1.1	•	1.9	1.0	1.8	1.3	1.0	0.8	0.8	1.2	1.4	1.0
Net Sales to Working Capital 32	15.9	•	36.2	48.3	9.9	12.7	14.5	•	47.9	11.4	6.4	12.1
Coverage Ratio 33	3.0	6.9	13.8	2.5	2.7	3.8	1.4	1.0	•	2.1	•	3.1
Total Asset Turnover 34	1.6	•	7.6	3.1	2.3	2.6	1.8	1.5	1.2	1.0	1.0	0.8
Inventory Turnover 35	23.2	•	71.0	35.3	27.0	43.9	17.5	15.4	16.7	14.7	8.9	21.9
Receivables Turnover 36	11.3	•	72.5	17.5	11.8	14.5	8.6	6.0	6.3	6.1	6.7	7.5
Total Liabilities to Net Worth 37	2.5	•	6.9	7.2	2.8	2.0	2.0	2.1	2.4	2.2	6.0	1.9
Current Assets to Working Capital 38	3.0	•	1.9	5.9	2.0	2.7	4.4	•	13.3	3.9	2.1	3.0
Current Liabilities to Working Capital 39	2.0	•	0.9	4.9	1.0	1.7	3.4	•	12.3	2.9	1.1	2.0
Working Capital to Net Sales 40	0.1	•	0.0	0.0	0.1	0.1	0.1	•	0.0	0.1	0.2	0.1
Inventory to Working Capital 41	0.1	•	0.1	0.1	0.0	0.2	0.2	•	0.8	0.2	0.1	0.1
Total Receipts to Cash Flow 42	3.3	3.4	3.2	3.0	3.7	4.5	2.9	4.7	4.7	3.4	2.8	3.1
Cost of Goods to Cash Flow 43	0.6	0.6	0.2	0.3	0.6	2.0	0.8	1.3	1.5	0.9	0.3	0.7
Cash Flow to Total Debt 44	0.7	•	2.7	1.2	0.9	0.9	0.9	0.5	0.4	0.4	0.4	0.4

Selected Financial Factors (in Percentages)

Debt Ratio 45	71.1	•	87.4	87.8	74.0	66.9	66.7	68.2	70.9	69.1	85.8	65.6
Return on Total Assets 46	9.9	•	52.8	18.2	9.7	9.0	2.2	2.5	•	7.1	•	9.1
Return on Equity Before Income Taxes 47	22.7	•	388.2	89.5	23.5	19.9	1.9	0.2	•	12.3	•	17.8
Return on Equity After Income Taxes 48	17.4	•	383.6	84.1	19.7	16.4	•	•	•	6.8	•	11.8
Profit Margin (Before Income Tax) 49	4.1	2.1	6.5	3.5	2.6	2.5	0.4	0.0	•	3.8	•	7.3
Profit Margin (After Income Tax) 50	3.1	1.6	6.4	3.3	2.2	2.1	•	•	•	2.1	•	4.9

Table II

Corporations with Net Income

MISC. HEALTH CARE AND SOCIAL ASSISTANCE

MONEY AMOUNTS AND SIZE OF ASSETS IN THOUSANDS OF DOLLARS

Item Description for Accounting Period 7/08 Through 6/09	Total	Zero Assets	Under 500	500 to 1,000	1,000 to 5,000	5,000 to 10,000	10,000 to 25,000	25,000 to 50,000	50,000 to 100,000	100,000 to 250,000	250,000 to 500,000	500,000 to 2,500,000	2,500,000 and over
Number of Enterprises 1	41559	9363	28239	2004	1582	199	78	32	17	25	12	10	0
Revenues ($ in Thousands)													
Net Sales 2	74006300	1478692	22770533	3513163	7370343	3016910	2456477	2155907	1624723	4597398	5346883	19675270	0
Interest 3	122792	64	1611	1022	3381	13276	5021	1911	3787	14590	6003	72127	0
Rents 4	18464	0	7098	0	4124	1437	148	12	496	699	3735	716	0
Royalties 5	38709	0	0	0	10967	0	0	0	22792	220	2693	2036	0
Other Portfolio Income 6	218635	18661	15655	3103	36691	43785	11490	279	1029	4339	22108	61498	0
Other Receipts 7	946368	26020	80712	24540	132572	191481	20868	9063	27062	87194	69846	277008	0
Total Receipts 8	75351268	1523437	22875609	3541828	7558078	3266889	2494004	2167172	1679889	4704440	5451268	20088655	0
Average Total Receipts 9	1813	163	810	1767	4778	16417	31974	67724	98817	188178	454272	2008866	•
Operating Costs/Operating Income (%)													
Cost of Operations 10	17.5	20.6	8.5	11.1	15.3	25.0	32.8	23.9	21.4	28.5	7.2	26.0	•
Salaries and Wages 11	29.6	16.8	32.7	31.9	39.4	29.4	22.4	32.9	31.9	26.5	34.3	22.9	•
Taxes Paid 12	3.7	3.3	4.7	4.7	4.2	3.1	2.7	3.5	3.3	3.3	3.2	2.8	•
Interest Paid 13	1.6	0.2	0.4	2.6	1.1	0.5	0.8	1.0	2.1	1.8	2.8	3.0	•
Depreciation 14	2.3	0.7	0.9	1.6	1.8	2.8	2.2	2.1	2.1	2.1	2.9	4.1	•
Amortization and Depletion 15	0.7	0.5	0.1	0.5	0.1	0.0	0.4	0.6	0.9	1.5	1.0	1.6	•
Pensions and Other Deferred Comp. 16	0.5	0.6	0.7	0.3	0.4	0.3	0.3	0.4	0.8	0.2	0.4	0.7	•
Employee Benefits 17	2.4	2.0	1.4	1.7	2.0	3.3	1.2	2.2	2.7	2.0	2.7	4.0	•
Advertising 18	0.5	0.4	0.7	0.6	0.5	0.8	0.5	0.4	0.4	0.4	0.2	0.4	•
Other Expenses 19	28.7	28.1	29.6	28.4	25.0	26.4	27.5	24.8	32.2	27.1	43.6	26.1	•
Officers' Compensation 20	5.2	12.0	11.7	7.1	4.4	3.7	2.2	2.1	1.7	0.9	0.6	0.8	•
Operating Margin 21	7.1	14.7	8.9	9.6	5.8	4.5	7.0	6.0	0.5	5.7	1.0	7.6	•
Operating Margin Before Officers' Comp. 22	12.4	26.8	20.6	16.7	10.3	8.2	9.2	8.1	2.1	6.6	1.6	8.4	•

Selected Average Balance Sheet ($ in Thousands)

Net Receivables 23	151	0	11	107	378	1529	3005	10475	12265	31186	82032	231060	•
Inventories 24	13	0	1	8	25	276	574	849	1379	2833	4676	18107	•
Net Property, Plant and Equipment 25	154	0	29	182	711	1056	2476	5979	7365	12982	62181	229677	•
Total Assets 26	1035	0	91	681	1738	6909	16285	32320	68200	156608	358975	2328990	•
Notes and Loans Payable 27	369	0	40	249	620	904	5718	10035	26827	45033	178541	806702	•
All Other Liabilities 28	286	0	18	101	362	2260	4132	9510	17230	41175	116047	683704	•
Net Worth 29	380	0	33	331	757	3745	6434	12774	24144	70400	64387	838584	•

Selected Financial Ratios (Times to 1)

Current Ratio 30	1.7	•	2.5	2.6	2.9	1.9	1.4	1.5	1.4	1.7	1.9	1.5	•
Quick Ratio 31	1.3	•	2.3	2.2	2.5	1.5	1.0	1.1	1.0	1.4	1.4	1.0	•
Net Sales to Working Capital 32	12.9	•	32.3	11.3	8.1	7.0	12.0	11.6	15.1	7.8	6.7	13.1	•
Coverage Ratio 33	6.6	94.3	25.9	5.0	8.6	25.4	12.4	7.2	2.8	5.5	2.0	4.2	•
Total Asset Turnover 34	1.7	•	8.9	2.6	2.7	2.2	1.9	2.1	1.4	1.2	1.2	0.8	•
Inventory Turnover 35	24.0	•	74.5	24.5	28.0	13.7	18.0	19.0	14.8	18.5	6.8	28.3	•
Receivables Turnover 36	11.2	•	69.2	14.4	14.6	9.5	8.3	6.6	5.2	6.6	6.8	7.0	•
Total Liabilities to Net Worth 37	1.7	•	1.7	1.1	1.3	0.8	1.5	1.5	1.8	1.2	4.6	1.8	•
Current Assets to Working Capital 38	2.4	•	1.7	1.6	1.5	2.1	3.4	3.0	3.7	2.5	2.1	3.2	•
Current Liabilities to Working Capital 39	1.4	•	0.7	0.6	0.5	1.1	2.4	2.0	2.7	1.5	1.1	2.2	•
Working Capital to Net Sales 40	0.1	•	0.0	0.1	0.1	0.1	0.1	0.1	0.1	0.1	0.1	0.1	•
Inventory to Working Capital 41	0.1	•	0.0	0.0	0.0	0.2	0.3	0.1	0.1	0.1	0.1	0.1	•
Total Receipts to Cash Flow 42	3.1	2.8	3.1	3.1	3.6	3.0	3.2	3.6	3.1	3.1	2.4	3.2	•
Cost of Goods to Cash Flow 43	0.5	0.6	0.3	0.3	0.5	0.7	1.1	0.9	0.7	0.9	0.2	0.8	•
Cash Flow to Total Debt 44	0.9	•	4.6	1.6	1.3	1.6	1.0	1.0	0.7	0.7	0.6	0.4	•

Selected Financial Factors (in Percentages)

Debt Ratio 45	63.3	•	63.4	51.4	56.4	45.8	60.5	60.5	64.6	55.0	82.1	64.0	•
Return on Total Assets 46	18.1	•	86.6	33.3	25.3	29.2	18.0	15.8	8.4	11.5	7.1	10.7	•
Return on Equity Before Income Taxes 47	41.8	•	227.8	54.9	51.4	51.7	41.9	34.5	15.3	20.8	20.3	22.6	•
Return on Equity After Income Taxes 48	35.9	•	225.6	53.3	48.2	48.1	36.2	27.6	11.9	15.1	15.5	15.4	•
Profit Margin (Before Income Tax) 49	8.9	17.8	9.4	10.4	8.4	12.8	8.6	6.5	3.9	8.0	2.9	9.6	•
Profit Margin (After Income Tax) 50	7.7	16.9	9.3	10.1	7.8	11.9	7.4	5.2	3.0	5.8	2.2	6.6	•

Table I

Corporations with and without Net Income

HOSPITALS, NURSING, AND RESIDENTIAL CARE FACILITIES

MONEY AMOUNTS AND SIZE OF ASSETS IN THOUSANDS OF DOLLARS

Item Description for Accounting Period 7/08 Through 6/09	Total	Zero Assets	Under 500	500 to 1,000	1,000 to 5,000	5,000 to 10,000	10,000 to 25,000	25,000 to 50,000	50,000 to 100,000	100,000 to 250,000	250,000 to 500,000	500,000 to 2,500,000	2,500,000 and over
Number of Enterprises **1**	18351	1785	12658	1280	2054	167	229	71	33	25	16	24	9
Revenues ($ in Thousands)													
Net Sales **2**	127827080	109850	7763165	3349164	11060541	1413469	6021252	4436078	3631264	5987165	6041581	26548273	51465278
Interest **3**	1047782	420	467	444	2281	1393	4992	5262	3814	8617	28394	260836	730863
Rents **4**	509308	0	0	0	424	0	3476	19041	2546	31020	18159	170858	263783
Royalties **5**	3	0	0	0	0	0	0	0	0	0	0	3	0
Other Portfolio Income **6**	871974	49957	113524	289	198	14244	33038	4919	57594	12405	5884	19796	560126
Other Receipts **7**	7834782	673	18772	4253	671190	6440	91236	80869	83841	396247	707916	501450	5271894
Total Receipts **8**	138090929	160900	7895928	3354150	11734634	1435546	6153994	4546169	3779059	6435454	6801934	27501216	58291944
Average Total Receipts **9**	7525	90	624	2620	5713	8596	26873	64031	114517	257418	425121	1145884	6476883
Operating Costs/Operating Income (%)													
Cost of Operations **10**	4.9	•	9.1	2.3	6.3	3.1	11.7	13.4	6.5	7.8	3.6	7.4	1.1
Salaries and Wages **11**	38.5	28.0	32.3	25.5	43.7	41.7	35.1	38.4	43.4	44.1	31.5	38.8	39.3
Taxes Paid **12**	4.7	6.5	4.4	4.0	6.7	5.5	5.7	3.9	5.8	5.9	4.4	4.8	4.1
Interest Paid **13**	5.1	4.5	1.1	0.7	1.3	1.4	1.9	1.5	2.0	1.6	3.8	4.1	8.8
Depreciation **14**	3.2	3.1	1.3	0.8	1.1	2.4	1.8	1.7	2.4	2.7	2.3	3.4	4.6
Amortization and Depletion **15**	0.7	0.1	0.2	0.1	0.1	0.2	0.2	0.2	0.5	0.2	1.0	1.1	0.8
Pensions and Other Deferred Comp. **16**	0.5	0.0	0.0	0.2	0.1	0.8	0.4	0.2	0.5	0.3	0.1	0.2	0.8
Employee Benefits **17**	4.4	1.5	1.6	2.4	3.1	4.8	4.2	3.2	3.7	4.1	2.7	4.0	5.8
Advertising **18**	0.4	1.1	0.5	0.5	0.3	1.2	0.2	0.3	0.4	0.4	0.2	0.4	0.4
Other Expenses **19**	42.2	112.4	38.2	60.6	37.2	37.1	37.2	37.6	38.0	38.7	69.8	38.8	42.8
Officers' Compensation **20**	1.1	5.6	7.8	3.8	1.5	1.3	1.0	0.8	0.8	0.5	0.4	0.4	0.3
Operating Margin **21**	•	•	3.6	•	•	0.6	0.6	•	•	•	•	•	•
Operating Margin Before Officers' Comp. **22**	•	•	11.4	2.8	1.9	1.9	1.6	•	•	•	•	•	•

Selected Average Balance Sheet ($ in Thousands)

Net Receivables 23	823	0	1	274	502	1717	3712	5715	16715	36141	51494	126543	760647
Inventories 24	13	0	0	2	2	11	103	172	741	1445	1324	3568	3548
Net Property, Plant and Equipment 25	2477	0	59	185	586	3407	5532	13304	23767	65697	125698	385308	2977857
Total Assets 26	7274	0	113	725	1971	6887	15316	34671	69520	159538	353323	1235109	8710033
Notes and Loans Payable 27	4586	0	127	399	1162	3767	8834	20143	35524	60726	200243	593728	6158501
All Other Liabilities 28	1703	0	32	285	672	2009	5606	10426	27324	49819	115577	276320	1790538
Net Worth 29	985	-46	41	137	1111	875	4101	6673	48993	37502	365060	760994	

Selected Financial Ratios (Times to 1)

Current Ratio 30	1.3	·	0.7	1.2	1.3	1.3	1.1	1.2	1.1	1.4	1.2	1.5	1.3
Quick Ratio 31	1.0	·	0.6	1.1	1.0	1.1	0.9	0.8	1.0	1.1	1.1	1.2	0.9
Net Sales to Working Capital 32	19.7	·	·	34.1	19.9	15.5	59.2	22.7	33.5	15.1	20.2	11.5	20.1
Coverage Ratio 33	1.4	·	5.8	·	4.4	2.5	2.5	1.8	1.1	1.7	·	1.0	1.5
Total Asset Turnover 34	1.0	·	5.4	3.6	2.7	1.2	1.7	1.8	1.6	1.5	1.1	0.9	0.7
Inventory Turnover 35	25.8	·	16934.4	37.1	138.0	23.2	30.0	48.7	9.6	12.9	10.1	22.9	18.3
Receivables Turnover 36	8.4	·	187.6	10.4	11.4	3.3	7.8	10.3	6.0	7.0	8.2	8.9	7.2
Total Liabilities to Net Worth 37	6.4	·	·	16.8	13.4	5.2	16.5	7.5	9.4	2.3	8.4	2.4	10.4
Current Assets to Working Capital 38	4.4	·	·	5.9	4.0	4.6	14.7	5.3	9.2	3.7	5.0	2.9	4.5
Current Liabilities to Working Capital 39	3.4	·	·	4.9	3.0	3.6	13.7	4.3	8.2	2.7	4.0	1.9	3.5
Working Capital to Net Sales 40	0.1	·	·	0.0	0.1	0.1	0.0	0.0	0.0	0.1	0.0	0.1	0.0
Inventory to Working Capital 41	0.0	·	·	0.0	0.0	0.0	0.2	0.1	0.2	0.1	0.0	0.0	0.0
Total Receipts to Cash Flow 42	2.7	2.2	3.2	1.9	3.1	3.2	2.9	2.9	3.3	3.1	2.1	3.1	2.4
Cost of Goods to Cash Flow 43	0.1	·	0.3	0.0	0.2	0.1	0.3	0.4	0.2	0.2	0.1	0.2	0.0
Cash Flow to Total Debt 44	0.4	·	1.2	2.0	0.9	0.5	0.6	0.7	0.5	0.7	0.6	0.4	0.3

Selected Financial Factors (in Percentages)

Debt Ratio 45	86.5	·	141.2	94.4	93.1	83.9	94.3	88.2	90.4	69.3	89.4	70.4	91.3
Return on Total Assets 46	7.1	·	34.7	·	16.1	4.3	8.1	5.0	3.5	4.2	·	3.8	8.5
Return on Equity Before Income Taxes 47	16.2	·	·	·	180.0	16.1	84.0	18.8	3.5	5.6	·	0.4	30.9
Return on Equity After Income Taxes 48	10.5	·	·	·	179.2	10.8	77.8	16.4	·	4.7	·	·	19.3
Profit Margin (Before Income Tax) 49	2.3	·	5.3	·	4.6	2.1	2.8	1.2	0.2	1.2	0.0	0.1	4.1
Profit Margin (After Income Tax) 50	1.5	·	5.1	·	4.6	1.4	2.6	1.1	·	1.0	·	·	2.6

Table II

Corporations with Net Income

HOSPITALS, NURSING, AND RESIDENTIAL CARE FACILITIES

MONEY AMOUNTS AND SIZE OF ASSETS IN THOUSANDS OF DOLLARS

Item Description for Accounting Period 7/08 Through 6/09	Total	Zero Assets	Under 500	500 to 1,000	1,000 to 5,000	5,000 to 10,000	10,000 to 25,000	25,000 to 50,000	50,000 to 100,000	100,000 to 250,000	250,000 to 500,000	500,000 to 2,500,000	2,500,000 and over
Number of Enterprises **1**	9271	353	6512	767	1337	51	150	•	18	16	8	13	•
Revenues ($ in Thousands)													
Net Sales **2**	84978042	85499	5330689	1934555	8642099	709639	4279224	•	2800240	3856334	4345415	13869522	•
Interest **3**	431797	370	392	176	1822	1284	4264	•	1636	5448	23499	87090	•
Rents **4**	309002	0	0	0	417	0	3442	•	650	13386	74	124131	•
Royalties **5**	3	0	0	0	0	0	0	•	0	0	0	3	•
Other Portfolio Income **6**	584453	47587	110761	289	175	14244	26078	•	2523	3415	1864	15812	•
Other Receipts **7**	6373781	88	17744	3016	635373	5222	50009	•	78020	301137	121921	244825	•
Total Receipts **8**	92677078	133544	5459586	1938036	9279886	730389	4363017	•	2883069	4179720	4492773	14341383	•
Average Total Receipts **9**	9996	378	838	2527	6941	14321	29087	•	160170	261232	561597	1103183	•
Operating Costs/Operating Income (%)													
Cost of Operations **10**	4.7	•	7.8	1.4	7.0	4.7	14.7	•	5.3	7.3	4.2	4.7	•
Salaries and Wages **11**	38.2	17.8	34.5	14.7	43.9	40.8	34.3	•	44.0	40.9	28.4	39.8	•
Taxes Paid **12**	4.5	3.6	4.1	1.8	6.6	5.6	5.8	•	6.0	6.0	4.3	4.8	•
Interest Paid **13**	4.9	3.1	0.5	0.2	1.0	0.9	1.4	•	1.6	1.4	2.0	3.3	•
Depreciation **14**	2.9	2.2	0.9	0.4	0.8	1.9	1.6	•	1.8	2.7	1.7	2.5	•
Amortization and Depletion **15**	0.6	0.1	0.0	0.1	0.1	0.3	0.2	•	0.2	0.3	0.7	1.0	•
Pensions and Other Deferred Comp. **16**	0.6	0.0	0.0	0.4	0.1	0.6	0.5	•	0.6	0.1	0.1	0.2	•
Employee Benefits **17**	4.5	0.5	1.7	1.0	3.3	4.4	4.2	•	4.3	4.0	2.3	4.4	•
Advertising **18**	0.4	1.4	0.5	0.1	0.3	2.0	0.2	•	0.4	0.4	0.2	0.4	•
Other Expenses **19**	40.2	56.3	30.4	68.5	34.8	28.0	32.9	•	34.3	41.4	55.2	37.1	•
Officers' Compensation **20**	1.3	6.4	9.2	4.5	1.6	2.4	1.0	•	0.9	0.6	0.4	0.6	•
Operating Margin **21**	•	8.6	10.4	7.0	0.5	8.5	3.2	•	0.7	•	0.3	1.2	•
Operating Margin Before Officers' Comp. **22**	•	15.0	19.6	11.4	2.1	10.9	4.2	•	1.6	•	0.8	1.8	•

Selected Average Balance Sheet ($ in Thousands)

	•	•	•	•	•	•	•	•	•	•	•	•
Net Receivables 23	1085	0	0	318	484	2086	3959	•	23810	37681	57802	135039
Inventories 24	18	0	0	0	2	1	124	•	812	1539	1660	4015
Net Property, Plant and Equipment 25	2710	0	33	138	396	1260	5690	•	22279	62913	124840	216994
Total Assets 26	9425	0	117	718	2033	6482	15205	•	69928	150660	345605	1041622
Notes and Loans Payable 27	5969	0	59	168	889	1421	8020	•	28035	55100	191869	391282
All Other Liabilities 28	1847	0	10	223	642	1408	5208	•	35598	45590	108876	289509
Net Worth 29	1609	0	48	327	501	3653	1978	•	6296	49970	44860	360832

Selected Financial Ratios (Times to 1)

	•	•	•	•	•	•	•	•	•	•	•	•
Current Ratio 30	1.5	•	3.0	2.2	2.1	2.4	1.4	•	1.1	1.4	1.3	1.7
Quick Ratio 31	1.2	•	2.6	2.1	1.4	2.2	1.1	•	1.0	1.1	1.1	1.4
Net Sales to Working Capital 32	14.6	•	18.8	9.0	10.0	7.0	15.4	•	37.2	14.8	21.0	9.2
Coverage Ratio 33	2.3	22.2	26.7	32.6	8.8	14.3	4.7	•	3.3	3.5	2.8	2.4
Total Asset Turnover 34	1.0	•	7.0	3.5	3.2	2.1	1.9	•	2.2	1.6	1.6	1.0
Inventory Turnover 35	24.1	•	10013.8	570.0	194.2	491.4	33.7	•	10.2	11.4	13.8	12.4
Receivables Turnover 36	8.7	•	173.0	8.1	13.3	3.5	7.9	•	6.5	7.7	9.5	6.3
Total Liabilities to Net Worth 37	4.9	•	1.4	1.2	3.1	0.8	6.7	•	10.1	2.0	6.7	1.9
Current Assets to Working Capital 38	3.1	•	1.5	1.8	1.9	1.7	3.8	•	8.9	3.7	4.7	2.4
Current Liabilities to Working Capital 39	2.1	•	0.5	0.8	0.9	0.7	2.8	•	7.9	2.7	3.7	1.4
Working Capital to Net Sales 40	0.1	•	0.1	0.1	0.1	0.1	0.1	•	0.0	0.0	0.0	0.1
Inventory to Working Capital 41	0.0	•	0.0	0.0	0.0	0.0	0.1	•	0.1	0.1	0.1	0.0
Total Receipts to Cash Flow 42	2.4	1.6	3.0	1.3	3.0	3.1	3.1	•	3.3	2.7	1.9	2.7
Cost of Goods to Cash Flow 43	0.1	•	0.2	0.0	0.2	0.1	0.4	•	0.2	0.2	0.1	0.1
Cash Flow to Total Debt 44	0.5	•	3.9	4.8	1.4	1.6	0.7	•	0.7	0.9	1.0	0.6

Selected Financial Factors (in Percentages)

	•	•	•	•	•	•	•	•	•	•	•	•
Debt Ratio 45	82.9	•	58.7	54.5	75.3	43.6	87.0	•	91.0	66.8	87.0	65.4
Return on Total Assets 46	10.9	•	93.5	25.9	28.2	26.3	12.4	•	11.6	7.7	9.0	8.1
Return on Equity Before Income Taxes 47	35.9	•	218.1	55.1	101.4	43.5	75.0	•	90.6	16.6	45.0	13.5
Return on Equity After Income Taxes 48	29.1	•	215.3	53.6	101.1	38.2	70.9	•	83.5	15.1	32.1	11.2
Profit Margin (Before Income Tax) 49	6.3	64.8	12.8	7.1	7.9	11.4	5.2	•	3.7	3.4	3.7	4.6
Profit Margin (After Income Tax) 50	5.1	54.9	12.7	6.9	7.8	10.0	4.9	•	3.4	3.1	2.6	3.8

Table I
Corporations with and without Net Income

OTHER ARTS, ENTERTAINMENT, AND RECREATION

MONEY AMOUNTS AND SIZE OF ASSETS IN THOUSANDS OF DOLLARS

Item Description for Accounting Period 7/08 Through 6/09	Total	Zero Assets	Under 500	500 to 1,000	1,000 to 5,000	5,000 to 10,000	10,000 to 25,000	25,000 to 50,000	50,000 to 100,000	100,000 to 250,000	250,000 to 500,000	500,000 to 2,500,000	2,500,000 and over
Number of Enterprises **1**	70697	16354	50963	1985	1008	201	59	48	23	28	18	10	0
Revenues ($ in Thousands)													
Net Sales **2**	4214306	1031770	17583284	4459428	3748632	1846810	1471612	1025659	1242129	3489333	4478166	7837483	0
Interest **3**	242801	192	6070	1339	6990	2472	2145	4957	3283	9902	73079	132373	0
Rents **4**	118504	2266	1717	1677	512	1359	0	691	155	4554	46866	58708	0
Royalties **5**	128200	2193	1550	388	0	0	0	1495	198	21603	94271	6502	0
Other Portfolio Income **6**	384674	2000	14473	74720	14332	9182	2732	8941	1668	4347	20597	231680	0
Other Receipts **7**	2333102	44614	325510	23234	13852	79984	2019	189002	106828	557345	855530	135185	0
Total Receipts **8**	51421587	1083035	17932604	4560786	3784318	1939807	1478508	1230745	1354261	4087084	5568509	8401931	0
Average Total Receipts **9**	727	66	352	2298	3754	9651	25059	25641	58881	145967	309362	840193	•
Operating Costs/Operating Income (%)													
Cost of Operations **10**	18.7	7.7	6.9	19.9	18.4	20.1	29.9	21.4	22.1	22.0	26.5	36.6	•
Salaries and Wages **11**	18.5	5.9	16.8	9.4	12.3	16.0	20.3	29.7	34.1	43.1	28.0	11.9	•
Taxes Paid **12**	3.6	2.6	2.2	2.7	3.5	2.5	2.5	2.6	3.4	2.8	10.8	4.4	•
Interest Paid **13**	1.8	1.3	0.5	0.5	0.6	2.1	1.0	1.0	1.6	3.4	4.1	4.5	•
Depreciation **14**	2.6	1.4	1.1	1.8	1.6	3.2	2.7	5.2	3.2	2.5	3.8	5.7	•
Amortization and Depletion **15**	1.0	0.6	0.1	0.1	0.1	0.1	0.1	0.7	0.3	4.4	2.5	2.4	•
Pensions and Other Deferred Comp. **16**	1.3	0.6	1.7	2.1	0.7	0.1	0.2	0.9	1.3	2.1	1.3	0.5	•
Employee Benefits **17**	1.1	0.8	0.5	0.7	0.5	0.6	1.4	2.4	1.7	2.1	2.7	1.2	•
Advertising **18**	2.1	1.6	0.8	3.8	1.3	3.5	0.9	2.2	3.0	4.0	1.6	3.6	•
Other Expenses **19**	38.6	70.1	50.2	26.1	29.6	41.1	27.4	51.0	33.0	24.4	31.4	31.2	•
Officers' Compensation **20**	11.5	8.7	16.7	27.6	16.1	6.1	9.6	2.2	10.1	3.3	1.8	1.3	•
Operating Margin **21**	•	•	2.5	5.2	15.5	4.7	3.9	•	•	•	•	•	•
Operating Margin Before Officers' Comp. **22**	10.7	7.4	19.2	32.8	31.6	10.8	13.5	•	•	•	•	•	•

Selected Average Balance Sheet ($ in Thousands)

	•	•	•	•	•	•	•	•	•	•	•	•
Net Receivables 23	35	0	4	12	107	290	2445	5180	4918	15107	30445	65090
Inventories 24	8	0	3	5	223	89	153	170	1292	1661	2087	3929
Net Property, Plant and Equipment 25	143	0	14	214	371	1728	4086	6436	11119	36835	82698	490036
Total Assets 26	515	0	63	697	1990	7180	14126	33247	66467	165550	361292	1323569
Notes and Loans Payable 27	255	0	67	271	889	4157	5228	10709	28493	74937	148055	610035
All Other Liabilities 28	170	0	16	172	311	2637	4471	13652	37495	82869	116005	387318
Net Worth 29	90	0	-19	254	790	386	4428	8885	479	7744	97232	326216

Selected Financial Ratios (Times to 1)

	•	•	•	•	•	•	•	•	•	•	•	•
Current Ratio 30	1.2	•	2.2	1.4	2.8	1.9	1.2	1.2	1.3	1.2	1.0	0.7
Quick Ratio 31	0.7	•	1.5	1.2	1.4	1.8	0.9	0.9	0.9	0.7	0.6	0.3
Net Sales to Working Capital 32	25.5	•	15.1	28.6	5.1	4.2	21.7	7.9	8.5	12.1	52.8	•
Coverage Ratio 33	4.2	3.7	10.4	15.7	30.5	5.5	5.3	1.5	•	1.9	3.3	2.0
Total Asset Turnover 34	1.3	•	5.5	3.2	1.9	1.3	1.8	0.6	0.8	0.8	0.7	0.6
Inventory Turnover 35	15.6	•	7.8	83.8	3.1	20.8	48.7	26.9	9.3	16.5	31.6	73.0
Receivables Turnover 36	19.4	•	123.3	102.9	33.7	20.0	9.6	4.3	10.4	6.9	11.5	11.2
Total Liabilities to Net Worth 37	4.7	•	•	1.7	1.5	17.6	2.2	2.7	137.7	20.4	2.7	3.1
Current Assets to Working Capital 38	7.2	•	1.8	3.7	1.6	2.1	5.2	5.1	4.0	5.6	25.6	•
Current Liabilities to Working Capital 39	6.2	•	0.8	2.7	0.6	1.1	4.2	4.1	3.0	4.6	24.6	•
Working Capital to Net Sales 40	0.0	•	0.1	0.0	0.2	0.2	0.0	0.1	0.1	0.1	0.0	•
Inventory to Working Capital 41	0.3	•	0.1	0.1	0.4	0.0	0.1	0.1	0.2	0.1	0.7	•
Total Receipts to Cash Flow 42	2.5	1.6	2.0	3.6	2.4	2.1	3.3	2.3	4.1	4.5	2.7	3.6
Cost of Goods to Cash Flow 43	0.5	0.1	0.1	0.7	0.4	0.4	1.0	0.5	0.9	1.0	0.7	1.3
Cash Flow to Total Debt 44	0.6	•	2.1	1.4	1.3	0.6	0.8	0.4	0.2	0.2	0.4	0.2

Selected Financial Factors (in Percentages)

	•	•	•	•	•	•	•	•	•	•	•	•
Debt Ratio 45	82.6	•	130.4	63.6	60.3	94.6	68.7	73.3	99.3	95.3	73.1	75.4
Return on Total Assets 46	10.3	•	27.2	25.4	31.6	14.9	9.5	1.0	•	4.8	9.5	5.4
Return on Equity Before Income Taxes 47	45.0	•	•	65.4	77.1	226.6	24.7	1.3	•	48.5	24.8	10.9
Return on Equity After Income Taxes 48	40.0	•	•	64.0	75.8	220.2	22.3	0.6	•	43.6	18.5	7.4
Profit Margin (Before Income Tax) 49	5.9	3.6	4.5	7.4	16.4	9.5	4.4	0.5	•	3.0	9.7	4.5
Profit Margin (After Income Tax) 50	5.3	1.0	4.4	7.2	16.1	9.2	4.0	0.3	•	2.7	7.2	3.1

Table II

Corporations with Net Income

OTHER ARTS, ENTERTAINMENT, AND RECREATION

MONEY AMOUNTS AND SIZE OF ASSETS IN THOUSANDS OF DOLLARS

Item Description for Accounting Period 7/08 Through 6/09		Total	Zero Assets	Under 500	500 to 1,000	1,000 to 5,000	5,000 to 10,000	10,000 to 25,000	25,000 to 50,000	50,000 to 100,000	100,000 to 250,000	250,000 to 500,000	500,000 to 2,500,000	2,500,000 and over
Number of Enterprises	1	35193	7362	25771	1252	590	•	34	21	12	13	14	•	0
Revenues ($ in Thousands)														
Net Sales	2	34187706	745538	10504268	3761925	3339388	•	1089669	505193	624504	1953441	3659478	•	0
Interest	3	206987	148	3610	554	6652	•	2082	4230	2715	2812	52021	•	0
Rents	4	101406	0	873	1677	512	•	0	691	0	4549	46866	•	0
Royalties	5	121619	325	0	369	0	•	0	0	198	19953	94271	•	0
Other Portfolio Income	6	339094	2000	3778	72588	4886	•	171	2283	1558	3728	13773	•	0
Other Receipts	7	1673105	82257	181779	18199	27902	•	14408	97068	55947	163864	848687	•	0
Total Receipts	8	36629917	830268	10694308	3855312	3379340	•	1106330	609465	684922	2148347	4715096	•	0
Average Total Receipts	9	1041	113	415	3079	5728	•	32539	29022	57077	165257	336793	•	•
Operating Costs/Operating Income (%)														
Cost of Operations	10	18.2	5.8	5.5	17.6	13.3	•	33.2	9.8	33.1	20.5	20.5	•	•
Salaries and Wages	11	16.8	4.0	17.7	8.8	11.9	•	20.1	26.9	17.5	30.9	29.5	•	•
Taxes Paid	12	3.7	2.8	2.3	2.8	3.4	•	2.6	1.9	2.0	2.8	12.8	•	•
Interest Paid	13	1.4	0.6	0.3	0.3	0.1	•	0.8	0.2	1.1	1.0	2.9	•	•
Depreciation	14	2.2	0.2	0.8	0.9	1.0	•	1.2	5.0	2.0	1.7	3.5	•	•
Amortization and Depletion	15	1.0	0.0	0.0	0.1	0.0	•	0.0	0.8	0.1	4.5	1.9	•	•
Pensions and Other Deferred Comp.	16	1.4	0.8	2.2	1.9	0.7	•	0.2	0.6	0.7	1.7	1.4	•	•
Employee Benefits	17	1.0	0.5	0.5	0.6	0.5	•	1.4	1.2	1.0	2.2	3.0	•	•
Advertising	18	2.3	1.5	1.0	4.2	1.4	•	0.8	1.8	2.6	4.4	1.8	•	•
Other Expenses	19	33.1	61.8	39.4	25.9	28.3	•	14.8	46.0	20.1	23.5	35.6	•	•
Officers' Compensation	20	12.0	10.1	17.4	28.7	17.8	•	11.8	2.2	7.7	2.6	2.1	•	•
Operating Margin	21	6.9	12.0	12.9	8.1	21.5	•	13.1	3.5	11.9	4.2	•	•	•
Operating Margin Before Officers' Comp.	22	18.9	22.1	30.3	36.8	39.3	•	24.9	5.8	19.6	6.8	•	•	•

Selected Average Balance Sheet ($ in Thousands)

		1	2	3	4	5	6	7	8	9	10	11	12	13
Net Receivables	23	46	0	4	12	172	•	1988	1842	•	2347	13792	34597	•
Inventories	24	12	0	2	1	365	•	162	263	•	1454	3229	2393	•
Net Property, Plant and Equipment	25	186	0	15	173	287	•	3862	2442	•	8792	35601	73815	•
Total Assets	26	720	0	65	737	2228	•	13276	32751	•	64862	153395	362053	•
Notes and Loans Payable	27	256	0	34	210	917	•	2081	3029	•	23537	46448	111179	•
All Other Liabilities	28	233	0	16	212	470	•	5101	14375	•	29862	69974	123393	•
Net Worth	29	231	0	14	315	841	•	6093	15347	•	11464	36973	127480	•

Selected Financial Ratios (Times to 1)

		1	2	3	4	5	6	7	8	9	10	11	12	13
Current Ratio	30	1.2	•	2.5	1.4	2.5	•	1.2	1.5	•	2.7	1.1	1.1	•
Quick Ratio	31	0.7	•	2.1	1.2	1.4	•	0.8	1.1	•	1.9	0.8	0.7	•
Net Sales to Working Capital	32	21.9	•	15.7	27.4	6.0	•	30.4	4.8	•	3.4	31.4	25.8	•
Coverage Ratio	33	11.0	41.7	45.3	35.4	228.8	•	19.8	100.9	•	20.3	14.9	5.7	•
Total Asset Turnover	34	1.3	•	6.3	4.1	2.5	•	2.4	0.7	•	0.8	1.0	0.7	•
Inventory Turnover	35	14.9	•	9.1	1046.1	2.1	•	65.6	9.0	•	11.9	9.5	22.4	•
Receivables Turnover	36	21.8	•	121.7	175.9	34.3	•	13.8	10.0	•	16.2	8.9	•	•
Total Liabilities to Net Worth	37	2.1	•	3.6	1.3	1.6	•	1.2	1.1	•	4.7	3.1	1.8	•
Current Assets to Working Capital	38	6.4	•	1.7	3.5	1.7	•	6.8	2.9	•	1.6	10.1	13.6	•
Current Liabilities to Working Capital	39	5.4	•	0.7	2.5	0.7	•	5.8	1.9	•	0.6	9.1	12.6	•
Working Capital to Net Sales	40	0.0	•	0.1	0.0	0.2	•	0.0	0.2	•	0.3	0.0	0.0	•
Inventory to Working Capital	41	0.3	•	0.1	0.0	0.4	•	0.0	0.1	•	0.2	0.4	0.2	•
Total Receipts to Cash Flow	42	2.4	1.3	2.1	3.3	2.2	•	3.6	1.6	•	2.6	3.2	2.2	•
Cost of Goods to Cash Flow	43	0.4	0.1	0.1	0.6	0.3	•	1.2	0.2	•	0.9	0.7	0.5	•
Cash Flow to Total Debt	44	0.8	•	3.9	2.2	1.9	•	1.3	0.9	•	0.4	0.4	0.5	•

Selected Financial Factors (in Percentages)

		1	2	3	4	5	6	7	8	9	10	11	12	13
Debt Ratio	45	68.0	•	78.1	57.2	62.2	•	54.1	53.1	•	82.3	75.9	64.8	•
Return on Total Assets	46	21.0	•	94.9	44.3	57.6	•	37.2	17.7	•	18.2	14.8	12.0	•
Return on Equity Before Income Taxes	47	59.5	•	422.9	100.5	151.8	•	77.0	37.5	•	98.0	57.2	28.1	•
Return on Equity After Income Taxes	48	55.7	•	420.5	98.7	149.7	•	73.9	36.6	•	95.5	55.0	22.0	•
Profit Margin (Before Income Tax)	49	14.1	23.4	14.7	10.6	22.6	•	14.6	23.9	•	21.6	14.1	13.7	•
Profit Margin (After Income Tax)	50	13.2	19.7	14.6	10.4	22.2	•	14.1	23.3	•	21.0	13.5	10.7	•

Table I

Corporations with and without Net Income

AMUSEMENT, GAMBLING, AND RECREATION INDUSTRIES

MONEY AMOUNTS AND SIZE OF ASSETS IN THOUSANDS OF DOLLARS

Item Description for Accounting Period 7/08 Through 6/09		Total	Zero Assets	Under 500	500 to 1,000	1,000 to 5,000	5,000 to 10,000	10,000 to 25,000	25,000 to 50,000	50,000 to 100,000	100,000 to 250,000	250,000 to 500,000	500,000 to 2,500,000	2,500,000 and over
Number of Enterprises	1	51728	8006	34233	4454	3905	534	337	151	46	32	11	16	3
Revenues ($ in Thousands)														
Net Sales	2	47969997	637188	7698838	3942202	6696357	3373121	2966679	2856125	1763492	2503618	2829187	7950537	4752653
Interest	3	518604	892	4826	6640	16194	4590	10898	8054	4907	26912	18677	38693	377322
Rents	4	165081	0	28290	4353	3322	17676	3741	4829	6057	4570	13094	51294	27854
Royalties	5	242811	0	0	3	16604	0	0	1544	107	35602	982	85972	101997
Other Portfolio Income	6	309858	41463	49515	13435	15061	4618	5463	10949	32198	56161	27017	26414	27565
Other Receipts	7	3688495	-29425	285906	700001	346304	251736	292718	125930	79055	127692	375670	988741	144165
Total Receipts	8	52894846	650118	8067375	4666634	7093842	3651741	3279499	3007431	1885816	2754555	3264627	9141651	5431556
Average Total Receipts	9	1023	81	236	1048	1817	6838	9731	19917	40996	86080	296784	571353	1810519
Operating Costs/Operating Income (%)														
Cost of Operations	10	22.0	15.3	21.5	12.3	31.1	20.1	29.8	23.4	12.1	24.9	41.4	8.3	28.5
Salaries and Wages	11	22.4	20.3	17.3	29.1	17.2	29.2	25.3	25.4	28.3	20.4	21.7	29.2	12.5
Taxes Paid	12	8.1	3.4	4.5	6.2	5.8	8.2	5.9	5.6	11.4	7.3	4.4	12.2	17.1
Interest Paid	13	5.8	2.6	0.9	2.3	3.8	3.8	3.5	3.1	3.7	5.6	6.7	10.7	16.5
Depreciation	14	8.3	5.6	5.5	4.9	6.4	7.2	9.8	10.5	8.8	11.1	9.5	11.5	9.7
Amortization and Depletion	15	0.9	0.5	0.2	0.4	0.5	0.7	0.5	0.8	1.0	1.0	1.4	1.2	2.2
Pensions and Other Deferred Comp.	16	0.3	0.0	0.1	0.5	0.2	0.7	0.2	0.3	0.3	0.5	0.5	0.1	0.3
Employee Benefits	17	1.6	0.5	1.1	1.0	1.7	1.0	2.5	1.7	2.0	2.2	1.5	2.1	2.0
Advertising	18	2.7	6.0	2.1	2.2	1.4	3.0	3.1	2.4	2.6	3.4	2.1	3.5	3.5
Other Expenses	19	36.4	55.5	45.2	52.4	32.7	34.9	29.3	30.7	35.1	33.4	28.0	42.3	17.8
Officers' Compensation	20	3.1	2.9	7.9	3.3	4.9	3.7	1.3	1.3	1.0	1.9	1.0	0.9	0.6
Operating Margin	21	•	•	•	•	•	•	•	•	•	•	•	•	•
Operating Margin Before Officers' Comp.	22	•	•	1.7	•	•	•	•	•	•	•	•	•	•

Selected Average Balance Sheet ($ in Thousands)

Net Receivables 23	86	6	38	119	511	828	1708	3541	9203	13222	47625	480974
Inventories 24	27	4	8	54	147	369	987	1575	2228	3225	26307	24145
Net Property, Plant and Equipment 25	705	51	406	1115	4784	9319	21720	40177	69782	185945	623895	1159708
Total Assets 26	1386	94	704	2003	6807	14858	35484	69139	151660	324090	1105880	4741374
Notes and Loans Payable 27	833	67	365	1450	4083	7045	10172	20730	69092	259116	761162	3077792
All Other Liabilities 28	290	20	91	374	1111	2612	8461	21004	42156	80404	279461	676189
Net Worth 29	263	7	248	179	1612	5201	16851	27404	40412	-15429	65258	987393

Selected Financial Ratios (Times to 1)

Current Ratio 30	1.0	1.4	1.4	1.3	0.9	1.1	1.2	1.1	1.5	0.6	0.5	1.0
Quick Ratio 31	0.7	1.1	1.1	1.0	0.7	0.8	0.8	0.8	1.2	0.4	0.3	0.9
Net Sales to Working Capital 32	•	27.7	20.5	14.9	•	24.3	13.3	24.6	6.6	•	•	39.0
Coverage Ratio 33	0.8	•	2.7	1.1	•	0.8	1.0	1.2	0.7	0.6	0.3	1.2
Total Asset Turnover 34	0.7	2.4	1.3	0.9	0.9	0.6	0.5	0.6	0.5	0.8	0.4	0.3
Inventory Turnover 35	7.5	12.0	13.3	9.8	8.7	7.1	4.5	3.0	8.7	33.0	1.6	18.7
Receivables Turnover 36	9.7	41.2	25.7	14.2	10.5	9.3	8.3	10.2	11.0	15.6	10.5	2.6
Total Liabilities to Net Worth 37	4.3	11.7	1.8	10.2	3.2	1.9	1.1	1.5	2.8	15.9	•	3.8
Current Assets to Working Capital 38	•	3.7	3.6	4.4	•	8.5	5.1	8.8	3.0	•	•	22.1
Current Liabilities to Working Capital 39	•	2.7	2.6	3.4	•	7.5	4.1	7.8	2.0	•	•	21.1
Working Capital to Net Sales 40	•	0.0	0.0	0.1	•	0.0	0.1	0.0	0.2	•	•	0.0
Inventory to Working Capital 41	•	0.4	0.2	0.4	•	0.6	0.8	1.0	0.3	•	•	0.8
Total Receipts to Cash Flow 42	4.4	4.3	2.4	4.8	4.4	4.6	4.6	4.1	5.2	6.9	4.5	5.9
Cost of Goods to Cash Flow 43	1.0	0.9	0.3	1.5	0.9	1.4	1.1	0.5	1.3	2.9	0.4	1.7
Cash Flow to Total Debt 44	0.2	0.6	0.8	0.2	0.3	0.2	0.2	0.2	0.1	0.1	0.1	0.1

Selected Financial Factors (in Percentages)

Debt Ratio 45	81.0	92.1	64.8	91.1	76.3	65.0	52.5	60.4	73.4	104.8	94.1	79.2
Return on Total Assets 46	2.9	•	7.7	3.5	•	1.7	1.6	2.4	2.0	3.1	1.6	6.7
Return on Equity Before Income Taxes 47	•	•	13.9	2.5	•	•	•	0.9	•	•	•	5.7
Return on Equity After Income Taxes 48	•	•	12.1	1.7	•	•	•	0.1	•	•	•	1.0
Profit Margin (Before Income Tax) 49	•	3.9	3.9	0.3	•	•	•	0.7	•	•	•	3.6
Profit Margin (After Income Tax) 50	•	3.4	3.4	0.2	•	•	•	0.1	•	•	•	0.6

Table II

Corporations with Net Income

AMUSEMENT, GAMBLING, AND RECREATION INDUSTRIES

MONEY AMOUNTS AND SIZE OF ASSETS IN THOUSANDS OF DOLLARS

Item Description for Accounting Period 7/08 Through 6/09		Total	Zero Assets	Under 500	500 to 1,000	1,000 to 5,000	5,000 to 10,000	10,000 to 25,000	25,000 to 50,000	50,000 to 100,000	100,000 to 250,000	250,000 to 500,000	500,000 to 2,500,000	2,500,000 and over
Number of Enterprises	1	23476	4580	14742	1932	1871	•	128	57	18	10	3	•	0
Revenues ($ in Thousands)														
Net Sales	2	21881203	400855	4436328	2189557	3859706	•	1422909	1270245	907405	758980	621361	•	0
Interest	3	133264	892	1276	4962	7027	•	2551	5019	1879	7851	6259	•	0
Rents	4	65734	0	25701	1531	143	•	610	2376	5664	260	9450	•	0
Royalties	5	8572	0	0	3	6919	•	0	1544	107	0	0	•	0
Other Portfolio Income	6	193353	38772	37049	2449	9281	•	2011	7083	30907	42381	1610	•	0
Other Receipts	7	1563118	3168	94625	135393	351345	•	208986	30402	26539	51212	72884	•	0
Total Receipts	8	23845244	443687	4594979	2333895	4234421	•	1637067	1316669	972501	860684	711564	•	0
Average Total Receipts	9	1016	97	312	1208	2263	•	12790	23099	54028	86068	237188	•	•
Operating Costs/Operating Income (%)														
Cost of Operations	10	19.4	12.8	20.0	11.4	31.2	•	28.0	19.9	9.3	19.9	2.5	•	•
Salaries and Wages	11	19.7	11.6	14.4	23.4	13.8	•	22.7	22.6	24.9	20.5	29.0	•	•
Taxes Paid	12	8.6	2.7	3.6	6.1	6.4	•	5.2	4.7	13.2	8.1	5.8	•	•
Interest Paid	13	3.2	4.2	0.8	2.0	2.5	•	3.0	1.3	2.8	3.3	3.1	•	•
Depreciation	14	6.8	6.4	4.9	4.8	3.8	•	8.4	8.5	8.8	6.9	20.6	•	•
Amortization and Depletion	15	0.5	0.0	0.2	0.2	0.4	•	0.1	0.1	0.3	0.7	1.6	•	•
Pensions and Other Deferred Comp.	16	0.2	0.0	0.0	0.2	0.1	•	0.1	0.3	0.4	0.4	0.1	•	•
Employee Benefits	17	1.4	0.7	0.5	0.8	1.8	•	2.3	1.1	1.5	2.8	1.6	•	•
Advertising	18	2.2	2.9	1.7	1.6	1.3	•	2.3	2.7	2.7	3.6	1.3	•	•
Other Expenses	19	32.0	47.0	41.6	37.5	31.1	•	26.9	27.6	30.1	27.2	35.8	•	•
Officers' Compensation	20	3.2	1.6	7.4	2.6	4.4	•	1.2	1.5	1.2	3.8	1.5	•	•
Operating Margin	21	2.8	10.2	5.0	9.5	3.3	•	•	9.7	4.9	2.7	•	•	•
Operating Margin Before Officers' Comp.	22	6.0	11.8	12.4	12.1	7.6	•	0.8	11.2	6.2	6.5	•	•	•

Selected Average Balance Sheet ($ in Thousands)

Net Receivables 23	57	0	11	46	171	590	1518	3662	15459	21696
Inventories 24	21	0	4	7	71	298	1439	632	1371	2185
Net Property, Plant and Equipment 25	584	0	65	493	922	9805	19309	47536	55969	193251
Total Assets 26	1104	0	121	758	2055	15019	35201	74878	146400	341555
Notes and Loans Payable 27	570	0	38	341	1074	7008	9137	26913	43923	135686
All Other Liabilities 28	151	0	26	70	387	2277	5542	11715	33590	89941
Net Worth 29	383	0	57	348	593	5733	20521	36249	68887	115927

Selected Financial Ratios (Times to 1)

Current Ratio 30	1.7	•	2.0	1.9	1.6	1.8	1.3	1.8	1.9	1.4
Quick Ratio 31	1.3	•	1.8	1.5	1.3	1.3	0.8	1.4	1.8	0.7
Net Sales to Working Capital 32	8.6	•	14.4	10.8	7.6	8.2	10.7	6.2	2.9	10.0
Coverage Ratio 33	4.7	6.0	12.1	9.1	6.3	5.9	10.9	5.3	5.9	4.8
Total Asset Turnover 34	0.8	•	2.5	1.5	1.0	0.7	0.6	0.7	0.5	0.6
Inventory Turnover 35	8.7	•	13.5	18.9	9.1	10.5	3.1	7.4	11.0	2.3
Receivables Turnover 36	9.1	•	30.4	28.4	11.3	16.4	10.1	12.4	5.9	•
Total Liabilities to Net Worth 37	1.9	•	1.1	1.2	2.5	1.6	0.7	1.1	1.1	1.9
Current Assets to Working Capital 38	2.4	•	2.0	2.2	2.6	2.2	3.9	2.3	2.1	3.5
Current Liabilities to Working Capital 39	1.4	•	1.0	1.2	1.6	1.2	2.9	1.3	1.1	2.5
Working Capital to Net Sales 40	0.1	•	0.1	0.1	0.1	0.1	0.1	0.2	0.3	0.1
Inventory to Working Capital 41	0.1	•	0.2	0.0	0.1	0.1	0.7	0.1	0.0	0.1
Total Receipts to Cash Flow 42	3.1	1.8	3.0	2.2	3.1	2.8	3.0	2.9	2.8	3.3
Cost of Goods to Cash Flow 43	0.6	0.2	0.6	0.3	1.0	0.8	0.6	0.3	0.6	0.1
Cash Flow to Total Debt 44	0.4	•	1.6	1.2	0.4	0.4	0.5	0.4	0.4	0.3

Selected Financial Factors (in Percentages)

Debt Ratio 45	65.3	•	53.1	54.1	71.1	61.8	41.7	51.6	52.9	66.1
Return on Total Assets 46	12.6	•	23.3	27.1	15.5	13.0	9.3	10.0	10.1	8.9
Return on Equity Before Income Taxes 47	28.5	•	45.6	52.5	45.0	28.3	14.4	16.7	17.8	20.6
Return on Equity After Income Taxes 48	25.6	•	44.3	49.7	44.4	26.3	12.8	15.1	17.7	13.4
Profit Margin (Before Income Tax) 49	11.7	20.9	8.6	16.1	12.9	14.6	13.3	12.0	16.1	11.6
Profit Margin (After Income Tax) 50	10.5	20.9	8.3	15.2	12.8	13.6	11.8	10.9	16.1	7.5

Table I

Corporations with and without Net Income

ACCOMMODATION

MONEY AMOUNTS AND SIZE OF ASSETS IN THOUSANDS OF DOLLARS

Item Description for Accounting Period 7/08 Through 6/09	Total	Zero Assets	Under 500	500 to 1,000	1,000 to 5,000	5,000 to 10,000	10,000 to 25,000	25,000 to 50,000	50,000 to 100,000	100,000 to 250,000	250,000 to 500,000	500,000 to 2,500,000	2,500,000 and over
Number of Enterprises **1**	35265	5224	16345	3873	7944	1166	404	139	64	36	25	30	13
Revenues ($ in Thousands)													
Net Sales **2**	93274449	2320729	4174005	1581442	9048132	3297814	4720979	3721539	3810779	6539377	5957018	7884436	40218198
Interest **3**	2121294	13688	653	3712	10437	4279	12636	18199	29171	39070	38452	298388	1652609
Rents **4**	813006	45589	1650	2204	2010	1488	12722	9378	9979	11867	31947	82131	602040
Royalties **5**	2493733	6593	0	0	0	0	1254	4	3027	3568	225494	34284	2219509
Other Portfolio Income **6**	1875323	6914	46470	767	52690	12649	20896	29038	4938	8989	4684	394306	1292985
Other Receipts **7**	9962034	-45462	49541	18089	108462	114956	141847	85212	80932	462322	221635	563700	8160799
Total Receipts **8**	110539839	2348051	4272319	1606214	9221731	3433186	4910334	3863370	3938826	7065193	6479230	9257245	54146140
Average Total Receipts **9**	3135	449	261	415	1161	2943	12154	27794	61544	196255	259169	308575	4165088
Operating Costs/Operating Income (%)													
Cost of Operations **10**	14.7	12.8	9.1	5.9	13.9	14.5	27.4	18.1	10.6	21.3	23.6	15.4	12.1
Salaries and Wages **11**	27.1	13.2	20.3	13.5	19.2	16.8	16.2	12.7	16.2	15.7	14.8	21.9	40.2
Taxes Paid **12**	6.9	5.6	8.1	8.5	7.0	6.2	3.8	4.3	3.8	3.6	3.8	10.7	8.0
Interest Paid **13**	10.4	6.0	2.5	9.7	9.1	9.5	4.6	3.9	3.9	2.0	2.9	16.4	15.0
Depreciation **14**	7.3	6.3	2.7	7.4	8.2	10.4	6.4	5.7	3.7	3.6	6.4	11.8	7.7
Amortization and Depletion **15**	0.9	0.3	0.2	0.4	0.5	0.4	0.3	0.2	0.2	0.2	0.4	2.2	1.3
Pensions and Other Deferred Comp. **16**	0.6	0.3	0.0	•	0.1	0.3	0.1	0.3	0.3	0.2	0.3	0.4	1.1
Employee Benefits **17**	2.7	0.7	0.4	0.4	1.3	1.8	2.2	1.1	2.5	1.4	1.0	2.6	4.3
Advertising **18**	3.3	2.3	1.8	1.3	1.8	1.4	2.2	2.0	3.3	4.2	3.5	4.2	4.0
Other Expenses **19**	42.8	61.7	59.6	55.8	36.7	41.4	42.7	55.7	62.5	56.1	48.5	33.5	36.8
Officers' Compensation **20**	1.3	2.2	2.5	3.0	3.0	2.1	1.0	1.2	0.6	0.4	1.7	0.9	0.8
Operating Margin **21**	•	•	•	•	•	•	•	•	•	•	•	•	•
Operating Margin Before Officers' Comp. **22**	•	•	•	•	2.1	•	•	•	•	•	•	•	•

Selected Average Balance Sheet ($ in Thousands)

Net Receivables 23	260	0	2	5	81	280	946	1719	4437	9622	24255	61309	342572
Inventories 24	103	0	2	3	13	18	122	463	810	2021	2637	14895	209148
Net Property, Plant and Equipment 25	3410	0	113	581	1637	4637	10794	21196	40767	81492	193764	511535	4976255
Total Assets 26	7402	0	161	731	2167	6455	15296	35785	73521	159658	339009	969481	13203472
Notes and Loans Payable 27	4577	0	156	654	1898	4849	10166	21128	34338	58017	150468	498304	8118836
All Other Liabilities 28	1612	0	32	64	137	964	2468	6054	12760	44124	56807	308569	2995371
Net Worth 29	1213	0	-27	13	132	642	2661	8603	26424	57518	131734	162608	2089266

Selected Financial Ratios (Times to 1)

Current Ratio 30	1.1	•	0.6	1.9	1.9	1.2	1.2	1.6	1.7	1.2	1.2	1.1	1.0
Quick Ratio 31	0.8	•	0.4	1.8	1.3	0.9	0.8	1.0	1.2	0.9	0.9	0.8	0.7
Net Sales to Working Capital 32	23.8	•	•	13.4	7.9	27.3	34.7	8.5	7.6	30.3	18.3	12.1	60.6
Coverage Ratio 33	1.2	•	•	0.5	1.1	0.9	0.3	0.6	•	0.7	1.6	0.8	1.5
Total Asset Turnover 34	0.4	•	1.6	0.6	0.5	0.4	0.8	0.7	0.8	1.1	0.7	0.3	0.2
Inventory Turnover 35	3.8	•	12.0	6.9	12.2	22.7	26.3	10.5	7.8	19.1	21.3	2.7	1.8
Receivables Turnover 36	9.5	•	137.4	29.1	17.4	9.0	12.4	15.5	12.0	15.8	10.9	4.8	7.5
Total Liabilities to Net Worth 37	5.1	•	•	56.7	15.4	9.1	4.7	3.2	1.8	1.8	1.6	5.0	5.3
Current Assets to Working Capital 38	8.6	•	•	2.1	2.1	7.0	7.4	2.6	2.4	7.4	5.9	8.4	25.9
Current Liabilities to Working Capital 39	7.6	•	•	1.1	1.1	6.0	6.4	1.6	1.4	6.4	4.9	7.4	24.9
Working Capital to Net Sales 40	0.0	•	•	0.1	0.1	0.0	0.0	0.1	0.1	0.0	0.1	0.1	0.0
Inventory to Working Capital 41	1.1	•	•	0.1	0.1	0.2	0.5	0.1	0.1	0.3	0.3	0.7	4.8
Total Receipts to Cash Flow 42	3.4	3.4	4.1	3.1	3.5	4.3	4.1	3.8	3.0	3.4	3.2	5.2	3.0
Cost of Goods to Cash Flow 43	0.5	0.4	0.4	0.2	0.5	0.6	1.1	0.7	0.3	0.7	0.8	0.8	0.4
Cash Flow to Total Debt 44	0.1	•	0.3	0.2	0.2	0.1	0.2	0.3	0.4	0.5	0.4	0.1	0.1

Selected Financial Factors (in Percentages)

Debt Ratio 45	83.6	•	116.7	98.3	93.9	90.1	82.6	76.0	64.1	64.0	61.1	83.2	84.2
Return on Total Assets 46	4.6	•	•	3.0	5.3	3.8	1.2	1.8	•	1.5	3.3	3.7	5.4
Return on Equity Before Income Taxes 47	5.4	•	46.3	•	9.4	•	•	•	•	•	3.3	•	12.0
Return on Equity After Income Taxes 48	1.4	•	47.1	•	7.3	•	•	•	•	•	0.9	•	7.3
Profit Margin (Before Income Tax) 49	2.5	•	•	•	1.1	•	•	•	•	•	1.8	•	8.1
Profit Margin (After Income Tax) 50	0.6	•	•	•	0.8	•	•	•	•	•	0.5	•	5.0

Table II
Corporations with Net Income

ACCOMMODATION

MONEY AMOUNTS AND SIZE OF ASSETS IN THOUSANDS OF DOLLARS

Item Description for Accounting Period 7/08 Through 6/09	Total	Zero Assets	Under 500	500 to 1,000	1,000 to 5,000	5,000 to 10,000	10,000 to 25,000	25,000 to 50,000	50,000 to 100,000	100,000 to 250,000	250,000 to 500,000	500,000 to 2,500,000	2,500,000 and over
Number of Enterprises **1**	13763	1384	5919	1569	4060	543	151	64	26	13	12	13	9
Revenues ($ in Thousands)													
Net Sales **2**	55178821	822300	1880675	705546	5256792	1450947	2235591	1641736	1165471	1136414	2554421	3724616	32604312
Interest **3**	1767416	6814	274	2985	9522	3094	7390	12048	16621	18523	28806	269003	1392336
Rents **4**	610322	4329	1650	0	1819	224	7689	5428	2781	7605	20497	36571	521730
Royalties **5**	1939737	0	0	0	0	0	0	4	367	0	225494	7260	1706612
Other Portfolio Income **6**	1773843	6914	43267	0	52287	12632	16822	25170	1082	2929	3485	370781	1238479
Other Receipts **7**	7393377	49351	28074	9360	73524	109220	31495	58677	25023	87511	151911	348770	6420453
Total Receipts **8**	68663516	889708	1953940	717891	5393944	1576117	2298987	1743063	1211345	1252982	2984614	4757001	43383922
Average Total Receipts **9**	4989	643	330	458	1329	2903	15225	27235	46590	96383	248718	365923	4875991
Operating Costs/Operating Income (%)													
Cost of Operations **10**	12.5	20.3	5.3	2.3	11.2	5.8	41.7	16.6	12.3	22.2	26.7	12.8	9.8
Salaries and Wages **11**	32.6	15.8	18.7	16.4	17.6	22.3	16.7	20.0	12.8	19.4	22.1	21.3	42.1
Taxes Paid **12**	8.0	7.8	6.8	9.5	6.4	8.2	4.3	6.2	5.1	5.6	4.3	13.8	8.4
Interest Paid **13**	9.2	1.6	2.1	8.1	7.8	9.8	3.3	3.8	3.9	2.1	2.5	9.3	11.6
Depreciation **14**	6.5	4.9	2.4	6.5	7.2	8.9	4.6	5.7	4.8	7.2	5.7	10.8	6.4
Amortization and Depletion **15**	0.9	0.3	0.0	0.5	0.5	0.4	0.1	0.3	0.2	0.2	0.3	1.8	1.2
Pensions and Other Deferred Comp. **16**	0.7	0.8	0.0	•	0.1	0.2	0.1	0.5	0.2	0.5	0.6	0.7	0.9
Employee Benefits **17**	3.3	0.9	0.6	0.5	0.9	1.8	0.7	1.9	2.2	2.9	1.2	1.6	4.7
Advertising **18**	3.9	3.8	2.2	1.2	1.4	1.7	1.1	2.8	4.7	5.5	4.4	3.3	4.7
Other Expenses **19**	35.6	35.8	50.5	43.0	33.6	31.4	21.5	37.7	50.6	29.2	33.7	31.5	36.2
Officers' Compensation **20**	1.1	0.0	2.3	3.5	3.4	2.2	1.1	1.6	0.7	0.8	2.8	1.2	0.5
Operating Margin **21**	•	8.0	9.1	8.5	9.8	7.3	4.6	2.9	2.5	4.2	•	•	•
Operating Margin Before Officers' Comp. **22**	•	8.0	11.4	12.0	13.2	9.6	5.7	4.5	3.2	5.0	•	•	•

Selected Average Balance Sheet ($ in Thousands)

Net Receivables 23	331	0	2	4	104	88	1612	2386	4397	7013	25094	40736	293632
Inventories 24	198	0	1	3	18	18	103	474	878	2805	2660	17277	257097
Net Property, Plant and Equipment 25	5142	0	149	568	1551	4435	9431	21123	36020	103727	183517	523790	5135576
Total Assets 26	11683	0	208	732	2198	6752	15593	35728	72841	170071	347240	1115003	13156915
Notes and Loans Payable 27	6217	0	146	538	1733	4015	8750	20106	31390	47912	128293	361615	7150611
All Other Liabilities 28	2428	0	24	17	129	636	1145	5057	11121	32668	54632	181602	3128164
Net Worth 29	3038	0	39	177	336	2100	5698	10565	30329	89490	164315	571786	2878140

Selected Financial Ratios (Times to 1)

Current Ratio 30	1.0	•	1.1	2.3	2.8	1.0	2.1	1.8	2.9	2.4	2.0	2.0	0.7
Quick Ratio 31	0.6	•	0.5	2.1	2.0	0.8	1.6	1.3	1.8	2.2	1.7	1.2	0.4
Net Sales to Working Capital 32	142.9	•	41.4	9.8	5.0	113.8	7.9	6.8	3.1	3.7	4.8	3.0	•
Coverage Ratio 33	2.4	10.9	7.1	2.3	2.6	2.6	3.3	3.4	2.7	7.8	6.1	3.1	2.1
Total Asset Turnover 34	0.3	•	1.5	0.6	0.6	0.4	0.9	0.7	0.6	0.5	0.6	0.3	0.3
Inventory Turnover 35	2.5	•	24.3	3.3	8.0	8.4	60.0	9.0	6.3	6.9	21.3	2.1	1.4
Receivables Turnover 36	8.5	•	129.6	49.8	14.8	11.0	9.5	10.3	7.7	4.9	10.4	•	3.6
Total Liabilities to Net Worth 37	2.8	•	4.4	3.1	5.5	2.2	1.7	2.4	1.4	0.9	1.1	1.0	3.6
Current Assets to Working Capital 38	47.2	•	7.9	1.8	1.5	26.8	1.9	2.2	1.5	1.7	2.0	2.0	•
Current Liabilities to Working Capital 39	46.2	•	6.9	0.8	0.5	25.8	0.9	1.2	0.5	0.7	1.0	1.0	•
Working Capital to Net Sales 40	0.0	•	0.0	0.1	0.2	0.0	0.1	0.1	0.3	0.3	0.2	0.3	•
Inventory to Working Capital 41	7.1	•	0.1	0.1	0.1	0.9	0.0	0.1	0.1	0.0	0.1	0.2	•
Total Receipts to Cash Flow 42	2.7	3.0	2.6	2.3	2.6	2.3	4.1	3.6	2.4	2.6	2.6	3.0	2.6
Cost of Goods to Cash Flow 43	0.3	0.6	0.1	0.1	0.3	0.1	1.7	0.6	0.3	0.6	0.7	0.4	0.3
Cash Flow to Total Debt 44	0.2	•	0.7	0.4	0.3	0.2	0.4	0.3	0.4	0.4	0.4	0.2	0.1

Selected Financial Factors (in Percentages)

Debt Ratio 45	74.0	•	81.5	75.8	84.7	68.9	63.5	70.4	58.4	47.4	52.7	48.7	78.1
Return on Total Assets 46	7.6	•	23.1	11.3	11.9	10.2	10.1	9.2	6.3	8.6	9.3	7.4	6.7
Return on Equity Before Income Taxes 47	17.1	•	107.4	26.0	47.8	20.3	19.2	21.8	9.5	14.2	16.5	9.9	16.2
Return on Equity After Income Taxes 48	13.0	•	105.8	25.5	46.2	19.3	17.6	19.5	8.4	11.6	12.4	6.8	11.3
Profit Margin (Before Income Tax) 49	12.9	16.2	13.0	10.2	12.4	15.9	7.4	9.0	6.4	14.5	12.7	19.7	12.9
Profit Margin (After Income Tax) 50	9.9	12.6	12.8	10.0	12.0	15.1	6.8	8.0	5.7	11.9	9.6	13.6	9.0

Table I

Corporations with and without Net Income

FOOD SERVICES AND DRINKING PLACES

MONEY AMOUNTS AND SIZE OF ASSETS IN THOUSANDS OF DOLLARS

Item Description for Accounting Period 7/08 Through 6/09		Total	Zero Assets	Under 500	500 to 1,000	1,000 to 5,000	5,000 to 10,000	10,000 to 25,000	25,000 to 50,000	50,000 to 100,000	100,000 to 250,000	250,000 to 500,000	500,000 to 2,500,000	2,500,000 and over
Number of Enterprises	1	257636	39373	190782	15575	10347	825	417	127	66	53	26	•	11
Revenues ($ in Thousands)														
Net Sales	2	340708996	7327261	101265050	27487290	42212489	10732947	11357846	7536235	8515188	12567363	12685669	•	62143705
Interest	3	956184	3768	15001	9242	20626	4137	14798	8924	4245	16533	31638	•	640169
Rents	4	649479	20890	17978	2953	26321	4026	6570	12183	10609	40091	69676	•	196374
Royalties	5	4434959	308359	8548	33	411	6292	33079	105598	64716	195255	550364	•	2032561
Other Portfolio Income	6	1805834	177488	176871	8295	71608	12473	9000	14998	4975	33586	61177	•	301298
Other Receipts	7	9760552	192702	718024	329281	473704	140723	235310	69359	94333	248628	133279	•	5564446
Total Receipts	8	358316004	8030468	102201472	27837094	42805159	10900598	11656603	7747297	8694066	13101456	13531803	•	70878553
Average Total Receipts	9	1391	204	536	1787	4137	13213	27953	61002	131728	247197	520454	•	6443505
Operating Costs/Operating Income (%)														
Cost of Operations	10	43.0	54.3	43.2	39.7	43.4	40.4	45.8	41.6	39.1	40.0	42.7	•	45.0
Salaries and Wages	11	18.9	11.2	16.8	20.0	17.4	20.8	18.4	19.6	18.6	22.8	21.2	•	19.0
Taxes Paid	12	3.9	3.9	4.1	4.0	3.5	3.3	3.8	4.0	3.0	3.8	3.8	•	4.1
Interest Paid	13	1.9	1.2	0.7	1.1	1.4	1.4	1.8	2.1	1.8	2.9	3.9	•	3.8
Depreciation	14	3.2	4.0	2.0	2.3	3.2	3.5	3.8	3.7	3.5	4.8	3.8	•	3.4
Amortization and Depletion	15	0.6	2.2	0.3	0.4	0.6	0.4	0.5	0.6	0.4	0.9	1.2	•	0.9
Pensions and Other Deferred Comp.	16	0.2	0.3	0.1	0.1	0.0	0.1	0.4	0.1	0.2	0.2	0.3	•	0.7
Employee Benefits	17	1.3	0.3	0.6	0.7	0.8	0.6	1.0	1.4	1.3	1.2	1.6	•	3.2
Advertising	18	2.4	3.4	1.7	2.3	2.9	3.4	3.3	3.1	2.0	2.6	2.6	•	2.1
Other Expenses	19	24.9	30.4	25.9	25.3	24.2	25.0	22.7	25.4	31.2	25.4	23.4	•	23.8
Officers' Compensation	20	2.4	2.5	4.8	3.8	2.4	1.4	1.4	1.1	0.8	0.9	0.5	•	0.4
Operating Margin	21	•	•	•	0.3	0.3	•	•	•	•	•	•	•	•
Operating Margin Before Officers' Comp.	22	•	•	4.5	4.1	2.6	1.1	•	•	•	•	•	•	•

Selected Average Balance Sheet ($ in Thousands)

Net Receivables 23	48	0	2	36	143	229	868	1484	5281	5548	18199	546516
Inventories 24	21	0	7	24	47	182	469	789	1779	3459	9678	142622
Net Property, Plant and Equipment 25	310	0	61	353	935	3546	7490	16899	34838	82727	133228	1638502
Total Assets 26	827	0	125	668	1867	6709	14709	34951	69358	155413	339403	7896632
Notes and Loans Payable 27	379	0	103	379	1055	3652	8292	18271	32068	74196	205580	2712133
All Other Liabilities 28	268	0	27	141	415	1467	3491	9135	17788	49479	97012	3019822
Net Worth 29	180	0	-5	149	398	1590	2926	7545	19502	31738	36812	2164678

Selected Financial Ratios (Times to 1)

Current Ratio 30	0.8	•	1.2	1.1	1.0	1.1	0.8	0.8	0.5	0.8	0.8	0.6
Quick Ratio 31	0.6	•	0.9	0.8	0.7	0.8	0.5	0.5	0.5	0.3	0.6	0.4
Net Sales to Working Capital 32	•	•	364.6	50.3	91.3	228.9	96.4	•	•	•	•	•
Coverage Ratio 33	2.3	•	1.9	2.4	2.2	2.0	0.9	1.0	1.2	0.6	1.4	3.2
Total Asset Turnover 34	1.6	•	4.2	2.6	2.2	1.9	1.9	1.7	1.9	1.5	1.4	0.7
Inventory Turnover 35	26.9	•	32.2	29.4	37.9	28.8	26.6	31.3	28.3	27.4	21.5	17.8
Receivables Turnover 36	28.8	•	214.6	47.7	35.8	72.4	33.3	33.7	23.2	42.5	30.5	10.9
Total Liabilities to Net Worth 37	3.6	•	•	3.5	3.7	3.2	4.0	3.6	2.6	3.9	8.2	2.6
Current Assets to Working Capital 38	•	•	23.7	5.1	11.0	27.7	14.0	•	•	•	•	•
Current Liabilities to Working Capital 39	•	•	22.7	4.1	10.0	26.7	13.0	•	•	•	•	•
Working Capital to Net Sales 40	•	•	0.0	0.0	0.0	0.0	0.0	•	•	•	•	•
Inventory to Working Capital 41	•	•	4.9	0.8	1.0	3.8	1.7	•	•	•	•	•
Total Receipts to Cash Flow 42	5.7	7.5	6.1	5.6	5.9	5.7	6.6	5.9	4.2	6.5	5.9	4.6
Cost of Goods to Cash Flow 43	2.4	4.1	2.6	2.2	2.6	2.3	3.0	2.4	1.7	2.6	2.5	2.1
Cash Flow to Total Debt 44	0.4	0.7	0.6	0.6	0.5	0.4	0.4	0.4	0.6	0.3	0.3	0.2

Selected Financial Factors (in Percentages)

Debt Ratio 45	78.2	•	104.2	77.8	78.7	76.3	80.1	78.4	71.9	79.6	89.2	72.6
Return on Total Assets 46	7.0	•	5.9	7.0	6.6	5.2	3.0	3.5	3.9	2.6	8.0	8.7
Return on Equity Before Income Taxes 47	18.3	•	•	18.4	17.0	10.9	•	•	1.8	•	21.8	21.7
Return on Equity After Income Taxes 48	12.3	•	•	17.1	16.3	9.8	•	•	0.4	•	13.1	14.0
Profit Margin (Before Income Tax) 49	2.5	•	0.7	1.6	1.7	1.3	•	•	0.3	0.3	1.6	8.3
Profit Margin (After Income Tax) 50	1.7	•	0.6	1.4	1.6	1.2	•	•	0.1	•	1.0	5.4

Table II

Corporations with Net Income

FOOD SERVICES AND DRINKING PLACES

MONEY AMOUNTS AND SIZE OF ASSETS IN THOUSANDS OF DOLLARS

Item Description for Accounting Period 7/08 Through 6/09	Total	Zero Assets	Under 500	500 to 1,000	1,000 to 5,000	5,000 to 10,000	10,000 to 25,000	25,000 to 50,000	50,000 to 100,000	100,000 to 250,000	250,000 to 500,000	500,000 to 2,500,000	2,500,000 and over
Number of Enterprises 1	118204	12740	90040	8201	6224	622	211	69	•	19	15	21	•
Revenues ($ in Thousands)													
Net Sales 2	232756099	5392653	60685580	17172843	29982905	8399470	6399831	4411029	•	4291808	7986457	24855260	•
Interest 3	779848	2672	8191	6144	12098	2063	3624	3590	•	5304	28733	130869	•
Rents 4	487337	20890	14264	41	25268	1999	1584	868	•	25170	49523	220727	•
Royalties 5	3653329	308359	8548	18	323	608	5817	48617	•	135648	465684	738559	•
Other Portfolio Income 6	1727735	177056	174167	5514	57256	10160	5404	11220	•	6552	56249	921461	•
Other Receipts 7	8553607	166730	548495	112295	288570	126373	178190	41698	•	200742	49798	1454847	•
Total Receipts 8	247957955	6068360	61439245	17296855	30366420	8540673	6594450	4517022	•	4665224	8636444	28321723	•
Average Total Receipts 9	2098	476	682	2109	4879	13731	31253	65464	•	245538	575763	1348653	•
Operating Costs/Operating Income (%)													
Cost of Operations 10	43.3	58.1	42.0	37.9	42.6	40.9	45.1	45.7	•	38.0	47.2	42.7	•
Salaries and Wages 11	18.3	9.0	16.3	21.3	16.9	19.7	19.4	15.7	•	22.9	20.5	23.7	•
Taxes Paid 12	3.7	3.2	3.9	4.2	3.3	3.2	3.2	3.5	•	3.7	3.4	3.3	•
Interest Paid 13	1.8	1.2	0.5	0.8	1.2	1.1	1.3	1.4	•	1.6	3.3	2.0	•
Depreciation 14	2.9	3.8	1.3	1.5	2.1	3.4	3.0	3.3	•	4.9	3.3	6.6	•
Amortization and Depletion 15	0.5	1.7	0.2	0.2	0.5	0.4	0.5	0.6	•	0.6	0.8	0.3	•
Pensions and Other Deferred Comp. 16	0.3	0.4	0.1	0.1	0.0	0.1	0.1	0.1	•	0.3	0.3	0.3	•
Employee Benefits 17	1.4	0.3	0.6	0.7	0.8	0.6	1.1	1.4	•	1.6	1.6	1.9	•
Advertising 18	2.3	4.1	1.6	1.8	3.0	3.4	3.1	2.9	•	2.7	2.7	2.8	•
Other Expenses 19	23.3	22.5	23.5	21.9	23.1	24.1	20.3	22.0	•	27.0	19.7	22.3	•
Officers' Compensation 20	2.3	2.3	5.0	3.9	2.6	1.3	1.6	1.1	•	0.9	0.5	0.7	•
Operating Margin 21	•	•	4.9	5.8	3.9	1.8	1.3	2.3	•	•	•	•	•
Operating Margin Before Officers' Comp. 22	2.2	•	9.9	9.7	6.4	3.1	2.9	3.3	•	•	•	•	•

Selected Average Balance Sheet ($ in Thousands)

	•	•	•	•	•	•	•	•	•	•	•	•
Net Receivables 23	82	0	2	42	219	225	1141	1602	•	6674	16934	37372
Inventories 24	34	0	8	29	55	181	607	852	•	4647	12402	25268
Net Property, Plant and Equipment 25	429	0	54	304	922	3691	6771	16333	•	79574	132732	566612
Total Assets 26	1287	0	130	664	1967	6775	14321	35824	•	158977	331627	1009327
Notes and Loans Payable 27	484	0	62	320	985	3362	6572	14962	•	57133	221890	301690
All Other Liabilities 28	413	0	27	131	369	1132	3166	7426	•	52998	94749	295552
Net Worth 29	390	0	42	213	614	2280	4583	13435	•	48847	14989	412085

Selected Financial Ratios (Times to 1)

	•	•	•	•	•	•	•	•	•	•	•	•
Current Ratio 30	0.8	•	1.7	1.9	1.4	1.2	1.2	1.0	•	0.7	0.9	0.8
Quick Ratio 31	0.6	•	1.1	1.3	1.1	0.9	0.7	0.7	•	0.5	0.6	0.4
Net Sales to Working Capital 32	•	•	34.0	19.1	24.9	50.5	54.7	564.3	•	•	•	•
Coverage Ratio 33	4.7	5.9	12.5	8.9	5.5	4.1	4.3	4.2	•	3.8	2.4	5.0
Total Asset Turnover 34	1.5	•	5.2	3.2	2.4	2.0	2.1	1.8	•	1.4	1.6	1.2
Inventory Turnover 35	25.2	•	37.2	27.1	37.7	30.6	22.5	34.3	•	18.5	20.3	20.0
Receivables Turnover 36	24.6	•	295.9	47.5	28.1	69.7	26.3	32.0	•	24.9	28.1	•
Total Liabilities to Net Worth 37	2.3	•	2.1	2.1	2.2	2.0	2.1	1.7	•	2.3	21.1	1.4
Current Assets to Working Capital 38	•	•	2.4	2.1	3.3	5.5	7.2	71.4	•	•	•	•
Current Liabilities to Working Capital 39	•	•	1.4	1.1	2.3	4.5	6.2	70.4	•	•	•	•
Working Capital to Net Sales 40	•	•	0.0	0.1	0.0	0.0	0.0	0.0	•	•	•	•
Inventory to Working Capital 41	•	•	0.4	0.3	0.2	0.8	1.1	7.8	•	•	•	•
Total Receipts to Cash Flow 42	4.9	5.2	4.9	5.1	5.1	5.2	5.6	5.0	•	4.1	5.9	5.3
Cost of Goods to Cash Flow 43	2.1	3.0	2.1	1.9	2.2	2.1	2.5	2.3	•	1.5	2.8	2.3
Cash Flow to Total Debt 44	0.4	•	1.6	0.9	0.7	0.6	0.6	0.6	•	0.5	0.3	0.4

Selected Financial Factors (in Percentages)

	•	•	•	•	•	•	•	•	•	•	•	•
Debt Ratio 45	69.7	•	68.1	67.9	68.8	66.3	68.0	62.5	•	69.3	95.5	59.2
Return on Total Assets 46	12.8	•	34.6	23.1	15.4	9.2	11.9	10.9	•	8.7	12.9	11.6
Return on Equity Before Income Taxes 47	33.4	•	99.8	63.9	40.5	20.7	28.6	22.1	•	20.9	167.3	22.7
Return on Equity After Income Taxes 48	27.4	•	98.0	62.2	39.7	19.7	25.7	20.9	•	16.1	130.5	15.5
Profit Margin (Before Income Tax) 49	6.6	6.2	6.1	6.5	5.2	3.5	4.3	4.6	•	4.5	4.7	7.9
Profit Margin (After Income Tax) 50	5.4	5.9	6.0	6.3	5.1	3.3	3.9	4.4	•	3.5	3.7	5.4

Table I

Corporations with and without Net Income

AUTOMOTIVE REPAIR AND MAINTENANCE

MONEY AMOUNTS AND SIZE OF ASSETS IN THOUSANDS OF DOLLARS

Item Description for Accounting Period 7/08 Through 6/09		Total	Zero Assets	Under 500	500 to 1,000	1,000 to 5,000	5,000 to 10,000	10,000 to 25,000	25,000 to 50,000	50,000 to 100,000	100,000 to 250,000	250,000 to 500,000	500,000 to 2,500,000	2,500,000 and over
Number of Enterprises	1	105190	17637	76778	7203	3263	219	54	18	9	5	4	0	0
Revenues ($ in Thousands)														
Net Sales	2	67655315	1538447	39250999	9563709	10191693	1178640	1055068	945936	1851063	475041	1604719	0	0
Interest	3	41497	1466	11510	6746	5430	1095	1014	4102	7321	1741	1073	0	0
Rents	4	19987	0	16223	320	919	450	635	665	46	118	612	0	0
Royalties	5	95403	0	0	0	0	0	1150	0	1488	49512	43254	0	0
Other Portfolio Income	6	136790	4146	17771	55775	4068	30092	5396	11618	6274	428	1224	0	0
Other Receipts	7	172388	3915	121557	5309	27028	-43651	12175	3075	8255	5026	29693	0	0
Total Receipts	8	68121380	1547974	39418060	9631859	10229138	1166626	1075438	965396	1874447	531866	1680575	0	0
Average Total Receipts	9	648	88	513	1337	3135	5327	19916	53633	208272	106373	420144	•	•
Operating Costs/Operating Income (%)														
Cost of Operations	10	51.6	43.6	50.1	54.7	58.7	52.1	39.0	51.9	38.0	40.6	58.6	•	•
Salaries and Wages	11	12.4	12.1	12.5	10.1	13.4	8.3	21.1	18.3	11.3	20.4	11.3	•	•
Taxes Paid	12	3.1	4.1	3.4	2.8	3.1	2.1	3.5	2.4	1.3	3.6	1.7	•	•
Interest Paid	13	1.3	0.5	0.8	2.3	1.7	3.0	1.0	2.4	0.8	9.0	3.6	•	•
Depreciation	14	2.1	3.6	1.6	2.9	2.3	3.0	4.1	4.7	1.5	3.1	2.2	•	•
Amortization and Depletion	15	0.4	0.5	0.2	0.7	0.5	0.5	0.2	1.1	0.4	4.5	2.8	•	•
Pensions and Other Deferred Comp.	16	0.1	0.0	0.1	0.1	0.2	0.0	0.2	0.3	0.2	0.6	0.4	•	•
Employee Benefits	17	1.1	0.5	1.1	1.3	0.8	1.2	1.6	1.1	1.3	1.8	2.2	•	•
Advertising	18	1.4	1.6	1.4	1.5	1.5	0.9	2.2	1.5	0.2	1.5	3.2	•	•
Other Expenses	19	19.9	39.1	19.7	19.3	12.5	23.4	23.3	19.1	45.1	22.9	20.2	•	•
Officers' Compensation	20	6.2	3.6	8.1	4.6	4.0	4.5	1.8	0.9	0.2	1.9	1.0	•	•
Operating Margin	21	0.4	•	1.2	•	1.3	1.0	2.0	•	•	•	•	•	•
Operating Margin Before Officers' Comp.	22	6.6	•	9.2	4.4	5.2	5.5	3.8	•	•	•	•	•	•

Selected Average Balance Sheet ($ in Thousands)

Net Receivables **23**	20	0	9	49	122	1455	1055	4023	13393	12332	10736
Inventories **24**	20	0	11	59	115	839	846	2159	2910	3927	33842
Net Property, Plant and Equipment **25**	91	0	38	307	853	1471	7115	15526	18768	39780	90430
Total Assets **26**	230	0	102	666	1658	6551	17718	31622	74241	194813	388513
Notes and Loans Payable **27**	138	0	75	490	845	2062	5982	15347	17691	105497	165727
All Other Liabilities **28**	54	0	34	117	207	1789	-132	5312	24899	46792	142562
Net Worth **29**	39	0	-7	58	606	2700	11268	10963	31651	42524	80224

Selected Financial Ratios (Times to 1)

Current Ratio **30**	1.4	•	1.2	1.4	2.1	1.5	1.6	1.2	1.5	1.2	1.0
Quick Ratio **31**	0.9	•	0.8	0.8	1.5	1.0	0.9	0.8	1.2	0.6	0.2
Net Sales to Working Capital **32**	30.3	•	68.2	26.1	11.9	6.5	9.5	30.5	19.7	17.5	•
Coverage Ratio **33**	1.8	•	3.0	1.1	2.0	1.0	4.9	0.3	2.3	1.2	0.4
Total Asset Turnover **34**	2.8	•	5.0	2.0	1.9	0.8	1.1	1.7	2.8	0.5	1.0
Inventory Turnover **35**	16.4	•	22.4	12.3	16.0	3.3	9.0	12.6	26.8	9.8	6.9
Receivables Turnover **36**	32.1	•	60.1	21.4	24.0	4.7	19.0	14.3	15.5	8.0	49.9
Total Liabilities to Net Worth **37**	4.9	•	•	10.4	1.7	1.4	0.5	1.9	1.3	3.6	3.8
Current Assets to Working Capital **38**	3.6	•	5.8	3.6	1.9	3.2	2.7	5.5	2.8	5.7	•
Current Liabilities to Working Capital **39**	2.6	•	4.8	2.6	0.9	2.2	1.7	4.5	1.8	4.7	•
Working Capital to Net Sales **40**	0.0	•	0.0	0.0	0.1	0.2	0.1	0.0	0.1	0.1	•
Inventory to Working Capital **41**	0.9	•	1.6	1.2	0.4	0.6	0.4	1.4	0.2	0.8	•
Total Receipts to Cash Flow **42**	7.1	5.9	7.1	7.4	10.3	6.8	4.7	12.7	2.4	7.4	9.9
Cost of Goods to Cash Flow **43**	3.7	2.6	3.6	4.1	6.0	3.5	1.8	6.6	0.9	3.0	5.8
Cash Flow to Total Debt **44**	0.5	•	0.7	0.3	0.3	0.2	0.7	0.2	2.0	0.1	0.1

Selected Financial Factors (in Percentages)

Debt Ratio **45**	83.1	•	106.8	91.2	63.5	58.8	34.2	65.3	57.4	78.2	79.4
Return on Total Assets **46**	6.6	•	12.1	5.1	6.2	2.4	5.6	1.3	5.0	5.4	1.5
Return on Equity Before Income Taxes **47**	17.5	•	•	6.3	8.3	•	6.8	•	6.6	4.5	•
Return on Equity After Income Taxes **48**	16.1	•	•	4.7	7.5	•	6.6	•	6.1	3.7	•
Profit Margin (Before Income Tax) **49**	1.1	•	1.6	0.3	1.6	•	3.9	•	1.0	2.0	•
Profit Margin (After Income Tax) **50**	1.0	•	1.6	0.2	1.5	•	3.8	•	0.9	1.7	•

Table II
Corporations with Net Income

AUTOMOTIVE REPAIR AND MAINTENANCE

MONEY AMOUNTS AND SIZE OF ASSETS IN THOUSANDS OF DOLLARS

Item Description for Accounting Period 7/08 Through 6/09	Total	Zero Assets	Under 500	500 to 1,000	1,000 to 5,000	5,000 to 10,000	10,000 to 25,000	25,000 to 50,000	50,000 to 100,000	100,000 to 250,000	250,000 to 500,000	500,000 to 2,500,000	2,500,000 and over
Number of Enterprises **1**	54483	6062	42796	3851	1558	167	31	9	•	•	0	0	0
Revenues ($ in Thousands)													
Net Sales **2**	40716331	589189	24504573	5165945	7024563	1060285	868944	208764	•	•	•	•	•
Interest **3**	26368	1464	7513	3698	3370	1088	995	608	•	•	0	0	0
Rents **4**	8103	0	7081	0	544	30	0	0	•	•	•	0	0
Royalties **5**	52150	0	0	0	0	0	1150	0	•	•	0	0	0
Other Portfolio Income **6**	91457	85	5168	55767	3283	15534	2734	7205	•	•	•	0	0
Other Receipts **7**	144489	41	71208	-223	22007	38682	6196	41	•	•	0	0	0
Total Receipts **8**	41038898	590779	24595543	5225187	7053767	1115619	880019	216618	•	•	•	0	0
Average Total Receipts **9**	753	97	575	1357	4527	6680	28388	24069	•	•	•	•	•
Operating Costs/Operating Income (%)													
Cost of Operations **10**	48.8	39.5	46.5	52.3	56.6	49.5	34.5	47.5	•	•	•	•	•
Salaries and Wages **11**	13.0	5.1	13.0	11.3	13.9	8.8	22.7	7.2	•	•	•	•	•
Taxes Paid **12**	3.2	2.5	3.3	3.1	3.1	2.1	3.7	2.4	•	•	•	•	•
Interest Paid **13**	0.9	0.2	0.5	2.1	0.7	3.1	0.4	2.4	•	•	•	•	•
Depreciation **14**	1.5	2.3	1.1	2.2	1.4	2.2	2.6	16.1	•	•	•	•	•
Amortization and Depletion **15**	0.3	0.5	0.1	0.9	0.2	0.5	0.2	0.1	•	•	•	•	•
Pensions and Other Deferred Comp. **16**	0.2	•	0.1	0.1	0.2	0.1	0.2	0.8	•	•	•	•	•
Employee Benefits **17**	1.1	1.0	1.0	1.2	0.9	1.3	1.4	2.3	•	•	•	•	•
Advertising **18**	1.6	0.7	1.6	1.1	1.7	0.9	2.3	1.4	•	•	•	•	•
Other Expenses **19**	17.8	33.7	19.2	15.3	12.2	23.0	24.3	19.4	•	•	•	•	•
Officers' Compensation **20**	6.1	2.3	7.5	4.3	4.4	4.6	1.7	1.7	•	•	•	•	•
Operating Margin **21**	5.6	12.2	6.0	6.2	4.7	3.9	6.0	•	•	•	•	•	•
Operating Margin Before Officers' Comp. **22**	11.7	14.6	13.6	10.5	9.1	8.5	7.8	0.3	•	•	•	•	•

Selected Average Balance Sheet ($ in Thousands)

Net Receivables 23	25	0	8	53	195	1817	1534	1251
Inventories 24	19	0	10	53	128	661	794	512
Net Property, Plant and Equipment 25	83	0	29	266	756	1711	7045	22173
Total Assets 26	227	0	96	647	1742	6807	15968	29438
Notes and Loans Payable 27	102	0	46	418	556	2175	4773	9716
All Other Liabilities 28	46	0	23	105	194	2295	2427	1335
Net Worth 29	80	0	27	124	992	2336	8768	18388

Selected Financial Ratios (Times to 1)

Current Ratio 30	1.9	•	1.8	1.9	2.9	1.5	1.6	1.3
Quick Ratio 31	1.4	•	1.4	1.2	2.2	1.1	1.2	1.1
Net Sales to Working Capital 32	17.0	•	26.6	16.3	9.3	5.9	11.1	18.6
Coverage Ratio 33	8.0	80.8	13.0	4.3	8.8	3.9	17.3	1.9
Total Asset Turnover 34	3.3	•	6.0	2.1	2.6	0.9	1.8	0.8
Inventory Turnover 35	19.0	•	28.0	13.2	19.9	4.8	12.2	21.5
Receivables Turnover 36	28.9	•	62.1	16.0	22.5	5.6	18.8	•
Total Liabilities to Net Worth 37	1.8	•	2.6	4.2	0.8	1.9	0.8	0.6
Current Assets to Working Capital 38	2.1	•	2.2	2.2	1.5	3.0	2.6	3.9
Current Liabilities to Working Capital 39	1.1	•	1.2	1.2	0.5	2.0	1.6	2.9
Working Capital to Net Sales 40	0.1	•	0.0	0.1	0.1	0.2	0.1	0.1
Inventory to Working Capital 41	0.4	•	0.5	0.5	0.3	0.4	0.2	0.4
Total Receipts to Cash Flow 42	5.7	3.0	5.4	5.8	7.7	4.4	4.0	10.1
Cost of Goods to Cash Flow 43	2.8	1.2	2.5	3.0	4.4	2.2	1.4	4.8
Cash Flow to Total Debt 44	0.9	•	1.5	0.4	0.8	0.3	1.0	0.2

Selected Financial Factors (in Percentages)

Debt Ratio 45	64.8	•	72.0	80.9	43.0	65.7	45.1	37.5
Return on Total Assets 46	23.9	•	41.5	18.9	15.0	11.3	13.6	3.6
Return on Equity Before Income Taxes 47	59.4	•	136.9	76.0	23.4	24.6	23.4	2.8
Return on Equity After Income Taxes 48	58.2	•	136.1	74.6	22.4	21.1	22.9	2.7
Profit Margin (Before Income Tax) 49	6.4	12.5	6.4	7.0	5.2	9.0	7.3	2.2
Profit Margin (After Income Tax) 50	6.2	12.5	6.4	6.9	4.9	7.8	7.2	2.2

Table I

Corporations with and without Net Income

OTHER REPAIR AND MAINTENANCE

MONEY AMOUNTS AND SIZE OF ASSETS IN THOUSANDS OF DOLLARS

Item Description for Accounting Period 7/08 Through 6/09		Total	Zero Assets	Under 500	500 to 1,000	1,000 to 5,000	5,000 to 10,000	10,000 to 25,000	25,000 to 50,000	50,000 to 100,000	100,000 to 250,000	250,000 to 500,000	500,000 to 2,500,000	2,500,000 and over
Number of Enterprises	1	60188	13656	42451	2193	1628	99	107	29	14	5	3	3	0
Revenues ($ in Thousands)														
Net Sales	2	44264124	893435	19142232	4749845	7099812	1664032	3406563	1708151	1624003	1133429	884608	1958012	0
Interest	3	103860	0	4941	5068	8952	3146	3840	2558	11372	896	2340	60747	0
Rents	4	17620	0	6979	252	1882	278	1625	423	5659	4	0	519	0
Royalties	5	74616	0	0	0	0	0	0	0	367	0	0	74249	0
Other Portfolio Income	6	87002	3443	4795	2323	57055	1045	4386	615	1038	1440	584	10279	0
Other Receipts	7	583948	585	41229	76493	42778	14466	26285	1569	6220	34904	926	338491	0
Total Receipts	8	45131170	897463	19200176	4833981	7210479	1682967	3442699	1713316	1648659	1170673	888458	2442297	0
Average Total Receipts	9	750	66	452	2204	4429	17000	32175	59080	117761	234135	296153	814099	•
Operating Costs/Operating Income (%)														
Cost of Operations	10	57.0	16.2	51.9	55.3	63.5	64.0	66.9	68.4	61.4	58.5	68.6	63.9	•
Salaries and Wages	11	11.9	4.9	14.7	10.2	8.5	9.5	10.7	11.7	10.2	15.1	5.9	9.2	•
Taxes Paid	12	2.2	1.5	2.5	2.5	2.1	1.5	1.8	2.0	1.3	2.1	1.8	1.8	•
Interest Paid	13	1.9	1.0	0.6	0.7	1.3	0.4	0.6	1.4	2.0	2.5	5.8	20.6	•
Depreciation	14	1.9	4.2	1.3	2.0	2.4	1.7	2.8	1.8	3.2	2.1	2.3	1.6	•
Amortization and Depletion	15	0.4	0.0	0.2	0.1	0.3	0.0	0.1	0.2	0.4	0.8	4.2	4.1	•
Pensions and Other Deferred Comp.	16	0.3	•	0.2	0.3	0.2	1.2	0.5	1.0	0.2	0.5	0.3	0.3	•
Employee Benefits	17	1.4	0.9	0.5	1.7	1.2	3.1	1.1	4.9	2.0	3.3	4.8	1.7	•
Advertising	18	0.7	1.3	0.9	0.8	0.4	0.4	0.5	0.2	1.0	0.2	0.1	1.4	•
Other Expenses	19	15.6	48.6	17.8	18.2	11.6	10.2	9.6	3.0	15.5	11.0	8.4	19.3	•
Officers' Compensation	20	5.2	9.4	6.7	8.0	4.3	5.7	2.0	1.5	1.0	0.5	2.8	0.9	•
Operating Margin	21	1.5	12.1	2.6	0.2	4.0	2.2	3.3	3.8	1.9	3.4	•	•	•
Operating Margin Before Officers' Comp.	22	6.7	21.5	9.3	8.2	8.4	7.9	5.4	5.3	2.9	3.9	•	•	•

Selected Average Balance Sheet ($ in Thousands)

Net Receivables **23**	66	0	12	143	417	1791	4662	13496	19812	42086	43666	267821
Inventories **24**	43	0	14	50	471	1409	4667	7869	11526	8157	3536	29558
Net Property, Plant and Equipment **25**	47	0	19	149	348	922	3351	5554	11875	30750	26938	35677
Total Assets **26**	393	0	75	663	2024	6555	16678	36317	71864	168905	349403	3114007
Notes and Loans Payable **27**	195	0	52	202	807	1312	5015	8669	25714	75866	198247	1832245
All Other Liabilities **28**	105	0	23	182	483	2026	4765	18474	26451	40018	50810	734794
Net Worth **29**	93	0	-1	279	734	3217	6897	9175	19699	53021	100346	546969

Selected Financial Ratios (Times to 1)

Current Ratio **30**	1.7	•	1.9	1.8	1.9	2.1	1.9	1.5	1.4	1.8	2.0	1.3
Quick Ratio **31**	1.1	•	1.3	1.1	1.0	1.3	1.1	1.0	0.7	1.1	1.6	1.0
Net Sales to Working Capital **32**	10.5	•	21.8	11.0	7.8	6.3	5.5	6.6	10.8	5.8	6.9	5.3
Coverage Ratio **33**	2.9	14.0	5.9	3.9	5.1	9.6	8.1	3.9	2.7	3.7	0.2	1.0
Total Asset Turnover **34**	1.9	•	6.0	3.3	2.2	2.6	1.9	1.6	1.6	1.3	0.8	0.2
Inventory Turnover **35**	9.8	•	17.1	23.8	5.9	7.6	4.6	5.1	6.2	16.3	57.2	14.1
Receivables Turnover **36**	11.2	•	29.6	17.8	9.6	8.1	6.8	5.1	6.3	4.2	2.7	4.9
Total Liabilities to Net Worth **37**	3.2	•	•	1.4	1.8	1.0	1.4	3.0	2.6	2.2	2.5	4.7
Current Assets to Working Capital **38**	2.4	•	2.1	2.2	2.2	1.9	2.1	2.8	3.6	2.2	2.0	4.3
Current Liabilities to Working Capital **39**	1.4	•	1.1	1.2	1.2	0.9	1.1	1.8	2.6	1.2	1.0	3.3
Working Capital to Net Sales **40**	0.1	•	0.0	0.1	0.1	0.2	0.2	0.2	0.1	0.2	0.1	0.2
Inventory to Working Capital **41**	0.6	•	0.6	0.4	0.9	0.5	0.8	0.9	1.3	0.2	0.1	0.2
Total Receipts to Cash Flow **42**	6.6	1.8	6.1	6.3	7.3	8.6	9.1	22.8	6.5	6.4	104.0	6.5
Cost of Goods to Cash Flow **43**	3.7	0.3	3.2	3.5	4.7	5.5	6.1	15.6	4.0	3.8	71.4	4.1
Cash Flow to Total Debt **44**	0.4	•	1.0	0.9	0.5	0.6	0.4	0.1	0.3	0.3	0.0	0.0

Selected Financial Factors (in Percentages)

Debt Ratio **45**	76.4	•	101.4	57.9	63.7	50.9	58.6	74.7	72.6	68.6	71.3	82.4
Return on Total Assets **46**	9.9	•	21.5	8.5	14.9	9.6	9.6	9.0	8.7	12.4	1.1	4.3
Return on Equity Before Income Taxes **47**	27.4	•	•	15.0	33.1	17.5	20.3	26.3	20.0	28.9	•	•
Return on Equity After Income Taxes **48**	23.7	•	•	12.2	31.0	11.6	14.9	20.2	16.6	18.2	•	•
Profit Margin (Before Income Tax) **49**	3.4	12.5	3.0	1.9	5.6	3.3	4.4	4.1	3.4	6.8	•	•
Profit Margin (After Income Tax) **50**	3.0	12.4	2.9	1.6	5.2	2.2	3.2	3.1	2.8	4.3	•	•

Table II

Corporations with Net Income

OTHER REPAIR AND MAINTENANCE

MONEY AMOUNTS AND SIZE OF ASSETS IN THOUSANDS OF DOLLARS

Item Description for Accounting Period 7/08 Through 6/09	Total	Zero Assets	Under 500	500 to 1,000	1,000 to 5,000	5,000 to 10,000	10,000 to 25,000	25,000 to 50,000	50,000 to 100,000	100,000 to 250,000	250,000 to 500,000	500,000 to 2,500,000	2,500,000 and over
Number of Enterprises **1**	34422	7562	24274	1313	1085	79	73	21	•	•	•	•	0
Revenues ($ in Thousands)													
Net Sales **2**	31501632	633452	13160577	3106023	5301764	1421005	2695242	1413892	•	•	•	•	0
Interest **3**	40763	0	3376	3610	6751	1880	3522	1961	•	•	•	•	0
Rents **4**	3677	0	26	0	1250	278	1625	0	•	•	•	•	0
Royalties **5**	820	0	0	0	0	0	0	0	•	•	•	•	0
Other Portfolio Income **6**	76096	2459	2934	1104	56071	1045	3016	615	•	•	•	•	0
Other Receipts **7**	285902	0	30771	470	37457	15090	18773	-627	•	•	•	•	0
Total Receipts **8**	31908890	635911	13197684	3111207	5403293	1439298	2722178	1415841	•	•	•	•	0
Average Total Receipts **9**	927	84	544	2370	4980	18219	37290	67421	•	•	•	•	•
Operating Costs/Operating Income (%)													
Cost of Operations **10**	54.9	12.8	46.9	52.2	64.8	64.3	65.7	65.5	•	•	•	•	•
Salaries and Wages **11**	12.2	3.8	16.9	8.2	6.6	9.3	11.9	8.1	•	•	•	•	•
Taxes Paid **12**	2.1	1.4	2.6	2.1	1.8	1.5	1.9	1.7	•	•	•	•	•
Interest Paid **13**	0.9	1.2	0.5	0.8	1.0	0.4	0.4	1.5	•	•	•	•	•
Depreciation **14**	1.6	4.3	1.0	2.4	1.8	1.6	1.7	1.8	•	•	•	•	•
Amortization and Depletion **15**	0.2	0.0	0.2	0.1	0.3	0.0	0.1	0.1	•	•	•	•	•
Pensions and Other Deferred Comp. **16**	0.4	•	0.3	0.4	0.2	1.3	0.5	0.3	•	•	•	•	•
Employee Benefits **17**	1.4	1.2	0.7	1.7	1.2	3.2	1.1	4.4	•	•	•	•	•
Advertising **18**	0.5	1.2	0.5	0.9	0.4	0.3	0.4	0.2	•	•	•	•	•
Other Expenses **19**	14.6	40.1	16.6	19.7	10.5	7.7	8.4	8.2	•	•	•	•	•
Officers' Compensation **20**	4.9	11.6	6.7	5.2	4.7	5.7	2.2	1.7	•	•	•	•	•
Operating Margin **21**	6.4	22.4	7.2	6.5	6.8	4.5	5.7	6.6	•	•	•	•	•
Operating Margin Before Officers' Comp. **22**	11.3	34.0	13.9	11.7	11.5	10.2	7.9	8.3	•	•	•	•	•

Selected Average Balance Sheet ($ in Thousands)

Net Receivables 23	78	0	12	61	427	2024	5533	14829
Inventories 24	57	0	15	25	553	1668	5705	7849
Net Property, Plant and Equipment 25	50	0	20	184	287	1000	2254	5644
Total Assets 26	314	0	88	639	2041	6469	17216	37884
Notes and Loans Payable 27	123	0	45	207	600	1309	3108	11329
All Other Liabilities 28	83	0	23	127	568	2000	5091	14848
Net Worth 29	108	0	20	305	873	3160	9017	11706

Selected Financial Ratios (Times to 1)

Current Ratio 30	2.1	•	2.5	2.2	2.0	1.9	2.4	1.6
Quick Ratio 31	1.4	•	1.7	1.2	1.1	1.2	1.4	1.0
Net Sales to Working Capital 32	9.0	•	16.9	11.6	7.4	7.8	4.5	7.2
Coverage Ratio 33	9.9	20.2	16.7	9.9	9.9	15.3	19.6	5.4
Total Asset Turnover 34	2.9	•	6.2	3.7	2.4	2.8	2.1	1.8
Inventory Turnover 35	8.8	•	16.5	49.2	5.7	6.9	4.3	5.6
Receivables Turnover 36	10.9	•	27.7	21.1	9.4	7.6	6.3	•
Total Liabilities to Net Worth 37	1.9	•	3.4	1.1	1.3	1.0	0.9	2.2
Current Assets to Working Capital 38	1.9	•	1.7	1.8	2.0	2.1	1.7	2.8
Current Liabilities to Working Capital 39	0.9	•	0.7	0.8	1.0	1.1	0.7	1.8
Working Capital to Net Sales 40	0.1	•	0.1	0.1	0.1	0.1	0.2	0.1
Inventory to Working Capital 41	0.5	•	0.5	0.1	0.8	0.6	0.6	0.8
Total Receipts to Cash Flow 42	5.3	1.7	4.9	4.6	6.2	8.5	8.0	8.1
Cost of Goods to Cash Flow 43	2.9	0.2	2.3	2.4	4.0	5.5	5.2	5.3
Cash Flow to Total Debt 44	0.8	•	1.6	1.5	0.7	0.6	0.6	0.3

Selected Financial Factors (in Percentages)

Debt Ratio 45	65.5	•	77.4	52.3	57.2	51.2	47.6	69.1
Return on Total Assets 46	24.8	•	49.1	27.5	23.2	17.2	15.1	14.6
Return on Equity Before Income Taxes 47	64.6	•	204.6	51.8	48.9	32.9	27.4	38.7
Return on Equity After Income Taxes 48	59.0	•	201.8	47.4	46.2	25.4	21.4	32.1
Profit Margin (Before Income Tax) 49	7.6	22.7	7.5	6.7	8.7	5.8	6.7	6.7
Profit Margin (After Income Tax) 50	7.0	22.5	7.4	6.1	8.2	4.5	5.2	5.6

Table I

Corporations with and without Net Income

PERSONAL AND LAUNDRY SERVICES

MONEY AMOUNTS AND SIZE OF ASSETS IN THOUSANDS OF DOLLARS

Item Description for Accounting Period 7/08 Through 6/09	Total	Zero Assets	Under 500	500 to 1,000	1,000 to 5,000	5,000 to 10,000	10,000 to 25,000	25,000 to 50,000	50,000 to 100,000	100,000 to 250,000	250,000 to 500,000	500,000 to 2,500,000	2,500,000 and over
Number of Enterprises **1**	154800	36918	106414	6433	4502	296	139	43	25	13	4	10	3
Revenues ($ in Thousands)													
Net Sales **2**	73580812	2941647	27693154	8405839	10494963	3220474	2253488	1664875	1637934	1587369	1271936	4810974	7598159
Interest **3**	139545	247	9606	3432	9767	2946	4586	8870	3054	5041	281	51939	39776
Rents **4**	63581	20	3529	2915	5703	1932	5601	851	670	3331	6988	19806	12235
Royalties **5**	136559	0	0	485	0	559	131	82	28	1674	0	88607	44994
Other Portfolio Income **6**	538958	94235	153968	18876	26432	4892	1341	4173	454	8330	2934	218541	4778
Other Receipts **7**	1618511	16470	237594	130287	470727	83844	88419	40844	23771	191319	727	262851	71662
Total Receipts **8**	76077966	3052619	28097851	8561834	11007592	3314647	2353566	1719695	1665911	1797064	1282866	5452718	7771604
Average Total Receipts **9**	491	83	264	1331	2445	11198	16932	39993	66636	138236	320716	545272	2590535
Operating Costs/Operating Income (%)													
Cost of Operations **10**	27.6	19.4	26.9	18.4	23.9	38.8	28.9	42.6	37.1	31.9	32.5	26.6	37.4
Salaries and Wages **11**	20.5	13.9	19.3	18.0	26.3	18.1	22.1	14.9	23.2	25.9	24.1	20.5	21.4
Taxes Paid **12**	3.5	3.9	3.2	3.1	5.0	3.7	2.9	2.4	3.3	3.6	2.4	4.3	3.3
Interest Paid **13**	2.1	3.9	1.1	1.7	2.3	1.5	2.0	1.5	3.4	3.0	3.2	6.1	2.9
Depreciation **14**	4.0	5.0	2.4	3.8	4.3	6.4	7.7	4.1	3.3	4.8	8.2	5.1	5.6
Amortization and Depletion **15**	1.1	2.1	0.4	0.4	0.6	0.3	0.7	0.6	1.0	2.0	6.0	5.9	1.2
Pensions and Other Deferred Comp. **16**	0.5	0.1	0.3	0.4	0.5	0.2	0.3	0.6	0.2	0.7	1.9	1.0	0.7
Employee Benefits **17**	1.5	0.7	0.9	0.9	1.7	1.2	2.7	1.8	2.4	3.0	1.7	3.3	2.7
Advertising **18**	1.8	1.4	2.2	1.5	1.6	2.7	1.9	1.6	1.6	1.7	0.4	2.6	0.7
Other Expenses **19**	32.6	51.7	33.0	44.7	34.1	23.4	29.2	26.6	27.4	36.0	19.7	26.0	21.4
Officers' Compensation **20**	5.7	7.8	9.0	6.9	5.5	2.2	2.2	1.9	1.6	2.1	0.5	0.8	0.7
Operating Margin **21**	•	•	1.4	0.0	•	1.7	•	1.6	•	•	•	•	2.2
Operating Margin Before Officers' Comp. **22**	4.7	•	10.4	6.9	•	3.9	1.5	3.5	•	•	•	•	2.9

Selected Average Balance Sheet ($ in Thousands)

Item													
Net Receivables 23	32	0	2	51	235	918	2560	6049	6784	19042	72360	125707	150517
Inventories 24	15	0	3	26	35	438	558	2598	2908	2522	22316	36846	247200
Net Property, Plant and Equipment 25	121	0	31	322	846	2846	5625	7414	22134	29644	179442	192104	1337421
Total Assets 26	363	0	75	691	1850	7059	15133	35798	72805	146363	421220	1007302	4749088
Notes and Loans Payable 27	163	0	59	378	962	2124	5630	9832	27560	44244	168688	401593	1452901
All Other Liabilities 28	112	0	15	127	427	2322	3980	15102	32750	86195	102824	361630	1693044
Net Worth 29	88	0	0	186	461	2613	5523	10864	12495	15924	149708	244078	1603143

Selected Financial Ratios (Times to 1)

Item													
Current Ratio 30	1.4	•	1.4	1.4	1.6	1.2	1.4	1.6	0.8	1.0	1.6	1.0	2.1
Quick Ratio 31	0.9	•	1.0	1.0	1.2	0.9	1.0	0.8	0.5	0.6	1.2	0.7	0.8
Net Sales to Working Capital 32	19.9	•	38.4	27.6	10.2	25.0	10.2	5.2	•	•	7.3	76.2	9.0
Coverage Ratio 33	2.2	•	3.7	2.1	0.6	4.1	2.9	4.3	0.2	0.5	1.1	3.0	2.6
Total Asset Turnover 34	1.3	•	3.5	1.9	1.3	1.5	1.1	1.1	0.9	0.8	0.8	0.5	0.5
Inventory Turnover 35	9.0	•	24.2	9.3	15.9	9.6	8.4	6.3	8.4	15.4	4.6	3.5	3.8
Receivables Turnover 36	16.4	•	102.8	24.6	10.0	11.5	5.9	7.5	11.8	7.7	5.4	5.4	16.0
Total Liabilities to Net Worth 37	3.1	•	193.2	2.7	3.0	1.7	1.7	2.3	4.8	8.2	1.8	3.1	2.0
Current Assets to Working Capital 38	3.8	•	3.3	3.8	2.6	6.2	3.4	2.8	•	•	2.6	36.5	1.9
Current Liabilities to Working Capital 39	2.8	•	2.3	2.8	1.6	5.2	2.4	1.8	•	•	1.6	35.5	0.9
Working Capital to Net Sales 40	0.1	•	0.0	0.0	0.1	0.0	0.1	0.2	•	•	0.1	0.0	0.1
Inventory to Working Capital 41	0.6	•	0.4	0.6	0.2	0.9	0.3	0.3	•	•	0.5	6.0	0.8
Total Receipts to Cash Flow 42	4.3	3.9	4.3	2.7	5.5	5.0	4.5	5.6	5.9	5.2	5.4	4.1	6.0
Cost of Goods to Cash Flow 43	1.2	0.8	1.2	0.5	1.3	1.9	1.3	2.4	2.2	1.6	1.8	1.1	2.2
Cash Flow to Total Debt 44	0.4	•	0.8	1.0	0.3	0.5	0.4	0.3	0.2	0.2	0.2	0.2	0.1

Selected Financial Factors (in Percentages)

Item													
Debt Ratio 45	75.6	•	99.5	73.1	75.1	63.0	63.5	69.7	82.8	89.1	64.5	75.8	66.2
Return on Total Assets 46	6.1	•	13.6	6.9	1.6	9.2	6.2	6.9	0.6	1.3	2.7	8.7	3.9
Return on Equity Before Income Taxes 47	13.4	•	1924.8	13.2	•	18.9	11.1	17.5	•	•	0.8	23.7	7.1
Return on Equity After Income Taxes 48	10.4	•	1901.4	12.4	•	17.9	9.7	14.8	•	•	0.8	15.6	4.5
Profit Margin (Before Income Tax) 49	2.5	•	2.8	1.9	•	4.5	3.8	4.9	•	•	0.4	12.0	4.5
Profit Margin (After Income Tax) 50	1.9	•	2.8	1.8	•	4.3	3.3	4.1	•	•	0.4	7.9	2.8

Table II

Corporations with Net Income

PERSONAL AND LAUNDRY SERVICES

MONEY AMOUNTS AND SIZE OF ASSETS IN THOUSANDS OF DOLLARS

Item Description for Accounting Period 7/08 Through 6/09	Total	Zero Assets	Under 500	500 to 1,000	1,000 to 5,000	5,000 to 10,000	10,000 to 25,000	25,000 to 50,000	50,000 to 100,000	100,000 to 250,000	250,000 to 500,000	500,000 to 2,500,000	2,500,000 and over
Number of Enterprises 1	77900	13708	57074	4036	2712	•	100	26	•	•	0	•	0
Revenues ($ in Thousands)													
Net Sales 2	50424834	1164975	18317069	6175622	7494759	•	1795849	1382424	•	•	0	•	0
Interest 3	97172	29	5532	2378	5885	•	3585	2188	•	•	0	•	0
Rents 4	47321	0	3128	1329	4225	•	5577	846	•	•	0	•	0
Royalties 5	97882	0	0	485	0	•	0	0	•	•	0	•	0
Other Portfolio Income 6	414591	25588	133486	10786	21911	•	1003	933	•	•	0	•	0
Other Receipts 7	810961	23180	130890	79476	59267	•	76345	24495	•	•	0	•	0
Total Receipts 8	51892761	1213772	18590105	6270076	7586047	•	1882359	1410886	•	•	•	•	•
Average Total Receipts 9	666	89	326	1554	2797	•	18824	54265	•	•	•	•	•
Operating Costs/Operating Income (%)													
Cost of Operations 10	25.5	11.3	26.8	15.3	20.9	•	31.7	47.3	•	•	•	•	•
Salaries and Wages 11	21.0	8.8	18.8	17.1	25.1	•	21.0	15.5	•	•	•	•	•
Taxes Paid 12	3.6	3.2	3.1	2.5	5.2	•	2.6	2.1	•	•	•	•	•
Interest Paid 13	1.7	1.0	0.8	1.4	1.8	•	1.2	1.0	•	•	•	•	•
Depreciation 14	3.1	1.1	1.8	2.7	2.5	•	6.2	2.4	•	•	•	•	•
Amortization and Depletion 15	1.0	0.6	0.3	0.5	0.7	•	0.3	0.6	•	•	•	•	•
Pensions and Other Deferred Comp. 16	0.5	0.0	0.3	0.4	0.4	•	0.3	0.6	•	•	•	•	•
Employee Benefits 17	1.5	0.4	0.7	0.6	1.4	•	2.9	1.9	•	•	•	•	•
Advertising 18	1.7	0.9	1.7	1.0	1.7	•	2.2	1.8	•	•	•	•	•
Other Expenses 19	29.5	42.6	28.7	47.4	31.9	•	26.9	20.1	•	•	•	•	•
Officers' Compensation 20	5.7	14.4	9.4	6.7	4.8	•	1.9	1.7	•	•	•	•	•
Operating Margin 21	5.3	15.8	7.5	4.5	3.6	•	2.7	5.1	•	•	•	•	•
Operating Margin Before Officers' Comp. 22	11.0	30.2	16.9	11.2	8.4	•	4.6	6.8	•	•	•	•	•

Selected Average Balance Sheet ($ in Thousands)

Net Receivables 23	45	0	3	62	215	2217	9207
Inventories 24	20	0	3	25	32	512	3607
Net Property, Plant and Equipment 25	141	0	29	276	693	5240	6376
Total Assets 26	454	0	79	653	1803	15057	36799
Notes and Loans Payable 27	177	0	46	324	765	3878	9181
All Other Liabilities 28	134	0	13	60	441	3560	15494
Net Worth 29	143	0	20	269	597	7618	12123

Selected Financial Ratios (Times to 1)

Current Ratio 30	1.5	•	2.2	2.1	1.8	1.6	1.5
Quick Ratio 31	1.0	•	1.8	1.6	1.3	1.1	1.1
Net Sales to Working Capital 32	16.3	•	21.3	13.6	10.0	8.4	7.6
Coverage Ratio 33	6.0	20.8	12.4	5.4	3.7	7.1	8.2
Total Asset Turnover 34	1.4	•	4.1	2.3	1.5	1.2	1.4
Inventory Turnover 35	8.1	•	31.7	9.3	18.2	11.1	7.0
Receivables Turnover 36	15.6	•	103.2	23.5	11.2	7.2	7.3
Total Liabilities to Net Worth 37	2.2	•	3.1	1.4	2.0	1.0	2.0
Current Assets to Working Capital 38	3.1	•	1.8	1.9	2.3	2.6	3.0
Current Liabilities to Working Capital 39	2.1	•	0.8	0.9	1.3	1.6	2.0
Working Capital to Net Sales 40	0.1	•	0.0	0.1	0.1	0.1	0.1
Inventory to Working Capital 41	0.4	•	0.2	0.2	0.1	0.3	0.5
Total Receipts to Cash Flow 42	3.7	2.3	3.7	2.2	4.8	4.0	5.1
Cost of Goods to Cash Flow 43	0.9	0.3	1.0	0.3	1.0	1.3	2.4
Cash Flow to Total Debt 44	0.6	•	1.5	1.8	0.5	0.6	0.4

Selected Financial Factors (in Percentages)

Debt Ratio 45	68.6	•	75.4	58.8	66.9	49.4	67.1
Return on Total Assets 46	14.2	•	39.8	17.4	10.1	10.5	11.8
Return on Equity Before Income Taxes 47	37.7	•	148.4	34.4	22.1	17.7	31.4
Return on Equity After Income Taxes 48	34.1	•	147.6	33.5	20.8	16.3	27.4
Profit Margin (Before Income Tax) 49	8.3	19.9	9.0	6.0	4.8	7.5	7.2
Profit Margin (After Income Tax) 50	7.5	19.8	9.0	5.9	4.5	6.9	6.2

Table I

Corporations with and without Net Income

RELIGIOUS, GRANTMAKING, CIVIC AND PROFESSIONAL ORGANIZATIONS

MONEY AMOUNTS AND SIZE OF ASSETS IN THOUSANDS OF DOLLARS

Item Description for Accounting Period 7/08 Through 6/09	Total	Zero Assets	Under 500	500 to 1,000	1,000 to 5,000	5,000 to 10,000	10,000 to 25,000	25,000 to 50,000	50,000 to 100,000	100,000 to 250,000	250,000 to 500,000	500,000 to 2,500,000	2,500,000 and over
Number of Enterprises **1**	50968	5461	38755	3881	2559	199	84	19	9	0	0	0	0
Revenues ($ in Thousands)													
Net Sales **2**	12012345	321646	4376670	1955904	3040023	558605	750551	430492	578454	0	0	0	0
Interest **3**	264369	6679	74374	58423	85471	14612	11090	6617	7103	0	0	0	0
Rents **4**	45912	0	8929	14374	11640	3605	4732	2206	427	0	0	0	0
Royalties **5**	4784	0	0	4656	0	126	0	1	0	0	0	0	0
Other Portfolio Income **6**	56758	0	17603	12211	10355	1573	9659	3865	1496	0	0	0	0
Other Receipts **7**	2543886	35963	1232297	518772	346648	156901	136165	57916	59221	0	0	0	0
Total Receipts **8**	14928054	364288	5709873	2564340	3494137	735422	912197	501097	646701	0	0	0	0
Average Total Receipts **9**	293	67	147	661	1365	3696	10859	26374	71856	•	•	•	•
Operating Costs/Operating Income (%)													
Cost of Operations **10**	15.7	6.6	8.7	22.3	15.2	7.1	30.6	21.5	37.4	•	•	•	•
Salaries and Wages **11**	15.0	10.2	5.5	10.6	24.0	21.0	23.8	29.5	28.8	•	•	•	•
Taxes Paid **12**	1.9	2.3	1.4	1.7	2.2	2.6	2.8	3.9	2.6	•	•	•	•
Interest Paid **13**	1.0	0.4	1.4	0.3	0.7	1.2	1.9	0.8	0.3	•	•	•	•
Depreciation **14**	2.0	1.6	0.9	1.9	2.0	5.8	3.8	3.9	3.4	•	•	•	•
Amortization and Depletion **15**	0.1	•	0.1	0.1	0.0	0.1	0.1	0.0	1.1	•	•	•	•
Pensions and Other Deferred Comp. **16**	0.4	•	0.0	0.1	0.3	0.3	2.0	1.5	1.8	•	•	•	•
Employee Benefits **17**	1.3	•	0.2	0.8	1.4	2.3	2.6	8.9	3.1	•	•	•	•
Advertising **18**	0.6	4.7	0.5	0.1	0.4	0.3	0.2	1.7	1.1	•	•	•	•
Other Expenses **19**	84.1	75.5	111.1	89.0	66.8	96.3	46.2	39.2	28.8	•	•	•	•
Officers' Compensation **20**	2.8	21.4	0.3	8.2	1.5	0.1	4.1	1.5	1.4	•	•	•	•
Operating Margin **21**	•	•	•	•	•	•	•	•	•	•	•	•	•
Operating Margin Before Officers' Comp. **22**	•	•	•	•	•	•	•	•	•	•	•	•	•

Selected Average Balance Sheet ($ in Thousands)

Net Receivables 23	21	0	6	43	141	349	1256	2205	11784
Inventories 24	1	0	0	0	8	24	290	734	329
Net Property, Plant and Equipment 25	72	0	9	69	481	2786	8713	12803	31701
Total Assets 26	313	0	104	695	1993	6419	15855	36306	87796
Notes and Loans Payable 27	39	0	24	40	186	542	2477	3631	5111
All Other Liabilities 28	75	0	18	139	492	2075	4003	12001	39186
Net Worth 29	198	0	62	516	1315	3802	9375	20675	43499

Selected Financial Ratios (Times to 1)

Current Ratio 30	3.1	•	4.3	4.9	3.0	1.4	1.6	1.7	1.5
Quick Ratio 31	2.8	•	3.9	4.6	2.7	1.1	1.2	1.0	1.3
Net Sales to Working Capital 32	1.7	•	1.6	1.2	1.3	3.1	5.2	3.7	6.5
Coverage Ratio 33	0.5	•	1.3	•	1.5	•	2.7	5.7	7.8
Total Asset Turnover 34	0.8	•	1.1	0.7	0.6	0.4	0.6	0.6	0.7
Inventory Turnover 35	26.4	•	124.3	393.9	22.1	8.2	9.4	6.6	73.0
Receivables Turnover 36	11.0	•	21.7	12.1	9.0	5.3	8.7	8.8	3.8
Total Liabilities to Net Worth 37	0.6	•	0.7	0.3	0.5	0.7	0.7	0.8	1.0
Current Assets to Working Capital 38	1.5	•	1.3	1.3	1.5	3.3	2.6	2.4	2.9
Current Liabilities to Working Capital 39	0.5	•	0.3	0.3	0.5	2.3	1.6	1.4	1.9
Working Capital to Net Sales 40	0.6	•	0.6	0.9	0.8	0.3	0.2	0.3	0.2
Inventory to Working Capital 41	0.0	•	0.0	0.0	0.0	0.0	0.1	0.2	0.0
Total Receipts to Cash Flow 42	1.5	2.1	1.1	1.4	1.9	2.3	2.3	2.8	4.2
Cost of Goods to Cash Flow 43	0.2	0.1	0.1	0.3	0.3	0.2	0.7	0.6	1.6
Cash Flow to Total Debt 44	1.4	•	2.5	2.0	0.9	0.5	0.6	0.5	0.3

Selected Financial Factors (in Percentages)

Debt Ratio 45	36.6	•	40.4	25.8	34.0	40.8	40.9	43.1	50.5
Return on Total Assets 46	0.4	•	1.9	•	0.7	•	2.9	2.8	1.6
Return on Equity Before Income Taxes 47	•	•	0.6	•	0.3	•	3.1	4.1	2.9
Return on Equity After Income Taxes 48	•	•	•	•	•	•	1.8	2.4	1.9
Profit Margin (Before Income Tax) 49	•	•	0.3	•	0.4	•	3.3	3.7	2.0
Profit Margin (After Income Tax) 50	•	•	•	•	•	•	1.9	2.2	1.3

RELIGIOUS, GRANTMAKING, CIVIC AND PROFESSIONAL ORGANIZATIONS

Table II
Corporations with Net Income

MONEY AMOUNTS AND SIZE OF ASSETS IN THOUSANDS OF DOLLARS

Item Description for Accounting Period 7/08 Through 6/09	Total	Zero Assets	Under 500	500 to 1,000	1,000 to 5,000	5,000 to 10,000	10,000 to 25,000	25,000 to 50,000	50,000 to 100,000	100,000 to 250,000	250,000 to 500,000	500,000 to 2,500,000	2,500,000 and over
Number of Enterprises **1**	24158	1056	18192	2919	1834	•	63	13	•	0	0	0	0
Revenues ($ in Thousands)													
Net Sales **2**	7249252	55651	2418393	1259019	1837992	•	666540	288845	•	0	0	0	0
Interest **3**	211396	4155	62290	48619	68475	•	9960	4498	•	0	0	0	0
Rents **4**	37261	0	5682	13116	10817	•	4732	2198	•	0	0	0	0
Royalties **5**	4783	0	0	4656	0	•	0	0	•	0	0	0	0
Other Portfolio Income **6**	54887	0	17099	12168	10150	•	9632	2983	•	0	0	0	0
Other Receipts **7**	1055544	7427	280670	256158	225161	•	130205	38434	•	0	0	0	0
Total Receipts **8**	8613123	67233	2784134	1593736	2152595	•	821069	336958	•	0	0	0	0
Average Total Receipts **9**	357	64	153	546	1174	•	13033	25920	•	•	•	•	•
Operating Costs/Operating Income (%)													
Cost of Operations **10**	16.1	•	8.6	12.1	15.0	•	29.7	29.4	•	•	•	•	•
Salaries and Wages **11**	13.7	•	4.2	7.9	18.9	•	24.8	28.3	•	•	•	•	•
Taxes Paid **12**	2.0	0.1	1.2	1.9	2.5	•	2.4	4.2	•	•	•	•	•
Interest Paid **13**	0.5	•	0.5	0.2	0.5	•	1.0	1.2	•	•	•	•	•
Depreciation **14**	1.5	0.2	0.9	0.6	1.8	•	2.7	2.7	•	•	•	•	•
Amortization and Depletion **15**	0.1	•	0.0	0.1	0.1	•	0.1	0.0	•	•	•	•	•
Pensions and Other Deferred Comp. **16**	0.5	•	•	0.1	0.0	•	2.3	1.7	•	•	•	•	•
Employee Benefits **17**	1.5	•	0.0	0.8	1.3	•	2.8	10.5	•	•	•	•	•
Advertising **18**	0.4	•	0.0	0.1	0.6	•	0.2	2.2	•	•	•	•	•
Other Expenses **19**	74.1	112.4	93.2	85.4	70.2	•	47.7	26.8	•	•	•	•	•
Officers' Compensation **20**	2.9	•	0.6	11.6	0.3	•	4.6	1.6	•	•	•	•	•
Operating Margin **21**	•	•	•	•	•	•	•	•	•	•	•	•	•
Operating Margin Before Officers' Comp. **22**	•	•	•	•	•	•	•	•	•	•	•	•	•

Selected Average Balance Sheet ($ in Thousands)

Net Receivables 23	26	0	5	29	109	1535	2047
Inventories 24	2	0	0	0	8	358	1013
Net Property, Plant and Equipment 25	67	0	11	31	293	6933	11916
Total Assets 26	444	0	151	676	1914	15838	36123
Notes and Loans Payable 27	24	0	9	20	95	1497	5208
All Other Liabilities 28	97	0	15	108	434	5032	8820
Net Worth 29	323	0	127	547	1384	9309	22095

Selected Financial Ratios (Times to 1)

Current Ratio 30	4.4	•	10.4	6.2	4.3	1.6	1.8
Quick Ratio 31	4.0	•	9.8	5.9	3.8	1.1	1.0
Net Sales to Working Capital 32	1.2	•	1.1	0.9	0.9	5.4	3.9
Coverage Ratio 33	12.6	•	12.1	39.2	11.8	6.0	7.4
Total Asset Turnover 34	0.7	•	0.9	0.6	0.5	0.7	0.6
Inventory Turnover 35	20.9	•	404.4	2447.9	19.5	8.8	6.4
Receivables Turnover 36	11.6	•	26.4	13.9	9.1	8.7	7.0
Total Liabilities to Net Worth 37	0.4	•	0.2	0.2	0.4	0.7	0.6
Current Assets to Working Capital 38	1.3	•	1.1	1.2	1.3	2.8	2.3
Current Liabilities to Working Capital 39	0.3	•	0.1	0.2	0.3	1.8	1.3
Working Capital to Net Sales 40	0.8	•	0.9	1.1	1.1	0.2	0.3
Inventory to Working Capital 41	0.0	•	0.0	0.0	0.0	0.1	0.3
Total Receipts to Cash Flow 42	1.5	1.1	1.3	1.4	1.6	2.1	3.6
Cost of Goods to Cash Flow 43	0.2	•	0.1	0.2	0.2	0.6	1.1
Cash Flow to Total Debt 44	1.6	•	4.3	2.5	1.2	0.8	0.4

Selected Financial Factors (in Percentages)

Debt Ratio 45	27.1	•	15.7	19.1	27.7	41.2	38.8
Return on Total Assets 46	4.1	•	5.7	3.9	3.3	3.9	5.4
Return on Equity Before Income Taxes 47	5.2	•	6.2	4.7	4.2	5.5	7.6
Return on Equity After Income Taxes 48	4.4	•	5.5	4.1	3.6	3.7	5.3
Profit Margin (Before Income Tax) 49	5.6	8.1	5.9	6.0	5.8	4.8	7.5
Profit Margin (After Income Tax) 50	4.7	6.6	5.2	5.1	5.0	3.3	5.3

Index

Index

S

Savings institutions, credit unions, and other depository credit intermediation, 279, 280
Scientific research and development services, 343, 344
Securities brokerage, 291, 292
Securities, commodity contracts, and other financial investments, 289-296
Security and commodity exchanges and other financial investment, 295, 296
Semiconductor and other electronic component,143, 144
Ship and boat building, 157, 158
Soap, cleaning compound, and toilet preparation, 91, 92
Soft drink and ice, 51, 52
Software publishers, 261, 262
Sound recording industries, 265, 266
Special trade contractors, 31-36
Specialized design services, 337, 338
Sporting goods, hobby, book, and music stores, 229, 230
Stock property and casualty companies (Form 1120-PC), 305, 306
Sugar and confectionery products, 39, 40
Support activities and fishing, hunting, and trapping, 5, 6
Support activities for mining, 15, 16

T

Telecommunications (wired, wireless, satellite, internet providers), 269, 270
Textile mills, 59, 60

Textile mills and textile product mills, 59-62
Textile product mills, 61, 62
Tobacco manufacturing, 57, 58
Transit and ground passenger transportation, 245, 246
Transportation and warehousing, 237-252
Transportation equipment manufacturing, 153-162
Travel arrangement and reservation services, 355, 356
Truck transportation, 243, 244

U

Utilities, 17-24

V

Ventilation, heating, A.C. & commercial refrigeration equip., 129, 130

W

Warehousing and storage, 251, 252
Waste management and remediation services, 359, 360
Water, sewage, and other systems, 21, 22
Water transportation, 241, 242
Wholesale electronic markets and agents and brokers, 201, 202
Wholesale trade, 167-202
Wholesale trade, durable goods, 167-182
Wholesale trade, nondurable goods, 183-202
Wineries and distilleries, 55, 56
Wood product manufacturing, 71, 72